Consumer Behaviour

A European Perspective

Visit the *Consumer Behaviour, 4th edition* Companion Website at
www.pearsoned.co.uk/solomon to find valuable **student**
learning material including:

- Video clips to contextualise your learning in the real world
- Multiple choice questions to test your learning
- Flashcards to test your understanding of key terms
- An online glossary to explain key terms
- An e study guide to check your understanding

Fourth
edition

Consumer Behaviour

A European Perspective

Michael Solomon

Gary Bamossy

Søren Askegaard

Margaret K. Hogg

FT Prentice Hall

FINANCIAL TIMES

An imprint of **Pearson Education**

Harlow, England • London • New York • Boston • San Francisco • Toronto • Sydney • Singapore • Hong Kong
Tokyo • Seoul • Taipei • New Delhi • Cape Town • Madrid • Mexico City • Amsterdam • Munich • Paris • Milan

Pearson Education Limited

Edinburgh Gate
Harlow
Essex CM20 2JE
England

and Associated Companies throughout the world

Visit us on the World Wide Web at:
www.pearsoned.co.uk

_____

First published by Prentice Hall Europe 1999
Second edition published 2002
Third edition published 2006
Fourth edition published 2010

© Prentice Hall Europe 1999
© Pearson Education 2002, 2006, 2010

The rights of Michael Solomon, Gary Bamossy, Søren Askegaard and Margaret K. Hogg
to be identified as authors of this work have been asserted by them in accordance with
the Copyright, Designs and Patents Act 1988.

Authorized adaptation from the United States edition, entitled CONSUMER BEHAVIOR, 8th Edition,
ISBN 0136015964 by Michael Solomon, published by Pearson Education, Inc, publishing as
Prentice Hall, Copyright © 2009.

ISBN: 978-0-273-71726-3

British Library Cataloguing-in-Publication Data
A catalogue record for this book is available from the British Library

Library of Congress Cataloging-in-Publication Data
Consumer behaviour : a European perspective / Michael Solomon . . . [et al.]. – 4th ed.
   p. cm.
  Includes bibliographical references and index.
   ISBN 978-0-273-71726-3 (pbk. : alk. paper) 1. Consumer behavior – Europe.
I. Solomon, Michael R. II. Title: Consumer behavior.
HF5415.33.E85S65 2010
658.8′342094—dc22

                            2009033199

10 9 8 7 6 5 4 3 2 1
14 13 12 11 10

Typeset in 9.5/12pt Palatino by 35
Printed and bound by Rotolito Lombarda, Italy

The publisher's policy is to use paper manufactured from sustainable forests.

Brief contents

Contents

Part A
Consumers in the marketplace

Chapter 1
An introduction to consumer behaviour

Chapter 2
A consumer society

Chapter 3
Shopping, buying and evaluating

Part B
How Consumers see the world and themselves

Part C
Consumers as decision-makers

Chapter 7
Learning and memory

Chapter 8
Attitudes

Part D
European consumers and their social groups

Supporting resources

Visit **www.pearsoned.co.uk/solomon** to find valuable online resources

Companion Website for students
- Video clips to contextualise your learning in the real world
- Multiple choice questions to test your learning
- Flashcards to test your understanding of key terms
- An online glossary to explain key terms
- An e study guide to check your understanding

For instructors
- Testbank of question material
- PowerPoint slides that can be downloaded and used for presentations
- Complete, downloadable Instructor's Manual

Also: The Companion Website provides the following features:
- Search tool to help locate specific items of content
- E-mail results and profile tools to send results of quizzes to instructors
- Online help and support to assist with website usage and troubleshooting

For more information please contact your local Pearson Education sales representative or visit **www.pearsoned.co.uk/solomon**

We wrote this book because we're fascinated by the everyday activities of people. The field of consumer behaviour is, to us, the study of how the world is influenced by the action of marketers. We're fortunate enough to be teachers and researchers (and occasionally consultants) whose work allows us to study consumers. Given that we're also consumers, we can find both professional and personal interest in learning more about how this process works. As consumers and future managers, we hope you find this study to be fascinating as well. Whether you're a student, manager, or professor, we're sure you can relate to the trials and tribulations associated with last-minute shopping, preparing for a big night out, agonizing over a purchase decision, fantasizing about a week skiing in the Swiss Alps, celebrating a holiday on the Cote d'Azur, or commemorating a landmark event, such as graduating from university, getting a driver's licence, or (dreaming about) winning the lottery.

Buying, having and being

Our understanding of this field goes beyond looking at the act of *buying* only, but extends to both *having* and *being* as well. Consumer behaviour is about much more than just buying things; it also embraces the study about how having (or not having) things affects our lives, and how our possessions influence the way we feel about ourselves and about each other – our state of being. In addition to understanding why people buy things, we also try to appreciate how products, services and consumption activities contribute to the broader social world we experience. Whether shopping, cooking, cleaning, playing football or hockey, lying on the beach, emailing or texting friends, or even looking at ourselves in the mirror, our lives are touched by the marketing system.

The field of consumer behaviour is young, dynamic and in flux. It is constantly being cross-fertilized by perspectives from many different disciplines. We have tried to express the field's staggering diversity in this text. Consumer researchers represent virtually every social science discipline, plus a few represent the physical sciences and the arts for good measure. From this melting pot has come a healthy debate among research perspectives, viewpoints regarding appropriate research methods, and even deeply held beliefs about what are and what are not appropriate issues for consumer researchers to study in the first place.

A European perspective on consumers and marketing strategy

The main objective for this new, fourth edition has been to significantly increase its relevance for European students and scholars, while retaining the accessibility, contemporary approach, and the level of excellence in the discussions of consumer behaviour theory and applications established over the last eight editions of Michael Solomon's *Consumer Behavior*. Based on the eighth American edition, we have tried to satisfy the need for a comprehensive consumer behaviour textbook with a significant European content. Hence, we have added illustrative examples and cases which are analyzed and discussed in a European consumer context, as well as numerous European scholarly references, including essays on the future of the field written by leading European Consumer Behavior scholars. The text also includes a number of advertisements of European origin so that the reader can visualize various elements in the marketing applications of consumer behaviour theory. These changes, which focus on European consumers and research, have been made throughout the book. However, the most substantial changes have been made in the chapters dealing with demographic groups, subcultures and lifestyles, where the American perspective provided in earlier editions of Solomon's text has been replaced with a European one. EU enlargement to the EU-27 has increased the population by 20 per cent, to 495 million people. At the same time, this significant increase in population has only raised EU Gross Domestic Production by 4.5 per cent. This fourth edition examines the demographics and social changes inherent in the structure of the new EU-27, and offers readers a variety of perspectives on European consumers' desires and aspirations. The new edition also offers many examples of the new opportunities and challenges in this marketplace, as well as discussing the implications and challenges of carrying out business strategies and developing tactics.

The internationalization of market structures makes it increasingly necessary for business people to acquire a clear perspective and understanding of cultural differences and similarities among consumers from various countries. One of the challenges of writing this book has been to develop materials which illustrate *local* as well as *pan-European* and *global* aspects of consumer behaviour. In this spirit, we have kept a number of American and other non-European examples to illustrate various similarities and differences on the global consumer scene. The book also emphasizes the importance of understanding consumers in formulating marketing strategy. Many (if not most) of the fundamental concepts of marketing are based on the practitioner's ability to understand people. To illustrate the potential of consumer research to inform marketing strategy, the text contains numerous examples of specific applications of consumer behaviour concepts by marketing practitioners.

Pedagogical features

Throughout the text there are numerous boxed illustrative examples which highlight particular aspects of the impact and informing role that consumer behaviour has on marketing activities. These colour-coded boxes are called:

● **Multicultural dimensions**,
● **Marketing opportunity**, and
● **Marketing pitfall**,

and represent examples from several European and global markets. There are several other features within each chapter to assist you in learning and reviewing this text, and to check and critically evaluate your understanding of topics; these include:

● an opening illustrative **vignette**,
● highlighted **key terms**,
● a **chapter summary**, and
● **Consumer behaviour challenge** questions.

To familiarize yourself with these features and how they will benefit your study from this text, they are reproduced and described in the Guided Tour on pages xviii–xxi.

Case study problems

The fourth edition has 18 new cases alongside four cases retained from the third edition, so 22 teaching cases in all! These cases were written by our European (and one Australian) colleagues who teach and research consumer behaviour. The case material covers various companies (e.g. IKEA; Tuborg; BMW and the Mini car), industries (e.g. the Portuguese port wine industry, the Turkish leisure industry, the Danish beer industry, the Finnish beauty products industry; and the UK telecommunications and funeral industries) and countries (e.g. Denmark, Finland, France, Germany, Greece, Portugal, Sweden, Spain, Turkey and the UK). The cases integrate the topics covered in the preceding chapters, and appear at the end of each Part. The questions at the end of each case study are designed to allow you to apply your understanding to real-life events and consumer behaviour activities; to develop your analytical skills; and to facilitate understanding of the different markets and cultural contexts across Europe. The questions often invite you to draw cross-cultural comparisons with your own consumer society.

Structure of the text

The structure of this textbook is simple: **Part A** opens with an overview chapter of the book and the discipline of consumer behaviour, and then provides chapters which place *you* in our contemporary culture of consuming (Chapter 2). The third chapter in this introductory section becomes more specific about you and your consumer behaviours, and describes how you navigate the retail world in which you make so many decisions

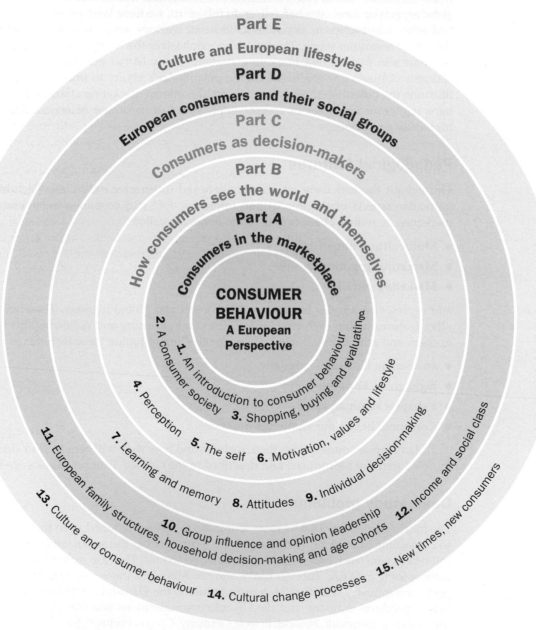

The Wheel of Consumer Behaviour

on a daily basis. In short, this opening section of the book is designed to give you a context of 'what is CB, what is consumer culture, and how do I fit into it?' The book's remaining 12 chapters move through a micro to a macro perspective on theory and applications of consumer behaviour. Think of the book as a sort of photograph album of consumer behaviour: each chapter provides a 'snapshot' of consumers, but the lens used to take each picture grows successively wider. The book begins with issues related to the individual consumer and expands its focus until it eventually considers the behaviours of large groups of people in their social settings. The topics covered correspond to the Wheel of Consumer Behaviour presented in the figure opposite.

Following the three introductory chapters, **Part B**, 'How consumers see the world and themselves' considers the consumer at the most micro level. It examines how the individual *perceives and receives* information from their immediate environment, how we use consumption as a tool in our life-long identity project of representing our *self*, and what *motives* are about (e.g. emerging new values around sustainability), and how we combine perceptions, sense of self, and motives to shape our *lifestyle(s)*.

Part C, 'Consumers as decision-makers', explores the ways in which consumers use the information they have acquired to learn and rely on memory, and to make decisions about consumption activities, both as individuals and as group members.

Part D, 'A portrait of European consumers', further expands the focus by considering how the consumer functions as a part of a larger social structure. No other consumer behaviour textbook offers as complete and up-to-date materials on the consumers of the EU-27 in this section (and the next). This structure includes the influence of different social groups to which the consumer belongs and/or identifies with, featuring social class, family, and age groups.

Finally, **Part E**, 'Culture and European lifestyles', completes the picture as it examines marketing's impact on mass culture. This discussion focuses on the relationship of marketing to the expression of cultural values and lifestyles, how products and services are related to rituals and cultural myths, and the interface between marketing efforts and the creation of art, music, and other forms of popular culture that are so much a part of our daily lives. It also includes a section on major cultural change processes, analyzed from the perspectives of globalization and postmodernism, and concludes by sketching in consumers' lives in the wider Europe.

Guided tour

4

Perception

Fabienne is a 35-year-old mother of two and works at the French National Railway Company's headquarters in Lyon Part Dieu. Twice a week she uses her two-hour lunch break to go to the nearby shopping centre, the biggest in Lyons. Today she had just two things in mind: a quick bite to eat and a present for her son, Georges-Hubert. As she enters the shopping centre she is immediately drawn to the appetizing aroma of pizza coming from a nearby fast food restaurant. She decides to stop and buy a slice and a small bottle of mineral water. Next she decides to go to a shop called Nature et Découvertes, a French firm following the style of the Californian Nature Company. She has never been there before, but Catherine, her 14-year-old daughter, says that all her friends are talking about it. It seems to be the perfect place to buy a small microscope for Georges-Hubert's birthday.

On entering the shop she is very surprised. As in all shops her eyes are immediately and highly stimulated, but what makes this shop different is that there is more to it than that: all five of her senses are appealed to. The background music lets Fabienne discover birdsong, the sound of the forest, nature itself. As she is able to handle the products, Fabienne can familiarize herself with new shapes, new materials. An appeal is also made to her sense of taste when she is offered a cup of herbal tea. Finally, the natural aromas from the woods and plants combined with synthetic aromatics recreate the delicious atmosphere of the undergrowth to appeal to her sense of smell.

Fabienne likes the shop very much and for half an hour loses all sense of time. She wanders round as if in a trance. When she finally goes to the cash desk she realizes that not only does she have the little microscope in her hands, but a candle as well, and a book on trees.

PATRICK HETZEL, University of Paris II, Panthéon-Assas

Opening vignette
Each chapter opens with a short, country-specific illustrative scenario, setting the scene for the chapter material and highlighting the interrelationships between the individual and his or her social realities.

PERSPECTIVES ON THE SELF

In the influential cyberpunk novel *Snow Crash*, author Neal Stephenson envisioned a virtual world, called the *Metaverse*, as a successor to the Internet. In the Metaverse, everyday people take on glamorous identities in a three-dimensional immersive digital world. The book's main character delivers pizza in RL, but in the Metaverse, he is a warrior prince and champion sword fighter.[30] The hugely popular *Matrix* movie trilogy paints a similar (though more sinister) picture of a world that blurs the lines between physical and digital reality.[31]

Today these fictional depictions come to life as we witness the tremendous growth of real-time, interactive virtual worlds that allow people to assume virtual identities in cyberspace. More than 9 million people worldwide belong to the virtual world of *Second Life*, more than 8 million play the online game *World of Warcraft*, and one-third of Korean adults belong to *CyWorld*. Add to that the millions more who play *The Sims Online* or who visit other computer-mediated environments (CMEs) such as *Webkinz*, *There*, *Whyville*, *Entropia Universe*, MTV's *Virtual Laguna Beach* (www.mtv.com/dyn/laguna_beach/vtb.jhtml) and so on and you are looking at a lot of serious role-playing.

On these sites people assume visual identities, or avatars, ranging from realistic versions of themselves to tricked-out versions with 'exaggerated' physical characteristics or winged dragons or superheroes. Researchers are just starting to investigate how these online selves will influence consumer behaviour and how the identities we choose in CMEs relate to our RL (or 'meat-world') identities. Already we know that when people take on avatar forms, they tend to interact with other avatars much as their meat-world selves interact with other RL people. For example, just as in the RL, males in *Second Life* leave more space between them when talking to other males versus females and they are less likely to maintain eye contact than females are. And when avatars get very close to one another, they tend to look away from each other – the norms of the RL are creeping into the virtual world.[32]

Consumer behaviour as I see it . . .

Interactive technologies have had a profound influence on consumer behaviour. Many people have found the WWW, which is essentially a medium of text and 2D images, sufficiently compelling to form social networks via e-mail, instant messaging, chatrooms, etc. They browse, they shop, they exchange information, develop meaningful relationships and worldwide cyber communities. So imagine the possibilities as we look toward the 3D Web, where Websites become enriched 3D virtual spaces within which digital representations of users, also known as avatars, can interact with others.

As avatars, we can represent ourselves in almost any way we choose, changing gender, skin colour, shape and even species at will. We may question that avatars are 'ushers of a post-human era' (Meadows, 2008) but through them we can explore new identities, new worlds and play any number of possible (or even impossible) selves, mixing fantasy and reality. I am excited by the potential and questions posed for consumer research. The sense of presence invoked by the immersive avatar experience is capable of producing reactions in participants similar to the real world, so throwing into sharp relief the drivers of behaviour and self-representation.

Kathy Keeling
Manchester Business
School, Manchester, UK

If we actively use clothes, appearance and possessions to construct and symbolize self and identity in the offline world, we should not be surprised that digital goods are used in the same way. But we have a limited understanding of how they are used in virtual worlds, as the technology offers boundless behavioural possibilities. Moreover, what is rare is valuable; the value of digital goods may be based on the difficulty of creation (programing/scripting) and so differ markedly from actual goods. Research questions arise on three fronts. First, issues of personal representation and identity. Humans are nothing if not social beings;

147

New to this edition
The **Consumer behaviour as I see it** feature asks leading academics to comment on key consumer behaviour theory, adding a valuable alternative viewpoint.

Marketing opportunity boxes show how consumer research informs marketing strategy, and the actual or potential application of consumer behaviour concepts by marketing practitioners.

Marketing pitfall boxes bring to life possible marketing situations or dilemmas that might arise due to cultural differences or lack of knowledge.

Multicultural dimensions boxes highlight cultural differences in consumer behaviour across countries and continents to drive home diversity across the globe.

Guided tour continued

Over 80 **Colour photographs** and company advertisements are integrated throughout the text to help bring consumer behaviour topics to life.

Consumer behaviour challenge
Each chapter ends with short, discursive-style questions to encourage critical examination of topics and issues. These can be used individually or as part of a group discussion.

Chapter summaries provide the key concepts and issues, along with a concise checklist of the topics and issues covered.

Key terms are given at the end of each chapter with page references highlighting the location of the key terms in the text.

Fully updated **Notes** at the end of each chapter provide readers with opportunities for further learning.

At the end of each part, detailed **Case studies** cover various companies, industries and countries, and integrate the topics from the preceding chapters. Questions then allow the reader to test his or her understanding against real-life events and consumer.

Case study 15

Good child, bad child: observing experiences of consumer socialization in a twenty-first century family

BEN KERRANE, Bradford University, UK

CONTEXT

Families play a large part in our lives. Indeed many decisions and purchases which we make in our adult lives are likely to be shaped and informed by our childhood experiences, and by the influence of family members. Within the family we learn to walk and talk, and how to interact with other people. We also learn about consumption in families: as children we may have been taken with our parents on many shopping trips; taught to save our pocket money and to carefully research our consumption choices; and we may have learnt how to influence the decisions of our parents and siblings. These experiences are part of the process of consumer socialization, from which we learn about consumption and acquire consumer skills. The family has therefore been described as the socialization unit, because it has such a tremendous influence on our consumption.

However, much of our current academic knowledge about families originates from research which was conducted in the 1960s and 1970s. These studies tended to concentrate on the experiences of husband and wives when collecting data. These studies also focused on nuclear families, comprising heterosexual couples who live in the same home with one or more children (biological or adopted). At the start of the twenty-first century many consumer researchers have called for family research to move beyond nuclear families.

Similarly, much of what we know about consumer socialization derives from research which was conducted some decades ago. This research characterized the family as being homogeneous, i.e. all the children in a family were believed to be treated in the same way by their parents. Earlier marketing research suggested that parents adopt a uniform socialization style and communication pattern when dealing with all their children.

The family story below paints a rather different picture of how children experience their family environments; and hints at some of the changes in our understanding of life in family settings.*

The name of this family and of the individual family members are fictional.

THE BALDWIN FAMILY STORY

Carole and Ray Baldwin got married two years ago. Before this they had spent several years cohabiting. They met following the death of Carole's first husband and the breakdown of Ray's first marriage. Carole and Ray both have children from their first marriages. Ray has two non-resident children, Jamie and Andrew, who live with their mother. Carole has four children from her first marriage; three are now fully-grown adults (George, Kathy and Marie) and live away from the family home. Carole's fourth child, Jessica (aged fourteen), lives with Carole and Ray in the new family home alongside Carole and Ray's biological child, Nina (aged five).

Carole and Ray have very different opinions of Jessica and Nina. Whilst Nina is clearly the apple of her parents' eyes, Jessica is often ostracized by her mother and stepfather, and she is frequently excluded from many family activities. As Carole comments, the couple believe that they have 'a good child [Nina] and a bad child [Jessica]', with Ray going even further, claiming that 'it's not a bad child; it's a pain in the arse child'. The roles of stepparents can be very unclear, and this seems to be the case for the Baldwin family with Ray adopting a disengaged parenting style towards his stepdaughter, Jessica. Ray chooses instead to spend much of his time with Nina, his biological daughter. For example, Ray and Nina are beginning to learn Spanish together after school.

Jessica is very aware of her mother's and her stepfather's favourable opinions of Nina. Jessica reckons that Nina 'doesn't have to ask for things off Mum, she just gets them'. The ways in which Jessica and Nina attempt to ask for things and influence their parents' behaviour, therefore differs dramatically. Jessica adopts a range of influence strategies in attempts to get her own way. These include the use of deal making, crying, and refusing to eat until she gets what she wants. Nina, in contrast, does not need to go to such great lengths.

In view of her parents' opinions, Jessica faces considerable parental resistance to her influence strategies. As a result she often uses violence and issues threats to try and get what she wants. She has realized that she stands little success in influencing her parents when she acts alone. Jessica realizes she needs to have Nina as an ally in her attempts to influence Carole and Ray. Nina, on the other hand, does not need to deploy such influence strategies. Her requests are regularly granted with minimal parental resistance. Ray, in particular, often buys Nina expensive products, much to her half-sister's annoyance. Indeed, Nina's consumption strategies differ from Jessica's, as she does not even need to ask for things. Carole and Ray often anticipate her desire for products, and purchase items for her without Nina having to instigate the process. For instance, Carole and Ray recently purchased a new mobile phone for Nina even though Jessica had been constantly asking for one for weeks before. Nina did not even ask to be bought a mobile phone. As Ray commented: 'No, Nina didn't ask for it, it was our treat. Jessica had been on at me for ages to get her one, but she goes about asking for things the wrong way. Nina just doesn't ask for things, but Jessica's like a dripping tap, and she goes on and on at you.'

Carole and Ray act as the gatekeepers of Nina and Jessica's consumption, having the ability to pay for what the children want. Carole and Ray are also therefore the recipients of their daughters' respective influence strategies, because they have the power (and money) to grant or reject their daughters' influence attempts. The relationship that the parents have with Nina and Jessica largely determines the success of the influence strategies the girls use. Realizing that alone she stands little chance of influencing her parents' decisions, Jessica recruits Nina to help her get what she wants, forming a coalition with Nina. The family recalled one occasion when Jessica wanted to purchase a toy that connected to Jessica's Sony PlayStation. Individually Jessica could not afford the toy. Jessica recognized that she would not be able to persuade her parents by herself to buy it for her. Jessica subsequently persuaded Nina to contribute towards the cost (even though Nina initially showed no interest in the product) to ensure that Jessica got the toy that she wanted. Realizing that Carole and Ray would not reject the wishes of their younger favourite daughter, and with Nina working as an intermediary for Jessica's influence strategy, Jessica got the toy that she wanted with minimal parental resistance.

Jessica, aware that her mother and stepfather spend a larger proportion of their time with her half-sister than with her, spends a great deal of time with her own friends. Consequently Jessica is often away from the family home. When Jessica is at home she spends a great deal of her time on the family computer, logged in to online chat rooms where she talks to her friends and surfs the Internet. For Jessica, her friends act as an important reference group, and they are often the source of lots of consumer information and advice. Whereas Nina is taken on shopping trips and on family days out, is involved and has an input in decisions relating to her family's consumption (particularly in terms of where they go on holiday), Jessica does not. The family, therefore, appears to be very important in Nina's consumer socialization, but plays a much less dominant role in Jessica's consumer socialization. This is perhaps not entirely surprising given Jessica's age, with adolescents often seeking consumption advice from their peers instead of their parents as it is rather uncool to be too closely associated with one's family's opinions and views as a teenager.

QUESTIONS

1 Jessica and Nina experience different environments within the family home. How and why? Identify and evaluate the features which distinguish the two environments experienced by Jessica and Nina.

2 How did the different treatment of Jessica and Nina affect their success in deploying influence strategies? How might their different experiences affect their consumer socialization?

3 Reflecting on your own family experiences, did your parents treat you and your siblings in a similar way? What influence strategies did you use to influence your parents/guardians? Do you think that these were effective, and if so, why?

4 How far can families be characterized as offering a homogeneous environment to children?

5 How far can the family be described as the socialization unit? Using evidence from the case, and elsewhere, justify your answer.

6 Why should marketers be interested in understanding family decision making, and in particular child consumers?

7 Traditional family decision making models assume that families have a nuclear family form.
(a) What impact might 'alternative' families have on such models?
(b) What role may other family members play in shaping family decision making and the socialization of children?

Further reading

Carlson, L., and Grossbart, S. (1988), 'Parent style and consumer socialization of children', Journal of Consumer Research, vol. 15: 77–94.

Carlson, L., Walsh, A., Laczniak, R.N., and Grossbart, S. (1994), 'Family communication patterns and marketplace motivations, attitudes, and behaviours of children and mothers', The Journal of Consumer Affairs, vol. 28(1): 25–53.

Gevens, M., Mast, G., and Pelsmacker, P. (2002), 'Children's influence on family purchase behaviour: The role of family structure', Asia Pacific Advances in Consumer Research, vol. 5: 130–135.

Acknowledgements

Many of our colleagues from the business world as well as from universities throughout Europe and beyond have made significant contributions to previous editions of this book by helping us identify important issues, and helping us think through them more clearly. We are grateful for their support, enthusiasm, and their willingness to share their knowledge with us. In addition, numerous colleagues developed European case materials and chapter-opening vignettes for this text, or provided valuable comments and feedback in the market research process and reviewing of manuscript drafts. To them, our special thanks:

Emma N. Banister, *Lancaster University, UK*

Carlos Ballesteros, *Universidad Pontificia Comillas, Madrid, Spain*

Suzanne C. Beckmann, *Copenhagen Business School, Denmark*

Kok Hoi Beh, *De Montfort University, Leicester, UK*

Russell W. Belk, *University of Utah, USA*

Matthias Bode, *University of Southern Denmark, Denmark*

Carlos Brito, *University of Porto, Portugal*

Marylyn Carrigan, *Open University, UK*

Janeen Arnold Costa, *Emerita, York University, Canada*

Teresa Davis, *University of Sydney, Australia*

Hanna-Kaisa Desavelle, *Tampere University of Technology, Finland*

Mandy Dixon, *Lancaster University, UK*

Basil Englis, *Berry College, Georgia, USA*

Burçak Ertimur, *University of California, Irvine, USA*

Jim Freund, *Lancaster University, UK*

Güliz Ger, *Bilkent University, Ankara, Turkey*

Andrea Groeppel-Klein, *University of Saarland, Germany*

Lampros Gkiouzepas, *Amaretto Group & Technological Educational Institute of Thessaloniki, Greece*

Patrick Hetzel, *University of Paris II, Panthéon-Assas, France*

Sally Hibbert, *Nottingham University Business School, UK*

Robert J.W. Hogg, *Bloomberg, London, UK*

Kalipso M. Karantinou, *Athens University of Economics and Business, Greece*

Kathy Keeling, *University of Manchester, UK*

Ben Kerrane, *Bradford University, UK*

Dannie Kjeldgaard, *University of Southern Denmark, Denmark*

Pauline Maclaran, *Royal Holloway College, University of London, UK*

Morven G. McEachern, *Lancaster University, UK*

Ilona Mikkonen, *Helsinki School of Economics, Finland*

Johanna Moisander, *Helsinki School of Economics, Finland*

Gabriele Morello, *GMA-Gabriele Morello and Associates, Palermo, Italy*

Stephanie O'Donohoe, *University of Edinburgh, Scotland*

Şahver Ömeraki, *Bilkent University, Ankara, Turkey*

Stijn van Osselaer, *Erasmus University, The Netherlands*

Jacob Östberg, *Stockholm University, Sweden*

Connie Pechmann, *University of California, Irvine, USA*

Lisa Peñaloza, *EDHEC, France*

Maria G. Piacentini, *Lancaster University, UK*

Linda Price, *University of Arizona, USA*

Effi Raftopoulou, *Keele University, UK*
Diego Rinallo, *Bocconi University, Milan, Italy*
Joonas Rokka, *Helsinki School of Economics, Finland*
Dominique Roux, *Université Paris 12, France*
Özlem Sandikci, *Bilkent University, Ankara, Turkey*
Tanja Schneider, *Oxford University, UK*
Jonathan Schroeder, *Exeter University, UK*
Laura Sierra, *Universidad Pontificia Comillas, Madrid, Spain*
Diana Storm, *University of Southern Denmark, Odense, Denmark*
Peter Svensson, *Lund University, Sweden*
Darach Turley, *Dublin City University, Ireland*
Sofia Ulver-Sneistrup, *Lund University, Sweden*
Carmelina Vela, *Universidad Pontificia Comillas, Madrid, Spain*
Alan Warde, *University of Manchester, UK*

We would also like to express our sincere thanks to our students in Denmark, the Netherlands and the UK who have proved to be valuable sources of ideas and examples throughout our work on this text. Special thanks, as well, to our Research Assistant, Laura Vallance (Lancaster University), for her expertise in identifying up-to-date material for the book; and also to Laura Salciuviene for her contributions to the online materials. Thanks also to our friends and colleagues at Syddansk Universitet, Odense Universitet, the Vrije Universiteit, Amsterdam, Georgetown University, and Lancaster University Management School for their support and inspiration throughout this project.

Gary, Søren and Margaret want to offer a special and personal word of thanks to Mike Solomon. While we were busy getting together the materials for this fourth European edition, Mike was already working hard on the manuscript for the eighth edition of *Consumer Behavior*. He shared materials with us as soon as they were ready, providing us with a pace and structure which kept us focused and on schedule! Mike was the perfect senior author – there when we needed something from him, and otherwise a positive source of energy and enthusiasm, coming from a comfortable distance. Ultimately, a great deal of synergy developed in our work together. We ended up sharing new materials, sources of research, and ideas in a mutual process of give and take. Thanks for giving us this opportunity to work with you, Mike.

Gary Bamossy would like to thank Anne Marie Parlevliet in Amsterdam for her excellent desk research on developments in The Netherlands and the EU. A special thanks to Janeen, Joost, Lieke and Jason – whose world views and consumption practices continue to amaze, amuse, inspire, and enlighten him. Søren Askegaard would like to thank Steen and Niels, his favourite fellow consumers, who perpetually tempted him to engage in a variety of leisurely consumption activities instead of revising this book. Margaret Hogg would like to say a very sincere 'thank you' to her sons, Daniel and Robert, and to her late husband, Richard, for their generous, unstinting and loving support since she started this project.

Finally, we would like to thank David Cox, our Acquisitions Editor, and the rest of the Pearson Education team for their understanding, support and guidance during this revision.

Publisher's acknowledgements

We are grateful to the following for permission to reproduce copyright material:

Figures

Figure 2.2 from Venkatesh, A., 'Ethnoconsumerism: A New Paradigm to Study Cultural and Cross-Cultural Consumer Behaviour', in J.A. Costa and G. Bamossy, eds, Marketing in a Multicultural World, copyright © 1995 by Sage Publications. Reprinted by permission of Sage Publications; Figure 3.7 from Venkatesh, A. (1998) 'Cybermarketscapes and Consumer Freedoms and Identities', European Journal of Marketing 32 (7/8), 664–76, used with permission; Figure 6.5 from Nielsen, N.A., Bech-Larsen, T. and Grunert, K.G. (1998) 'Consumer Purchase Motives and Product Perceptions: A Laddering Study on Vegetable Oil in Three Countries', *Food Quality and Preference* 9(6), 455–66, with permission from Elsevier Science; Figure 9.1 from http://www.eaca.be/_upload/documents %5CMedia%20Consumption%20in%20EU%2025%20updated.pdf, nVision/Future Foundation; Figure 9.2 from *Journal of Personality and Social Psychology*, 1980, 38, 311–22. Copyright © 1980 by the American Psychological Association. Adapted with permission. Figure 9.14 from Stobbe, L., 2 August 2007, Fraunhofer Institute for Reliability and Microintegration IZM, http://www.izm.fraunhofer.de/EN/ About/index.jsp, Preparatory Studies "Televisions" (Lot 5) Final Report on Task 3 "Consumer Behaviour and Local Infrastructure" (TREN/D1/40 lot 5-2005); Figure 10.5 adapted from Feick, L. and Price, L. (1987) 'The Market Maven: A Diffuser of Market-place Information', *Journal of Marketing* 51 (January), 83–7; Figure 14.4 based on Mick, D.G., DeMoss, M. and Faber, R.J. (1990) *Latent Motivations and Meanings of Self-Gifts*, research report, Centre of Retailing Education and Research, University of Florida; Figure 15.13 adapted from Peñalosa, L. (1994) Atravesando Fronteras/Border Crossings: A Critical Ethnographic Exploration of the Consumer Acculturation of Mexican Immigrants, *Journal of Consumer Research* 21 (June), 32–54; Figure 15.4 from Dominated Consumer Acculturation: The Social Construction of Migrant Women's Consumer Identity Projects in a Turkish Squatter, *Journal of Consumer Research*, 34, 53 (Ustuner, T. and Holt, D.B. 2007), © University of Chicago Press. The University is not responsible for the accuracy of the translation from English.

Tables

Table 2.1 adapted from Trusting, Complex, Quality Conscious or Unprotected? Constructing the Food Consumer in Different European National Contexts, *Journal of Consumer Culture*, 7, 379–402 (Halkier, B. *et al.* 2007), Bente Halkier, Lotte Holm, Mafalda Domingues, Paolo Magaudda, Annemette Nielsen, Laura Terragni, Journal of Consumer Culture (Vol. 7, Issue Number 3), pp. 379–402, copyright © 2007 by SAGE publications. Reprinted by permission of SAGE; Table 3.1 from http://www. retail-index.com/HomeSearch/RetailinEuropedatabaseEnglish/FoodRetailersinEuropeandworldwide.aspx, Veraart Research; Table 8.1 from An investigation of the relationships between beliefs about an object and the attitude toward that object, *Human Relations*, 16, 233–40 (Fishbein, M. 1963), Fishbein, M., Human Relations (16) pp. 233–40, copyright © SAGE publications 1963. Reprinted by permission of SAGE; Table 9.2 from Bloch, P.H., Sherell, D.L. and Ridgway, N. (1986) 'Consumer Research: An Extended Framework', *Journal of Consumer Research* 13 (June), 120; Table 9.3 from On the psychology of Loss Aversion: Possession, Valence and Reversals of the Endowment Effect, *Journal of Consumer Research*, 34, Table 1370 (Brenner, L., Rottenstreich, Y., Sood, S. and Bilgin, B. 2007), © University of Chicago Press. The University is not responsible for the accuracy of the translation from English; Tables 9.6 and 9.7 from http://www.ft.com/cms/s/0/abdf3546-0cf4-11dd-86df-0000779fd2ac.html, © Millward Brown Optimor (including data from BrandZ, Datamonitor and Bloomberg); Table 10.1 adapted from Whan Park, C. and Parker Lessig, V. (1977) 'Students and Housewives: Differences in Susceptibility to Reference Group Influence', Journal of Consumer Research 4 (September), 102; Table 11.1 adapted from Gilly, M.C. and Enis, B.M. (1982) 'Recycling the Family Life Cycle: A Proposal for Redefinition' in A.A. Mitchell, (ed.) *Advances in Consumer Research*, 9, 274; Table 13.1 from Rook, D.W. (1985) 'The Ritual Dimension of Consumer Behaviour', *Journal of Consumer Research* 12 (December), 251–64; Table 14.2 from Ruth, J.A., Otnes, C.C. and Brunel, F.F. (1999) 'Gift Receipt and the reformulation of interpersonal relationships' Journal of Consumer Research 25 (March), 385–402; Table 14.4 from Bottled Water: The Pure Commodity in the Age of Branding, *Journal of Consumer Culture*, 6, 304 (Wilk, R. 2006), Richard Wilk, Journal of Consumer Culture (Vol. 6, Issue Number 3) p. 304 copyright 2006 © by SAGE publications. Reprinted by permission of SAGE; Table 14.5 from Foxhall, G.R. and Bhate, S. (1993) 'Cognitive Style and Personal Involvement as Explicators of Innovative Purchasing of Health Food Brands', *European Journal of*

Marketing, 27(2), 5–16, MCB UP Ltd.; Table 15.5 from Davison, J.A. and Grab, E. (1993) 'The Contributions of Advertising Testing to the Development of Effective International Advertising: The KitKat Case Study' Marketing and Research Today (February), 15–24, GfK AG Germany; Figures on pages 361 to 363 by permission of BT.

Text

Article on page 218 from E-commerce: EBay changes aim for fewer critics and more sellers *The Guardian*, 20 August 2008 (Gibson, O.), Copyright Guardian News & Media Ltd. 2008; Article on pages 600–1 from Once bitten . . . The science of nanotechnology, 26 March 2008 (Boggan, S.); Article on page 590 from Consumers hold key to securing the net, 4 July 2008 (Pritchard, S.), Copyright Guardian News & Media Ltd. 2008.

The Financial Times

Article on page 617 from Valley view: The IT world pokes its head in the cloud, 9 July 2008 (Nuttall, C.); Article on pages 590–1 from Staying connected: Technology on holiday, 8 August 2008 (Taylor, P.).

In some instances we have been unable to trace the owners of copyright material, and we would appreciate any information that would enable us to do so.

Picture Credits

The publisher would like to thank the following for their kind permission to reproduce their photographs:

(Key: b-bottom; c-centre; l-left; r-right; t-top)

www.adbusters.org: 51; Advertising Savants: 550; Alamy Images: Martin Dalton 399; Stockfolio 217; OnWhite 422; AT&T Archives and History Centre; Bianco Footwear Danmark A/S: 149; BooneOakley Advertising: 133; Campbell Soup Company: 124; Canal/ACB-Contrapunto BBDO Ad Agency: 516t; Caroline Penhoat: 516b; Carte bleue: 477; Church & Dwight Co., Inc.: 322; Corbis: Image Source 215; CHARLES JEAN MARC/CORBIS SYGMA 73r; Danny Lehman 594; James Leynse 313l; Richard T. Nowitz 313r; Mark Peterson 606; Neal Preston 531; Arnd Wiegmann/Reuters 73l; SIME 79; David Cox: 565; Diesel S.p.A.: 564; DiMassimo, Inc.: 202; Gary Bamossy: 279, 434; Getty Images: 388, 591; AFP 16, 122, 197; Carl Schneider 408; M.N. Chan 45; Taxi/Getty Images 521; Goldsmith/Jeffrey and Bodyslimmers: 156; Google, Inc.: 406; Hewlett-Packard Development Company, L.P.: 69; IAC Search and Media, Inc. 2009. All rights reserved: 342; Ilan Rubin, D'Adda, Lorenzini Vigorelli, BBDO S.p.A.: 153; Jacek Wolowski, Grey Worldwide Warszawa: 346b; Junta Islamica: 240; iParty Corp: 343; Maidenform, Inc.: 562; Courtesy: Mary Boone Gallery, New York: Copyright: Barbara Kruger 1987, 60; Oliver Toscani, Benetton Group S.p.A.: 119; Peter Byron/Photo Researchers, Inc.: 84; Procter & Gamble Nederland B.V.: 123; Professor Robert Kozinets: 208; Michael Corridore: 64; Robson Brown Advertising: 547; Saga Publishing Ltd.: 443; S,C,P,F . . . , Patricia Luján, Carlitos. Photo: Biel Capllonch: 579; Sunkist Growers Inc. Sunkist is a registered trademark of © 2005 Sunkist Growers, Inc., Sherman Oaks, CA 91923, USA. All rights reserved: 125; Susan Goldman/The Image Works/TopFoto: 390; Swisspatat: 193; Tesco Stores Ltd.: 75; The Advertising Archives: 41, 42, 43, 52, 63, 68, 126, 136, 158, 161, 163, 168, 178, 180, 181, 184, 200, 213, 217, 252, 255, 265, 267, 298, 300, 301, 303, 333, 339, 346, 347t, 386t, 394, 398, 435, 465, 514, 602; The University of Miami, from Page-Wood, E.S., Kaufman, C.J. and Lane, P.M. (1990) 'The Art of Time', Proceedings of the Academy of Marketing Science © Academy of Marketing Science: 70; Toyota Singapore and Saatchi & Saatchi Ltd.: 254; United States Postal Service. USPS Corporate Signature is a trademark owned by the United States Postal Service. Used with permission. All rights reserved: 316; Volkswagen Group: 368; Volswagen of the Netherlands: 216; Volkswagen of South Africa: 63; Jan Burwick, the German National Committee for UNICEF and Springer & Jacoby Fuenfte Werbeagentur GmbH & Co. KG: 20; American Association of Advertising Agencies: 21.

All other images © Pearson Education.

Picture Research by: Debra Weatherley

Every effort has been made to trace the copyright holders and we apologise in advance for any unintentional omissions. We would be pleased to insert the appropriate acknowledgement in any subsequent edition of this publication.

About the authors

Michael R. Solomon, Ph.D., joined the Haub School of Business at Saint Joseph's University in Philadelphia as Professor of Marketing in 2006, where he also serves as Director of the Center for Consumer Research. From 1995 to 2006, he was the Human Sciences Professor of Consumer Behavior at Auburn University. Prior to joining Auburn he was Chairman of the Department of Marketing in the School of Business at Rutgers University, New Brunswick, New Jersey.

Professor Solomon's primary research interests include consumer behaviour and lifestyle issues, branding strategy, the symbolic aspects of products, the psychology of fashion, decoration and image, services marketing, and the development of visually oriented online research methodologies. He currently sits on the Editorial Boards of the *Journal of Consumer Behaviour*, the *European Business Review*, and the *Journal of Retailing*, and he recently completed a six-year term on the Board of Governors of the Academy of Marketing Science.

In addition to this book, he is also the co-author of the widely used textbook *Marketing: Real People, Real Decisions*. Professor Solomon frequently appears on television and radio shows such as *The Today Show*, *Good Morning America*, Channel One, The Wall Street Journal Radio Network, and National Public Radio to comment on consumer behaviour and marketing issues.

Gary J. Bamossy, Ph.D., is Professor of Marketing at the McDonough School of Business, Georgetown University, in Washington D.C. From 1985 to 1999 he was on the Faculty of Business and Economics at the Vrije Universiteit, Amsterdam, as *Hoogleraar, Marktkunde* (Professor of Marketing), and Director of Business Research for the VU's participation at the Tinbergen Research Institute. Prior to his appointment at Georgetown, he was Director of the Global Business Program and a member of the marketing faculty at the University of Utah (1999–2005).

Professor Bamossy's primary research interests are on the global diffusion of material culture, and on sustainable consumption. He has published numerous articles on these and related topics in academic journals and as chapters in research books. He has given invited lectures on materialism and sustainable consumption issues at universities, companies, and government agencies in North America, Europe, and Asia, and his work has been funded by the Dutch Science Foundation (KNAW), the Marketing Science Institute, the Davidson Institute (University of Michigan) and the Anglo-Dutch Scholar Forum. Together with Prof. W.F. van Raaij, Dr Bamossy co-chaired the first European conference for the Association for Consumer Research, in Amsterdam. For the past several years, Dr Bamossy has served as an Invited Member by The Bank of Sweden, to nominate a candidate for the Nobel Memorial Prize in Economic Sciences.

Professor Bamossy is a frequent contributor to the mass media. His research has been quoted or written about in the *Wall Street Journal Europe*, *The Washington Post*, *The Los Angeles Times*, *The Atlanta Journal Constitution*, The Associated Press, National Public Radio, CBS Television, *Fox News*, and CBS Radio.

Søren Askegaard entered the atmosphere the same year as Yuri Gagarin left it. After wanting to be a postman for most of his childhood, he is now Professor of Marketing at the University of Southern Denmark. He has a postgraduate Diploma in Communication Studies from the Sorbonne University, Paris and Ph.D. in Business Studies from Odense University, 1993.

He served as head of the Department of Marketing at the University of Southern Denmark from 2003 to 2005, and he remains director of the BSc and MSc programmes of international business and modern languages at the university.

Professor Askegaard has given invited lectures at universities in Europe, North America, Asia and Latin America. He has served on a dozen programme committees for scientific conferences and been the co-organizer of the 2003 Cross-Cultural Research Conference in Jamaica, and the 2007 Conference on Consumer Behaviour and Marketing Communications in La Londe, France. He has been visiting professor at the following universities for shorter or longer periods of time: Bilkent University, Turkey, ESSEC, Université de Savoie, ESC Clermont-Ferrand

and Université de Lille 2, France and Lund University, Sweden. In the USA, he has been a Fulbright scholar at the University of California, Irvine, and a distinguished visiting professor at Suffolk University, Boston.

Professor Askegaard is currently associate editor at *The Journal of Consumer Research*, the leading scientific journal for research in consumer behaviour. He also serves on the editorial boards for four other journals. His research has been published in numerous international journals and anthologies. For his research accomplishment he has received three research awards, including the Danish Marketing Association's Research Award.

He co-founded the research-business collaboration network *Brand Base*, which organizes collaborative events between consumer researchers and the business environment. *Brand Base* currently has more than 100 member organizations. For this he was rewarded the Danish Academy for Business research Award for communication of research to the Danish society and business community in 2008. He also serves as the honorary consul of France in Odense, Denmark.

His research has been widely quoted by the mass media in Denmark, where he is a frequent commentator on consumer and market issues. His research has also been featured in the Swedish media and on BBC4.

Professor Askegaard's research interests generally are in the field of consumer culture theory and commercial symbolism. He is generally interested in debunking what is known as 'common sense', and he likes to act as a 'Martian' in his own society (as well as other societies), in order to catch a glimpse of all the funny little – and not-so-little – things we do (and consume!), while thinking that it is 'perfectly normal'.

Margaret K. Hogg holds the Chair of Consumer Behaviour and Marketing in the Department of Marketing at Lancaster University Management School (LUMS). She read for an M.A. (Hons.) in Politics and Modern History at Edinburgh University; postgraduate studies in History at the Vrije Universiteit, Amsterdam; an M.A. in Business Analysis at Lancaster University; and a Ph.D. in Consumer Behaviour and Retailing at Manchester Business School. She worked for six years in marketing with 'K Shoes' in Kendal. She spent eight years at Manchester School of Management (MSM), UMIST before moving to LUMS in May 2004.

Professor Hogg's main areas of research interests are around the issues of identity, self and consumption within consumer behaviour. Her work has appeared in refereed journals including the *Journal of Advertising* (forthcoming), *Journal of Business Research, Journal of Marketing Management, European Journal of Marketing, International Journal of Advertising, Journal of Services Marketing, Journal of Consumer Policy, Marketing Management Journal, Advances in Consumer Research and Consumption, Markets and Culture*. She edited six volumes of papers on Consumer Behaviour in the Sage Major Works series (2005 and 2006) and has co-authored numerous book chapters. Professor Hogg regularly presents papers at international conferences including European Marketing Academy (EMAC), US, European and Asia-Pacific meetings of the Association for Consumer Research (ACR), the Society for Consumer Psychology (SCP) and AMA Marketing and Public Policy. She has given numerous seminar papers as an invited speaker (e.g. in Australia, New Zealand and Europe). She is a regular reviewer for the UK Economic and Social Research Council (ESRC) and for the Social Sciences and Humanities Research Council of Canada, as well as for the *Journal of Consumer Culture, Journal of Consumer Research, European Journal of Marketing, Journal of International Business Studies, Services Industry Journal, International Marketing Review, International Journal of Bank Marketing, International Journal of New Product Design and Innovation Management*. She has been on the conference programme committees for US and European meetings of the Association for Consumer Research (ACR).

Professor Hogg currently holds an award under the French Agence Nationale de la Recherche (ANR/Programme Blanc) for two studies as part of Professor Dominique Roux's (Paris XII) project on New Approaches to Consumer Resistance (NACRE). She has taught extensively on consumer behaviour at undergraduate and postgraduate level, and supervised and examined a wide range of Ph.D. students.

Consumers in the marketplace

This introductory part comprises three chapters. The first chapter previews much of what this book is about and gives an overview of the field of consumer behaviour. It examines how the field of marketing is influenced by the actions of consumers, and also how we as consumers are influenced by marketers. It also surveys consumer behaviour as a discipline of enquiry, and describes some of the different approaches that researchers use in order better to understand what makes consumers behave as they do. The second chapter takes a look at contemporary consumer culture and, more particularly, its globalization tendencies. It digs deeper into how marketing and culture are intertwined in contemporary societies and raises the important issue of the meaning of consumer goods for consumers. The third chapter looks at the consumer in the marketplace, through its investigation of the modern ritual of the shopping process. It also looks at various contemporary retail environments, and the roles they play in consumers' social lives.

1

An introduction to consumer behaviour

Nathalie is working at her computer. It is early autumn and the beginning of a new term at her Danish university. Time for getting new books and study materials. As a second-year student, she is not surprised to find that several of the required books are still unavailable at the campus bookshop.

She goes online to check if she can get her books from one of the Internet bookshops. She uses her favourite portal (**www.jubii.dk**) to check out the Scandinavian bookshops, which she thinks might be able to deliver the books faster than their international competitors. None of them have all of the books in stock that she needs, and she really feels that she should get all of the books from the same store. On an impulse, Nathalie visits a student shop which sells used books and provides search facilities for Barnes & Noble. She searches for a couple of the titles she is looking for, but the search facility does not seem to work. For a moment, she considers putting some of her used books up for sale, then decides not to let herself be distracted, and moves on to the UK version of **Amazon.com**. She has heard from friends that prices are a little steeper here (relative to the other internet bookshops), but she knows this site well by now. Besides, the books she wants are in stock and can be delivered in about a week, maybe less. Considering that the chances of the books she needs appearing in the campus bookshop on time seem pretty slim, Nathalie decides to go ahead and buy them now online.

While she fills out the order form, she tries to plan where to go next. She and her friend are looking for an interesting topic for a course project and she wants to look in the social science section of **www.yahoo.com** for some inspiration. Also, she wants to visit a few of her favourite sites for news, music and travel. 'A little information update before meeting the girls this afternoon for coffee,' she thinks to herself. She clicks 'OK' to her order confirmation and is glad to have that out of the way. She navigates her way to **yahoo.com** and starts her search. All the while, she is thinking to herself that it would be nice to spend a little time checking out the latest in fashion and beauty tips; a little treat to herself while she still has some time on her hands. Suddenly Nathalie remembers that there were a couple of study plans to print out from the university Website – and a few e-mails to answer. She checks her e-mail account and is a little surprised to see that she has received so much mail today – seems like everybody just realized that summer is over and wants to get started on new projects. It makes her feel joyful, even sort of invigorated . . .

DIANA STORM, University of Southern Denmark, Odense, Denmark

CONSUMPTION IN EUROPE? THE EUROPEAN CONSUMER?

This is a book about consumer behaviour, written from a European perspective. But what does that mean exactly? Obviously, to write about a 'European' consumer or a 'European's consumer behaviour' is problematic. Some of the general theory about the psychological or sociological influences on consumer behaviour may be common to all Western cultures. On the one hand, some theories may be culturally specific. Certain groups of consumers do show similar kinds of behaviour across national borders, and research on consumers in Europe suggests that we even use our understanding of the consumption environment to make sense of the foreign cultures we are visiting.[1] On the other hand, the ways in which people live their consumption life vary greatly from one European country to another, and sometimes even within different regions of the same country. As a student of consumer behaviour, you might want to ask yourself: 'In which consumption situations do I seem to have a great deal in common with fellow students from other European countries? And in what ways do I seem to resemble more closely my compatriots? In what ways do subcultures in my country exert a strong influence on my consumption patterns, and how international are these subcultures?' To add to the complexity of all this, the EU continues to expand, adding new members and now comprises 27 countries (EU-27) and 495 million consumers.[2] These 'new' European consumers come from vastly different economic and political circumstances, and each has their own unique historical and cultural development. Much more on these consumers' aspirations and consumption behaviours will be reviewed in chapters in Part D of this text, 'A portrait of European consumers'.

This book is about consumer behaviour theory in general, and we will illustrate our points with examples from various European markets as well as from the United States and other countries. Each chapter features 'Multicultural dimensions' boxes which spotlight international aspects of consumer behaviour. From both a global and a pan-European perspective, these issues will be explored in depth in Chapters 2, 13 and 14.

Consumer behaviour: people in the marketplace

You can probably relate to at least some general aspects of Nathalie's behaviour. This book is about people like Nathalie. It concerns the products and services they buy and use, and the ways these fit into their lives. This introductory chapter briefly describes some important aspects of the field of consumer behaviour, including the topics studied, who studies them, and some of the ways these issues are approached by consumer researchers.

But first, let's return to Nathalie: the sketch which started the chapter allows us to highlight some aspects of consumer behaviour that will be covered in the rest of the book.

- As a consumer, Nathalie can be described and compared to other individuals in a number of ways. For some purposes, marketers might find it useful to categorize Nathalie in terms of her age, gender, income or occupation. These are some examples of descriptive characteristics of a population, or *demographics*. In other cases, marketers would rather know something about Nathalie's interests in fashion or music, or the way she spends her leisure time. This sort of information often comes under the category *psychographics*, which refers to aspects of a person's lifestyle and personality. Knowledge of consumer characteristics plays an extremely important role in many marketing applications, such as defining the market for a product or deciding on the appropriate techniques to employ when targeting a certain group of consumers.

- Nathalie's purchase decisions are heavily influenced by the opinions and behaviours of her friends. A lot of product information, as well as recommendations to use or avoid particular brands, is picked up in conversations among real people, rather than by way of television commercials, magazines or advertising messages. The bonds among Nathalie's group of friends are in part cemented by the products they all use. There is also pressure on each group member to buy things that will meet with the group's approval, and often a price to pay in the form of group rejection or embarrassment when one does not conform to others' conceptions of what is good or bad, 'in' or 'out'.

- As a member of a large society, people share certain cultural values or strongly held beliefs about the way the world should be structured. Other values are shared by members of *subcultures*, or smaller groups within the culture, such as ethnic groups, teens, people from certain parts of the country, or even 'Hell's Angels'. The people who matter to Nathalie – her *reference group* – value the idea that women in their early twenties should be innovative, style-conscious, independent and up front (at least a little). While many marketers focus on either very young targets or the thirty-somethings, some are recognizing that another segment which is attracting marketers' interest is the rapidly growing segment of older (50+) people.[3]

- When browsing through the websites, Nathalie is exposed to many competing 'brands'. Many offerings did not grab her attention at all; others were noticed but rejected because they did not fit the 'image' with which she identified or to which she aspired. The use of *market segmentation strategies* means targeting a brand only to specific groups of consumers rather than to everybody – even if that means that other consumers will not be interested or may choose to avoid that brand.

- Brands often have clearly defined *images* or 'personalities' created by product advertising, packaging, branding and other marketing strategies that focus on positioning a product a certain way or by certain groups of consumers adopting the product. One's leisure activities in particular are very much lifestyle statements: it says a lot about what a person is interested in, as well as something about the type of person they would like to be. People often choose a product offering, a service or a place, or subscribe to a particular idea, because they like its image, or because they feel its 'personality' somehow corresponds to their own. Moreover, a consumer may believe that by buying and using the product, its desirable qualities will somehow magically 'rub off'.

- When a product succeeds in satisfying a consumer's specific needs or desires, as **http://www.amazon.co.uk** did for Nathalie, it may be rewarded with many years of *brand* or *store loyalty*, a bond between product or outlet and consumer that may be very difficult for competitors to break. Often a change in one's life situation or self-concept is required to weaken this bond and thus create opportunities for competitors.

- Consumers' evaluations of products are affected by their appearance, taste, texture or smell. We may be influenced by the shape and colour of a package, as well as by more subtle factors, such as the symbolism used in a brand name, in an advertisement, or even in the choice of a cover model for a magazine. These judgments are affected by – and often reflect – how a society feels that people should define themselves at that point in time. Nathalie's choice of a new hairstyle, for example, says something about the type of image women like her want to project. If asked, Nathalie might not be able to say exactly why she considered some websites and rejected others. Many product meanings are hidden below the surface of the packaging, the design and advertising, and this book will discuss some of the methods used by marketers and social scientists to discover or apply these meanings.

- **Amazon.co.uk** has a combined American and international image that appeals to Nathalie. A product's image is often influenced by its *country of origin*, which helps to determine its 'brand personality'. In addition, our opinions and desires are increasingly shaped by input from around the world, thanks to rapid advancements in communications and transportation systems (witness the Internet!). In today's global culture, consumers often prize products and services that 'transport' them to different locations and allow them to experience the diversity of other cultures. Clearly, the Internet has changed many young Europeans' consumer behaviours. Global music sales continues to fall, with Germany, Denmark, France, Sweden, Belgium, Greece and Ireland all having double digit decreases in sales of recorded music. While music sales fall, young European consumers seem to be searching the Internet for another form of 'shopping', with 50 per cent of 'singles' reporting visiting a dating Website at least once in the past year.[4]

▶ The field of **consumer behaviour** covers a lot of ground: it is the study of the processes involved when individuals or groups select, purchase, use or dispose of products, services, ideas or experiences to satisfy needs and desires. Consumers take many forms, ranging from a 6-year-old child pleading with her mother for wine gums to an executive in a large corporation deciding on an extremely expensive computer system. The items that are consumed can include anything from tinned beans to a massage, democracy, rap music, and even other people (the images of rock stars, for example). Needs and desires to be satisfied range from hunger and thirst to love, status or even spiritual fulfilment. There is a growing interest in consumer behaviour, not only in the field of marketing but from the social sciences in general. This follows a growing awareness of the increasing importance of consumption in our daily lives, in our organization of daily activities, in our identity formation, in politics and economic development, and in the flows of global culture, where consumer culture seems to spread, albeit in new forms, from North America and Europe to other parts of the world. This spread of consumer culture via marketing is not always well received by social critics and consumers, as we shall see in subsequent chapters.[5] Indeed, consumption can be regarded as playing such an important role in our social, psychological, economic, political and cultural lives that today it has become the 'vanguard of history'.[6]

Consumers are actors on the marketplace stage

▶ The perspective of **role theory**, which this book emphasizes, takes the view that much of consumer behaviour resembles actions in a play,[7] where each consumer has lines, props and costumes that are necessary to a good performance. Since people act out many different roles, they may modify their consumption decisions according to the particular 'play' they are in at the time. The criteria that they use to evaluate products and services in one of their roles may be quite different from those used in another role.

Another way of thinking about consumer roles is to consider the various 'plays' that the consumer may engage in. One classical role here is the consumer as a 'chooser' – somebody who, as we have seen with Nathalie, can choose between different alternatives and explores various criteria for making this choice. But the consumer can have many other things at stake than just 'making the right choice'. We are all involved in a communication system through our consumption activities, whereby we communicate our roles and statuses. We are also sometimes searching to construct our identity, our 'real selves', through various consumption activities. Or the main purpose of our consumption might be an exploration of a few of the many possibilities the market has to offer us, maybe in search of a 'real kick of pleasure'. On the more serious side, we might feel victimized by fraudulent or harmful offerings, and we may decide to take action against such risks from the marketplace by becoming active in consumer movements. Or we may react against the authority of the producers by co-opting their products, and turning them into something else, as when military boots all of a sudden became 'normal' footwear for peaceful women. We may decide to take action as 'political consumers' and boycott products from companies or countries whose behaviour does not meet our ethical or environmental standards. Hence, as consumers we can be choosers, communicators, identity-seekers, pleasure-seekers, victims, rebels and activists – sometimes simultaneously.[8]

Figure 1.1 Some issues that arise during stages in the consumption process

Consumer behaviour is a process

In its early stages of development, the field was often referred to as *buyer behaviour*, reflecting an emphasis on the interaction between consumers and producers at the time of purchase. Marketers now recognize that consumer behaviour is an ongoing *process*, not merely what happens at the moment a consumer hands over money or a credit card and in turn receives some good or service.

▶ The **exchange**, in which two or more organizations or people give and receive something of value, is an integral part of marketing.[9] While exchange remains an important part of consumer behaviour, the expanded view emphasizes the entire consumption process, which includes the issues that influence the consumer before, during and after a purchase. Figure 1.1 illustrates some of the issues that are addressed during each stage of the consumption process.

Consumer behaviour involves many different actors

A consumer is generally thought of as a person who identifies a need or desire, makes a purchase and then disposes of the product during the three stages in the consumption process. In many cases, however, different people may be involved in the process. The *purchaser* and *user* of a product may not be the same person, as when a parent chooses clothes for a teenager (and makes selections that can result in 'fashion suicide' from the teenager's point of view). In other cases, another person may act as an *influencer*, providing recommendations for (or against) certain products without actually buying or using them. For example, a friend, rather than a parent, accompanying a teenager on a shopping trip may pick out the clothes that they decide to purchase.

Finally, consumers may be organizations or groups in which one person may make the decisions involved in purchasing products that will be used by many, as when a purchasing agent orders the company's office supplies. In other organizational situations, purchase decisions may be made by a large group of people – for example, company accountants, designers, engineers, sales personnel and others – all of whom will have a say in the various stages of the consumption process. As we will see in Chapter 11, one important organization is the family, where different family members play pivotal roles in decision-making regarding products and services used by all.

CONSUMERS' IMPACT ON MARKETING STRATEGY

Surfing cool Websites is a lot of fun. But, on the more serious side, why should managers, advertisers, and other marketing professionals bother to learn about consumer behaviour?

Very simply, *understanding consumer behaviour is good business*. The basic marketing concept states that firms exist to satisfy needs. Marketers can only satisfy these needs to the extent that they understand the people or organizations who will use the products and services they are trying to sell.

Consumer response is the ultimate test of whether a marketing strategy will succeed. Thus, a marketer should incorporate knowledge about consumers into every facet of a successful marketing plan. Data about consumers help organizations to define the market and identify threats to and opportunities for a brand. And, in the wild and wacky world of marketing, nothing is forever: this knowledge also helps to ensure that the product continues to appeal to its core market.

The Sony Walkman is a good example of a successful product that needed to update its image – especially since the company faces fierce competition from the incredibly popular Apple iPod. Although Sony revolutionized the mobile music experience and sold almost 300 million Walkmans in the process, today's teens see portable cassette players as dinosaurs (assuming they have even heard of cassettes!). The company's advertising agency followed 125 teens to see how they use products in their day-to-day lives. Based on this consumer research, Sony relaunched the product with a removable 'Memory Stick' instead of a cassette player so it works with MP3 files.[10]

Market segmentation: to whom are we marketing?

▶ Whether within or across national boundaries, effective **market segmentation** delineates segments whose members are similar to one another in one or more characteristics and different from members of other segments. Depending on its goals and resources, a company may choose to focus on just one segment or several, or it may ignore differences among segments by pursuing a mass market strategy. In the Internet-based market, **Amazon.com** tries to reach multiple segments at the same time, while Google News UK focuses on being a search engine for information and news for consumers in the United Kingdom.[11]

In many cases, it makes a lot of sense to target a number of market segments. The likelihood is that no one will fit any given segment description exactly, and the issue is whether or not consumers differ from our profile in ways that will affect the chances of their adopting the products we are offering.

Many segmentation variables form the basis for slicing up a larger market, and a great deal of this book is devoted to exploring the ways marketers describe and characterize different segments. The segmentation variables listed in Table 1.1 are grouped into four categories, which also indicate where in the book these categories are considered in more depth.

While consumers can be described in many ways, the segmentation process is valid only when the following criteria are met:

- Consumers within the segment are similar to one another in terms of product needs, and these needs are different from consumers in other segments.

- Important differences among segments can be identified.

Table 1.1 Variables for market segmentation

Category	Variables	Location of discussion
Demographics	Age	Chapter 11
	Gender	Chapter 5
	Social class, occupation, income	Chapter 12
	Ethnic group, religion	Chapter 13
	Stage in life	Chapter 11
	Purchaser vs. user	Chapter 10
Geographic	Region	Chapter 13
	Country differences	Chapters 2, 15
Psychographic	Self-concept, personality	Chapter 5
	Lifestyle	Chapters 13, 14, 15
Behavioural	Brand loyalty, extent of usage	Chapter 8
	Usage situation	Chapter 9
	Benefits desired	Chapter 6

- The segment is large enough to be profitable.
- Consumers in the segment can be reached by an appropriate marketing mix.
- The consumers in the segment will respond in the desired way to the marketing mix designed for them.

▶ **Demographics** are statistics that measure observable aspects of a population, such as birth rate, age distribution or income. The national statistical agencies of European countries and pan-European agencies such as EuroStat[12] are major sources of demographic data on families, but many private firms gather additional data on specific population groups. The changes and trends revealed in demographic studies are of great interest to marketers, because the data can be used to locate and predict the size of markets for many products, ranging from mortgages to baby food to health care for senior aged consumers.

In this book, we will explore many of the important demographic variables that make consumers the same as, or different from, others. We'll also consider other important
▶ characteristics that are not so easy to measure, such as **psychographics** – differences in consumers' personalities and tastes which can't be measured objectively. For now, let's summarize a few of the most important demographic dimensions, each of which will be developed in more detail in later chapters. However, a word of caution is needed here. The last couple of decades have witnessed the growth of new consumer segments that are less dependent on demographics and more likely to borrow behavioural patterns and fashions across what were formerly more significant borders or barriers. It is now not so uncommon to see men and women, or grandmothers and granddaughters, having similar tastes. Hence, useful as they might be, marketers should beware of using only demographic variables to predict consumer tastes.

Age

Consumers in different age groups have very different needs and wants, and a better understanding of the ageing process of European consumers will continue to be of great importance to marketers as well as public policy decision-makers.[13] While people who belong to the same age group differ in many other ways, they do tend to share a set of values and common cultural experiences that they carry throughout life.[14] *Marie Claire*, the French magazine that is published in 25 editions and 14 languages, has noticed that its circulation and readership has fallen in past years, due primarily to not keeping pace with its younger readers and their reading habits. In the past, article length was typically nine to ten pages, and what is now desired is two to five pages. Rather than concentrating on serious articles on contemporary women's issues, the newer and younger readership is looking for something more fun and entertaining. Finding the balance of 'fun' (e.g. 'Four Celebs, secrets to fabulous legs') and 'serious' (e.g. 'The role of the veil in Islamic dress') has been the challenge in bridging women readers of different age groups.[15]

Gender

Many products, from fragrances to footwear, are targeted at men or women. Differentiating by sex starts at a very early age – even nappies are sold in pink-trimmed versions for girls and blue for boys. As proof that consumers take these differences seriously, market research has revealed that many parents refuse to put baby boys in pink nappies![16]

One dimension that makes segmenting by gender so interesting is that the behaviours and tastes of men and women are constantly evolving. In the past most marketers assumed that men were the primary decision-makers for car purchases, but this perspective is changing with the times.

Sometimes, the gender segmentation can be an unintended product of an advertising strategy. Wranglers launched a European campaign featuring macho Wild West values such as rodeo riding, after an earlier campaign, featuring a supermodel, had made their sales of jeans to women grow 400 per cent but put men off their brand.[17]

 Marketing opportunity

Websites for women

Segmenting by gender is alive and well in cyberspace.[18] In France, for example, a group of women started the country's first women's electronic magazine and Web portal called **Newsfam.com**. These entrepreneurs are hoping to reproduce the success of American sites like **iVillage.com** and **Women.com**.[19] To underscore the idea that men and women differ in their tastes and preferences (the French would say *vive la différence!*), a Website for high-tech products called **Hifi.com** opened a sister site just for women called **herhifi.com**. Within two years, **herhifi.com** was out of business, as the firm's notion that women would respond to a 'female' site for information on hi fi equipment just did not seem to have any value to women.

Family structure

A person's family and marital status is yet another important demographic variable, since this has such a big effect on consumers' spending priorities. Young bachelors and newly-weds are the most likely to take exercise, go to wine bars and pubs, concerts and the cinema and to consume alcohol. Families with young children are big purchasers of health foods and fruit juices, while single-parent households and those with older children buy more junk food. Home maintenance services are most likely to be used by older couples and bachelors.[20] Chapter 11 provides an overview of European family structures, and the diversity of what constitutes 'family' and 'households' throughout Europe.

Social class and income

People in the same social class are approximately equal in terms of their incomes and social status. They work in roughly similar occupations and tend to have similar tastes in music, clothing and so on. They also tend to socialize with one another and share many ideas and values.[21] The distribution of wealth is of great interest to marketers, since it determines which groups have the greatest buying power and market potential. As the number of member states of Europe continues to grow, the consumer behaviour implications of social class and income categories continues to grow as well! More on this dynamic construct of our European populace in Chapter 12.

BUY AN L300 VAN.

Marketers are paying increasing attention to demographic changes throughout Europe, and particularly with respect to changing income levels in Eastern Europe.

Mitsubishi

Race and ethnicity

Immigrants from various countries in Africa and Asia are among the fastest-growing ethnic groups in Europe. As our societies grow increasingly multicultural, new opportunities develop to deliver specialized products to racial and ethnic groups, and to introduce other groups to these offerings.

Sometimes, this adaptation is a matter of putting an existing product or service into a different context. For example, in Great Britain there is a motorway service station and cafeteria targeted at the Muslim population. It has prayer facilities, no pork menus and serves *halal* meat.[22] And now, Turks in Berlin do not have to rely solely on the small immigrants' greengroceries and kiosks known from so many other European cities. A Turkish chain has opened the first department store in Berlin, carrying Turkish and Middle Eastern goods only, catering to both the large Turkish population as well as to other immigrant groups and Germans longing for culinary holiday memories. As one of the fastest growing segments in the European food market, halal foods now has its own on-going marketing research organizations and media outlets for European managers and consumers.[23]

11

Multicultural dimensions

As we will discuss shortly, people can express their self and their cultural and religious belonging through consumption patterns. At times, this has led to cultural clashes, as in an example involving France or Denmark, where young Muslim women's wearing of headscarves either in school or at work has been debated for several years, and has even led to legislation prohibiting the wearing of 'conspicuous religious symbols' in French public schools.[24] Wearing a headscarf is criticized for being a religious statement, which should not be allowed in the explicitly secular French public schools, as a sign of oppression of women or as incompatible with the 'modern' image of the employing company. Similarly, there is debate in The Netherlands, long known for its tolerance of expression, as to whether female police officers who

are Islamic should be allowed to wear the headscarf in public.[25] Clearly, a headscarf is not just a headscarf. There are at least four culturally bound ways of displaying this controversial textile: the 'Italian way', known from stars of the 1950s and 1960s such as Sophia Loren, Claudia Cardinale or Gina Lollobrigida on the back seats of scooters and revived by nostalgia movements; the 'women's lib' way, with the knot in the back as displayed by many Scandinavian women in the 1970s; the 'German Hausfrau' version with a bow in the front; and the much-disputed Muslim version. In Turkey, one may see a lot of women wearing headscarves, but one can tell from the way they are tied whether this is a religious expression from a religious woman or rather an expression of a cultural tradition, and as such more a rural than a religious reference.[26]

Geography

In Europe, most of the evidence points to the fact that cultural differences persist in playing a decisive role in forming our consumption patterns and our unique expressions of consumption. At the same time, global competition tends to have a homogenizing effect in some markets such as music, sports, clothing and entertainment, and multinational companies such as Sony, Pepsi, Nintendo, Nike and Levi Strauss continue to dominate or play important roles in shaping markets.[27] With the creation of the single European market, many companies have begun to consider even more the possibilities of standardized marketing across national boundaries in Europe. The increasing similarity of the brands and products available in Europe does not mean that the consumers are the same, however! Variables such as personal motivation, cultural context, family relation patterns and rhythms of everyday life, all vary substantially from country to country and from region to region. And consumption of various product categories is still very different.

To sum up, a European segmentation must be able to take into consideration:

● consumption which is common across cultures (the global or regional, trends, lifestyles and cultural patterns that cross borders); and

● consumption which is specific to different cultural groups (differences in values, lifestyles, behavioural patterns, etc. among different cultures and subcultures).

▲ **Marketing opportunity**

New segments

Marketers have come up with so many ways to segment consumers – from the overweight to overachievers – that you might think they had run out of segments. Hardly. Changes in lifestyle and other characteristics of the population are constantly creating new opportunities. The following are some 'hot' market segments.

The gay community
In more and more societies, the gay minority is becoming increasingly visible. New media featuring homosexual lifestyles and the consumption patterns attached to them flourish and marketers claim that the gay community is as attractive a marketing niche as many other subcultures and that this group forms

a 'hungry target'.[28] For example, in the marketing of Copenhagen as a tourist destination, the gay community has been explicitly chosen as one of the target markets. The gay segment tends to be economically upmarket and is frequently involved in travelling and short holidays to metropolitan areas. So the tourist board has tried to reach it through specific marketing activities targeted at gay environments in Europe. Recently, London has emerged as 'more than a destination' tourist spot for gays, based on the city's overall welcome to gays, which is not focused on just one specific area or neighbourhood. The government-funded 'visitbritain' Website targets gay visitors, touting Britain as the 'United Queendom'.[29]

Single females

A worldwide study by Young and Rubicam has discovered a new and interesting market segment, that of well-educated, intelligent women who choose to stay single and pursue their life and career goals without husband or children. Furthermore, they represent heavy-spending consumers. They are reportedly brand-loyal and highly influenced by their friends in terms of consumption choices. The way to reach this attractive consumer group is to speak to their feelings of independence and self-respect.[30]

Disabled people

In the wake of legislation on the rights of disabled people, some marketers are starting to take notice of the estimated 10 to 15 per cent of the population who have some kind of disability. Initiatives include special phone numbers for hearing-impaired customers and assistance services for disabled people. IBM and Nissan have also used disabled actors in their advertising campaigns.[31] Mattel Inc., which produces Barbie, launched a sister doll, Becky, in a wheelchair – a reflection of the growing awareness of the disabled population in society.

Even then, the problem of specifying the relevant borders arises. Cultural borders do not always follow national borders. Although national borders are still very important for distinguishing between cultures, there may be important regional differences within a country, as well as cultural overlap between two countries.[32] Add to this the significant trends of immigration across Europe (mostly East to West) and the import of foreign (often American) cultural phenomena, and you begin to understand why it is very difficult to talk about European countries as being culturally homogeneous. For example, it is important to distinguish between, say, Dutch *society* with all its multicultural traits and Dutch *culture*, which may be one, albeit dominant, cultural element in Dutch society. Furthermore, Dutch culture (as is the case with all cultures) is not a *static* but a *dynamic* phenomenon, which changes over time and from contact, interaction and integration with other cultures.

Relationship marketing: building bonds with consumers

Marketers are carefully defining customer segments and listening to people as never before. Many of them have realized that the key to success is building lifetime relationships between brands and customers. Marketers who believe in this philosophy – so-called

▶ **relationship marketing** – are making an effort to keep in touch with their customers on a regular basis, and are giving them reasons to maintain a bond with the company over time. Various types of membership of retail outlets, petrol companies and co-operative movements illustrate this. One co-operative chain offers reductions to its members on such diverse goods as travelling, clothing, home appliances, electronics and garden furniture.[33] A new trend is to form consortia of diverse companies from different sectors, such as supermarkets, banks, petrol retailers, telecommunications and the entertainment and leisure industry. The consortium then issues a loyalty card to help secure a stable clientele.[34]

Some companies establish these ties by offering services that are appreciated by their customers. Many companies donate a small percentage of the purchase price to a charity such as the Red Cross or the World Wildlife Fund, or for the care of the poor and marginalized in society. This cements the relationship by giving customers an additional reason to continue buying the company's products year after year.

Another revolution in relationship building is being brought to us by courtesy of
▶ **database marketing**. This involves tracking consumers' buying habits by computer and
crafting products and information tailored precisely to people's wants and needs.

Keeping close tabs on their customers allows database marketers to monitor their
preferences and communicate with those who show an interest in their products or
services. Information is passed to the appropriate division for follow-up. DVD online
rental companies such as ScreenSelect in the UK and Web.DE in Germany are testing
a system that makes recommendations based on a consumer's prior rentals and offers
special promotions based on these choices.[35] However, some consumers feel threatened
by this kind of surveillance and resist such marketing efforts. Hence, attempts have been
made to ensure that database marketing conforms to the requirements of respondent
confidentiality.[36]

MARKETING'S IMPACT ON CONSUMERS

For better or worse, we live in a world that is significantly influenced by marketers. We
are surrounded by marketing stimuli in the form of advertisements, shops and products
competing for our attention and our cash. Much of what we learn about the world is
filtered by marketers, whether through conspicuous consumption depicted in glamorous
magazine advertising or via the roles played by family figures in TV commercials. Ads
show us how we ought to act with regard to recycling, alcohol consumption and even the
types of house or car we aspire to. In many ways we are at the mercy of marketers, since
we rely on them to sell us products that are safe and perform as promised, to tell us the
truth about what they are selling, and to price and distribute these products fairly.

The global consumer

As of 2006, the majority of people on earth live in urban centres – the number of mega-
cities, defined as urban centres of 10 million or more, is projected to grow to 26 in 2015.[37]
One highly visible – and controversial – by-product of sophisticated marketing strategies
▶ is the movement towards a **global consumer culture**, in which people are united by
their common devotion to brand-name consumer goods, film stars and rock stars.[38] Some
products in particular have become so associated with an American lifestyle that they
are prized possessions around the world. In Chapters 2, 13, and 14 we will pay special
attention to the good and bad aspects of this cultural homogenization.[39] On the other
hand, popular culture continues to evolve as products and styles from different cultures
mix and merge in new and interesting ways. For example, although superstars from the
US and the UK dominate the worldwide music industry, there is a movement afoot to
include more diverse styles and performers. In Europe, local music acts are grabbing
a larger share of the market and pushing international (that is, English-speaking) acts
down the charts. Revenue from Spanish-language music has quadrupled in five years.

We owe much of this interconnectedness and global consumer perspective to exciting
new developments in technology that allow us to link with companies – and with each
other – regardless of our physical locations. Indeed, our old model of sitting in front of a
▶ PC to surf the Web will soon disappear like the horse and buggy. **U-commerce** is the use
of *ubiquitous networks* that will slowly but surely become a part of us, whether in the form
of wearable computers or customized advertisements beamed to us on our cell phones
('Hey, you're walking by McDonald's. Come on in for today's burger special').[40]

▶ Many products already carry a plastic **RFID tag** containing a computer chip and a tiny
antenna that lets the chip communicate with a network. Grocery items will tell the store
what needs to be restocked and which items are past their expiration dates, and your
house will know when you're pulling into the driveway as it turns on the lights and
starts your favourite music before you walk in the door.

The rise of global marketing means that even small companies are looking to expand overseas – and this increases the pressure to understand how customers in other countries are the same or different from those in one's own country. In the restaurant industry, for example, Shakey's pizza restaurants are mushrooming in the Philippines, and food from the International House of Pancakes is selling like hotcakes in Tokyo. But menu changes are sometimes called for to please local palates: Schlotzky's in Malaysia offers Smokey Mountain Chicken Crunch with 'half-virgin' chicken, and diners at Bob's Big Boy in Thailand snap up Tropical Shrimp, deep fried with 'exotic breading'. This book will pay special attention to the good and bad aspects of this cultural homogenization.

Virtual consumption and the power of crowds

There is little doubt that the digital revolution is one of the most significant influences on consumer behaviour, and the impact of the Web will continue to expand as more and more people around the world log on. Many of us are avid Web surfers, and it is hard to imagine a time when texting, MP3 files, iPhones, or BlackBerrys were not an accepted part of daily life.

Electronic marketing has increased convenience by breaking down many of the barriers caused by time and location. You can shop 24/7 without leaving home, you can read today's newspaper without getting drenched picking up a hard copy in a rainstorm, and you don't have to wait for the 6:00 P.M. news to find out what the weather will be like tomorrow – at home or around the globe. And, with the increasing use of handheld devices and wireless communications, you can get that same information – from stock quotes to the weather – even when you're away from your computer.[41]

▶ And, it's not all about businesses selling to consumers (**B2C e-commerce**). The cyberspace explosion has created a revolution in consumer-to-consumer activity (**C2C**
▶ **e-commerce**): welcome to the new world of *virtual brand communities*. Just as e-consumers are not limited to local retail outlets in their shopping, they are not limited to their local communities when looking for friends or fellow fans of wine, hip-hop, or skateboarding.

Picture a small group of local collectors who meet once a month at a local diner to discuss their shared interests over coffee. Now multiply that group by thousands, and include people from all over the world who are united by a shared passion for sports memorabilia, Barbie dolls, Harley-Davidson motorcycles, refrigerator magnets, or *MMOGs* (massive multiplayer online games) such as *World of Warcraft*. The Web also provides an easy way for consumers around the world to exchange information about their experiences with products, services, music, restaurants, and movies. The Hollywood Stock Exchange (**hsx.com**) offers a simulated entertainment stock market where traders predict the 4-week box office revenues for each film. **Amazon.com** encourages shoppers to write reviews of books. The popularity of chat rooms where consumers can go to discuss various topics with like-minded 'Netizens' around the world grows every day, as do immersive virtual worlds such as *Second Life*, *Entropia Universe*, *There.com*, and *Kaneva*. News reports tell us of the sometimes wonderful and sometimes horrific romances that have begun on the Internet as people check out potential mates on sites such as **Match.com** or **Lavalife** (in a typical month, 26 million people visit online dating sites!).[42]

A 'cousin' of the global consumer is the much debated Euro-consumer. Marketing researchers are heavily involved in a debate about the possibilities of finding market segments that are European rather than national in character. In a study on the consumption of luxury goods, it was concluded that one could draw a demographic portrait of the average European consumer of luxury goods. However, important differences between the countries were also detected. Consumers who expressed more positive attitudes towards cultural change were also more likely to consume luxury goods, independent of their demographics and social class.[43] Given these findings, it is questionable how much is gained from working with the concept of the Euro-consumer in terms of segment description. For a product such as cars, which intuitively and in terms of functionality

Marketers develop relationships with consumers by constructing meanings which go way beyond the utilitarian value of the product. The American basketball player LaBron James is a globally-known 'product', offering an emotional (even mythical) value to consumers.

Getty Images/AFP

would seem relatively easy to market as a European-wide product, the models still appear in a variety of versions to suit particular national needs and wants.

In the next chapter, we will take a look at the cultural dimensions of marketing and its impact on consumers. The relationship between marketing and consumption in a globalizing and increasingly unsustainable consumer society raises some real ethical issues. Right now, however, we will turn our attention to some of the more specifically ethical issues in the direct relationship between marketers and consumers.

Marketing ethics

In business, conflicts often arise between the goal to succeed in the marketplace and the desire to conduct business honestly and maximize the well-being of consumers by providing them with safe and effective products and services. Some people argue that by the time people reach university, secondary school or are actually employed by companies, it is a little late to start teaching them ethics! Still, many universities and corporations are now focusing very intently on teaching and reinforcing ethical behaviour.

Prescribing ethical standards of conduct

Professional organizations often devise a code of ethics for their members. For example, European or national consumer protection laws or various national marketing associations' codes of ethics provide guidelines for conduct in many areas of marketing practice. These include:

- Disclosure of all substantial risks associated with a product or service.
- Identification of added features that will increase the cost.
- Avoidance of false or misleading advertising.
- Rejection of high-pressure or misleading sales tactics.
- Prohibition of selling or fund-raising under the guise of conducting market research.

Socially responsible behaviour

Whether intentionally or not, some marketers do violate their bond of trust with consumers. In some cases these actions are illegal, as when a manufacturer deliberately mislabels the contents of a package or a retailer adopts a 'bait-and-switch' selling strategy, whereby consumers are lured into the store with promises of inexpensive products with the sole intention of getting them to switch to higher-priced goods. A similar problematic issue of the luring of consumers is the case of misleading claims, for instance on food product labels.[44] For example, what about a label such as '100 per cent fat-free strawberry jam'?

In other cases, marketing practices have detrimental effects on society even though they are not explicitly illegal. The introduction of so-called alcopops, a mix of alcohol and soda or lemonade, targeted more or less explicitly at the teen market, has caused considerable debate in various European countries. Following negative press coverage, sales have gone down in Sweden and the UK, and the two largest retail chains in Denmark withdrew these drinks from their product range.[45] Others have run into difficulties by sponsoring commercials depicting groups of people in an unfavourable light to get the attention of a target market. One may recall the heated debate as to whether Benetton's advertising campaigns are attempts to sensitize consumers to the world's real problems, as the company contends, or to exploit unfortunate people – as in the ads depicting an AIDS victim, a dead Croat soldier or a ship packed with Albanian refugees – in order to sell more Benetton clothing.[46]

Faced with the rising phenomenon of the 'political consumer' – a consumer who expresses their political and ethical viewpoints by selecting and avoiding products from companies which are antithetical to these viewpoints – the industry is increasingly coming to realize that ethical behaviour is also good business in the long run, since the trust and satisfaction of consumers translates into years of loyalty from customers. However, many problems remain. Throughout this book, ethical issues related to the practice of marketing are highlighted. Special boxes headed 'Marketing pitfall' feature dubious marketing practices or the possible adverse effects on consumers of certain marketing strategies.

▼ Marketing pitfall

Women for s@le! The charge against abuse of marketing techniques has taken on new dimensions with the rise of the Internet. Would you like to buy a Latvian girl for escort service? Or a Russian bride by mail order? The trade in women from Eastern Europe, Asia or Latin America has reached new heights with the easier contact made possible by the Internet. Obvious problems are created by the difficulty of distinguishing between serious marriage bureaus or au pair agencies on the one side and organized traders of women for various kinds of prostitution services on the other. According to human rights organizations, many women who believe that they are going to marry the prince of their lives end up as 'sexual services workers', sometimes under slavery-like conditions.[47]

Public policy and consumerism

Public concern for the welfare of consumers has been an issue since at least the beginning of the twentieth century. This is normally referred to as **consumer policy**. Partly as a result of consumers' efforts, many national and international agencies have been established to oversee consumer-related activities. Consumers themselves continue to have a lively interest in consumer-related issues, ranging from environmental concerns, such as pollution caused by oil spills or toxic waste, the use of additives and genetically manipulated material in food and so on, to excessive violence and sex on television.

Consumer research and consumer welfare

The field of consumer behaviour can play an important role in improving our lives as consumers.[48] Many researchers play a role in formulating or evaluating public policies, such as ensuring that products are labelled accurately, that people can comprehend

Table 1.2 Ten principles of consumer protection in the EU

- **Buy what you want, where you want.**
  Whether you physically go to a different EU country for shopping, or whether you order goods over the phone, Internet, or by post, you should not have to pay customs duty or additional VAT on those purchases.

- **If it doesn't work, send it back.**
  Under EU law, if a product you buy does not conform to the agreement you made with the seller at the time of purchase, you can take it back and have it repaired or replaced. Alternatively, you can ask for a price reduction, or a complete refund of your money. This applies for up to two years after you take delivery of the product.

- **High safety standards for food and consumer goods.**
  Food safety is based on the principle that consumers need to look at the whole of the 'food chain' in order to ensure safety. EU food safety laws therefore regulate how farmers produce food (including what chemicals they use when growing plants and what they feed their animals), how food is processed, what colourings and additives can be used in it and how it is sold. The EU's safety laws on other consumer goods (toys, cosmetics, electrical equipment, etc.) are also strict.

- **Know what you are eating.**
  How can you find out what's in your food? Just look at the information on the package! EU laws on food labelling enable you to know what you are eating. Full details of the ingredients used to make a food product must be given on the label, along with details of any colouring, preservatives, sweeteners and other chemical additives used. EU food labelling laws regulate which products can be called 'organic' and the use of names associated with quality products from particular European regions – for example, if it is labeled *Prosciutto di Parma* you can be sure the ham comes from Parma, if it is labelled *Kalamata* you can be sure the olives are from Kalamata.

- **Contracts should be fair to consumers.**
  EU law says that unfair contract terms are prohibited. Irrespective of which EU country you sign such a contract in, EU law protects you from unfair contract terms.

- **Sometimes consumers can change their mind.**
  As a general principle, you can cancel a contract made by a doorstep salesperson within seven days. EU law also protects you, as a consumer, when you buy from mail order, Internet or telesales companies and other 'distance sellers'.

- **Making it easier to compare prices.**
  How do you compare the price of two different brands of breakfast cereal when one comes in a 375g box and the other in a 500g box? EU law requires supermarkets to give you the 'unit price' of products – for example, how much they cost per kilo or per litre – to help make it easier for you to decide which one is best value for money.

- **Consumers should not be misled.**
  Advertising that misleads or deceives consumers is prohibited under EU law. In addition, when you are dealing with telesales, mail order or online retailers, sellers must be open and honest with you. EU law requires them to give you full details of who they are, what they are selling, how much it costs (including taxes and delivery charges) and how long it will take for them to deliver it.

- **Protection while you are on holiday.**
  Package tour operators must have arrangements in place to get you home should they go bankrupt while you are on holiday. They must also offer you compensation if your holiday does not correspond to what they promised in their brochure. Last, but by no means least, EU law makes it easier for you to take your furry friends on holiday with you. Once your veterinarian has issued your cat, dog or ferret with one of the new 'pet passports' your pet can travel with you to any EU country.

- **Effective redress for cross-border disputes.**
  Consumer interests should be promoted and defended, particularly in view of the increasing complexity of the markets in which they operate. The scope and size of markets has grown enormously over the last few years, not least due to the introduction of the euro, the development of e-commerce and increased intra-EU mobility. Recognising consumers as essential, responsible economic agents in the internal market is one of the key principles of European consumer policy. Consumers should be empowered to make informed choices about the goods and services that they purchase.

Source: versions of the brochure are available in 20 European languages at: **http://europa.eu.int/comm/consumers/cons_info/10principles_en.htm**

important information presented in advertising, or that children are not exploited by programme-length toy commercials masquerading as television shows.

Of course, to a large degree consumers are dependent on their governments to regulate and police safety and environmental standards. The extent of supervision may depend on such factors as the national political and cultural climate. Debates within the EU concerning regulation of the use of pesticides and food additives are examples here. In addition, a country's traditions and beliefs may make it more sympathetic to one or the other point of view expressed by consumers or producers. For example, the cross-Atlantic debate concerning market acceptance of genetically modified food products has also given rise to research about consumers' attitudes toward the acceptability and labelling of such products.[49]

Promoting consumers' rights, prosperity and well-being are core values of the European Union (EU), and this is reflected in its laws. Membership of the European Union ensures additional protection for consumers. Table 1.2 describes ten basic principles of how EU law protects you, as a consumer, no matter where you are in the EU. What is described is the minimum level of protection all EU countries should, according to EU law, give consumers. The details of exactly what your rights are – and how you can apply them – will vary from country to country depending on how they have implemented the EU rules in their national law. You should note that national consumer protection laws may – in some cases – give you a higher level of protection.

▶ There is also a growing movement to develop knowledge about **social marketing**, which attempts to encourage such positive behaviours as increased literacy and to discourage negative activities such as drink-driving.[50] A project in Sweden aimed at curbing adolescent drinking illustrates social marketing at work. The Swedish Brewers' Association is investing 10 million Skr (about $7.5 million) in a co-operative effort with the Swedish Non-Violence Project to change teens' attitudes to alcohol consumption. Consumer researchers working on the project discovered that Swedish adolescents freely admit that they 'drink in order to get drunk' and enjoy the feeling of being intoxicated, so persuading them to give up alcohol is a formidable task. However, the teens reported that they are also afraid of losing control over their own behaviour, especially if there is a risk of their being exposed to violence. And while worries about the long-term health effects of drinking don't concern this group (after all, at this age many believe they will

This German ad for Unicef makes a statement about the problem of child labour.

© German National Committee for UNICEF and Springer & Jacoby Fuenfte Werbeagentur GmbH & Co. KG. Photo: Jan Burwick live forever), female adolescents reported a fear of becoming less attractive as a result of prolonged alcohol consumption.

Based on these findings, the group commissioned to execute this project decided to stress a more realistic message of 'Drink if you want to, but within a safe limit. Don't lose control, because if you do, you might get yourself into violent situations'. They made up the motto 'Alco-hole in your head' to stress the importance of knowing one's limits. This message is being emphasized along with strong visual images that appear on billboards, in video spots that depict situations involving young drinkers getting out of control, and in school presentations given by young people who will be credible role models for teens.[51]

DO MARKETERS MANIPULATE CONSUMERS?

One of the most common and stinging criticisms of marketing is that marketing techniques (especially advertising) are responsible for convincing consumers that they 'need' many material goods and that they will be unhappy and somehow inferior if they do not have these 'necessities'. The issue is complex, and one that is certainly worth considering: do marketers give people what they want, or do they tell people what they ought to want?

Philosophers have approached this issue when considering the concept of free will. It has been argued that in order to claim that consumers are acting autonomously in response to ads, the capacity for free will and free action must be present. That is, the consumer must be capable of deciding *independently* what to do, and not be prevented from carrying out that decision. This, it has been argued, is probably true for purely informative advertising, where only the product or store information required to make a rational decision is provided, whereas the case for advertising where imagery or underlying motivations are tapped is not as clear.[52] Such a view presupposes that informative advertising is somehow more objective than imagery-based advertising. But functionality and utility are also important images of a specific cultural context that uses references to our reason to seduce us.[53] Three issues related to the complex relationship between marketing practices and consumers' needs are considered here.

Do marketers create artificial needs?

The marketing system has come under fire from both ends of the political spectrum. On the one hand, some conservative traditionalists believe that advertising contributes to the moral breakdown of society by presenting images of hedonistic pleasure. On the other hand, some leftists argue that the same misleading promises of material pleasure function to buy off people who would otherwise be revolutionaries working to change the system.[54] Through advertising, then, the system creates demand that only its products can satisfy.

One possible response to such criticism is that a need is a basic biological motive, while a want represents one way that society has taught us that the need can be satisfied. For example, while thirst is biologically based, we are taught to want Coca-Cola to satisfy that thirst rather than, say, goat's milk. Thus, the need is already there: marketers simply recommend ways to satisfy it. A basic objective of advertising is to create awareness that these needs exist, rather than to create them.

However, marketers are important engineers of our environment. And beyond the level of banality, needs are always formed by the social environment. Thus, in a sense, needs are always 'artificial' because we are interested in needs only in their social form. Alternatively, needs are never artificial because they are always 'real' to the people who feel them. 'Needs' are something we are socialized to have. In the case of the Coca-Cola vs. goat's milk example, it should be remembered that we do not eat and drink solely to satisfy a biological need. We eat and drink for a number of reasons, all of them embedded

DESPITE WHAT SOME PEOPLE THINK, ADVERTISING CAN'T MAKE YOU BUY SOMETHING YOU DON'T NEED.

Some people would have you believe that you are putty in the hands of every advertiser in the country.

They think that when advertising is put under your nose, your mind turns to oatmeal.

It's mass hypnosis. Subliminal seduction. Brain washing. Mind control. It's advertising.

And you are a pushover for it.

It explains why your kitchen cupboard is full of food you never eat.

Why your garage is full of cars you never drive.

Why your house is full of books you don't read, TV's you don't watch, beds you don't use, and clothes you don't wear.

You don't have a choice. You are forced to buy.

That's why this message is a cleverly disguised advertisement to get you to buy land in the tropics.

Got you again, didn't we? Send in your money.

ADVERTISING

ANOTHER WORD FOR FREEDOM OF CHOICE.

American Association of Advertising Agencies

This ad was created by the American Association of Advertising Agencies to counter charges that ads create artificial needs.

American Association of Advertising Agencies

in our cultural context. What is the need of a sofa? A TV? A car? A textbook on consumer behaviour? Thus, a better response would be that marketers do not create artificial needs, but they do contribute heavily to the socialization of people in contemporary society and thus to the establishment of the *social* system of needs. Consequently, marketers must take a share of responsibility for the development of society.

Is advertising necessary?

As the social commentator Vance Packard wrote nearly 50 years ago, 'Large-scale efforts are being made, often with impressive success, to channel our unthinking habits, our purchasing decisions, and our thought processes by the use of insights gleaned from psychiatry and the social sciences.'[55] The economist John Kenneth Galbraith believed that radio and television are important tools to accomplish this manipulation of the masses. Since virtually no literacy is required to use these media, they allow repetitive and compelling communications to reach almost everyone.

Goods are arbitrarily linked to desirable social attributes. One influential critic even argued that the problem is that we are not materialistic enough – that is, we do not sufficiently value goods for the utilitarian functions they deliver, but instead focus on the irrational value of goods for what they symbolize. According to this view, 'Beer would be enough for us, without the additional promise that in drinking it we show ourselves to be manly, young at heart, or neighbourly. A washing machine would be a useful machine to wash clothes, rather than an indication that we are forward-looking or an object of envy to our neighbours.'[56]

Such arguments seem somewhat outdated at the beginning of the twenty-first century, when advertising has been embraced as an art form in itself. Today, children are brought up to be both consumers and readers of advertising. A predominantly functional approach to consumption, as in the former planned economies of Eastern Europe, did not make people happier, nor did it prevent them from establishing mythologies about other goods, such as the scarce and expensive ones from the West. Advertisers, just like marketers, are important communicators. Their importance must be accompanied by a sense of responsibility concerning the social and individual effect of their messages.

Do marketers promise miracles?

Consumers are led to believe via advertising that products have magical properties; they will do special and mysterious things for them that will transform their lives. They will be beautiful, have power over others' feelings, be successful, be relieved of all ills, and so on. In this respect, advertising functions as mythology does in primitive societies: it provides simple, anxiety-reducing answers to complex problems. Is this a problem in itself?

Yes and no. The consumer is not an automaton that will react in a predefined way to certain stimuli. On the other hand, we are all partly socialized by the market and its messages. So, whereas the manipulative effectiveness of advertising is often overstated, there is little doubt that advertising creates and changes patterns of consumption. This is especially so in the new market economies, where the population does not maintain the same distance from and critical attitude to advertising messages and imagery.

But the effect is in general more subtle than simple manipulative persuasion. In most cases, advertisers simply do not know enough about people to manipulate them directly. Consider that the failure rate for new products ranges from 40 to 80 per cent. The main effect of advertising may often be found on the more general level, in the promotion of the idea that your self and your personal relationships, your success and your image all depend on your consumer choices.

CONSUMER BEHAVIOUR AS A FIELD OF STUDY

Although people have been consumers for a very long time, it is only recently that consumption per se has been the focus of formal study. In fact, while many business schools now require that marketing students take a consumer behaviour course, most universities and business schools did not even offer such a course until the 1970s. Much of the impetus for the attention now being given to consumer behaviour was the realization by many business people that the consumer really *is* the boss.

Interdisciplinary influences on the study of consumer behaviour

Consumer behaviour is a very new field and, as it grows, it is being influenced by many different perspectives. Indeed, it is hard to think of a field that is more interdisciplinary. People with a background in a very wide range of fields – from psychophysiology to literature – can now be found doing consumer research. Consumer researchers are employed by universities, manufacturers, museums, advertising agencies and governments. Professional groups, such as the Association for Consumer Research, have been formed since the mid-1970s, and European academics and practitioners are major contributors to the growing literature on consumer behaviour.

Figure 1.2 The pyramid of consumer behaviour

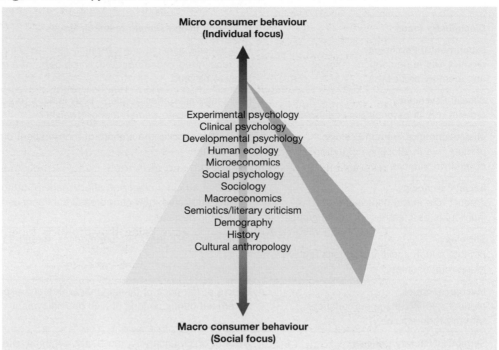

Researchers approach consumer issues from different perspectives. You might remember a fable about blind men and an elephant. The gist of the story is that each man touched a different part of the animal, and, as a result, the descriptions each gave of the elephant were quite different. This analogy applies to consumer research as well. A similar consumer phenomenon can be studied in different ways and at different levels depending on the training and interests of the researchers studying it.

Figure 1.2 covers some of the disciplines in the field and the level at which each approaches research issues. These disciplines can be loosely characterized in terms of their focus on micro vs. macro consumer behaviour topics. The fields closer to the top of the pyramid concentrate on the individual consumer (micro issues), while those towards the base are more interested in the aggregate activities that occur among larger groups of people, such as consumption patterns shared by members of a culture or subculture (macro issues).

The issue of strategic focus

Many people regard the field of consumer behaviour as an applied social science. Accordingly, the value of the knowledge generated has traditionally been measured in terms of its ability to improve the effectiveness of marketing practice. Recently, though, some researchers have argued that consumer behaviour should not have a strategic focus at all; the field should not be a 'handmaiden to business'. It should instead focus on understanding consumption for its own sake, rather than because the knowledge can be applied by marketers.[57] This view is probably not held by most consumer researchers, but it has encouraged many to expand the scope of their work beyond the field's traditional focus on the purchase of consumer goods. And it has certainly led to some fierce debates among people working in the field! In fact, it can also be argued that business gets better research from non-strategic research projects because they are unbiased by strategic goals. Take a relatively simple and common consumer object like the women's

Table 1.3 Interdisciplinary research issues in consumer behaviour

Disciplinary focus	Magazine usage sample research issues
Experimental Psychology: product role in perception, learning and memory processes	How specific aspects of magazines, such as their design or layout, are recognized and interpreted; which parts of a magazine are most likely to be read
Clinical Psychology: product role in psychological adjustment	How magazines affect readers' body images (e.g. do thin models make the average woman feel overweight?)
Microeconomics/Human Ecology: product role in allocation of individual or family resources	Factors influencing the amount of money spent on magazines in a household
Social Psychology: product role in the behaviours of individuals as members of social groups	Ways that ads in a magazine affect readers' attitudes towards the products depicted; how peer pressure influences a person's readership decisions
Sociology: product role in social institutions and group relationships	Pattern by which magazine preferences spread through a social group
Macroeconomics: product role in consumers' relations with the marketplace	Effects of the price of fashion magazines and expense of items advertised during periods of high unemployment
Semiotics/Literary Criticism: product role in the verbal and visual communication of meaning	Ways in which underlying messages communicated by models and ads in a magazine are interpreted
Demography: product role in the measurable characteristics of a population	Effects of age, income and marital status of a magazine's readers
History: product role in societal changes over time	Ways in which our culture's depictions of 'femininity' in magazines have changed over time
Cultural Anthropology: product role in a society's beliefs and practices	Ways in which fashions and models in a magazine affect readers' definitions of masculine vs. feminine behaviour (e.g. the role of working women, sexual taboos)

magazine, found in every culture in a variety of versions. How much is there to say about the 'simple' act of buying such a magazine? Well, quite a lot. Table 1.3 lists some potential issues relevant for the marketing of or advertising in women's magazines which can be researched based on the variety of disciplines influencing consumer research.

This more critical view of consumer research has led to the recognition that not all consumer behaviour and/or marketing activity is necessarily beneficial to individuals or to society. As a result, current consumer research is likely to include attention to the 'dark side' of consumer behaviour, such as addiction, prostitution, homelessness, shoplifting or environmental waste. This activity builds upon the earlier work of researchers who, as we have seen, have studied consumer issues related to public policy, ethics and consumerism.

The issue of two perspectives on consumer research

One general way to classify consumer research is in terms of the fundamental assumptions the researchers make about what they are studying and how to study it. This set
▶ of beliefs is known as a **paradigm**. Like other fields of study, consumer behaviour is

Table 1.4 Positivist vs. interpretivist approaches to consumer behaviour

Assumptions	Positivist approach	Interpretivist approach
Nature of reality	Objective, tangible Single	Socially constructed Multiple
Goal	Prediction	Understanding
Knowledge generated	Time-free Context-independent	Time-free Context-independent
View of causality	Existence of real causes	Multiple, simultaneous shaping events
Research relationship	Separation between researcher and subject	Interactive, co-operative, with researcher being part of phenomenon under study

Source: Adapted from Laurel A. Hudson and Julie L. Ozanne, 'Alternative ways of seeking knowledge in consumer research', *Journal of Consumer Research* 14 (March 1988): 508–21. Reprinted with the permission of The University of Chicago Press.

dominated by a paradigm, but some believe it is in the middle of a *paradigm shift*, which occurs when a competing paradigm challenges the dominant set of assumptions.

The basic set of assumptions underlying the current dominant paradigm is called ▶ **positivism**. This perspective has significantly influenced Western art and science since the late sixteenth century. It emphasizes that human reason is supreme and that there is a single, objective truth that can be discovered by science. Positivism encourages us to stress the function of objects, to celebrate technology and to regard the world as a rational, ordered place with a clearly defined past, present and future. Some feel that positivism puts too much emphasis on material well-being, and that its logical outlook is dominated by an ideology that stresses the homogeneous views of a predominantly Western and male culture.

▶ The newer paradigm of **interpretivism** questions these assumptions. Proponents of this perspective argue that our society places too much emphasis on science and technology, and that this ordered, rational view of consumers denies the complexity of the social and cultural world in which we live. Interpretivists stress the importance of symbolic, subjective experience, and the idea that meaning is in the mind – that is, we each construct our own meanings based on our unique and shared cultural experiences, so that there are no single right or wrong references. To the value we place on products, because they help us to create order in our lives, is added an appreciation of consumption as a set of diverse experiences.

The major differences between these two perspectives are summarized in Table 1.4.

In addition to the cross-cultural differences in consumer behaviour discussed earlier, it is also clear that research styles differ significantly between Europe and North America and also within European countries. For example, studies have shown that European researchers tend to consider the cultural dimension much more than their American counterparts.[58] Further, two special sessions at a European consumer research conference revealed that there seem to be important differences between the way consumer behaviour is conceived in Germany and the UK, for example.[59] A recent and more 'bridging' perspective on approaches to the study of consumer research argues that the study of particular consumption contexts are not an end in themselves, but rather that studying human behaviour in a consumption context is useful for generating new constructs and theoretical insights. This approach, consumer culture theory (CCT), embraces a variety of methodological approaches (used by both positivist and interpretivist), and recognizes that managers can make use of multiple methods to better understand trends in the marketplace, such as the complexities of lifestyle, multicultural marketing, and how consumers use media as part of their lives.[60]

Consumer research is still moving on. From its original emphasis on buying behaviour and the factors influencing the decision-making process, the field gradually widened to become a study of consumer behaviour in a more general sense, also taking into consideration what happened before and after the purchase. After the introduction of the interpretivist approach, a broader research perspective has included many new and non-psychological facets in the increasingly complex portraits of consumers. And it can be argued that the field increasingly looks beyond the single individual and their social background and environment to describe and analyze the complex relationships that

▶ have led us to start characterizing our present society as a **consumer society**.[61] The facts of living in a consumer society and being surrounded by consumer culture permeate this book but will be dealt with in more detail in Chapters 2 and 13.

Consumer behaviour as I see it . . .

Our world is fraught with international conflict that leads people to feel angry at other countries. This anger is sometimes made manifest in the decisions consumers make about what to buy. Consumer decisions, in other words, can depend on more than just the material value of a product, or how good consumers think the product is. They can depend upon how people feel about the country where the product was made.

Professor Jill Klein
INSEAD

My research over the last ten years has examined how feelings about a producing country affect the willingness to buy. Specifically, my colleagues and I have examined how **animosity** – the remnants of antipathy toward another country due to past military, political or economic conflicts – affects consumer behaviour. Consumers in France who are angry at the United States because of the war in Iraq are less likely to buy US brands than those who are not angry. Consumers in Australia who were angry at the French for testing nuclear weapons in the South Pacific, stopped buying French products. This is not just a temporary phenomenon. Animosity can affect consumer decisions decades after the negative events took place. Some consumers in China remain angry with the Japanese because of the Japanese invasion in the 1930s. Those consumers are less likely to own Japanese products. Dutch consumers who are still angry at Germany because of World War II, are less likely to purchase German products. Japanese consumers who remain angry with the United States for dropping the atomic bomb on Hiroshima and Nagasaki still shun American products. Animosity can even affect how consumers feel about buying products from within their own country. Southerners in the United States whose anger still lingers from the Civil War prefer to purchase products produced in the south rather than the north.

Consumers who avoid products from a country that angers them do not necessarily feel that these products are necessarily poor in quality. Consumers in the United States who feel angry with Japan over the bombing of Pearl Harbor hold the quality of Japanese products in high regard. They see these products as strong in workmanship, value and reliability. But their animosity keeps them from purchasing Japanese goods. Thus, improving perceptions of product quality will not appease the angry consumer.

International conflict has many dire consequences, as we can see on our television screens on a daily basis. From a consumer behaviour standpoint, these tensions have the additional effect that consumers may avoid the products of the offending country. And just as the conflicts of decades ago still have an impact on current consumer choices, the conflicts of today will probably cast their shadow on consumption decisions for decades to come.

CHAPTER SUMMARY

- Consumer behaviour is the study of the processes involved when individuals or groups select, purchase, use or dispose of products, services, ideas or experiences to satisfy needs and desires.

- A consumer may purchase, use and/or dispose of a product, but these functions may be performed by different people. In addition, consumers may be thought of as role players who need different products to help them play their various parts.

- Market segmentation is an important aspect of consumer behaviour. Consumers can be segmented along many dimensions, including product usage, demographics (the objective aspects of a population, such as age and sex) and psychographics (psychological and life-style characteristics). Emerging developments, such as the new emphasis on relationship marketing and the practice of database marketing, mean that marketers are much more attuned to the wants and needs of different consumer groups.

- Marketing activities exert an enormous impact on individuals. Consumer behaviour is relevant to our understanding of both public policy issues (e.g. ethical marketing practices) and of the dynamics of popular culture.

- The Web is transforming the way consumers interact with companies and with each other. Online commerce allows us to locate obscure products from around the world, and consumption communities provide forums for people to share opinions and product recommendations. Potential problems accompany these benefits, including the loss of privacy and the deterioration of traditional social interactions as people log more time online.

- It is often said that marketers create artificial needs. Although this criticism is over-simplified, it is true that marketers must accept their share of the responsibility for how society develops and what is considered necessary to have and what is acceptable, nice and fun to do within society.

- The field of consumer behaviour is interdisciplinary: it is composed of researchers from many different fields who share an interest in how people interact with the marketplace. These disciplines can be categorized by the degree to which their focus is micro (the individual consumer) or macro (the consumer as a member of groups or of the larger society).

- There are many perspectives on consumer behaviour, but research orientations can roughly be divided into two approaches. The positivist perspective, which currently dominates the field, emphasizes the objectivity of science and the consumer as a rational decision-maker. The interpretivist perspective, in contrast, stresses the subjective meaning of the consumer's individual experience and the idea that any behaviour is subject to multiple interpretations rather than one single explanation.

► KEY TERMS

B2C e-commerce (p. 15)

C2C e-commerce (p. 15)

Consumer behaviour (p. 6)

Consumer policy (p. 17)

Consumer society (p. 26)

Database marketing (p. 14)

Demographics (p. 9)

Exchange (p. 7)

Global consumer culture (p. 14)

Interpretivism (p. 25)

Market segmentation (p. 8)

Paradigm (p. 24)

Positivism (p. 25)

Psychographics (p. 9)

Relationship marketing (p. 13)

RFID tag (p. 14)

Role theory (p. 6)

Social marketing (p. 19)

U-commerce (p. 14)

▶ CONSUMER BEHAVIOUR CHALLENGE

1 This chapter states that people play different roles and that their consumption behaviours may differ depending on the particular role they are playing. State whether you agree or disagree with this perspective, giving examples from your own life.

2 Some researchers believe that the field of consumer behaviour should be a pure, rather than an applied, science. That is, research issues should be framed in terms of their scientific interest rather than their applicability to immediate marketing problems. Do you agree?

3 In recent years, there has been a large debate about the influence that Internet shopping will have on our consumer lives. Try listing the changes that you personally have made in your buying and consumption patterns due to e-commerce. Compare these changes with changes experienced by other people from various social groups, e.g. somebody from your parents' generation, an IT freak, or somebody with a lower educational background.

4 Name some products or services that are widely used by your social group. State whether you agree or disagree with the notion that these products help to form bonds within the group, and support your argument with examples from your list of products used by the group.

5 Although demographic information on large numbers of consumers is used in many marketing contexts, some people believe that the sale of data on customers' incomes, buying habits and so on constitutes an invasion of privacy and should be banned. Comment on this issue from both a consumer's and a marketer's point of view.

6 List the three stages in the consumption process. Describe the issues that you considered in each of these stages when you made a recent important purchase.

7 State the differences between the positivist and interpretivist approaches to consumer research. For each type of inquiry, give examples of product dimensions that would be more usefully explored using that type of research over the other.

8 What aspects of consumer behaviour are likely to be of interest to a financial planner? To a university administrator? To a graphic arts designer? To a social worker in a government agency? To a nursing instructor?

9 Select a product and brand that you use frequently and list what you consider to be the brand's determinant attributes. Without revealing your list, ask a friend who is approximately the same age but of the opposite sex to make a similar list for the same product (the brand may be different). Compare and contrast the identified attributes and report your findings.

10 Collect ads for five different brands of the same product. Report on the segmentation variables, target markets and emphasized product attributes in each ad.

For additional material see the companion website at **www.pearsoned.co.uk/solomon**

NOTES

1. Andrea Davies, James Fitchett and Avi Shankar, 'An Ethnoconsumerist Enquiry into International Consumer Behaviour', in Darach Turley and Stephen Brown, eds, *European Advances in Consumer Research: All Changed, Changed Utterly?* 6 (Valdosta, GA: Association for Consumer Research, 2003): 102–7.

2. Eurostat: Europe in Figues, Eurostat yearbook, 2008, available at: http://epp.eurostat.ec.europa.eu/cache/ITY_OFFPUB/KS-SF-08-081/EN/KS-SF-08-081-EN.PDF

3. Older Consumers in the Spotlight, April 2004, accessed at: http://www.cmdglobal.com/database/U/UFO/Understanding_Fifties_and_Over

4. Kay Larsen, 'Global music sales fell in 2003, but 2nd half softened in the drop' *Wall Street Journal* (8 April 2003): B6; Gabi Ouwerkerk and Hotze Zijlstra, 'Vlinders op internet', *De Telegraaf* (4 January 2005), http://www2.telegraaf.nl/i-mail/16940401/Vlinders_op_internet.html; 'Online Dating Revenues Soar in Europe', Jupiter Research,

http://www.onlinedatingmagazine.com/news2006/onlinedatingrevenues.html

5. Mike Featherstone, ed., *Global Culture. Nationalism, Globalization, and Modernity* (London: Sage, 1990). For a critical review of the effects and reception of (American style) marketing, see Johansson, Johny K., *In Your Face: How American Marketing Excess Fuels Anti-Americanism* (Upper Saddle River, NJ: Financial Times Prentice Hall, 2004).

6. Daniel Miller, 'Consumption as the Vanguard of History', in D. Miller, ed., *Acknowledging Consumption* (London: Routledge, 1995): 1–57.

7. Erving Goffman, *The Presentation of Self in Everyday Life* (Garden City, NY: Doubleday, 1959); George H. Mead, *Mind, Self, and Society* (Chicago: University of Chicago Press, 1934); Michael R. Solomon, 'The role of products as social stimuli: A symbolic interactionism perspective', *Journal of Consumer Research* 10 (December 1983): 319–29.

8. Yiannis Gabriel and Tim Lang, *The Unmanageable Consumer* (London: Sage, 1995).

9. Frank Bradley, *Marketing Management: Providing, Communicating and Delivering Value* (London: Prentice-Hall, 1995).

10. Evan Ramstad, 'Walkman's Plan for Reeling in the Ears of Wired Youths', *Wall Street Journal Interactive Edition* (18 May 2000).

11. http://news.google.com/news?ned=uk (accessed 25 July 2005).

12. http://epp.eurostat.ec.europa.eu/portal/page?_pageid=1090,30070682,1090_33076576&_dad–portal&_schema–PORTAL

13. Päivi Munter and Norma Cohen, 'Ageing populations "will create crippling debt"', *Financial Times* (31 March 2004).

14. Natalie Perkins, 'Zeroing in on consumer values', *Ad Age* (22 March 1993): 23. See also: 'Ageing, Children, and Gender Issues', *European Public Health Alliance*, 2008, http://www.epha.org/r/37

15. Charles Goldsmith and Anne-Michelle Morice, '*Marie Claire* wants to add some fun', *Wall Street Journal* (12 April 2004): B-1.

16. Jennifer Lawrence, 'Gender-specific works for diapers – almost too well', *Ad Age* (8 February 1993): S-10 (2); see also: Dixon, John, 'On Discourse and Dirty Nappies', *Theory & Psychology*, vol. 14 no. 2, 167–189 (2004).

17. 'Wrangler ad ropes in men', *Marketing* (27 March 1997).

18. 'Gender Gap Alive and Well Online' BBC News, http://news.bbc.co.uk/2/hi/technology/4555370.stm

19. Amy Barrett, 'Site blends frivolous, serious to draw French women online', *Wall Street Journal Interactive Edition* (11 April 2000).

20. Charles M. Schaninger and William D. Danko, 'A conceptual and empirical comparison of alternative household life cycle models', *Journal of Consumer Research* 19 (March 1993): 580–94; Robert E. Wilkes, 'Household life-cycle stages, transitions, and product expenditures', *Journal of Consumer Research* 22(1) (June 1995): 27–42.

21. Richard P. Coleman, 'The continuing significance of social class to marketing', *Journal of Consumer Research* 10 (December 1983): 265–80.

22. BBS Radio (4 January 1997).

23. *Information* (26 September 2000): 11; see also: Kerstin Hilt, 'Mail order firm ships a taste of home', *Deutsche Welle* (29 December 2004), http://www.dw-world.de/dw/article/0,1564,1441829,00.html. See also: *The Halal Journal*, http://www.halaljournal.com/artman/publish_php/cat_index_66.php

24. See http://en.wikipedia.org/wiki/French_law_to_ban_conspicuous_religious_symbols for an overview of conspicuous religious symbols in French schools (2005).

25. Verhaar, O. and Saharso, S., 'The Weight of Context: Headscarves in Holland', *Ethical Theory and Moral Practice*, vol. 7, 2, nr. 4, 2004, pp. 179–95.

26. Özlem Sandikci and Güliz Ger, 'Fundamental Fashions: The Cultural Politics of the Turban and the Levi's', paper presented at the 2000 Association for Consumer Research Conference, Salt Lake City (19–22 October 2000).

27. Jean-Claude Usunier, *Marketing Across Cultures*, 4th edn (London: Prentice-Hall, 2005).

28. Søren Askegaard and Tage Koed Madsen, 'The local and the global: homogeneity and heterogeneity in food consumption in European regions', *International Business Review* 7(6) (1998): 549–68.

29. *Information* (4 February 1997); Vanessa Thorpe, 'London becomes Europe's pink capital', *The Observer* (9 January 2005), http://media.guardian.co.uk/site/story/0,14173,1386236,00.html; see also: 'Hello Sailors: The United Queendom Wants You', *The Sunday Times* (5 February 2006).

30. *Markedsføring* 18 (7 September 2000): 16.

31. *Markedsføring* 17 (25 August 2000): 8.

32. Richard Vezina, Alain d'Astous and Sophie Deschamps, 'The Physically Disabled Consumer: Some Preliminary Findings and an Agenda for Future Research', in F. Hansen, ed., *European Advances in Consumer Research* 2 (Provo, UT: Association for Consumer Research, 1995): 277–81.

33. *Samvirke* 3 (March 1997).

34. 'Play your cards right', *Marketing* (17 April 1997): 32–3.

35. http://www.screenselect.co.uk/visitor/home.html and http://web.de/, 2005.

36. Barry Leventhal, 'An approach to fusing market research with database marketing', *Journal of the Market Research Society* 39(4) (1997): 545–58.

37. Brad Edmondson, 'The dawn of the megacity', *Marketing Tools* (March 1999): 64.

38. For a discussion of this trend, see Russell W. Belk, 'Hyperreality and globalization: Culture in the age of Ronald McDonald', *Journal of International Consumer Marketing* 8(3/4) (1995): 23–37.

39. For a fully fledged study of this process, see Tom O'Dell, *Culture Unbound. Americanization and Everyday Life in Sweden* (Lund: Nordic Academic Press, 1997).

40. Richard T. Watson, Leyland F. Pitt, Pierre Berthon and George M. Zinkhan, 'U-Commerce: Expanding the Universe of Marketing', *Journal of the Academy of Marketing Science* 30 (2002): 333–47.

41. Some material in this section was adapted from Michael R. Solomon and Elnora W. Stuart, *Welcome to Marketing.Com: The Brave New World of E-Commerce* (Upper Saddle River, NJ: Prentice Hall, 2000).

42. Patricia Winters Lauro, 'Marketing Battle for Online Dating', *New York Times on the Web* (27 January 2003).

43. Bernard Dubois and Gilles Laurent, 'Is there a Euro Consumer for Luxury Goods?', in W.F. van Raaij and G. Bamossy, eds, *European Advances in Consumer Research* 1 (Provo, UT: Association for Consumer Research, 1993): 58–69.

44. R. Pearce, 'Social responsibility in the marketplace: assymetric information in food labelling', *Business Ethics: A European Review* 8(1) (1999): 26–36.

45. 'Alcopop sales dry up for Diageo', 19 February 2004, BBC News, http://news.bbc.co.uk/2/hi/business/3503589.stm

46. Pasi Falk, 'The Advertising Genealogy', in P. Sulkunen, J. Holmwood, H. Radner and G. Schulze, eds, *Constructing the New Consumer Society* (London: Macmillan, 1997): 81–107.

47. *Information* (2–3 September 2000): 11; Victor Malarek, *The Natashas: The New Global Sex Trade Book* (Viking Canada, 2003); see also: 'New crackdown on sex trafficking', 2007 October 3, *BBC News*, http://news.bbc.co.uk/2/hi/uk_news/7024646.stm

48. For scientific consumer research and discussions related to public policy issues, there is a special European journal, the *Journal of Consumer Policy* (available in university libraries).

49. G.K. Hadfield and D. Thompson, 'An information-based approach to labeling bio-technology consumer products', *Journal of Consumer Policy* 21 (1998): 551–78; H. Sheehy, M. Legault and D. Ireland, 'Consumers and biotechnology: A synopsis of survey and focus group research', *Journal of Consumer Policy* 21 (1998): 359–86.

50. See Philip Kotler and Alan R. Andreasen, *Strategic Marketing for Nonprofit Organizations*, 7th edn (Englewood Cliffs, NJ: Prentice Hall, 2008); Jeff B. Murray and Julie L. Ozanne, 'The critical imagination: Emancipatory interests in consumer research', *Journal of Consumer Research* 18 (September 1991): 192–44; William D. Wells, 'Discovery-oriented consumer research', *Journal of Consumer Research* 19.(March 1993): 489–504.

51. Bertil Swartz, '"Keep Control": The Swedish Brewers' Association Campaign to Foster Responsible Alcohol Consumption Among Adolescents', paper presented at the ACR Europe Conference, Stockholm, June 1997; Anna Oloffson, Ordpolen Informations AB, Sweden, personal communication, August 1997.

52. Roger Crisp, 'Persuasive advertising, autonomy, and the creation of desire', *Journal of Business Ethics* 6 (1987): 413–18.

53. Søren Askegaard and A. Fuat Firat, 'Towards a Critique of Material Culture, Consumption and Markets' in S. Pearce, ed., *Experiencing Material Culture in the Western World* (London: Leicester University Press, 1997): 114–39.

54. William Leiss, Stephen Kline and Sut Jhally, *Social Communication in Advertising: Persons, Products & Images of Well-Being* (Toronto: Methuen, 1986); Jerry Mander, *Four Arguments for the Elimination of Television* (New York: William Morrow, 1977).

55. Vance Packard, *The Hidden Persuaders* (London: Longmans Green, 1957).

56. Raymond Williams, 'Advertising: The Magic System', in *Problems in Materialism and Culture* (London: New Left Books, 1962).

57. Morris B. Holbrook, 'The Consumer Researcher Visits Radio City: Dancing in the Dark', in E.C. Hirschman and M.B. Holbrook, eds, *Advances in Consumer Research* 12 (Provo, UT: Association for Consumer Research, 1985): 28–31.

58. Jean-Claude Usunier, 'Integrating the Cultural Dimension into International Marketing', Proceedings of the Second Conference on the Cultural Dimension of International Marketing (Odense: Odense University, 1995): 1–23.

59. Hansen, ed., *European Advances in Consumer Research* 2.

60. Eric J. Arnould and Craig J. Thompson, 'Consumer culture theory (CCT): Twenty years of research', *Journal of Consumer Research* 31 (March 2005): 868–82.

61. Per Østergaard and Christian Jantzen, 'Shifting Perspectives in Consumer Research: From Buyer Behaviour to Consumption Studies' in S.C. Beckmann and R. Elliott, eds, *Interpretive Consumer Research* (Copenhagen: Copenhagen Business School Press, 2000): 9–23.

2

A consumer society

Six weeks before St Valentine's Day, called Lovers' Day in Turkey, Ayşe starts planning for that special romantic evening. She remembers that last year she and her husband could not find a table in any restaurant in Ankara, all hotels and restaurants had been fully booked and florists had run out of red roses. So she acts early and makes a reservation for two at a good restaurant. She starts window shopping for a gift that she would like to receive. She sees a St Valentine's Day Swatch that she really likes. Two weeks before Lovers' Day, she starts asking her husband what he is thinking of getting her. She takes him to the shopping centre and shows him the St Valentine's Day Swatch and tells him that she'd like that *very* much. On Lovers' Day Ayşe's husband remembers that he has not yet bought anything, goes to get the St Valentine's Day Swatch – only to discover that the shop has run out of them. Instead he buys a much more expensive Swatch. When he comes home, he finds his wife, dressed up ready to go out for dinner. Excited, she closes her eyes and puts her arm forward, confident that he will put a watch around her wrist. And he does. But when she opens her eyes and sees that it is not the St Valentine's Day Swatch, she is upset – and furious. She bursts into tears; they have an argument; and Ayşe goes to the bedroom and takes off her nice clothes. They spend the evening at home, in separate rooms, not talking to each other. 'Some Lovers' Day!' she thinks.

Later, Ayşe tells the story to her friends, some of whom think it's very funny . . .

GÜLIZ GER, Bilkent University, Ankara

CONSUMER CULTURE

The opening vignette illustrates two of the processes related to changes in consumer societies that are discussed in this chapter, globalization and the importance of consumption in structuring our lives. Lovers' Day started to be celebrated in Turkey about a decade ago, first by exchanging cards among school friends. It has become more widespread in the last few years, mostly among the urban middle class who now exchange gifts and make a special evening of it. St Valentine's Day, appropriated as Lovers' Day, is taking root among married and unmarried couples in this Muslim country where traditional norms of respectability did not allow dating – dating is not what 'nice' girls were supposed to do, and many from conservative or lower-middle class families still frown on it. Beyond globalization, we can also see how important consumption is in the creation of a meaningful relationship and a meaningful cultural event such as St Valentine's Day. In fact, in contemporary modern society, it is hard to think of many kinds of social behaviour that do not involve consumption in one form or another. Consumption activities provide both meaning and structure to the way we live. Brands are becoming ubiquitous signs of the importance of symbolic meanings in the marketplace. These are some of the processes we will deal with in this chapter.

New books and art exhibitions witness the increasing importance of consumption, branding and advertising in our societies.[1] To some extent, consumption replaces politics as a way of running a community. In 2000, it was announced that Huntington Beach, a Los Angeles suburb, had made Coca-Cola the official drink of the community. For $600,000 per year the company will exclude Pepsi and other soft drinks from official buildings and put up drink dispensers and advertisements all over the city. The city council initiated the deal, saying it was an alternative to higher taxes.[2]

▶ Many people use the notion of the **consumer society** in order to describe the current type of social organization in the economically-developed world. This is not only because we live in a world full of things, which we obviously do, but also because the most decisive step in the construction of consumer society is the new role of consumption activities. We used to define ourselves primarily based on our role in the production process, i.e., our work. Increasingly, however, it is more decisive for our personal and social identities how we consume instead of what we do for a living. The plethora of goods and their varieties in range and styles allows consumption choices to become clear (or sometimes purposefully ambiguous) statements about our personality, our values, aspirations, sympathies and antipathies, and our way of handling social relations.

Modern consumer society is thus characterized by consumption-based identities, but other related features of a consumer society include many of the other topics discussed in this book: shopping as leisure activity combined with the variety of shopping possibilities including shopping centres (the new 'temples of consumption'), easier access to credit, the growing attention to brand images and the communicative aspects of product and packaging as well as the pervasiveness of promotion, the increasing political organization of consumers in groups with a variety of purposes and the sheer impossibility of trying not to be a consumer and still participating in ordinary social life.[3] Things do matter.[4]

Popular culture

▶ When it is said that contemporary culture is a **consumer culture**, we do not only refer to the central role of consumption in all of our daily activities. We also underline the basic relationship between market forces, consumption processes and the basic characteristics of what we normally understand by 'a culture'. As we shall see, whether we talk about high culture (such as the fine arts etc.) or popular culture, our contemporary culture is basically something 'to be consumed'. Whether we talk about our way of travelling around, our styles of dressing, our music, our spectacles and sports events, tourism, fashion, popular music and sports are deeply commercialized consumer markets.[5] We consume 'spaces' and 'places' both in our cities when we are enjoying their commercial and/or cultural areas and offerings as well as on holidays; we are constantly consuming different styles and fashions, not only in clothing but also in food, home appliances, garden and interior design, music and so on and so forth. Marketing sometimes seems to exert a self-fulfilling prophecy on popular culture. As commercial influences on popular culture increase, marketer-created symbols make their way into our daily lives to a greater degree. Historical analyses of plays, best-selling novels and the lyrics of hit songs, for example, clearly show large increases in the use of brand names over time.[6]

▶   **Popular culture**, the music, films, sports, books and other forms of entertainment consumed by the mass market, is both a product of and an inspiration for marketers. Our lives are also affected in more fundamental ways, ranging from how we acknowledge social events such as marriages, deaths or holidays to how we view societal issues such as air pollution, gambling and addiction. The football World Cup, Christmas shopping, tourism, newspaper recycling, cigarette smoking and Barbie dolls are all examples of products and activities that touch many of us in our lives.

Marketing's role in the creation and communication of popular culture is especially emphasized in this book. This cultural influence is hard to ignore, although many people fail to appreciate the extent to which their view of the world – their film and music icons, the latest fashions in clothing, food and interior design, and even the physical features that they find attractive or not in sexual partners – is influenced by the marketing system.

Consider the product characters that marketers use to create a personality for their products. From the Michelin Man to Ronald McDonald, popular culture is peopled with fictional heroes. In fact, it is likely that more consumers will recognize characters such as these than can identify former (or present!) prime ministers, captains of industry or artists. These characters may not exist, but many of us feel that we 'know' them, and they certainly are effective *spokes-characters* for the products they promote.

THE MEANING OF THINGS

For better or worse, we live in a world that is significantly influenced by marketers. We are surrounded by marketing stimuli in the form of advertisements, shops and products competing for our attention and our cash. Much of what we learn about the world is filtered by marketers, whether through conspicuous consumption depicted in glamorous magazine advertising or via the roles played by family figures in TV commercials. Ads show us how we ought to act with regard to recycling, alcohol consumption and even the types of house or car we aspire to. In many ways we are heavily influenced by and depend upon marketers, since we rely on them to sell us products that are safe and perform as promised, to tell us the truth about what they are selling, and to price and distribute these products fairly.

The meaning of consumption

One of the fundamental premises of consumer behaviour is that people often buy products not for what they do, but for what they *mean*.[7] This principle does not imply that a product's primary function is unimportant, but rather that the roles products play

▶   and the **meaning** that they have in our lives go well beyond the tasks they perform. The deeper meanings of a product may help it to stand out from other, similar goods and services – all things being equal, a person will choose the brand that has an image (or even a personality!) consistent with their underlying ideas. While this text takes multiple perspectives on how consumers view products in their lives, one of the recurring themes throughout is that consumer goods are an important medium in European society, that goods and services are loaded with both public and private meanings, and that we as consumers are constantly drawing meanings out of our possessions and using them to construct our domestic and public worlds.

Research has demonstrated that the cultural symbolism of product meanings influence physiological processes such as taste. When we think we adhere to the values represented by a product or a brand, we also think that it tastes better.[8] So such cultural symbols are very powerful and product meanings are to some extent self-fulfilling. Athletes swear by their favourite brand and may lose self-confidence and perform poorly if they cannot wear it, although objectively speaking they cannot run faster or jump higher if they are wearing Nikes rather than Reeboks. These archrivals are marketed in terms of their image – meanings that have been carefully crafted with the help of legions of rock stars, athletes, slickly produced commercials – and many millions of dollars. So, when you buy a Nike 'Swoosh' you may be doing more than choosing footwear – you may also be making a lifestyle statement about the type of person you are, or want to be. For a relatively simple item made of leather and laces, that's quite a feat!

As Figure 2.1 shows, meaning transfer is largely accomplished by such marketing vehicles as the advertising and fashion industries, which associate products with symbolic qualities. These goods, in turn, impart their meanings to consumers through different forms of ritual and are used to create and sustain consumer identities. We will take a much closer look at how these rituals work in Chapter 13 and at the fashion system in Chapter 14. In this chapter, the model serves the more general purpose of underlining the importance of meaning for understanding contemporary consumption.

One can make the objection to the model in Figure 2.1, that there is a feedback arrow missing between the individual consumer and the cultural values and symbols. Cultural values and symbols obviously only exist in so far as people enact and use them. Therefore, it is also important to remind ourselves that the advertising and fashion industries, even though they are highly influential, are not dictatorial in establishing product meanings. We all give a helping hand. In a sense, in consumer society we are all 'lifestyle experts' to some degree, and many of us are trying to assert our uniqueness by mixing and matching styles and products that we can find in the marketplace. In a very existential sense,

Figure 2.1 The movement of meaning

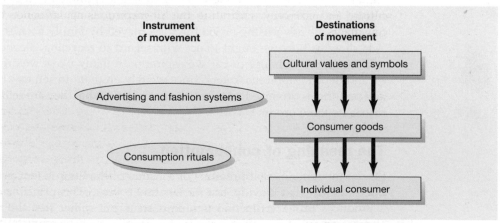

Source: Adapted from Grant McCracken, 'Culture and consumption: A theoretical account of the structure and movement of the cultural meaning of consumer goods', *Journal of Consumer Research* 13 (June 1986): 72. Reprinted with permission of The University of Chicago Press.

Figure 2.2 Relationship between culture and economy

I. Pre-modern

No distinction between Culture and Economy. One implies the other

II. Modern

Culture and Economy are separate

Economy is accorded a superior status because of its relevance to the creation of 'productive' value

ECONOMY   Culture

Production   Consumption

III. Postmodern-postindustrial

New perspectives on the relationship between Culture and Economy

Culture subsumes Economy

CULTURE

Economy	Government	Ideology
Education	Family	
Institutions	Production	Consumption
Symbolic systems		

Source: Alladi Venkatesh, 'Ethnoconsumerism: A New Paradigm to Study Cultural and Cross-Cultural Consumer Behavior', in J.A. Costa and G. Bamossy, eds, *Marketing in a Multicultural World* (Thousand Oaks, CA: Sage, 1995).

we can say that we are what we consume, an issue we will discuss in more detail in Chapter 5 on consumption and the self.

Consumer society, then, is a society where the social life is organized less around our identities as producers or workers in the production system, and more according to our roles as consumers in the consumption system. This expresses a relatively new idea. Until recently, many researchers treated culture as a sort of variable that would explain differences in what they saw as the central dimension in society: economic behaviour. However, in our post-industrial society it has become increasingly evident that the principles of economy are themselves expressions of a specific kind of culture. Figure 2.2 provides an overview of this evolving approach to the relationship between culture and economy, indicating the all-encompassing influence that culture has on consumers.

Cultural categories

▶ Meanings that are imparted to products reflect underlying **cultural categories**, which correspond to the basic ways we characterize the world.[9] Our culture makes distinctions between different times of the day, such as between leisure and work hours, as well as other differences, such as between genders, occasions, groups of people, and so on. The fashion system provides us with products that signify these categories. For example, the clothing industry gives us clothing to denote certain times (evening wear, resort wear), it differentiates between leisure clothes and work clothes, and it promotes masculine, feminine or unisex styles.[10] Goods, then are 'signs of the times' in which we live. The 'rocket designs' in the fifties reflected the belief in the technological progress of that era. Political figures (and their relatives) and what they represent are also potential style icons. One of the first examples indicating the rise of consumer society was Jackie Kennedy, and a very contemporary example is Michelle Obama becoming a style icon even before she had officially become the 'First Lady'. Her stylish and professional outfits have greatly stimulated sales of 'affordable luxury' clothing for working women in America.[11] What is important to retain, then, is that meanings of consumer goods and their designs are not universal but relative to given social and historical contexts or, to put it simply, are bound to particular times and particular places.

What do we do, when we consume? Product meanings in use

If consumption is not just about solving practical problems, but is also about the personal, and cultural meanings ascribed to the consumption practices, then it raises the important question about the cultural purposes of consumption. For example, we do not just eat because we are hungry, since most eating behaviours are linked to a myriad of cultural meanings and rituals. We will take a closer look at this in Chapter 13, but for now consider a more general explanation of consumption practices. In a fine proposal of a theory to answer this question, one consumer researcher has developed a classification scheme in an attempt to explore the different ways that products and experiences can provide meaning to people.[12] This consumption typology was derived from a two-year analysis of supporters of a baseball team in the US, but it is easily transferable to both the European context and to other types of consumption as well. But focusing on an event such as a baseball match – or to make it more familiar to Europeans a football match – is a useful reminder that when we refer to consumption, we are talking about intangible experiences, ideas and services (the thrill of a goal or the antics of a team mascot) in addition to tangible objects (like the food and drink consumed at the stadium). This analysis identified four distinct types of consumption activities:

1 *Consuming as experience* – when the consumption is a personal emotional or aesthetic goal in itself. This would include activities like the pleasure derived from learning how to interpret the offside rule, or appreciating the athletic ability of a favourite player.

2 *Consuming as integration* – using and manipulating consumption objects to express aspects of the self. For example, some fans express their solidarity with the team by identifying with, say, the mascot and adopting some of its characteristic traits. Attending matches in person rather than watching them on TV allows the fan to integrate their experience more completely with their self – the feeling of 'having been there'.

3 *Consuming as classification* – the activities that consumers engage in to communicate their association with objects, both to self and to others. For example, spectators might dress up in the team's colours and buy souvenirs to demonstrate to others that they are diehard fans. Unfortunately, the more hard core express their contempt for opponents' supporters violently. There is a profound 'us' and 'them' dichotomy present here.

4 *Consuming as play* – consumers use objects to participate in a mutual experience and merge their identities with that of a group. For example, happy fans might scream in unison and engage in an orgy of jumping and hugging when their team scores a goal – this is a different dimension of shared experience compared with watching the game at home.

It is important to realize that these categories are not mutually exclusive, and that consumption activities may have traits of several or all of these aspects. On the other hand, one aspect may dominate in the understanding of one particular consumption situation.

Even though this typology takes its point of departure in the consumption of baseball, it is easy to see how it can be applied to other types of consumption as well. You can drive/consume your car for the experience of it, just you and your car and the feeling of the oneness of the driver and the machine, or you can drive it as an extended self, an confirmation of your personality (maybe it is an eco-friendly VW Lupo that serves to underline your environmental consciousness). You can drive your car based on the playful togetherness and the freedom of movement it gives to you and your friends. And finally, it is hard to think of a car that does not in some sense classify its driver, be it a cheerfully painted Citroën 2CV, a sporty convertible Mini or a black Mercedes Benz 500 SE.[13]

A BRANDED WORLD

One of the most important ways in which meaning is created in consumer society is
▶ through the **brand**. Although defining exactly what a brand is, is a complex task,[14] the point of departure is that it refers to those strategic processes whereby managers try to create and sustain meanings attached to products, services, organizations, etc. The problem arises when we add that the brand is not limited by these strategically intended meanings but possibly first and foremost come to life in the minds of consumers. Hence, what the brand means is ultimately decided by the consumer, not by the brand manager. In the twenty-first century, there has been a tremendous growth in the interest in brands, whether product brands or corporate brands, and their increasing importance as vehicles of meaning for people/consumers. Few people will raise an eyebrow at the suggestion that a university, a school, a kindergarten, a politician, a sports club or even a type of sports can be thought of in terms of being a brand. In fact, today, it is not unheard of to think about oneself as a brand, that must compete in the marketplace for friends, partners, jobs, success, etc.[15]

As we have already seen in Chapter 1, the hallmark of marketing strategies at the beginning of the twenty-first century is an emphasis on building relationships with customers. The nature of these relationships can vary, and these bonds help us to understand some of the possible meanings products have for us. Here are some of the types of relationship a person may have with a brand:[16]

- *Self-concept attachment*: the product helps to establish the user's identity.
- *Nostalgic attachment*: the product serves as a link with a past self.
- *Interdependence*: the product is a part of the user's daily routine.
- *Love*: the product elicits bonds of warmth, passion or other strong emotion.

Brand identities are thus potentially very closely intertwined with consumer identities[17] and brands can elicit deep emotional engagement from consumers.[18] Even brands we do not like can be very important to us, because we often define ourselves in opposition to what we do not like.[19]

One of the 'discoveries' of consumer research in the twenty-first century is that consumers increasingly organize communities based on their consumption of and
▶ attachment to particular brands, so-called **brand communities**.[20] Such brand communities can range from core members of 'social clubs' or organizations to 'felt' memberships of some imagined community. For example, drivers of the Swedish produced Saab cars in the US considered each other somehow linked through their Saab ownership, and many have adopted the habit of greeting other Saab drivers whom they meet in the traffic regardless of the fact that they are complete strangers. Just the fact that they drive the same brand of cars makes the Saab owners feel part of a special group of people set apart from the rest of society: a brand community. Memberships of brand

communities can also be very important in conveying a sense of authenticity and confirmation of one's identity as a member of some (youth) subculture oriented towards consumption of a particular style of fashion or type of music.[21] Brand communities do not have to be about expensive products such as computers or cars. A very active virtual brand community has formed around the hazelnut-based spread Nutella, where consumers online write or talk about and expose themselves in Nutella consumption situations and share their funniest or happiest 'Nutella moments'.[22] Some consumers form communities around brands, but some consumer communities form their own brands. Communities around Websites such as *outdoorseiten.net* and *skibuilders.com* have engaged in developing equipment and branding based on what community members felt was lacking in the marketplace.[23] We will return to brand devotion and community building in Chapter 13.

Experience economy

Some marketers have suggested that the contemporary economy can be characterized as an **experience economy**.[24] They argue that the competition among different market offers has driven producers to distinguish otherwise almost identical product first through the services attached to acquiring the product but now increasingly through differentiating the experience that comes along with consuming the product. This historical shift, it is argued, can be exemplified through the consumption of a birthday cake. Historically, the standard way of creating a birthday party for one's child has gone from buying the ingredients for making a cake, buying a cake at the baker's/confectioner's shop, buying the cake as well as a number of other objects supposedly providing a thematized birthday (a Spiderman birthday, a ghost birthday, a Barbie birthday) to buying the whole birthday party at the local McDonald's, the local toy store, the local zoo or any other provider of a 'complete birthday experience'. To the extent that consumers demand and companies provide more and more 'total experiences', we live in an experience economy.

Some of the most notable providers of consumable experiences are theme parks and amusement parks, such as the Disneylands, Legolands, Parc Asterix or other thematized spaces of leisurely consumption. But experience economy has also found its way to more mundane consumption activities. Even banks have tried different ways of turning the bank services into an experience. One Danish bank, in addition to the café corner, provided particular rooms with photos from around the world and an airplane-wing shaped table for talks about financing travels and provided about 30 different packages of brochures and information visualizing their product offers. If you were to talk about a loan for building or reconstructing a house, the information came in a box shaped and coloured like a brick. If discussing investments and savings, the box had the shape of a gold bar. If you were financing the acquisition of a house or an apartment, the box came disguised as a moving box.[25]

Postmodernism

Many of the themes that we address in this book, such as the dominance of the brand (over whatever reality lies behind it), the possibility of engineering reality in the experience economy or the blurring of the fashion picture, have been linked to major social changes. One proposed summary term for this change is **postmodernism** – one of the most widely discussed and disputed terms in consumer research in the past decade and a half.[26]

Postmodernists argue that we live in period where the modern order, with its shared beliefs in certain central values of modernism and industrialism, is breaking up. Examples of these values include the benefits of economic growth and industrial

production, and the infallibility of science. In opposition to currently held views, postmodernism questions the search for universal truths and values, and the existence of
► objective knowledge.[27] Thus a keyword is **pluralism**, indicating the co-existence of various truths, styles and fashions. Consumers (and producers) are relatively free to combine elements from different styles and domains to create their own personal expression. This pluralism, it is argued, has significant consequences for how we regard theories of marketing and consumer behaviour. Most significantly, pluralism does not mean that anything goes in terms of method or theory, but it does mean that no single theory or method can pretend to be universal in its accounting for consumer behaviour or marketing practices.[28]

There have been several attempts to sum up features of postmodernism and their implications for contemporary market conditions.[29] Together with pluralism, one European researcher has suggested that postmodernism can be described by six key features:[30]

1 *Fragmentation*. The splitting up of what used to be simpler and more mass oriented, exemplified by the ever-growing product ranges and brand extensions in more and more specialized variations. The advertising media have also become fragmented, with increasingly specialized TV channels, magazines, radio stations and Websites for placing one's advertising.

2 *De-differentiation*. Postmodernists are interested in the blurring of distinctions between hierarchies such as 'high and low culture', 'advertising and programming' or 'politics and show business'. Examples would be the use of artistic works in advertising and the celebration of advertising as artistic works. Companies such as Coca-Cola, Nike and Guinness have their own museums. The blurring of gender categories also refers to this aspect of postmodernism.

▲ Marketing opportunity

In London, the vodka brand Absolut has opened a bar where the temperature is maintained artificially at minus 5 degrees. This cold environment evokes the imagery consumers have of Sweden, the vodka brand's country of origin, and the clear, crystalline feeling that drinking the vodka should convey. Equipped with a cape and gloves, consumers can sip their vodka from a glass made of ice, a truly glacial experience.[31] The company also rebuilds a hotel made of ice and snow every year in northern Sweden, complete with rooms, dining and meeting facilities, a sauna and, of course, another icebar for tasting the famous vodka.[32] The brand has thus recreated a hyperreal world in the image of its own 'crystal clear and icy' brand identity. In the contemporary experience economy, this promises to be one of a kind. Are you tempted?

► 3 *Hyperreality* refers to the spreading of simulations and the 'making real of what was just a fantasy'. Disneyland (and other theme parks) are quintessentially hyperreal. Marketers are among the prime creators of hyperreality.[33] But consumers contribute too! Film director Quentin Tarantino lets some of his main characters in *Pulp Fiction* smoke a fictitious 'Red Apple' cigarette brand, which later appears on an advertising billboard in *Kill Bill*. Merchandise for this fictitious brand has subsequently been made real by certain consumers, presumably devoted Tarantino fans captured by the coolness of Red Apples smokers Butch Coolidge (Bruce Willis) and Mia Wallace (Uma Thurman), through the production of, e.g., tee shirts and ashtrays featuring the otherwise fictitious Red Apple brand![34]

▼ Marketing pitfall

Sometimes companies may fall victim to their own hyperreality. It is the dream of many producers to create a strong brand with a solid position in cultural life. But as they do so, their brand images are incorporated into the general cultural sign system, and the company loses control over the signs attached to the brand name. For example, the name 'Barbie' today is much more than a brand name – it has almost become a name for a personality type. When a Danish pop group, Aqua, enjoyed a huge success with the song 'Barbie', which contained lyrics alluding to the personal life of this hyperreal personality (e.g. 'you can dress my hair, undress me everywhere'), Mattel Inc. was not amused. It sued the pop group for abuse of the Barbie name and for destroying the pure and positive image of Barbie's world created through a long range of expensive campaigns. This is yet another example of the blurring of marketing and popular culture, and the question is: can you patent culture?[35]

4 *Chronology*. This refers to the consumer's nostalgic search for the authentic and a preoccupation with the past.[36] A postmodern way of looking at the same phenomenon is *retro branding* conceptualized as 'the revival or relaunch of a brand from a prior historical period that differs from nostalgic brands by the element of updating'.[37] Retro brands are of relevance here as well because 'these revived brands invoke brand heritage which triggers personal and communal nostalgia'.[38]

▶ 5 ***Pastiche***. A recent book on postmodern marketing is a pastiche of a novel. This novel's content is in itself a pastiche since it is a thinly veiled 'copy' of Dan Brown's bestseller, *The Da Vinci Code*, complete with murders, suspense, and a sectarian society that acts as a keeper of the ultimate secret. The book, *The Marketing Code*, basically uses the format of the novel to discuss various marketing techniques, promoting the view that marketing is an art form rather than a science.[39] Such playful and ironic mixing of existing categories and styles is typical of pastiche.

The seventeenth-century Danish landmark of the 'round tower' of Copenhagen has been recreated (in a slightly smaller version) in the simulated Danish environment of Solvang, California, founded as a 'little Denmark' by Danish immigrants in the nineteenth century, but gradually becoming more of a hyperreal theme park under the influence of marketing in the postwar period. The tower in Solvang houses a local pizza restaurant: Tower Pizza, of course!

Photo: Søren Askegaard

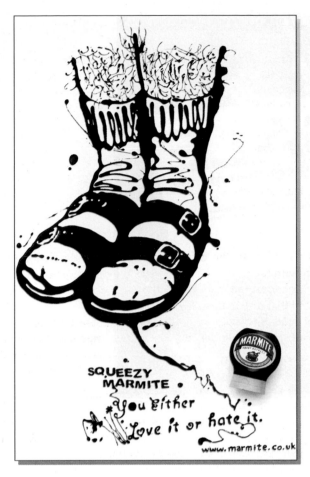

Self-parody is one postmodern approach to communication.
The Advertising Archives

6 *Anti-foundationalism*. This last feature of postmodern marketing efforts refers not to parody but to an outright 'anti-campaign campaign'. For example, campaigns encouraging the receiver of the message *not* to take notice of the message since somebody is trying to seduce and take advantage of them, as seen in the photo above.

Postmodernism has also been attached to such themes as the ability of readers to see through the hype of advertising.[40] This may suggest that we are becoming more skilled consumers and readers/interpreters of advertising, recognizing ads as hyperreal persuasion or seduction attempts which do not intend to reflect our own daily experiences. Younger consumers especially may be prone to detect and enjoy the self-referencing or intertextuality of advertising.[41] Here, the self-consciousness of the brand as a brand and the ambivalence that follows from it is seen as the entertaining aspect of contemporary marketing.[42]

GLOBAL CONSUMER CULTURE

Consumer culture is becoming increasingly globalized, and brands have becomes signs of a global ideology of cultural (and commercial!) value and power.[43] In fact, the tempting imagery of contemporary consumer culture and marketing, the prime vehicles that bring this imagery about, may be considered some of the most important drivers of ▶ globalization. The process of **globalization** has attracted a tremendous amount of interest in the last couple of decades. But learning about the relationship between the global and the local in the practices of other cultures is more than just interesting – it is an essential

This advert for HSBC illustrates how a global company addresses a global issue by respecting localities.

The Advertising Archives

task for any company that wishes to expand its horizons and become part of the international or global marketplace at the beginning of the new millennium.

▶   This viewpoint represents an **etic perspective**, which focuses on commonalities across cultures. An etic approach assumes that there are common, general categories and measurements which are valid for all cultures under consideration. One such etic study identified four major clusters of consumer styles when they looked at data from the US, the UK, France, and Germany: *price-sensitive consumers*, *variety seekers*, *brand-loyal consumers*, and *information seekers*.[44] On the other hand, many marketers choose to study and

▶   analyze a culture using an **emic perspective**, which attempts to explain a culture based on the cultural categories and experiences of the insiders. For example, cultures vary sharply in the degree to which references to sex and nudity (and other controversial issues) are permitted. One study analyzed responses to advertising for 'controversial products', including potentially offensive ads related to sexual behaviour such as ads for condoms, female contraceptives, underwear and (prevention of) sexually transmitted diseases. It was found that results for what was deemed controversial differed highly between the UK and New Zealand on the one hand and Turkey and Malaysia on the other. While negative reactions to sexual references differed, racist imagery was ranked among the most offensive in all samples. Good that we can agree on something like that![45]

A global consumer?

It is often asserted that global marketing works well with affluent people who are 'global citizens' and who are exposed to ideas from around the world through their travels, business contacts and media experiences, and as a result share common tastes.[46] One sector that comes across as inherently 'global' is the market for luxury goods, with its highly standardized and aesthetisized marketing campaigns and its cosmopolitan target market.

Still, a recent study distinguished between a European type of luxury brands, based more on history, rarity and craftsmanship and an American type of luxury brands based on storytelling, marketing imagery and marketing finesse.[47] The differing business cultures, we can assume, also cover differences in the cultural meaning of luxury products across the Atlantic Ocean. Furthermore, differences in the perception and valorization of the concept of 'performance' (an important notion in many contemporary marketing campaigns) has led to different responses to the same advertisement in countries such as the US, Germany, France, Spain and Thailand.[48]

Another 'global segment' that is often referred to is young people whose tastes in music and fashion are strongly influenced by international pop culture broadcasting many of the same images and sounds to multiple countries.[49] On the other hand, one recent study of the global youth culture concluded that although similar existential conditions existed, including the search for an identity and the feeling of being a member of a global youth consumer culture, the way these similar existential conditions are lived out in reality varies a lot from context to context.[50]

A large-scale study with consumers in 41 countries identified the characteristics people associate with global brands, and it also measured the relative importance of those dimensions when consumers buy products.[51] The researchers grouped consumers who evaluate global brands in the same way and they identified four major segments:

1 *Global citizens.* The largest segment (55 per cent of consumers) uses the global success of a company as a signal of quality and innovation. At the same time, they are concerned about whether companies behave responsibly on issues such as consumer health, the environment, and worker rights.

2 *Global dreamers.* The second-largest segment, at 23 per cent, consists of consumers who see global brands as quality products and readily buy into the myths they author. They are not nearly as concerned with social responsibility as are the global citizens.

This ad is targeting an allegedly global segment of cool, young (wealthy?) cosmopolitans.

The Advertising Archives

3 *Antiglobals.* Thirteen per cent of consumers are sceptical that transnational companies deliver higher-quality goods. They dislike brands that preach American values and do not trust global companies to behave responsibly. They try to avoid doing business with transnational firms.

4 *Global agnostics.* The remaining 9 per cent of consumers don't base purchase decisions on a brand's global attributes. Instead, they evaluate a global product by the same criteria they use to judge local brands and don't regard its global nature as meriting special consideration.

▼ Marketing pitfall

The language barrier is one problem confronting marketers who wish to break into foreign markets. One technique that is used to avoid this problem is where a translated ad is retranslated into the original language by a different interpreter to catch errors. Some specific translation obstacles that have been encountered around the world include the following:[52]

- Wrigley's Spearmint Gum reads as 'Shark's sperm' in some east European countries.
- When Vauxhall launched its Nova model in Spain, it realized that the name meant 'Doesn't go' in Spanish.

- Also in Spain, Mitsubishi discovered that its four-wheel-drive model Pajero would be known as 'Wanker'.
- When Rolls-Royce introduced its Silver Mist model in Germany, it found that the word 'mist' is translated as 'excrement'. Similarly, Sunbeam's hair curling iron, called the Mist-Stick, translated as 'manure wand'. To add insult to injury, 'Vicks' is German slang for sexual intercourse, so that the company's name had to be changed to Wicks in this market.

Coca-Colonization: exporting Western lifestyles

The West (and especially the US) is a *net exporter* of popular culture. Western symbols in the form of images, words and products have diffused throughout the world. This influence is eagerly sought by many consumers, who have learned to equate Western lifestyles in general and the English language in particular with modernization and sophistication. As a result, people around the world are being exposed to a blizzard of Western products that are attempting to become part of local lifestyles.

The allure of Western consumer culture has spread as people in other societies slowly but surely falls under the spell of far-reaching advertising campaigns, contact with tourists and the desire to form attachments with other parts of the world. This attraction sometimes results in bizarre permutations of products and services, as they are modified to be compatible with local customs. For example, in addition to traditional gifts of cloth, food and cosmetics, Nigerian Hausa brides receive cheap quartz watches although they cannot tell the time.[53] As indicated by this and many other examples, many formerly isolated cultures now incorporate Western objects into their traditional practices. In the process, the meanings of these objects are transformed and adapted to local tastes (at times in seemingly bizarre ways). Sometimes the process enriches local cultures; sometimes it produces painful stresses and strains the local society.

The most evident contemporary showcase for studying the impact of a rapid introduction of consumer culture is China. In the 1970s, the Chinese strove to attain what they called the 'three bigs': bikes, sewing machines and wristwatches. This wish list was later modified to become the 'new big six', adding refrigerators, washing machines and televisions. The list was then expanded with *colour* televisions, cameras and video recorders.[54] The Chinese consumer culture of 2009 and the history behind it is described below.

Mainland China is one of the newest markets opening up to Western business and culture. When McDonald's opened in China in the early 1990s, their new Beijing restaurant became their largest outlet in the world with more than 700 seats and 1,000 employees. Hong Kong Disneyland opened their $1.8 billion park in September 2005. They expect to attract 5.6 million visitors in their first year, drawing a third of these from mainland China (http://money.cnn.com/2005/09/11/news/international/disney_hk.reut/).

Getty Images/M.N. Chan

Consumer behaviour as I see it . . .

In a 1979 movie called The China Syndrome, *a meltdown in an American nuclear reactor threatened to bore a hole through the earth to China. Today, there are much faster ways to reach China by e-mail, text messaging, satellite television, podcasts, and other such technologies. The year before* The China Syndrome *opened in theatres, China opened its doors to the world through a group of strategically positioned special economic zones. Deng Xiaoping had replaced Mao Zedong and 'market socialism' was beginning to replace the centralized planning of communism. Deng came to the special economic zone city of Shenzhen, across the border from Hong Kong, and pronounced a revolutionary new slogan. In sharp contrast to the old mottoes urging Chinese people to sacrifice and carry the revolution forward by hard work and austere consumption, the new slogan read: 'To Get Rich Is Glorious'.*

Professor Russell Belk
York University

This was the beginning of an outward-looking China that initiated a still-continuing period of remarkable economic growth toward becoming the world's largest economy (something it should achieve by 2026 given its current rates of growth). It was also the start of an equally profound consumer revolution in China as the market-directed economy took hold. Especially in China's large cities, a prosperous new middle class arose along with a number of millionaires and a few billionaires. From drab stores, identical Sun Yat-Sen ('Mao') jackets, and advertising-free public spaces,

Consumer behaviour as I see it . . . (continued)

Chinese consumer culture burst onto the scene in these cities in a spectacular way. China quickly became a natural laboratory in which we might observe the effects of consumerism, materialism, and dramatic changes in material lifestyles.

What sorts of effects are we seeing from these changes in Chinese consumption? One effect that seems apparent is that besides its nouveau riche consumers, China as a nation might be regarded as a nouveau riche country, with all the reckless and brash spending this implies. Shanghai now has more skyscrapers than New York City. Beijing totally revamped itself for the 2008 Olympics. And Shenzhen is now virtually indistinguishable from Hong Kong, except for its three large amusement parks, including Window on the World with its replica of the Eiffel Tower, indoor ski mountain, and reconstructions of many famous world monuments and icons. It is said that the national bird of China is the construction crane. Whereas Japan remains the world's largest market for luxury brands such as Luis Vuitton, Prada, and Chanel, Chinese consumption of such brands is not far behind and is growing rapidly. And for those who can't yet afford such brands, there is an array of counterfeits that are graded 'A', 'B' and 'C' according to how perfectly they replicate the originals. There is also a category called 'clones' that are virtually indistinguishable from the real thing. In an eight-country study posing consumer 'ethical dilemmas' that included buying counterfeit goods, Giana Eckhardt, Tim Devinney, and I found that Chinese consumers stood out by failing to see any ethical problem with such behaviour. They instead insisted that the famous brands were unethical because their prices were so outrageous. If the clever Chinese could find a way to right the balances with copies, then good for them, our Chinese interviewees said.

Something else that has changed in China is advertising. When advertising returned to China in the late 1970s, it was initially unemotional, informational, and utilitarian in its appeals. But 30 years later, Nan Zhou and I found that Chinese advertising has become much more similar to Western advertising, including its use of many Caucasian models. This prompted a study that is currently underway examining portrayals of beauty and skin colour in several Asian countries. Early results suggest that although lighter skin colour is held to be extremely important in these countries, this is not entirely because of a desire to look more Western or to attain a globalized standard of beauty. There are also distinctly Asian traditions of whiteness, such as those of Japanese geishas and Chinese opera. But the study also raises important questions about globalism, race, and nationalism.

In studies I have done with Güliz Ger, we found that consumer materialism (believing that consumer goods are the major source of happiness in life) tends to increase during periods of sudden economic growth. Such growth appears to upset the status quo with regard to social prestige, and consumer goods increase in importance as a way to shore up or increase social status. The current China syndrome involving conspicuous consumption, luxury goods, counterfeit goods, and volatile standards of beauty seems to be a key example of such a status scramble. At the same time, the formerly flat Chinese income distribution is becoming more polarized through extremes of wealth and poverty that differ between urban and rural areas, coastal and non-coastal areas, dominant and minority ethnic groups, and eastern and western China. Thirty years is enough to see some of the effects of the consumer revolution in China, but the natural experiment is far from over. And we have only to contrast the consumer boom in pre-communist Shanghai of the 1930s versus the Chinese cultural revolution of the 1960s to realize that conditions can change dramatically in an equally short period of time. Today, as China joins the global consumer society, it is showing a fascinating amalgam of tastes. For example, Chinese rap music and Chinese opera both flourish. A secular version of Western Christmas is becoming popular (mostly as a couples holiday like Valentine's Day in the West), but it is not nearly as popular as the Chinese New Year, also known as the Spring Festival. And various regional Chinese cuisines continue to dominate even as the flood of Western fast foods continues to spread. One popular Chinese fast food chain, California Beef Noodle King, serves only Chinese foods and has no counterpart in the West. From a consumer behaviour perspective China may well be the most interesting place on earth.

Consumption of global products and symbols: Japanese motorcyclists with 'chopped' bikes, jackets, jeans and that 'rebel' look.

Harley Davidson, Inc.

In contrast to China, the Japanese have already become accustomed to a bounty of consumer goods. Still, the Japanese are particularly enthusiastic borrowers of Western culture. American music and films are especially popular, perhaps because they are the best way to experience US lifestyles and popular culture.

The Japanese often use Western words as a shorthand for anything new and exciting, even if they do not understand their meaning. The resulting phenomenon is known as 'Japlish',[55] where new Western-sounding words are merged with Japanese. Cars are given names like Fairlady, Gloria and Bongo Wagon. Consumers buy *deodoranto* (deodorant) and *appuru pai* (apple pie). Ads urge shoppers to *stoppu rukku* (stop and look), and products are claimed to be *yuniku* (unique).[56] For an interesting and revealing Website which features dozens of well-known Western celebrities doing commercials for Japanese media, spend some time at Japander![57]

The lure of Western consumption styles and the brands that carry this message have been some of the most effective tools in spreading Western-style consumer culture across the globe. But these tools are now used in order to maintain a particular cultural identity. Branding strategies are used by increasingly strong Asian managers in order to construct a universe of 'Asianness' that can be used to construct local brand value in the booming Asian markets. The Asia portrayed in these campaigns is not the traditional one of peasants working in rice fields but a modern, booming and busting self-confident transnational (not a priori tied to a specific country) Asian world. The result is a branding style that reinforces pride and self-confidence in the Asian region.[58]

▶ Multicultural dimensions

When Marvel Comics launched 'Spiderman India', the first ethnic adaptation of the popular comic book series, the writers turned Peter Parker of New York City into Pavitr Prabhakar of Mumbai. Mary Jane became Meera Jain, and the villainous Norman Osbourne (aka the Green Goblin) is Nalin Oberoi. Spiderman changed from a semitragic figure representing the dangers of scientific experimentation into a hero trying to navigate a modern India still steeped in Hindu mysticism.[59]

Emerging consumer cultures in transitional economies

China and India are not the only emerging consumer societies. After the collapse of communism, eastern Europeans emerged from a long winter of deprivation of consumer goods into a springtime of abundance. The picture is not all rosy, however, since attaining consumer goods is not easy for many in **transitional economies**, where the economic system is still 'neither fish nor fowl', and governments ranging from Vietnam to Romania struggle with the difficult adaptation from a controlled, centralized economy to a free market system. [60] These problems stem from such factors as the unequal distribution of income among citizens, as well as striking rural–urban differences in expectations and values. The key aspect of a transitional economy is the rapid change required in social, political and economic dimensions as the populace is suddenly exposed to global communications and external market pressures. One study investigated how poor villagers migrating to a larger Turkish city coped with becoming acculturated to consumer society. The study basically concluded that these consumers-to-be would select one of three coping strategies. They would either shut out the whole modern consumer lifestyle altogether, trying to perpetuate village life in the poor shantytown outside the city, or collectively embrace the dreams proposed by consumer society by adopting ritualized consumption practices to the best of their humble means. A final strategy consists in giving up on both projects, which leads to shattered identities for the consumers involved, neither being able to maintain the traditional identity, nor to adopt a consumer identity. [61] Such transitional process can have heartbreaking consequences. In Turkey one researcher met a rural consumer, a mother who deprived her child of nutritious milk from the family's cow and instead sold it in order to be able to buy sweets for her child because 'what is good for city kids is also good for my child'. [62]

Some of the consequences of the transition to capitalism thus include a loss of confidence and pride in the local culture, as well as alienation, frustration and an increase in stress as leisure time is sacrificed to work ever harder to buy consumer goods. The yearning for the trappings of Western material culture is perhaps most evident in parts of eastern Europe, where citizens who threw off the shackles of communism now have direct access to coveted consumer goods from the US and western Europe – if they can afford them. One analyst observed, '. . . as former subjects of the Soviet empire dream it, the American dream has very little to do with liberty and justice for all and a great deal to do with soap operas and the Sears Catalogue'. [63]

Glocalization

Based on these discussions, we are now able to reflect a little more on the character of the globalization process. The conclusion we can safely draw is that globalization is always inevitably a **glocalization** since all global phenomena exist and become meaningful in a local context. Even completely similar McDonald's restaurants, just to take one obvious example, have different meanings and play different roles for consumers when placed in Chicago, Bordeaux, Moscow or Middlesbrough. Globalization may even engender an increased focus on the local. [64] An anthropological study of developments in the British food culture revealed four different types of food consumption that are all consequences of globalization. [65] The first is the *global food* culture, represented mainly by the ubiquitous fast food of burgers and pizzas, convenience products like instant coffee, etc. that are found everywhere and belong nowhere in particular. Secondly, *expatriate food* refers to the search for authentic meals and products from other cultures – 'Indian','Mexican', Thai, etc. Thirdly, *nostalgia food* represents a search for local authenticity – in Britain, for example, Stilton cheese, sticky toffee puddings – from the local cultural heritage that is under pressure from globalization. Finally, *creolization* of food involves blending various traditions into new ones, such as Chinese dishes omitting ingredients considered unappetizing in Western culture, spiced down Indonesian food in the Netherlands, or Indianized versions of sandwiches. Similar processes are found in all European cultures.

It is interesting to note that all four are related to globalization trends, but only global food leads to a tendency to standardize consumption patterns. We may consider these tendencies as relevant for all types of consumption, not just for consumption of food. So whether we look at retailing, interior decoration, tourism or musical tastes, we may find at least these four tendencies, taking the notion of globalization beyond the interpretation of it as homogenization. It also includes the increasing awareness of other styles and tastes, and the search for 'exotic authenticity', as well as the incorporation of this 'exoticism' into local habits and consumption styles. And finally, the exposure to all this 'otherness' often makes consumers more aware of their own cultural roots, and the tastes and consumption styles that they would define as 'our own'. All these offers of old and new, strange and familiar, authentic and creolized, tend to coexist in the marketplace. Therefore, it is not so strange that some authors discuss globalization more in terms of fragmentation than in terms of homogenization.[66]

THE POLITICS OF CONSUMPTION

The issue of postmodernism and the suggestion that the focus on consumption in our current culture is basically a way of securing meaning and continuity through our private consumer lives in times where continuity is no longer provided by society[67] might suggest that consumption has become an independent sphere of playful self-realization without too much depth or seriousness attached to it. However, not all is well in consumer society and the globalization of consumer culture makes these problems even clearer because we can, so to speak, 'study the problems as they aggravate'. Many critics have attacked consumer society for a variety of reasons: that it erodes cultural differences, that it creates superficial and inauthentic forms of social interaction and that it inspires competition and individualism rather than solidarity and community. While many of these assertions may or may not bear close scrutiny,[68] consumer society in general does represent some serious challenges for our future development, not least in terms of the pressure on the environment.

The pressure of consumer society is not only felt on the environment but also on the
▶ individual consumer, sometimes with negative outcomes. **Compulsive buying** is a physiological and/or psychological dependency on products or services. While most people equate addiction with drugs, virtually any product or service can be seen as relieving some problem or satisfying some need to the point where reliance on it becomes extreme. Even the act of shopping itself is an addictive experience for some consumers.[69] Such compulsive consumption has been on the rise in Western societies throughout the last decades. But there is reason to believe that consumers in newly marketized economies are even more vulnerable. For example, evidence from Germany indicates that the rise of compulsive buying behaviour is bigger in the newly marketized parts of central and eastern Europe compared with the western parts.[70] Finally, over-consumption should not be regarded strictly as an individual failure, but may also be viewed as a structural problem that has evolved in our affluent, consumer society.[71]

The central role of consumption in today's society has also led to an increasing interest in the social and political consequences of consumer society. The aggravating environmental crisis, the linkages between over-consumption and climate change, the unsustainability of many consumption practices, and a feeling that a consumer orientation has turned politics into marketing and branding – all these factors contribute to the feeling that consumer society is not a care- and risk-free lifestyle. Some critics have
▶ coined the term **affluenza**[72] to account for the negative sides of a society over-focused on its consumption. The recent animated success movie from Pixar, *Wall-E*, is based on a grim projection of a future world as a victim of affluenza.

▶ It has been suggested that we live in a **risk society**, where our ways of manufacturing goods are increasingly producing just as many and even more 'bads' or risks,[73] risks that the consumer will have to take into account in their decision-making. Lots of these risks are linked to our consumption processes, whether they concern something we eat or drink, chemicals in the paint and surface coating of various construction materials, the content of phtalates (plasticizers) in toys and so on. The sense of risks is compounded by recurring food scandals such as the addition of melanine in Chinese milk products which severely has lowered consumer confidence in many foods 'made in China'[74] or the many scandals surrounding meat (for example the BSE scandal) or classifications of wine or olive oil.

One example of a product type where such risks have made consumers sceptical about the benefits suggested to them by the industry is that of genetically manipulated organisms (GMO). One fear expressed by consumers in a study of acceptance or rejection of GMO foods in Sweden and Denmark was of too great a concentration of power in a few giant corporations dominating both research and industry.[75] Similar results were found for several European countries in a cross-national study. Testing consumer attitudes and purchase intentions regarding GMO foods, it was concluded that an overall rejection of the technology as such was found in Denmark, Germany, the UK and Italy.[76] In connection with this study, various types of information material were also tested, some more informative, some more emotional, in order to estimate the potential of informational campaigns in changing negative attitudes. But whatever data was given to the consumers, it only made their attitude *more* negative, something which points to the deep-seated nature of this scepticism among European consumers. Instead, the demand for organic produce has increased tremendously in several European countries over the last few years. And annual growth rates around 20 per cent are expected in both the British and American markets as we move towards 2010.[77]

The political consumer

The discussion above points to an increasing awareness of the political and moral consequences of consumption choices among many consumers. Consumers are not just individuals responsible solely for the private outcomes of their choices, they are also social citizens with social responsibilities.[78] How consumers feel these responsibilities and act upon them depends largely on how they perceive the robustness of nature in the face of so many consumers who intervene and use resources[79] but also on their beliefs regarding technology and its role for society.[80] This social and moral consciousness means that what started out predominantly as a green consumer is gradually being followed by, or perhaps

▶ is turning into, a **political consumer**.[81] The political consumer uses their buying pattern as a weapon against companies they don't like and in support of the companies that reflect values similar to the consumer's own. This consumer type selects products according to the company's ethical behaviour, which includes respect for human rights, animal protection, environmental friendliness and support for various benevolent causes.

Although consumer boycott of, for example, South African produce during the apartheid regime has been known for some time, the term 'the political consumer' was first coined in Denmark in the 1990s following consumer protests against the dumping of a drilling platform in the North Sea and against France for its nuclear testing in the Pacific.[82] Today, political consumers are found in all countries, but significant differences are also found. One EU-based study, TRUSTINFOOD, concluded, that Norwegian food consumers could generally be framed as trusting, Danish as complex, Italian as quality conscious and Portuguese as unprotected. Some results from that study are reproduced in Table 2.1.

The political consumer is supported by such agencies as the Vancouver-based Adbusters,[83] which engages in twisting campaigns from major companies that, for some reason, have come under their spotlight for immoral or harmful behaviour. For example, they made a spoof on the well-known Coca-Cola polar bear campaign by depicting a

Table 2.1 Political consumption activities among food consumers in four European countries (percentage of population) (all results: p = <0.0001)

	Norway N = 1002	Denmark N = 1005	Italy N = 2006	Portugal N = 1000
During last 12 months, I have been involved in the following activities:				
Refused to buy food types or brands to express opinion about a political or social issue	21%	35%	24%	25%
Bought particular food to support their sale	31%	38%	21%	14%
Participated in organized consumer boycott	3%	4%	13%	6%

Source: Adapted from Bente Halkier *et al*.: 'Trusting, complex, quality conscious or unprotected? Constructing the food consumer in different European national contexts', *Journal of Consumer Culture*, 7(3), 2007: 379–402.

family of bears on a tiny ice floe, with the sign: 'Enjoy Climate Change' written in that well-known type from the Coca-Cola logo, thereby protesting against the company's use of ozone-harming gases in its vending machines.[84] This kind of 'peaceful' rebelliousness against what is seen as control over our minds and imagination by major companies is called *culture jamming*.[85] Vigilante marketing is also emerging where new ads and ideas for campaigns appear without either client or agency involvement. These are often generated by freelances, fans or agencies looking for work.[86]

The global brands are generally the target of such consumer activism. A recent study examined consumers' experiences of the global coffee shop chain Starbucks.[87] The authors

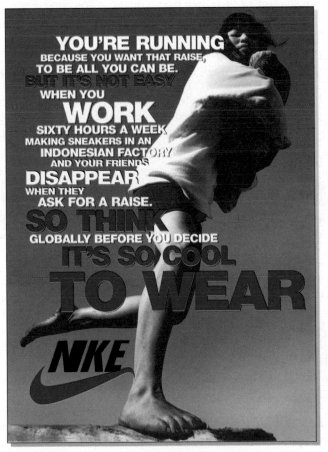

This Adbusters campaign against exploitation of cheap labour in Indonesia highlights the role of the major corporation, Nike, and uses its logo and line 'to be all you can be' to create individual awareness of the global impact of big corporations (and individual consumer choice of running shoe) on newly emerging economies and their labour forces.

Courtesy of www.adbusters.org

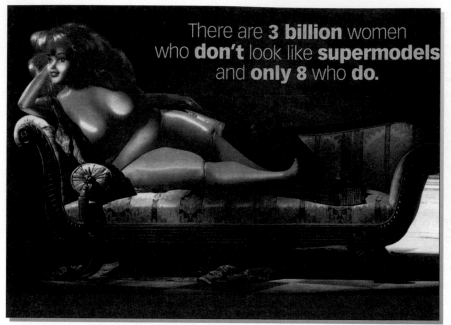

There are **3 billion** women who **don't** look like **supermodels** and **only 8** who **do**.

The Body Shop's Ruby, a Barbie-lookalike doll but with considerably rounder forms, introduced in order to fight the tyranny of thinness and impossible body ideal of the supermodels which are reinforced by Barbie's shape. The version you see here was not used, because Mattel claimed that Ruby had too much facial similarity with Barbie, hence another version was produced. See for example www.imforanimals.com/images/people/ruby_poster.jpg (accessed 9 January 2009).

The Advertising Archives

concluded that although Starbucks has created a lot of followers in and outside the US who see Starbucks as the quintessential cool café environment, it also has produced significant consumer resistance among consumers who perceive Starbucks as inauthentic and no better in terms of the café culture than McDonald's is for the global food culture. As such, they must fight a negative shadow of their own brand image, a so-called *doppelgänger brand image*.[88]

Not all companies are on the defensive, though. Companies such as The Body Shop are founded on the idea of natural and non-animal-tested products and a maximum of environmental concern. But their concerns are becoming directed towards a broader array of social values. They took up the debate over beauty ideals by introducing 'Ruby', a Barbie-lookalike doll but one with considerably rounder forms, in order to fight the tyranny of thinness and the impossible body ideal of the supermodels which are also endorsed by Barbie's shape. The reaction was predictable: Mattel Inc., the producers of Barbie, took out an injunction against The Body Shop because Ruby's face was too like Barbie's.

Consumer boycotts

As we have seen, we live in a period when many consumers are becoming increasingly aware that their consumption pattern is part of a global political and economic system, to the extent that they become political consumers. Sometimes a negative experience can trigger an organized and devastating response, as when a consumer group organizes a *boycott* of a company's products. These efforts can include protests against everything from investing in a politically undesirable country (as when Carlsberg and Heineken both withdrew their investments from Myanmar following protests against this support for a repressive regime), to efforts to discourage consumption of products from certain companies or countries (as during the boycott of French wines and other products during the nuclear testing in the Pacific in 1996, an action which was especially strongly felt in The Netherlands and in the Scandinavian countries). Four factors are found to predict boycott participation:

1 the desire to make a difference
2 the scope for self-enhancement
3 counterarguments that inhibit boycotting and
4 the cost to the boycotter of constrained consumption.[89]

Boycotts are not always effective – studies show that normally only a limited per-centage of a country's consumers participate in them. However, those who do are disproportionately vocal and well educated, so they are a group companies especially do not want to alienate. One increasingly popular solution used by marketers is to set up a joint task force with the boycotting organization to try to iron out the problem. In the US, McDonald's used this approach with the Environmental Defense Fund, which was concerned about its use of such things as polystyrene containers, bleached paper and antibiotics in food. The company agreed to test a composting programme, to switch to plain brown bags and to eliminate the use of antibiotics in such products as poultry.[90]

Corporate social responsibility

Parallel to the changing consumer attitudes towards the political and environmental role of marketplace behaviour, consumption as well as production, changing attitudes among companies and businesses can be traced as they recognize the changing nature of their ► customer. **Corporate social responsibility (CSR)** has become increasingly prominent in companies' provision of and stakeholders' approaches to buying goods and services. CSR addresses two kinds of commercial responsibility: 'commercial responsibilities (that is running their businesses successfully) and social responsibilities (that is their role in society and the community)'.[91] CSR Europe is the leading European business network for corporate social responsibility with over 60 leading multinational corporations as members '. . . [committed to helping] companies integrate CSR into the way they do business every day'.[92] One large-scale EU sponsored survey concluded that the public's key priority for companies is a demonstration of corporate citizenship (e.g. quality and service; human health and safety; being open and honest) rather than just charitable or community giving.'[93] In turn the study also identified 'the active conscious consumer' or 'socially responsible activists' (SR activists) who were defined 'as those people how have participated in five or more socially responsible activities in the last twelve months'. Across Europe more than a quarter are activists. In Switzerland, Sweden and Belgium the proportion rises to two in five. In contrast, only around one in ten could be classified in this way in Germany, France, Portugal and Italy.

The growing attention to CSR has not prevented a series of business scandals in various countries emerging with the growing financial and economic crisis. This has also caused new reflections on the consumer society and the pitfalls and benefits that may emerge. It is too early to tell, but the fall in real estate value and risks of unemployment could contribute to a severe drop in consumer spending. This might also lead to a questioning of the consumer society as we know it. We can ask ourselves: 'Is it likely that some of the happy-go-lucky attitudes and expectations concerning ever-increasing consumption opportunities will be challenged by new consumer attitudes oriented towards values of modesty?'

▼ Marketing pitfall

The Swedish-owned company Vattenfall which offers energy and heat in several European countries have tried to profile themselves as a highly environmentally-conscious corporation through large campaigns promoting imagery of unspoiled nature and through organizing a petition among consumers for imposing a global cost on CO_2 production. But at the same time, their own plans for expanding energy and heat production based on coal in countries such as Germany, and alleged behind-the-scenes activities for watering down upcoming agreements on climate change, have severely damaged this attempt.[94] Accusations of such so-called 'green-washing' of activities have recently also hit the fair trade organization Max Havelaar, when a TV documentary revealed that the working conditions in their tea plantations were hardly any better than in conventional commercially driven plantations.[95] The moral is: There are increasing demands of keeping one's path very clean, if a company is promoting itself through some form of corporate social responsibility.

CHAPTER SUMMARY

- We live in a *consumer society*, where more and more of our personal identities and the relationships between people are mediated through consumption. Consumer society is thus characterized by a consumer culture.

- The core of consumer culture is that consumption goes far beyond solving practical and utilitarian problems. Consumer society has become a reality when consumption becomes more a matter of *cultural meaning* and less a matter of utility. Consumption is first and foremost a way of creating meaningful lives in the context of personal identity and social relationships. Consumption, branding and marketing have become some of the prime reflectors of current cultural values, norms, and social roles. Economy and cultures of consumption are thus closely intertwined.

- We increasingly live in an *experience economy* that provides not only goods and services but complete staged events, or experiences, for the consumers.

- Experience economy can be linked to *postmodernism*, which involves processes of social change in an era where the 'grand truths' of modernism, such as scientific knowledge or the progressiveness of economic growth, are no longer taken for granted. Postmodernism includes social processes such as fragmentation, de-differentiation, hyperreality, chronology, pastiche and anti-foundationalism.

- The increasing political and moral significance of consumption has given birth to the *political consumer*, who 'votes with their shopping basket' in an attempt to influence companies to care for the natural as well as the human environment, adding issues such as human rights to the set of dimensions that influence purchases.

- Followers of an *etic perspective* believe that the same universal messages will be appreciated by people in many cultures. Believers in an *emic perspective* argue that individual cultures are too unique to permit such standardization: marketers instead must adapt their approaches to be consistent with local values and practices. Attempts at global marketing have met with mixed success: in many cases this approach is more likely to work if the messages appeal to basic values and/or if the target markets consist of consumers who are more internationally rather than locally oriented.

- The Western world is a net exporter of popular culture. Consumers around the world have eagerly adopted Western products, especially entertainment, vehicles and items that are linked symbolically to a uniquely Western lifestyle (e.g. Marlboro, Levi's, BMW, Nestlé). Despite or because of the continuing 'Americanization' or 'Westernization' of cultures in the world, some consumers are alarmed by this influence, and are instead emphasizing a return to local products and customs.

- It is appropriate to consider the process of globalization as one of the most central in understanding the development of consumer society. But it is also important to bear in mind that globalization should almost always be considered as *glocalization*, due to the complex interactions between the global and the local that follows from it.

▶ KEY TERMS

Affluenza (p. 49)	Globalization (p. 41)
Brand (p. 37)	Glocalization (p. 48)
Brand communities (p. 37)	Hyperreality (p. 39)
Compulsive buying (p. 49)	Meaning (p. 33)
Consumer culture (p. 32)	Pastiche (p. 40)
Consumer society (p. 32)	Pluralism (p. 39)
Corporate social responsibility (CSR) (p. 53)	Political consumer (p. 50)
Cultural categories (p. 35)	Popular culture (p. 33)
Emic perspective (p. 42)	Postmodernism (p. 38)
Etic perspective (p. 42)	Risk society (p. 50)
Experience economy (p. 38)	Transitional economies (p. 48)

▶ CONSUMER BEHAVIOUR CHALLENGE

1 Try to consider some of your own patterns and behaviour in the light of the different types of consumption practices: experience, integration, play and classification. What do you conclude?

2 Reflect on your and your friends' consumption patterns in the same light. What do you see?

3 Try to consider your personal relationship to brands. Select one that you are absolutely positive about. How would you characterize your relationship to that brand? And then one you are absolutely negative about; what is your relationship to that? Which personal and cultural factors might explain your brand relationships?

4 Find three examples of how experience economy, i.e. the staging of complete consumer experiences, has altered some market offerings that you know about.

5 Try to collect advertisements that reflect the postmodern features of fragmentation, de-differentiation, hyperreality, chronology, pastiche and anti-foundationalism.

6 What role does the globalization process play in your personal consumption profile? After reflecting on that, take a walk in your nearest shopping area and look for signs of the global and the local. What is from 'somewhere else'? What is distinctively local? Are there mixtures, or are these two domains separate? Can you identify any *hegemonic brandscapes*?

7 Try to identify processes of glocalization in your own consumption patterns? And in your shopping neighbourhood?

8 Is the 'political consumer' a fad or a new and growing challenge and/or opportunity for marketers and producers? Discuss.

9 Go to your local supermarket to check the selection of politically correct products (organic produce, fair trade products, etc.). How are they presented in the store? What does that say about the way these products are regarded?

10 What do you think about boycotts as consumers' response to what is perceived as companies' unethical behaviour?

11 Identify and assess the importance of corporate social responsibility for companies, consumers and government policy.

For additional material see the companion website at www.pearsoned.co.uk/solomon

NOTES

1. Jane Pavitt, 'The art of marketing', *Marketing* (19 October 2000).
2. *Markedsføring* 7 (1999): 12.
3. Celia Lury, *Consumer Culture* (New Brunswick, NJ: Rutgers University Press, 1996). Another excellent book on the rise of consumer culture is Don Slater, *Consumer Culture and Modernity* (Cambridge: Polity Press, 1997).
4. Daniel Miller, 'Why Some Things Matter', in D. Miller, ed., *Material Cultures: Why Some Things Matter* (London: UCL Books, 1998): 3–21.
5. Steven Miles, *Consumerism – as a Way of Life* (London: Sage 1998).
6. T. Bettina Cornwell and Bruce Keillor, 'Contemporary Literature and the Embedded Consumer Culture: The Case of Updike's Rabbit', in Roger J. Kruez and Mary Sue MacNealy, eds, *Empirical Approaches to Literature and Aesthetics: Advances in Discourse Processes* 52 (Norwood, NJ: Ablex Publishing Corporation, 1996): 559–72; Monroe Friedman, 'The changing language of a consumer society: Brand name usage in popular American novels in the postwar era', *Journal of Consumer Research* 11 (March 1985): 927–37; Monroe Friedman, 'Commercial influences in the lyrics of popular American music of the postwar era', *Journal of Consumer Affairs* 20 (Winter 1986): 193.
7. Sidney J. Levy, 'Symbols for sale', *Harvard Business Review* 37 (July–August 1959): 117–24.
8. Michael W. Allen, Richa Gupta and Arnaud Monnier, 'The interactive effect of cultural symbols and human values on taste evaluation', *Journal of Consumer Research*, vol. 35 (August 2008): 294–308.
9. Grant McCracken, 'Culture and consumption: A theoretical account of the structure and movement of the cultural meaning of consumer goods', *Journal of Consumer Research* 13 (June 1986): 71–84.
10. One example of such a cultural category is the definition of being 'a real woman'. For a cultural analysis of female identity and consumption of lingerie, see Christian Jantzen, Per Østergaard and Carla Sucena Vieira, 'Becoming a woman to the backbone. Lingerie consumption and the experience of female identity', *Journal of Consumer Culture*, vol. 6 no. 2, (2006): 177–202.
11. 'Michelle Obama: Fashion's New Darling?' Wall Street Journal online edition, June 19 2008. http://online.wsj.com/article/SB121389326494088867.html, accessed 16 January 2009, see also http://www.youtube.com/watch?v=S66ZeMTKj88 and David Hauslaib, 'Michelle Obama to Dictate Fashion in Upcoming Years', http://www.jossip.com/michelle-obama-to-dictate-fashion-in-upcoming-years-20090109/
12. Douglas B. Holt, 'How consumers consume: a typology of consumption practices', *Journal of Consumer Research* 22(1) (June 1995): 1–16.
13. For a recent study on consumer and car cultures, see Paul Hewer, Douglas Brownlie, Steven Treanor, Pauline Ferguson and Susan Hamilton, 'Peeps, Beemers and Scooby-doos; Exploring Community Value amongst Scottish Car Cruisers', in A.Y. Lee and D. Soman, eds, *Advances in Consumer Research*, vol. XXXV (Duluth, MN: Association for Consumer Research, 2008): 429–38.
14. Stephen Brown, 'Ambi-Brand Culture', in J. Schroeder and M. Salzer-Mörling, eds, *Brand Culture* (London: Routledge: 2006): 50–66.
15. Michael Solomon, Greg Marshall and Elnora Stuart, *Marketing. Real People, Real Choices* (Prentice Hall 2006).
16. Susan Fournier, 'Consumers and their brands. Developing relationship theory in consumer research', *Journal of Consumer Research* 24 (March 1998): 343–73.
17. Fabian F. Csaba and Anders Bengtsson, 'Rethinking Identity in Brand Management' in J. Schroeder and M. Salzer-Mörling, eds, *Brand Culture* (London: Routledge, 2006): 118–35.
18. Elisabeth A. Pichler and Andrea Hemetsberger, 'Driven by Devotion – How Consumers Interact with their Objects of Devotion', in A.Y. Lee and D. Soman, eds, *Advances in Consumer Research*, vol. XXXV (Duluth, MN: Association for Consumer Research, 2008): 439–43.
19. Margaret Hogg and Emma Banister, 'Dislikes, distastes and the undesired self: Conceptualising and exploring the role of the undesired end state in consumer experience', *Journal of Marketing Management*, vol. 17 no. 1–2 (2001): 73–104; Emma Banister and Margaret Hogg, 'Negative symbolic consumption and consumers' drive for self-esteem: The case of the fashion industry', *European Journal of Marketing*, vol. 38 no. 7 (2004): 850–68.
20. Albert Muñiz and Thomas O'Guinn, 'Brand communities', *Journal of Consumer Research*, vol. 27 no. 4 (2001): 412–32.
21. Richard Elliott and Andrea Davies, 'Symbolic Brands and Authenticity of Identity Performance', in J. Schroeder and M. Salzer-Mörling, eds, *Brand Culture* (London: Routledge, 2006): 155–70.
22. Bernard Cova and Stefano Pace, 'Brand community of convenience products: New forms of customer empowerment – the case "my Nutella The Community"', *European Journal of Marketing*, vol. 40 no. 9/10 (2006): 1087–105. See also www.nutellaville.it
23. Johann Füller, Marius Luedicke and Gregor Jawecki, 'How Brands Enchant: Insights from Observing Community Driven Brand Creation', in A.Y. Lee and D. Soman, eds, *Advances in Consumer Research* (Duluth, MN: Association for Consumer Research, 2008): 359–66.
24. B. Joseph Pine and James Gilmore, 'Welcome to the experience economy', *Harvard Business Review* (July/August 1998): 97–105.
25. www.brandbase.dk/arrangementer/reportager/oplevelsesokonomi-for-alle-pengene, accessed 8 January 2009.
26. Two special issues of *International Journal of Research in Marketing* 10(3) (1993) and 11(4) (1994), both edited by A. Fuat Firat, John F. Sherry Jr and Alladi Venkatesh, have been decisive for the introduction of themes of postmodernism in marketing and consumer research.
27. Craig J. Thompson, 'Modern truth and postmodern incredulity: A hermeneutic deconstruction of the metanarrative of "scientific truth" in marketing research', *International Journal of Research in Marketing* 10(3) (1993): 325–38.
28. Christina Goulding, 'Issues in representing the postmodern consumer', *Qualitative Market Research: An International Journal*, vol. 6 no. 3 (2003): 152–59.
29. See, for example, A. Fuat Firat and Alladi Venkatesh, 'Postmodernity: The age of marketing', *International Journal of Research in Marketing* 10(3) (1993): 227–49; James Ogilvy, 'This postmodern business', *Marketing and Research Today* (February 1990): 4–22; W. Fred van Raaij, 'Postmodern consumption', *Journal of Economic Psychology* 14 (1993): 541–63.

30. Stephen Brown, *Postmodern Marketing* (London: Routledge, 1995): 106ff.

31. www.belowzerolondon.com/icebar/index.html, accessed 4 December 2008.

32. www.icehotel.com, accessed 4 December 2008.

33. Fuat Firat and Venkatesh, 'Postmodernity: The age of marketing', *op. cit.*

34. Laurent Muzellec, 'Ceci n'est pas une brand. Postmodernism and Brand Management', paper presented at the 36th EMAC Conference (Reykjavik 2007).

35. Eric Arnould and Søren Askegaard, 'HyperCulture: The Next Stage in the Globalization of Consumption', paper presented at the 1997 Annual Association for Consumer Research Conference in Denver, Colorado, 16–19 October.

36. Aurélie Kessous and Elyette Roux, 'A semiotic analysis of nostalgia as as connection to the past', *Qualitative Market Research. An International Journal*, vol. 11 no. 2 (2008): 192–212.

37. Stephen Brown, Robert V. Kozinets and John F. Sherry Jr, 'Teaching old brands new tricks: Retro branding and the revival of brand meaning', *Journal of Marketing* 67 (July 2003): 19–33.

38. Brown, Kozinets and Sherry Jr, 'Teaching old brands new tricks', *ibid.*

39. Stephen Brown, *The Marketing Code*, (London: Cyan Books, 2006).

40. Richard Elliott, Susan Eccles and Michelle Hodgson, 'Recoding gender representations: Women, cleaning products, and advertising's "New Man"', *International Journal of Research in Marketing* 10(3) (1993): 311–24.

41. Stephanie O'Donohoe, 'Raiding the postmodern pantry: Advertising intertextuality and the young adult audience', *European Journal of Marketing* 31(3/4) (1997): 234–53.

42. Stephanie O'Donohoe, 'Living with ambivalence: Attitudes towards advertising in postmodern times', *Marketing Theory*, vol. 1 no. 1 (2001): 91–108.

43. Søren Askegaard, 'Brands as a Global Ideoscape', in J. Schroeder and M. Salzer-Mörling, eds, *Brand Culture*, (London: Routledge, 2006): 91–102.

44. Martin McCarty, Martin I. Horn, Mary Kate Szenasy, and Jocelyn Feintuch, 'An exploratory study of consumer style: Country differences and international segments', *Journal of Consumer Behaviour* 6, no. 1 (2007): 48.

45. David Waller, Kim-Shyan Fam and B. Zafer Erdigan, 'Advertising of controversial products: A cross-cultural study', *Journal of Consumer Marketing*, vol. 22 no. 1 (2005): 6–13.

46. See, for example, Craig Thompson and Siok Kuan Tambyah, 'Trying to be cosmopolitan', *Journal of Consumer Research*, vol. 26 no. 3 (1999): 214–41.

47. Jean-Noël Kapferer, 'The Two Business Cultures of Luxury Brands', in J. Schroeder and M. Salzer-Mörling, eds, *Brand Culture*, (London: Routledge, 2006): 67–76.

48. Sandra Diehl, Ralf Terlutter and Barbara Mueller, 'The Influence of Culture on Responses to the Globe Dimension of Performance Orientation in Advertising Messages – Results from the US, Germany, France, Spain, and Thailand', in A.Y. Lee and D. Soman, eds, *Advances in Consumer Research*, vol. XXXV (Duluth, MN: Association for Consumer Research, 2008): 269–75.

49. See also Ulf Hannerz, 'Cosmopolitans and Locals in World Culture', in Mike Featherstone, ed., *Global Culture* (London: Sage, 1990): 237–52.

50. Dannie Kjeldgaard and Søren Askegaard, 'The glocalization of youth culture: The global youth segment as structures of common difference', *Journal of Consumer Research*, vol. 33 no. 2 (2006): 231–47.

51. Douglas B. Holt, John A. Quelch, and Earl L. Taylor, 'How global brands compete', *Harvard Business Review* (September 2004): 68–75.

52. 'Abroadminded', *Marketing* (24 April 1997): 20–1.

53. Eric J. Arnould and Richard R. Wilk, 'Why Do the Natives Wear Adidas? Anthropological Approaches to Consumer Research', in Elisabeth C. Hirschman and Morris B. Holbrook, eds, *Advances in Consumer Research* 12 (Provo, UT: Association for Consumer Research, 1985): 748–52.

54. David K. Tse, Russell W. Belk and Nan Zhou, 'Becoming a consumer society: A longitudinal and cross-cultural content analysis of print ads from Hong Kong, the People's Republic of China, and Taiwan', *Journal of Consumer Research* 15 (March 1989): 457–72; see also Annamma Joy, 'Marketing in modern China: An evolutionary perspective', *CJAS* (June 1990): 55–67, for a review of changes in Chinese marketing practices since the economic reforms of 1978.

55. See: http://www.tokyotales.com/japlish/ (accessed 30 July 2005).

56. John F. Sherry Jr and Eduardo G. Camargo, '"May your life be marvelous": English language labeling and the semiotics of Japanese promotion', *Journal of Consumer Research* 14 (September 1987): 174–88.

57. http://www.japander.com/japander/zz.htm (accessed 30 July 2005).

58. Julien Cayla and Giana Eckhardt, 'Asian brands and the shaping of a transnational imagined community', *Journal of Consumer Research*, vol. 35 no. 2 (2008), 216–30.

59. Jason Overdorf, 'Comics: Off to Save Mumbai', *Newsweek* (2 August 2004): 15.

60. Material in this section adapted from Güliz Ger and Russell W. Belk, 'I'd like to buy the world a Coke: Consumptionscapes of the "less affluent world"', *Journal of Consumer Policy* 19(3) (1996): 271–304; Russell W. Belk, 'Romanian Consumer Desires and Feelings of Deservingness', in Lavinia Stan, ed., *Romania in Transition* (Hanover, NH: Dartmouth Press, 1997): 191–208; see also Güliz Ger, 'Human development and humane consumption: Wellbeing beyond the good life', *Journal of Public Policy and Marketing* 16(1) (1997): 110–25.

61. Tuba Üstüner and Douglas B. Holt, 'Dominated consumer acculturation: The social Construction of poor migrant women's consumer identity projects in a Turkish squatter', *Journal of Consumer Research*, vol. 34 no. 1 (2007): 41–56.

62. Güliz Ger, 'The positive and negative effects of marketing on socioeconomic development: The Turkish case', *Journal of Consumer Policy* 15 (1992): 229–54.

63. Erazim Kohák, 'Ashes, ashes . . . Central Europe after forty years', *Daedalus* 121 (Spring 1992): 197–215, at 219, quoted in Belk, 'Romanian Consumer Desires and Feelings of Deservingness', *op. cit.*

64. Søren Askegaard and Dannie Kjeldgaard, 'Here, there and everwhere: Place branding and gastronomic glocalization in a macromarketing perspective', *Journal of Macromarketing*, vol. 27 no. 2 (2007): 138–47.

65. Allison James, 'Cooking the Books: Global or Local Identities in Contemporary British Food Cultures?' in David Howes, ed., *Cross-Cultural Consumption* (London: Routledge, 1996): 77–92.

66. A. Fuat Firat, 'Globalization of fragmentation – a framework for understanding contemporary global markets', *Journal of International Marketing* 5(2) (1997): 77–86. See also

T. Bettina Cornwell and Judy Drennan, 'Cross-cultural consumer/consumption research: Dealing with issues emerging from globalization and fragmentation', *Journal of Macromarketing*, vol. 24 no. 2 (2004): 108–21.

67. Zygmunt Bauman, 'Consuming Life', *Journal of Consumer Culture*, vol. 1 no. 1 (2001): 9–29.

68. Daniel Miller, 'Consumption as the Vanguard of History', in D. Miller, ed., *Acknowledging Consumption* (London: Routledge, 1995): 1–57; see also Cornelia Dröge, Roger Calantone, Madhu Agrawal and Robert Mackay, 'The consumption culture and its critiques: A framework for analysis', *Journal of Macromarketing* (Fall 1993): 32–45.

69. Richard Elliott, 'Addictive consumption: Function and fragmentation in postmodernity', *Journal of Consumer Policy* 17 (1994): 159–79; Thomas C. O'Guinn and Ronald J. Faber, 'Compulsive buying: A phenomenological exploration', *Journal of Consumer Research* 16 (1989): 147–57.

70. Michael Neuner, Gerhard Raab and Lucia A. Reisch, 'Compulsive Buying as a Consumer Policy Issue in East and West Germany', in K.G. Grunert and J. Thøgersen, eds, *Consumers, Policy and the Environment* (New York: Springer, 2005): 89–114.

71. Hans Kjellberg, 'Market practices and over-consumption', *Consumption, Markets and Culture*, vol. 11 no. 2 (2008): 151–67.

72. John de Graaf, David Wann, and Thomas H. Naylor, *Affluenza. The All-Consuming Epidemic* (San Francisco: Berrett-Koehler Publishers, 2001).

73. Ulrich Beck, *Risk Society* (London: Sage Publications, 1992).

74. http://blogs.wsj.com/chinajournal/2008/10/01/seeking-sources-of-information-on-melamine-tainted-food/20090118.

75. Karin Ekström and Søren Askegaard, 'Daily Consumption in Risk Society: The Case of Genetically Modified Foods', in S. Hoch and R. Meyer, eds, *Advances in Consumer Research* 27 (Provo, UT: Association for Consumer Research, 2000): 237–43.

76. Lone Bredahl, 'Determinants of Consumer Attitudes and Purchase Intentions with Regard to Genetically Modified Foods – Results from a Cross-National Survey', MAPP Working Paper no. 69 (Aarhus: The Aarhus School of Business, 2000).

77. www.ota.com/organic/mt/business.html and 'UK retailers see strong demand for organic food', (20 June 2007) (http://uk.reuters.com/article/electionsNews/idUKL2057297620070621) both accessed 18 November 2008.

78. Liisa Uusitalo, 'Consumers as Citizens – Three Approaches to Collective Consumer Problems', in K.G. Grunert and J. Thøgersen, eds, *Consumers, Policy and the Environment*, (New York: Springer, 2005): 127–50. See also Yannis Gabriel and Tim Lang, *The Unmanageable Consumer*, 2nd ed. (London: Sage, 2006).

79. Suzanne Beckmann, 'In the Eye of the Beholder: Danish Consumer-Citizens and Sustainability', in K.G. Grunert and J. Thøgersen, eds, *Consumers, Policy and the Environment*, *op. cit.*: 265–99.

80. On consumers and their ideologized narratives about technology, see Robert V. Kozinets, 'Technology/ideology: How ideological fields influence consumers' technology narratives', *Journal of Consumer Research*, vol. 34 no. 6 (2008): 865–81.

81. Bente Halkier, 'Consequences of the politicization of consumption: The example of environmentally friendly consumption practices', *Journal of Environmental Policy and Planning* 1 (1999): 25–41.

82. Richard Jones, 'Challenges to the notion of publics in public relations: Implications of the risk society for the discipline', *Public Relations Review*, vol. 28 no. 1 (2002): 49–62.

83. http://www.adbusters.org/home/ (accessed 30 July 2005).

84. www.cokespotlight.org; see also www.adbusters.org and www.corpspotlight.org (accessed 30 July 2005).

85. Kalle Lasn, 'Culture Jamming', in J.B. Schor and D.B. Holt, eds, *The Consumer Society Reader* (New York: The New Press, 2000): 414–32.

86. Nat Ives, 'Advertising: Unauthorized campaigns used by unauthorized creators become a trend', *New York Times* (23 December 2004); see www.gomotron.com and www.MadisonAveNew.com for posting suggestions for companies such as Coca-Cola, Mitsubishi Motors, North American and Alltel (accessed 30 July 2005).

87. Craig J. Thompson and Zeynep Arsel, 'The Starbucks brandscape and consumers' (anticorporate) experiences of glocalization', *Journal of Consumer Research* 31 (December 2004): 631–42.

88. Craig J. Thompson, Aric Rindfleisch and Zeynep Arsel, Emotional branding and the strategic value of the doppelgänger brand image', *Journal of Marketing*, vol. 70 no. 1 (2006): 50–64.

89. Jill Gabrielle Klein, N. Craig Smith and Andrew John, 'Why we boycott: Consumer motivation for boycott participation', *Journal of Marketing*, vol. 68 (July 2004): 92–109.

90. Marcus Mabry, 'Do Boycotts Work?' *Newsweek* 3 (6 July 1992): 35; 'McDonald's antibiotic project: No more playing chicken with antibiotics', retrieved 16 July 2005 at: http://www.environmentaldefense.org/partnership_project.cfm?subnav=project_fullstory&projectID=1.

91. MORI, 'Stakeholder dialogue: consumer attitude' (November 2000), http://www.csreurope.org/whatwedo/consumerattitudes_page408.aspx.

92. CSR Europe website, http://www.csreurope.org (accessed 15 March 2005).

93. MORI, 'Stakeholder dialogue: consumer attitudes', *op. cit.*

94. 'Vattenfall vasker kulsort energi grøn', *Information*, 14 November 2008.

95. 'The Bitter Taste of Tea', TV documentary, Denmark's Radio TV, 26 November 2008, accessed 8 January 2009 on www.dr.dk/Dr1/dokumentar/2008/1120141500.htm

3

Shopping, buying and evaluating

Grace's digital tuner in her television was on the blink. Or, at least, that was the diagnosis offered by the television engineer she had called out to look at her television. She had two choices. Either she could invest in a new TV, which sounded like an attractive but expensive option. Or she could buy one of the new digiboxes, which could act as an alternative digital tuner for her TV. That sounded like a cheaper option, but possibly more complicated in the long run. The young engineer was very reassuring. All the digiboxes came as 'plug and play'. All that was necessary was to change over the aerial connection, and then connect the TV to the digibox using a Scart lead. Scart leads could be temperamental. They needed to be aligned exactly, which meant that it could be fiddly to get the connection to work. But it should all be pretty straightforward. What should she do? Grace was keen to try the simpler and cheaper option. Partly because her TV set was not very old, and the young engineer argued that her cathode ray model would still have a sharper picture than many of the new fashionable HD plasma flatscreen TVs. Partly because her sustainability principles strongly pushed her towards this alternative. However, she was nervous about making everything work. She'd heard before about 'everything is simple, it's just plug and play', but she'd learnt that was not always true. The engineer recommended popping along to the local Tesco Extra store and buying one of their digiboxes. She did a little bit of Web surfing for her homework, visiting a couple of her favourite online browsing sites (e.g. **microsoftdirect.com** and **kelkoo.com**). Then she went along to her local Tesco, where she was overwhelmed by the array of choice. In order to be on the safe side she decided to visit the television section of a very reputable department store, John Lewis ('Never knowingly undersold'). She wandered around their display, and still felt confused. A sales assistant approached, so she asked his advice about which model to choose. Essentially it seemed, you got what you paid for. She decided to purchase the most expensive digibox that they stocked, reasoning that a top branded purchase from a top department store was the best combination for reducing all the risks. She brought it home, took it out of the box and began setting it up. This proved to be more difficult than she'd hoped. She had to resort to recalling the original engineer to get him to make the Scart lead plug in properly so that the digibox would play. As her earlier experiences with new technology had suggested, so much indeed for 'plug and play' . . .

INTRODUCTION

Grace's story highlights the range of dilemmas many consumers face when making consumption choices (more on consumer decision-making in Chapter 9, and the difficulties faced by Daniel when choosing amongst different televisions), and how consumers try and manage different types of perceived risk. Grace's dilemma also highlights the importance of the purchase situation and the post-purchase evaluation (was it the right choice?). On top of this, the experience of service linked to the act of purchasing and evaluating the purchase play central roles. In a British poll, 80 per cent of consumers said that they would change suppliers if they were unhappy with the service; and 86 per cent said that they expected better service currently than they did five years ago.[1] Furthermore, the issue of environmental friendliness is becoming more and more important for many purchase decisions, just as it was for Grace, who was keen to limit any potential damage to the environment by dumping a television set which still potentially had years of useful life left in it. Whereas European households currently keep their TVs for between 10 and 15 years, it is predicted that there will be a faster turnover in sales because of the improving technology (e.g. flat panel televisons, high definition video and digital broadcasting). In addition, the cost of repairs is increasing, so that consumers are more likely to buy a new television set rather than repair an old one, which means that more sets are likely to be discarded and accumulated for recycling in the future, with all the associated environmental pressures (see Chapter 6 for more debates about sustainability as a core consumer value and consumers' disposal options).[2]

Grace's experience illustrates some of the concepts to be discussed in this chapter. Making a purchase is often not a simple, routine matter of going to a shop and choosing something. As illustrated in Figure 3.1, a consumer's choices are affected by many personal factors, such as mood, time pressure and the particular situation or context for which the product is needed. In some situations, like the purchase of a car or a home, the salesperson or the reference group (which we will discuss in Chapter 10) play a pivotal role in the final choice. And today people are using the Web to arm themselves with product and price information before they even enter a store[3] (note Daniel's preliminary search for televisions via the Internet in the opening vignette of Chapter 9), which puts added pressure on retailers to deliver the value customers expect.

Barbara Kruger, 'I shop therefore I am'.

Copyright Barbara Kruger, Courtesy: Mary Boone Gallery, New York

Figure 3.1 Issues related to purchase and post-purchase activities

The store environment also exerts a major influence: shopping is like a stage performance, with the customer involved either as a member of the audience or as an active participant. The quality of the performance is affected by the other *cast members* (salespeople or other shoppers), as well as by the *setting* of the play (the image of a particular store and the 'feeling' it imparts) and *props* (store fittings and promotional material which try to influence the shopper's decisions).

In addition, the consumer activity per se occurs *after* a product has been purchased and brought home. After using a product, the consumer must decide whether or not they are satisfied with it. The satisfaction process is especially important to marketers, who realize that the key to success is not selling a product once, but rather forging a relationship with the consumer so that they will continue to buy in the future. Finally, just as Grace thought about the recycling of her television, we must also consider how consumers go about disposing of products and how secondary markets (e.g. eBay; second-hand car dealers) often play a pivotal role in product acquisition. This chapter considers many issues related to purchase and post-purchase phenomena.

ANTECEDENT STATES

A person's mood or physiological condition at the time of purchase can have a major impact on what is bought and can also affect how products are evaluated.[4] One reason for this is that behaviour is directed towards certain goal states, as will be discussed in Chapter 6. In addition, the person's particular social identity, or the role that is being played at a given time, will be influential.[5]

Situational effects: mood and consumption situations

A consumer's mood will have an impact on purchase decisions. For example, stress can reduce a consumer's information-processing and problem-solving abilities.[6] Two dimensions determine whether a shopper will react positively or negatively to a store environment: *pleasure* and *arousal*. A person can enjoy or not enjoy a situation, and they can feel stimulated or not. As Figure 3.2 indicates, different combinations of pleasure and arousal levels result in a variety of emotional states. For example, an arousing situation can be either distressing or exciting, depending on whether the context is positive or negative (e.g. a street riot vs. a street festival). Maintaining an upbeat mood in a pleasant context is one factor behind the success of theme parks such as Disneyland, which try to provide consistent doses of carefully calculated stimulation to patrons.[7]

A specific mood is some combination of pleasure and arousal. For example, the state of happiness is high in pleasantness and moderate in arousal, while elation would be high

Figure 3.2 Dimensions of emotional states

Source: James Russell and Geraldine Pratt, 'A description of the affective quality attributed to environment', *Journal of Personality and Social Psychology* 38 (August 1980): 311–22.

in both dimensions.[8] In general, a mood state (either positive or negative) biases judgments of products and services in that direction.[9] Put simply, consumers like things better when they are in a good mood (this may explain the popularity of the business lunch).

Moods can be affected by store design, the weather or other factors specific to the consumer. In addition, music and television programming can affect mood; this has important consequences for commercials.[10] When consumers hear happy music or watch happy programmes, they have more positive reactions to commercials and products, especially when the marketing appeals are aimed at arousing emotional reactions.[11]

A *consumption situation* is defined by factors over and above the characteristics of the person and of the product. Situational effects can be behavioural (such as entertaining friends) or perceptual (being depressed, or feeling pressed for time).[12] Common sense tells us that people tailor their purchases to specific occasions or that the way we feel at a specific time affects what we feel like buying or doing.

One reason for this variability is that the role a person plays at any time is partly determined by their *situational self-image*: 'Who am I right now?' (see also Chapter 5).[13] Someone trying to impress his girlfriend by playing the role of 'man about town' may spend more lavishly, ordering champagne rather than beer and buying flowers – purchases he would never consider when he is with his male friends in a pub and playing the role of 'one of the boys'. As this example demonstrates, knowledge of what consumers are doing at the time a product is consumed may improve predictions of product and brand choice.[14]

Situational segmentation

By systematically identifying important usage situations, market segmentation strategies can be developed to position products that will meet the specific needs arising from these situations. Many product categories are amenable to this form of segmentation. The South African ad for Volkswagen, opposite, emphasizes the versatility of the Volkswagen people carrier bus for different situations.[15]

Situations can be used to fine-tune a segmentation strategy. By mapping context (e.g. skiing vs. sunbathing for a protective sunscreen) against users (children; fair-skinned vs. dark-skinned men or women) a matrix can be constructed that identifies specific product features that should be emphasized for each situation[16]. Our brand loyalty may also be dependent on the situation. French research has demonstrated how our brand loyalty

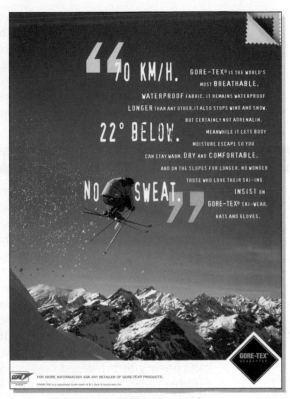

(*Left*) This Burberry ad shows the situational context for the consumption of their products, notably in social settings and by upper class, young adult consumers. (The Advertising Archives)

(*Right*) Clothing choices often are heavily influenced by the situation in which they need to be worn. (The Advertising Archives)

within product categories such as fruit juice, cheese or coffee depends on whether our situation is one of the following: shopping for a party for friends, running out of the product ourselves, or the shop having run out of stock.[17]

A study of 2,500 online customers[18] identified 'occasion-based segmentation'. Using variables such as length of session, time spent on each page of the website, and the

This South African ad for Volkswagen emphasizes that brand criteria can differ depending upon the situation in which the product will be used.

Courtesy of Volkswagen of South Africa

user's familiarity with the site, seven different occasions were identified which could be classified into two groups. First, the group Loitering, Information Please and Surfing, spent between 33 and 70 minutes online, and was more likely to purchase. The second group, Quickies, Just the Facts, Single Mission and Do It Again, remained online for much shorter periods. 'It's only by decoding the type of occasion – such as gathering product information – that marketers can fully harness the web's interactive powers by aiming messages and offers at the right place at the right time.'[19]

SOCIAL AND PHYSICAL SURROUNDINGS

A consumer's physical and social environment can make a big difference in affecting their motives for product purchase and also product evaluation. Important cues include the number and type of other consumers, as well as dimensions of the physical environment. Decor, smells (the use of scents in the retail environment can increase the pleasure and hedonic values derived from shopping)[20] and even temperature can significantly influence consumption.

▶ In addition to physical cues, many of a consumer's purchase decisions are significantly affected by the groups or social settings in which these occur (as we shall see in Chapter 10). In some cases, the presence or absence of **co-consumers**, the other patrons in a setting, can be a determinant attribute (see the discussion in Chapter 9) and function as a product attribute, as when an exclusive resort or boutique promises to provide privacy to privileged customers. At other times, the presence of others can have positive value. A sparsely attended football match or an empty bar, in contrast, can be depressing sights.

Many stores and services (like airlines) try to differentiate themselves in terms of the physical environments they offer, touting such amenities as comfort and space.
Courtesy of Qantas Airlines and M&C Saatchi

The presence of large numbers of people in a consumer environment increases arousal levels, so a consumer's subjective experience of a setting tends to be more intense. This polarization can be both positive and negative. While the experience of other people creates a state of arousal, the consumer's actual experience depends on their *interpretation of* and *reaction to* this arousal. Crowding may result in avoidance (leaving the store earlier), aggressiveness (rushing others), opportunism (using the extra time to find bargains) or self-blame (for coming into the store at the wrong hour).[21] It is important, therefore, to distinguish between *density* and *crowding*. Density refers to the actual number of people occupying a space, while the psychological state of crowding exists only if a negative affective state occurs as a result of this density.[22] For example, 100 students packed into a classroom designed for 75 may result in an unpleasant situation for all concerned, but the same number of people jammed together at a party occupying a room of the same size might just make for a great party.

In addition, the *type* of consumers who patronize a store or service can serve as a store attribute; and the *type* of consumers who use a product can influence evaluations. We may infer something about a store by examining its customers. For this reason, some restaurants require men to wear a jacket for dinner, and bouncers at some 'hot' nightspots hand-pick patrons from the queue based on whether they have the right 'look' for the club.

Temporal factors

Time is one of consumers' most precious and limiting resources. Recent research indicates that there are significant time–money differences when consumers use heuristics ('rules-of-thumb for problem solving learnt by experiment or trial and error' [Merriam-Webster **http://www.merriam-webster.com/dictionary/heuristic**]) for decision-making. i.e. 'decisions related to time rather than money foster an enhanced use of heuristics' which suggests that although time and money seem to be economically equivalent, they are in fact psychologically different[23] (see Chapter 9). Our perspectives on time can affect many stages of decision making and consumption, such as needs that are stimulated, the amount of information search we undertake and so on. Common sense tells us that more careful information search and deliberation occurs when we have the luxury of taking our time.

Economic time

Time is an economic variable; it is a resource that must be divided among activities.[24] Consumers try to maximize satisfaction by allocating time to the appropriate combination of tasks. Of course, people's allocation decisions differ. An individual's priorities
▶ determine their **time style**.[25] Time style incorporates dimensions like economic time, past orientation, future orientation, time submissiveness and time anxiety.[26] Research identified four dimensions of time: social, temporal, planning, and polychromic orientation. The social dimension refers to individuals' categorization of time as either 'time for me' or 'time with/for others'. The temporal orientation depicts the relative significance individuals attach to past, present or future. The planning orientation dimension alludes to different time management styles varying on a continuum from analytic to spontaneous. And lastly, polychromic orientation denotes doing-one-thing-at-a-time versus multitasking time styles. These multiple dimensions of time style push and pull individuals in different directions, which ultimately lead to psychological conflicts. From these dimensions, five emergent symbolic metaphors of time were proposed,[27] which reflected different perspectives on time and the process by which the perspective was created:

1 *'Time is a pressure cooker*: Women who personify this metaphor are usually analytic in their planning, other oriented, and monochronic in their time styles. They treat shopping in a methodical manner and they often feel under pressure and in conflict.

2 *Time is a map*: Women who exemplify this metaphor are usually analytic planners, have a future temporal orientation and a polychronic time style. They often engage in extensive information search and in comparison shopping.

3 *Time is a mirror*: Women who come under this metaphor are also analytic planners and have a polychromic orientation. However, they have a past temporal orientation. Due to their risk averseness in time use, these women are usually loyal to products and services they know and trust.

4 *Time is a river*: Women whose time styles can be described through this metaphor are usually spontaneous in their planning orientation and have a present focus. They go on unplanned, short and frequent shopping trips undertaken on impulse.

5 *Time is feast*: These women are analytic planners who have a present temporal orientation. They view time as something to be consumed in the pursuit of sensory pleasure and gratification and, hence, they are motivated by hedonic and variety seeking desires in their consumption behavior.'[28]

Some of the implications for consumer behaviour which flowed from this research[29] included the following:

1 'There are major differences in individuals' attitudes and behaviors in relation to shopping across the five temporal metaphors.

2 These symbolic metaphors are also associated with differences in individuals' consumption of leisure, food habits, expenditure of time and money on keeping up with appearances.

3 In the domain of food habits, women who exemplify time as a feast metaphor demonstrated preference for fresh and novel ingredients, while women that fit with the mirror metaphor were more inclined towards convenience food choices.

4 Individuals who placed emphasis on keeping up with their appearances coupled with their social orientation were found to spend more time and money on their presentation of self and their material possessions.'[30]

▶ Many consumers believe they are more pressed for time than ever before, a feeling called **time poverty**. This feeling may, however, be due more to perception than to fact. People may simply have more options for spending their time and feel pressured by the weight of it all. European research showed that women aged 15 to 24 spent more time on average on personal care, studying and unpaid work (e.g. cooking, cleaning, caring for children) than young men of the same age (15 to 24) who spent more time in paid work and leisure activities (e.g. sports, watching TV and playing computer games) (see Figure 3.3).[31]

Figure 3.3 How young women and men aged 15–24 spend their time

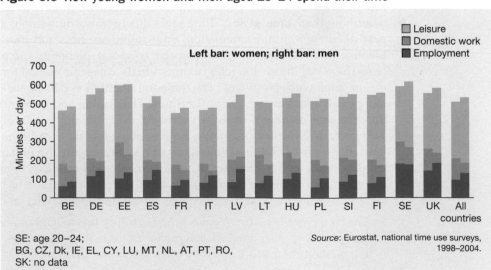

SE: age 20–24;
BG, CZ, DK, IE, EL, CY, LU, MT, NL, AT, PT, RO, SK: no data

Source: Eurostat, national time use surveys, 1998–2004.

Source: *The life of women and men in Europe: A Statistical Portrait* – 2008 edition, Fig. 39 page 48, European Commission/Eurostat Luxembourg: Cat. No. KS-80-07-135-EN-N website http://ec.europa.eu/eurostat.

For some interesting (and revealing!) data on how we spend our time, see http://ec.europa.eu/eurostat[32] and Figures 3.4 and 3.5.

This sense of *time poverty* has made consumers very responsive to marketing innovations that allow them to save time. New online business concepts based on improved delivery are popping up all over the Web. Delivery of videos, groceries, or dry cleaning to customers' doors are a few of the time-saving online possibilities.[33] In Hong Kong rush-hour commuters no longer need to stand and queue to buy Underground tickets. Instead, a scanner automatically reads an Octopus card and automatically deducts the fare from their account. The card doesn't even require contact to be read, so people can just pass their entire bag over the scanner and race to catch their trains.[34]

Figure 3.4 Time spent by women and men, aged 25–44, on paid work and unpaid domestic work

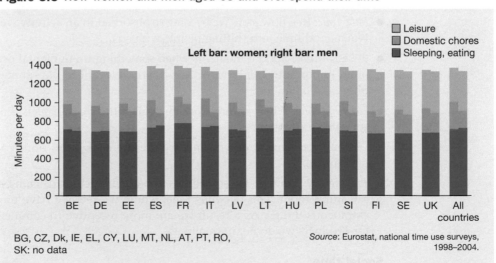

BG, CZ, Dk, IE, EL, CY, LU, MT, NL, AT, PT, RO, SK: no data

Source: Eurostat, national time use surveys, 1998–2004.

Sourcc: *The life of women and men in Europe: A Statistical Portrait* – 2008 edition, Fig. 121 page 111, European Commission/Eurostat Luxembourg: Cat. No. KS-80-07-135-EN-N website http://ec.europa.eu/eurostat.

Figure 3.5 How women and men aged 65 and over spend their time

BG, CZ, Dk, IE, EL, CY, LU, MT, NL, AT, PT, RO, SK: no data

Source: Eurostat, national time use surveys, 1998–2004.

Source: *The life of women and men in Europe: A Statistical Portrait* – 2008 edition, Fig. 158 page 147, European Commission/Eurostat Luxembourg: Cat. No. KS-80-07-135-EN-N website http://ec.europa.eu/eurostat.

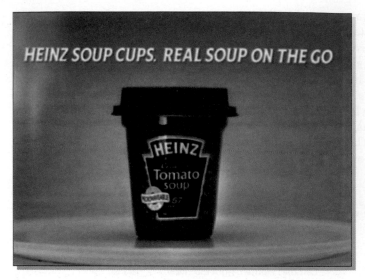

HEINZ SOUP CUPS. REAL SOUP ON THE GO

Time poverty is creating opportunities for many new products (like portable soups) that let people multitask.

The Advertising Archives

 Net profit

With the increase in time poverty, researchers are also noting a rise in *polychronic activity*, where consumers do more than one thing at a time.[35] One area where this type of activity is especially prevalent is eating. Many consumers often do not allocate a specific time to dining, but do something else while eating. As one food industry executive commented, 'We've moved beyond grazing and into gulping.'[36] On the other hand, counter-trends of slow food are also found among other segments. A new 'slow food movement' originating in Italy and spreading via France to several European countries and even the United States witnesses a cultural resistance to the disappearance of cooking and eating a meal as a social event.[37]

Psychological time

The fluidity of time is important for marketers to understand, because we are more likely to be in a consuming mood at some times rather than others. We can identify time categories in terms of when people are likely to be receptive to marketing messages:[38]

- *Flow time*: In a flow state we become so absorbed in an activity we notice nothing else. Not a good time to be hitting people with ads.

- *Occasion time*: Special moments when something monumental occurs, such as a birth or an important job interview. Ads clearly relevant to the situation will be given our undivided attention.

- *Deadline time*: When we are working against the clock. This is the worst time to catch someone's attention.

- *Leisure time*: During down time, we are more likely to notice ads and perhaps try new things.

- *Time to kill*: Waiting for something to happen such as catching a plane or sitting in a waiting room. This is bonus time, where we feel we have the luxury to focus on extraneous things. As a result we are more receptive to commercial messages, even for products we do not normally use.

Social time

Social time has been proposed as an important but overlooked time dimension in consumer behaviour.[39] Social time refers to the time in relation to social processes and

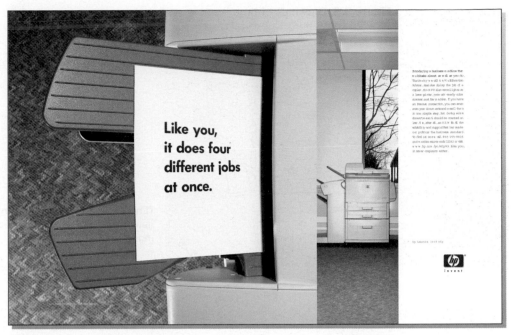

Multitasking has become a way of life for many of us.
Hewlett-Packard Development Company, L.P.

rhythms and schedules in society. It takes into account how determined our lives are by interrelated temporal phenomena, such as working hours, opening hours, eating hours and other institutionalized schedules.

To most Western consumers, time is something that is neatly compartmentalized: we wake up in the morning, go to school or work, come home, eat, go out, go to bed, then do it all over again. This perspective is called linear separable time (or Christian time): events proceed in an orderly sequence and different times are well defined: 'There's a time and a place for everything.' In this worldwide 'modernized' conception of time, there is a clear sense of past, present and future, and the present is preferred to the past, whereas the future is generally rated better than the present.[40] Many activities are performed as the means to an end that will occur at a future point, as when people 'save for a rainy day'.

But even in North European and American cultures, the very linear and compartmentalized chronological time is not hegemonic.[41] When groups of university students were asked to draw a picture of time, the resulting sketches (Figure 3.6) illustrated some of these different temporal perspectives.[42] The drawing at the top represents procedural time: there is a lack of direction from left to right and little sense of past, present and future. The two drawings in the middle denote cyclical time, with regular cycles designated by markers. The bottom drawing represents linear time, with a segmented time line moving from left to right in a well-defined sequence.

Some products and services are believed to be appropriate for certain times and not for others. Some products crossing cultural borders are also crossing over from consumption at one time of day to another time of day. In its home country of Italy, the cappuccino is known as a breakfast coffee. Now it has become popular all over Europe, and in these new markets it is drunk at all times of the day whenever a plain cup of coffee would traditionally have been appropriate. So the cappuccino has moved from a 'breakfast time' category to a more general 'coffee time' category.[43]

Figure 3.6 Drawings of time

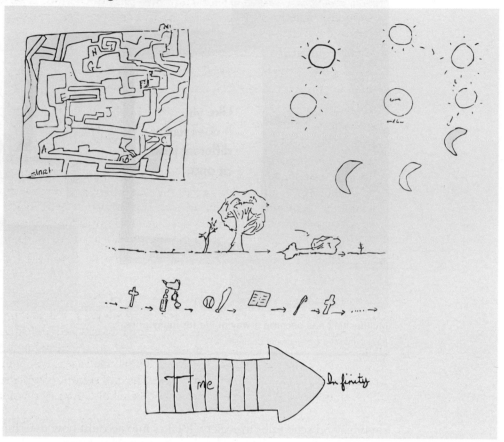

Source: Esther S. Page-Wood, Carol J. Kaufman and Paul M. Lane, 'The Art of Time', *Proceedings of the Academy of Marketing Science* (1990).

SHOPPING: MOTIVATIONS AND EXPERIENCES

People often shop even though they do not necessarily intend to buy anything at all, whereas others have to be dragged to the shopping centre. Shopping is a way to acquire needed products and services, but social motives for shopping are also important. Retailers need to understand the variety of shopping motivations because these all affect how consumers evaluate different aspects of their retail experience such as atmospherics, promotion and marketing communications.[44] One scholar has suggested that shopping activities have a lot to do with love and caring for significant others, to the extent that shopping can be seen as a person's (often the mother's) personal sacrifice of time and devotion for the well-being of the family.[45]

Other scholars distinguish between shopping as an activity performed for utilitarian (functional or tangible) or hedonic (pleasurable or intangible) reasons.[46] These different motives are illustrated by scale items used by researchers to assess people's underlying reasons for shopping. One item that measures hedonic value is: 'During the trip, I felt the excitement of the hunt.' When that type of sentiment is compared to a functionally related statement such as: 'I accomplished just what I wanted to on this shopping trip', the contrast between these two dimensions is clear.[47] European research identified the following hedonic shopping motives:[48]

● *Anticipated utility*: Desire for innovative products, expectations of benefits or hedonistic states which will be provided by the product to be acquired.

- *Role enactment*: Taking on the culturally prescribed roles regarding the conduct of shopping activity, such as careful product and price comparisons, possibly discussed with other shoppers.

- *Choice optimization*: Desire to find the absolutely best buy.

- *Negotiation*: To seek economic advantages and sports-like pleasure through bargaining interactions with sellers in a 'bazaar atmosphere'.

- *Affiliation*: Shopping centres are a natural place to affiliate. The shopping arcade has become a central meeting place for teenagers. It also represents a controlled, secure environment for other groups, such as the elderly.

- *Power and authority*: Entering a power game with the sales personnel and maybe feeling superior to the personnel. As every salesperson knows, some people love the experience of being waited on, even though they may not necessarily buy anything. One men's clothing salesman offered this advice: 'Remember their size, remember what you sold them last time. Make them feel important! If you can make people feel important, they are going to come back. Everybody likes to feel important!'[49]

- *Stimulation*: Searching for new and interesting things offered in the marketplace – shopping just for fun.

▶ Consumers can also be segmented in terms of their **shopping orientation**, or general attitudes about shopping. These orientations may vary depending on the particular product categories and store types considered. Many people feel insecure about shopping for a car (many women, for instance, feel quite intimidated by car showrooms), but they may love to browse in record shops. Our feelings about shopping are also influenced by the culture in which we live. Several shopping types have been identified, although the following list does not cover the whole range of possibilities:[50]

- *The economic shopper*: a rational, goal-oriented shopper who is primarily interested in maximizing the value of their money.

- *The personalized shopper*: a shopper who tends to form strong attachments to store personnel ('I shop where they know my name').

- *The ethical shopper*: a shopper who likes to help out the underdog and will support local shops rather than chain stores.

- *The apathetic shopper*: one who does not like to shop and sees it as a necessary but unpleasant chore.

- *The recreational shopper*: a person who views shopping as a fun, social activity – a preferred way to spend leisure time.

 ## Multicultural dimensions

Who loves to shop the most? In a survey of women around the world, over 60 per cent said they enjoy shopping for clothes in every country except Hong Kong, where only 39 per cent responded so positively. The 'Born to Shop' prize goes to Latin Americans: over 80 per cent of women in countries like Brazil and Colombia agree that clothes shopping is a favourite activity. Other high-scoring countries include France, Italy and Japan. In comparison, only 61 per cent of American women said they like or love to go clothes shopping. Reflecting the casual trend that's swept the country in recent years, the survey indicates that American women are more likely to say that they are not as interested in clothing as they used to be, are more willing to be slightly underdressed at a party rather than slightly overdressed, and are more willing to wear one comfortable outfit all day long rather than change clothes to fit each occasion. Almost everywhere in the world, women agreed that store displays are the most important source of information about clothing. Two exceptions are German women, who ranked fashion magazines highest, and Mexican women, who reported that their families are the best place to learn about what to wear.[51]

Given what we said above, however, one type of shopper is missing from this list: *the hate-to-shop shopper*. They are emerging from research on a variety of examples of the aversive side of shopping, including the hassle of finding a parking space, shopping with a girl- or boyfriend with completely different shopping motivations, dealing with the fact that just when you've made a purchase you find something better or less expensive, or coping with intruding 'Can-I-help-you?' sales assistants.[52]

Trends in the purchase environment

We see bumper stickers and T-shirts everywhere: 'Shop 'til you drop', 'When the going gets tough, the tough go shopping', 'Born to shop'. Like it or not, shopping is a major activity for many consumers. The competition for shoppers among retailers is getting tougher, especially in the face of the economic downturn that has followed the credit crunch. In the UK alone such familiar retailing brands as Woolworths have closed down as they lost sales in a falling market, and as they lost touch with their consumers. Retailers must now offer something extra to lure shoppers, whether that something is excitement or, increasingly, just plain bargains.[53] 'Grocery shopping in Europe, North America and indeed around the world is changing in two main ways. Firstly, shoppers' attitudes towards the different elements of the retail offer are shifting. And secondly, these changing attitudes are encouraging the development of new forms of retail channel which shoppers are using in new and different ways.'[54]

Another European trend is the increase of trade from kiosks (for instance in Greece), and from smaller stores with extended opening hours carrying a small selection of daily goods as well as snack products, sweets, newspapers, etc., sometimes more or less like the 7–11 concept imported from the US. In many countries, such kiosks are well established and are often run by Middle Eastern or North African immigrants. But in countries such as Finland, where the introduction of kiosks is more recent, it has created a new feature in the retail channel system.[55]

In order to be able to compete in the European single market, many retail chains have undergone an internationalization process. The ten biggest companies controlled 30 per cent of the turnover in daily goods in Europe in the mid to late 1990s, and the concentration was growing fast at the end of the 1990s.[56] By 2007 (Table 3.1) the French-owned Carrefour had emerged as the top food retailer in Europe, and the second largest

Table 3.1 Top food retailers in Europe[57] (Turnover in Europe 2007 in billion euros)

	Retailer	Turnover
1	Carrefour	68.4
2	Metro	60.5
3	Tesco	59.6 (2008)
4	Schwarz	45.6
5	Rewe	41 e
6	Edeka	37.8
7	Aldi	36 e
8	Auchan	34 e
9	ITM	31.6
10	E.Leclerc	30 e
11	Sainsbury	24.7
12	Wal-Mart	18.2 (2008)
13	Casino	25.8
14	Tengelmann	18.9
15	Morrison	18.2

© 2008 www.retail-index.com

Internationalization of retail brands, illustrated by these outlets for the low-cost German grocery retailer Lidl, in Lodz, Poland (left), and France (above).

distribution company in the world operating globally; its main markets are in Europe, Latin America and Asia. With over 50 per cent of its business deriving from outside France, and growing markets in Poland and Turkey (as well as China and Brazil), it aims to support local suppliers by sourcing locally in so far as it can, depending on the country.[58] German-owned Metro Group was the second biggest food retailer in Europe. Its Cash and Carry business showed over 14 per cent sales growth in Eastern Europe for the first half of 2008, with particularly strong growth in the Czech Republic, Poland, Russia and the Ukraine. This was in comparison with declining sales in Portugal and the UK.[59] Tesco, at third in the Table, has an expanding international presence and its European ventures have been into the Czech Republic, Hungary, Poland, Slovakia and Turkey.[60]

Store loyalty

Faced with a turbulent retailing environment, including economic recession, retailers highly value store-loyal consumers. Consumers now have an abundance of choices regarding where to shop, including electronic alternatives, which have proved particularly attractive in the economic downturn. Sales online held up well in the traditional pre-Christmas trading period in 2008 for instance, compared with consumer expenditure in high street stores in the UK in the same period. People tend not to be as store-loyal as they once were.[61] Since the 1990s Tesco have gained a reputation for their very effective exploitation of the information gathered via their store loyalty Clubcards. Clubcard's quarterly mailings are so carefully customized that the company prints over 4 million variations for each mailing.[62] Research suggests that loyalty programmes, properly designed and targeted, can serve five goals: 'keep customers from defecting; win greater share of wallet; prompt customers to make additional purchases; yield insights into customer behaviour; and help turn a profit.'[63] 'Levers of loyalty' were identified as: first, the divisibility of rewards (i.e. redeemable points divided into attractive size clusters, e.g. two lots of 5,000 points rather than one set of 10,000 points); secondly, sense of momentum for the members; nature of rewards (more hedonic than utilitarian in emphasis); thirdly, expansion of relationship (by encouraging the customer to buy more *different* products rather than simply more of the same product); and fourthly, combined-currency flexibility (i.e. spending the alternative currencies represented by points such as air miles in smaller amounts in combination with cash purchase of an air ticket is more attractive than spending a lot of air miles in one go).[64] However, the same researchers warn of the dangers of designing schemes which reward the disloyal; reward volume over profit; give too much away in terms of profit margin; and promise more than can be delivered.[65]

E-COMMERCE: CLICKS VS. BRICKS

As more and more Websites pop up to sell everything from fridge magnets to cars, marketers continue to debate how this **cyberspace** marketplace in the online world will affect how they conduct business.[66] The European online buying population is well over 100 million,[67] with obvious differences between the older and younger segments (see Chapter 15 for a discussion of the changing patterns of Internet access and online shopping across Europe). A Swedish survey indicated that searching for product and service information were more important aspects of Internet behaviour than actual purchases (note Daniel's behaviour in the opening vignette for Chapter 9). In 2000 only 9 per cent of consumers wanted to buy food online (and a mere 1 per cent had actually tried it), and even the highest scoring purchase types like travel and ticket purchase did not exceed 30 per cent at that point.[68] However, the last ten years have seen e-commerce take off globally so that the e-market is increasingly important. By 2008 'more than 85 per cent of the world's online population had used the Internet to make a purchase, increasing the market for online shopping by 40 per cent in the past two years.'[69]

For marketers, the growth of online commerce is a sword that cuts both ways: on the one hand, they can reach customers around the world even if they are physically located 100 miles from nowhere. On the other hand, their competition now comes not only from the shop across the street, but from thousands of Websites spanning the globe. A second problem is that offering products directly to consumers has the potential to cut out the middleman – the loyal store-based retailers who carry the firm's products and who sell them at a marked-up price.[70] The 'clicks vs. bricks' dilemma is raging in the marketing world.

Many online shopping sites offer time-saving convenience. This French ad for a shopping/home delivery website says, 'stop the muscle training on Saturdays . . . yes, this is total laziness. But so what?'

Jean & Montmarin, Paris

So, can you have your cake and eat it too? Coca-Cola thinks so, with its new 'think local, act local' strategy based on a philosophy of getting closer to the consumers. A Danish–Swedish–Norwegian–Finnish (probably as local as Coca-Cola gets!) campaign featuring an Indiana Jones-inspired adventure quiz has as its primary purpose to get teenagers to log on to the Coca-Cola Website in order to participate in a quiz with adventurous travels as prizes. 'If we want to communicate on the teens' premises, we have to make an active use of the Internet and SMS media', says one executive.[71] This is also becoming true for US teenagers who were slower than other teenagers to adopt mobile phones for text messaging.[72] Another possibility for reaching the youth markets is product placement in the chat rooms. For example, a virtual rose given to a fellow chatterer could be from a branded chain of florists. Or the chat environment can be constructed as a cruise ship with various branded services and games available for the chatterers.[73] But more serious organizations have also demonstrated their abilities to utilize the net. A Danish anti-cancer organization supporting research and cancer patients has a Website where visitors can give a small gift by clicking on a button. Immediately, 'thank you' appears with six banners referring to sponsoring companies, encouraging the visitor to visit the sponsors. This format has produced a much higher rate of banner-clicking than normal commercial banners.[74]

So, what makes e-commerce sites successful? According to a survey by NPD Online, 75 per cent of online shoppers surveyed said that good customer service would make them shop at the site again.[75] A study of how online grocery shoppers negotiated three different store layouts, freeform, grid and racetrack,[76] indicated that they found the freeform layout most useful for finding shopping list products within the store, and also by far the most entertaining to use. They also found the grid layout much easier to use than the other layouts.[77] Another study suggested that 'four factors were predictive of customer judgments about quality and satisfaction, customer loyalty and attitudes towards a website (see Table 3.2):

- *Website design.* This covers all elements of the customer's experience at the website including navigation, information search, order processing, appropriate personalization and product selection.

E-commerce sites like Tesco give shoppers the option of shopping without leaving home.

http://www.tesco.com. Courtesy of Tesco Stores Limited

Table 3.2 eTailQ items: measuring customer satisfaction with Websites

Factor	Customer judgement
Website design	1 The Website provides in-depth information.
	2 The site doesn't waste my time.
	3 It is quick and easy to complete this transaction at this Website.
	4 The level of personalization at this site is about right, not too much or too little.
	5 This Website has good selection.
Fulfilment/reliability	6 The product that came was represented accurately by the Website.
	7 You get what you ordered from this site.
	8 The product is delivered by the time promised by the company.
Security/privacy	9 I feel like my privacy is protected at this site.
	10 I feel safe in my transactions with this Website.
	11 The Website has adequate security features.
Customer service	12 The company is willing and ready to respond to customer needs.
	13 When you have a problem, the Website shows a sincere interest in solving it.
	14 Inquiries are answered promptly.

Source: Based on Mary Wolfinbarger and Mary C. Gilly, 'eTailQ: Dimensionalizing, measuring and predicting etail quality', *Journal of Retailing* 79 (2003): Table 4. Reproduced by permission.

- *Fulfillment/reliability*. This involves, firstly, the accurate display and description of a product so that what customers receive is what they thought they ordered; and secondly, the delivery of the right product within the time frame promised.

- *Privacy/security*. This involves the security surrounding credit card payments and the privacy of shared information.

- *Customer service*. This needs to be responsive, helpful and willing service with a quick response time to customer enquiries.'[78]

Many successful e-tailers are learning that using technology to provide extra value for customers is attracting and keeping customers. A variety of online banking services are becoming very popular.[79] And estate agents can provide much more information, floor plans and more appealing photographs of homes for sale as well as virtual guided tours, for example, than has been possible through the traditional print media. In a similar way companies such as Expedia have offered potential customers virtual tours of holiday destinations including pictures of hotel rooms and beaches.[80] Interactive TV is letting home viewers provide input to the videos played on MTV and to play along on *Who Wants to Be a Millionaire?* Soon MTV viewers will be able to use their remote controls to purchase the CDs that go with the music videos they are seeing. In Germany, the most successful application of interactive television (after home shopping) is the call-in quiz show, which combines television and telephone.[81]

Figure 3.7 depicts, the major domains in the development of consumer possibilities in cyberspace. Consumer experiences in cyberspace can be analyzed according to two dimensions: *telepresence* and *bricolage*.[82] Telepresence expresses the degree to which the consumer feels immersed in the virtual environment, the time spent there and the positive feelings generated, whereas bricolage (a French word meaning 'getting by with whatever is at hand') is an indication of the interactive medium's possibilities for the consumer to be in control of the information gathered and used, presumably leading to a higher degree of involvement in and retention of the information.

However, all is not perfect in the virtual world. E-commerce does have its limitations. Security is one important concern. We hear horror stories of consumers whose credit cards and other identity information have been stolen. While an individual's financial

Figure 3.7 Everyday life of a consumer in cyberspace

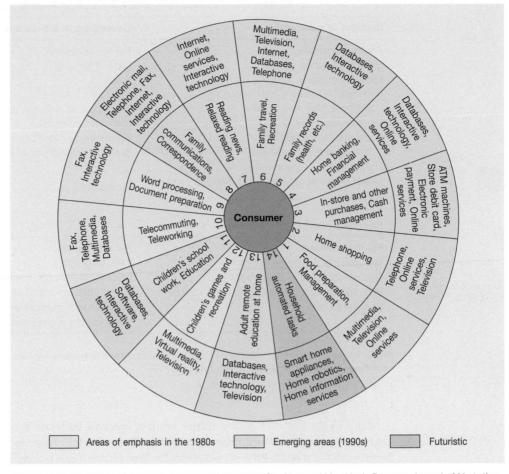

Source: Alladi Venkatesh, 'Cybermarketscapes and consumer freedoms and identities', *European Journal of Marketing* 32(7/8) (1998): 664–76. Used by permission.

liability in most theft cases is limited to approximately €60 or £55, the damage to one's credit rating can last for years.

Other limitations of e-commerce relate to the actual shopping experience. While it may be satisfactory to buy a computer or a book on the Internet, buying clothing and other items in which touching the item or trying it on is essential may be less attractive. Lack of tactile input (feeling material; smelling a bouquet) is one the major factors which deters consumers from using the Internet for buying goods. One study established that consumers with a higher need for tactile inputs tended not to use the Internet so much for product purchase; and men tend to exhibit less need for tactile input than women when evaluating products.[83] Even though most companies have very liberal returns policies, consumers can still get stuck with large delivery and return postal charges for items where the material does not hang properly, or they don't fit, or they simply aren't the right colour. However, a potentially interesting counter-example to this is the purchase of wedding dresses online, where customers have the opportunity to co-design their dresses. This was a particularly attractive opportunity for customers who were already comfortable with technology and already owned personal technological devices; have already bought formal clothes online; and regularly spend time online.[84] Some of the pros and cons of e-commerce are summarized in Table 3.3. It is clear that traditional shopping isn't quite dead yet.

Table 3.3 Pros and cons of e-commerce

Benefits of e-commerce	Limitations of e-commerce
For the consumer	**For the consumer**
Shop 24 hours a day	Lack of security
Less travelling	Fraud
Can receive relevant information in	Can't touch items
seconds from any location	Exact colours may not reproduce on
More choice of products	computer monitors
More products available to	Expensive to order and then return
less-developed countries	Potential breakdown of human relationships
Greater price information	
Lower prices so that less affluent can purchase	
Participate in virtual auctions	
Fast delivery	
Electronic communities	
For the marketer	**For the marketer**
The world is the marketplace	Lack of security
Decreases costs of doing business	Must maintain site to reap benefits
Very specialized businesses can be successful	Fierce price competition
Real-time pricing	Conflicts with conventional retailers
	Legal issues not resolved

Source: Adapted from Michael R. Solomon and Elnora W. Stuart, *Welcome to Marketing.Com: The Brave New World of E-Commerce* (Englewood Cliffs, NJ: Prentice Hall, 2001).

Many of the winners in the future retail scene will be those who can create a high degree of synergy between their online and offline outlets.[85] There is already evidence of the rewards for retailers who successfully link offline with online because the fastest-growing trend in consumer behaviour is combining patronage of offline company outlets (shops and/or mail order catalogues or car dealerships) with online company Websites.[86]

Bricks-and-mortar retailers will need to work hard to give shoppers something they can not get (yet anyway) in the virtual world – a stimulating or pleasant environment in which to browse with sensory appeals not available online.[87] They will need to build emotional bonds with their customers through imaginative and entertaining retail design and merchandising strategies.[88] Now let's consider how they are doing that.

SERVICESCAPES: RETAILING AS THEATRE

Shopping can no longer be regarded as a simple act of purchasing.[89] A retail culture has arisen,[90] where the act of shopping has taken on new entertainment and/or experiential dimensions as retailers compete for customers' attention, not to mention their loyalty. The act of shopping ties into a number of central existential aspects of human life such as sexuality.[91] Furthermore, the customer may be regarded not as a passive recipient of the offerings of the purchase environment but rather as an active co-creator of this very environment and the meanings attached to it,[92] in a situation analogous to the focus among 'marketing mavens' (see Chapter 10) on flexibility in the area of product supply and tailormade marketing mixes for the individual consumer.[93] One of the most obvious trends in the retailing sector in Europe is the construction of shopping centres, often modelled on American prototypes. Once introduced into an area, shopping centres often bring with them a whole new combination of leisure activities, shopping and social encounters in safe environments.[94]

Hard Rock Café: one of the oldest and most well-established themed consumer environments.
© SIME/Corbis

Shopping centres have tried to gain the loyalty of shoppers by appealing to their social motives as well as providing access to desired goods. It is now typical to find such features as children's rides and climbing walls in a suburban shopping centre. As one retailing executive put it, 'Malls are becoming the new mini-amusement parks.'[95] The importance of creating a positive, vibrant and interesting image has led innovative marketers to blur the line between shopping and the theatre. Shopping centres and individual stores have to create environments that stimulate people and allow them to shop and be entertained at the same time.[96] The Hard Rock Café, established in London over 25 years ago, now has over 45 restaurants around the world, and has become a sort of pilgrimage place in itself. The classic European counterpart to the American mall is the department store.[97] The first department stores can be seen as marking the introduction of a modern consumer culture, nourished by dreams of abundance.[98] The following are a few examples of 'performers' in the retailing theatre:

- A Dutch internet bank, ING, has turned the ground floor of its office in Toronto, Canada, into a stylish café, complete with counter, armchairs, sofas and background music. But in addition to the variety of coffees, the chalkboard behind the counter announces interest rates in various savings accounts and other banking information.[99]

- The Powerscourt Townhouse Centre in Dublin succeeded in merging a variety of styles and features, including a grand piano on a stage in the central hall, to make a sort of new version of a Victorian marketplace atmosphere. Unlike the mall of America, it does not appear as a carefully planned environment but rather a happy blend of many consumption opportunities including an Italian restaurant, a modern hairstylist, an antique shop, etc. in a stylish classical setting.[100]

The quest to entertain means that many stores are going all-out to create imaginative environments that transport shoppers to fantasy worlds or provide other kinds of stimulation. This strategy is called **retail theming**. Innovative merchants today use four basic kinds of theming techniques:

- *Landscape themes* rely upon associations with images of nature, earth, animals and the physical body. Bass Pro Shops, for example, create a simulated outdoor environment including pools stocked with fish.

- *Marketscape themes* build upon associations with man-made places. An example is the Venetian Hotel in Las Vegas that lavishly recreates parts of the Italian city.

- *Cyberspace themes* are built around images of information and communications technology. eBay's retail interface instils a sense of community among its vendors and traders.

- *Mindscape themes* draw upon abstract ideas and concepts, introspection and fantasy, and often possess spiritual overtones. At the Seibu store in Tokyo, shoppers enter as neophytes at the first level. As they progress through the physical levels of the store each is themed to connote increasing levels of consciousness until they emerge at the summit as completed shoppers.[101]

▶ Cutting-edge retailers are figuring out that they need to convert a store into a **being space** that resembles a commercial living room where we can go to relax, be entertained, hang out with friends, escape the everyday, or even learn. When you think of being spaces, Starbucks will probably come to your mind. The coffee chain's stated goal is to become our 'third place', where we spend the bulk of our time in addition to home and work. Starbucks led the way when it fitted out its stores with comfy chairs and WiFi. Another example is Borders bookstores which creates a similar 'sitting room' environment with comfortable sofas and easy chairs so that you can sit and read your newspaper or book with a leisurely cup of coffee. But there are many other marketers who are meeting our needs for exciting commercial spaces – no matter what those needs are.

▶ **Pop-up stores** are appearing in many forms around the world. Typically these are makeshift installations that do business only for a few days or weeks, and then disappear before they get old. Some interesting examples from around the world include the following:

- American Apparel opened a 45-day pop-up store in New York featuring daily spontaneous events like karaoke, dreidel spinning, and mariachi performances.

- The Swatch Instant Store appeared in London, Paris, Barcelona, Amsterdam and Berlin. The stores sold limited edition watches; as soon as the masses discovered a store it closed.

- Caravan is a fashion boutique on wheels that turns up at appointed times in different New York locations to offer a mix of hip clothing, accessories, gift items, and art to fashionistas who are 'on the inside'.[102]

- In The Netherlands, Dommelsch Beer organized pop-up concerts featuring well-known performers. Fans could enter barcodes they found on cans, beer bottles and coasters on the brewer's Website to discover dates and locations.

- Nintendo set up a Pokémon theme park for six months in Nagoya, Japan. From there it moved on to other cities for three-month stints.

- At the LG Wash Bar in Paris, visitors could enjoy music and a drink while doing their laundry. Staff helped customers with their laundry, demonstrating the equipment as needed. Every Tuesday customers who dressed from head to toe in white got free 'Whiter than white' ('Plus Blanc que Blanc') cocktails.[103]

Spectacular consumption environments represent another example of servicescapes, where the emphasis is on *play*, and the co-creation of the experience by the producer and the consumer. Recent research within a themed retail environment, the ESPN Zone Chicago, examined the agency of the consumer in this type of environment and how the use of technology affected consumers' sense of reality. Consumers seemed to exercise creative control over the spectacular environment by using technology and their bodies to produce parts of the spectacle, and to create and alter space, suggesting a dialectical relationship between producers and consumers. The researchers identified two ludic (play related) elements that help us understand the role of *play* in consumption environments:

1 '*Liminoid Real Estate*: This refers to the creation of new worlds through consumer play, which consumers interpret as different realities. This notion of transcendent surrender provides a link between play and religion, ritual, sacrifice and the sacred.

2 *The Obverse Panapticon*: This refers to physical structures that are designed in a way that appeals to exhibitionistic desires of consumers by enabling them to be observed by others.'[104]

Consumer behaviour as I see it . . .

Professor Pauline Maclaran
Royal Holloway College, University of London

How do people make sense of the spaces and places around them, what is the difference between space and place, and how do spaces become places? To me these are fascinating questions that have been relatively overlooked in consumer research. Places, such as retail centres, restaurants, pubs and other consumption scapes, are much more than spatial co-ordinates or dots on a map. As places become intimately associated with life's events (whether routine or unique), they come to represent symbols of the experiences concerned. Places perform many socio cultural functions that go unacknowledged in traditional marketing management texts where the 'P' of place is just another element of the marketing mix. Places can make us feel secure; they can evoke nostalgic memories; they can excite and stimulate; they can bind us to old friends or lead us to new ones. We form bonds with places that we know and they can often perform an important social role. Consider the pensioner who goes to her local supermarket everyday just to find a friendly face with whom to exchange a smile; or the young man who sits at the bar counter telling his woes to the patient bartender. A space thus becomes a place when it becomes invested with meanings by those who use it. Our relationships with places are dynamic, however, and the meaning that places hold for us changes and evolves as we move through the life course.

My research often looks at how consumption intersects with spaces and places. For example, one of my studies, about a refurbishment of a festival marketplace, showed the deep emotional attachments that many people held for the centre, and how it was also tied in with their sense of self. They believed it held a special ambience that differentiated it strongly from normal high street shopping. As the refurbishment took place, and the centre moved towards mainstream retailing, consumers complained that it could now be anywhere and that it had lost its special ambience. Many consumers were very angry at the changes, believing that a unique place had been sacrificed to the encroaching forces of globalization and, indeed, that a part of their heritage had been taken away. They blamed the management of the centre and dissatisfaction with the new minimalist look only served to increase their nostalgia for the old centre which had once symbolized for them the antithesis of high street shopping.

This example also illustrates how marketers and consumers are involved in joint cultural production of spaces and how marketers need to be aware of the important social role they play in the organization of such spaces. Their relationships with consumers are enhanced by judicious use of marketing activities within the spaces concerned. When marketers overlook this social role their marketing activities may actually subvert, rather than support, consumers' interest in a particular space. In particular, it highlights the importance for management of understanding the meaning systems that consumers create around consumption scapes and how these may be very powerful and enduring.

Store image

With so many stores competing for customers, how do consumers select one rather than another? Like products, we can think of stores as having 'personalities'. Some stores have very clearly defined images (either good or bad). Others tend to blend into the crowd. They may not have anything distinctive about them and may be overlooked for

▶ this reason. This personality, or **store image**, is composed of many different factors. The design and general image of the store is central to the perception of the goods displayed there, whether we are talking about fashion,[105] food products[106] or any other type of good. Store features, coupled with such consumer characteristics as shopping orientation, help to predict which shopping outlets people will prefer.[107] Some of the important dimensions of a store's profile are location, merchandise suitability and the knowledge and congeniality of the sales staff.[108]

These features typically work together to create an overall impression. When shoppers think about stores, they may not say, 'Well, that place is fairly good in terms of convenience, the salespeople are acceptable, and services are good.' They are more likely to say, 'That place gives me the creeps', or 'I always enjoy shopping there.' Consumers evaluate

▶ stores in terms of both their specific attributes *and* a global evaluation, or the **store gestalt** (see Chapter 4).[109] This overall feeling may have more to do with such intangibles as interior design and the types of people one finds in the store than with aspects such as returns policies or credit availability. As a result, some stores are likely to be consistently in consumers' evoked sets (see Chapter 9), whereas others will never be considered.[110]

Atmospherics

Because a store's image is now recognized as a very important aspect of the retailing mix,

▶ store designers pay a lot of attention to **atmospherics**, or the 'conscious designing of space and its various dimensions to evoke certain effects in buyers'.[111] These dimensions include colours, scents and sounds. For any store or any shopping centre, one may think of this process as a careful *orchestration* of the various elements, each playing its part to form a whole.[112]

A store's atmosphere in turn affects what we buy. In one study researchers who asked shoppers how much pleasure they were feeling five minutes after they entered a store predicted the amount of time and money they spent there.[113] To boost the entertainment value of shopping (and to lure online shoppers back to bricks-and-mortar stores), some

▶ retailers now offer **activity stores** that let consumers participate in the production of the products or services they buy there. At a chain of stores catering to preteen girls called Club Libby Lu, for instance, girls enter a fantasyland environment where they dress as princesses and mix their own fragrances.[114]

Many elements of store design can be cleverly controlled to attract customers and produce desired effects on consumers. Light colours impart a feeling of spaciousness and serenity, and signs in bright colours create excitement. One study found that brighter in-store lighting influenced people to examine and handle more merchandise.[115]

In addition to visual stimuli, all sorts of cues can influence behaviours.[116] For example, music can affect eating habits. A study found that diners who listened to loud, fast music ate more food. In contrast, those who listened to Mozart or Brahms ate less and more slowly. The researchers concluded that diners who choose soothing music at mealtimes can increase weight loss by at least five pounds a month![117] Classical music can have a positive effect on consumers' evaluation of store atmosphere.[118]

In-store decision-making

Despite all their efforts to 'pre-sell' consumers through advertising, marketers are increasingly recognizing the significant degree to which many purchases are strongly influenced by the store environment. Women tell researchers, for example, that store displays are one of the major information sources they use to decide what clothing to buy.[119] A Danish survey indicated that nine out of ten customers did not plan the purchase of at least one-third of the goods they acquired.[120] The proportion of unplanned purchases is even higher for other product categories such as food – it is estimated that about two out of every three supermarket purchases are decided in the aisles. And people with lists are just as likely to make spontaneous purchases as those without them.[121] Marketers are scrambling to engineer purchasing environments in order to increase the likelihood that they will be in contact with consumers at the exact time they make a decision. This strategy even applies to drinking behaviour: Diageo, the world's largest liquor company, discovered that 60 per cent of bar customers do not know what they will drink until seconds before they place their orders. To make it more likely that the customer's order will include Smirnoff vodka, Johnnie Walker Scotch or one of its other brands, Diageo launched its Drinks Invigoration Team to increase what it calls its 'share of throat'. The Dublin-based team experimented with bar 'environments', bottle-display techniques and how to match drinks to customers' moods. For example, the company researchers discovered that bubbles stimulate the desire for spirits, so it developed bubble machines to put in the back of bars. Diageo has even categorized bars into types and is identifying the types of drinkers – and the drinks they prefer – who frequent each. These include 'style bars', where cutting-edge patrons like to sip fancy fresh-fruit martinis, and 'buzz bars', where the clientele is receptive to a drink made of Smirnoff and energy brew Red Bull.[122]

Spontaneous shopping

When a shopper is prompted to buy something in a shop, one of two different processes may be at work: *unplanned buying* may occur when a person is unfamiliar with a store's layout or perhaps when under some time pressure; or, a person may be reminded to buy something by seeing it on a store shelf. About one-third of unplanned buying has been attributed to the recognition of new needs while within the store.[123]

Impulse buying

▶ In contrast, impulse buying occurs when the person experiences a sudden urge that they cannot resist. For this reason, so-called impulse items such as sweets and chewing gum are conveniently placed near the checkout. Similarly, many supermarkets have installed wider aisles to encourage browsing, and the widest tend to contain products with the highest margin. Low mark-up items that are purchased regularly tend to be stacked high in narrower aisles, to allow shopping trolleys to speed through.[124] A more recent high-tech tool has been added to encourage impulse buying: a device called 'The Portable Shopper', a personal scanning gun which allows customers to ring up their own purchases as they shop. The gun was initially developed for Albert Heijn, the Netherlands' largest grocery chain, to move customers through the store more quickly. It is now in use in over 150 supermarkets worldwide.[125]

One particular type of occasion where a lot of impulse buying goes on is in the seasonal sales, which appeal especially to younger and price-conscious shoppers according to one British study.[126] In general, shoppers can be categorized in terms of how much advance planning they do. *Planners* tend to know what products and specific brands they will buy beforehand, *partial planners* know they need certain products, but do not decide on specific brands until they are in the store, and *impulse purchasers* do no advance planning whatsoever.[127]

Point-of-purchase stimuli

Because so much decision-making apparently occurs while the shopper is in the purchasing environment, retailers are beginning to pay more attention to the amount of information in their stores, as well as to the way it is presented. It has been estimated that impulse purchases increase by 10 per cent when appropriate displays are used. Consumers' images

of a good-value-for-money purchase are in many cases not induced by careful price examinations but by powerful and striking in-store information.[128] That explains why US
▶ companies spend more than $13 billion each year on **point-of-purchase stimuli (POP)**. A POP can be an elaborate product display or demonstration, a coupon-dispensing machine, or someone giving out free samples of a new perfume in the cosmetics aisles. Research indicated that European consumers responded more positively to spray samplers than to vials and plugs in the promotion campaign for a fragrance. 'Both fragrance marketers and retailers confirm[ed] that spray samplers successfully entice customers to try, experience and buy an upscale product. The sprays are able to effectively communicate the feel, gesture and essence of a brand' and are now being increasingly tried out in the US as an effective way of getting consumers to try a new fragrance.[129] Winning consumers in the store with packaging and displays is regarded as 'the first moment of truth'.[130]

Much of the growth in point-of-purchase activity has been in new electronic technologies.[131] Videotronic, a German hardware producer, has specialized in compact in-store video displays. The newest feature is a touch-screen selection with various pieces of information which eventually provoke scent to be produced.[132] Some shopping trolleys have a small screen that displays advertising, which is keyed to the specific areas of the store through which the trolley is wheeled.[133] New interactive possibilities seem to enhance the effectiveness of POP information systems,[134] although the effect of in-store advertising and other POP continues to be difficult to assess. High-tech solutions such as hand-held computers which will process filmed as well as alphanumerical data are used by Reebok to show whether their in-store efforts are used correctly and which type works best in comparison with competitors.[135]

In-store *displays* are another commonly used device to attract attention in the store environment. While most displays consist of simple racks that dispense the product and/or related coupons, some highlight the value of regarding retailing as theatre by supplying the 'audience' with elaborate performances and scenery. In the UK market for construction toys, Lego has long dominated, with Meccano a distant second. However,

Smart retailers recognize that many purchase decisions are made at the time the shopper is in the store. That's one reason why grocery carts sometimes resemble billboards on wheels.

Peter Byron/Photo Researchers, Inc.

by using an aggressive POP strategy, K'Nex came close to a 20 per cent market share in 1996 from a standing start that same year.[136]

Place-based media

Advertisers are also being more aggressive about hitting consumers with their messages, wherever they may be. *Place-based media* is a specialized medium that has grown in popularity: it targets consumers based on the locations in which the message is delivered. Tesco followed Wal-Mart and installed TV in 300 stores where 'in between news clips, recipe tips and beauty advice, the screens will show ads for products in the aisles'.[137] In 2007 dunnhumby relaunched Tesco's in-store TV screens to provide a more tailored content proposition.[138] Twentieth Century Fox has negotiated a partnership deal with shopping centres owned by US General Growth Properties for the promotion of its films using methods which range from banners, posters, window stickers to tray liners and ad placements in eating areas.[139] Even MTV is in on the act: its Music Report, shown in record stores, is a two-hour 'video capsule' featuring video spots and ads for music retailers and corporate sponsors. An MTV executive observed, 'They're already out there at the retail environment. They're ready to spend money.'[140] A Dutch CD retailer, Free Record Shop, has installed a device that permits shoppers to compile and burn their own CD in-store. Consumers can select up to 74 minutes of music and are charged a per-song amount (up to €1.23). The teens are delighted about this legal way of making personalized compilations. The company planned to spread the system to their other stores in The Netherlands, Belgium, Norway and France.[141]

The salesperson

One of the most important in-store factors is the salesperson, who attempts to influence the buying behaviour of the customer.[142] This influence can be understood in terms of ► **exchange theory**, which stresses that every interaction involves an exchange of value. Each participant gives something to the other and hopes to receive something in return.[143]

What 'value' does the customer look for in a sales interaction? There are a variety of resources a salesperson might offer. For example, they might offer expertise about the product to make the shopper's choice easier. Alternatively, the customer may be reassured because the salesperson is an admired or likeable person whose tastes are similar and who is seen as someone who can be trusted.[144] A long stream of research attests to the impact of a salesperson's appearance on sales effectiveness. In sales, as in much of life, attractive people appear to hold the upper hand.[145] In addition, it's not unusual for service personnel and customers to form fairly warm personal relationships; these have been termed *commercial* friendships (think of all those patient bartenders who double as therapists for many people). Researchers have found that commercial friendships are similar to other friendships in that they can involve affection, intimacy, social support, loyalty and reciprocal gift giving. They also work to support marketing objectives such as satisfaction, loyalty and positive word-of-mouth.[146]

A buyer/seller situation is like many other dyadic encounters (two-person groups); it is a relationship where some agreement must be reached about the roles of each participant, when a process of *identity negotiation* occurs.[147] For example, if the salesperson immediately establishes themself as an expert, they are likely to have more influence over the customer through the course of the relationship. Some of the factors that help to determine a salesperson's role (and relative effectiveness) are their age, appearance, educational level and motivation to sell.[148]

In addition, more effective salespeople usually know their customers' traits and preferences better than do ineffective salespeople, since this knowledge allows them to adapt their approach to meet the needs of the specific customer.[149] The ability to be adaptable is especially vital when customers and salespeople differ in terms of their *interaction styles*.[150] Consumers, for example, vary in the degree of assertiveness they bring to interactions. At one extreme, non-assertive people believe that complaining is not socially acceptable and may be intimidated in sales situations. Assertive people are more likely to stand up for themselves in a firm but non-threatening way. Aggressives may resort to rudeness and threats if they do not get their way.[151]

POST-PURCHASE SATISFACTION

▶ **Consumer satisfaction/dissatisfaction (CS/D)** is determined by the overall feelings, or attitude, a person has about a product after it has been purchased. Consumers engage in a constant process of evaluating the things they buy as they integrate these products into their daily consumption activities.[152] Despite evidence that customer satisfaction is steadily declining in many industries, good marketers are constantly on the lookout for sources of dissatisfaction so that they can improve.[153] Customer satisfaction has a real impact on profitability: a study conducted among a large sample of Swedish consumers found that product quality affects customer satisfaction, which in turn results in increased profitability among firms who provide quality products.[154] Quality is more than a marketing 'buzzword'.

Perceptions of product quality

Just what do consumers look for in products? The answer's easy: they want quality and value. Especially because of foreign competition, claims of product quality have become strategically crucial to maintaining a competitive advantage.[155] Consumers use a number of cues to infer quality, including brand name, price, and even their own estimates of how much money has been put into a new product's advertising campaign.[156] These cues, as well as others such as product warranties and follow-up letters from the company, are often used by consumers to relieve perceived risk and assure themselves that they have made smart purchase decisions.[157]

This ad for Audi relies on a claim about quality based on technical excellence in engineering and design.
The Advertising Archives

Figure 3.8 Customer expectation zones: managing quality expectations

The importance of expectations

Satisfaction or dissatisfaction is more than a reaction to the actual performance quality of a product or service. First of all, satisfaction is not just a matter of functional but also of the hedonic performance of the product – something which may be more difficult for the producer to ensure beforehand. When we buy a book, we don't expect that the pages will come loose or fall out.[158]

Satisfaction, then, is highly influenced by prior expectations regarding all aspects
► of quality. According to the **expectancy disconfirmation model**, consumers form beliefs about product performance based on prior experience with the product and/or communications about the product that imply a certain level of quality.[159] When something performs the way we thought it would, we may not think much about it. If, on the other hand, it fails to live up to expectations, negative affect may result. Furthermore, if performance happens to exceed our expectations, we are satisfied and pleased.

To understand this perspective, think about different types of restaurants. People expect to be provided with sparkling, clear glassware at high-class restaurants, and they might become upset if they discover a grimy glass. On the other hand, we may not be surprised to find fingerprints on our mug at a local 'greasy spoon'; we may even shrug it off because it contributes to the 'charm' of the place. An important lesson emerges for marketers from this perspective: don't over-promise if you can't deliver.[160]

This perspective underscores the importance of *managing expectations* – customer dissatisfaction is usually due to expectations exceeding the company's ability to deliver. Figure 3.8 illustrates the alternative strategies a firm can choose in these situations. When confronted with unrealistic expectations about what it can do, the firm can either accommodate these demands by improving the range or quality of products it offers, alter the expectations, or perhaps even choose to abandon the customer if it is not feasible to meet their needs.[161] Expectations are altered, for example, when waiters tell patrons in advance that the portion size they have ordered will not be very big, or when new car buyers are warned of strange smells they will experience during the running-in period. A firm can also under-promise, as when Xerox inflates the time it will take for a service rep to visit. When the rep arrives a day earlier, the customer is impressed.

One approach to customer satisfaction, known as the *Kano-model*, operates with three kinds of expectation: basis, performance and enthusiasm expectations. The first includes the implicit and taken-for-granted qualities expected from a product. If these are not satisfied, the product will never be able to live up to the customer's requirements, but even if fulfilled, they do not profile the product because these qualities are taken for granted as a minimum. For the performance expectations satisfaction is proportional to how well the product lives up to the expectations. Such quality requirements are often specified and articulated by the customer. As for enthusiasm-related product features, it is wrong to call them expectations since their essential character is that they are *not* expected by the customer. Therefore, such positive surprises can lead to a very great feeling of satisfaction, since the product quality was even better than expected.[162] Furthermore, research evidence indicates that product experience is important for customer satisfaction. When people have no experiences they are relatively easy to satisfy, but with growing experience they become harder to satisfy. Then, when they reach a certain level of experience, satisfaction again becomes easier to obtain, since consumers are now 'experts' and this facilitates choice and generates more realistic expectations.[163]

Satisfaction levels are determined not only by the product purchased but also by the expectations about the quality of alternatives that were *not* purchased. In other words, the higher the expectations about unselected alternatives, the lower the level of satisfaction with the chosen good.[164] A general conclusion which one should draw from such a discussion is that consumer goals may be multiple and the product or service offer so complex to evaluate that any measurement of satisfaction must be used with caution.[165]

Quality and product failures

The power of quality claims is most evident when a company's product fails. Here, consumers' expectations are dashed and dissatisfaction results. In these situations, marketers must immediately take steps to reassure customers. When the company confronts the problem truthfully, consumers are often willing to forgive and forget, as was the case with Perrier when traces of benzene were found in the water. When the company appears to be dragging its heels or covering up, on the other hand, consumer resentment will grow, as occurred during Union Carbide's chemical disaster in India, the massive Alaskan oil spill caused by the tanker *Exxon Valdez* or corporate scandals such as the collapse of Enron. The EC has seen a significant rise in national notifications of unsafe non-food products in the last few years (Figure 3.9). Germany (12%); Greece (8%); Slovakia (8%); Hungary (8%) and Spain (8%) were the source of 44% of the national notifications to the EC (Figures 3.10 and 3.11).[166] Of national notifications to the EC, 70% related to: toys (31%); motor vehicles (15%); electrical appliances (12%); lighting equipment (6%); and cosmetics (6%) (Figure 3.12). 'More than one out of three products notified in 2007 was either a toy or a childcare article/children's equipment, thus confirming that child safety is a top-ranking priority for market surveillance authorities.'[167]

Figure 3.9 The total number of notifications to EC Health and Consumer Protectorate (2004–2007)*

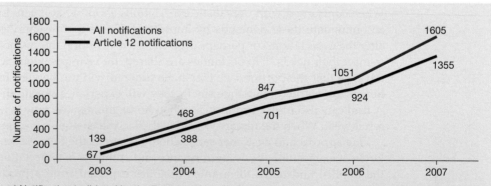

* Notification 'validated by the European Commission has risen steeply during the last few years. In the fourth year of application of the revised GPSD [General Product Safety], the number of notifications has more than tripled from 468 in 2004 to 1605 in 2007'.

Source: 'Keeping European Consumers Safe', 2007 Annual Report on the operation of the Rapid Alert System for non-food consumer products, European Communities Health and Consumer Protection Directorate General, Luxembourg, 2008: 15.

Figure 3.10 The total number of notifications by country (%) of unsafe products to EC Health and Consumer Protectorate (2007)

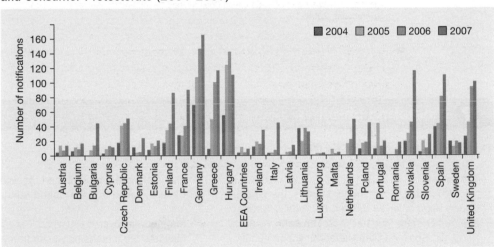

Source: 'Keeping European Consumers Safe', 2007 Annual Report on the operation of the Rapid Alert System for non-food consumer products, European Communities Health and Consumer Protection Directorate General, Luxembourg, 2008: 17.

Figure 3.11 Number of notifications by notifying country of unsafe products to EC Health and Consumer Protectorate (2004–2007)

Source: 'Keeping European Consumers Safe', 2007 Annual Report on the operation of the Rapid Alert System for non-food consumer products, European Communities Health and Consumer Protection Directorate General, Luxembourg, 2008: 18.

Acting on dissatisfaction

If a person is not happy with a product or service, what can be done? Reasons for complaining include bad service, unsafe products, failure to respect consumer legislation, and lack of transparency or availability of information.[168] Essentially, a consumer can take one or more possible courses of action:[169]

1 *Voice response*: The consumer can appeal directly to the retailer for redress (e.g. a refund).

2 *Private response*: Express dissatisfaction about the store or product to friends and/or boycott the store. As will be discussed in Chapter 10, negative word-of-mouth (WOM) can be very damaging to a retailer's reputation.

3 *Third-party response*: The consumer can take legal action against the merchant, register a complaint with the Ombudsman, or perhaps write a letter to a newspaper (e.g. the weekly consumer complaints page in *The Guardian*'s *G2* section).

Figure 3.12 The five most frequently notified product categories of unsafe products to EC Health and Consumer Protectorate (2007)

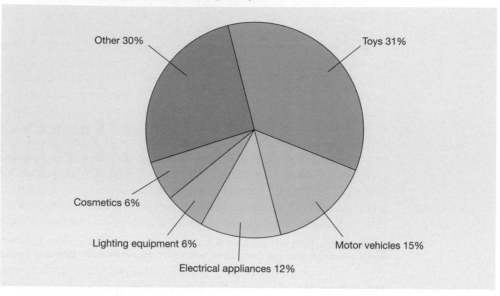

Source: 'Keeping European Consumers Safe', 2007 Annual Report on the operation of the Rapid Alert System for non-food consumer products, European Communities Health and Consumer Protection Directorate General, Luxembourg, 2008: 19.

▼ Marketing pitfall

Danger in everyday items

Toothpaste
'In 2007, during the summer months, the European Commission received through the RAPEX system information from Member States (notably France, Romania, Spain and the United Kingdom) about batches of Chinese toothpaste distributed in the EU containing diethylene glycol (DEG), a chemical component often used in anti-freeze and as a solvent. The levels of DEG detected in the batches of toothpaste varied and in certain cases reached up to 9 per cent. As the notified toothpastes could pose a serious risk to the health and safety of consumers (mostly children, who are likely to ingest toothpaste, and individuals with kidney or liver disease), they were immediately withdrawn from the market and recalled from consumers by the market surveillance authorities of the Member States. Several of the Chinese toothpastes with DEG found on the EU market were counterfeit goods. Following the action and measures taken in Europe, Chinese authorities banned the use of DEG in toothpaste and closed down a number of local manufacturers. Chinese toothpastes containing DEG were also found in many other countries around the world, including Canada, Japan and the United States.

Magnets in toys
Magnets are increasingly used in toys for their play and educational value. In recent years, they have become more powerful and can also be detached more easily, because the construction techniques used so far have sometimes turned out to be inadequate for the countless ways in which magnets are now used in toys. Either loose or otherwise detached from the toy, magnets can be swallowed or inhaled by a child, hence posing life-threatening risks. When more than one magnet is swallowed, the magnets can attract each other and cause intestinal perforation, infection or blockage, which can be fatal. A number of accidents, either deadly or requiring major surgery, involving magnets in toys, were reported worldwide in the course of 2006 and 2007. During the summer of 2007, over 18 million magnetic toys were recalled globally, and a significant number of these toys were found on the European market.'[170]

A number of factors influence which route is taken. The consumer may in general be assertive or meek. Action is more likely to be taken for expensive products such as household durables, cars and clothing than for inexpensive products.[171] If the consumer does not believe that the store will respond positively to a complaint, the person will be more likely to switch brands than fight.[172] Ironically, marketers should *encourage* consumers to complain to them: people are more likely to spread the word about unresolved negative experiences to their friends than they are to boast about positive occurrences.[173] Consumers are more likely to spread negative information about a bad service than they are to spread information about a successful complaint handling. Complaint management is thus not as good an alternative as high-quality service in the first place.[174] In addition, consumers who are satisfied with a store are more likely to complain; they take the time to complain because they feel connected to the store. Older people are more likely to complain, and are much more likely to believe the store will actually resolve the problem. Shoppers who get their problems resolved feel even *better* about the store than if nothing went wrong.[175] A variety of factors affect consumers' willingness to complain including different national systems for consumer protection; consumers' perception of the likelihood of success; and consumers' different expectations of the outcome of a complaint. Within the EU, 'country-level analysis suggests that consumers living in northern Europe are more likely to launch a complaint than other Europeans. A socio-economic analysis of results indicates that citizens with higher education levels tend to be more assertive if they are not satisfied with their purchases and proceed to launch a complaint (21%)'.[176] A sense of the scale of potential complainants can be grasped from Figures 3.13 and 3.14.[177]

Figure 3.13 Percentage of consumers who have made any kind of formal complaint to a seller/provider – % of yes

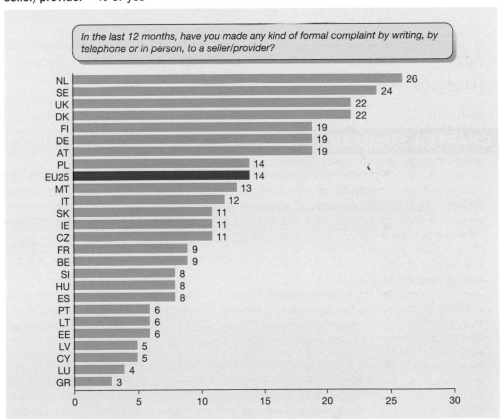

Data Source: Special Eurobarometer 252 – Consumer protection in the Internal Market, 2006.

Source: *The Consumer Markets Scoreboard Monitoring Consumer Outcomes in the Single Market*, COM (2008) 31, European Communities, Luxembourg, 2008, Figure 1: 18.

Figure 3.14 Satisfaction with complaint handling – % of yes

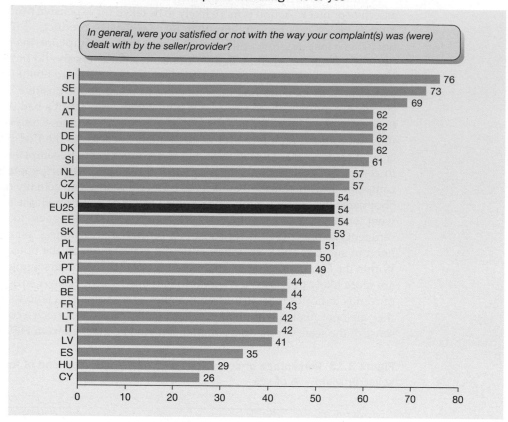

In general, were you satisfied or not with the way your complaint(s) was (were) dealt with by the seller/provider?

FI	76
SE	73
LU	69
AT	62
IE	62
DE	62
DK	62
SI	61
NL	57
CZ	57
UK	54
EU25	54
EE	54
SK	53
PL	51
MT	50
PT	49
GR	44
BE	44
FR	43
LT	42
IT	42
LV	41
ES	35
HU	29
CY	26

Data Source: Special Eurobarometer 252 – Consumer protection in the Internal Market, 2006.

Source: *The Consumer Markets Scoreboard: Monitoring Consumer Outcomes in the Single Market,* COM (2008) 31, European Communities, Luxembourg, 2008, Figure 4: 20.

CHAPTER SUMMARY

- Factors operating at the time of purchase can dramatically influence the consumer decision-making process. Many factors over and above the quality of the product or service influence the outcome of an actual transaction.

- *The act of purchase* is affected by many factors. These include the consumer's antecedent state (e.g. their mood, time pressure, or disposition toward shopping). Time is an important resource that often determines how much effort and search will go into a decision. Our moods are influenced by the degree of pleasure and arousal a store environment creates.

- *The usage context* of a product can be a basis for segmentation; consumers look for different product attributes, depending on the use to which they intend to put their purchase. The presence or absence of other people (co-consumers) – and the types of people they are – can also affect a consumer's decisions.

- The shopping experience is a pivotal part of the purchase decision. In many cases, retailing is like theatre – the consumer's evaluation of stores and products may depend on the type of 'performance' they witness. The actors (e.g. salespeople), the setting (the store environment), and props (e.g. store displays) influence this evaluation. Like a brand personality a number of factors such as perceived convenience, sophistication, and the expertise of salespeople determine *store image*. With increasing competition from non-store alternatives, creating a positive shopping experience has never been more important. Online shopping is growing in importance, and this new way to acquire products has both good (e.g. convenience) and bad (e.g. security) aspects.

- In addition to what a shopper already knows or believes about a product, the information that a store or a Website provides can strongly influence their purchase decisions. Because we don't make many purchase decisions until we're actually in the store, *point-of-purchase* (POP) stimuli are very important sales tools. These include product samples, elaborate package displays, place-based media, and in-store promotional materials such as 'shelf talkers'. POP stimuli are particularly useful in promoting impulse buying, which happens when a consumer yields to a sudden urge for a product.

- A salesperson can be the crucial link between interest in a product and its actual purchase. The consumer's encounter with a salesperson is a complex and important process. The outcome can be affected by such factors as the salesperson's similarity to the customer and their perceived credibility.

- Marketers need to be concerned about a consumer's evaluations of a product after they buy it as well as before. A person's overall feelings about the product after they buy it determine *consumer satisfaction/dissatisfaction*. Many factors influence our perceptions of product quality, including price, brand name, and product performance. Our degree of satisfaction often depends on the extent to which a product's performance is consistent with our prior expectations of how well it will function.

▶ KEY TERMS

Activity stores (p. 82)
Atmospherics (p. 82)
Being space (p. 80)
Co-consumers (p. 64)
Consumer satisfaction/dissatisfaction (CS/D) (p. 86)
Cyberspace (p. 74)
Exchange theory (p. 85)
Expectancy disconfirmation model (p. 87)

Impulse buying (p. 83)
Point-of-purchase stimuli (POP) (p. 84)
Pop-up stores (p. 80)
Retail theming (p. 79)
Shopping orientation (p. 71)
Store gestalt (p. 82)
Store image (p. 82)
Time poverty (p. 66)
Time style (p. 65)

▶ CONSUMER BEHAVIOUR CHALLENGE

1 Discuss some of the motivations for shopping described in the chapter. How might a retailer adjust their strategy to accommodate these motivations? What is the difference between unplanned buying and impulse buying?

2 Do you think shopping motives might be different between online and offline shopping? If so, why? What are the pros and cons of e-commerce?

3 What are some positive and negative aspects of requiring employees who interact with customers to wear some kind of uniform or to impose a dress code in the office?

4 Think about exceptionally good and bad salespeople you have encountered in the past. What qualities seem to differentiate them?

5 List the five stages of a long-term service relationship. How can a practitioner of

▶ CONSUMER BEHAVIOUR CHALLENGE (*continued*)

relationship marketing incorporate each stage into their strategy?

6 What factors help determine store image? What are the two dimensions that determine whether we will react positively or negatively to a purchase environment? Describe the difference between density and crowding. Why is this relevant in purchase environments?

7 The store environment is heating up as more and more companies put their promotional resources into point-of-purchase efforts. Shoppers are now confronted by videos at the checkout, computer monitors attached to their shopping trolleys, and so on. Place-based media expose us to ads in non-shopping environments. Do you feel that these innovations are unacceptably intrusive? At what point might shoppers rebel and demand some peace while shopping? Do you see any market potential in the future for stores that 'counter-market' by promising a 'hands-off' shopping environment?

8 Find a spectacular consumption environment and examine how consumers' play is encouraged and constrained by producers. How is technology used by producers and consumers in this environment to create and alter the sense of reality and space in this spectacular environment? If you don't have a spectacular consumption environment near you, consider these questions (and the associated research findings) about the co-creation of meaning between producers and consumers within the context of the online world, e.g. computer games.

9 Discuss the concept of 'time style'. Based on your own experiences, how might consumers be segmented in terms of their time styles?

10 What is time poverty, and how might it influence our purchase decisions?

11 Recent research (among American married and single women without children) has shown that there are major differences in individuals' attitudes and behaviours in relation to shopping across five metaphors of time: pressure cooker, map, mirror, river, and feast. Consider how these temporal metaphors might vary across households (e.g. married with children); age (e.g. empty nest households); and culture.

12 Conduct naturalistic observation at a local mall or shopping centre. Sit in a central location and observe the activities of mall staff and customers. Keep a log of the non-retailing activity you observe (special performances, exhibits, socializing, etc.). Does this activity enhance or detract from business conducted at the mall or shopping centre? As malls become more like high-tech game rooms, how valid is the criticism that shopping areas are only encouraging more loitering by teenage boys, who do not spend a lot in stores and simply scare away other customers?

13 Use the first five items from the eTailQ tool in Table 3.2 on p. 76 to compare and contrast six Websites in two different product and service categories by their Website design. Are there any other aspects of these Websites' design which you might want to include in this comparison? Compare your extra items with the full range of eTailQ items (Table 2 in Wolfinbarger and Gilly 2003: 188–9).[178]

14 Select three competing clothing stores in your area and conduct a store image study for each one. Ask a group of consumers to rate each store on a set of attributes and plot these ratings on the same graph. Based on your findings, are there any areas of competitive advantage or disadvantage you could bring to the attention of store management? (This technique is described in Chapter 8.)

15 How do a consumer's prior expectations about product quality influence their satisfaction with the product after they buy it? List three actions a consumer can take if they are dissatisfied with a purchase.

16 Discuss and critique the view that 'shoppers who blend store, mail order catalogues and Websites spend more.'[179]

17 New interactive tools are being introduced that allow surfers on sites such as landsend.com to view apparel product selections on virtual models in full, 360-degree rotational view. In some cases, the viewer can modify the bodies, face, skin colouring and hairstyles of these models. In others, the consumer can project their *own* likeness into the space by scanning a photo into a 'makeover' programme.[180] Visit landsend.com or another site that offers a personalized model. Surf around. Try on some clothes. How was your experience? How helpful was this model? When you shop for clothes online, would you rather see how they look on a body with dimensions the same as yours, or on a different body? What advice can you give Website designers who are trying to personalize these shopping environments by creating lifelike models to guide you through the site?

18 Choy and Loker (2004)[181] explored and classified Internet sites supporting the wedding industry and the purchase of a wedding gown in their study of mass customization. They identified four major categories: marketing, browsing, advice and customizing. Choose another industry (e.g. mother and baby; travel; leisure; pets; music) and classify the Websites according to their characteristics and strategies. What categories can you identify?

19 The mall of the future will most likely be less about purchasing products than about exploring them in a physical setting. This means that retail environments will have to become places to build brand images, rather than just places to sell products. What are some strategies stores can use to enhance the emotional/sensory experiences they give to shoppers?

20 Identify three people who own the same technological product (e.g. electric coffeemaker; satnav; DVD recorder; Apple 3G iPhone). Then, observe them as they actually use the appliance. Based on these experiences, what recommendations might you make to the designer of a new appliance that would improve customers' experience with the product?

For additional material see the companion website at **www.pearsoned.co.uk/solomon**

NOTES

1. 'Consumers hit at poor service', *Marketing* (5 December 1996): 4.
2. Lutz Stobbe EuP Preparatory Studies 'Televisions' (Lot 5) Final Report on Task 3 'Consumer Behaviour and Local Infrastructure' (TREN/D1/40 lot 5–2005), compiled by Deutsche Umwelthilfe and Fraunhofer IZM, contractor: Fraunhofer Institute for Reliability and Microintegration, IZM, Berlin, 2 August 2007: 15–6.
3. Brian T. Ratchford, Debabrata Talukdar and Myung-Soo Lee, 'The impact of the internet on consumers' use of information sources for automobiles: A re-inquiry', *Journal of Consumer Research* 34 (June 2007): 111–119.
4. Laurette Dube and Bernd H. Schmitt, 'The Processing of Emotional and Cognitive Aspects of Product Usage in Satisfaction Judgments', in Rebecca H. Holman and Michael R. Solomon, eds, *Advances in Consumer Research* 18 (Provo, UT: Association for Consumer Research, 1991): 52–6; Lalita A. Manrai and Meryl P. Gardner, 'The Influence of Affect on Attributions for Product Failure', in *ibid.*: 249–54.
5. Peter J. Burke and Stephen L. Franzoi, 'Studying situations and identities using experimental sampling methodology', *American Sociological Review* 53 (August 1988): 559–68.
6. Kevin G. Celuch and Linda S. Showers, 'It's Time To Stress *Stress*: the Stress-Purchase/Consumption Relationship', in Holman and Solomon, eds, *Advances in Consumer Research* 18: 284–9; Lawrence R. Lepisto, J. Kathleen Stuenkel and Linda K. Anglin, 'Stress: An Ignored Situational Influence', in *ibid.*: 296–302.
7. See Eben Shapiro, 'Need a little fantasy? A bevy of new companies can help', *New York Times* (10 March 1991): F4.
8. John D. Mayer and Yvonne N. Gaschke, 'The experience and meta-experience of mood', *Journal of Personality and Social Psychology* 55 (July 1988): 102–11.
9. Meryl Paula Gardner, 'Mood states and consumer behavior: A critical review', *Journal of Consumer Research* 12 (December 1985): 281–300; Scott Dawson, Peter H. Bloch and Nancy M. Ridgway, 'Shopping motives, emotional states, and retail outcomes', *Journal of Retailing* 66 (Winter 1990): 408–27; Patricia A. Knowles, Stephen J. Grove and W. Jeffrey Burroughs, 'An experimental examination of mood states on retrieval and evaluation of advertisement and brand information', *Journal of the Academy of Marketing Science* 21 (April 1993): 135–43; Paul W. Miniard, Sunil Bhatla and Deepak Sirdeskmukh, 'Mood as a determinant of postconsumption product evaluations: Mood effects and their dependency on the affective intensity of the consumption experience', *Journal of Consumer Psychology* 1 (1992) 2: 173–95; Mary T. Curren and Katrin R. Harich, 'Consumers' mood states: The mitigating influence of personal relevance on product evaluations', *Psychology and Marketing* 11(2) (March/April 1994): 91–107; Gerald J. Gorn, Marvin E. Goldberg and Kunal Basu, 'Mood, awareness, and product evaluation', *Journal of Consumer Psychology* 2(3) (1993): 237–56.
10. Gordon C. Bruner, 'Music, mood, and marketing', *Journal of Marketing* 54 (October 1990): 94–104; Basil G. Englis, 'Music Television and its Influences on Consumers, Consumer Culture, and the Transmission of Consumption Messages', in Holman and Solomon, eds, *Advances in Consumer Research* 18: 111–14; see also Steve Oakes, 'Examining the Relationships Between Background

Musical Tempo and Perceived Duration Using Different Versions of a Radio Ad', in B. Dubois, T. Lowrey, L.J. Shrum and M. Vanhuele, eds, *European Advances in Consumer Research* 4 (Provo, UT: Association of Consumer Research, 1999): 40–4.

11. Marvin E. Goldberg and Gerald J. Gorn, 'Happy and sad TV programs: How they affect reactions to commercials', *Journal of Consumer Research* 14 (December 1987): 387–403; Gorn, Goldberg and Basu, 'Mood, awareness, and product evaluation': 237–56; Curren and Harich, 'Consumers' mood states'.

12. Pradeep Kakkar and Richard J. Lutz, 'Situational Influence on Consumer Behavior: A Review', in Harold H. Kassarjian and Thomas S. Robertson, eds, *Perspectives in Consumer Behavior*, 3rd edn (Glenview, IL: Scott, Foresman, 1981): 204–14.

13. Carolyn Turner Schenk and Rebecca H. Holman, 'A Sociological Approach to Brand Choice: The Concept of Situational Self-Image', in Jerry C. Olson, ed., *Advances in Consumer Research* 7 (Ann Arbor, MI: Association for Consumer Research, 1980): 610–14.

14. Russell W. Belk, 'An exploratory assessment of situational effects in buyer behavior', *Journal of Marketing Research* 11 (May 1974): 156–63; U.N. Umesh and Joseph A. Cote, 'Influence of situational variables on brand-choice models', *Journal of Business Research* 16(2) (1988): 91–9; see also J. Wesley Hutchinson and Joseph W. Alba, 'Ignoring irrelevant information: Situational determinants of consumer learning', *Journal of Consumer Research* 18 (December 1991): 325–45.

15. Peter R. Dickson, 'Person–situation: segmentation's missing link', *Journal of Marketing* 46 (Fall 1982): 56–64.

16. See Peter R. Dickson, *ibid*.: 62.

17. Bernard Dubois and Gilles Laurent, 'A Situational Approach to Brand Loyalty', in E. Arnould and L. Scott, eds, *Advances in Consumer Research* 26 (Provo, UT: Association for Consumer Research, 1999): 657–63.

18. Booz-Allen Hamilton's Digital Consumer Project and Nielsen/NetRatings reported in Laura Mazur, 'Web marketers must now adapt to the occasion', *Marketing* (29 May 2003): 16 (http://search.epnet.com/login.aspx?direct=true&db=buh&an=10029509).

19. Laura Mazur, 'Web marketers must now adapt to the occasion', *op. cit.*

20. Anja Stöhr, 'Air-Design: Exploring the Role of Scents in Retail Environments', in B. Englis and A. Olofsson, eds, *European Advances in Consumer Research* 3 (Provo, UT: Association for Consumer Research, 1998): 126–32.

21. Delphine Dion, 'A Theoretical and Empirical Study of Retail Crowding', in Dubois, Lowrey, Shrum and Vanhuele, eds, *European Advances in Consumer Research* 4: 51–7.

22. Daniel Stokols, 'On the distinction between density and crowding: Some implications for future research', *Psychological Review* 79 (1972): 275–7.

23. Ritesh Saini and Ashwani Monga, 'How I decide depends on what I spend: Use of heuristics is greater for time than for money', *Journal of Consumer Research* 34 (April 2008): 921.

24. Carol Felker Kaufman, Paul M. Lane and Jay D. Lindquist, 'Exploring more than 24 hours a day: A preliminary investigation of polychronic time use', *Journal of Consumer Research* 18 (December 1991): 392–401.

25. Laurence P. Feldman and Jacob Hornik, 'The use of time: An integrated conceptual model', *Journal of Consumer Research* 7 (March 1981): 407–19; see also Michelle M. Bergadaa,

26. 'The role of time in the action of the consumer', *Journal of Consumer Research* 17 (December 1990): 289–302.

27. Jean-Claude Usunier and Pierre Valette-Florence, 'Individual time orientation: A psychometric scale', *Time and Society* 3(2) (1994): 219–41.

27. June Cotte, S. Ratneshwar and David Glen Mick, 'The times of their lives: Phenomenological and metaphorical characteristics of consumer timestyles', *Journal of Consumer Research* 31 (September 2004): 333–45.

28. June Cotte, S. Ratneshwar and David Glen Mick, *ibid*.

29. *Ibid*.

30. June Cotte, S. Ratneshwar and David Glen Mick, *ibid*.

31. 'The life of women and men in Europe: A statistical portrait – 2008 edition': 47–49, European Commission/Eurostat Luxembourg: Cat. No. KS-80-07-135-EN-N, http://ec.europa.eu/eurostat

32. The life of women and men in Europe: A statistical portrait – 2008 edition: 111–113, European Commission/Eurostat Luxembourg: Cat. No. KS-80-07-135-EN-N, website http://ec.europa.eu/eurostat

33. Jared Sandberg, 'NoChores.com', *Newsweek* (30 August 1999): 30(2).

34. 'Plugged in: Hong Kong embraces the Octopus Card', *The New York Times on the Web* (8 June 2002).

35. Kaufman, Lane and Lindquist, 'Exploring more than 24 hours a day', *op. cit.*

36. Quoted in 'Fast food? It just isn't fast enough anymore', *New York Times* (6 December 1989): A1.

37. John P. Robinson, 'Time squeeze', *Advertising Age* (February 1990): 30–3.

38. David Lewis and Darren Bridger, *The Soul of the New Consumer: Authenticity – What We Buy and Why in the New Economy* (London: Nicholas Brealey Publishing, 2000).

39. Sigmund Grønmo, 'Concepts of Time: Some Implications for Consumer Research', in Thomas K. Srull, ed., *Advances in Consumer Research* 16 (Provo, UT: Association for Consumer Research 1989): 339–45.

40. Gabriele Morello and P. van der Reis, 'Attitudes towards time in different cultures: African time and European time', *Proceedings of the Third Symposium on Cross-Cultural Consumer and Business Studies* (Honolulu: University of Hawaii, 1990); Gabriele Morello, 'Our attitudes towards time', *Forum* 96/2 (European Forum for Management Development, 1996): 48–51.

41. Gary Davies, 'What should time be?' *European Journal of Marketing* 28(8/9) (1994): 100–13.

42. Esther S. Page-Wood, Carol J. Kaufman and Paul M. Lane, 'The art of time', in *Proceedings of the Academy of Marketing Science* (1990).

43. Søren Askegaard and Tage Koed Madsen, 'The local and the global: Traits of homogeneity and heterogeneity in European food cultures', *International Business Review* 7(6) (1998): 549–68; for a thorough discussion of food culture, see Claude Fischler, *L'Homnivore* (Paris: Odile Jacob, 1990).

44. Mark J. Arnold and Kristy E. Reynolds, 'Hedonic shopping motivations', *Journal of Retailing* 79 (2003): 90–1.

45. Daniel Miller, *A Theory of Shopping* (Cambridge: Polity Press, 1998).

46. For a scale that was devised to assess these dimensions of the shopping experience, see Barry J. Babin, William R. Darden and Mitch Griffin, 'Work and/or fun: Measuring hedonic and utilitarian shopping value', *Journal of Consumer Research* 20 (March 1994): 644–56.

47. *Ibid.*
48. Adapted from Andrea Groeppel-Klein, Eva Thelen and Christoph Antretter, 'The Impact of Shopping Motives on Store Assessment', in Dubois, Lowrey, Shrum and Vanhuele, eds, *European Advances in Consumer Research* 4: 63–72.
49. Quoted in Robert C. Prus, *Making Sales: Influence as Interpersonal Accomplishment* (Newbury Park, CA: Sage Library of Social Research, Sage, 1989): 225.
50. Gregory P. Stone, 'City shoppers and urban identification: Observations on the social psychology of city life', *American Journal of Sociology* 60 (1954): 36–45; Danny Bellenger and Pradeep K. Korgaonkar, 'Profiling the re-creational shopper', *Journal of Retailing* 56(3) (1980): 77–92.
51. 'A Global Perspective . . . on Women and Women's Wear', *Lifestyle Monitor* 14 (Winter 1999/2000): Cotton Inc., 8–11.
52. Stephen Brown and Rhona Reid, 'Shoppers on the Verge of a Nervous Breakdown', in S. Brown and D. Turley, eds, *Consumer Research: Postcards from the Edge* (London: Routledge, 1997): 79–149.
53. Nina Gruen, 'The retail battleground: Solutions for today's shifting marketplace', *Journal of Property Management* (July–August 1989): 14.
54. http://www.datamonitor.com/industries/research/?pid=DMCM4619&type=Report accessed April 25 2008.
55. Personal communication with a Finnish reviewer.
56. 'Slaget om Europa', *Jyllands Posten* (12 February 1997).
57. http://www.retail-index.com/HOMESEARCH/FoodRetailers/tabid/3496/Default.aspx accessed 20 August 2008.
58. http://www.carrefour.com/cdc/group/our-group/ accessed 20 August 2008.
59. http://www.metrogroup.de/servlet/PB/menu/1179530_l2/index.htm accessed 20 August 2008.
60. http://www.tescocorporate.com/publiclibs/tesco/International.pdf; for an interview with Sir Terry Leahy (CEO of Tesco) discussing the Group's international strategy see http://w3.cantos.com/08/tesco-804-0lvon/interviews.php?task=view&type=video&i=1&med=asx&cnt=bb&url=http://w3.cantos.com/08/tesco-804-0lvon/video/tsco-d005-bb-v-5.asx accessed 20 August 2008.
61. Arieh Goldman, 'The shopping style explanation for store loyalty', *Journal of Retailing* 53 (Winter 1977–8): 33–46, 94; Robert B. Settle and Pamela L. Alreck, 'Hyperchoice shapes the marketplace', *Marketing Communications* (May 1988): 15.
62. Joseph C. Nunes and Xavier Dreze, 'Your loyalty program is betraying you', *Harvard Business Review* April 2006: 126.
63. Joseph C. Nunes and Xavier Dreze, 'Your loyalty program is betraying you', *Harvard Business Review* April 2006: 124–131, 125–128.
64. Joseph C. Nunes and Xavier Dreze, 'Your loyalty program is betraying you', *Harvard Business Review* April 2006: 128–9.
65. Joseph C. Nunes and Xavier Dreze, 'Your loyalty program is betraying you', *Harvard Business Review* April 2006: 129–131.
66. Some material in this section was adapted from Michael R. Solomon and Elnora W. Stuart, *Welcome to Marketing.Com: The Brave New World of E-Commerce* (Upper Saddle River, NJ: Prentice Hall, 2001).
67. Seema Williams, David M. Cooperstein, David E. Weisman and Thalika Oum, 'Post-web retail', *The Forrester Report*, Forrester Research, Inc., September 1999; Catherine Arnold, 'Across the pond', *Marketing News* (28 October 2002): 3.
68. Mikael Lundström, 'E-handel inget för svensson', *Info* 8 (2000): 52–4.
69. The Nielsen Company Press Release 'Over 875 Million Consumers Have Shopped Online – the Number of Internet Shoppers Up 40 per cent in Two Years' http://www.earthtimes.org/articles/show/over-875-million-consumers-have-shopped-online--the-number,263812.shtml accessed 20 August 2008.
70. Rebecca K. Ratner, Barbara E. Kahn and Daniel Kahneman, 'Choosing less-preferred experiences for the sake of variety', *Journal of Consumer Research* 26 (June 1999): 1–15.
71. *Markedsføring* (25 November 2000): 18.
72. Ellen Sheng, 'Advertisers sharpen their targeting', *WSJ Online* (27 October 2004).
73. *Markedsføring* (25 September 2000): 22.
74. *Markedsføring* (9 November 2000): 14.
75. Jennifer Gilbert, 'Customer service crucial to online buyers', *Advertising Age* (13 September 1999): 52.
76. 'The grid layout is a rectangular arrangement of displays and long aisles that generally run parallel to one another. The freeform layout is a free-flowing and asymmetric arrangement of displays and aisles, employing a variety of different sizes, shapes and styles of display. In the racetrack/boutique layout, the sales floor is organized into individual, semi-separate areas, each built around a particular shopping theme', Adam P. Vrechopolous, Robert M. O'Keefe, Georgios I. Doukidis and George J. Siomkos, 'Virtual store layout: An experimental comparison in the context of grocery retail', *Journal of Retailing* 80 (2004): 13–22.
77. *Ibid.*
78. Mary Wolfinbarger and Mary C. Gilly, 'eTailQ: Dimensionalizing, measuring and predicting etail quality', *Journal of Retailing* 79 (2003): 183–98. Their article provides a useful managerial tool (eTailQ) for assessing the quality of virtual stores.
79. Datamonitor predicted that by the end of 2003 almost 60 million European consumers would bank online; Laura Mazur, 'Web marketers must now adapt to the occasion', *Marketing* (29 May 2003): 16 (http://search.epnet.com/login.aspx?direct=true&db=buh&an=10029509).
80. Bob Tedeschi, 'More e-commerce sites aim to add "sticky" content', *NYT Online* (9 August 2004).
81. Kevin J. O'Brien, 'German quiz shows thrive as contestants stay home', *NYT Online* (9 August 2004).
82. Chuan-Fong Shih, 'Conceptualizing consumer experiences in cyberspace', *European Journal of Marketing* 32(7/8) (1998): 655–63.
83. Alka Varma Citrin, Donald E. Stern, Eric R. Spangenberg and Michael J. Clark, 'Consumer need for tactile input: An internet retailing challenge', *Journal of Business Research* 56 (2003): 915–22. See also Joann Peck and Terry L. Childers, 'Individual differences in haptic information processing: The need for touch scale', *Journal of Consumer Research* 30 (December 2003): 430–42, whose scale includes both instrumental and autotelic factors which differentiate between need for touch as part of the pre-purchase decision-making process, and the need for touch as an end in itself. The importance of touch (particularly as an end in itself) points to this as a potential barrier to the use of e-commerce by some consumers across all product groups.

84. Rita Choy and Suzanne Loker, 'Mass customization of wedding gowns: Design involvement on the internet', *Clothing and Textiles Research Journal* 22(1&2) (2004): 79–87.

85. *Markedsføring* (17 February 2000): 20.

86. Kortney Stringer, 'Shoppers who blend store, catalog, web spend more', *The Wall Street Journal Online* (3 September 2004): A7.

87. Marc Gobé, *Emotional Branding: The New Paradigm for Connecting Brands to People* (New York: Allworth Press, 2001): xxv.

88. *Ibid.*

89. An excellent collection of articles on this topic is found in Pasi Falk and Colin Campbell, eds, *The Shopping Experience* (London: Sage, 1997).

90. C. Gardner and J. Sheppard, *Consuming Passion: The Rise of Retail Culture* (London: Unwin Hyman, 1989).

91. Stephen Brown, 'Sex "n" Shopping', Working Paper 9501 (University of Stirling: Institute for Retail Studies, 1995); see also Stephen Brown, 'Consumption Behaviour in the Sex "n" Shopping Novels of Judith Krantz: A Poststructuralist Perspective', in Kim P. Corfman and John G. Lynch, Jr., eds, *Advances in Consumer Research* 23 (Provo, UT: Association for Consumer Research, 1996): 43–8.

92. Véronique Aubert-Gamet, 'Twisting servicescapes: Diversion of the physical environment in a re-appropriation process', *International Journal of Service Industry Management* 8(1) (1997): 26–41.

93. Stephen Brown, *Postmodern Marketing* (London: Routledge, 1995), discussion on pp. 50ff.; Lars Thøger Christensen and Søren Askegaard, 'Flexibility in the marketing organization: The ultimate consumer orientation or Ford revisited?' *Marketing Today and for the 21st Century*, Proceedings of the XIV EMAC Conference, ed. Michelle Bergadaà (Cergy-Pontoise: ESSEC, 1995): 1507–14.

94. Turo-Kimmo Lehtonen and Pasi Mäenpää, 'Shopping in the East Centre Mall', in Falk and Campbell, eds, *The Shopping Experience*: 136–65.

95. Quoted in Jacquelyn Bivins, 'Fun and mall games', *Stores* (August 1989): 35.

96. Sallie Hook, 'All the retail world's a stage: Consumers conditioned to entertainment in shopping environment', *Marketing News* 21 (31 July 1987): 16.

97. David Chaney, 'The department store as a cultural form', *Theory, Culture and Society* 1(3) (1983): 22–31.

98. Cecilia Fredriksson, 'The Making of a Swedish Department Store Culture', in Falk and Campbell, eds, *The Shopping Experience*: 111–35.

99. 'ING uses the soft sell for online banking unit', *Wall Street Journal* (17 October 2000): A18.

100. Pauline Maclaran and Lorna Stevens, 'Romancing the Utopian Marketplace', in S. Brown, A.M. Doherty and B. Clarke, eds, *Romancing the Market* (London: Routledge, 1998): 172–86.

101. Millie Creighton, 'The Seed of Creative Lifestyle Shopping: Wrapping Consumerism in Japanese Store Layouts', in ed. John F. Sherry Jr., *Servicescapes: The Concept of Place in Contemporary Markets* (Lincolnwood, IL: NTC Business Books, 1998): 199–228.

102. http://www.newyorkcool.com/archives/2007/September/fashion_Caravan.htm accessed 20 August 2008.

103. March 2007 Trend Briefing, http://www.trendwatching.com/briefing/ accessed 2007; Amy Johannes, 'Choice Hotels Launches Upscale Brand Via Pop-Up Hotel Suite', *PROMO Xtra* (8 January 2007).

104. Robert V. Kozinets, John F. Sherry, Diana Storm, Adam Duhachek, Krittinee Nuttavuthisit and Benet DeBerry-Spence, 'Ludic agency and retail spectacle', *Journal of Consumer Research* 31 (December 2004): 658–72.

105. Patrick Hetzel and Veronique Aubert, 'Sales Area Design and Fashion Phenomena: A Semiotic Approach', in van Raaij and Bamossy, eds, *European Advances in Consumer Research* 1: 522–33.

106. Søren Askegaard and Güliz Ger, 'Product-Country Images as Stereotypes: A Comparative Analysis of the Image of Danish Food Products in Germany and Turkey', *MAPP Working Paper* 45 (Aarhus: The Aarhus School of Business, 1997).

107. Susan Spiggle and Murphy A. Sewall, 'A choice sets model of retail selection', *Journal of Marketing* 51 (April 1987): 97–111; William R. Darden and Barry J. Babin, 'The role of emotions in expanding the concept of retail personality', *Stores* 76 (April 1994) 4: RR7–RR8.

108. Most measures of store image are quite similar to other attitude measures, as discussed in Chapter 5. For an excellent bibliography of store image studies, see Mary R. Zimmer and Linda L. Golden, 'Impressions of retail stores: A content analysis of consumer images,' *Journal of Retailing* 64 (Fall 1988): 265–93.

109. *Ibid.*

110. Spiggle and Sewall, 'A choice sets model of retail selection', *op. cit.*

111. Philip Kotler, 'Atmospherics as a marketing tool,' *Journal of Retailing* (Winter 1973–74): 10; Anna Mattila and Jochen Wirtz, 'Congruency of scent and music as a driver of in-store evaluations and behavior', *Journal of Retailing* 77 (Summer 2001): 273–89; J. Duncan Herrington, 'An Integrative Path Model of the Effects of Retail Environments on Shopper Behavior', in Robert L. King, ed., *Marketing: Toward the Twenty-First Century* (Richmond, VA: Southern Marketing Association, 1991): 58–62; see also Ann E. Schlosser, 'Applying the functional theory of attitudes to understanding the influence of store atmosphere on store inferences', *Journal of Consumer Psychology* 7(4) (1998): 345–69.

112. Fabian Csaba and Søren Askegaard, 'Malls and the Orchestration of the Shopping Experience in a Historical Perspective', in Arnould and Scott, eds, *Advances in Consumer Research* 26: 34–40.

113. Robert J. Donovan, John R. Rossiter, Gilian Marcoolyn, and Andrew Nesdale, 'Store atmosphere and purchasing behavior', *Journal of Retailing* 70, no. 3 (1994): 283–94.

114. Alice Z. Cuneo, 'Malls seek boost with "activity" stores', *Advertising Age* (21 July 2003): 6.

115. Charles S. Areni and David Kim, 'The influence of in-store lighting on consumers' examination of merchandise in a wine store', *International Journal of Research in Marketing* 11(2) (March 1994): 117–25.

116. Jean-Charles Chebat, Claire Gelinas Chebat and Dominique Vaillant, 'Environmental background music and in-store selling', *Journal of Business Research* 54 (2001): 115–23; Judy I. Alpert and Mark I. Alpert, 'Music influences on mood and purchase intentions', *Psychology and Marketing* 7 (Summer 1990): 109–34.

117. Brad Edmondson, 'Pass the meat loaf', *American Demographics* (January 1989): 19.

118. Dhruv Grewal, Julie Baker, Michael Levy and Glenn B. Voss, 'The effects of wait expectations and store atmosphere evaluations on patronage intentions in service-intensive retail store', *Journal of Retailing* 79 (2003): 259–68.

119. 'Through the looking glass', *Lifestyle Monitor* 16 (Fall/Winter 2002).

120. 'Butikken er en slagmark', *Berlingske Tidende* (15 July 1996): 3.

121. Jennifer Lach, 'Meet you in aisle three', *American Demographics* (April 1999): 41.

122. Ernest Beck, 'Diageo attempts to reinvent the bar in an effort to increase spirits sales', *The Wall Street Journal* (23 February 2001).

123. Easwar S. Iyer, 'Unplanned purchasing: Knowledge of shopping environment and time pressure', *Journal of Retailing* 65 (Spring 1989): 40–57; C. Whan Park, Easwar S. Iyer and Daniel C. Smith, 'The effects of situational factors on in-store grocery shopping', *Journal of Consumer Research* 15 (March 1989): 422–33.

124. Michael Wahl, 'Eye POPping persuasion', *Marketing Insights* (June 1989): 130.

125. 'Zipping down the aisles', *New York Times Magazine* (6 April 1997).

126. Peter McGoldrick, Erica J. Betts and Kathleen A. Keeling, 'Antecedents of Spontaneous Buying Behaviour During Temporary Markdowns', in Arnould and Scott, eds, *Advances in Consumer Research* 26: 26–33.

127. Cathy J. Cobb and Wayne D. Hoyer, 'Planned versus impulse purchase behavior', *Journal of Retailing* 62 (Winter 1986): 384–409; Easwar S. Iyer and Sucheta S. Ahlawat, 'Deviations from a Shopping Plan: When and Why Do Consumers Not Buy as Planned?' in Melanie Wallendorf and Paul Anderson, eds, *Advances in Consumer Research* 14 (Provo, UT: Association for Consumer Research, 1987): 246–9.

128. Andrea Groeppel-Klein, 'The Influence of the Dominance Perceived at the Point-of-Sale on the Price-Assessment', in Englis and Olofsson, eds, *European Advances in Consumer Research* 3: 304–11.

129. Dennis Desrochers, 'European consumers respond to spray samplers', *Global Cosmetic Industry* 171(16) (June 2003): 28.

130. Chairman-CEO A.G. Laffley, quoted in Jack Neff, 'P&G boosts design's role in marketing', *Advertising Age* (9 February 2004): 52.

131. William Keenan, Jr., 'Point-of-purchase: From clutter to technoclutter', *Sales and Marketing Management* 141 (April 1989): 96.

132. *Markedsføring* 13 (1999): 24.

133. Cyndee Miller, 'Videocart spruces up for new tests', *Marketing News* (19 February 1990): 19; William E. Sheeline, 'User-friendly shopping carts', *Fortune* (5 December 1988): 9.

134. Bernard Swoboda, 'Multimedia Customer Information Systems at the Point of Sale: Selected Results of an Impact Analysis', in Englis and Olofsson, eds, *European Advances in Consumer Research* 3: 239–46.

135. 'Effective demands', *Marketing* (5 December 1996): 34–8.

136. 'A never-ending toy story', *Marketing* (5 December 1996): 33.

137. Erin White, 'Look up for new products in aisle 5: In-store TV advertising gains traction globally; Timely pitch at shoppers', *The Wall Street Journal Online* (23 March 2004): B11.

138. http://www.talkingretail.com/industry_announcements/6076/dunnhumby-relaunches-Tesco-in-.ehtml

139. Merissa Marr, 'Fox to pitch its movies at the mall as TV-ad costs escalate: Studio says new approach avoids broadcast clutter', *The Wall Street Journal Online* (15 July 2004): B6.

140. Cyndee Miller, 'MTV "Video Capsule" features sports for music retailers, corporate sponsors', *Marketing News* (3 February 1992): 5.

141. 'Dutch shop lets clients burn own CDs', *Wall Street Journal* (14 November 2000): B10.

142. See Robert B. Cialdini, *Influence: Science and Practice*, 2nd edn (Glenview, IL: Scott, Foresman, 1988).

143. Richard P. Bagozzi, 'Marketing as exchange', *Journal of Marketing* 39 (October 1975): 32–9; Peter M. Blau, *Exchange and Power in Social Life* (New York: Wiley, 1964); Marjorie Caballero and Alan J. Resnik, 'The attraction paradigm in dyadic exchange', *Psychology and Marketing* 3(1) (1986): 17–34; George C. Homans, 'Social behavior as exchange', *American Journal of Sociology* 63 (1958): 597–606; Paul H. Schurr and Julie L. Ozanne, 'Influences on exchange processes: Buyers' preconceptions of a seller's trustworthiness and bargaining toughness', *Journal of Consumer Research* 11 (March 1985): 939–53; Arch G. Woodside and J.W. Davenport, 'The effect of salesman similarity and expertise on consumer purchasing behavior', *Journal of Marketing Research* 8 (1974): 433–6.

144. Paul Busch and David T. Wilson, 'An experimental analysis of a salesman's expert and referent bases of social power in the buyer–seller dyad', *Journal of Marketing Research* 13 (February 1976): 3–11; John E. Swan, Fred Trawick Jr., David R. Rink and Jenny J. Roberts, 'Measuring dimensions of purchaser trust of industrial salespeople', *Journal of Personal Selling and Sales Management* 8 (May 1988): 1.

145. For a study in this area, see Peter H. Reingen and Jerome B. Kernan, 'Social perception and interpersonal influence: Some consequences of the physical attractiveness stereotype in a personal selling setting', *Journal of Consumer Psychology* 2 (1993): 25–38.

146. Linda L. Price and Eric J. Arnould, 'Commercial friendships: Service provider–client relationships in context', *Journal of Marketing* 63 (October 1999): 38–56.

147. Mary Jo Bitner, Bernard H. Booms and Mary Stansfield Tetreault, 'The service encounter: Diagnosing favorable and unfavorable incidents', *Journal of Marketing* 54 (January 1990): 7–84; Robert C. Prus, *Making Sales* (Newbury Park, CA: Sage, 1989); Arch G. Woodside and James L. Taylor, 'Identity Negotiations in Buyer–Seller Interactions', in Elizabeth C. Hirschman and Morris B. Holbrook, eds, *Advances in Consumer Research* 12 (Provo, UT: Association for Consumer Research, 1985): 443–9.

148. Barry J. Babin, James S. Boles and William R. Darden, 'Salesperson stereotypes, consumer emotions, and their impact on information processing', *Journal of the Academy of Marketing Science* 23(2) (1995): 94–105; Gilbert A. Churchill Jr., Neil M. Ford, Steven W. Hartley and Orville C. Walker Jr., 'The determinants of salesperson performance: A meta-analysis', *Journal of Marketing Research* 22 (May 1985): 103–18.

149. Siew Meng Leong, Paul S. Busch and Deborah Roedder John, 'Knowledge bases and salesperson effectiveness: A script-theoretic analysis', *Journal of Marketing Research* 26 (May 1989): 164; Harish Sujan, Mita Sujan and James R. Bettman, 'Knowledge structure differences between more effective and less effective salespeople', *Journal of Marketing Research* 25 (February 1988): 81–6; Robert Saxe and Barton Weitz, 'The SOCCO scale: A measure of the customer orientation of salespeople', *Journal of Marketing Research* 19 (August 1982): 343–51; David M. Szymanski, 'Determinants of selling effectiveness: The importance of

declarative knowledge to the personal selling concept', *Journal of Marketing* 52 (January 1988): 64–77; Barton A. Weitz, 'Effectiveness in sales interactions: A contingency framework,' *Journal of Marketing* 45 (Winter 1981): 85–103.

150. Jagdish M. Sheth, 'Buyer–Seller Interaction: A Conceptual Framework,' in Beverlee B. Anderson, ed., *Advances in Consumer Research* 3 (Cincinnati, OH: Association for Consumer Research, 1976): 382–6; Kaylene C. Williams and Rosann L. Spiro, 'Communication style in the salesperson–customer dyad', *Journal of Marketing Research* 22 (November 1985): 434–42.

151. Marsha L. Richins, 'An analysis of consumer interaction styles in the marketplace,' *Journal of Consumer Research* 10 (June 1983): 73–82.

152. Rama Jayanti and Anita Jackson, 'Service Satisfaction: Investigation of Three Models', in Holman and Solomon, eds, *Advances in Consumer Research* 18: 603–10; David K. Tse, Franco M. Nicosia and Peter C. Wilton, 'Consumer satisfaction as a process', *Psychology and Marketing* 7 (Fall 1990): 177–93. For a treatment of satisfaction issues from a more interpretive perspective, see Susan Fournier and David Mick, 'Rediscovering satisfaction,' *Journal of Marketing* 63 (October 1999): 5–23.

153. Constance L. Hayes, 'Service takes a holiday', *New York Times* (23 December 1998): C1.

154. Eugene W. Anderson, Claes Fornell and Donald R. Lehmann, 'Customer satisfaction, market share, and profitability: Findings from Sweden', *Journal of Marketing* 58(3) (July 1994): 53–66.

155. Robert Jacobson and David A. Aaker, 'The strategic role of product quality', *Journal of Marketing* 51 (October 1987): 31–44; for a review of issues regarding the measurement of service quality, see J. Joseph Cronin Jr. and Steven A. Taylor, 'Measuring service quality: A reexamination and extension', *Journal of Marketing* 56 (July 1992): 55–68.

156. Anna Kirmani and Peter Wright, 'Money talks: Perceived advertising expense and expected product quality', *Journal of Consumer Research* 16 (December 1989): 344–53; Donald R. Lichtenstein and Scot Burton, 'The relationship between perceived and objective price-quality', *Journal of Marketing Research* 26 (November 1989): 429–43; Akshay R. Rao and Kent B. Monroe, 'The effect of price, brand name, and store name on buyers' perceptions of product quality: An integrative review', *Journal of Marketing Research* 26 (August 1989): 351–7.

157. Shelby Hunt, 'Post-transactional communication and dissonance reduction', *Journal of Marketing* 34 (January 1970): 46–51; Daniel E. Innis and H. Rao Unnava, 'The Usefulness of Product Warranties for Reputable and New Brands,' in Holman and Solomon, eds, *Advances in Consumer Research* 18: 317–22; Terence A. Shimp and William O. Bearden, 'Warranty and other extrinsic cue effects on consumers' risk perceptions', *Journal of Consumer Research* 9 (June 1982): 38–46.

158. Mia Stokmans, 'The Relation Between Postpurchase Evaluations and Consumption Experiences of Hedonic Products: A Case of Reading Fiction', in Englis and Olofsson, eds, *European Advances in Consumer Research* 3: 139–45.

159. Gilbert A. Churchill Jr. and Carol F. Surprenant, 'An investigation into the determinants of customer satisfaction', *Journal of Marketing Research* 19 (November 1983): 491–504; John E. Swan and I. Frederick Trawick, 'Disconfirmation of expectations and satisfaction with a retail service', *Journal of Retailing* 57 (Fall 1981): 49–67;

Peter C. Wilton and David K. Tse, 'Models of consumer satisfaction formation: An extension', *Journal of Marketing Research* 25 (May 1988): 204–12; for a discussion of what may occur when customers evaluate a new service for which comparison standards do not yet exist, see Ann L. McGill and Dawn Iacobucci, 'The Role of Post-Experience Comparison Standards in the Evaluation of Unfamiliar Services,' in John F. Sherry Jr. and Brian Sternthal, eds, *Advances in Consumer Research* 19 (Provo, UT: Association for Consumer Research, 1992): 570–8; William Boulding, Ajay Kalra, Richard Staelin and Valarie A. Zeithaml, 'A dynamic process model of service quality: From expectations to behavioral intentions', *Journal of Marketing Research* 30 (February 1993): 7–27.

160. John W. Gamble, 'The expectations paradox: The more you offer customers, the closer you are to failure', *Marketing News* (14 March 1988): 38.

161. Jagdish N. Sheth and Banwari Mittal, 'A framework for managing customer expectations', *Journal of Market Focused Management* 1 (1996): 137–58.

162. Franz Bailom, Hans H. Hinterhuber, Kurt Matzler and Elmar Sauerwein, 'Das kano-modell der kundenzufriedenheit', *Marketing ZFP* 2 (2nd quarter 1996): 117–26.

163. Marit G. Engeset, Kjell Grønhaug and Morten Heide, 'The impact of experience on customer satisfaction as measured in direct surveys', in *Marketing for an Expanding Europe*, Proceedings of the 25th EMAC Conference, eds Berács, Bauer and Simon: 403–17.

164. Andreas Herrmann, Frank Huber and Christine Braunstein, 'A Regret Theory Approach to Assessing Customer Satisfaction when Alternatives are Considered', in Dubois, Lowrey, Shrum and Vanhuele, eds, *European Advances in Consumer Research* 4: 82–8.

165. Kjell Grønhaug and Alladi Venkatesh, 'Products and services in the perspectives of consumer socialisation', *European Journal of Marketing* 21(10) (1987); Folke Ölander, 'Consumer Satisfaction – A Sceptic's View', in H.K. Hunt, ed., *Conceptualization and Measurement of Consumer Satisfaction and Dissatisfaction* (Cambridge, MA: Marketing Science Institute, 1977): 453–88.

166. 'Keeping European Consumers Safe', *2007 Annual Report on the operation of the Rapid Alert System for non-food consumer products*, European Communities Health and Consumer Protection Directorate General, Luxembourg 2008: 15–7.

167. 'Keeping European Consumers Safe', *2007 Annual Report on the operation of the Rapid Alert System for non-food consumer products*, European Communities Health and Consumer Protection Directorate General, Luxembourg 2008: 36–7.

168. *The Consumer Markets Scoreboard: Monitoring Consumer Outcomes in the Single Market*, COM (2008) 31, European Communities, Luxembourg 2008: 17.

169. Mary C. Gilly and Betsy D. Gelb, 'Post-purchase consumer processes and the complaining consumer', *Journal of Consumer Research* 9 (December 1982): 323–8; Diane Halstead and Cornelia Droge, 'Consumer Attitudes Toward Complaining and the Prediction of Multiple Complaint Responses', in Holman and Solomon, eds, *Advances in Consumer Research* 18: 210–16; Jagdip Singh, 'Consumer complaint intentions and behavior: Definitional and taxonomical issues,' *Journal of Marketing* 52 (January 1988): 93–107.

170. 'Keeping European Consumers Safe', *2007 Annual Report on the operation of the Rapid Alert System for non-food consumer*

products, European Communities Health and Consumer Protection Directorate General, Luxembourg 2008: 19.

171. Alan Andreasen and Arthur Best, 'Consumers complain – does business respond?', *Harvard Business Review* 55 (July/August 1977): 93–101.

172. Ingrid Martin, 'Expert–Novice Differences in Complaint Scripts', in Holman and Solomon, eds, *Advances in Consumer Research* 18: 225–31; Marsha L. Richins, 'A multivariate analysis of responses to dissatisfaction', *Journal of the Academy of Marketing Science* 15 (Fall 1987): 24–31.

173. John A. Schibrowsky and Richard S. Lapidus, 'Gaining a competitive advantage by analysing aggregate complaints', *Journal of Consumer Marketing* 11 (1994) 1: 15–26.

174. Veronica Liljander, 'Consumer Satisfaction with Complaint Handling Following a Dissatisfactory Experience with Car Repair', in Dubois, Lowrey, Shrum and Vanhuele, eds, *European Advances in Consumer Research* 4: 270–5.

175. Tibbett L. Speer, 'They complain because they care', *American Demographics* (May 1996): 13–14.

176. *The Consumer Markets Scoreboard: Monitoring Consumer Outcomes in the Single Market*, COM (2008) 31, European Communities, Luxembourg, 2008: 17.

177. Special Eurobarometer 252, Consumer Protection in the Internal Market 2006, Figure 1, *The Consumer Markets Scoreboard: Monitoring Consumer Outcomes in the Single Market*, COM (2008) 31, European Communities, Luxembourg.

178. Mary Wolfinbarger and Mary C. Gilly, 'eTailQ: Dimensionalizing, measuring and predicting etail quality', *Journal of Retailing* 79 (2003): 183–98.

179. See Kortnery Stringer, 'Shoppers who blend store, catalog, web spend more', *The Wall Street Journal Online* (3 September 2004): A7 for a detailed discussion of these issues.

180. William Echison, 'Designers climb onto the virtual catwalk', *Business Week* (11 October 1999): 164.

181. Rita Choy and Suzanne Loker, 'Mass customization of wedding gowns: Design involvement on the internet', *Clothing and Textiles Research Journal* 22(1&2) (2004): 79–87.

Case study 1

'Small is beautiful': the Mini brand community

PAULINE MACLARAN, Royal Holloway College, London University, UK

KOK HOI BEH, De Montfort University, Leicester, UK

Associated with rebel culture in the swinging '60s, the Mini has been the most popular British car ever produced. Despite the fact that it ceased production in 2000, the Mini still has a huge following of loyal fans around the world. They maintain their Minis with extreme devotion, ensuring their cars remain in prime condition on our UK roads, where they serve as a continual reminder of the iconic status of this little car that we have all come to love. Significantly, BMW, who bought the Mini brand as part of their takeover of Rover, were able to trade on this nostalgia when they launched the new MINI (spelt with capitals to differentiate it from the classic Mini) in 2001. To understand the passion that these loyal fans hold for the original Mini, we need to understand the car's history and its evolution into a cultural icon.

The Mini was first launched by the British Motor Corporation (BMC) in 1959, in response to increasing competition from the German manufactured 'bubble cars', small three-wheelers that were highly economic to run at a time when fuel prices were soaring following the Suez Crisis. The Mini's designer, Sir Alex Issigonis, introduced several innovative features, and, in particular, the use of front wheel drive, to allow for more passenger and luggage space and to overcome the car's limitations of size.

The Mini quickly became the quintessential fashion item of the '60s. With its cheeky straplines, such as 'You don't need a big one to be happy. Happiness is Mini shaped', it enabled a then young baby boom generation to rebel against parental values (Filby, 1981). It epitomized perfectly the hedonistic, fun-seeking youth culture that the '60s heralded (Broderick, Maclaran and Ma, 2003). Throughout this decade the Mini was continually associated with major celebrities of the time – Michael Caine, Peter Sellers, Ringo Starr, Britt Ekland, Lulu and a host of others – many of whom had specially customized models (Beh, 2009). Fashion designer Mary Quant, whose famous mini skirt was another iconic symbol of the '60s, appeared in many photos alongside her Mini car. The Mini's subversive connotations were further enhanced when Marianne Faithful drove to Mick Jagger's drugs trial in her Mini, and George Harrison's psychedelic Mini appeared in the Beatles' *Magical Mystery Tour* (Beh, 2009). In 1969 the Mini's notoriety was ensured when it played a starring role in *The Italian Job*, a film about a gold bullion robbery that featured what has now become a classic car chase. The robbers used three Minis to make their dramatic and 'nippy' escape from the police, which included racing down a set of steps and many other daring stunts. This film was remade in 2003 using the new MINI.

The Mini's image was further enhanced by the launches of the Mini Cooper (in 1961) and the more powerful Mini Cooper S (in 1963). These high-performance versions of the Mini attracted many international rally drivers that gave the car a racy image. This was strongly reinforced when the Mini Cooper S won the Monte Carlo Rally in 1964, 1965 and 1967. In addition, well-known daredevil racers such as Niki Lauda, Enzo Ferrari and Steve McQueen drove Mini Coopers.

At the height of its popularity the Mini was exported to markets around the world, including South Africa, Australia, New Zealand and Japan (where it still has a very loyal following). From the early 1980s onwards, however, sales of the Mini declined, as newer small car designs, such as the Ford Fiesta and Volkswagen Polo, captured the popular imagination. Although production volumes decreased significantly in response to this declining demand, special editions of the Mini were launched thereafter at regular intervals. This gave the car a niche market allure and exclusivity that enhanced its sense of style and appeal as a collector's item.

Through its wealth of associations with pop, style and sporting icons, the Mini has become a cultural icon that stands for fun, happiness and individuality. Its loyal fans often creatively theme the car's interior, exterior and even their own attire and take pride in the fact that no two [themed] Minis are the same. For example, one passionate devotee, who drives a pink-painted Mini, dresses all in pink and has pink accessories for both herself and her car when she attends regular Mini events. The Mini's faithful followers constitute a brand community in that they relate to each other through their ownership of a Mini, regardless of traditional community markers, such as geographic location, age, gender, class or ethnicity (Muniz and O'Guinn, 2001).

There are over 150 Mini clubs alone in the UK and many others around the world, particularly in Italy and Japan (Beh, 2009). These clubs were set up by groups of Mini enthusiasts in order to meet with each other, swop advice, exchange parts, tell stories and enjoy themselves. They also communicate online where many Mini cyber communities are now flourishing. The Internet enables members to transcend their own locality and communicate about their passion with other likeminded *aficionados* of the Mini from around the globe. Wherever members of the Mini community go, nationally or internationally, they can be assured of a welcome from other Mini owners. The three markers of community identified by Muniz and O'Guinn (2001) – consciousness of kind; moral responsibility; rituals and tradition – are very evident in the way Mini owners behave towards each other.

1 CONSCIOUSNESS OF KIND

This refers to the essential connection that members feel towards one another, a sense of 'we-ness' that engenders deep bonds through their shared passion for the brand. Two interconnected mechanisms engender consciousness of kind, 'legitimacy' and 'oppositional brand loyalty'. Legitimacy is the process by which the community recognize their identity and distinguish between 'true' members, peripheral members, and those who are not members at all. Oppositional brand loyalty gives the community member a sense of distinctiveness from those who do not belong. Normally this would be against other competitive brands. However, the launch of the new BMW MINI has created additional grounds for an oppositional loyalty which is not so much inter-brand as it is *intra*-brand (Beh, 2009). Many Mini clubs do not permit new Mini owners to join. There are several reasons why many Mini brand community members feel that the BMW MINI is not a true Mini. First, many members feel that the design of the new MINI does not retain the authenticity of the orginal Mini, and they are indignant that the two designs should be associated. Second, the MINI is no longer British and there is a sense of betrayal. Frequent contributors to the Mini Internet discussion boards refer to BMW as 'British Motor Wreckers', and a 'foreign imposter' (Beh, 2009). A third reason, according to certain members, is that the new MINI does not permit the same level of individual customization and creative expression. Members have expressed negative feelings towards the BMW MINI with car stickers such as: '100 per cent FREE OF B.M.W. PARTS' and 'REAL MINI BEWARE OF IMITATION.'

2 MORAL RESPONSIBILITY

Mini community members feel a deep sense of responsibility not only to other members, but also to the community as a whole. They have two important communal missions. The first of these is the recruiting, integrating and retaining of members to ensure the continued existence of the club. Members spread the word about their passion for the Mini with a missionary zeal that has been noted in other brand communities such as the 'Cult of Macintosh' (Belk and Tumbat, 2003). The second communal mission is internal and is based on assisting members to care for their Minis in order to ensure a thriving community. For example, Mini drivers always stop to help each other if they see a Mini that has broken down (but they do not stop for a BMW MINI). They place great emphasis on a felt obligation to lend tools or exchange parts in order to help maintain each other's Minis.

3 RITUALS AND TRADITIONS

Holding regular events to celebrate the history of the brand reinforces the Mini community's sense of identity and allows certain rituals and traditions to evolve as members share stories about their experiences of the Mini. Mini events are colourful pageants where members parade and display their customized Minis to each other. Car accessories become ritual artefacts to assist these performances and the sales of Mini collectibles are an important part of this ritualized behaviour. Other unwritten traditions have evolved over the years, such as flashing headlights and waving when two Minis pass on the road. Interestingly, non-brand- and brand-related rituals sometimes become mutually reinforcing, as when a member receives Mini-related birthday and Christmas presents.

From the above analysis we can see how the relationships between Mini owners meet the essential criteria for being considered a community. The Mini brand community has been going through a certain amount of turmoil in recent years. Similar to the Apple Newton brand community (Muniz and Schau, 2005), some members felt abandoned when production of the original Mini ceased in 2000. Many others experienced a sense of betrayal when BMW commenced production of what they saw as a very different MINI. We suggest that much of the BMW MINI's success is due to the fact that the Mini brand community, acting independently from marketers, has kept the core values of the original Mini brand alive for nearly 50 years, values that once again resonate with a new generation of MINI owners.

QUESTIONS

1 What do you think are the key influences that enabled the Mini car to become a cultural icon?

2 In what ways has the launch of the new BMW MINI destabilized the Mini brand community?

3 How do you think the opposition between fans of the BMW MINI and the original Mini might be resolved in the future?

4 Identify a brand community and assess it with respect to the three markers of community identified by Muniz and O'Guinn (2001), i.e. consciousness of kind; moral responsibility; and rituals and traditions.

Sources

Beh, K.H. (2009) 'Unity in Diversity? Identity, Relationship and Cultural Context in the Mini Brand Community', unpublished doctoral dissertation, De Montfort University.

Belk, R.W. and Tumbat, G. (2003) 'The Cult of Macintosh (Video)', in D. Turley and S. Brown (eds), *European Advances in Consumer Research*, vol. 6, Provo, UT: Association for Consumer Research.

Broderick, A., Maclaran, P. and Ma, P. (2003) 'Brand meaning negotiation and the role of the online community: a Mini case study', *Journal of Customer Behaviour*, vol. 2(1): 75–104.

Filby, P. (1981) *Amazing Mini*, UK: Haynes Publishing.

Muniz, A.M. and Schau, H.J. (2005) 'Religiosity in the abandoned Apple Newton brand community,' *Journal of Consumer Research*, vol. 31 (March): 737–747.

Muniz, A.M. and O'Guinn, T.C. (2001) 'Brand community', *Journal of Consumer Research*, 27 (March): 412–432.

How different is different? IKEA's challenge to appeal to local tastes globally

SOFIA ULVER-SNEISTRUP and PETER SVENSSON, Lund University, Sweden

INTRODUCTION

In an interview in 2005, an IKEA manager described the IKEA business in the following words:

In a way our business is people's *tastes*, how things look. And that's a quite difficult thing for us here in America where the taste is quite traditional [. .]
I *do* think IKEA should have an opinion about what we could call 'good taste' is. In the long run we want to attract more and more customers but we also want to educate our markets too, educate them to like IKEA and to share *our* points of view when it comes to home decoration.

The customers referred to above are not customers in general, but the lower income segments in the United States. Although IKEA continuously faces the problem of different taste preferences among consumers in different markets, as indeed do all global brands, in some markets this difference in taste preferences is a more serious threat to IKEA's global expansion than in others. Thus, in the United States IKEA has struggled for years with American low income consumers holding on to tastes for traditional and conventional styles, whereas the majority of IKEA's priority range is Scandinavian modern and mostly patronized by the more dynamic middle class. This tension between IKEA's global range strategy on the one hand and local consumers' taste resistance on the other, highlights the following general theoretical and practical problems, representing three perspectives from which global marketing can be discussed:

1 *From a consumer perspective*: how do different consumer markets, and consumers within these markets, adapt to and/or resist global brands' taste instructions in different ways?
2 *From a management perspective*: how should these differences be managed across the marketing mix?
3 *From an ethical/political perspective*: how far should a company go in terms of trying to change local cultural tastes?

Needless to say, in marketing practice these questions are not separated from but are actualized in every marketing decision. In order to understand these issues better, in this case study we draw upon research carried out in three different countries (USA, Sweden, Turkey) both among IKEA management and among IKEA consumers (Ulver-Sneistrup, 2008).

CONSUMER PERSPECTIVE: THE EXAMPLE OF INDIVIDUALISTIC CONSUMPTION

In 30 interviews with middle-class consumers from different age groups in their homes in Turkey, Sweden and USA, styles were often seen to be materially different but the ways of talking about preferred versus despised tastes seemed to be quite similar. For instance, in general consumers celebrated the virtue of being individualistic in their consumption and having a unique style. However, among the Swedish and US consumers, 'being individualistic' meant something rather different from what was meant by the consumers from Turkey.

The Turkish respondents emphasized the value of having the courage to break with the strong traditions and conventions held by family, relatives and older generations. One man said that:

[Regular] Turkish people prefer two couches, two or three. They also want to buy single armchairs. I don't know why they prefer that. Look, *we* don't have that! . . . And also, a typical piece of furniture is a *garderobe*, something like this [drawing a *garderobe*]. A big piece with doors on it, some shelves and they put a lot of money into that. And they think that if there's not a piece of furniture like this in the living-room, the living-room will be empty! [Laughter] This is a *must* for them! [Laughter] I don't know why they prefer it. They put all the stuff in it. Cups, mugs, I don't know all the stuff they put in there! [Laughter] So they buy something like this, it's a *must*, it's a *must*! This is Turkish culture, I can say that . . . Most people are not rich in Turkey, and when they try to get married, oh, it's not easy to get married in Turkey! [Laughter] Because you have to rent, rent a flat, buy furniture, and also you have to choose furniture that your parents like because they help their children to buy the furniture [laughter]! Also they will have some visitors because of their parents – because they have lots of relatives – for example, so you will have a lot of guests coming to see your house. 'What's happening here?' [Laughter] So this is a very important point for Turkish people. We don't have an isolated life. So lots of people, they prefer to choose furniture that everybody can like, you know. Half that they prefer and half that their relatives or other people prefer. They prefer to combine them, this feeling.

(Turkish male, 30)

Hence, going to IKEA to buy a set of furniture shown in the IKEA catalogue was seen as quite rebellious, as IKEA's room-sets were considered to be quite a contrast to the Turkish norms and conventions on how to furnish a home. For example, a Turkish sitting-room (a *salon*) should, according to traditional conventions, consist of a three-person couch, a two-person couch and at least two armchairs in the same elegant style. IKEA seldom offers a sofa with an accompanying large set. Neither do they offer the heavy, large and ornamented cupboards in dark wood with glass doors (*vitrines*) that are close to mandatory in the Turkish *salons*. In the interviews, the middle-class Turkish consumers emphasized that it was high status among the new generations within the pro-European Turkish elite, to have the courage to move away from the old conventions and to buy complete 'room solutions' such as those presented in advertisements and catalogues by modern retailers like IKEA.

In contrast, among the respondents from Sweden and USA, 'individuality' meant something completely different from the views expressed by the Turkish respondents. In Sweden and USA, imitating room sets in catalogues from mass producers like IKEA was seen as the plain opposite to rebellion. An American woman explained that:

When I say 'common' I would mean – I would say common or uninspired . . . regular people, regular people who, primarily blue-collar, working-class . . . young, very young professionals. Uhm, it's not high income bracket. Definitely. Uhm, except the high-income bracket people will come there and furnish an apartment for their child . . . or furnish a dorm-room there . . . things like that. So definitely not an intellectual crowd *at all* . . . The idea that that place [IKEA] gives – *allows* people to have . . . I don't know . . . style who would not normally have style, is a new concept. And now, somebody graduating from college can walk in there and just get a room, I mean their whole apartment can be set up relatively cheaply. Like *anybody* can do it. *Anybody* can do it!

(American female, 35)

Buying prefabricated room sets, as presented by the marketing communications of large global brands like IKEA, was considered to show a lack of imagination and ultimately a lack of individuality and uniqueness. Instead, these consumers preferred anti-commercial 'eclectic', 'authentic' and 'historical' styles. That is, styles that the Turkish consumers thought were too close to the preferences held by their own grandparents, *or* – if the styles were too historical and rural in their expressions – too similar to the less educated and lower income groups' tastes.

Hence, in the American and Swedish homes, 'individuality' was expressed by mixing styles, such as old with new, cheap with expensive, dark with light, commercial with vintage and colonial with modern. In the fieldwork in Turkish homes, in contrast, 'individuality' was expressed through the entirely modern style solutions offered by companies such as IKEA. Still, what the respondents from the three countries *did* have in common was that they all perceived themselves to be 'individualistic' and anti-traditional consumers, different from the masses, and genuinely unique.

MANAGEMENT PERSPECTIVE: THE EXAMPLE OF SOCIAL GATHERINGS

At the time of writing, IKEA, the Swedish home furnishing retailer with the mission to 'create a better everyday life for the many people' has almost 300 stores in 35 countries globally (**IKEA.com**, 2008). The global marketing strategy in terms of global/local standardization or adaptation is continuously under evaluation and incessantly debated within the organization (IKEA manager interview, 2005). Meanwhile, various standardization and adaptation strategies continue to be mixed and combined across the marketing mix. For example, the popular IKEA catalogue is standardized globally but does carry some local adaptations (e.g. front covers, products in focus on central pages, etc.) based on global product range strategy in combination with the specific market's choice of range. Some products are globally mandatory to offer in the stores and some are not. Manuals by Inter IKEA Systems provide mandatory guidelines for its local managers about how to present the IKEA brand in external and internal communication; and yet advertisements, TV commercials, showrooms and Websites are adapted for the local markets and stores.

The general idea behind IKEA's US strategy of targeting the lower income classes is founded on two arguments linked, first, to the IKEA 'identity' (its range) and secondly, to the business idea (to offer function and design at a reasonable price to many people). The famous IKEA idea of 'democratic design' is based on targeting lower income groups, but it is also assumed to carry some additional economic advantages: (1) the lower income groups make lower demands on service than higher income groups; (2) the lower income groups welcome IKEA furniture into all rooms of their home whereas the higher income groups generally treat IKEA as more 'transitional' and for the lower-profile rooms of the home; and (3) the low income market is larger than the higher income market.

However, IKEA's strategy of *driving* the market in terms of tastes rather than being market-*driven* entails some problems. As mentioned earlier, the lower income markets are assumed to be less dynamic and open to change than the middle-class market. Consequently, the educative strategy needs to be long-term and focus persistently on lower income classes' exposure to Scandinavian and modern styles over time. According to the IKEA managers interviewed in the study, this can be accomplished by emphasizing, and even exaggerating, the range which internally is called 'traditional' style and actually only constitutes 20 per cent of the total range – to make it look as if it constitutes 40 per cent to give the impression that this style is more dominant so as to attract people to the store. Once inside the store shoppers are presented, early on, with traditional styles, but the rest of the items displayed tend to derive from the more 'modern' range which constitutes 80 per cent of IKEA's total product. This way, consumers visiting the IKEA store will immediately come across the traditional styles that they are already attracted to, but at the same time they are exposed to the attractive showrooms and settings of modern Scandinavian living. The idea is that this exposure will educate the consumers into a way of thinking (and taste) that fits well with the IKEA product range. As one IKEA manager put it:

> The more inclusive we try to be, the more it is about giving people the *courage* and to . . . yes, that's perhaps where it turns into what we could call 'education'. We also know – another thing we know about our customers, and perhaps even more about our *potential* customers, is that once we expose them to IKEA, then many of them . . . because we have done a lot of focus groups, etc., and some exercises where we have invited customers and non-customers to the stores on guided tours, and it is almost always the same result. If we only get them to the store, a large majority really likes the experience. So, that's one key.
>
> (IKEA manager)

Being 'inclusive' towards the lower income groups also means, as the IKEA manager makes clear, speaking to consumers with an IKEA voice but in a way that the target group wants to listen to. This has consequences for the global versus local marketing strategies, where ethnic groups and women are prioritized as target groups within the larger low income group. In terms of the ethnic groups for example, IKEA has hired advertising and media agencies who are experts on specific ethnic communities (e.g. on the Turkish community in Berlin, and on the Mexican community in Los Angeles) and know how and where to communicate with these groups (e.g. for the Mexican community via Hispanic soap operas on TV). Part of the strategy is to slightly adapt the room settings in the ads and in the stores to the preferences expressed by these ethnic groups. For instance in the Mexican case, IKEA undertook ethnographic research within these communities and found that specific lifestyle aspects had a large impact on why IKEA furniture was seldom chosen by this group. One of these aspects was that IKEA's image of room settings was seldom adapted to larger groups of people. The IKEA ethnographers found that, in the Mexican communities, gatherings at home often included more than ten people, mixing families, friends and generations. Moreover, the colours often portrayed in IKEA's images were perceived to be quite cold and unwelcoming.

Hence, to be more inclusive, the local IKEA store interior designers created room settings that were vastly more Mexican in style, showing smart space solutions for large dinner parties with many chairs, and textiles and kitchen work space in hues of warm terracotta colours. At the same time IKEA launched local TV commercials in Spanish, broadcast only during the soap operas watched by the targeted Hispanic groups. The overall campaign was successful and set an example within IKEA globally for the local adaptation of marketing campaigns.

FROM AN ETHICAL/POLITICAL PERSPECTIVE: HOME VIOLATORS OR TASTE TEACHERS?

It is impossible to discuss global marketing enterprises such as that of IKEA without commenting on the ethical and political issues involved. The scope of this case study does not allow us to elaborate on the notions of ethics and politics at length. For the sake of the discussion we will just use ethics as an entry point into questions regarding the extent of IKEA's global responsibility that far transcends the usual financial and legal considerations. By 'politics' is meant the exercise of power through IKEA's global marketing strategies.

Globalization is a key notion in this respect. The process by which we see a world society is emerging is not just the result of an autonomous historical force, outside of and beyond the control of human activity and decision making. Corporations are not bystanders and passive observers of external globalization movements. On the contrary, globalization involves changes in the relationships between regions, nations and markets worldwide. Organizations – such as IKEA – have an active part in these globalization processes. In effect, IKEA is a paramount example of an organization that brings together the economic, political and cultural aspects of globalization in one business idea. The export of Swedish-made furniture is not only about the global flow of goods; it is also, as discussed above, about the export of values, preferences and taste. The export of furniture and taste moreover carries with it political effects on the ideological power relations between regions, nations and perhaps even class. In that sense, the global marketing of IKEA furniture can be seen as a good example of what Pierre Bourdieu refers to as 'symbolic power' or 'symbolic violence' (Bourdieu, 1992;

Bourdieu and Passeron, 1996), i.e. the ways in which symbols and representations are involved in the exercise of power. In the educative endeavour performed by IKEA strategists, to persuade potential customers about their room sets, a certain representation of 'the home' is imposed upon and reproduced for the target market. The marketing of Scandinavian home style and fashion to Hispanic consumer segments in USA, for instance, goes to the heart of the fundamental question of what a home is and how the social space is to be organized in everyday, domestic life. In the example of Mexican consumers discussed above, the pivotal question asked and answered by the IKEA ethnographers was: How many people make up a social gathering? In other words, the marketing of IKEA here touched upon very fundamental cultural categories such as 'space', 'room' and 'group'.

The symbolic power (or violence), found in the tension between standardization and adaptation, creates difficult (and interesting) ethical challenges for the global marketer. These issues are quite familiar to us from the practice of colonialization. The relationship between colonizer and colonized appears to be of a similar kind to that between IKEA as educator and the consumer as student of taste. The enterprise of colonialization also involved the export, also violent but in a slightly different sense of the term, of values and tastes.

Ethical issues of this cultural-political kind are obviously devoid of simple solutions or decision models. What is important, however, is to acknowledge their existence. Their solutions can only be produced in concrete and practical marketing situations.

However, culture should not be seen as a static set of values and practices, and the relationship between global standardization and adaptation is hardly as simple as that between an authoritarian colonizer and an oppressed colonized. Culture exists in incessant change and transformation. In so far as globalization has resulted in an increased volume of encounters between different cultures, values, styles and tastes, some researchers have argued that in these meetings, hybrids emerge, in between, as it were, the colonizer and the colonized (see Bhabha, 1994). In these hybrid amalgams resides potential resistance against colonial power. This may also be the case for the business of global IKEA. In domestic practices, such as the above-mentioned social gatherings, hybrid forms of using (consuming) the home and furnishing can appear. These hybridities are hard to predict and beyond the reach and control of IKEA's marketing management activities.

QUESTIONS

1 How would you describe IKEA's strategies to overcome the problem that the American market prefers the part of the range that IKEA does not actually want to emphasize?

2 How do *you* think IKEA should manage it? Should they change their own product range or should they change (educate) the consumers? Why?

3 How can consumers' tastes be seen as related to social class?

4 How can IKEA's market driving strategy across markets be seen from this perspective on differing consumer tastes?

5 How can IKEA manage the paradox that consumers in different parts of the world may celebrate the same themes (e.g. in this case 'individuality') when they talk, but at the same time *mean* completely different things in practice?

6 Discuss IKEA's objective to 'educate' consumers globally into northern European tastes from an ethical perspective. What are the political implications (i.e. power effects) of this conception of marketing as education?

7 Do you think some socio-historical settings are more prone to encourage resistance between older and younger generations than others? If you think so, then why?

8 Discuss how homes around the globe will look in the future, depending on whether or not IKEA succeeds with their objective to educate 'the many people' on how to furnish a home tastefully.

Sources

Bhabha, H.K. (1994) *The Location of Culture*, London: Routledge.

Bourdieu, P. and Passeron, J. (1996) *Reproduction*, London: Sage.

Bordieu, P. (1992) *Language and Symbolic Power*, Cambridge: Polity Press.

Ulver-Sneistrup, S. (2008) *Status-Spotting – A Consumer Cultural Exploration into Ordinary Status Consumption of 'Home' and Home Aesthetics*, PhD Dissertation, Lund: Lund Business Press.

How second-hand consumption re-enchants and empowers the consumer's life

DOMINIQUE ROUX, Université Paris 12, France

Anne and Philippe first got to know each other in the Paris area in the 1980s. Now in their 40s, they are married with two children aged 12 and 15. Anne works as a management controller for a leading French car manufacturer and Philippe as a Telecom engineer.

When they met, they were both comfortably-off middle-class junior managers. Because of Philippe's work, they moved for a short period to the north of France. During that time, they discovered the 'Grande Braderie' of Lille, an annual discount market dating back to the fairs of the Middle Ages, which attracts thousands of participants and exhibitors each year from the French-Belgian frontier area. They were astounded and quite won over in the course of a night spent bargain-hunting among the 70 kilometres of streets displaying goods of every imaginable kind. They also made a point at weekends of visiting the various second-hand sales that were advertised as taking place in the villages of the Lille region. Both practical and pleasurable, such occasions provided the opportunity to get to know the area, as well as for picking up decorative household knick-knacks, clothes, or tools, according to their mood at the time. In this region, second-hand sales were such a common occurrence that it seemed quite natural to go there and wander around on the lookout for bargains.

Undoubtedly, the most striking memory Anne has of this period was acquiring her wedding dress. She didn't want to buy it in a traditional shop, where the dresses all seemed the same – not necessarily unattractive, but banal. One Sunday they were in a charming village 10 kilometres from Lille, when Anne, without having planned on doing so, found herself standing in front of a market stall where, hanging from the sunshade, was an Empire-style wedding dress. Intrigued, she stared at it for a long time, admiring its pure straight lines, embellished by fine lace facing and pearls stitched to the bodice. She was irresistibly attracted to it, but not daring to imagine she might be married in a dress bought at a flea market, she turned it over and over, disbelievingly. The stall-holder offered it to her for the equivalent of €15, a price that seemed ridiculous, exciting and very appealing, in that the dress appeared to be in perfect condition. What's more, to Anne's experienced eye it looked to be her size. After asking Philippe's opinion – he found the idea rather amusing – she finally left with what she would later come to think of as a trophy. Years later, the famous 'flea-market wedding dress' had become something of a fetish object, to the extent that Anne had recounted 'the legend' to her daughters, promising to bequeath it to them when they got married.

The following year, with Philippe's training complete, the return to the Paris area left them feeling depressed. They were struck by the absence of second-hand markets, something they had not been aware of before they left. They also wondered why such events did not exist or seemed unknown in Paris. By way of compensation, during their holidays, they would have no hesitation in making a detour of several kilometres to rummage through a second hand store signposted along a country road. Anne always managed to find some pieces of old lace, and Philippe antiquarian books.

When their first daughter was born, friends passed on baby clothes they had no further use for. Anne had also retrieved the clothes her mother had saved from her childhood, and which she was happy to see her daughter wearing.

Then, to their great surprise, two or three years later, a number of second-hand markets made their appearance in the Paris area. Anne and Philippe were delighted by this development, and began to believe that the pleasures of their Lille years would again be part of their daily life. At the same time, second-hand stores started opening up here and there, and they would often make a tour of them at random. Anne especially liked looking for decorative items for the house, but more than anything, such places were like great caves, full of treasure. One would never know what one might find there. They were permeated with an antiquated atmosphere, and Anne loved the untidy profusion of abandoned objects. Sometimes pathetic but often touching, these fragments of personal histories seemed always to be part and parcel of the dust that covered them. Every now and then, in Paris, she would push open the door of a second-hand clothes shop, and admire the originality of the somewhat outdated dresses and beautifully cut ladies' suits. The clothes were all different, each item unique. Clearly they had been worn very little. A woman had once loved them, then cast them aside. Anne found things there that she never saw in regular clothes shops, items that seemed attractive precisely because they weren't available through the standard distribution channels. By wearing these clothes, she too could feel herself to be unique and different. She would also buy lots of things for her children, pretty little outfits that were practically unworn.

Philippe, for his part, appreciated finding useful items. He often had a clear idea of what he was looking for. 'What was the point of rushing to the supermarket?' he said. Second-hand markets and stores were full of things people no longer wanted and which were still in perfect working order. Why pay more, why buy at high prices when high quality goods were thrown out? Often the products sold at hypermarkets did not appear to be any more appealing or effective than others that had already been used and proved their worth. He was also particularly sensitive to waste, and to the consumption race that seemed to him to be as futile as it was harmful. His financial commitment to humanitarian causes – donations that he made every year to various charities – went hand-in-hand with respect for resources and a concern for the preservation of objects as much as with the labour that had produced them. It was by no means unusual for him, on the days allocated for the disposal of bulky objects, to collect various items of furniture, electrical equipment or computers from the Paris streets and pavements. He would salvage the components and test them out. He liked to say that from three discarded bikes he had reconstructed one for his daughter. He did this not out of necessity but through conviction, finding ridiculous all the waste and incompetence that led people to throw things away without even trying to repair them. Increasingly, Philippe has begun purchasing on the Internet. Second-hand sales sites enable him to find out-of-print old books, which he collects, as well as CDs and DVDs.

Anne and Philippe were aware they were increasingly avoiding the standard distribution channels. They still did their day-to-day shopping in hypermarkets, and bought certain products new for convenience, security or when appropriate. But very often they preferred to wait, compare and find better value for money or something more original. Their approach was in part one of economic calculation, but allied to the pleasure of being resourceful. This feeling of being smarter arose to some extent from the sense of making better buying choices for themselves and of using their resources intelligently, but also from the moral satisfaction of not contributing to overall wastage. At the age of 40, with a settled life and materially well-off, they did not feel they were changing the world, but rather were living in a different way in terms of consumption. The increase in the various channels of exchange between private individuals and second-hand goods in general gave them great pleasure, since it enabled them to re-enchant their life as consumers while reclaiming a whole domain of freedom.

QUESTIONS

1 What factors do consumers consider when comparing second-hand distribution channels, either favourably or unfavourably, with traditional channels?

2 Would you say that Anne and Philippe have the same motivations toward second-hand shopping? What distinguishes them or brings them together in terms of their profiles (e.g. attitudes; values; perceptions)?

3 Do certain alternative distribution channels seem to cater better for certain types of motivation rather than others? Which features of the different channels respond best to which orientations?

4 In what respects can second-hand exchanges between consumers be said to enhance their power? In your opinion does this constitute a long-term threat to traditional channels?

Port wine: ruby, tawny, white and the premiums

CARLOS BRITO, University of Porto, Portugal

Port is a fortified wine named after Porto, the second-largest Portuguese city, where it has traditionally been shipped from. However, port begins its life in the Douro Valley which starts some 100km east of Porto (or Oporto in its anglicized form), and extends as far as the Spanish border. The valley is an administratively demarcated region where an estimated 30,000 farmers produce what is considered to be one of the great wines of the world.

The three most popular styles of port are ruby, tawny and white. The first is a young wine, somewhat full-bodied and fruity, with an open red colour. It is usually bottled after three years' ageing in wood and it is ready for drinking immediately. It is usually consumed after dinner as a dessert wine. It goes very well with cheese, chocolate and dried fruits. Tawny is also a red wine but is aged longer than ruby. The wine becomes smoother, and acquires a brownish and lighter style. Tawny is considered the most 'versatile' of ports: it can be appreciated both as a dessert wine and as an aperitif (preferably chilled). In this case it goes very well with pâté, smoked ham and nuts. White port is, as its name suggests, made only with white grapes, and can be sweet or dry. After ageing usually three to five years in concrete vats, it is consumed chilled as an aperitif or summer drink. A good example is Portonic, a long drink made up of equal parts of white port and tonic water, served over ice with a slice of lemon.

Average port prices in 2007

Types of port	Average price (euros/litre)
Standard port	
Ruby	3.35
Tawny	3.34
White	3.55
Special categories	
Vintage	18.38
Late bottled vintage	6.68
With indication of age	11.69

Source: Port and Douro Wines Institute.

In addition to these basic types, there are several special categories which correspond to the premium wines. Their prices are much higher than for a standard port. This is because their quality in terms of flavour and colour is better. However, there are also other reasons.

First, the maturation process is longer and more complex which tends to increase cost. Secondly, there are intangible aspects related to port: history and culture. As a matter of fact, a bottle of port does not only include wine in the strictest sense. It also embodies the history of port which, in many respects, is linked to the history of Portugal over the past four centuries. And it also carries all of the social, cultural and geographical factors related to the environment of the Douro Valley, a region that was declared a world heritage site by UNESCO. This means that when setting the price of port, especially premium ports, the shipping-houses know that consumers value such intangible aspects.

Vintage, late bottled vintage and port with an indication of age are some of the best categories of port. The aristocrat of the wines is vintage port since it is produced with grapes of an outstanding year. It is bottled two years after the harvest and it matures in the bottle thereafter. Ten years is generally the absolute minimum, but 15 or 20 years might be needed. Vintage port and cheese are considered to have been created to be consumed together. An excellent example of this is the most classical and British combination: Stilton and Vintage.

Late bottled vintage (LBV) is also port of a single year but with a lower quality than vintage. It is bottled between the fourth and the sixth year after the harvest. New-style LBVs (which are becoming the majority) are filtered before bottling, and do not need further maturation in the bottle. Enjoy it during the meal, for example, with roasted duck or as a dessert wine with a wide range of chocolate of different textures.

Port with an indication of age can be 10, 20, 30 years old or, rarely, over 40 years old. These ages, it should be noted, are average ages, and the old wines in the blend gain enormously from being refreshed by the addition of younger wine. These wines are aged in the cask and should not be further aged in the bottle. Ten-year-old port is fresh and fruity; the older ports are progressively nuttier, with less overt fruit. These ports are particularly pleasant when accompanying fresh fruit, light puddings, ice creams and not very rich cakes. They are also splendid as a digestive after coffee, when one enjoys the contentment that follows a good meal.

PORT TRADE

Although port is produced in the Douro Valley, only a very small amount is shipped from there. In fact, almost all port produced in the Valley is transported during the spring following the vintage to Porto, where shippers' lodges are located. On arriving there, the wine is analyzed in laboratories, tasted and classified. Then it matures for at least three years before being ready for commercialization.

There are dozens of shipping-houses. Some of them are descendants of old British families established in Porto in the early eighteenth century. Croft, Warre and Taylor, Fladgate & Yeatman are examples of firms over 300 years old. Alongside the houses owned by the British families, there are important Portuguese owned companies such as Real Companhia Velha and Ferreira. Some multinationals related to the drinks business have also taken a position in the sector. This is the case with Gran Cruz, owned by the multinational Martiniquaise.

Traditionally, nationality differences have been connected with distinct market orientations. In general, the Portuguese sector has dominated the home market along with very strong positions in France and Belgium. On the other hand, the British shippers have dominated the after-dinner segment, where quality and brand prestige are important factors in consumers' preferences. The United Kingdom has been the largest market for premium ports, though in recent years this segment has grown considerably in some other countries such as the United States and Canada.

THE MARKETS

Although port is shipped to more than 100 countries, its sales are highly concentrated in just a few markets. The top four (France, Portugal, The Netherlands and the United Kingdom) account for almost two-thirds of total sales.

Each market has its own characteristics, and it is interesting to note that the top four countries are representative of distinct patterns of consumer behaviour.

France is the leading market, accounting for almost a quarter of total sales of port. Its profile is very typical: consumers are in general interested in cheap and young ports, and have little or no brand loyalty. Most trade is conducted via distributors who retail under their own labels. In general, price is the critical factor in securing contracts. For the shipping-house, this means uncertainty about orders, low profit margins, and minimal influence over the market.

Port trade in 2007

Markets	Sales		Price
	10³ euros	%	Euros/litre
France	89,369	22.1	3.48
Portugal	61,662	15.2	4.80
Netherlands	50,757	12.6	3.45
United Kingdom	49,826	12.3	4.81
Belgium	41,690	10.3	3.60
USA	29,437	7.3	7.38
Canada	18,241	4.5	8.49
Germany	13,655	3.4	3.67
Denmark	7,535	1.9	5.47
Spain	6,917	1.7	4.57
Others	35,124	8.7	5.60
Total	404,213	100.0	4.29

Source: Port and Douro Wines Institute.

The Netherlands is the third leading market and has a similar profile. Consumers prefer cheap, standard quality ports imported by distributors who retail under their own labels. However, the Dutch market has grown considerably over the past few years, compared with France whose sales have remained at a steady level.

In contrast to these countries, the United Kingdom, the fourth top market, has traditionally been the largest market for premium ports. Special categories of port represent the majority of the total volume consumed there. Although vintage is considered to be the symbol of the British market, consumers are now moving towards lighter ports such as old tawny. For this reason, most shippers have launched new types of port in this segment, e.g. Cockburn's Special Reserve Tawny, Graham's 40-year-old tawny, and Croft's Distinction. But even these more standard ports are, in general, very good quality. As a result, their price is higher than the average price of standard ports shipped to France and The Netherlands. Nevertheless, a significant part of port distributed in the United Kingdom is under the purchasers' own label, which reduces, to some extent, the shippers' control over the market.

Portugal, the second leading market accounting for 15.2 per cent of total sales, is neither a low quality nor a premium market. Consumers tend to prefer standard quality ports, particularly tawny and white port. Shippers' well-known brands have had a major impact on consumer preferences, although recent cases of heavy advertising and aggressive discounts have also succeeded in influencing consumer preferences.

Each market for port has its own differential characteristics. One of the idiosyncrasies of the Portuguese market has to do with the reasons for buying port. A significant part of buying is for gift-giving, inasmuch as it is common to give a bottle of port on special occasions such as anniversaries, parties and, especially, at Christmas. This fact has important consequences. First, almost every family has at least one bottle of port at home – but did not buy it. Rather, it was given by someone else. This means that for a majority of consumers, the port they drink was chosen by someone else. Marketing strategies are affected by this fact. For instance, bottles, cases and labels are designed to take into account that in most instances port is bought as a gift. A good example of this is the form of the exterior packaging. Quite often bottles of port are sold inside a wooden or paper box. In addition to being a protective covering, its objective is to create promotional value since consumers tend to pay more for the appearance and prestige of better packages. But there is another interesting aspect. Square cases are more valued than round cases – because it is easier to wrap a square case.

France, Portugal, The Netherlands and the United Kingdom are just four out of dozens of markets for port. In each one, consumer behaviour is different. This is undoubtedly one of the major challenges faced by the companies that produce and trade port: a great product with many offerings.

QUESTIONS

1 What are the factors which influence product evaluation and choice in this case study?

2 Assume you are a marketing manager for the Portuguese market of a large port shipping-house. Suggest some guidelines for an ad to promote a standard white port.

3 Use the port wine case to illustrate the concept of glocalization.

4 Discuss how you might market port in your own country.

How consumers see the world and themselves

The second part deals with the questions of 'who am I?' and 'how do I see the world'. Building on the initial themes set out in the first part, these chapters examine how consumers' perceptions affect their understanding and interpretation of the market place, how they use consumption in constructing their sense of self, and how motivations, values and lifestyles affect their consumption.

4

Perception

Fabienne is a 35-year-old mother of two and works at the French National Railway Company's headquarters in Lyon Part Dieu. Twice a week she uses her two-hour lunch break to go to the nearby shopping centre, the biggest in Lyons. Today she had just two things in mind: a quick bite to eat and a present for her son, Georges-Hubert. As she enters the shopping centre she is immediately drawn to the appetizing aroma of pizza coming from a nearby fast food restaurant. She decides to stop and buy a slice and a small bottle of mineral water. Next she decides to go to a shop called Nature et Découvertes, a French firm following the style of the Californian Nature Company. She has never been there before, but Catherine, her 14-year-old daughter, says that all her friends are talking about it. It seems to be the perfect place to buy a small microscope for Georges-Hubert's birthday.

On entering the shop she is very surprised. As in all shops her eyes are immediately and highly stimulated, but what makes this shop different is that there is more to it than that: all five of her senses are appealed to. The background music lets Fabienne discover birdsong, the sound of the forest, nature itself. As she is able to handle the products, Fabienne can familiarize herself with new shapes, new materials. An appeal is also made to her sense of taste when she is offered a cup of herbal tea. Finally, the natural aromas from the woods and plants combined with synthetic aromatics recreate the delicious atmosphere of the undergrowth to appeal to her sense of smell.

Fabienne likes the shop very much and for half an hour loses all sense of time. She wanders round as if in a trance. When she finally goes to the cash desk she realizes that not only does she have the little microscope in her hands, but a candle as well, and a book on trees.

PATRICK HETZEL, University of Paris II, Panthéon-Assas

INTRODUCTION

We live in a world overflowing with sensations. Wherever we turn, we are bombarded by a symphony of colours, sounds and odours. Some of the 'notes' in this symphony occur naturally, such as the barking of a dog, the shadows of the evening sky or the heady smell of a rose bush. Others come from people; the person sitting next to you might have dyed blonde hair, bright pink jeans, and be wearing enough perfume to make your eyes water.

Marketers certainly contribute to this commotion. Consumers are never far from advertisements, product packages, radio and television commercials, and advertising hoardings that clamour for their attention. Each of us copes with this bombardment by paying attention to some stimuli and screening out others. When we do make a decision to purchase, we are responding not only to these influences but to our interpretations of them. The aim of Nature et Découvertes is to open the doors to the emotions, to a sense of wonder, to get in touch with one's capacity for pleasure. Unlike many other sales outlets there is a determined motivation to create sensory effects to the utmost, to play on all five senses simultaneously. In a situation like this, the appeal is not so much to Fabienne's mind as to her perceptions, her emotions.

This chapter focuses on the process of perception, in which sensations are absorbed by the consumer and used to interpret the surrounding world. After discussing the stages of this process, the chapter examines how the five senses (sight, smell, sound, touch and taste) affect consumers. It also highlights some of the ways in which marketers develop products and communications that appeal to the senses.

The chapter emphasizes that the way in which a marketing stimulus is presented plays a role in determining whether the consumer will make sense of it or even notice it at all. The techniques and marketing practices that make messages more likely to be noticed are discussed. Finally, the chapter discusses the process of interpretation, in which the stimuli that are noticed by the consumer are organized and assigned meaning.

THE PERCEPTUAL PROCESS

As you sit in a lecture hall, you may find your attention shifting. One minute you are concentrating on the lecture, and in the next, you catch yourself daydreaming about the weekend ahead before you realize that you are missing some important points and tune back into the lecture.

People undergo stages of information processing in which stimuli are input and stored. However, we do not passively process whatever information happens to be present. Only a very small number of the stimuli in our environment are ever noticed. Of these, an even smaller number are attended to. And the stimuli that do enter our consciousness are not processed objectively. The meaning of a stimulus is interpreted by the individual, who is influenced by their unique biases, needs and experiences. These three stages of *exposure (or sensation)*, *attention* and *interpretation* make up the process of perception. The stages involved in selecting and interpreting stimuli are illustrated in Figure 4.1, which provides an overview of the perceptual process.

From sensation to perception

▶ **Sensation** refers to the immediate response of our sensory receptors (e.g. eyes, ears, nose,
▶ mouth, fingers) to such basic stimuli as light, colour and sound. **Perception** is the process by which these stimuli are selected, organized and interpreted. We process raw data (sensation); however, the study of perception focuses on what we add to or take away from these sensations as we assign meaning to them.

Figure 4.1 An overview of the perceptual process

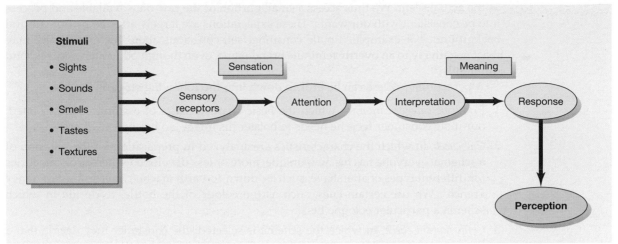

The subjective nature of perception is demonstrated by a controversial advertisement developed for Benetton. Because a black man and a white man were handcuffed together, the ad was the target of many complaints about racism after it appeared in magazines and on hoardings, even though the company has a reputation for promoting racial tolerance. People interpreted it to mean that the black man had been arrested by a white man.[1] Even though both men are dressed identically, people's prior assumptions shaped the ad's meaning. Of course, the company's goal was exactly that: to expose us to our own perceptual prejudice through the ambiguity of the photo.

▶   Such interpretations or assumptions stem from **schemas**, or organized collections of beliefs and feelings. That is, we tend to group the objects we see as having similar characteristics, and the schema to which an object is assigned is a crucial determinant of how we choose to evaluate this object at a later time.

The perceptual process can be illustrated by the purchase of a new aftershave. We have learned to equate aftershave with romantic appeal, so we search for cues that (we believe) will increase our attractiveness. We make our selection by considering such

One in a series of controversial ads from Benetton, trying to expose our prejudice to ourselves.

Handcuffs – © Copyright 1989 Benetton Group S.p.A. Photo: Oliviero Toscani

119

factors as the image associated with each alternative and the design of the bottle, as well as the actual scent. We thus access a small portion of the raw data available and process it to be consistent with our wants. These expectations are largely affected by our cultural background. For example, a male consumer self-conscious about his masculinity may react negatively to an overtly feminine brand name, even though other men may respond differently.[2]

A perceptual process can be broken down into the following stages:[3]

1 *Primitive categorization*, in which the basic characteristics of a stimulus are isolated: our male consumer feels he needs to bolster his image, so he chooses aftershave.

2 *Cue check*, in which the characteristics are analyzed in preparation for the selection of a schema: everyone has his own unique, more or less developed schemas or categories for different types of aftershave, such as 'down-to-earth macho', 'mysterious' or 'fancy French'. We use certain cues, such as the colour of the bottle, to decide in which schema a particular cologne fits.

3 *Confirmation check*, in which the schema is selected: the consumer may decide that a brand falls into his 'mysterious' schema.

4 *Confirmation completion*, in which a decision is made as to what the stimulus is: the consumer decides he has made the right choice, and then reinforces this decision by considering the colour of the bottle and the interesting name of the aftershave.

Such experiences illustrate the importance of the perceptual process for product positioning. In many cases, consumers use a few basic dimensions to categorize competing products or services, and then evaluate each alternative in terms of its relative standing on these dimensions.

▶ This tendency has led to the use of a very useful positioning tool – a **perceptual map**. By identifying the important dimensions and then asking consumers to place competitors within this space, marketers can answer some crucial strategic questions, such as which product alternatives are seen by consumers as similar or dissimilar, and what opportunities exist for new products that possess attributes not represented by current brands. Figure 4.2 offers a perceptual map of the iconic Burberry brand, showing its 'old' position from the 1980s and 1990s, and the shift in perceptions of the brand in more recent years.

Figure 4.2 Perceptual map of the Burberry brand, relative to competitors

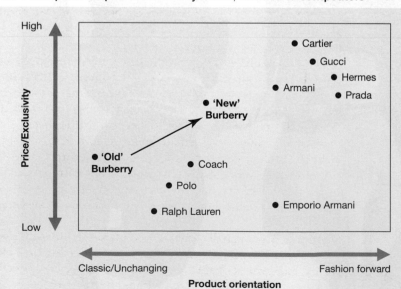

▲ Marketing opportunity

While working in his olive grove in the rugged mountains near the Andalusian town of Jaén last fall, Juan Manuel Melero Aibar was approached by a man admiring one of his olive trees. After years of close pruning to optimize production, the tree resembled a very large bonsai. The stranger, Mr Aibar recalls, told him he could get €50,000 for it at auction. What piqued the potential buyer's interest in the tree wasn't the circumference of its trunk, which measured eight meters, or its yield of olives, roughly 600 kilograms every other year. It was the tree's age – estimated by a representative from the Agriculture Department at 1,200 to 1,500 years.

Mr Aibar decided not to sell his tree, and the stranger gave up trying to convince him to part with it. But a growing number of other farmers in the region have been less reluctant to cash in on theirs. Trees considered 'ancient' – more than 500 years old – can sell for several thousand euros apiece.

Olive trees, called olivos in Spanish and said originally to have been planted on the Iberian peninsula by the Romans, have stood witness to much of Spain's history. Today the country's vast groves make it the world's largest producer of olive oil. Many of these olive trees have a striking visual appeal: gnarled, thick trunks with cropped branches and silvery-green leaves. Landscape architects seek out old trees with aesthetic personality, or to suit a particular buyer's garden. Now, with a 10-year building boom along Spain's southern coast, from Tarifa to Valencia, the trees – often uprooted by developers – are finding new homes in Spain and abroad as yard ornaments.

Buyers usually are not interested in the fruit the trees produce. They want works of landscape art. 'Olives are in their prime in terms of production capacity at 25 to 40 years old,' says Charles Butler Mackay, an olive grower in Jaén and publisher of the Olive Oil Gazette, an online journal of the olive business. 'That's centuries ago.' To farmers, this is reason enough to sell the trees; if they aren't adding to their annual yield – and are worth thousands of euros – why not offload them?

Most of the old trees are replanted in tourist areas, especially exclusive golf courses such as Monte Mayor and La Zagaleta courses in Malaga, to add a look of regional authenticity. Aaron Mount, owner of Ancient Olive Trees, a California-based transplant service that moves trees from Europe and Latin America to the US, says, 'When resorts and hotels open, they want to look established from day one. An old tree helps create that feel.'

A substantial number of trees are sold each year to individuals looking to adorn private gardens. Mr Mount says the appeal to buyers is the one-of-a-kind status they offer. 'Olive trees are like antiques,' he says. 'There is a story tied to each one, in this case stories that cover kingdoms rising and falling.'[4]

SENSORY SYSTEMS

External stimuli, or sensory inputs, can be received on a number of channels. We may see an advertising hoarding, hear a jingle, feel the softness of a cashmere sweater, taste a new flavour of ice cream or smell a leather jacket.

The inputs picked up by our five senses constitute the raw data that generate many types of responses. For example, sensory data emanating from the external environment (hearing a song on the radio) can generate internal sensory experiences when the song on the radio triggers a young man's memory of his first dance and brings to mind the smell of his date's perfume or the feel of her hair on his cheek.

Sensory inputs evoke historical imagery, in which events that actually occurred are recalled. Fantasy imagery results when an entirely new, imaginary experience is the ▶ response to sensory data. These responses are an important part of **hedonic consumption**, or the multi-sensory, fantasy and emotional aspects of consumers' interactions with products.[5] The data that we receive from our sensory systems determine how we respond to products.

Although we usually trust our sensory receptors to give us an accurate account of the external environment, new technology is making the linkage between our senses and reality more questionable. Computer-simulated environments, or *virtual reality*, allow surgeons to 'cut into' a person without drawing blood or an architect to see a building design from different perspectives. This technology, which creates a three-dimensional

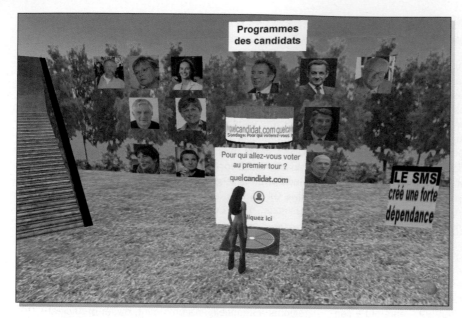

Virtual reality.

Getty Images/AFP

perceptual environment which the viewer experiences as being virtually real, is already being adapted to everyday pursuits, such as virtual reality games.

Enterprising business people will no doubt continue to find new ways to adapt this technology for consumers' entertainment – perhaps by developing 'virtual catalogues' which allow a person to browse through a shop without leaving their armchair. Until that time, though, we are mostly affected by marketers' ability to manipulate real sensory inputs along five distinct channels. In this section, we will take a brief look at some of the processes involved in the business applications of sensory stimuli.

Vision

Marketers rely heavily on visual elements in advertising, store design and packaging. Meanings are communicated on the visual channel through a product's size, styling, brightness and distinctiveness compared with competitors.

Colour in the marketplace

Colours are rich in symbolic value and cultural meanings. For example, the display of red, white and blue evokes feelings of patriotism for both British and French people. Such powerful cultural meanings make colour a central aspect of many marketing strategies. Colour choices are made with regard to packaging, advertising, and even shop fittings. Indeed, there is evidence to suggest that some colours (particularly red) are arousing while others (such as blue) are relaxing. The power of colours to evoke positive and negative feelings makes this an important consideration in advertising design. Like the colour of your teeth? Europeans have recently paid attention to a new route to pearly white teeth. Tooth whiteners (peroxide strips) in the European Union will soon be available with a 6 per cent solution (the current limit is 0.1 per cent), and this reworking of the EC Cosmetic Directive will allow consumers to switch from costly dental treatments to off-the-shelf treatments. What does having white teeth suggest to you?[6]

A special use of colour was introduced in a TV commercial by the brand Circle Coffee. This showed an orange circle with a coffee bean inside while the voiceover told the viewer to stare at the bean for 30 seconds; then, when the screen went black, a blue circle 'magically' appeared on the screen. This illusion is created by the perceptual law of complementary colours – a fitting illusion, given that another of the company's coffee brands is Blue Circle.[7]

The ability of colours to 'colour' our expectations is frequently exploited by marketers. Recently, marketers of products from beer and soft drinks to deodorant and petrol have launched new 'clear' products, which are intended to convey such qualities as purity and simplicity as a counter to overelaborate product claims.[8] Green, too, has been gaining in popularity as consumers' ecological consciousness has grown. In fact, the use of green to suggest an environmentally progressive or responsible company or product has recently come under more critical view by European consumers as 'greenwashing', the (false or misleading) portraying of environmentally-friendly attributes.[9]

Today colour is a key issue in package design. But the choice used to be made casually. The familiar Campbell's Soup can was produced in red and white because a company executive liked the football kit at a particular university! Now colour is a serious business, and companies frequently employ consultants to assist in these decisions. Osram Sylvania, the North American arm of Germany's Siemans AG has recently introduced bright and colourful icons to each of its 270 product packages in their retail automotive aftermarket of lighting. The package colour schemes denote levels of brightness, downroad sight distances, and increased peripheral vision.[10]

Some colour combinations come to be so strongly associated with a particular corporation that they become known as the company's livery, and the company may even be granted exclusive use of the colours. Eastman Kodak is one such company and has successfully protected its yellow, black and red in court. As a rule, however, this protection is granted only if there is the possibility that consumers might be confused about what they are buying if a competitor uses the same colour combination.[11]

Since the number of competing brands has proliferated for many types of products, colour can be a critical spur to sales. When introducing a white cheese as a 'sister product' to an existing blue Castello cheese, a Danish company launched it in a red package and under the name of Castello Bianco. The red package was chosen for maximum visibility and signal effect. Although taste tests were very positive, sales were disappointing. A semiotic analysis of consumer interpretations showed that the red packaging and the name gave the consumers the wrong association about the product type and its degree

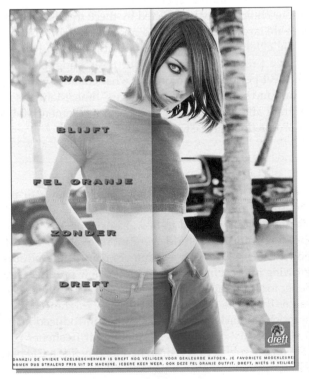

The text in the ad reads: 'Where would the bright orange be without Dreft?' Orange is the national colour of The Netherlands, so the ad simultaneously underlines the colour-protecting qualities of the product and, through the national colour code, refers to the strength of the Dutch nation.

Procter & Gamble Nederland B.V.

The slight changes in the design of Campbell's canned soups illustrate the company's efforts to keep the central, traditional features of the brand packaging while making sure that the product does not begin to look dated.

Campbell Soup Company

of sweetness (due to associations with the vermouth Martini Bianco). It was relaunched in a white packaging and with the name 'white Castello', and almost immediately sales figures more than doubled.[12]

In a given year, certain colours appear to be 'hot' and show up over and over again in clothing, home furnishings, cars, and so on. But favourite colours disappear as fast as they come, to be replaced by another set of 'hot' colours the next year or season.

Consumers' colour choices may be affected by these trends. One simple reason is that consumers' choices are largely limited by the colours available in the stores. Few people, however, realize the extent to which these 'hot' colours result from choices made by industry insiders, in a process known as colour forecasting. Colour experts in various consulting groups meet periodically to predict what colours will best reflect a season in one year's, five years' and sometimes even ten years' time. Members make colour predictions based on cultural and social trends, and these recommendations are then used by manufacturers in production forecasting.[13]

Smell

Odours can stir emotions or create a calming feeling. They can invoke memories or relieve stress. One study found that consumers who viewed ads for either flowers or chocolate and who also were exposed to flowery or chocolaty odours spent more time processing the product information and were more likely to try different alternatives within each product category.[14] Many consumers control the odours in their environments and this growing interest has spawned a lot of new products since Glade marketed the first air freshener to suburban families in 1956. Today, younger people are at the forefront of scented air as they take advantage of plug-ins, fragrance fans, diffusers, and potpourri. Sensing a growing market, Procter & Gamble introduced Febreze air products in 2004 and appealed to twentysomethings by making air freshener products seem cool – Scentstories is a Febreze dispenser P&G designed to look like a CD player, complete with 'stop' and 'play' buttons that radiate scents rather than music.[15]

Consumers' love of fragrances has contributed to a very large industry. Because this market is extremely competitive (30–40 new scents are introduced each year) and expensive (it costs an average of £30 million to introduce a new fragrance), manufacturers are scrambling to find new ways to expand the use of scents and odours in our daily lives. While traditional floral scents, such as rose and jasmine, are still widely used, newer fragrances feature such scents as melon peach (Elizabeth Arden's *Sunflowers*) and a blend of peach, mandarin orange, waterlily and white cloud rose (*Sun Moon Stars* by Karl Lagerfeld).[16] A later trend, supported by the marketing efforts of, among others, Calvin Klein, are perfumes positioned as unisex. In addition to the perfume market, home fragrance products, consisting primarily of potpourri, room sprays and atomizers, drawer liners, sachets and scented candles, represent important markets. But the use of smell goes further than that. An association of employers in the wood industry used a scratch'n'sniff card to convince potential apprentices of the advantages of smell in the wood industry compared with other professions.[17]

Sound

Music and sound are also important to marketers. Consumers spend vast amounts of money each year on compact discs and cassettes, advertising jingles maintain brand awareness and background music creates desired moods.[18] In a novel development, greetings card manufacturers are prospering by selling consumers the ability to send their own sounds to others: Hallmark Cards Inc. sells 'Recordable Greetings Cards' that allow the sender to record a personal 10-second message on a microchip. The message plays automatically when the card is opened.[19] There is also evidence that the literal sound that one makes when pronouncing a brand's name can influence perceptions of the product's attributes. English-language speaking consumers infer that brands containing the vowel sound of short 'i' are lighter than brands containing the vowel sound of 'a'.[20]

Many aspects of sound affect people's feelings and behaviours. One British company stresses the importance of the sound a packaging gives when opened, after having watched consumers open, close and reopen it several times during a test, clearly also listening to the right sound of the opening procedure.[21] Two areas of research that have widespread applications in consumer contexts are the effects of background music on mood and the influence of speaking rate on attitude change and message comprehension.

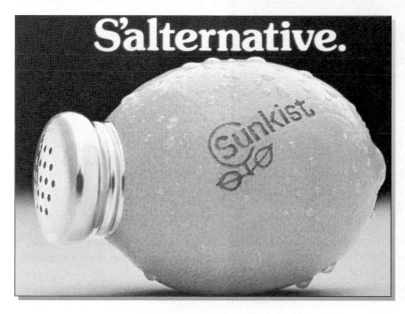

This ad metaphorically illustrates the natural quality and taste sensation of a lemon as a substitute for salt.

Sunkist Growers, Inc.

Muzak is heard by millions of people every day. This so-called 'functional music' is played in stores, shopping centres and offices either to relax or stimulate consumers. There is general agreement that muzak contributes to the well-being and buying activities of customers, but no scientific proof exists. *Time compression* is a technique used by broadcasters to manipulate perceptions of sound. It is a way to pack more information into a limited time by speeding up an announcer's voice in commercials. The speaking rate is typically accelerated to about 120 to 130 per cent of normal. Most people fail to notice this effect.

The evidence for the effectiveness of time compression is mixed. It has been shown to increase persuasion in some situations but to reduce it in others. One explanation for a positive effect is that the listener uses a person's speaking rate to infer whether the speaker is confident; people seem to think that fast talkers must know what they are talking about. Another explanation is that the listener is given less time to elaborate on the assertions made in the commercial. The acceleration disrupts normal responses to the ad and changes the cues used to form judgements about its content. This change can either hinder or facilitate attitude change, depending on other conditions.[22]

Touch

Although relatively little research has been done on the effects of tactile stimulation on consumer behaviour,[23] common observation tells us that this sensory channel is important. Consider the classic, contoured Coca-Cola bottle. The bottle was designed approximately 90 years ago to satisfy the request of a US bottler for a soft drink container that people could identify even in the dark. Touch has even been shown to be a factor in sales interactions. There are considerable cultural differences in the world as well as within Europe concerning the appropriate amount and kind of touching in interpersonal interactions. In general, northern Europeans touch less than their southern European

Just as fabrics are prized for their texture, some drinks are presented as having a luxurious 'feel'. This ad for Velvet Hot Chocolate links the chocolate drink to a well known brand of chocolate, and ties them together as 'irresistible'.

The Advertising Archives

Table 4.1 Tactile oppositions to fabrics

Perception	Male	Female	
High-class	Wool	Silk	Fine
Low-class	Denim	Cotton	↕
	Heavy	Light	Coarse

counterparts. Many British think the French shake hands for too long.[24] Sensations that reach the skin, whether from a luxurious massage or the bite of a winter wind, stimulate or relax us. Researchers even have shown that touch can influence sales interactions. In one study, diners whom waitstaff touched gave bigger tips, and the same researchers reported that food demonstrators in a supermarket who lightly touched customers had better luck in getting shoppers to try a new snack product and to redeem coupons for the brand.[25] Britain's Asda grocery chain removed the wrapping from several brands of toilet tissue in its stores so that shoppers could feel and compare textures. The result, the retailer says, was soaring sales for its own in-store brand, resulting in a 50 per cent increase in shelf space for the line.[26]

Tactile cues have symbolic meaning. People associate the textures of fabrics and other products with underlying product qualities. The perceived richness or quality of the material in clothing, bedding or upholstery is linked to its 'feel', whether it is rough or smooth, soft or stiff. A smooth fabric such as silk is equated with luxury, while denim is considered practical and durable. The vibration of a mobile phone against the owner's body signals a personal telephone call coming in, as well as some degree of respect about not disturbing others in the area. Some of these tactile/quality associations are summarized in Table 4.1. Fabrics that are composed of rare materials or that require a high degree of processing to achieve their smoothness or fineness tend to be more expensive and thus are seen as being classier. Similarly, lighter, more delicate textures are assumed to be feminine. Roughness is often positively valued for men, while smoothness is sought by women.

Taste

Our taste receptors contribute to our experience of many products. Sensory analysis is used to account for the human perception of sensory product qualities. One study used sensory analysis to assess butter biscuits: the crispness, buttery-taste, rate of melt, density, 'molar packing' (the amount of biscuit that sticks to the teeth) and the 'notes' of the biscuit, such as sweetness, saltiness or bitterness.[27]

Food companies go to great lengths to ensure that their products taste as they should. Philips' highly successful Senseo coffee machine produces a creamy head of foam on the top of a cup of home-brewed coffee.[28] Companies may use a group of 'sensory panellists' as tasters. These consumers are recruited because they have superior sensory abilities, and are then given six months' training. Or they rely on lay people, i.e. ordinary consumers. In a blind taste test, panellists rate the products of a company and its competitors on a number of dimensions. The results of such studies are important to discover both different consumer preferences and, thus, different consumer segments, and the positioning of a company or a brand in terms of the most important sensory qualities of the product.[29]

Are blind taste tests worth their salt? While taste tests often provide valuable information, their results can be misleading when it is forgotten that objective taste is only one component of product evaluation. The most famous example of this mistake concerns New Coke, Coca-Cola's answer to the Pepsi Challenge.[30] The new formulation was preferred to Pepsi in blind taste tests (in which the products were not identified) by an average of 55 per cent to 45 per cent in 17 markets, yet New Coke ran into problems when it replaced the older version. People do not buy a cola for taste alone; they are buying intangibles like brand image as well.

Sometimes taste test failures can be overcome by repositioning the product. For example, Vernor's ginger ale did poorly in a taste test against leading ginger ales. When the research team introduced it as a new type of soft drink with a tangier taste, it won easily. As an executive noted, 'People hated it because it didn't meet the preconceived expectations of what a ginger ale should be.'[31]

SENSORY THRESHOLDS

If you have ever blown a dog whistle and watched pets respond to a sound you cannot hear, you will know that there are some stimuli that people simply are not capable of perceiving. And, of course, some people are better able to pick up sensory information than are others.

▶ The science that focuses on how the physical environment is integrated into our personal, subjective world is known as **psychophysics**. By understanding some of the physical laws that govern what we are capable of responding to, this knowledge can be translated into marketing strategies.

The absolute threshold

When we define the lowest intensity of a stimulus that can be registered on a sensory
▶ channel, we speak of a threshold for that receptor. The **absolute threshold** refers to the minimum amount of stimulation that can be detected on a sensory channel. The sound emitted by a dog whistle is too high to be detected by human ears, so this stimulus is beyond our auditory absolute threshold. The absolute threshold is an important consideration in designing marketing stimuli. A hoarding might have the most entertaining story ever written, but this genius is wasted if the print is too small for passing motorists to read it.

The differential threshold

▶ The **differential threshold** refers to the ability of a sensory system to detect changes or differences between two stimuli. A commercial that is intentionally produced in black and white might be noticed on a colour television because the intensity of colour differs from the programme that preceded it. The same commercial being watched on a black-and-white television would not be seen as different and might be ignored altogether.

The issue of when and if a change will be noticed is relevant to many marketing situations. Sometimes a marketer may want to ensure that a change is noticed, such as when merchandise is offered at a discount. In other situations, the fact that a change has been made is downplayed, as in the case of price increases or when the size of a product, such as a chocolate bar, is decreased.

A consumer's ability to detect a difference between two stimuli is relative. A whispered conversation that might be unintelligible on a noisy street can suddenly become public and embarrassing knowledge in a quiet library. It is the relative difference between the decibel level of the conversation and its surroundings, rather than the loudness of the conversation itself, that determines whether the stimulus will register.

▶ The minimum change in a stimulus that can be detected is also known as the **JND**, which stands for 'just noticeable difference'. In the nineteenth century, Ernst Weber, a psychophysicist, found that the amount of change that is necessary to be noticed is related

to the original intensity of the stimulus. The stronger the initial stimulus, the greater the
▶ change must be for it to be noticed. This relationship is known as **Weber's Law**. Many
companies choose to update their packages periodically, making small changes that will
not necessarily be noticed at the time. When a product icon is updated, the manufacturer
does not want people to lose their identification with a familiar symbol.

PERCEPTUAL SELECTION

Although we live in an 'information society', we can have too much of a good thing.
Consumers are often in a state of sensory overload, exposed to far more information
than they are capable of or willing to process. People in a noisy, crowded bar or party for
several hours may feel the need to step outside periodically to take a break. A consumer
can experience a similar feeling of being overwhelmed after being forced to sift through
the claims made by hundreds of competing brands. Further, the competition for our
attention is increasing steadily with the increasing number of exposures to television
commercials and other types of advertising.

Because the brain's capacity to process information is limited, consumers are very
▶ selective about what they pay attention to. **Perceptual selectivity** means that people
attend to only a small portion of stimuli to which they are exposed. Consumers practise
a form of psychic economy, picking and choosing among stimuli, to avoid being overwhelmed by *advertising clutter*. This over-abundance of advertising stimuli highlights
two important aspects of perceptual selectivity as they relate to consumer behaviour:
exposure and attention.

▼ Marketing pitfall

Consumers and marketers are increasingly annoyed
by advertising clutter. Advertising professionals feel
that the proliferation of ads in both traditional media
as well as non-traditional locations, such as in
cinemas and on TV monitors in doctors' waiting
rooms, is threatening the quality of their work.
They fear that consumers will be so bombarded
by competing stimuli that they won't be in a receptive
frame of mind when their messages are transmitted.
Consumers are also fed up. More and more surveys
reveal that it takes a very good ad to avoid consumer
boredom and hold the attention: either a good joke,
nice aesthetics – whatever these are – or some real
information.

Exposure

▶ **Exposure** is the degree to which people notice a stimulus that is within range of their
sensory receptors. Consumers concentrate on certain stimuli, are unaware of others, and
even go out of their way to ignore some messages. An experiment by a bank illustrates
consumers' tendencies to miss or ignore information in which they are not interested.
After a law was passed in America requiring banks to explain details about money
transfer in electronic banking, the Northwestern National Bank distributed a pamphlet
to 120,000 of its customers at considerable cost to provide the required information
– hardly exciting bedtime reading. In 100 of the leaflets, a phrase in the middle of the
pamphlet offered the reader $10.00 just for finding that paragraph. Not a single person
claimed it.[32]

Selective exposure

Experience, which is the result of acquiring stimulation, is one factor that determines
how much exposure to a particular stimulus a person accepts. Perceptual filters based on
consumers' past experiences influence what we decide to process.

129

Perceptual vigilance is a factor in selective exposure. Consumers are more likely to be aware of stimuli that relate to their current needs. These needs may be conscious or unconscious. A consumer who rarely notices car ads will become very much more conscious of them when they are in the market for a new car. A newspaper ad for a fast food restaurant that would otherwise go unnoticed becomes significant when one glances at the paper during a five o'clock class.

The advent of the video recorder has allowed consumers armed with remote control fast-forward buttons to be much more selective about which TV messages they are exposed to. By 'zipping', viewers fast-forward through commercials when watching their favourite programmes. A video recorder marketed by Mitsubishi can remove the need for zipping. It distinguishes between the different types of TV signals used to broadcast programmes and commercials and automatically pauses during ads. Witness also the market success of TIVO in the UK, and other European markets, where 'tivo' has become a verb, as in, 'I just tivo'ed it instead of watching'.[33]

Zipping has enhanced the need for advertising creativity. Interesting commercials do not get zipped as frequently. Evidence indicates that viewers are willing to stop fast-forwarding to watch an appealing or novel commercial. In addition, longer commercials and those that keep a static figure on the screen (such as a brand name or a logo) appear to counteract the effects of zipping; they are unaffected by a speed increase, since the figure remains in place.[34]

Adaptation

▶ Another factor affecting exposure is **adaptation**, or the degree to which consumers continue to notice a stimulus over time. The process of adaptation occurs when consumers no longer pay attention to a stimulus because it is so familiar.[35] Almost like drug addiction, a consumer can become 'habituated' and require increasingly stronger 'doses' of a stimulus for it to continue to be noticed. For example, a consumer on the way to work might read a new advertising hoarding, but after a few days it becomes part of the passing scenery.

Several factors can lead to adaptation:

- *Intensity*: Less intense stimuli (e.g. soft sounds or dim colours) habituate because they have less of a sensory impact.
- *Duration*: Stimuli that require relatively lengthy exposure in order to be processed tend to habituate because they require a long attention span.
- *Discrimination*: Simple stimuli tend to habituate because they do not require attention to detail.
- *Exposure*: Frequently encountered stimuli tend to habituate as the rate of exposure increases.
- *Relevance*: Stimuli that are irrelevant or unimportant will habituate because they fail to attract attention.

Attention

▶ **Attention** is the degree to which consumers focus on stimuli within their range of exposure. Because consumers are exposed to so many advertising stimuli, marketers are becoming increasingly creative in their attempts to gain attention for their products. Some successful advertisers such as Apple, Nike, Gap and Dyson have created a visual identity with their television ads, and then deliver more detailed product information in other places, such as websites and newspaper stories in which third party experts provide independent reviews.[36]

A dynamic package is one way to gain this attention. Some consulting firms have established elaborate procedures to measure package effectiveness, using such instruments as an angle metre, which measures package visibility as a shopper moves down the aisle and views the package from different angles. Also, data from eye-tracking tests, in which consumers' eye movements as they look at packages and ads are followed and measured, can result in subtle but powerful changes that influence their impact. Eye-tracking tests are also used to evaluate in-store displays.[37]

Countering advertising clutter

Many marketers are attempting to counter the sensory overload caused by advertising clutter in order to call attention to their products. One expensive strategy involves buying large blocks of advertising space in order to dominate consumers' attention. IBM has experimented with buying two or three consecutive full-page newspaper ads. And Coca-Cola once bought a full five-minute block of TV commercial time on Danish television shortly before Christmas.

Other companies are using 'bookend ads', where a commercial for one product is split into parts that are separated by commercials for other products. The first part creates conflict, and the second resolves it. This technique motivates the viewer to keep watching in order to get the rest of the story. For example, a TV commercial for Tuborg's special Christmas brew beer showed a cartoon Santa Claus in his sleigh going from one side of the screen to the other. After a couple of other commercials, he reappears, this time meeting a Tuborg delivery van going in the opposite direction. He quickly turns his sleigh round and follows the van as Tuborg wishes everybody a merry Christmas and a happy new year.

Some advertisers have taken to printing part of their ads upside down to get the reader's attention. Perhaps reflecting differences in level of cultural involvement in advertising, the editor of the *Starch-Tested Copy* newsletter noted, 'I find people don't like to work at reading their ads! Americans don't like it. There's a disorienting aspect they find uncomfortable. The English, on the other hand, like it.'[38]

Another solution has been to put ads in unconventional places, where there will be less competition for attention. These include the backs of supermarket shopping trolleys, pedestrian underpasses, floors of sports stadiums and even films, as the growing interest in product placement has shown.[39] More obscure places where advertisements can be found are public toilets,[40] petrol pump handles and on the steps in the London Underground.[41] And, of course, runner Linford Christie's specially designed contact lenses with the Puma logo created a lot of publicity.[42] An executive at Campbell's Soup, commenting on the company's decision to place ads in church bulletins, noted, 'We have to shake consumers up these days in order to make them take notice . . . Television alone won't do that. Now we have to hit them with our ads where they shop and play and on their way to work.'[43] Of course, such a policy may backfire if people are getting more and more weary of the difficulty of finding advertising-free moments in their life.

Creating contrast

When many stimuli are competing to be noticed, one will receive attention to the extent that it differs from those around it. Stimuli that fall into unpredictable patterns often command a lot of attention. Size and colour differences are also powerful ways to achieve contrast. A black-and-white object in a colour ad is quite noticeable, as is a block of printed type surrounded by large amounts of white space. The size of the stimulus itself in contrast to the competition is also important.

An increasingly frequent way of creating contrast is by using advertising clichés and then giving them a twist. A mortgage company used the cliché of a homecoming soldier and the young waiting wife to advertise new restoration loans. After seeing the woman gazing out of the window and the soldier in the troop transport, he is shown finally arriving – only to hit his head hard on a low-hanging beam.[44] In general, self-referential advertisements where sympathy and credibility are created by mocking advertising or other cultural stereotypes are becoming more common.[45]

INTERPRETATION: DECIDING WHAT THINGS MEAN

▶ Interpretation refers to the meaning that people assign to sensory stimuli. Just as people differ in terms of the stimuli that they perceive, the eventual assignment of meanings to these stimuli varies as well. Two people can see or hear the same event, but their interpretation of it may be completely different.

▶ Consumers assign meaning to stimuli based on the *schema*, or set of beliefs, to which the stimulus is assigned. During a process known as priming, certain properties of a stimulus are more likely to evoke a schema than others. As evidenced by the case of Castello cheese quoted earlier, a brand name can communicate expectations about product attributes and colour consumers' perceptions of product performance by activating a schema. One somewhat disturbing example of how this works comes from America. Children aged 3 to 5 who ate McDonald's French fries served in a McDonald's bag overwhelmingly thought they tasted better than those who ate the same fries out of a plain white bag. Even carrots tasted better when they came out of a McDonald's bag – more than half the children preferred them to the same carrots served in a plain package![46]

▶ Stimulus ambiguity occurs when a stimulus is not clearly perceived or when it conveys a number of meanings. In such cases, consumers tend to project their own wishes and desires to assign meaning. Although ambiguity in product advertisements is normally seen as undesirable to marketers, it is frequently used creatively to generate contrast, paradox, controversy or interest. For example, a popular ad for Benson & Hedges cigarettes featured a group of people sitting around a dinner table, while a man wearing only pyjama bottoms stands in the background. This ambiguous character yielded valuable publicity for the company as people competed to explain the meaning of the mysterious 'pyjama man'.

Stimulus organization

People do not perceive a single stimulus in isolation. Our brains tend to relate incoming sensations to imagery of other events or sensations already in our memory based on some fundamental organizational principles. A number of perceptual principles describe how stimuli are perceived and organized.

 Marketing opportunity

Companies such as the Anglo-Dutch Unilever and France's Picard are attempting to change consumer perceptions of frozen foods. In supermarkets across the UK, it is the chiller cabinet rather than the freezer that increasing numbers of shoppers head for first. The chilled food section is where much of the innovation in convenience food is happening and where manufacturers compete most aggressively for space. Chilled food is perceived by the consumer as fresher and healthier. But, cry the champions of frozen food, it is food picked or prepared and immediately frozen that keeps its nutritional value, and does not rely on preservatives in the way that some chilled or ambient (tinned) food does. In the UK, frozen food already faces increasingly stiff competition from the chilled pretender, and suffers from stigma. 'In the UK, frozen food is seen as an inferior product, and consumer perception of freshness is warped. Frozen food is seen as the last resort, eaten when you can't get to the shops, or fed to the children.' This is less true in the other seven countries where the company operates. 'Perception of frozen food in southern Europe is that it is modern, so they have fewer hang-ups,' says Andrew Beattie, Unilever's Rotterdam-based marketing director for frozen foods.[47] Critical to the development of new perceptions regarding frozen foods is newly designed logo and packaging, with a warmer, more contemporary design, which implies that the food is the product of natural sunlight rather than factory freezing, and more pleasant lighting in the freezer area. In France, the main reasons for the surge in 'surgelé' (as frozen food is called) are two-career couples, children with overcommitted activities, and the desire to avoid spending whatever leisure time there is chopping, dredging and sautéing. In 1960, the French consumed only 2kg of frozen food products per year, while in 2001, this figure has gone up to over 30kg. Shopping for frozen packages in an antiseptic, ultra-white Picard store or in similar aisles at France's national supermarket chains may lack romance, but it is reliable.[48]

Figure 4.3 Principles of stimulus organization derived from gestalt psychology

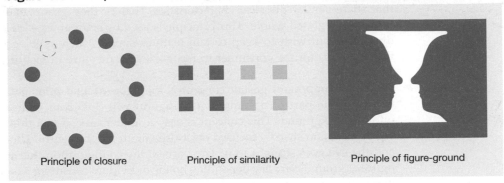

Principle of closure   Principle of similarity   Principle of figure-ground

The gestalt

▶ These principles are based on work in gestalt psychology, a school of thought maintaining that people derive meaning from the totality of a set of stimuli, rather than from any individual stimulus. The German word 'Gestalt' roughly means 'whole', 'pattern' or 'configuration', and this perspective is best summarized by the saying, 'the whole is greater than the sum of its parts'. A piecemeal perspective that analyzes each component of the stimulus separately will be unable to capture the total effect. The gestalt perspective provides several principles relating to the way stimuli are organized. Three of these principles, or perceptual tendencies, are illustrated in Figure 4.3.

▶ The gestalt principle of closure implies that consumers tend to perceive an incomplete picture as complete. That is, we tend to fill in the blanks based on our prior experience. This principle explains why most of us have no trouble reading a neon sign, even if one or two of its letters are burned out, or filling in the blanks in an incomplete message. The principle of closure is also at work when we hear only part of a jingle or theme. Utilization of the principle of closure in marketing strategies encourages audience participation, which increases the chance that people will attend to the message.

This billboard for Wrangler jeans makes creative use of the figure-ground principle.
BooneOakley Advertising

▶   The **principle of similarity** tells us that consumers tend to group together objects that share similar physical characteristics. That is, they group like items into sets to form an integrated whole. This principle is used by companies who have extended product lines, but wish to keep certain features similar, such as the shape of a bottle, so that it is easy for the consumer to recognize that they are in fact buying a shampoo of brand X.

▶   Another important gestalt concept is the **figure-ground principle** (see Wrangler ad), in which one part of a stimulus (the figure) will dominate while other parts recede into the background. This concept is easy to understand if one thinks of a photograph with a clear and sharply focused object (the figure) in the centre. The figure is dominant, and the eye goes straight to it. The parts of the configuration that will be perceived as figure or ground can vary depending on the individual consumer as well as other factors. Similarly, in marketing messages that use the figure-ground principle, a stimulus can be made the focal point of the message or merely the context that surrounds the focus.

The role of symbolism in interpretation

When we try to make sense of a marketing stimulus, whether a distinctive package, an elaborately staged television commercial or perhaps a model on the cover of a magazine, we do so by interpretation of its meaning in the light of associations we have with these images. For this reason much of the meaning we take away is influenced by what we make of the symbolism we perceive. After all, on the surface many marketing images have virtually no literal connection to actual products. What does a cowboy have to do with a bit of tobacco rolled into a paper tube? How can a celebrity such as the football star Gary Lineker enhance the image of a potato crisp, or can Jamie Oliver do a good job for Sainsbury's?[49]

▶   For assistance in understanding how consumers interpret the meanings of symbols, some marketers are turning to a field of study known as **semiotics**, which examines the correspondence between signs and symbols and their role in the assignment of meaning.[50] Semiotics is important to the understanding of consumer behaviour, since consumers use products to express their social identities. Products have learned meanings, and we rely on advertising to work out what those meanings are. As one set of researchers put it, 'advertising serves as a kind of culture/consumption dictionary; its entries are products, and their definitions are cultural meanings'.[51]

According to the semiotician Charles Sanders Peirce, every message has three basic components: an object, a sign and an interpretant. A marketing message such as a Marlboro
▶   ad can be read on different levels. On the lowest level of reading, the **object** would be the
▶   product that is the focus of the message (Marlboro cigarettes). The **sign** is the sensory imagery that represents the intended meanings of the object (the contents of the ad, in
▶   this case, the cowboy). The **interpretant** is the meaning derived (this man smokes these cigarettes). But this man is not any man. He is a cowboy – and not just any cowboy. The interpretant 'man (cowboy) smoking these cigarettes' in itself becomes a sign, especially since we have already seen many examples of these ads from this company. So, on the second, connotative level, this sign refers to the fictive personality of 'the Marlboro Man', and its interpretant consists of all the connotations attached to the Marlboro Man, for example his being a 'rugged, individualistic American'. On the third level, called the ideological level, the interpretant of the 'rugged, individualistic American' becomes a sign for what is stereotypically American. So its object is 'America', and the interpretant all the ideas and characteristics that we might consider as typically and quintessentially American. This semiotic relationship is shown in Figure 4.4. By means of such a chain of meanings, the Marlboro ad both borrows from and contributes to reinforcing a fundamental 'myth of America'.

From the semiotic perspective of Peirce, signs are related to objects in one of three ways. They can resemble objects, be connected to them with some kind of causal or other relation, or be conventionally tied to them.

Figure 4.4 Relationship of components in semiotic analysis of meaning

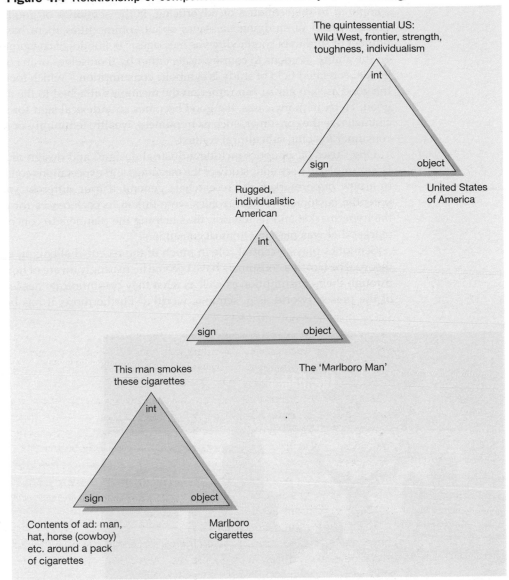

▶ [52]An **icon** is a sign that resembles the product in some way (e.g. Apple Computers
▶ uses the image of an apple to represent itself). An **index** is a sign that is connected to a
product because they share some property (e.g. the pine tree on certain cleaning products
▶ conveys the shared property of fresh, natural scent). A **symbol** is a sign that is related
to a product through purely conventional associations (e.g. the Mercedes star which in
addition to the Mercedes-Benz company provides associations with German industrial
quality and ingenuity).

The use of symbols provides a powerful means for marketers to convey product
attributes to consumers. For example, expensive cars, designer fashions and diamond
jewellery – all widely recognized symbols of success – frequently appear in ads to
associate products with affluence or sophistication. The rhetoric of advertising is an
additional field of analysis which has been useful for the discussion of how advertising
communicates its messages.[53] Semiotic analysis of ads has been connected to product
and brand life-cycles in order to establish some guidelines about when to use the most
complex advertising forms.[54]

One aspect of the semiotics of consumption, which used to be relatively neglected compared to the semiotics of advertising, is the semiotics of goods as such. In recent years, instead of studying messages about commodities there has been an increased number of studies of commodities as messages.[55] Semiotics of consumer goods, then, focus on the ability of goods to communicate either by themselves or in connection with other goods. A related field of study is symbolic consumption,[56] which focuses not so much on the good as sign per se, but rather on the meanings attached to the act of consuming the good. Here, in many cases, the good becomes an indexical sign for some attributes that characterize the consumer, such as trendiness, wealth, femininity or others that place the consumer in some subcultural context.

Other uses of semiotics include industrial design[57] and design of distribution outlets. For example, in a semiotic study of the meanings and expectations consumers would attach to a new hypermarket, the researchers generated four different value profiles among potential customers. These profiles were linked to preferences for different designs of the hypermarket and its interior, thus helping the planners to conceive a type of hypermarket that was pleasing to most consumers.[58]

Semiotics plays a central role in much of the recent challenging consumer behaviour theory. The fact that consumers have become increasingly aware of how they communicate through their consumption as well as what they communicate has led to the designation of the present world as a 'semiotic world'.[59] Furthermore, it has been argued that we

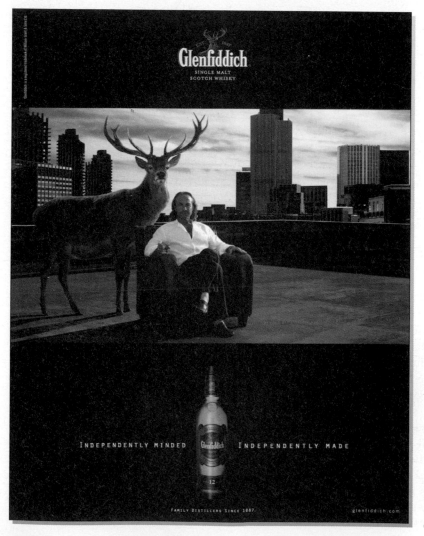

An illustration of how to read an advertisement semiotically.
The Advertising Archives

feel more confident in creating our own messages rather than just following what is proposed by marketing or fashion statements. This tendency to eclecticism means that we are increasingly likely to match things, such as articles of clothing, furniture or even lifestyles that traditionally have not been perceived as fitting together.

As we have already argued, one of the hallmarks of modern advertising is that it creates a condition where advertising is becoming self-referential. An increasing number of ads and commercials are referring, often ironically or tongue-in-cheek, to other advertisements, and thus creating a universe of their own, which in many ways is independent from the goods actually advertised. Advertising thus becomes an art in itself and is appreciated as such rather than as deceptive information about products.[60] **Hyperreality** refers to the becoming real of what is initially simulation or 'hype'.[61] Advertisers create new relationships between objects and interpretants by inventing new connections between products and benefits, such as equating Marlboro cigarettes with the American frontier spirit.[62] To a large extent, over time the relationship between the symbol and reality is increasingly difficult to discern, and the 'artificial' associations between advertisement symbols, product symbols and the real world may take on a life of their own.

For example, Tasters' Choice coffee perfected the concept of an ongoing series of 'soap opera' commercials where a romantic relationship is slowly cultivated between two actors, a commercial form later adopted by other coffee brands such as Nestlé's Gold Blend.

Hyperreality will be discussed again in the final chapter of the book because it has been linked to the concept of postmodernism, the idea that we are living in a period of radical cultural change where certain hitherto dominant features and assumptions of modern societies are challenged.

Consumer behaviour as I see it . . .

How much would you be willing to pay for a knitted cap? Perhaps $13,200? That's how much a music fan paid for a cap worn on stage by U2's guitarist, The Edge. And – would someone really pay £90,100 for a ten-year-old BMW with 70,000 miles on it? That's what a sport fan shelled out for the car formerly owned by football star David Beckham.

It's interesting that, even though two knitted caps or two cars may look and perform exactly the same, one can be worth ten thousand times more than the other. Although there's little or no perceptual difference between a car owned by a celebrity and one sold on a used-car lot, why are people willing to pay more for the one driven by the star?

Professor Kent Grayson
Northwestern University

The answer comes from an American philosopher named Charles Peirce, who founded a school of thought called 'semiotics' in the late 1800s. As Peirce noted, when we perceive things, we don't just simply allow sights, sounds and smells to come directly into our senses from the outside world. Instead, we're always filtering and interpreting this information in relation to other things and experiences in our lives. For example, when someone asks us to buy a product, we think not only about whether the product is similar in appearance to other products (what Peirce called iconicity) but also how the product is physically connected to other things (indexicality) and what the product means to us and to other people (symbolism).

In other words, although two different knitted caps may be quite iconic (similar in appearance), they can still have very different marketplace values because their indexicality is different: one cap is connected to The Edge and the other isn't. Because of this difference, the symbolism is also different – the cap worn by the U2 guitarist means something different to an identical cap sold in a department store. So if you're ever at a music concert and the singer throws you something that you sell for a mint on eBay . . . you can thank Charles Peirce's semiotics.

CHAPTER SUMMARY

- Perception is the process by which physical sensations such as sights, sounds and smells are selected, organized and interpreted. The eventual interpretation of a stimulus allows it to be assigned meaning. A perceptual map is a widely used marketing tool which evaluates the relative standing of competing brands along relevant dimensions.

- Marketing stimuli have important sensory qualities. We rely on colours, odours, sounds, tastes and even the 'feel' of products when forming evaluations of them.

- Not all sensations successfully make their way through the perceptual process. Many stimuli compete for our attention, and the majority are not noticed or comprehended.

- People have different thresholds of perception. A stimulus must be presented at a certain level of intensity before it can be detected by sensory receptors. In addition, a consumer's ability to detect whether two stimuli are different (the differential threshold) is an important issue in many marketing contexts, such as changing a package design, altering the size of a product or reducing its price.

- Some of the factors that determine which stimuli (above the threshold level) are perceived are the amount of exposure to the stimulus, how much attention it generates and how it is interpreted. In an increasingly crowded stimulus environment, advertising clutter occurs when too many marketing-related messages compete for attention.

- A stimulus that is attended to is not perceived in isolation. It is classified and organized according to principles of perceptual organization. These principles are guided by a gestalt, or overall, pattern. Specific grouping principles include closure, similarity and figure-ground relationships.

- The final step in the process of perception is interpretation. We make sense of the world through the interpretation of signs: icons, indexes and symbols. This interpretation is often shared by others, thus forming common languages and cultures. The degree to which the symbolism is consistent with our previous experience affects the meaning we assign to related objects. Every marketing message contains a relationship between the product, the sign or symbol, and the interpretation of meaning. A semiotic analysis involves the correspondence between message elements and the meaning of signs.

- Signs function on several levels. The intended meaning may be literal (e.g. an icon like a street sign with a picture of children playing). The meaning may be indexical; it relies on shared characteristics (e.g. the horizontal stripe in a stop sign means do not pass beyond this). Finally, meaning can be conveyed by a symbol, where an image is given meaning by convention or by agreement by members of a society (e.g. stop signs are octagonal, while give way signs are triangular).

▶ KEY TERMS

Absolute threshold (p. 128)

Adaptation (p. 130)

Attention (p. 130)

Differential threshold (p. 128)

Exposure (p. 129)

Figure-ground principle (p. 134)

Gestalt psychology (p. 133)

Hedonic consumption (p. 121)

Hyperreality (p. 137)

Icon (p. 135)

Index (p. 135)

Interpretant (p. 134)

Interpretation (p. 132)

JND (p. 128)

Object (p. 134)

Perception (p. 118)

Perceptual map (p. 120)

Perceptual selectivity (p. 129)

Priming (p. 132)

Principle of closure (p. 133)

Principle of similarity (p. 134)

Psychophysics (p. 128)

Schema (p. 119)

Semiotics (p. 134)

Sensation (p. 118)

Sign (p. 134)

Stimulus ambiguity (p. 132)

Symbol (p. 135)

Weber's Law (p. 129)

▶ CONSUMER BEHAVIOUR CHALLENGE

1 Many studies have shown that our sensory detection abilities decline as we grow older. Discuss the implications of the absolute threshold for marketers attempting to appeal to the elderly.

2 Interview three to five male and three to five female friends regarding their perceptions of both men's and women's fragrances. Construct a perceptual map for each set of products. Based on your map of perfumes, do you see any areas that are not adequately served by current offerings? What (if any) gender differences did you obtain regarding both the relevant dimensions used by raters and the placement of specific brands along these dimensions?

3 Assume that you are a consultant for a marketer who wants to design a package for a new premium chocolate bar targeted to an affluent market. What recommendations would you provide in terms of such package elements as colour, symbolism and graphic design? Give the reasons for your suggestions.

4 Do you believe that marketers have the right to use any or all public spaces to deliver product messages? Where would you draw the line in terms of places and products that should be restricted?

5 Find one ad that is rich in symbolism and perform a semiotic analysis of it. Identify each type of sign used in the ad and the product qualities being communicated by each. Comment on the effectiveness of the signs that are used to communicate the intended message.

6 Using magazines archived in the library, track the packaging of a specific brand over time. Find an example of gradual changes in package design that may have been below the JND.

7 Collect a set of current ads for one type of product (e.g. personal computers, perfumes, laundry detergents or athletic shoes) from magazines, and analyze the colours employed. Describe the images conveyed by different colours, and try to identify any consistency across brands in terms of the colours used in product packaging or other aspects of the ads.

8 Look through a current magazine and select one ad that captures your attention over the others. Give the reasons why.

9 Find ads that utilize the techniques of contrast and novelty. Give your opinion of the effectiveness of each ad and whether the technique is likely to be appropriate for the consumers targeted by the ad.

For additional material see the companion website at **www.pearsoned.co.uk/solomon**

NOTES

1. Kim Foltz, 'Campaign on harmony backfires for Benetton', *New York Times* (20 November 1989): D8.

2. For an overview of Unilever's successful Axe/Lynx after-shave campaign, see: http://axeads.blogspot.com/2007/04/bomchickawahwah-france.html; also, as part of the masculine perceptions that Axe is trying to portray, the company has enlisted the help of Husky Injection Molding company, to rework the packaging of Axe. See: 'Unilever chooses Husky hot runners for redesigned Axe Lynx closure', at http://www.husky.ca/abouthusky/news/content-1085-106.html

3. Jerome S. Bruner, 'On perceptual readiness', *Psychological Review* 64 (March 1957): 123–52.

4. Synder, William R., *Wall Street Journal* (18 April 2008), http://online.wsj.com/article/SB120846638155724155.html

5. Elizabeth C. Hirschman and Morris B. Holbrook, 'Hedonic consumption: Emerging concepts, methods, and propositions', *Journal of Marketing* 46 (Summer 1982): 92–101.

6. Clare Dowdy, 'Hollywood smiles spread across Europe', *Financial Times* (17 March 2004), http://news.ft.com/servlet/ContentServer?pagename=FT.com/StoryFT/FullStory&c=StoryFT&cid=1079419714360&p=1057562408029.

7. *Markedsføring* 1 (1995): 18.

8. 'Crystal clear persuasion', *Tufts University Diet and Nutrition Letter* (January 1993): 1.

9. See up-to-date examples of greenwashing at: http://www.sourcewatch.org/index.php?title=Greenwashing/Europe

10. 'Sylvania's enlightened redesign overhauls 270 items, embracing sustainability' at: http://www.shelfimpact.com/archives/2008/09/sylvanias_enlightened_redesign_1.php

11. Meg Rosen and Frank Alpert, 'Protecting your business image: The Supreme Court rules on trade dress', *Journal of Consumer Marketing* 11(1) (1994): 50–5.

12. 'Ny emballage og nyt navn fordoblede salget', *Markedsføring* 12 (1992): 24.

13. See: http://www.fashiontrendsetter.com/content/color_trends/2007/lenzing-ss-2009.html for colour predictions.

14. Deborah J. Mitchell, Barbara E. Kahn, and Susan C. Knasko, 'There's something in the air: Effects of congruent or incongruent ambient odor on consumer decision-making', *Journal of Consumer Research* 22 (September 1995): 229–38; for a review of olfactory cues in store environments, see also Eric R. Spangenberg, Ayn E. Crowley, and Pamela W. Henderson, 'Improving the store environment: Do olfactory cues affect evaluations and behaviors?', *Journal of Marketing* 60 (April 1996): 67–80.

15. Thom Forbes, 'P&G Noses Its Way into Youthful Air Freshener Market' (3 January 2007), available from mediapost.com, accessed 3 January 2007.

16. Suein L. Hwang, 'Seeking scents that no one has smelled', *The Wall Street Journal* (10 August 1994): B12.

17. 'En duft af træ', *Markedsføring* 13 (1996): 6.

18. Gail Tom, 'Marketing with music', *Journal of Consumer Marketing* 7 (Spring 1990): 49–53; J. Vail, 'Music as a marketing tool', *Advertising Age* (4 November 1985): 24.

19. Joan E. Rigdon, 'Hallmark cards can send a message that's a real earful for a loved one', *The Wall Street Journal* (5 November 1993): A5I.

20. N.T. Tavassoli and Y.H. Lee, 'The differential interaction of auditory and visual advertising elements within Chinese and English', *Journal of Marketing Research* 40(4) (November 2003): 468–80.

21. *Marketing* (3 April 1997).

22. For research in time compression, see James MacLachlan and Michael H. Siegel, 'Reducing the costs of television commercials by use of time compression', *Journal of Marketing Research* 17 (February 1980): 52–7; James MacLachlan, 'Listener perception of time compressed spokespersons', *Journal of Advertising Research* 2 (April/May 1982): 47–51; Danny L. Moore, Douglas Hausknecht and Kanchana Thamodaran, 'Time compression, response opportunity, and persuasion', *Journal of Consumer Research* 13 (June 1986): 85–99.

23. J. Peck and T.L. Childers, 'Individual differences in haptic information processing: The "need for touch" scale', *Journal of Consumer Research* 30(3) (2003): 430–42.

24. Jean-Claude Usunier, *Marketing Across Cultures* (Pearson, 2005).

25. Jacob Hornik, 'Tactile stimulation and consumer response', *Journal of Consumer Research* 19 (December 1992): 449–58.

26. Sarah Ellison and Erin White, ' "Sensory" marketers say the way to reach shoppers is the nose', *Advertising* (24 November 2000): 1–3.

27. Anne C. Bech, Erling Engelund, Hans Jørn Juhl, Kai Kristensen and Carsten Stig Poulsen, 'QFood. Optimal Design of Food Products', *MAPP Working Paper* no. 19 (Aarhus: The Aarhus School of Business, 1994); Hans Jørn Juhl, 'A Sensory Analysis of Butter Cookies – An Application of Generalized Procrustes Analysis', *MAPP Working Paper* no. 20 (Aarhus: The Aarhus School of Business, 1994).

28. Richard Tomkins, 'Products that aim for your heart', *Financial Times* (28 April 2005), http://news.ft.com/cms/s/d92c1660-b809-11d9-bc7c-00000e2511c8.html. Senseo has been so successful with this new product that they have a website for several European countries. See: http://www.senseo.com/content/default.html.

29. Andreas Scharf, 'Positionierung neuer bzw. modifizierter Nahrungsund Genußmittel durch integrierte Marktund Sensorik-forschung', *Marketing ZFP* 1 (1st quarter 1995): 5–17.

30. See Tim Davis, 'Taste tests: Are the blind leading the blind?' *Beverage World* (April 1987) 3: 43.

31. Quoted in Davis, *ibid.*: 44.

32. '$10 sure thing', *Time* (4 August 1980): 51.

33. David Kilburn, 'Japanese VCR edits out the ads', *Advertising Age* (20 August 1990): 16. For TIVO in the UK, go to http://archive.tivocommunity.com/tivo-vb/history/forum/14-1.html. TIVO's corporate website: http://www.tivo.com/0.0.asp (accessed 5 August 2005). See also: Lamb, Gregory M., 'Screen wars: stealing TV's "eyeball" share', *Christian Science Monitor*, 15 August 2008, at: http://features.csmonitor.com/innovation/2008/08/15/screen-wars-stealing-tv%E2%80%99s-%E2%80%98eyeball%E2%80%99-share/

34. Craig Reiss, 'Fast-forward ads deliver', *Advertising Age* (27 October 1986) 2: 3; Steve Sternberg, 'VCR's: impact and implications', *Marketing and Media Decisions* 22 (December 1987) 5: 100.

35. Martin O'Neill and Adrian Palmer, 'The Effects of Survey Timing Upon Visitor Perceptions of Destination Service Quality', in Darach Turley and Stephen Brown (eds), *European Advances in Consumer Research: All Changed, Changed Utterly?* 6 (Valadosta, GA: Association for Consumer Research, 2003): 37–41.

36. Gary Silverman, 'Image is everything in attention wars', *Financial Times* (17 January 2005), http://news.ft.com/cms/s/23a18ba4-68b3-11d9-9183-00000e2511c8,ft_acl=ftalert_ftarc_ftcol_ftfree_ftindsum_ftmywap_ftprem_ftspecial_ftsurvey_ftworldsub_ftym.

37. 'It's all in the mind', *Marketing* (27 March 1997): 31–4.

38. Quoted in Stuart Elliott, 'When up is down, does it sell?' *New York Times* (21 February 1992) 2: D1.

39. 'Reklamer i det skjulte', *Markedsføring* 7 (1996): 28.

40. 'Toilet ads', *Marketing* (5 December 1996): 11.

41. 'Rare media well done', *Marketing* (16 January 1997): 31.

42. Christian Alsted and Hanne Hartvig Larsen, 'Toward a semiotic typology of advertising forms', *Marketing and Semiotics. Selected Papers from the Copenhagen Symposium*, Hanne Hartvig Larsen, David Glen Mick and Christian Alsted (eds) (Copenhagen: Handelshøjskolens forlag, 1991): 75–103.

43. Stephen Tompkins, 'By your adverts ye shall be known', http://news.bbc.co.uk/2/hi/uk_news/magazine/4244958.stm (14 September 2005).

44. 'Realkredit for mennesker', *Markedsføring* 4 (1996): 10.

45. Stephen Brown, *Postmodern Marketing* (London: Routledge, 1995); see also: (2005) 'The modern rules of advertising?' http://news.bbc.co.uk/2/hi/uk_news/magazine/4204412.stm

46. Bakalar Nicholas, 'If It Says McDonald's, Then It Must Be Good', *New York Times Online Edition*, accessed 14 August 2007.

47. Clare Dowdy, 'A fresh look inside the shop freezer', *Financial Times* (24 March 2004), http://news.ft.com/servlet/ContentServer?pagename=FT.com/StoryFT/FullStory&c=StoryFT&cid=1079419893700&p=1059480266913.

48. Elaine Sciolino, 'Foie gras in the freezer? Just don't tell anyone!', *The New York Times* (19 December 2002), http://www.nytimes.com/2002/12/19/international/europe/19PARI.html?ex=1041353523&ei=1&en=4560794b5f85c27c.

49. Apparently, many consumers think the answer is 'No!' See http://news.bbc.co.uk/2/hi/talking_point/3270473.stm for a discussion on whether celebrities should endorse 'junk food'. See also: (Spring 2008) 'Using celebrities to endorse products: What NOT to do', http://www.pannone-services.com/Subscription-Management/documents/celeritas/Spring-2008.htm

50. See David Mick, 'Consumer research and semiotics: Exploring the morphology of signs, symbols, and significance', *Journal of Consumer Research* 13 (September 1986): 196–213.

51. Teresa J. Domzal and Jerome B. Kernan, 'Reading advertising: The what and how of product meaning', *Journal of Consumer Marketing* 9 (Summer 1992): 48–64, at 49.

52. Winfried Nöth, *Handbook of Semiotics* (London: Sage, 1994); David Mick, 'Consumer research and semiotics', *op. cit.*; Charles Sanders Peirce, in Charles Hartshorne, Paul Weiss and Arthur W. Burks (eds), *Collected Papers* (Cambridge, MA: Harvard University Press, 1931–58).

53. Jacques Durand, 'Rhetorical Figures in the Advertising Image', in Jean Umiker-Sebeok (ed.), *Marketing and Semiotics. New Directions in the Study of Signs for Sale* (Berlin: Mouton de Gruyter, 1987): 295–318.

54. Alsted and Larsen, 'Toward a semiotic typology of advertising forms', *op. cit.*

55. Winfried Nöth, 'The language of commodities. Groundwork for a semiotics of consumer goods', *International Journal of Research in Marketing* 4 (1988): 173–86.

56. See the early introduction of the field: Elizabeth C. Hirschman and Morris B. Holbrook (eds), *Symbolic Consumer Behavior* (Ann Arbor, MI: Association for Consumer Research, 1981).

57. Odile Solomon, 'Semiotics and marketing. New directions in industrial design applications', *International Journal of Research in Marketing* 4 (1988): 201–15.

58. *Ibid.*

59. James Ogilvy, 'This postmodern business', *Marketing and Research Today* (February 1990): 4–22.

60. Chantal Cinquin, 'Homo Coca-Colens: From Marketing to Semiotics and Politics', in Umiker-Sebeok (ed.), *Marketing and Semiotics, op. cit.*: 485–95.

61. A. Fuat Firat and Alladi Venkatesh, 'Postmodernity: The age of marketing', *International Journal of Research in Marketing* 10(3) (1993): 227–49.

62. Jean Baudrillard, *Simulations* (New York: Semiotext(e), 1983).

5

The self

Gareth, a marketing director, is a happily married man, and his two children aged ten and nine provide immense joy in his life. However, at 42 he feels younger than his years, and somewhat anxious about his totally family-oriented life – he has a nice house, a magnificent garden and takes regular family holidays in rural France. But he has begun to feel the loss of his previous, extravagant, carefree life, one in which he perceived himself to be a well-dressed, admired individual of good taste and discernment who always turned heads when he entered the room. He is apprehensive that his 'Gareth the family man' role has totally taken over his life's spirit. It's a life he loves and one which has his complete commitment, but one which he also views as 'prudent and sensible'.

Some months into the development of these feelings, Gareth is contacted by his company's personnel department about replacing his company car. Three years earlier he had selected a sensible Audi 80 with the needs of the family in mind. In the meantime, his wife has bought a Volvo Estate, which is always used for family travel. He has an exorbitant budget allocated to car purchase, due to his long-term commitment and excellent contribution to company performance over the last 18 months. As a result he can select almost any car he desires. After a prolonged search and extensive thought he decides on a Porsche Boxster.

The Porsche Boxster, a well-designed and admired car for the driver of good taste and discernment, has the image of a sporty, confident, powerful individual. The current press campaign displays a successful 30-something man being admired at the traffic lights, in the office car parks *and* at the local school collecting his children. Whilst driving home Gareth plays his CD collection at full volume, exceeds the legal speed limit when he believes it is 'safe' to do so, and generally feels more like the much-revered Gareth who graduated some 20 years ago. Now to consider trying some of those men's cosmetics and moisturizers that he's read so much about lately in *Maxim*, *GQ*, *Esquire* and *FHM* magazines . . .

CAROLYN STRONG, University of Bath

Gareth is not alone in feeling that his self-image and possessions affect his 'value' as a person. Consumers' insecurities about their appearance are rampant: it has been estimated that 72 per cent of men and 85 per cent of women are unhappy with at least one aspect of their appearance.[1] Even among married couples, the sense of presenting one's self is guarded. When it comes to being naked in front of one's partner, one-third of women are too shy to take their clothes off in front of their husband. In the same study, 80 per cent of women reported having real difficulty in showering or changing clothes in front of other women in the gym.[2] Reflecting this discontent, new cosmetics for men and new clinical 'beauty procedures' have grown rapidly in Europe in the past few years, and revenues for men's cosmetics are projected to approach €1 billion![3] Many products, from cars to aftershave, are bought because the person is trying to highlight or hide some aspect of the self. In this chapter, we will focus on how consumers' feelings about themselves shape their consumption habits, particularly as they strive to fulfil their society's expectations about how a male or female should look and act.

Does the self exist?

The 1980s were called the 'Me Decade' because for many this time was marked by an absorption with the self. While it seems natural to think about each consumer having a self, this concept is actually a relatively new way of regarding people and their relationship to society. The idea that each human life is unique, rather than a part of a group, developed in late medieval times (between the eleventh and fifteenth centuries in Europe). The notion that the self is an object to be pampered is even more recent. In addition, the emphasis on the unique nature of the self is much greater in Western societies.[4] Many Eastern cultures by contrast stress the importance of a collective self, where the person's identity is derived in large measure from their social group.

Both Eastern and Western cultures see the self as divided into an inner, private self and an outer, public self. But where they differ is in terms of which part is seen as the 'real you'. The West tends to subscribe to an independent construal of the self which emphasizes the inherent separateness of each individual. Non-Western cultures, in contrast, tend to focus on an interdependent self where one's identity is largely defined by the relationships one has with others.[5]

For example, a Confucian perspective stresses the importance of 'face' – others' perceptions of the self and maintaining one's desired status in their eyes. One dimension of face is *mien-tzu* – reputation achieved through success and ostentation. Some Asian cultures developed explicit rules about the specific garments and even colours that certain social classes and occupations were allowed to display, and these live on today in Japanese style manuals which provide very detailed instructions for dressing and for addressing a particular individual.[6] That orientation is at odds with such Western practices as 'casual Fridays', which encourage employees to express their unique selves. To illustrate these cross-cultural differences further, a recent Roper Starch Worldwide survey compared consumers in 30 countries to see which were the most and least vain. Women living in Venezuela topped the charts: 65 per cent said they thought about their appearance all the time.[7] Other high-scoring countries included Russia and Mexico. In the UK, a study of image consciousness showed that women in Liverpool check their appearance up to 71 times a day, while men check their appearance up to 66 times daily. Overall, London was the most 'image conscious' city in the survey.[8]

The self can be understood from many different theoretical vantage points. As you will read about in Chapter 6, a psychoanalytical or Freudian perspective regards the self as a system of competing forces riddled with conflict. Chapter 7 (Learning and Memory) discusses the point that behaviourists tend to regard the self as a collection of conditioned responses. From a cognitive orientation, the self is an information-processing system, an organizing force that serves as a nucleus around which new information is processed.[9]

Self-concept

▶ The **self-concept** refers to the beliefs a person holds about their attributes, and how they evaluate these qualities. While one's overall self-concept may be positive, there are certainly parts of the self that are evaluated more positively than others. For example, Gareth felt better about his professional identity than he did about his pending 'middle age' identity.

Components of the self-concept

The self-concept is a very complex structure. It is composed of many attributes, some of which are given greater emphasis when the overall self is being evaluated. Attributes of self-concept can be described along such dimensions as their content (for example, facial attractiveness vs. mental aptitude), positivity or negativity (i.e. self-esteem), intensity, stability over time and accuracy (that is, the degree to which one's self-assessment corresponds to reality).[10] As we will see later in the chapter, consumers' self-assessments can be quite distorted, especially with regard to their physical appearance.

Self-esteem

Self-esteem refers to the positivity of a person's self-concept. People with low self-esteem do not expect that they will perform very well, and they will try to avoid embarrassment, failure or rejection. In developing a new line of snack cakes, for example, Sara Lee found that consumers low in self-esteem preferred portion-controlled snack items because they felt they lacked self-control.[11] In contrast, people with high self-esteem expect to be successful, will take more risks and are more willing to be the centre of attention.[12] Self-esteem is often related to acceptance by others. As you probably remember, teenagers who are members of high-status groups have higher self-esteem than their excluded classmates.[13] Alberto-Culver uses a self-esteem appeal to promote a new product that reflects our changing society: Soft & Beautiful Just for Me Texture Softener, an alternative to hair pressing or relaxing. It is targeted to Caucasian mothers who don't know how to care for the hair of their multiracial children who have 'hair texture' issues. The self-esteem portion of the campaign, dubbed 'Love Yourself. Love Your Hair', includes a website, **texturesoftener.com** that offers 'conversation starters' to help parents find ways to talk to their daughters about self-image.[14]

Marketing communications can influence a consumer's level of self-esteem. Exposure to ads can trigger a process of *social comparison*, where the person tries to evaluate their self by comparing it to the people depicted in these artificial images. This form of comparison appears to be a basic human motive, and many marketers have tapped into this need by supplying idealized images of happy, attractive people who just happen to be using their products.

The social comparison process was illustrated in a study which showed that female college students do tend to compare their physical appearance with advertising models. Furthermore, study participants who were exposed to beautiful women in advertisements afterwards expressed lowered satisfaction with their own appearance, as compared to controls.[15] Another study demonstrated that young women's perceptions of their own body shapes and sizes can be altered after being exposed to as little as 30 minutes of television programming.[16] Finally, in what would seem to be a counter-intuitive finding, a recent study showed that while female subjects felt badly about themselves after viewing ads with thin female models, they also evaluated the brands being paired with the thin models more highly. Further, the subjects who saw ads depicting normal weight models did not feel bad about themselves, but they did rate the brands lower.[17]

Self-esteem advertising attempts to change product attitudes by stimulating positive feelings about the self.[18] One strategy is to challenge the consumer's self-esteem and then show a linkage to a product that will provide a remedy. Sometimes compliments are derived by comparing the person to others. One recent European advertising campaign even took to comparing different European nationalities, with the focus on self-esteem. British women face a stereotype: they are the plump ones on the beaches of Europe. Until now, that image has been fodder for jokes – not an advertising campaign. Slim-Fast, the diet brand, is running ads that rally British women to lose weight or lose face to sexier Continental counterparts in France, Spain and Sweden. One Slim-Fast ad is a photo of a French model and reads, 'I love British women. They make me look great.' Another spot shows a gorgeous Spanish woman: 'Face it, British women, it's not last year's bikini getting smaller.' One proposed ad read: 'You've got to be brave to share the beach with me.' After focus groups found it too insulting, the advertising agency softened the copy by making it more collective. It became: 'British women are so brave sharing the beach with us.' They also dropped the line, 'I bet your boyfriend thinks I look great in this.'[19]

Real and ideal selves

Self-esteem is influenced by a process where the consumer compares their actual standing on some attribute to some ideal. A consumer might ask, 'Am I as attractive as
▶ I would like to be?' 'Do I make as much money as I should?' and so on. The **ideal self**
▶ is a person's conception of how they would like to be, while the **actual self** refers to our more realistic appraisal of the qualities we have or lack. We choose some products because we think they are consistent with our actual self, whereas we buy others to help us to reach more of an ideal standard. And we often engage in a process of
▶ **impression management** where we work hard to 'manage' what others think of us by strategically choosing clothing and other cues that will put us in a good light.[20]

The ideal self is partly moulded by elements of the consumer's culture, such as heroes or people depicted in advertising who serve as models of achievement or appearance.[21] Products may be purchased because they are believed to be instrumental in helping us achieve these goals. Some products are chosen because they are perceived to be consistent with the consumer's actual self, while others are used to help reach the standard set by the ideal self. In a recent study looking at the willingness of young healthy adults to take (legal) drugs to enhance their social, emotional, and cognitive traits, people were much more reluctant to take drugs which promised to enhance traits that they considered fundamental to their self identity (social comfort), and more likely to take drugs which were viewed as being less central to their self identity, such as performance enhancing drugs for memory. Advertising messages which promoted 'enabling' rather than 'enhancing' were more favourably received as well. Apparently, boosting one's ability to concentrate is more easily accepted than boosting one's mood![22]

Fantasy: bridging the gap between the selves

While most people experience a discrepancy between their real and ideal selves, for some consumers this gap is larger than for others. These people are especially good targets for
▶ marketing communications that employ *fantasy* appeals.[23] A **fantasy** or daydream is a self-induced shift in consciousness, which is sometimes a way of compensating for a lack of external stimulation or of escaping from problems in the real world.[24] Many products and services are successful because they appeal to consumers' tendency to fantasize. These marketing strategies allow us to extend our vision of ourselves by placing us in unfamiliar, exciting situations or by permitting us to try interesting or provocative roles. And with today's technology, like Dove's Real Beauty campaign[25] or the virtual digitized preview from the plastic surgeon's PC of how your new face-lift will probably look, consumers can experiment before taking the plunge in the real world.

Multiple selves

In a way, each of us is really a number of different people – your mother probably would not recognize the 'you' that emerges while you're on holiday with a group of friends! We have as many selves as we do different social roles. Depending on the situation, we act differently, use different products and services, and we even vary in terms of how much we like ourselves. A person may require a different set of products to play a desired role: she may choose a sedate, understated perfume when she is being her professional self, but splash on something more provocative on Saturday night as she becomes her *femme fatale* self. The dramaturgical perspective on consumer behaviour views people much like actors who play different roles. We each play many roles, and each has its own script, props and costumes.[26]

The self can be thought of as having different components, or *role identities*, and only some of these are active at any given time. Some identities (e.g. husband, boss, student) are more central to the self than others, but other identities (e.g. stamp collector, dancer or advocate for greater equality in the workplace) may be dominant in specific situations.[27] For example, executives in a survey undertaken in the US, the UK and some Pacific Rim countries said that different aspects of their personalities come into play depending on whether they are making purchase decisions at home or at work. Not surprisingly, they report being less time-conscious, more emotional and less disciplined in their home roles.[28]

Virtual identity

The thousands of personal Websites people create to make statements about themselves relate to the motivation to project a version of the self (perhaps an idealized one) into popular culture. A study investigated why consumers create personal websites and how those Web space strategies compare to the self-presentation strategies we use in real life. The authors found that events such as a graduation or promotion trigger many of these personal sites; other prominent causes include a desire for personal growth (mastering of technology, search for a job, etc.), or *advocacy* (homage to a favourite artist or product). The creators choose every element of the site carefully, selecting images and text that symbolize something about their self-identity, and many of them digitize their physical selves as part of their self-presentation. Also the sites often reveal intimate aspects of the self that people wouldn't necessarily share in real life (RL).[29]

Author's personal correspondence with Xin Zhao, 2007.

In the influential cyberpunk novel *Snow Crash*, author Neal Stephenson envisioned a virtual world, called the *Metaverse*, as a successor to the Internet. In the Metaverse, everyday people take on glamorous identities in a three-dimensional immersive digital world. The book's main character delivers pizza in RL, but in the Metaverse, he is a warrior prince and champion sword fighter.[30] The hugely popular *Matrix* movie trilogy paints a similar (though more sinister) picture of a world that blurs the lines between physical and digital reality.[31]

▶ Today these fictional depictions come to life as we witness the tremendous growth of real-time, interactive virtual worlds that allow people to assume **virtual identities** in cyberspace. More than 9 million people worldwide belong to the virtual world of *Second Life*, more than 8 million play the online game *World of Warcraft*, and one-third of Korean adults belong to *CyWorld*. Add to that the millions more who play *The Sims Online* or who visit other computer-mediated environments (CMEs) such as *Webkinz*, *There*, *Whyville*, *Entropia Universe*, MTV's *Virtual Laguna Beach* (**www.mtv.com/ontv/dyn/laguna_beach/vlb.jhtml**) and so on and you are looking at a lot of serious role-playing.

▶ On these sites people assume visual identities, or **avatars**, ranging from realistic versions of themselves to tricked-out versions with 'exaggerated' physical characteristics or winged dragons or superheroes. Researchers are just starting to investigate how these online selves will influence consumer behaviour and how the identities we choose in CMEs relate to our RL (or 'meat-world') identities. Already we know that when people take on avatar forms, they tend to interact with other avatars much as their meat-world selves interact with other RL people. For example, just as in the RL, males in *Second Life* leave more space between them when talking to other males versus females and they are less likely to maintain eye contact than females are. And when avatars get very close to one another, they tend to look away from each other – the norms of the RL are creeping into the virtual world.[32]

Consumer behaviour as I see it . . .

Interactive technologies have had a profound influence on consumer behaviour. Many people have found the WWW, which is essentially a medium of text and 2D images, sufficiently compelling to form social networks via e-mail, instant messaging, chatrooms, etc. They browse, they shop, they exchange information, develop meaningful relationships and worldwide cyber communities. So imagine the possibilities as we look toward the 3D Web, where Websites become enriched 3D virtual spaces within which digital representations of users, also known as avatars, can interact with others.

Kathy Keeling
Manchester Business School, Manchester, UK

As avatars, we can represent ourselves in almost any way we choose, changing gender, skin colour, shape and even species at will. We may question that avatars are 'ushers of a post-human era' (Meadows, 2008) but through them we can explore new identities, new worlds and play any number of possible (or even impossible) selves, mixing fantasy and reality. I am excited by the potential and questions posed for consumer research. The sense of presence invoked by the immersive avatar experience is capable of producing reactions in participants similar to the real world, so throwing into sharp relief the drivers of behaviour and self-representation.

If we actively use clothes, appearance and possessions to construct and symbolize self and identity in the offline world, we should not be surprised that digital goods are used in the same way. But we have a limited understanding of how they are used in virtual worlds, as the technology offers boundless behavioural possibilities. Moreover, what is rare is valuable; the value of digital goods may be based on the difficulty of creation (programing/scripting) and so differ markedly from actual goods. Research questions arise on three fronts. First, issues of personal representation and identity. Humans are nothing if not social beings;

Consumer behaviour as I see it . . . (continued)

in these virtual yet social worlds, what shapes or constrains the choice of avatar appearance from the almost limitless possibilities? How is identity negotiated once we have chosen our display of avatar characteristics? Is avatar appearance accepted as a reliable and accurate symbolism of the user or partially or wholly discounted? What can the individual's choice of avatar and digital possessions tell us about emotional desires or cultural notions of the self? Do virtual experiences and identity exploration contribute to changes in the offline self?

Second, we might imagine opportunities for modification or transformation of customer–business relationships in virtual worlds. The use of an avatar or the presence of other avatars will change the processes of customer interaction in contrast to most e-retailing, e.g. you can easily go shopping with a friend in virtual worlds. How best can business use avatars to connect with customers and consumers to augment purchase and consumption experiences? Does a trial virtual purchase lead to a real-world purchase, or will it depress offline consumption?

Third, we should choose carefully in applying existing theoretical models of consumer behaviour to the virtual world context where people have multiple representations of themselves (perhaps in different genders) can fly (with or without wings), change their body shape, eye colour, skin colour (try the purple) at will, and/or inhabit their (and others') fantasy worlds. How can theories of cognitive processing, motivation and social psychology inform our understanding? Virtual worlds promise unique opportunities for exploring and experimenting with consumer behaviour, as well as testing the boundaries of our present understanding and theories. It's going to be an interesting journey.

Symbolic interactionism

If each person potentially has many social selves, how does each develop and how do we decide which self to 'activate' at any point in time? The sociological tradition of symbolic interactionism stresses that relationships with other people play a large part in forming the self.[33] This perspective maintains that people exist in a symbolic environment, and the meaning attached to any situation or object is determined by the interpretation of these symbols. As members of society, we learn to agree on shared meanings. Thus, we 'know' that a red light means stop, or that McDonald's 'golden arches' mean fast food.

Like other social objects, the meanings of consumers themselves are defined by social consensus. The consumer interprets their own identity, and this assessment is continually evolving as they encounter new situations and people. In symbolic interactionist terms, we *negotiate* these meanings over time. Essentially the consumer poses the question: 'Who am I in this situation?' The answer to this question is greatly influenced by those around us: 'Who do *other people* think I am?' We tend to pattern our behaviour on the perceived expectations of others in a form of *self-fulfilling prophecy*. By acting the way we assume others expect us to act, we may confirm these perceptions. This pattern of self-fulfilling behaviour is often expressed in our 'gendered roles', as we will see later in this chapter.

The looking-glass self

Some stores are testing a new interactive mirror that doubles as a high-resolution digital screen. When you choose an article of clothing, the mirror superimposes it on your reflection so that you can see how it would look on you. A camera relays live images of you modelling your virtual outfit to an Internet site where your friends can log to instant message (IM) you to tell you what they think; their comments pop up on the side of the mirror for you to read. They can also select virtual items for you to try on that will be reflected in the 'magic' mirror.[34] This process of imagining the reactions of others towards us is known as 'taking the role of the other', or the looking-glass self.[35] According to this view, our desire to define ourselves operates as a sort of psychological

THE STILETTO EFFECT

BIANCO.®
FOOTWEAR

While this Bianco Footwear ad is making a visually playful metaphor which likens the 'Stiletto Effect' of the model's legs to the stiletto heel of the shoes, an additional message to female consumers is also part of the ad – the message that thin is fashionable.

Bianco Footwear Danmark A/S

sonar: we take readings of our own identity by 'bouncing' signals off others and trying to project what impression they have of us. The looking-glass image we receive will differ depending upon whose views we are considering.

Like the distorted mirrors in a funfair, our appraisal of who we are can vary, depending on whose perspective we are taking and how accurately we are able to predict their evaluations of us. A successful man like Gareth may have doubts about his role as a middle-aged 'family man' as it conflicts with his earlier self-image as dapper and carefree (whether these perceptions are true or not). A self-fulfilling prophecy may be at work here, since these 'signals' can influence Gareth's actual behaviour. If he does not believe he is dapper, he may choose clothing and behaviour that actually make him less dapper. On the other hand, his self-confidence in a professional setting may cause him to assume that others hold his 'executive self' in even higher regard than they actually do (we've all known people like that!).

Self-consciousness

There are times when people seem to be painfully aware of themselves. If you have ever walked into a class in the middle of a lecture and noticed that all eyes were on you, you can understand this feeling of *self-consciousness*. In contrast, consumers sometimes behave with shockingly little self-consciousness. For example, people may do things in a stadium, a riot or a student party that they would never do if they were highly conscious of their behaviour.[36]

Some people seem in general to be more sensitive to the image they communicate to others (on the other hand, we all know people who act as if they are oblivious to the impression they are making). A heightened concern about the nature of one's public 'image' also results in more concern about the social appropriateness of products and consumption activities.

Several measures have been devised to measure this tendency. Consumers who score high on a scale of *public self-consciousness*, for example, are also more interested in clothing and are heavier users of cosmetics.[37] A similar measure is *self-monitoring*. High self-monitors are more attuned to how they present themselves in their social environments, and their product choices are influenced by their estimates of how these items will be perceived by others.[38] Self-monitoring is assessed by consumers' extent of agreement with such items as 'I suppose I put on a show to impress or entertain others', or 'I would probably make a good actor'.[39] High self-monitors are more likely than low self-monitors to evaluate products consumed in public in terms of the impressions they make on others.[40] Similarly, other research has looked at aspects of *vanity*, such as a fixation on physical appearance or on the achievement of personal goals. Perhaps not surprisingly, groups like body-builders and fashion models tend to score higher on this dimension.[41]

CONSUMPTION AND SELF-CONCEPT

By extending the dramaturgical perspective a bit further, it is easy to see how the consumption of products and services contributes to the definition of the self. For an actor to play a role convincingly, they need the correct props, stage setting and so on. Consumers learn that different roles are accompanied by *constellations* of products and activities which help to define these roles.[42] Some 'props' are so important to the roles we play that they can be viewed as a part of the *extended self*, a concept to be discussed shortly.

Products that shape the self: you are what you consume

Recall that the reflected self helps to shape self-concept, which implies that people see themselves as they imagine others see them. Since what others see includes a person's clothing, jewellery, furniture, car and so on, it stands to reason that these products also help to determine the perceived self. A consumer's products place them in a social role, which helps to answer the question, 'Who am I *now*?'

People use an individual's consumption behaviours to help them make judgements about that person's social identity. In addition to considering a person's clothes, grooming habits, and such like, we make inferences about personality based on a person's choice of leisure activities (squash vs. soccer), food preferences (vegetarians vs. 'steak and chips' people), cars or home decorating choices. People who are shown pictures of someone's sitting room, for example, are able to make surprisingly accurate guesses about their personality.[43] In the same way that a consumer's use of products influences others' perceptions, the same products can help to determine their *own* self-concept and social identity.[44]

A consumer exhibits *attachment* to an object to the extent that it is used by that person to maintain their self-concept.[45] Objects can act as a sort of security blanket by reinforcing our identities, especially in unfamiliar situations. For example, students who decorate their room or house with personal items are less likely to drop out. This coping process may protect the self from being diluted in an unfamiliar environment.[46]

The use of consumption information to define the self is especially important when an identity is yet to be adequately formed, something that occurs when a consumer plays a new or unfamiliar role. **Symbolic self-completion theory** predicts that people who have an incomplete self-definition tend to complete this identity by acquiring and displaying symbols associated with it.[47] Adolescent boys may use 'macho' products like cars and cigarettes to bolster their developing masculinity: these items act as a 'social crutch' to be leaned on during a period of uncertainty about identity.

Loss of self

The contribution of possessions to self-identity is perhaps most apparent when these treasured objects are lost or stolen. One of the first acts performed by institutions that want to repress individuality and encourage group identity, such as prisons or convents, is to confiscate personal possessions.[48] Victims of burglaries and natural disasters commonly report feelings of alienation, depression or of being 'violated'. One consumer's comment after being robbed is typical: 'It's the next worse thing to being bereaved; it's like being raped.'[49] Burglary victims exhibit a diminished sense of community, reduced sense of privacy and take less pride in their house's appearance than do their neighbours.[50]

The dramatic impact of product loss is highlighted by studying post-disaster conditions, when consumers may literally lose almost everything but the clothes on their backs following a fire, hurricane, flood or earthquake. Some people are reluctant to undergo the process of recreating their identity by acquiring all new possessions. Interviews with disaster victims reveal that some are reluctant to invest the self in new possessions and so become more detached about what they buy. This comment from a woman in her fifties is representative of this attitude: 'I had so much love tied up in my things. I can't go through that kind of loss again. What I'm buying now won't be as important to me.'[51]

Self/product congruence

Because many consumption activities are related to self-definition, it is not surprising to learn that consumers demonstrate consistency between their values and the things they buy.[52] **Self-image congruence models** predict that products will be chosen when their attributes match some aspect of the self.[53] These models assume a process of cognitive matching between these attributes and the consumer's self-image.[54]

While results are somewhat mixed, the ideal self appears to be more relevant as a comparison standard for highly expressive social products such as perfume. In contrast, the actual self is more relevant for everyday, functional products. These standards are also likely to vary by usage situation. For example, a consumer might want a functional, reliable car to commute to work everyday, but a flashier model with more 'zing' when going out on a date in the evening. Sadly, there are examples of people using products by which the goal of enhancing the ideal self ends up conflicting with and damaging the actual self. The body-building craze that swept through the US and the north-east of England resulted in an increasing number of young men using anabolic steroids for body-building. This steroid use may 'bulk up' the physique (and provide a faster attainment of the ideal self), but it also damages the actual self, since the steroids cause male infertility.[55]

Research tends to support the idea of congruence between product usage and self-image. One of the earliest studies to examine this process found that car owners' ratings of themselves tended to match their perceptions of their cars – drivers of the sporty Pontiac model saw themselves as more active and flashier than did Volkswagen drivers.[56] Congruity has also been found between consumers and their most preferred brands of beer, soap, toothpaste and cigarettes relative to their least preferred brands, as well as between consumers' self-images and their favourite shops.[57] Some specific attributes that have been found to be useful in describing some of the matches between consumers and products include rugged/delicate, excitable/calm, rational/emotional and formal/informal.[58]

While these findings make some intuitive sense, we cannot blithely assume that consumers will always buy products whose characteristics match their own. It is not clear that consumers really see aspects of themselves in down-to-earth, functional products that do not have very complex or human-like images. It is one thing to consider a brand personality for an expressive, image-oriented product like perfume and quite another to impute human characteristics to a toaster.

Another problem is the old 'chicken-and-egg' question: do people buy products because the products are seen as similar to the self, or do they *assume* that these products must be similar because they have bought them? The similarity between a person's self-image and the images of products purchased does tend to increase with ownership, so this explanation cannot be ruled out.

The extended self

As noted earlier, many of the props and settings consumers use to define their social roles in a sense become a part of their selves. Those external objects that we consider a part of us comprise the **extended self**. In some cultures, people literally incorporate objects into the self – they lick new possessions, take the names of conquered enemies (or in some cases ate them) or bury the dead with their possessions.[59] We don't usually go that far, but many people do cherish possessions as if they were a part of them. Many material objects, ranging from personal possessions and pets to national monuments or landmarks, help to form a consumer's identity. Just about everyone can name a valued possession that has a lot of the self 'wrapped up' in it, whether it is a treasured photograph, a trophy, an old shirt, a car or a cat. Indeed, it is often possible to construct a pretty accurate 'biography' of someone just by cataloguing the items on display in their bedroom or office.

In one study on the extended self, people were given a list of items that ranged from electronic equipment, facial tissues and television programmes to parents, body parts and favourite clothes. They were asked to rate each in terms of its closeness to the self. Objects were more likely to be considered a part of the extended self if 'psychic energy' was invested in them by expending effort to obtain them or because they were personalized and kept for a long time.[60] A recent exploration of the conflicts Muslim women who choose to wear headscarves experience illustrates how even a simple piece of cloth reflects a person's aesthetic, political, and moral dimensions.[61] The Turkish women in the study expressed the tension they felt in their ongoing struggle to reconcile ambiguous religious principles that simultaneously call for modesty and beauty. Society sends Muslim women contradictory messages in modern-day Turkey. Although the Koran denounces waste, many of the companies that produce religious headscarves introduce new designs each season and, as styles and tastes change, the women are encouraged to purchase more scarves than necessary. Moreover, the authors point out that a wearer communicates her fashion sense by the fabrics she selects and by the way she drapes and ties her scarf. In addition, veiling sends contradictory images about the proper sex roles of men and women. On the one hand, women who cover their heads by choice feel a sense of empowerment. On the other, the notion that Islamic law exhorts women to cover themselves lest they threaten men's self-restraint and honour is a persistent sign that men exert control over women's bodies and restrict their freedom. As a compromise solution Nike designed a uniform for observant women in Somalia who want to play sports without abandoning the traditional *hijab* (a robe that wraps around the head and loosely drapes over the entire body). The company streamlined the garment so that volleyball players could move but still keep their bodies covered.[62]

In an important study on the self and possessions, four levels of the extended self were described. These range from very personal objects to places and things that allow people to feel like they are rooted in their larger social environments:[63]

- *Individual level*. Consumers include many of their personal possessions in self-definition. These products can include jewellery, cars, clothing and so on. The saying 'You are what you wear' reflects the belief that one's things are a part of what one is.
- *Family level*. This part of the extended self includes a consumer's residence and its furnishings. The house can be thought of as a symbolic body for the family and often is a central aspect of identity.
- *Community level*. It is common for consumers to describe themselves in terms of the neighbourhood or town from which they come. For farming families or residents with close ties to a community, this sense of belonging is particularly important.
- *Group level*. Our attachments to certain social groups can be considered a part of self. A consumer may feel that landmarks, monuments or sports teams are a part of the extended self.

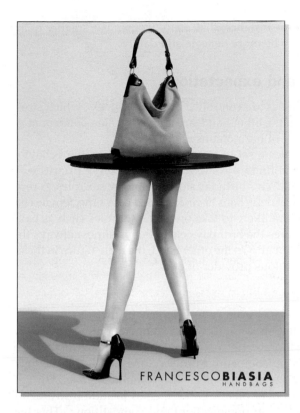

This Italian ad demonstrates that our favourite products are part of the extended self.

D'Adda, Lorenzini, Vigorelli, BBDO S.p.A. Photo: Ilan Rubin

GENDER ROLES

Sexual identity is a very important component of a consumer's self-concept. People often conform to their culture's expectations about how those of their gender should act, dress, speak and so on. Of course, these guidelines change over time, and they can differ radically across societies. Some societies are highly dichotomized, with little tolerance for deviation from gender norms. In other societies this is not the case, and greater freedom in behaviour, including behaviour stemming from sexual orientation, is allowed. In certain societies, lip-service is paid to gender equality, but inequalities are just under the surface; in others, there is greater sharing of power, of resources and of decision-making. To the extent that our culture is everything that we learn, then virtually all aspects of the consumption process must be affected by culture. It is not always clear to what extent sex differences are innate rather than culturally shaped – but they are certainly evident in many consumption decisions.[64]

Consider the gender differences market researchers have observed when comparing the food preferences of men and women. Women eat more fruit, men are more likely to eat meat. As one food writer put it, 'Boy food doesn't grow. It is hunted or killed.' Men are more likely to eat Frosted Flakes or Corn Flakes, while women prefer multigrain cereals. Men are more likely than women to consume soft drinks, while women account for the bulk of sales of bottled water. The sexes also differ sharply in the quantities of food they eat: when researchers at Hershey's discovered that women eat smaller amounts of sweets, the company created a white chocolate confection called Hugs, one of the most successful food launches of all time.

Gender differences in socialization

A society's assumptions about the proper roles of men and women are communicated in terms of the ideal behaviours that are stressed for each sex (in advertising, among other

153

places). It is likely, for instance, that many women eat smaller quantities because they have been 'trained' to be more delicate and dainty.

Gender goals and expectations

▶ In many societies, males are controlled by **agentic goals**, which stress self-assertion and
▶ mastery. Females, on the other hand, are taught to value **communal goals**, such as affiliation and the fostering of harmonious relations.[65]

Every society creates a set of expectations regarding the behaviours appropriate for men and women, and finds ways to communicate these priorities. This training begins very young: even children's birthday stories reinforce sex roles. A recent analysis showed that while stereotypical depictions have decreased over time, female characters in children's books are still far more likely to take on nurturant roles such as baking and gift-giving. The adult who prepares the birthday celebration is almost always the mother – often no adult male is present at all. On the other hand, the male figure in these stories is often cast in the role of a miraculous provider of gifts.[66]

Macho marketers?

Marketing has historically been defined largely by men, so it still tends to be dominated by male values. Competition rather than co-operation is stressed, and the language of warfare and domination is often used. Strategists often use distinctly masculine concepts: 'market penetration' or 'competitive thrusts', for example. Marketing articles in academic journals also emphasize agentic rather than communal goals. The most pervasive theme is power and control over others. Other themes include instrumentality (manipulating people for the good of an organization) and competition.[67] This bias may diminish in years to come, as more marketing researchers begin to stress such factors as emotions and aesthetics in purchase decisions, and as increasing numbers of women graduate in marketing.

Gender vs. sexual identity

Sex role identity is a state of mind as well as body. A person's biological gender (i.e.
▶ male or female) does not totally determine whether they will exhibit **sex-typed traits**, or characteristics that are stereotypically associated with one sex or the other. A consumer's subjective feelings about their sexuality are crucial as well.[68]

Unlike maleness and femaleness, masculinity and femininity are *not* biological characteristics. A behaviour considered masculine in one culture may not be viewed as such in another. For example, the norm in northern Europe, and in Scandinavia in particular, is that men are stoic, while cultures in southern Europe and in Latin America allow men to show their emotions. Each society determines what 'real' men and women should and should not do.

Sex-typed products

Many products also are *sex-typed*: they take on masculine or feminine attributes, and consumers often associate them with one sex or another.[69] The sex-typing of products is often created or perpetuated by marketers (e.g. Princess telephones, boys' and girls' toys, and babies' colour-coded nappies). Even brand names appear to be sex-typed: those containing alphanumerics (e.g. Formula 409, 10W40, Clorox 2) are assumed to be technical and hence masculine.[70] Our gender also seems to influence the instrumentality of the products we buy. Studies have shown that men tend to buy instrumental and leisure items impulsively, projecting independence and activity, while women tend to buy symbolic and self-expressive goods concerned with appearance and emotional aspects of self. Other research has shown, for example, that men take a more self-oriented approach to buying clothing, stressing its use as expressive symbols of personality and functional benefits, whilst women have 'other-oriented' concerns, choosing to use clothes as symbols of their social and personal interrelatedness with others.[71]

Androgyny

▶ Masculinity and femininity are not opposite ends of the same dimension. **Androgyny** refers to the possession of both masculine and feminine traits.[72] Researchers make a distinction between *sex-typed people*, who are stereotypically masculine or feminine, and *androgynous people*, whose mixture of characteristics allows them to function well in a variety of social situations.

Differences in sex-role orientation can influence responses to marketing stimuli, at least under some circumstances.[73] For example, research evidence indicates that females are more likely to undergo elaborate processing of message content, so they tend to be more sensitive to specific pieces of information when forming a judgement, while males are more influenced by overall themes.[74] In addition, women with a relatively strong masculine component in their sex-role identity prefer ad portrayals that include non-traditional women.[75] Some research indicates that sex-typed people are more sensitive to the sex-role depictions of characters in advertising, although women appear to be more sensitive to gender role relationships than are men.

In one study, subjects read two versions of a beer advertisement, couched in either masculine or feminine terms. The masculine version contained phrases like 'X Beer has the strong aggressive flavour that really asserts itself with good food and good company . . .' while the feminine version made claims like 'Brewed with tender care, X Beer is a full-bodied beer that goes down smoothly and gently . . .' People who rated themselves as highly masculine or highly feminine preferred the version that was described in (respectively) very masculine or feminine terms.[76] Sex-typed people in general are more concerned with ensuring that their behaviour is consistent with their culture's definition of gender appropriateness.

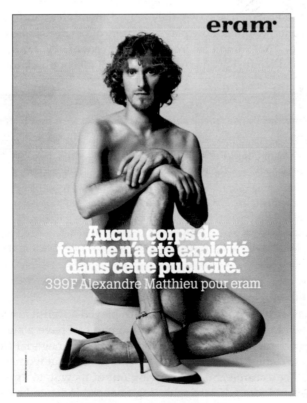

This French shoe ad pokes fun at ads that demean women by proclaiming: 'No woman's body was exploited in the making of this advertisement.'
Eram and Devarrieuxvillaret Ad Agency

155

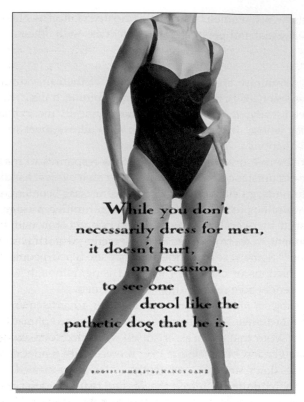

This ad illustrates the 'men-bashing' approach taken by some advertisers who are trying to appeal to women.

Advertising Age (1994). Photo courtesy of Goldsmith/Jeffrey and Bodyslimmers

Female gender roles

Gender roles for women are changing rapidly. Social changes, such as the dramatic increase in the proportion of women in waged work, have led to an upheaval in the way women are regarded by men, the way they regard themselves and in the products they choose to buy. Modern women now play a greater role in decisions regarding tradition-ally male purchases. For example, more than 60 per cent of new car buyers under the age of 50 are female, and women even buy almost half of all condoms sold.[77]

 Multicultural dimensions

Each society determines what 'real' men and women should and should not do and it communicates these expectations. For example, as part of a campaign to sell a new shaver to China's growing ranks of young urban professional men, Philips Electronics developed an Internet campaign featuring a trio of slinky secret agents who dispense tips on shaving, romance, and success. The young women, collectively called 'My Secret Weapon', are modelled on *Charlie's Angels*: black-clad Jennifer helps with career networking, sultry Angelina dishes out romantic tips, and martini-sipping party girl Victoria offers guidance on social matters. According to the company's marketing research, many single Chinese men do not get this kind of advice at home, so Philips is trying to satisfy a need for guidance – and hopefully sell a bunch of shavers in the process.[78]

Segmenting women

In the 1949 movie *Adam's Rib*, Katherine Hepburn played a stylish and competent lawyer. This film was one of the first to show that a woman can have a successful career and still be happily married. Today, the evolution of a new managerial class of women has forced marketers to change their traditional assumptions about women as they target this growing market. For example, Suzuki is going out of its way to appeal to the growing number of women in India who are achieving financial independence and buying their own cars. Its Zen Estilo (*Estilo* means 'style' in Spanish) model comes in eight colours, including 'purple fusion', 'virgin blue' and 'sparkling olive'.[79] Ironically, it seems that in some cases marketers have overcompensated for their former emphasis on women as housewives. Many attempts to target the vast market of females employed outside the home tend to depict all these women in glamorous, executive positions. This portrayal ignores the fact that the majority of women do not hold such jobs, and that many work because they have to, rather than for self-fulfilment. This diversity means that not all women should be expected to respond to marketing campaigns that stress professional achievement or the glamour of the working life.

Whether or not they work outside the home, many women have come to value greater independence and respond positively to marketing campaigns that stress the freedom to make their own lifestyle decisions. American Express has been targeting women for a long time, but the company found that its 'Do you know me?' campaign did not appeal to women as much as to men. A campaign aimed specifically at women featured confident women using their American Express cards. By depicting women in active situations, the company greatly increased its share of the women's credit card market.[80]

Cheesecake: the depiction of women in advertising

As implied by the ads for Virginia Slims cigarettes – 'You've come a long way, baby!' – attitudes about female sex roles changed remarkably during the twentieth century. Still, women continue to be depicted by advertisers and the media in stereotypical ways. Analyses of ads in such magazines as *Time*, *Newsweek*, *Playboy* and even *Ms.* have shown that the large majority of women included were presented as sex objects (so-called 'cheesecake' ads) or in traditional roles.[81] Similar findings have been obtained in both the UK and the US.[82] One of the biggest culprits may be rock videos, which tend to reinforce traditional women's roles.

Ads may also reinforce negative stereotypes. Women are often portrayed as stupid, submissive or temperamental, or as sexual objects who exist solely for the pleasure of men. An ad for Newport cigarettes illustrated how the theme of female submission may be perpetuated. The copy 'Alive with pleasure!' was accompanied by a photo of a woman in the woods, playfully hanging from a pole being carried by two men. The underlying message may be interpreted as two men bringing home their captured prey.[83]

Although women continue to be depicted in traditional roles, this situation is changing as advertisers scramble to catch up with reality. For example, the highly successful Dove Real Beauty campaign has significantly changed women's perceptions of what is 'beautiful', particularly with respect to the notion of beauty and natural ageing. The campaign shows women in various roles, and at varying ages, and the notion of 'beauty' is central to the discussions.[84] Women are now as likely as men to be central characters in television commercials. But while males are increasingly depicted as spouses and parents, women are still more likely than men to be seen in domestic settings. Also, about 90 per cent of all narrators in commercials are male. The deeper male voice is apparently perceived as more authoritative and credible.[85]

Some ads now feature *role reversal*, where women occupy traditional men's roles. In other cases, women are portrayed in romantic situations, but they tend to be more sexually dominant. Ironically, current advertising is more free to emphasize traditional female traits now that sexual equality is becoming more of an accepted fact. This freedom is demonstrated in a German poster for a women's magazine. The caption reads, 'Today's women can sometimes show weakness, because they are strong'.

Male sex roles

While the traditional conception of the ideal male as a tough, aggressive, muscular man who enjoys 'manly' sports and activities is not dead, society's definition of the male role is evolving. Starting in the late 1990s, men were allowed to be more compassionate and to have close friendships with other men. In contrast to the depiction of macho men who do not show feelings, some marketers were promoting men's 'sensitive' side. An emphasis on male bonding was the centrepiece of many ad campaigns, especially for beers.[86] Just as for women, however, the true story is more complicated than that. Indeed, ▶ scholars of **masculinism** study the male image and the complex cultural meanings of masculinity.[87] Like women, men receive mixed messages about how they are supposed to behave and feel. No doubt one of the biggest marketing buzzwords over the past few ▶ years is the **metrosexual**, a straight, urban male who is keenly interested in fashion, home design, gourmet cooking, and personal care. For another take on the presentation and fashion of males, and the evolution to the 'retrosexual' see the case 'Being a Real Man About Town' at the end of this Part. A gay writer named Mark Simpson actually coined the term way back in a 1994 article when he 'outed' British soccer star and pop icon David Beckham as a metrosexual. Simpson noted that Beckham is 'almost as famous for wearing sarongs and pink nail polish and panties belonging to his wife, Victoria (aka Posh from the Spice Girls), as he is for his impressive ball skills.'[88]

Some analysts argue that men are threatened because they do not necessarily recognize themselves in the powerful male stereotypes against which feminists protest.[89] One study examined how American men pursue masculine identities through their everyday consumption. The researchers suggest that men are trying to make sense out of three different models of masculinity that they call *breadwinner*, *rebel*, and *man-of-action hero*, as they figure out just who they are supposed to be. On the one hand, the breadwinner model draws from the American myth of success and celebrates respectability, civic virtues, pursuit of material success, and organized achievement. The rebel model, on the other hand, emphasizes rebellion, independence, adventure, and potency. The man-of-action hero is a synthesis that draws from the better of the other two models.[90]

One consequence of the continual evolution of sex roles is that men are concerned as never before with their appearance. Men spend $7.7 billion on grooming products globally each year. A wave of male cleansers, moisturizers, sunscreens, depilatories, and

REO certainly has a clearly targeted market for their new cologne. Does this exclusive brand positioning make good business sense to you? Why or why not?

The Advertising Archives

body sprays is washing up on US shores, largely from European marketers. L'Oréal Paris reports that men's skincare products is now its fastest-growing sector. In Europe, 24 per cent of men younger than age 30 use skincare products – and 80 per cent of young Korean men do.[91]

Beefcake: the depiction of men in advertising

Men as well as women are often depicted in a negative fashion in advertising. They frequently come across as helpless or bumbling. As one advertising executive put it, 'The woman's movement raised consciousness in the ad business as to how women can be depicted. The thought now is, if we can't have women in these old-fashioned traditional roles, at least we can have men being dummies.'[92]

Just as advertisers are criticized for depicting women as sex objects, so the same accusations can be made about how males are portrayed – a practice correspondingly known as 'beefcake'.[93] An advertising campaign for Sansabelt trousers featured the theme, 'What women look for in men's pants.' Ads featured a woman who confides, 'I always lower my eyes when a man passes [pause] to see if he's worth following.' One female executive commented, 'Turnabout is fair play . . . If we can't put a stop to sexism in advertising . . . at least we can have some fun with it and do a little leering of our own.'[94]

Gay and lesbian consumers

Gay and lesbian consumers are still largely ignored by marketers. This situation is starting to change, however, as some marketers are acknowledging the upmarket demographic profile of these consumers.[95] IKEA, the Swedish furniture retailer with outlets throughout Europe and in several major US cities, broke new ground by running a TV spot featuring a gay male couple purchasing a dining-room table at the shop.[96] Other major companies making an effort to market to homosexuals include AT&T, Anheuser-Busch, Apple Computers, Benetton, Philip Morris, Seagram and Sony.[97] Gay consumers can even get their own credit card – a Rainbow Visa card issued by Travelers Bank USA. Using tennis star Martina Navratilova as spokeswoman, such groups as the National Center for Lesbian Rights are benefited by users of the card. The card allows people who don't qualify based on income to apply with a same-sex partner.[98]

The percentage of the population that is gay and lesbian is difficult to determine, and efforts to measure this group have been controversial.[99] However, the respected research company Yankelovich Partners Inc., which has tracked consumer values and attitudes since 1971 in its annual Monitor survey, now includes a question about sexual identity in its survey. This study was virtually the first to use a sample that reflects the population as a whole instead of polling only smaller or biased groups (such as readers of gay publications) whose responses may not be representative of all consumers. About 6 per cent of respondents identified themselves as gay/homosexual/lesbian.

As civil rights gains are made by gay activists, the social climate is becoming more favourable for firms targeting this market segment.[100] In one of the first academic studies in this field, the conclusion was that gays and lesbians did not qualify as a market segment because they did not satisfy the traditional criteria of being identifiable, accessible and of sufficient size.[101] Subsequent studies have argued that the segmentation criteria rely on outdated assumptions regarding the nature of consumers, marketing activities and the ways in which media are used in the contemporary marketplace. Here, the argument is that identifiability is an unreliable construct for socially subordinated groups, and really is not the issue anyway. How marketers segment (by race, ethnicity, gender or, in this case, sexuality) is not as important as whether the group itself expresses consumption patterns in identifiable ways. Similarly, the accessibility criterion continues with the assumption of active marketers who contact passive consumers. This criterion also needs to take into account the dramatic changes in media over the past two decades, in particular the use of speciality media by marketers to access special-interest segments.

159

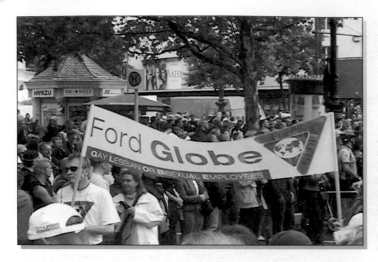

As gays and lesbians continue to become more socially intergrated into the mainstream of European cultures, many companies (large and small) are also becoming more visible and open in their support of this social movement. This photo, taken at the Gay & Lesbian Parade in Berlin in June 2001, shows the involvement and support of Ford in the day's celebrations.

Gay consumers are also active web surfers: the website **Gay.com** attracts 1 million consumers a month. As many as 65 per cent of gay and lesbian internet users go online more than once a day and over 70 per cent make purchases online.[102] Finally, sufficient size assumes separate campaigns are necessary to reach each segment, an assumption that ignores consumers' ability and willingness to explore multiple media.[103]

At least in some parts of the US and Europe, homosexuality appears to be becoming more mainstream and accepted.[104] Mattel even sells an Earring Magic Ken doll, complete with *faux*-leather vest, lavender mesh shirt and two-tone hair (though the product has become a favourite of gay men, the company denied it was targeted at that group).

▲ Marketing opportunity

Lesbian consumers have recently been in the cultural spotlight, perhaps due in part to the actions of such high-profile cultural figures as Martina Navratilova, singers k.d. lang and Melissa Etheridge, and actress Ellen DeGeneres. Whatever the reason, American Express, Stolichnaya vodka, Atlantic Records and Naya bottled water are among those corporations now running ads in lesbian publications (an ad for American Express Travellers Cheques for Two shows two women's signatures on a cheque). Acting on research that showed that lesbians are four times as likely to own one of their cars, Subaru of America recently began to target this market as well.[105]

BODY IMAGE

 A person's physical appearance is a large part of their self-concept. **Body image** refers to a consumer's subjective evaluation of their physical self. As was the case with the overall self-concept, this image is not necessarily accurate. A man may think of himself as being more muscular than he really is, or a woman may think she is fatter than is the case. In fact, it is not uncommon to find marketing strategies that exploit consumers' tendencies to distort their body images by preying upon insecurities about appearance, thereby creating a gap between the real and the ideal physical self and, consequently, the desire to purchase products and services to narrow that gap.

Body cathexis

 A person's feelings about their body can be described in terms of **body cathexis**. Cathexis refers to the emotional significance of some object or idea to a person, and some parts

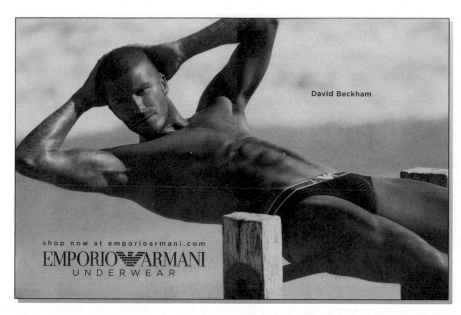

David Beckham

shop now at emporioarmani.com

EMPORIO ARMANI
UNDERWEAR

As suggested by this Emporio Armani ad, a global perspective on ideals of beauty is resulting in more ways to be considered attractive.

The Advertising Archives

of the body are more central to self-concept than others. One study of young adults' feelings about their bodies found that these respondents were most satisfied with their hair and eyes and had least positive feelings about their waists. These feelings were related to consumption of grooming products. Consumers who were more satisfied with their bodies were more frequent users of such 'preening' products as hair conditioner, hairdryers, aftershave, artificial tanning products, toothpaste and pumice soap.[106] In a large-scale study of older women in six European countries, the results showed that women would like to 'grow old beautifully', and that they were prepared to follow diets, exercise and use cosmetics to reach this goal. Wrinkles were the biggest concern, and Greek and Italian women were by far the most concerned about how to combat ageing, with northern European women expressing more agreement with the statement that ageing was natural and inevitable.[107]

Ideals of beauty

A person's satisfaction with the physical image they present to others is affected by how closely that image corresponds to the image valued by their culture. In fact, infants as young as two months show a preference for attractive faces.[108] An **ideal of beauty** is a particular model, or exemplar, of appearance. Ideals of beauty for both men and women may include physical features (big breasts or small, bulging muscles or not) as well as clothing styles, cosmetics, hairstyles, skin tone (pale vs. tan) and body type (petite, athletic, voluptuous, etc.).

Is beauty universal?

Recent research indicates that preferences for some physical features over others are 'wired in' genetically, and that these reactions tend to be the same among people around the world. Specifically, people appear to favour features associated with good health and youth, attributes linked to reproductive ability and strength. Men are also more likely to use a woman's body shape as a sexual cue, and it has been theorized that this is because feminine curves provide evidence of reproductive potential. During puberty a typical female gains almost 15kg of 'reproductive fat' around hips and thighs which supplies the approximately 80,000 extra calories needed for pregnancy. Most fertile women have waist:hip ratios of 0.6:0.8, an hourglass shape that happens to be the one men rank highest. Even though preferences for total weight change, waist:hip ratios tend to stay in

161

this range – even the super-thin model Twiggy (who pioneered the 'waif' look decades before Kate Moss) had a ratio of 0.73.[109] Other positively valued female characteristics include a higher forehead than average, fuller lips, a shorter jaw and a smaller chin and nose. Women, on the other hand, favour men with a heavy lower face, those who are slightly above average height and those with a prominent brow.

Of course, the way these faces are 'packaged' still varies enormously, and that is where marketers come in. Advertising and other forms of mass media play a significant role in determining which forms of beauty are considered desirable at any point in time. An ideal of beauty functions as a sort of cultural yardstick. Consumers compare themselves to some standard (often advocated by the fashion media) and are dissatisfied with their appearance to the extent that it does not match up to it. These mass media portrayals have been criticized not only on social grounds, but on issues of health as well. In a study of New Zealand print advertisements over the period 1958–88, the findings confirmed that advertising models became thinner and less curvaceous over the 30-year period, resulting in contemporary models being approximately 8.5kg lighter than they would be if they had the same body shape as models of the late 1950s. To achieve the currently fashionable body shape, a young woman of average height would have to weigh approximately 42kg, which is far below the recommended level for good health.[110] Clearly, what constitutes 'beauty' for women involves a number of complex relationships – a recent study in The Netherlands found that Dutch women consider friendliness, self-confidence, happiness and humour are the most important pillars of female beauty, while only 2 per cent found 'pretty' a description for female beauty. A majority of the over 3,200 women in the study felt that the media's depiction of the 'ideal' female beauty was unrealistic. Most of the women in the study complained slightly of their weight and the shape of their body.[111]

Ideals of beauty over time

While beauty may be only skin deep, throughout history and across cultures women in particular have worked very hard to attain it. They have starved themselves, painfully bound their feet, inserted plates into their lips, spent countless hours under hairdryers, in front of mirrors and beneath ultraviolet lights, and have undergone breast reduction or enlargement operations to alter their appearance and meet their society's expectations of what a beautiful woman should look like.

Periods of history tend to be characterized by a specific 'look', or ideal of beauty. American history can be described in terms of a succession of dominant ideals. For example, in sharp contrast to today's emphasis on health and vigour, in the early 1800s it was fashionable to appear delicate to the point of looking ill. The poet John Keats described the ideal woman of that time as 'a milk white lamb that bleats for man's protection'. Other looks have included the voluptuous, lusty woman as epitomized by Lillian Russell, the athletic Gibson Girl of the 1890s, and the small, boyish flapper of the 1920s as exemplified by Clara Bow.[112]

Throughout much of the nineteenth century, the desirable waistline for American women was 18 inches, a circumference that required the use of corsets pulled so tight that they routinely caused headaches, fainting fits, and possibly even the uterine and spinal disorders common among women of the time. While modern women are not quite as 'strait-laced', many still endure such indignities as high heels, body waxing, eye-lifts and liposuction. In addition to the millions spent on cosmetics, clothing, health clubs and fashion magazines, these practices remind us that – rightly or wrongly – the desire to conform to current standards of beauty is alive and well.

The ideal body type of Western women has changed radically over time, and these changes have resulted in a realignment of *sexual dimorphic markers* – those aspects of the body that distinguish between the sexes. For example, analyses of the measurements of *Playboy* centrefolds over a 20-year period from 1958 to 1978 show that these ideals became thinner and more muscular. The average hip measurement went from 36 inches

☐ fat?
☐ fit?

Does true beauty only squeeze into size 8?

campaignforrealbeauty.co.uk ❧ *Dove*

The Dove campaign emphasizes that our ideals about beauty, and what is beautiful, vary over time, place and age.
The Advertising Archives

in 1958 to just over 34 inches in 1978. Average bust size shrank from almost 37 inches in 1958 to about 35 inches in 1978.[113]

The first part of the 1990s saw the emergence of the controversial 'waif' look, where successful models (notably Kate Moss) were likely to have bodies resembling those of young boys. More recently, the pendulum seems to be shifting back a bit, as the more buxom 'hourglass figure' popular in the 1950s (exemplified by the Marilyn Monroe ideal) has reappeared.[114] One factor leading to this change has been the opposition to the use of super-thin models by feminist groups and healthcare experts, who charge that these role models encourage starvation diets and eating disorders among women who want to emulate the look.[115] These groups have advocated boycotts against companies like Coca-Cola and Calvin Klein who have used wafer-thin models in their advertising. Some protesters have even taken to pasting stickers over these ads that read, 'Feed this woman', or 'Give me a cheeseburger'.

We can also distinguish among ideals of beauty for men in terms of facial features, musculature and facial hair – who could confuse Tom Cruise with Mr Bean? In fact, one national survey which asked both men and women to comment on male aspects of appearance found that the dominant standard of beauty for men is a strongly masculine, muscled body – though women tend to prefer men with less muscle mass than men themselves strive to attain.[116] Advertisers appear to have the males' ideal in mind – a study of men appearing in advertisements found that most sport the strong and muscular physique of the male stereotype.[117]

Working on the body

Because many consumers are motivated to match up to an ideal appearance, they often go to great lengths to change aspects of their physical selves. From cosmetics to plastic surgery, tanning salons to diet drinks, a multitude of products and services are directed towards altering or maintaining aspects of the physical self in order to present a desirable appearance. It is difficult to overstate the importance of the physical self-concept (and the desire by consumers to improve their appearance) to many marketing activities.

Sizeism

As reflected in the expression 'you can never be too thin or too rich', many Western societies have an obsession with weight. Even primary school children perceive obesity as worse than being disabled.[118] The pressure to be slim is continually reinforced both by advertising and by peers. Americans in particular are preoccupied by what they weigh. They are continually bombarded by images of thin, happy people.

How realistic are these appearance standards? In Europe, the public discourse on appearance and body weight is becoming more active and visible, particularly with respect to the weight of European children. Of the 77 million children in the EU, 14 million are overweight. In 2005, the EU planned to launch a 'platform' on diet, physical activity and health as a public policy approach to the issue of weight. Obesity is especially acute in Mediterranean countries, underscoring concerns that people in the southern region are turning away from the traditional diet of fish, fruits and vegetables to fast food, high in fat and refined carbohydrates.[119] Still, many consumers focus on attaining an unrealistic ideal weight, sometimes by relying on height and weight charts which show what one should weigh. These expectations are communicated in subtle ways. Even fashion dolls, such as the ubiquitous Barbie, reinforce the ideal of thinness. The dimensions of these dolls, when extrapolated to average female body sizes, are unnaturally long and thin.[120] In spite of Americans' obsession about weight, as a country they continue to have a greater percentage of obesity in the general population relative to all European countries, as shown in Figure 5.1. Within Europe, female and male consumers aged 15 to 24 from Malta, Germany, and England lead the EU in measures of obesity.[121]

Want to calculate your own body mass index? Go to **http://www.consumer.gov/ weightloss/bmi.htm#BMI** and fill in your personal data.

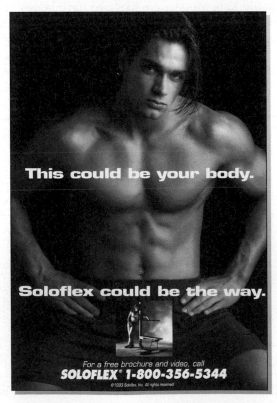

Could this really be your body? Physical self-concept and improving one's appearance are important motivations in consumer behaviour.

Soloflex, Inc.

Figure 5.1 Distribution of young men and women according to body mass index, 2004

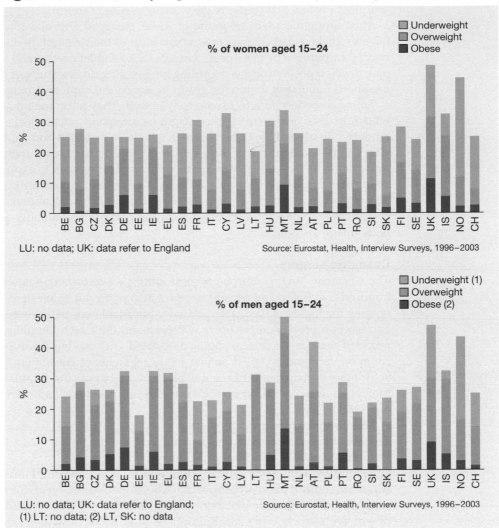

LU: no data; UK: data refer to England   Source: Eurostat, Health, Interview Surveys, 1996–2003

LU: no data; UK: data refer to England;   Source: Eurostat, Health, Interview Surveys, 1996–2003
(1) LT: no data; (2) LT, SK: no data

Source: The life of women and men in Europe: A statistical portrait, 2008.

Body image distortions

While many people perceive a strong link between self-esteem and appearance, some consumers unfortunately exaggerate this connection even more, and sacrifice greatly to attain what they consider to be a desirable body image. Women tend to be taught to a greater degree than men that the quality of their bodies reflects their self-worth, so it is not surprising that most major distortions of body image occur among females.

Men do not tend to differ in ratings of their current figure, their ideal figure and the figure they think is most attractive to women. In contrast, women rate both the figure they think is most attractive to men and their ideal figure as much thinner than their actual figure.[122] In one survey, two-thirds of college women admitted resorting to unhealthy behaviour to control weight. Advertising messages that convey an image of slimness help to reinforce these activities by arousing insecurities about weight.[123]

A distorted body image has been linked to the rise in in eating disorders, which are particularly prevalent among young women. People with anorexia regard themselves as fat, and starve themselves in the quest for thinness. This condition may be accompanied by bulimia, which involves two stages: first, binge eating occurs (usually in private), where more than 5,000 calories may be consumed at one time. The binge is then followed by induced vomiting, abuse of laxatives, fasting and/or overly strenuous exercise – a 'purging' process that reasserts the woman's sense of control.

Most eating disorders are found in white, teenaged girls and students. Victims often have brothers or fathers who are hypercritical of their weight. In addition, binge eating may be encouraged by one's peers. Groups such as athletic teams and social clubs at school may develop positive norms regarding binge eating. In one study of a female social club, members' popularity within the group increased the more they binged.[124]

Eating disorders do affect some men as well. They are common among male athletes who must also conform to various weight requirements, such as jockeys, boxers and male models.[125] In general, though, most men who have distorted body images consider themselves to be too light rather than too heavy: society has taught them that they must be muscular to be masculine. Men are more likely than women to express their insecurities about their bodies by becoming addicted to exercise. In fact, striking similarities have been found between male compulsive runners and female anorexics. These include a commitment to diet and exercise as a central part of one's identity and susceptibility to body image distortions.[126]

Cosmetic surgery

The Cosmetic Surgery Europe website (**http://www.cosmetic-surgery-europe.com/**) lists hundreds of clinics, and several websites also point out to Western Europeans that the options for highly skilled, safe and very affordable cosmetic surgery can be found in Eastern European countries such as Poland and the Czech Republic. There is no longer much (if any) psychological stigma associated with having this type of operation: it is commonplace and accepted among many segments of consumers.[127] In fact, men now account for as many as 20 per cent of plastic surgery patients. Popular operations include the implantation of silicon pectoral muscles (for the chest) and even calf implants to fill out 'chicken legs'.[128]

Many women turn to surgery either to reduce weight or to increase sexual desirability. The use of liposuction, where fat is removed from the thighs with a vacuum-like device, has almost doubled since it was introduced in the US in 1982.[129] Some women believe that larger breasts will increase their allure and undergo breast augmentation procedures. Although some of these procedures have generated controversy due to possible negative side effects, it is unclear whether potential medical problems will deter large numbers of women from choosing surgical options to enhance their (perceived) femininity. The importance of breast size to self-concept resulted in an interesting and successful marketing strategy undertaken by an underwear company. While conducting focus groups on bras, an analyst noted that small-chested women typically reacted with hostility when discussing the subject. They would unconsciously cover their chests with their arms as they spoke and felt that their needs were ignored by the fashion industry. To meet this overlooked need, the company introduced a line of A-cup bras called 'A-OK' and depicted wearers in a positive light. A new market segment was born. Other companies are going in the opposite direction by promoting bras that create the illusion of a larger cleavage. In Europe and the US, both Gossard and Playtex are aggressively marketing specially designed bras offering 'cleavage enhancement' which use a combination of wires and internal pads to create the desired effect. Recently, the market for women's bras has had to contend with at least one natural development: unaugmented breasts (no surgery) are getting bigger by themselves, as a result of using the pill and changes in diet. The average cup size in Britain has grown from 34B to 36C over the past 30 years, and bra designers such as Bioform and Airotic, and retailers such as Knickerbox and Victoria's Secret, have all responded with new product offerings to meet what they consider to be a long-term market trend.[130]

Body decoration and mutilation

The body is adorned or altered in some way in every culture. Decorating the self serves a number of purposes.[131]

- *To separate group members from non-members.* The Chinook Indians of North America used to press the head of a newborn baby between two boards for a year, permanently altering its shape. In our society, teenagers go out of their way to adopt distinctive hair and clothing styles that will distinguish them from adults.

- *To place the individual in the social organization.* Many cultures engage in rites of passage at puberty when a boy symbolically becomes a man. Young men in Ghana paint their bodies with white stripes to resemble skeletons to symbolize the death of their child status. In Western culture, this rite may involve some form of mild self-mutilation or engaging in dangerous activities.

- *To place the person in a gender category.* The Tchikrin Indians of South America insert a string of beads in a boy's lip to enlarge it. Western women wear lipstick to enhance femininity. At the turn of the century, small lips were fashionable because they represented women's submissive role at that time.[132] Today, big, red lips are provocative and indicate an aggressive sexuality. Some women, including a number of famous actresses and models, have collagen injections or lip inserts to create large, pouting lips (known in the modelling industry as 'liver lips').[133]

- *To enhance sex-role identification.* Wearing high heels, which podiatrists agree are a prime cause of knee and hip problems, backaches and fatigue, can be compared with the traditional Oriental practice of foot-binding to enhance femininity. As one doctor observed, 'When they [women] get home, they can't get their high-heeled shoes off fast enough. But every doctor in the world could yell from now until Doomsday, and women would still wear them.'[134]

- *To indicate desired social conduct.* The Suya of South America wear ear ornaments to emphasize the importance placed in their culture on listening and obedience. In Western society gay men may wear an earring to signal how they expect to be identified.

- *To indicate high status or rank.* The Hidates Indians of North America wear feather ornaments that indicate how many people they have killed. In our society, some people wear glasses with clear lenses, even though they do not have eye problems, to increase their perceived intellectual or fashion status.

- *To provide a sense of security.* Consumers often wear lucky charms, amulets, rabbits' feet and so on to protect them from the 'evil eye'. Some modern women wear a 'mugger whistle' around their necks for a similar reason.

Tattoos

Tattoos – both temporary and permanent – are a popular form of body adornment.[135] This body art can be used to communicate aspects of the self to onlookers and may serve some of the same functions that other kinds of body painting do in primitive cultures. In fact, much of the recent literature and discourse on tattoos centres on the theme of users as 'Modern Primitives'.[136] Tattoos (from the Tahitian *ta-tu*) have deep roots in folk art. Until recently, the images were crude and were primarily either death symbols (e.g. a skull), animals (especially panthers, eagles and snakes), pin-up women or military designs. More current influences include science fiction themes, Japanese symbolism and tribal designs.

A tattoo may be viewed as a fairly risk-free (?) way of expressing an adventurous side of the self. Tattoos have a long history of association with people who are social outcasts. For example, the faces and arms of criminals in sixth-century Japan were tattooed as a way of identifying them, as were Massachusetts prison inmates in the nineteenth century. These emblems are often used by marginal groups, such as bikers or Japanese *yakuze* (gang members), to express group identity and solidarity. In Europe today, the growth of tattoos on individuals of all ages and social classes can be seen both as a form of communication, and a growth in commodification. European consumers are more and more often using their own skin as part of their expression of consumer culture.[137]

Body decoration can be permanent, or (hopefully!) temporary, in order to distinguish oneself, shock others, signify group membership, or express a particular mood or message.

The Advertising Archives

Body piercing

Decorating the body with various kinds of metallic inserts has evolved from a practice associated with some fringe groups to become a popular fashion statement. Piercings can range from a hoop protruding from a navel to scalp implants, where metal posts are inserted in the skull (do not try this at home!). Publications such as *Piercing Fans International Quarterly* are seeing their circulations soar and Websites featuring piercings and piercing products are attracting numerous followers. This popularity is not pleasing to hard-core piercing fans, who view the practice as a sensual consciousness-raising ritual and are concerned that now people just do it because it is trendy. As one customer waiting for a piercing remarked, 'If your piercing doesn't mean anything, then it's just like buying a pair of platform shoes.'[138]

CHAPTER SUMMARY

■ Consumers' *self-concepts* are reflections of their attitudes towards themselves. Whether these attitudes are positive or negative, they will help to guide many purchase decisions; products can be used to bolster self-esteem or to 'reward' the self.

■ Many product choices are dictated by the similarity the consumer perceives between their personality and attributes of the product. The *symbolic interactionist perspective* on the self implies that each of us actually has many selves, and a different set of products is required as props to play each. Many things other than the body can also be viewed as part of the self. Valued objects, car, homes and even attachments to sports teams or national monuments are used to define the self, when these are incorporated into the extended self.

■ A person's *sex-role identity* is a major component of self-definition. Conceptions about masculinity and femininity, largely shaped by society, guide the acquisition of 'sex-typed' products and services.

■ Advertising and other media play an important role in socializing consumers to be male and female. While traditional women's roles have often been perpetuated in advertising depictions, this situation is changing somewhat. The media do not always portray men accurately either.

■ Sometimes these activities are carried to an extreme, as people try too hard to live up to cultural ideals. One example is found in eating disorders, where women in particular become obsessed with thinness.

■ A person's conception of their body also provides feedback to self-image. A culture communicates certain ideals of beauty, and consumers go to great lengths to attain these. Many consumer activities involve manipulating the body, whether through dieting, cosmetic surgery or tattooing.

▶ KEY TERMS

Actual self (p. 145)	Impression managment (p. 145)
Agentic goals (p. 154)	Looking-glass self (p. 148)
Androgyny (p. 155)	Masculinism (p. 158)
Avatars (p. 147)	Metrosexual (p. 158)
Body cathexis (p. 160)	Self-concept (p. 144)
Body image (p. 160)	Self-image congruence models (p. 151)
Communal goals (p. 154)	Sex-typed traits (p. 154)
Extended self (p. 152)	Symbolic interactionism (p. 148)
Fantasy (p. 145)	Symbolic self-completion theory (p. 150)
Ideal of beauty (p. 161)	Virtual identities (p. 147)
Ideal self (p. 145)	

▶ CONSUMER BEHAVIOUR CHALLENGE

1 How might the creation of a self-conscious state be related to consumers who are trying on clothing in changing rooms? Does the act of preening in front of a mirror change the dynamics by which people evaluate their product choices? Why?

2 Is it ethical for marketers to encourage infatuation with the self?

3 List three dimensions by which the self-concept can be described.

4 Compare and contrast the real vs. the ideal self. List three products for which each type of self is likely to be used as a reference point when a purchase is considered.

5 Watch a series of ads featuring men and women on television. Try to imagine the characters with reversed roles (the male parts played by women, and vice versa). Can you see any differences in assumptions about sex-typed behaviour?

6 To date, the bulk of advertising targeted at gay consumers has been placed in exclusively gay media. If it was your decision, would you consider using mainstream media to reach gays, who constitute a significant proportion of the general population? Or, bearing in mind that members of some targeted segments have serious objections to this practice, especially when the product (e.g. alcohol, cigarettes) may be viewed as harmful in some way, do you think gays should be singled out at all by marketers?

CONSUMER BEHAVIOUR CHALLENGE (*continued*)

7 Do you agree that marketing strategies tend to have a male-oriented bias? If so, what are some possible consequences for specific marketing activities?

8 Construct a 'consumption biography' of a friend or family member. Make a list of and/or photograph their favourite possessions, and see if you or others can describe this person's personality just from the information provided by this catalogue.

9 Some consumer advocates have protested at the use of super-thin models in advertising, claiming that these women encourage others to starve themselves in order to attain the 'waif' look. Other critics respond that the media's power to shape behaviour has been overestimated, and that it is insulting to people to assume that they are unable to separate fantasy from reality. What do you think?

For additional material see the companion website at **www.pearsoned.co.uk/solomon**

NOTES

1. Daniel Goleman, 'When ugliness is only in patient's eye, body image can reflect mental disorder', *New York Times* (2 October 1991): C13. See also: Duncan Robertson (2007), 'Too Shy to Strip in Front of a Man' www.dailymail.co.uk/news/article-445068/Too-shy-strip-man.html

2. Duncan Robertson, 'Too Shy to Strip in Front of a Man', *Daily Mail*, 28 March 2007, based on a survey of 3,500 women for SHUC, a bathroom equipment company www.dailymail.co.uk/news/article-445068/Too-shy-strip-man.html

3. Tatiana Boncompagni, 'Newest wrinkle in the anti-ageing war', *Financial Times* (12 March 2004), http://news.ft.com/servlet/ContentServer?pagename=FT.com/StoryFT/FullStory&c=StoryFT&cid=1078381734673&p=1016625900932; Rhymer Rigby, 'Grooming the male market', *Financial Times* (3 February 2004), http://news.ft.com/servlet/ContentServer?pagename=FT.com/StoryFT/FullStory&c=StoryFT&cid=1073281521382&p=1059480266913

4. Harry C. Triandis, 'The self and social behavior in differing cultural contexts', *Psychological Review* 96 (1989) 3: 506–20; H. Markus and S. Kitayama, 'Culture and the self: Implications for cognition, emotion, and motiva-tion', *Psychological Review* 98 (1991): 224–53.

5. Markus and Kitayama, 'Culture and the self', *ibid*.

6. Nancy Wong and Aaron Ahuvia, 'A Cross-Cultural Approach to Materialism and the Self', in Dominique Bouchet, ed., *Cultural Dimensions of International Marketing* (Denmark, Odense University, 1995): 68–89.

7. Lisa M. Keefe, 'You're so vain', *Marketing News* (28 February 2000): 8.

8. 'Liverpool named most vain city in England', 11 April 2007, http://www.liveleak.com/view?i=769_1194208373

9. Anthony G. Greenwald and Mahzarin R. Banaji, 'The self as a memory system: Powerful, but ordinary', *Journal of Personality and Social Psychology* 57 (1989)1: 41–54; Hazel Markus, 'Self Schemata and Processing Information About the Self', *Journal of Personality and Social Psychology* 35 (1977): 63–78.

10. Morris Rosenberg, *Conceiving the Self* (New York: Basic Books, 1979); M. Joseph Sirgy, 'Self-concept in consumer behavior: A critical review', *Journal of Consumer Research* 9 (December 1982): 287–300.

11. Emily Yoffe, 'You are what you buy', *Newsweek* (4 June 1990): 59. See also: (2008) 'Therapy hoe for eating disorders', http://news.bbc.co.uk/2/hi/health/7779468.stm. See also: http://www.eatingdisorderexpert.co.uk/

12. Roy F. Baumeister, Dianne M. Tice and Debra G. Hutton, 'Self-presentational motivations and personality differences in self-esteem', *Journal of Personality* 57 (September 1989): 547–75; Ronald J. Faber, 'Are Self-Esteem Appeals Appealing?' *Proceedings of the 1992 Conference of the American Academy of Advertising*, ed. Leonard N. Reid (1992): 230–5.

13. B. Bradford Brown and Mary Jane Lohr, 'Peer-group affiliation and adolescent self-esteem: An integration of ego identity and symbolic-interaction theories', *Journal of Personality and Social Psychology* 52 (1987) 1: 47–55.

14. Christine Bittar, 'Alberto-Culver Ties Hair Relaxer to Self-Esteem', available from www.mediapost.com, accessed 2007 February 15. See also: http://texturesoftener.com/

15. Marsha L. Richins, 'Social comparison and the idealized images of advertising', *Journal of Consumer Research* 18 (June 1991): 71–83; Mary C. Martin and Patricia F. Kennedy, 'Advertising and social comparison: Consequences for female preadolescents and adolescents', *Psychology and Marketing* 10 (November/December 1993) 6: 513–30.

16. Philip N. Myers Jr. and Frank A. Biocca, 'The elastic body image: The effect of television advertising and programming on body image distortions in young women', *Journal of Communication* 42 (Summer 1992): 108–33.

17. Kees, Jeremy, Karen Becker-Olsen, and Milos Mitric (2008), 'The Use of Thin Models in Advertising: The Moderating Effect of Self-Monitoring on Females' Body Esteem and Food Choices', in John Kozup, Charles R. Taylor, and Ronald Paul Hill (eds), *Marketing and Public Policy Proceedings* (Philadelphia, PA).

18. Jeffrey F. Durgee, 'Self-esteem advertising', *Journal of Advertising* 14 (1986) 4: 21.

19. Erin White and Deborah Ball, 'Slim-Fast pounds home tough talk ads aimed at U.K. women offer steady diet of

barbs to encourage weight loss', *The Wall Street Journal* (28 May 2004): B3.

20. For the seminal treatment of this process, *cf.* Erving Goffman, *The Presentation of Self in Everyday Life* (New York: Doubleday, 1959).

21. Sigmund Freud, *New Introductory Lectures in Psychoanalysis* (New York: Norton, 1965).

22. Jason Riis, Joseph P. Simmons, and Geoffrey P. Goodwin (2008), 'Preferences for enhancement pharmaceuticals: The reluctance to enhance fundamental traits', *Journal of Consumer Research* 35 (October 2008): 495–508.

23. Harrison G. Gough, Mario Fioravanti and Renato Lazzari, 'Some implications of self versus ideal-self congruence on the revised adjective check list', *Journal of Personality and Social Psychology* 44 (1983) 6: 1214–20.

24. Steven Jay Lynn and Judith W. Rhue, 'Daydream believers', *Psychology Today* (September 1985): 14.

25. http://campaignforrealbeauty.co.uk (accessed 5 August 2005).

26. Erving Goffman, *The Presentation of Self in Everyday Life* (Garden City, NY: Doubleday, 1959); Michael R. Solomon, 'The role of products as social stimuli: A symbolic interactionism perspective', *Journal of Consumer Research* 10 (December 1983): 319–29.

27. Yinlong Zhang, and L.J. Shrum (2009) 'The influence of self construal on impulsive consumption', *Journal of Consumer Research*, 35, 5 (February 2009): 838–50.

28. Julie Skur Hill, 'Purchasing habits shift for execs', *Advertising Age* (27 April 1992): 1–16.

29. Hope Jensen Schau and Mary Gilly, 'We are what we post? Self-presentation in personal web space', *Journal of Consumer Research* 30 (December 2003): 385–404.

30. Neal Stephenson, *Snow Crash* (New York: Bantam Books, 1992).

31. Jeffrey Wang, Xin Zhao, X., and Gary Bamossy (2008), 'The Sacred and Profane in On-Line Gaming' in *Virtual Social Identity and Consumer Behavior*, M. Solomon and N. Wood (eds) (M.E. Shapre: London, in press).

32. Svensson, Peter, 'Study: Virtual Men Are Standoffish Too', *MyFox 21* (February 2007), www.myfoxkccom/myfox/pages/News/Detail, accessed 22 February 2007.

33. George H. Mead, *Mind, Self and Society* (Chicago: University of Chicago Press, 1934).

34. Natasha Singer, 'If the Mirror Could Talk (It Can)', *New York Times Online* (18 March 2007), accessed 18 March 2007.

35. Charles H. Cooley, *Human Nature and the Social Order* (New York: Scribner's, 1902).

36. J.G. Hull and A.S. Levy, 'The organizational functions of the self: An alternative to the Duval and Wicklund model of self-awareness', *Journal of Personality and Social Psychology* 37 (1979): 756–68; Jay G. Hull, Ronald R. Van Treuren, Susan J. Ashford, Pamela Propsom and Bruce W. Andrus, 'Self-consciousness and the processing of self-relevant information', *Journal of Personality and Social Psychology* 54 (1988) 3: 452–65.

37. Arnold W. Buss, *Self-Consciousness and Social Anxiety* (San Francisco: W.H. Freeman, 1980); Lynn Carol Miller and Cathryn Leigh Cox, 'Public self-consciousness and makeup use', *Personality and Social Psychology Bulletin* 8 (1982) 4: 748–51; Michael R. Solomon and John Schopler, 'Self-consciousness and clothing', *Personality and Social Psychology Bulletin* 8 (1982) 3: 508–14.

38. Morris B. Holbrook, Michael R. Solomon and Stephen Bell, 'A re-examination of self-monitoring and judgments

of furniture designs', *Home Economics Research Journal* 19 (September 1990): 6–16; Mark Snyder and Steve Gangestad, 'On the nature of self-monitoring: matters of assessment, matters of validity', *Journal of Personality and Social Psychology* 51 (1986): 125–39.

39. Snyder and Gangestad, 'On the nature of self-monitoring', *ibid.*

40. Timothy R. Graeff, 'Image congruence effects on product evaluations: The role of self-monitoring and public/private consumption', *Psychology and Marketing* 13(5) (August 1996): 481–99.

41. Richard G. Netemeyer, Scot Burton and Donald R. Lichtenstein, 'Trait aspects of vanity: Measurement and relevance to consumer behavior', *Journal of Consumer Research* 21 (March 1995): 612–26.

42. Michael R. Solomon and Henry Assael, 'The forest or the trees? A gestalt approach to symbolic consumption', in Jean Umiker-Sebeok, ed., *Marketing and Semiotics: New Directions in the Study of Signs for Sale* (Berlin: Mouton de Gruyter, 1987): 189–218.

43. Jack L. Nasar, 'Symbolic meanings of house styles', *Environment and Behavior* 21 (May 1989): 235–57; E.K. Sadalla, B. Verschure and J. Burroughs, 'Identity symbolism in housing', *Environment and Behavior* 19 (1987): 599–687.

44. Douglas B. Holt and Craig J. Thompson, 'Man-of-action heroes: The pursuit of heroic masculinity in everyday consumption', *Journal of Consumer Research* 31 (September 2004): 425–40; Michael R. Solomon, 'The role of products as social stimuli: A symbolic interactionism perspective', *Journal of Consumer Research* 10 (December 1983): 319–28; Robert E. Kleine III, Susan Schultz-Kleine and Jerome B. Kernan, 'Mundane consumption and the self: A social-identity perspective', *Journal of Consumer Psychology* 2 (1993) 3: 209–35; Newell D. Wright, C.B. Claiborne and M. Joseph Sirgy, 'The Effects of Product Symbolism on Consumer Self-Concept', in John F. Sherry Jr. and Brian Sternthal, eds, *Advances in Consumer Research* 19 (Provo, UT: Association for Consumer Research, 1992): 311–18; Susan Fournier, 'A Person Based Relationship Framework for Strategic Brand Management', Ph.D. dissertation, University of Florida, 1994.

45. A. Dwayne Ball and Lori H. Tasaki, 'The role and measurement of attachment in consumer behavior', *Journal of Consumer Psychology* 1 (1992) 2: 155–72.

46. William B. Hansen and Irwin Altman, 'Decorating personal places: A descriptive analysis', *Environment and Behavior* 8 (December 1976): 491–504.

47. R.A. Wicklund and P.M. Gollwitzer, *Symbolic Self-Completion* (Hillsdale, NJ: Lawrence Erlbaum, 1982).

48. Erving Goffman, *Asylums* (New York: Doubleday, 1961).

49. Quoted in Floyd Rudmin, 'Property crime victimization impact on self, on attachment, and on territorial dominance', *CPA Highlights, Victims of Crime Supplement* 9 (1987) 2: 4–7.

50. Barbara B. Brown, 'House and Block as Territory', paper presented at the Conference of the Association for Consumer Research, San Francisco, 1982.

51. Quoted in Shay Sayre and David Horne, 'I Shop, Therefore I Am: The Role of Possessions for Self Definition', in Shay Sayre and David Horne, eds, *Earth, Wind, and Fire and Water: Perspectives on Natural Disaster* (Pasadena, CA: Open Door Publishers, 1996): 353–70. Recently in Germany, the 'loss of self' was taken to the ultimate extreme when a 43-year-old German from Berlin advertised on the internet that he would like to be eaten. His ad was answered and,

with his consent, he was cut into pieces, frozen and placed in the freezer next to the takeaway pizza. See: 'Cannibal to face murder charge at retrial', *The Guardian* (23 April 2005), http://www.guardian.co.uk/international/story/0,,1468373,00.html.

52. Deborah A. Prentice, 'Psychological correspondence of possessions, attitudes, and values', *Journal of Personality and Social Psychology* 53 (1987) 6: 993–1002.

53. Sak Onkvisit and John Shaw, 'Self-concept and image congruence: Some research and managerial implications', *Journal of Consumer Marketing* 4 (Winter 1987): 13–24. For a related treatment of congruence between advertising appeals and self-concept, see George M. Zinkhan and Jae W. Hong, 'Self-Concept and Advertising Effectiveness: A Conceptual Model of Congruency, Conspicuousness, and Response Mode', in Rebecca H. Holman and Michael R. Solomon, eds, *Advances in Consumer Research* 18 (Provo, UT: Association for Consumer Research, 1991): 348–54.

54. C.B. Claiborne and M. Joseph Sirgy, 'Self-Image Congruence as a Model of Consumer Attitude Formation and Behavior: A Conceptual Review and Guide for Further Research', paper presented at the Academy of Marketing Science Conference, New Orleans, 1990.

55. Liz Hunt, 'Rise in infertility linked to craze for body building', *The Independent* (12 July 1995): 12; Paul Kelso, Duncan Mackay and Matthew Taylor, 'From gym to club to school: the shock spread of steroid abuse', *The Guardian* (14 November 2003), http://www.guardian.co.uk/uk_news/story/0,,1084792,00.html. See also: 'Anabolic Steroids, Use and Abuse', (July 2006) http://menshealth.about.com/cs/fitness/a/anab_steroids.htm

56. Al E. Birdwell, 'A study of influence of image congruence on consumer choice', *Journal of Business* 41 (January 1964): 76–88; Edward L. Grubb and Gregg Hupp, 'Perception of self, generalized stereotypes, and brand selection', *Journal of Marketing Research* 5 (February 1986): 58–63.

57. Ira J. Dolich, 'Congruence relationship between self-image and product brands', *Journal of Marketing Research* 6 (February 1969): 80–4; Danny N. Bellenger, Earle Steinberg and Wilbur W. Stanton, 'The congruence of store image and self image as it relates to store loyalty', *Journal of Retailing* 52 (1976) 1: 17–32; Ronald J. Dornoff and Ronald L. Tatham, 'Congruence between personal image and store image', *Journal of the Market Research Society* 14 (1972) 1: 45–52.

58. Naresh K. Malhotra, 'A scale to measure self-concepts, person concepts, and product concepts', *Journal of Marketing Research* 18 (November 1981): 456–64.

59. Ernest Beaglehole, *Property: A Study in Social Psychology* (New York: Macmillan, 1932).

60. M. Csikszentmihalyi and Eugene Rochberg Halton, *The Meaning of Things: Domestic Symbols and the Self* (Cambridge, MA: Cambridge University Press, 1981).

61. Sandikci, Özlem and Güliz Ger, 'Aesthetics, Ethics and Politics of the Turkish Headscarf', *Clothing As Material Culture*, S. Kuechler, D. Miller (eds): 61–82 (London: Berg Publisher, 2005).

62. Marc Lacey, 'Where Showing Skin Doesn't Sell, a New Style Is a Hit', *New York Times Online* (20 March 2006).

63. Russell W. Belk, 'Possessions and the extended self', *Journal of Consumer Research* 15 (September 1988): 139–68.

64. Janeen Arnold Costa, 'Introduction', in J.A. Costa, ed., *Gender Issues and Consumer Behavior* (Thousand Oaks, CA: Sage, 1994).

65. Joan Meyers-Levy, 'The influence of sex roles on judgment', *Journal of Consumer Research* 14 (March 1988): 522–30.

66. Kimberly J. Dodson and Russell W. Belk, 'Gender in Children's Birthday Stories', in Janeen Costa, ed., *Gender, Marketing, and Consumer Behavior* (Salt Lake City, UT: Association for Consumer Research, 1996): 96–108.

67. Elizabeth C. Hirschman, 'A Feminist Critique of Marketing Theory: Toward Agentic-Communal Balance', working paper, School of Business, Rutgers University, New Brunswick, NJ, 1990.

68. Eileen Fischer and Stephen J. Arnold, 'Sex, gender identity, gender role attitudes, and consumer behavior', *Psychology and Marketing* 11 (March/April 1994) 2: 163–82.

69. Kathleen Debevec and Easwar Iyer, 'Sex Roles and Consumer Perceptions of Promotions, Products, and Self: What Do We Know and Where Should We Be Headed', in Richard J. Lutz, ed., *Advances in Consumer Research* 13 (Provo, UT: Association for Consumer Research, 1986): 210–14; Joseph A. Bellizzi and Laura Milner, 'Gender positioning of a traditionally male-dominant product', *Journal of Advertising Research* (June/July 1991): 72–9.

70. Janeen Arnold Costa and Teresa M. Pavia, 'Alphanumeric brand names and gender stereotypes', *Research in Consumer Behavior* 6 (1993): 85–112.

71. Helga Dittmar, Jane Beattie and Susanne Friese, 'Gender identity and material symbols: Objects and decision considerations in impulse purchases', *Journal of Economic Psychology* 16 (1995): 491–511; Jason Cox and Helga Dittmar, 'The functions of clothes and clothing (dis)satisfaction: A gender analysis among British students', *Journal of Consumer Policy* 18 (1995): 237–65.

72. Sandra L. Bem, 'The measurement of psychological androgyny', *Journal of Consulting and Clinical Psychology* 42 (1974): 155–62; Deborah E.S. Frable, 'Sex typing and gender ideology: Two facets of the individual's gender psychology that go together', *Journal of Personality and Social Psychology* 56 (1989) 1: 95–108.

73. See D. Bruce Carter and Gary D. Levy, 'Cognitive aspects of early sex-role development: The influence of gender schemas on preschoolers' memories and preferences for sex-typed toys and activities', *Child Development* 59 (1988): 782–92; Bernd H. Schmitt, France Le Clerc and Laurette Dube-Rioux, 'Sex typing and consumer behavior: A test of gender schema theory', *Journal of Consumer Research* 15 (June 1988): 122–7.

74. Carol Gilligan, *In a Different Voice: Psychological Theory and Women's Development* (Cambridge, MA: Harvard University Press, 1982); Joan Meyers-Levy and Durairaj Maheswaran, 'Exploring differences in males' and females' processing strategies', *Journal of Consumer Research* 18 (June 1991): 63–70.

75. Lynn J. Jaffe and Paul D. Berger, 'Impact on purchase intent of sex-role identity and product positioning', *Psychology and Marketing* (Fall 1988): 259–71; Lynn J. Jaffe, 'The unique predictive ability of sex-role identity in explaining women's response to advertising', *Psychology and Marketing* 11 (September/October 1994) 5: 467–82.

76. Leila T. Worth, Jeanne Smith and Diane M. Mackie, 'Gender schematicity and preference for gender-typed products', *Psychology and Marketing* 9 (January 1992): 17–30.

77. Julie Candler, 'Woman car buyer – don't call her a niche anymore', *Advertising Age* (21 January 1991): S-8; see also Robin Widgery and Jack McGaugh, 'Vehicle message appeals and the new generation woman', *Journal of*

Advertising Research (September/October 1993): 36–42; Blayne Cutler, 'Condom mania', *American Demographics* (June 1989): 17.

78. Jonathan Cheng, 'Shaver's Cutting-Edge China Campaign Trio of Women Dispense Grooming Tips for Guys in Philips Web Effort', *Wall Street Journal* (4 May 2007): B3.

79. Eric Bellman, 'Suzuki's Stylish Compacts Captivate India's Women', *Wall Street Journal* (11 May 2007): B1.

80. B. Abrams, 'American Express is gearing new ad campaign to women', *Wall Street Journal* (4 August 1983): 23.

81. 'Ads' portrayal of women today is hardly innovative', *Marketing News* (6 November 1989): 12; Jill Hicks Ferguson, Peggy J. Kreshel and Spencer F. Tinkham, 'In the pages of *Ms.*: Sex role portrayals of women in advertising', *Journal of Advertising* 19 (1990) 1: 40–51.

82. Richard Elliott, Abigail Jones, Andrew Benfield and Matt Barlow, 'Overt sexuality in advertising: A discourse analysis of gender responses', *Journal of Consumer Policy* 18 (1995): 187–217; Sonia Livingstone and Gloria Greene, 'Television advertisements and the portrayal of gender', *British Journal of Social Psychology* 25 (1986): 149–54; for one of the original articles on this topic, see L.Z. McArthur and B.G. Resko, 'The portrayal of men and women in American television commercials', *Journal of Social Psychology* 97 (1975): 209–20.

83. Richard Edel, 'American dream vendors', *Advertising Age* (9 November 1988): 153.

84. http://campaignforrealbeauty.co.uk (accessed 5 August 2005).

85. Daniel J. Brett and Joanne Cantor, 'The portrayal of men and women in U.S. television commercials: A recent content analysis and trends over 15 years', *Sex Roles* 18 (1988): 595–609.

86. Gordon Sumner, 'Tribal rites of the American male', *Marketing Insights* (Summer 1989): 13.

87. Barbara B. Stern, 'Masculinism(s) and the Male Image: What Does It Mean to Be a Man?' in Tom Reichert and Jacqueline Lambiase, eds, *Sex in Advertising: Multidisciplinary Perspectives on the Erotic Appeal* (Mahwah, NJ: Erlbaum, 2003).

88. 'Defining Metro sexuality', *Metrosource* (September/October/November 2003).

89. Rinallo, Diego, 'Metro/Fashion/Tribes of men: Negotiating the boundaries of men's legitimate consumption', in B. Cova, R. Kozinets & A. Shankar (eds), *Consumer Tribes: Theory, Practice, and Prospects* (Elsevier/Butterworth-Heinemann, 2007).

90. Douglas B. Holt and Craig J. Thompson, 'Man-of-action heroes: The pursuit of heroic masculinity in everyday consumption', *Journal of Consumer Research* 31 (September): 425–40.

91. Vivian Manning-Schaffel, 'Metrosexuals: A Well-Groomed Market?' www.brandchannel.com, accessed 22 May 2006.

92. Quoted in Jennifer Foote, 'The ad world's new bimbos', *Newsweek* (25 January 1988): 44.

93. Maples, 'Beefcake marketing', *op. cit.*

94. Quoted in Lynn G. Coleman, 'What do people really lust after in ads?', *Marketing News* (6 November 1989): 12.

95. For an up-to-date census on gay European consumers, see: http://www.glcensus.org/ Riccardo A. Davis, 'Marketers game for gay events', *Advertising Age* (30 May 1994): S-1 (2); Cyndee Miller, 'Top marketers take bolder approach in targeting gays', *Marketing News* (4 July 1994): 1 (2); see also Douglas L. Fugate, 'Evaluating the US male homosexual

and lesbian population as a viable target market segment', *Journal of Consumer Marketing* 10(4) (1993) 4: 46–57; Laura M. Milner, 'Marketing to Gays and Lesbians: A Review', unpublished manuscript, the University of Alaska, 1990.

96. Kate Fitzgerald, 'IKEA dares to reveal gays buy tables, too', *Advertising Age* (28 March 1994): 3(2); Miller, 'Top marketers take bolder approach in targeting gays': 1(2); Paula Span, 'ISO the gay consumer', *Washington Post* (19 May 1994): D1 (2).

97. Kate Fitzgerald, 'AT&T addresses gay market', *Advertising Age* (16 May 1994): 8.

98. James S. Hirsch, 'New credit cards base appeals on sexual orientation and race', *Wall Street Journal* (6 November 1995): B1 (2).

99. Projections of the incidence of homosexuality in the general population are often influenced by assumptions of the researchers, as well as the methodology they employ (e.g. self-report, behavioural measures, fantasy measures). For a discussion of these factors, see Edward O. Laumann, John H. Gagnon, Robert T. Michael and Stuart Michaels, *The Social Organization of Homosexuality* (Chicago: University of Chicago Press, 1994).

100. Lisa Peñaloza, 'We're here, we're queer, and we're going shopping! A critical perspective on the accommodation of gays and lesbians in the U.S. marketplace', *Journal of Homosexuality* 31(1/2) (1966): 9–41.

101. Fugate, 'Evaluating the U.S. male homosexual and lesbian population as a viable target market segment'. See also Laumann, Gagnon, Michael and Michaels, *The Social Organization of Homosexuality*.

102. Laura Koss-Feder, 'Out and about', *Marketing News* (25 May 1998): 1(2); Rachel X. Weissman, 'Gay market power', *American Demographics* 21 (June 1999) 6: 32–3.

103. Peñaloza, 'We're here, we're queer, and we're going shopping!' *op. cit.*

104. For an up-to-date overview of gay consumption, lifestyle and markets, see: http://www.gayeuro.com/

105. Michael Wilke, 'Subaru adds lesbians to niche marketing drive', *Advertising Age* (4 March 1996): 8. See also: http://lesbianlife.about.com/od/otherfunstuff/tp/LesbianCars.htm for the top ten brands of cars purchased by gay women.

106. Dennis W. Rook, 'Body Cathexis and Market Segmentation', in Michael R. Solomon, ed., *The Psychology of Fashion* (Lexington, MA: Lexington Books, 1985): 233–41.

107. 'Nederlandse vrouw krijt lachend rimpels', *De Telegraaf* (26 April 1997): TA5.

108. Jane E. Brody, 'Notions of beauty transcend culture, new study suggests', *New York Times* (21 March 1994): A14.

109. Geoffrey Cowley, 'The biology of beauty', *Newsweek* (3 June 1996): 61–6.

110. Michael Fay and Christopher Price, 'Female body-shape in print advertisements and the increase in anorexia nervosa', *European Journal of Marketing* 28 (1994): 12.

111. 'Vrouwen hebben complexe relatie met schoonheid' ('Women have a complex relationship with beauty') *De Telegraaf* (31 January 2005), http://www2.telegraaf.nl/binnenland/17688091/_Vrouwen_hebben_complexe_relatie_met_schoonheid_.html.

112. Lois W. Banner, *American Beauty* (Chicago: The University of Chicago Press, 1980); for a philosophical perspective, see Barry Vacker and Wayne R. Key, 'Beauty *and* the beholder: The pursuit of beauty through commodities', *Psychology and Marketing* 10 (November/December 1993) 6: 471–94.

113. David M. Garner, Paul E. Garfinkel, Donald Schwartz and Michael Thompson, 'Cultural expectations of thinness in women', *Psychological Reports* 47 (1980): 483–91.

114. Kathleen Boyes, 'The new grip of girdles is lightened by lycra', *USA Today* (25 April 1991): 6D.

115. Stuart Elliott, 'Ultrathin models in Coca-Cola and Calvin Klein campaigns draw fire and a boycott call', *New York Times* (26 April 1994): D18; Cyndee Miller, 'Give them a cheeseburger', *Marketing News* (6 June 1994): 1 (2).

116. Jill Neimark, 'The beefcaking of America', *Psychology Today* (November/December 1994): 32 (11).

117. Richard H. Kolbe and Paul J. Albanese, 'Man to man: A content analysis of sole-male images in male-audience magazines', *Journal of Advertising* 25(4) (Winter 1996): 1–20.

118. 'Girls at 7 think thin, study finds', *New York Times* (11 February 1988): B9.

119. Beth Carney, 'In Europe, the fat is in the fire', *Business Week* (8 February 2005), http://www.businessweek.com/bwdaily/dnflash/feb2005/nf2005028_5771_db016.htm?chan=gb. For a comprehensive report on obesity in the EU, go to http://www.iotf.org (accessed 5 August 2005).

120. Elaine L. Pedersen and Nancy L. Markee, 'Fashion dolls: Communicators of ideals of beauty and fashion', paper presented at the international Conference on Marketing Meaning, Indianapolis, 1989; Dalma Heyn, 'Body hate', *Ms.* (August 1989): 34; Mary C. Martin and James W. Gentry, 'Assessing the internalization of physical attractiveness norms', *Proceedings of the American Marketing Association Summer Educators' Conference* (Summer 1994): 59–65.

121. 'So Germans can be gourmets too', *The Economist* (9 December 2000): 57. See also The European Commission, Eurostat, and 'International survey: Teens fattest in the U.S.', CNN (6 January 2004), http://www.cnn.com/2004/HEALTH/parenting/01/05/obese.teens.ap/index.html.

122. Debra A. Zellner, Debra F. Harner and Robbie I. Adler, 'Effects of eating abnormalities and gender on perceptions of desirable body shape', *Journal of Abnormal Psychology* 98 (February 1989): 93–6.

123. Robin T. Peterson, 'Bulimia and anorexia in an advertising context', *Journal of Business Ethics* 6 (1987): 495–504.

124. Christian S. Crandall, 'Social contagion of binge eating', *Journal of Personality and Social Psychology* 55 (1988): 588–98.

125. Judy Folkenberg, 'Bulimia: Not for women only', *Psychology Today* (March 1984): 10.

126. Eleanor Grant, 'The exercise fix: What happens when fitness fanatics just can't say no?' *Psychology Today* 22 (February 1988): 24.

127. Annette C. Hamburger and Holly Hall, 'Beauty quest', *Psychology Today* (May 1988): 28.

128. Emily Yoffe, 'Valley of the silicon dolls', *Newsweek* (26 November 1990): 72.

129. Keith Greenberg, 'What's hot: Cosmetic surgery', *Public Relations Journal* (June 1988): 23.

130. 'Bra wars', *The Economist* (2 December 2000): 64.

131. Ruth P. Rubinstein, 'Color, Circumcision, Tattoos, and Scars', in Solomon, ed., *The Psychology of Fashion*: 243–54; Peter H. Bloch and Marsha L. Richins, 'You look "mahvelous": The pursuit of beauty and marketing concept', *Psychology and Marketing* 9 (January 1992): 3–16.

132. Sondra Farganis, 'Lip service: The evolution of pouting, pursing, and painting lips red', *Health* (November 1988): 48–51.

133. Michael Gross, 'Those lips, those eyebrows: New face of 1989 (new look of fashion models)', *New York Times Magazine* (13 February 1989): 24.

134. Quoted in 'High heels: Ecstasy's worth the agony', *New York Post* (31 December 1981).

135. Dannie Kjeldgaard and Anders Bengtsson (2005), 'Consuming the Fashion Tattoo', *Advances in Consumer Research* 32, Geeta Menon and Akshay R. Rao, eds (Duluth, MN: Association for Consumer Research): 172–7.

136. Mike Featherstone, ed., *Body Modification* (Thousand Oaks, CA: Sage, 2000); Anne M. Velliquette and Jeff B. Murray, 'The New Tattoo Subculture', in *Mapping the Social Landscape: Readings in Sociology*, ed. Susan Ferguson (Mountain View, CA: Mayfield, 1999): 56–68; Anne M. Velliquette, Jeff B. Murray and Elizabeth H. Creyer, 'The Tattoo Renaissance: An Ethnographic Account of Symbolic Consumer Behavior', in Joseph W. Alba and J. Wesley Hutchinson, eds, *Advances in Consumer Research* 25 (Provo, UT: Association for Consumer Research, 1998): 461–7; Anne M. Velliquette, 'Modern Primitives: The Role of Product Symbolism in Lifestyle Cultures and Identity', dissertation, University of Arkansas Press, 2000; Margo DeMello, *Bodies of Inscription: A Cultural History of the Modern Tattoo Community* (Durham, NC: Duke University Press, 2000); Anne Veliquette and Gary Bamossy, 'Modern Primitives: The Role of the Body and Product Symbolism in Lifestyle Cultures and Identity', in Andrea Groppel-Klein and Franz-Rudolf Esch, eds, *European Advances in Consumer Research* 5 (Valdosta, GA: Association for Consumer Research, 2001): 21–2.

137. Jonathan Schroeder, 'Branding the Body: Skin and Consumer Communication', in Darach Turley and Stephen Brown, eds, *European Advances in Consumer Research: All Changed, Changed Utterly?* 6 (Valdosta, GA: Association for Consumer Research 2003): 23; Maurice Patterson and Richard Elliott, 'Harsh Beauty: The Alternative Aesthetic of Tattooed Women', in Turley and Brown, eds, *European Advances in Consumer Research* 6: 23; Dannie Kjeldgaard and Anders Bengtsson, 'Acts, Images, and Meaning of Tattooing', in Turley and Brown, eds, *European Advances in Consumer Research* 6: 24; Jonathan Schroeder and Janet Borgerson, 'Skin Signs: The Epidermal Schema in Contemporary Marketing Communications', in Turley and Brown, eds, *European Advances in Consumer Research* 6: 26; Roy Langer, 'SKINTWO: (Un)covering the Skin in Fetish Carnivals', in Turley and Brown, eds, *European Advances in Consumer Research* 6: 27.

138. Quoted in Wendy Bounds, 'Body-piercing gets under America's skin', *Wall Street Journal* (4 April 1994): B1 (2), B4.

6

Motivation, values and lifestyle

Rufus and his Italian girlfriend, Adrienne, have just found a table for lunch at a small, family-run restaurant in Kolonaki. The restaurant was recommended by the *Observer* travel section[1] for its 'warm, cosy, bistro-like atmosphere'; as well as its 'simple Greek food at amazing prices in Athens' poshest neighbourhood'. It had been Rufus' turn to choose where to eat as Adrienne had suggested the Cretan restaurant where they had had dinner the previous night. Rufus studies the menu hard. Rufus is reflecting on what a man will do for love. Adrienne is keen that they both eat healthily. She's not yet managed to persuade him to follow her conversion to vegetarianism. However, she's slowly but surely persuading him to give up burgers and pizzas for healthier, preferably organic, fare; and swop his beer drinking for wine. At least while they are on holiday he can hide from tofu and the other vegan delights which confront him as the menu choices at their favourite local café when he visits her in Bergamo. The café has just started offering 'veggie' alternatives to its usual rich Bergamasque cuisine of casconcelli (pasta stuffed with sausagemeat), all types of charcuterie, game and rabbit.

Adrienne is still prepared to eat dairy products, so she is not a vegan. She argues that eating this way not only cuts out unwanted fat, but is also good for the environment. Just Rufus' luck to fall head-over-heels for a green, organic-food-eating environmentalist who is into issues of sustainability. As Rufus gamely tries to decide between the stuffed artichokes with red pepper vinaigrette and the grilled, marinated zucchini, he wonders if he might be able to choose the soutzoukakia smyrneika (meatballs cooked with cumin, cinnamon and garlic in a tomato sauce) – after all, they are on holiday and in Greece?

INTRODUCTION

As a lacto-ovo-vegetarian (rather than a lacto-vegetarian or a vegan),[2] Adrienne certainly is not alone in believing that eating organic foods are good for the body, the soul and the planet.[3] 'About one quarter of the 6.5 billion people who live on our planet enjoy a mostly vegetarian diet.'[4] In 2002 there were about 12 million vegetarians in Europe,[5] and this number has been growing steadily. There has been a lively debate in Europe about genetically modified foods compared with the US, although genetic modification for medical purposes has not met with such widespread hostility in Europe. Consumers see 'functional foods as placed midway on the combined "naturalness–healthiness continuum" from organically processed to genetically modified'[6] but tend to remain unconvinced that genetically modified foods can offer any significant health benefits.[7] However, concerns about adult, and more especially childhood, obesity means that diet has become a burning issue for many European governments.[8] It is obvious our menu choices have deep-seated consequences.

The forces that drive people to buy and use products are generally straightforward, as when a person chooses what to have for lunch. As hard-core vegans demonstrate, however, even the consumption of basic food products may also be related to wide-ranging beliefs regarding what is appropriate or desirable. Among the more general population there are strong beliefs about genetically modified foods, which have proved difficult to alter via information campaigns.[9] In some cases, these emotional responses create a deep commitment to the product. Sometimes people are not even fully aware of the forces that drive them towards some products and away from others. Often a person's *values* – their priorities and beliefs about the world – influence these choices. Choices are not always straightforward. Often there are tradeoffs to be made.

 Marketing opportunity

Clashing values? No easy answers for consumers

Consumers are often faced with a clash between values, for instance between ethical behaviour, environmentalism and/or sustainability (of which more below) and the need to manage a family budget. Of new parents, for instance, 42 per cent regularly express concerns about formula milk, disposable nappies and baby food. However, bringing up a green baby can cost, on average, more than £700 (about €770) extra a year if parents don't choose standard food and equipment for their new baby. The cost of standard items during the first year of a baby's life is £835 (about €920) (according to a report by Family Investments) compared with £1,532 (about €1,685) for organic or ethical nappies, baby food, clothes and products like baby oil.

Disposable nappies represent the largest cost item as newborns get through about 2,000 nappies in their first 12 months of life. The annual cost of ordinary nappies is about £380 (about €420) compared with £802 (about €885) for eco-disposables (according to the Women's Environmental Network). However, many green parents try and use cloth nappies, which work out at about £500 (about €550) for the first year, once the costs of purchasing and home laundering the nappies are taken into account. But green parents haven't finished then. They still face the choice of landfill versus water usage (and issues around the new virtual water footprint,[10] of which more below). There really are no easy answers for consumers.[11]

To understand motivation is to understand *why* consumers do what they do. Why do some people choose to bungee jump off a bridge (which is close to being an important rite of passage for young Europeans on their gap year visiting New Zealand) while others choose to do gardening for their relaxation;[12] whilst still others spend their leisure time online playing games or visiting the virtual world of secondlife.com? Whether to quell the pangs of hunger like Rufus and Adrienne, kill boredom, or to attain some deep spiritual experience, we do everything for a reason, even if we can't always articulate what that reason is. Marketing students are taught from Day One that the goal of marketing is to satisfy consumers' needs. However, this insight is useless unless we can discover *what* those needs are and *why* they exist. A beer commercial once asked, 'Why ask why?' In this chapter, we'll find out.

THE MOTIVATION PROCESS: A PSYCHOLOGICAL PERSPECTIVE

▶ **Motivation** refers to the processes that cause people to behave as they do. From a
▶ *psychological perspective* motivation occurs when a **need** is aroused that the consumer wishes to satisfy. Once a need has been activated, a state of tension exists that drives the consumer to attempt to reduce or eliminate the need. This need may be *utilitarian* (a desire to achieve some functional or practical benefit, as when Adrienne eats green vegetables for nutritional reasons) or it may be *hedonic* (an experiential need, involving emotional responses or fantasies, as when Rufus thinks longingly about the rich Bergamasquan cuisine of charcuterie and game). The distinction between the two is,
▶ however, a matter of degree. The desired end-state is the consumer's **goal**. Marketers try to create products and services that will provide the desired benefits and permit the consumer to reduce this tension.

Whether the need is utilitarian or hedonic, a discrepancy exists between the consumer's present state and some ideal state. This gulf creates a state of tension. The magnitude of this tension determines the urgency the consumer feels to reduce the tension. This degree
▶ of arousal is called a **drive**. A basic need can be satisfied in any number of ways, and the specific path a person chooses is influenced both by their unique set of experiences and by the values instilled by cultural, religious, ethnic or national background. In Adrienne's case, her Italian upbringing means that breakfast is not a particularly important meal. Lunch, with her mother's home-cooked food, is normally her main meal of the day, and for supper she will usually prepare something lighter for herself.[13]

▶ These personal and cultural factors combine to create a **want**, which is one manifestation of a need. For example, hunger is a basic need that must be satisfied by all; the lack of food creates a tension state that can be reduced by the intake of such products as paella, bouillabaisse, pasta, cheeses, smoked herring, chocolate biscuits or bean sprouts. The specific route to drive reduction is culturally and individually determined. Once the goal is attained, tension is reduced and the motivation recedes (for the time being). Motivation can be described in terms of its *strength*, or the pull it exerts on the consumer, and its *direction*, or the particular way the consumer attempts to reduce motivational tension.

MOTIVATIONAL STRENGTH

The degree to which a person is willing to expend energy to reach one goal as opposed to another reflects their underlying motivation to attain that goal. Many theories have been advanced to explain why people behave the way they do. Most share the basic idea that people have some finite amount of energy that must be directed towards certain goals. A conceptual distinction has been made between goal setting and goal striving.[14] Recent research has extended Bagozzi and Dhokalia's modelling of goals by examining consumers' willingness to *persistently* strive to achieve goals. In a study of assisted reproductive technologies, the researchers identify the important interplay between culture and cognition in affecting consumers' persistence in achieving goals, in this case the highly emotional goal of parenthood.[15]

POWER IS NOTHING WITHOUT CONTROL. **PIRELLI**

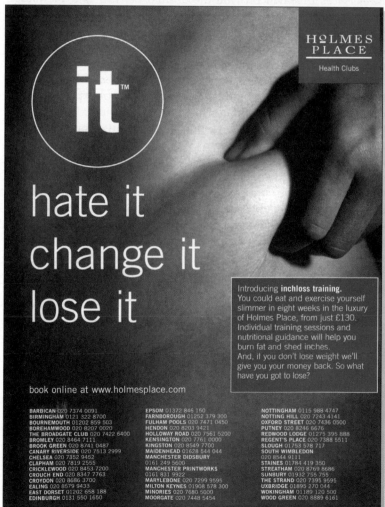

it™

hate it
change it
lose it

HOLMES PLACE
Health Clubs

Introducing **inchloss training.**
You could eat and exercise yourself
slimmer in eight weeks in the luxury
of Holmes Place, from just £130.
Individual training sessions and
nutritional guidance will help you
burn fat and shed inches.
And, if you don't lose weight we'll
give you your money back. So what
have you got to lose?

book online at www.holmesplace.com

BARBICAN 020 7374 0091
BIRMINGHAM 0121 322 8700
BOURNEMOUTH 01202 859 503
BOREHAMWOOD 020 8207 0020
THE BROADGATE CLUB 020 7422 6400
BROMLEY 020 8464 7111
BROOK GREEN 020 8741 0487
CANARY RIVERSIDE 020 7513 2999
CHELSEA 020 7352 9462
CLAPHAM 020 7819 2555
CRICKLEWOOD 020 8453 7200
CROUCH END 020 8347 7763
CROYDON 020 8686 3700
EALING 020 8579 9433
EAST DORSET 01202 658 188
EDINBURGH 0131 550 1650

EPSOM 01372 846 150
FARNBOROUGH 01252 379 300
FULHAM POOLS 020 7471 0450
HENDON 020 8203 9421
HOLLOWAY ROAD 020 7561 5200
KENSINGTON 020 7761 0000
KINGSTON 020 8549 7700
MAIDENHEAD 01628 544 044
MANCHESTER DIDSBURY
0161 249 5600
MANCHESTER PRINTWORKS
0161 831 9922
MARYLEBONE 020 7299 9595
MILTON KEYNES 01908 578 300
MINORIES 020 7680 5000
MOORGATE 020 7448 5454

NOTTINGHAM 0115 988 4747
NOTTING HILL 020 7243 4141
OXFORD STREET 020 7436 0500
PUTNEY 020 8246 6676
REDWOOD LODGE 01275 395 888
REGENT'S PLACE 020 7388 5511
SLOUGH 01753 578 717
SOUTH WIMBLEDON
020 8544 9111
STAINES 01784 419 350
STREATHAM 020 8769 8686
SUNBURY 01932 755 755
THE STRAND 020 7395 9595
UXBRIDGE 01895 270 044
WOKINGHAM 01189 120 500
WOOD GREEN 020 8889 6161

(*Above*) Pirelli uses the sport metaphor
of world-class competition to emphasize
motivation and top performance.

The Advertising Archives

(*Left*) This ad for health clubs and
exercise regimes shows men an undesired
state (lack of muscle tone and fitness,
as dictated by contemporary Western
culture), and suggests a solution to the
problem of spare inches around the waist
(purchase of health club membership in
order to attain a fit and healthy body).

The Advertising Archives

Biological vs. learned needs

Early work on motivation ascribed behaviour to *instinct*, the innate patterns of behaviour that are universal in a species. This view is now largely discredited. The existence of an instinct is difficult to prove or disprove. The instinct is inferred from the behaviour it is supposed to explain (this type of circular explanation is called a *tautology*).[16] It is like saying that a consumer buys products that are status symbols because they are motivated to attain status, which is hardly a satisfactory explanation.

Drive theory

▶ **Drive theory** focuses on biological needs that produce unpleasant states of arousal (e.g. your stomach grumbles during the first lecture of the day – you missed breakfast). We are motivated to reduce the tension caused by this arousal. Tension reduction has been proposed as a basic mechanism governing human behaviour.

In a marketing context, tension refers to the unpleasant state that exists if a person's consumption needs are not fulfilled. A person may be grumpy or unable to concentrate very well if they haven't eaten. Someone may be dejected or angry if they cannot afford that new car they want. This state activates goal-oriented behaviour, which attempts to reduce
▶ or eliminate this unpleasant state and return to a balanced one called **homeostasis**.

Those behaviours that are successful in reducing the drive by satisfying the underlying need are strengthened and tend to be repeated. (This *reinforcement* aspect of the learning process will be discussed in Chapter 7.) Your motivation to leave your lecture early to buy a snack would be greater if you hadn't eaten in the previous 24 hours than if you had eaten breakfast only two hours earlier. If you did sneak out and experienced indigestion after, say, wolfing down a packet of crisps, you would be less likely to repeat this behaviour the next time you wanted a snack. One's degree of motivation, then, depends on the distance between one's present state and the goal.

Drive theory, however, runs into difficulties when it tries to explain some facets of human behaviour that run counter to its predictions. People often do things that *increase* a drive state rather than decrease it. For example, people may delay gratification. If you know you are going out for a five-course dinner, you might decide to forgo a snack earlier in the day even though you are hungry at that time. And, as we shall see in the discussion of desire, the most rewarding thing may often be the tension of the drive state itself rather than its satisfaction. It's not the kill, it's the thrill of the chase.

Expectancy theory

Most explanations of motivation currently focus on cognitive rather than biological factors
▶ in order to understand what drives behaviour. **Expectancy theory** suggests that behaviour is largely pulled by expectations of achieving desirable outcomes – *positive incentives* – rather than being pushed from within. We choose one product over another because we expect this choice to have more positive consequences for us. Thus the term *drive* is used here more loosely to refer to both physical and cognitive, i.e. learned, processes.

MOTIVATIONAL DIRECTION

Motives have direction as well as strength. They are goal oriented in that they drive us to satisfy a specific need. Most goals can be reached by a number of routes, and the objective of a company is to convince consumers that the alternative it offers provides the best chance to attain the goal. For example, a consumer who decides that they need a pair of jeans to help them reach their goal of being accepted by others can choose among Levi's, Wranglers, Diesel, Calvin Klein, Pepe, Gap, Hugo Boss, Stone Island and many other alternatives, each of which promises to deliver certain functional as well as symbolic benefits.

A technical product can satisfy hedonic desires.

The Advertising Archives

Needs vs. wants

The specific way a need is satisfied depends on the individual's unique history, learning experiences and their cultural environment. The particular form of consumption used to satisfy a need is termed a want. For example, two classmates may feel their stomachs rumbling during a lunchtime lecture. If neither person has eaten since the night before, the strength of their respective needs (hunger) would be about the same. However, the way each person goes about satisfying this need might be quite different. The first person may be a vegetarian like Adrienne who fantasizes about large bowls of salad, whereas the second person like Rufus might be equally aroused by the prospect of a large plateful of Greek meatballs in tomato sauce.

Types of needs

A start to the discussion of needs and wants can best be illustrated by considering two basic types of need. People are born with a need for certain elements necessary to maintain life, such as food, water, air and shelter. These are called *biogenic needs.* People have many other needs, however, that are not innate. We acquire *psychogenic needs* as we become members of a specific culture. These include the need for status, power, affiliation, and so on. Psychogenic needs reflect the priorities of a culture, and their effect on behaviour will vary in different environments. For example, an Italian consumer may be driven to devote a good portion of their income to products that permit them to display their individuality, whereas their Scandinavian counterpart may work equally hard to ensure that they do not stand out from their group.

This distinction is revealing because it shows how difficult it is to distinguish needs from wants. How can we tell what part of the motivation is a psychogenic need and what part is a want? Both are profoundly formed by culture, so the distinction is problematic at best. As for the biogenic needs, we know from anthropology that satisfaction of these needs leads to some of the most symbolically rich and culturally based activities of humankind. The ways we want to eat, dress, drink and provide shelter are far more interesting to marketers than our need to do so. And, in fact, human beings need very little in the strict sense of the word. Charles Darwin was astonished to see the native Americans of Tierra del Fuego sleep naked in the snow. Hence, the idea of satisfaction of biogenic needs is more or less a given thing for marketing and consumer research because it is on the most basic level nothing more than a simple prerequisite for us to be here. Beyond that level, and of much greater interest (and challenge) to marketers, is a concept embedded in culture such as wants.[17]

As we have seen, another traditional distinction is between the motivation to satisfy either utilitarian or hedonic needs. The satisfaction of *utilitarian needs* implies that consumers will emphasize the objective, tangible attributes of products, such as fuel economy in a car; the amount of fat, calories, and protein in a hamburger; and the durability of a pair of denim jeans. *Hedonic needs* are subjective and experiential. Here, consumers might rely on a product to meet their needs for excitement, self-confidence, fantasy, and so on. Of course, consumers can be motivated to purchase a product because it provides *both* types of benefits. For example, a mink coat might be bought because it feels soft against the skin, because it keeps one warm through the long cold winters of northern Europe, and because it has a luxurious image. But again the distinction tends to hide more than it reveals, because functionality can bring great pleasure to people and is an important value in the modern world.[18]

We expect today's technical products to satisfy our needs – instantly.
The Advertising Archives

MOTIVATIONAL CONFLICTS

A goal has *valence*, which means that it can be positive or negative. A positively valued goal is one towards which consumers direct their behaviour; they are motivated to *approach* the goal and will seek out products that will help them to reach it. However, not all behaviour is motivated by the desire to approach a goal. As we will see in the discussion of negative reinforcement (Chapter 7), consumers may instead be motivated to *avoid* a negative outcome.[19] They will structure their purchases or consumption activities to reduce the chances of attaining this end result. For example, many consumers work hard to avoid rejection, a negative goal. They will stay away from products that they associate with social disapproval. Products such as deodorants and mouthwash frequently rely on consumers' negative motivation by depicting the onerous social consequences of underarm odour or bad breath.

Because a purchase decision can involve more than one source of motivation, consumers often find themselves in situations where different motives, both positive and negative, conflict with one another.[20] Because marketers are attempting to satisfy consumers' needs, they can also be helpful by providing possible solutions to these dilemmas. As shown in Figure 6.1, three general types of conflicts can occur: approach–approach; approach–avoidance and avoidance–avoidance.

Approach–approach conflict

▶ In an **approach–approach conflict**, a person must choose between two desirable alternatives. As a student, Adrienne might be torn between going home for the holidays or going on a skiing trip with friends. Or, she might have to choose between two CDs.

▶ The **theory of cognitive dissonance** is based on the premise that people have a need for order and consistency in their lives and that a state of tension is created when beliefs or behaviours conflict with one another. The conflict that arises when choosing between two alternatives may be resolved through a process of *cognitive dissonance reduction*, where people are motivated to reduce this inconsistency (or dissonance) and thus eliminate unpleasant tension.[21]

A state of dissonance occurs when there is a psychological inconsistency between two or more beliefs or behaviours. It often occurs when a consumer must make a choice

Figure 6.1 Three types of motivational conflict

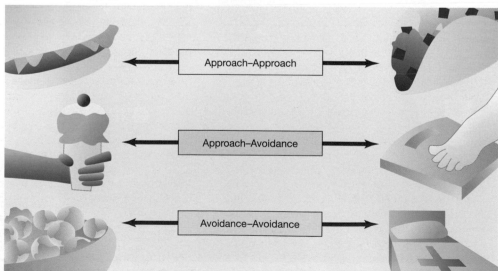

between two products, where both alternatives usually possess both good and bad qualities. By choosing one product and not the other, the person gets the bad qualities of the chosen product and loses out on the good qualities of the one not chosen.

This loss creates an unpleasant, dissonant state that the person is motivated to reduce. People tend to convince themselves, after the fact, that the choice they made was the right one by finding additional reasons to support the alternative they chose, or perhaps by 'discovering' flaws with the option they did not choose (sometimes we call this 'rationalization'). A marketer can resolve an approach–approach conflict by bundling several benefits together. For example, many low calorie products claim that they have 'all the taste' *and* 'half the calories', e.g. Muller Light Yoghurts,[22] 'deliciously thick and creamy tasting and still fat free', allowing the consumer to avoid having to choose between better taste and fewer calories.

Approach–avoidance conflict

Many of the products and services we desire have negative consequences attached to them as well. We may feel guilty or ostentatious when buying a status-laden product such as a fur coat, or we might feel like a glutton when contemplating a box of chocolates.

 When we desire a goal but wish to avoid it at the same time, an **approach–avoidance conflict** exists. Some solutions to these conflicts include the proliferation of fake furs, which eliminate guilt about harming animals to make a fashion statement; and the success of low calorie and diet foods, such as those produced by Weight Watchers, that promise good food without the calories (weight-watchers.com). Some marketers counter consumer resistance to overconsumption and spending by promising more (benefits) from less, as in an Audi advertisement (in 2000), whereas other marketers try to overcome guilt by convincing consumers that they deserve luxuries (such as when the model for L'Oréal cosmetics states, 'Because I'm worth it!'). Sometimes consumers go outside the conventional marketplace to satisfy their needs, wants and desires, for instance drag-racing in Moscow where young Russian car fanatics fulfil their drive for thrill-seeking outside the law.[23]

▲ Marketing opportunity

Men's changing skincare practices

The promotion of men's skincare products has to counter similar issues around approach and avoidance. Men's attitudes to anti-ageing products have changed significantly between 2005 and 2007. A Mintel report on anti-ageing products argued that 'Men in general have shown that they are much more open to using products that enhance personal appearance',[24] as also suggested by Diego Rinallo below, in his discussion of changing views of masculinity. Male anti-ageing products appeal beyond the elite niche and across the age range from 18 to 50 as well as to baby boomers keen to keep looking young in the workplace whilst countering the effects of increasing maturity on their skin (e.g. deep lines). The products are marketed differently so that words such as 'active', 'powerful', 'fight', and 'defend' are used to promote the idea to men of fighting bad skin or defending against age (e.g. wrinkle defence) rather

than positioning the products as 'anti-ageing' as would be the case with women. However, at the same time men have to avoid being seen as feminine by adopting careful grooming habits which traditionally have been viewed as inappropriate for male gender positioning.[25] L'Oréal's website for men, for instance, talks about skincare technology[26] and clinical research into the evolution of the characteristics of men's skin over time, as well as offering diagnosis online and recommended products to deal with crow's feet; forehead wrinkles; laughter lines; sagging lower face; and under-eye bags.[27] The emphasis throughout is on validating the acceptability of the idea of men taking care of themselves and their skins by using male skincare products; and implicitly countering potential male fears that using creams and lotions might be perceived as detracting from their masculinity.

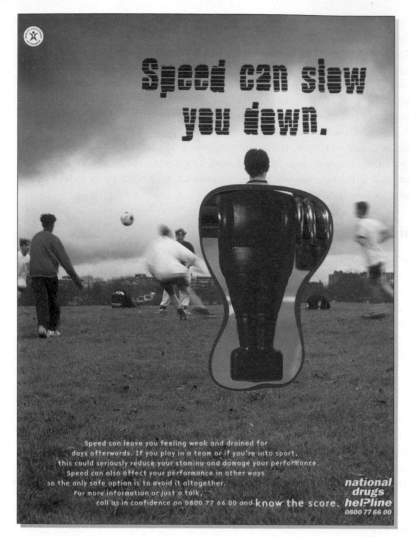

The Partnership for a Drug-Free America points out the negative consequences of drug addiction for those who are tempted to start.

The Advertising Archives

Avoidance–avoidance conflict

Sometimes consumers find themselves 'caught between a rock and a hard place'. They may face a choice between two undesirable alternatives, for instance the option of either investing more money into an old car with more repairs or buying a new one. Marketers
▶ frequently address an **avoidance–avoidance conflict** with messages that stress the unforeseen benefits of choosing one option (e.g. by emphasizing special credit plans to ease the pain of new car payments).

CLASSIFYING CONSUMER NEEDS

Much research has been done on classifying human needs. On the one hand, some psychologists have tried to define a universal inventory of needs that could be traced systematically to explain virtually all behaviour. One such effort, developed by Henry Murray, delineates a set of 20 psychogenic needs that (sometimes in combination) result in specific behaviours. These needs include such dimensions as *autonomy* (being independent), *defendance* (defending the self against criticism), and even *play* (engaging in pleasurable activities).[28]

Murray's needs structure serves as the basis for a number of widely used personality tests such as the Thematic Apperception Technique (TAT) and the Edwards' Personal Preference Schedule (EPPS). In the TAT, test subjects are shown four to six ambiguous pictures and are asked to write answers to four questions about the pictures. These questions are: (1) What is happening? (2) What has led up to this situation? (3) What is being thought? (4) What will happen? Each answer is then analyzed for references to certain needs and scored whenever that need is mentioned. The theory behind the test is that people will freely project their own subconscious needs onto the stimulus. By getting their responses to the picture, you are really getting at the person's true needs for achievement or affiliation or whatever other need may be dominant. Murray believed that everyone has the same basic set of needs, but that individuals differ in their priority ranking of these needs.[29]

Specific needs and buying behaviour

Other motivational approaches have focused on specific needs and their ramifications for behaviour. For example, individuals with a high *need for achievement* strongly value personal accomplishment.[30] They place a premium on products and services that signify success because these consumption items provide feedback about the realization of their goals. These consumers are good prospects for products that provide evidence of their achievement. One study of working women found that those who were high in achievement motivation were more likely to choose clothing they considered businesslike, and less likely to be interested in apparel that accentuated their femininity.[31] Some other important needs that are relevant to consumer behaviour include the following:

- *Need for affiliation* (to be in the company of other people):[32] this need is relevant to products and services that are 'consumed' in groups and alleviate loneliness, such as team sports, bars and shopping centres.

- *Need for power* (to control one's environment):[33] many products and services allow consumers to feel that they have mastery over their surroundings, ranging from cars with 'souped up' engines and loud sound systems that impose the driver's musical tastes on others, to luxury resorts that promise to respond to every whim of their pampered guests.

- *Need for uniqueness* (to assert one's individual identity):[34] products can satisfy this need by pledging to accentuate a consumer's distinctive qualities. For example, Cachet perfume claims to be 'as individual as you are'.

Maslow's hierarchy of needs

One influential approach to motivation was proposed by the psychologist Abraham Maslow. Maslow's approach is a general one, originally developed to understand personal growth and the attainment of 'peak experiences'.[35] Maslow formulated a hierarchy of biogenic and psychogenic needs, in which certain levels of motives are specified. This *hierarchical* approach implies that the order of development is fixed – that is, a certain level must be attained before the next, higher one is activated. Marketers have embraced this perspective because it (indirectly) specifies certain types of product benefits people might be looking for, depending on the different stages in their development and/or their environmental conditions.[36] However, as we shall see it contains many problems, and we shall devote space to it here because it is a 'standard' in marketing knowledge rather than because we believe in its theoretical and practical value.

Maslow's levels are summarized in Figure 6.2. At each level, different priorities exist in terms of the product benefits a consumer is looking for. Ideally, an individual progresses up the hierarchy until their dominant motivation is a focus on 'ultimate' goals, such as justice and beauty. Unfortunately, this state is difficult to achieve (at least on a

Figure 6.2 Levels of need in the Maslow hierarchy

regular basis); most of us have to be satisfied with occasional glimpses, or *peak experiences*. One study of men aged 49 to 60 found respondents engaged in three types of activities to attain self-fulfillment:

1 *sport and physical activity*;

2 *community and charity*; and

3 *building and renovating*.

Regardless of whether these activities related to their professional work, these so-called *magnetic points* gradually took the place of those that were not as fulfilling.[37]

The implication of Maslow's hierarchy is that one must first satisfy basic needs before progressing up the ladder (i.e. a starving man is not interested in status symbols, friend-ship or self-fulfilment).[38] This suggests that consumers value different product attributes depending upon what is currently available to them.

The application of this hierarchy by marketers has been somewhat simplistic, especially as the same product or activity can satisfy a number of different needs. Sex, for example, is characterized as a basic biological drive. While this observation is true throughout most of the animal kingdom, it is obviously a more complicated phenomenon for humans. Indeed, this activity could conceivably fit into every level of Maslow's hierarchy. A sociobiologist, who approaches human behaviour in terms of its biological origins, might argue that reproductive behaviour provides security because it ensures continuation of a person's gene pool and the provision of children to care for the person in old age. Sex can also express love and affiliation at the belongingness level. In addition, sex is often used as a vehicle to attain status, domination over another and to satisfy ego needs; it can be a significant determinant of self-respect. Finally, a sexual experience can be self-actualizing in that it may provide an ecstatic, transcendental experience. The same thing could be said for almost any kind of consumer experience. Similarly, while eating is certainly necessary for our survival, it can also be very much a social act (belongingness); a status act as in the consumption of champagne or other expensive wines and fine cuisine and dining experiences; and an act through which the gourmet cook or the caring and nurturing parent can obtain self-actualization. The house gives us shelter, but is also a security device, a home for the family, a status object and a space for actualizing our personal aspirations and aesthetic tastes.[39] Another example would be gardening, which has been found to satisfy needs at every level of the hierarchy:[40]

- *Physiological*: 'I like to work in the soil.'
- *Safety*: 'I feel safe in the garden.'
- *Social*: 'I can share my produce with others.'
- *Esteem*: 'I can create something of beauty.'
- *Self-actualization*: 'My garden gives me a sense of peace.'

Another problem with taking Maslow's hierarchy too literally is that it is culture-bound. The assumptions of the hierarchy may be restricted to a highly rational, materialistic and individualistic Western culture. People in other cultures may question the order of the levels as specified. A religious person who has taken a vow of celibacy would not necessarily agree that physiological needs must be satisfied before self-fulfilment can occur. Neither do all people in Western cultures seem to live according to Maslow's hierarchy. In fact, spiritual survival can be seen as a stronger motivator than physical survival, as can be seen from patriots or freedom fighters giving their life for the idea of nation, political or religious fanatics for their beliefs, or suicidal people drawing the consequence of a 'spiritual death' by ending their physical lives.[41]

Similarly, many Asian cultures value the welfare of the group (belongingness needs) more highly than needs of the individual (esteem needs). The point is that Maslow's hierarchy, while widely applied in marketing, is only helpful to marketers in so far as it reminds us that consumers may have different need priorities in different consumption situations and at different stages in their lives – not because it exactly specifies a consumer's progression up the ladder of needs. It also does not take account of the cultural formation of needs.

HIDDEN MOTIVES: THE PSYCHOANALYTICAL PERSPECTIVE

A motive is an underlying reason for behaviour and not something researchers can see or easily measure. The same behaviour can be caused by a configuration of different motives. To compound the problem of identifying motives, the consumer may be unaware of the actual need/want they are attempting to satisfy, or alternatively they may not be willing to admit that this need exists. Because of these difficulties, motives must often be *inferred* by the analyst. Although some consumer needs undoubtedly are utilitarian and fairly straightforward, some researchers feel that a great many purchase decisions are not the result of deliberate, logical decisions. On the contrary, people may do things to satisfy motives of which they are not even aware.

Sigmund Freud had a profound, if controversial, impact on many basic assumptions about human behaviour. His work changed the way we view such topics as adult sexuality, dreams and psychological adjustment. **Freudian theory** developed the idea that much of human behaviour stems from a fundamental conflict between a person's desire to gratify their physical needs and the necessity to function as a responsible member of society. This struggle is carried out in the mind among three systems. (Note that these systems do not refer to physical parts of the brain.)

The *id* is entirely oriented towards immediate gratification – it is the 'party animal' of the mind. It operates according to the pleasure principle: behaviour is guided by the primary desire to maximize pleasure and avoid pain. The *id* is selfish and illogical.

It directs a person's psychic energy towards pleasurable acts without regard for the consequences.

The *superego* is the counterweight to the *id*. This system is essentially the person's conscience. It internalizes society's rules (especially as communicated by parents) and works to prevent the *id* from seeking selfish gratification.

Finally, the *ego* is the system that mediates between the *id* and the *superego*. It is in a way a referee in the fight between temptation and virtue. The *ego* tries to balance these two opposing forces according to the reality principle. It finds ways to gratify the *id* that will be acceptable to the outside world. These conflicts occur on an unconscious level, so the person is not necessarily aware of the underlying reasons for their behaviour.

Some of Freud's ideas have also been adapted by consumer researchers. In particular, his work highlights the potential importance of unconscious motives underlying purchases. The implication is that consumers cannot necessarily tell us their true motivation for choosing a product, even if we can devise a sensitive way to ask them directly. The Freudian perspective also hints at the possibility that the *ego* relies on the symbolism in products to compromise between the demands of the *id* and the prohibitions of the *superego*. The person channels their unacceptable desires into acceptable outlets by using products that signify these underlying desires. This is the connection between product symbolism and motivation: the product stands for, or represents, a consumer's true goal, which is socially unacceptable or unattainable. By acquiring the product, the person is able to vicariously experience the forbidden fruit.

Motivational research

The first attempts to apply Freudian ideas to understand the deeper meanings of products and advertisements were made in the 1950s as a perspective known as ▶ **motivational research** was developed. This approach was largely based on psychoanalytic (Freudian) interpretations, with a heavy emphasis on unconscious motives. A basic assumption is that socially unacceptable needs are channelled into acceptable outlets. Product use or avoidance is motivated by unconscious forces which are often determined in childhood.

This form of research relies on *depth interviews* probing deeply into each person's purchase motivations. These can be derived only after questioning and interpretation on the part of a carefully trained interviewer. This work was pioneered by Ernest Dichter, a psychoanalyst who was trained in Vienna in the early part of the twentieth century (see Table 6.1). Dichter conducted in-depth interview studies on over 230 different products, and many of his findings have been incorporated into marketing campaigns.[42] For example, Esso (or Exxon) for many years reminded consumers to 'Put a Tiger in Your Tank', after Dichter found that people responded well to powerful animal symbolism containing vaguely suggestive overtones.

Criticisms of motivational research

Motivational research has been attacked for two quite different reasons. Some feel it does not work, while others feel it works *too* well. On the one hand, social critics attacked this school of thought for giving advertisers the power to manipulate consumers.[43] On the other hand, many consumer researchers felt the research lacked sufficient rigour and validity, since interpretations were subjective and indirect.[44] Because conclusions are based on the analyst's own judgement and are derived from discussions with a small number of people, some researchers are doubtful about the degree to which these results can be generalized to a large market. In addition, because the original motivational researchers were heavily influenced by orthodox Freudian theory, their interpretations usually carried strong sexual overtones. This emphasis tends to overlook other plausible causes for behaviour.

The positive side of motivational research

Motivational research had great appeal at least to some marketers for several reasons, some of which are detailed here. Motivational research tends to be less expensive than large-scale, quantitative survey data because interviewing and data processing costs are relatively small.

The knowledge derived from motivational research may help in the development of marketing communications that appeal to deep-seated needs and thus provide a more powerful hook to relate a product to consumers. Even if they are not necessarily valid for all consumers in a target market, these insights can be valuable when used in an exploratory way. For example, the rich imagery that may be associated with a product can be used creatively when developing advertising copy.

Some of the findings seem intuitively plausible after the fact. For example, motivational studies concluded that coffee is associated with companionship, that people avoid prunes because they remind them of old age, and that men fondly equate the first car they owned as a young man with the onset of their sexual freedom.

Table 6.1 Major motives for consumption as identified by Ernest Dichter

Motive	
Power – masculinity virility	Power: sugary products and large breakfasts (to charge oneself up), bowling, electric trains, hot rods, power tools Masculinity virility: coffee, red meat, heavy shoes, toy guns, buying fur coats for women, shaving with a razor
Security	Ice cream (to feel like a loved child again), full drawer of neatly ironed shirts, real plaster walls (to feel sheltered), home baking, hospital care
Eroticism	Sweets (to lick), gloves (to be removed by woman as a form of undressing), a man lighting a woman's cigarette (to create a tension-filled moment culminating in pressure, then relaxation)
Moral purity – cleanliness	White bread, cotton fabrics (to connote chastity), harsh household cleaning chemicals (to make housewives feel moral after using), bathing (to be equated with Pontius Pilate, who washed blood from his hands), oatmeal (sacrifice, virtue)
Social acceptance	Companionship: ice cream (to share fun), coffee Love and affection: toys (to express love for children), sugar and honey (to express terms of affection) Acceptance: soap, beauty products
Individuality	Gourmet foods, foreign cars, cigarette holders, vodka, perfume, fountain pens
Status	Scotch, ulcers, heart attacks, indigestion (to show one has a high-stress, important job!); carpets (to show one does not live on bare earth like peasants)
Femininity	Cakes and biscuits, dolls, silk, tea, household curios
Reward	Cigarettes, sweets, alcohol, ice cream, biscuits
Mastery over environment	Kitchen appliances, boats, sporting goods, cigarette lighters
Disalienation (a desire to feel connectedness to things)	Home decorating, skiing, morning radio broadcasts (to feel 'in touch' with the world)
Magic – mystery	Soups (having healing powers), paints (change the mood of a room), carbonated drinks (magical effervescent property), vodka (romantic history), unwrapping of gifts

Source: Adapted from Jeffrey F. Durgee, 'Interpreting Dichter's Interpretations: An Analysis of Consumption Symbolism in *The Handbook of Consumer Motivation*', *Marketing and Semiotics: Selected Papers from the Copenhagen Symposium*, ed. Hanne Hartvig-Larsen, David Glen Mick and Christian Alsted (Copenhagen: Handelshøjskolens forlag, 1991).

Despite its drawbacks, motivational research continues to be employed as a useful diagnostic tool. Its validity is enhanced, however, when it is used in conjunction with other research techniques available to the consumer researcher.

CONSUMER DESIRE

▶ More recently, researchers have begun to discuss the importance of the concept of **desire** for understanding consumer behaviour. Desire as a motivational construct is quite revolutionary, since it turns the attention away from satisfaction and over to the thrills of the process of desiring.[45] This potentially opens up a better understanding of consumer insatiability than can be provided by needs and wants. Desire, furthermore, better captures the seductive spirit of the positioning of many contemporary brands and the deep feelings involved in consumer goods' contribution to the formation of consumers' self-images. Because emotions, unruly passions and bodily cravings and pleasures are so central to the experience of desiring, desire reintroduces the bodily aspect of motivation without reducing it to biogenic needs.[46] On the contrary, the concept of desire also emphasizes that, even though desires, needs and wants are felt psychologically, the concept of society (often called 'the Other' in the literature on desire) is very central to the understanding of desire. Thus, desire would refer to the *sociogenic* nature of needs.[47]

An example of a collage used to explore consumer desire.

A Dutch respondent's collage emphasises this person's conception of paradise as a place where there is interpersonal harmony and concern for the environment.

One study of consumer desires in Denmark, Turkey and the US concluded that desires were much more profound than wants, that desire is cyclical and basically insatiable, and that what is desired is more often various kinds of social relationship mediated by consumption experiences than consumption in itself.[48] The study used collages among other techniques to explore consumer desire, and the collage opposite illustrates some of the featured findings: that desire is positive but potentially harmful if out of control (the balance, the fight with one's own shadow) and can lead to impossible dreams (the ugly man and the model) or to excess and violation of norms (Hugh Grant and the prostitute). Desire is one way of dealing with very passionate consumers, stressing the very emotional and sometimes irrational side of consumer behaviour. If consumer desire is investigated from a more rationalizing and cognitive psychological perspective, it tends to be dealt with under the term consumer *involvement*.

CONSUMER INVOLVEMENT

Do consumers form strong relationships with products and services? People can become pretty attached to products. As we have seen, a consumer's motivation to attain a goal increases their desire to expend the effort necessary to acquire the products or services they believe will be instrumental in satisfying that goal. However, not everyone is motivated to the same extent – one person might be convinced they can't live without the latest Apple iPhone, while another is perfectly happy with their three year-old LG.

▶ **Involvement** is defined as 'a person's perceived relevance of the object based on their inherent needs, values, and interests'.[49] The word *object* is used in the generic sense and refers to a product (or a brand), an advertisement, or a purchase situation. Consumers can find involvement in all these *objects*. Figure 6.3 shows that because involvement is a motivational construct, different antecedents can trigger it. These factors can be something about the person, something about the object, or something about the situation, which can combine to determine the consumer's motivation to process product-related information at a given point in time. When consumers are intent on doing what they can to satisfy a need, they will be motivated to pay attention and process any information felt to be relevant to achieving their goals.

On the other hand, a person may not bother to pay any attention to the same information if it is not seen as relevant to satisfying some need. Adrienne, for instance, who prides

Figure 6.3 Conceptualizing components of involvement

ANTECEDENTS OF INVOLVEMENT

POSSIBLE RESULTS OF INVOLVEMENT

Person factors
- needs
- importance
- interest
- values

Object or stimulus factors
- differentiation of alternatives
- source of communication
- content of communication

Situational factors
- purchase/use
- occasion

INVOLVEMENT

With advertisements

With products

With purchase decisions

Elicitation of counter-arguments to ads

Effectiveness of ad to induce purchase

Relative importance of the product class

Perceived differences in product attributes

Preference for a particular brand

Influence of price on brand choice

Amount of information search

Time spent deliberating alternatives

Type of decision rule used in choice

INVOLVEMENT = f (Person, Situation, Object)

The level of involvement may be influenced by one or more of these factors. Interactions among persons, situation, and object factors are likely to occur.

herself on her knowledge of the environment and green issues, may read everything she can find about the subject, while another person may skip over this information without giving it a second thought.

Involvement can be viewed as the motivation to process information.[50] To the degree that there is a perceived linkage between a consumer's needs, goals or values and product knowledge, the consumer will be motivated to pay attention to product information. When relevant knowledge is activated in memory, a motivational state is created that drives behaviour (e.g. shopping). As felt involvement with a product increases, the consumer devotes more attention to ads related to the product, exerts more cognitive effort to understand these ads, and focuses more attention on the product-related information in them.[51] However, this kind of 'rational' involvement may be the exception rather than the rule.[52]

Levels of involvement: from inertia to passion

The type of information processing that will occur thus depends on the consumer's level of involvement. It can range from *simple processing*, where only the basic features of a message are considered, all the way to *elaboration*, where the incoming information is linked to one's pre-existing knowledge system.[53]

Inertia

We can think of a person's degree of involvement as a continuum, ranging from absolute lack of interest in a marketing stimulus at one end to obsession at the other. Consumption at the low end of involvement is characterized by **inertia**, where decisions are made out of habit because the consumer lacks the motivation to consider alternatives. At the high end of involvement, we can expect to find the type of passionate intensity reserved for people and objects that carry great meaning for the individual. For the most part a

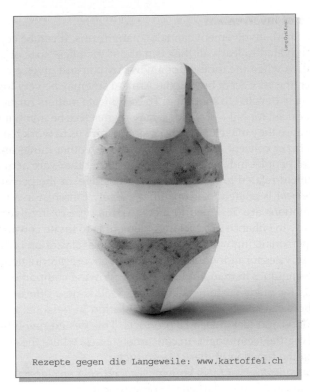

Rezepte gegen die Langeweile: www.kartoffel.ch

The Swiss Potato Board is trying to increase involvement with its product. The ad reads, 'Recipes against boredom'.

Swisspatat

consumer's involvement level with products falls somewhere in the middle, and the marketing strategist must determine the relative level of importance to understand how much elaboration of product information will occur.

When consumers are truly involved with a product, an ad or a Website, they enter what has been called a **flow state**. This state is the Holy Grail of **Web** designers who want to create sites that are so entrancing that the surfer loses all track of time as they become engrossed in the site's contents (and hopefully buys things in the process!). The Web is 'a part of the Internet accessed through a graphical user interface and containing documents often connected by hyperlinks' [**http://www.merriam-webster.com/dictionary/world+wide+web**]. Flow is an optimal experience characterized by:

- a sense of playfulness;
- a feeling of being in control;
- concentration and highly focused attention;
- mental enjoyment of the activity for its own sake;
- a distorted sense of time;
- a match between the challenge at hand and one's skills.[54]

⚠ Marketing opportunity

Cult products

Cult products command fierce consumer loyalty, devotion – and maybe even worship by consumers who are very highly involved with a brand. These items take many forms, from Apple products and Harley-Davidson motorcycles to Barbie dolls and Manchester United football strips.

The many faces of involvement

As previously defined, involvement can take many forms. It can be cognitive, as when a 'Web-head' is motivated to learn all they can about the latest spec of a new multimedia PC, or emotional, as when the thought of a new Armani suit gives a clothes horse goose pimples.[55] Further, the very act of buying the Armani suit may be very involving for people who are passionately devoted to shopping. To complicate matters further, advertisements, such as those produced for Nike or Adidas, may themselves be involving for some reason (for example, because they make us laugh, cry, or inspire us to work harder). It seems that involvement is a fuzzy concept, because it overlaps with other things and means different things to different people. Indeed, the consensus is that there are actually several broad types of involvement related to the product, the message, or the perceiver.[56]

Product involvement is related to a consumer's level of interest in a particular product. Many sales promotions are designed to increase this type of involvement. Perhaps the most powerful way to enhance product involvement is to invite consumers to play a role ▶ in designing or personalizing what they buy. **Mass customization** is the personalization of products and services for individual customers at a mass-production price.[57] Improved manufacturing techniques in many industries are allowing companies to produce made-to-order products for many customers at a time. Dell is now offering customized paint jobs on its notebooks, as part of the design revolution in personal computers aimed at giving a unique look and feel to Dell IT products. This design revolution recognizes the changing role of digitial technologies in consumers' lives, where the emphasis is as much on the form as on the function of these IT products. [58]

Message-response involvement (also known as *advertising involvement*), refers to the consumer's interest in processing marketing communications.[59] Television is considered a low-involvement medium because it requires a passive viewer who exerts relatively little control (remote control 'zapping' notwithstanding) over content. In contrast, print is often seen as a high-involvement medium. The reader is actively involved in processing the information and is able to pause and reflect on what they have read before moving on.[60] We'll discuss the role of message characteristics in changing attitudes in Chapter 8.

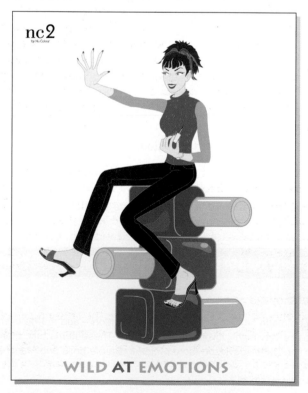

Many marketing messages, such as this ad for a cosmetics company in Taiwan, focus on emotions rather than cognitions.

Pao&Paws Ad Agency

Marketing opportunity

Marketers are experimenting with novel ways to increase consumers' involvement with different product and message formats. Smart marketers are waking up to the idea that their most avid fans are a great resource – rather than ignoring their suggestions, they know they need to take them seriously. This input is certainly clear to producers who develop movies based upon cherished comic book characters or other stories such as *Star Wars* or *Lord of the Rings*. When director Ang Lee hinted that in his movie version *The Hulk* might not wear his trademark purple pants – or any pants at all – devotees of the comic character bombarded the Web with protests and threats of a boycott. Guess what? When the movie was released, The Hulk was indeed sporting his familiar attire.[61]

The quest to heighten message involvement is fuelling the rapid growth of **interactive mobile marketing** where consumers participate in real-time promotional campaigns via their trusty cell phones, usually by text-messaging entries to on-air TV contests. These strategies are very popular in the UK, for example, where revenue from phone and text-messaging services for TV programmes bring in almost half a billion dollars (over 680 million euros) a year. Viewers sent over 500,000 text-message votes within two days during the reality show *Big Brother*.[62]

Purchase situation involvement refers to differences that may occur when buying the same object for different contexts. Here the person may perceive a great deal of social risk or none at all. For example, when you want to impress someone you may try to buy a brand or a product with a certain image that you think reflects good taste. When you have to buy a gift for someone in an obligatory situation, like a wedding gift for a cousin you do not really like, you may not care what image the gift portrays. Or you may actually pick something cheap that reflects your desire to distance yourself from that cousin. Again, some smart retailers are waking up to the value of increasing purchase situation involvement by appealing to hedonic shoppers who are looking to be entertained or otherwise engaged in addition to just 'buying stuff'.[63] We saw how they are doing this via the creation of themed retailing venues and other strategies in Chapter 3.

Ego involvement (sometimes described as *enduring involvement*) refers to the importance of a product to a consumer's self-concept. This concept implies a high level of social risk: the prospect of the product not performing its desired function may result in embarrassment or damage to the consumer's self-concept (Chapter 5 is devoted to the importance of the self-concept for consumer behaviour issues). For example, Adrienne's vegetarianism and interest in green issues are clearly an important part of her self-identity (her choice of organic foods is said to have high sign value). This type of involvement is independent of particular purchase situations. It is an ongoing concern related to the self and often hedonic or experiential experiences (the emotions felt as a result of using products).[64]

Measuring involvement

The measurement of involvement is important for many marketing applications. For example, research evidence indicates that a viewer who is more involved with a television show will also respond more positively to commercials contained in that show, and that these spots will have a greater chance of influencing their purchase intentions.[65] The many conceptualizations of involvement have led to some confusion about the best way to measure the concept. One of the most widely used measures of the state of involvement are the scales in Zaichkowsky's (1994) Personal Involvement Inventory.[66]

Teasing out the dimensions of involvement

Two French researchers devised a scale to measure the antecedents of product involvement, arguing that no single component of involvement is predominant.[67] Recognizing that consumers can be involved with a product because it is a risky purchase and/or its use reflects on or affects the self, they advocate the development of an *involvement profile* containing five components:[68]

195

1 The personal interest a consumer has in a product category, its personal meaning or importance.

2 The perceived importance of the potential negative consequences associated with a poor choice of product (risk importance).

3 The probability of making a bad purchase.

4 The pleasure value of the product category.

5 The sign value of the product category (how closely it is related to the self).[69]

Segmenting by involvement levels

A measurement approach of this nature allows consumer researchers to capture the diversity of the involvement construct, and it also provides the potential to use involvement as a basis for market segmentation. For example, a yoghurt manufacturer might find that even though its product is low in sign value for one group of consumers, it might be highly related to the self-concept of another market segment, such as health food enthusiasts or avid dieters. The company could adapt its strategy to account for the motivation of different segments to process information about the product. These variations are discussed in Chapter 8. Note also that involvement with a product class may vary across cultures.[70]

Strategies to increase involvement

Although consumers differ in their level of involvement with respect to a product message, marketers do not just have to sit back and hope for the best. By being aware of some basic factors that increase or decrease attention, they can take steps to increase the likelihood that product information will get through. A marketer can boost consumers' motivations to process relevant information by using one or more of the following techniques:[71]

● *Appeal to the consumers' hedonic needs*. For example, ads using sensory appeals generate higher levels of attention.[72]

● *Use novel stimuli, such as unusual cinematography, sudden silences, or unexpected movements in commercials*. One ad for the British firm Egg Banking stated, 'Cats always land on their paws', and then two researchers in white lab coats dropped a kitten off a rooftop – never to see it again (animal rights activists were not amused).[73]

● *Use prominent stimuli, such as loud music and fast action, to capture attention in commercials*. In print formats, larger ads increase attention. Also, viewers look longer at coloured pictures as opposed to black and white.

● *Include celebrity endorsers to generate higher interest in commercials*. (We will discuss this strategy in Chapter 8.)

● *Build a bond with consumers by maintaining an ongoing relationship with them*. The routes to cultivating brand loyalty will be discussed further in Chapter 9.

● *The Internet has provided companies with new possibilities for creating loyalty bonds with customers*. For example, girls can customize their own doll at Mattel's My Design Website, located at **www.barbie.com/mydesign**. They can specify her skin tone, hair and eye colour and outfits. They can also name the doll, and she comes with a personality profile they can tailor from choices on the Website.[74]

CONSUMER-GENERATED CONTENT (CGC)

▶ **Consumer-generated content**, where ordinary people voice their opinions about products, brands, and companies on blogs, podcasts and social networking sites like Facebook and MySpace, and even film their own commercials that thousands view on sites like

Fountain of youth: a total of 1,360 students in Leuven, Belgium, create a new world record for the greatest number of simultaneous Mentos fountains, achieved by dropping a Mentos mint into a bottle of Coke.

Getty Images/AFP

YouTube, is probably the biggest marketing phenomenon of the last few years (even bigger than the iPhone). Have you checked out one of those crazy Mentos/Diet Coke videos yet? At least 800 of them flooded the Internet after people discovered that when you drop the quarter-size mint sweets into bottles of Diet Coke you get a geyser that shoots 20 feet into the air. Needless to say, Mentos got a gusher of free publicity out of the deal too,[75] including a world record in Leuven when 1,360 students created the greatest number of simultaneous Mentos fountains (fountains of youth).[76] 'The explosion in Consumer Generated Media over the last year means that this reliance on word of mouth, over other forms of referral, looks set to increase.'[77] Advertisers will probably spend '$1.4 billion (nearly 1 billion euros) in 2008 to place ads on social networking sites, with that number predicted to rise to $2.6 billion (over 1.7 billion euros) by 2012.'[78] This important trend helps to define the so-called era of Web 2.0; the rebirth of the Internet as a social, interactive medium from its original roots as a form of one-way transmission from producers to consumers.

Although many marketers find this change threatening because they are now forced to 'share' ownership of their brands with users, this new form of user participation is here to stay. The reality is that companies can no longer rely solely upon a 'push method' to inform their customers about their products; there is now a vibrant two-way dialogue that allows consumers to contribute their evaluations of products within their respective Web communities. Consumers are embracing this trend for several reasons: the technology is readily available and inexpensive to use; Internet access allows any surfer to become (somewhat of) an expert on anything in a matter of hours (see Chapter 15 for discussion of European consumers' access to the Internet and their e-skills); and people trust their peers' opinions more than they do those of big companies (more on this in Chapter 10).[79] So, marketers need to accept this new reality of consumer-generated content – even when they don't necessarily like what customers have to say about their brands. Here are a just few of the many consumer-generated campaigns we have seen recently:[80]

- Lucasfilm made clips of *Star Wars* available to fans on the Internet to *mash up* (remix) at will to celebrate the 30th anniversary of the epic's release. Working with an easy-to-use editing program fans can cut, add to and retool the clips. Then they can post their creations to blogs or social networking sites like MySpace.

- Now that TV spin-offs from the *Star Trek* series have ended, bereft fans are filling the void by banding together to make their own episodes. Up to two dozen of these fan-made

Star Trek projects are in various stages of completion, depending what you count as a fully-fledged production. You can view a Scottish production at **www.ussintrepid.org.uk**. A Los Angeles group has filmed more than 40 episodes, some of which explore gay themes the original didn't get near (check out **www.hiddenfrontier.com**). A Texas-based group resurrected a ship whose crew was turned into salt in an episode of the original series (**www.starshipexeter.com**).

● Danish *Vores Øl* ('Our Beer') claims to be the world's first open-source brew. The brewer publishes the recipe under a 'Creative Commons' licence, meaning that anyone can use *Vores Øl*'s name. As long as home brewers publish the recipe under the same licence, they're free to make money from their versions of the brand.

● Honda UK is sponsoring a new blog network, **2TalkAbout.com**, that lets audiences publish their views on well-known brands as well as respond to other people's views. Although the online community is completely independent from Honda, its engineers and associates will regularly log on to contribute to and respond to feedback, giving users direct access to the brand.

▼ Marketing pitfall

Chevrolet learned the hard way about the downside of giving control over its brands to consumers. The carmaker introduced a Website allowing visitors to take existing video clips and music, insert their own words and create a customized 30-second commercial for the 2007 *Chevrolet Tahoe*. The idea was to generate interest for the *Tahoe* by encouraging satisfied drivers to circulate videos of themselves around the Web. Sure enough, plenty of videos circulated – but many of the messages for the gas-hungry SUV weren't exactly flattering. One ad used a sweeping view of the *Tahoe* driving through a desert. 'Our planet's oil is almost gone,' it said. 'You don't need GPS to see where this road leads.' Another commercial asked: 'Like this snowy wilderness? Better get your fill of it now. Then say hello to global warming.'

A spokeswoman for Chevrolet said, 'We anticipated that there would be critical submissions. You do turn over your brand to the public, and we knew that we were going to get some bad with the good. But it's part of playing in this space.'[81]

VALUES

▶ Generally speaking, a **value** can be defined as a belief about some desirable end-state that transcends specific situations and guides selection of behaviour.[82] Thus, values are general and different from attitudes in that they do not apply to specific situations only. A person's set of values plays a very important role in their consumption activities, since many products and services are purchased because (it is believed) they will help us to attain a value-related goal. Two people can believe in the same behaviours (for example, vegetarianism) but their underlying belief systems may be quite different (animal activism vs. health concerns). The extent to which people share a belief system is a function of individual, social and cultural forces. Advocates of a belief system often seek out others with similar beliefs, so that social networks overlap and as a result believers tend to be exposed to information that supports their beliefs (e.g. environmentalists rarely socialize with factory farmers).[83]

Core values

▶ Every culture has a set of **core values** that it imparts to its members.[84] For example, people in one culture might feel that being a unique individual is preferable to sub-ordinating one's identity to the group, while another group may emphasize the virtues of group membership. In many cases, values are universal. Who does not desire health, wisdom or world peace? But on the other hand, values can vary across cultures and do change over time. In Japan young people are working hard to adopt Western values and behaviours – which explains why the current fashion for young people is bleached, blond hair, chalky make-up and a deep tan. Government policies have encouraged this type of consumer spending. However, changing patterns of consumption have increased feelings of personal liberation among the younger generation. They are now challenging many of the values of the past as shown, for instance, by the increasing school drop-out rate, which has grown by 20 per cent since 1997.[85] Similar concerns about the consequences of what is often called a value crisis are also discussed in European societies. Likewise, one may wonder what happened to the traditional Scandinavian modesty – in both Denmark and Sweden people are now showing more willingness to share their private lives with thousands of others in either talk shows or docu-soaps of the *Big Brother* variety.

▶ Multicultural dimensions

Take the core value of cleanliness – everyone wants to be clean, but some societies are more fastidious than others and won't accept products and services that they think cut corners. Italian women on average spend 21 hours a week on household chores other than cooking – compared with just four hours for Americans, according to Procter & Gamble's research. They wash kitchen and bathroom floors at least four times a week, Americans just once. They typically iron nearly all their washing, even socks and sheets, and they buy more cleaning supplies than do women elsewhere.

So, they should be ideal customers for cleaning products, right? That's what Unilever thought when it launched its all-purpose Cif spray cleaner there, but it flopped. Similarly, P&G's best-selling Swiffer Wet Mop failed quite spectacularly. Both companies underestimated this market's desire for products that are tough cleaners, not timesavers. Only about 30 per cent of Italian households have dishwashers because many women don't trust machines to get dishes as clean as they can get them by hand, manufacturers say. Many of those who have machines tend to thoroughly rinse the dishes before loading them in the machine. The explanation for this value: after World War II, Italy remained a poor country until well into the 1960s, so labour-saving devices like washing machines that had become popular in wealthy countries arrived late. Italian women joined the workforce later than

many other European women and in smaller numbers. While younger women increasingly work outside the home, they still spend nearly as much time as their mothers did on housework.

When Unilever did research to find out why Italians didn't take to Cif, they found that these women weren't convinced that a mere spray would do the job on tough kitchen grease; or that one product would adequately clean different surfaces (it turns out that 72 per cent of Italians own more than eight different cleaning products). The company reformulated the product and reintroduced it with different varieties instead of as an all-in-one cleaning product. It also made the bottles 50 per cent bigger because Italians clean so frequently; and changed its advertising to emphasize the product's cleaning strength rather than its convenience. P&G also reintroduced its Swiffer. This time they added beeswax and included a Swiffer duster that is now a best seller. It sold five million boxes in the first eight months, twice the company's forecasts.[86] This is in comparison with the UK where 'consumer preference tends to shuffle between the task-specific and multi-purpose cleaners when it comes to purchasing surface cleaners'.[87] In the face of difficult economic conditions, UK consumers are increasingly driven by the need to watch budgets in making their choice amongst cleaning products,[88] so that the goal of cleanliness has to be offset against the goal of affordability and managing the household budget.

Value systems

▶ Every culture is characterized by its members' endorsement of a **value system**. These end-states may not be equally endorsed by everyone, and in some cases values may even seem to contradict one another (e.g. Westerners in general appear to value both conformity and individuality, and seek to find some accommodation between the two). Nonetheless, it is usually possible to identify a general set of *core values* which uniquely define a culture.

How do we find out what a culture values? We term the process of learning the beliefs
▶ and behaviours endorsed by one's own culture **enculturation**. In contrast, we call the process of learning the value system and behaviours of another culture (often a priority for

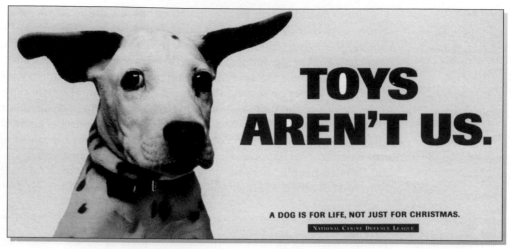

Many advertisements appeal to people's values to persuade them to change or modify their behaviours.

The Advertising Archives

▶ those who wish to understand consumers and markets in foreign countries) **acculturation**.[89] *Socialization agents* including parents, friends, and teachers impart these beliefs to us. Another important type of agent is the media; we learn a lot about a culture's priorities by looking at the values communicated by advertising. Sales strategies, for example, differ significantly between the US and China. American commercials are more likely to present facts about products and suggestions from credible authorities, while Chinese advertisers tend to focus more on emotional appeals without bothering too much to substantiate their claims. American ads tend to be youth-oriented, while Chinese ads are more likely to stress the wisdom of older people.[90] Italians don't like online publicity because online ads represent obstacles as they try to navigate a Website. Nearly 70 per cent of Italians interviewed complained that the publicity was a violation of their privacy, and about 40 per cent found online advertising invasive.[91]

Core values must be understood in the local context – that is, the meaning of the values changes when the cultural context shifts. This is a serious challenge to the idea that it is possible to compare value systems by studying the rankings of universal sets of values across countries.

Consumer behaviour as I see it . . .

One of my ongoing research interests is fashion, which I consider an interesting setting in which to explore how consumer values and lifestyles are evolving. Being Italian and living in Milan, my foreign colleagues regularly say that I'm definitely in the right place. One recent development is that fashion increasingly speaks to men. In the past, women were the only targets of companies in the fashion and beauty businesses. After the French Revolution men renounced fashion – on the basis of the cultural principle that judgement of a man's worth should be based on accomplishments rather than on simple appearance. In the 1980s, however, fashion designers like Armani, Versace, Dolce & Gabbana, Calvin Klein – to name just a few prominent examples – started employing muscular and handsome male models in their ads who were far from the average-looking guy next door. Such beauty ideals, which are shaped by gay aesthetics, are difficult (not to say impossible) to achieve for most men. In some cases, these images were rejected

Dr Diego Rinallo
Bocconi University, Milan

by male consumers for being unrealistic or even exploitative of psychological fragilities. However, many male consumers are seduced by these beautiful representations of masculinity, which stimulate consumer narcissism and lead men to look at themselves and other men as objects of beauty. People who are now in their twenties and early thirties have grown up immersed in a media environment full of these hyper-real images of masculinity, which have influenced male consumer aesthetics. Young straight men, increasingly, look like gay men, particularly when living in metropolitan areas. Accordingly, fashion involvement is no longer a predominantly female trait.

However, the fashion-conscious guy may face stigma – particularly outside big cities. Sure, men have to abide by minimum requirements to be socially accepted. However, there are boundaries that cannot be crossed without risks. Men who spend too much time and money on looking beautiful or adopt extreme fashions to attract attention to their physical appearance may be considered unmanly: vain, superficial, effeminate, and even gay. In contexts characterized by homophobia, such evaluations engender negative social consequences. Even those fashion innovators who would like to experiment with new products and styles are constrained by the fear of being misjudged or made fun of by family, friends, and acquaintances. These facts show that important aspects of consumer behaviour – such as consumer involvement and the acquisition of expertise regarding certain product categories – may be shaped by cultural norms about what is gender appropriate for men and women. Such norms are internalized by consumers and, in cases of transgressions, actively sanctioned through the judgemental gaze of relevant others.

As early fashion theorists have often reminded us, fashion is based on ambivalence between two opposing needs: expressing individuality on the one hand, and being socially accepted on the other. In Italy, people are often said to be obsessed with bella figura (literally, a good figure, which can be roughly translated as making a good impression). Bella figura in fashion requires standing out in the crowd, but without going to the extreme. Virtue resides in the middle, according to an old Latin proverb. However, the 'middle' is socially constructed and marketers, through their mass production of visual images of beauty, constantly try to redefine it. Outside of Italy, national cultural differences may play important roles in configuring what constitutes excess in men's fashion and physical appearance. I leave male readers to ponder the limits of an acceptable involvement with fashion and beauty in their own country and social milieu.

How can marketers target fashion-involved men in an effective way? In my view, all marketing mix elements can be deployed for this purpose. Male models in advertising should be beautiful, but not impossibly so, in order to avoid consumer rejection. Celebrity endorsers should be selected on the basis of what they have achieved, rather than just on their looks. In addition, promotion, product design, distribution channels and price should in general help male consumers avoid social criticism while indulging in narcissism. For example, a cheap moisturizing cream bought in a supermarket may be much more socially acceptable than an expensive, top brand purchased at a cosmetics counter in an up-market department store; an anti-wrinkle cream may be redefined as 'regenerating' and its use linked to special circumstances ('I wouldn't buy it, but my skin needs to be fresh for tomorrow's meeting with my boss').

Applications of values to consumer behaviour

Despite their importance, values have not been as widely applied to direct examinations of consumer behaviour as might be expected. One reason is that broad-based concepts such as freedom, security, or inner harmony are more likely to affect general purchasing patterns rather than to differentiate between brands within a product category. For this reason, some researchers have found it convenient to make distinctions among broad-based *cultural values* such as security or happiness; *consumption-specific values* such as convenient shopping or prompt service; and *product-specific values* such as ease of use or durability, that affect the relative importance people in different cultures place on possessions.[92] However, such a distinction may border on abusing the value concept, since it is normally taken to represent the most general and profound level in the social psychological hierarchy.

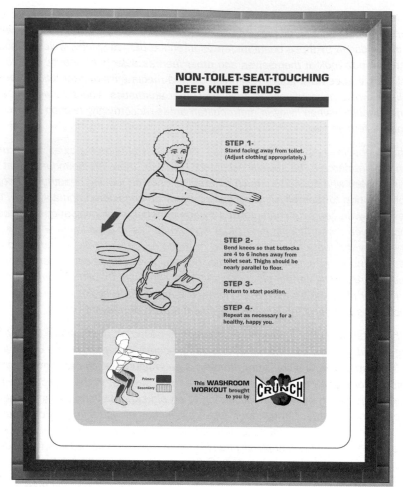

Cleanliness is a
core value in many
cultures.

DiMassimo, Inc.

A recent study of product-specific values looked in depth at Australians who engage in extreme sports like surfing, snowboarding and skateboarding. The researchers identified four dominant values that drove brand choice: freedom, belongingness, excellence and connection. For example, one female surfer they studied embraced the value of belongingness. She expressed this value by wearing popular brands of surfing apparel even when these major brands had lost their local roots by going mainstream. In contrast, another surfer in the study valued connection; he expressed this by selecting only locally-made brands and going out of his way to support local surfing events.[93]

While some aspects of brand image such as sophistication tend to be common across cultures, others are more likely to be relevant in specific places. The characteristic of peacefulness is valued to a larger extent in Japan, while the same holds true for passion in Spain and ruggedness in the US.[94] Because values drive much of consumer behaviour (at least in a very general sense), we might say that virtually all consumer research ultimately is related to the identification and measurement of values. This process can take many forms, ranging from qualitative research techniques such as ethnography to quantitative techniques such as laboratory experiments and large-scale surveys. This section will describe some specific attempts by researchers to measure cultural values and apply this knowledge to marketing strategy.

A number of companies track changes in values through large-scale surveys. For instance, one Young and Rubicam study tracked the new segment of single, professional career women without any ambitions of having a family. They are among the highest consuming segments and are characterized by central values such as freedom and independence.[95]

Many companies use value inventories in order to adapt their strategies. SAS, the airline, which for a long time addressed 'hard values' of their key segment, business travellers, realized that this segment had started to express more informal and 'softer' values, and they changed their communication profile accordingly.[96]

Such ideas are reflected in a relatively recent theory of consumer value. According to this theory, value for a consumer is the consumer's evaluation of a consumer object in terms of which general benefit the consumer might get from consuming it.[97] As such, the value at stake in consumption is tied much more to the consumption experience than to general existential values of the person. Thus, it is suggested that the consumer experience may generate eight distinct types of consumer value:

1 *Efficiency*: referring to all products aimed at providing various kinds of convenience for the consumer.

2 *Excellence*: addressing situations where the experience of quality is the prime motivation.

3 *Status*: when the consumer pursues success and engages in impression management and conspicuous consumption.

4 *(Self-)Esteem*: situations where the satisfaction of possessing is in focus, as is the case with materialism.

5 *Play*: the value of having fun in consuming.

6 *Aesthetics*: searching for beauty in one's consumption e.g. designer products, fashion or art.

7 *Ethics*: referring to motivations behind consumption, e.g. morally or politically correct consumption choices.

8 *Spirituality*: experiencing magical transformations or sacredness in the consumption, as felt by devoted collectors.[98]

The Rokeach Value Survey

▶ The psychologist Milton Rokeach identified a set of **terminal values**,[99] or desired end-states, that apply (to various degrees) to many different cultures. The *Rokeach Value*
▶ *Survey*, a scale used to measure these values, also includes a set of **instrumental values**,[100] which are composed of actions needed to achieve these terminal values.[101] These sets of values have been used in many studies, for example to investigate the changes in the value system of post-Soviet Russia.[102]

Some evidence indicates that differences on these global values do translate into product-specific preferences and differences in media usage. Nonetheless, marketing researchers have not widely used the Rokeach Value Survey.[103] One reason is that our society is evolving into smaller and smaller sets of *consumption micro-cultures* within a larger culture, each with its own set of core values.

The List of Values (LOV)

▶ The **List of Values** identifies nine consumer values which can be related to differences in consumption behaviours. It includes the following values: sense of belonging, fun and enjoyment in life, excitement, warm relationships with others, self-fulfilment, being well respected, a sense of accomplishment, self-respect and security. A comparative study of French and German consumers which used this instrument found that the values of sense of belonging and self-respect were much more popular in Germany, whereas the values of fun and enjoyment in life, self-fulfilment and self-accomplishment were chosen as the most important values in France significantly more often.[104]

However, it should be noted that the cross-cultural validity of such value instruments is, at best, difficult to obtain since, as we have already said, the meaning of values may differ significantly in different cultural contexts.[105] For example, the LOV did not do very well in a test of its cross-cultural validity.[106]

Figure 6.4 The motivational domains of the Schwartz value survey

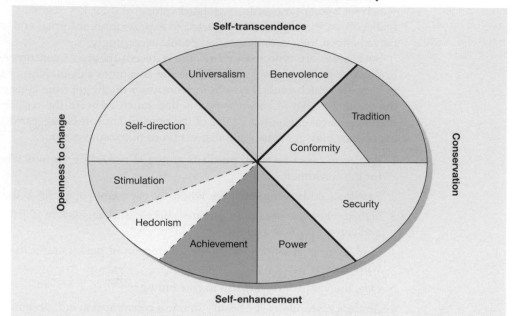

Schwartz value survey

This very elaborate set of values, containing 56 different values organized in ten so-called motivational domains, has been demonstrated to be among the more cross-culturally valid set of instruments.[107] The structuring of values in interrelated motivational domains provides a theoretical framework for this approach to values which many researchers find more satisfactory compared to other value inventories. More specifically, it has been demonstrated to distinguish between cultures[108] and types of media consumption behaviour[109] better than the traditional dichotomy of individualism and collectivism. The values are located in a space demarcated by the poles 'openness to change' vs. 'conservation' and 'self-transcendence' vs. 'self-enhancement'. These dimensions seem relatively universal for a lot of syndicated lifestyle and value surveys. A mapping of the motivational domains can be seen in Figure 6.4. The Schwartz value survey was used to profile Danish consumers with environmentally friendly attitudes and behaviour, where it turned out that such values as 'protecting the environment' and 'unity with nature' but also 'mature love', 'broadminded' and 'social justice' characterized the 'green' segment, whereas values such as 'authority', 'social power', 'national security' and 'politeness' were the values most characteristic of the non-green segment.[110]

THE MEANS–END CHAIN MODEL

▶ Another research approach that incorporates values is termed a **means–end chain model**. This approach assumes that people link very specific product attributes (indirectly) to terminal values: we choose among alternative means to attain some end state we value (such as freedom or safety). Thus, we value products to the extent that they provide the

▶ means to some end we desire. Through a technique called **laddering**, consumers' associations between specific attributes and general consequences are uncovered. Consumers are helped to climb up the 'ladder' of abstraction that connects functional product attributes with desired end-states.[111] Based upon consumer feedback, researchers create *hierarchical value maps* that show how specific product attributes get linked to end-states (see Figure 6.5).

Figure 6.5
Hierarchical
value maps for
vegetable oil in
three countries

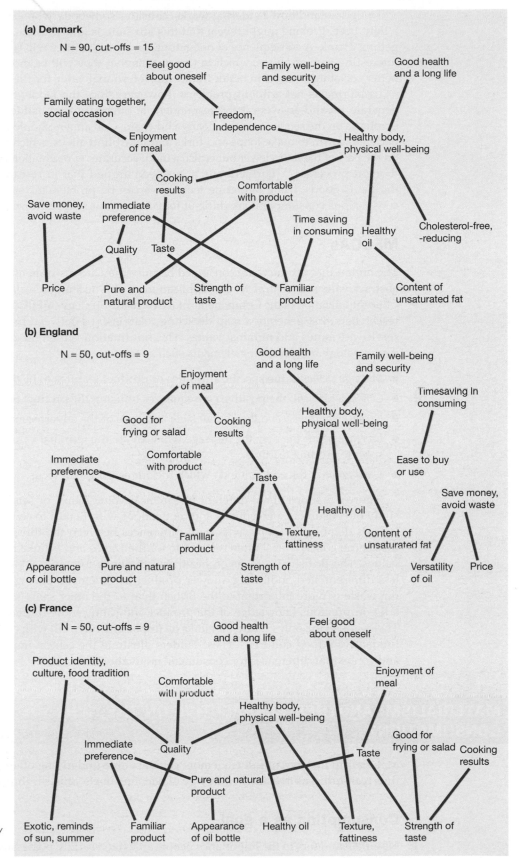

(a) Denmark

N = 90, cut-offs = 15

(b) England

N = 50, cut-offs = 9

(c) France

N = 50, cut-offs = 9

Source: N.A. Nielsen,
T. Bech-Larsen and
K.G. Grunert,
'Consumer purchase
motives and product
perceptions:
a laddering study on
vegetable oil in three
countries', *Food Quality
and Preference* 9(6)
(1998): 455–66.

To understand how laddering works, consider somebody who expresses a liking for a light beer. Probing might reveal that this attribute is linked to the consequence of not getting drunk. A consequence of not getting drunk is that they will be able to enjoy more interesting conversations, which in turn means that they will be more sociable. Finally, better sociability results in better friendship, a terminal value for this person.[112]

Laddering is not without problems, however, since the laddering technique might generate invalid answers if the respondent is pushed up the ladder by too strong an emphasis on the sequence in the means–end chain. Consumers should be allowed to jump back and forth, to make loops and forks and take blind alleys, which requires more skill on the part of the interviewer but is also a more accurate representation of the respondent's thought processes.[113] Furthermore, it has been argued that in researching the demand for status goods, using laddering techniques can be problematic since motivations for conspicuous consumption are difficult for consumers to express or reveal.[114]

MECCAs

The notion that products are consumed because they are instrumental in attaining more abstract values is central to one application of this technique, called the Means–End Conceptualization of the Components of Advertising Strategy (MECCAs). In this approach, researchers first generate a map depicting relationships between functional product or service attributes and terminal values. This information is then used to develop advertising strategy by identifying elements such as the following:[115]

- *Message elements*: the specific attributes or product features to be depicted.
- *Consumer benefit*: the positive consequences of using the product or service.
- *Executional framework*: the overall style and tone of the advertisement.
- *Leverage point*: the way the message will activate the terminal value by linking it with specific product features.
- *Driving force*: the end value on which the advertising will focus.

Figure 6.5 shows three different hierarchical value maps, or sets of ladders, from a study of consumers' perceptions and motivations with regard to cooking oils. The three ladders demonstrate some important differences between the three markets. Health is the central concept most often referred to for the Danes and is linked to several personal values. The British also focus on health but the links to personal values are fewer and less differentiated, indicating a lower product involvement. Saving money and avoiding waste is more important to the British than to the other samples. The French focus a lot on previous knowledge of the product, indicating more routine with buying oils. Theirs is also the only culture that links oil (especially olive oil) with cultural identity and fundamental food culture.[116] These ladders illustrate the central importance of cultural and contextual differences for consumers' motivation structures.

MATERIALISM: ANOTHER PERSPECTIVE ON THE 'WHY' OF CONSUMPTION?

Materialism may be considered a more general value underlying other consumer values, thus reassuring us that an obvious way of realizing one's values is through consumption.

Consumption as a goal

Materialism refers to the importance people attach to worldly possessions. Westerners in general (and Americans in particular) are often stereotyped as being members of a highly materialistic society where people often gauge their worth and that of others in terms of how much they own.

Materialists are more likely to value possessions for their status and appearance-related meanings, whereas those who do not emphasize this value tend to prize products that connect them to other people or that provide them with pleasure in using them.[117] As a result, products valued by high materialists are more likely to be publicly consumed and to be more expensive.[118] The priorities of materialism tend to emphasize the well-being of the individual versus the group, which may conflict with family or religious values. That conflict may help to explain why people with highly material values tend to be less happy.[119] A recent study has identified the important role that self-esteem plays in potentially explaining the variation in levels of materialism amongst children and adolescents. Results indicated that materialism increased from middle childhood to early adolescence (between 8 and 13 years old) and decreased from early adolescence onwards (between 13 and 18). Increasing levels of materialism amongst 8- to 13-year-olds was linked to declining levels of self-esteem in this age group. The researchers argue that 'a drop in self-esteem experienced by many children as they enter adolescence triggers a focus on material goods, primarily as a means of self-enhancement. As self-esteem rebounds in late adolescence, the need for self-enhancement of any sort, including the use of material goods, declines along with a decrease in materialistic orientation.'[120]

In Europe, we often take the existence of an abundance of products and services for granted, until we remember how recent many of these developments are; and how subject these developments are to economic conditions, e.g. the market downturn towards the end of 2008. The widespread ownership of cars, freezers, telephones and televisions is all a post-1950s phenomenon. Nowadays many young people could not imagine a life without cell phones, iPods and other creature comforts. In fact, one way to think about marketing is as a system that provides a certain standard of living to consumers. To some extent, then, our lifestyles are influenced by the standard of living we have come to expect and desire. However, there is evidence that how much money we have does not relate directly to happiness: 'as long as people are not battling poverty, they tend to rate their happiness in the range of 6 or 7, or higher, on a 10-point scale'.[121] The latest World Values survey rated Denmark as the happiest country in the world, followed by other European countries: Iceland (4), Northern Ireland (5), Ireland (6) Switzerland (7), the Netherlands (8) and Austria (10).[122]

Of course, not everyone stresses the value of materialism to the same degree. Individual differences have been found among consumers in terms of this emphasis. One approach partitions the value of materialism into three categories: success, centrality and happiness.[123] Cross-cultural differences in materialism have also been analyzed. One study of 12 countries resulted in the following ranking in degree of materialism from highest to lowest: Romania, US, New Zealand, Ukraine, Germany, Turkey, Israel, Thailand, India, UK, France and Sweden.[124] From these results, several conclusions can be drawn. First of all, materialism is not directly linked to affluence, as has often been proposed. On the contrary, some of the most materialistic cultures are the ones where most consumers (feel that they) lack a lot of things. But this obviously is not the only explanation, since the US, New Zealand and Germany score relatively high as well, and India scores low. Since neither wealth, 'Western-ness', nor any other single variable can explain these differences, it must be concluded that materialism is a consequence of several factors, including such things as social stability, access to information, reference models, as well as historical developments and cultural values.

This study was followed up by another based on qualitative depth interviews, adding more insight into consumers' different ways of coping with their own materialism, which was generally perceived as something negative. Basically, two ways of dealing with materialism were found, justifying versus excusing oneself: either you condemn materialism and provide an explanation why your personal materialism is a particularly good one, or you admit to being a 'bad' materialist but provide an excuse for being so.[125]

Participants at the anti-corporate Burning Man Festival find novel ways to express their individuality.

Courtesy of Professor Robert Kozinets

Large numbers of consumers are trying to reduce their reliance on possessions by ▶ **downshifting**. This means learning to get by with less, avoiding the use of credit cards, and in extreme cases living totally 'off the grid' without using commercial services. Other evidence of the disenchantment among some people with a culture dominated by materialist values and big corporations shows up in events that promote uniqueness and anti-corporate statements. Probably the most prominent movement in the US is the annual Burning Man project. This is a week-long annual anti-market event, where thousands of people gather at Black Rock Desert in Nevada to express themselves and proclaim their emancipation from Corporate America. The highlight of the festival involves the burning of a huge figure of a man made out of wood that symbolizes the freedom from market domination. Ironically, some critics point out that even this high-profile anti-market event is being commercialized as it becomes more popular each year.[126]

SUSTAINABILITY: A NEW CORE VALUE?

Are European consumers finally going green – for real? In a US 2007 survey, fully 8 in 10 US consumers said they believe it is important to buy green brands and products from green companies, and that they will pay more to do so. The US consumer's focus on personal health is merging with a growing interest in global health. Some analysts call ▶ this new value **conscientious consumerism**.[127]

Who is driving this change in the US? Marketers in the US point to a segment of ▶ consumers who practice **LOHAS** – an acronym for 'lifestyles of health and sustainability'.

This label refers to people who worry about the environment, want products to be produced in a sustainable way, and who spend money to advance what they see as their personal development and potential. These so-called 'Lohasians' (others refer to this segment as *Cultural Creatives*) represent a great market for products such as organic foods, energy-efficient appliances, and hybrid cars as well as alternative medicine, yoga tapes, and eco-tourism. One organization that tracks this group estimates they make up about 16 per cent of the adults in the US, or 35 million people; it values the market for socially conscious products at over $200 billion.[128]

 Marketing segmentation

UK consumers and pro-environmental behaviours

In the UK the government has identified 12 headline goals for pro-environmental behaviours which focus on personal transport, eco-products and three aspects of the home: energy, water, and waste (see Figure 6.6). Drawing on extensive research Defra (the UK Department of Environment, Food and Rural Affairs)[129] developed a segmentation model which divided consumers into seven clusters based on attitudes and beliefs about the environment, environmental issues and behaviours: positive greens; waste watchers; concerned consumers; sideline supporters; cautious participants; stalled starters; and honestly disengaged. Figure 6.7 maps these segments along the dimensions 'willingness to act' and 'ability to act'. 'It is apparent that segments 1, 2 and 3 offer the most potential in terms of their ability to act, though there are very different motivations and barriers.'[130] Figure 6.8 identifies which segments might do what, in terms of the government's headline pro-environmental goals, linked to the segments' respective ability and willingness to act.[131]

Figure 6.6 12 UK government headline behaviour goals (pro-environmental behaviours)

Source: Defra Report 'A framework for pro-environmental behaviours' (Jan 2008) London http://www.defra.gov.uk/evidence/social/behaviour/ page 5, accessed August 16 2008.

Figure 6.7 The seven population segments

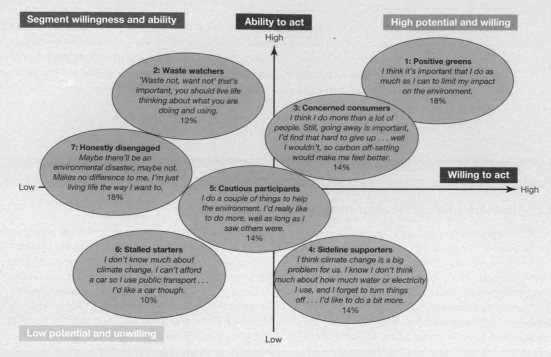

Source: Defra Report 'A framework for pro-environmental behaviours' (Jan 2008) London
http://www.defra.gov.uk/evidence/social/behaviour/ p. 8, accessed August 16 2008.

Figure 6.8 Acceptability of headline goals by segment

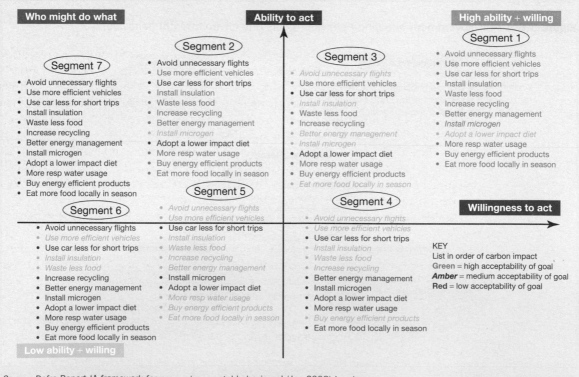

Source: Defra Report 'A framework for pro-environmental behaviours' (Jan 2008) London
http://www.defra.gov.uk/evidence/social/behaviour/ p. 9, accessed August 16 2008.

Marketers and retailers are responding with thousands of new eco-friendly products and programmes. L'Oréal acquired The Body Shop. Kellogg introduced organic versions of some of its best-selling cereals like Rice Krispies. We are seeing a significant increase in products with better-for-you positioning, but new products that take an ethical stance are also driving this trend, whether the claim links to fair trade, sustainability, or ecological friendliness. Whereas in the past it was sufficient for companies to offer recyclable products, this new movement is creating a whole new vocabulary as consumers begin to 'vote with their forks' by demanding food, fragrances and other items that are made with no *GMOs* (genetically modified ingredients); hormone-free; no animal clones; no animal testing; locally grown; and cage-free, to name a few.[132]

 Marketing opportunity

As mainstream marketers recognize this change, they are starting to alter their practices to satisfy desires for healthy and earth-friendly products. Here are some recent examples:

- H&M is selling clothes made from organic cotton fabrics to fashion-conscious shoppers. Gap introduced an organic cotton T-shirt for men in more than 500 of its US stores[133]
- Procter & Gamble is reducing the size of its packaging for its liquid detergent. It is switching to a double concentrate formula to serve its $4 billion North American liquid detergent market. Its competitor Unilever launched its concentrated liquid detergent 'Small and Mighty' in the US in 2005, which it estimates reduces packaging by more than 40 per cent, water usage by about 60 per cent, and shipping volumes by 60 per cent.[134]
- Airplanes are notorious for their huge carbon footprints (i.e. the pollutants they expel into the atmosphere), but even the aerospace industry is going green. European plane maker Airbus calls its massive A380 superjumbo 'the gentle green giant' because, with 550 people onboard, it burns less fuel per passenger than a small car. Its promotional materials show a silhouette of the largest commercial jetliner ever made set against images of dolphins, rain forests and fishing boats on a misty pond. An Airbus spokesperson introduced the behemoth at a 2007 air show with the claim that Airbus is '. . . saving the planet, one A380 at a time.'[135]

Not content to wait for companies to change their practices, ordinary consumers are taking action. Many are joining numerous organizations like Slow Food to agitate for lifestyle changes. One such movement called 'Local First' stresses the value of buying locally made products. This group (some members call themselves 'locavores') values small community businesses, but it is also reacting to the waste it sees occurring as people import things they need from long distances.[136]

Still other consumers are rebelling against the huge market for bottled water. They object to the fact that some brands come from as far away as Fiji. These imports create pollution because of the tanker ships that have to cart them halfway around the world and the waste from millions of discarded plastic bottles.[137]

The environmental effect of an object seemingly as innocent as a plastic water bottle ▶ points to the concern that many now have about the size of their **carbon footprint**. This measures in units of carbon dioxide the impact that human activities have on the environment in terms of the amount of greenhouse gases they produce. The average American is responsible for 9.44 tons of CO_2 per year![138] A carbon footprint comes from the sum of two parts, the direct/primary footprint and the indirect/secondary footprint:

▶ 1 The **primary footprint** is a measure of our direct emissions of CO_2 from the burning of fossil fuels including domestic energy consumption and transportation (e.g. car and plane).

▶ 2 The **secondary footprint** is a measure of the indirect CO_2 emissions from the whole lifecycle of products we use – those associated with their manufacture and eventual breakdown.[139]

Thousands of consumers are using services like Climate Clean and TerraPass that sell them *greenhouse gas offsets (GHG)*. These businesses enable individuals and businesses to reduce their GHG emissions by offsetting, reducing or displacing the GHG to another place, typically where it is more economical to do so. GHG offsets typically include renewable energy, energy efficiency, and methane capture that reduce the emission of gases scientists tell us contribute to global warming. For example, if your company flies you to another city for a business trip, it might purchase an 'offset' equal to the amount of emissions the airplane created to get you there.[140]

▶ Another emerging environmental issue for the developed world is the **virtual water footprint** which represents how much water is required to produce a product: 'when virtual water is taken into account, consumers in developed nations are leaving a large water footprint not just in their own countries but across the globe too'.[141] In the case of the UK, for instance, under 40 per cent of the country's total footprint is met from its own resources; more than 60 per cent is met by the rest of the world. 'A can of fizzy drink might contain 0.35 litres of water, for instance, yet it also requires about 200 litres to grow and process the sugar that goes into it.'[142] This means that the average Briton consumes about 4,645 litres of water a day once these hidden factors are included. World Water Forum experts are 'increasingly talking of fresh water as "the new oil"'.[143]

▶ Definitions

'**Virtual water**: alternatively called 'embedded', is water that has been used in the production of food and fibres. Includes resources also for irrigation, processing and packaging of produce.

Water footprint: amount of virtual and visible water used by a country, businesses or individuals.

External water footprint: quantity of virtual water deriving from other countries in imported goods.

Green water: that which derives directly from rainfall or from the soil. Generally replenished, but climate change will alter patterns of rainfall and there could be a decline in many parts of the world.

Blue water: withdrawn from ground-water or surface reserves. In many areas blue water is being used faster than nature replenishes it.'[144]

▶ Marketing challenge

'Ecological footprint: from environmental pressures to impacts

▶ An **ecological footprint** provides a useful indicator of the degree to which a country's consumption is sustainable. Resources consumed to meet the country's demand for food, energy and goods are translated into equivalent land area in hectares per capita to provide those resources and to absorb emissions such as CO_2 without permanent change. These can then be compared to the total global available bio-capacity per person. Countries whose footprint significantly exceeds the global available bio-capacity (1.8 hectares per person in 2003) can be considered to have unsustainable consumption and production patterns.

One of the main concerns about production or consumption activities is the environmental impact that they cause. Environmental pressures include: emissions of air pollutants such as greenhouse gases, solid waste and waste water production, releases of toxic substances to air, soil and water, consumption of resources beyond reproductive capacities and conversion of natural land into built-up areas. These cause changes in environmental conditions which in turn lead to impacts on human beings, ecosystems and infrastructures. Environmental pressures can be expressed in terms of quantities of pollutants discharged, weights or volumes of resources extracted or material consumed, volumes of fish or timber harvested, or, at the most aggregated level, presented as material flows in tonnes. However, with current knowledge, pressures from production or consumption cannot easily be converted into information on specific environmental impacts. As a general rule of thumb, the higher the use of materials, energy and land, the higher the resulting impacts on the environment. However, more research is needed to express environmental impacts and link them to specific environmental pressures. By 2003 Eastern Europe (excluding Moldova) and all the Southeastern European countries (except for Albania) showed indications of unsustainable consumption and production. Russia had a footprint which was twice the available global bio-capacity per capita, though they still remained below the average figure for EU-25. The majority of the population in Western Europe and increasingly in Central Europe has access to "reasonable" income levels and can afford goods and services which exceed their basic needs, so that the focus in these countries is on the environmental pillar of sustainability i.e. improving efficiency of production and using economic incentives and various other means to orient consumption towards less pressure-intensive goods and services. In contrast, for much of Southeastern Europe and Eastern Europe issues revolve around the social pillar of sustainability because significant segments of the population live in poverty, and in rural areas do not have reliable access to basic needs such as clean water, household energy and adequate nutrition.'[145]

PRODUCT DISPOSAL

How do our changing consumer values around sustainability and environmentalism affect our consumer behaviour when disposing of products? Consumers must often dispose of things, either because they have fulfilled their designated functions, or possibly because they no longer fit with consumers' views of themselves. Because people often form strong attachments to products, the decision to dispose of something can be a painful one. One function performed by possessions is to serve as anchors for our identities: our past lives on in our things.[146] Although some people have more trouble than others in discarding things, even a 'magpie' does not keep everything. Concern about the environment coupled with a need for convenience has made ease of product disposal a key attribute in categories from razors to nappies.

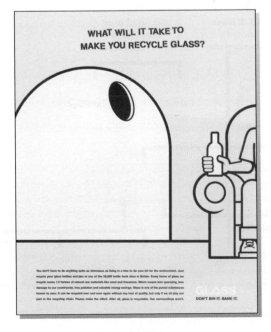

This British ad promotes the recycling of glass.
The Advertising Archives

Disposal options

When a consumer decides that a product is no longer of use, several choices are available. The person can either (1) keep the item, (2) temporarily dispose of it, or (3) permanently dispose of it. In many cases, a new product is acquired even though the old one still functions.[147] Figure 6.9 provides an overview of consumers' disposal options. Compared with the original scheme, we have added the opportunity of 'to be recycled' in the lower left corner. This is interesting because it bears witness to the fact that thinking about recycling as a 'natural' thing to do is a rather recent occurrence. The issue of product disposal is doubly vital because of its enormous public policy implications. We live in a throwaway society, which creates problems for the environment and also results in a great deal of unfortunate waste.

Training consumers to recycle has become a priority in many countries. Japan recycles about 40 per cent of its rubbish, and this relatively high rate of compliance is partly due to the social value the Japanese place on recycling: citizens are encouraged by dustbin lorries that periodically rumble through the streets playing classical music or children's songs.[148] Companies continue to search for ways to use resources more efficiently, often at the prompting of activist consumer groups. For example, McDonald's restaurants bowed to pressure by eliminating the use of styrofoam packages, and its outlets in Europe experimented with edible breakfast plates made of maize.[149]

► In the US, lateral cycling is literally a lifestyle for some people with an anti-consumerist
► bent who call themselves freegans (this label is a takeoff on *vegans*, who shun all animal products). Freegans are modern-day scavengers who live off discards as a political statement against corporations and consumerism. They forage through supermarket trash and eat the slightly bruised produce or just-expired canned goods that are routinely thrown out, and negotiate gifts of surplus food from sympathetic stores and restaurants. Freegans dress

Figure 6.9 Consumers' disposal options

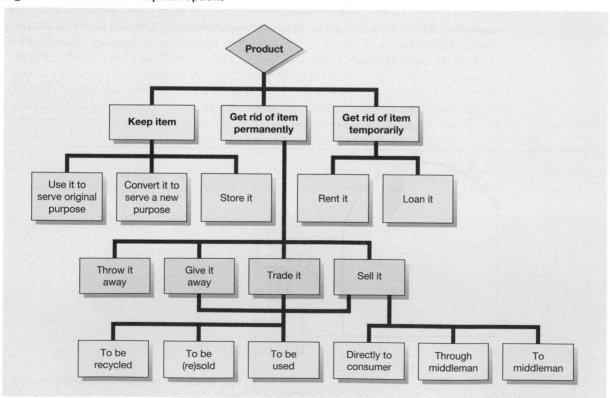

Source: Adapted from Jacob Jacoby, Carol K. Berning and Thomas F. Dietvorst, 'What about disposition?' *Journal of Marketing* 41 (April 1977): 23.

Xmas tree recycling.
Corbis/Image Source

in castoff clothes and furnish their homes with items they find on the street. They get the word on locations where people are throwing out a lot of stuff (end-of-semester dorm cleanouts are a prime target) by checking out postings at **freecycle.org** where users post unwanted items; and at so-called *freemeets*, flea markets where no one exchanges money.[150]

A study examined the relevant goals consumers have in recycling. It used a means–end chain analysis of the type described on p. 204 to identify how specific instrumental goals are linked to more abstract terminal values. The most important lower-order goals identified were 'avoid filling up landfills', 'reduce waste', 'reuse materials' and 'save the environment'. These were linked to the terminal values of 'promote health/avoid sickness', 'achieve life-sustaining ends' and 'provide for future generations'. Another study reported that the perceived effort involved in recycling was the best predictor of whether people would go to the trouble – this pragmatic dimension outweighed general attitudes toward recycling and the environment in predicting intention to recycle.[151] By applying such techniques to study recycling and other product disposal behaviours, it will be easier for social marketers to design advertising copy and other messages that tap into the underlying values that will motivate people to increase environmentally responsible behaviour.[152]

▼ Marketing pitfall

As if other kinds of waste were not bad enough, one consequence of our infatuation with new technology is working out what to do with the things that quickly become obsolete. Now even discarded mobile phones are becoming a problem as customers rapidly switch among mobile services and upgrade to new models. One popular solution seems to be to ship unwanted electronic waste such as old computer monitors and circuit boards to the Third World. As much as 50 to 80 per cent of electronic waste collected for recycling in the US is placed on container ships and sent to China, India, Pakistan or other developing countries, where it is reused or recycled under largely unregulated conditions. Recycling industries in these places often use young children to handle cathode ray tubes filled with lead and other toxic substances. The EU is so concerned about the problem that it is moving toward requiring manufacturers to take cradle-to-grave responsibility for their products.[153]

This Dutch ad says: 'And when you've had enough of it, we'll clear it away nicely.'

Courtesy of Volkswagen of The Netherlands

Lateral cycling: junk vs. 'junque'

Interesting consumer processes occur during lateral cycling, where already-purchased objects are sold to others or exchanged for yet other things. Many purchases are made second-hand, rather than new. The reuse of other people's things is especially important in our throwaway society because, as one researcher put it, 'there is no longer an "away" to throw things to'.[154]

Flea markets, garage sales, classified advertisements, bartering for services, hand-me-downs, car-boot sales, charity shops and the black market all represent important alternative marketing systems that operate alongside the formal marketplace.

The Internet has revolutionized the lateral cycling process, as millions of people flock to eBay to buy and sell their 'treasures'. This phenomenally successful online auction site started as a trading post for Beanie Babies and other collectibles. Now two-thirds of the site's sales are for practical goods. eBay expects to sell $2 billion worth of used cars and $1 billion worth of computers a year. Coming next are event tickets, food, industrial equipment and property.[155] However, eBay has recently hit a slight hiccup with the award by a French court against the company of €38.6 million in damages to 'LVMH, the luxury giant behind Louis Vuitton and Christian Dior for negligence in allowing the sale of fake bags and clothes, and of perfume that it was not licensed to sell. The ruling comes hot on the heels of a judgment by another French court that ordered eBay to pay 20,000 euros to Hermès for allowing the sale of fake bags. L'Oréal has lawsuits pending against eBay in five European countries, including the UK, and there is another filed by Tiffany in the US. As part of its case, LVMH presented evidence to the court that of the 300,000 products purporting to be Louis Vuitton or Christian Dior sold on the site in the second quarter of 2006, 90 per cent were fakes.'[156]

Ironically, an economic slowdown is good news for auction sites like eBay, because it is the kind of business that prospers when other businesses aren't doing well. As one

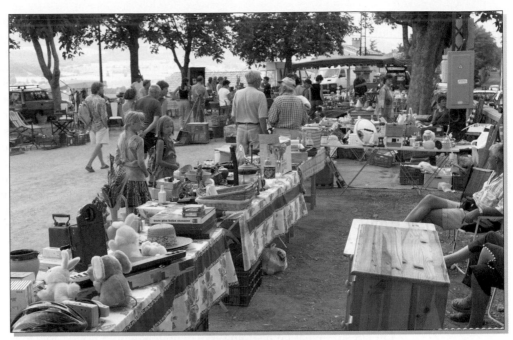

Flea markets are an important form of lateral cycling.
Alamy/Stockfolio

analyst explained, 'The interesting thing about eBay is that it may benefit because some people may choose not to buy something new, like a computer or consumer electronics.' Hobbies and crafts also are selling strongly, which may be due to the number of people staying at home rather than travelling.

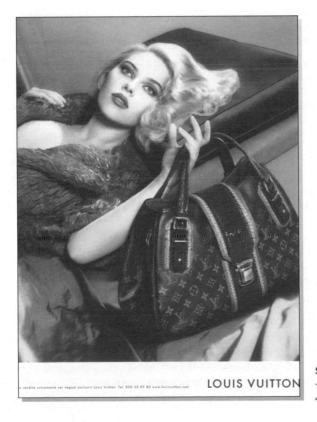

Scarlett Johanssen, Louis Vuitton.
The Advertising Archives

▶ **Freecycling** is the practice of giving away useful but unwanted goods to keep them out of landfills and maybe to help someone less fortunate in the process. Free recycling – which already existed in a number of forms offline, for example, jumble sales and donations to charity shops and church institutions (such as the Salvation Army) – has emerged online with the establishment of **www.freecycle.org** by a consumer in Tucson, Arizona, keen to give away a queen-size bed and some packaged peanuts. What started as an email circular to friends turned into a Website for the exchange of unwanted items. 'Free, legal and appropriate for all ages': these are the only constraints on what is offered via the site. At **freecycle.org**, roughly three million people from more than 70 countries exchange unwanted items.[157]

Despite its success, there's sometimes a bittersweet quality to eBay. Some of the sellers are listing computers, fancy cars, jewellery and other luxury items because they desperately need the money. As one vendor explained when he described the classic convertible he wanted to sell, 'I am out of money and need to pay my rent, so my toys have to be sold.' The site witnessed a particularly strong surge in these kinds of messages following 9/11 when many people were laid off in the wake of a sluggish economy. In the words of an accountant who lost his job, 'Things were bad before, and then they got really bad after the bombings. Everything completely dried up.' Noting that he used to sell merchandise on eBay as a hobby but is now forced to sell some of his own possessions, including his BMW and his wife's jewellery, he commented, 'If it weren't for eBay, I'm not sure what I'd be doing. We definitely would not be able to pay the bills.'[158]

While traditional marketers have paid little attention to the second-hand market,[160] factors such as concern about the environment, demands for quality and cost and fashion consciousness are conspiring to make these 'secondary' markets more important.[161]

▶ Economic estimates of this **underground economy** range from 3 to 30 per cent of the GNP of the US and up to 70 per cent of the GDP of other countries. Interest in antiques, period accessories and specialized magazines catering for this niche is increasing, e.g. Lassco (London Architectural Salvage and Supply Company) is a reclamation business.

 Marketing update

'eBay changes aim for fewer critics and more sellers

Selling £30bn worth of goods a year globally and visited by two out of every three internet shoppers in the UK monthly, eBay has been lauded as one of the great success stories of the internet age. But it has endured a rocky year. When Louis Vuitton won a high-profile French court case over fake goods, analysts questioned its capacity for growth and some of its hitherto loyal band of sellers staged an open revolt over changes to its fee structure. As it faces a wave of renewed competition from online competitors like Amazon and so-called "bricks and clicks" players such as Tesco combining shops and the internet, eBay UK will today unveil several changes it says are designed to help those entrepreneurs make the most of fixed-price sales.

Upfront fees for listing items will be slashed and the fee for a successful sale will be increased in an effort to get buyers to list a wider range of goods and increase choice. Sellers will receive discounts on those fees and better search listings according to the volume of sales and quality of service . . . Though today's changes may appear inconsequential to non-users of the site, for its 15 million monthly visitors – and in particular to the 178,000 bedroom entrepreneurs who have been able to quit their jobs to trade on eBay full time – they are crucial. "We've been on this path for the last few years," said Clare Gilmartin, director of marketplaces for eBay in the UK. "There's no doubt this year has seen some very, very bold changes – necessarily so and entirely reflective of what our buyers and sellers want". She said that the shift from auction sales to fixed price was an indication of how online retailing had matured, growing from 1 per cent to 17 per cent of the overall market in the nine years since eBay launched in Britain. "I don't think anything can surpass eBay in terms of choice. But e-commerce is now mainstream. We see our competitive set as a broad one – anywhere where a buyer can buy stuff online. That might be Amazon or the more traditional bricks and clicks. But the big advantage we have is choice – mums sitting alongside entrepreneurs, sitting alongside big retailers." '[159]

▶ 'Reclaimers are not, strictly speaking, antique dealers, and very definitely not junk merchants . . . they are not in the business of plundering the past, they are in the business of rescuing large lumps of history from the wrecking ball . . . reclaiming is . . . part of the current craze for "collectables" (architectural salvage is big on eBay).'[162] Other growth areas include markets for used computers and ski swaps, where used ski equipment is exchanged. A new generation of second-hand shopkeepers is developing markets for everything from used office equipment to cast-off kitchen sinks. Many are non-profit ventures started with government funding. These efforts remind us that recycling is actually the last step in the familiar mantra of the environmental movement: reduce, reuse, recycle.[163] Only if no use is found for an item should it be shredded and made into something else.

If our possessions do indeed come to be a part of us, how do we bring ourselves to part with these precious items? Some researchers recently examined the ways consumers
▶ practise **divestment rituals**, where they take steps to gradually distance themselves from things they treasure so that they can sell them or give them away (more on rituals in Chapter 13). As they observed people getting items ready to be sold at garage sales, the researchers identified these rituals:

- *Iconic transfer ritual*: taking pictures and videos of objects before selling them.
- *Transition-place ritual*: putting items in an out-of-the-way location such as a garage or attic before disposing of them.
- *Ritual cleansing*: washing, ironing, and/or meticulously wrapping the item.[164]

The 'why' of consumption

As we have seen in this chapter, there are many reasons why we want to engage in consumption activities. One of the main lessons to retain is probably that the 'why?' question cannot stand alone, but must be asked with reference to a number of other questions such as 'who?' indicating personal, group and cultural differences; 'when?' and 'where?' indicating situational and contextual differences; 'how?' pointing to the reflexive and emotional processes involved; and finally 'what' kind of consumption items and consumer behaviour are we talking about? These dimensions, which are all to some extent addressed later in this book, are illustrated in Figure 6.10.

Figure 6.10 Contextualizing the 'why' of consumption

Source: Adapted from S. Ratneshwar, D.G. Mick and C. Huffman, 'Introduction', in S. Ratneshwar, D.G. Mick and C. Huffman, eds, *The Why of Consumption* (London: Routledge, 2000): 1–8.

CHAPTER SUMMARY

- It is important for marketers to recognize that products can satisfy a range of consumer needs. Marketers try to satisfy consumer needs, but the reasons people purchase any product can vary widely. The identification of consumer motives is an important step in ensuring that a product will satisfy appropriate needs. Traditional approaches to consumer behavior have focused on the abilities of products to satisfy rational needs (utilitarian motives), but hedonic motives (e.g., the need for exploration or for fun) also play a key role in many purchase decisions. Hence there has been a shift away from talking about needs towards talking about goals, wants and desires.

- As Maslow's hierarchy of needs demonstrates, the same product can satisfy different needs, depending on the consumer's state at the time. In addition to his objective situation (e.g., have basic physiological needs already been satisfied?), we must also consider the consumer's degree of involvement with the product.

- The way we evaluate and choose a product depends upon our degree of involvement with the product, the marketing message, and/or the purchase situation. Product involvement can range from very low, where purchase decisions are made via inertia, to very high, where consumers form very strong bonds with what they buy. In addition to considering the degree to which consumers are involved with a product, marketing strategists also need to assess their extent of involvement with marketing messages and with the purchase situation.

- Our deeply held culturally-informed values dictate the types of products and services we seek out or avoid. Values are basic, general principles used to judge the desirability of end-states. Underlying values often drive consumer motivations. Products thus take on meaning because they are seen as being instrumental in helping the person to achieve some goal that is linked to a value, such as individuality or freedom.

- All cultures form a value system which sets them apart from other cultures. Each culture is characterized by a set of core values to which many of its members adhere. Some researchers have developed lists to account for such value systems and used them in cross-cultural comparisons.

- One approach to the study of values is the means–end chain, which tries to link product attributes to consumer values via the consequences that usage of the product will have for the consumer.

- Since consumers are not necessarily able or willing to communicate their underlying desires to marketers, various other techniques such as projective tests (e.g. collages) can be employed to assess desires indirectly.

- Consumers vary in the importance they attach to worldly possessions, and this orientation in turn has an impact on their priorities and behaviours. *Materialism* refers to the importance people attach to worldly possessions. Materialism may be considered a more general value underlying other consumer values, thus reassuring us that an obvious way of realizing one's values is through consumption. There are indications of a value shift within a sizable portion of the different population groups – and this is currently often accompanied by much greater interest in environmentally sustainable products and services.

- Consumer behaviours around getting rid of products which we no longer need or want are a major concern both to marketers and to public policymakers. *Product disposal* is an increasingly important problem. Recycling is one option that will become more crucial as consumers' environmental awareness grows. *Lateral cycling* occurs when we buy, sell or barter second-hand objects.

► KEY TERMS

Acculturation (p. 200)
Approach–approach conflict (p. 182)
Approach–avoidance conflict (p. 183)
Avoidance–avoidance conflict (p. 184)
Carbon footprint (p. 211)
Conscientious consumerism (p. 208)
Consumer-generated content (CGC) (p. 196)
Core values (p. 198)
Cult products (p. 193)
Desire (p. 190)
Divestment rituals (p. 219)
Downshifting (p. 208)
Drive (p. 177)
Drive theory (p. 179)
Ecological footprint (p. 212)
Enculturation (p. 199)
Expectancy theory (p. 179)
Flow state (p. 193)
Freecycling (p. 218)
Freegans (p. 214)
Freudian theory (p. 187)
Goal (p. 177)
Homeostasis (p. 179)
Inertia (p. 192)
Instrumental values (p. 203)

Interactive mobile marketing (p. 195)
Involvement (p. 191)
Laddering (p. 204)
Lateral cycling (p. 214)
List of Values (LOV) (p. 203)
LOHAS (p. 208)
Mass customization (p. 194)
Materialism (p. 206)
Means–end chain model (p. 204)
MECCAs (p. 206)
Motivation (p. 177)
Motivational research (p. 188)
Need (p. 177)
Primary footprint (p. 211)
Reclaimers (p. 219)
Secondary footprint (p. 211)
Terminal values (p. 203)
Theory of cognitive dissonance (p. 182)
Underground economy (p. 218)
Value (p. 198)
Value system (p. 199)
Virtual water footprint (p. 212)
Want (p. 177)
Web (p. 193)

► CONSUMER BEHAVIOUR CHALLENGE

1 What is motivation, and how is motivation relevant to consumer behaviour?

2 Describe three types of motivational conflicts, citing an example of each from current marketing campaigns.

3 Consumer researchers have the right to probe into the consumer's unconscious. Is this a violation of privacy, or just another way to gather deep knowledge of purchase motivations?

4 What is the difference between a want and a desire? Think about your own feelings and try to describe the differences.

5 Devise separate promotional strategies for an article of clothing, each of which stresses one of the levels of Maslow's hierarchy of needs.

6 What is consumer involvement? Give examples of the three types of consumer involvement. How do these types of involvement relate to motivation?

7 Collect a sample of ads that appeals to consumers' values. What value is being communicated in each ad, and how is this done? Is this an effective approach to designing a marketing communication?

8 What is your conception of paradise? Construct a collage consisting of images you personally associate with paradise, and compare the results with those of your classmates. Do you detect any common themes?

9 Construct a hypothetical means–end chain model for the purchase of a bouquet of roses. How might a florist use this approach to construct a promotional strategy?

10 Describe how a man's level of involvement with his car would affect how he is influenced by different marketing stimuli. How might you design a strategy for a line of car batteries for a segment of low-involvement consumers, and how would this strategy differ from your attempts to reach a segment of men who are very involved in working on their cars?

11 Interview members of a celebrity fan club. Describe their level of involvement with the 'product' and devise some marketing opportunities to reach this group.

12 'High involvement is just a fancy term for expensive.' Do you agree?

13 'University students' concerns about ethics, sustainability, the environment, carbon footprints, genetically modified foods, and vegetarianism are just passing fads; a way to look "cool".' Do you agree?

14 Assess the role of materialism in consumer behaviour. Think about some of the excuses or explanations you have used towards yourself or towards others for materialistic wants. How do they correspond to the explanations and excuses accounted for here?

15 'Although more money delivers big increases in happiness when you are poor, each extra dollar makes less difference once your basic needs have been met.'[165] Debate this viewpoint in class.

16 Compose a three-line summary of the main argument(s) in Andrew Oswald's (1999) 'A Non-technical Introduction to the Economics of Happiness' (http://www2.warwick.ac.uk/fac/soc/economics/staff/faculty/oswald/intro.pdf). Evaluate the relevance of Oswald's findings for (a) consumer behaviour researchers; (b) marketing managers devising a strategy for the marketing of a product or service.

17 Visit the *Business Week* website http://images.businessweek.com/ss/08/08/ 0819_happiest_countries/index.htm. Read the latest report by the World Value Survey of the happiest countries. Identify and discuss the key features used to assess happiness in the descriptions of these European countries. How would you describe and evaluate your own society using these criteria?

18 Some market analysts see a shift in values among young people. They claim that this generation has not had a lot of stability in their lives. They are fed up with superficial relationships, and are yearning for a return to tradition. This change is reflected in attitudes toward marriage and family. One survey of 22–24-year-old women found that 82 per cent thought motherhood was the most important job in the world. *Brides* magazine reports a swing towards traditional weddings – 80 per cent of brides today are tossing their garters. Daddy walks 78 per cent of them down the aisle.[166] So, what do you think about this? Are young people indeed returning to the values of their parents (or even their grandparents)? How have these changes influenced your perspective on marriage and family? Find statistics that demonstrate the changing patterns of marriage and cohabitation across Europe. Why and how might these changing patterns of household and family formation be important for consumer behaviour researchers and marketing managers?

19 The movement away from a 'disposable consumer society' towards one that emphasizes creative recycling creates many opportunities for marketers. Can you identify some?

20 Interview people who are selling items at a flea market or garage sale. Ask them to identify some items to which they had a strong attachment. Then, see if you can prompt them to describe one or more divestment rituals they went through as they prepared to offer these items for sale.

For additional material see the companion website at **www.pearsoned.co.uk/solomon**

1. *Observer* Travel, 'Readers' Guide to Athens', 25 March 2006: 10.
2. For detailed definitions of different types of vegetarianism see http://www.vegsoc.org/info/definitions.html
3. See Susan Baker, Keith E. Thompson and Julia Engelken, 'Mapping the values driving organic food choice: Germany vs the UK', *European Journal of Marketing* 38 (2004): 995ff. Their study showed that although there were similarities between German and UK consumers of organic products in terms of values related to health, well-being and enjoyment, there were differences in terms of product attributes linked to achieving these values. A major difference was that UK consumers did not necessarily link organic food with the environment.
4. Vegetarian Society quickfacts1: http://www.youngveggie.org/Information/quick%20facts1.pdf accessed 22 August 2008.
5. Jess Halliday, 'The market for vegetarian supplements' Nutra Ingredients.com free newsletter, 20 January 2006, http://www.nutraingredients.com/news/ng.asp?n=65255-vegetarian-supplements
6. Tino Bech-Larsen and Klaus G. Grunert, 'The Influence of Tasting Experience and Health Benefits on Nordic Consumers' Rejection of Genetically Modified Foods', in Andrea Groppel-Klein and Franz-Rudolf Esch, eds, *European Advances in Consumer Research* 5 (Valdosta, GA: Association for Consumer Research, 2001): 11–14.
7. *Ibid.*
8. Laura Smith, 'Childhood obesity fuelled by cartoons', *The Guardian* (24 February 2005): 5.
9. Bech-Larsen and Grunert, 'The Influence of Tasting Experience and Health Benefits', *op. cit.*: 11–14.
10. Editorial comment, 'Water: Go against the flow', *The Guardian*, 20 August 2008: 30, http://www.guardian.co.uk/commentisfree/2008/aug/20/water.food
11. Hilary Osborne, 'The parent trap: bringing up a green baby may save the planet but it can cost the earth', *The Guardian*, 16 Mary 2007, http://www.guardian.co.uk/money/2007/mar/16/ethicalliving accessed 23 August 2008.
12. Paul Hewer, 'Consuming Gardens: Representations of Paradise, Nostalgia and Postmodernism', in Darach Turley and Stephen Brown, eds, *European Advances in Consumer Research* 6 (Valdosta, GA: Association for Consumer Research, 2003): 327–31.
13. http://www.study-in-italy.it/about/eating.html
14. Richard Bagozzi and Utpal Dholakia, 'Goal setting and goal striving in consumer behavior', *Journal of Marketing* 63 (October 1999): 19–23.
15. Eileen Fischer, Cele C. Otnes and Linda Tuncay, 'Pursuing parenthood: Integrating cultural and cognitive perspectives on persistent goal striving', *Journal of Consumer Research* 34 (December 2007): 425–40.
16. Robert A. Baron, *Psychology: The Essential Science* (Needham, MA: Allyn & Bacon, 1989).
17. Jean Baudrillard, 'La genèse idéologique des besoins', *Cahiers internationaux de sociologie* 47 (1969): 45–68.
18. Søren Askegaard and A. Fuat Firat, 'Towards a Critique of Material Culture, Consumption, and Markets', in S. Pearce, ed., *Experiencing Material Culture in the Western World* (London: Leicester University Press, 1997): 114–39.
19. See for instance the discussion in Emma N. Banister and Margaret K. Hogg, 'Negative symbolic consumption and consumers' drive for self-esteem: the case of the fashion industry', *European Journal of Marketing* 38(7) (2004): 850–68.
20. Thomas Kramer and Song-Oh yoon, 'Approach-Avoidance Motivation and the Use of affect as Information,' *Journal of Consumer Psychology* 17, no. 2 (2007): 128–38.
21. Leon Festinger, *A Theory of Cognitive Dissonance* (Stanford, CA: Stanford University Press, 1957).
22. http://www.visit4info.com/advert/Muller-Light-Yoghurt-Muller-Yoghurt-Fromage-Frais-Range/55309#
23. Jeannie Whalen, 'Meet the leader of the pack: Moscow's drag-racing queen Katya Karenina organizes illicit matches under the nose of the city police force', *The Wall Street Journal* (9 December 2002) jeanne.whalen@wsj.com.
24. Laura Petrecca, 'Men arm themselves with anti-aging weapons: Market for skincare grows as guys try to look younger', *USA Today*, 15 April 2008, Section Monday: 03b. http://web.ebscohost.com/ehost/detail?vid=4&hid=13&sid=5de66170-66ee-4147-917c-371186bca3ab%40sessionmgr9&bdata=JnNpdGU9ZWhvc3QtbGl2ZQ%3d%3d#db=a9h&AN=J0E041378452108 accessed 22 August 2008.
25. Laura Petrecca, 'Men arm themselves with anti-aging weapons: Market for skincare grows as guys try to look younger', *USA Today*, 15 April 2008, Section Monday: 03b. http://web.ebscohost.com/ehost/detail?vid=4&hid=13&sid=5de66170-66ee-4147-917c-371186bca3ab%40sessionmgr9&bdata=JnNpdGU9ZWhvc3QtbGl2ZQ%3d%3d#db=a9h&AN=J0E041378452108 accessed 22 August 2008.
26. http://www.lorealmen.com/ accessed 22 August 2008.
27. http://www.lorealparis.co.uk/minisites/menexpert/ accessed 22 August 2008.
28. See Paul T. Costa and Robert R. McCrae, 'From catalog to classification: Murray's needs and the five-factor model', *Journal of Personality and Social Psychology* 55 (1988): 258–65; Calvin S. Hall and Gardner Lindzey, *Theories of Personality*, 2nd edn (New York: Wiley, 1970); James U. McNeal and Stephen W. McDaniel, 'An analysis of need-appeals in television advertising', *Journal of the Academy of Marketing Science* 12 (Spring 1984): 176–90.
29. Michael R. Solomon, Judith L. Zaichkowsky, and Rosemary Polegato, *Consumer Behaviour: Buying, Having, and Being – Canadian Edition* (Scarborough, Ontario: Prentice Hall Canada, 1999).
30. See David C. McClelland, *Studies in Motivation* (New York: Appleton-Century-Crofts, 1955).
31. Mary Kay Ericksen and M. Joseph Sirgy, 'Achievement Motivation and Clothing Preferences of White-Collar Working Women', in Michael R. Solomon, ed., *The Psychology of Fashion* (Lexington, MA: Lexington Books, 1985): 357–69.
32. See Stanley Schachter, *The Psychology of Affiliation* (Stanford, CA: Stanford University Press, 1959).
33. Eugene M. Fodor and Terry Smith, 'The power motive as an influence on group decision making', *Journal of Personality and Social Psychology* 42 (1982): 178–85.
34. C.R. Snyder and Howard L. Fromkin, *Uniqueness: The Human Pursuit of Difference* (New York: Plenum, 1980).
35. Abraham H. Maslow, *Motivation and Personality*, 2nd edn (New York: Harper & Row, 1970).
36. A more recent integrative view of consumer goal structures and goal-determination processes proposes six discrete levels of goals wherein higher-level (vs. lower-level) goals

are more abstract, more inclusive and less mutable. In descending order of abstraction, these goal levels are life themes and values, life projects, current concerns, consumption intentions, benefits sought and feature preferences. See Cynthia Huffman, S. Ratneshwar and David Glen Mick, 'Consumer Goal Structures and Goal-Determination Processes, An Integrative Framework', in S. Ratneshwar, David Glen Mick and Cynthia Huffman, eds, *The Why of Consumption* (London: Routledge, 2000): 9–35.

37. Henry, Paul (2006), 'Magnetic points for lifestyle shaping: The contribution of self-fulfillment, aspirations and capabilities', *Qualitative Market Research* 9(2): 170.

38. See, however, Primo Levi, *If This Is A Man* (London: Abacus by Sphere Books, 1987); his discussion of the importance of friendship for surviving extreme conditions of deprivation; and his description of the loss of his concentration camp friend and companion Alberto: 161.

39. Woodward, Ian (2001), 'Domestic objects and the taste epiphany: A resource of consumption methodology', *Journal of Material Culture* 6(2): 115–36.

40. Study conducted in the Horticulture Department at Kansas State University, cited in 'Survey tells why gardening's good', *Vancouver Sun* (12 April 1997): B12; see also Paul Hewer and Douglas Brownlie (2006), 'Constructing "Hortiporn": On the Aesthetics of Stylized Exteriors', *Advances in Consumer Research* 33(1).

41. Richard Maddock, 'A Theoretical and Empirical Substructure of Consumer Motivation and Behaviour', in Flemming Hansen, ed., *European Advances in Consumer Research* 2 (Provo, UT: Association for Consumer Research, 1995): 29–37.

42. Ernest Dichter, *A Strategy of Desire* (Garden City, NY: Doubleday, 1960); Ernest Dichter, *The Handbook of Consumer Motivations* (New York: McGraw-Hill, 1964); Jeffrey J. Durgee, 'Interpreting Dichter's Interpretations: An Analysis of Consumption Symbolism in *The Handbook of Consumer Motivations*', *Marketing and Semiotics. Selected Papers from the Copenhagen Symposium*, ed. Hanne Hartvig Larsen, David G. Mick and Christian Alsted (Copenhagen: Handelshøjskolens forlag 1991): 52–74; Pierre Martineau, *Motivation in Advertising* (New York: McGraw-Hill, 1957).

43. Vance Packard, *The Hidden Persuaders* (New York: D. McKay, 1957).

44. Harold Kassarjian, 'Personality and consumer behavior: A review', *Journal of Marketing Research* 8 (November 1971): 409–18.

45. Richard Elliott, 'Existential consumption and irrational desire', *European Journal of Marketing* 31(3/4) (1997): 285–96.

46. Russell W. Belk, Güliz Ger and Søren Askegaard, 'The Missing Streetcar Named Desire', in Ratneshwar, Mick and Huffman, eds, *The Why of Consumption*: 98–119.

47. Robert Bocock, *Consumption* (London: Routledge 1993).

48. Russell W. Belk, Güliz Ger and Søren Askegaard, 'Consumer Desire in Three Cultures', in D. MacInnis and M. Brucks, eds, *Advances in Consumer Research* 14 (Provo, UT: Association for Consumer Research, 1997): 24–8.

49. Judith Lynne Zaichkowsky, 'Measuring the involvement construct in marketing', *Journal of Consumer Research* 12 (December 1985): 341–52.

50. Andrew Mitchell, 'Involvement: A Potentially Important Mediator of Consumer Behaviour', in William L. Wilkie, ed., *Advances in Consumer Research* 6 (Provo, UT: Association for Consumer Research, 1979): 191–6.

51. Richard L. Celsi and Jerry C. Olson, 'The role of involvement in attention and comprehension processes', *Journal of Consumer Research* 15 (September 1988): 210–24.

52. Ton Otker, 'The highly involved consumer: A marketing myth?' *Marketing and Research Today* (February 1990): 30–6.

53. Anthony G. Greenwald and Clark Leavitt, 'Audience involvement in advertising: Four levels', *Journal of Consumer Research* 11 (June 1984): 581–92.

54. Mihaly Csikszentmihalyi, *Flow: The Psychology of Optimal Experience* (New York: HarperCollins, 1991); Donna L. Hoffman and Thomas P. Novak, 'Marketing in hypermedia computer-mediated environments: Conceptual foundations', *Journal of Marketing* (July 1996), 60, 50–68.

55. Judith Lynne Zaichkowsky, 'The Emotional Side of Product Involvement', in Paul Anderson and Melanie Wallendorf, eds, *Advances in Consumer Research* 14 (Provo, UT: Association for Consumer Research): 32–5.

56. For a recent discussion of interrelationship between situational and enduring involvement, see Marsha L. Richins, Peter H. Bloch and Edward F. McQuarrie, 'How enduring and situational involvement combine to create involvement responses', *Journal of Consumer Psychology* 1(2) (1992): 143–53. For more information on the involvement construct see 'Special issue on involvement' *Psychology and Marketing* 10(4) (July/August 1993).

57. Joseph B. Pine II and James H. Gilmore, *Markets of One – Creating Customer-Unique Value through Mass Customization* (Boston: Harvard Business School Press, 2000); www.managingchange.com/masscust/overview.htm, accessed 30 May 2005.

58. http://search.ft.com/ftArticle?queryText=personalization&y=4&aje=false&x=16&id=070913000705&ct=0 accessed 26 April 2008 http://adfarm.mediaplex.com/ad/fm/54649?mpt=5640053&mpvc= accessed 27 April 2008.

59. Rajeev Batra and Michael L. Ray, 'Operationalizing Involvement as Depth and Quality of Cognitive Responses', in Alice Tybout and Richard Bagozzi, eds, *Advances in Consumer Research* 10 (Ann Arbor, MI: Association for Consumer Research, 1983): 309–13.

60. Herbert E. Krugman, 'The impact of television advertising: Learning without involvement', *Public Opinion Quarterly* 29 (Fall 1965): 349–56.

61. Scott Bowles, 'Fans Use Their Muscle to Shape The Movie', *USA Today* (June 20, 2003): 2A.

62. Li Yuan, 'Television's New Joy of Text Shows With Vote by Messaging Are on the Rise as Programmers Try To Make Live TV Matter', *Wall Street Journal* (20 July 2006): B1.

63. Mark J. Arnold, Kristy E. Reynolds, 'Hedonic shopping motivations', *Journal of Retailing* 79 (2003): 77–95.

64. Marsha L. Richins and Peter H. Bloch, 'After the new wears off: The temporal context of product involvement', *Journal of Consumer Research* 13 (September 1986): 280–5.

65. Kevin J. Clancy, 'CPMs must bow to "involvement" measurement', *Advertising Age* (20 January 1992): 26.

66. Judith Lynne Zaichkowsky, 'The Personal Involvement Inventory: Reduction, revision, and application to advertising', *Journal of Advertising* 23(4) (December 1994): 59–70.

67. Gilles Laurent and Jean-Noël Kapferer, 'Measuring consumer involvement profiles', *Journal of Marketing Research* 22 (February 1985): 41–53.

68. Gilles Laurent and Jean-Noël Kapferer, 'Measuring consumer involvement profiles', *Journal of Marketing Research* 22 (February 1985): 41–53; this scale was validated on an

American sample as well, see William C. Rodgers and Kenneth C. Schneider, 'An empirical evaluation of the Kapferer–Laurent consumer involvement profile scale', *Psychology & Marketing* 10 (July/August 1993): 333–45. For an English translation of this scale see Jean-Noël Kapferer and Gilles Laurent, 'Further evidence on the consumer involvement profile: Five antecedents of involvement', *Psychology and Marketing* 10 (July/August 1993): 347–56.

69. Gilles Laurent and Jean-Noël Kapferer, 'Measuring consumer involvement profiles', *Journal of Marketing Research* 22 (February 1985): 45, Table 3.

70. Culture clash experienced by one of the authors.

71. David W. Stewart and David H. Furse, 'Analysis of the impact of executional factors in advertising performance', *Journal of Advertising Research* 24 (1984): 23–26; Deborah J. MacInnis, Christine Moorman and Bernard J. Jaworski, 'Enhancing and measuring consumers' motivation, opportunity, and ability to process brand information from ads', *Journal of Marketing* 55 (October 1991): 332–53.

72. Morris B. Holbrook and Elizabeth C. Hirschman, 'The experiential aspects of consumption: Consumer fantasies, feelings, and fun', *Journal of Consumer Research* 9 (September 1982): 132–40.

73. Elaine Sciolino, 'Disproving notions, raising a fury', *The New York Times on the Web* (21 January 2003).

74. K. Oanh Ha, 'Have it your way', *Montgomery Advertiser* (9 November 1998): 2D.

75. Suzanne Vranica and Chad Terhune, 'Mixing Diet Coke and Mentos Makes a Gusher of Publicity', *Wall Street Journal* (June 12, 2006): B1.

76. 'Fountain of youth', eyewitness picture by Sven Dillen/EPA in *The Guardian*, 23 April 2008: 22–3.

77. The Nielsen Company Press Release 'Over 875 Million Consumers Have Shopped Online – the Number of Internet Shoppers Up 40 per cent in Two Years', http://www.earthtimes.org/articles/show/over-875-million-consumers-have-shopped-online--the-number,263812.shtml accessed 20 August 2008.

78. Knowledge@Wharton, 'Fast Forward: Tech Giants Scramble for Bigger Piece of Growing Online Ad Market', 23 July 2008, http://knowledge.wharton.upenn.edu/

79. Donaton, Scott (May 2006), 'How to thrive in new world of user-created content: Let go', *Advertising Age* 77(18), 38; 'Interactive: User-generated – cheap, but is it safe to let go?' *Marketing Week* (May 2006): 40–41; Wasserman, Todd (June 2006), 'Intelligence gathering', *Brandweek* 47(25): S8–S18.

80. Julie Bosman, 'Chevy Tries a Write-Your-Own-Ad Approach, and the Potshots Fly', New York Times (4 April 2006); Suzanne Vranica, 'Marketers' new idea: Get the consumer to design the ads', *Wall Street Journal* (14 December 2005): B1; William M. Bulkeley, 'CNN posts user-generated content – got a better letter opener? Staples solicits inventive ideas from the public for products it can brand, sell exclusively', *Wall Street Journal* (13 July 2006): B1; Norman Madden, 'Forget creatives: Pepsi has Chinese consumers', *The World*, November 2006: 48; Nina M. Lentini, 'Pepsi to let one consumer design 500 million cans' (5 April 2007), *Marketing Daily*, mediapost.com; Sarah McBride, 'Make-it-yourself "Star Wars" Lucasfilm will post clips from film saga on the web, inviting fans to edit at will', *Wall Street Journal* (24 May 2007): B1; Stuart Elliott, 'Forget Spartacus, I am Fresno state', *New York Times* (22 May 2007); May 2006 Trend Briefing, http://www.trendwatching.com/briefing/ (accessed 27 June 2007); Danny Hakim, ' "Star Trek" fans, deprived of a show, recreate the franchise on digital video', *New York Times* (18 June 2006).

81. Julie Bosman, 'Chevy tries a write-your-own-ad approach, and the potshots fly', *New York Times* (April 4, 2006).

82. Shalom H. Schwartz and Warren Bilsky, 'Toward a universal psychological structure of human values', *Journal of Personality and Social Psychology* 53 (1987): 550–62.

83. Ajay K. Sirsi, James C. Ward and Peter H. Reingen, 'Microcultural analysis of variation in sharing of causal reasoning about behavior', *Journal of Consumer Research* 22 (March 1996): 345–72.

84. Richard W. Pollay, 'Measuring the cultural values manifest in advertising', *Current Issues and Research in Advertising* (1983): 71–92.

85. Howard W. French, 'Vocation for dropouts is painting Tokyo red', *New York Times on the Web* (5 March 2000).

86. Deborah Ball, 'Women in Italy Like to Clean but Shun the Quick and Easy: Convenience Doesn't Sell When Bathrooms Average Four Scrubbings a Week', *Wall Street Journal* (April 25, 2006): A1.

87. Serena Jian, 'Brand Watch: Rapid Innovation keeps Cillit Bang ahead of the competition', 1 July 2008, http://www.euromonitor.com/Brand_Watch_Rapid_innovation_keeps_Cillit_Bang_ahead_of_the_competition accessed 11 August 2008.

88. Serena Jian, 'Brand Watch: Rapid Innovation keeps Cillit Bang ahead of the competition', *ibid.*

89. See for instance the discussion of acculturation issues and British South East Asian women in A.M. Lindridge, M.K. Hogg and M. Shah, 'Imagined multiple worlds: How South Asian women in Britain use family and friends to navigate the "border crossings" between household and societal contexts', *Consumption, Markets and Culture* 7(3) (September 2004): 211–38.

90. Carolyn A. Lin, 'Cultural values reflected in Chinese and American television advertising', *Journal of Advertising* 30 (Winter 2001): 83–94.

91. Sante J. Achille, 'Italians dislike online publicity', http://www.multilingual-search.com/italians-dislike-online-publicity/22/07/2008 accessed 20 August 2008.

92. Donald E. Vinson, Jerome E. Scott and Lawrence R. Lamont, 'The role of personal values in marketing and consumer behaviour', *Journal of Marketing* 41 (April 1977): 44–50; John Watson, Steven Lysonski, Tamara Gillan and Leslie Raymore, 'Cultural values and important possessions: A cross-cultural analysis', *Journal of Business Research* 55 (2002): 923–31.

93. Quester, Pascale, Michael Beverland and Francis Farrelly (2006), 'Brand-personal values fit and brand meanings: Exploring the role individual values play in ongoing brand loyalty in extreme sports subcultures', *Advances in Consumer Research* 33(1).

94. Jennifer Aaker, Veronica Benet-Martinez and Jordi Garolera, 'Consumption symbols as carriers of culture: A study of Japanese and Spanish brand personality constructs', *Journal of Personality and Social Psychology* (2001).

95. *Markedsføring* (25 August 2000): 8. See also Amelia Hill and Anushka Asthana, 'She's young, gifted and ahead of you at the till', *Observer* (2 January 2005): 7, http://observer.guardian.co.uk/uk_news/story/0,6903,1382042,00.html which describes 10 million twenty-to-thirty somethings in UK 'who are the new darlings of the retailers and politicians want their vote'. They are key decision makers and spenders in homeware stores.

96. *Markedsføring* (12 November 1999): 2.

97. Morris B. Holbrook, *Consumer Value* (London: Routledge, 1999).

98. *Ibid.* This book contains a chapter by various consumer researchers on each of the value types.

99. A comfortable life; an exciting life; a sense of accomplishment; a world at peace; a world of beauty; equality; family security; freedom; happiness; inner harmony; mature love; national security; pleasure; salvation; self-respect; social recognition; true friendship; and wisdom.

100. Ambitious; broad-minded; capable; cheerful; clean; courageous; forgiving; helpful; honest; imaginative; independent; intellectual; logical; loving; obedient; polite; responsible; and self-controlled.

101. Milton Rokeach, *Understanding Human Values* (New York: The Free Press, 1979); see also J. Michael Munson and Edward McQuarrie, 'Shortening the Rokeach Value Survey for Use in Consumer Research', in Michael J. Houston, ed., *Advances in Consumer Research* 15 (Provo, UT: Association for Consumer Research, 1988): 381–86.

102. Jacques-Marie Aurifeille, 'Value Changes and Their Marketing Implications: A Russian Survey', in W.F. van Raaij and G. Bamossy, eds, *European Advances in Consumer Research* 1 (Provo, UT: Association for Consumer Research, 1993): 249–61.

103. B.W. Becker and P.E. Conner, 'Personal values of the heavy user of mass media', *Journal of Advertising Research* 21 (1981): 37–43; Scott Vinson and Lamont Vinson, 'The role of personal values in marketing and consumer behavior': 44–50.

104. Pierre Valette-Florence, Suzanne C. Grunert, Klaus G. Grunert and Sharon Beatty, 'Une comparaison franco-allemande de l'adhésion aux valeurs personnelles', *Recherche et Applications en Marketing* 6(3) (1991): 5–20.

105. Klaus G. Grunert, Suzanne C. Grunert and Sharon Beatty, 'Cross-cultural research on consumer values', *Marketing and Research Today* 17 (1989): 30–9.

106. Suzanne C. Grunert, Klaus G. Grunert and Kai Kristensen, 'Une méthode d'estimation de la validité interculturelle des instruments de mesure: Le cas de la mesure des valeurs des consommateurs par la liste des valeurs LOV', *Recherche et Applications en Marketing* 8(4) (1993): 5–28. Beatty, Kahle, Homer and Misra, 'Alternative measurement approaches to consumer values': 181–200; Lynn R. Kahle and Patricia Kennedy, 'Using the List of Values (LOV) to understand consumers', *Journal of Consumer Marketing* 2 (Fall 1988): 49–56; Lynn Kahle, Basil Poulos and Ajay Sukhdial, 'Changes in social values in the United States during the past decade', *Journal of Advertising Research* 28 (February/March 1988): 35–41; see also Wagner A. Kamakura and Jose Alfonso Mazzon, 'Value segmentation: A model for the measurement of values and value systems', *Journal of Consumer Research* 18 (September 1991): 28; Jagdish N. Sheth, Bruce I. Newman and Barbara L. Gross, *Consumption Values and Market Choices: Theory and Applications* (Cincinnati: South-Western Publishing Co., 1991).

107. Shalom H. Schwartz and Warren Bilsky, 'Toward a theory of universal content and structure of values: Extensions and cross-cultural replications', *Journal of Personality and Social Psychology* 58 (1990): 878–91; Shalom H. Schwartz, 'Universals in the Content and Structure of Values: Theoretical Advance and Empirical Test in 20 Countries', in M. Zanna, ed., *Advances in Experimental Social Psychology* 25 (San Diego, CA: Academic Press, 1992): 1–65.

108. Shalom H. Schwartz, 'Beyond Individualism/Collectivism: New Cultural Dimensions of Values' in U. Kim *et al.*, eds, *Individualism and Collectivism* (Thousand Oaks, CA: Sage, 1994): 85–119.

109. Sarah Todd, Rob Lawson and Haydn Northover, 'Value Orientation and Media Consumption Behavior', in B. Englis and A. Olofsson, eds, *European Advances in Consumer Behaviour* 3 (Provo, UT: Association for Consumer Research): 328–32.

110. Suzanne C. Grunert and Hans Jørn Juhl, 'Values, environmental attitudes, and buying of organic foods', *Journal of Economic Psychology* 16 (1995): 39–62.

111. Thomas J. Reynolds and Jonathan Gutman, 'Laddering theory, method, analysis, and interpretation', *Journal of Advertising Research* (February/March 1988): 11–34; Beth Walker, Richard Celsi and Jerry Olson, 'Exploring the Structural Characteristics of Consumers' Knowledge', in Melanie Wallendorf and Paul Anderson, eds, *Advances in Consumer Research* 14 (Provo, UT: Association for Consumer Research, 1986): 17–21.

112. Andreas Hermann, 'Wertorientierte produktund werbegestaltung', *Marketing ZFP* 3 (3rd quarter 1996): 153–63.

113. Klaus G. Grunert and Suzanne C. Grunert, 'Measuring subjective meaning structures by the laddering method: Theoretical considerations and methodological problems', *International Journal of Research in Marketing* 12(3) (1995): 209–25. This volume of *IJRM* is a special issue on means–end chains and the laddering technique.

114. Roger Mason, 'Measuring the Demand for Status Goods: An Evaluation of Means–End Chains and Laddering', in Hansen, ed., *European Advances in Consumer Research* 2: 78–82.

115. Thomas J. Reynolds and Alyce Byrd Craddock, 'The application of the MECCAS model to the development and assessment of advertising strategy: A case study', *Journal of Advertising Research* (April/May 1988): 43–54.

116. N.A. Nielsen, T. Bech-Larsen and K.G. Grunert, 'Consumer purchase motives and product perceptions: A laddering study on vegetable oil in three countries', *Food Quality and Preference* 9(6) (1998): 455–66.

117. Marsha L. Richins, 'Special possessions and the expression of material values', *Journal of Consumer Research* 21 (December, 1994): 522–33.

118. *Ibid.*

119. James E. Burroughs and Aric Rindfleisch, 'Materialism and well-being: A conflicting values perspective', *Journal of Consumer Research* 29 (December 2002): 348ff.

120. Lan Nguyen Chaplin and Deborah Roedder John, 'Growing up in a Material World: Age Differences in Materialism in Children and Adolescents', *Journal of Consumer Research* 34 (December 2007): 490.

121. Daniel Kahneman cited in Benedict Carey, 'TV time, unlike child care, ranks high in mood study', *NYTimes.com* (3 December 2004); see also Richard Tomkins, 'Materialism damages well-being,' *Financial Times* (27 November 2003), http://news.ft.com/servlet/ContentServer?pagename=FT.com/StoryFT/FullStory&c=StoryFT&cid=1069493548137&p=1012571727088

122. Matt Mabe 'Got Warm Feelings?' Business Week report on World Values Survey on the happiest countries, 20 August 2008, http://images.businessweek.com/ss/08/08/0819_happiest_countries/index.htm accessed 22 August 2008.

123. Marsha L. Richins and Scott Dawson, 'A consumer values orientation for materialism and its measurement: Scale

development and validation', *Journal of Consumer Research* 20 (December 1992).

124. Güliz Ger and Russell Belk, 'Cross-cultural differences in materialism', *Journal of Economic Psychology* 17 (1996): 55–77.

125. Güliz Ger and Russell Belk, 'Accounting for materialism in four cultures', *Journal of Material Culture* 4(2) (1999): 183–204.

126. Robert V. Kozinets, 'Can consumers escape the market? Emancipatory illuminations from burning man', *Journal of Consumer Research* 29 (June 2002): 20–38; see also Douglas B. Holt, 'Why do brands cause trouble? A dialectical theory of consumer culture and branding', *Journal of Consumer Research* 29 (June 2002): 70–90.

127. Emily Burg, 'Whole Foods Is Consumers' Favorite Green Brand', *Marketing Daily*, mediapost.com (10 May 2007).

128. www.lohas.com/about.htm, accessed 30 June 2007.

129. http://www.defra.gov.uk/

130. Defra Report, 'A framework for pro-environmental behaviours' (January 2008) London, http://www.defra.gov.uk/evidence/social/behaviour/ : 8, accessed 16 August 2008.

131. Defra Report, 'A framework for pro-environmental behaviours' (January 2008) London, http://www.defra.gov.uk/evidence/social/behaviour/, accessed 16 August 2008.

132. Adrienne W. Fawcett, 'Conscientious Consumerism Drives Record New Product Launches in 2006', *New York Timesimes.com/magazine* (24 January 2007).

133. Sarah Mahoney, 'Putting Green In Vogue: Organic Clothes Get Hot', *Marketing Daily*, www.mediapost.com (17 April 2007).

134. P&G going green Liquid detergents will come in smaller packaging with double concentrate as the company moves to become enviro-friendly, according to a published report, *CNNMoney.com* (2 May 2007).

135. Quoted in Lynn Lunsford and Daniel Michaels, 'On Paris's Jet Runways, Green Is the New Gray', *The Wall Street Journal Online Edition* (22 June 2007).

136. Mya Frazier, Farmstands vs. Big Brands: With Consumers Interested in Locally Produced Goods, Marketers Scramble to Get in on a Movement Going Mainstream, advertisingage.com (5 June 2007).

137. Cecilia M. Vega, 'Mayor to cut off flow of city money for bottled water', http://sfgate.com/cgi-bin/article.cgi?f=/c/a/2007/06/22/BAGE8QJVIL1.DTL (22 June 2007).

138. http://green.yahoo.com/index.php?q=action, accessed 30 June 2007.

139. http://www.carbonfootprint.com/carbon_footprint.html, accessed 30 June 2007.

140. http://www.climateclean.net/, accessed 30 June 2007; http://www.terrapass.com/, accessed 30 June 2007.

141. Editorial, 'Water: Go Against the Flow', *The Guardian*, 20 August 2008: 30, http://www.guardian.co.uk/commentisfree/2008/aug/20/water.food, accessed 20 August 2008.

142. *Ibid.*

143. Felicity Lawrence, 'Revealed: the massive scale of UK's water consumption', *The Guardian*, 20 August 2008: 1, http://www.guardian.co.uk/environment/2008/aug/20/water.food1, accessed 20 August 2008.

144. Felicity Lawrence, ' UK adds to drain on global water sources', Special Report, *The Guardian*, 20 August 2008: 9, http://www.guardian.co.uk/environment/2008/aug/20/water.food, accessed 20 August 2008.

145. European Environment Agency, 'Sustainable consumption and production in South East Europe and Eastern Europe, Caucasus and Central Asia: Joint UNEP-EEA report on the opportunities and lessons learned', Copenhagen and Geneva EEA Report 3/2007 Box 2.1: 30, 31.

146. Russell W. Belk, 'The Role of Possessions in Constructing and Maintaining a Sense of Past,' in Marvin E. Goldberg, Gerald Gorn and Richard W. Pollay, eds, *Advances in Consumer Research* 17 (Provo, UT: Association for Consumer Research, 1989): 669–76.

147. Jacob Jacoby, Carol K. Berning and Thomas F. Dietvorst, 'What about disposition?' *Journal of Marketing* 41 (April 1977): 22–8.

148. Mike Tharp, 'Tchaikovsky and toilet paper', *U.S. News and World Report* (December 1987): 62; B. Van Voorst, 'The recycling bottleneck', *Time* (14 September 1992): 52–4; Richard P. Bagozzi and Pratibha A. Dabholkar, 'Consumer recycling goals and their effect on decisions to recycle: A means–end chain analysis,' *Psychology and Marketing* 11 (July/August 1994): 313–40.

149. 'Finally, something at McDonald's you can actually eat', *UTNE Reader* (May/June 1997): 12.

150. Steven Kurutz, 'Not Buying It', *nytimes.com* (21 June 2007).

151. Debra J. Dahab, James W. Gentry, and Wanru Su, 'New Ways to Reach Non-Recyclers: An Extension of the Model of Reasoned Action to Recycling Behaviors', paper presented at the meetings of the Association for Consumer Research, 1994.

152. Bagozzi and Dabholkar, 'Consumer recycling goals and their effect on decisions to recycle', *op. cit.*; see also L.J. Shrum, Tina M. Lowrey and John A. McCarty, 'Recycling as a marketing problem: A framework for strategy development,' *Psychology and Marketing* 11 (July/August 1994): 393 416; Dahab, Gentry and Su, 'New Ways to Reach Non-Recyclers', *op. cit.*

153. John Markoff, 'Technology's toxic trash is sent to poor nations', *The New York Times on the Web*, 25 February 2002; 'Recycling phones to charities, not landfills', *The New York Times on the Web*, 26 October 2002.

154. John F. Sherry Jr., 'A socio-cultural analysis of a Midwestern American flea market', *Journal of Consumer Research* 17 (June 1990): 13–30.

155. Saul Hansell, 'Meg Whitman and eBay, net survivors', *The New York Times on the Web*, 5 May 2002.

156. Jess Cartner-Morley, 'In search of the real deal', *The Guardian*, 2 July 2008, http://www.guardian.co.uk/technology/2008/jul/02/ebay.consumeraffairs, accessed 20 August 2008.

157. Rob Walker, 'Unconsumption', *New York Times Magazine* (7 January 2007): 19; Tina Kelley, 'Socks? With Holes? I'll Take It', *New York Times on the Web*, 16 March 2004.

158. Quoted in Stephanie Stoughton, 'Unemployed Americans turn to e-Bay to make money', *The Boston Globe*, 16 October 2001.

159. Owen Gibson, 'E-commerce: Ebay changes aim for fewer critics and more sellers', *The Guardian*, 20 August 2008, http://www.guardian.co.uk/business/2008/aug/20/ebay.efinance, accessed 20 August 2008.

160. However, see E.A. Greenleaf, 'Reserves, regret, and rejoicing in open English auctions', *Journal of Consumer Research* 31 (September 2004): 264–73 for a study of consumer behaviour within the context of English auctions, with specific reference to sellers' seeking to minimize regret and maximize rejoicing when setting reserve prices.

161. Allan J. Magrath, 'If used product sellers ever get organized, watch out', *Marketing News*, 25 June 1990: 9; Kevin McCrohan and James D. Smith, 'Consumer participation

in the informal economy', *Journal of the Academy of Marketing Science* 15 (Winter 1990): 62.

162. John Sutherland, 'The price of nostalgia', *Guardian G2*, 28 March 2005: 5 (http://www.guardian.co.uk/g2/story/0,,1446610,00.html).

163. 'New kind of store getting more use out of used goods', *Montgomery Advertiser*, 12 December 1996: 7A.

164. John L. Lastovicka and Karen V. Fernandez, 'Three paths to disposition: The movement of meaningful possessions to strangers', *Journal of Consumer Research* 31 (March 2005): 813–23.

165. Tomkins, 'Materialism damages well-being', *op. cit.*

166. Helene Stapinski, 'Y Not Love?' *American Demographics*, February 1999: 62–8.

Consuming ethically? Exploring the dilemmas facing ethical consumers

MORVEN G MCEACHERN, Lancaster University, UK

MARYLYN CARRIGAN, Open University, UK

CONTEXT

This case study provides some insights into how ethics fit (but not always comfortably) into the ethically-conscious consumers' overall framework of decision making, where they are trying to achieve certain goals (e.g. local sourcing of products, environmentally friendly practices; fair trade) but simultaneously have to balance ethical choices with the challenges of everyday life.

THE ETHICAL MARKETPLACE

Ethical spending in the UK has doubled since 2002 (Co-operative Bank, 2007), with the result that companies who possess a substantial and growing share of this market have now become acquisition targets in order to extend the brand portfolios of large multinationals. More than 3,000 products also now carry the Fairtrade logo, and supermarkets including Tesco, Sainsbury's and Marks & Spencer are eager to prove their Fairtrade credentials. Examples of moves into the ethical branding arena include the likes of: L'Oréal and its takeover of The Bodyshop; Unilever's purchase of Ben & Jerry's; Horizon Organic Holding's takeover of Rachel's Dairy; and Cadbury Schweppes and its acquisition of Green & Black's. An additional branding strategy has been one of brand line extension, one undertaken by large multinationals such as Kraft Foods Inc. and Nestlé's launch of their Fairtrade coffee brand 'Partners' Blend'. Neither Kraft nor Nestlé are renowned for their ethical activities, but both recognize the added value of such ethical links, given that a recent Co-operative Group survey revealed 80 per cent of consumers are prepared to pay a little more to be reassured about the ethics of a product (Butler, 2008). Yet, such moves have raised criticism in the marketplace. Although the Fairtrade logo appears prominently in Starbucks outlets, only 4 per cent of Starbucks coffee is Fairtrade; Green & Black's only uses Fairtrade cocoa in one of its chocolate bars – Maya Gold – and for Nestlé, despite their fierce promotion of Partners' Blend, it only represents 0.02 per cent of the multinational's coffee purchases. Some campaigners saw this as a sell-out by Fairtrade, while others thought it was a useful exercise to expose Nestlé as expedient and tokenistic, given none of its other 8,500 products are Fairtrade. The Fairtrade organization is unrepentant, stating that they need to engage firms like Nestlé on commercial grounds, and lock Fairtrade into their core business. As yet, no definitive understanding exists as to how consumers cope when negotiating the potential ethical conflicts embedded within such purchasing decisions and whether these practices have impacted (if at all) upon the perceptions, attitudes and purchase behaviour of ethically-conscious consumers.

DILEMMAS FOR AN ETHICAL CONSUMER

While there are many positive signs that the market for ethical products is growing, consumers are still faced with a variety of choices in trying to 'consume ethically' in the marketplace. Complex attitudes, inclinations and lifestyle goals underpin ethical consumption choices. Early exploratory research suggests that there is a group of consumers that fall between the ethical practices of Voluntary Simplifiers (aka 'Principled Pioneers') and Beginner Voluntary Simplifiers (aka 'Onlookers') (Szmigin, Carrigan and McEachern, 2008). This group chooses 'to consume with sensitivity' by 'selecting ethical alternatives' (Szmigin and Carrigan, 2006: 609) when faced with a number of 'competing priorities, paradoxical outcomes, and the nature of compromises reached in real decision processes' (McDonald et al., 2006: 529) when making ethical consumption choices. Even though consumers may have socially responsible attitudes, it does not necessarily mean they make ethical purchases, or boycott unethical firms; rationales for purchasing may be in transition or flux; their underlying tensions and competing values may not always be resolved consistently; and/or their consumption behaviour can be unpredictable and heavily context dependent.

EXPLORING THE DILEMMAS

Many consumers perceive limits to their ethical behaviours arising from time, convenience and cost, even though they have an 'ethical' orientation towards consumption (Szmigin, Carrigan and McEachern, 2008).

Tesco spoiling the high street – that is something I'm concerned about but at the end of the day, everybody needs the convenience of a Tesco unless you are in the fortunate position to have all the time in the world.

(Amanda)

I'd rather choose organic and fair trade, I mean if I had loads of money that is, I would buy it all the time.

(Sheena)

Unlike more mainstream consumers who may seek out information only in more complex decision environments, ethically-motivated consumption is often accompanied with a stronger desire towards seeking out product and manufacturer information regardless of the decision-making complexity (Berry and McEachern, 2005). Similarly, many ethical consumers emphasize the importance of information sharing via informal channels and appear increasingly reliant on word of mouth/mouse communications between friends, family and work colleagues. Such communications can be particularly influential upon anti-consumption, de-consumption and boycott behaviour.

Ethical consumers often hold mixed views about multinationals' acquisition of established ethical brands and their brand extensions. This consumer ambivalence highlights the potential paradoxes inherent within many forms of ethical purchasing behaviour (Szmigin, Carrigan and McEachern, 2008).

On one side it's good because at the end of the day it is benefiting somebody . . . it's better than nothing . . . but on the other hand they might be just doing it to pull the wool over people's eyes.

(Maurice)

Some ethically-inclined consumers are prepared to tentatively accept some mainstream manufacturers such as Cadburys moving into the ethical marketplace (via their acquisition of Green & Black's) (Szmigin, Carrigan and McEachern, 2008). This reveals a certain degree of flexibility in their perceptions of who can be believed/trusted as being ethical.

With Sainsbury's . . . they are doing them because consumers are asking for these products . . . that's not the right reason for doing it but if it has the right result, is there a problem with that? . . . Companies like Nestlé, I guess it does bother me because there are other areas of their treatment of workers and people . . . that actually are appalling, so just to put a badge on this and say this is OK, that does irritate me.

(Caroline)

Inevitably the arrival of brands much-maligned for their unethical business practices, such as Starbucks, Nestlé and Unilever, into the ethical market has led to angry criticism, particularly of organizations such as the Fairtrade Foundation for allowing retailers to gain ethical credentials for a very limited commitment

(Butler, 2008). Mainstream brands that have adopted ethical credentials can be seen as lacking in authenticity because of the perceived gap between the ethical values recently associated with the brand and the activities of the corporation. There is some evidence of resistance by ethically-conscious consumers to what they perceive as a cynical attempt to lure them into the Nestlé brand family (Szmigin, Carrigan and McEachern, 2008).

I'd rather stick to brands I trust as being Fairtrade and it's established and that's what they're based on . . . just putting in one ethical product is just sort of cashing in.

(Hannah)

It's just a contradiction in terms . . . it's got to go deeper than that.

(Peter)

Research (Kozinets and Handelman, 1998; Thompson and Arsel, 2004) among ethical consumers commonly reveals their expressions of strong dislike and distaste for a group of brands (i.e. Nike, Nestlé, McDonald's, Esso, Starbucks). However, the intensity of dislike and apathy towards such brands is not always a strong indicator of boycott behaviour. Some UK consumers demonstrated significant flexibility in their resistance to or avoidance of the same products and brands whose ethical credentials they criticized (Szmigin, Carrigan and McEachern, 2008). Brand resistance and/or avoidance can also be undermined by the needs and/or wants of a consumer's family members/partners (Slater and Miller, 2007). However much ethically-conscious consumers dislike Nestlé or desire to serve a greater good, many are willing to put aside their principles to accommodate the needs of their loved ones, highlighting the compromises people have to reach in day-to-day decision making (Szmigin, Carrigan and McEachern, 2008).

We would like to acknowledge the involvement of Professor Isabelle Szmigin in the research study and data set from which the quotes used in this case study were sourced.

QUESTIONS

1 Identify and evaluate what kind(s) of consumption and/or purchasing behaviour differentiate an ethically-conscious consumer in the marketplace from more mainstream consumers.

2 Why do you think an 'attitude–behaviour' gap exists between the intentions and the actions of many ethically-aware consumers?

3 Within the context of your own country, discuss the various barriers to ethical purchasing behaviour. Comment as to how these barriers differ (if at all) from the UK context described in the case study.

4 Why do you think some brands find it particularly hard to convince shoppers of their ethical credentials?

Sources

Berry, Hannah and McEachern, Morven G. (2005), 'Informing Ethical Consumers' in *The Ethical Consumer*, Harrison, R., Newholm, T. and Shaw, D. (eds) (Sage Publications, London): 69–87.

Butler, S. (2008), 'Good intentions, or just pandering to the consumer?' *The Guardian*, 27 February: 5.

Co-operative Bank (2007), *The Ethical Consumerism Report* (Manchester): December.

Kozinets, Robert. V. and Handelman, Jay (1998), 'Ensouling consumption: a netnographic exploration of the meaning of boycotting behaviour', *Advances in Consumer Research*, 25: 475–480.

McDonald, S., Oates, C.J., Young, C.W. and Hwang, K. (2006), 'Toward sustainable consumption: Researching voluntary simplifiers', *Psychology & Marketing*, 23(6): 515–534.

Slater, D. and Miller, D. (2007), 'Moments and Movements in the study of consumer culture: a discussion between Daniel Miller and Don Slater', *Journal of Consumer Culture*, 7(5): 5–23.

Szmigin, Isabelle and Carrigan, Marylyn (2005), 'Exploring the dimensions of ethical consumption', *Advances in Consumer Research*, vol. 7, Karin M. Ekström and Helene Brembeck (eds) (MN: Association for Consumer Research): 608–613.

Szmigin, Isabelle, Carrigan, Marylyn and McEachern, Morven G. (2008), 'Flexibility, dissonance and the conscious consumer', *Advances in Consumer Research* (European Conference of the Association for Consumer Research, Milan): July.

Thompson, Craig. J. and Zeynep Arsel (2004), 'The Starbucks brandscape and consumers' (anticorporate) experiences of glocalization', *Journal of Consumer Research*, 31: 631–642.

Being a real man about town: the challenge of the 'new masculinity'

JACOB ÖSTBERG, Stockholm University School of Business, Sweden

Stockholm, like most other reasonably large cities, has a rich nightlife. Also, like most other reasonably large cities, the people at the centre of the Stockholm nightlife circuit are convinced that the particular nightlife in the city is spectacular; more akin to Paris, London, New York or LA than other similarly sized cities such as, heaven forbid, Copenhagen. Especially, they are convinced that Stockholm has a unique sense of fashion and style that is surmounted by only the hippest of the hip. Be that as it may. What is a given, however, is that the activities in and around the nightclubs in Stockholm are gaining a fair share of attention in both mainstream and specialized media. Not least various Internet sites, with as many as 340,000 unique visitors per month,* which are chronicling everyone's whereabouts on the nightclub circuit. Most notably they are publishing thousands of pictures every week where the lucky ones whose photos get published are given a chance to show the world what an exquisite sense of style they have. The chance to get your image displayed to thousands of viewers is, however, a double-edged sword. On the one hand you have a fantastic opportunity to make an impact, but on the other hand you only have a flash of a moment to make that impression. The challenge is to communicate *who you are* clearly and distinctly without overdoing it and becoming a parody. Needless to say, fervent image management activities are taking place in these locations.

One group who finds this especially challenging is those people aspiring to be connected to the old elite in Sweden. Whether they are indeed old aristocrats is beside the point, the interesting issue is that there is a rather large group on the Stockholm nightclub scene that affiliate themselves with some sort of faux-aristocracy, claiming lineage to the old aristocratic families or, at least, being on a first name basis with the princesses or the prince of Sweden. The members of this group have traditionally been expressing their masculine identities through knowledge and practice of refined consumption, and have thus set themselves apart from the masses by being more stylish.

In the last couple of years, however, it has been proposed that we see a 'new hegemonic masculinity' (Patterson and Elliott, 2002), which includes a feminization of masculinity, and invites men from all social positions to partake in the carnival of consumption in ways previously reserved predominantly for female consumers (Schroeder and Zwick, 2004). Due to this change in mainstream masculinity, the traditional elite – who have long been concerned with appearances and express their masculine identities through a knowledge and practice of refined consumption – is challenged in their roles as tastemakers *par excellence* (Osgerby, 2001). The advent of popular-culture outlets for new gender ideologies – such as the TV show *Queer Eye for the Straight Guy*, self-help books such as *The Metrosexual Guide to Style*, not to mention the abundant availability of men's lifestyle magazines and, increasingly, blogs – make the cultural capital previously reserved for the higher social classes available to the masses. Consequently, the legacy of the traditional elite is challenged. The question is, how do young men from social groups that have historically paid particular attention to appearance respond to the popularization – and perhaps vulgarization – of their traditional consumption codes? What strategies are utilized by the traditional elite to strengthen their sense of masculinity in light of this new, allegedly feminized, consumption ethos?

DEFENDERS OF TIMELESS STABILITY: THE RETROSEXUALS

The first characteristic of the traditional elite's consumption is that they do not regard themselves as representing something new, or as following contemporary trends. Instead, they see themselves as defenders of stability and providing a timeless, classic (and classy) masculinity as an alternative to all the currently available fast-moving consumer fads. They are characterized more by conservatism and a willingness to uphold – what they perceive to be – traditional values, than the more rebellious traits usually upheld by similar youth constellations (cf. Hodkinson, 2002). Instead of manifesting their identity by rebelling against the parent generation,

* www.stureplan.se

they act in a rebellious fashion by trying to resurrect conservative values of an imagined past. They are thus escaping the temporality of contemporary, faddish consumption, of which they would regard the new feminized masculine consumption as a prime example, by attaching themselves to a timeless ethos of style. In the online communities, references are made many times to how they – the traditional elite – do things with style, whereas others – particularly the new elite – lack the ability, both economically and culturally, to be stylish. One principal way for them to distinguish their consumption from that of the new elite is to frame the latter's consumption behaviours as overly conscious or even girlish; if one *really* has style, one rarely has to show it in the explicit way utilized by the new elite. One of the official tastemakers of the Stockholm nightclub scene, Roland-Philippe Krezschmar, fashion editor of the webpage 'Stureplan: La publication glamoreuse, superfashion et tres exclusif', strongly suggests that when it comes to style, just buying a fancy outfit won't cut it, you need some depth and history in your closet, you need to be a 'retrosexual':

> It is not until you have 7 suits, 7 pairs of shoes and 21 shirts [. . .], that you can start experimenting with jeans, t shirts, slacks, sneakers and jackets. You are smart, so you never go for fashion-fashion, but for the timeless classics. Call it preppy, call it carefree, call it retrosexual . . .

The oh-so-stylish Mr Krezschmar continues by drawing lines between those who have understood what style is and the others who are just anxiously following the lead of whoever is portrayed as the fashion guru of the day:

> . . . The retrosexual man, when it comes to appearance, is a man who is strategic, long-term, and smart. It's all about investing in one's lifelong success, not about day trading with one's appearance. It's about being confidently relaxed in oneself and not about being a fashion-poof who dances to Tom Ford's pipe. It's about Ralph Lauren but not Karl Lagerfeld, Adrian Brody but not Kevin Federline, Bernard Arnault but not Donald Trump. It's about men with class, finesse, and natural panache.

In this way, the traditional elite express that they do not *need* brands and fashion to show that they are stylish. Instead, this quality seems to be almost inherent in who they are. The crux of the matter is that the traditional elite wants to at least imagine that this comes naturally to them, while it might be hard for onlookers to know who is just posing and who was born that way. Despite their calls to stay true to the eternal codes of style rather than follow the whims of fashion, what is stylish at any given point of time is constantly changing. Distinguishing the exclusive classic style from the marketized version available to the masses is becoming increasingly hard. A few years ago, the Spanish company *Zara* introduced a new line of suits that catered to the stylish gentleman. One of the features was that the cuffs could be unbuttoned, traditionally a sign that the jacket was made by a tailor. The elite used to wear one button unbuttoned to subtly signal to the likeminded that they were wearing an expensive jacket. On the *Zara* suits there was a little tag explaining this behaviour to the prospective buyers and thus giving away the secret code. When these codes are spread to the masses the elite has to adapt. The following quote, taken from a Webpage catering to the ones more interested in classic style than fashion,* illustrates how the elite has to vulgarize their old behaviours in order to stay one step ahead of the crowd:

> When struck by the urge to undo a jacket sleeve button, walk quickly to a large public men's room. Unbutton and roll up your sleeves and wash your hands. Then dry your hands and button the sleeves again. You'll demonstrate that your sleeve buttons work to many men without embarrassing yourself and after a few repetitions the urges will cease.

CONNECTING TO A GLOBAL ELITE

Another common denominator for what is deemed stylish, and thus a suitable blueprint for the construction of masculinity, is that it should be connected to what other, imagined, groups of similar consumers around the world are engaging in. In this way, the traditional elite tries to escape the spatial restrictions of their present consumption by attaching themselves to an imagined community of global cosmopolitans. By viewing these global soulmates as their points of reference rather than the upward-striving new elitists, or at least the ones posing as such, they manage to downplay the similarities between their respective consumption behaviours. Again, they have to walk a thin line to be able to show off in a manner that can easily be decoded from a snapshot posted on a webpage, while not coming across as overtly conscious about appearing in a particular way. The trick is to frame others' behaviours as vulgar and one's own as sophisticated. One behaviour that has been used in such a manner lately is the spraying of champagne, an activity that perhaps could come across as always unsophisticated. But no, apparently it all depends on *how* you do it. If you spray it for effect, to get as much attention as possible, you are not getting it right, you have to adopt the right blasé attitude to make it look like it is just something that needs to be done. Again, the fashionable Webpage 'Stureplan' shows how it should be done by alluding to the really stylish people in faraway places with this description followed by a dozen pictures of people pouring champagne into the

* asuitablewardrobe.dynend.com

pool at the nightclub *Le Cave de Roy* in St Tropez: 'What do the real players look like in St Tropez, New York or Shanghai? Yes, you guessed it – like real men, not like overgrown teenagers.' How vulgar it is to ostentatiously spray champagne. You then come across as an attention-seeking teenager dying for the world to pay attention to you. To be stylish, in the right cosmopolitan manner, you should just turn the bottle upside-down and casually let the liquid glide from the ($100) bottle at its own pace.

QUESTIONS

1 Discuss the groups of consumers described in this case from the perspective of lifestyles.

2 What (if any) is the difference between style, as defined by the traditional elite, and fashion?

3 What challenges are there for companies trying to market to groups of consumers who strive to be elitists?

EXERCISE

1 The group of consumers described in this case is symbolically fighting over the right to define what should be deemed masculine and stylish. Try to come up with other examples of consumption domains where groups of consumers are fighting over the right to define what's hot and what's not.

Sources

Hodkinson, Paul (2002), *Goth: Identity, style and subculture* (Oxford and New York: Berg).

Osgerby, Bill (2001), *Playboys in paradise: Masculinity, youth and leisure-style in modern America* (Oxford and New York: Berg).

Patterson, Maurice and Elliott, Richard (2002), 'Negotiating masculinities: Advertising and the inversion of the male gaze', *Consumption, Markets and Culture*, 5(3): 231–246.

Schroeder, Jonathan E. and Zwick, Detlev (2004), 'Mirrors of masculinity: Representation and identity in advertising images', *Consumption, Markets and Culture*, 7(1): 21–52.

Global brand strategies and local meaning making: contesting ideals of beauty

JOONAS ROKKA, Helsinki School of Economics, Finland

HANNA-KAISA DESAVELLE, Tampere University of Technology, Finland

INTRODUCTION

Beauty is strongly linked to 'naturalness' which means really a straight-out-of-the-sauna cleanliness, it isn't natural beauty anymore if one needs to work hard for it or use a lot of make up to obtain a natural look.

Natural beauty is encapsulated in freshness and Nordic luminousness. It is not only about physical appearance but real naturalness combined with joy and a positive attitude. It is like the Finnish Elovena girl from the oatmeal porridge package who is hard working, healthy, fresh-faced and blond[e] – a real natural Finnish beauty!

The ideal form of this beauty is something that comes about spontaneously, without effort. It needs to be understood as something that is available to everyone. It does not stem from extreme measures e.g. dieting, exercise or painful bodily modifications. A beautiful person doesn't need to wear any make up either. A real Miss Finland – there is joy and softness. And she's not being tortured and skinny!

The body and the healthiness of the body are essential aspects of beauty. 'Being fit' translates into beauty, though only within limits: overt athleticism; 'testosterone babes'; or 'body builders' do not equate with natural beauty.

Authenticity and genuineness are important features of natural beauty. But they cannot be attained through photoshopping and the artificial manipulation of images. This picture [L'Oréal's ad] has been tampered with . . . but all ads are! A photoshopped woman can sometimes be beautiful but it is not the same! Silicone doll-like Pamela Anderson or Paris Hilton are just horrible.

What does the above extract tell us about Finnish women's views of beauty? It illustrates how Finnish women interpret global media images. The Finnish respondents draw on memories of a mythic girl, Elovena, from a Finnish oatmeal brand from the 1920s and compare her with the photoshopped global celebrities of the twenty-first century that they see in the media. What we are interested in here is how consumers draw on both global and local cues to understand beauty ideals. Using data from Finnish female consumers, we discuss the interrelationship between the specific cultural context (in this case, Finland) and global advertising messages in understanding what constitutes beauty.

CONTEXT

Beauty consists of a multibillion euro business, broadly encompassing industries from fast moving consumer goods, through to cosmetics, healthcare, fashion, and entertainment. Beauty is iconized by models and endorsers in global advertising and other media. The global beauty industry has been criticized for shaping and forming the ideals of beauty, using massive marketing campaigns which promote almost uniform, and often unrealistic, beauty ideals. Beauty, i.e. physical, bodily appearance, is also an omnipresent feature across many other areas of industry and business activity.

Some companies, such as Dove, have turned the global mainstream conception of beauty to their advantage. In their campaign for 'Real Beauty', Dove has decisively taken a position against the production of unrealistic beauty stereotypes with thought-provoking ads and global societal efforts (**www.campaignforrealbeauty.com**). Through this highly successful advertising campaign Dove has taken important steps towards the creation of alternative beauty conceptions in the global media. They emphasize the multiplicity of shapes and forms that beauty can take by identifying the conspicuous role of photoshopping in advertising and print media in their communications. The Finnish consumers' attraction to the Dove campaign can be understood in terms of equality values; beauty is promoted as available to everyone. Everybody can potentially be a model, a role which has traditionally been restricted to a very few men and women, and conditional on their possessing certain rare physical qualities. In the last few years a number of Finnish marketers have introduced their own versions of real beauty campaigns. Some recent examples include the Finnish clothing retailer Seppälä, and a supermarket chain's monthly customer magazine *Pirkka*. For example Seppälä's campaign, 'Be the supermodel of your own life', launched in 2006 depicts young 'ordinary' women and men modelling in television ads as well as in their catalogue (**www.seppala.fi**).

FINNISH CONSUMERS NEGOTIATING BEAUTY

The interpretation of beauty by Finnish women in our data demonstrate interestingly how consumers draw from global cultural flows, such as international women's magazines, to make sense of their own everyday lives and identities. The global advertising plays a key role in circulating and streaming complex repertoires of images around the world. These images are often times played out as role models and sources of aspiration for consumers, but they are also being contested and negotiated differently in various cultural surroundings.

One of the most prominent ways of approaching beauty in the Finnish discourse was through the idea of 'naturalness' which was strongly linked to Finnishness, and to Finnish ideals of beauty. Naturalness has previously been identified as an important form of commercial fashion discourse. However, this commercialized 'natural look' is not to be equated with naturally transpiring or an easily obtained state of being, but it is rather another form of beauty ideal which one has to work to attain. In the Finnish context, on the other hand, naturalness needs to be understood differently; the ideal form of naturalness is something that comes about spontaneously, without effort. The natural ideal, which on the superficial level is manifested as a particular type of nondescript appearance, stems from certain mental characteristics that derive from the Scandinavian-Protestant world view (i.e. modesty, equality, value of labour).

The emphasis on 'naturalness' in the Finnish beauty discourse can also be seen as rooted in the prominence of nature and symbols of nature in different spheres of Finnish life. Finns have made sense of their national identity and homeland through the conceptualization of nature as the biological and ecological elements (soil, water, air, animals, and plants) in their organic state, i.e. not affected by human presence. For example, the Finnish national anthem 'Maamme' ('Our Land') praises the Finnish land and scenery whereas other national anthems in Europe (for instance, France or Poland) can be seen as rather belligerent. The Finnish euro coins do not feature buildings or statesmen, but cloudberries and whooper swans. Therefore, considering the beauty narrative as understood by Finnish women, it is increasingly obvious that consumers' local socio-cultural and historical contexts provide resources for consumers' consumption practices of images and meaning making from images.

Finnish consumers are very familiar with, and often very influenced by, Americanized media and popular culture. They are part of the global marketplace, recognizing international advertising campaigns; identifying celebrities and evaluating their public images; and assessing the advertisers' motives in trying to influence consumers. At the same time, Finnish consumers are also influenced by their own specific cultural context, with its own sources of socio-historical meanings and myths. These local cultural resources inform Finnish consumers' ways of understanding and making sense of advertising images. The image of the Elovena-girl, for example, can be traced all the way back to the mythical female characters prominent both in literature and in arts, such as Lady Aino in the Finnish national epic *Kalevala** and embodied in the national artist Akseli Gallen-Kallela's paintings. Therefore, whilst the global cultural flows represented by international advertising campaigns do play an important role in providing symbolic resources and materials for Finnish (and other European) consumers, they are not the only resources that consumers call on when they interpret beauty ideals from advertising. Consumers are also embedded in and open to their own cultural context, which potentially accentuates local interpretations of beauty ideals, such as in the case of the Finnish women and the above-mentioned ideals which surround naturalness.

The Finnish cosmetics company Lumene Group provides an interesting and long-term example of a marketing strategy which incorporated aspects of nature and Nordic beauty. The origin of the Lumene Group can be traced back over 60 years to 1948, and the Lumene cosmetics line was introduced in 1970. The cosmetics brand Lumene is the market leader in the Finnish cosmetics market, and other important markets include Russia, USA, Scandinavia and the Baltic countries. (About Lumene Group: **www.lumenegroup.com/default.asp?docId=12987**.) Nature and naturalness are omnipresent in Lumene group's corporate narrative from mission and vision all the way to R&D. For example, the company Website describes Lumene's core competence and the origin of the brand name as follows:

> Only Lumene has the unique know-how and technology for utilizing the most precious parts of Arctic plants . . . Lumene was named after the sparkling blue Lake Lummenne in Kuhmoinen in the Finnish Lake District. Our inspiration is pure, crystal clear and thrives in the white summer nights of the North . . . Lumene glorifies inner well-being and radiance. It is clean. Crisp. Pure. Natural.

(Our story: **www.lumene.com/default.asp?docId=22447**)

These ideals are embodied in the products and marketing strategies. For example, Lumene uses Finnish berries and plants such as cloudberries or

---

* The Finnish national epic compiled by Elias Lönnrot from folk poetry in 1835 to 1849.

plantain as raw materials in some of their leading product lines. In addition, elements of nature are reflected in product names such as 'Arctic Duet Mineral eye shadow', 'Cranberry Kiss lipstick', 'Berryfun lipgloss', 'Lumene Blueberry mascaras', 'Organic Linen' or 'Arctic Aqua' skincare line. Advertising campaigns also draw strongly on the 'natural' and 'Nordic' aspects of beauty both in written and visual terms. The Lumene slogan or tagline for international markets is 'The Secret of Arctic Nature' and for the domestic market it is 'The Secret of Nordic Nature'. The international Website promotes Lumene Blueberry Mascaras by 'Dramatic Volume with the force of nature'. In the Finnish market, the campaign for the new Natural Code product line calls for using 'Nature's Code for Beauty' with the help of 100 per cent Finnish plantain. The visual marketing material is strongly based on landscapes depicting, for example, elements of water, forest, berries and plants. Also, an interesting point to take into consideration is that until very recently the diverse advertising campaigns used almost exclusively blonde endorsers, who were traditionally seen as the reflection of Finnish or Nordic beauty.

Based on the previous discussion which identified the importance of naturalness and symbols of nature in the negotiation of the meaning of beauty by Finnish consumers, one could easily conclude that Lumene achieves unanimous acceptance among the Finnish consumers. Even though highly successful in Finland, consumers' interpretation of the Finnish company as inspired by Nordic natural beauty is not uniformly positive.

> Well this is just like . . . Lumene always aims at that kind of really boring ads where there's always some blondie who is so Scandinavian looking that she is like not wearing any make-up at all. I think it is so boring!
> (Henna, 25)

> Well this is just so boring [referring to Lumene's ad].
> (Sini, 26)

It is important to emphasize that the various negotiation processes used to arrive at notions of the Finnish ideal of beauty involve contradictory aspects. The same consumers who praise 'naturalness' as being the founding principle of their beauty conception can partly disclaim it even within their own beauty discourses, e.g. by seeing the emphasis on Scandanavian blonde beauty in the Lumene campaign as boring.

Therefore, however common and everyday the notions of Finnish beauty might be, including its dimensions such as naturalness, these notions need to be understood as multilayered and partly contradictory conceptions that can disguise diverse cultural meanings. From here, we can see that beauty remains a rather fluid notion with constantly changing interpretations,

as well as often being contradictory but not necessarily mutually exclusive constructions. Diverse ideals and ideologies related to beauty circulate in mass mediated culture as 'raw ingredients' that consumers draw upon to construct their identities. Consumers in their everyday lives are not merely exposed to beauty and its ideals, but they are performing beauty by reproducing, negotiating, mirroring, contesting, reformulating, and transmitting voluntarily or involuntarily symbolically-related actions including make-up and hairstyles, dressing-up, brand choices, and leisure activities.

THE GLOBALIZATION OF BEAUTY IDEALS?

So should we see the Finnish consumers as victims of Western or American cultural imperialism propelled by the entertainment media? It has been widely argued that globalization has become synonymous with the formation of uniform consumption habits, homogenizing tastes and ultimately the erasure of local cultures to the point where we can almost start talking about a global consumer culture – at least at the superficial level in terms of visual signs. In this argument the mass media, or the 'mediascape' (e.g. advertising, television, film industry, leisure activities, sports, literature, and news), is seen as a key vehicle in spreading global cultural flows such as trends, fashion or music. The mass-mediated messages, including advertising, tend to promote relatively unified, typically Westernized or Americanized, tastes and norms around a variety of domains, activities, industries and products. Therefore, many Western and other consumers can be seen as acculturated into the global cultural flows in addition to their local cultural environment. People all over the world seem to be consuming the same foods, watching the same TV shows and movies, listening to the same music, and wearing the same clothing and make-up brands. Does this mean that the notions about what constitutes 'beauty' are also coalescing around the world? What do you think?

This case is written on the basis of the authors' previous work where full references can be found: Rokka, J., Desavelle, H-K & Mikkonen, I. (2008), Negotiating beauty: Local readings of global cultural flows, *Latin American Advances in Consumer Research*, vol. 2.

QUESTIONS AND CLASS EXERCISE

Bring to class different magazines as elicitation material; and then consider the following questions in small groups.

Take some time (5–10 mins) to leaf through the magazines and mark images that represent beauty or different aspects of beauty to you.

Discuss and share in your small group the following questions. Feel free to comment on others' views and pose your own additional questions.

- What represents beauty or being beautiful to you in the chosen images?
- What inspires shared 'global' understanding of beauty in the representations?
- What do you consider to be specific to your own culture in the advertisements – such as cultural myths or icons?
  - How would you describe your consumption habits (practices, time consumption, products used) in terms of: global, local or glocal?
- Think about current ad campaigns (or examples given in the text). Can you find interesting illustrations where the campaign plays on global or local myths, symbolic endorsers, metaphors, and discourses?
  - What makes you interpret them as global rather than local?
  - Do you find them compelling?
  - Are other forms of media intertwined in these advertising campaigns e.g. movies, music, television, current societal issues?

- What do you perceive the role of advertising to be vs. other media in promulgating beauty ideals?
  - Look around you: what else, in addition to a human being, inspires beauty?
- Dove has been praised and criticized – what kind of ideals does it promote?
  - Does your local context have its own 'Dove spin-offs'?
- Naturalness can also be understood as a global trend in recent marketing campaigns – broadly speaking, health, food, design, and even fashion industries tend to adapt strategies employing it. Why do you think naturalness has come to play such an important role for consumers?
  - Can you give examples of campaigns or companies that tap into the naturalness trend?
- Discuss how and to what extent (global) companies should take into consideration local specificities in their branding strategies?

Consumption and immigration: the distribution of the *Halal* brand in Spain

CARLOS BALLESTEROS, CARMELINA VELA and LAURA SIERRA, Universidad Pontificia Comillas, Madrid, Spain

Zahara has the same problem every time she goes to the supermarket. In addition to the difficulty which faces all housewives in drawing up a shopping list, she has to spend half her precious time checking the labels on the products she wishes to buy. Just as if she were buying pharmaceuticals, this mother of a Muslim family must scrutinize the labels of all the food products she purchases to ensure that nothing that is considered as *Haram* (forbidden) by her religion will end up on her dinner table. For the 1,130,000 Muslims living in Spain, this is not an easy task. The religious restrictions imposed on the consumption of foodstuffs means that in many cases the consumption of even everyday items can represent a challenge to their spiritual beliefs.

Islam teaches that before eating meat, a good Muslim must be sure that the animal has been sacrificed without suffering and under certain conditions. These conditions are difficult to verify when you don't live in a Muslim country. However, some organizations have responded to the significant opportunity represented by some 13 million* consumers throughout the EU. They have begun providing products produced in accordance with religious regulations, aimed specifically at this market. Thus, for Zahara and her family, it is becoming much easier to buy foodstuffs which conform to their religious beliefs.

THE ENVIRONMENT: THE IMMIGRANT POPULATION IN SPAIN

At the beginning of the twentieth century, Spain was a population exporter. A large number of Spaniards left the country, travelling to the north of Europe and Latin America for political and economic reasons. Today, history has reversed itself. Spain has become a receiver of population with an immigrant community of approximately 9.1 per cent. Immigration has significant social and economic repercussions, modifying the character of the host country. The market is transformed through the appearance of new and diverse needs of new multicultural communities.

It is difficult to gather accurate information regarding this phenomenon. The most reliable information is probably that of the Municipal Register. Between 1992 and 2000 the growth in immigration was fairly steady. From 2000 onwards this growth may be described as exponential, as demonstrated by the figure below.

Growth in immigration, in thousands of persons

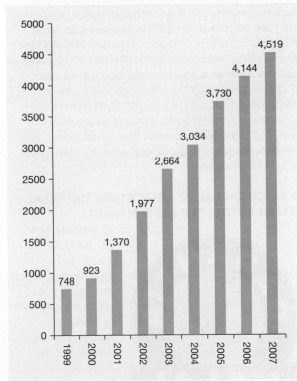

Source: Explotación estadística INE, 'Revisión del Padrón municipal 2007', *Evolución de los extranjeros residentes. España en Cifras 2003–04*, www.ine.es, online publications, date of publication 02.04 (20 May 2004).

* Report, 'Muslims in the European Union, discrimination and Islamophobia', EUMC 2006: 29.

Immigrants by nationality

Nationality	Number	% of total foreign population
Moroccans	621,295	0.14
Romanians	510,000	0.11
Ecuadorians	434,673	0.10
British	322,005	0.07
Colombians	291,676	0.06
Argentines	272,985	0.06
Germans	222,066	0.05

Source: INE, Explotación estadística del Padrón, 1 January 2007, op. cit.

The Municipal Register gives a total of 4,519,554 immigrants in 2007, which implies that in just four years the number of immigrants in Spain almost doubled. There are almost two million more people than in 2003. The largest percentage of immigrants come from Morocco, followed by Romania, Ecuador, the UK, Colombia, Argentina and Germany, as shown in the table above.

The supermarkets, hypermarkets and other distribution companies are adapting some of their product lines to meet the gastronomic needs of the immigrant population. In Spain, a change is occurring among the large food distribution companies. They are beginning to note the increased demand for foreign products. A report of the Vth Semana de Alimentación, held in Madrid in October 2003, revealed that the Spanish Ibero-American food market had a turnover of some €25 million. Demand grew in particular for basic food products such as corn flour, cane sugar, tropical fruits, guayaba based sweets and malt beverages. However, this adaptation is more complicated when religious requirements need to be taken into account.

A SPECIFIC CASE OF ADAPTATION: THE *HALAL* BRAND ENTERS THE HYPERMARKET

As we have seen, Zahara looks for quality and healthy products for herself and her family which are prepared or produced according to the precepts of the Koran without this becoming an additional economic burden. For Zahara, it is essential to know the process

Source: Explotación estadística del Padrón, 1 January 2007, op. cit.

from the slaughterhouse to the supermarket, what is now known as the 'traceability system'. Muslims are often doubtful about the origins of food, particularly as it is difficult to find the necessary information regarding the origin of meat and how and by whom it was sacrificed.

However, it has become increasingly easy to find these products. Alcampo, Carrefour and Eroski, three of the principal food distributors in Spain, have recently started stocking items bearing the *Halal Guarantee* in their product lines (June 2004), particularly in those cities with significant Muslim communities. This introduction, which has not been associated with price increases, was also accompanied during the early months by free consumer information in order to familiarize consumers with the brand. Some of the most prominent meat producers in Spain, such as El Pozo or Casademont, now include this type of guarantee with some of their products.

The *Halal Guarantee* is a brand created by the Halal Institute of the Islamic Council of Spain in order to identify those products which meet the conditions required by Islamic law. Thus, in addition to fresh meat, it controls the production process of other manufactured food products; e.g. dairy products, biscuits, prepared meats, products containing lactic acids, and even non-alcoholic beer. This brand has been regulated by law for more than 15 years. In Spain there are approximately 100 Spanish companies* whose products now bear this quality guarantee.

The two sectors where this label principally applies are:

1 *Food producers and/or processors or beverage companies*. In this case, the *Halal* label guarantees that:
  - products are free of any substance or ingredient which may be forbidden (*Haram*), or any component derived from a forbidden animal
  - if a product is produced, manufactured and/or stored, the tools or machinery used are in accordance with the stipulations of Islamic law as well as Spanish health regulations
  - these food products do not come into contact with substances or products which are forbidden during their production, manufacture, processing, storage or transport
  - in the case of fresh meats, the animals have been sacrificed in accordance with Islamic law
  - in the case of beverages, these do not contain alcohol.

2 *Service sector establishments*. In this case it signifies that they meet the conditions required by Muslims in terms of food, places dedicated to prayer and facilities necessary to perform ablutions.

* http://institutohalal.wordpress.com/2007/06/25/listado-completo-de-empresas-certificadas-halal/

However, Zahara and her family may be the victims of false guarantees or possible fraud. While the Islamic Institute is the only entity officially authorized by the Spanish government to provide this guarantee, many products are sold with a *Halal* label which was not granted by the Institute. Spain is the only European country with a certifying institution and, at certain times of the year, many North African immigrants cross Spain from Belgium, Holland and France, *en route* to their countries of origin on the so-called *Ruta del Estrecho*. This has been the source of some problems.

In August 2004, the Institute sued a well-known chain of service stations 'for the illegitimate use of the *Halal* label and for consumer fraud'. It also sought the removal of the signs announcing the sale of *Halal* products in its service stations, specifically those on the 'Route' mentioned above. According to the company, it was not offering food produced or prepared by Spanish companies according to the precepts of the Koran but selling products from various countries and for this reason they were not eligible for the guarantee label. A simple case of unfair competition? A monopolistic drive by the Institute? A fraud by producers trying to sell something as pure which in fact isn't?

The truth is that many places sell a wide range of products bearing the *Halal* label (be it official or not). For Zahara and her family and the rest of the Muslim community resident in Spain (and by extension, in Europe), it is becoming easier to find foodstuffs which meet their religious beliefs, values and consumption habits.

QUESTIONS

1 Investigate if a case similar to that of Zahara has occurred in your community. Are there cultures and groups that require special products because of their beliefs?

2 Consider the repercussions on consumption caused by religious norms in other religions such as Judaism, Christianity, Buddhism, Sikhism, Hinduism.

3 Reflect on the future of immigration in Spain (or another country) and the consequences this may have on sectors other than the food industry, e.g. banking and money transfers to other countries, holidays, customs of dress, and opinions on advertising.

4 Do you believe that a company should anticipate the specific needs of an immigrant community or should it wait until their number becomes significant?

5 Debate the issues around acculturation, and the flow of influences between immigrant and host communities.

6 What new consumption trends or situations may arise out of the second or third generation of immigrants as compared to the first?

Part E
Culture and European lifestyles

Part D
European consumers and their social groups

**Part C
Consumers as decision-makers**

Part B
How consumers see the world and themselves

Part A
Consumers in the marketplace

**CONSUMER
BEHAVIOUR**
A European
Perspective

Consumers as decision-makers

This Part explores how individuals make choices and discusses many of the internal influences involved in the process of consumer decision-making. Chapter 7 considers how decisions are affected by what we have learnt and what we have remembered. Chapter 8 provides an overview of how attitudes are formed and changed; and also discusses how influences such as advertising affect our consumer choices and our predisposition to make certain consumption decisions. Chapter 9 focuses on the basic sequence of steps we undergo when making a decision.

Learning and memory

Mario Rossi is a 60-year-old Italian insurance man, and still very active in his field. He is a pleasant, sociable and easygoing fellow, and has made a very good career for himself. Together with his wife and four children, he lives in a comfortable flat in the suburbs of Rome. Although Rome is full of historical sites to visit, Mario is a staunch nature-lover, and he prefers to 'get back to nature' in his free time.

Mario's dog, Raphael, recognizes the sound of his master's old Fiat drawing up outside as he arrives home late after work, and Raphael begins to get excited at the prospect of having his master back home. Mario's 'first love' was a Fiat 126, and in spite of his good income he keeps the old car running. Relaxing and sipping a glass of Chianti is just what he needs after a hard day's work. The pieces of furniture in his sitting room, and even his television set, are not the latest models, but he likes it that way – the old objects give him a sense of security. Slowly unwinding, he looks forward to spending the weekend with his family and friends at his house in the countryside. He grew up there, and is very attached to the old villa and everything in it.

He often imagines what it will be like when he retires, when he will be able to live there permanently, surrounded by his family. It will be like the good old days, when he was a boy and life was uncomplicated, less chaotic. He pictures them all sitting around the table enjoying a leisurely meal (with pasta, of course!) made from home-grown produce, and afterwards sitting together.

This peaceful fantasy is in stark contrast to the reality of last weekend. His two eldest sons had gone off to a football match. The youngest ones restlessly complained about the fact that there was still such a slow Internet connection in the house, and then went into another room to settle down in front of the television for what they called an afternoon's entertainment!

GABRIELE MORELLO, GMA-Gabriele Morello and Associates, Palermo, Italy

INTRODUCTION

▶ **Learning** refers to a relatively permanent change in behaviour which comes with experience. This experience does not have to affect the learner directly: we can learn vicariously by observing events that affect others.[1] We also learn even when we are not trying to do so. Consumers, for example, recognize many brand names and can hum many product jingles, even for those product categories they themselves do not use. This casual, unintentional acquisition of knowledge is known as *incidental learning*. Like the concept of perception discussed in an earlier chapter, learning is an ongoing process. Our knowledge about the world is constantly being revised as we are exposed to new stimuli and receive feedback that allows us to modify behaviour in other, similar situations. The concept of learning covers a lot of ground, ranging from a consumer's simple association between a stimulus such as a product logo (such as Coca-Cola) and a response (e.g. 'refreshing soft drink') to a complex series of cognitive activities (like writing an essay on learning for a consumer behaviour exam). Psychologists who study learning have advanced several theories to explain the learning process. These range from those focusing on simple stimulus–response associations to perspectives that regard consumers as complex problem-solvers who learn abstract rules and concepts by observing others. Understanding these theories is important to marketers as well, because basic learning principles are at the heart of many consumer purchase decisions. In this chapter we will explore how learned associations among feelings, events and products – and the memories they evoke – are an important aspect of consumer behaviour.

BEHAVIOURAL LEARNING THEORIES

▶ **Behavioural learning theories** assume that learning takes place as the result of responses to external events. Psychologists who subscribe to this viewpoint do not focus on internal thought processes. Instead, they approach the mind as a 'black box' and emphasize the observable aspects of behaviour, as depicted in Figure 7.1. The observable aspects consist of things that go into the box (the stimuli, or events perceived from the outside world) and things that come out of the box (the responses, or reactions to these stimuli).

This view is represented by two major approaches to learning: classical conditioning and instrumental conditioning. People's experiences are shaped by the feedback they receive as they go through life. Similarly, consumers respond to brand names, scents, jingles and other marketing stimuli based on the learned connections they have formed over time. People also learn that actions they take result in rewards and punishments, and this feedback influences the way they respond in similar situations in the future. Consumers who are complimented on a product choice will be more likely to buy that brand again, while those who get food poisoning at a new restaurant will not be likely to patronize it in the future.

Figure 7.1 The consumer as a 'black box': a behaviourist perspective on learning

Marketing opportunity

Popcorn, and perhaps body odour, are the scents usually associated with a trip to the movies. But in a European cinema, you might just smell bread, chocolate or whatever else an advertiser wants you to.

A company called Cinescent is giving marketers the chance to pump out the scent of their brands in German theatres, where it first tested the technology for Beiersdorf's Nivea. For the test, a specially made 60-second spot showed a typical sunny beach scene, with people lying around on deck chairs or sunbathing on towels while waves crashed and seagulls cried in the background. As people wondered what the ad was for, the scent of Nivea sun cream permeated the cinema, and a Nivea logo appeared on screen along with the words, 'Nivea. The scent of summer'. The results were significant: cinema exit polls showed a 515 per cent rise in recall for the Nivea ad compared with moviegoers who saw the spot without the scent. The same ad, when combined with only a subliminal whiff of scent, scored a 25 per cent lift. Cinescent works by pumping smells through the cinema's air-conditioning system to distribute a scent that covers other odours without being overpowering. Using this method, much finer fragrance molecules reach the audience, minimizing the allergy and irritation

problems encountered by previous attempts, when smells were dispensed via boxes located among the audience.

Mike Hope-Milne, enterprise director at Pearl & Dean, which sells cinema advertising, is so impressed by the German results that he is bringing the technology to the UK. 'We are talking to a handful of clients, including sun cream, bread, coffee, perfume, air fresheners and chocolate manufacturers. It is most cost-effective when working with scent-based products that have the scent oils already to hand,' he said.

One of the advertisers lined up is a car manufacturer that wants to promote its Cabriolet version by evoking the smell of fresh country air and newly cut grass. The argument is that scents provide a dynamic psychological and emotional trigger that can be invaluable to brands.

Mr Hope-Milne is also hoping to drum up new business with the technology, noting that three of the companies he's talking to have never advertised in cinemas before. 'It's encouraging people to reappraise the medium,' he said. He said the Cinescent idea works best when advertising a product that appeals to a broad audience. 'Perfume is probably a bit of a risk and is better off using sampling.'[2]

Classical conditioning

▶ **Classical conditioning** occurs when a stimulus that elicits a response is paired with another stimulus that initially does not elicit a response on its own. Over time, this second stimulus causes a similar response because it is associated with the first stimulus. This phenomenon was first demonstrated in dogs by Ivan Pavlov, a Russian physiologist doing research on digestion in animals.

Pavlov induced classically conditioned learning by pairing a neutral stimulus (a bell) with a stimulus known to cause a salivation response in dogs (he squirted dried meat powder into their mouths). The powder was an unconditioned stimulus (UCS) because it was naturally capable of causing the response. Over time, the bell became a conditioned stimulus (CS): it did not initially cause salivation, but the dogs learned to associate the bell with the meat powder and began to salivate at the sound of the bell only. The drooling of these canine consumers over a sound, now linked to feeding time, was a conditioned response (CR), just as Mario's dog Raphael begins to get excited hearing his master's Fiat 126 coming close to home.

This basic form of classical conditioning primarily applies to responses controlled by the autonomic (e.g. salivation) and nervous (e.g. eye blink) systems. That is, it focuses on visual and olfactory cues that induce hunger, thirst or sexual arousal. When these cues are consistently paired with conditioned stimuli, such as brand names, consumers may learn to feel hungry, thirsty or aroused when later exposed to the brand cues.

Classical conditioning can have similar effects for more complex reactions, too. Even a credit card becomes a conditioned cue that triggers greater spending, especially since it is a stimulus that is present only in situations where consumers are spending money. People learn that they can make larger purchases when using credit cards, and they also have been found to leave larger tips than they do when using cash.[3] Small wonder that American Express reminds us, 'Don't leave home without it.' Conditioning effects are more likely to occur after the conditioned and unconditioned stimuli have been paired a number of times.[4] Repeated exposures increase the strength of stimulus–response associations and prevent the decay of these associations in memory.

▶ Conditioning will not occur or will take longer if the CS is only occasionally presented with the UCS. One result of this lack of association may be extinction, which occurs when the effects of prior conditioning are reduced and finally disappear. This can occur, for example, when a product is overexposed in the marketplace so that its original allure is lost. The Lacoste polo shirt, with its distinctive crocodile logo, is a good example of this effect. When the once-exclusive crocodile started to appear on baby clothes and many other items, it lost its cachet and was soon replaced by other contenders, such as the Lauren polo player.[5]

▶ Stimulus generalization refers to the tendency of stimuli similar to a CS to evoke similar, conditioned responses.[6] Pavlov noticed in subsequent studies that his dogs would sometimes salivate when they heard noises that only resembled a bell (e.g. keys jangling). People react to other, similar stimuli in much the same way that they responded to an original stimulus. A chemist shop's bottle of own-brand mouthwash deliberately packaged to resemble Listerine mouthwash may evoke a similar response among consumers who assume that this 'me-too' product shares other characteristics of the original. These 'lookalikes' tactics work, and companies have targeted well-known brands ranging from Unilever's Blue Band margarine, and Calvé peanut butter, to Hermès scarves. Similar colours, shapes and designs are all stimuli which consumers organize and interpret, and up to a point, these tactics are perfectly legal.[7]

▶ Stimulus discrimination occurs when a stimulus similar to a CS is not followed by a UCS. In these situations, reactions are weakened and will soon disappear. Part of the learning process involves making a response to some stimuli but not to other, similar stimuli. Manufacturers of well-established brands commonly urge consumers not to buy 'cheap imitations' because the results will not be what they expect.

Operant conditioning

▶ Operant conditioning, also known as instrumental conditioning, occurs as the individual learns to perform behaviours that produce positive outcomes and to avoid those that yield negative outcomes. This learning process is most closely associated with the psychologist B.F. Skinner, who demonstrated the effects of instrumental conditioning by teaching animals to dance, pigeons to play ping-pong, and so on, by systematically rewarding them for desired behaviours.[8]

While responses in classical conditioning are involuntary and fairly simple, those in instrumental conditioning are made deliberately to obtain a goal and may be more complex. The desired behaviour may be learned over a period of time, as intermediate actions are rewarded in a process called *shaping*. For example, the owner of a new shop may award prizes to shoppers just for coming in, hoping that over time they will continue to drop in and eventually buy something.

Also, classical conditioning involves the close pairing of two stimuli. Instrumental learning occurs as a result of a reward received following the desired behaviour and takes place over a period in which a variety of other behaviours are attempted and abandoned because they are not reinforced. A good way to remember the difference is to keep in mind that in instrumental learning the response is performed because it is instrumental to gaining a reward or avoiding a punishment. Consumers over time come to associate with people who reward them and to choose products that make them feel good or satisfy some need.

Operant conditioning (instrumental learning) occurs in one of three ways. When
► the environment provides **positive reinforcement** in the form of a reward, the response
is strengthened, and appropriate behaviour is learned. For example, a woman who is
complimented after wearing Obsession perfume will learn that using this product has
► the desired effect, and she will be more likely to keep buying the product. **Negative
reinforcement** also strengthens responses so that appropriate behaviour is learned. A
perfume company, for example, might run an ad showing a woman sitting alone on
a Saturday night because she did not use its fragrance. The message to be conveyed is
that she could have avoided this negative outcome if only she had used the perfume. In
contrast to situations where we learn to do certain things in order to avoid unpleasant-
► ness, **punishment** occurs when a response is followed by unpleasant events (such as
being ridiculed by friends for wearing an offensive-smelling perfume). We learn not to
repeat these behaviours.

When trying to understand the differences between these mechanisms, keep in
mind that reactions from a person's environment to behaviour can be either positive or
negative and that these outcomes or anticipated outcomes can be applied or removed.
That is, under conditions of both positive reinforcement and punishment, the person
receives a reaction after doing something. In contrast, negative reinforcement occurs when
a negative outcome is avoided: the removal of something negative is pleasurable and
hence is rewarding. Finally, when a positive outcome is no longer received, extinction
is likely to occur, and the learned stimulus–response connection will not be maintained
(as when a woman no longer receives compliments on her perfume). Thus, positive
and negative reinforcement strengthen the future linkage between a response and an
outcome because of the pleasant experience. This tie is weakened under conditions of
both punishment and extinction because of the unpleasant experience. The relationships
among these four conditions are easier to understand by referring to Figure 7.2.

An important factor in operant conditioning is the set of rules by which appropriate
reinforcements are given for a behaviour. The issue of what is the most effective
reinforcement schedule to use is important to marketers, because it relates to the amount
of effort and resources they must devote to rewarding consumers in order to condition
desired behaviours.

- *Fixed-interval reinforcement*. After a specified period has passed, the first response that
  is made brings the reward. Under such conditions, people tend to respond slowly
  immediately after being reinforced, but their responses speed up as the time for the
  next reinforcement approaches. For example, consumers may crowd into a store for
  the last day of its seasonal sale and not reappear again until the next one.

- *Variable-interval reinforcement*. The time that must pass before reinforcement is delivered
  varies around some average. Since the person does not know exactly when to expect
  the reinforcement, responses must be performed at a consistent rate. This logic is
  behind retailers' use of so-called secret shoppers – people who periodically test for
  service quality by posing as customers at unannounced times. Since store employees
  never know exactly when to expect a visit, high quality must be constantly maintained.

- *Fixed-ratio reinforcement*. Reinforcement occurs only after a fixed number of responses.
  This schedule motivates people to continue performing the same behaviour over and
  over again. For example, a consumer might keep buying groceries at the same store in
  order to earn a gift after collecting 50 books of trading stamps.

- *Variable-ratio reinforcement*. The person is reinforced after a certain number of responses,
  but they do not know how many responses are required. People in such situations tend
  to respond at very high and steady rates, and this type of behaviour is very difficult
  to extinguish. This reinforcement schedule is responsible for consumers' attraction to
  slot machines. They learn that if they keep feeding money into the machine, they will
  eventually win something (if they don't go broke first).

Figure 7.2 Four types of learning outcome

Cognitive learning theory

▶ **Cognitive learning** occurs as a result of mental processes. In contrast to behavioural theories of learning, cognitive learning theory stresses the importance of internal mental processes. This perspective views people as problem-solvers who actively use information from the world around them to master their environment. Supporters of this viewpoint also stress the role of creativity and insight during the learning process.

The issue of consciousness

A lot of controversy surrounds the issue of whether or when people are aware of their learning processes. While behavioural learning theorists emphasize the routine, automatic nature of conditioning, proponents of cognitive learning argue that even these simple effects are based on cognitive factors: that is, expectations are created that a stimulus will be followed by a response (the formation of expectations requires mental activity). According to this school of thought, conditioning occurs because subjects develop conscious hypotheses and then act on them.

On the one hand, there is some evidence for the existence of non-conscious procedural knowledge. People apparently do process at least some information in an automatic, passive way, which is a condition that has been termed mindlessness.[9] When we meet someone new or encounter a new product, for example, we have a tendency to respond to the stimulus in terms of existing categories, rather than taking the trouble to formulate different ones. Our reactions are activated by a trigger feature, some stimulus that cues us towards a particular pattern. For example, men in one study rated a car in an ad as superior on a variety of characteristics if a seductive woman (the trigger feature) was present in the ad, despite the fact that the men did not believe the woman's presence actually had an influence.[10] A recent study which reviewed the literature on knowledge (a meta-analysis) took the approach of looking at what consumers' know, versus what they think they know. Results suggest that we are better at having objective knowledge about products (as opposed to services), and that we have a stronger sense of subjective knowledge (what we think we know) when the information comes to us from an expert in the product category.[11] Ultimately, our ability to retrieve information comes from our actual knowledge, as well as from what we think we know.

Nonetheless, many modern theorists are beginning to regard some instances of conditioning as cognitive processes, especially where expectations are formed about the linkages between stimuli and responses. Indeed, studies using masking effects, in which it is difficult for subjects to learn CS/UCS associations, show substantial reductions in conditioning.[12] For example, an adolescent girl may observe that women on television and in real life seem to be rewarded with compliments and attention when they smell nice and wear alluring clothing. She works out that the probability of these rewards occurring is greater when she wears perfume and deliberately wears a popular scent to obtain the pay-off of social acceptance.

Observational learning

▶ **Observational learning** occurs when people watch the actions of others and note the reinforcements they receive for their behaviours. This type of learning is a complex process: people store these observations in memory as they accumulate knowledge, perhaps using this information at a later point to guide their own behaviours. This process of imitating the behaviour of others is called modelling. For example, a woman shopping for a new kind of perfume may remember the reactions a friend received when wearing a certain brand several months earlier, and she will base her behaviour on her friend's actions. In order for observational learning in the form of modelling to occur, four conditions must be met (see Figure 7.3).[13]

1 The consumer's attention must be directed to the appropriate model who, for reasons of attractiveness, competence, status or similarity, it is desirable to emulate.

2 The consumer must remember what is said or done by the model.

3 The consumer must convert this information into actions.

4 The consumer must be motivated to perform these actions.

Figure 7.3 Components of observational learning

MARKETING APPLICATIONS OF LEARNING PRINCIPLES

Understanding how consumers learn is very important to marketers. After all, many strategic decisions are based on the assumption that consumers are continually accumulating information about products and that people can be 'taught' to prefer some alternatives over others.

Behavioural learning applications

Many marketing strategies focus on the establishment of associations between stimuli and responses. Behavioural learning principles apply to many consumer phenomena, ranging from the creation of a distinctive brand image to the perceived linkage between a product and an underlying need.

How marketers take advantage of classical conditioning principles

The transfer of meaning from an unconditioned stimulus to a conditioned stimulus explains why 'made-up' brand names like Marlboro, Coca-Cola or IBM can exert such powerful effects on consumers. The association between the Marlboro Man and the cigarette is so strong that in some cases the company no longer even includes the brand name in its ad. When nonsense syllables (meaningless sets of letters) are paired with such evaluative words as beauty or success, the meaning is transferred to the nonsense syllables. This change in the symbolic significance of initially meaningless words shows that complex meanings can be conditioned. Recent studies have shown that attitudes formed through classical conditioning are enduring.[14]

▶ These conditioned associations are crucial to many marketing strategies that rely on the creation and perpetuation of positive brand equity, in which a brand has strong positive associations in a consumer's memory and commands a lot of loyalty as a result.[15] As we will see in the next chapter, a product with brand equity holds a tremendous advantage in the marketplace.

Repetition   One advertising researcher argues that more than three exposures are wasted. The first creates awareness of the product, the second demonstrates its relevance to the consumer, and the third serves as a reminder of the product's benefits.[16] However,

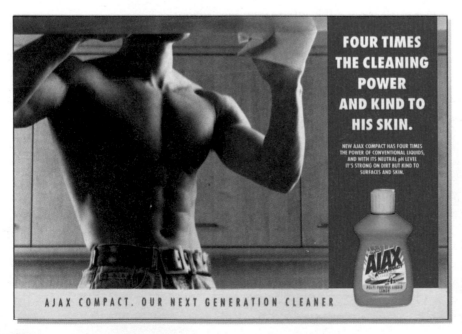

FOUR TIMES THE CLEANING POWER AND KIND TO HIS SKIN.

NEW AJAX COMPACT HAS FOUR TIMES THE POWER OF CONVENTIONAL LIQUIDS, AND WITH ITS NEUTRAL pH LEVEL IT'S STRONG ON DIRT BUT KIND TO SURFACES AND SKIN.

AJAX COMPACT. OUR NEXT GENERATION CLEANER

Advertising often pairs a product with a positive stimulus (the attractive male model), or to a positive outcome (kind to his skin).
The Advertising Archives

even this bare-bones approach implies that repetition is needed to ensure that the consumer is actually exposed to (and processes) the ad at least three times. Marketers attempting to condition an association must ensure that the consumers they have targeted will be exposed to the stimulus a sufficient number of times.

On the other hand, it is possible to have too much of a good thing. Consumers can become so used to hearing or seeing a marketing stimulus that they cease to pay attention to it (see Chapter 4). This problem, known as advertising wear-out, can be reduced by varying the way in which the basic message is presented.

Conditioning product associations   Advertisements often pair a product with a positive stimulus to create a desirable association. Various aspects of a marketing message, such as music, humour or imagery, can affect conditioning. In one study, subjects who viewed a slide of pens paired with either pleasant or unpleasant music were more likely later to select the pen that appeared with pleasant music.[17]

The order in which the conditioned stimulus and the unconditioned stimulus is presented can affect the likelihood that learning will occur. Generally speaking, the unconditioned stimulus should be presented prior to the conditioned stimulus. The technique of backward conditioning, such as showing a soft drink (the CS) and then playing a jingle (the UCS), is generally not effective.[18] Because sequential presentation is desirable for conditioning to occur, classical conditioning is not very effective in static situations, such as in magazine ads, where (in contrast to TV or radio) the marketer cannot control the order in which the CS and the UCS are perceived.

Just as product associations can be formed, so they can be extinguished. Because of the danger of extinction, a classical conditioning strategy may not be as effective for products that are frequently encountered, since there is no guarantee they will be accompanied by the CS. A bottle of Pepsi paired with the refreshing sound of a carbonated beverage being poured over ice may seem like a good example of conditioning. Unfortunately, the product would also be seen in many other contexts where this sound was absent, reducing the effectiveness of the conditioning.

By the same reasoning, a novel tune should be chosen over a popular one to pair with a product, since the popular song might also be heard in many situations in which the product is not present.[19] Music videos in particular may serve as effective UCSs because they often have an emotional impact on viewers and this effect may transfer to ads accompanying the video.[20]

Applications of stimulus generalization   The process of stimulus generalization is often central to branding and packaging decisions that attempt to capitalize on consumers' positive associations with an existing brand or company name, as exemplified by a hairdressing establishment called United Hairlines.[21] In one 20-month period, Procter & Gamble introduced almost 90 new products. Not a single product carried a new brand name. In fact, roughly 80 per cent of all new products are actually extensions of existing brands or product lines.[22] Strategies based on stimulus generalization include the following:

- *Family branding*, in which a variety of products capitalize on the reputation of a company name. Companies such as Campbell's, Heinz, Philips and Sony rely on their positive corporate images to sell different product lines.

- *Product line extensions*, in which related products are added to an established brand. Dole, which is associated with fruit, was able to introduce refrigerated juices and juice bars, while Sun Maid went from raisins to raisin bread. Other recent extensions include Woolite rug cleaner, and the various models of Nike Air shoes.[23]

- *Licensing*, in which well-known names are 'rented' by others. This strategy is increasing in popularity as marketers try to link their products and services with well established figures. Companies as diverse as McDonald's, Disney, Vogue, and Harley-Davidson have authorized the use of their names on products.

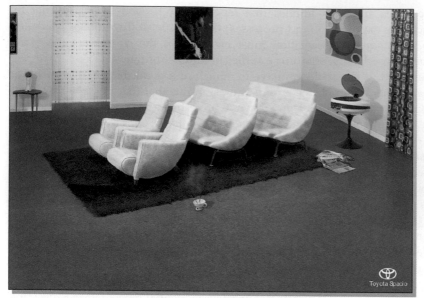

Many marketing strategies focus on the establishment of associations between stimuli and responses. Associating products with the imagery of riding in a Toyota with one's comfortable, modern living room is one example of this stimulus–response application.

Used with permission of Toyota Singapore and Saatchi & Saatchi Ltd.

- Marketers are increasingly capitalizing on the public's enthusiasm for films[24] and popular TV programmes by developing numerous *product tie-ins*.
- *Lookalike packaging*, in which distinctive packaging designs create strong associations with a particular brand. This linkage is often exploited by makers of generic or private-label brands who wish to communicate a quality image by putting their products in very similar packages. As one chemist chain store executive commented, 'You want to tell the consumer that it's close to the national brand. You've got to make it look like, within the law, close to the national brand. They're at least attracted to the package.'[25]

Applications of stimulus discrimination An emphasis on communicating a product's distinctive attributes vis-à-vis its competitors is an important aspect of positioning, in which consumers learn to differentiate a brand from its competitors (see Chapter 4). This is not always an easy task, especially in product categories where the brand names of many of the alternatives look and sound alike. For example, one survey showed that many consumers have a great deal of trouble distinguishing between products sold by the top computer manufacturers. With a blur of names like OmniPlex, OptiPlex, Premmia, Premium, ProLinea, ProLiant, etc., this confusion is not surprising.[26]

Companies with a well-established brand image try to encourage stimulus discrimination by promoting the unique attributes of their brands: the constant reminders for American Express Travellers Cheques: 'Ask for them by name . . .' On the other hand, a brand name that is used so widely that it is no longer distinctive becomes part of the public domain and can be used by competitors, as has been the case for such products as aspirin, cellophane, yo-yos and escalators.

How marketers take advantage of instrumental conditioning principles

Principles of instrumental conditioning are at work when a consumer is rewarded or punished for a purchase decision. Business people shape behaviour by gradually reinforcing consumers for taking appropriate actions. For example, a car dealer might encourage a reluctant buyer to try sitting in a showroom model, then suggest a test drive, and so on.

Marketers have many ways of reinforcing consumers, ranging from a simple thank you after a purchase to substantial rebates and follow-up phone calls. For example, a life insurance company obtained a much higher rate of policy renewal among a group of new customers who received a thank you letter after each payment compared to a control group that did not receive any reinforcement.[27]

► A popular technique known as **frequency marketing** reinforces regular purchasers by giving them prizes with values that increase along with the amount purchased. This operant learning strategy was pioneered by the airline industry, which introduced 'frequent-flyer' programmes in the early 1980s to reward loyal customers. Well over 20 per cent of food stores now offer trading stamps or some other frequent-buyer promotion. Manufacturers in the fast-moving consumer goods (FMCG) category also make use of this technique in food stores. For example, Douwe Egberts, the coffee manufacturer owned by Sara Lee, offers stamps which can be saved and redeemed for a whole range of coffee-related products such as espresso makers, service sets and coffee grinders, including their classic (and nostalgic) hand coffee grinder.

In some industries, these reinforcers take the form of clubs, including a Hilton Hotel Club. Club members usually earn bonus points to set against future purchases, and some get privileges such as magazines and free telephone numbers and sometimes even invitations to exclusive outings.

How marketers take advantage of cognitive learning principles

Consumers' ability to learn vicariously by observing how the behaviour of others is reinforced makes the lives of marketers much easier. Because people do not have to be directly reinforced for their actions, marketers do not necessarily have to reward or punish them for purchase behaviours. Instead, they can show what happens to desirable models who use or do not use their products and know that consumers will often be motivated

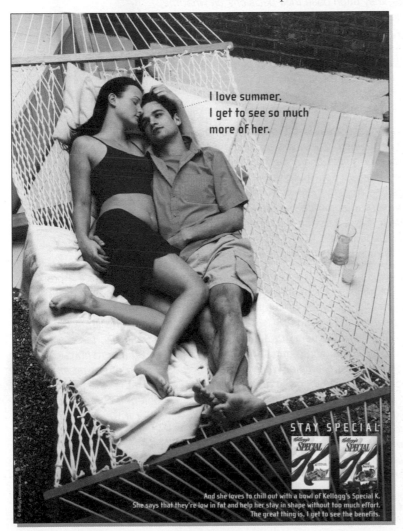

I love summer.
I get to see so much
more of her.

STAY SPECIAL

And she loves to chill out with a bowl of Kellogg's Special K.
She says that they're low in fat and help her stay in shape without too much effort.
The great thing is, I get to see the benefits.

This cereal ad illustrates the principle of vicarious reinforcement. The model uses the product and is shown reaping the reward – the approval of her boyfriend.

The Advertising Archives

to imitate these actions at a later time. For example, a perfume commercial may depict a woman surrounded by a throng of admirers who are providing her with positive reinforcement for using the product. Needless to say, this learning process is more practical than providing the same personal attention to each woman who actually buys the perfume!

Consumers' evaluations of models go beyond simple stimulus–response connections. For example, a celebrity's image is often more than a simple reflexive response of good or bad: it is a complex combination of many attributes.[28] In general, the degree to which a model will be emulated depends upon their social attractiveness. Attractiveness can be based upon several components, including physical appearance, expertise or similarity to the evaluator.

These factors will be addressed further in Chapter 8, which discusses personal characteristics that make a communication's source more or less effective in changing consumers' attitudes. In addition, many applications of consumer problem-solving are related to ways in which information is represented in memory and recalled at a later date. This aspect of cognitive learning is the focus of Part C.

Consumer behaviour as I see it . . .

Tie it to the brand

When consumers decide to buy products, they often base their decisions on what they have learned about those products. Thus, it is important to understand how people learn about products. My research has shown that a lot of the learning consumers do is based on relatively simple processes not unlike the ones we see in rats and pigeons. Luckily, more and more research suggests that rats and pigeons are not nearly as stupid as people sometimes think they are. It turns out that even very simple learning rules can lead to quite sophisticated behaviour. When they learn, it's almost as if rats and pigeons are performing regression analyses, for example.

Stijn van Osselaer
Rotterdam School
of Management,
Erasmus University

With my co-authors Chris Janiszewski and Joseph Alba, I have documented how many of these rat-like learning processes play out when consumers learn about brands.* For example, when rats repeatedly encounter a light and a tone presented together followed by the appearance of food, they learn to anticipate the appearance of food as soon as the light and tone are presented (together). However, when after those learning trials the light or the tone is presented separately, there is only a weak anticipatory response. This is quite smart. It is almost as if the rats are doing some sophisticated reasoning about the cause of the food's appearance. Was it the light that caused the food to appear or the tone? Because light and tone were always presented together, you can't really know.

In our lab, we found that people do something similar with brands. If a marketer always presents the brand name together with information about a product characteristic such as an ingredient, the presence of the ingredient decreases learning of the connection between the brand and its benefits. For example, if you say that Calvé brand peanut butter tastes great because it has 97 per cent peanuts, people don't learn the relationship between the brand name (Calvé) and the benefit (tastes great) very well. Basically, the brand name (Calvé) is like the light, the ingredient (97 per cent peanuts) is like the tone, and the benefit (tastes great) is like the appearance of the food in the rat example. What happens is that instead of having all your brand equity in the brand name, your locus of equity shifts, in part, to the ingredient. That is, the brand equity is no longer mostly in the brand name itself, but in an ingredient. This is a problem if competitors can also claim the ingredient (e.g. if Aldi peanut butter also has 97 per cent peanuts) or if you want to introduce a new product (e.g. Calvé chocolate spread) that doesn't contain the ingredient. The bottom line is clear: you need to make sure people learn that the brand name (and not its ingredients) is the main predictor of the product's benefits. This can be done by focusing your advertising on the brand and what it does for consumers (e.g. provide a great taste) instead of focusing on ingredients.

* van Osselaer, Stijn M.J. (2008), 'Associative Learning and Consumer Decisions', in *Handbook of Consumer Psychology*, Curtis P. Haugtvedt, Paul M. Herr and Frank R. Kardes, eds, New York, Erlbaum: 699–729.

THE ROLE OF LEARNING IN MEMORY

▶ Memory involves a process of acquiring information and storing it over time so that it will be available when needed. Contemporary approaches to the study of memory employ an information-processing approach. They assume that the mind is in some ways like a computer: data are input, processed and output for later use in revised form. In the
▶ encoding stage, information is entered in a way the system will recognize. In the storage stage, this knowledge is integrated with what is already in memory and 'warehoused'
▶ until needed. During retrieval, the person accesses the desired information.[29] The memory process is summarized in Figure 7.4.

As suggested by Mario's memories and musings at the beginning of the chapter, many of our experiences are locked inside our heads, and we maintain those memories and recall those experiences if prompted by the right cues. Marketers rely on consumers to retain information they have learned about products and services, trusting that it will later be applied in situations where purchase decisions must be made. During the consumer decision-making process, this internal memory is combined with external memory – which includes all the product details on packages in shopping lists, and through other marketing stimuli – to permit brand alternatives to be identified and evaluated.[30] Research supports the idea that marketers can distort a consumer's recall of a product experience. What we think we 'know' about products can be influenced by advertising messages to which we are exposed after using them. This *post-experience advertising* is more likely to alter actual memories when it is very similar or activates memories about the actual experience. For example, advertising can make a remembered product experience more favourable than it actually was.[31]

Encoding of information for later retrieval

The way information is encoded or mentally programmed helps to determine how it will be represented in memory. In general, incoming data that are associated with other information already in memory stand a better chance of being retained. For example, brand names that are linked to physical characteristics of a product category (such as Coffee-mate creamer or Sani-flush toilet bowl cleaner) or that are easy to visualize (e.g. Tide, or Omo detergent) tend to be more easily retained in memory than more abstract brand names.[32] Today, one of the biggest memory problems relates to our need to retain the numerous passwords we have to remember to function in our high-tech society. In fact, one in nine consumers keeps their passwords written down in electronic form – making the whole system so insecure that government regulators require online banks to add more layers of authentication. A company called Cogneto recently introduced a new service aimed at eliminating passwords by substituting what it calls 'pass thoughts'. These are based on how each person's unique memory works. The company's software asks you some personal questions and then it looks at how you answered (How long did you take? Where did your cursor hover while responding?) to create retrieval cues you won't need to actively remember.[33]

Figure 7.4 The memory process

Types of memory

A consumer may process a stimulus simply in terms of its sensory meaning, such as its colour or shape. When this occurs, the meaning may be activated when the person sees a picture of the stimulus. We may experience a sense of familiarity on seeing an ad for a new snack food we recently tasted, for example.

In many cases, though, meanings are encoded at a more abstract level. *Semantic meaning* refers to symbolic associations, such as the idea that rich people drink champagne or that fashionable men wear an earring.

Episodic memories are those that relate to events that are personally relevant, such as Mario's.[34] As a result, a person's motivation to retain these memories will be strong. Couples often have 'their song' that reminds them of their first date or wedding. The memories that might be triggered upon hearing this song would be quite different and unique for them.

Commercials sometimes attempt to activate episodic memories by focusing on experiences shared by many people. Recall of the past may have an effect on future behaviour. A university fund-raising campaign can get higher donations by evoking pleasant memories. Some especially vivid associations are called *flashbulb* memories. These are usually related to some highly significant event. One method of conveying product information is through a *narrative* or a story. Much of the social information that an individual acquires is represented in memory this way. Therefore, utilizing this method in product advertising can be an effective marketing technique. Narratives persuade people to construct a mental representation of the information they are viewing. Pictures aid in this construction and allow for a more developed and detailed mental representation.[35]

Memory systems

According to the information-processing perspective, there are three distinct memory systems: sensory memory, short-term memory (STM) and long-term memory (LTM). Each plays a role in processing brand-related information. The interrelationships of these memory systems are summarized in Figure 7.5.

▶ **Sensory memory** permits storage of the information we receive from our senses. This storage is very temporary: it lasts a couple of seconds at most. For example, a person might be walking past a bakery and get a brief, but enticing, whiff of bread baking inside. While this sensation would only last for a few seconds, it would be sufficient to allow the person to determine if they should investigate further. If the information is retained for

Figure 7.5 Relationships among memory systems

further processing, it passes through an attentional gate and is transferred to short-term memory.

▶ **Short-term memory** also stores information for a limited period of time, and its capacity is limited. Similar to a computer, this system can be regarded as working memory: it holds the information we are currently processing. Verbal input may be stored acoustically (in terms of how it sounds) or semantically (in terms of its meaning).

The information is stored by combining small pieces into larger ones in a process known as 'chunking'. A chunk is a configuration that is familiar to the person and can be manipulated as a unit. For example, a brand name can be a chunk that summarizes a great deal of detailed information about the brand.

Initially, it was believed that STM was capable of processing five to nine chunks of information at a time, and for this reason phone numbers were designed to have seven digits.[36] It now appears that three to four chunks is the optimum size for efficient retrieval (seven-digit phone numbers can be remembered because the individual digits are chunked, so we may remember a three-digit exchange as one piece of information).[37]

▶ **Long-term memory** is the system that allows us to retain information for a long period of time. In order for information to enter into long-term memory from short-term memory, elaborative rehearsal is required. This process involves thinking about the meaning of a stimulus and relating it to other information already in memory. Marketers sometimes assist in the process by devising catchy slogans or jingles that consumers repeat on their own.

Storing of information in memory

Relationships among the types of memory are a source of some controversy. The traditional perspective, known as multiple-store, assumes that STM and LTM are separate systems. More recent research has moved away from the distinction between the two types of memory, instead emphasizing the interdependence of the systems. This work argues that, depending upon the nature of the processing task, different levels of processing occur that activate some aspects of memory rather than others. These approaches

▶ are called **activation models of memory**.[38] The more effort it takes to process information (so-called deep processing), the more likely it is that information will be placed in long-term memory.

Activation models propose that an incoming piece of information is stored in an associative network containing many bits of related information organized according to some set of relationships. The consumer has organized systems of concepts relating to brands, stores, and so on.

Knowledge structures

▶ These storage units, known as **knowledge structures**, can be thought of as complex spiders' webs filled with pieces of data. This information is placed into nodes, which are connected by associative links within these structures. Pieces of information that are seen as similar in some way are chunked together under some more abstract category. New, incoming information is interpreted to be consistent with the structure already in place.[39] According to the hierarchical processing model, a message is processed in a bottom-up fashion: processing begins at a very basic level and is subject to increasingly complex processing operations that require greater cognitive capacity. If processing at one level fails to evoke the next level, processing of the ad is terminated, and capacity is allocated to other tasks.[40]

Links form between nodes as an associative network is developed. For example, a consumer might have a network for 'perfumes'. Each node represents a concept related to the category. This node can be an attribute, a specific brand, a celebrity identified with a perfume, or even a related product. A network for perfumes might include concepts like the names Chanel, Obsession and Charlie, as well as attributes like sexy and elegant.

Figure 7.6 An associative network for perfumes

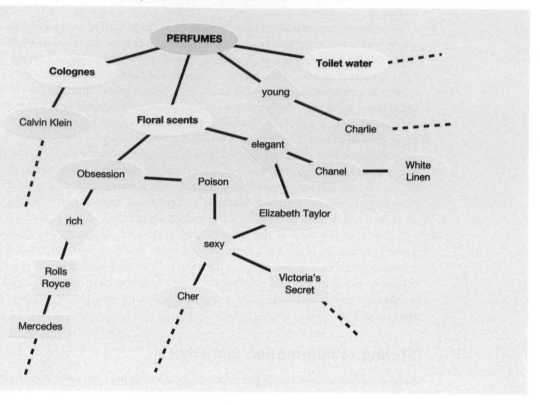

When asked to list perfumes, the consumer would recall only those brands contained
in the appropriate category. This group constitutes that person's evoked set. The task
of a new entrant that wants to position itself as a category member (e.g. a new luxury
perfume) is to provide cues that facilitate its placement in the appropriate category. A
sample network for perfumes is shown in Figure 7.6.

Spreading activation

A meaning can be activated indirectly: energy spreads across nodes at varying levels
of abstraction. As one node is activated, other nodes associated with it also begin to be
triggered. Meaning thus spreads across the network, bringing up concepts including
competing brands and relevant attributes that are used to form attitudes towards the
brand.

This process of spreading activation allows consumers to shift back and forth between
levels of meaning. The way a piece of information is stored in memory depends upon the
type of meaning assigned to it. This meaning type will, in turn, determine how and when
the meaning is activated. For example, the memory trace for an ad could be stored in one
or more of the following ways:

- *Brand-specific*: in terms of claims made for the brand.
- *Ad-specific*: in terms of the medium or content of the ad itself.
- *Brand identification*: in terms of the brand name.
- *Product category*: in terms of how the product works, where it should be used, or
  experiences with the product.
- *Evaluative reactions*: in terms of whether 'that looks like fun'.[41]

Levels of knowledge

Knowledge is coded at different levels of abstraction and complexity. Meaning concepts are individual nodes (e.g. elegant). These may be combined into a larger unit, called a *proposition* (also known as a belief). A proposition links two nodes together to form a more complex meaning, which can serve as a single chunk of information. For example, a proposition might be that 'Chanel is a perfume for elegant women'.

▶ Propositions are, in turn, integrated to produce a complex unit known as a **schema**. A schema is a cognitive framework that is developed through experience. Information that is consistent with an existing schema is encoded more readily.[42] The ability to move up and down between levels of abstraction greatly increases processing flexibility and efficiency. For this reason, young children, who do not yet have well-developed schemas, are not able to make efficient use of purchase information compared with older children.[43]

One type of schema that is relevant to consumer behaviour is a script, a sequence of procedures that is expected by an individual. For example, consumers learn service scripts that guide expectations and purchasing behaviour in business settings. Consumers learn to expect a certain sequence of events, and they may become uncomfortable if the service departs from the script. A service script for your visit to the dentist might include such events as (1) driving to the dentist, (2) reading old magazines in the waiting room, (3) hearing your name called and sitting in the dentist's chair, (4) having the dentist probe your teeth, (5) having the dentist scale and polish your teeth, and so on. This desire to follow a script helps to explain why such service innovations as automatic bank machines and self-service petrol stations have met with resistance by some consumers, who have trouble adapting to a new sequence of events.[44]

Retrieving of information for purchase decisions

Retrieval is the process whereby information is accessed from long-term memory. As evidenced by the popularity of the board game *Trivial Pursuit*, or the television programme *Who Wants to Be a Millionaire?* people have a vast quantity of information stored in their heads that is not necessarily available on demand. Although most of the information entered in long-term memory does not go away, it may be difficult or impossible to retrieve unless the appropriate cues are present.

Factors influencing retrieval

Individual cognitive or physiological factors are responsible for some of the differences we see in retrieval ability among people.[45] Some older adults consistently display inferior recall ability for current items, such as prescription drug instructions, although they may recall events that happened to them when they were younger with great clarity.[46] The recent popularity of puzzles, such as Sudoku, and centres that offer 'mental gymnastics' attest to emerging evidence that we can keep our retrieval abilities sharp by exercising our minds just as we keep our other muscles toned by working out on a regular basis.

Other factors that influence retrieval are situational; they relate to the environment in which the message is delivered. Not surprisingly, recall is enhanced when we pay more attention to the message in the first place. Some evidence indicates that we can retrieve information about a *pioneering brand* (the first brand to enter a market) more easily from memory than we can for *follower brands* because the first product's introduction is likely to be distinctive and, for the time being, no competitors divert our attention.[47] In addition, we are more likely to recall descriptive brand names than those that do not provide adequate cues as to what the product is.[48]

Not surprisingly, the way a marketer presents their message influences the likelihood
▶ we will be able to recall it later. The **spacing effect** describes the tendency for us to recall printed material more effectively when the advertiser repeats the target item periodically rather than presenting it repeatedly in a short time period.[49] The viewing environment of a marketing message also affects recall. For example, General Electric found that its

commercials fared better in television shows with continuous activity, such as stories or dramas, compared to variety shows or talk shows that are punctuated by a series of acts.[50] Finally, a large-scale analysis of TV commercials found that viewers recall commercials shown first in a series of ads better than those they see last.[51]

▶ Some advertisers today are experimenting with **bitcoms** that try to boost viewers' retention of a set of ads inserted within a TV show (we call this a *commercial pod*). In a typical bitcom, when the pod starts, a stand-up comedian (perhaps an actor in the show itself) performs a small set that leads into the actual ads. This is one way that marketers are trying to integrate a show's contents with commercial messages and increase viewers' involvement with advertising.[52]

State-dependent retrieval In a process termed state-dependent retrieval, people are better able to access information if their internal state is the same at the time of recall as it was when the information was learned.

This phenomenon, called the *mood congruence effect*, underscores the desirability of matching a consumer's mood at the time of purchase when planning exposure to marketing communications. A consumer is more likely to recall an ad, for example, if their mood or level of arousal at the time of exposure is similar to that in the purchase environment. By recreating the cues that were present when the information was first presented, recall can be enhanced.[53]

Familiarity and recall As a general rule, prior familiarity with an item enhances its recall. Indeed, this is one of the basic goals of marketers who are trying to create and maintain awareness of their products. The more experience a consumer has with a product, the better use that person is able to make of product information.[54]

However, there is a possible fly in the ointment: as noted earlier in the chapter, some evidence indicates that overfamiliarity can result in inferior learning and/or recall. When consumers are highly familiar with a brand or an advertisement, they may attend to fewer attributes because they do not believe that any additional effort will yield a gain in knowledge.[55] For example, when consumers are exposed to the technique of radio replay, where the audio track from a television ad is replayed on the radio, they do very little critical, evaluative processing and instead mentally replay the video portion of the ad.[56]

Salience and recall The salience of a brand refers to its prominence or level of activation in memory. As noted in Chapter 4, stimuli that stand out in contrast to their environment are more likely to command attention, which, in turn, increases the likelihood that they will be recalled. Almost any technique that increases the novelty of a stimulus also improves recall (a result known as the von Restorff effect).[57] This effect explains why unusual advertising or distinctive packaging tends to facilitate brand recall.[58]

As we saw in Chapter 4, introducing a surprise element in an ad can be particularly effective. This strategy aids recall even if the stimulus is not relevant to the factual information being presented.[59] In addition, so-called mystery ads, where the brand is not identified until the end, are more effective at building associations in memory between the product category and that brand – especially in the case of novel brands.[60]

Pictorial vs. verbal cues There is some evidence for the superiority of visual memory over verbal memory, but this advantage is unclear because it is more difficult to measure recall of pictures.[61] However, the available data indicate that information presented in pictorial form is more likely to be recognized later.[62] Certainly, visual aspects of an ad are more likely to grab a consumer's attention. In fact, eye-movement studies indicate that about 90 per cent of viewers look at the dominant picture in an ad before they bother to view the copy.[63]

While pictorial ads may enhance recall, however, they do not necessarily improve comprehension. One study found that television news items presented with illustrations (still pictures) as a backdrop result in improved recall for details of the news story, even though understanding of the story's content does not improve.[64] Visual imagery can be especially effective when it includes verbal cues that relate to the consumer's existing knowledge.

Factors influencing forgetting

Marketers obviously hope that consumers will not forget their products. However, in a poll of more than 13,000 adults, over half were unable to remember any specific ad they had seen, heard or read in the previous 30 days.[65] Forgetting is obviously a problem for marketers.

Early memory theorists assumed that memories fade due to the simple passage of time. In a process of decay, the structural changes in the brain produced by learning

▶ simply go away. Forgetting also occurs due to *interference*: as additional information is learned, it displaces the earlier information.

Stimulus–response associations will be forgotten if the consumers subsequently learn new responses to the same or similar stimuli in a process known as *retroactive interference*. Or prior learning can interfere with new learning, a process termed *proactive interference*. Since pieces of information are stored in memory as nodes that are connected to one another by links, a meaning concept that is connected by a larger number of links is more likely to be retrieved. But, as new responses are learned, a stimulus loses its effectiveness in retrieving the old response.[66]

These interference effects help to explain problems in remembering brand information. Consumers tend to organize attribute information by brand.[67] Additional attribute information regarding a brand or similar brands may limit the person's ability to recall old brand information. Recall may also be inhibited if the brand name is composed of frequently used words. These words cue competing associations and result in less retention of brand information.[68]

In one study, brand evaluations deteriorated more rapidly when ads for the brand appeared with messages for 12 other brands in the same category than when the ad was shown with ads for 12 dissimilar products.[69] By increasing the salience of a brand, the recall of other brands can be impaired.[70] On the other hand, calling a competitor by name can result in poorer recall for one's own brand.[71]

Finally, a phenomenon known as the *part-list cueing effect* allows marketers to utilize the interference process strategically. When only a portion of the items in a category are presented to consumers, the omitted items are not as easily recalled. For example, comparative advertising that mentions only a subset of competitors (preferably those that the marketer is not very worried about) may inhibit recall of the unmentioned brands with which the product does not compare favourably.[72]

Products as memory markers

Products and ads can themselves serve as powerful retrieval cues. Indeed, the three types of possessions most valued by consumers are furniture, visual art and photos. The most common explanation for this attachment is the ability of these things to summon memories of the past.[73] Products are particularly important as markers when our sense of past is threatened, as when a consumer's current identity is challenged due to some change in role caused by divorce, moving, graduation, and so on.[74] Products have mnemonic qualities that serve as a form of external memory by prompting consumers to retrieve episodic memories. For example, family photography allows consumers to create their own retrieval cues, with the 11 billion amateur photos taken annually forming a kind of external memory bank for our culture.

Researchers are just beginning to probe the effects of autobiographical memories on buying behaviour. These memories appear to be one way that advertisements create emotional responses: ads that succeed in getting us to think about our own past also appear to get us to like these ads more – especially if the linkage between the nostalgia experience and the brand is strong.[75]

The marketing power of nostalgia

Marketers often resurrect popular characters and stories from days gone by; they hope that consumers' fond memories will motivate them to revisit the past. We had a 1950s revival in the 1970s, and consumers in the 1980s got a heavy dose of memories from the 1960s. Today, it seems that popular characters only need to be gone for a few years before someone tries to bring them back. That is the case with the Teletubbies, four characters a BBC television show introduced in 1997 that were aimed at children ages 3 and under. Ragdoll, the British company that owns the rights to these lovable (yet strangely creepy) creatures, brought them back with features including a trivia quiz, podcasts, and a website at **taketheteletubbiestest.com**.[76] What emotions do these characters evoke in you?

► **Nostalgia** describes a bittersweet emotion where we view the past with both sadness and longing.[77] References to 'the good old days' are increasingly common, as advertisers call up memories of youth – and hope these feelings will translate to what they are selling today.

Many European companies are making use of nostalgic appeals, some of which are based on the not-too-distant past. Berlin's Humboldt University and City Museum have staged a fashion show of the 1960s, displaying clothes, appliances and posters from the communist era. The show, entitled *Ostalgie*, which is a play on words for 'East Nostalgia' in the German language, gave a nostalgic view of a time when goods might have been shoddy but when there was no unemployment or homelessness. There is growing interest in the Trabant (the joke used to be that you could double the value of a Trabant by filling it with sand) which has resulted in the Son of Trabant, built in the same factory where they used to build the original. Likewise, Western European multinationals are relaunching local brands of East European origin in response to a backlash against the incursion of foreign products. From cigarettes to yoghurt, multinationals are trying to lure consumers by combining yesteryear's product names with today's quality. Local brands like Nestlé's Chokito or Unilever's Flora margarine brands are now among the companies' best-selling products in Eastern European markets.

Considerable care goes into the production values of campaigns which are intended to evoke nostalgia. Mulino Bianco, the Italian producer of cakes, biscuits and cereals, carefully developed a campaign depicting the quiet aspects of rural life to increase sales of cakes, which are typically served only on special occasions. The campaign showed a white farmhouse on a green hill, next to a watermill. Parents, children and friends are shown in a slow, relaxed, informal atmosphere, far from the hectic urban commitments of work. The object was to evoke a relationship between 'the good old days' and cakes, and to present cakes as genuine food to be eaten every day during normal meals. In Italy, where the tension to escape from the hectic urban life is high, the campaign was quite successful. In France, where eating habits are different, and the appeal to rural life is weaker, the same campaign was not successful.[78]

Marketing opportunity (?)

In affluent New Ireland, rural pubs are so yesterday

For generations, Carney's, the only pub in this tiny village in western Ireland, had been the place to strike up a romance, celebrate a birth or mourn a death – or just sip a pint of Guinness among friends near a warm fire on a damp day.

So when Carney's shut down last year after more than a century in business, Teresa Tuttle, 62, took it hard. 'Where can we go after a funeral? After work? Where would we all meet?' she recalled thinking, shaking her head in her kitchen, not far from the pub. The 'closed' sign abruptly posted on Carney's door – and on the doors of 1,000 rural Irish pubs in the past

three years – was another sign of the profound lifestyle changes that have accompanied the country's dizzying rise to affluence. 'It was like a sudden death in the family,' said Anthony Scanlan, 51, a farmer who lives near Carney's. 'Everything has changed in Ireland. It's as fast as New York around here.'

As recently as the 1980s, young people had to leave Ireland to find work and millionaires were as rare as hen's teeth, as the Irish say. But by 2005, according to the Bank of Ireland, the country of 4 million people had 30,000 residents worth more than a million euros, or about $1.5 million. A year later, the number of millionaires had jumped another 10 per cent. Ireland's per-capita income is now among the highest in the world, surpassing those in the United States, Sweden and Japan, according to the World Bank.

Wealth has given the Irish more options and less time – a bad combination for the local pub. More people are spending sunny weekends in Spain rather than evenings of 'craic', as good times and conversation are known, down at the pub.

Smoking bans in pubs and stricter drunken-driving laws have also played a role in the decline, said Michael O'Keefe, a spokesman for the Vintners group. He said some pub owners are serving lattes along with beer and whiskey in an attempt to cater to changing tastes. 'Twenty years ago, if you asked a barman for a cappuccino, he would have looked at you as if you had two heads,' O'Keefe said.

Some shrug off the closures, saying Ireland had too many pubs anyway. Many say they are delighted there are more fine restaurants and upscale coffee shops. But others, particularly older people, lament the decline of a touchstone, a place that linked neighbours, a seat near the fire where their fathers and grandfathers chatted before them. 'Be absolutely assured that people don't want to return to the days of poverty,' O'Hara said. 'But,' she added, 'there is a question of how much we are losing as a result of prosperity . . . a nostalgia for simpler times when people had more time for each other.'[79]

Memory and aesthetic preferences

In addition to liking ads and products that remind us of our past, our prior experiences also help to determine what we like now. Some recent research indicates that people's tastes in such products as films and clothing are influenced by what was popular during certain critical periods of their youth. For example, liking for specific songs appears to be related to how old a person was when those songs were popular: on average, songs that were popular when an individual was 23 to 24 years old are the most likely

The Gillette brand has always positioned itself as innovative. This 'innovative' brand association is learned, and reinforced, over their customers' lifetime.

The Advertising Archives

to be favoured.[80] In the US, the Nickelodeon cable network programmes its *Nick at Nite* segment, which features repeats, by selecting the shows that were highly rated when its major audience was 12 years old.[81] Similar programming strategies are followed by several satellite stations throughout Europe (Tisza tennis shoes, anyone? Or how about some Ludwik brand laundry detergent?).[82] In addition, it seems that men form preferences for women's clothing styles that were in vogue when these men were in their early twenties.[83]

More generally, many marketers understand that life-long brand loyalties are formed at a fairly early age: they view the battle for the hearts (and wallets) of students and young adults as a long-term investment. These age-related preferences will be further addressed in Chapter 11.

Measuring memory for advertising

Because advertisers pay so much money to place their messages in front of consumers, they are naturally concerned that people will actually remember these messages at a later point. It seems that they have good reason to be concerned. In one study, less than 40 per cent of television viewers made positive links between commercial messages and the corresponding products; only 65 per cent noticed the brand name in a commercial; and only 38 per cent recognized a connection to an important point.[84]

More worryingly, only 7 per cent of television viewers can recall the product or company featured in the most recent television commercial they watched. This figure represents less than half the recall rate recorded in 1965 and may be attributed to such factors as the increase of 30- and 15-second commercials, the highly fragmented media consumption of consumers in the twenty-first century, and the practice of airing television commercials in clusters rather than in connection with single-sponsor programmes.[85]

Recognition vs. recall

One indicator of good advertising is, of course, the impression it makes on consumers. But how can this impact be defined and measured? Two basic measures of impact are recognition and recall. In the typical recognition test, subjects are shown ads one at a time and asked if they have seen them before. In contrast, free recall tests ask consumers to produce independently previously acquired information and then perform a recognition test on it.

Under some conditions, these two memory measures tend to yield the same results, especially when the researchers try to keep the viewers' interest in the ads constant.[86] Generally, though, recognition scores tend to be more reliable and do not decay over time in the way recall scores do.[87] Recognition scores are almost always better than recall scores because recognition is a simpler process and more retrieval cues are available to the consumer.

Both types of retrieval play important roles in purchase decisions. Recall tends to be more important in situations where consumers do not have product data at their disposal, and so they must rely upon memory to generate this information.[88] On the other hand, recognition is more likely to be an important factor in a store, where consumers are confronted with thousands of product options and information (i.e. where external memory is abundantly available) and where the task may simply be to recognize a familiar package. Unfortunately, package recognition and familiarity can have a negative consequence in that warning labels may be ignored, since their existence is taken for granted and not really noticed.[89]

The Starch Test

A widely used commercial measure of advertising recall for magazines is called the Starch Test, a syndicated service founded in 1932. This service provides scores on a number of aspects of consumers' familiarity with an ad, including such categories as

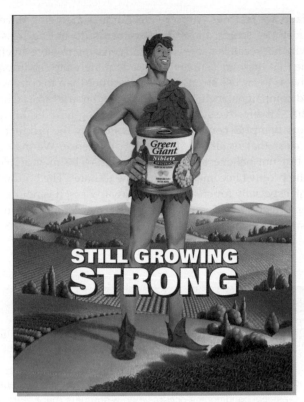

A picture is worth a thousand words. Product icons – like the Jolly Green Giant who has appeared in ads and on packaging for more than 30 years – are a significant factor in product recognition.

The Advertising Archives

'noted', 'associated' and 'read most'. It also scores the impact of the component parts of an overall ad, giving such information as 'seen' for major illustrations and 'read some' for a major block of copy.[90] Such factors as the size of the ad, whether it appears towards the front or the back of the magazine, if it is on the right or left page, and the size of illustrations play an important role in affecting the amount of attention given to an ad as determined by Starch scores.

Problems with memory measures

While the measurement of an ad's memorability is important, the ability of existing measures to assess these dimensions accurately has been criticized for several reasons.

▶ **Response biases** Results obtained from a measuring instrument are not necessarily due to what is being measured, but rather to something else about the instrument or the respondent. This form of contamination is called a **response bias**. For example, people tend to give 'yes' responses to questions regardless of what is asked. In addition, consumers are often eager to be 'good subjects' by pleasing the experimenter. They will try to give the responses they think they are looking for. In some studies, the claimed recognition of bogus ads (ads that have not been seen before) is almost as high as the recognition rate of real ads.[91]

Memory lapses People are also prone to forgetting information unintentionally. Typical problems include omitting (the leaving out of facts), averaging (the tendency to 'normalize' things and not report extreme cases), and telescoping (the inaccurate recall of time).[92] These distortions call into question the accuracy of various product usage databases that rely upon consumers to recall their purchase and consumption of food and household items. In one study, for example, people were asked to describe what portion of various foods – small, medium or large – they ate in a normal meal; however, different definitions of 'medium' were used (e.g. 185ml vs. 375ml). Regardless of the measurement specified, about the same number of people claimed they normally ate medium portions.[93]

Memory for facts vs. feelings Although techniques are being developed to increase the accuracy of memory scores, these improvements do not address the more fundamental issue of whether recall is necessary for advertising to have an effect. In particular, some critics argue that these measures do not adequately tap the impact of 'feeling' ads where the objective is to arouse strong emotions rather than to convey concrete product benefits. Many ad campaigns, including those for Hallmark cards, Chevrolet and Pepsi, use this approach.[94] An effective strategy relies on a long-term build-up of feeling rather than on a one-shot attempt to convince consumers to buy the product.

Also, it is not clear that recall translates into preference. We may recall the benefits touted in an ad but not believe them. Or the ad may be memorable because it is so obnoxious, and the product becomes one we 'love to hate'. The bottom line is that while recall is important, especially for creating brand awareness, it is not necessarily sufficient to alter consumer preferences. To accomplish this, marketers need more sophisticated attitude-change strategies. These issues will be discussed in Chapter 8.

CHAPTER SUMMARY

- Learning is a change in behaviour that is caused by experience. Learning can occur through simple associations between a stimulus and a response or via a complex series of cognitive activities.

- Behavioural learning theories assume that learning occurs as a result of responses to external events. Classical conditioning occurs when a stimulus that naturally elicits a response (an unconditioned stimulus) is paired with another stimulus that does not initially elicit this response. Over time, the second stimulus (the conditioned stimulus) comes to elicit the response as well.

- This response can also extend to other, similar, stimuli in a process known as stimulus generalization. This process is the basis for such marketing strategies as licensing and family branding, in which a consumer's positive associations with a product are transferred to other contexts.

- Operant or instrumental conditioning occurs as the person learns to perform behaviours that produce positive outcomes and avoid those that result in negative outcomes. While classical conditioning involves the pairing of two stimuli, instrumental learning occurs when reinforcement is delivered following a response to a stimulus. Reinforcement is positive if a reward is delivered following a response. It is negative if a negative outcome is avoided by not performing a response. Punishment occurs when a response is followed by unpleasant events. Extinction of the behaviour will occur if reinforcement is no longer received.

- Cognitive learning occurs as the result of mental processes. For example, observational learning takes place when the consumer performs a behaviour as a result of seeing someone else performing it and being rewarded for it.

- Memory refers to the storage of learned information. The way information is encoded when it is perceived determines how it will be stored in memory. The memory systems known as sensory memory, short-term memory and long-term memory each play a role in retaining and processing information from the outside world.

- Information is not stored in isolation, it is incorporated into knowledge structures, where it is associated with other related data. The location of product information in associative networks and the level of abstraction at which it is coded help to determine when and how this information will be activated at a later time. Some factors that influence the likelihood of retrieval include the level of familiarity with an item, its salience (or prominence) in memory and whether the information was presented in pictorial or written form.

- Products also play a role as memory markers: they are used by consumers to retrieve memories about past experiences (autobiographical memories) and are often valued for their ability to do this. This function also contributes to the use of nostalgia in marketing strategies.

- Memory for product information can be measured through either recognition or recall techniques. Consumers are more likely to recognize an advertisement if it is presented to them than to recall one without being given any cues.

▶ **KEY TERMS**

Activation models of memory (p. 259)

Behavioural learning theories (p. 246)

Bitcoms (p. 262)

Brand equity (p. 252)

Classical conditioning (p. 247)

Cognitive learning (p. 250)

Encoding (p. 257)

Evoked set (p. 260)

Extinction (p. 248)

Frequency marketing (p. 255)

Interference (p. 263)

Knowledge structures (p. 259)

Learning (p. 246)

Long-term memory (p. 259)

Memory (p. 257)

Negative reinforcement (p. 249)

Nostalgia (p. 264)

Observational learning (p. 251)

Operant conditioning (p. 248)

Positive reinforcement (p. 249)

Punishment (p. 249)

Response bias (p. 267)

Retrieval (p. 257)

Schema (p. 261)

Sensory memory (p. 258)

Short-term memory (p. 259)

Spacing effect (p. 261)

Stimulus discrimination (p. 248)

Stimulus generalization (p. 248)

Storage (p. 257)

▶ **CONSUMER BEHAVIOUR CHALLENGE**

1 Identify three patterns of reinforcement and provide an example of how each is used in a marketing context.

2 Describe the functions of short-term and long-term memory. What is the apparent relationship between the two?

3 Devise a 'product jingle memory test'. Compile a list of brands that are or have been associated with memorable jingles, such as Opal Fruits or Heinz Baked Beans. Read this list to friends, and see how many jingles are remembered. You may be surprised at the level of recall.

4 Identify some important characteristics for a product with a well-known brand name. Based on these attributes, generate a list of possible brand extension or licensing opportunities, as well as some others that would be unlikely to be accepted by consumers.

5 Collect some pictures of 'classic' products that have high nostalgia value. Show these pictures to consumers and allow them to make free associations. Analyze the types of memories that are evoked, and think about how these associations might be employed in a product's promotional strategy.

For additional material see the companion website at www.pearsoned.co.uk/solomon

NOTES

1. Robert A. Baron, *Psychology: The Essential Science* (Boston: Allyn & Bacon, 1989).

2. Emma Hall (2008), 'What's that Smell in the Movie Theatre? It's an Ad', *Adage*, 24 July 2008, http://adage.com/article?article_id=129864

3. Richard A. Feinberg, 'Credit cards as spending facilitating stimuli: A conditioning interpretation', *Journal of Consumer Research* 13 (December 1986): 348–56.

4. R.A. Rescorla, 'Pavlovian conditioning: It's not what you think it is', *American Psychologist* 43 (1988): 151–60; Elnora W. Stuart, Terence A. Shimp and Randall W. Engle, 'Classical conditioning of consumer attitudes: Four experiments in an advertising context', *Journal of Consumer Research* 14 (December 1987): 334–9; Terence A. Shimp, Elnora W. Stuart and Randall W. Engle, 'A program of classical conditioning experiments testing variations in the conditioned stimulus and context', *Journal of Consumer Research* 18(1) (June 1991): 1–12.

5. 'Anemic crocodile', *Forbes* (15 August 1994): 116.

6. Baron, *Psychology, op. cit.*

7. Caitlin Ingrassia, 'Counterfeiter, imitators: fine line, *The Wall Street Journal* (16 January 2004), http://online.wsj.com/article/0,,SB107421653820930400,00.html?mod=article-outset-box; see also: 'AH moet twee verpakkingen aanpassingen' (video), *RTL Nieuws* (28 April 2005), http://www.rtl.nl/actueel/rtlnieuws/video/

8. For a comprehensive approach to consumer behaviour based on operant conditioning principles, see Gordon R. Foxall, 'Behavior analysis and consumer psychology', *Journal of Economic Psychology* 15 (March 1994): 5–91. Foxall also sets out some consumer behaviour based on a neo-behaviourist perspective. By identifying environmental determinants, he develops four classes of consumer behaviour: *accomplishment*, *pleasure*, *accumulation* and *maintenance*. For an extensive discussion on this approach, see the entire special issue of Gordon R. Foxall, 'Science and interpretation in consumer behavior: A radical behaviourist perspective', *European Journal of Marketing* 29(9) (1995): 3–99.

9. Ellen J. Langer, *The Psychology of Control* (Beverly Hills, CA: Sage, 1983); Klaus G. Grunert, 'Automatic and strategic processes in advertising effects', *Journal of Marketing* 60 (1996): 88–91.

10. Robert B. Cialdini, *Influence: Science and Practice*, 2nd edn (New York: William Morrow, 1984).

11. Jay P. Carlson, Leslie H. Vincent, David M. Hardesty, and William O. Bearden (2009) 'Objective and subjective knowledge relationships: A quantitative analysis of consumer research findings', *Journal of Consumer Research* 35 (February 2009): 864–76.

12. Chris T. Allen and Thomas J. Madden, 'A closer look at classical conditioning', *Journal of Consumer Research* 12 (December 1985): 301–15.

13. Albert Bandura, Social Foundations of Thought and Action: A Social Cognitive View (Englewood Cliffs, NJ: Prentice Hall, 1986); Baron, *Psychology, op. cit.*

14. Allen and Madden, 'A closer look at classical conditioning', *op. cit.*; Chester A. Insko and William F. Oakes, 'Awareness and the conditioning of attitudes', *Journal of Personality and Social Psychology* 4 (November 1966): 487–96; Carolyn K. Staats and Arthur W. Staats, 'Meaning established by classical conditioning', *Journal of Experimental Psychology* 54 (July 1957): 74–80; Randi Priluck Grossman and Brian D. Till, 'The persistence of classically conditioned brand attitudes', *Journal of Advertising* 21(1) (Spring 1998): 23–31.

15. Stijn M.J. van Osselaer and Joseph W. Alba, 'Consumer learning and brand equity', *Journal of Consumer Research* 27(1) (June 2000): 1–16; Kevin Lane Keller, 'Conceptualizing, measuring, and managing customer-based brand equity', *Journal of Marketing* 57 (January 1993): 1–22; Patrick Bawise, 'Brand equity: Snark or boojum?' *International Journal of Research in Marketing* 10 (1993): 93–104; W. Fred van Raaij and Wim Schoonderbeer, 'Meaning Structure of Brand Names and Extensions', in W. Fred van Raaij and Gary J. Bamossy, eds, *European Advances in Consumer Research* 1 (Provo, UT: Association for Consumer Research, 1993): 479–84; Gil McWilliam, 'The Effect of Brand Typology on Brand Extension Fit: Commercial and Academic Research Findings', in van Raaij and Bamossy, eds, *European Advances in Association for Consumer Research* 1: 485–91; Elyette Roux and Frederic Lorange, 'Brand Extension Research: A Review', in van Raaij and Bamossy, eds, *European Advances in Consumer Research* 1: 492–500; 'The art of perception', *Marketing* (28 November 1996): 25–9.

16. Herbert Krugman, 'Low recall and high recognition of advertising', *Journal of Advertising Research* (February/March 1986): 79–86.

17. Gerald J. Gorn, 'The effects of music in advertising on choice behavior: A classical conditioning approach', *Journal of Marketing* 46 (Winter 1982): 94–101.

18. Calvin Bierley, Frances K. McSweeney and Renee Vannieuwkerk, 'Classical conditioning of preferences for stimuli', *Journal of Consumer Research* 12 (December 1985): 316–23; James J. Kellaris and Anthony D. Cox, 'The effects of background music in advertising: A reassessment', *Journal of Consumer Research* 16 (June 1989): 113–18.

19. Frances K. McSweeney and Calvin Bierley, 'Recent developments in classical conditioning', *Journal of Consumer Research* 11 (September 1984): 619–31.

20. Basil G. Englis, 'The Reinforcement Properties of Music Videos: "I Want My . . . I Want My . . . I Want My . . . MTV" ' (paper presented at the meetings of the Association for Consumer Research, New Orleans, 1989).

21. 'Giving bad puns the business', *Newsweek* (11 December 1989): 71.

22. Bernice Kanner, 'Growing pains – and gains: Brand names branch out', *New York* (13 March 1989): 22.

23. Peter H. Farquhar, 'Brand equity', *Marketing Insights* (Summer 1989): 59.

24. Product Placements in film and TV programmes is also a very common marketing approach to building learning and awareness, and to associate a product or service with a particular actor, or popular cultural event. Go to: http://www.brandchannel.com/brandcameo_films.asp?movie_year=2009#movie_list to see just how prevalent this practice is for films.

25. Quoted in 'Look-alikes mimic familiar packages', *New York Times* (9 August 1986): D1; 'Action fails to match spirit of lookalike law', *Marketing* (27 March 1997): 19.

26. Laurie Hays, 'Too many computer names confuse too many buyers', *Wall Street Journal* (29 June 1994): B1 (2 pp.).

27. Blaise J. Bergiel and Christine Trosclair, 'Instrumental learning: Its application to customer satisfaction', *Journal of Consumer Marketing* 2 (Fall 1985): 23–8.

28. Terence A. Shimp, 'Neo-Pavlovian Conditioning and Its Implications for Consumer Theory and Research', in Thomas S. Robertson and Harold H. Kassarjian, eds, *Handbook of Consumer Behavior* (Englewood Cliffs, NJ: Prentice Hall, 1991).

29. K.K. Desai and Wayne Hoyer, 'Descriptive characteristics of memory-based consideration sets: Influence of usage occasion frequency and usage location familiarity', *Journal of Consumer Research* 27(3) (December 2000): 309–23; R.C. Atkinson and R.M. Shiffrin, 'Human Memory: A Proposed System and Its Control Processes', in K.W. Spence and J.T. Spence, eds, *The Psychology of Learning and Motivation: Advances in Research and Theory* (New York: Academic Press, 1968): 89–195.

30. James R. Bettman, 'Memory factors in consumer choice: a review', *Journal of Marketing* (Spring 1979): 37–53. For a study that explored the relative impact of internal versus external memory on brand choice, see Joseph W. Alba, Howard Marmorstein and Amitava Chattopadhyay, 'Transitions in preference over time: The effects of memory on message persuasiveness', *Journal of Marketing Research* 29 (November 1992): 406–17. For other research on memory and advertising, see H. Shanker Krishnan and Dipankar Chakravarti, 'Varieties of Brand Memory Induced by Advertising: Determinants, Measures, and Relationships', in David A. Aaker and Alexander L. Biel, eds, *Brand Equity and Advertising: Advertising's Role in Building Strong Brands* (Hillsdale, NJ: Lawrence Erlbaum Associates, 1993): 213–31; Bernd H. Schmitt, Nader T. Tavassoli and Robert T. Millard, 'Memory for print ads: Understanding relations among brand name, copy, and picture', *Journal of Consumer Psychology* 2(1) (1993): 55–81; Marian Friestad and Esther Thorson, 'Remembering ads: The effects of encoding strategies, retrieval cues, and emotional response', *Journal of Consumer Psychology* 2(1) (1993): 1–23; Surendra N. Singh, Sanjay Mishra, Neeli Bendapudi and Denise Linville, 'Enhancing memory of television commercials through message spacing', *Journal of Marketing Research* 31 (August 1994): 384–92.

31. Kathryn R. Braun, 'Postexperience advertising effects on consumer memory', *Journal of Consumer Research* 25 (March 1999): 319–34; See also: Gal Zauberman, Rebecca K. Ratner, and B. Kyu Kim (2008), 'Memories as assets: Strategic memory protection in choice over time', *Journal of Consumer Research* 35 (February 2009): 715–28.

32. Kim Robertson, 'Recall and recognition effects of brand name imagery', *Psychology and Marketing* 4 (Spring 1987): 3–15.

33. Datta, Saheli, 'A Mind-Reading Security Check', *Business 2.0* (April 2007): 39.

34. Endel Tulving, 'Remembering and knowing the past', *American Scientist* 77 (July/August 1989): 361.

35. Rashmi Adaval and Robert S. Wyer, Jr, 'The role of narratives in consumer information processing', *Journal of Consumer Psychology* 7(3) (1998): 207–46.

36. George A. Miller, 'The magical number seven, plus or minus two: Some limits on our capacity for processing information', *Psychological Review* 63 (1956): 81–97.

37. James N. MacGregor, 'Short-term memory capacity: Limitation or optimization?' *Psychological Review* 94 (1987): 107–8.

38. See Catherine A. Cole and Michael J. Houston, 'Encoding and media effects on consumer learning deficiencies in the elderly', *Journal of Marketing Research* 24 (February 1987): 55–64; A.M. Collins and E.F. Loftus, 'A spreading activation theory of semantic processing', *Psychological Review* 82 (1975): 407–28; Fergus I.M. Craik and Robert S. Lockhart, 'Levels of processing: A framework for memory research', *Journal of Verbal Learning and Verbal Behavior* 11 (1972): 671–84.

39. Walter A. Henry, 'The effect of information-processing ability on processing accuracy', *Journal of Consumer Research* 7 (June 1980): 42–8.

40. Anthony G. Greenwald and Clark Leavitt, 'Audience involvement in advertising: Four levels', *Journal of Consumer Research* 11 (June 1984): 581–92. See also: Anirban Mukhopadhyay, Jaideep Sengupta, and Suresh Ramanathan (2008), 'Recalling past temptations: An information processing perspective on the dynamics of self control', *Journal of Consumer Research* 35 (December 2008): 586–99.

41. Kevin Lane Keller, 'Memory factors in advertising: The effect of advertising retrieval cues on brand evaluations', *Journal of Consumer Research* 14 (December 1987): 316–33. For a discussion of processing operations that occur during brand choice, see Gabriel Biehal and Dipankar Chakravarti, 'Consumers' use of memory and external information in choice: Macro and micro perspectives', *Journal of Consumer Research* 12 (March 1986): 382–405.

42. Susan T. Fiske and Shelley E. Taylor, *Social Cognition* (Reading, MA: Addison Wesley, 1984).

43. Deborah Roedder John and John C. Whitney Jr, 'The development of consumer knowledge in children: A cognitive structure approach', *Journal of Consumer Research* 12 (March 1986): 406–17.

44. Michael R. Solomon, Carol Surprenant, John A. Czepiel and Evelyn G. Gutman, 'A role theory perspective on dyadic interactions: The service encounter', *Journal of Marketing* 49 (Winter 1985): 99–111.

45. S. Danziger, S. Moran, and V. Rafaely, 'The influence of ease of retrieval on judgment as a function of attention to subjective experience', *Journal of Consumer Psychology* 16(2) (2006): 191–95.

46. Roger W. Morrell, Denise C. Park, and Leonard W. Poon, 'Quality of instructions on prescription drug labels: Effects on memory and comprehension in young and old adults', *The Gerontologist* 29 (1989): 345–54.

47. Frank R. Kardes, Gurumurthy Kalyanaram, Murali Chandrashekaran, and Ronald J. Dornoff, 'Brand retrieval, consideration set composition, consumer choice, and the pioneering advantage' (unpublished manuscript, University of Cincinnati: Ohio, 1992).

48. Judith Lynne Zaichkowsky and Padma Vipat, 'Inferences from Brand Names', paper presented at the European meeting of the Association for Consumer Research, Amsterdam, June 1992.

49. H. Noel, 'The spacing effect: Enhancing memory for repeated marketing stimuli', *Journal of Consumer Psychology* 16(3) (2006): 306–20; for an alternative explanation, see S.L. Appleton-Knapp, R.A. Bjork, and T.D. Wickens, 'Examining the spacing effect in advertising: Encoding variability, retrieval processes, and their interaction', *Journal of Consumer Research* 32(2) (2005): 266–76.

50. Herbert E. Krugman, 'Low recall and high recognition of advertising', *Journal of Advertising Research* (February–March 1986): 79–86.

51. Rik G.M. Pieters and Tammo H.A. Bijmolt, 'Consumer memory for television advertising: A field study of duration, serial position, and competition effects', *Journal of Consumer Research* 23 (March 1997): 362–72.

52. David Goetzl, 'Turner: We'll Get Your Brand into Our Programming', *Marketing Daily*, available from mediapost.com, accessed 14 March 2007.

53. Margaret G. Meloy, 'Mood-driven distortion of product information', *Journal of Consumer Research* 27(3) (December 2000): 345–59.

54. Eric J. Johnson and J. Edward Russo, 'Product familiarity and learning new information', *Journal of Consumer Research* 11 (June 1984): 542–50.

55. Eric J. Johnson and J. Edward Russo, 'Product Familiarity and Learning New Information', in Kent Monroe, ed., *Advances in Consumer Research* 8 (Ann Arbor, MI: Association for Consumer Research, 1981): 151–5; John G. Lynch and Thomas K. Srull, 'Memory and attentional factors in consumer choice: Concepts and research methods', *Journal of Consumer Research* 9 (June 1982): 18–37.

56. Julie A. Edell and Kevin Lane Keller, 'The information processing of coordinated media campaigns', *Journal of Marketing Research* 26 (May 1989): 149–64.

57. Lynch and Srull, 'Memory and attentional factors in consumer choice', *op. cit.*

58. Joseph W. Alba and Amitava Chattopadhyay, 'Salience effects in brand recall', *Journal of Marketing Research* 23 (November 1986): 363–70; Elizabeth C. Hirschman and Michael R. Solomon, 'Utilitarian, Aesthetic, and Familiarity Responses to Verbal Versus Visual Advertisements', in Thomas C. Kinnear, ed., *Advances in Consumer Research* 11 (Provo, UT: Association for Consumer Research, 1984): 426–31.

59. Susan E. Heckler and Terry L. Childers, 'The role of expectancy and relevancy in memory for verbal and visual information: What is incongruency?' *Journal of Consumer Research* 18 (March 1992): 475–92.

60. Russell H. Fazio, Paul M. Herr and Martha C. Powell, 'On the development and strength of category-brand associations in memory: The case of mystery ads', *Journal of Consumer Psychology* 1(1) (1992): 1–13.

61. Hirschman and Solomon, 'Utilitarian, aesthetic, and familiarity responses to verbal versus visual advertisements', *op. cit.*

62. Terry Childers and Michael Houston, 'Conditions for a picture-superiority effect on consumer memory', *Journal of Consumer Research* 11 (September 1984): 643–54; Terry Childers, Susan Heckler and Michael Houston, 'Memory for the visual and verbal components of print advertisements', *Psychology and Marketing* 3 (Fall 1986): 147–50.

63. Werner Krober-Riel, 'Effects of Emotional Pictorial Elements in Ads Analyzed by Means of Eye Movement Monitoring', in Kinnear, ed., *Advances in Consumer Research* 11: 591–6.

64. Hans-Bernd Brosius, 'Influence of presentation features and news context on learning from television news', *Journal of Broadcasting and Electronic Media* 33 (Winter 1989): 1–14.

65. Raymond R. Burke and Thomas K. Srull, 'Competitive interference and consumer memory for advertising', *Journal of Consumer Research* 15 (June 1988): 55–68.

66. *Ibid.*

67. Johnson and Russo, 'Product Familiarity and Learning New Information', *op. cit.*

68. Joan Meyers-Levy, 'The influence of brand names association set size and word frequency on brand memory', *Journal of Consumer Research* 16 (September 1989): 197–208.

69. Michael H. Baumgardner, Michael R. Leippe, David L. Ronis and Anthony G. Greenwald, 'In search of reliable persuasion effects: II. Associative interference and persistence of persuasion in a message-dense environment', *Journal of Personality and Social Psychology* 45 (September 1983): 524–37.

70. Alba and Chattopadhyay, 'Salience effects in brand recall', *op. cit.*

71. Margaret Henderson Blair, Allan R. Kuse, David H. Furse and David W. Stewart, 'Advertising in a new and competitive environment: persuading consumers to buy', *Business Horizons* 30 (November/December 1987): 20.

72. Lynch and Srull, 'Memory and attentional factors in consumer choice', *op. cit.*

73. Russell W. Belk, 'Possessions and the extended self', *Journal of Consumer Research* 15 (September 1988): 139–68.

74. Russell W. Belk, 'The Role of Possessions in Constructing and Maintaining a Sense of Past', in Marvin E. Goldberg, Gerald Gorn and Richard W. Pollay, eds, *Advances in Consumer Research* 16 (Provo, UT: Association for Consumer Research, 1990): 669–78.

75. Hans Baumgartner, Mita Sujan and James R. Bettman, 'Autobiographical memories, affect and consumer information processing', *Journal of Consumer Psychology* 1 (January 1992): 53–82; Mita Sujan, James R. Bettman and Hans Baumgartner, 'Influencing consumer judgments using autobiographical memories: A self-referencing perspective', *Journal of Marketing Research* 30 (November 1993): 422–36.

76. Stuart Elliott, 'Remember the Teletubbies? The Brand Owner Hopes So', *New York Times Online Edition* (26 March 2007). Take the test at: http://www.teletubbies.co.uk/en/teletubby-test.asp

77. Susan L. Holak and William J. Havlena, 'Feelings, fantasies, and memories: An examination of the emotional components of nostalgia', *Journal of Business Research* 42 (1998): 217–26.

78. Gabriella Stern, 'VW hopes nostalgia will spur sales of retooled Beetle, fuel US comback', *Wall Street Journal, Europe* (7 May 1997): 4; 'Ostalgie for the day when they'd never had it so good', *The Independent* (10 February 1997); Almar Latour, 'Shelf wars', *Central European Economic Review* 4 (Dow Jones, May 1997); G. Morello, *The Hidden Dimensions of Marketing* (Amsterdam: Vrije Universiteit, 1993): 13.

79. Jordan, Mary, 'In Affluent New Ireland, Rural Pubs are so Yesterday', *Washington Post*, 2008 April 25, http://www.washingtonpost.com/wp-dyn/content/article/2008/04/24/AR2008042403855.html?hpid=topnews

80. Morris B. Holbrook and Robert M. Schindler, 'Some exploratory findings on the development of musical tastes', *Journal of Consumer Research* 16 (June 1989): 119–24.

81. Randall Rothenberg, 'The past is now the latest craze', *New York Times* (29 November 1989): D1.

82. Susan Holak, Alexei Matveev, and William J. Havlena, (2006) 'Nostalgia in post-socialist Russia: Exploring applications to advertising strategy', *Journal of Business Research* 61(2) (February 2008): 172–78.

83. See Morris B. Holbrook, 'Nostalgia and consumption preferences: Some emerging patterns of consumer tastes', *Journal of Consumer Research* 20 (September 1993): 245–56;

Robert M. Schindler and Morris B. Holbrook, 'Critical periods in the development of men's and women's tastes in personal appearance', *Psychology and Marketing* 10(6) (November/December 1993): 549–64; Morris B. Holbrook and Robert M. Schindler, 'Age, sex, and attitude toward the past as predictors of consumers' aesthetic tastes for cultural products', *Journal of Marketing Research* 31 (August 1994): 412–22.

84. 'Only 38 per cent of T.V. audience links brands with ads', *Marketing News* (6 January 1984): 10.

85. 'Terminal television', *American Demographics* (January 1987): 15.

86. Richard P. Bagozzi and Alvin J. Silk, 'Recall, recognition, and the measurement of memory for print advertisements', *Marketing Science* (1983): 95–134.

87. Adam Finn, 'Print ad recognition readership scores: An information processing perspective', *Journal of Marketing Research* 25 (May 1988): 168–77.

88. Bettman, 'Memory factors in consumer choice', *op. cit.*

89. Mark A. deTurck and Gerald M. Goldhaber, 'Effectiveness of product warning labels: effects of consumers' information processing objectives', *Journal of Consumer Affairs* 23(1) (1989): 111–25.

90. Finn, 'Print ad recognition readership scores', *op. cit.*

91. Surendra N. Singh and Gilbert A. Churchill Jr., 'Response-bias-free recognition tests to measure advertising effects', *Journal of Advertising Research* 29 (June/July 1987): 23–36.

92. William A. Cook, 'Telescoping and memory's other tricks', *Journal of Advertising Research* 27 (February/March 1987): 5–8.

93. 'On a diet? Don't trust your memory', *Psychology Today* (October 1989): 12.

94. Hubert A. Zielske and Walter A. Henry, 'Remembering and forgetting television ads', *Journal of Advertising Research* 20 (April 1980): 7–13.

8

Attitudes

It's Saturday evening, and Leah, Lynn and Nicki are hanging out at Nicki's flat in Manchester. While waiting to go out on the town, they are doing some channel-surfing. Leah clicks to the sports channel and the three friends see there's a football game on, being televised from Switzerland. Portugal plays against Turkey. Leah has been a fan for as long as she can remember – perhaps as a result of having three older brothers and growing up in a house which had Manchester United souvenirs in every room. She loves the subtle intensity of the game, of any game – the traps, the moves, the way players make it look easy to move a ball around a huge field as if it were a small patch of grass. Further, she's proud of Manchester United's rich history as a club, and its success as a business operation. But don' ask her opinion of having her beloved team's ownership taken over by some American businessman who doesn't even understand the game![1] Nicki's a glutton for thrills and chills – at least when it comes to the national team: she converted to football after seeing the England team beat Germany 5–1 in a qualifying game for the 2002 World Cup. But this time the English team did not qualify, and so she is somewhat less interested. Lynn, on the other hand, doesn't know a corner kick from a penalty kick. For her, the most interesting part of the match was the footage being shown of the Portuguese player Christiano Ronaldo's spectacular playing skills. She thinks he is the cutest thing – and even considered asking her boyfriend to get a haircut like Ronaldo's. Still, soccer doesn't really ring her chimes – but as long as she gets to hang out with her girlfriends she doesn't really care if they watch non-contact sports like football or contact sports like *Celebrity Big Brother*!

THE POWER OF ATTITUDES

All over Europe, football has a long and rich tradition, but as a sport it has been dominated by male patronage at the stadiums and male viewership on the television. A long running campaign for the Danish national betting corporation plays on the widespread attitude that women are not into football. With the pay-off line 'There's so much that women do not understand', the humourous TV spots illustrate female misunderstandings of a variety of expressions in football jargon, thereby maintaining an image of football as a male domain (or refuge?). Not so in the US, where attitudes towards the game are much more positive towards women's football.

On the other hand, football clubs, sports gear producers and other market agents generally welcome female consumers among their ranks. For example, Leah is just the kind of fan sponsoring companies like Nike, Gatorade and Adidas hope will turn more women into an ongoing source of football fanaticism. It is obvious that a variety of hero myths are necessary in order to mobilize such new fan groups. However, following Beckham's, Ronaldo's and others' stardom as male sex symbols rather than as footballers, certain people belive that too much focus is moving away from the sport and onto something which should be secondary. According to this attitude, it is one (acceptable) thing to use the hero myth to sell something related to the sport,[2] it is another to sell something completely unrelated to the sport.

Any which way, football is big business, but how it operates in the life of the single consumer is very much a question of attitude, as we have seen with Leah, Nicki and Lynn. As you'll see throughout this chapter and this book, attitudes can vary significantly along gender lines, and from one culture to another. Attitudes obviously also vary over time. Since most of us are also consuming banking services and other financial products, we may be able to relate to the attitudinal statement, 'I have confidence in the financial sector'. How would that rate in an attitude measurement in the autumn of 2007 versus the autumn of 2008? Effectively, part of the problem is exactly that the shift in attitudes vis-à-vis the financial sector is provoking much lower degrees of confidence which in itself aggravates the crisis.

▶ The term **attitude** is widely used in popular culture. You might be asked, 'What is your attitude towards abortion?' A parent might scold, 'Young man, I don' like your attitude.' Some bars even euphemistically refer to Happy Hour as 'an attitude adjustment period'. For our purposes, though, an attitude is a lasting, general evaluation of people (including oneself), objects, advertisements or issues.[3] Anything towards which one has
▶ an attitude is called an **attitude object (A$_o$)**.

This chapter will consider the contents of an attitude, how attitudes are formed, how they can be measured, and review some of the surprisingly complex relationships between attitudes and behaviour. Both as a theoretical concept, and as a tool to be used in the marketplace, the notion and dynamics of attitudes remain one of the most studied and applied of all behavioural constructs.[4] In the final part of chapter, we will take a closer look at how attitudes can be changed – certainly an issue of prime importance to marketers.

THE FUNCTION OF ATTITUDES

▶ The **functional theory of attitudes** was initially developed by the psychologist Daniel Katz to explain how attitudes facilitate social behaviour.[5] According to this pragmatic approach, attitudes exist because they serve a function for the person. That is, they are determined by a person's motives. Consumers who expect that they will need to deal with similar information at a future time will be more likely to start forming attitudes in anticipation of this event.[6]

Two people can each have the same attitude towards an object for very different reasons. As a result, it can be helpful for a marketer to know why an attitude is held before attempting to change it. The following are attitude functions as identified by Katz:

- *Utilitarian function*. The utilitarian function is related to the basic principles of reward and punishment. We develop some of our attitudes towards products simply on the basis of whether these products provide pleasure or pain. If a person likes the taste of a cheeseburger, that person will develop a positive attitude towards cheeseburgers. Ads that stress straightforward product benefits (e.g. you should drink Diet Coke 'just for the taste of it') appeal to the utilitarian function.

- *Value-expressive function*. Attitudes that perform a value-expressive function express the consumer' central values or self-concept. A person forms a product attitude not because of its objective benefits, but because of what the product says about them as a person (e.g. 'What sort of woman reads *Elle*?'). Value-expressive attitudes are highly relevant to lifestyle analyzes, where consumers cultivate a cluster of activities, interests and opinions to express a particular social identity.

- *Ego-defensive function*. Attitudes that are formed to protect the person, from either external threats or internal feelings, perform an ego-defensive function. An early marketing study indicated that housewives in the 1950s resisted the use of instant coffee because it threatened their conception of themselves as capable homemakers.[7] Products that promise to help a man project a 'macho' image (e.g. Marlboro cigarettes) may be appealing to his insecurities about his masculinity. Another example of this function is deodorant campaigns that stress the dire, embarrassing consequences of underarm odour.

- *Knowledge function*. Some attitudes are formed as the result of a need for order, structure or meaning. This need is often present when a person is in an ambiguous situation or is confronted with a new product (e.g. 'Bayer wants you to know about pain relievers').

An attitude can serve more than one function, but in many cases a particular one will be dominant. By identifying the dominant function a product serves for consumers (i.e. what benefits it provides), marketers can emphasize these benefits in their communications and packaging. Ads relevant to the function prompt more favourable thoughts about what is being marketed and can result in a heightened preference for both the ad and the product.

One American study determined that for most people coffee serves more of a utilitarian function than a value-expressive function. As a consequence, subjects responded more positively to copy for a fictitious brand of coffee that read, 'The delicious, hearty flavour and aroma of Sterling Blend coffee comes from a blend of the freshest coffee beans' (i.e. a utilitarian appeal) than they did to copy that read, 'The coffee you drink says something about the type of person you are. It can reveal your rare, discriminating taste' (i.e. the value-expressive function). In European countries with a strong 'coffee culture', such as Germany, the Benelux and Scandinavian countries, ads are more likely to stress the value-expressive function, in which the more social and ritualistic aspects of coffee consumption are expressed.[8]

As we saw in the experiences of the three Manchester women watching a football game, the importance of an attitude object may differ quite a bit for different people. Understanding the attitude' centrality to an individual and to others who share similar characteristics can be useful to marketers who are trying to devise strategies that will appeal to different customer segments. A study of football game attendance illustrates that varying levels of commitment result in different fan 'profiles'.[9] The study identified three distinct clusters of fans:[10]

- One cluster consisted of the real diehard fans like Leah who were highly committed to their team and who displayed an enduring love of the game. To reach these fans, the researchers recommended that sports marketers should focus on providing them with greater sports knowledge and relate their attendance to their personal goals and values.

- A second cluster was like Nicki – their attitudes were based on the unique, self-expressive experience provided by the game. They enjoyed the stimulation of cheering for a team and the drama of the competition itself. These people are more likely to be 'brand switchers', fair-weather fans who shift allegiances when the home team no longer provides the thrills they need. This segment can be appealed to by publicizing aspects of the visiting teams, such as advertising the appearance of stars who are likely to give the fans a game they will remember.

- A third cluster was like Lynn – they were looking for camaraderie above all. These consumers attend games primarily to take part in small-group activities such as a pre- or post-game party which may accompany the event. Marketers could appeal to this cluster by providing improved peripheral benefits, such as making it easier for groups to meet at the stadium, improving parking, and offering multiple-unit pricing.

The ABC model of attitudes and hierarchies of effects

Most researchers agree that an attitude has three components: affect, behaviour and cognition. **Affect** refers to the way a consumer feels about an attitude object. **Behaviour** involves the person's intentions to do something with regard to an attitude object (but, as will be discussed later, an intention does not always result in an actual behaviour). **Cognition** refers to the beliefs a consumer has about an attitude object. These three components of an attitude can be remembered as the **ABC model of attitudes**.

This model emphasizes the interrelationships between knowing, feeling and doing. Consumers' attitudes towards a product cannot be determined simply by identifying their beliefs about it. For example, a researcher may find that shoppers 'know' a particular digital camera has a 10X optical zoom lens, auto-focus and can also shoot *QuickTime Movies*, but such findings do not indicate whether they feel these attributes are good, bad or irrelevant, or whether they would actually buy the camera.

While all three components of an attitude are important, their relative importance will vary depending upon a consumer's level of motivation with regard to the attitude object. Attitude researchers have developed the concept of a **hierarchy of effects** to explain the relative impact of the three components. Each hierarchy specifies that a fixed sequence of steps occurs en route to an attitude. Three different hierarchies are summarized in Figure 8.1.

Figure 8.1 Three hierarchies of effects

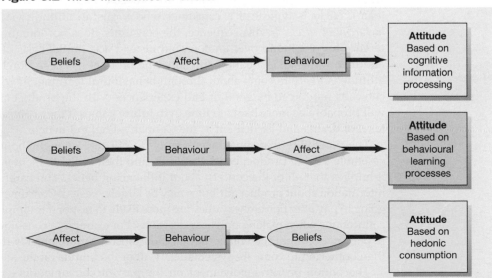

The standard learning hierarchy

Leah' positive attitude towards football closely resembles the process by which most attitudes have been assumed to be constructed. A consumer approaches a product decision as a problem-solving process. First, they form beliefs about a product by accumulating knowledge (beliefs) regarding relevant attributes. Next, the consumer evaluates these beliefs and forms a feeling about the product (affect).[11] Over time, Leah assembled information about the sport, began to recognize the players, and learned which teams were superior to others. finally, based on this evaluation, the consumer engages in a relevant behaviour, such as buying the product or supporting a particular team by wearing its shirt. This careful choice process often results in the type of loyalty displayed by Leah: the consumer 'bonds' with the product over time and is not easily persuaded to experiment with other brands. The standard learning hierarchy assumes that a consumer is highly involved in making a purchase decision.[12] The person is motivated to seek out a lot of information, carefully weigh alternatives, and come to a thoughtful decision. As we saw in Chapter 6, this process is likely to occur if the decision is important to the consumer or in some way central to the consumer's self-concept. If you understand the level of fan support for Manchester United, then you will appreciate just how central Leah's attitudes about football (or, in this case, Manchester United) are for her.

While attitudes that Leah holds towards Manchester United may be well understood to be positive, it is not always an easy and straightforward task to assume that any related product purchases she makes will be consistent with her positive attitudes towards the team. Imagine that Leah is considering the purchase of some Nike football shoes for herself, and as part of gathering information about the shoes, she comes across an article on globalization, and Nike's use of outsourcing the labour for making football shoes to factories in low labour cost countries such as Vietnam. Leah's attitudes towards globalization, coupled with her own cognitive beliefs about the labour conditions in these factors may in fact lead her to have a negative affect towards the Nike shoes. At the same time, Leah's attitude towards buying a well-made football shoe at a very competitive price might be quite positive! So possibly she is likely to still buy the shoes. In a different context, it has been shown that satisfaction with the brand's performance is more directly related to brand loyalty than corporate image.[13]

The low-involvement hierarchy

In contrast to Leah, Nicki's interest in the attitude object (football) is at best lukewarm. She is not particularly knowledgeable about the sport, and she may have an emotional response to an exciting game but not to a specific team (excluding the English national team). Nicki is typical of a consumer who forms an attitude via the *low-involvement hierarchy of effects*. In this sequence, the consumer does not initially have a strong preference for one brand over another, but instead acts on the basis of limited knowledge and then forms an evaluation only after the product has been purchased or used.[14] The attitude is likely to come about through behavioural learning, in which the consumer's choice is reinforced by good or bad experiences with the product after purchase. Nicki will probably be more likely to tune in to future games if they continue to have the same level of drama and excitement as the Germany–England match.

The possibility that consumers simply do not care enough about many decisions to assemble a set of product beliefs carefully and then evaluate them is important, because it implies that all of the concern about influencing beliefs and carefully communicating information about product attributes may be largely wasted. Consumers are not necessarily going to pay attention anyway; they are more likely to respond to simple stimulus–response connections when making purchase decisions. For example, a consumer choosing between paper towels might remember that 'Brand X absorbs more quickly than Brand Y', rather than bothering to compare systematically all of the brands on the shelf.

The notion of low involvement on the part of consumers is a bitter pill for some marketers to swallow. Who wants to admit that what they market is not very important

While Leah may have very positive attitudes towards soccer, and for the soccer boot made by one of her favourite brands, Nike, she still needs to sort out her conflicting attitudes towards globalization, and labour practices, which Nike and other shoe manufacturers use.

Photo: Gary Bamossy

or involving? A brand manager for, say, a brand of chewing gum or cat food may find it hard to believe that consumers do not put that much thought into purchasing their product because they themselves spend many of their waking (and perhaps sleeping) hours thinking about it.

For marketers, the ironic silver lining to this low-involvement cloud is that, under these conditions, consumers are not motivated to process a lot of complex brand-related information. Instead, they will be swayed by principles of behavioural learning, such as the simple responses caused by conditioned brand names, point-of-purchase displays, and so on. This results in what we might call the *involvement paradox*: the less important the product is to consumers, the more important are many of the marketing stimuli (e.g. packages, jingles) that must be devised to sell it.

The experiential hierarchy

In recent years researchers have begun to stress the significance of emotional response as a central aspect of an attitude. According to the experiential hierarchy of effects, consumers act on the basis of their emotional reactions (just as Lynn enjoys watching TV with her friends, regardless of what is on). Although the factors of beliefs and behaviour are recognized as playing a part, a consumer's overall evaluation of an attitude object is considered by many to be the core of an attitude.

This perspective highlights the idea that attitudes can be strongly influenced by intangible product attributes such as package design, and by consumers' reactions to accompanying stimuli such as advertising and even the brand name. As an example, consider one Swedish study which underlined the importance of the book covers with sexually charged images in the forming of the attitude towards the book.[15] As discussed in Chapter 6, resulting attitudes will be affected by consumers' hedonic motivations, such as how the product makes them feel or the fun its use will provide. Numerous studies indicate that the mood a person is in when exposed to a marketing message influences how the ad is processed, the likelihood that the information presented will be remembered, and how the person will feel about the advertised item and related products in the future.[16] Furthermore, feelings may not be uniform, as we saw with Leah: Manchester United and Nike shoes. They can be mixed positive and negative. There are indications that people with Eastern cultural background are better at accepting mixed emotions in the formation of an attitude than Westerners, since they have a less dichotomizing way

'Smokers are more sociable than others . . . while it lasts.' This Norwegian ad represents the many anti-smoking campaigns running in European markets.

John Hopkins Bloomberg School of Public Health

of looking at life, and instead understand the balancing of contradictory principles, as seen in the principle of yin and yang.[17]

One important debate about the experiential hierarchy concerns the independence of cognition and affect. On the one hand, the *cognitive–affective model* argues that an affective judgement is the last step in a series of cognitive processes. Earlier steps include the sensory registration of stimuli and the retrieval of meaningful information from memory to categorize these stimuli.[18]

On the other hand, the *independence hypothesis* takes the position that affect and cognition involve two separate, partially independent systems; affective responses do not always require prior cognitions.[19] The number one song in the 'Top Ten' hit parade may possess the same attributes as many other songs (dominant bass guitar, raspy vocals, persistent downbeat), but beliefs about these attributes cannot explain why one song becomes a classic while another sharing the same characteristics ends up in the bargain bin at the local record shop. The independence hypothesis does not eliminate the role of cognition in experience. It simply balances this traditional, rational emphasis on calculated decision-making by paying more attention to the impact of aesthetic, subjective experience. This type of holistic processing is more likely to occur when the product is perceived as primarily expressive or delivers sensory pleasure rather than utilitarian benefits.[20]

There is more to marketing than product attitudes

Marketers who are concerned with understanding consumers' attitudes have to contend with an even more complex issue: in decision-making situations, people form attitudes towards objects other than the product itself that can influence their ultimate selections. One additional factor to consider is attitudes towards the act of buying in general or attitudes towards a particular shop.[21] As we will see later in the chapter, sometimes people are reluctant, embarrassed or just too lazy to expend the effort to obtain a desired product or service. In addition, consumers' reactions to a product, over and above their feelings about the product itself, are influenced by their evaluations of its advertising. Our evaluation of a product can be determined solely by our appraisal of how it is depicted in marketing communications – that is, we do not hesitate to form attitudes about products we have never even seen personally, much less used.

▶ The **attitude towards the advertisement (A$_{ad}$)** is defined as a predisposition to respond in a favourable or unfavourable manner to a particular advertising stimulus during a particular exposure occasion. Determinants of A_{ad} include the viewer's attitude towards the advertiser, evaluations of the ad execution itself, the mood evoked by the ad and the degree to which the ad affects the viewer's arousal levels.[22] A viewer's feelings about the context in which an ad appears can also influence brand attitudes. For example, attitudes about an ad and the brand depicted will be influenced if the consumer sees the ad while watching a favourite TV programme.[23] The effects demonstrated by A_{ad} emphasize the importance of an ad's entertainment value in the purchase process.[24]

The feelings generated by advertising can have a direct impact on brand attitudes. Commercials can evoke a wide range of emotional responses, from disgust to happiness. Further, there is evidence that emotional responses will vary from one group of consumers to another. In an empirical study of students and housewives in Belgium and Holland, the results showed that the Belgians were more positive towards the hedonic and sociocultural aspects of advertising than their Dutch counterparts. In the UK, Ford's ad campaign research on the Ford Ka, which is targeting an image-oriented market, showed it annoyed 41 per cent of 55 to 64-year-olds, compared with only 18 per cent of 25 to 34-year-olds. These feelings can be influenced both by the way the ad is done (i.e. the specific advertising execution) and by the consumer's reactions to the advertiser's motives. For example, many advertisers who are trying to craft messages for adolescents and young adults are encountering problems because this age group, having grown up in a 'marketing society', tends to be sceptical about attempts to persuade them to buy things.[25] These reactions can, in turn, influence memory for advertising content.[26] At least three emotional dimensions have been identified in commercials: pleasure, arousal and intimidation.[27] Specific types of feelings that can be generated by an ad include the following:[28]

- *Upbeat feelings*: amused, delighted, playful.
- *Warm feelings*: affectionate, contemplative, hopeful.
- *Negative feelings*: critical, defiant, offended.

▼ Marketing pitfall

Is there a European attitude towards humour in advertising?

One of the reasons the use of humour is so widespread is that it is such a versatile tool. 'It has a surprisingly broad range of applications. It can act as a razor-sharp discriminator, allowing advertisers to address very tightly defined demographic and attitudinal segments, but because humour is universal it can also act as a catch-all, a way of appealing to everyone,' says advertising psychologist David Lewis.

Humour may be universal, but few nations use it to the extent it is used in the UK. Research carried out three years ago by the University of Luton into the devices used in beer advertising found that 88 per cent of British beer ads used humour, compared with a third of Dutch beer ads and only 10 per cent of German beer commercials. Brits' reliance on humour reflects historic and cultural factors peculiar to this country, say commentators. A major ingredient is our antipathy to 'the sell', argues writer and communications consultant Paul Twivy, who has written comedy scripts for television and run a major advertising agency. 'It's a feature of the British malaise. We are embarrassed about the hard sell. Germany for instance has a tradition of revering engineering, so they are quite happy to talk unironically about product quality. We on the other hand still look down on commerce and value amateurism and effortless success in a way that can be traced back to the nineteenth century. So humour which entertains is a way of selling, while not being seen to sell.' Others say that it reflects a narrow range of emotional responses and attitudes within the national culture. 'Other countries are much more open about expressing a wide range of attitudes. We tend to be repressed and self-deprecating and consider it rude to wear our emotions on our sleeve. So we use humour as a way of not expressing what we really feel,' says Andy Nairn, joint planning director at advertising agency Miles Calcraft Briginshaw Duffy. 'The upshot is that American advertising, for instance, has a much wider emotional repertoire than British, using joy, love, ambition and desire in a way that would simply make British audiences gag.'[29] How do you respond to humorous ads from different countries in Europe? Do they all strike you as 'funny', and does the approach improve your attitude towards the advertiser'?

FORMING ATTITUDES

We all have lots of attitudes, and we do not usually question how we got them. No one is born with the conviction that, say, Pepsi is better than Coke or that heavy metal music liberates the soul. Where do these attitudes come from?

An attitude can form in several different ways, depending on the particular hierarchy of effects in operation. It can occur because of classical conditioning, in which an attitude object, such as the name Pepsi, is repeatedly paired with a catchy jingle ('You're in the Pepsi Generation . . .'). Or it can be formed through instrumental conditioning, in which consumption of the attitude object is reinforced (Pepsi quenches the thirst). Alternatively, the learning of an attitude can be the outcome of a very complex cognitive process. For example, a teenager may come to model the behaviour of friends and media endorsers, such as Beyoncé, who drink Pepsi because they believe that this will allow them to fit in with the desirable lifestyle Pepsi commercials portray.

It is thus important to distinguish between types of attitudes, since not all are formed the same way.[30] A highly brand-loyal consumer like Leah, the Manchester United fan, has an enduring, deeply-held positive attitude towards an attitude object, and this involvement will be difficult to weaken. On the other hand, another consumer like Nicki, who likes the drama and excitement more than the subtle aspects of soccer, may have a mildly positive attitude towards a product but be quite willing to abandon it when something better comes along. This section will consider the differences between strongly and weakly held attitudes and briefly review some of the major theoretical perspectives that have been developed to explain how attitudes form and relate to one another in the minds of consumers.

Levels of commitment to an attitude

Consumers vary in their commitment to an attitude, and the degree of commitment is related to their level of involvement with the attitude object.[31] Consumers are more likely to consider brands that engender strong positive attitudes.[32] Let's look at three (increasing) levels of commitment:

- *Compliance.* At the lowest level of involvement, compliance, an attitude is formed because it helps in gaining rewards or avoiding punishments from others. This attitude is very superficial: it is likely to change when the person's behaviour is no longer monitored by others or when another option becomes available. A person may drink Pepsi because that is the brand the café sells and it is too much trouble to go elsewhere for a Coca-Cola.

- *Identification.* A process of identification occurs when attitudes are formed in order for the consumer to be similar to another person or group. Advertising that depicts the social consequences of choosing some products over others is relying on the tendency of consumers to imitate the behaviour of desirable models, cf. chapter 10 on group influences.

- *Internalization.* At a high level of involvement, deep-seated attitudes are internalized and become part of the person's value system. These attitudes are very difficult to change because they are so important to the individual. For example, many consumers had strong attitudes towards Coca-Cola and reacted very negatively when the company attempted to switch to the New Coke formula. This allegiance to Coke was obviously more than a minor preference for these people: the brand had become intertwined with their social identities, taking on patriotic and nostalgic properties.

The consistency principle

Have you ever heard someone say, 'Pepsi is my favourite soft drink. It tastes terrible', or 'I love my husband. He's the biggest idiot I've ever met'? If we disregard the use of irony, perhaps not very often, because these beliefs or evaluations are not consistent with one another. According to the **principle of cognitive consistency**, consumers value harmony among their thoughts, feelings and behaviours, and they are motivated to maintain uniformity among these elements. This desire means that, if necessary, consumers will change their thoughts, feelings or behaviours to make them consistent with their other experiences. The consistency principle is an important reminder that attitudes are not formed in a vacuum. A significant determinant of the way an attitude object will be evaluated is how it fits with other, related attitudes already held by the consumer.

▼ Marketing pitfall

World falls out of love with US brands?

'It is no accident that 64 of the most valuable 100 global brands, as measured by Interbrand, are owned by US companies. For more than half a century, the US and its products have stood for progress, glamour and freedom in the minds of consumers around the world. Yet there seems to be a growing challenge for US companies in the attitudes of people such as John McInally, a Scottish management consultant living in Brussels, whose boycott of US products goes as far as asking that his four-year-old son not be given Coca-Cola at birthday parties. "I used to have a lot of respect for America; now there is mostly fear," says Mr McInally. "You feel pretty powerless, but the one thing you can do is stop buying American products."

There is little doubt that there are more Mr McInallys in the world today than there were before Abu Ghraib

and Guantánamo Bay became household names. Poll after poll has shown that allegations of human rights abuses and the failure to find weapons of mass destruction in Iraq have tarnished the international reputation of the US.

Yet geopolitics seems to be easily left behind when shoppers get to the till. Those activists who express their anger at the US through conscious boycotts of its companies remain a small minority. The bigger question worrying the business world is whether the opinion poll data point to a more subtle tarnishing of US brands in the minds of millions of ordinary consumers. If the American dream played such an important role in the growth of iconic US brands, what happens if significant numbers of consumers begin to think of the US as a bit of a nightmare?'[33]

GMI poll of international consumers' attitudes towards US brands

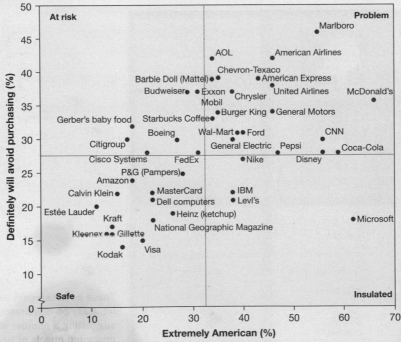

Impact on buying intentions and brand perceptions of consumers who said there had been a negative change in their willingness to purchase American goods as a result of US foreign policy and military action*

* GMI poll of 8,000 international consumers conducted one week after US elections, Nov 2004.

Source: Interbrand, and Dan Roberts, 'Is the world falling out of love with US brands?' Financial Times, 30 December 2004.

Cognitive dissonance theory revisited

In Chapter 6, we discussed the role played by cognitive dissonance when consumers are trying to choose between two desired products. Cognitive dissonance theory has other important ramifications for attitudes, since people are often confronted with situations in which there is some conflict between their attitudes and behaviours.[34]

The theory proposes that, much like hunger or thirst, people are motivated to reduce this negative state by making things fit with one another. The theory focuses on situations where two cognitive elements are inconsistent with one another.

A cognitive element can be something a person believes about themselves, a behaviour they perform or an observation about their surroundings. For example, the two cognitive elements 'I know smoking cigarettes causes cancer' and 'I smoke cigarettes' are dissonant. This psychological inconsistency creates a feeling of discomfort that the smoker is motivated to reduce. The magnitude of dissonance depends upon both the importance and the number of dissonant elements.[35] In other words, the pressure to reduce dissonance is more likely to be observed in high-involvement situations in which the elements are more important to the individual.

Dissonance reduction can occur by either eliminating, adding or changing elements. For example, the person could stop smoking (eliminating) or remember Great-Aunt Sophia, who smoked until the day she died at age 90 (adding). Alternatively, they might question the research that links cancer and smoking (changing), perhaps by believing industry-sponsored studies that try to refute this connection.

Dissonance theory can help to explain why evaluations of a product tend to increase after it has been purchased, i.e. post-purchase dissonance. The cognitive element 'I made a stupid decision' is dissonant with the element 'I am not a stupid person', so people tend to find even more reasons to like something after buying it.

A field study performed at a horse race demonstrates post-purchase dissonance. Gamblers evaluated their chosen horses more highly and were more confident of their success after they had placed a bet than before. Since the gambler is financially

These advertisement examples play ironically on dissonance theory by suggesting a number of allegedly unwanted effects of beer drinking that consumers might actually still accept as consequences of their beer drinking. What is your attitude towards the ads?

committed to the choice, they reduce dissonance by increasing the attractiveness of the chosen alternative relative to the unchosen ones.[36] One implication of this phenomenon is that consumers actively seek support for their purchase decisions, so marketers should supply them with additional reinforcement to build positive brand attitudes.

While the consistency principle works well in explaining our desire for harmony among thoughts, feelings and behaviours, and subsequently in helping marketers understand their target markets, it is not a perfect predictor of the way in which we hold seemingly *related* attitudes, as we saw in the case of Leah's attitudes towards soccer, Nike and labour practices in our globalized economy.

Self-perception theory

Do attitudes necessarily change following behaviour because people are motivated to
▶ feel good about their decisions? **Self-perception theory** provides an alternative explanation of dissonance effects.[37] It assumes that people use observations of their own behaviour to determine what their attitudes are, just as we assume that we know the attitudes of others by watching what they do. The theory states that we maintain consistency by inferring that we must have a positive attitude towards an object if we have bought or consumed it (assuming that we freely made this choice).

Self-perception theory is relevant to the low-involvement hierarchy, since it involves situations in which behaviours are initially performed in the absence of a strong internal attitude. After the fact, the cognitive and affective components of attitude fall into line. Thus, buying a product out of habit may result in a positive attitude towards it after the fact – namely, why would I buy it if I didn't like it?

Self-perception theory helps to explain the effectiveness of a sales strategy called the
▶ **foot-in-the-door technique**, which is based on the observation that a consumer is more likely to comply with a request if they have first agreed to comply with a smaller request.[38] The name of this technique comes from the practice of door-to-door selling, when the salesperson was taught to plant their foot in a door so the prospect could not slam it shut. A good salesperson knows that they are more likely to get an order if the customer can be persuaded to open the door and talk. By agreeing to do so, the customer has established that they are willing to listen. Placing an order is consistent with this self-perception. This technique is especially useful for inducing consumers to answer surveys or to donate money to charity. Such factors as the time lag between the first and second requests, the similarity between the two requests, and whether the same person makes both requests have been found to influence their effectiveness.[39]

Social judgement theory

▶ **Social judgement theory** assumes that people assimilate new information about attitude objects in the light of what they already know or feel.[40] The initial attitude acts as a frame of reference, and new information is categorized in terms of this existing standard. Just as our decision that a box is heavy depends in part on other boxes we have lifted, so we develop a subjective standard when making judgements about attitude objects.

One important aspect of the theory is the notion that people differ in terms of the
▶ information they will find acceptable or unacceptable. They form **latitudes of acceptance and rejection** around an attitude standard. Ideas that fall within a latitude will be favourably received, while those falling outside this zone will not. There are plenty of examples of how latitudes of acceptance and rejection are influencing marketing practices and consumers' behaviour in Europe: recently, childhood obesity has become an alarming European issue, prompting the Belgian parliament's ban of Coca-Cola machines in Belgium's elementary schools.[41] Similar steps have been taken in other countries as well. Likewise, European attitudes towards smoking have clearly evolved towards a latitude of rejection – providing GlaxoSmithKline with the opportunity to launch new anti-smoking products such as nicotine replacement gums and patches.[42] Furthermore, a positive attitude towards consumption of nicotine replacement therapy has been

shown to be the single most influential factor in establishing a behavioural desire to quit smoking.[43] Nowadays, in more and more European countries, pubs, bars, restaurants and other public facilities have faced new legislation banning smoking in public rooms. The widespread acceptance of this legislation, also among smokers, reflects these changing attitudes towards smoking.

Messages that fall within the latitude of acceptance tend to be seen as more consistent with one's position than they actually are. This process is called an *assimilation effect*. On the other hand, messages falling in the latitude of rejection tend to be seen as even further from one's position than they actually are, resulting in a *contrast effect*.[44]

Balance theory

▶ **Balance theory** considers relations among elements a person might perceive as belonging together.[45] This perspective involves relations (always from the perceiver's subjective point of view) among three elements, so the resulting attitude structures are called *triads*. Each triad contains (1) a person and their perceptions of (2) an attitude object and (3) some other person or object.

These perceptions can be positive or negative. More importantly, people *alter* these perceptions in order to make relations among them consistent. The theory specifies that people desire relations among elements in a triad to be harmonious, or balanced. If they are not, a state of tension will result until perceptions are changed and balance is restored.

Elements can be perceived as going together in one of two ways. They can have a *unit relation*, where one element is seen as belonging to or being a part of the other (something like a belief), or a *sentiment relation*, where the two elements are linked because one has expressed a preference (or dislike) for the other. A couple might be seen as having a positive sentiment relation. If they marry, they will have a positive unit relation. The process of divorce is an attempt to sever a unit relation.

To see how balance theory might work, consider the following scenario:

- Monica would like to go out with Anthony, who is in her consumer behaviour class. In balance theory terms, Monica has a positive sentiment relation with Anthony.

- One day, Anthony attends class wearing clothing that allows his fellow students to see his tattoo. Anthony has a positive unit relation with the tattoo. It belongs to him and is literally a part of him.

- Monica does not like tattooed men. She has a negative sentiment relation with tattoos.

According to balance theory, Monica faces an unbalanced triad, and she will experience pressure to restore balance by altering some aspect of the triad, as shown in Figure 8.2. She could, for example, decide that she does not like Anthony after all. Or her liking for Anthony could prompt a change in her attitude towards tattoos. Finally, she could choose to 'leave the field' by thinking no more about Anthony and his controversial tattoo. Note that while the theory does not specify which of these routes will be taken, it does predict that one or more of Monica's perceptions will have to change in order to achieve balance. While this distortion is an oversimplified representation of most attitude processes, it helps to explain a number of consumer behaviour phenomena.

Balance theory reminds us that when perceptions are balanced, attitudes are likely to be stable. On the other hand, when inconsistencies are observed we are more likely to observe changes in attitudes. Balance theory also helps to explain why consumers like to be associated with positively valued objects. Forming a unit relation with a popular product (buying and wearing fashionable clothing or driving a high-performance car) may improve one's chances of being included as a positive sentiment relation in other people' triads.

This 'balancing act' is at the heart of celebrity endorsements, in which marketers hope that the star's popularity will transfer to the product or when a nonprofit organization

Figure 8.2 Alternative routes to restoring balance in a triad

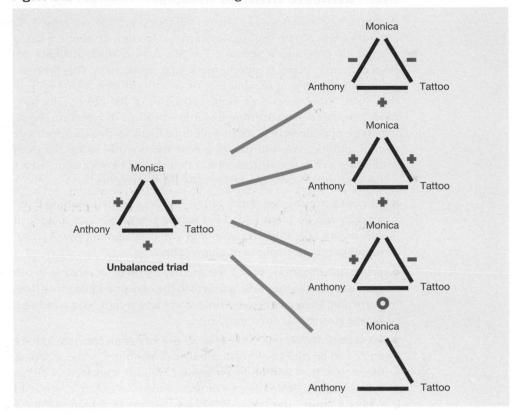

gets a celebrity to discourage harmful behaviours.[46] We will consider this strategy in more detail towards the end of the chapter. For now, it pays to remember that creating a unit relation between a product and a star can backfire if the public's opinion of the celebrity endorser shifts from positive to negative. This happened when Pepsi pulled an ad featuring Madonna after she released a controversial music video involving religion and sex and when celebrity bad girl Paris Hilton got busted. The strategy can also cause trouble if people question the star–product unit relation: this happened when the late singer Michael Jackson, who also did promotions for Pepsi, subsequently confessed that he did not drink soda at all.

ATTITUDE MODELS

A consumer's overall evaluation of a product sometimes accounts for the bulk of their *attitude* towards it. When market researchers want to assess attitudes, it can often be sufficient for them simply to ask the consumer, 'How do you feel about Heineken?' or 'How do you feel about the eventual acceptance of a European constitution?'

However, as we saw earlier, attitudes can be a lot more complex than that. One problem is that a product or service may be composed of many attributes or qualities – some of which may be more important than others to particular people. Another problem is that a person's decision to act on their attitude is affected by other factors, such as whether it is felt that buying a product will meet with approval of friends or family (if Leah's closest friends are strongly opposed to using cheap labour for the making of Nike soccer boots, this may be a key reason for her not to buy Nike). For these reasons, attitude models have been developed that try to specify the different elements that might work together to influence people's evaluations of attitude objects.

Multi-attribute attitude models

A simple response does not always tell us everything we need to know about why the consumer has certain feelings towards a product or about what marketers can do to change the consumer's attitude. For this reason, **multi-attribute attitude models** have been extremely popular among marketing researchers. This type of model assumes that a consumer's attitude (evaluation) of an attitude object (A_o) will depend on the beliefs they have about several or many attributes of the object. The use of a multi-attribute model implies that an attitude towards a product or brand can be predicted by identifying these specific beliefs and combining them to derive a measure of the consumer's overall attitude. We will describe how these work, using the example of a consumer evaluating a complex attitude object that should be very familiar: a university.

Basic multi-attribute models specify three elements:[47]

- *Attributes* are characteristics of the A_o. Most models assume that the relevant characteristics can be identified. That is, the researcher can include those attributes that consumers take into consideration when evaluating the A_o. For example, scholarly reputation is an attribute of a university.

- *Beliefs* are cognitions about the specific A_o (usually relative to others like it). A belief measure assesses the extent to which the consumer perceives that a brand possesses a particular attribute. For example, a student might have a belief that Oxford colleges have a strong academic standing.

- *Importance weights* reflect the relative priority of an attribute to the consumer. Although an A_o can be considered on a number of attributes, some will be more important than others (i.e. they will be given greater weight), and these weights are likely to differ across consumers. In the case of universities, for example, one student might stress the school's library resources, while another might assign greater weight to the social environment in which the university is located.

Measuring attitude elements

Suppose a supermarket chain wanted to measure shoppers' attitudes towards its retail outlets. The firm might administer one of the following types of attitude scales to consumers by mail, phone or in person.[48]

Single-item scales   One simple way to assess consumers' attitudes towards a store or product is to ask them for their general feelings about it. Such a global assessment does not provide much information about specific attributes, but it does give managers some sense of consumers' overall attitudes. This single-item approach often uses a Likert scale, which measures respondents' overall level of agreement or feelings about an attitude statement.

How satisfied are you with your grocery store?

☐ Very satisfied   ☐ Somewhat satisfied   ☐ Satisfied   ☐ Not at all satisfied

Multiple-item batteries   Attitude models go beyond such a simple measure, since they acknowledge that an overall attitude may often be composed of consumers' perceptions about multiple elements. For this reason, many attitude measures assess a set of beliefs about an issue and combine these reactions into an overall score. For example, the supermarket might ask customers to respond to a set of Likert scales and combine their responses into an overall measure of store satisfaction:

1 My supermarket has a good selection of produce.
2 My supermarket maintains sanitary conditions.
3 I never have trouble finding exotic foods at my supermarket.

☐ Agree strongly   ☐ Agree somewhat   ☐ Neither agree nor disagree   ☐ Disagree somewhat   ☐ Disagree strongly

The *semantic-differential scale* is useful for describing a person's set of beliefs about a company or brand, and it is also used to compare the images of competing brands. Respondents rate each attribute on a series of rating scales, where each end is anchored by adjectives or phrases, such as this one:

My supermarket is
Dirty 1—2—3—4—5—6—7 Clean

Semantic-differential scales can be used to construct a profile analysis of the competition, where the images of several stores or products can be compared visually by plotting the mean ratings for each object on several attributes of interest. This simple technique can help to pinpoint areas where the product or store diverges sharply from the competitors (in either a positive or a negative way).

The Fishbein model

The most influential multi-attribute model is the Fishbein model, named after its primary developer.[49] The model measures three components of attitude.

1 *Salient beliefs* people have about an A_o (those beliefs about the object that are considered during evaluation).

2 *Object-attribute linkages*, or the probability that a particular object has an important attribute.

3 *Evaluation* of each of the important attributes.

Note, however, that the model makes some assumptions that may not always be warranted. It assumes that we have been able to specify adequately all the relevant attributes that, for example, a student will use in evaluating their choice about which college to attend. The model also assumes that they will go through the process (formally or informally) of identifying a set of relevant attributes, weighing them and summing them. Although this particular decision is likely to be highly involving, it is still possible that their attitude will be formed by an overall affective response (a process known as *affect-referral*).

By combining these three elements, a consumer's overall attitude towards an object can be computed. (We will see later how this basic equation has been modified to increase its accuracy.) The basic formula is

$$A_{ijk} = \sum B_{ijk} I_{ik}$$

where i = attribute; j = brand; k = consumer; I = the importance weight given attribute i by consumer k; B = consumer k's belief regarding the extent to which brand j possesses attribute i; and A = a particular consumer k's attitude score for brand j.

The overall attitude score (A) is obtained by multiplying a consumer's rating of each attribute for all the brands considered by the importance rating for that attribute.

To see how this basic multi-attribute model might work, let's suppose we want to predict which digital camera a young girl is likely to buy. Sandra has now has reduced her choice to three alternatives. Since she must now decide between these, we would first like to know which attributes Sandra will consider in forming an attitude towards each camera. We can then ask Sandra to assign a rating regarding how well each camera performs on each attribute and also determine the relative importance of the attributes to her. An overall attitude score for each camera can then be computed by summing scores on each attribute (after weighing each by its relative importance). These hypothetical ratings are shown in Table 8.1. Based on this analysis, it seems that Sandra has the most favourable attitude towards Nikon Coolpix.

Strategic applications of the multi-attribute model

Imagine you are the director of marketing for Minolta, another brand that Sandra is considering. How might you use the data from this analysis to improve your image?

Table 8.1 The basic multi-attribute model: Sandra's camera decision

Attribute (i)	Importance (I)	Beliefs (b)		
		Canon Digital Ixus	Minolta Dimage F100	Nikon Coolpix
Price	6	5	3	7
Brand reputation	5	5	5	7
Size	4	5	4	6
No. of pixels	3	5	3	6
Type of screen	2	2	2	3
Zoom	1	3	4	1
Attitude score		97	76	126

Note: These hypothetical ratings are scored from 1 to 10, and higher numbers indicate 'better' standing on an attribute. For a negative attribute (e.g. price), higher scores indicate that the camera is believed to have 'less' of that attribute (i.e. to be cheaper).

Capitalize on relative advantage   If one's brand is viewed as being superior on a particular attribute, consumers like Sandra need to be convinced that this particular attribute is an important one. For example, while Sandra rates Minolta's zoom highly, she does not believe this attribute is a very important one for a camera. As Minolta's marketing director, you might emphasize the importance of good zoom in terms of the increased possibilities and pleasures that the camera offers.

Strengthen perceived product/attribute linkages   A marketer may discover that consumers do not equate their brand with a certain attribute. This problem is commonly addressed by campaigns that stress the product's qualities to consumers (e.g. 'new and improved'). Sandra apparently does not think much of Minolta's screen, nor its pixel resolution quality. You might develop an informational campaign to improve these perceptions (e.g. 'Little-known facts about Minolta cameras').

Add a new attribute   Product marketers frequently try to create a distinctive position from their competitors by adding a product feature. Minolta might try to emphasize some unique aspect, such as an improved technique for linking the camera with a cell phone's MMS function.

Influence competitors' ratings   Finally, you might try to decrease the positive rating of competitors. This type of action is the rationale for a strategy of comparative advertising forbidden in many countries. One tactic might be to publish an ad that lists the prices for a number of cameras, as well as their attributes with which Minolta can be favourably compared, as the basis for emphasizing the value for money obtained when buying a Minolta.

DO ATTITUDES PREDICT BEHAVIOUR?

Although multi-attribute models have been used by consumer researchers for many years, they have been plagued by a major problem: in many cases, knowledge of a person's attitude is not a very good predictor of behaviour. In a classic demonstration of 'do as I say, not as I do', many studies have obtained a very low correlation between a person's reported attitude towards something and their actual behaviour towards it. Some researchers have been so discouraged that they have questioned whether attitudes are of any use at all in understanding behaviour.[50] This questionable linkage can be a big headache for advertisers when consumers love a commercial yet fail to buy the product.

A Norwegian charity won an award for a popular advertising campaign on which it spent 3 million Nkr (£300,000), only to find that it resulted in just 1.7 million Nkr in donations.[51]

The extended Fishbein model

The original Fishbein model, which focused on measuring a consumer's attitude towards a product, has been extended in a number of ways to improve its predictive ability. The revised version is called the **theory of reasoned action**.[52] The model is still not perfect, but its ability to predict relevant behaviour has been improved.[53] Some of the modifications to this model are considered here.

Intentions vs. behaviour

Many factors might interfere with actual behaviour, even if the consumer's intentions are sincere. They might save up with the intention of buying a stereo system. In the interim, though, any number of things – being made redundant or finding that the desired model is out of stock – could happen. It is not surprising, then, that in some instances past purchase behaviour has been found to be a better predictor of future behaviour than is a consumer's behavioural intention.[54] The theory of reasoned action aims to measure behavioural intentions, recognizing that certain uncontrollable factors inhibit prediction of actual behaviour.

Social pressure

The theory acknowledges the power of other people in influencing behaviour. Many of our behaviours are not determined in isolation. Much as we may hate to admit it, what we think others would like us to do may be more relevant than our own individual preferences.

In the case of Sandra's camera choice, note that she is very positive about purchasing a less expensive model. However, if she feels that this choice would be unpopular (perhaps her friends will think she is mad), she might ignore or downgrade this preference when making her final decision. A new element, the subjective norm (SN), was thus added to include the effects of what we believe other people think we should do. The value of SN is arrived at by including two other factors: (1) the intensity of a normative belief (NB) that others believe an action should be taken or not taken, and (2) the motivation to comply (MC) with that belief (i.e. the degree to which the consumer takes others' anticipated reactions into account when evaluating a course of action or a purchase).

Attitude towards buying

The model now measures **attitude towards the act of buying (A_{act})**, rather than only the attitude towards the product itself. In other words, it focuses on the perceived consequences of a purchase. Knowing how someone feels about buying or using an object proves to be more valid than merely knowing the consumer's evaluation of the object itself.[55]

To understand this distinction, consider a problem that might arise when measuring attitudes towards condoms. Although a group of college students might have a positive attitude towards condom use, does this necessarily predict that they will buy and use them? A better prediction would be obtained by asking the students how likely they are to buy condoms. While a person might have a positive A_o towards condoms, A_{act} might be negative due to the embarrassment or the trouble involved. Different shopping contexts, such as seasonal sales are also met with different attitudes, since consumers weigh the benefits and costs of such sales differently. One factor to consider is whether such sales are actually sales or just a marketing trick. In order to improve the trustworthiness and therefore the positive attitude, it has been suggested that shops produce a 'seasonal sales charter', promising good ethical conduct in their sales policies.[56]

Finally, in these days when more and more shopping takes place online, it is also useful to consider yet another attitude type: attitude toward the site (A_{site}). One study concluded, however, that affect (mood state based mainly on interactivity and aesthetics of the Website) was more influential in producing purchase intentions than the attitude toward the Website.[57]

Obstacles to predicting behaviour

Despite improvements to the Fishbein model, problems arise when it is misapplied. In many cases the model is used in ways for which it was not intended or where certain assumptions about human behaviour may not be warranted.[58] Other obstacles to predicting behaviour are as follows:

1 The model was developed to deal with actual behaviour (e.g. taking a slimming pill), not with the outcomes of behaviour (e.g. losing weight) which are assessed in some studies.

2 Some outcomes are beyond the consumer's control, such as when the purchase requires the co-operation of other people. For instance, someone might seek a mortgage, but this intention will be worthless if they cannot find a banker to give them one.

3 The basic assumption that behaviour is intentional may be invalid in a variety of cases, including those involving impulsive acts, sudden changes in one's situation, novelty-seeking or even simple repeat-buying. One study found that such unexpected events as having guests, changes in the weather or reading articles about the health qualities of certain foods exerted a significant effect on actual behaviours.[59]

4 Measures of attitude often do not really correspond to the behaviour they are supposed to predict, either in terms of the A_o or when the act will occur. One common problem is a difference in the level of abstraction employed. For example, knowing a person's attitude towards sports cars may not predict whether they will purchase a Porsche 911. It is very important to match the level of specificity between the attitude and the behavioural intention.

5 A similar problem relates to the time-frame of the attitude measure. In general, the longer the time between the attitude measurement and the behaviour it is supposed to assess, the weaker the relationship will be. For example, predictability would improve markedly by asking consumers the likelihood that they would buy a house in the next week as opposed to within the next five years.

6 Attitudes formed by direct, personal experience with an A_o are stronger and more predictive of behaviour than those formed indirectly, such as through advertising.[60] According to the attitude accessibility perspective, behaviour is a function of the person's immediate perceptions of the A_o in the context of the situation in which it is encountered. An attitude will guide the evaluation of the object, but only if it is activated from memory when the object is observed. These findings underscore the importance of strategies that induce trial (e.g. by widespread product sampling to encourage the consumer to try the product at home, by taste tests, test drives, etc.) as well as those that maximize exposure to marketing communications.

 Marketing pitfall

Free the carp?

For Joseph Vladsky, the insight came one December evening in Warsaw at a supermarket packed with Christmas shoppers. While walking past the fish department, he saw something that stopped him in his tracks. There, in white plastic tubs, were carp – more carp, it seemed, than water. Some were floating belly up. A group of shoppers peered eagerly into the tubs, selecting the main course for their holiday supper. Shop assistants in stained aprons fished out the chosen carp, tossed them onto scales, then dropped them, still flopping, into plastic bags. If asked, the shop assistants would kill the carp with a quick blow to the head from a thick wooden stick or metal pipe. 'Christmas is supposed to be a joyful time,' Mr Vladsky recalls thinking. 'But then you go to the market, and there's a tank of fish, dying, being killed. How terrible.'

Carp have graced east European holiday tables since the seventeenth century, when Christian monks first recognized the Asian import as a substitute for meatless feasts. Hundreds of years later, having carp for Christmas came to symbolize defiance of Communist rule. Today, Polish consumers still buy their carp live, and deliver the fatal blow at home, letting the fish swim out their final days in the family bathtub. Lately, however, sales have been stagnant, even though the price has fallen more than 30 per cent over the past three years. Newly affluent Poles seem to prefer salmon or mahi-mahi. Others simply hate

waiting for the carp to get out of the bathtub and into the oven (there is a lingering smell in the tub!), and then there are those like Mr Vladsky who object to the seasonal slaughter. Recent media coverage by the Animal Protection Society regarding the inhumane and insanitary conditions surrounding 'Christmas Carp' have slowed the consumption of carp. In Mr Vladsky's case, his children became so attached to the carp in their friend's bathtub that they gave them names, and started treating them as pets. Slowly, attitudes towards killing live carp for Christmas are changing . . .[61]

Question: *How would you apply Fishbein's (no pun intended) multi-attribute model to predict future behaviour of Polish consumption of carp, given the changing attitudes described above?*

▶ Multicultural dimensions

The theory of reasoned action has primarily been applied in the West. Certain assumptions inherent in the model may not necessarily apply to consumers from other cultures. Several of the following diminish the universality of the theory of reasoned action:

- The model was developed to predict the performance of any voluntary act. Across cultures, however, many consumer activities, ranging from taking exams and entering military service to receiving an inoculation or even choosing a marriage partner, are not necessarily voluntary.
- The relative impact of subjective norms may vary across cultures. For example, Asian cultures tend to value conformity and face-saving, so it is possible that subjective norms involving the anticipated reactions of others to the choice will have an even

greater impact on behaviour for many Asian consumers.
- The model measures behavioural intentions and thus presupposes that consumers are actively anticipating and planning future behaviours. The intention concept assumes that consumers have a linear time sense, i.e. they think in terms of past, present and future. As will be discussed in a later chapter, this time perspective is not held by all cultures.
- A consumer who forms an intention is (implicitly) claiming that they are in control of their actions. Some cultures tend to be fatalistic and do not necessarily believe in the concept of free will. Indeed, one study comparing students from the US, Jordan and Thailand found evidence for cultural differences in assumptions about fatalism and control over the future.[62]

Trying to consume

Other theorists have proposed different perspectives on the attitude–behaviour connection. For example, a recent model its authors call the multiple pathway anchoring and adjustment (MPAA) model emphasizes multiple pathways to attitude formation, including outside-in (object-centered) and inside-out (person-centered) pathways.[63]

Another perspective tries to address some of these problems by focusing instead on consumers' goals and what they believe they have to do to attain them. The **theory of trying** states that the criterion of behaviour in the reasoned action model should be replaced with *trying* to reach a goal.[64] This perspective recognizes that additional factors might intervene between intent and performance – both personal and environmental barriers might prevent the individual from attaining the goal. For example, a person who intends to lose weight may have to deal with numerous issues: they may not believe they are capable of slimming down, they may have a roommate who loves to cook and who leaves tempting goodies lying around the apartment, their friends may be jealous of their

Figure 8.3 Theory of trying

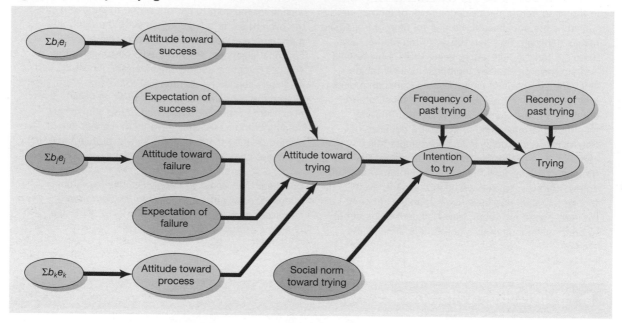

attempts to diet and encourage them to pig out, or they may be genetically predisposed to obesity and cutting down on calories simply will not produce the desired results.

The theory of trying includes several new components that attempt to account for the complex situations in which many factors either help or hurt our chances of turning intentions into actions, as Figure 8.3 shows. These factors include the amount of control the person has over the situation, their expectations of success or failure in achieving the goal, social norms related to attaining the goal, and their attitude toward the process of trying (i.e. how the action required to attain the goal makes them feel, regardless of the outcome). Still other new variables include the frequency and recency of past trying of the behaviour – for example, even if a person does not have specific plans to go on a diet in the next month, the frequency with which they have tried to do so in the recent past (and the success – however fleeting – they may have experienced) would be the best predictor of future attempts to shed some pounds. To predict whether someone would try to lose weight, here are a few sample issues that a researcher might address:

- *Past frequency*: how many times in the past year did the person try to lose weight?
- *Recency*: did they try to lose weight in the past week?
- *Beliefs*: did they believe they would be healthier if they lost weight?
- *Evaluations of consequences*: did they believe their girlfriend/boyfriend would be happier if they succeeded in losing weight? Did they believe their friends would make fun of them if they tried but failed to lose weight?
- *The process*: would the diet make them uncomfortable or depressed?
- *Expectations of success and failure*: did they believe it likely that they would be able to lose weight if they tried?
- *Subjective norms toward trying*: would the people who are important to them approve of their efforts to lose weight?

Tracking attitudes over time

An attitude survey is like a snapshot taken at a single point in time. It may tell us a lot about the position of a person, issue or object at that moment, but it does not permit

Table 8.2 Recycling rate of container glass (%)

Country	1990	1995	1996	1997	1998	1999	2000	2001	2002	2003	2004
Austria	60	n.a.	n.a.	88	86	84	84	83	87	86	88
Belgium	59	67	66	75	n.a.	n.a.	87	88	95	88	90
Denmark	40	63	66	70	63	63	65	65	76	71	75
Finland	46	50	63	62	69	78	89	91	92	73	72
France	41	70	50	52	55	55	55	55	55	58	58
Germany	54	75	79	79	81	81	83	87	90	88	91
Greece	16	35	29	26	27	25	26	27	27	30	24
Ireland	19	39	46	38	37	35	40	55	58	59	61
Italy	49	53	53	34	37	41	40	55	58	59	61
Netherlands	66	80	81	82	85	91	78	78	78	81	76
Norway	34	75	75	76	81	83	85	88	88	86	90
Portugal	23	42	42	44	42	42	40	34	35	38	39
Spain	27	32	35	37	41	40	31	33	36	38	41
Sweden	35	61	72	76	84	84	86	84	87	92	96
Switzerland	61	85	89	91	91	93	91	92	94	96	96
Turkey	30	12	13	20	31	25	24	24	23	22	24
United Kingdom	21	27	22	23	24	26	29	34	34	36	44

n.a. = Not available

Source: FEVE (European Container Glass Federation); *Consumers in Europe: Facts and figures*, Eurostat, Theme 3: Population and Social Statistics (Luxembourg, 2001).

many inferences about progress made over time or any predictions about possible future changes in consumer attitudes. To accomplish these tasks, it is necessary to develop an attitude-tracking programme. This activity helps to increase the predictability of behaviour by allowing researchers to analyze attitude trends over an extended period of time. It is more like a film than a snapshot. For example, a longitudinal survey conducted by Eurostat of Europeans' attitudes regarding recycling behaviour shows how attitudes can shift over a decade of time, and across countries. Table 8.2 shows the results of a large-scale study carried out in 17 countries. The percentage of respondents reporting that they recycle container glass tends to be growing over the past decade, but at uneven rates, and at very different starting points for each country in the EU.

These results would suggest that even as Europe moves towards a more integrated union with a common currency, consumers from individual countries vary in their recycling attitudes.[65]

Tracking studies

Attitude tracking involves the administration of an attitude survey at regular intervals. Preferably, the same methodology will be used each time so that results can be reliably compared. Several services, such as Gallup, the Henley Centre or the Yankelovich Monitor, track consumer attitudes over time.

This activity can be extremely valuable for strategic decision-making. For example, one financial services firm monitored changes in consumer attitudes towards one-stop banking centres. Although a large number of consumers were enthusiastic about the idea when it was first introduced, the number of people who liked the concept did not increase over time despite the millions of dollars invested in advertising to promote the centres. This finding indicated some problems with the way the concept was being presented, and the company decided to 'go back to the drawing board', and eventually came up with a new way to communicate the advantages of this service.

Changes to look for over time

Some of the dimensions that can be included in attitude tracking include the following:

- *A focus on changes in different age groups.* Attitudes tend to change as people age (a life-cycle effect), and this will be of continual interest to government and business as the demographic profile of Europe continues to get older. More on this in Chapter 13. In addition, cohort effects occur; that is, members of a particular generation (e.g. teens, generation X, or the elderly) tend to share certain outlooks. Also, historical effects can be observed as large groups of people are affected by profound cultural changes (for example, the democratization of eastern European countries, and their admission to the EU).

- *Scenarios about the future.* Consumers are frequently tracked in terms of their future plans, confidence in the economy, and so on. These measures can provide valuable data about future behaviour and yield insights for public policy.

- *Identification of change agents.* Social phenomena can change people's attitudes towards basic consumption activities over time, as when consumers' willingness to buy fur products shifts. Or people's likelihood of seeking divorce may be affected by such facilitators as changes in the legal system that make this easier, or by inhibitors, such as the prevalence of AIDS and the value of two salaries in today's economy.[66]

PERSUADING CONSUMERS TO CHANGE ATTITUDES

As consumers we are constantly bombarded by messages inducing us to change our attitudes. These persuasion attempts can range from logical arguments to graphic pictures, and from intimidation by peers to exhortations by celebrity spokespeople. And, communications flow both ways – the consumer may seek out information sources in order to learn more about these options, for instance by surfing the Net. The increasing choice of ways to access marketing messages is changing the way we think about persuasion attempts. Our focus will be on some basic aspects of communication that specifically help to determine how and if attitudes will be created or modified. This objective relates to

▶ **persuasion**, which refers to an active attempt to change attitudes. Persuasion is, of course, the central goal of many marketing communications.

Consumer behaviour as I see it . . .

Television networks increasingly try to include educational content in the plots of their television shows, particularly in shows for young people. The networks view this as a public service and call it 'entertainment education'. Previously the networks aired public service announcements at the commercial breaks, typically late at night to minimize the loss in paid advertising revenue. Now the networks prefer entertainment education because it reaches prime-time viewers, and they believe that messages in television shows are more credible and persuasive. If your favourite television actors tell you something within their show, you listen, or so they believe.

Connie Pechmann
University of California, Irvine

I study the effects of different types of educational messages on young people. I go into high schools and arrange for students to be released from a class, watch one type of educational show, and then complete a survey. I test television shows that try to discourage youths from smoking. In a typical show, attractive youths smoke but their friends disapprove and tell them to quit. I found this works; it makes viewers less likely to light up. However, in other shows, the reaction to the smoking is more mixed; some people approve while others disapprove. This doesn't work. Also many shows include a short epilogue before the closing credits in which the characters reappear and restate their antismoking message. This boomerangs or actually encourages viewers to light up because they don't want television characters telling them what to do.

Consumers: ad readers or ad users?

In a traditional communications model, advertising is essentially viewed as the process of transferring information to the buyer before a sale. As such, there is a 'real' meaning of the ad based on the intentions of the sender of the message. This meaning can then be transferred to the consumer, if the message is clear enough and the medium is easy to get access to. In other words, if there is not too much 'noise' (as it was called!) on the line, the message should pass undistorted to the consumer. In this perspective, the power of creating the content of the message lies exclusively with the sender.[67]

Is this an accurate picture of the way we relate to marketing communications? In ▶ **reader-response theory**,[68] it is argued that it is better to conceive of the communication process as consisting of two communicators, both actively engaged in a process of making sense in and of some message. Instead of the 'machine-like' transmission of information, advertising must be understood as a particular type of communication, a particular genre, and it is understood and interpreted by consumers using particular strategies. Persuading consumers through advertising is not a technical but a cultural process.[69] In other words, when there is uncertainty about how consumers understand and interpret ads, this cannot be explained by 'noise' disturbing the 'real message', but must instead be understood based on consumers' own personal and cultural backgrounds.[70]

▶ Proponents of **uses and gratification theory** add to this argument that consumers are an active, goal-directed audience who draw on mass media as a resource to satisfy needs. Instead of asking what media do *for* or *to* people, they ask what people do *with* the media.[71] Research with young people in the UK finds that they rely on advertising for many gratifications, including entertainment (some report that the 'adverts' are better than the programmes), escapism, play (some report singing along with jingles, others make posters out of magazine ads), and self-affirmation (ads can reinforce their own values or provide role models).[72]

Credibility and attractiveness

Regardless of whether a message is received by passive or, as it seems, more active consumers, common sense tells us that the same words uttered or written by different people can have very different effects. Research on *source effects* has been carried out for more than 50 years. By attributing the same message to different sources and measuring the degree of attitude change that occurs after listeners hear it, it is possible to determine which aspects of a communicator will induce attitude change.[73] Two particularly important source characteristics are *credibility* and *attractiveness*.[74]

▶ **Source credibility** refers to a source's perceived expertise, objectivity or trustworthiness. This characteristic relates to consumers' beliefs that a communicator is competent, and is willing to provide the necessary information to evaluate competing products adequately. A credible source can be particularly persuasive when the consumer has not yet learned much about a product or formed an opinion of it.[75] The decision to pay an expert or a celebrity to promote a product can be a very costly one, but researchers have concluded that on average the investment is worth it simply because the announcement of an endorsement contract is often used by market analysts to evaluate a firm's potential profitability, thereby affecting its expected return. On average, then, the impact of endorsements appears to be so positive that it offsets the cost of hiring the spokesperson.[76]

▶ **Source attractiveness** refers to the source's perceived social value. This quality can emanate from the person's physical appearance, personality, social status, or their similarity to the receiver (we like to listen to people who are like us). A compelling source has great value and endorsement deals are constantly in the works. Even dead sources can be attractive: the great-grandson of the artist Renoir is putting his famous ancestor's name on bottled water, and the Picasso family licensed their name to the French car maker Citroën.[77] The use of celebrity endorsers is an expensive but commonly used strategy.

Celebrity endorsement in advertising.
The Advertising Archives

While a celebrity endorsement strategy is expensive, it can pay off handsomely.[78] Celebrities increase awareness of a firm's advertising and enhance both company image and brand attitudes.[79] Tiger Woods is now the richest endorser in sports history, with an estimated income of $62 million per year (not counting the money he makes actually winning golf tournaments!).[80] More generally, star power works because celebrities represent *cultural meanings* – they symbolize important categories such as status and social class (a 'business icon' such as Bill Gates), gender (a 'manly man' like Mel Gibson, or a strong feminine character, such as Reebok's endorser, Venus Williams),[81] age (the boyish Brad Pitt or the mature and serene Sean Connery) and even personality types (the noble humanitarian George Clooney). Ideally, the advertiser decides what meanings the product should convey (that is, how it should be positioned in the marketplace), and then chooses a celebrity who has come to evoke that meaning. The product's meaning thus moves from the manufacturer to the consumer, using the star as a vehicle.[82]

 Multicultural dimensions

Does this work for you?

Park Jin Sung combs through a rack of button-down shirts at a clothes shop in Seoul. After close examination, he picks out one in light blue that has a stiff, narrow collar and buttons spaced just right, so that the top two can be left open without exposing too much chest. 'Bill would wear this. The collar on this other one is too floppy. Definitely not Bill's style,' Mr Park says. William H. Gates, Chairman of Microsoft Corp., may not be considered the epitome of chic in Europe, but in Seoul, Korea, he is a serious style icon. Young South Koreans believe that 'dressing for success' means copying Mr Gates's wardrobe, down to his round, tortoise-shell glasses, unpolished shoes and wrinkle-free trousers.[83] While Bill Gates doesn't even try to be an endorser of style in Korea, or elsewhere, some celebrities choose to maintain their credibility by endorsing products only in other countries. Many celebrities who do not do many American advertisements appear frequently in Japan. Mel Gibson endorses Asahi beer, Sly Stallone appears for Kirin beer, Sean Connery plugs Ito hams and the singer Sheena was featured in ads for Shochu liquor – dressed in a kimono and wig. Even the normally reclusive comedian and film director Woody Allen featured in a campaign for a large Tokyo department store.[84] **Japander.com** is a website where consumers can see Hollywood stars in Japanese commercials: George Clooney advertising Toyota cars (2001); Harrison Ford promoting Kirin beer (mid 1990s); and Brad Pitt selling blue jeans (late 1990s).[85]

Hype vs. buzz: the corporate paradox

Obviously many marketers spend lavishly to create marketing messages that they hope will convince hordes of customers that they are the best. There's the rub – in many cases ▶ they may be trying too hard! We can think of this as the **corporate paradox** – the more involved a company appears to be in the dissemination of news about its products, the less credible it becomes.[86] As we will see in Chapter 10, consumer word-of-mouth ▶ is typically the most convincing kind of message. As Table 8.3 shows, **buzz** is word- ▶ of-mouth that is viewed as authentic and generated by customers. In contrast, **hype** is dismissed as inauthentic – corporate propaganda planted by a company with an axe to grind. So, the challenge to marketers is to get the word out and about without it looking like they are trying too hard.

The now-famous *Blair Witch Project* that led many viewers to believe the fictional treatment was in fact a real documentary demonstrated the power of a brand that seems as if it is not one. Some marketers are trying to borrow the veneer of buzz by mounting 'stealth' campaigns that seem as if they are untouched by the corporate world. *Buzz building* has become the new mantra for many companies that recognize the power of underground word-of-mouth.[87] Indeed, a small cottage industry has sprung up as some firms begin to specialize in the corporate promotion business by planting comments on Websites which are made to look as if they originated from actual consumers. Consider one example:

● When RCA records wanted to create a buzz around teen pop singer Christina Aguilera, they hired a team of young people to swarm the Web and chat about her on popular teen sites like **alloy.com**, **bolt.com** and **gurl.com**. Posing as fans, they posted entries raving about her new material. Just before one of her albums was launched, RCA also hired a direct marketing company to e-mail electronic postcards filled with song snippets and biographical information to 50,000 Web addresses.[88] The album quickly went to No. 1 in the charts.

As powerful as these tactics are, they have the potential to poison the well in a big way. Web surfers, already sceptical about what they see and hear, may get to the point where they assume every 'authentic' site they find is really a corporate front. Until then, however, buzz building online is growing strongly. Still, there is no beating the impact of a marketing message that really does originate with product users.

Table 8.3 Hype versus buzz

Hype	Buzz
Advertising	Word-of-Mouth
Overt	Covert
Corporate	Grass-roots
Fake	Authentic
Scepticism	Credibility

Types of message appeals

The *way* something is said can be as significant as *who* says it. A persuasive message can tug at the heartstrings or scare you, make you laugh, make you cry or leave you ▶ yearning to learn more, depending on the appeal used. In this section, we will briefly review the major alternatives available to communicators who wish to appeal to a message recipient.

The first alternative often considered is whether to use rational or emotional appeals; or, in other words, appeal to the head or to the heart? As with the other types of appeals, there is no single given 'right' or 'wrong' answer to this question. The answer always depends upon the nature of the product, the type of relationship consumers have with it, and the current competitive situation in the market. Although they are hard to gauge, it has not prevented researchers from trying to predict the precise effects of rational vs. emotional appeals. Even if recall of ad contents tends to be better for 'thinking' ads than for 'feeling' ads, conventional measures of advertising effectiveness (e.g. day-after recall) may not be adequate to assess cumulative effects of emotional ads. These open-ended measures are oriented towards cognitive responses, and feeling ads may be penalized because the reactions are not as easy to articulate.[89]

Echoing the widely held belief that 'sex sells', many marketing communications – for everything from perfumes to cars – feature heavy doses of erotic suggestions that range

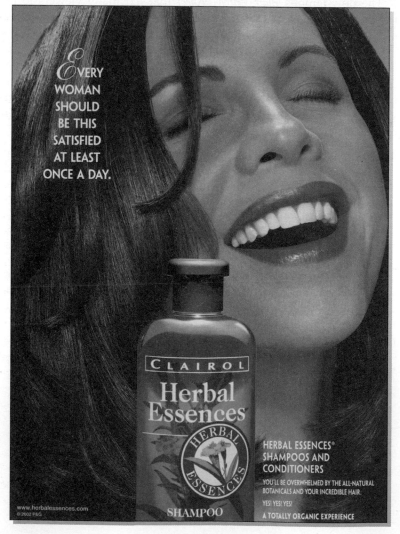

Shampoo ad employing a sexual appeal.
The Advertising Archives

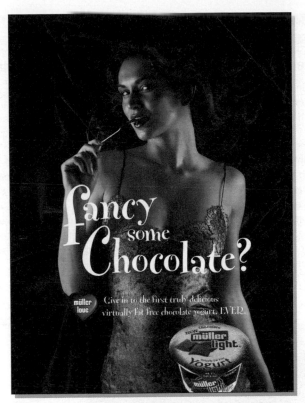

An ad employing a sexual appeal.
The Advertising Archives

from subtle hints to blatant displays of flesh. Of course, the prevalence of sex appeals varies from country to country. American firms run ads abroad that would not go down well in the US. For example, a recent 'cheeky' ad campaign designed to boost the appeal of American-made Lee Jeans among Europeans features a series of bare buttocks. The messages are based on the concept that if bottoms could choose jeans, they would opt for Lee: 'Bottoms feel better in Lee Jeans'.[90]

Does sex work? Although the use of sex does appear to draw attention to an ad, it may actually be counter-productive to the marketer. Ironically, a provocative picture can be *too* effective; it attracts so much attention that it hinders processing and recall of the ad's other contents, such as the brand. Some researchers also suggest that strong use of sexual appeals are generally received negatively.[91] In one survey, an overwhelming 61 per cent of the respondents said that sexual imagery in a product's ad made them less likely to buy it.[92] However, as in all attitude measurements, it is important to remember that such statements are highly influenced by the moral picture that consumers like to present, not only to the researcher, but also to themselves.

And what about humour? Does humour work? Overall, humorous advertisements do get attention. One study found that recognition scores for humorous alcohol ads were better than average. However, the verdict is mixed as to whether humour affects recall or product attitudes in a significant way.[93] One function it may play is to provide a source of *distraction*. A funny ad inhibits the consumer from *counter-arguing* (thinking of reasons why they don't agree with the message), thereby increasing the likelihood of message acceptance.[94]

Humour is more likely to be effective when the brand is clearly identified and the funny material does not 'swamp' the message. This danger is similar to that of beautiful models diverting attention from copy points. Furthermore, subtle humour is usually better, as it presents the product or brand as 'clever'. Finally, the humour can make fun of the brand (and its producers), something which makes them appear as 'more cool', but generally not of the potential consumer.

▲ Marketing opportunity

Marketing with double entendres – sex *and* humour: opportunity or pitfall?

'Virgin Atlantic Airways is hoping business travelers will say, "Oh, behave!" after seeing a cheeky new commercial, which uses bawdy British humour to spoof soft-core pornography.

The jest even extends to the choice of media for the parody, which will appear where the intended audience watches actual soft-core pornography, on the sex-oriented entertainment channels of the closed-circuit television systems in hotel rooms. The spoof, almost 10 minutes long, promotes Virgin Atlantic's "Upper Class Suite" service on flights between London and New York. Though there is no nudity or profanity, there is enough wink-wink, nudge-nudge japery to fill a fourth Austin Powers film. First, there is the title, "Suite &

Innocent", then come woodenly acted characters with names like Miles High, Big Ben and Summer Turbulence, who deliver dialogue replete with double entendres about "your first time" on board and enjoying "several inches more" of legroom.

The plot, such as it is, is centered on a buxom blonde, the chief executive of a lingerie company, who enjoys a business trip from New York to London in a Virgin Atlantic Upper Class Suite. In one scene, a venture capitalist she meets on board offers to invest in her company, and as he writes a cheque for $100 million, she recites aloud each zero by moaning, "Oh, oh, oh, oh." '[95]

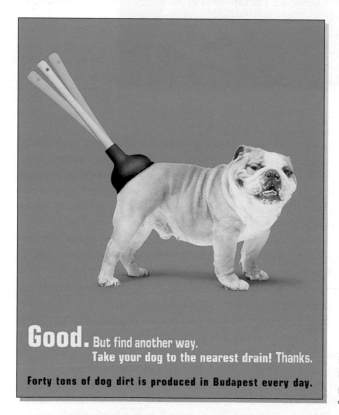

Good. But find another way.
Take your dog to the nearest drain! Thanks.

Forty tons of dog dirt is produced in Budapest every day.

Humourous ads like this one from Budapest grab our attention.

McCann-Erickson, New York

Fear appeals highlight the negative consequences that can occur unless the consumer changes a behaviour or an attitude. This strategy is widespread: fear appeals are used in over 15 per cent of all television ads.[96] The arousal of fear is a common tactic for social policy issues, such as encouraging consumers to change to a healthier lifestyle by stopping smoking, using contraception, taking more exercise, eating a more balanced diet, drinking without driving (by relying on a designated driver in order to reduce physical risk to themselves or others). It can also be applied to social risk issues by threatening one's success with the opposite sex, career and so on. One French study made a direct comparison of fear appeals, guilt appeals and shame appeals in terms of persuading consumers to refrain from excessive alcohol consumption; fear and shame were found to have the biggest persuasive impact.[97]

Does fear work? Fear appeals, it has been argued, are usually most effective when only a moderate amount of fear is induced and when a solution to the problem is presented.[98] If the threat is too great, the audience tends to deny that it exists as a way to rationalize the danger. Consumers will tune out of the ad because they can do nothing to solve the problem.[99] This approach also works better when source credibility is high.[100]

Some of the research on fear appeals may be confusing a threat (the literal content of a message, such as saying 'engage in safe sex or die') with fear (an emotional response to the message). According to this argument, greater fear does result in greater persuasion – but not all threats are equally effective because different people will respond differently to the same threat. Therefore, the strongest threats are not always the most persuasive because they may not have the desired impact on the perceiver. For example, raising the spectre of AIDS is about the strongest threat that can be delivered to sexually active young people – but this tactic is only effective if they believe they will get the disease. Because many young people (especially those who live in fairly affluent areas) do not believe that 'people like them' will be exposed to the AIDS virus, this strong threat may not actually result in a high level of fear.[101] The bottom line is that more precise measures of actual fear responses are needed before definitive conclusions can be drawn about the impact of fear appeals on consumption decisions.

Fear, humour, or any other communicative strategy – most of them remind us that marketers today are storytellers, who supply visions of reality similar to those provided by authors, poets and artists. These communications take the form of stories often because the product benefits they describe are intangible and must be given tangible meaning by expressing them in a form that is concrete and visible. Advertisers (consciously or not) rely on various literary devices to communicate these meanings. To do this, they often use metaphors, which involves placing two dissimilar things in a close relationship by expressing one thing in terms of another. 'Love is a battlefield' is one

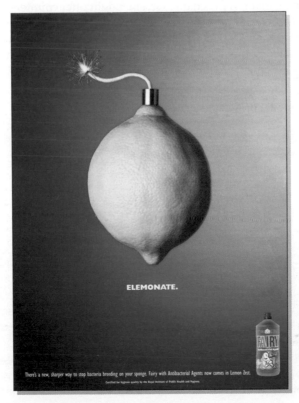

ELEMONATE.

There's a new, sharper way to stop bacteria breeding on your sponge. Fairy with Antibacterial Agents now comes in Lemon Zest.

Certified for hygienic quality by the Royal Institute of Public Health and Hygiene.

Fairy uses the metaphor of 'lighting the fuse and blowing the germs away' in its sales pitch for Lemon Fairy with its antibacterial agents.

The Advertising Archives

example of metaphor. 'Argument is war' is another.[102] Such usage of metaphors is both an expression of and a development of some of those cultural values and symbols used by the advertising industry in connection with providing meaning to a product or brand, as we saw in Figure 2.1.

The elaboration likelihood model

Some major features of the persuasion process, like the qualities of the source and the appeals have been discussed. Which aspect has more impact in persuading consumers to change their attitudes? Should marketers worry more about *what* is said, or *how* it is said and *who* says it?

The answer is, it depends. Variations in a consumer's level of involvement, as discussed in Chapter 6, result in the activation of very different cognitive processes when a message is received. Research indicates that this level of involvement will determine which aspects of a communication are processed. The situation appears to resemble a traveller who comes to a fork in the road: one or the other path is chosen, and this choice has a big impact on the factors that will make a difference in persuasion attempts.

▶ The elaboration likelihood model (ELM) assumes that once a consumer receives a message they begin to process it.[103] Depending on the personal relevance of this information, one of two routes to persuasion will be followed. Under conditions of high involvement, the consumer takes the *central route* to persuasion. Under conditions of low involvement, a *peripheral route* is taken instead. This model is shown in Figure 8.4.

The central route to persuasion

When the consumer finds the information in a persuasive message to be relevant or somehow interesting, they will carefully attend to the message content. The person is likely actively to think about the arguments presented and generate *cognitive responses* to these arguments. On hearing a radio message warning about drinking alcohol while pregnant, an expectant mother might say to herself, 'She's right. I really should stop drinking alcohol now that I'm pregnant.' Or, she might offer counter-arguments, such as, 'That's a load of nonsense. My mother had a cocktail every night when she was pregnant with me, and I turned out OK.' If a person generates counter-arguments in response to a message, it is less likely that they will yield to the message, whereas the generation of further supporting arguments by the consumer increases the probability of compliance.[104]

Figure 8.4 The elaboration likelihood model of persuasion

Source: From *Consumer Behavior*, 2nd edn, by John C. Mowen, Macmillan Publishing Company.

The central route to persuasion is likely to involve the traditional hierarchy of effects, as discussed earlier in the chapter. Beliefs are carefully formed and evaluated, and the resulting strong attitudes will be likely to guide behaviour. The implication is that message factors, such as the quality of arguments presented, will be important in determining attitude change. Prior knowledge about a topic results in more thoughts about the message and also increases the number of counter-arguments.[105]

The peripheral route to persuasion

In contrast, the peripheral route is taken when the person is not motivated to think deeply about the arguments presented. Instead, the consumer is likely to use other cues in deciding on the suitability of the message. These cues might include the product's package, the attractiveness of the source, or the context in which the message is presented. Sources of information extraneous to the actual message content are called *peripheral cues* because they surround the actual message.

The peripheral route to persuasion highlights the paradox of low involvement discussed in Chapter 6: when consumers do not care about a product, the stimuli associated with it increase in importance. The implication here is that low-involvement products may be purchased chiefly because the marketer has done a good job in designing a 'sexy' package, choosing a popular spokesperson, or perhaps just creating a pleasant shopping environment.

Support for the ELM model

The ELM model has received a lot of research support.[106] In one study, undergraduates were exposed to one of several mock advertisements for Break, a new brand of low-alcohol beer. Using the technique of *thought listing*,[107] they were asked to provide their thoughts about the ads, which were later analyzed.[108] Three independent variables crucial to the ELM model were manipulated.

1 *Message-processing involvement*: some subjects were motivated to be highly involved with the ads. They were promised a gift of low-alcohol beer for participating in the study and were told that the brand would soon be available in their area. Low-involvement subjects were not promised a gift and were told that the brand would be introduced in a distant area.

2 *Argument strength*: one version of the ad used strong, compelling arguments to drink Break (e.g. 'Break contains one-half of the amount of alcohol of regular beers and, therefore, has fewer calories than regular beer'), whereas the other listed only weak arguments (e.g. 'Break is just as good as any other regular beer').

3 *Source characteristics*: ads contained a photo of a couple drinking the beer, but their relative social attractiveness was varied by their dress, their posture and nonverbal expressions, and the background information given about their educational achievements and occupations.

Consistent with the ELM model, high-involvement subjects had more thoughts related to the ad messages than did low-involvement subjects, who devoted more cognitive activity to the sources used in the ad. The attitudes of high-involvement subjects were more likely to be swayed by powerful arguments, whereas the attitudes of low-involvement subjects were more likely to be influenced by the ad version using attractive sources. The results of this study, paired with numerous others, indicate that the relative effectiveness of a strong message and a favourable source depends on consumers' level of involvement with the product being advertised.

It is important to remember, however, that the same communications variable can be both a central and a peripheral cue, depending on its relation to the attitude object. The physical attractiveness of a model might serve as a peripheral cue in a car commercial, but her beauty might be a central cue for a product such as shampoo, where the product's benefits are directly tied to enhancing attractiveness.[109]

CHAPTER SUMMARY

- An attitude is a predisposition to evaluate an object or product positively or negatively.

- Social marketing refers to attempts to change consumers' attitudes and behaviours in ways that are beneficial to society as a whole.

- Attitudes are made up of three components: beliefs, affect and behavioural intentions.

- Attitude researchers traditionally assumed that attitudes were learned in a predetermined sequence, consisting first of the formation of beliefs (cognitions) regarding an attitude object, followed by an evaluation of that object (affect) and then some action (behaviour). Depending on the consumer's level of involvement and the circumstances, though, attitudes can result from other hierarchies of effects.

- A key to attitude formation is the function the attitude plays for the consumer (e.g. is it utilitarian or ego-defensive?).

- One organizing principle of attitude formation is the importance of consistency among attitudinal components – that is, some parts of an attitude may be altered to conform with others. Such theoretical approaches to attitudes as cognitive dissonance theory, balance theory and congruity theory stress the vital role of consistency.

- The complexity of attitudes is underscored by multi-attribute attitude models, in which sets of beliefs and evaluations are identified and combined to predict an overall attitude. Factors such as subjective norms and the specificity of attitude scales have been integrated into attitude measures to improve predictability.

- *Persuasion* refers to an attempt to change consumers' attitudes.

- Two important characteristics that characterize a message source are its *attractiveness* and *credibility*. Although celebrities are often used with the purpose of enhancing these characteristics, their credibility is not always as strong as marketers hope. Marketing messages that consumers perceive as buzz (that are authentic and consumer-generated) tend to be more effective than those they categorize as hype (that are inauthentic, biased and company-generated).

- Some elements of a message that help to determine its effectiveness in terms of attitude change are whether an emotional or a rational appeal is employed and whether the message includes fear, humour or sexual references.

- The relative influence of the source versus the message depends on the receiver's level of involvement with the communication. The *elaboration likelihood model* specifies that a less involved consumer will more likely be swayed by source effects, whereas a more involved consumer will be more likely to attend to and process components of the actual message.

▶ KEY TERMS

ABC model of attitudes (p. 277)

Affect (p. 277)

Appeal (p. 300)

Attitude (p. 275)

Attitude object (A_o) (p. 275)

Attitude towards the act of buying (A_{act}) (p. 291)

Attitude towards the advertisement (A_{ad}) (p. 280)

Balance theory (p. 286)

Behaviour (p. 277)

Buzz (p. 299)

Cognition (p. 277)

Corporate paradox (p. 299)

Elaboration likelihood model (ELM) (p. 304)

Foot-in-the-door technique (p. 285)

Functional theory of attitudes (p. 275)

Hierarchy of effects (p. 277)

Hype (p. 299)	Self-perception theory (p. 285)
Latitudes of acceptance and rejection (p. 285)	Social judgement theory (p. 285)
	Source attractiveness (p. 297)
Multi-attribute attitude models (p. 288)	Source credibility (p. 297)
Persuasion (p. 296)	Theory of reasoned action (p. 291)
Principle of cognitive consistency (p. 282)	Theory of trying (p. 293)
Reader-response theory (p. 297)	Uses and gratification theory (p. 297)

▶ CONSUMER BEHAVIOUR CHALLENGE

1 Contrast the hierarchies of effects outlined in the chapter. How will strategic decisions related to the marketing mix be influenced by which hierarchy is operative among target consumers?

2 List three functions played by attitudes, giving an example of how each function is employed in a marketing situation. To examine European countries' attitudes towards a wide variety of issues, go to the website: http://europa.eu.int/en/comm/dg10/ infcom/epo/eo.html. Which sorts of attitudes expressed in different countries seem utilitarian, value-expressive or ego-defensive? Why?

3 Think of a behaviour exhibited by an individual that is inconsistent with their attitudes (e.g. attitudes towards cholesterol, drug use or even buying things to attain status or be noticed). Ask the person to elaborate on why they do the behaviour, and try to identify the way the person has resolved dissonant elements.

4 Using a series of semantic-differential scales, devise an attitude survey for a set of competing cars. Identify areas of competitive advantage or disadvantage for each model you incorporate.

5 Construct a multi-attribute model for a set of local restaurants. Based on your findings, suggest how restaurant managers can improve their establishments' image using the strategies described in the chapter.

6 A government agency wants to encourage the use of designated drivers by people who have been drinking. What advice could you give the organization about constructing persuasive communications? Discuss some factors that might be important, including the structure of the communications, where they should appear, and who should deliver them. Should fear appeals be used, and if so, how?

7 Why would a marketer consider saying negative things about their product? When is this strategy feasible? Can you find examples of it?

8 Create a list of celebrities who match up with products in your country. What are the elements of the celebrities and products that make for a 'good match'? Why? Which celebrities have a global or European-wide appeal, and why?

For additional material see the companion website at **www.pearsoned.co.uk/solomon**

NOTES

1. 'It' a funny old game', *The Economist* (10 February 2001): 57–8.
2. See for example Sven Bergvall and Mikolaj Dymek, 'Uncovering Sport Game Covers – The Consumption of Video Game Packages', in K. Ekström and H. Brembeck (eds), *European Advances in Consumer Research*, vol. 7 (Valdosta, GA: Association for Consumer Research, 2007): 310–16.
3. Robert A. Baron and Donn Byrne, *Social Psychology: Understanding Human Interaction*, 5th edn (Boston: Allyn & Bacon, 1987).
4. D. Albarracín, B.T. Johnson and M.P. Zanna (eds), *The Handbook of Attitudes* (Mahwah, NJ: Erlbaum, 2005); see also: J.R. Priester, D. Nayakankuppan, M.A. Fleming and J. Godek, 'The A(2)SC(2) model: The influence of attitudes and attitude strength on consideration set choice', *Journal of Consumer Research* 30(4) (2004): 574–87 for a study on how the strength of attitudes influences and guides a consumer's consideration of brands.
5. Daniel Katz, 'The functional approach to the study of attitudes', *Public Opinion Quarterly* 24 (Summer 1960):

163–204; Richard J. Lutz, 'Changing brand attitudes through modification of cognitive structure', *Journal of Consumer Research* 1 (March 1975): 49–59.

6. Russell H. Fazio, T.M. Lenn and E.A. Effrein, 'Spontaneous attitude formation', *Social Cognition* 2 (1984): 214–34.

7. Mason Haire, 'Projective techniques in marketing research', *Journal of Marketing* 14 (April 1950): 649–56.

8. Sharon Shavitt, 'The role of attitude objects in attitude functions', *Journal of Experimental Social Psychology* 26 (1990): 124–48; see also J.S. Johar and M. Joseph Sirgy, 'Value-expressive versus utilitarian advertising appeals: When and why to use which appeal', *Journal of Advertising* 20 (September 1991): 23–34.

9. For the original work that focused on the issue of levels of attitudinal commitment, see H.C. Kelman, 'Compliance, identification, and internalization: Three processes of attitude change', *Journal of Conflict Resolution* 2 (1958): 51–60.

10. Lynn R. Kahle, Kenneth M. Kambara and Gregory M. Rose, 'A functional model of fan attendance motivations for college football', *Sports Marketing Quarterly* 5(4) (1996): 51–60.

11. For a study that found evidence of simultaneous causation of beliefs and attitudes, see Gary M. Erickson, Johny K. Johansson and Paul Chao, 'Image variables in multi-attribute product evaluations: Country-of-origin effects', *Journal of Consumer Research* 11 (September 1984): 694–9.

12. Michael Ray, 'Marketing Communications and the Hierarchy-of-Effects', in P. Clarke (ed.), *New Models for Mass Communications* (Beverly Hills, CA: Sage, 1973): 147–76.

13. Jung Chae Suh & Youjae Yi, 'When brand attitudes affect the customer satisfaction-loyalty relation: The moderating role of product involvement', *Journal of Consumer Psychology* 16(2): 145–55.

14. Herbert Krugman, 'The impact of television advertising: Learning without involvement', *Public Opinion Quarterly* 29 (Fall 1965): 349–56; Robert Lavidge and Gary Steiner, 'A model for predictive measurements of advertising effectiveness', *Journal of Marketing* 25 (October 1961): 59–62.

15. Magnus Söderlund, 'Judging Fiction Books by the Cover: An Examination of the Effects of Sexually Charged Cover Images', in S. Borghini, M.A. McGrath and C.C. Otnes (eds), *European Advances in Consumer Research* 8 (Duluth, MN: Association for Consumer Research, 2008): 500–4.

16. For some studies on this topic see Andrew B. Aylesworth and Scott B. MacKenzie, 'Context is key: The effect of program-induced mood on thoughts about the ad', *Journal of Advertising*, 27(2) (Summer 1998): 15–17 (at 15); Angela Y. Lee and Brian Sternthal, 'The effects of positive mood on memory', *Journal of Consumer Research* 26 (September 1999): 115–28; Michael J. Barone, Paul W. Miniard and Jean B. Romeo, 'The influence of positive mood on brand extension evaluations', *Journal of Consumer Research* 26 (March 2000): 386–401. For a study that compared the effectiveness of emotional appeals across cultures, see Jennifer L. Aaker and Patti Williams, 'Empathy versus pride: The influence of emotional appeals across cultures', *Journal of Consumer Research* 25 (December 1998): 241–61.

17. See for example, Özlem H. Sanaktekin, 'Moderating Role of Valence Sequence in the Mixed Affective Approach', in S. Borghini, M.A. McGrath and C.C. Otnes (eds), *European Advances in Consumer Research* 8 (Duluth, MN: Association for Consumer Research, 2008): 150–54.

18. Punam Anand, Morris B. Holbrook and Debra Stephens, 'The formation of affective judgments: The cognitive –

affective model versus the independence hypothesis', *Journal of Consumer Research* 15 (December 1988): 386–91; Richard S. Lazarus, 'Thoughts on the relations between emotion and cognition', *American Psychologist* 37(9) (1982): 1019–24.

19. Robert B. Zajonc, 'Feeling and thinking: Preferences need no inferences', *American Psychologist* 35(2) (1980): 151–75.

20. Banwari Mittal, 'The role of affective choice mode in the consumer purchase of expressive products', *Journal of Economic Psychology* 4(9) (1988): 499–524.

21. Dirk Morschett, Bernhard Swoboda and Hanna Schramm-Klein, 'Shopping Orientations as Determinants of Attitude Towards Food Retailers and Perception of Store Attributes', in K. Ekström and H. Brembeck (eds), *European Advances in Consumer Research* 7 (Duluth, MN: Association for Consumer Research, 2006): 160–67.

22. Scot Burton and Donald R. Lichtenstein, 'The effect of ad claims and ad context on attitude toward the advertisement', *Journal of Advertising* 17(1) (1988): 3–11; Karen A. Machleit and R. Dale Wilson, 'Emotional feelings and attitude toward the advertisement: The roles of brand familiarity and repetition', *Journal of Advertising* 17(3) (1988): 27–35; Scott B. Mackenzie and Richard J. Lutz, 'An empirical examination of the structural antecedents of attitude toward the ad in an advertising pretesting context', *Journal of Marketing* 53 (April 1989): 48–65; Scott B. Mackenzie, Richard J. Lutz and George E. Belch, 'The role of attitude toward the ad as a mediator of advertising effectiveness: A test of competing explanations', *Journal of Marketing Research* 23 (May 1986): 130–43; Darrel D. Muehling and Russell N. Laczniak, 'Advertising's immediate and delayed influence on brand attitudes: Considerations across message-involvement levels', *Journal of Advertising* 17(4) (1988): 23–34; Mark A. Pavelchak, Meryl P. Gardner and V. Carter Broach, 'Effect of Ad Pacing and Optimal Level of Arousal on Attitude Toward the Ad', in Rebecca H. Holman and Michael R. Solomon (eds), *Advances in Consumer Research* 18 (Provo, UT: Association for Consumer Research, 1991): 94–9. Some research evidence indicates that a separate attitude is also formed regarding the brand name itself: see George M. Zinkhan and Claude R. Martin Jr, 'New brand names and inferential beliefs: Some insights on naming new products', *Journal of Business Research* 15 (1987): 157–72.

23. John P. Murry Jr., John L. Lastovicka and Surendra N. Singh, 'Feeling and liking responses to television programs: An examination of two explanations for media-context effects', *Journal of Consumer Research* 18 (March 1992): 441–51.

24. Barbara Stern and Judith Lynne Zaichkowsky, 'The impact of entertaining advertising on consumer responses', *Australian Marketing Researcher* 14 (August 1991): 68–80; Mark Ritson, 'Polysemy: The Multiple Meanings of Advertising' in Darach Turley and Stephen Brown, eds, *European Advances in Consumer Research: All Changed, Changed Utterly?* 6 (Valdosta, GA: Association for Consumer Research, 2003): 341; Stefano Puntoni, Mark Ritson and Lan Nguyen, 'The Multiple Meanings of a TV Ad' in Turley and Brown (eds), *European Advances in Consumer Research: All Changed, Changed Utterly* 6: 432; Magnus Soderlund, 'The Smiling Female Model in Ads: Does She Really Make a Difference?' in Turley and Brown (eds), *European Advances in Consumer Research: All Changed, Changed Utterly* 6: 343; Karolina Brodin and Mark Ritson, 'The Impact of

Advertising Interaction on Advertising Polysemy' in Turley and Brown (eds), *European Advances in Consumer Research: All Changed, Changed Utterly* 6: 343.

25. For a study examining the impact of scepticism on advertising issues, see David M. Boush, Marian Friestad and Gregory M. Rose, 'Adolescent skepticism toward TV advertising and knowledge of advertiser tactics', *Journal of Consumer Research* 21 (June 1994): 165–75; see also Lawrence Feick and Heribert Gierl, 'Skepticism about advertising: A comparison of East and West German consumers', *International Journal of Research in Marketing* 13 (1996): 227–35; Rik Pieters and Hans Baumgartner, 'The Attitude Toward Advertising of Advertising Practitioners, Homemakers and Students in The Netherlands and Belgium', in W. Fred van Raaij and Gary J. Bamossy (eds), *European Advances in Consumer Research* 1 (Provo, UT: Association for Consumer Research, 1993): 39–45.

26. Basil G. Englis, 'Consumer Emotional Reactions to Television Advertising and Their Effects on Message Recall', in S. Agres, J.A. Edell and T.M. Dubitsky (eds), *Emotion in Advertising: Theoretical and Practical Explorations* (Westport, CT: Quorum Books, 1990): 231–54.

27. Morris B. Holbrook and Rajeev Batra, 'Assessing the role of emotions as mediators of consumer responses to advertising', *Journal of Consumer Research* 14 (December 1987): 404–20.

28. Marian Burke and Julie Edell, 'Ad reactions over time: Capturing changes in the real world', *Journal of Consumer Research* 13 (June 1986): 114–18.

29. Alex Benady, 'Advertisers' funny business', *Financial Times* (17 February 2004), http://news.ft.com/servlet/ContentServer?pagename=FT.com/StoryFT/FullStory&c=StoryFT&cid=1075982574327&p=1012571727085.

30. Kelman, 'Compliance, identification, and internalization', *op. cit.*: 51–60.

31. See Sharon E. Beatty and Lynn R. Kahle, 'Alternative hierarchies of the attitude–behaviour relationship: The impact of brand commitment and habit', *Journal of the Academy of Marketing Science* 16 (Summer 1988): 1–10.

32. J.R. Priester, D. Nayakankuppan, M.A. Fleming, and J. Godek, 'The A(2)SC(2) model: The influence of attitudes and attitude strength on consideration set choice', *Journal of Consumer Research* 30(4) (2004): 574–87.

33. Dan Roberts, 'Is the world falling out of love with U.S. brands?' *Financial Times* (30 December 2004), http://news.ft.com/cms/s/502f6994-59d5-11d9-ba09-00000e2511c8.html.

34. Leon Festinger, *A Theory of Cognitive Dissonance* (Stanford, CA: Stanford University Press, 1957).

35. Chester A. Insko and John Schopler, *Experimental Social Psychology* (New York: Academic Press, 1972).

36. Robert E. Knox and James A. Inkster, 'Postdecision dissonance at post time', *Journal of Personality and Social Psychology* 8(4) (1968): 319–23.

37. Daryl J. Bem, 'Self-Perception Theory', in Leonard Berkowitz (ed.), *Advances in Experimental Social Psychology* (New York: Academic Press, 1972): 1–62.

38. Jonathan L. Freedman and Scott C. Fraser, 'Compliance without pressure: the foot-in-the-door technique', *Journal of Personality and Social Psychology* 4 (August 1966): 195–202; for further consideration of possible explanations for this effect, see William DeJong, 'An examination of self-perception mediation of the foot-in-the-door effect', *Journal of Personality and Social Psychology* 37 (December

1979): 221–31; Alice M. Tybout, Brian Sternthal and Bobby J. Calder, 'Information availability as a determinant of multiple-request effectiveness', *Journal of Marketing Research* 20 (August 1988): 280–90.

39. David H. Furse, David W. Stewart and David L. Rados, 'Effects of foot-in-the-door, cash incentives and follow-ups on survey response', *Journal of Marketing Research* 18 (November 1981): 473–8; Carol A. Scott, 'The effects of trial and incentives on repeat purchase behavior', *Journal of Marketing Research* 13 (August 1976): 263–9.

40. Muzafer Sherif and Carl I. Hovland, *Social Judgment: Assimilation and Contrast Effects in Communication and Attitude Change* (New Haven, CT: Yale University Press, 1961).

41. 'Cola geweerd uit Belgische basisscholen', *De Telegraaf* (4 January 2005), http://www2.telegraaf.nl/buitenland/16939271/Cola_geweerd_uit_Belgische_basisscholen.html.

42. Andrew Jack, 'GSK launches a5m NiQuitin marketing drive', *Financial Times* (10 January 2005), http://news.ft.com/cms/s/042bcb56-62ad-11d9-8e5d-00000e2511c8.html; Peter John, 'Wetherspoon to stub out smoking in its 650 pubs', *Financial Times* (25 January 2005), http://news.ft.com/cms/s/2b37e7d8-6e75-11d9-a60a-00000e2511c8.html.

43. Edward Shiu, Louise M. Hassan, Jennifer A. Thomson and Deirdre Shaw, 'An Empirical Examination of the Extended Model of Goal-Directed Behaviour: Assessing the Role of Behavioural Desire', in S. Borghini, M.A. McGrath and C.C. Otnes (eds), *European Advances in Consumer Research* 8 (Duluth, MN: Association for Consumer Research, 2008): 66–79.

44. Joan Meyers-Levy and Brian Sternthal, 'A two-factor explanation of assimilation and contrast effects', *Journal of Marketing Research* 30 (August 1993): 359–68.

45. Fritz Heider, *The Psychology of Interpersonal Relations* (New York: Wiley, 1958).

46. Debra Z. Basil and Paul M. Herr, 'Attitudinal balance and cause-related marketing: An empirical application of balance theory', *Journal of Consumer Psychology* 16(4) (2006): 391–403.

47. William L. Wilkie, *Consumer Behavior* (New York: Wiley, 1986).

48. A number of criteria beyond the scope of this book are important in evaluating methods of attitude measurement, including such issues as reliability, validity and sensitivity. For an excellent treatment of attitude-scaling techniques, see David S. Aaker and George S. Day, *Marketing Research*, 4th edn (New York: Wiley, 1990).

49. Martin Fishbein, 'An investigation of the relationships between beliefs about an object and the attitude toward that object', *Human Relations* 16 (1983): 233–40.

50. Allan Wicker, 'Attitudes versus actions: The relationship of verbal and overt behavioral responses to attitude objects', *Journal of Social Issues* 25 (Autumn 1969): 65.

51. Laura Bird, 'Loved the ad. May (or may not) buy the product', *Wall Street Journal* (7 April 1994): B1 (2 pp.); 'Which half?' *The Economist* (8 June 1996): 80.

52. Icek Ajzen and Martin Fishbein, 'Attitude–behavior relations: A theoretical analysis and review of empirical research', *Psychological Bulletin* 84 (September 1977): 888–918.

53. Morris B. Holbrook and William J. Havlena, 'Assessing the real-to-artificial generalizability of multi-attribute attitude models in tests of new product designs', *Journal of*

Marketing Research 25 (February 1988): 25–35; Terence A. Shimp and Alican Kavas, 'The theory of reasoned action applied to coupon usage', *Journal of Consumer Research* 11 (December 1984): 795–809.

54. Richard P. Bagozzi, Hans Baumgartner and Youjae Yi, 'Coupon Usage and the Theory of Reasoned Action', in Holman and Solomon (eds), *Advances in Consumer Research* 18: 24–7; Edward F. McQuarrie, 'An alternative to purchase intentions: The role of prior behavior in consumer expenditure on computers', *Journal of the Market Research Society* 30 (October 1988): 407–37; Arch G. Woodside and William O. Bearden, 'Longitudinal Analysis of Consumer Attitude, Intention, and Behavior Toward Beer Brand Choice', in William D. Perrault Jr (ed.), *Advances in Consumer Research* 4 (Ann Arbor, MI: Association for Consumer Research, 1977): 349–56.

55. Michael J. Ryan and Edward H. Bonfield, 'The Fishbein Extended Model and consumer behavior', *Journal of Consumer Research* 2 (1975): 118–36.

56. Christine Gonzalez and Michaël Korchia, 'Attitudes Toward Seasonal Sales: An Exploratory Analysis of the Concept and its Antecedents', in K. Ekström and H. Brembeck (eds), *European Advances in Consumer Research* 7 (Duluth, MN: Association for Consumer Research, 2006): 485–94.

57. Anis Allagui and Jean-Francois Lemoine, 'Web Interface and Consumers' Buying Intention in e-Tailing: Results from and Online Experiment', in S. Borghini, M.A. McGrath and C.C. Otnes (eds), *European Advances in Consumer Research* 8 (Duluth, MN: Association for Consumer Research 2008): 24–30.

58. Blair H. Sheppard, Jon Hartwick and Paul R. Warshaw, 'The theory of reasoned action: A meta-analysis of past research with recommendations for modifications and future research', *Journal of Consumer Research* 15 (December 1988): 325–43.

59. Joseph A. Cote, James McCullough and Michael Reilly, 'Effects of unexpected situations on behavior–intention differences: A garbology analysis', *Journal of Consumer Research* 12 (September 1985): 188–94.

60. Russell H. Fazio, Martha C. Powell and Carol J. Williams, 'The role of attitude accessibility in the attitude-to-behavior process', *Journal of Consumer Research* 16 (December 1989): 280–8; Robert E. Smith and William R. Swinyard, 'Attitude–behavior consistency: The impact of product trial versus advertising', *Journal of Marketing Research* 20 (August 1983): 257–67.

61. Elizabeth Williamson, 'Free the carp? That's one way to get them out of the bathtub', *Wall Street Journal* (22 December 2000): A1.

62. Joseph A. Cote and Patriya S. Tansuhaj, 'Culture Bound Assumptions in Behavior Intention Models', in Thom Srull (ed.), *Advances in Consumer Research* 16 (Provo, UT: Association for Consumer Research, 1989): 105–9.

63. Joel B. Cohen and Americus Reed, 'A multiple pathway anchoring and adjustment (MPAA) model of attitude generation and recruitment', *Journal of Consumer Research* 33 (June 2006): 1–15.

64. Richard P. Bagozzi and Paul R. Warshaw, 'Trying to consume', *Journal of Consumer Research* 17 (September 1990): 127–40.

65. In terms of the relative importance of structural conditions (equipment) and attitudes in determining recycling behaviour, see also Folke Ölander and John Thøgersen, 'The A-B-C of Recycling', in K. Ekström and H. Brembeck (eds), *European Advances in Consumer Research* 7 (Duluth, MN: Association for Consumer Research, 2006): 297–307.

66. Matthew Greenwald and John P. Katosh, 'How to track changes in attitudes', *American Demographics* (August 1987): 46.

67. For a good introduction to various classical perspectives on human communication, see R. Aubrey Fischer, *Perspectives on Human Communication* (New York: Macmillan, 1978).

68. See for example Umberto Eco, *The Role of the Reader*, (Bloomington: Indiana University Press, 1979).

69. See for example Linda M. Scott, 'The Bridge from Text to Mind: Adapting Reader-Response Theory to Consumer Research', *Journal of Consumer Research* 21 (December 1994): 461–80.

70. David G. Mick and Claus Buhl, 'A meaning-based model of advertisement experiences', *Journal of Consumer Research* 19 (December 1992): 317–38.

71. First proposed by Elihu Katz, 'Mass communication research and the study of popular culture: An editorial note on a possible future for this journal', *Studies in Public Communication* 2 (1959): 1–6. For a more recent discussion of this approach, see Stephanie O'Donohoe, 'Advertising uses and gratifications', *European Journal of Marketing* 28(8/9) (1994): 52–75.

72. Mark Ritson and Richard Elliott, 'The social uses of advertising: an ethnographic study of adolescent advertising audiences', *Journal of Consumer Research* 25(3) (December 1999): 260–78.

73. Carl I. Hovland and W. Weiss, 'The influence of source credibility on communication effectiveness', *Public Opinion Quarterly* 15 (1952): 635–50.

74. Herbert Kelman, 'Processes of opinion change', *Public Opinion Quarterly* 25 (Spring 1961): 57–78; Susan M. Petroshuis and Kenneth E. Crocker, 'An empirical analysis of spokesperson characteristics on advertisement and product evaluations', *Journal of the Academy of Marketing Science* 17 (Summer 1989): 217–26.

75. S. Ratneshwar and Shelly Chaiken, 'Comprehension's role in persuasion: The case of its moderating effect on the persuasive impact of source cues', *Journal of Consumer Research* 18 (June 1991): 52–62.

76. Jagdish Agrawal and Wagner A. Kamakura, 'The economic worth of celebrity endorsers: An event study analysis', *Journal of Marketing* 59 (July 1995): 56–62.

77. Kruti Trivedi, 'Great-grandson of artist Renoir uses his name for marketing blitz', *The Wall Street Journal Interactive Edition* (2 September 1999).

78. Judith Graham, 'Sponsors line up for rockin' role', *Advertising Age* (11 December 1989): 50.

79. Michael A. Kamins, 'Celebrity and noncelebrity advertising in a two-sided context', *Journal of Advertising Research* 29 (June–July 1989): 34; Joseph M. Kamen, A.C. Azhari and J.R. Kragh, 'What a spokesman does for a sponsor', *Journal of Advertising Research* 15(2) (1975): 17–24; Lynn Langmeyer and Mary Walker, 'A First Step to Identify the Meaning in Celebrity Endorsers', in Rebecca H. Holman and Michael R. Solomon (eds), *Advances in Consumer Research* 18 (Provo, UT: Association for Consumer Research, 1991): 364–71.

80. Vranica and Walker, 'Tiger Woods switches watches', *op. cit.*

81. Joseph Pereira, 'Reebok serves up tennis star in new ads', *Wall Street Journal* (18 January 2001): B2.

82. Grant McCracken, 'Who is the celebrity endorser? Cultural foundations of the endorsement process', *Journal of Consumer Research* 16(3) (December 1989): 310–21.

83. Choi Hae Won, 'Bill Gates, style icon? Oh yes – in Korea, where geek is chic', *Wall Street Journal* (4 January 2001): A1.

84. Marie Okabe, 'Fading yen for foreign stars in ads', *Singapore Straits Times* (1986).

85. Erin White, 'Found in translation? Stars who make ads overseas recoil at internet exposure: Mr DiCaprio fights back', *The Wall Street Journal* (20 September 2004): B1.

86. This section is based upon a discussion in Michael R. Solomon, *Conquering Consumerspace: Marketing Strategies for a Branded World* (New York: AMACOM, 2003); see also David Lewis and Darren Bridger, *The Soul of the New Consumer: Authenticity – What We Buy and Why in the New Economy* (London: Nicholas Brealey Publishing, 2000).

87. Jeff Neff, 'Pressure points at IPG', *Advertising Age* (December 2001): 4.

88. Wayne Friedman, 'Street marketing hits the internet', *Advertising Age* (May 2000): 32; Erin White, 'Online buzz helps album skyrocket to top of charts', *The Wall Street Journal Interactive Edition* (5 October 1999): available from www.wsj.com.

89. H. Zielske, 'Does day-after recall penalize "feeling" ads?' *Journal of Advertising Research* 22 (1982): 19–22.

90. Allessandra Galloni, 'Lee's cheeky ads are central to new European campaign', *Wall Street Journal Online* (15 March 2002).

91. Michael S. LaTour and Tony L. Henthorne, 'Ethical judgments of sexual appeals in print advertising', *Journal of Advertising* 23(3) (September 1994): 81–90.

92. Rebecca Gardyn, 'Where's the lovin'?' *American Demographics* (February 2001): 10.

93. Thomas J. Madden, 'Humor in Advertising: An Experimental Analysis' (working paper, no. 83–27, University of Massachusetts, 1984); Thomas J. Madden and Marc G. Weinberger, 'The effects of humor on attention in magazine advertising', *Journal of Advertising* 11(3) (1982): 8–14; Weinberger and Spotts, 'Humor in U.S. versus U.K. TV commercials;' see also Ashesh Mukherjee and Laurette Dubé, 'The Use of Humor in Threat-Related Advertising', unpublished manuscript, McGill University, June 2002.

94. David Gardner, 'The distraction hypothesis in marketing', *Journal of Advertising Research* 10 (1970): 25–30.

95. Stuart Elliott, 'Marketing with double entendres', *NYT Online* (4 October 2004).

96. Lynette S. Unger and James M. Stearns, 'The Use of Fear and Guilt Messages in Television Advertising: Issues and Evidence', in Patrick E. Murphy *et al.* (eds), *1983 AMA Educators' Proceedings* (Chicago: American Marketing Association, 1983): 16–20.

97. Imene Becheur, Hayan Dib, Dwight Merunka and Pierre Valette-Florence, 'Emotions of Fear, Guilt or Shame in Anti-Alcohol Messages: Measuring Direct Effects on Persuasion and the Moderating Role of Sensation Seeking', in S. Borghini, M.A. McGrath and C.C. Otnes (eds), *European Advances in Consumer Research* 8 (Duluth, MN: Association for Consumer Research, 2008): 99–108.

98. Michael L. Ray and William L. Wilkie, 'Fear: The potential of an appeal neglected by marketing', *Journal of Marketing* 34 (1970) 1: 54–62.

99. Ibid.

100. Brian Sternthal and C. Samuel Craig, 'Fear appeals: Revisited and revised', *Journal of Consumer Research* 1 (December 1974): 22–34.

101. Prof. Herbert J. Rotfeld, Auburn University, personal communication, 9 December 1997; Herbert J. Rotfeld, 'Fear appeals and persuasion: assumptions and errors in advertising research', *Current Issues and Research in Advertising* 11(1) (1988): 21–40; Michael S. LaTour and Herbert J. Rotfeld, 'There are threats and (maybe) fear-caused arousal: Theory and confusions of appeals to fear and fear arousal itself', *Journal of Advertising* 26(3) (Fall 1997): 45–59.

102. For a classical discussion of the importance of metaphors in our culture, see George Lakoff and Mark Johnson, *Metaphors We Live By* (University of Chicago Press, 1980).

103. Richard E. Petty, John T. Cacioppo and David Schumann, 'Central and peripheral routes to advertising effectiveness: The moderating role of involvement' *Journal of Consumer Research* 10(2) (1983): 135–46.

104. Jerry C. Olson, Daniel R. Toy and Philip A. Dover, 'Do cognitive responses mediate the effects of advertising content on cognitive structure?' *Journal of Consumer Research* 9(3) (1982): 245–62.

105. Julie A. Edell and Andrew A. Mitchell, 'An Information Processing Approach to Cognitive Responses,' in S.C. Jain (ed.), *Research Frontiers in Marketing: Dialogues and Directions* (Chicago: American Marketing Association, 1978).

106. See Mary Jo Bitner and Carl Obermiller, 'The Elaboration Likelihood Model: Limitations and Extensions in Marketing', in Elizabeth C. Hirschman and Morris B. Holbrook (eds), *Advances in Consumer Research* 12 (Provo, UT: Association for Consumer Research, 1985): 420–5; Meryl P. Gardner, 'Does attitude toward the ad affect brand attitude under a brand evaluation set?', *Journal of Marketing Research* 22 (1985): 192–98; C.W. Park and S.M. Young, 'Consumer response to television commercials: The impact of involvement and background music on brand attitude formation', *Journal of Marketing Research* 23 (1986): 11–24; Petty, Cacioppo and Schumann, 'Central and peripheral routes to advertising effectiveness'; for a discussion of how different kinds of involvement interact with the ELM, see Robin A. Higie, Lawrence F. Feick and Linda L. Price, 'The Importance of Peripheral Cues in Attitude Formation for Enduring and Task-Involved Individuals', in Holman and Solomon (eds), *Advances in Consumer Research* 18: 187–93.

107. For a recent extension of this technique, see Yanliu Huang and J. Wesley Hutchinson, 'Counting every thought: Implicit measures of cognitive responses to advertising', *Journal of Consumer Research* 35 (June 2008): 98–118.

108. J. Craig Andrews and Terence A. Shimp, 'Effects of involvement, argument strength, and source characteristics on central and peripheral processing in advertising', *Psychology and Marketing* 7 (Fall 1990): 195–214.

109. Richard E. Petty, John T. Cacioppo, Constantine Sedikides and Alan J. Strathman, 'Affect and persuasion: a contemporary perspective', *American Behavioral Scientist* 31(3) (1988): 355–71.

311

9

Individual decision-making

Daniel is really frustrated. There's no way he is going to keep on watching TV on his small portable, out-of-date black-and-white set. It was bad enough trying to see the graphics of the possible answers to questions on *Who Wants to Be a Millionaire?* The final straw was when he could barely tell Spain from Germany during the UEFA Cup final (June 2008). When he finally went next door – in total exasperation – to watch the second half on Lily's new HDTV, he really realized what he had been missing out on. Budget or not, it was time to act: a man has to get his priorities right, especially as he felt he was miles behind all his friends in getting the latest digital television technology.

Where to start looking? The Web, naturally. Daniel does a quick search on YouTube (**http://www.youtube.com**) for HDTVs, and then checks out an independent online consumer guide (**http://www.hdtvorg.co.uk/**) – there's no point in slogging around the high street shops at this early stage. After narrowing down his options, he ventures out to look at the possible HDTVs which he has identified. He knows he will get some good advice at the small specialist high street retailer about the merits of particular brands so he decides to start there; and then he can hunt around for the best buy by visiting a couple of comparison-shopping Websites such as Kelkoo and PriceRunner (**http://www.pricerunner.co.uk/**). He reckons he'll probably find the most affordable models at one of the out-of-town 'big shed' retailers. At the local specialist retailer, Daniel goes straight to the television section, where he can browse quietly. Eventually, one of the sales assistants asks him if he wants any help. Daniel asks some questions, and gets some useful advice and tips about what features to think about when making his purchase; and one or two recommendations about current good buys. Before leaving the shop, Daniel asks the salesperson to write down the model names and numbers (and prices) for him. At this point Daniel does some more searching online, this time visiting the manufacturers' and brand Websites in order to compare the respective features of the different models more carefully. Daniel then visits one of the out-of-town 'big shed' retailers. When he gets there he heads for the Video Zone at the back – barely noticing the rows of toasters, microwave ovens and stereos on his way. Within minutes, a smiling salesperson in a cheap suit accosts him. Daniel reckons that these guys don't know what they're talking about, and they're just out to make a sale, no matter what. Anyway, he has already collected all the information he needs for making his decision.

Daniel starts to look at the new HDTVs. He knew his friend Christopher had a set by Prime Wave that he really liked, and his fellow hockey player, Hannah, had warned him to stay away from the Kamashita. Although Daniel finds a Prime Wave model loaded with features such as a sleep timer, on-screen programming menu, cable compatible tuner, and picture-in-picture, he chooses the less-expensive Precision 2000X because it has one feature that really catches his fancy: stereo broadcast reception; and it had been highly recommended by the high street specialist retailer.

Later that day, Daniel is a happy man as he sits in his armchair, watching Wimbledon. If he's going to be a couch potato, he's going to do it in style . . . next up, the Tour de France, followed by the motor racing.

CONSUMERS AS PROBLEM-SOLVERS

A consumer purchase is a response to a problem, which in Daniel's case is the perceived need for a new TV, partly because his existing TV is too old; and partly because he feels he has fallen behind with the trends. Certainly, a third of all households within the EU15 own digital TVs, with the UK (60 per cent) and Ireland (40 per cent) far above the average, so Daniel is probably right to feel that he has not kept up with the Joneses. Central and Eastern Europe, in comparison to Western Europe, have much lower rates of adoption of digital television (see Figure 9.1).[1]

Figure 9.1 Proportion of households with digital TV

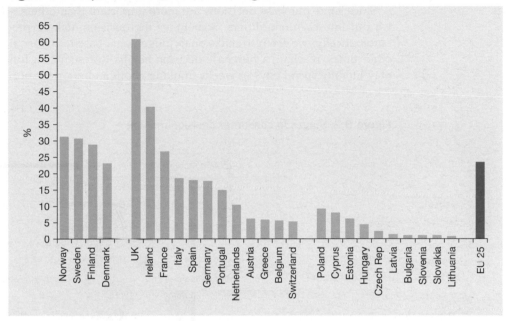

Data Source: nVision/Future Foundation (2006), Media Consumption in the EU 25 – How new media is affecting television, radio and newspapers, London.

Source: Lutz Stobbe EuP Preparatory Studies 'Televisions' (Lot 5) Final Report on Task 3 'Consumer Behaviour and Local Infrastructure' (TREN/D1/40 lot 5-2005), Compiled by Deutsche Umwelthilfe and Fraunhofer IZM, Contractor: Fraunhofer Institute for Reliability and Microintegration, IZM, Berlin 2 August 2007 p. 18.

Daniel's situation is similar to that encountered by consumers virtually every day of their lives (even deciding not to make any decision is still a decision). Daniel realizes that he wants to make a purchase, and he goes through a series of steps in order to
▶ make it. These steps can be described as: (1) problem recognition, (2) **information search**, (3) evaluation of alternatives, and (4) product choice. After the decision is made, the

Two of the most powerful global brands for 2008.

quality of that decision affects the final step in the process, when learning occurs based on how well the choice worked out. This learning process influences the likelihood that the same choice will be made the next time the need for a similar decision occurs. There is also evidence that suggests that 'more optimistic expectations of future goal pursuit . . . have a greater impact on immediate choices'.[2]

Figure 9.2 provides an overview of this decision-making process (and Professor Suzanne C. Beckmann offers a critique of this five stage model below). This chapter begins by considering various approaches consumers use when faced with a purchase decision. We then focus on three of the steps in the decision process: how we recognize the problem, or need for a product; how we search for information about product choices; and the ways in which we evaluate alternatives to arrive at a decision. Chapter 3 considered influences in the actual purchase situation, as well as the person's satisfaction with the decision.

Since some purchase decisions are more important than others, the amount of effort we put into each one differs. Sometimes the decision-making process is done almost automatically; we seem to make snap judgements based on very little information. At other times, reaching a purchase decision begins to resemble a full-time job. A person may literally spend days or weeks thinking about an important purchase such as a new

Figure 9.2 Stages in consumer decision-making

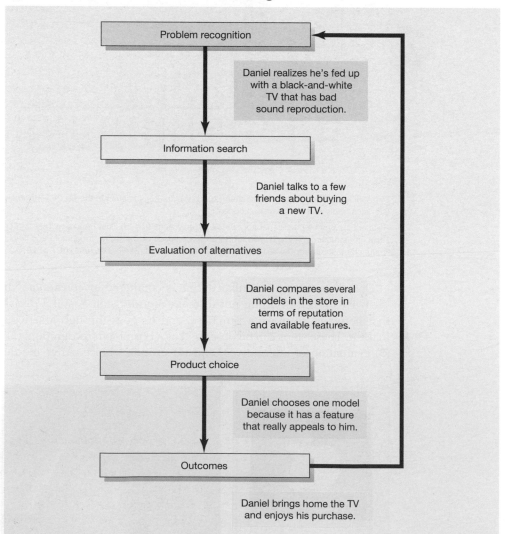

home, even to the point of obsession. This intensive decision-making process becomes even more complicated in today's environment where we have so many options from which to choose. Ironically, for many modern consumers one of the biggest problems they face is not having *too few* choices but having *too many*. We describe this profusion

▶ of options as **consumer hyperchoice**, a condition where the large number of available options forces us to make repeated choices that may drain psychological energy while decreasing our abilities to make smart decisions.[3]

Perspectives on decision-making

▶ Traditionally, consumer researchers have approached decision-making from a **rational perspective**. In this view, people calmly and carefully integrate as much information as possible with what they already know about a product, painstakingly weighing the pluses and minuses of each alternative, and arriving at a satisfactory decision. This traditional decision-making perspective incorporates the *economics of information* approach to the search process; it assumes that consumers will gather as much data as they need in order to make an informed decision. Consumers form expectations of the value of additional information and continue to search to the extent that the rewards of doing so (what economists call the *utility*) exceed the costs. This utilitarian assumption also implies that the person will collect the most valuable units of information first. They will absorb additional pieces only to the extent that they think they will add to what they already know.[4] In other words, people will put themselves out to collect as much information as possible, as long as the process of gathering it is not too onerous or time-consuming.[5]

This process implies that steps in decision-making should be carefully studied by marketing managers in order to understand how consumers obtain information, how consumers form beliefs, and what criteria consumers use to make product or service choices. Companies can then develop products or services that emphasize the appropriate attributes, and marketers can tailor promotional strategies to deliver the types of information consumers are most likely to desire, via the best channels, and in the most effective formats.[6]

How valid is this perspective? Professor Beckmann acknowledges the value and limitations of this perspective, and illustrates some of the complexities involved in consumer decision-making in her commentary (see below). While consumers do follow these decision-making steps when making some purchases, such a rational process does not accurately portray many of our purchase decisions.[7] Consumers simply do not go through this elaborate sequence every time they buy something. If they did, their entire lives would be spent making such decisions, leaving them with very little time to enjoy the things they eventually decide to buy. Some of our consumption behaviours simply don't seem 'rational' because they don't always seem to serve a logical purpose (e.g. people who break the law to collect the eggs of the osprey (a rare bird) in Scotland even though the eggs have no (legal) monetary value).[8] Other purchase behaviours are undertaken with virtually no advance planning at all (e.g. impulsively grabbing that tempting bar of chocolate at the checkout till while waiting to pay for groceries in the supermarket). Still other actions are actually contrary to those predicted by rational models. For example,

▶ **purchase momentum** occurs when these initial impulses actually increase the likelihood that we will buy even more (instead of less as our needs are satisfied), almost as if we get caught up in a spending spree.[9]

Researchers are now beginning to realize that decision-makers actually possess a repertoire of strategies. A consumer evaluates the effort required to make a particular choice, and then they choose a strategy best suited to the level of effort required. This sequence of events is known as *constructive processing*. Rather than using a big stick to kill an ant, consumers tailor their degree of cognitive 'effort' to the task at hand.[10] When the task requires a well-thought-out, rational approach, we'll invest the brainpower required for the decision. Otherwise, we look for short cuts or fall back upon learned responses that 'automate' these choices. Researchers are also beginning to understand the role that controlling the information flow can have on consumers' decisions, as increased control leads to increased performance. These new insights promise to be particularly important in the new online environments where 'marketers have the potential to integrate interactive communication systems back into mass communication'[11] where controlling the information flow can particularly influence the quality of consumers' decisions, memory, knowledge and confidence.[12] Research on information structure (the amount of information in a choice set) is also relevant in the new electronic marketplaces, where consumers are regularly faced with information overload when making decisions.[13] One study suggests that: 'consumers adapt their acquisition of information in response to changes in information structure. When a choice set contains more information per element, fewer acquisitions are made, more time is spent per acquisition, and customers are more selective in their information acquisition.'[14] Other recent research has identified how consumers integrate the Internet into other product information sources such as retailers and media during their search for information. Car buyers, for instance, often use the manufacturer and dealer Internet sources to substitute for more traditional information search via visits to car dealerships.[15] Daniel also used the Internet for informal information gathering, and then for price searching when looking for his new HDTV, thus integrating the Net into his search activities.

This ad for the US Postal Service presents a problem, illustrates the decision-making process and offers a solution.

Some decisions are made under conditions of low involvement, as discussed in Chapter 3. In many of these situations, our decision is a learned response to environmental cues (see Chapter 7), as when we decide to buy something on impulse that is being promoted as a special offer in a shop. A concentration on these types of decisions ▶ can be described as the **behavioural influence perspective**. Under these circumstances, managers must concentrate on assessing the characteristics of the environment that influence members of a target market,[16] such as the design of a retail outlet or whether a package is enticing.

In other cases, consumers are highly involved in a decision, but still we cannot explain their selections entirely rationally. For example, the traditional approach is hard pressed to explain a person's choice of art, music, or even a partner. In these cases, no single ▶ quality may be the determining factor. Instead, the **experiential perspective** stresses the *Gestalt*, or totality (see Chapter 4), of the product or service.[17] Marketers in these areas focus on measuring consumers' affective responses to products or services and developing offerings that elicit appropriate subjective reactions.

Consumer behaviour as I see it . . .

Individual decision-making

Professor Suzanne C. Beckmann
Copenhagen Business School, Denmark

The five stage-model of decision-making (Figure 9.2) is the core of the classic view on consumer behaviour, based on the idea that a consumer is an information processing 'machine'. Although certainly helpful in structuring this sequence by putting the various events in boxes connected by arrows, the model is not really useful in understanding real life consumer decisions. For one simple reason: neither problem recognition nor information search nor evaluation of alternatives nor product choice take place in isolation from each other and without the impact of any external influences. Human beings are social beings, and the number of 'problems' that are truly individual are quite few and far between, and are mostly related to biological needs. It is obvious that consumers' interaction with others – family, friends, peers – will to a large extent determine where to search for information, which features to look for when evaluating alternatives, and what ultimately to buy. Hence, much of the consumer research at our department uses the classical model as a background, but not as a driver, for study designs.

There is for instance the complexity issue. How do consumers decide between products in a world full of brands, when confronted with so much information? Lots of information does not necessarily mean that choices are easier or quicker to make for the individual consumer. Take the case of grocery shopping for example. And how do consumers incorporate other aspects such as health, pleasure or status into their decision-making process? One group at our department works with 'supra-complex' decision-making in the food market, suggesting that the construct of perceived complexity will help us in better understanding how consumers actually make use of informational cues. And why is health and nutrition information more often than not overlooked? We distinguish between four levels of perceived complexity, with price being the least complex of all the indicators. The Danish label 'Varefakta' is an example of the next level of complexity, because it contains core objective information on product content, but it is not a quality label. The third situation relates to product labels provided by producers such as 'light' or 'natural' that are used by consumers as a surrogate when they are evaluating products. And the highest level of complexity is reached when all these other informational cues are supplemented by labels concerning fair trade, ecology or energy saving. Admittedly, it is the individual consumer who perceives complexity in decision-making but it is the environment, the interaction with others and societal requirements that increase this complexity.

Consumer behaviour as I see it . . . (continued)

Consumers are not only consumers but have many different roles in daily life vis-à-vis other people. And these roles are played out in different situations. How they are played out depends to a large degree on personality, values and beliefs. Therefore, another group at our department has developed 'CUBEicle thinking' = customer universe based execution for designing marketing strategies. The core idea is to know the customer type combined with a certain role and a certain situation or context and to plot this into a Necker 3-D cube-type graphic. Consider air transportation as an example: a woman arriving at the airport with her briefcase on the way to a business meeting has different needs and expectations about what the airport should offer her whilst waiting for the departure of her flight compared with the same woman arriving a few days later with her two small children and on her way on holiday with her young family. The challenge of this approach is to determine exactly the content of the three sides of the cube which takes account of all the individual and social determinants of decision-making.

A third example of our research is our studies on brand relevance. We assume that there are situations where brands are less relevant than in others. One important dimension here is product category, i.e. not all categories necessarily have the same brand relevance for all consumers. One of our findings is that brand loyalty competes with store loyalty in out-of-stock situations: certain consumers will switch supermarket when their preferred brand in a category is not available, while others will be prepared to substitute with another brand. Yet, this behaviour is dependent on category, since the propensity for store switching is greater, for instance, in the case of shampoo than it is for marinated herring. While the decision to switch or not to switch is made individually at the point of purchase, the drivers for this decision could very well be other people within the decision-making unit: 'I know that my husband doesn't care which brand of marinated herring I buy' versus 'My daughter will be furious if I bring home the wrong shampoo.'

Types of consumer decisions

One helpful way to characterize the decision-making process is to consider the amount of effort that goes into the decision each time we must make it. Consumer researchers have found it convenient to think in terms of a continuum, which is anchored at one end by habitual decision-making and at the other extreme by extended problem-solving. Many decisions fall somewhere in the middle and so we characterize these as limited problem solving. This continuum is presented in Figure 9.3.

Figure 9.3 A continuum of buying decision behaviour

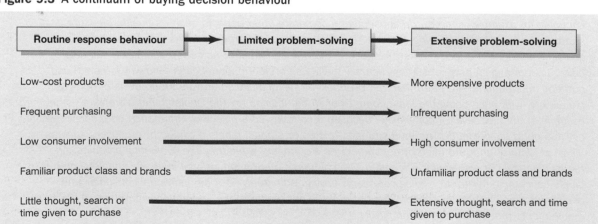

Table 9.1 Characteristics of limited vs. extended problem-solving

	Limited problem-solving	Extended problem-solving
Motivation	Low risk and involvement	High risk and involvement
Information search	Little search Information processed passively In-store decision likely	Extensive search Information processed actively Multiple sources consulted prior to store visits
Alternative evaluation	Weakly held beliefs Only most prominent criteria used Alternatives perceived as basically similar Non-compensatory strategy used	Strongly held beliefs Many criteria used Significant differences perceived among alternatives Compensatory strategy used
Purchase	Limited shopping time; may prefer self-service Choice often influenced by store displays	Many outlets visited if necessary Communication with store personnel often desirable

Extended problem-solving

▶ Decisions involving **extended problem-solving** correspond most closely to the traditional decision-making perspective. As indicated in Table 9.1, we usually initiate this careful process when the decision we have to make relates to our self-concept (see Chapter 5), and we feel that the outcome may be risky in some way. In that case we try to collect as much information as possible, both from our memory (internal search) and from outside sources such as Google or YouTube (as Daniel did when looking for information about HDTVs) (external search). Based on the importance of the decision, we carefully evaluate each product alternative, often considering the attributes of one brand at a time and seeing how each brand's attributes shape up to some set of desired characteristics or outcomes that we hope to achieve through our choice.

Limited problem-solving

▶ **Limited problem-solving** is usually more straightforward and simple. In this case we are not nearly as motivated to search for information or to evaluate each alternative rigorously. Instead, we are likely to use simple *decision rules* to choose among alternatives. These cognitive short cuts (more about these later) enable consumers to fall back on general guidelines, instead of having to start from scratch every time we need to make a decision.

Habitual decision-making

Both extended and limited problem-solving modes involve some degree of information search and deliberation, though they vary in the degree to which we engage in these

▶ activities. At the other end of the choice continuum, however, lies **habitual decision-making**; choices that we make with little or no conscious effort. Many purchase decisions are so routinized that we may not realize we have made them until we look in our shopping trolleys. We make these choices with minimal effort and without conscious control; researchers call this process *automaticity*.[18]

While this kind of thoughtless activity may seem dangerous at worst or stupid at best, it is actually quite efficient in many cases. The development of habitual, repetitive behaviour allows consumers to minimize the time and energy spent on mundane purchase decisions. On the other hand, habitual decision-making poses a problem when a marketer tries to introduce a new way of doing an old task. In this case consumers must be convinced to 'unfreeze' their former habit and replace it with a new one – perhaps by using digital banking rather than the local branch of the bank; or using an ATM machine instead of a live bank teller; or switching to self-service petrol pumps instead of being served by an attendant.

Steps in the decision-making process

Daniel did not suddenly wake up and crave a new HDTV. He went through several steps between feeling the need for a better quality television picture for watching sporting fixtures, and actually purchasing a new television. Let's review the basic steps in this process.

PROBLEM RECOGNITION

▶ **Problem recognition** occurs whenever we see a significant difference between our current state of affairs and some desired or ideal state. We realize that to get from here to there we need to solve a problem, which may be large or small, simple or complex. A person who unexpectedly runs out of petrol on the motorway or autobahn has a problem, as does the person who becomes dissatisfied with the image of their car, even though there may be nothing mechanically wrong with it. Although the quality of Daniel's TV had not changed, for example, his *standard of comparison* has altered, and he was confronted with a desire he did not have prior to watching his friend Lily's HDTV.

Problem creation

Figure 9.4 shows that a problem can arise in one of two ways. As in the case of the person who runs out of petrol, the quality of the consumer's *actual state* can sometimes move downwards or decrease (*need recognition*). On the other hand, as in the case of the person who craves a high performance car, the consumer's *ideal state* can move upward (*opportunity recognition*). Either way, a gulf occurs between the actual state and the ideal state.[19] In Daniel's case, a problem was perceived as a result of opportunity recognition; his ideal state in terms of the television reception and viewing quality that he wanted.

Need recognition can occur in several ways. A person's actual state can decrease if they run out of a product, or if they buy a product that doesn't adequately satisfy their needs, or if they realize that they have a new need or desire (e.g. buying a house

Figure 9.4 Problem recognition: shifts in actual or ideal states

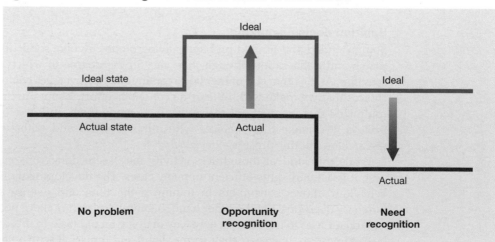

| No problem | Opportunity recognition | Need recognition |

can set off an avalanche of other choices, because many new things will be needed to furnish the house – assuming that there's any money left over). In contrast, opportunity recognition often occurs when we're exposed to different or better-quality products. This happens because our circumstances have somehow changed, as when an individual goes to university or gets a new job. As our frame of reference shifts, we make purchases to adapt to the new environment.

Marketers' role in problem creation

While problem recognition can and does occur naturally, this process is often spurred by marketing efforts. In some cases, marketers attempt to create *primary demand*, where consumers are encouraged to use a product or service regardless of the brand they choose. Such needs are often encouraged in the early stages of a product's life cycle, as, for example, when microwave ovens were first introduced. *Secondary demand*, where consumers are prompted to prefer a specific brand instead of others, can occur only if primary demand already exists. At this point, marketers must convince consumers that a problem can be best solved by choosing their brand over others in the same category.

INFORMATION SEARCH

Once a problem has been recognized, consumers need adequate information to resolve it. Information search is the process by which the consumer surveys their environment for appropriate data to make a reasonable decision. In this section we will review some of the factors this search involves.

Types of information search

A consumer may recognize a need and then search the marketplace for specific information (a process called *pre-purchase search*). On the other hand, many consumers, especially veteran shoppers, enjoy browsing just for the fun of it, or because they like to stay up-to-date on what's happening in the marketplace. Those shopaholics are engaging in *ongoing search*.[20] Some differences between these two search modes are described in Table 9.2.

Table 9.2 A framework for consumer information search

	Pre-purchase search	Ongoing search
Determinants	Involvement in the purchase Market environment Situational factors	Involvement with the product Market environment Situational factors
Motives	Making better purchase decisions	Building a bank of information for future use Experiencing fun and pleasure
Outcomes	Increased product and market knowledge Better purchase decisions Increased satisfaction with the purchase outcome	Increased product and market knowledge, leading to • future buying efficiencies • personal influences Increased impulse buying Increased satisfaction from search and other outcomes

Source: Peter H. Bloch, Daniel L. Sherrell and Nancy M. Ridgway, 'Consumer search: An extended framework', *Journal of Consumer Research* 13 (June 1986): 120. Reprinted with permission by The University of Chicago Press.

Internal vs. external search

Information sources can be roughly broken down into two kinds: internal and external. As a result of prior experience and simply living in a consumer culture, each of us often has some degree of knowledge about many products already in our memory. When confronted with a purchase decision, we may engage in *internal search* by scanning our own memory bank to assemble information about different product alternatives (see Chapter 7). Usually, though, even the most market-aware of us needs to supplement this knowledge with external search, by which we obtain the information from advertisements, friends, or just plain people-watching. A study in Finland recently demonstrated how what our neighbours buy impacts our own decision making. The researchers discovered that when one of a person's ten nearest neighbours bought a car, the odds that they would buy a car of the same make during the next week and a half jumped 86 per cent. The effect was even stronger for used car purchases – low-income families and those who lived in rural areas were more likely to be influenced by their neighbours than were wealthy Helsinki residents. They explained this finding in terms of the information value of these choices – because used cars are less reliable, a neighbour's endorsement of one kind over others might carry more weight.[21]

Deliberate vs. 'accidental' search

Our existing knowledge of a product may be the result of *directed learning*: on a previous occasion we might already have searched for relevant information or experienced some of the alternatives. A parent who bought a birthday cake for one child last month, for example, probably has a good idea of the best kind to buy for another child this month.

Alternatively, we may acquire information in a more passive manner. Even though a product may not be of direct interest to us right now, exposure to advertising, packaging, sales promotion and viral marketing activities may result in *incidental learning*. Mere exposure over time to conditioned stimuli and observations of others results in the learning of much material that may not be needed for some time, if ever. For marketers, this is one of the benefits of steady, 'low-dose' advertising, as they establish and maintain product associations until the time we need them.[22]

This ad for Arm & Hammer demonstrates the strategy of identifying new problems an existing product can solve.

Church & Dwight Co., Inc.

In some cases, we may be so expert about a product category (or at least believe we are) that no additional search is undertaken. Frequently, however, our own existing state of knowledge is not sufficient to make an adequate decision, and we must look elsewhere for more information. The sources we consult for advice vary. They may be impersonal and marketer-dominated sources, such as retailers, retailers' websites and catalogues; they may be friends and family members; or they may be unbiased third parties such as *Which?* magazine or other consumer reports which are published in a number of European countries.[23]

Marketing opportunity

Tangled web

Of course, Internet search engines (especially Google) are huge players now when it comes to searching. Yahoo found that consumers spend 10 per cent more for televisions and digital cameras they buy in stores when they research these purchases online first using a search engine, and people who use these engines consult twice as many information sources as those who don't.[24]

When we search online for product information, we're a perfect target for advertisers because we're declaring our desire to make a purchase. Recognizing this, many companies pay **search engines** to show ads to users who have searched for their brand names. However, when DoubleClick (an online marketing company) looked closely at what people search for, it found that searches including brand names account for a small share of our queries. Instead, most pre-purchase searches use only generic terms, like 'hard drive'. Consumers tend to make these searches early on, and then conduct a small flurry of brand-name queries right

before buying.[25] The Internet is increasingly integrated into overall search strategies.[26] Hence Daniel's iteration between online and offline sources of information as he assessed the variety of choices available to him before purchasing his new HDTV. There is also evidence of migration from printed sources of objective information to online sources of objective information.[27] 'However, possibly because friends/relatives convey different types of information, the Internet does not appear to have a significant effect on the use of friends/relatives as a source [of information].'[28] However, Nielsen's latest research suggests where friends and relatives are important is in suggesting Websites to try 'recommendations from fellow consumers – whether they are people they know or fellow online shoppers – play an enormous role in the decision-making process. The explosion in Consumer Generated Media over the last year means that this reliance on word of mouth, over other forms of referral, looks set to increase.'[29]

The economics of information

The traditional decision-making perspective incorporates the *economics-of-information* approach to the search process: it assumes that consumers will gather as much data as needed to make an informed decision. Consumers form expectations of the value of additional information and continue to search to the extent that the rewards of doing so (what economists call the *utility*) exceed the costs. This utilitarian assumption also implies that the most valuable units of information will be collected first. Additional pieces will be absorbed only to the extent that they are seen to be adding to what is already known.[30] In other words, people will put themselves out to collect as much information as possible, as long as the process of gathering it is not too onerous or time-consuming, as we saw with Daniel's search for information about HDTVs.[31]

Do consumers always search rationally?

This assumption of rational search is not always supported. As we've seen, consumers don't necessarily engage in a rational search process where they carefully identify every alternative before choosing one they prefer. The amount of external search that we do for most products is surprisingly small, even when we would benefit by having more information. For example, lower-income shoppers, who have more to lose by making a bad purchase, actually search *less* prior to buying than more affluent people do.[32]

Like Daniel, some consumers typically visit only one or two stores and often don't seek out unbiased information sources prior to making a purchase decision, especially when there is little time to do so.[33] This pattern is especially prevalent for decisions regarding durable goods such as appliances or cars, even when these products represent significant investments. There is also some evidence that even having information available on the package does not necessarily mean that consumers make use of it. Environmentally friendly products in Finland are beginning to carry the Nordic Environmental Label to assist consumers in their choice of environmentally safe products. In a study which asked Finnish consumers to evaluate detergent and batteries choices, little use was made of and little trust was placed in the 'green label' on the packages, in spite of the positive attitudes that Finnish citizens have towards the environment. The results suggest that marketers have a long way to go in order to provide clear, easily comprehensible and unbiased information regarding 'green' products.[34]

This tendency to avoid external search is less prevalent when consumers consider the purchase of symbolic items, such as clothing. In those cases, not surprisingly, people tend to do a fair amount of external search, although most of it involves seeking the opinions of peers.[35] Although the stakes may be lower financially, people may see these self-expressive decisions as having dire social consequences if they make the wrong choice. The level of perceived risk, a concept to be discussed shortly, is high.

In addition, consumers are often observed to engage in *brand switching*, even if their current brand satisfies their needs.[36] Sometimes, it seems that people simply like to try new things – we crave variety as a form of stimulation or to reduce boredom. **Variety seeking**, the desire to choose new alternatives over more familiar ones, even influences us to switch from our favourite products to ones we like less. This can occur even before we become *satiated*, or tired of our favourite product. Research supports the idea that we are willing to trade enjoyment for variety because the unpredictability itself is rewarding.

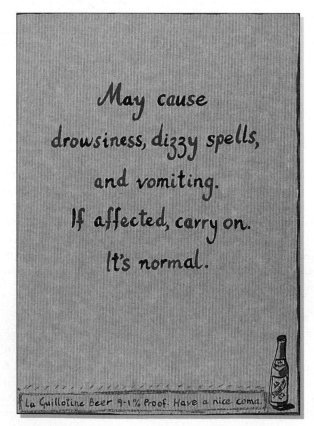

This Singaporean beer ad reminds us that not all product decisions are made rationally.

Variety seeking is a choice strategy that occurs as a result of pleasurable memories of ringing the changes.[37] Variety seeking is especially likely to occur when we are in a good mood, or when there is relatively little stimulation elsewhere in our environment.[38] In the case of foods and beverages, variety seeking can occur due to a phenomenon known as *sensory-specific satiety*. Put simply, this means the pleasantness of a recently consumed food item drops, while the pleasantness of uneaten foods remains unchanged.[39] So even though we have favourites, we still like to sample other possibilities. Ironically, consumers may actually switch to less-preferred options for variety's sake even though they enjoy the more familiar option more. On the other hand, when the decision situation is ambiguous or when there is little information about competing brands, we tend to opt for the safe choice by selecting familiar brands and maintaining the status quo. Figure 9.5 shows the brand attributes consumers consider most important when choosing among alternatives, according to a survey *Advertising Age* conducted.

Figure 9.5 *Advertising Age poll*: importance of brand attitudes

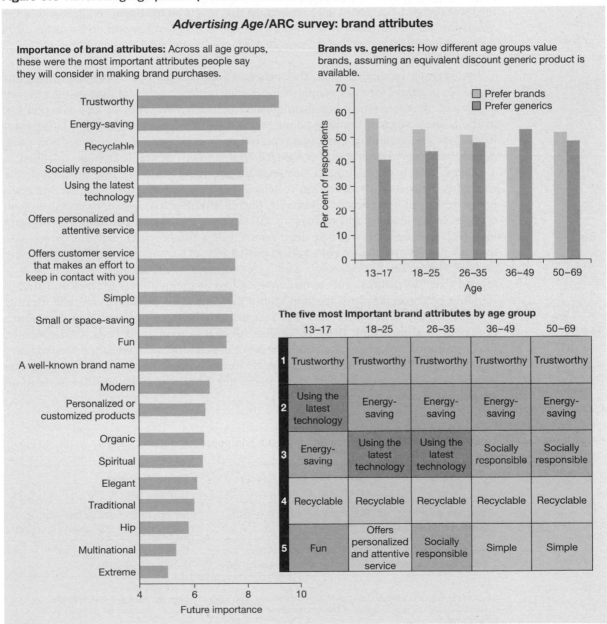

Brand familiarity influences confidence about a brand, which in turn affects purchase intention.[40] Still, the tendency of consumers to shift brand choices over time means that marketers can never relax in the belief that once they have won a customer, they are necessarily theirs forever.[41]

Biases in the decision-making process

Consider the following scenario: you've been given a free ticket to an important football match. At the last minute, though, a sudden snowstorm makes getting to the football ground somewhat dangerous. Would you still go? Now, assume the same game and snowstorm, except this time you paid a lot of money for the ticket. Would you go?

▶ Analyses of people's responses to this situation and to other similar puzzles illustrates principles of **mental accounting**. This process demonstrates that the way we pose a problem (we call this *framing*) and whether it's phrased in terms of gains or losses, influences our decisions.[42] In this case, researchers found that people are more likely to risk their personal safety in the storm if they paid for the football ticket than if it was a freebie. Only the most diehard fan would fail to recognize that this is an irrational choice, because the risk is the same regardless of whether or not you got a great bargain on the ticket. This decision-making bias is called the *sunk-cost fallacy* – having paid for something makes us reluctant to waste it.

Loss aversion is another bias. This means we emphasize our losses more than our gains. For example, for most people losing money is more *unpleasant* than gaining money is *pleasant*. A recent study has distinguished between two types of loss aversion (or, as the authors suggest thinking about aversion in this context, as either loss sensitivity or loss exaggeration). First, one type of loss aversion focuses on losses and gains defined in terms of desirability or valence. In this case a desirable change is defined as a valence gain (e.g. passing an examination; surviving surgery), and an undesirable change is defined as a valence loss (catching a cold; being in a car crash; having one's house destroyed by a tornado). Secondly, the other type of loss aversion concentrates on changes in possessions and ownership. Giving up a possession becomes a 'possession loss' (e.g. the removal of a bad debt; removal of a tumour; although this possession loss can also involve the loss of a valued possession such as house or money). Receiving an item represents a 'possession gain' (e.g. winning a scholarship). From here, it is argued that this distinction between types of loss aversion allows for a clearer understanding of possession loss aversion within the context of consumer decision-making.

▶ The **Psychology of Loss Aversion (PLA)** particularly helps to predict 'opposite patterns of staying and switching between choices involving goods and bads. Consequently, PLA can simultaneously explain both the traditional endowment effect (i.e. the tendency to value more highly an item that is already in one's possession) and also the fact that people may sometimes strongly desire to switch from a current negative state to an alternative negative state' (see Table 9.3).[43]

Table 9.3 Example of valence gains/losses and possession gains/losses

	Possession gain (receiving an item)	Possession loss (giving up an item)
Valence gain (positive changes)	Receiving an attractive item (e.g. winning $100)	Giving up an unattractive item (e.g. giving up the speeding ticket)
Valence loss (negative changes)	Receiving an unattractive item (e.g. receiving a speeding ticket)	Giving up an attractive item (e.g. losing $100)

Source: Lyle Brenner, Yuval Rottenstreich, Sanjay Sood and Baler Bilgin, 'On the psychology of loss aversion: Possession, valence, and reversals of the endowment effect', *Journal of Consumer Research* 34 (October 2007): Table 1: 370.[44]

▶ **Prospect theory**, which describes how people make choices, finds that utility is a function of gains and losses. Our sense of risk differs when we face options involving gains versus those involving losses.[45]

To illustrate this bias, consider the following choices. For each, would you take the safe bet or choose to gamble?

- *Option 1.* You're given €100 and then offered a chance to flip a coin: heads you win €30; tails you lose €30.
- *Option 2.* You're given a choice of getting €100 outright, or accepting a coin flip that will win you either €115 or €85.

In one study, 70 per cent of those given Option 1 chose to gamble, compared to just 43 per cent of those offered Option 2. Yet, the odds are the same for both options! The difference is that people prefer 'playing with the house money'; they are more willing to take risks when they perceive they're using someone else's resources. So, contrary to a rational decision-making perspective, we value money differently depending on its source. This explains why someone might choose to spend a big bonus on some frivolous purchase, but they would never consider taking that same amount out of their savings account for this purpose.

Finally, research in mental accounting demonstrates that extraneous characteristics of the choice situation can influence our selections, even though they wouldn't *if* we were totally rational decision-makers. As one example, participants in a survey were provided with one of two versions of this scenario:

You are lying on the beach on a hot day. All you have to drink is iced water. For the last hour you have been thinking about how much you would enjoy a nice cold bottle of your favourite brand of beer. A companion gets up to go and make a phone call and offers to bring back a beer from the only nearby place where beer is sold (either a fancy resort hotel or a small, run-down grocery store, depending on the version you're given). They say that the beer might be expensive and so asks how much you are willing to pay for it . . . What price do you tell them?

In this survey, the median price given by participants who were in the fancy resort version was $2.65 (about €2), but those given the grocery store version were only willing to pay $1.50 (just over €1)! In both versions the consumption act is the same, the beer is the same, and no 'atmosphere' is consumed because the beer is being brought back to the beach.[46] So much for rational decision-making!

Recent work has examined the role of emotions in decision-making. One study looked at 'the pain of paying'; and argued that immediate emotions experienced at the point of choice could affect consumer behaviour. These researchers examined the emotion of 'pain of paying' and identified that the 'anticipatory pain of paying drives "tightwads" to spend less than they would ideally spend. "Spendthrifts", by contrast, experience too little pain of paying and typically spend more than they would ideally like to spend.'[47]

How much search occurs?

As a general rule, search activity is greater when the purchase is important, when we have more of a need to learn more about the purchase, and/or when the relevant information is easily obtained and utilized.[48] Consumers differ in the amount of search they tend to undertake, regardless of the product category in question. All things being equal, younger, better-educated people who enjoy the shopping/fact-finding process tend to conduct more information search. Women are more inclined to search than men are, as are those who place greater value on style and the image they present.[49] A recent study of information search in high technology markets suggested that use of information channels can be segmented by age and education, with older consumers accessing information channels with less complex information compared with more highly educated consumers who tend to search all information channels. In addition, 'during each segment of the search consumers tend to use multiple sources of information'.[50]

Figure 9.6 The relationship between amount of information search and product knowledge

The consumer's prior expertise

Should prior product knowledge make it more or less likely that consumers will engage in search? The answer to this question is not as obvious as it first appears. Product experts and novices use very different procedures during decision-making. Novices who know little about a product should be the most motivated to find out more about it. However, experts are more familiar with the product category, so they should be able to better understand the meaning of any new product information they might acquire.

So, who searches more? The answer is neither: search tends to be greatest among those consumers who are *moderately knowledgeable* about the product. There is an inverted-U relationship between knowledge and external search effort, as shown in Figure 9.6. People with very limited expertise may not feel they are capable of searching extensively. In fact, they may not even know where to start. Daniel, who did spend a lot of time researching his purchase, is only partly representative of this situation. He used the Web to do some research at the beginning, and again after he'd visited a specialist store for advice. At that point, he'd largely made up his mind and so went to the second store to make his final purchase where the prices were very competitive. In other respects Daniel resembled other shoppers with very limited expertise who typically limit their search by looking at only a few brands with which they are already familiar; and focus on only a small number of product features. They usually also tend to limit their visits to stores.[51]

The *type* of search undertaken by people with varying levels of expertise differs as well. Because experts have a better sense of what information is relevant to the decision, they tend to engage in *selective search*, which means their efforts are more focused and efficient. In contrast, novices are more likely to rely on the opinions of others and to rely on 'non-functional' attributes, such as brand name and price, to distinguish among alternatives. They may also process information in a 'top-down' rather than a 'bottom-up' manner, focusing less on details than on the big picture. For instance, they may be more impressed by the sheer amount of technical information presented in an ad than by the actual significance of the claims made.[52]

Perceived risk

As a rule, purchase decisions that involve extensive search also entail some kind of ▶ **perceived risk**, or the belief that the product has potentially negative consequences from using or not using the product or service. Perceived risk may be present if the product is expensive or is complex and difficult to understand, or if the brand is unfamiliar. Mood effects on consumers' attitudes and perceptions about risk are stronger when brands are unfamiliar.[53] Perceived risk can also be a factor when a product choice is visible to others and we run the risk of embarrassment if we make the wrong choice.[54]

▼ Marketing pitfall

In recent years, some researchers have started to focus on the plight of consumers who really have trouble searching – because they have difficulty reading. When we do consumer research, we typically assume that our respondents are fully literate so they are able to find information, identify products, and conduct transactions with few problems. However, it's worth noting that, in fact, more than half of the US population reads at or below the equivalent of sixth-grade school level (i.e. 11 or 12 years of age) – and that roughly half are unable to master specific aspects of shopping. In the UK this would represent national curriculum levels 3 and 4 (entry level 3 of the core curriculum for literacy) and constitutes about 3.5 million people aged between 16 and 65 in the UK.[55] This fact reminds us to think more about the low-literate consumer who is at a big disadvantage in the marketplace. Some of these people (whom researchers term *social isolates*) cope with the stigma of illiteracy by avoiding situations where they will have to reveal this problem. They may avoid eating at a restaurant with an unfamiliar menu, for example. Low-literate consumers rely heavily on visual cues, including brand logos and store layouts, to navigate in retail settings, but they often make mistakes when they select similarly packaged products (for example, brand line extensions). They also encounter problems with *innumeracy* (understanding numbers); many low-literate people have difficulty knowing, for example, whether they have enough money to purchase the items in their cart and are vulnerable to being cheated out of the correct amount of change due. Not surprisingly, these challenges create an emotional burden for low-literate consumers, who experience stress, anxiety, fear, shame, and other negative emotions before, during, and after they shop.[56] Some groups of European consumers are equally vulnerable in the marketplace (see Table 9.4). (For a discussion of levels of e-skills amongst European consumers see Chapter 15.)

Table 9.4 Percentage of students with low performance in reading, mathematical and scientific literacy, 2003

	Reading ([1])		Maths ([1])		Scientific ([2])	
	Girls	Boys	Girls	Boys	Girls	Boys
BE	13.0	22.4	15.7	17.2	15.4	17.5
CZ	15.0	23.5	18.1	15.1	12.1	11.2
DK	12.7	20.5	17.4	13.4	24.7	20.6
DE	16.3	28.1	21.4	21.4	18.2	19.0
IE	7.7	14.3	18.7	15.0	12.8	13.4
EL	18.5	32.5	41.9	35.8	22.3	21.0
ES	14.5	27.9	23.4	22.5	18.7	19.6
FR	12.1	23.5	16.5	16.8	15.6	17.7
IT	17.2	31.1	34.0	29.7	20.9	21.6
LV	11.6	25.0	23.1	24.4	15.8	18.7
LU	17.1	28.5	23.4	20.0	21.8	21.1
HU	14.9	25.5	23.9	22.2	14.0	15.5
NL	8.6	14.3	11.7	10.2	11.6	10.6
AT	13.1	28.2	18.4	19.2	16.7	20.2
PL	10.3	23.4	21.4	22.7	17.4	17.9
PT	15.1	29.5	31.3	28.7	23.1	23.9
SK	18.6	30.9	22.0	18.0	17.6	16.1
FI	2.4	9.0	6.2	7.3	4.6	6.9
SE	8.8	17.7	17.9	16.7	16.6	15.7
UK	:	:	:	:	:	:
HR	:	:	:	:	:	:
TR	27.8	44.1	55.8	40.0	38.3	38.9
IS	9.5	26.9	11.5	18.3	13.5	18.7
LI	8.0	12.7	14.4	10.2	13.3	11.0
NO	11.3	24.8	21.1	20.6	20.5	22.0
CH	11.8	21.2	15.7	13.4	15.8	15.3

UK: Response rate too low
([1]) Level 1 or below (below 421 score points)
([2]) Below 400 score points

Source: Eurostat, *The life of women and men in Europe*, 2008 edition, KS-80-07-135-EN-C European Commission, Luxembourg, Annex Table 15: 158.

Figure 9.7 lists five kinds of risk – including objective (e.g. physical danger) and subjective factors (e.g. social embarrassment) – as well as the products that tend to be affected by each type. As this figure notes, perceived risk is less of a problem for consumers who have greater 'risk capital' because they have less to lose from a poor choice. For example, a highly self-confident person might worry less about the social risk inherent in a product, whereas a more vulnerable, insecure consumer might be reluctant to take a chance with a product or brand that might not be seen as cool and thus not be accepted by peers. Within the EU complaints about the physical risks associated with consumer products are particularly related to the categories of toys, motor vehicles, electrical appliances, lighting equipment, cosmetics, children's equipment, clothing and household appliances (Figure 9.8).[57] The five most reported risk categories were injuries (23%);

Figure 9.7 Five types of perceived risk

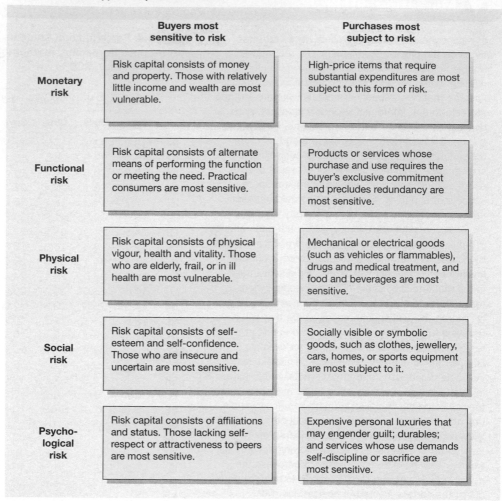

Figure 9.8 Notifications by type of risk of unsafe non-food products to EC Health and Consumer Protectorate (2007)

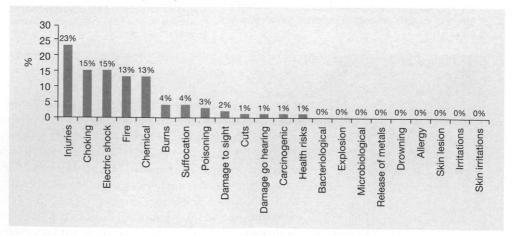

Source: *Keeping European Consumers Safe*, 2007 Annual Report on the operation of the Rapid Alert System for non-food consumer products, European Communities Health and Consumer Protection Directorate General, Luxembourg, 2008: 21.

choking (15%); electric shock (15%); fire (13%); and chemical risk (13%) (Figures 9.9 and 9.10). There was a pattern to the combination of particular products with certain risks, e.g. toys are associated with the risk of choking; vehicles, electrical appliances and lighting equipment with the risk of fire; and cosmetics with chemical risks.[58] Nuts and fish attracted the most notifications in the food product category (Figure 9.11).

Figure 9.9 Five most frequently notified types of risk of unsafe non-food products to EC Health and Consumer Protectorate (2007)

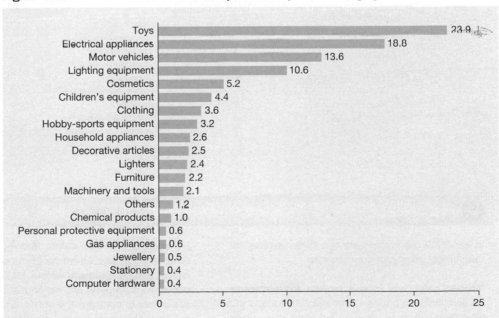

Source: *Keeping European Consumers Safe*, 2007 Annual Report on the operation of the Rapid Alert System for non-food consumer products, European Communities Health and Consumer Protection Directorate General, Luxembourg, 2008: 21.

Figure 9.10 'Serious risk' notifications by non-food product category – in %

Category	Value
Toys	23.9
Electrical appliances	18.8
Motor vehicles	13.6
Lighting equipment	10.6
Cosmetics	5.2
Children's equipment	4.4
Clothing	3.6
Hobby-sports equipment	3.2
Household appliances	2.6
Decorative articles	2.5
Lighters	2.4
Furniture	2.2
Machinery and tools	2.1
Others	1.2
Chemical products	1.0
Personal protective equipment	0.6
Gas appliances	0.6
Jewellery	0.5
Stationery	0.4
Computer hardware	0.4

Data Source: Rapex 2006 Annual Report.

Source: *The Consumer Markets Scoreboard Monitoring Consumer Outcomes in the Single Market*, COM (2008) 31, European Communities, Luxembourg, 2008, Figure 25: 38.

Figure 9.11 Notifications by product category (foodstuffs) – in %

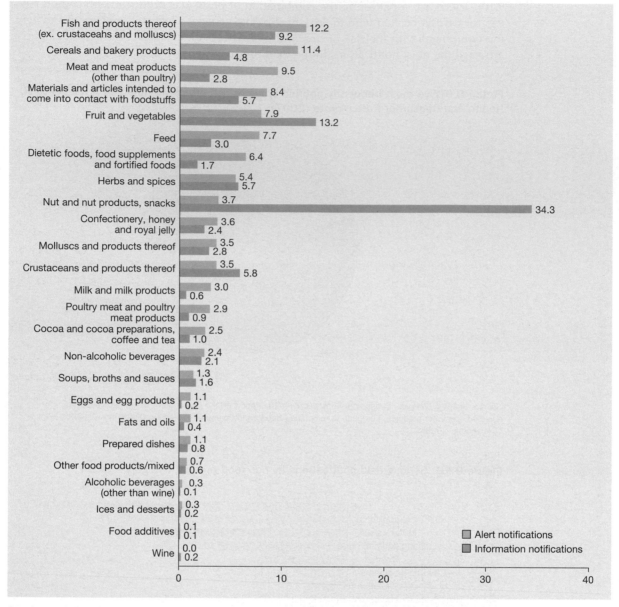

Data Source: Rasff 2006 Annual Report.

Source: *The Consumer Markets Scoreboard Monitoring Consumer Outcomes in the Single Market*, COM (2008) 31, European Communities, Luxembourg, 2008, Figure 26: 38.

▶ Marketing – Report from the front line

In her 2007 report the European Commissioner for Consumers, Meglena Kuneva wrote:

'Product safety is a shared concern and a shared responsibility. In our new economy, a product's journey from factory floor to supermarket shelf often spans the entire globe. This is why effective governance of product safety is such a critical issue today. There can

be no compromise on safety. And yet, there is no such thing as a risk-free environment. As consumers, we expect that the products we buy for ourselves and our families are safe and we should not have to worry about how to distinguish a safe product from an unsafe one. It is the job of public authorities, regulators and businesses to jointly manage the risks of this new economy and make sure that all products are safe.

The year 2007 will certainly be remembered for its "summer of recalls", involving toothpastes tainted with chemicals and dangerous toys. However, we should be more worried by silence than by activity because alerts and crises always come with a lesson for us to learn. And indeed, those events have clearly shown us that 2007 will mark the turning point for global product safety. These recalls have prompted greater awareness of our entire product safety system and have strengthened our determination to improve that system through a renewed vision of the opportunities that we can seize together with our major trading partners to raise consumer safety across the world . . . In 2007 . . . significantly more dangerous products were detected and neutralised by businesses and national authorities than in the year before . . . The exchange of RAPEX [EU Rapid Alert System] information with China has revealed tremendous capacity and potential for improving product safety upstream in the supply chain and in fostering a culture of safety and market surveillance outside Europe . . . [and] international cooperation tools on product safety.'[59]

EVALUATION OF ALTERNATIVES

Much of the effort we put into a purchase decision occurs at the stage in which a choice must be made from the available alternatives. This may not be easy; modern consumer society abounds with choices. In some cases, there may be literally hundreds of different brands (as in cigarettes) or different variations of the same brand (as in shades of lipstick), each clamouring for our attention.

Identifying alternatives

How do we decide which criteria are important, and how do we narrow down product alternatives to an acceptable number and eventually choose one instead of the others?

This BT Cellnet ad appeals to the need for social recognition and approbation from peer groups.

The Advertising Archives

Figure 9.12 Identifying alternatives: getting in the game

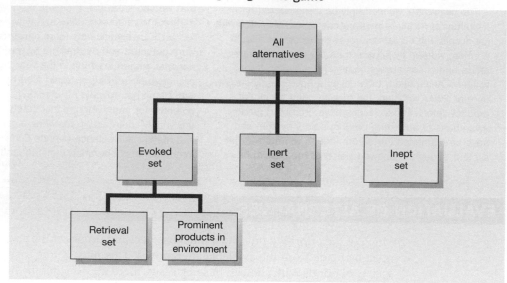

The answer varies depending upon the decision-making process we are using. A consumer engaged in extended problem-solving may carefully evaluate several brands, whereas someone making a habitual decision may not consider any alternatives to their normal brand. Furthermore, some evidence indicates that we do more extended processing in situations that arouse negative emotions due to conflicts among the available choices. This is most likely to occur when there are difficult trade-offs, for example, when a person must choose between the risks involved in undergoing a heart bypass operation versus the potential improvement in their life if the operation is successful.[60]

▶   We call the alternatives a consumer knows about their **evoked set**; and the ones they
▶ actually consider their **consideration set** (because often we do not seriously consider every single brand in a category because of issues such as price, a prior negative experience, and so on).[61] The evoked set comprises those products already in memory (the retrieval set), plus those prominent in the retail environment. For example, recall that Daniel did not know much about the technical aspects of HDTVs, and he had only a few major brands in memory. Of these, two were acceptable possibilities and one was not. The alternatives that the consumer is aware of but would not consider buying are their *inept set*, while those not under consideration at all comprise the *inert set*. You can easily guess in which set a marketer wants its brand to appear! These categories are depicted in Figure 9.12.

Consumers often include a surprisingly small number of alternatives in their evoked set. One study combined results from several large-scale investigations of consumers' evoked sets. It found that people overall include a small number of products in these sets, although this amount varies by product category and across countries.[62]

For obvious reasons, a marketer who finds that their brand is not in their target market's evoked set has cause to worry. You don't often get a second chance to make a good first impression. A consumer is not likely to place a product in his evoked set after they have already considered it and rejected it. Indeed, we are more likely to add a new brand to the evoked set than one that we had previously considered but passed over, even after a marketer has provided additional positive information about the brand.[63] For marketers, consumers' unwillingness to give a rejected product a second chance underlines the importance of ensuring that it performs well from the time it is introduced.

Product categorization

Remember that when consumers process product information, they do not do so in a vacuum. Instead, they evaluate a product stimulus in terms of what they already know about a product or other similar ones. A person evaluating a particular digital camera will most likely compare it with other digital cameras rather than to a 35mm camera, and would be unlikely to compare it with a DVD player or iPod. Since the category in which a product is placed determines the other products it will be compared with, *categorization* is a crucial determinant of how a product is evaluated.

The products in a consumer's evoked set are likely to share some similar features. This process can either help or hurt a product, depending on what people compare it with. For example, in one survey about 25 per cent of consumers said they would be less likely to buy a product made of hemp if they know it is derived from the same plant from which marijuana comes (but without the latter's effects). When faced with a new product, consumers refer to their already existing knowledge in familiar product categories to form new knowledge.[64]

It is important to understand how consumers cognitively represent this information in a **knowledge structure**, a set of beliefs and the way we organize these beliefs in our minds.[65] We discussed these knowledge structures in Chapter 7.[66]

Levels of categorization

Not only do people group things into categories, but these groupings occur at different levels of specificity. Typically, we represent a product in a cognitive structure at one of three levels. To understand this idea, consider how someone might respond to these questions about an ice-cream: what other products share similar characteristics, and which would be considered as alternatives to eating an ice-cream?

These questions may be more complex than they first appear. At one level, an ice-cream is similar to an apple, because both could be eaten as a dessert. At another level, an ice-cream is similar to a slice of pie, because both are eaten for dessert and both are fattening. At still another level, an ice-cream is similar to an ice-cream sundae – both are eaten for dessert, are made of ice cream and are fattening.

It is easy to see that the items a person associates with, say, the category 'fattening dessert' influence the choices they will make for what to eat after dinner. The middle level, known as the *basic level category*, is typically the most useful in classifying products, because at this level the items we group together tend to have a lot in common with each other, but still permit us to consider a broad enough range of alternatives. The broader *super-ordinate category* is more abstract, whereas the more specific *subordinate category* often includes individual brands.[67] These three levels are depicted in Figure 9.13.

Figure 9.13 Levels of abstraction in categories of dessert

Of course, not all items fit equally well into a category. Apple pie is a better example of the subordinate category 'pie' than is rhubarb pie, even though both are types of pie. Apple pie is thus more *prototypical*, and would tend to be considered first, especially by category novices. In contrast, pie experts will tend to have knowledge about both typical and atypical category examples.[68]

Strategic implications of product categorization

The way we categorize products has many strategic implications. This process affects which products consumers will compare with our product and also the criteria they will use to decide if they like us or our competitors.

Product positioning

The success of a *positioning strategy* often hinges on the marketer's ability to convince the consumer that their product should be considered within a given category. For example, the orange juice industry tried to reposition orange juice as a drink that could be enjoyed all day long ('It's not just for breakfast anymore'). On the other hand, soft drinks companies are now attempting the opposite by portraying carbonated drinks as suitable for breakfast consumption. They are trying to make their way into consumers' 'breakfast drink' category, along with orange juice, grapefruit juice and coffee. Of course, this strategy can backfire, as PepsiCo discovered when it introduced Pepsi A.M. and positioned it as a coffee substitute. The company did such a good job of categorizing the drink as a morning beverage that customers wouldn't drink it at any other time, and the product failed.[69]

Identifying competitors

At the abstract, super-ordinate level, many different product forms compete for membership. The category 'entertainment' might comprise both bowling and the ballet, but not many people would consider the substitution of one of these activities for the other. Products and services that on the surface are quite different, however, actually compete with each other at a broad level for consumers' discretionary cash. While bowling or ballet may not be a likely trade-off for many people, it is feasible, for example, that a symphony orchestra might try to lure away season ticket-holders to the ballet by positioning itself as an equivalent member of the category 'cultural event'.[70]

We are often faced with choices between non-comparable categories, where we cannot directly relate the attributes of one category to those in another category (the old problem of comparing apples and oranges). When we can create an overlapping category that encompasses both items (for instance, entertainment, value, usefulness) and then rate each alternative in terms of that superordinate category comparison, the process is easier.[71]

Exemplar products

As we saw with the case of apple pie versus rhubarb, if a product is a really good example of a category, it is more familiar to consumers and they more easily recognize and recall it.[72] The characteristics of category exemplars tend to exert disproportionate influence on how people think of the category in general.[73] In a sense, brands that are strongly associated with a category 'call the shots' by defining the evaluative criteria that should be used to evaluate all category members.

Being a bit less than prototypical is not necessarily a bad thing, however. Products that are moderately unusual within their product category may stimulate more information processing and positive evaluations, because they are neither so familiar that we will take them for granted nor so different that we will not consider them at all.[74] A brand that is strongly discrepant may occupy a unique niche position, whereas those that are moderately discrepant remain in a distinct position within the general category.[75]

Locating products

Product categorization also can affect consumers' expectations regarding the places where they can locate a desired product. If products do not clearly fit into categories (is a carpet furniture?), this may diminish our ability to find them or work out what they are meant to do, once we have found them. For instance, a frozen dog food that had to be thawed and cooked failed in the market, partly because people could not adapt to the idea of buying dog food in the 'frozen foods for people' section of their supermarkets.

PRODUCT CHOICE: SELECTING AMONG ALTERNATIVES

Once we assemble and evaluate the relevant options in a category, we have to choose one.[76] Recall that the decision rules guiding choice can range from very simple and quick strategies to complicated processes requiring much attention and cognitive processing.[77] The choice can be influenced by integrating information from sources such as prior experience with the product or a similar one, information present at the time of purchase, and beliefs about the brands that have been created by advertising.[78]

Our job isn't getting any easier as we often find that there are more and more features to evaluate. We deal with 50-button remote controls, digital cameras with hundreds of mysterious features and book-length manuals, and cars with dashboard systems worthy
▶ of the space shuttle. Experts call this spiral of complexity **feature creep**, also known as
▶ **feature fatigue** or **feature bloat**.[79] As evidence that the proliferation of gizmos is counterproductive, Philips Electronics found that at least half of returned products have nothing wrong with them – consumers simply couldn't figure out how to use them! What's worse, on average the person spent only 20 minutes trying to figure out how to use the product before giving up.

Why don't companies avoid this problem? One reason is that when we look at a new product in a store we tend to think that the more features there are, the better. It is only once we get the product home and try to use it that we realize the virtues of simplicity. We tend to rely on indirect experience when choosing products, so that before using a product our preference tends to be for many features and capabilities. It is only after we have had direct experience of a product that we tend to prefer simpler products that we find easier to use.[80] In one study,[81] consumers chose among three models of a digital device that varied in terms of how complex each was. More than 60 per cent chose the one with the most features. Then, the participants got the chance to choose from up to 25 features to customize their product – the average person chose 20 of these add-ons. But when they actually used the devices, it turns out that the large number of options only frustrated them – they ended up being much happier with the simpler product. As the saying goes, 'Be careful what you wish for . . .'[82]

Evaluative criteria

When Daniel was looking at different HDTVs, he focused on one or two product features and completely ignored several others. He narrowed down his choices by only considering two specific brand names, and from the Prime Wave and Precision models, he chose one that featured stereo capability. A survey carried out by different European manufacturers showed that they had identified a range of criteria used by consumers in Germany, Netherlands and Czech Republic when choosing televisions. Purchase price, design and technology emerged as key considerations for consumer decision-making in this product category (Figure 9.14).[83]
▶ **Evaluative criteria** are the dimensions we use to judge the merits of competing options. In comparing alternative products, Daniel could have chosen from among any number of criteria, ranging from very functional attributes ('does this TV have a remote

Figure 9.14 Importance of aspects in the buying decision for TVs (weighting by seven TV producers)

Data source: Manufacturers' questionnaires from Germany, Netherlands and Czech Republic.

Source: Lutz Stobbe, EuP Preparatory Studies 'Televisions' (Lot 5) Final Report on Task 3 'Consumer Behaviour and Local Infrastructure' (TREN/D1/40 lot 5-2005), compiled by Deutsche Umwelthilfe and Fraunhofer IZM, contractor: Fraunhofer Institute for Reliability and Microintegration, IZM, Berlin, 2 August 2007: 5.

control?') to experiential ones ('does this TV's sound reproduction make me imagine I'm in a concert hall?').

Another important point is that criteria on which products *differ* from one another carry more weight in the decision process than do those where the alternatives are *similar*. If all brands being considered rate equally well on one attribute (e.g. if all TVs come with remote control), consumers will have to find other reasons to choose one over another.

▶ **Determinant attributes** are the features we actually use to differentiate among our choices.

Reflecting consumers' renewed interest in ethical and sustainable marketing (see Chapter 6) it makes sense that a company's reputation for social responsibility is emerging as one of the most important determinant attributes when people choose among brands. Each year Harris Interactive and *The Wall Street Journal* conduct a survey and rank corporate reputations on 20 attributes in 6 categories: financial performance, social responsibility, workplace environment, quality of products and services, vision and leadership, and emotional appeal.[84] Although Microsoft has its share of critics, in 2007 it achieved the number one ranking – helped to a large extent by founder Bill Gates' philanthropy. The company beat Johnson & Johnson into number two place, although their emotionally appealing baby products business had kept Johnson & Johnson in first place for 7 consecutive years. However, the corporate world's overall reputation remains dismal as new scandals continue to emerge, e.g. Parmalat, Madoff, and Satyam.[85] About 69 per cent of respondents graded corporate America's reputation as either 'not good' or 'terrible'.

Marketers can play a role in educating consumers about which criteria should be used as determinant attributes. For example, research indicated that many consumers view the use of natural ingredients as a determinant attribute. The result was promotion of toothpaste made from baking soda, which the company, Church & Dwight, already manufactured for its Arm & Hammer brand.[86] The decision about which attributes to use is the result of *procedural learning*, in which a person undergoes a series of cognitive steps before making a choice. These steps include identifying important attributes, remembering whether competing brands differ on those attributes, and so on. In order for a marketer to recommend a new decision criterion effectively, their communication should convey three pieces of information:[87]

1 It should point out that there are significant differences among brands on the attribute.

2 It should supply the consumer with a decision-making rule, such as *if* (deciding among competing brands), *then* . . . (use the attribute as a criterion).

This advert for Powerade uses a series of explicit appeals linked to different evaluation criteria such as endurance, speed, energy and co-ordination.

The Advertising Archives

3 It should convey a rule that can be easily integrated with how the person has made this decision in the past. Otherwise, the recommendation is likely to be ignored because it requires too much mental work.

Neuromarketing: how your brain reacts to alternatives

Is there a 'buy button' in your brain? Some corporations are teaming up with neuroscientists to find out.[88] **Neuromarketing** uses *functional magnetic resonance imaging* (or *MRI*), a brain-scanning device that tracks blood flow as we perform mental tasks. In recent years, researchers have discovered that regions in the brain, such as the amygdala, the hippocampus, and the hypothalamus, are dynamic switchboards that blend memory, emotions, and biochemical triggers. These interconnected neurons shape the ways that fear, panic, exhilaration, and social pressure influence our choices.

Scientists know that specific regions of the brain light up in these scans to show increased blood flow when a person recognizes a face, hears a song, makes a decision, or senses deception. Now they are trying to harness this technology to measure consumers' reactions to movie trailers, choices about automobiles, the appeal of a pretty face, and loyalty to specific brands. British researchers recorded brain activity as shoppers toured a virtual store. They claim to have identified the neural region that becomes active when a shopper decides which product to pluck from a supermarket shelf. DaimlerChrysler took brain scans of men as they looked at photos of cars and confirmed that sports cars activated their reward centres. The company's scientists found that the most popular vehicles – the Porsche- and Ferrari-style sports cars – triggered activity in a section of the brain they call the *fusiform face area*, which governs facial recognition. A psychiatrist who ran the study commented, 'They were reminded of faces when they looked at the cars. The lights of the cars look a little like eyes.'

A study that took brain scans of people as they drank competing soft drink brands illustrates how loyalty to a brand affects our reactions, even at a very basic, physiological level. When the researchers monitored brain scans of 67 people who took a blind taste test of Coca-Cola and Pepsi, each soft drink lit up the brain's reward system, and the participants were evenly split as to which drink they preferred – even though three out of four participants *said* they preferred Coke. When told they were drinking Coke, the regions of the brain that control memory lit up, and this activation drowned out the area that simply reacts to taste cues. In this case, Coke's strong brand identity trumped the sensations coming from respondents' taste receptors.

In another study, researchers reported that pictures of celebrities triggered many of the same brain circuits as images of shoes, cars, chairs, wristwatches, sunglasses, handbags, and water bottles. All of these objects set off a rush of activity in a part of the cortex that neuroscientists know links to a sense of identity and social image. The scientists also identified types of consumers based on their responses. At one extreme were people whose brains responded intensely to 'cool' products and celebrities with bursts of activity but who didn't respond at all to 'uncool' images. They dubbed these participants 'cool fools,' likely to be impulsive or compulsive shoppers. At the other extreme were people whose brains reacted only to the unstylish items, a pattern that fits well with people who tend to be anxious, apprehensive, or neurotic. Many researchers remain sceptical about how helpful this technology will be for consumer research. If indeed researchers can reliably track consumers' brand preferences by seeing how their brains react, there may be many interesting potential opportunities for new research techniques that rely on what we (or at least our brains) do rather than what we say.

▲ Marketing opportunity

Cybermediaries

As anyone who has ever typed a phrase like 'home theatres' into a search engine like Google knows, the Web delivers enormous amounts of product and retailer information in seconds. In fact (remembering the earlier discussion of the problem of hyperchoice) the biggest problem Web surfers face these days is narrowing down their choices, not increasing them. In cyberspace, simplification is key. Some people even use Web filters like **intermute.com** to remove soundtracks, pop-up frames and other distractions from the sites they find.

With the tremendous number of Websites available, and the huge number of people surfing the Web each day, how can people organize information and decide where to click? One type of business that is growing to meet this demand is called a **cybermediary**. This is an intermediary that helps to filter and organize online market information so that customers can identify and evaluate alternatives more efficiently.[89] Cybermediaries take different forms.[90]

- *Directories* and *portals* such as **Yahoo!** or **fashionmall.com** are general services that tie together a large variety of different sites.

- *Website evaluators* reduce the risk to consumers by reviewing sites and recommending the best ones. For example, Point Communications selects sites that it designates as 'Top 5 per cent' of the Web.

Forums, fan clubs and *user groups* offer product-related discussions to help customers sift through options (more on this in Chapter 10). It is becoming clear that customer product reviews are a key driver of satisfaction and loyalty. In one large survey, about half of the respondents who bought an item from a major Website remembered seeing customer product reviews. This group's satisfaction with the online shopping experience was five per cent higher than for shoppers who did not recall customer reviews.[91] Another advantage of cybermediaries is that consumers get to experience a much wider array of options – and at the same time products such as movies, books, and CDs that are not 'blockbusters' are more likely to sell.

- *Financial intermediaries* authorize payments from buyers to sellers. Payment systems include the electronic equivalents to credit card charges (PayPal).

▶ - **Intelligent agents** are sophisticated software programs that use *collaborative filtering* technologies to learn from past user behaviour in order to recommend new purchases. For example, when you let **Amazon.com** suggest a new book, it is using an intelligent agent to suggest novels based on what you and others like you have bought in the past. This approach was introduced in 1995 (the Stone Ages in Web time!) by firefly to make recommendations for taste-based products like music, books and films.[92] Now, a variety of shopping 'bots' (automated tasks run by software applications) are available to act as online purchasing shopping agents, including **clickthebutton.com**, **mysimon.com**, **dealtime.com** and Ask Jeeves. Collaborative filtering is still in its infancy. In the next few years, expect to see many new Web-based methods developed to simplify the consumer decision-making process. Now if only someone could come up with an easier way to pay for all the great stuff you find courtesy of shopping bots!

Researchers are working hard to understand how consumers go about finding information online, and in particular how they react to and integrate recommendations they receive from different kinds of online agents in their own product choices. An ▶ **electronic recommendation agent** is a software tool that tries to understand a human decision-maker's multi-attribute preferences for a product category by asking the user to communicate their preferences. Based on that data, the software then recommends a list of alternatives sorted by the degree that they fit these criteria. Some findings now emerging include the following:[93]

- Consumers who consult recommendation agents select the recommended products twice as often as those who do not.

- The extent to which a consumer has agreed with the agent on past recommendations influences the likelihood they will accept the advice.

- Recommendation agents have a greater impact on decisions when consumers feel the decision is risky, for example, if the consequences of making a poor decision are high or if the item is expensive.

- When a recommendation agent asks the consumer about their preferences for a particular product attribute, the consumer will weigh up that attribute more when making an actual product choice.

Heuristics: mental short cuts

Do we actually perform complex mental calculations every time we make a purchase decision? Of course not! When we are not relying on a Website to steer us to the right place, we often use other decision rules to simplify our choices. For example, Daniel relied on certain assumptions as substitutes for a prolonged information search. In particular, he assumed the selection at the out-of-town big shed retailer would be more than sufficient, so he did not bother to investigate any of its competitors. This assumption served as a short cut to more extended information processing.[94] Daniel could have chosen a heuristic approach based either on compromise or anchoring. A compromise strategy might have involved following one of the options used by his friends in choosing a new HDTV, e.g. Hannah might have done an exhaustive Web-based search; Lily might have visited every high street and out of town stockist; and Christopher might

Ask Jeeves, one of the popular search engines/shopping 'bots' available on the web to simplify the consumer decision-making process via online searches.

have read all the independent consumer reports. Daniel's compromise would have been to have done some Web-searching, visited one high street retailer, and then made a purchase after visiting just one large out-of-town stockist.[95] Alternatively, Daniel could have pursued anchoring (Tversky and Kahneman, 1974),[96] i.e. 'the tendency to rely heavily, or anchor, on one piece of information in order to arrive at a decision'.[97]

▶ Especially when limited problem-solving occurs prior to making a choice, we often fall back on **heuristics**, or mental rules-of-thumb that lead to a speedy decision. These rules range from the very general ('Higher-priced products are higher-quality products' or 'Buy the same brand I bought last time') to the very specific ('Buy Silver Spoon, the brand of sugar my mother always bought').[98] Recent research has 'demonstrated that decision making is more heuristic in situations that involve spending time rather than money'.[99]

Sometimes these short cuts may not be in our best interests. A consumer who personally knows one or two people who have had problems with a particular make of car, for example, might assume they would have similar trouble with it rather than taking the time to find out that it has an excellent repair record.[100] The influence of such assumptions may be enhanced if the product has an unusual name, which makes it *and* the experiences with it more distinctive.[101]

Relying on a product signal

One short cut we often use is to infer hidden dimensions of products from attributes we ▶ can observe. In these cases the visible element acts as a **product signal** that communicates some underlying quality. This explains why someone trying to sell a used car takes great pains to be sure the car's exterior is clean and shiny. Potential buyers often judge the vehicle's mechanical condition by its appearance, even though this means they may drive away in a shiny, clean death trap.[102]

When we only have incomplete product information, we often base our judgements on our beliefs about *co-variation*; the associations we have among events that may or may not actually influence one another.[103] For example, a consumer may judge product quality

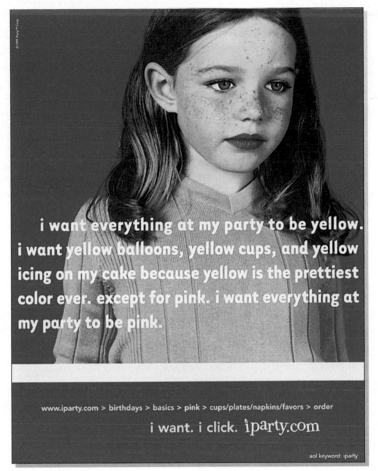

Consumers often simplify choices by using heuristics such as automatically choosing a favourite colour or brand.

iParty Corp.

by the length of time a manufacturer has been in business. Other signals or attributes consumers tend to believe co-exist with good or bad products include well-known brand names, country of origin, price and the retail outlets that carry the product.

Market beliefs: is it better if I have to pay more for it?

We are constantly forming assumptions about companies, products and stores. These market beliefs then become the short cuts that guide our decisions – regardless of whether or not these beliefs are accurate.[104] Recall, for instance, that Daniel chose to shop at a large 'electronics supermarket' because he *assumed* the prices would be more competitive there than at a specialized shop; and Grace from Chapter 3 also ended paying the top price to reduce her sense of risk in her purchase of a digibox. A large number of ▶ **market beliefs** have been identified. Some of these are listed in Table 9.5. How many do you share?

Do higher prices mean higher quality? The assumption of a *price–quality relationship* is one of the most pervasive market beliefs.[105] Novice consumers may in fact consider price as the *only* relevant product attribute (e.g. Grace from Chapter 3). Experts also consider this information, although they tend to use price for its informational value, especially for products (e.g. virgin wool) they know vary widely in quality. When this quality level is more standard or strictly regulated (e.g. Harris Tweed sports jackets), experts do not weigh price in their decisions. For the most part, this belief is justified; you do tend to get what you pay for. However, let the buyer beware: the price–quality relationship is not always justified.[106]

Table 9.5 Common market beliefs

Brand	All brands are basically the same.
	Generic products are just name brands sold under a different label at a lower price.
	The best brands are the ones that are purchased the most.
	When in doubt, a national brand is always a safe bet.
Store	Specialized shops are good places to familiarize yourself with the best brands; but once you know what you want, it's cheaper to buy it at a discount outlet.
	A store's character is reflected in its window displays.
	Salespeople in specialized shops are more knowledgeable than other sales personnel.
	Larger stores offer better prices than small stores.
	Locally-owned stores give the best service.
	A store that offers a good value on one of its products probably offers good values on all of its items.
	Credit and return policies are most lenient at large department stores.
	Stores that have just opened usually charge attractive prices.
Prices/Discounts/Sales	Sales are typically run to get rid of slow-moving merchandise.
	Stores that are constantly having sales don't really save you money.
	Within a given store, higher prices generally indicate higher quality.
Advertising and sales promotion	'Hard-sell' advertising is associated with low-quality products.
	Items tied to 'giveaways' are not good value (even with the freebie).
	Coupons represent real savings for customers because they are not offered by the store.
	When you buy heavily advertised products, you are paying for the label, not for higher quality.
Product/Packaging	Largest-sized containers are almost always cheaper per unit than smaller sizes.
	New products are more expensive when they're first introduced; prices tend to settle down as time goes by.
	When you are not sure what you need in a product, it's a good idea to invest in the extra features, because you'll probably wish you had them later.
	In general, synthetic goods are lower in quality than goods made of natural materials.
	It's advisable to stay away from products when they are new to the market; it usually takes the manufacturer a little time to sort out the bugs.

Source: Adapted from Calvin P. Duncan, 'Consumer Market Beliefs: A Review of the Literature and an Agenda for Future Research', in Marvin E. Goldberg, Gerald Gorn and Richard W. Pollay, eds, *Advances in Consumer Research* 17 (Provo, UT: Association for Consumer Research, 1990): 729–35.

Country of origin as a product signal

Modern consumers choose among products made in many countries. European consumers may buy Portuguese, Italian or Brazilian shoes, Japanese cars, clothing imported from Taiwan, or microwave ovens built in South Korea. A product's 'address' matters. Consumers' reactions to these imports are mixed. In some cases, people have come to assume that a product made overseas is of better quality (cameras, cars), whereas in other cases the knowledge that a product has been imported tends to lower perceptions of product quality (apparel).[107] In general, people tend to rate their own country's products more favourably than do foreigners, and products from industrialized countries are rated better than are those from developing countries.

▶ As briefly discussed in Chapter 8 when we were talking about persuasive communication, a product's **country of origin** in some cases is an important piece of information

Figure 9.15 Notifications by country of origin of unsafe non-food products to EC Health and Consumer Protectorate (comparison 2004–2007)

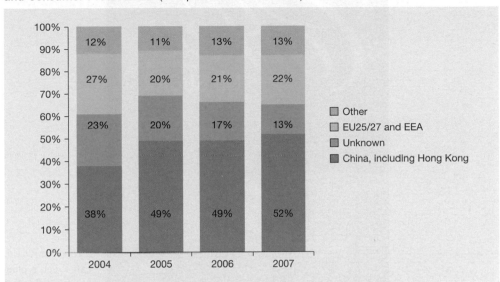

Source: *Keeping European Consumers Safe*, 2007 Annual Report on the operation of the Rapid Alert System for non-food consumer products, European Communities Health and Consumer Protection Directorate General, Luxembourg, 2008: 25.

in the decision-making process.[108] A product's origin, then, is often used as a signal of quality. Certain items are strongly associated with specific countries, and products from those countries often attempt to benefit from these linkages. Sometimes, however, the country of origin can act as a negative signal. Recent reports of poor experiences with goods has undermined some national manufacturing reputations. In a recent EC report China (including Hong Kong) accounted for over half of the notifications in 2007 (compared with 49 per cent in 2006) of substandard non-food products. In addition to its status as a major exporter to the EU, China also attracted increased attention because of a series of high-profile product recalls during 2007 (Figure 9.15).[109]

 Marketing pitfall

'High-level recalls and global product safety

In 2007, over 18 million toys were recalled globally during the summer because of magnetic parts that became loose, thereby posing life threatening risks to children. This recall was coupled with almost 2 million toys being pulled off the shelves because of excessive levels of lead in their paint. A few months before, toothpaste tainted with diethylene glycol, a thickener used in brake fluids and anti-freeze, was found on the European market. As all products originated from China, and even though it was made very clear that the risk posed by the magnetic toys lay with their design and not with their country of origin, questions about the 'Made in China' brand were asked and, more importantly, the confidence of consumers was affected . . . In 2007, 700 RAPEX [EU's Rapid Alert System[110]]

notifications concerned products of Chinese origin, including Hong Kong. This figure corresponds to 52 per cent of all notifications and confirms the important share and, at the same time, the slow growth of dangerous products 'Made in China' and found in Europe, as compared to 2006 data. In October 2007, undoubtedly because of the special campaign to check the safety of Chinese-made toys in the run-up to the holiday season sales, there was an all-time high of 179 RAPEX notifications. During the same month, 69 per cent of all serious risk notifications concerned Chinese products. In this respect, it is also important to bear in mind that almost 80 per cent of all toys on the European market are imported from China.'[111]

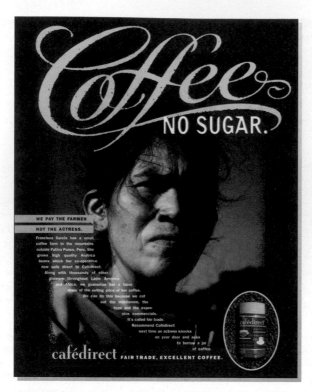

cafédirect, a pioneer company in ethical business, is associated with three major coffee-producing countries: Peru, Costa Rica and Mexico.

The Advertising Archives

Countries, in their turn, can be very protective of product names which potentially provide them with an important competitive advantage in winning customers. The EU has been trying to achieve a global trade agreement to protect some of its product names such as champagne and wines like Beaujolais, chianti and Madeira; cheeses such as Roquefort, Feta and Gorgonzola; as well as meat products like Parma ham and Mortadella sausages. This has been opposed in some non-EU countries where these names are seen ► as generic.[112] Country of origin can function as a **stereotype** – a knowledge structure based on inferences across products. These stereotypes may be biased or inaccurate, but they do play a constructive role in simplifying complex choice situations.[113]

Recent evidence indicates that learning of a product's country of origin is not necessarily good or bad. Instead, it has the effect of stimulating the consumer's interest in the product to a greater degree. The purchaser thinks more extensively about the product and evaluates it more carefully.[114] The origin of the product can thus act as a product attribute that combines with other attributes to influence evaluations.[115] In addition, the consumer's own expertise with the product category moderates the effects of this attribute. When other information is available, experts tend to ignore country-of-origin information, whereas novices continue to rely on it. However, when other information is unavailable or ambiguous, both experts and novices will rely on this attribute to make a decision.[116]

► **Ethnocentrism** is the tendency to prefer products or people of one's own culture to those from other countries. Ethnocentric consumers are likely to feel it is wrong to buy products from other countries, particularly because of the negative effect this may have on the domestic economy. Marketing campaigns stressing the desirability of 'buying American' in the US are more likely to appeal to this consumer segment. The Consumer Ethnocentrism Scale (CETSCALE) measures this trait. Ethnocentric consumers agree with statements such as:

● purchasing foreign-made products is un-American,
● curbs should be put on all imports,
● American consumers who purchase products made in other countries are responsible for putting their fellow Americans out of work.[117]

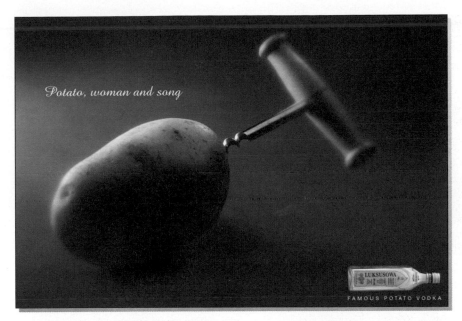

Some countries are strongly associated with certain types of alcoholic products. This Polish ad plays on these stereotypes.

Grey Worldwide Warszawa. Photo: Jacek Wolowski

Americans are not the only people who display ethnocentrism. Citizens of many countries tend to feel that their native products are superior (just ask a French person to choose between French or Californian wines). The scale for testing for ethnocentrism (CETSCALE) was originally developed in the US, and its applicability in other cultural contexts such as Spain has been examined.[118]

Choosing familiar brand names: loyalty or habit?

Branding is a marketing strategy that often functions as a heuristic. When you fall in love with a brand, it may be your favourite for a lifetime. People form preferences for a favourite brand, and then they literally may never change their minds in the course of a lifetime. In a study of the market leaders in 30 product categories by the Boston Consulting Group, it was found that 27 of the brands that were number one in 1930 in the US remain at the top today. These include such perennial American favourites as Ivory Soap, Campbell's Soup and Gold Medal Flour.[119] As this study demonstrates, some brands in a sense are well known because they are well known; we assume that if so many people choose a product, it must be good. Clearly, choosing a well-known

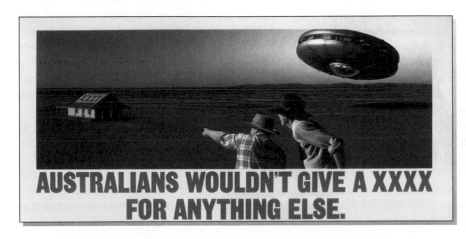

This advertisement illustrates Australian ethnocentrism by emphasizing the importance placed by Australian consumers on drinking their own 'XXXX' beer, as opposed to any other beverage.

The Advertising Archives

Table 9.6 The Brandz top 100 most powerful brands compiled by Millward Brown Optimor

Position	Brand	Brand value 08	BV 07	BV 06	Brand contribution	Brand momentum	Change in brand value	Position change
1	Google	86,057	66,434	37,445	3	5	30%	=
2	GE (General Electric)	71,379	61,880	55,834	2	10	15%	=
3	Microsoft	70,887	54,951	62,039	3	7.5	29%	=
4	Coca-Cola[1]	58,208	49,612	46,545	4	9	17%	=
5	China Mobile	57,225	41,214	39,168	3	10	39%	=
6	IBM	55,335	33,572	36,084	2	8.5	65%	3
7	Apple	55,206	24,728	15,976	3	9	123%	9
8	McDonald's	49,499	33,138	28,985	3	7	49%	3
9	Nokia	43,975	31,670	26,538	3	5	39%	3
10	Marlboro	37,324	39,166	38,510	3	6.5	−5%	−4

Source: Salvador Davoudi, 'Market trends: strong names beat the market', **ft.com**, 20 April 2008, **http://www.ft.com/cms/s/0/abdf3546-0cf4-11dd-86df-0000779fd2ac.html**, accessed 24 August 2008.

brand name is a powerful heuristic. A recent study has applied cultural theory to understanding how brands become icons over time.[120]

A brand that exhibits that kind of staying power is treasured by marketers, and for good reason. Brands that dominate their markets are as much as 50 per cent more profitable than their nearest competitors.[121] In a survey of global brands, Interbrand and *Business Week* identified the importance for companies of building 'communities around their products and services creating "cult brands" that enable customers to feel as if they own the brand. Cutting-edge technology companies did well as four of the top five biggest gainers in brand value are from the tech sector, while long-established brands such as Coca-Cola, Disney and Ford actually lost brand value. The overall number of American companies on the list dropped from 64 to 58.'[122]

Consumers' attachments to certain brands, such as Marlboro, Coca-Cola and Levi's, are so powerful that this loyalty is often considered as a positive product attribute in and of itself. Brand equity can actually be quantified in terms of *goodwill*, defined as the difference between the market value and the book value of a brand. The British company Grand Metropolitan recorded the brand names it had acquired on its balance sheets, including these intangible assets in its financial reports to shareholders.[123] In 1992, Marlboro was the most valuable brand name in the world, valued at $31.2 billion.[124] By 2004, Marlboro was the tenth most valuable brand name in the world, valued at $22.13 billion, with Coca-Cola leading the world's brands and valued at $67.39 billion.[125]

A recent study has identified the emergence of Google as the most powerful and valuable global brand for the second year running (see Table 9.6). Apart from Nokia, which has risen three places to number 9, other European brands with a global presence within the top 50 included Vodafone (11); BMW (17); Louis Vuitton (19); Tesco (25); Porsche (28); SAP (29); HSBC (35); Mercedes (36); L'Oréal (38); Deutsche Bank (42); ING (43); Carrefour (44); Siemens (47); Banco Santander (48); Orange (50).[126] Ranking of the most powerful brands in Europe are shown in Table 9.7.

However, there are growing concerns about the impact of geopolitics on some of the iconic US brands in European markets (e.g. Germany and France) where Coca-Cola, Marlboro, McDonald's, Wal-Mart, Disney and Gap have all reported weak or falling sales, though the companies also point to local factors.[127] A survey of 8,000 consumers in eight countries showed strong evidence of the potential influence of politics on consumer behaviour, with 20 per cent of European and Canadian consumers saying that they would refrain from buying US brands because of US foreign policy.[128]

Table 9.7 The Brandz top 20 by brand value for Europe (incl. UK) compiled by Millward Brown Optimor 2008

Position	Brand	BV 08	BC	BM
1	Nokia	43,975	3	5
2	Vodafone	36,962	2	4.5
3	BMW	28,015	4	7
4	Louis Vuitton	25,739	5	10
5	Tesco	23,208	4	7
6	Porsche	21,718	5	10
7	SAP	21,669	2	6.5
8	HSBC	18,479	2	5
9	Mercedes	18,044	4	6.5
10	L'Oréal	16,459	4	7
11	Deutsche Bank	15,104	1	2.5
12	ING	15,080	2	5
13	Carrefour	15,057	3	4.5
14	Siemens	14,665	2	4.5
15	Banco Santander	14,549	2	1.5
16	Orange	14,093	2	4
17	Marks & Spencer	11,600	3	9.5
18	UBS	11,220	2	5.5
19	H&M	11,182	2	4.5
20	Hermès	9,631	5	10

BV = Brand Value: 'the dollar value of each brand in the ranking is the sum of all future earnings that that brand can be expected to generate, discounted to present day value.'

BC = Brand contribution: 'this is the degree to which brand equity actually plays a role in generating earnings'

BM[129] = Brand momentum: 'an index from 1 to 10, where 10 indicates the greatest likelihood of future growth. Brands with above average growth rates have a momentum of above five, while those with below-average growth rates have a momentum of less than five'.[130]

Source: Salvador Davoudi, 'Market trends: strong names beat the market', **ft.com**, 20 April 2008, http://www.ft.com/cms/s/0/abdf3546-0cf4-11dd-86df-0000779fd2ac.html, accessed 24 August 2008.

Inertia

Many people tend to buy the same brand just about every time they go shopping. This consistent pattern is often due to **inertia** – we buy a brand out of habit merely because it requires less effort. If another product is introduced that is for some reason easier to buy (for instance, it is cheaper or the original product is out of stock), we will not hesitate to change our minds. A competitor who is trying to change a buying pattern based on inertia often can do so rather easily, because the shopper won't hesitate to jump to the new brand if it offers the right incentive. When we have little to no underlying commitment to a particular brand, marketers find it easy to 'unfreeze' our habit when they use promotional tools such as point-of-purchase displays, extensive couponing, or noticeable price reductions. Some analysts predict that we are going to observe this kind of fickle behaviour more and more as consumers flit from one brand to the next. Indeed, one industry observer labels this variety-seeking consumer a *brand slut*; she points out that from 2004 to 2007 the number of women who say a manufacturer's brand name is very influential in their decision to buy a beauty product decreased by 21 percentage points to stand at 19 per cent.[131]

Brand loyalty: a 'friend', tried and true

This kind of fickleness or promiscuity will not occur if true **brand loyalty** exists. In contrast to inertia, brand loyalty describes repeat purchasing behaviour that reflects a *conscious* decision to continue buying the same brand.[132] For brand loyalty to exist, a pattern of repeat purchase must be accompanied by an underlying positive attitude towards the brand, rather than simply buying the same brand out of habit. Brand loyalty may be initiated by customer preference based on objective reasons, but after the brand has existed for a long time and is heavily advertised it can also create an emotional attachment, either by being incorporated into the consumer's self-image or because it is associated with prior experiences.[133] Purchase decisions based on brand loyalty also become habitual over time, though in these cases the underlying commitment to the product is much firmer.

Compared to inertia, a situation in which the consumer passively accepts a brand, a brand-loyal consumer is actively (sometimes passionately) involved with their favourite. Because of the emotional bonds that can come about between brand-loyal consumers and products, 'true-blue' users react more vehemently when these products are altered, redesigned or withdrawn.[134] Recall, for example, when Coca-Cola replaced its tried-and-true formula with New Coke in the 1980s.

A decade ago, marketers struggled with the problem of *brand parity*, which refers to consumers' beliefs that there are no significant differences among brands. For example, one survey at that time found that more than 70 per cent of consumers worldwide believed that all paper towels, all soaps and all crisps are alike.[135] Some analysts even proclaimed the death of brand names, predicting that private label or generic products that offered the same value for less money would kill off the tried-and-true products.

However, the reports of this death appear to be premature – major brands are making a dramatic comeback. Brand sluts aside, today branding is king. Some attribute this renaissance to information overload (as mentioned by Suzanne C. Beckmann above) – with too many alternatives (many of them unfamiliar names) to choose from, people seem to be looking for a few clear signals of quality. Following a period in the late 1980s and early 1990s when people had strong doubts about the ability of large companies to produce quality products, more recent surveys indicate consumers are slowly beginning to trust major manufacturers again.[136] Brand names are very much alive.

 Net profit

Brand loyalty lives – online. Many brand fans create personal Web pages that trumpet their allegiance to one or more favourite products. These pages may take the form of passionate essays or perhaps photo albums that show in vivid detail the ways the page creator uses the product. Many of them include external links that provide reams of additional details about the featured products. A study of these personal Web pages found that the brands referenced range from common software and net application products to entertainment/entertainers (fan sites), clothing, financial/governmental/political organizations, restaurants and even household goods. In addition to providing a fascinating glimpse into how far people will go to express their allegiance to favourite products (yes, even to appliances!), these personal online 'shrines' to favourite products are potentially a great untapped resource for marketers that want to locate brand-loyal followers who will help them to spread the word in cyberspace.[137]

Decision rules we use when we care

We have seen that we use different rules to choose among competing products depending on the decision's complexity and how important the choice is to us. Sometimes we use a simple heuristic, but at other times we carefully weigh alternatives. We can describe the processes we use when we are giving more thought to these decisions by dividing the types of rules we use into two categories: *compensatory* and *non-compensatory*. To aid the discussion of some of these rules, Table 9.8 summarizes the attributes of the HDTV sets Daniel considered. It is now possible to see how some of these rules result in different brand choices.

Table 9.8 Hypothetical alternatives for an HDTV

Attribute	Importance ranking	Brand ratings		
		Kamashita	Prime Wave	Precision
Size of screen	1	Excellent	Excellent	Excellent
Stereo broadcast capability	2	Good	Poor	Excellent
Brand reputation	3	Poor	Excellent	Excellent
On-screen programming	4	Poor	Excellent	Poor
Cable-ready capability	5	Good	Good	Good
Sleep timer	6	Good	Excellent	Poor

Non-compensatory decision rules

▶ We use **non-compensatory decision rules** when we feel that a product with a low standing on one attribute cannot compensate for this flaw by doing better on another attribute. Simple non-compensatory decision rules are therefore short cuts to making choices. In other words we simply eliminate all options that do not meet some basic standards. A consumer like Daniel who uses the decision rule, 'Only buy well-known brand names', would not consider a new brand, even if it were equal or superior to existing ones. When people are less familiar with a product category or are not very motivated to process complex information, they tend to use simple, non-compensatory rules, which are summarized below:[138]

The lexicographic rule When a person uses *the lexicographic rule*, they select the brand that is the best on the most important attribute selected. If they feel two or more brands are equally good on that attribute, the consumer then compares them on the second most important attribute. This selection process goes on until the tie is broken. In Daniel's case, because both the Prime Wave and Precision models were tied on his most important attribute (screen size), he chose the Precision because of its rating on this second most important attribute – its stereo capability.

The elimination-by-aspects rule Using the elimination-by-aspects rule, the buyer also evaluates brands on the most important attribute. In this case, though, they impose specific cut-offs. For example, if Daniel had been more interested in having a sleep timer on his HDTV (if that had had a higher importance ranking), he might have stipulated that his choice 'must have a sleep timer'. Because the Prime Wave model had one and the Precision did not, he would have chosen the Prime Wave.

The conjunctive rule Whereas the two former rules involve processing by attribute, the *conjunctive rule* entails processing by brand. As with the elimination-by-aspects procedure, the decision-maker establishes cut-offs for each attribute. They choose a brand if it meets all of the cut-offs, while failure to meet any one cut-off means they will reject it. If none of the brands meet all of the cut-offs, they may delay the choice, change the decision rule, or modify the cut-offs they choose to apply.

If Daniel had stipulated that all attributes had to be rated 'good' or better, he would not have been able to choose any of the options. He might then have modified his decision rule, conceding that it was not possible to attain these high standards in the price range he was considering. In this case, Daniel might decide that he could live without on-screen programming, so he would again consider the Precision model.

▶ Compensatory decision rules

Unlike non-compensatory decision rules, compensatory decision rules give a product a chance to make up for its shortcomings. Consumers who employ these rules tend to be more involved in the purchase and so they are willing to exert the effort to consider the entire picture in a more exacting way. The willingness to let good and bad product qualities balance out can result in quite different choices. For example, if Daniel had not been concerned about having stereo reception, he might have chosen the Prime Wave model. But because this brand doesn't feature this highly ranked attribute, it doesn't stand a chance when he uses a non-compensatory rule.

Two basic types of compensatory rules have been identified. When they use the *simple additive rule*, the consumer merely chooses the alternative that has the largest number of positive attributes. This choice is most likely to occur when their ability or motivation to process information is limited. One drawback to this approach for the consumer is that some of these attributes may not be very meaningful or important. An ad containing a long list of product benefits may be persuasive, despite the fact that many of the benefits included are actually standard within the product class and are not determinant attributes at all.

The *weighted additive rule* is a more complex version.[139] When using this rule, the consumer also takes into account the relative importance of positively rated attributes, essentially multiplying brand ratings by importance weights. If this process sounds familiar, it should. The calculation process strongly resembles the multi-attribute attitude model described in Chapter 8.

Recent research argues that the difficulties faced by consumers in making decisions derives not just from the evaluation and trading off of different attributes (as described by the different decision rules above), but also derives from some degree of incompatibility between the *task* of choosing itself, and the valence of the alternatives within the decision set. When the consumer experiences conflict between the task of choosing and the valence of the alternatives then they face greater difficulties in making decisions; and take longer to make the decision. In the case of Daniel, for instance, if he had been faced with choices between HDTVs that he had not liked, then this would have compounded the difficulty involved in the task itself, i.e. making a decision. When all of the alternatives are unattractive, then decision-making increases in difficulty. The conflict Daniel would have faced in making a decision, when confronted by alternatives that he did not like, would have been heightened because he was faced with making a choice that he did not wish to make; and he would have taken longer to make a decision.[140]

CHAPTER SUMMARY

- Consumer decision making is a central part of consumer behaviour, but the way we evaluate and choose products (and the amount of thought we put into these choices) varies widely, depending on such dimensions as the degree of novelty or risk related to the decision.

  We almost constantly need to make decisions about products. Some of these decisions are very important and entail great effort, whereas we make others on a virtually automatic basis. The decision-making task is further complicated because of the sheer number of decisions we need to make in a marketplace environment characterized by consumer hyper choice.

  Perspectives on decision making range from a focus on habits that people develop over time to novel situations involving a great deal of risk in which consumers must carefully collect and analyze information prior to making a choice. Many of our decisions are highly automated and we make them largely by habit. This trend is accelerating as marketers begin to introduce smart products that enable silent commerce, where the products literally make their own purchase decisions (e.g. a malfunctioning appliance that contacts the repair person directly).

- A decision is actually composed of a series of stages that results in the selection of one product over competing options. A typical decision process involves several steps. The first is problem recognition, where we realize we must take some action. This recognition may occur because a current possession malfunctions or perhaps because we have a desire for something new.

■ Once the consumer recognizes a problem and sees it as sufficiently important to warrant some action, they begin the process of information search. This search may range from simply scanning their memory to determine what they have done before to resolve the same problem to extensive fieldwork where they consult a variety of sources to amass as much information as possible. In many cases, people engage in surprisingly little search. Instead, they rely on various mental short cuts, such as brand names or price, or they may simply imitate others' choices.

■ In the evaluation of alternatives stage, the product alternatives a person considers comprise their evoked set. Members of the evoked set usually share some characteristics; we categorize them similarly. The way the person mentally groups products influences which alternatives they will consider, and usually we associate some brands more strongly with these categories (i.e. they are more prototypical).

■ Our access to online sources is changing the way we decide what to buy. The World Wide Web has changed the way many of us search for information. Today, our problem is more likely to involve weeding out excess detail rather than searching for more information. Comparative search sites and intelligent agents help to filter and guide the search process. We may rely on cybermediaries, such as Web portals, to sort through massive amounts of information as a way to simplify the decision-making process.

■ Research in the field of behavioural economics illustrates that decision making is not always strictly rational. Principles of mental accounting demonstrate that the way a problem is posed (called framing) and whether it is put in terms of gains or losses influences what we decide.

■ When the consumer eventually must make a product choice from among alternatives, they use one of several decision rules. Non-compensatory rules eliminate alternatives that are deficient on any of the criteria we have chosen. Compensatory rules, which are more likely to be applied in high-involvement situations, allow us to consider each alternative's good and bad points more carefully to arrive at the best overall choice.

■ Very often, we use heuristics, or mental rules-of-thumb, to simplify decision making. In particular, we develop many market beliefs over time. One of the most common beliefs is that we can determine quality by looking at the price. Other heuristics rely on well-known brand names or a product's country of origin as signals of product quality. When we consistently purchase a brand over time, this pattern may be the result of true brand loyalty or may be simply due to inertia because it is the easiest thing to do.

▶ KEY TERMS

Behavioural influence perspective (p. 317)

Brand loyalty (p. 349)

Compensatory decision rules (p. 351)

Consideration set (p. 334)

Consumer hyperchoice (p. 315)

Country of origin (p. 344)

Cybermediary (p. 340)

Determinant attributes (p. 338)

Electronic recommendation agent (p. 341)

Ethnocentrism (p. 346)

Evaluative criteria (p. 337)

Evoked set (p. 334)

Experiential perspective (p. 317)

Extended problem-solving (p. 319)

Feature bloat (p. 337)

Feature creep (p. 337)

▶ KEY TERMS

Feature fatigue (p. 337)

Habitual decision-making (p. 319)

Heuristics (p. 342)

Inertia (p. 349)

Information search (p. 313)

Intelligent agents (p. 341)

Knowledge structure (p. 335)

Limited problem-solving (p. 319)

Low-literate consumer (p. 329)

Market beliefs (p. 343)

Mental accounting (p. 326)

Neuromarketing (p. 339)

Non-compensatory decision rules (p. 351)

Perceived risk (p. 328)

Problem recognition (p. 320)

Product signal (p. 342)

Prospect theory (p. 327)

Psychology of Loss Aversion (PLA) (p. 326)

Purchase momentum (p. 315)

Rational perspective (p. 315)

Search engines (p. 323)

Stereotype (p. 346)

Variety seeking (p. 324)

▶ CONSUMER BEHAVIOUR CHALLENGE

1 What is the difference between the behavioral influence and experiential perspectives on decision making? Give an example of the type of purchase that each perspective would help to explain.

2 If people are not always rational decision-makers, is it worth the effort to study how purchasing decisions are made? What techniques might be employed to understand experiential consumption and to translate this knowledge into marketing strategy?

3 What is prospect theory? Does it support the argument that we are rational decision makers?

4 Give an example of the sunk-cost fallacy.

5 Describe the difference between a super-ordinate category, a basic level category, and a subordinate category. What is an example of an exemplar product?

6 Describe the relationship between a consumer's level of expertise and how much they are likely to search for information about a product.

7 List three types of perceived risk, and give an example of each.

8 List three product attributes that can be used as quality signals and provide an example of each.

9 Explain the 'evoked set'. Why is it difficult to place a product in a consumer's evoked set after it has already been rejected? What strategies might a marketer use in an attempt to accomplish this goal?

10 Define the three levels of product categorization described in the chapter. Diagram these levels for a health club.

11 How does a brand function as a heuristic?

12 Describe the difference between inertia and brand loyalty.

13 Discuss two different non-compensatory decision rules and highlight the difference(s) between them. How might the use of one rule versus another result in a different product choice?

14 Choose a friend or parent who shops for groceries on a regular basis and keep a log of their purchases of common consumer products during the term. Can you detect any evidence of brand loyalty in any categories based on consistency of purchases? If so, talk to the person about these purchases. Try to determine if their choices are based on true brand loyalty or on inertia. What techniques might you use to differentiate between the two?

15 Form a group of three. Pick a product and develop a marketing plan based on each of the three approaches to consumer decision-making: rational, experiential and behavioural influence. What are the major differences in emphasis among the three perspectives? Which is the most likely type of problem-solving activity for the product you have selected? What characteristics of the product make this so?

16 Find a person who is about to make a major purchase. Ask that person to make a chronological list of all the information sources consulted prior to making a decision. How would you characterize the types of sources used (i.e. internal versus external, media versus personal, etc.)? Which sources appeared to have the most impact on the person's decision?

17 Perform a survey of country-of-origin stereotypes. Compile a list of five countries and ask people what products they associate with each. What are their evaluations of the products and likely attributes of these different products? The power of a country stereotype can also be demonstrated in another way. Prepare a brief description of a product, including a list of features, and ask people to rate it in terms of quality, likelihood of purchase, and so on. Make several versions of the description, varying only the country from which it comes. Do ratings change as a function of the country of origin?

18 Ask a friend to 'talk through' the process they used to choose one brand rather than others during a recent purchase. Based on this description, can you identify the decision rule that was most likely employed?

19 Technology has the potential to make our lives easier by reducing the amount of clutter we need to work through in order to access the information on the Internet that really interests us. On the other hand, perhaps intelligent agents that make recommendations based only on what we and others like us have chosen in the past limit us – they reduce the chance that we will stumble upon something (e.g. a book on a topic we've never heard of, or a music group that's different from the style we usually listen to). Will the proliferation of shopping bots make our lives too predictable by only giving us more of the same? If so, is this a problem?

20 Read Rust, Thompson and Hamilton's article in *Harvard Business Review* (February 2006: 98ff) on 'Defeating feature fatigue'. Summarize their main arguments and examples into a paragraph. Working in groups of three, write a brief for a marketing manager, first, explaining why consumers prefer capability to usability; secondly, identifying the disadvantages for both consumers and managers of consumers' tendency to prefer capability to usability; and thirdly, suggesting strategies that managers might adopt to counter feature fatigue amongst consumers.

21 'Too many features can make a product overwhelming for consumers and difficult to use' (Thompson, Rust and Hamilton, 2005: 431 [Debora V. Thompson, Rebecca W. Hamilton and Roland T. Rust, 'Feature fatigue: when product capabilities become too much of a good thing', *Journal of Marketing Research* 42 (November 2005): 431–442]. Debate this in class, using the material on adoption and diffusion from Chapter 14. How might marketing managers overcome barriers to adoption of their technically sophisticated products?

22 Give one of the scenarios described in the section on biases in decision-making to 10 to 20 people. How do the results you obtain compare with those reported in the chapter?

23 Think of a product you recently shopped for online. Describe your search process. How did you become aware you wanted/needed the product? How did you evaluate alternatives? Did you end up buying online? Why, or why not? What factors would make it more or less likely that you would buy something online rather than in a traditional store?

24 Consider the five types of perceived risk in Figure 9.7 within the context of making a decision to purchase a new diamond. Review the following Websites, and discuss the kinds of risk you would consider in buying a diamond on the Web: **www.diamond.com**, **www.mondera.com**, **www.bluenile.com**.

25 Find examples of electronic recommendation agents on the Web. Evaluate these – are they helpful? What characteristics of the sites you locate are likely to make you buy products you wouldn't have bought on your own?

26 It is increasingly clear that many postings on blogs and product reviews on Websites are fake

CONSUMER BEHAVIOUR CHALLENGE (*continued*)

or are posted there to manipulate consumers' opinions. For example, a mini-scandal erupted in 2007 when the press learned that the CEO of Whole Foods had regularly been blasting competitor Wild Oats on blogs under a pseudonym.[141] How big a problem is this if consumers are increasingly looking to consumer-generated product reviews to guide their purchase decisions? What steps, if any, can marketers take to nip this problem in the bud?

27 Visit the EC Website with video briefings about systems of consumer protection in the EC: http://ec.europa.eu/dgs/health_consumer/press/index_en.htm#consumers. Debate in class the reasons why there is increasing concern about 'keeping consumers safe'; and how far is it the role of national governments or international institutions (like the EC) to undertake this? What about the traditional view of the consumer's responsibility, i.e. buyer beware or *caveat emptor*?

For additional material see the companion website at **www.pearsoned.co.uk/solomon**

NOTES

1. Lutz Stobbe, EuP Preparatory Studies, 'Televisions' (Lot 5) Final Report on Task 3 'Consumer Behaviour and Local Infrastructure' (TREN/D1/40 lot 5-2005), compiled by Deutsche Umwelthilfe and Fraunhofer IZM (contractor: Fraunhofer Institute for Reliability and Microintegration, IZM: Berlin) (2 August 2007): 18.

2. Ying Zhang, Ayelet Fishback and Ravi Dhar, 'When thinking beats doing: The role of optimistic expectations in goal-based choice', *Journal of Consumer Research* 34 (December 2007): 567.

3. David Glen Mick, Susan M. Broniarczyk, and Jonathan Haidt, 'Choose, choose, choose, choose, choose, choose, choose: Emerging and prospective research on the deleterious effects of living in consumer hyperchoice', *Journal of Business Ethics* 52 (2004): 207–11; see also Barry Schwartz, *The Paradox of Choice: Why More Is Less* (New York: Ecco, 2005).

4. Itamar Simonson, Joel Huber, and John Payne, 'The relationship between prior brand knowledge and information acquisition order', *Journal of Consumer Research* 14 (March 1988): 566–78.

5. John R. Hauser, Glenn L. Urban, and Bruce D. Weinberg, 'How consumers allocate their time when searching for information', *Journal of Marketing Research* 30 (November 1993): 452–66; George J. Stigler, 'The economics of information', *Journal of Political Economy* 69 (June 1961): 213–25. For a set of studies focusing on online search costs, see John G. Lynch, Jr, and Dan Ariely, 'Wine online: Search costs and competition on price, quality, and distribution', *Marketing Science* 19(1) (2000): 83–103.

6. John C. Mowen, 'Beyond consumer decision making', *Journal of Consumer Marketing* 5(1) (1988): 15–25.

7. Richard W. Olshavsky and Donald H. Granbois, 'Consumer decision making – fact or fiction', *Journal of Consumer Research* 6 (September 1989): 93–100.

8. Chris Marks, 'As two osprey nests are raided, fears that thieves see Scotland as a soft option', *Daily Mail* (14 May 2002).

9. Ravi Dhar, Joel Huber, and Uzma Khan, 'The Shopping Momentum Effect', paper presented at the Association for Consumer Research, Atlanta, Georgia, October 2002.

10. James R. Bettman, 'The Decision Maker Who Came in from the Cold' (presidential address), in Leigh McAllister and Michael Rothschild (eds), *Advances in Consumer Research* 20 (Provo, U.T.: Association for Consumer Research, 1993): 7–11; John W. Payne, James R. Bettman and Eric J. Johnson, 'Behavioral decision research: A constructive processing perspective', *Annual Review of Psychology* 4 (1992): 87–131; J.R. Bettman, M.F. Luce and J.W. Payne 'Constructive consumer choice processes', *Journal of Consumer Research* 25(3) (December 1998): 187–217; for an overview of recent developments in individual choice models, see Robert J. Meyer and Barbara E. Kahn, 'Probabilistic Models of Consumer Choice Behavior', in Thomas S. Robertson and Harold H. Kassarjian (eds), *Handbook of Consumer Behavior* (Upper Saddle River, N.J.: Prentice Hall, 1991): 85–123.

11. Dan Ariely, 'Controlling the information flow: Effects on consumers' decision making and preferences', *Journal of Consumer Research*, 27 (September 2000): 245; John Deighton, 'The future of interactive marketing', *Harvard Business Review* 74(6) (1996): 151–62.

12. Ariely, 'Controlling the information flow' *ibid.*: 233–48.

13. Nicholas H. Lurie, 'Decision making in information-rich environments: The role of information structure', *Journal of Consumer Research* 30 (March 2004): 473–86.

14. Nicholas H. Lurie, 'Decision making in information-rich environments: The role of information structure', *Journal of Consumer Research* 30 (March 2004): 484–5.

15. Brian T. Ratchford, Debabrata Talukdar and Myung-Soo Lee, 'The impact of the internet on consumers' use of information sources for automobiles: A re-inquiry', *Journal of Consumer Research* 34 (June 2007): 111–9.

16. Mowen, 'Beyond consumer decision making', *op. cit.*

17. The Fits-Like-a-Glove (FLAG) framework is a new decision-making perspective that views consumer decisions as a

holistic process shaped by the person's unique context: see Douglas E. Allen, 'Toward a theory of consumer choice as sociohistorically shaped practical experience: The fits-like-a-glove (FLAG) framework', *Journal of Consumer Research* 28 (March 2002): 515–32.

18. Joseph W. Alba and J. Wesley Hutchinson, 'Dimensions of consumer expertise', *Journal of Consumer Research* 13 (March 1988): 411–54.

19. Gordon C. Bruner III and Richard J. Pomazal, 'Problem recognition: The crucial first stage of the consumer decision process', *Journal of Consumer Marketing* 5(1) (1988): 53–63.

20. Peter H. Bloch, Daniel L. Sherrell and Nancy M. Ridgway, 'Consumer search: An extended framework', *Journal of Consumer Research* 13 (June 1986): 119–26.

21. Peter H. Bloch, Daniel L. Sherrell, and Nancy M. Ridgway, 'Consumer search: An extended framework', *Journal of Consumer Research* 13 (June 1986): 119–26.

22. Girish Punj, 'Presearch decision making in consumer durable purchases', *Journal of Consumer Marketing* 4 (Winter 1987): 71–82.

23. H. Beales, M.B. Jagis, S.C. Salop and R. Staelin, 'Consumer search and public policy', *Journal of Consumer Research* 8 (June 1981): 11–22.

24. Laurie Petersen, 'Study Places Value On Marketing At Consumer Research Stage', *Marketing Daily* (27 June 2007): www.medipost.com.

25. Alex Mindlin, 'Buyers Search Online, but Not by Brand', *New York Times* (13 March 2006).

26. Brian T. Ratchford, Debabrata Talukdar and Myung-Soo Lee, 'The impact of the internet on consumers' use of information sources for automobiles: A re-inquiry', *op. cit.*

27. Brian T. Ratchford, Debabrata Talukdar and Myung-Soo Lee, 'The Impact of the Internet on Consumers' Use of Information Sources for Automobiles: A Re-Inquiry', *op. cit.*: 112.

28. *Ibid.*

29. The Nielsen Company Press Release, 'Over 875 Million Consumers Have Shopped Online – the Number of Internet Shoppers Up 40 per cent in Two Years', http://www.earthtimes.org/articles/show/over-875-million-consumers-have-shopped-online--the-number,263812.shtml, accessed 20 August 2008.

30. Itamar Simonson, Joel Huber and John Payne, 'The relationship between prior brand knowledge and information acquisition order', *Journal of Consumer Research* 14 (March 1988): 566–78.

31. John R. Hauser, Glen L. Urban and Bruce D. Weinberg, 'How consumers allocate their time when searching for information', *Journal of Marketing Research* 30 (November 1993): 452–66; George J. Stigler, 'The economics of information', *Journal of Political Economy* 69 (June 1961): 213–25; for a set of studies focusing on online search costs see John G. Lynch Jr. and Dan Ariely, 'Wine Online: Search Costs and Competition on Price, Quality, and Distribution' (unpublished manuscript, Duke University).

32. Cathy J. Cobb and Wayne D. Hoyer, 'Direct observation of search behavior', *Psychology and Marketing* 2 (Fall 1985): 161–79.

33. Sharon E. Beatty and Scott M. Smith, 'External search effort: An investigation across several product categories', *Journal of Consumer Research* 14 (June 1987): 83–95; William L. Moore and Donald R. Lehmann, 'Individual differences in search behavior for a nondurable', *Journal of Consumer Research* 7 (December 1980): 296–307.

34. Kiel and Layton, 'Dimensions of consumer information seeking behavior'; see also Srinivasan and Ratchford, 'An empirical test of a model of external search for automobiles'; Mari Niva, Eva Heiskanen and Päivi Timonen, 'Environmental information in consumer decision making', *National Consumer Research Centre* (Helsinki, July 1996).

35. David F. Midgley, 'Patterns of interpersonal information seeking for the purchase of a symbolic product', *Journal of Marketing Research* 20 (February 1983): 74–83.

36. Cyndee Miller, 'Scotland to U.S.: "This Tennent's for you"', *Marketing News* (29 August 1994): 26.

37. Rebecca K. Ratner, Barbara E. Kahn and Daniel Kahneman, 'Choosing less-preferred experiences for the sake of variety', *Journal of Consumer Research* 26 (June 1999): 1–15.

38. Satya Menon and Barbara E. Kahn, 'The impact of context on variety seeking in product choices', *Journal of Consumer Research* 22 (December 1995): 285–95; Barbara E. Kahn and Alice M. Isen, 'The influence of positive affect on variety seeking among safe, enjoyable products', *Journal of Consumer Research* 20 (September 1993): 257–70.

39. J. Jeffrey Inman, 'The Role of Sensory-Specific Satiety in Consumer Variety Seeking Among Flavors' (unpublished manuscript, A.C. Nielsen Center for Marketing Research, University of Wisconsin-Madison, July 1999).

40. Michael Laroche, Chankon Kim and Lianxi Zhou, 'Brand familiarity and confidence as determinants of purchase intention: An empirical test in a multiple brand context', *Journal of Business Research* 37 (1996): 115–20.

41. Barbara E. Kahn, 'Understanding Variety-Seeking Behavior From a Marketing Perspective', unpublished manuscript, University of Pennsylvania, University Park, 1991; Leigh McAlister and Edgar A. Pessemier, 'Variety-seeking behavior: An interdisciplinary review', *Journal of Consumer Research* 9 (December 1982): 311–22; Fred M. Feinberg, Barbara E. Kahn and Leigh McAlister, 'Market share response when consumers seek variety', *Journal of Marketing Research* 29 (May 1992): 228–37; Kahn and Isen, 'The influence of positive affect on variety seeking among safe, enjoyable products', *op. cit.*

42. Gary Belsky, 'Why smart people make major money mistakes', *Money* (July 1995): 76; Richard Thaler and Eric J. Johnson, 'Gambling with the house money or trying to break even: The effects of prior outcomes on risky choice', *Management Science* 36 (June 1990): 643–60; Richard Thaler, 'Mental accounting and consumer choice', *Marketing Science* 4 (Summer 1985): 199–214.

43. Lyle Brenner, Yuval Rottenstreich, Sanjay Sood and Baler Bilgin, 'On the Psychology of Loss Aversion Aversion: Possession, Valence, and Reversals of the Endowment Effect', *Journal of Consumer Research* 34 (October 2007): 376.

44. Lyle Brenner, Yuval Rottenstreich, Sanjay Sood and Baler Bilgin, 'On the Psychology of Loss Aversion Aversion: Possession, Valence, and Reversals of the Endowment Effect', *Journal of Consumer Research* 34 (October 2007): 370, Table 1.

45. Daniel Kahneman and Amos Tversky, 'Prospect theory: An analysis of decision under risk,' *Econometrica* 47 (March 1979): 263–91; Timothy B. Heath, Subimal Chatterjee and Karen Russo France, 'Mental accounting and changes in price: The frame dependence of reference dependence', *Journal of Consumer Research* 22(1) (June 1995): 90–7.

46. Quoted in Thaler, 'Mental accounting and consumer choice', *op. cit.*: 206.

47. Scott I. Rick, Cynthia E. Cryder and George Loewenstein, 'Tightwads and Spendthrifts', *Journal of Consumer Research* 34 (April 2008): 767.

48. Girish N. Punj and Richard Staelin, 'A model of consumer search behavior for new automobiles', *Journal of Consumer Research* 9 (March 1983): 366–80.

49. Cobb and Hoyer, 'Direct observation of search behavior', *op. cit.*; Moore and Lehmann, 'Individual differences in search behavior for a nondurable', *op. cit.*; Punj and Staelin, 'A model of consumer search behavior for new automobiles', *op. cit.*

50. Judi Strebel, Tulin Erdem and Joffre Swait, 'Consumer search in high technology markets: Exploring the use of traditional information channels', *Journal of Consumer Psychology* 14(1 and 2) (2004): 96–104.

51. James R. Bettman and C. Whan Park, 'Effects of prior knowledge and experience and phase of the choice process on consumer decision processes: A protocol analysis', *Journal of Consumer Research* 7 (December 1980): 234–48.

52. Alba and Hutchinson, 'Dimensions of consumer expertise'; Bettman and Park, 'Effects of prior knowledge and experience and phase of the choice process on consumer decision processes', *op. cit.*; Merrie Brucks, 'The effects of product class knowledge on information search behavior', *Journal of Consumer Research* 12 (June 1985): 1–16; Joel E. Urbany, Peter R. Dickson and William L. Wilkie, 'Buyer uncertainty and information search', *Journal of Consumer Research* 16 (September 1989): 208–15.

53. Alexander Fedorikhin and Catherine A. Cole, 'Mood effects on attitudes, perceived risk and choice: Moderators and mediators', *Journal of Consumer Psychology*, 14(1 and 2) (2004): 2–12.

54. For a discussion of 'collective risk', where consumers experience a reduction in perceived risk by sharing their exposure with others who are also using the product or service, see an analysis of Hotline, an online file-sharing community in Markus Geisler, 'Collective Risk', working paper, Northwestern University, March 2003.

55. DfES Skills for Life national needs and impact survey 2003, http://www.literacytrust.org.uk/database/stats/adultstats.html and http://www.literacytrust.org.uk/Policy/adultlevels.html, accessed 23 August 2008.

56. Natalie Ross Adkins and Julie L. Ozanne, 'The low literate consumer', *Journal of Consumer Research* 32(1) (2005): 93; Madhubalan Viswanathan, Jose Antonio Rosa, and James Edwin Harris, 'Decision making and coping of functionally illiterate consumers and some implications for marketing management', *Journal of Marketing* 69(1) (2005): 15.

57. 'Keeping European Consumers Safe', 2007 Annual Report on the operation of the Rapid Alert System for non-food consumer products, European Communities Health and Consumer Protection Directorate General, Luxembourg, 2008 page 10; see also weekly updates: http://ec.europa.eu/consumers/dyna/rapex/create_rapex.cfm?rx_id=196

58. *Ibid.*: 20.

59. 'Keeping European Consumers Safe', Foreword to the 2007 Annual Report on the operation of the Rapid Alert System for non-food consumer products, European Communities Health and Consumer Protection Directorate General, Luxembourg, 2008: 3; note that the RAPEX weekly overviews can be consulted at http://ec.europa.eu/rapex; the EC's General Product Safety Directiv (GPSD) is available at: http://eur-lex.europa.eu/LexUriServ/LexUriServ.do?uri=CELEX:32001L0095:EN:NOT and the Guidelines at: http://ec.europa.eu/consumers/safety/rapex/guidelines_states_en.htm; sectoral directives are available at the EUR-Lex website: http://eur-lex.europa.eu/ and include coverage of toys, cosmetics and cars.

60. Mary Frances Luce, James R. Bettman and John W. Payne, 'Choice processing in emotionally difficult decisions', *Journal of Experimental Psychology: Learning, Memory, and Cognition* 23 (March 1997): 384–405; example provided by Prof. James Bettman, personal communication, 17 December 1997.

61. Some research suggests that structural elements of the information available, such as the number and distribution of attribute levels, will influence how items in a consideration set are processed; *cf.* Nicholas H. Lurie, 'Decision making in information-rich environments: The role of information structure', *Journal of Consumer Research* 30 (March 2004): 473–86.

62. John R. Hauser and Birger Wernerfelt, 'An evaluation cost model of consideration sets', *Journal of Consumer Research* 16 (March 1990): 393–408.

63. Robert J. Sutton, 'Using empirical data to investigate the likelihood of brands being admitted or readmitted into an established evoked set', *Journal of the Academy of Marketing Science* 15 (Fall 1987): 82.

64. Cyndee Miller, 'Hemp is latest buzzword', *Marketing News* (17 March 1997): 1.

65. Alba and Hutchinson, 'Dimensions of consumer expertise'; Joel B. Cohen and Kunal Basu, 'Alternative models of categorization: Toward a contingent processing framework', *Journal of Consumer Research* 13 (March 1987): 455–72.

66. Robert M. McMath, 'The perils of typecasting', *American Demographics* (February 1997): 60.

67. Eleanor Rosch, 'Principles of Categorization', in E. Rosch and B.B. Lloyd (eds), *Recognition and Categorization* (Hillsdale, N.J.: Erlbaum, 1978).

68. Michael R. Solomon, 'Mapping product constellations: A social categorization approach to symbolic consumption', *Psychology and Marketing* 5(3) (1988): 233–58.

69. McMath, 'The perils of typecasting', *op. cit.*

70. Elizabeth C. Hirschman and Michael R. Solomon, 'Competition and Cooperation Among Culture Production Systems', in Ronald F. Bush and Shelby D. Hunt (eds), *Marketing Theory: Philosophy of Science Perspectives* (Chicago: American Marketing Association, 1982): 269–72.

71. Michael D. Johnson, 'The differential processing of product category and noncomparable choice alternatives', *Journal of Consumer Research* 16 (December 1989): 300–9.

72. Mita Sujan, 'Consumer knowledge: Effects on evaluation strategies mediating consumer judgments', *Journal of Consumer Research* 12 (June 1985): 31–46.

73. Rosch, 'Principles of categorization', *op. cit.*

74. Joan Meyers-Levy and Alice M. Tybout, 'Schema congruity as a basis for product evaluation', *Journal of Consumer Research* 16 (June 1989): 39–55.

75. Mita Sujan and James R. Bettman, 'The effects of brand positioning strategies on consumers' brand and category perceptions: Some insights from schema research', *Journal of Marketing Research* 26 (November 1989): 454–67.

76. See William P. Putsis Jr and Narasimhan Srinivasan, 'Buying or just browsing? The duration of purchase deliberation', *Journal of Marketing Research* 31 (August 1994): 393–402.

77. Robert E. Smith, 'Integrating information from advertising and trial: Processes and effects on consumer response

to product information', *Journal of Marketing Research* 30 (May 1993): 204–19.

78. *Ibid.*

79. Roland T. Rust, Debora V. Thompson and Rebecca W. Hamilton, 'Defeating feature fatigue', *Harvard Business Review* 84 (February 2006): 100.

80. Rebecca W. Hamilton and Debora Viana Thompson, 'Is there a substitute for direct experience? Comparing consumers' preferences after direct and indirect product experiences', *Journal of Consumer Research* 34 (December 2007): 546–55.

81. Debora V. Thompson, Rebecca W. Hamilton and Roland T. Rust, 'Feature fatigue: when product capabilities become too much of a good thing', *Journal of Marketing Research* 42 (November 2005): 431–42; Roland T. Rust, Debora V. Thompson and Rebecca W. Hamilton, 'Defeating feature fatigue', *op. cit.*: 98–107.

82. Robert E. Smith, 'Integrating information from advertising and trial: Processes and effects on consumer response to product information', *op. cit.*

83. Lutz Stobbe, EuP Preparatory Studies, 'Televisions' (Lot 5) Final Report on Task 3 'Consumer Behaviour and Local Infrastructure' (TREN/D1/40 lot 5-2005), compiled by Deutsche Umwelthilfe and Fraunhofer IZM (contractor: Fraunhofer Institute for Reliability and Microintegration, IZM: Berlin) (2 August 2007): 5.

84. James Surowiecki, 'Feature Presentation', *The New Yorker* (28 May 2007), accessed 23 May 2007, www.NewYorker.com

85. Sikka, Prem, 'Sleeping watchdogs', http://www.guardian.co.uk/commentisfree/2009/jan/14/corporatefraud, accessed 14 January 2009.

86. Jack Trout, 'Marketing in tough times', *Boardroom Reports* 2 (October 1992): 8.

87. Amna Kirmani and Peter Wright, 'Procedural learning, consumer decision making and marketing communication', *Marketing Letters* 4(1) (1993): 39–48.

88. *Ibid.*

89. Michael Porter, *Competitive Advantage* (New York: Free Press, 1985).

90. Material in this section adapted from Michael R. Solomon and Elnora W. Stuart, *Welcome to Marketing.com: The Brave New World of E-Commerce* (Englewood Cliffs, NJ: Prentice Hall, 2001).

91. 'Customer Product Reviews Drive Online Satisfaction and Conversion', available from www.mediapost.com, accessed 24 January 2007.

92. Phil Patton, 'Buy here, and we'll tell you what you like', *The New York Times on the Web* (22 September 1999).

93. Kristin Diehl, 'When two rights make a wrong: Searching too much in ordered environments', *Journal of Marketing Research* 42 (August 2005): 313–22; Andrew D. Gershoff, Ashesh Mukherjee, and Anirban Mukhopadhyay, 'Consumer acceptance of online agent advice: Extremity and positivity effects', *Journal of Consumer Psychology* 12(1 and 2) (2003): 161–70; Vanitha Swaminathan, 'The impact of recommendation agents on consumer evaluation and choice: The moderating role of category risk, product complexity, and consumer knowledge', *Journal of Consumer Psychology* 12(1 and 2) (2003): 93–101; Gerald Haubl and Kyle B. Murray, 'Preference construction and persistence in digital marketplaces: The role of electronic recommendation agents', *Journal of Consumer Psychology* 13(1 and 2) (2003): 75–91; Dan Ariely, John G. Lynch, Jr, and Manuel Aparicio IV, 'Learning by collaborative and individual-based recommendation agents', *Journal of Consumer Psychology* 14(1 and 2) (2004): 81–95; Sylvain Senecal and Jacques Nantel, 'The influence of online product recommendations on consumers' online choices', *Journal of Retailing* 80 (2004): 159–69.

94. Robert A. Baron, *Psychology: The Essential Science* (Boston: Allyn & Bacon, 1989); Valerie S. Folkes, 'The availability heuristic and perceived risk', *Journal of Consumer Research* 15 (June 1989): 13–23; Daniel Kahneman and Amos Tversky, 'Prospect theory: An analysis of decision under risk', *Econometrica* 47 (1979): 263–91.

95. Example developed from Ritesh Saini and Ashwani Monga, 'How I decide depends on what I spend: Use of heuristics is greater for time than for money', *Journal of Consumer Research* 34 (April 2008): 914–22.

96. Amos Tversky and Daniel Kahneman, 'Judgment under uncertainty: Heuristics and biases', *Science* 27, 185 (September 1974): 1124–131.

97. Ritesh Saini and Ashwani Monga, 'How I decide depends on what I spend', *op. cit.*: 915.

98. Wayne D. Hoyer, 'An examination of consumer decision making for a common repeat purchase product', *Journal of Consumer Research* 11 (December 1984): 822–9; Calvin P. Duncan, 'Consumer Market Beliefs: A Review of the Literature and an Agenda for Future Research,' in Marvin E. Goldberg, Gerald Gorn and Richard W. Pollay (eds), *Advances in Consumer Research* 17 (Provo, U.T.: Association for Consumer Research, 1990): 729–35; Frank Alpert, 'Consumer market beliefs and their managerial implications: An empirical examination', *Journal of Consumer Marketing* 10(2) (1993): 56–70.

99. Ritesh Saini and Ashwani Monga, 'How I Decide Depends on What I Spend', *op. cit.*: 920.

100. Michael R. Solomon, Sarah Drenan and Chester A. Insko, 'Popular induction: When is consensus information informative?' *Journal of Personality* 49(2) (1981): 212–24.

101. Folkes, 'The availability heuristic and perceived risk', *op. cit.*

102. Beales *et al.*, 'Consumer search and public policy', *op. cit.*

103. Gary T. Ford and Ruth Ann Smith, 'Inferential beliefs in consumer evaluations: An assessment of alternative processing strategies', *Journal of Consumer Research* 14 (December 1987): 363–71; Deborah Roedder John, Carol A. Scott and James R. Bettman, 'Sampling data for covariation assessment: The effects of prior beliefs on search patterns', *Journal of Consumer Research* 13 (June 1986): 38–47; Gary L. Sullivan and Kenneth J. Berger, 'An investigation of the determinants of cue utilization', *Psychology and Marketing* 4 (Spring 1987): 63–74.

104. Duncan, 'Consumer market beliefs', *op. cit.*

105. Chr. Hjorth-Andersen, 'Price as a risk indicator', *Journal of Consumer Policy* 10 (1987): 267–81.

106. David M. Gardner, 'Is there a generalized price–quality relationship?' *Journal of Marketing Research* 8 (May 1971): 241–3; Kent B. Monroe, 'Buyers' subjective perceptions of price', *Journal of Marketing Research* 10 (1973): 70–80.

107. Durairaj Maheswaran, 'Country of origin as a stereotype: Effects of consumer expertise and attribute strength on product evaluations', *Journal of Consumer Research* 21 (September 1994): 354–65; Ingrid M. Martin and Sevgin Eroglu, 'Measuring a multi-dimensional construct: Country image', *Journal of Business Research* 28 (1993): 191–210; Richard Ettenson, Janet Wagner and Gary Gaeth, 'Evaluating the effect of country of origin and the "Made in the

U.S.A." campaign: A conjoint approach', *Journal of Retailing* 64 (Spring 1988): 85–100; C. Min Han and Vern Terpstra, 'Country-of-origin effects for uni-national and bi-national products', *Journal of International Business* 19 (Summer 1988): 235–55; Michelle A. Morganosky and Michelle M. Lazarde, 'Foreign-made apparel: Influences on consumers' perceptions of brand and store quality', *International Journal of Advertising* 6 (Fall 1987): 339–48.

108. See Richard Jackson Harris, Bettina Garner-Earl, Sara J. Sprick and Collette Carroll, 'Effects of foreign product names and country-of-origin attributions on advertisement evaluations', *Psychology and Marketing* 11 (March/April 1994): 129–45; Terence A. Shimp, Saeed Samiee and Thomas J. Madden, 'Countries and their products: A cognitive structure perspective', *Journal of the Academy of Marketing Science* 21 (Fall 1993): 323–30.

109. 'Keeping European Consumers Safe', 2007 Annual Report on the operation of the Rapid Alert System for non-food consumer products, European Communities Health and Consumer Protection Directorate General, Luxembourg, 2008: 24.

110. http://ec.europa.eu/consumers/safety/rapex/index_en.htm, accessed 24 August 2008.

111. 'Keeping European Consumers Safe', *op. cit.*: 31–3.

112. 'EU steps up global battle over Parma ham, Roquefort cheese', *NYT online* (28 August 2003).

113. Durairaj Maheswaran, 'Country of origin as a stereotype: Effects of consumer expertise and attribute strength on product evaluations', *Journal of Consumer Research* 21 (September 1994): 354–65.

114. Sung-Tai Hong and Robert S. Wyer Jr, 'Effects of country-of-origin and product-attribute information on product evaluation: An information processing perspective', *Journal of Consumer Research* 16 (September 1989): 175–87; Marjorie Wall, John Liefeld and Louise A. Heslop, 'Impact of country-of-origin cues on consumer judgments in multi-cue situations: A covariance analysis', *Journal of the Academy of Marketing Science* 19(2) (1991): 105–13.

115. Wai-Kwan Li and Robert S. Wyer Jr, 'The role of country of origin in product evaluations: Informational and standard-of-comparison effects', *Journal of Consumer Psychology* 3(2) (1994): 187–212.

116. Maheswaran, 'Country of origin as a stereotype', *op. cit.*

117. Items excerpted from Terence A. Shimp and Subhash Sharma, 'Consumer ethnocentrism: Construction and validation of the CETSCALE', *Journal of Marketing Research* 24 (August 1987): 282.

118. Teodoro Luque-Martinez, Jose-Angel Ibanez-Zapata and Salvador del Barrio-Garcia, 'Consumer ethnocentrism measurement – an assessment of the reliability and validity of the CETSCALE in Spain', *European Journal of Marketing* 34(11/12) (2000): 1353ff.

119. Richard W. Stevenson, 'The brands with billion-dollar names', *New York Times* (28 October 1988): A1.

120. Douglas B. Holt, *How Brands Become Icons: The Principles of Cultural Branding* (Boston: Harvard Business School Press, 2004).

121. Ronald Alsop, 'Enduring brands hold their allure by sticking close to their roots', *The Wall Street Journal*, centennial edn (1989): B4.

122. *BusinessWeek*/Interbrand's Annual Ranking of 'The best global brands', press release, *BusinessWeekOnline* archive, www.businessweek.com (22 July 2004).

123. 'What's in a name?' *The Economist* (27 August 1988): 62.

124. Stuart Elliott, 'What's in a name? Perhaps billions', *New York Times* (12 August 1992): D6.

125. Interbrand, cited in Dan Roberts, 'Is the world falling out of love with US brands?' *Financial Times* (30 December 2004) http://news.ft.com/cms/s/502f6994-59d5-11d9-ba09-00000e2511c8.html.

126. Source: Salvador Davoudi, 'Market trends: strong names beat the market', ft.com, 20 April 2008, http://www.ft.com/cms/s/0/abdf3546-0cf4-11dd-86df-0000779fd2ac.html, accessed 24 August 2008.

127. Roberts, 'Is the world falling out of love with US brands?' *op. cit.*

128. *Ibid.*

129. For explanation of methodology see: Joanna Seddon 'methodology: how the ranking table is compiled', 20 April 2008, ft.com, http://www.ft.com/cms/s/0/aec2532e-0cf4-11dd-86df-0000779fd2ac,dwp_uuid=9b7f008c-0d17-11dd-b90a-0000779fd2ac.html, accessed 24 August 2008.

130. Joanna Seddon, 'Methodology', *op. cit.*

131. Greg Morago, 'Envy: The Brand Sluts – Many Who Covet Their Retailers' Garb No Longer Look at the Logo', *Hartford Courant on the Web* (1 January 2007).

132. Jacob Jacoby and Robert Chestnut, *Brand Loyalty: Measurement and Management* (New York: Wiley, 1978).

133. Anne B. Fisher, 'Coke's brand loyalty lesson', *Fortune* (5 August 1985): 44.

134. Jacoby and Chestnut, *Brand Loyalty*, *op. cit.*

135. Ronald Alsop, 'Brand loyalty is rarely blind loyalty', *The Wall Street Journal* (19 October 1989): B1.

136. Betsy Morris, 'The brand's the thing', *Fortune* (4 March 1996): 72(8).

137. Hope Jensen Schau and Mary C. Gilly, 'We are what we post: The presentation of self in personal webspace', *Journal of Consumer Research* 30 (December 2003): 385–404; Hope Schau, Temple University, personal communication, March 2003.

138. C. Whan Park, 'The effect of individual and situation-related factors on consumer selection of judgmental models', *Journal of Marketing Research* 13 (May 1976): 144–51.

139. Joseph W. Alba and Howard Marmorstein, 'The effects of frequency knowledge on consumer decision making', *Journal of Consumer Research* 14 (June 1987): 14–25.

140. Anish Nagpal and Parthasarathy Krishnamurthy, 'Attribute conflict in consumer decision making: The role of task compatibility', *Journal of Consumer Research* 34 (February 2008): 696–705.

141. David Kesmodel and John R. Wilke, 'Whole Foods Is Hot, Wild Oats a Dud – So Said "Rahodeb" Then Again, Yahoo Poster Was a Whole Foods Staffer, the CEO to Be Precise', *Wall Street Journal* (12 July 2007): A1.

How research into consumer attitudes led to the creation of the O2 brand

JIM FREUND, Lancaster University Management School, UK

'... this case is emblematic of how brand engineering can transform not just the metrics of a business, but the morale of its staff, the esteem of its public, its ability to sustain competitive advantage and its potential to deliver future earnings.'

'It only works if it all works: How troubled BT Cellnet transformed into thriving O2', VCCP, O2's advertising agency in *Advertising Works 13* (UK Institute of Practitioners in Advertising)

BACKGROUND

In 2000 BT (the trading name of British Telecommunications plc) was keeping a careful eye on the rapidly changing global mobile market. There were several strong international mobile network operators, but two brands in particular looked as though they were on course to become truly global: Vodafone and Orange.

Vodafone was known for its great size and had a strong brand and reputation among business users. Orange, on the other hand, was particularly strong among consumers and had, since its creation in 1984, been known as a mould-breaking brand, with its daring abstract name, and its brilliant strapline – 'The future's bright, the future's Orange' – which summarized the essence of the Orange brand: optimism.

By permission of BT

BT owned shares in many mobile companies around the world, and had a controlling share in mobile network operators in four European countries; but each of these four controlled businesses traded under a different brand:

> **BT Cellnet** in the UK
> **Esat Digifone** in the Republic of Ireland
> **Viag Interkom** in Germany
> **Telfort** in the Netherlands

In July 2000 BT formed a global mobile division called BT Wireless to manage all these diverse wireless interests. It was clear that considerable integration benefits could be realized by creating a single international mobile brand that could compete with the likes of Vodafone and Orange.

RESEARCH

A global research programme was commissioned by BT's Group Brand Team to understand what users felt about the current mobile brands, and understand what characteristics this new brand should have to appeal to those customers. The research examined the existing quantitative brand tracking in each country, and then qualitative research, consisting of focus groups with consumers and in-depth interviews with business customers, was carried out. The research was conducted in the UK, Germany, Ireland, the Netherlands, Spain, Japan and the USA.

Japan was included in the research because it was ahead of Europe in terms of both the development of mobile technology and services, and consumer adoption of these new applications. And the USA was included because of its potential as a marketplace and because it had a very different perspective from Europe and Asia and a much more fragmented set of competing brands.

If the rebranding was going to go ahead, BT Cellnet in the UK was going to be the most important country at launch, not only because the brand owner was based there, but because it was financially the biggest of the companies that would be rebranded, therefore the risk of getting it wrong was the greatest.

The main research findings were:

1 Mobiles had become an essential tool and were highly integrated into people's lives. People could no longer imagine life without their mobile and 'would feel naked without it' (see slide (Figure 1) from research debrief).
2 The physical handset brands, especially Nokia, were more emotionally involving than the network brands. Handsets encapsulate the benefit, whereas networks were generally seen as being associated with the monthly bill, the price you pay.
3 Desirable characteristics for a new mobile brand were found to be 'Liberating', 'Cool' and 'Tomorrow'.

4 Overall, there was little loyalty among customers to the four owned brands. Each of the four brands had quite a different image from the others, and only one of them – Digifone – was seen as being positive on both functional and emotional characteristics. BT was not well known by consumers outside the UK, and so should probably not be used as an element in the new brand. BT Cellnet in the UK was seen as an older brand and as being more for business customers than for consumers. The name Cellnet was seen as functional and pretty boring (Cellular-Network).

The fact that none of the existing brands were particularly strong opened the door to taking the big risk of rebranding them all. The fear was that the rebranding could be expensive and disrupting, might not be accepted by the customers and the media, and could damage the business of some or all of the companies. But the upside was that the new brand could revitalize all of the businesses, and create an integrated new European business that could soon become much greater than the sum of its parts.

Figure 1

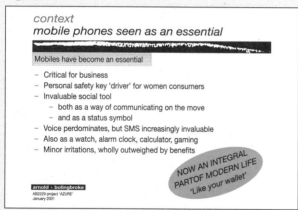

By permission of BT

Figure 2

By permission of BT

Figure 3

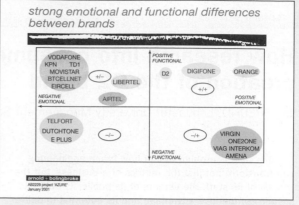

By permission of BT

NEW BRAND

Once the evidence of this major research programme had been accepted, there was the exciting prospect (and anxiety) of creating a major new European communications brand. A pitch was arranged between four design agencies. The brief was written to inspire different thinking and create a truly original but relevant new brand name and visual identity. The agencies were told about the research findings and the new brand was described as follows:

It's serious. It's simple. It's global. It's cool.

It gets things done.

It makes you feel you can always get around things. Unless you leave it behind – then you're stuffed.

It's a very powerful thing to have – socially, at work, and just for the fun of it.

It's essential equipment for the modern world.

As regards the name, the requirement in the brief was:

Short is beautiful.

Real words are best.

Works globally.

Reflects the simplicity and power of the brand.

This brief led first to the name idea, 'Oxygen', which was evolved into 'O2' and the core idea: Essential for life. The winning agency Lambie-Nairn initially presented ideas in the pitch which included the bubbles in water as a way of visualizing the invisible element O2.

In that pitch presentation the O2 logo was written using a font that was metallic silver in colour and looked solid, as though it was made of mercury. This prototype O2 logo was designed to contrast with the fluidity of the water and oxygen imagery, and to represent graphically the solidity of the handset that had been found to be so popular with consumers in contrast to the intangible qualities of the network.

This metallic logo was at first intended for use with various background colours including red, green and blue.

The pitch was unanimously awarded to Lambie-Nairn for transforming the strategic thinking and customer insights into a brilliant creative solution. Over the following weeks the early ideas were debated, researched, and developed. The metallic logo was changed to plain white and was set in the Frutiger font – this was done so as not to distract from the impact of the main idea – the freshness and vitality of O2 as depicted by the images of bubbles in blue water. For the same reason, the other background colours were also dropped.

What remained was a short, intriguing, original name, and a compelling and single-minded visual idea, based on a well-researched customer insight. Like the new mobile services, it felt liberating and refreshing; it was everywhere; it was essential for life. The new name, visuals and brand ideas were tested among the various audiences and countries of interest. Some groups of customers in certain markets found the new name and branding too cold or abstract, and felt that people wouldn't get the link between oxygen and mobility; but other groups were very enthusiastic about the new name and graphics, especially younger consumers. The branding team felt it was an acceptable risk to push ahead with the O2 brand, as it was considered more important to appeal strongly to some demographic groups, rather than to avoid offending any group.

Various factors have since made O2 into a multi-billion pound brand: their extremely consistent application of the name and visual identity across their entire range of marketing communications, products, and shops; their inspired use of sponsorship as a brand-building medium; their focus on keeping their existing customers happy rather than chasing new ones; their bold targeting of younger customers without alienating older ones; and their high standards of treatment of their employees – and all of this latter activity was set off on the right footing with the creation of a brand and identity that was original, relevant and based on customer insight.

This case study contains some important lessons in branding:

1 Take great care and adequate time to make the right naming and branding decisions at the outset of a venture.
2 Base your new brand on a strong idea.
3 The creative process occurs in a haphazard series of steps or leaps forward, e.g. new research insights or name ideas or visuals or core brand ideas can each spark off new ways of improving the other elements to build a coherent and integrated solution.
4 Sometimes elements of a solution that seem important and relevant need to be eliminated in order not to dilute and distract from the main idea. Less is often more.
5 Test your ideas on the audience at each stage – but don't be afraid occasionally to ignore parts of their feedback if you have a good reason to do so.
6 Once you have a great idea, be single-minded and ruthless in applying it and nothing else. O2's rallying cry for marketing communications is, 'It only works if it all works'.

'They have done a superb job. They have done a superb job on branding.'

Hans Snook, founder of Orange, *The Times*, February 2004.

QUESTIONS

1 What mobile brands operate in your country? Which ones are global and which ones are local? What are their strengths and weaknesses from a customer's point of view? Can you draw a positioning map which will draw out the main differences between the competing brands?

2 Can you think of any major brands that have rebranded and entirely changed their name and identity? Was the rebranding successful, or not? Did they just change the surface of the brand (how it looks, what it's called, the campaigns), or did the entire philosophy of the brand change (the services and products, pricing, distribution, the way they treat customers, brand personality, tone of voice).

3 Do you believe that qualitative or quantitative stakeholder research is most important to inform the process of creative development?

4 Set yourself a branding and naming challenge: select a product or service category that you are interested in (e.g. perfumes, mobile networks, beer) in your country. Imagine that you're rebranding one of the biggest brands in that category. Try to come up with the new brand including the name, the logo, the design look and feel, a strapline, and a definition of what the new brand should mean to its customers. What customer insight is your new brand based on? Will it use any elements from the existing brand, or do you believe you need to take the risk to kill off the old brand and launch a completely new brand? How is the new or revised brand positioned differently from the other brands?

Fear, guilt and shame: the use of emotions in advertising to change public behaviour

EFFI RAFTOPOULOU, Keele University, UK

Advertisers have always used a range of techniques to attract attention, increase the memorability of advertisements, create particular brand associations and ultimately sell their products or services to consumers. The use of emotion appeals in adverts has been quite popular as advertisers have always believed that the stimulation of emotions can exert a strong influence on audiences. The strength of the emotion generated by an ad is thought to be directly linked to consumers' reactions to adverts. Advertisements are frequently quite entertaining, funny, sexy or moving. However, advertising is not only about creating positive emotions. Advertisements also employ negative emotions, such as fear, shock, embarrassment, guilt or shame.

Despite the prominence of emotions in adverts, their effectiveness has been questioned by researchers, e.g. whether or not consumers actually feel the emotions intended by advertising (Campbell, 1995; Englis, 1990). In addition, advertisers have also been accused of manipulation by playing on people's emotions. This has been particularly the case with advertisements that draw upon negative emotions.

NEGATIVE EMOTIONS IN ADVERTISEMENTS

Negative emotion appeals have been used by commercial organizations. The (in)famous Benetton advertising campaigns in the 1990s is a particularly prominent example. The Benetton campaign drew on such hot topics as religion, homosexuality and AIDS in order to shock viewers. Negative emotional appeals are also frequently employed in charity and public sector advertising. Recent examples from the UK include an advertisement aimed at convincing people to stop smoking. The ad showed a hook going through a woman's mouth to represent the addiction to smoking. Another advertisement against child abuse depicts a scared little girl sitting in her room, listening out for the sound of approaching footsteps (presumably of a potential abuser).

Such advertising campaigns are often notorious for attracting a significant number of complaints from viewers disturbed by the images. The Advertising Standards Authority (ASA, UK) is typical of the organizations that seek to regulate advertisements as well as other promotional activities. The ASA are often faced with decisions about whether or not certain appeals are acceptable. The aforementioned anti-smoking advert, for example, has received the highest number of complaints in 2007 from viewers disturbed by the graphic imagery (Advertising Standards Authority and Committee of Advertising Practice, 2007). Similarly, an advert that showed a woman slapping her husband in a furniture shop also drew complaints from the public.

The Code of Advertising Practice states clearly that fear, violent images or distress should not be used without good reason or disproportionately; and that advertisers should avoid causing distress or offence to members of the public. However, this can be often a rather subjective call, particularly in cases where guilt, shame or embarrassment appeals are used. In view of the mounting criticism of advertising's manipulative tactics (e.g. Campbell, 1995; Cotte, Coulter and Moore, 2005), the question arises about whether or not such types of appeals should be used at all by advertisers in order to promote a product, service or a particular behaviour.

In this case study we examine a campaign against benefit fraud, which plays on emotions in a more subtle and indirect way. We begin by outlining the historical background of the campaign; and then we describe some of the ads used in the campaign which employed negative emotions such as fear and guilt.

THE BACKGROUND

The campaign against benefit fraud was commissioned by the Department for Work and Pensions (DWP) in the UK. The issue of benefit fraud was particularly important for the Labour government from when it came to power in 1997. Benefit fraud was seen as an important problem for the DWP as it was estimated that around £2 billion are lost every year through fraud and error in the system, 60 per cent of which relate to claims for Income Support, Jobseeker's Allowance and Housing Benefit (House of Commons Committee of Public Accounts, 2003). Benefit fraud remains an ongoing problem. The latest report from the Audit Commission (May 2008) revealed a record £140 million of fraud and overpayments by local councils in England, up by 26 per cent on the previous year. This included £24 million in housing benefit fraud in this period (http://www.guardian.co.uk/money/2008/may/20/ scamsandfraud.localgovernment).

On coming to power the Labour government tried to establish a strategy for the consistent evaluation and prevention of fraud. An influential report prepared by Lord Grabiner (2000) on the 'informal economy', argued that publicity and in particular advertising, should be used in order to change the culture of tolerance that sustains fraud. More specifically, it was suggested that advertising could be used in order, first, to further publicize the benefit fraud hotline that had been in operation since 1997; and secondly to change attitudes towards benefit fraud and show its consequences to the general public.

May 2000 saw the launch of the pilot campaign for benefit fraud. This campaign ran in the North West until November 2000 (National Audit Office, 2003). During July 2000, the first independent benefit fraud website was also launched. The same advertising campaign was launched nationally (February 2001), following evaluation of the pilot. The campaign has had several phases since then, with some changes in its advertising material and website.

In 2005, a strategy document, 'Reducing Fraud in the Benefit System' (DWP, 2005), argued that the benefit fraud campaign (characterized as a campaign of deterrence) had achieved its goals of influencing public attitudes towards fraud and of raising awareness. The DWP proclaimed that the Targeting Fraud campaign would continue, with the aim of warning fraudsters and deterring potential cheats. The Benefit Fraud Hotline would remain as a medium for the deterrence of fraudsters.

So far, there are conflicting opinions about the campaign's effectiveness. Whereas an independent report suggests some viewers of the pilot perceived benefit fraud as easier to commit (DSS, Targeting Fraud Campaign Evaluation, 2001), the Minister of DSS claimed that evaluation results were encouraging (Rooker J. Hansard, 26 April 2001).

The 'Reducing Fraud in the Benefit System' report (DWP, 2005) suggests that campaign evaluation (on the fifth wave of the campaign) shows that the belief that the government takes benefit fraud seriously has strengthened, and attitudes against those who deliberately cheat the system have hardened. In addition it suggests that each phase of the campaign has led to a significant increase in the number of calls from the public about suspected fraud to the National Benefit Fraud Hotline. The DWP claims that the reduction in benefit fraud and error from 1998 until 2005 was 41 per cent (DWP, 2005), although the referrals from the website and the telephone hotline slowed down by 25 per cent in 2001–2 (the year when the campaign was most heavily promoted) as did the rate in the reduction of fraud (House of Commons Committee of Public Accounts, 2003).

The campaign has attracted a lot of attention in the media with several articles in the newspapers and a TV programme (*Panorama* programme on government advertising on BBC, 26 May 2002). The campaign also generated discussion in Parliament (e.g. 26 October 2001, 25 April 2001). What made this campaign so significant for the media and politicians was that it demonstrated the increasing reliance of the UK government on advertising rather than on any other form of publicity (National Audit Office, 2003). In addition, the government was reportedly, during that time period, the biggest spender on advertising in the UK. This DWP campaign on benefit fraud received the highest funding from the government in 2000–1 (£3.442 million) (Cozens, 2001).

DESCRIPTION OF THE CAMPAIGN

The campaign makes use of a number of different media including the Internet, television, radio, press and outdoor advertisements. The main aims of this campaign are, first, to create a climate of intolerance towards benefit fraud and to undermine its social acceptability; and secondly to warn fraudsters or people that may be thinking about committing fraud that they will be caught and punished (DWP, 2005: 14). The target audiences are, therefore, not only benefit fraudsters or potential fraudsters but also the public, who may not perceive fraud as a real crime or may potentially assist fraudsters (National Audit Office, 2003).

A large number of the benefit fraud adverts depict a similar scene: a person, who is presumably a benefit fraudster, is pictured in a work setting. Usually this involves some type of seasonal or temporary work, e.g. decorating a house, working as a waitress at a seaside café, or working at a fairground. The viewer observes the situation through the camera lens and the person in the advert seems to be unaware of the fact that they are being observed. A white spotlight is beamed at the central person in the ad. The cheat is captured in the spotlight, and the potential fraudster is shown at the centre of what appears to be a target (rather like a darts board). A caption underneath the adverts establishes the context for the situation by stating that it is benefit fraud not to declare employment; and that the DWP monitors and investigates benefit fraud. The advert then gives people who want to report fraud details of the confidential hotline and website.

This particular campaign therefore works on a rather subtle emotional level. It creates a sense of surveillance by suggesting the monitoring and targeting of benefit fraudsters or of people that are thinking of committing fraud. The aim is to prevent the benefit cheats. The white spotlight-target signifies that the fraudster has been caught in the act, creating a sense that fraudsters cannot escape the vigilance of the authorities. The ad also seeks to deter potential fraudsters. Furthermore, the most recent adverts used the logo: 'No ifs, no buts', signalling a firmness and strictness towards benefit fraudsters.

CONCLUDING THOUGHTS

This campaign is one of the many advertising campaigns used by the government in order to try and solve social problems. It seems that the use of advertising for these purposes is an increasingly common practice in a number of countries. Since these campaigns concern important social issues and deep-seated attitudes, it is particularly important to ensure that appropriate and ethical advertising practices are adopted, particularly in the use of emotional appeals in the campaign messages.

QUESTIONS

1 Make a list of campaigns that are aimed at solving (or ameliorating) social problems. Which elements make these campaigns effective (or not)?

2 Is the use of emotional appeals in advertisements that help in the solution of social problems justified and if so, why (or if not, why not)?

3 What are the merits of using emotion campaigns in this context? What may be the potential adverse consequences?

4 The campaign on benefit fraud uses emotions (such as fear and guilt) in a rather subtle way. Discuss the ethical issues that may arise from this use of emotions; and assess the need for regulation of the use of emotions in marketing campaigns.

Sources

Advertising Standards Authority and Committee of Advertising Practice (2007), 'Advertising Standards Authority Annual Report 2007–8', http://www.asa.org.uk/NR/rdonlyres/F1CB4D0C-74BB-4B6E-8F48-01BA2465957D/0/Annual_Statement_20072008.pdf.

Campbell, M.C. (1995), 'When attention-getting advertising tactics elicit consumer inferences of manipulative intent', *Journal of Consumer Psychology*, 4, 3: 225–254.

Cotte, J., Coulter, R.A. and Moore, M. (2005), 'Enhancing or disrupting guilt: the role of ad credibility and perceived manipulative intent', *Journal of Business Research*, vol. 58, i. 3: 361–368.

Cozens, C. (2001), 'Labour's 172 Advertising Campaigns', *The Guardian*, 26 April.

Department for Work and Pensions (2005), *Reducing Fraud in the Benefit System: Achievements and Ambitions*, London.

Englis, B.G. (1990), 'Consumer Emotional Reactions to Television Advertising and Their Effects on Message Recall', in Agres, S.J., Edell, J.A. and Dubitsky, T.M. (eds), *Emotion in advertising: theoretical and practical explorations* (New York, Quorum Books).

House of Commons Committee of Public Accounts (2003), 'Tackling Benefit Fraud: Thirty First Report of Session 2002–3', The Stationery Office, Lordon.

Lord Grabiner Q.C. (2000), 'The Informal Economy', The Public Enquiry Unit, HM Treasury, London.

National Audit Office (2003), 'Government Advertising', The Stationery Office, London.

What do consumers do with advertising?
This lemon is a bomb: how consumers read rhetorical visual imagery in advertising

LAMPROS GKIOUZEPAS, Amaretto Group, Technological Educational Institute of Thessaloniki, Greece

CONTEXT

This case study explores some of the issues faced by advertisers in creating visual metaphors in ads, and by consumers in interpreting visual metaphors in ads. Advertisers seem to use visual metaphors – like verbal metaphors – to make indirect claims about their brands. They have to make a number of decisions, e.g. about metaphorical terms; visual syntax; representation techniques; and the accompanying text. Consumers in their turn, as readers, have to recognize the relevance of the ad; to choose among alternative readings; and decide whether or not they should disregard counter-intuitive meanings.

DAPHNE'S READING OF THE VISUAL METAPHOR IN THE ELEMONATE AD

Relevance

While Daphne was initially baffled by the ad visual of the lemon as an exploding bomb it did not strike her that the ad was merely a tragic advertising gaffe. Daphne felt sure that there was a reason for such a bizarre image and it was up to her to figure it out. Her *presumption* was that the ad visual was *relevant* in some way. Actually, she believes that every ad carries such a *promise of relevance*.

INTERPRETING THE VISUAL IMAGERY

To start with, Daphne was rather puzzled about the significance of merging a real lemon with the top of a salt cellar (Sunkist, p. 125, Chapter 4). Then, she noticed that another lemon was about to explode (*Fairy*, p. 303, Chapter 8). A fuse was burning on the top of this second lemon. The headline for that ad 'explained' that this was because *Fairy* detergent can *elemonate* when it is used for washing-up. This was the first clue, and from here it did not take Daphne long to start working out the meaning of what – at first sight – seemed to be a rather strange image of an exploding lemon.

Visual syntax*

Fusing a lemon with a bomb might be one way to link these two objects together. Simply placing a lemon next to a bomb on a single page might be another way to point to a relationship between them (Figure 1). It seems, however, that the visual syntax (i.e. the way the objects within the ad are organized visually in relation to each other) differs in each case. In the first case, the advertiser is physically merging the two objects (see also Figure 2). This might be the equivalent of having the advertising say that the lemon *is* a bomb. In the second case, the advertiser seems to adopt a more subtle syntax. The objects are depicted

Figure 1 Lemon and bomb placed side by side

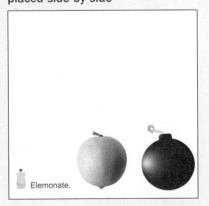

Elemonate.

Figure 2 Lemon and bomb merged

Elemonate.

Figure 3 Lemon resembling a bomb

Elemonate.

* Visual syntax relates to the rules for ordering and combining visual elements in an advertisement so that the ads are comprehensible to consumers who read and interpret the adverts.

Figure 4 Cars replacing a pair of shoes

Leather as standard. The Passat Highline from only £19,160 rrp.

Volkswagen Group

in their entirety, separated from each other. It might be that the advertiser now says that the lemon *is like* a bomb. Still another way to present this metaphor visually might be to place lemons in such a way as to resemble the shape of a bomb. In this third case, the bomb is not physically present. Our fictitious reader, Daphne, would only have understood this point from the shape of the lemons (as they resembled the roundness of bombs in their physical appearance, rather than the more usual conical shapes of lemons). In this case it would be as if the advertiser had implicitly described lemons in terms of a bomb, but by exercising a certain amount of discretion never mentioned the word *bomb* explicitly by name. Similarly, the lemon's dried stalk could also be made to function like a fuse. The advertiser just had to make it burn (Figure 3). Alternatively, the lemon might prominently replace a bomb inside a wooden box stacked with explosive devices, fuses, and other bombs. Here, the advertiser does not describe the bomb or mention its name but gives away all its 'friends and acquaintances'. Volkswagen seems to adopt this latter visual syntax in its ad for the Passat Highline (Figure 4).

Recognition and visual representation

If the choices involved in the figurative use of the image of a lemon seem obscure, the skills required to understand such ads are probably even more complex. Daphne needs to be familiar with the objects to understand that what is visually depicted refers to a lemon, a bomb, a salt cellar or a pair of shoes. This might seem a case of elementary perception and recognition ability for Daphne, but this cannot be safely assumed for every reader. In addition, it is not even certain that Daphne has understood these objects in the same way as the advertiser does. The reading process becomes particularly demanding when some of the objects are only partially depicted or merely suggested by the rest of the visual. In the Passat ad, for example, the pair of shoes is not physically present in the picture. Daphne has to be familiar not only with the missing object (the shoes) but with an extended array of associated items and combinations, such as shoe boxes and labels, as well as the neat alignment of a new pair of shoes in their box, carefully wrapped up in tissue paper.

In addition, the viewer has to be accustomed to the representation technique used by the advertiser. Photographic records of the world might seem to be the easiest pictures for Daphne to read. And yet, even in the case of photography, slight variations in the camera angle used to depict objects might make their recognition more or less difficult. This implies that some angles of vision might be easier to understand than others. For instance, a picture of a lemon (standing upright) might come closer to an accepted norm than another picture of a lemon (where only the top of the lemon is visible). The importance of such prototypical views, in helping us understand the visual syntax of ads, is illustrated by the picture of the lemon in the *Fairy* ad. The lemon standing upright (Figure 5) or lying on its side is usually easier to identify as a lemon, compared with when only the top of the lemon is visible (Figure 6). In this respect, the Passat ad

Figure 5 A straight on view of a Lemon

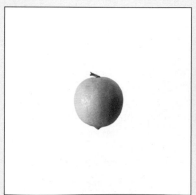

Figure 6 A top view of a Lemon

seems to be at a disadvantage because the pair of shoes never appear in the ad, they are 'absent' and can only be construed from hints and careful interpretation of the visual syntax. Furthermore, the car is shown in a rather unusual position. Importantly for the Passat, its sales are not as entirely dependent upon recognition of the product (drawing on the ad) at the point of purchase, compared with fast moving consumer products. For a product like *Fairy*, recognition is important as consumers walk along the aisles of the supermarket choosing their preferred product for cleaning dishes.

INTERPRETATION

Daphne almost instantly inferred that what the advertiser implied was that the lemon had some of the (fatal) properties of a bomb. However, it seemed to Daphne that if it were not for her knowing that *Fairy* apparently does not sell bombs, the visual metaphor alone could be understood the other way around. That is, she could have understood the bomb in terms of the lemon; even if this just meant that the bomb was to be seen as a fresh one. Daphne, knowing the detergent product category and the brand, *Fairy*, decided against this rather bizarre interpretation. Nonetheless, she had to suppress some of the other properties that could be 'transferred' from the bomb and the lemon to the advertised product. For example, it crossed her mind that the detergent could be harsh for the skin. Both the explosive power of a bomb and the acidity of a lemon can bear testimony to this effect after all. Although nothing prevented her from drawing such inferences, Daphne thought that this was not what the advertiser wanted to convey to the reader. This interpretation did not seem legitimate to her.

Daphne also inferred that the detergent must be suitable for heavy professional use. The comparison with the bomb also suggested to her that *Fairy* could tackle tough stains. Furthermore, Daphne expected that this product would help her to do the washing-up faster. However, an additional interpretation could be that the dishes needed to soak in the detergent for a while in order to be completely clean, just as one has to wait a while before a bomb with a slow-burning fuse explodes. For some reason, Daphne also thought that the detergent should produce rich foam. Daphne had already drawn quite a few inferences about the ad's meaning but she was not quite sure which one to believe or what was actually its main message.

Anchored in text

The 'elemonate' title in the *Fairy* ad had already provided a very clear hint about the meaning of the ad visual. The combination of a noun (*lemon*) and a verb (*eliminate*) produced a new word, which was clearly anomalous and yet still comprehensible. Daphne could work out from the word 'elemonate' that the detergent had some eliminating properties, and that also, somehow, lemon was responsible for these eliminating properties. Lemon had been a cleaning agent in many societies before the invention of detergents. However, Daphne still sensed that she had not fully uncovered the ad's main message. At this point, the verbal part of the ad came to her rescue. Daphne read, at the bottom of the ad, that *Fairy* can stop bacteria breeding on the sponge. The ad's main message was much clearer now. It might even be that the ad was so clear now that too much information had been given away, which might threaten the satisfaction that readers might derive from working out the solution implicitly posed by the ad (i.e. the role of lemon in eliminating dirt, odours and germs) without too much help. The solution was contained in fine print so that Daphne did not notice these extra clues to the puzzle in the ad at the beginning. Daphne regarded this as the final solution to the visual puzzle but she was unsure whether or not she was entitled to retain her other inferences or even draw yet more meanings from the ad.

Substantiation

The connections and the links that Daphne had to comprehend did not seem to stop either with understanding the combination of words or with interpreting what the synthesis of objects meant. The ad clearly implied a relationship between the lemon and the dish-washing detergent. Specifically, the ad seemed to propose that the lemon, somehow, stands for the advertised brand. This type of metonymical association is yet another instance of figurative 'language', where the whole is represented by the use of an associated element. Such a link might seem evident, but, in fact, Daphne remained clueless as to its real nature. For example, Daphne wondered whether the liquid detergent contains either a real lemon; or an artificial added lemon aroma; or just some of the ingredients of lemon. Or maybe the lemon and the liquid detergent bear no real relationship to each other? Although the advertiser could visually link the advertised product directly to the bomb, the advertiser preferred that the relationship between the bomb-like destructive powers of the detergent (towards dirt and germs) should be mediated by a lemon. Daphne, sceptical as she was, wondered whether it might be just as plausible for the consumer to believe in the detergent's power to stop bacteria when this is presented through the lemon, regardless of the nature of such an association between a lemon and the brand.

More visual connotations

The decisions which advertisers make when choosing visual objects for ads do not seem to depend solely on the product attributes that need to be communicated.

Put another way, the message in this ad might not just be all about communicating the antibacterial power of a detergent. A highly prominent metaphorical object might also affect the mood of the ad as a whole. For example, the tone of an ad using a bomb might look aggressive. The choice did look threatening to Daphne. She would have preferred *Fairy* to use the magic power of a fairy as a gentler way to communicate its antibacterial action. However, on second thoughts, she wandered whether using the magic power of a fairy would have made the ad less realistic and thus less persuasive. Although she did not fully understand the link between the lemon and the detergent product, she thought that the link between a fairy and *Fairy* brand would have been even more irrational. She also thought, on the spur of the moment, that a plain white background would make the ad look more classy, rather like the Passat ad. She had always liked minimalist art.

QUESTIONS

1 Do you believe that all the product inferences drawn by Daphne are justified? Why did negative product attributes not prevail in her interpretation of the ad? Which communication model better supports your answer?

2 Text that explains a rhetorical visual might direct the interpretation of a visual. What might be the consequences of explaining either too much or too little to consumers in terms of ad liking, persuasion, and comprehension?

3 Collect examples of advertisements that use visual metaphors and try to identify the different ways used to visually link two objects. Can you classify them into meaningful categories? (*Hint:* think of the three ways suggested for combining pictures of lemons and bombs in the discussion of visual syntax above.) Consider how each category could

affect important consumer responses such as attention, comprehension, ad liking, and elaboration.

4 What is meant by syntax? (*Hint:* look up a definition in **http://dictionary.reference.com/browse/syntax**.) What is meant by visual syntax? What rules do you think advertising has to obey in order for consumers to be able to read the advertisements and understand them?

5 Choose one ad from the examples you collected of ads which use visual metaphors and analyze the meaning as Daphne did for the elemonate ad, e.g. relevance; visual syntax; visual representation; interpretation; verbal syntax (anchored in the text); substantiation; more visual connotations. Does the ad you've found meet the key criteria of marketing managers, i.e. does it communicate the brand message effectively? If so, why? If not, why not?

Sources

Forceville, Charles (1996), *Pictorial Metaphor in Advertising* (London: Routledge).

Larsen, Val, David Luna, and Laura A. Peracchio (2004), 'Points of view and pieces of time: A taxonomy of image attributes', *Journal of Consumer Research*, 31(1): 102–11.

McQuarrie, Edward F. and David Glen Mick (1999), 'Visual rhetoric in advertising: Text-interpretive, experimental, and reader-response analyses', *Journal of Consumer Research*, 26(1): 37–54.

McQuarrie, Edward F. and Barbara J. Phillips (2005), 'Indirect persuasion in advertising', *Journal of Advertising*, 34(2): 7–20.

Phillips, Barbara J. (2000), 'The impact of verbal anchoring on consumer response to image ads', *Journal of Advertising*, 29(1): 15–24.

Pracejus, John W., Douglas G. Olsen, and Thomas C. O'Guinn (2006), 'How nothing became something: White space, rhetoric, history, and meaning', *Journal of Consumer Research*, 33(1): 82–90.

Scott, Linda M. (1994), 'Images in advertising: The need for a theory of visual rhetoric', *Journal of Consumer Research*, 21(2): 252–73.

Sperber, Dan and Deirdre Wilson (1986), *Relevance: Communication and Cognition* (Oxford: Blackwell).

Hidden motives: is consumer behaviour shaped by fairy tale archetypes?

ANDREA GROEPPEL-KLEIN, University of Saarland, Germany

ARCHETYPES AND CONSUMER BEHAVIOUR

Ernest Dichter and Vance Packard were convinced that consumer behaviour is shaped by hidden motives, which can be detected by using psychoanalytical research. For instance, Ernest Dichter argued that whenever consumers eat ice cream, in fact what they are trying to do is to satisfy the innate need for 'security'. These psychoanalytical findings (derived from 'research on the couch' rather than from experimental research in a laboratory) have attracted controversy because they do not fit into 'exact' positivistic research paradigms with respect to inter-subjective perceived comprehensibility. This has meant that consumer behaviour researchers have tended to neglect these research findings. However, current progress in neuro(physio)logical research and modern brain imaging technologies has started to allow us to shed some light on unconscious processes and instincts, thus offering the possibility of validating psychoanalytical research today which was originally undertaken by Sigmund Freud many decades ago.

Jung's archetypal psychology also belongs to this group of psychoanalytical research about consumer behaviour. Carl G. Jung (1875–1961) was influenced by his mentor Sigmund Freud, but developed his own ideas – and in contrast to Freud, Jung was not such a staunch supporter of experimental or neurological research. Following Jung's theory (1954/1959 a, b), the psyche can be divided into three parts. Part one is the conscious mind termed the 'ego'. Closely related to the ego is the second part, the 'personal unconscious' that includes anything not presently conscious. The personal unconscious includes both memories that can easily be brought to mind and those that have been suppressed for some reason. Jung's third part of the psyche is called the 'collective unconscious', and it is this element that makes his theory stand out from others.

Jung's collective unconscious can be characterized as the 'psychic inheritance' or as the kind of knowledge with which all human beings are born. The individual is never directly aware of this collective reservoir of experiences, but it can indirectly influence personal feelings and behaviour. Effects that illustrate the functioning of the collective unconscious are experiences of first love, of déjà vu and the immediate recognition and understanding of certain myths. The content of the collective unconscious is characterized by so-called 'archetypes' that represent inborn and universal ways of perceiving and comprehending the world, and which provide individuals with 'wisdom' about the past and predispose people to experience the world as their ancestors did. Thus, archetypes have an instinctive or biological function (Veen, 1994) and act as regulators and stimulators. As inherent experiences of the human species, they are stable across time and societies, but can be culturally coded in typical iconic representations (Hirschman, 2000). Characters from myths or fairy tales can act as such representations.

The variety of archetypal images is substantial. In this case study special attention is devoted to (1) the hero, who is characterized as a man who can master all challenges in life and is able to rescue an unhappy or threatened woman, and (2) the innocent maiden-archetype (referred to as 'Cinderella-Archetype'), the young and beautiful woman, who lives in distress or misery and is rescued by a gallant prince who promises her a wonderful life free of worry and care.

ARCHETYPES AND ADVERTISING CAMPAIGNS

Walle (1986, 22) argues that archetypes 'constitute valuable tools for practitioners such as strategic planners of promotional campaigns', because archetypal advertising resonates from innate human universals and focuses on innate needs. Actually, a content analysis of advertisements in German magazines and newspapers shows that many brands (even prestigious credit institutions or sophisticated newspapers) use archetypal motives like brave heroes, innocent maidens like 'Cinderella', or pictures associated with such fairy tales as The Frog Prince, or animal archetypes like the 'faithful horse' or the 'lion' in their marketing communications.

However, do advertising campaigns that are shaped by archetypal myths really appeal to all consumers? As a counter-argument, the feminist movement (e.g. Enns, 1994: 73; Lauter and Rupprecht, 1985) believes that, on the one hand, the greater the prevalence of fairy tales about heroic men and needy women, the more difficult it will be for women to change stereotypical role expectations. On the other hand, currently, more and more students are female; they often achieve better examination results than their male colleagues and more and more women are gaining high career positions. Thus, the Cinderella-archetype may be called into question by women's current experience, or is even changing. The book *The Cinderella Complex* (Dowling, 1981) questions the abdication of women's power to males and asks why, in the old fairy tales, we never hear about what happens to the young Cinderella after she marries the prince. Will she really be happy and satisfied with a spouse role or will there be a tendency to break out of the repressive castle existence? To summarize, we could question whether a modern young woman still believes that she needs to do no more with her life than find a gallant prince who will take care of her. In other words: do typical archetypes like 'Cinderella' or 'Sleeping Beauty' really reflect women's ideals and can they therefore be used successfully in advertising strategies?

In this context, a relationship between personality variables and preferred archetypes can be assumed. Holbrook and Olney (1995) found that people vary in the degree to which they are attracted either by romanticism or by classicism. These findings could lead to the assumption that individual levels of romanticism also influence the perceived appeal of different archetypes such as Cinderella-like figures, or Sleeping Beauty.

In our study (for details see Groeppel-Klein, Domke and Bartmann, 2005), we investigate whether archetypes like 'Cinderella' or 'Sleeping Beauty' cause positive attitudes and unconscious responses. In order to gain insights into the more or less unconscious reactions of test persons, we measured *phasic arousal* evoked by archetypal stimuli. From a psycho-physiological perspective, arousal is a fundamental feature of behaviour. It can be defined as the basic neurophysiological process underlying all activity in the human organism. Thus, arousal is the basis of emotions, motivation, information processing, and behavioural reactions (Bagozzi, Gopinath and Nyer, 1999). Basically, a distinction can be made between tonic and phasic arousal. Tonic arousal refers to a relatively long-term state of consciousness. Phasic arousal arises in response to specific stimuli, resulting in short-term variations in the arousal level. It indicates a ready state of the body for reaction and is closely related to attention, that is, enhanced sensitivity of the organism to relevant stimuli and stimuli processing (Boucsein, 1992).

Empirical studies emphasize the relevance of phasic arousal in marketing communication. (Groeppel-Klein and Baun, 2001). *Arousal* is an important factor in *predicting approach behaviour*. Furthermore, since consumers cannot willingly influence their arousal reactions, it is either a valid indicator of *unconscious reactions* or a detection mechanism for social desirability articulation biases – on condition that arousal is measured accurately. In contrast to verbal methods, psychophysiological measures such as heart rate, electroencephalogram (EEG), and electrodermal reaction (EDR) are the most valid indicators, since *deliberately influencing* the test results obtained from these methods is almost impossible. In addition, EDR (Boucsein, 1992: 263) is considered to be the most sensitive indicator of arousal that could be relevant to behaviour and can be recorded *simultaneously* with the perception of a stimulus. Due to these advantages, we employed EDR as indicator. EDR is founded on the psycho-physiological fact that increasing arousal leads to increasing sweat gland activity of our hand palms, and even the very smallest psychological change can be detected (Boucsein, 1992). The hydration depends on external and internal factors and leads to electric conductivity of the skin, thus making it possible to measure it by means of two electrodes attached to the skin. The amplitude (measured in η-Siemens) describes the strength of each phasic arousal reaction. The intensity of perceived arousal over a certain *period of time* can be received by summing all single amplitudes so as to obtain the *total amplitude* that is the most important phasic arousal parameter in experiments.

EXPERIMENTAL STUDIES

Archetypal advertising focuses on innate needs. This would suggest that a message that is compatible with innate desires or desired behaviour will evoke higher arousal than one that is less focused on these innate drives. Thus, we can hypothesise whether a TV commercial or a movie that uses a typical fairy tale archetype (like Cinderella) will evoke higher phasic arousal reactions than films without this archetype. Furthermore, the question arises if all people show similar responses, or if different personalities are more or less attracted by Cinderella-archetypes.

We tested our hypotheses in two empirical studies. The first study was conducted in October and November 2004 in a lecture room at our university. First, students were chosen randomly and asked if they were interested in participating in an advertising experiment. Then, the participants completed a general questionnaire about their personal attitudes towards career, family, self-concept, self-esteem, and romanticism. Students were told that we wanted to arrange a typical advertising situation, in which films are normally interrupted by TV commercials. Before being presented with different TV commercials, one test person was attached to the EDR electrodes and asked to relax and to watch the film just as in a cinema or at home. Only one commercial used an archetypal myth: the story takes place in a typical enchanted 'fairy tale castle'. The prince wants to rescue and wake up Sleeping Beauty, but all kissing attempts fail. Only the aroma and flavour of a cookie (named 'Prinzenrolle') works, so that Sleeping Beauty is finally enraptured by her rescuer.

During EDR registration, markers were set on the registered data whenever a new commercial started, and another one when the scene from the movie began. Thus, the arousal reaction of each commercial and of the movie could be registered. After showing the TV commercials, half the sample (randomly chosen) was presented with the last scene of *Pretty Woman* whereas the other half watched a sequence from *Gone With The Wind*. Actually, we chose these two films because, on the one hand, the Cinderella 'archetype has shaped movies such as *Pretty Woman*' (Waters, 2003), whereas on the other hand, Scarlett O'Hara (as we established through an Internet search) is characterized as a 'woman, who fought with her sweat and blood to keep her family's plantation, a woman who overcame every war and obstacle' (unknown reviewer, **www.target.com**) and 'her incredible tenacity makes her a contender' (Isaacs, 2004: 4). Thus, viewing the movie was also part of the experiment though participants were not aware of it. Afterwards, EDR test persons were detached from the electrodes, and completed the second part of the questionnaire, including items measuring attitude towards the ad, the brand, and the movie.

The second study was conducted in February 2005, with an experimental design and questionnaire comparable to those of Study 1. In contrast to our first study, half the sample (randomly chosen) was exposed to the archetypal TV commercial 'Sleeping Beauty' ('Prinzenrolle'), whereas the other half was exposed to a more informational TV commercial of 'Prinzenrolle', that shows a group of cooks (called the 'cookie experts') with white coats and long chefs' hats preparing hot chocolate sauce for their delicious cookies. This experimental design was chosen in order to find out if the archetypal TV commercial of 'Prinzenrolle' was indeed more effective than a more informational spot for the same brand. Furthermore, the Calgon spot of Study 1 was replaced by a commercial also advertising cookies (with the brand name 'Hanuta'). This clip shows a female fencer fighting with one of the famous three musketeers. She wins and gets the 'Hanuta'. This commercial was chosen, on the one hand, to present a tough and fearless *female* actor and, on the other hand, to show an additional 'sweets' spot to examine whether arousal reactions were simply evoked by this special *product category*. After presenting the TV commercials, half the sample viewed the last scene of *Pretty Woman* whereas the other half watched a

sequence from *Erin Brockovich*. Scarlett O'Hara (Study 1) is probably one of the most prominent examples of a fearless female character. However, *Gone With The Wind* was shot before World War II and is set in the American Civil War, whereas *Pretty Woman* was produced in 1990 and features a modern *zeitgeist*. Furthermore, Julia Roberts is one of the most popular actresses in Hollywood, and the arousal reaction to *Pretty Woman* might simply be due to her charisma. Therefore, in the second study, we wanted to control a potential 'Julia Roberts artefact', and compared *Pretty Woman* to another movie starring Julia Roberts as Erin Brockovich, who is characterized as 'an inspirational reminder of the power of the human spirit. Her passion, tenacity, and steadfast desire to fight for the rights of the underdog defied the odds' (**www.erinbrockovich.com**).

RESULTS

The first study compares the archetypal TV commercial ('Sleeping Beauty', brand 'Prinzenrolle') with four other non-archetypal commercials, and demonstrates significantly higher arousal for the archetypal spot (Figure 1). In Study 2, we controlled for whether the famous brand name or the product category might be responsible for the arousal reactions, with the result that the archetypal spot evokes a significantly higher level of arousal (Figure 2) and a more positive attitude towards the ad than the informational spot for this brand than the 'Hanuta' spot.

The movie presenting a typical Cinderella archetype as a character (*Pretty Woman*) was compared with movies presenting brave, aggressive and selfish female characters (Study 1: Scarlett O'Hara, *Gone With The Wind*; Study 2: *Erin Brockovich*). The results show

Figure 1 Study 1 – Arousal differences between commercials

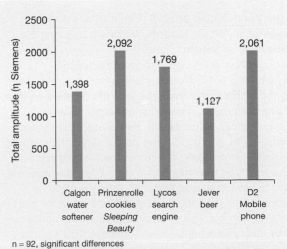

n = 92, significant differences

Figure 2 Study 2 – Arousal differences between, cookie commercials

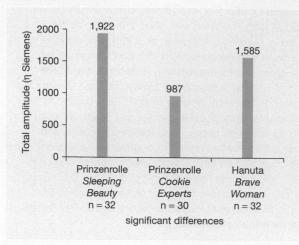

Figure 3 Arousal differences between films

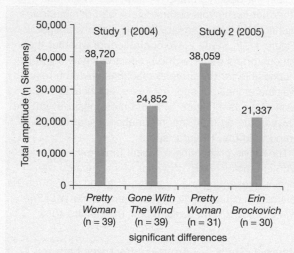

significantly higher arousal (Figure 3) and a more favourable attitude towards the movie featuring the Cinderella archetype.

In our first study, we also investigated the relationship between personality types and responses to the archetypal commercial and the different movies. Using statements measuring attitudes towards career, family, romanticism, self-concept clarity and self-esteem, we found three personality groups among female test persons. Women in the first segment are characterized by romanticism (they enjoy daydreaming and believe in love at first sight), they want to be protected by their future husband and yearn for a life without worries. Though they are quite self-confident, they still have an unclear self-concept. This segment is called 'optimistic daydreamers'. The second group (called 'cool self-made women') considers it important

to believe in facts rather than dreams, and always likes to keep a cool head. They have a clear self-concept and high self-esteem. The third cluster ('self-condemned losers') has an extremely negative score on 'high self-esteem'. These women perceive themselves as failures, and have no self-confidence at all. They are neither energetic nor career-oriented, nor do they have any optimistic daydreams as to how they could change their lives. However, they want to be protected in life. Regarding the archetypal commercial, arousal and assessment of the commercial differ significantly between the three female groups ('optimistic daydreamers' showed very positive responses). The results of the arousal responses with respect to *Pretty Woman* yielded no significant differences between the three clusters. Does this mean that even cool-headed women unconsciously cannot avoid being affected by the *Pretty Woman* story?

DISCUSSION

It is interesting that today one can find advertising campaigns containing typical fairy tale characters across different countries. Some examples: there is a commercial for the Swiss brand 'Chocolat Frey' showing a unicorn, a commercial for the German brand 'Prinzenrolle' showing 'Sleeping Beauty', the US brand 'Capital One' uses the 'Frog Prince' and a Canadian social campaign against eating disorders reinterprets *Hansel and Gretel*. Furthermore, CanTeen, an Australian organization that helps people who suffer from cancer, also uses a fairy tale (*Rapunzel*) to encourage people not to give up or to feel depressed when they lose their hair after chemotherapy ('Life is not always a fairy tale'). Do fairy tales console people, can they work as an 'anchor' or are they simply used to evoke attention?

QUESTIONS

1 Explain the notion of 'archetypes'.

2 In our studies EDR was used as an indicator to measure 'phasic arousal'. Please explain the 'arousal construct' and how EDR measurement works. Why was this method used?

3 Discuss the relationship between personality traits and preference for 'Cinderella archetypes' from a female *and* a male perspective. Women's emancipation might also have changed men's expectations and philosophy about life. Analogously, we could question whether men are still attracted by the hero-scheme. Does a man always feel capable of mastering all obstacles, and is he really keen on assuming responsibility for his wife and family, or does the hero-claim rather lead to a feeling of being burdened? How would you measure gender differences?

4 Do you agree with Walle (1986: 22), who describes archetypes as constituting 'valuable tools for practitioners such as strategic planners of promotional campaigns'?

EXERCISES

1 Conduct a content analysis of current advertising campaigns in newspapers and magazines published in your country. Do you also find archetypal ads?

2 Jung referred to archetypes as kind of knowledge with which all human beings are born. Search for current advertising campaigns in *different* countries. Do you find similar archetypes when comparing international campaigns?

3 Have a look at the products included in archetypal campaigns. Do you think that archetypal images are appropriate for all product categories or do you see limitations?

4 Imagine you were a researcher with the task of analyzing the effects of archetypes in advertising campaigns, but you have no opportunity to use EDR measurement. Which methods would you use alternatively to find out whether or not consumer behaviour is shaped by archetypes?

5 Discuss the relevance of new brain imaging technologies to consumer research. Do you think that psychoanalytical research may be validated one day by these new methods?

Sources

Bagozzi, Richard P., Mahesh Gopinath, and Prashanth U. Nyer (1999), 'The role of emotions in marketing', *Journal of the Academy of Marketing Science*, 27 (Spring): 184–206.

Boucsein, Wolfram (1992), *Electrodermal Activity* (New York, London: Plenum Press).

Dowling, Colette (1981), *The Cinderella Complex: Women's Hidden Fear of Independence* (New York: Summit Books).

Enns, Carolyn Zerbe (1994), 'Archetypes and gender: Goddesses, warriors, and psychological health', *Journal of Counseling & Development*, 73 (November/December): 127–133.

Freud, Sigmund (1933), *New Introductory Lectures on Psychoanalysis* (New York: Norton).

Groeppel-Klein, Andrea and Dorothea Baun (2001), 'The Role of Customers' Arousal for Retail Stores – Results from An Experimental Pilot Study Using Electrodermal Activity as Indicator', in *Advances in Consumer Research*, vol. 28, Mary C. Gilly and Joan Meyers-Levy (eds) (Provo, UT: Association for Consumer Research): 412–419.

Groeppel-Klein, Andrea, Anja Domke, and Benedikt Bartmann (2006), 'Pretty Woman or Erin Brockovich? Unconscious and conscious reactions to commercials and movies shaped by fairy tale archetypes – results from two experimental studies', *Advances in Consumer Research*, vol. 33, Cornelia Pechmann and Linda L. Price (eds) (Duluth, MN: Association for Consumer Research): 163–174.

Hirschman, Elizabeth C. (2000), 'Consumers' use of intertextuality and archetypes', *Advances in Consumer Research*, vol. 27, Stephen J. Hoch and Robert J. Meyer (eds) (Provo, UT: Association for Consumer Research): 57–63.

Holbrook, Morris B. and Thomas J. Olney (1995), 'Romanticism and wanderlust: An effect of personality on consumer preference', *Psychology & Marketing*, 12(3): 207–222.

Isaacs, Susan (2004), 'Brave Dames and Wimpettes', http://www.susanisaacs.com/bib/brave_dames.php.

Jung, Carl Gustav (1954/1959a), 'The archetypes and the collective unconscious', *The Collected Works of C.G. Jung*, vol. 9, Part I, ed. Sir Herbert Read, Michael Fordham, and Gerhard Adler, New York: Bollingen, Pantheon, 3–41.

Jung, Carl Gustav (1954/1959b), 'Psychological Aspects of The Mother Archetype,' in *The Collected Works of C.G. Jung*, vol. 9, Part I, Sir Herbert Read, Michael Fordham, and Gerhard Adler (eds) (New York: Bollingen, Pantheon): 75–110.

Jung, Carl Gustav (1961), *Memories, Dreams, Reflections* (New York: Random House).

Lauter, Estella and Carol Schreier Rupprecht (1985), *Feminist Archetypal Theory* (Knoxville: University of Tennessee Press).

Veen, Steve Vander (1994), 'The consumption of heroes and the hero hierarchy of effects', *Advances in Consumer Research*, vol. 21, Chris T. Allen and Deborah Roedder John (eds) (Provo, UT: Association for Consumer Research): 332–336.

Walle, Alf (1986), 'Archetypes, athletes and advertising', *Journal of Consumer Marketing*, 3 (November): 21–29.

Waters, Jen (2003), 'Cinderella. A Biography of An Archetype', *Washington Times*, 31 May 2003.

From lamb's fry, three eggs and bacon to processed cereal: Kellogg's transforms the Australian breakfast landscape in the post-war years

TERESA DAVIS, University of Sydney, Australia

TANJA SCHNEIDER, James Martin Institute, Oxford University, UK

This is the story of how Kellogg's Australia set about changing the breakfast menu at Australian tables over the course of half a century. By tracking Kellogg's marketing campaign in *Australian Women's Weekly*, we can identify the cultural change that took place in Australians' breakfast eating practices.

In 1925 Joel S. Mitchell, an American sales representative of the Kellogg's company in the United States, was sent to Australia to introduce breakfast cereal to the Australian palate. He was faced with no mean task. Breakfast was an important family meal before the working day began. Cultural traditions of a 'sit–down' cooked meal was well established in urban and regional households. This traditional meal was prepared and served in much the same way as early settlers in the fledgling Federation at the turn of the century had done. Breakfast consisted of fried or scrambled eggs with cured meats such as bacon, ham or sausage. Alternatively, lamb meat would be served on the side (usually pan fried) with the eggs. Toasted bread, butter, jam or fruit preserves were also served. The traditional 'cooked' breakfast of lamb's fry or eggs and bacon was served in most Australian households. The cultural barriers to changes in eating patterns were still strong. Australia in the pre-Second World War era ate as their ancestors from the UK had eaten – a diet high in protein and carbohydrate. The protein was largely from fresh meat and fish with carbohydrate from bread and potatoes. The Australian economy was also based on a strong primary industry for meat, wool and dairy. The flourishing meat, dairy and poultry industries were urging Australians to 'eat more eggs' 'drink more milk' and that 'red meat was good for growing bodies'. This combined with the imperative to nurture healthy workers and citizens to keep the sparsely populated country but flourishing economy running. Public health policy favoured fresh Australian produce.

In the quarter century after 1925 Kellogg's made little headway in the Australian breakfast market. The early advertisements for Kellogg's All-Bran used a 'health food' approach. However, this was beginning to change after the Second World War. Breakfast and food patterns were changing; as were perceptions of cereals as a 'health food' and bread substitute – consumed largely by the health conscious and elderly/sick.

Social, political and economic trends were in Kellogg's favour. First, the post-war industrial boom represented a bonanza for food manufacturers. Economic prosperity, combined with women being freed from participating in the wartime economy (since the men had returned from war to the peacetime work places), helped food preparation and consumption to become more varied. Secondly, the post-war migration of European groups brought new traditions of eating which influenced the way Australians now ate. The Italians, Greeks, Turkish and Portuguese brought traditions of Continental baked breads as well as new habits in the consumption of coffee and other beverages. Thirdly, the American war alliance had seen large numbers of American soldiers spend time in Australia and 'war brides' brought new 'American' consumption habits to Australia.

The admiration of the American ways of consuming can be clearly seen in the editorials of popular magazines of the time such as the *Australian Women's Weekly* which included recipe columns such as 'American Medley' (5 May 1951: 57). This introduced exotic new fruit such as avocados (described as a 'delicately flavoured tropical fruit'. On 1 August 1951 (49) the same magazine has a recipe section titled 'Californian Style'. The introduction reads, 'The recipes on this page will be included in the menus of the gala dinners for our California Fiesta Fashion parades in Melbourne, Sydney and Adelaide. These are dishes for which the famous Brown Derby Restaurants of California are noted.' Suddenly, all things American were very popular. Continental seven-minute soups advertised their products with: 'In a few short weeks Continental Chicken Noodle soup has taken Australia by storm. Direct from the tables of America, Continental costs less . . . tastes better than any other soup.'

Being an American company producing processed cereals now became easier for Kellogg's. The cultural barriers to processed foods were weakening. Their advertisement for Kellogg's Cornflakes in the *Australian Women's Weekly* (27 January 1951: 48) shows a very different 'positioning'. It is clearly no longer just a 'health food' but a real, nutritious substitute for the traditional breakfast. The experts say so, and the cost comparisons are clear. Economic and efficient, the product appeals to the post-war consumer who is still cost conscious but looking for convenience. The advertisement uses a visual which clearly conveys the nutritional content of the product, e.g. the spoon in the middle of the bowl of cornflakes says without ambiguity, 'One third of your daily food needs . . .' The word 'BIG' reassures consumers about this seemingly 'light' breakfast doing the job of the hefty traditional cooked breakfast.

Subsequent Kellogg's advertisements for breakfast cereals in the 1960s and 1970s stopped using the positioning: 'cereal as substitute for cooked breakfast' and moved to the theme of the nutrition and vitamins that the cereal delivered to consumers. A 1961 advertisement for Kellogg's Cornflakes said, 'Nutritious! Kelloggs! Many More Vitamins than the Whole grain itself' (April 1961, *Australian Women's Weekly*), thereby suggesting it was even more nutritious than the whole grain by itself.

By 1971 Kellogg's was using joint promotions, e.g. with the milk industry for International Milk Day. Kellogg's Cornflakes delivers: 'double goodness, double health – milk and Kellogg's Cornflakes are full of Nutrition!' (2 June 1971) followed by a list of all the vitamins it contains (niacin, riboflavin, etc. . . .). No longer does Kellogg's have to convince the consumer of the suitability of cereal as a substitute for a cooked breakfast, their message is much more about the nutritive advantages of eating this cereal over others for breakfast. In the two decades after the 1950s, cereal for breakfast became the norm. The cooked breakfast of the pre-war era was reserved for weekends and special breakfasts. Everyday cereal consumption had become established breakfast practice.

In the early 1980s Kellogg's All Bran and Bran Buds cereals used the new notion of 'fibre'. The visual (2 December 1981: 88, 89, *Australian Women's Weekly*) is of a large bowl of cereal with fruit on top of it on one full page. The second page has a title, 'The alternatives are not so attractive'. It goes on to describe in the copy 'Varicose veins, Gallstones, Coronaries, are some of the serious health disorders a growing number of researchers believe are linked to the lack of fibre in diet . . .' A Dr Denis Burkitt is introduced as an expert who extols the virtues of fibre and its magical properties. Then the ad asks, 'how to get your daily fibre? Kellogg's All Bran and Bran Buds

breakfast cereals . . . the fibre contained in both All Bran and Bran Buds passes directly through the digestive system . . .' During the 1980s the shift was to the new wonder component 'fibre', but this was recommended as part of a healthy breakfast diet. But again the assumption that these are 'breakfast cereals' is clear. The health claims and benefits are no longer about the economy of substituting cereal for a cooked breakfast, or the convenience or even the nutrition of the many vitamins that cereals contain, but simply the new element of 'fibre'.

Thus, by analyzing Kellogg's advertising campaign in *Australian Women's Weekly* over a century, we can identify the cultural change that took place in the period following the Second World War (up to the present day) in Australians' breakfast eating practices. This cannot be entirely attributed to Kellogg's products. However, some of the social, political and economic conditions of the post-war period made it the 'right' time for processed breakfast cereals to take over the 'breakfast market' in a significant way. Australian cereal companies – such as Sanitarium, Uncle Toby's and Kellogg's – have the majority of the breakfast market in Australia. Commercial success grows out of understanding and taking advantage of such major changes in lifestyle and consumption patterns. Kellogg's presented their products as viable breakfast alternatives which helped shape and change how breakfast as a meal was consumed. Thus, the major socio-cultural shifts Australia has seen in the post-war period – peacetime economic prosperity, the changing role of women, and an acceptance of American food habits learnt during wartime – helped Kellogg's ride a wave of change that established it firmly in the Australian marketplace.

QUESTIONS

1 Was Kellogg's merely 'riding' certain post-war socio-cultural changes or actually influencing and changing the way Australians had traditionally eaten breakfast?

2 What are some of the 'cultural' factors that may have made Kellogg's entry into the Australian market easier than it may have been in some European countries at the same time?

3 Think of one example in your own country of such a cultural shift in food habits. Reflect on and enumerate the reasons why, in your example, the changes were resisted or embraced by the consumers.

4 Consider the entry of American processed cereal products to your country and compare the trajectory of change in breakfast mealtimes – examine how and why these changes may have happened – was it related to social, economic or cultural changes?

5 George Ritzer (1995) has used the term 'MacDonaldization' of society (others have used words such as 'Cococolonization' and 'Disneyfication' or even 'Globalization') to describe a particular trend of late capitalistic consumption that promotes a standardized, efficiency-optimizing process of production. Is there a backlash from consumers to such trends in food production and consumption? Identify, describe and assess examples that counter the terms described above, such as 'the slow food movement', etc.

Sources

Kellog's Australia website: http://www.kelloggs.com.au/DisplayPage.asp?PageID=413&sectionid=2&PageCopyID=19660

Sanitarium Australia website: http://www.sanitarium.com.au/company/history.html

Davis, T. and Schneider, T. (2005), 'Making Sense of Health Foods: A Socio-historical Analysis of Post war Magazine Advertising in Australia', in *Interdisciplinary Perspectives in Food Studies*, M. Koc, R. MacRae and K. Bronson (McGraw-Hill Ryers, Toronto): 47–58.

Schneider, T. and Davis, T., '(Trans-)forming appetites: Breakfast and nutrition discourses in the *Australian Women's Weekly* 1951–2001' (forthcoming article in *Consumption Markets and Culture*, 2010).

European consumers and their social groups

The chapters in this Part consider some of the social influences that help to determine who we are, with an emphasis on the various subcultures to which we belong. Chapter 10 looks at the influences that groups have on our consumer behaviour, and the particular influences that opinion leaders provide in our consumption deliberations. Chapter 11 provides a discussion of family structures in Europe, and identifies the many instances in which our purchase decisions are made in conjunction with the family. The chapter also points out the strong influence that age has on our behaviours as consumers, with an emphasis on the bonds we share with others who were born at roughly the same time. Chapter 12 focuses on factors that define our social classes, and how membership of a social class exerts a strong influence on what we buy with the money we make.

10

Group influence and opinion leadership

Bobbie tries to play sport just about every day. The obsession that started with football has expanded to include cricket, tennis and squash (depending on the season). He will happily skip a lecture to play in a university football league, especially the 11-a-side league on a Wednesday afternoon. The original team that Bobbie played for has now become his closest circle of friends, and they always celebrate an important victory with a heavy night out, with the importance of the health benefits of sport relegated to a poor second against the joys of a great team spirit.

Recently Bobbie decided he needed new football boots, since the ends of his old trusty Puma boots had both split open, letting in rain, mud and whatever else happened to be lying around on the football pitch. He has also got a bit sick of his mates telling him he looks like he is wearing tramp's shoes, as his boots are just so worn out. In the university matches there is a certain amount of prestige to be upheld. Since he had had his boots for so long, however, he feels he deserves some new ones.

Bobbie's mates had rather mixed things to say about Nike football boots. Bobbie was tempted by the Nike Air Legend II FGC boot, which also offered customization by NIKEid. But Bobbie really wondered if he could justify spending quite that much money out of his student budget on football boots. His friend Pete had found that Nike Air Legends hadn't offered as much support as he had wanted, so Bobbie decided those probably would not suit him. He would have liked to have stayed with Puma boots but there wasn't really the choice that he was looking for in their current offering. So that left Adidas (possibly Copa Mundial or the Predators), Umbro or maybe the T90s from the Nike range. Adidas represented his final choice (there was no point even considering other brands which his mates would start ribbing him about). The next decision was whether or not to get screw-in studs or moulded studs. Screw-ins invariably fell out in Bobbie's experience, however much you tightened them, whereas moulded studs stayed in and looked pretty flashy as well. However, Bobbie had seen fellow team-mates with moulded studs falling over constantly on wet, muddy pitches, and since English pitches were frequently muddy Bobbie decided he had to go for screw-ins, despite the fact he would have to buy a set of replacement studs. The only thing Bobbie had to do now was to buy the flashiest pair that none of his mates had so that he could impress them. After all, you want to stand out in the crowd, to be individual and different, but maybe not *too* different . . .

R.J.W. HOGG, Bloomberg, London

INTRODUCTION

Football is central to Bobbie's identity as a sports-loving student, and his team-mates influence many of his buying decisions for sports kit. Humans are social animals. We all belong to groups, try to please others and pick up cues about how to behave by observing the actions of those around us. In fact, our desire to 'fit in' or to identify with desirable individuals or groups is the primary motivation for many of our consumption behaviours. We often go to great lengths to please the members of a group whose acceptance we covet;[1] and to avoid the groups with which we do not wish to be associated.[2]

This chapter focuses on how other people, whether fellow footballers and team-mates, co-workers, friends and family or just casual acquaintances, influence our purchase decisions. It considers how our preferences are shaped by our positive group memberships, as well as by our dissociative reference groups, by our desire to please or be accepted by others, even by the actions of famous people whom we've never met. Finally, it explores why some people are more influential than others in affecting consumers' product preferences, and how marketers go about finding those people and enlisting their support in the persuasion process.

REFERENCE GROUPS

Bobbie's football team is an important part of his identity, and this membership influences many of his buying decisions. Bobbie doesn't model himself on just *any* footballer – only the people with whom he really identifies can exert that kind of influence. For example, Bobbie primarily identifies with other sport enthusiasts, especially football players. The English Football League represents one of Bobbie's most important *reference groups* whilst the English Rugby Union represents one of his dissociative groups.

▶ A **reference group** is 'an actual or imaginary individual or group conceived of having significant relevance upon an individual's evaluations, aspirations, or behaviour'.[3] Reference groups influence consumers in three ways. These influences, *informational*, *utilitarian*, and *value-expressive*, are described in Table 10.1.

Types of reference groups

Although two or more people are normally required to form a group, the term *reference group* is often used a bit more loosely to describe *any* external influence that provides social cues.[4] The referent may be a cultural figure and have an impact on many people (e.g. Nelson Mandela, Madonna or football stars like the winner of FIFA Footballer of the Year 2009 Cristiano Ronaldo) or a person or group whose influence only operates in the consumer's immediate environment (e.g. Bobbie's various football teams, 5-a-side and 11-a-side). Reference groups that affect consumption can include parents, fellow football enthusiasts and team members, classmates, other leisure activity enthusiasts, a political party or even sports clubs such as Manchester United and bands such as U2 and Coldplay.

Some groups and individuals exert a greater influence than others and affect a broader range of consumption decisions. For example, our parents may play a pivotal role in forming our values toward many important issues, such as attitudes about marriage
▶ and the family or where to go to university. We call this **normative influence** – that is, the reference group helps to set and enforce fundamental standards of conduct. In contrast,
▶ a Harley-Davidson club or Manchester United fan club exerts **comparative influence**, whereby decisions about specific brands or activities are affected.[5]

Table 10.1 Three forms of reference group influence

Informational influence	The individual seeks information about various brands from an association of professionals or independent group of experts.
	The individual seeks information from those who work with the product as a profession.
	The individual seeks brand-related knowledge and experience (such as how Brand A's performance compares to Brand B's) from those friends, neighbours, relatives or work associates who have reliable information about the brands.
	The brand the individual selects is influenced by observing a seal of approval of an independent testing agency (such as *Good Housekeeping*).
	The individual's observation of what experts do (such as observing the type of car that police drive or the brand of television that repairers buy) influences their choice of a brand.
Utilitarian influence	So that they satisfy the expectation of fellow work associates, the individual's decision to purchase a particular brand is influenced by their preferences.
	The individual's decision to purchase a particular brand is influenced by the preferences of people with whom they have social interaction.
	The individual's decision to purchase a particular brand is influenced by the preferences of family members.
	The desire to satisfy the expectations that others have of them has an impact on the individual's brand choice.
Value-expressive influence	The individual feels that the purchase or use of a particular brand will enhance the image others have of them.
	The individual feels that those who purchase or use a particular brand possess the characteristics that they would like to have.
	The individual sometimes feels that it would be nice to be like the type of person that advertisements show using a particular brand.
	The individual feels that the people who purchase a particular brand are admired or respected by others.
	The individual feels that the purchase of a particular brand would help show others what they are or would like to be (such as an athlete, successful business person, good parent, etc.).

Source: Adapted from C. Whan Park and V. Parker Lessig, 'Students and housewives: Differences in susceptibility to reference group influence', *Journal of Consumer Research* 4 (September 1977): 102. Reprinted with permission of The University of Chicago Press.

Formal vs. informal groups

A reference group can take the form of a large, formal organization that has a recognized structure, regular meeting times and officers. Or it can be small and informal, such as a group of friends or students living in a university hall of residence. Marketers tend to have more control over their influencing of formal groups because they are more easily identifiable and accessible.

In general, small, informal groups exert a more powerful influence on individual consumers. These groups tend to be more involved in our day-to-day lives and to be more important to us, because they are high in normative influence. Larger, formal groups tend to be more product or activity-specific and thus are high in comparative influence.

▶ Membership vs. aspirational reference groups

Some reference groups consist of people we actually know; whereas others are composed of people we can either *identify with* or admire. These people are likely to be successful business people, athletes, performers, or whosoever appeals to us. Not surprisingly, many marketing efforts that specifically adopt a reference group appeal concentrate

This Marks & Spencer's advertising campaign used non-celebrities to endorse its message, 'Exclusively For Everyone'.
The Advertising Archives

on highly visible, widely admired figures (such as well-known athletes or performers) and link these people to brands so that the products they use or endorse also take on this aspirational quality.[6]

Identificational reference groups
Because we tend to compare ourselves with those who are similar to us, many promotional strategies include 'ordinary' people whose consumption activities provide informational social influence. How can we predict which people you know will become
▶ part of your **identificational membership reference group**? Several factors make it more likely:

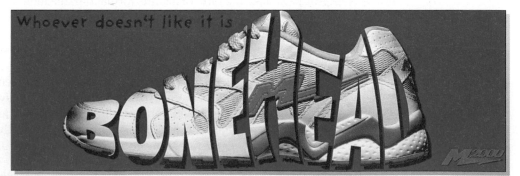

Many products, especially those targeted at young people, are often touted as a way to take the inside track to popularity. This Brazilian shoe ad proclaims: 'Anyone who doesn't like them is a nerd.'

- *Propinquity*: As physical distance between people decreases and opportunities for inter- action increase, relationships are more likely to form. We call this physical nearness *propinquity*. An early study on friendship patterns in a housing complex showed this factor's strong effects: residents were much more likely to be friends with the people next door than with those who lived only two doors away. Furthermore, people who lived next to a staircase had more friends than those at the ends of a corridor (presumably, they were more likely to 'bump into' people using the stairs).[7] Physical structure has a lot to do with who we get to know and how popular we are.

- *Mere exposure*: We come to like persons or things simply as a result of seeing them more often, which social scientists call the *mere exposure phenomenon*.[8] Greater frequency of contact, even if unintentional, may help to determine one's set of local referents. The same effect holds when evaluating works of art or even political candidates.[9] One study predicted 83 per cent of the winners of political primaries solely by the amount of media exposure given to candidates.[10]

- *Group cohesiveness*: Cohesiveness refers to the degree to which members of a group are attracted to each other and how much each values their group membership. As the value of the group to the individual increases, so too does the likelihood that the group will influence their consumption decisions. Smaller groups tend to be more cohesive because in larger groups the contributions of each member are usually less important or noticeable. By the same token, groups often try to restrict membership to a select few, which increases the value of membership to those who are admitted. Exclusivity of membership is a benefit often promoted by credit card companies, book clubs and so on, even though the actual membership base might be fairly large.

Positive vs. negative reference groups

Reference groups may exert either a positive or a negative influence on consumption behaviours. In most cases, we model our behaviour to be consistent with what we think the group expects us to do. Sometimes however we also deliberately do the opposite if we want to distance ourselves from other people or groups who function as **avoidance** or **dissociative groups**. We may carefully study the dress or mannerisms of a disliked group and scrupulously avoid buying anything that might identify us with that group. Many consumers find it difficult to express what they want whereas they can quite clearly express what they do not want. In fact, some researchers suggest that the phenomenon of distaste is much more decisive for our consumption choices but harder to study than tastes, since our choices are quite obvious compared to all the non-selected alternatives.[11] For example, rebellious adolescents often resent parental influence and may deliberately do the opposite of what their parents would like as a way of making a statement about their independence. As Romeo and Juliet discovered, nothing makes a partner more attractive than a little parental opposition.

The motivation to distance oneself from a negative reference group can be as or more powerful than the desire to please a positive group.[12] That is why advertisements occa- sionally show an undesirable person using a competitor's product to subtly make the point that you can avoid winding up like *that* kind of person by staying away from the products they buy. As a once-popular book reminded us, 'Real men *don't* eat quiche!'[13] Today, others have adapted this avoidance group appeal to point out the ways we define ourselves by not consuming some products or services. For example, a T-shirt for sale on a computer-oriented Website proudly proclaims, 'Real Men Don't Click Help'. Recent research suggests that 'dissociative reference groups have a greater impact on consumers' self-brand connections, product evaluations, and choices than do products associated with out-groups more generally'.[14] The Web has encouraged the rise of a new kind of group – **anti-brand communities** (more on brand communities below, see p. 391). These groups coalesce around a celebrity, store or brand – but in this case they're united by their disdain for it.

▼ **Marketing pitfall**

Brand bullying

'Recent research by one of the major UK teaching unions has found that "children who cannot afford to buy the latest brands and fashions face bullying and ridicule by their peers", as well as isolation and exclusion. Teachers also feel that there has been "a significant rise in the influence of marketing and advertising on children". Dr Mary Bousted (general secretary of the Association of Teachers and Lecturers) said that "Children feel under immense pressure to look right and having the key brands is part of that. Advertising and marketing have made our society increasingly image-conscious and our children are suffering the consequences. Schools and colleges should be places where children feel equal, but it is virtually impossible for schools to protect their pupils from the harsher aspects of these commercial influences". 93 per cent of teachers questioned said that "brands are the top influence on what children buy, followed by friends and logos".'[15]

Virtual communities

▶ Before the Web was widely accessible most **membership reference groups** consisted of people who had face-to-face contact. Now, it is possible to share interests with people whom you have never met – and probably never will. Have you ever heard of Little Boots? No? Well, this singer 'hasn't released record yet, at least not properly, just a couple of downloads and an old-fashioned seven-inch vinyl single, limited to 300 copies' and yet she was named Sound of 2009 in the annual BBC poll of music industry insiders, critics and broadcasters.[16] Evidence of the power of the Internet where she launched her first song in February 2008 via an anonymous MySpace page.

Little Boots: her career launch into the music industry illustrates the power of the internet in reaching consumers electronically.

Getty Images

► A **virtual community of consumption** is a collection of people who interact online to share their enthusiasm for and knowledge of a specific consumption activity. Like brand communities (see below) these groups grow up around an incredibly diverse set of interests – everything from Barbie dolls to fine wine. However, members remain anonymous because they only interact with each other in cyberspace. Still, these groups can and do make their voices heard. In one recent effort, nearly 14,000 people banded together on Facebook to beg Cadbury Schweppes to bring back Wispa, a chocolate bar the company discontinued in 2003. Sure enough, Cadbury announced in late 2007 that it was reintroducing the chocolate bar.[17]

Virtual communities come in many different forms:[18]

- *Multi-user dungeons (MUD)*. Originally, these were environments where players of fantasy games met. Now they refer to any computer-generated environment where people interact socially through the structured format of role- and game-playing.

- In a game called EverQuest, on any given night up to 50,000 people can be found roaming around a fantasy land in cyberspace. This is known as a 'massively multi-player game', which combines the stunning graphics of advanced gaming with the social scene of a chat room.[19] Realizing that the average online player logs 17 hours per week, firms like Sony, Microsoft and Sega are building their own virtual worlds to get a piece of the action. As one game company executive put it, 'This is not a genre of game but a break-through new medium. It provides a completely new social, collaborative shared experience. We're basically in the Internet community business.'[20]

- *Rooms*, *rings* and *lists*. These include internet relay chat (IRC), otherwise known as *chat rooms*. *Rings* are organizations of related home pages, and *lists* are groups of people on a single mailing list who share information.

- *Boards*. Online communities can be organized around interest-specific electronic bulletin boards. Active members read and post messages sorted by date and subject. There are boards devoted to musical groups, films, wine, cigars, cars, comic strips, even fast food restaurants.

► - *Blogs*. The newest and fastest growing form of online community is the **weblog**, or *blog*. These online personal journals are building an avid following among Internet users who like to dash off a few random thoughts, post them on a Website and read similar musings by others. For example, one site (**www.livejournal.com**) signed up 690,000 registered users in four years and added another 1,100 every day. A new blogger puts
► in their offering every 40 seconds, so this burgeoning **blogosphere** (the name given to the universe of active weblogs) is starting to look like a force to be reckoned with. The BBC has developed blogs around some of its most popular news programmes and commentators (e.g. the Business Editor Robert Peston's blog on the credit crunch and economic downturn **http://www.bbc.co.uk/blogs/thereporters/robertpeston/**), inviting listeners and viewers to join in debates about topical issues; and many newspapers (e.g. *The Guardian*, *Daily Telegraph*, *Le Monde*) also engage their readers via blogs.[21]

Other than the more global sites at, for example, **geocities.com**, there is a proliferation of national community sites for specific consumer profiles. In Denmark, for example, there are sites for teenage girls (**surfergirl.dk**), for themes such as relationships (**lovefinder.dk**), or an extremely popular site for medical problems (**netdoktor.dk**). In the UK there are many sites including those for parents (**newmother.co.uk**; **parentlineplus.org.uk/**); health issues (**netdoctor.co.uk**); and consumers (**consumeractiongroup.co.uk**).

Virtual communities are still a fairly recent phenomenon, but their impact on individuals' product preferences promises to be huge. These loyal consumers are essentially working together to form their tastes, evaluate product quality and even negotiate for better deals with producers. They place great weight on the judgements of their fellow members. Recent research has identified the important role played by social capital within

Role-playing computer games involve thousands of players worldwide in interactive, online communities.

© Susan Goldman/The Image Works/Topfoto

virtual communities, parallel to the role of social capital within face-to-face communities, and emphasizing the increasing importance of consumer-to-consumer exchanges within the consumption process.[22]

While consumption communities are largely a grass-roots phenomenon founded by consumers for other consumers, these community members can be reached by marketers – if they are careful not to alienate members by being too aggressive or 'commercial'. Using newsgroup archives and search engines, companies can create a detailed profile of any individual consumer who has posted information. Firms like Warner Brothers form communities with fans around the world. The company noticed that many fans of Bugs Bunny, Batman and the Tazmanian Devil were downloading images and sound clips onto their personal Web pages and then selling ad space on those pages. Instead of suing its fans, Warner created an online community called ACME City that builds home pages for registered members. Many corporate-sponsored sites build home pages for new members and ask for nothing in return except personal information on a registration form. They can use this information to fine-tune the online experience by making advertising, contests and rewards programmes more relevant.

How do people get drawn into consumption communities? Internet users tend to progress from asocial information gathering ('lurkers' are surfers who like to watch but don't participate) to increasingly affiliative social activities. At first they will merely browse the site but later they may well be drawn into active participation.

The intensity of identification with a virtual community depends on two factors. The first is that the more central the activity is to a person's self-concept, the more likely they will be to pursue active membership in a community. The second is that the intensity of the social relationships the person forms with other members of the virtual community helps to determine the extent of their involvement. As Figure 10.1 shows, combining these two factors creates four distinct member types:

1 *Tourists* lack strong social ties to the group, and maintain only a passing interest in the activity.

2 *Minglers* maintain strong social ties, but are not very interested in the central consumption activity.

3 *Devotees* express strong interest in the activity, but have few social attachments to the group.

4 *Insiders* exhibit both strong social ties and strong interest in the activity.

Figure 10.1 Virtual communities

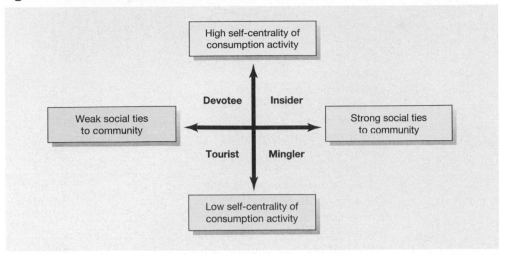

Source: Adapted from Robert V. Kozinets, 'E-tribalized marketing: the strategic implications of virtual communities of consumption', *European Management Journal* 17(3) (June 1999): 252–64.

Devotees and insiders are the most important targets for marketers who wish to exploit communities for promotional purposes. They are the heavy users of virtual communities. And, by reinforcing usage, the community may upgrade tourists and minglers to insiders and devotees.[23] But marketers have only scratched the surface of this intriguing new virtual world. Consumer researchers are working on techniques to help them understand what is going on in cyberspace. Some use a technique they call **netnography**, which adapts ethnographic techniques anthropologists use to study real-life cultures when they 'live with the native people' to virtual communities.[24] For example, a team of Chinese researchers did a netnography of beauty product enthusiasts to understand how Chinese consumers interact with each other to share their passion for cosmetics.[25]

More generally, e-commerce sites know that consumers give more weight to the opinions of real people, so they are finding ways to let these opinions be included on their Websites. This trend of posting customer reviews was started by **Amazon.com** in 1995. Now, sellers of computers and other high-priced products post customer reviews.[26] A great idea – but in a highly publicized lawsuit Amazon was accused of charging publishers to post positive reviews on the site. The company had to offer refunds for all books it recommended and now Amazon tells customers when a publisher has paid for a prominent display on its site.[27]

A basic topic for discussion is: who owns the Net? The outcome of a legal case against the music exchange service Napster, ruling that it was illegal to organize even non-profitable exchange of music files among its users, tends to point in the direction that cyberspace can be patented and owned. However, the reaction among hard-core virtual community people seems to be that there will always be ways of circumventing such attempts to stop the free flow of information within the virtual communities. The problem for Warner Brothers and many other producers of cultural products is that on the one hand they like (for good pecuniary reasons) the iconic cult status their products may obtain (e.g. Harry Potter), but on the other they do not fully appreciate that part of the love for cultural products is sharing them with other devotees.[28] The big question remains, within as well as outside cyberspace: who owns culture?

Brand communities and tribes

Some marketing researchers are embracing a new perspective on reference groups as they identify groups built around a shared allegiance to a product or activity. A **brand community** is a set of consumers who share a set of social relationships based upon usage of or interest in a product. Unlike other kinds of communities, these members typically do not live near each other – and they often meet only for brief periods at

▶ organized events called **brand-fests**, such as those sponsored by Jeep, Saturn or Harley-Davidson. These brand-fests help owners to 'bond' with fellow enthusiasts and strengthen their identification with the product as well as with others they meet who share their passion.

Researchers find that people who participate in these events feel more positive about the products as a result and this enhances brand loyalty. They are more forgiving than others of product failures or lapses in service quality, and less likely to switch brands even if they learn that competing products are as good or better. Furthermore, these community members become emotionally involved in the company's welfare, and they often serve as brand missionaries by carrying its marketing message to others.[29]

▶ The notion of a **consumer tribe** is similar to a brand community; it is a group of people who share a lifestyle and who can identify with each other through a shared allegiance to an activity or a product. Although these tribes are often unstable and short-lived, at least for a time members identify with others through shared emotions, moral beliefs, styles of life, and of course the products they jointly consume as part of their tribal affiliation.

▶ Some companies, especially those that are more youth oriented, are using **tribal marketing** to link their product to the needs of a group as a whole. Many tribes devoted to activities like skateboarding or football are youth oriented, and we will talk more about these in Chapter 15. However, there are also plenty of tribes with older members, such as car enthusiasts who gather to celebrate such cult products (see Chapter 6) as the Citroën and Mini Cooper in Europe and the Ford Mustang in the US.[30]

▶ Other research has identified **communities of practice** as a potentially valuable way of understanding and interpreting group behaviour. Communities of practice are 'an aggregate of people who come together around mutual engagement in an endeavour'.[31] Developed from work in socio-linguistics, communities of practice are usually defined by three characteristics: 'mutual engagement; a joint enterprise; and a shared repertoire'.[32] A study of Bolton schoolgirls showed how consumption symbols (e.g. Rockport shoes) could be combined with other social symbols (e.g. language) in order to create meanings related to group identity:[33] 'we are surrounded by stylistic material, and as long as we can position ourselves in relation to the sources of that material, and attribute meaning to it, we can use it'.[34]

When reference groups are important

Reference group influences are not equally powerful for all types of products and consumption activities. For example, we are not as likely to take others' preferences into account when we choose products that are not very complex, that are low in perceived risk or that we can try before we buy.[35] In addition, knowing what others prefer may influence us at a general level. At times they may determine the use of certain products rather than others (owning or not owning a computer, eating junk food versus healthy food), whereas at other times they may have specific effects on brand decisions within a product category (wearing Levi's jeans versus Diesel jeans, or smoking Marlboro cigarettes instead of a national brand).

Two dimensions that influence the degree to which reference groups are important are whether we will consume the item publicly or privately and whether it is a luxury or a necessity. As a rule, reference group effects are more robust for purchases that are (1) luxuries rather than necessities (e.g. yachts), because products that we buy using discretionary income are subject to individual tastes and preferences, whereas necessities do not offer this range of choices; and (2) socially conspicuous or visible to others (e.g. living room furniture or clothing), because we do not tend to be swayed as much by the opinions of others if no one but ourselves will ever see what we buy.[36] The relative effects of reference group influences on some specific product classes are shown in Figure 10.2.

Figure 10.2 Relative effects of reference groups

Source: Adapted from William O. Bearden and Michael J. Etzel, 'Reference group influence on product and brand purchase decisions', *Journal of Consumer Research* 9 (September 1982): 185. Reprinted with permission of The University of Chicago Press.

This obviously does not mean that a reference group cannot exert influence on the consumption of private necessities.

The power of reference groups

Why are reference groups so persuasive? The answer lies in the potential power they wield over us. **Social power** refers to 'the capacity to alter the actions of others'.[37] To the degree that you are able to make someone else do something, whether they do it willingly or not, you have power over that person. The following classification of *power bases* can help us to distinguish among the reasons why a person can exert power over another, the degree to which the influence is allowed voluntarily, and whether this influence will continue to have an effect in the absence of the power source.[38]

Referent power

If a person admires the qualities of a person or a group, they try to imitate those qualities by copying the referent's behaviours (choice of clothing, cars, leisure activities) as a guide to forming consumption preferences, just as Bobbie's sporting friends and football team-mates affected his preferences. Prominent people in all walks of life can affect people's consumption behaviours by virtue of product endorsements (e.g. top model Cindy Crawford for Omega watches), distinctive fashion statements (e.g. Madonna's use of lingerie as outerwear), or championing causes (e.g. Brigitte Bardot's campaigning against fur or Lance Armstrong's work for cancer). **Referent power** is important to many marketing strategies because consumers voluntarily modify what they do and buy to identify with a referent.

Information power

A person can have **information power** simply because they know something others would like to know. Editors of trade publications such as *Women's Wear Daily* in the fashion industry often possess power due to their ability to compile and disseminate information that can make or break individual designers or companies. People with information power are able to influence consumer opinion by virtue of their (assumed) access to the 'truth'.

Legitimate power

Sometimes power is granted to people by virtue of social agreements, such as the authority given to the police, border security officers at airports and ports, and the armed forces.

▶ The **legitimate power** conferred by a uniform is recognized in many consumer contexts, including teaching hospitals, in which medical students don white coats to enhance their aura of authority with patients, and organizations such as banks, where tellers' uniforms communicate trustworthiness.[39] Marketers may 'borrow' this form of power to influence consumers. For example, an ad featuring a model wearing a nurse's uniform can add an aura of legitimacy or authority to the presentation of the product as seen in TV advertising campaigns in the babies' nappy market.

Expert power

To attract the casual Internet user, US Robotics signed up British physicist Stephen Hawking to endorse its modems. A company executive commented, 'We wanted to generate trust. So we found visionaries who use US Robotics technology, and we let them tell the consumer how it makes their lives more productive.' Hawking, who has Lou Gehrig's (motor neurone) disease and speaks via a synthesizer, said in one TV spot, 'My body may be stuck in this chair, but with the Internet my mind can go to the

▶ end of the universe.'[40] **Expert power** such as that possessed by Hawking is derived from possessing specific knowledge about a content area; it helps to explain the weight many of us assign to reviews of restaurants, books, films, cars and so on by critics who specialize in evaluating products on our behalf.[41] This power base also underlies the appeal of television shows, where panels of authorities – often a mix of journalists and

Every cigarette we smoke makes
fatty deposits stick in our arteries.

We'll help you give up before you clog up completely.   bhf.org.uk

This anti-tobacco advertisement draws on the legitimate and expert power represented by The British Heart Foundation, and combines it with stark images of the effects which smoking has on arteries – and thus on our health – to create a strong anti-smoking message.

The Advertising Archives

professional experts – discuss issues of interest to consumers. However the advent of blogs and open source references such as Wikipedia means that it is increasingly difficult to tell who is an expert; and professional reviewers and critics are increasingly seeing blogs as sources of competition[42].

▶ Reward power

A person or group with the means to provide positive reinforcement (see Chapter 7) has **reward power**. The reward may be the tangible kind, as occurs when an employee is given a pay rise. Or, the reward may be intangible: social approval or acceptance is often what is exchanged in return for moulding one's behaviour to a group or buying the products expected of group members. However, this kind of power is perhaps wearing thin in advertising, since an overexploitation of reward arguments has left such campaigns with little credibility. The Sprite soft drink campaign under the slogan 'Image is nothing, thirst is everything, obey your thirst' makes fun of other commercials' use of reward power in their slogans. Other commercials suggest that something more basic than thirst is being rewarded by drinking their product (i.e. image needs). Sprite is playing off this idea by emphasizing that the basic need is thirst and not anything associated with image. However, the slogan in itself paradoxically promises a reward in the form of an image – of somebody who does not fall for cheap tricks.[43]

▶

Coercive power

We exert **coercive power** when we influence someone by social or physical intimidation. While coercive power is often effective in the short term, it does not tend to produce permanent attitudinal or behavioural change. Surveillance of some sort is usually required to make people do something they do not wish to do. Fortunately, coercive power is rarely

▶ Multicultural dimensions

Norms change slowly over time, but there is general agreement within a society about which ones should be obeyed, and we adjust our way of thinking to conform to these norms. A powerful example is the change in attitudes towards smoking since the 1960s, when this practice was first linked with health concerns such as cancer and emphysema. By the mid-1990s, some communities in the US had outlawed smoking in public places. New York City did this in 2002. The Netherlands banned smoking from many public places in January 2004; Eire banned smoking in all public places in March 2004; Norway banned smoking in restaurants and bars in June 2004; Italy banned smoking in public places in January 2005; and Scotland introduced a ban in June 2006, followed by England in July 2007. In October 2003 the French government raised the price of cigarettes by 20 per cent in an attempt to cut levels of smoking; banned smoking in public places such as hospitals and government buildings in July 2007; and then extended the ban on smoking to include bars, cafés, restaurants, hotels and night clubs with effect from January 2008. In Germany the ban on smoking in public places was introduced in January 2008, but met with some resistance.[44] Siggi Ermer (chairman of Germany's largest anti-tobacco lobby) argued that 'The smoking ban is a failure, it hasn't worked in the same way that it has in Italy, France and Britain. The difference is that there in each case you have a clear law that has put in place an absolute ban. Here we have a host of laws and major interpretation problems'.[45]

Much of the motivation to begin smoking at an early age is due to peer pressure; the alluring advertising images of smokers as cool, sexy or mature help to convince many young people that beginning the habit is a path to social acceptance. Because the power of advertising to influence attitudes is widely recognized, some groups have tried to fight fire with fire by creating anti-smoking ads that depict smoking as an ugly habit that turns people off.

Are these ads effective? One study of non-smoking seventh graders examined their perceptions of smokers after being exposed to both cigarette ads and anti-smoking ads. Results were promising: the researchers found that those who saw the anti-smoking ads were more likely to rate smokers lower in terms of both personal appeal and common sense. These findings imply that it is possible to use advertising to debunk myths about the glamour of smoking, especially if used in tandem with other health education efforts.[46]

employed in marketing situations, unless you count those annoying calls from telemarketers. However, elements of this power base are evident in fear appeals, intimidation in personal selling, and campaigns that emphasize the negative consequences that can occur if people do not use a product.

CONFORMITY

In every age there are those who 'march to the beat of their own drum'. However, most people tend to follow society's expectations regarding how they should act and look ▶ (with a little improvisation here and there, of course). **Conformity** refers to a change in beliefs or actions as a reaction to real or imagined group pressure. In order for a society ▶ to function, its members develop **norms,** or informal rules that govern behaviour. If such a system of agreements and rules did not evolve, chaos would result. Imagine the confusion if a simple norm such as sitting down to attend class did not exist.

We conform in many small ways every day – even though we don't always realize it. Unspoken rules govern many aspects of consumption. In addition to norms regarding appropriate use of clothing and other personal items, we conform to rules that include gift-giving (we expect birthday presents from loved ones and get upset if they do not materialize), sex roles (men were often expected to pick up the bill on a first date, though this convention is changing) and personal hygiene (we are expected to shower or bathe regularly to avoid offending others).

Types of social influence

Just as the bases for social power can vary, so the process of social influence operates in several ways.[47] Sometimes a person is motivated to model the behaviour of others because this mimicry is believed to yield rewards such as social approval or money. At other times, the social influence process occurs simply because the person honestly does not *know* the correct way to respond and is using the behaviour of the other person or ▶ group as a cue to ensure that they are responding correctly.[48] **Normative social influence** occurs when a person conforms to meet the expectations of a person or group.

▶   In contrast, **informational social influence** refers to conformity that occurs because the group's behaviour is taken as evidence of reality: if other people respond in a certain way in an ambiguous situation, we may mimic their behaviour because this appears to be the correct thing to do.[49]

Reasons for conformity

Conformity is not an automatic process, and many factors contribute to the likelihood that consumers will pattern their behaviour after others.[50] Among the factors that affect the likelihood of conformity are the following:

● *Cultural pressures*: Different cultures encourage conformity to a greater or lesser degree. The American slogan 'Do your own thing' in the 1960s reflected a movement away from conformity and towards individualism. In contrast, Japanese society is characterized by the dominance of collective well-being and group loyalty over individuals' needs. Most European societies are situated somewhere between these two, in this respect, 'extreme' cultures. In an analysis of the reading of a soft drinks TV commercial, Danish consumers stressed the group solidarity that they saw in the ad, an aspect not mentioned at all by the American sample.[51]

● *Fear of deviance*: The individual may have reason to believe that the group will apply *sanctions* to punish nonconforming behaviours. It is not unusual to observe adolescents shunning a peer who is 'different' or a corporation or university passing over a person for promotion because they are not a 'team player'.

- *Commitment*: The more people are dedicated to a group and value their membership in it, the more motivated they are to do what the group wants. Rock groupies and followers of religious sects may do anything that is asked of them, and terrorists (or martyrs and freedom fighters, depending on the perspective) may be willing to die for the good of their cause. According to the *principle of least interest*, the person that is least committed to staying in a relationship has the most power, because that party doesn't care as much if the other person rejects them.[52]

- *Group unanimity*, *size*, and *expertise*: As groups gain in power, compliance increases. It is often harder to resist the demands of a large number of people than just a few, and this difficulty is compounded when the group members are perceived to know what they are talking about.

- *Susceptibility to interpersonal influence*: This trait refers to an individual's need to have others think highly of them. This enhancement process is often accompanied by the acquisition of products the person believes will impress their audience and by the tendency to learn about products by observing how others use them.[53] Consumers who are low on this trait have been called *role-relaxed*; they tend to be older, affluent and to have high self-confidence. Based on research identifying role-relaxed consumers, Subaru created a communications strategy to reach these people. In one commercial, a man is heard saying, 'I want a car . . . Don't tell me about wood panelling, about winning the respect of my neighbours. They're my neighbours. They're not my heroes.'

Social comparison: 'How am I doing?'

Informational social influence implies that sometimes we look to the behaviour of others to provide a yardstick about reality. **Social comparison theory** asserts that this process occurs as a way of increasing the stability of one's self-evaluation, especially when physical evidence is unavailable.[54] Social comparison even applies to choices for which there are no objectively correct answers. Such stylistic decisions as tastes in music and art are assumed to be a matter of individual choice, yet people often assume that some choices are 'better' or more 'correct' than others.[55] If you have ever been responsible for choosing the music to play at a party, you can probably appreciate the social pressure involved in choosing the right 'mix'.

Although people often like to compare their judgements and actions with those of others, they tend to be selective about precisely who they will use as benchmarks. Similarity between the consumer and others used for social comparison boosts confidence that the information is accurate and relevant (though we may find it more threatening to be outperformed by someone similar to ourselves).[56] We tend to value the views of obviously dissimilar others only when we are reasonably certain of our own.[57]

Social comparison theory has been used to explore the effects of advertising images on women's self-perceptions of their physical attractiveness and their levels of self-esteem.[58] Many early studies showed that social comparison, when studied in terms of only self evaluation, is likely to have a negative effect on self-esteem. However, the incorporation of the specific goal (self-evaluation; self-improvement; or self-enhancement)[59] suggests that social comparison can have either positive or negative effects on self-feelings depending on the goal for social comparison.[60] One study suggests that the direction of spontaneous social comparison and social evaluation processes may be determined by fairly subtle cues. Whereas most advertising research suggests that comparisons with idealized models lead to contrast, this study found evidence that comparisons can also lead to assimilation of standards into the self-evaluation.[61]

In general people tend to choose a *co-oriented peer*, or a person of equivalent standing, when performing social comparison. For example, a study of adult cosmetics users found that women were more likely to seek information about product choices from

This advert for deoderant illustrates a message appeal based on conforming to the unspoken rule about personal hygiene in many societies.

The Advertising Archives

similar friends to reduce uncertainty and to trust the judgements of similar others.[62] The same effects have been found for evaluations of products as diverse as men's suits and coffee.[63]

Tactical requests

How do we increase the likelihood that a person will conform to our wishes? The way a request for compliance is phrased or structured can make a difference. One well-known sales tactic is known as the *foot-in-the-door technique*, where the consumer is first asked a small request and then is 'hit' for something bigger.[64] This term is adapted from door-to-door selling. Experienced salespeople know that they are much more likely to make a sale if they first convince a customer to let them into the house to deliver their sales pitch. Once the person has agreed to this small request, it is more difficult to refuse a larger one, since the consumer has legitimized the salesperson's presence by entering into a dialogue. The salesperson is no longer a threatening stranger at the door.

Other variations on this strategy include the *low-ball technique*, where a person is asked a small favour and is informed after agreeing to it that it will be very costly, or the *door-in-the-face technique*, where a person is first asked to do something extreme (a request that is usually refused) and is then asked to do something smaller. In each of these cases, people tend to go along with the smaller request, possibly because they feel guilty about denying the larger one.[65]

Group effects on individual behaviour

With more people in a group, it becomes less likely that any one member will be singled out for attention. People in larger groups, or those in situations where they are unlikely to be identified, tend to focus less attention on themselves, so normal restraints on behaviour are reduced. You may have observed that people sometimes behave more wildly at fancy dress parties, at hen or stag parties or partying on, for example, charter holidays, than they would normally do. This phenomenon is known as **de-individuation**. This is a process in which individual identities get submerged within a group and a special situation.

▶ Multicultural dimensions

University parties sometimes illustrate the dark side of de-individuation when students are encouraged by their peers to consume almost superhuman volumes of alcohol in group settings. About 4.5 million young people in the US are estimated to be alcohol-dependent or problem drinkers. Binge drinking among university students is reaching epidemic proportions. In a two-week period, 42 per cent of all college students engage in binge drinking (more than five drinks at a time) versus 33 per cent of their non-university counterparts. One in three students drinks primarily to get drunk, including 35 per cent of university women. For most, social pressure to abandon all inhibitions is the culprit.[66] Binge drinking is also increasingly recognized as a problem in the UK,[67] and not only among university students.[68]

▶ **Social loafing** happens when we do not devote as much effort to a task when our contribution is part of a larger group effort.[69] Waiting staff are painfully aware of social loafing: people who eat in groups tend to tip less per person than when they are eating alone.[70] For this reason, many restaurants automatically add on a fixed gratuity for groups of six or more.

▶ There is some evidence that decisions made by groups differ from those that would be made by each individual on their own. The **risky shift** refers to the observation that in many cases, group members show a greater willingness to consider riskier alternatives following group discussion than they would if members made individual decisions with no discussion.[71] Psychologists propose several explanations for this increased riskiness. One possibility is that something similar to social loafing occurs. As more people are involved in a decision, each individual is less accountable for the outcome, resulting in *diffusion of responsibility*.[72] The practice of placing blanks in at least one of the rifles used by a firing squad is one way of diffusing each soldier's responsibility for the death of a prisoner because it is never certain who actually shot them. Another explanation is termed the *value hypothesis* which states that our culture values risky behaviour, so when people make decisions in groups they conform to this expectation.[73]

▶ Research evidence for the risky shift is mixed. A more general finding is that group discussion tends to increase **decision polarization**. Therefore, whichever direction the group members were leaning towards before discussion began – whether towards a risky choice or towards a more conservative choice – becomes even more extreme in that

Costumes hide our true identities and encourage de-individuation.

Alamy/Martin Dalton

direction after discussion. Group discussions regarding product purchases tend to create a risky shift for low-risk items, but they yield more conservative group decisions for high-risk products.[74]

Shopping patterns

Even shopping behaviour changes when people do it in groups. For example, people who shop with at least one other person tend to make more unplanned purchases, buy more and cover more areas of a store than those who go alone.[75] These effects are due to both normative and informational social influence. Group members may buy something to gain the approval of the others, or the group may simply be exposed to more products and stores by pooling information with the group. For these reasons, retailers are well advised to encourage group shopping activities.

 Multicultural dimensions

The institution of home shopping parties, as epitomized by Tupperware, capitalizes on group pressure to boost sales.[76] A company representative makes a sales presentation to a group of people who have gathered in the home of a friend or acquaintance. This format is effective because of informational social influence. Participants model the behaviour of others who can provide them with information about how to use certain products, especially since the home party is likely to be attended by a relatively homogeneous group

(e.g. neighbourhood housewives) that serves as a valuable benchmark. Normative social influence also operates because others can easily observe our actions. Pressures to conform may be particularly intense and may escalate as more and more group members begin to 'cave in' (this process is sometimes termed the *bandwagon effect*). In addition, these parties may activate de-individuation and/or the risky shift. As consumers get caught up in the group, they may find themselves willing to try new products they would not normally consider.

▶   These same dynamics underlie the latest variation on the Tupperware **home shopping parties'** technique: the Botox party. The craze for Botox injections that paralyze facial nerves to reduce wrinkles (for three to six months anyway) is being fuelled by gatherings where dermatologists or plastic surgeons redefine the definition of house calls. For patients, mixing cocktail hour with cosmetic injections takes some of the anxiety out of the procedure. Egged on by the others at the party, as many as ten patients can be 'de-wrinkled' in an hour. An advertising executive who worked on the Botox marketing strategy explained that the membership reference group appeal is more effective than the traditional route of using a celebrity spokesperson to promote the injections in advertising: 'We think it's more persuasive to think of your next-door neighbour using it.'[77] The only hitch is that after you get the injections your face is so rigid that your friends can't tell if you're smiling.

Resistance to influence

Many people pride themselves on their independence, unique style, or ability to resist the best efforts of salespeople and advertisers to buy products.[78] Indeed, individuality should be encouraged by the marketing system: innovation creates change and demand for new products and styles.

Anti-conformity vs. independence

It is important to distinguish between *independence* and *anti-conformity*; in anti-conformity, defiance of the group is the actual object of behaviour.[79] Some people will go out of their way *not* to buy whatever happens to be in fashion. Indeed, they may spend a lot of time and effort to ensure that they will not be caught 'in style'. This behaviour is a bit of a paradox, because in order to be vigilant about not doing what is expected, one must always be aware of what is expected. In contrast, truly independent people are oblivious to what is expected; they 'march to the beat of own drum'.

Reactance and the need for uniqueness

People have a deep-seated need to preserve freedom of choice. When they are threatened with a loss of this freedom, they try to overcome this loss. This negative emotional state
▶ is termed **reactance**, and results when we are deprived of our freedom to choose.[80] This feeling can drive us to value forbidden things even if they wouldn't be that interesting to us otherwise. For example, efforts to censor books, television shows or rock music because some people find the content objectionable may result in an *increased* desire for these products by the public.[81] Similarly, extremely overbearing promotions that tell consumers they must or should use a product may lose customers in the long run, even those who were already loyal to the advertised brand. Reactance is more likely to occur when the perceived threat to one's freedom increases and as the threatened behaviour's importance to the consumer also increases.

If you have ever arrived at a party wearing the same outfit as someone else, you know how upsetting it can be, a reaction resulting from a search for uniqueness.[82] Consumers who have been led to believe they are not unique are more likely to try to compensate by increasing their creativity, or even to engage in unusual experiences. In fact, this is one explanation for the purchase of relatively obscure brands. People may try to establish a unique identity by deliberately *not* buying market leaders.

This desire to carve out a unique identity was the rationale behind Saab's shift from stressing engineering and safety in its marketing messages to appealing to people to 'find your own road'. According to a Saab executive, 'Research companies tell us we are moving into a period where people feel good about their choices because it fits their own self-concept rather than social conventions.'[83]

WORD-OF-MOUTH COMMUNICATION

Despite the abundance of formal means of communication (such as newspapers, magazines and television), much information about the world is conveyed by individuals on an informal basis.[84] If you think carefully about the content of your own conversations in the course of a normal day, you will probably agree that much of what you discuss with friends, family members or co-workers is product-related: whether you compliment someone on her dress and ask her where she bought it, recommend a new restaurant to a friend, or complain to your neighbour about the shoddy treatment you got at the
▶ bank, you are engaging in **word-of-mouth communication (WOM)**. Recall, for example, that Bobbie's choice of football boots was directly initiated by comments and suggestions from his friends and team-mates. This kind of communication can be an efficient marketing tool. When the film *The Blair Witch Project* became a big success, it was almost assured beforehand because of the pre-premiere WOM sparked by a good Website and heavy exploitation of the blurring of reality and fiction.

Information obtained from those we know or talk to directly tends to be more reliable and trustworthy than that received through more formal channels and, unlike advertising, it is often backed up by social pressure to conform to these recommendations.[85] Another factor in the importance of WOM is the decline in people's faith in institutions. As traditional endorsers are becoming increasingly problematical to use, celebrities because they can be unreliable and classical authority figures because of the withering of their authority, and, indeed, as people are becoming more cynical about all sorts of commercial communications, they turn to sources which they feel are above commercial exploitation: friends and family.[86] The importance of personal, informal product communication to marketers is further underscored by one advertising executive, who stated, 'Today, 80 per cent of all buying decisions are influenced by someone's direct recommendations.'[87] In one survey, 69 per cent of interviewees said they relied on a personal referral at least once over the course of a year to help them choose a restaurant, 36 per cent reported they used referrals to decide on computer hardware and software, and 22 per cent got help from friends and associates to decide where to travel.[88] Recent research however has challenged the traditional assumption that consumers weigh negative word-of-mouth more heavily than positive word of mouth where judgement and choice are concerned. These researchers suggest that negative word of mouth will be outweighed in cases where consumers positively evaluate the agent (the agent could be *inter alia* a friend, family member, online poster, or professional critic) who is the source of the word of mouth. This means that if the consumer judges the agent as having similar tastes to their own or as being a suitable source of information, then the consumer will potentially weigh that agent's positive evaluation more heavily than negative word of mouth from other sources.[89]

The dominance of WOM

In the 1950s communications theorists began to challenge the assumption that advertising primarily determines what we buy. As a rule, advertising is more effective when it reinforces our existing product preferences than when it tries to create new ones.[90] Studies in both industrial and consumer purchase settings underline the idea that, although information from impersonal sources is important for creating brand awareness, consumers rely on word-of-mouth in the later stages of evaluation and adoption.[91] Quite simply, the more positive information consumers get about a product from peers, the more likely they will be to adopt the product.[92]

The influence of others' opinions is at times even more powerful than one's own perceptions. In one study of furniture choices, consumers' estimates of how much their friends would like the furniture was a better predictor of purchase than their *own* evaluations.[93]

Factors encouraging WOM

Product-related conversations can be motivated by a number of factors:[94]

- A person might be highly involved with a type of product or activity and get pleasure in talking about it. Computer hackers, avid birdwatchers, football fans and 'fashion plates' seem to share the ability to steer a conversation towards their particular interests.

- A person might be knowledgeable about a product and use conversations as a way to let others know it. Thus, word-of-mouth communication sometimes enhances the ego of the individual who wants to impress others with their expertise.

- A person might initiate such a discussion out of genuine concern for someone else. We are often motivated to ensure that people we care about buy what is good for them, do not waste their money, and so on.

- One way to reduce uncertainty about the wisdom of a purchase is to talk about it. Talking gives the consumer an opportunity to generate more supporting arguments for the purchase and to garner support for this decision from others.

Most WOM campaigns happen spontaneously, as a product begins to develop a regional or a sub-cultural following, but occasionally a 'buzz' is created intentionally. For example, when launching a new brand of beer, called Black Sheep, bottles were distributed and maximum exposure to opinion leaders in the trade ensured in order to pave the way for a massive word-of-mouth effect, intended as the vehicle for carrying the new brand towards success.[95] A similar *word-of-mouth advertising* technique was used when a group of opinion leaders, or 'influencers', was used to market services in the insurance market.[96]

Guerrilla marketing

To promote their hip hop albums, Def Jam and other labels started building a buzz months before a release, leaking advance copies to DJs who put together 'mix tapes' to sell on the street. If the kids seemed to like a song, *street teams* then pushed it to club DJs. As the official release date neared, these groups of fans started slapping up posters around the inner city. They plastered telephone poles, sides of buildings and car windscreens with promotions announcing the release of new albums by artists such as Public Enemy, Jay-Z, DMX or L.L. Cool J.[97]

► These streetwise strategies started in the mid-1970s, when pioneering DJs promoted their parties through graffiti-style flyers. This type of grass-roots effort epitomizes **guerrilla marketing**, promotional strategies that use unconventional locations and intensive word-of-mouth campaigns to push products. As Ice Cube observed, 'Even though I'm an established artist, I still like to leak my music to a kid on the street and let him duplicate it for his homies before it hits radio.'[98]

Today, big companies are buying into guerrilla marketing strategies in a big way. Coca-Cola did it for a Sprite promotion, Nike did it to build interest in a new shoe model.[99] Upmarket fashion companies are adopting this strategy, in order to offer shoppers a different retailing experience compared with conventional retail outlets. Comme des Garçons Guerrilla Store opened in New York in February 2004: '[I]n the first example of provisional retailing by an established fashion house, the store plans to close in a year even if it is making money. All 20 stores that the Tokyo-based company plans to open by next year, including one in Brooklyn in September [2004], will adopt the same guerrilla strategy, disappearing after a year.'[100]

When RCA Records wanted to create a buzz around teen pop singer Christina Aguilera, they hired a team of young people to swarm the Web and chat about her on popular teen sites. They posted information casually, sometimes sounding like fans. Just before one of her albums debuted, RCA also hired a direct marketing company to e-mail electronic postcards filled with song snippets and biographical information to 50,000 Web addresses.[101] Guerrilla marketing delivers: the album quickly went to No. 1 in the charts.

Viral marketing

Many students are big fans of Hotmail, a free email service. But there's no such thing as a free lunch: Hotmail inserts a small ad on every message sent, making each user a salesperson. The company had 5 million subscribers in its first year and continues
► to grow exponentially.[102] **Viral marketing** refers to the strategy of getting customers to sell a product on behalf of the company that creates it. This approach is particularly well suited to the Web, since emails circulate so easily. According to a study by Jupiter Communications, only 24 per cent of consumers say they learn about new Websites in magazine or newspaper ads. Instead, they rely on friends and family for new site recommendations, so viral marketing is their main source of information about new sites.[103] The chief executive of **Gazooba.com**, a company that creates viral marketing promotions, observed that 'the return mail address of a friend is a brand that you trust'.[104] Obviously, given what was discussed above, there may be some ethical problems and limitations as to how much marketers can infiltrate what is otherwise a network of friends/fans, before this particular 'brand that you trust' is no longer trusted.

The film *A.I.* (Artificial Intelligence) launched an elaborate viral marketing campaign by listing a credit at the end of the film for Jeanine Salla, who was described as a 'sentient machine therapist'. Curious viewers who typed in her name into the Google search engine got back a list of Web addresses and they eventually got drawn into a futuristic murder mystery where characters (including robots) from the film e-mailed and voice mailed them with clues. The campaign generated more than 3 million sessions, and 28 per cent of the visitors remained online for more than half an hour.[105]

Efficiency of WOM

Interpersonal transmissions can be quite rapid. The producers of *Batman* showed a trailer to 300 Batman fans months before its release to counteract widespread anger about the casting of Michael Keaton as the hero. The film-makers attribute the film's eventual huge success to the positive word-of-mouth that quickly spread following the screening.[106]

WOM is especially powerful in cases where the consumer is relatively unfamiliar with the product category. Such a situation would be expected in cases where the product is new (e.g. medication to prevent hair loss) or is technologically complex (e.g. DVD recorders). As one example, the strongest predictor of a person's intention to buy a residential solar water heating system was found to be the number of solar heating users the person knew.[107]

Negative WOM

Word-of-mouth is a two-edged sword that can cut both ways for marketers. Informal discussions among consumers can make or break a product or store. Furthermore, consumers weigh **negative word-of-mouth** more heavily than they do positive comments. According to one study, 90 per cent of unhappy customers will not do business with a company again. Each of these people is likely to share their grievance with at least nine other people, and 13 per cent of these disgruntled customers will go on to tell *more than 30* people of their negative experience.[108]

Especially when we're considering a new product or service, we're likely to pay more attention to negative information than positive information and tell others of our nasty experience.[109] Some consumers may even use negative WOM in order to restore their own positive self-image, for example in cases where a product offering is judged not to have corresponded to the person's self-image. Instead of blaming oneself for a misjudgment which would harm self-images of rationality and being in control, negative WOM may be the outcome.[110] Research shows that negative WOM reduces the credibility of a firm's advertising and influences consumers' attitudes toward a product as well as their intention to buy it.[111] And negative WOM is even easier to spread online. Many dissatisfied customers and disgruntled former employees have been 'inspired' to create Websites just to share their tales of woe with others. For example, a Website for people to complain about the Dunkin' Donuts chain became so popular the company bought it in order to control the bad press it was getting. It grew out of a complaint by the original owner because he could not get skimmed milk for his coffee.[112]

In an in-depth study of 40 complaint Websites such as **walmartsucks.com**, the authors use *protest-framing theory* that sociologists developed to understand how people define a social situation to others in order to influence their behaviour.[113] They identify three basic subframes, or themes:

1 *Injustice*: consumer protestors frequently talk about their repeated attempts to contact the company, only to be ignored.

2 *Identity*: posters characterize the violator (often top management) as evil, rather than simply wrong.

3 *Agency*: individual Website creators try to create a collective identity for those who share their anger with a company. They evoke themes of crusades and heroism to rally others to believe that they have the power to change the *status quo* in which companies can wrong consumers without retribution.

Rumours

▶ A **rumour** can be very dangerous, especially when it is false. In the 1930s, 'professional rumourmongers' were hired to organize word-of-mouth campaigns to promote clients'

Figure 10.3 The transmission of misinformation. These drawings provide a classic example of the distortions that can occur as information is transmitted from person to person. As each person reproduces the figure, it gradually changes from an owl to a cat

Source: Kenneth J. Gergen and Mary Gergen, *Social Psychology* (New York: Harcourt Brace Jovanovich, 1981): p. 365. Adapted from F.C. Bartlett, *Remembering* (Cambridge: Cambridge University Press, 1932).

products and criticize those of competitors.[114] As information is transmitted among consumers, it tends to change. The resulting message usually does not resemble the original at all.

Social scientists who study rumours have examined the process by which information gets distorted. The British psychologist Frederic Bartlett used the method of *serial reproduction* to examine how content mutates. A subject is asked to reproduce a stimulus, such as a drawing or a story. Another subject is given this reproduction and asked to copy that, and so on. This technique is shown in Figure 10.3. The figure illustrates how the message changes as it is reproduced. Bartlett found that distortions almost inevitably follow a pattern: they tend to change from ambiguous forms to more conventional ones as subjects try to make them consistent with pre-existing schemas. He called this process *assimilation*, and he noted that it often occurs as people engage in *levelling*, when they omit details to simplify the structure, or *sharpening*, when they exaggerate prominent details.

In general, people have been shown to prefer transmitting good news rather than bad, perhaps because they like to avoid unpleasantness or dislike arousing hostility. However, this reluctance does not appear to occur when companies are the topic of conversation. Corporations such as Procter & Gamble and McDonald's have been the subjects of rumours about their products, sometimes with marked effects on sales.

Rumours are thought to reveal the underlying fears of a society. While rumours sometimes die out by themselves, in other instances a company may take direct action to

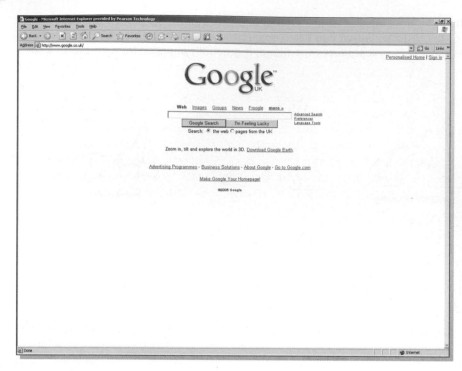

The Google search engine finds many matches for key word searches. For instance, the elaborate viral marketing campaign for the film *A.I.* (Artificial Intelligence) was based around key word searches on Google for 'Jeanine Salla' (described on page 403).

Used with permission from Google, Inc.

counteract them. A French margarine was rumoured to contain contaminants, and the company addressed this in its advertising by referring to the story as 'The rumour that costs you dearly'.[115]

Consumer behaviour as I see it . . .

We're told that people nowadays are becoming less similar to each other and that, as a result, markets are becoming more fragmented. In such a world it becomes harder to make general statements about consumers. However, despite this trend, one such statement still holds: some day each of us is going to die – and we know it. But why mention death in this chapter on groups? Well, much of my own research has sought to explore possible interfaces between consumer behaviour and mortality, death, and mourning, and much of this consumer behaviour inevitably takes place in a social context.

I think that three topics in this area hold particular promise for consumer researchers in the years ahead. First is the impact of impending death on people's consumption. Pavia and Mason's study is an insightful example.[116] Faced with a terminal diagnosis, do consumers, for example, renew or cancel their gym subscription, purchase a new car or hold on to their existing model, take that dream holiday or stay at home? The answer would appear to be that consumer behaviour can both influence and be influenced by such medical conditions. The second area concerns those left behind after the recent loss of a loved one. Working with my research colleague, Dr Stephanie O'Donohoe, I've come to see how the journey through grief can involve a number of demanding and often poignant consumer decisions: whether to hold a burial or cremation, whether to sell the family home and downsize, when and how to dispose of the dead person's possessions. The third area takes a broader time horizon to examine memorializing consumer behaviour. Survivors invest more money, time and emotion in deciding on headstones and anniversary celebrations, for example, than they do in many of their more routine purchases. Very often consumers who can least afford it spend the most. Is this form

Professor Darach Turley
Dublin City University, Ireland

of consumer behaviour simply repaying the dead person or might it have more to do with keeping their memory alive? Might it even be a means of working on relationships with those who are no longer with us physically?

So to return to my original question, why discuss bereaved consumers in a chapter on groups? People seem unhappy talking about death and uncomfortable meeting those touched by it. In turn, those who have lost a loved one recently often sense this unease in others and experience a certain social isolation, a feeling of being out of step with mainstream society through no fault of their own. In this sense they can be seen as an involuntary aversion group. This chapter also looks at opinion leadership (below). Typically the opinion leader is seen as a living person; however, our encounters with bereaved persons suggests that some people can continue to exercise leadership on consumer choices, especially on family decisions, from beyond the grave.

OPINION LEADERSHIP

Although consumers get information from personal sources, they tend not to ask just *anyone* for advice about purchases. If you decide to buy a new stereo, you will most likely seek advice from a friend who knows a lot about sound systems. This friend may own a sophisticated system, or they may subscribe to specialized magazines such as *Stereo Review* and spend free time browsing through electronics stores. On the other hand, you may have another friend who has a reputation for being stylish and who spends their free time reading fashion and lifestyle magazines and shopping at trendy boutiques. While you might not bring up your stereo problem with them, you may take them with you to shop for a new wardrobe.

This so-called opinion leadership is an important influence on a brand's popularity in many categories. The market for sports accessories is among these, where both celebrity endorsements (see Chapter 8) and sponsorship are major marketing tools used to form opinions. The American Gatorade sports drink company made its entrance on the British market on an exclusive opinion leadership basis, sponsoring sports events and professionals like the captain of the national cricket team, but without any major promotion of the product itself. This suspense strategy created curiosity, interest and enquiries, and probably pre-shaped a lot of opinion leaders' opinions about the product before its major launch in distribution outlets.[117]

The nature of opinion leadership

Everyone knows people who are knowledgeable about products and whose advice is taken seriously by others. These individuals are **opinion leaders**. An opinion leader is a person who is frequently able to influence others' attitudes or behaviours.[118] Some people's recommendations carry more weight than others.

Opinion leaders are extremely valuable information sources because they have the social power discussed earlier in this chapter:

- They are technically competent and thus are convincing because they possess expert power.[119]

- They have pre-screened, evaluated and synthesized product information in an unbiased way, so they possess knowledge power.[120] Unlike commercial endorsers, opinion leaders do not represent the interests of one company. They are more credible because they have no 'axe to grind'.

- They tend to be socially active and highly interconnected in their community.[121]

- They are likely to hold offices in community groups and clubs and to be active outside of the home. As a result, opinion leaders often have legitimate power by virtue of their social standing.

- They tend to be similar to the consumer in terms of their values and beliefs, so they possess referent power. Note that although opinion leaders are set apart by their interest or expertise in a product category, they are more convincing to the extent that they are *homophilous* rather than *heterophilous*. **Homophily** refers to the degree that a pair of individuals is similar in terms of education, social status and beliefs.[122]

- Effective opinion leaders tend to be slightly higher in terms of status and educational attainment than those they influence but not so high as to be in a different social class.

- Opinion leaders are often among the first to buy new products, so they absorb much of the risk. This experience reduces uncertainty for others who are not as courageous. Furthermore, whereas company-sponsored communications tend to focus exclusively on the positive aspects of a product, the hands-on experience of opinion leaders makes them more likely to impart *both* positive and negative information about product performance.

Whereas individual behavioural and psychological traits are the most important in identifying opinion leaders, there are some indications that opinion leadership does not function the same way in different cultures. For example, there are cultural differences in how much people rely on impersonal vs. personal information. In a study of opinion leadership in 14 European countries plus the US and Canada, the countries most characterized by the use of impersonal information-seeking (from consumer magazines, etc.) were Denmark, Norway, Sweden and Finland, whereas the countries least characterized by impersonal information-seeking were Italy, Portugal and Spain.[123]

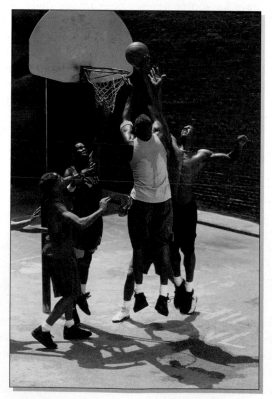

Opinion leadership is a big factor in the marketing of athletic shoes. Many styles first become popular in the inner city and then spread by word-of-mouth.

Carl Schneider/Getty Images, Inc.

The extent of an opinion leader's influence

When marketers and social scientists initially developed the concept of the opinion leader, they assumed that certain influential people in a community would exert an overall impact on group members' attitudes. Later work, however, began to question the assumption that there is such a thing as a *generalized opinion leader*, somebody whose recommendations we seek for all types of purchases. Very few people are capable of being expert in a number of fields. Sociologists distinguish between those who are *monomorphic*, or expert in a limited field, and those who are *polymorphic*, or expert in several fields.[124] Even opinion leaders who are polymorphic, however, tend to concentrate on one broad domain, such as electronics or fashion.

Research on opinion leadership generally indicates that although opinion leaders do exist for multiple product categories, expertise tends to overlap across similar categories. It is rare to find a generalized opinion leader. An opinion leader for home appliances is likely to serve a similar function for home cleaners but not for cosmetics. In contrast, a *fashion opinion leader* whose primary influence is on clothing choices, may also be consulted for recommendations on cosmetics purchases, but not necessarily on microwave ovens.[125] Most recently two researchers have run simulations which suggest that opinion leaders or **influentials** (to give them their other name) are indeed likely under certain circumstances 'to be disproportionately responsible for triggering large-scale "cascades" of influence'.[126] However, this effect of opinion leaders or influentials tends to be the exception rather than the rule. Their computer simulation suggested that 'most social change is driven not by influentials but by easily influenced individuals influencing other easily influenced individuals'.[127] They concluded that 'influentials are only modestly more important than average individuals'[128] and thus influentials are less central to the process of diffusion of innovations or early adoption than hitherto assumed.[129]

Opinion leaders vs. other consumer types

Early conceptions of the opinion leader role also assumed a static process: the opinion leader absorbs information from the mass media and in turn transmits data to opinion receivers. This view has turned out to be overly simplified; it confuses the functions of several different types of consumers. Furthermore, research has shown some evidence that the flow of influence is not one-way but two-way, so that opinion leaders are influenced by the responses of their followers.[130] This would reflect a more complex communication situation as discussed in Chapter 8.

Opinion leaders may or may not be purchasers of the products they recommend. Early purchasers are known as *innovators* (see Chapter 14). Opinion leaders who are also early purchasers have been termed **innovative communicators**. One study identified a number of characteristics of male university students who were innovative communicators for fashion products. These men were among the first to buy new fashions, and their fashion opinions were incorporated by other students into their own clothing purchases. Other characteristics of these men included:[131]

- They were socially active.
- They were appearance-conscious and narcissistic (i.e. they were quite fond of themselves and self-centered).
- They were involved in rock culture.
- They were heavy magazine readers.
- They were likely to own more clothing, and a broader range of styles, than other students.
- Their intellectual interests were relatively limited.

Opinion leaders also are likely to be **opinion seekers**. They are generally more involved in a product category and actively search for information. As a result, they are more likely to talk about products with others and to solicit others' opinions as

Figure 10.4 Updated opinion leadership model

well.[132] Contrary to the static view of opinion leadership, most product-related conversation does not take place in a 'lecture' format in which one person does all of the talking. A lot of product-related conversation is prompted by the situation and occurs in the context of a casual interaction rather than as formal instruction.[133] One study, which found that opinion seeking is especially high for food products, revealed that two-thirds of opinion seekers also view themselves as opinion leaders.[134] This updated view of interpersonal product communication is contrasted with the traditional view in Figure 10.4.

The market maven

Consumers who are expert in a product category may not actively communicate with others, whereas other consumers may have a more general interest in talking about ▶ all sorts of purchases. A **market maven** is a person who likes to transmit marketplace information of all types. Market mavens are not necessarily interested in certain products and may not necessarily be early purchasers of products; they are just interested in staying on top of what is happening in the marketplace. They come closer to the function of a generalized opinion leader because they tend to have a solid overall knowledge of how and where to procure products. Researchers use the following scale items (Figure 10.5), to which respondents indicate how much they agree or disagree, to identify market mavens.[135]

The surrogate consumer

In addition to everyday consumers who are instrumental in influencing others' purchase decisions, a class of marketing intermediary called the **surrogate consumer** often ▶ influences what we buy. A surrogate consumer is a person whom we hire to provide input into purchase decisions. Unlike the opinion leader or market maven, the surrogate is usually compensated for their advice.

Interior designers, stockbrokers or professional shoppers can all be thought of as surrogate consumers. Whether or not they actually make the purchase on behalf of the consumer, surrogates' recommendations can be enormously influential. The consumer, in essence, relinquishes control over several or all decision-making functions, such as information search, the evaluation of alternatives, or the actual purchase. For example, a client may commission an interior designer to update their house, and a broker may be entrusted to make crucial buy/sell decisions on behalf of investors. The involvement

Figure 10.5 Scale items used to identify market mavens

1. I like introducing new brands and products to my friends.

2. I like helping people by providing them with information about many kinds of products.

3. People ask me for information about products, places to shop, or sales.

4. If someone asked me where to get the best buy on several types of products, I could tell him or her where to shop.

5. My friends think of me as a good source of information when it comes to new products or sales.

6. Think about a person who has information about a variety of products and likes to share this information with others. This person knows about new products, sales, stores, and so on, but does not necessarily feel he or she is an expert on one particular product. How well would you say this description fits you?

Source: Adapted from Lawrence Feick and Linda Price, 'The market maven: A diffuser of marketplace information', *Journal of Marketing* 51 (January 1987): 83–7.

of surrogates in a wide range of purchase decisions tends to be overlooked by many marketers, who may be mistargeting their communications to end-consumers instead of to the surrogates who are actually sifting through product information and deciding among product alternatives.[136]

Identifying opinion leaders

Because opinion leaders are so central to consumer decision-making, marketers are quite interested in identifying influential people for a product category. In fact, many ads are intended to reach these influentials rather than the average consumer, especially if the ads contain a lot of technical information.

Professional opinion leaders

Perhaps the easiest way to find opinion leaders is to target people who are paid to give expert opinions. *Professional opinion leaders* are people such as doctors or scientists who obtain specialized information from technical journals and other practitioners.

Marketers who are trying to gain consumer acceptance for their products sometimes find it easier to try to win over professional opinion leaders, who (they hope) will, in turn, recommend their products to customers. A case in point is the effort by Roc SA, maker of Europe's leading brand of hypoallergenic lotions, to break into the lucrative American market for skincare products. Instead of competing head-to-head with the lavish consumer advertising of Revlon or Estée Lauder, the French company decided first to gain medical acceptance by winning over pharmacists and dermatologists. In 1994 the company began advertising in medical journals, and the product was distributed to dermatologists and to pharmacies patronized by patients of dermatologists. A free telephone number was established to provide interested consumers with the names of pharmacies carrying the range.[137]

Of course, this approach may backfire if it is carried to an extreme and compromises the credibility of professional opinion leaders. In several countries, the medical industry has a dubious reputation of 'bribing' doctors with invitations to product presentations disguised as conferences, often held in glamorous places. A recent examination of registers of gifts and donations to doctors in the UK showed the scale of sponsorship by pharmaceutical companies of all-expenses-paid conference trips around the world ran into millions of pounds.[138]

Consumer opinion leaders

Since most opinion leaders are everyday consumers and are not formally included in marketing efforts, they are harder to find. A celebrity or an influential industry executive is by definition easier to locate. They have national or at least regional visibility or may be listed in published directories. In contrast, opinion leaders tend to operate at the local level and may influence five to ten consumers rather than an entire market segment. In some cases, companies have tried to identify influentials and involve them directly in their marketing efforts, hoping to create a 'ripple effect' as these consumers sing the company's praises to their friends. Many department stores, for instance, sponsor fashion panels, usually composed of adolescent girls, who provide input into fashion trends, participate in fashion shows and so on.

Because of the difficulties involved in identifying specific opinion leaders in a large market, most attempts to do so instead focus on exploratory studies. Researchers aim to identify the profile of a representative opinion leader and then generalize these insights to the larger market. This knowledge helps marketers target their product-related information to appropriate settings and media. For example, one attempt to identify financial opinion leaders found that these consumers were more likely to be involved in managing their own finances and tended to use a computer to do so. They were also more likely to follow their investments on a daily basis and to read books and watch television shows devoted to financial issues.[139]

The self-designating method

The most commonly used technique to identify opinion leaders is simply to ask individual consumers whether they consider themselves to be opinion leaders.

However, there are obvious problems with self-designation. While respondents who report a greater degree of interest in a product category are more likely to be opinion leaders, the results of surveys intended to identify *self-designated opinion leaders* must be viewed with some scepticism. Some people have a tendency to inflate their own import-ance and influence, whereas others who really are influential might not admit to this quality or be conscious of it.[140] Just because we transmit advice about products does not mean other people *take* that advice. For someone to be considered a bona fide opinion leader, opinion seekers must actually heed their advice. An alternative is to select certain group members (*key informants*) who in turn are asked to identify opinion leaders. The success of this approach hinges on locating those who have accurate knowledge of the group and on minimizing their response biases (the tendency to inflate one's own influence on the choices of others).

The self-designating method is not as reliable as a more systematic analysis (in which we can verify individual claims of influence by asking others whether the person is really influential), but it does have the advantage of being easy to apply to a large group of potential opinion leaders. In some cases not all members of a community are surveyed. Figure 10.6 shows one of the measurement scales researchers use for this kind of self-designation.

Sociometry

A web-based service has been created that is based on the popular play *Six Degrees of Separation*. The basic premise of the plot is that everyone on the planet is separated by only six other people. The website (**www.sixdegrees.com**) allows a person to register and provide names and email addresses of other people, so that when the user needs to network a connection is made with others in the database.

▶ This site is a digital version of more conventional **sociometric methods**, which trace communication patterns among group members and allow researchers systematically to map out the interactions that take place among group members. By interviewing participants and asking them to whom they go for product information, researchers can identify those who tend to be sources of product-related information. This method is the

Figure 10.6 A revised and updated version of the opinion leadership scale

Please rate yourself on the following scales relating to your interactions with friends and neighbours regarding _____.

1. In general, do you talk to your friends and neighbours about _____:

   very often   *never*
   | 5 | 4 | 3 | 2 | 1 |

2. When you talk to your friends and neighbours about _____ do you:

   give a great deal of information   *give very little information*
   | 5 | 4 | 3 | 2 | 1 |

3. During the past six months, how many people have you told about a new _____?

   told a number of people   *told no one*
   | 5 | 4 | 3 | 2 | 1 |

4. Compared with your circle of friends, how likely are you to be asked about new _____?

   very likely to be asked   *not at all likely to be asked*
   | 5 | 4 | 3 | 2 | 1 |

5. In discussion of new _____, which of the following happens most?

   you tell your friends about _____   *your friends tell you about* _____
   | 5 | 4 | 3 | 2 | 1 |

6. Overall in all of your discussions with friends and neighbours are you:

   often used as a source of advice   *not used as a source of advice*
   | 5 | 4 | 3 | 2 | 1 |

Source: Adapted from Terry L. Childers, 'Assessment of the psychometric properties of an opinion leadership scale', *Journal of Marketing Research* 23 (May 1986): 184–8; and Leisa Reinecke Flynn, Ronald E. Goldsmith and Jacqueline K. Eastman, 'The King and Summers opinion leadership scale: revision and refinement', *Journal of Business Research* 31 (1994): 55–64.

most precise, but it is very hard and expensive to implement because it involves very close study of interaction patterns in small groups. For this reason, sociometric techniques are best applied in a closed, self-contained social setting, such as in hospitals, prisons, and army bases, where members are largely isolated from other social networks.

A sociometric study on obesity provides a striking example of how our social networks influence our consumption behaviors. The researchers analyzed a sample of more than 12,000 people who participated in the Framingham Heart Study, which closely documented their health from 1971 to 2003. They discovered that obesity can spread from person to person, much like a virus (we'll talk more about how consumer trends spread in this way in Chapter 14). The investigators knew who was friends with whom as well as who was a spouse or sibling or neighbour, and they knew how much each person weighed at various times over three decades so they could reconstruct what happened over the years if study participants became obese. Guess what? When one person gains weight, close friends tend to gain weight, too – a person's chances of being obese if a close friend put on the pounds increased by 57 per cent. The friend's influence remained even if they lived hundreds of miles away. The researchers explained this 'social contagion' effect by speculating that when our best friends get fat, this alters our perception of normal body weight so we are not as concerned when we put on a few pounds as well. The moral of the story: Hang out with thin people[141].

Many professionals (e.g. accountants, lawyers) and services marketers (e.g. cleaning services) depend primarily on word-of-mouth to generate business. In many cases consumers recommend a service provider to a friend or fellow worker, and in other cases business people will make recommendations to their customers. For example, only 0.2 per cent of respondents in one study reported choosing a physician based on advertising. Advice from family and friends was the most widely used criterion.[142]

We use sociometric analyses to better understand *referral behaviour* and to locate strengths and weaknesses in terms of how one's reputation flows through a community.[143] *Network analysis* focuses on communication in social systems, considers the relations among people in a *referral network*, and measures the *tie strength* among them. Tie strength refers to the nature of the bond between people. It can range from strong primary (e.g.

one's partner) to weak secondary (e.g. an acquaintance whom one rarely sees). A strong tie relationship may be thought of as a primary reference group; interactions are frequent and important to the individual.

While strong ties are important, weak ties can perform a *bridging function*. This type of connection allows a consumer access between sub-groups. For example, you might have a regular group of friends who serve as a primary reference group (strong ties). If you have an interest in tennis, say, one of these friends might introduce you to a group of people who play on the tennis team at the local club. As a result, you gain access to their valuable expertise through this bridging function. This referral process demonstrates the strength of weak ties.[144]

CHAPTER SUMMARY

- Others, especially those who possess some kind of social power, often influence us. We belong to or admire many different groups and a desire for them to accept us often drives our purchase decisions. Individuals or groups whose opinions or behaviour are particularly important to consumers are reference groups. Both formal and informal groups influence the individual's purchase decisions, although such factors as the conspicuousness of the product and the relevance of the reference group for a particular purchase determine how influential the reference group is.

- Individuals have influence in a group to the extent that they possess social power; types of social power include information power, referent power, legitimate power, expert power, reward power, and coercive power.

- We seek out others who share our interests in products or services. Brand communities unite consumers who share a common passion for a product. Brand-fests, when companies organize to encourage this kind of community, can build brand loyalty and reinforce group membership.

- We are motivated to buy or use products in order to be consistent with what other people do. We conform to the desires of others for two basic reasons: (1) People who model their behaviour on others because they take others' behaviour as evidence of the correct way to act are conforming because of informational social influence, and (2) those who conform to satisfy the expectations of others or to be accepted by the group are affected by normative social influence. Group members often do things they would not do as individuals because their identities become merged with the group; they become de-individuated.

- The things that other consumers tell us about products (good and bad) are often more influential than the advertising we see. Much of what we know about products we learn through word-of-mouth (WOM) communication rather than formal advertising. We tend to exchange product-related information in casual conversations. Guerrilla marketing strategies try to accelerate the WOM process by enlisting consumers to help spread the word.

- Although WOM often is helpful for making consumers aware of products, it can also hurt companies when damaging product rumors or negative WOM occurs.

- Online technologies are accelerating the impact of word-of-mouth communication. The Web has greatly amplified consumers' abilities to be exposed to numerous reference groups. Virtual consumption communities are composed of people who are united by a common bond – enthusiasm about or knowledge of a specific product or service. Emerging marketing strategies try to leverage the potential of the Web to spread information from consumer to consumer extremely quickly. Viral marketing techniques enlist individuals to tout products, services, Websites, and so on to others on behalf of companies. A new mode of online communication called blogging allows consumers to easily post their thoughts about products for others to see.

■ Social networking is changing the way companies and consumers interact. Social networking, where members post information about themselves and make contact with others who share similar interests and opinions, represents a change in the way we think about marketing. As Web 2.0 continues to develop, companies and consumers increasingly interact directly. The wisdom of crowds perspective argues that, under the right circumstances, groups are smarter than the smartest people in them. If this is true, it implies that large numbers of consumers can predict successful products.[145] In a sense, a lot of social networking sites let their members dictate purchase decisions.

■ Opinion leaders who are knowledgeable about a product and whose opinions are highly regarded tend to influence others' choices. Specific opinion leaders are somewhat hard to identify, but marketers who know their general characteristics can try to target them in their media and promotional strategies. Other influencers include market mavens, who have a general interest in marketplace activities, and surrogate consumers, who are compensated for their advice about purchases.

▶ KEY TERMS

Anti-brand communities (p. 387)

Aspirational reference groups (p. 385)

Avoidance reference groups (p. 387)

Blogosphere (p. 389)

Brand community (p. 391)

Brand-fests (p. 392)

Coercive power (p. 395)

Communities of practice (p. 392)

Comparative influence (p. 384)

Conformity (p. 396)

Consumer tribe (p. 392)

Decision polarization (p. 399)

De-individuation (p. 398)

Dissociative reference groups (p. 387)

Expert power (p. 394)

Guerrilla marketing (p. 403)

Home shopping parties (p. 400)

Homophily (p. 408)

Identificational membership reference group (p. 386)

Influentials (p. 409)

Information power (p. 393)

Informational social influence (p. 396)

Innovative communicators (p. 409)

Legitimate power (p. 394)

Market maven (p. 410)

Membership reference group (p. 385)

Negative word-of-mouth (p. 404)

Netnography (p. 391)

Normative influence (p. 384)

Normative social influence (p. 396)

Norms (p. 396)

Opinion leader (p. 407)

Opinion seekers (p. 409)

Reactance (p. 401)

Reference group (p. 384)

Referent power (p. 393)

Reward power (p. 395)

Risky shift (p. 399)

Rumour (p. 404)

Social comparison theory (p. 397)

Social loafing (p. 399)

Social power (p. 393)

Sociometric methods (p. 412)

Surrogate consumer (p. 410)

Tribal marketing (p. 392)

Viral marketing (p. 403)

Virtual community of consumption (p. 389)

Weblog (p. 389)

Word-of-mouth communication (WOM) (p. 401)

▶ CONSUMER BEHAVIOUR CHALLENGE

1 Compare and contrast the five bases of power described in the text. Which are most likely to be relevant for marketing efforts?

2 Why is referent power an especially potent force for marketing appeals? What factors help to predict whether or not reference groups will be a powerful influence on a person's purchase decisions?

3 Identify the differences between a membership and an aspirational reference group. Give an example of each.

4 What is a brand community, and why is it of interest to marketers? Describe the four types of virtual community members identified in this chapter; and assess their relevance to marketers.

5 Evaluate the strategic soundness of the concept of guerrilla marketing. For what types of product categories is this strategy most likely to be a success?

6 Discuss some factors that determine the amount of conformity likely to be observed among consumers.

7 Define de-individuation. Does de-individuation cause binge drinking? What can or should be done to discourage this type of behaviour?

8 What is the risky shift? How does this affect going shopping with friends? See if you can demonstrate risky shift. Get a group of friends together and ask each privately to rate the likelihood, on a scale from 1 to 7, that they would try a controversial new product (e.g. a credit card that works with a chip implanted in a person's wrist). Then ask the group to discuss the product and rate the idea again. If the average rating changes from the first rating, you have just observed a risky shift.

9 Under what conditions are we more likely to engage in social comparison with dissimilar others versus similar others? How might this dimension be used in the design of marketing appeals?

10 Discuss some reasons for the effectiveness of home shopping parties as a selling tool. What other products might be sold this way? Are home shopping parties, which put pressure on friends and neighbour to buy, ethical?

11 Discuss some factors that influence whether membership groups will have a significant influence on a person's behaviour.

12 Why is word-of-mouth communication often more persuasive than advertising? Which is more powerful, positive or negative word of mouth?

13 Is there such a thing as a generalized opinion leader? What is likely to determine if an opinion leader will be influential with regard to a specific product category? How can marketers use opinion leaders to help them promote their products or services?

14 The adoption of a certain brand of shoe or apparel by athletes can be a powerful influence on students and other fans. Should secondary school and university coaches be paid to determine what brand of athletic equipment their players will wear?

15 The power of unspoken social norms often becomes obvious only when these norms are violated. To witness this result firsthand, try one of the following: stand facing the back wall in a lift; serve dessert before the main course; offer to pay cash for dinner at a friend's home; wear pyjamas to class; or tell someone not to have a nice day.

16 Identify a set of avoidance groups for your peers. Can you identify any consumption decisions that are made with these groups in mind?

17 Identify fashion opinion leaders at your university or business school. Do they fit the profile discussed in the chapter?

18 What are sociometric techniques? Conduct a sociometric analysis within your hall of residence or neighbourhood. For a product category such as music or cars, ask each individual to identify other individuals with whom they share information. Systematically trace all of these avenues of communication, and identify opinion leaders by locating individuals who are repeatedly named as providing helpful information.

19 The strategy of *viral marketing* gets customers to sell a product to other customers on behalf of the company. That often means convincing your friends to climb on the bandwagon, and sometimes you get a small percentage return

(or other reward) if they end up buying something.[146] Some might argue that means you are selling out your friends (or at least selling to your friends) in exchange for a marketing reward. Others might say you are just sharing the wealth with those you care about. Have you been involved in viral marketing by passing along names of your friends or sending them to a Website such as **hotmail.com**? If so, what happened? How do you feel about this practice? Discuss the pros and cons of viral marketing.

20 Trace a referral pattern for a service provider such as a hair stylist by tracking how clients came to choose them. See if you can identify opinion leaders who are responsible for referring several clients to the businessperson. How might the service provider take advantage of this process to grow their business?

For additional material see the companion website at **www.pearsoned.co.uk/solomon**

NOTES

1. Joel B. Cohen and Ellen Golden, 'Informational social influence and product evaluation', *Journal of Applied Psychology* 56 (February 1972): 54–59; Robert E. Burnkrant and Alain Cousineau, 'Informational and normative social influence in buyer behavior', *Journal of Consumer Research* 2 (December 1975): 206–15; Peter H. Reingen, 'Test of a list procedure for inducing compliance with a request to donate money', *Journal of Applied Psychology* 67 (1982): 110–18.

2. Katherine White and Darren, W. Dahl, 'To be or not to be? The influence of dissociative reference groups on consumer preferences', *Journal of Consumer Psychology* 16 (2006:4): 404–414; Katherine White and Darren W. Dahl, 'Are all out-groups created equal? Consumer identity and dissociative influence', *Journal of Consumer Research* 34 (December 2007): 525–36.

3. C. Whan Park and V. Parker Lessig, 'Students and housewives: Differences in susceptibility to reference group influence', *Journal of Consumer Research* 4 (September 1977): 102–10.

4. Kenneth J. Gergen and Mary Gergen, *Social Psychology* (New York: Harcourt Brace Jovanovich, 1981).

5. Harold H. Kelley, 'Two Functions of Reference Groups', in Harold Proshansky and Bernard Siedenberg (eds), *Basic Studies in Social Psychology* (New York: Holt, Rinehart & Winston, 1965): 210–14.

6. A. Benton Cocanougher and Grady D. Bruce, 'Socially distant reference groups and consumer aspirations', *Journal of Marketing Research* 8 (August 1971): 79–81.

7. L. Festinger, S. Schachter and K. Back, *Social Pressures in Informal Groups: A Study of Human Factors in Housing* (New York: Harper, 1950).

8. R.B. Zajonc, H.M. Markus and W. Wilson, 'Exposure effects and associative learning', *Journal of Experimental Social Psychology* 10 (1974): 248–63.

9. D.J. Stang, 'Methodological factors in mere exposure research', *Psychological Bulletin* 81 (1974): 1014–25; R.B. Zajonc, P. Shaver, C. Tavris and D. Van Kreveid, 'Exposure, satiation and stimulus discriminability', *Journal of Personality and Social Psychology* 21 (1972): 270–80.

10. J.E. Grush, K.L. McKeogh and R.F. Ahlering, 'Extrapolating laboratory exposure research to actual political elections', *Journal of Personality and Social Psychology* 36 (1978): 257–70.

11. Richard Wilk, 'A critique of desire: Distaste and dislike in consumer behavior', *Consumption, Culture and Markets* 1(2) (1997): 175–96; see also Pierre Bourdieu, *Distinction: A Social Critique of the Judgement of Taste* (London: Routledge, 1984); E.N. Banister and M.K. Hogg, 'Negative symbolic consumption and consumers' drive for self-esteem: The case of the fashion industry', *European Journal of Marketing* 7 (2004): 850–68; B.S. Turner and J. Edmunds, 'The distaste of taste: Bordieu, cultural capital and the Australian postwar elite', *Journal of Consumer Culture* 2(2) (2002): 219–40.

12. Basil G. Englis and Michael R. Solomon, 'To be and not to be: Reference group stereotyping and *The Clustering of America*', *Journal of Advertising* 24 (Spring 1995): 13–28; Michael R. Solomon and Basil G. Englis, 'I Am Not, Therefore I Am: The Role of Anti-Consumption in the Process of Self-Definition', Special Session at the Association for Consumer Research meetings, October 1996, Tucson, Arizona.

13. Bruce Feirstein, *Real Men Don't Eat Quiche* (New York: Pocket Books, 1982); www.auntiefashions.com, accessed 31 December 2002.

14. Katherine White and Darren W. Dahl, 'Are all out-groups created equal? Consumer identity and dissociative influence', *Journal of Consumer Research* 34 (December 2007): 525.

15. Natasha Gilbert, 'Brand new bullying in fashion', *Guardian.co.uk* (11 August 2008): 10, http://www.guardian.co.uk/education/2008/aug/11/bullying.schools1/print, accessed 11 August 2008.

16. Petridis, Alexis, 'I've done so much embarrassing stuff it's untrue', http://www.guardian.co.uk/music/2009/jan/10/little-boots-interview-pop-music, accessed 14 January 2009.

17. Eric Pfanner, 'Taste of Victory: Online Outcry Revives a Chocolate Bar', *New York Times Online* (27 August 2007), accessed 27 August 2007.

18. This typology is adapted from material presented in Robert V. Kozinets, 'E-tribalized marketing: The strategic implications of virtual communities of consumption', *European Management Journal* 17(3) (June 1999): 252–64.

19. Tom Weber, 'Net's hottest game brings people closer', *Wall Street Journal Interactive Edition* (20 March 2000).

20. Quoted in Marc Gunther, 'The newest addiction', *Fortune* (2 August 1999): 122–4, at 123.

21. http://www.bbc.co.uk/blogs/theeditors/; http://www.bbc.co.uk/blogs/pm/; http://blogs.guardian.co.uk/index.html; http://blogs.telegraph.co.uk/; http://www.lemonde.fr/web/blogs/0,39-0,48-0,0.html

22. Charla Mathwick, Caroline Wiertz and Ko De Ruyter, 'Social capital production in a virtual P3 community', *Journal of Consumer Research* 34 (April 2008): 832–49.

23. Kozinets, 'E-tribalized marketing', *op. cit.*

24. Robert V. Kozinets, 'Click to connect: Netnography and tribal advertising', *Journal of Advertising Research* 46(3) (2006): 279–88.

25. Stella Yiyan Li and Kineta H. Hung, 'Netnographic study of a community of beauty product enthusiasts in China', *Advances in Consumer Research* 33(1) (2006).

26. Bob Tedeschi, 'Online retailers find that customer reviews build loyalty', *New York Times on the Web* (6 September 1999).

27. 'Bookseller offers refunds for advertised books', *Opelika-Auburn News* (11 February 1999): A11.

28. *Information* (14 February 2001): 2.

29. James H. McAlexander, John W. Schouten and Harold F. Koenig, 'Building brand community', *Journal of Marketing* 66 (January 2002): 38–54; Albert Muniz and Thomas O'Guinn, 'Brand community', *Journal of Consumer Research* (March 2001): 412–32.

30. Veronique Cova and Bernard Cova, 'Tribal aspects of postmodern consumption research: The case of French in-line roller skaters', *Journal of Consumer Behavior* 1 (June 2001): 67–76.

31. Penelope Eckert and Sally McConnell-Ginet, 'Think practically and look locally: Language and gender as community-based practice', *Annual Review of Anthropology* (1992): 461–90, at 464, cited in Emma Moore, 'Approaches to Identity: Lesson from Sociolinguistics', Seminar paper, Customer Research Academy, Manchester School of Management, UMIST, UK (22 April 2004): 2.

32. Etienne Wenger, *Communities of Practice: Learning, Meaning and Identity* (Cambridge: Cambridge University Press, 1998), cited in Moore, 'Approaches to Identity', *op. cit.*

33. Emma Moore, 'Learning Style and Identity: A Sociolinguistic Analysis of a Bolton High School', unpublished Ph.D. dissertation, University of Manchester (2003).

34. Penelope Eckert, 'Constructing Meaning in Socio-linguistic Variation', paper presented at the Annual Meeting of the American Anthropological Association, New Orleans, USA (November 2002) (accessible at www.stanford.edu/~eckert/AAA02.pdf), cited in Moore 'Approaches to Identity', *op. cit.*: 3.

35. Jeffrey D. Ford and Elwood A. Ellis, 'A re-examination of group influence on member brand preference', *Journal of Marketing Research* 17 (February 1980): 125–32; Thomas S. Robertson, *Innovative Behavior and Communication* (New York: Holt, Rinehart & Winston, Inc., 1980): ch. 8.

36. William O. Bearden and Michael J. Etzel, 'Reference group influence on product and brand purchase decisions', *Journal of Consumer Research* 9 (1982): 183–94.

37. Gergen and Gergen, *Social Psychology*, *op. cit.*: 312.

38. J.R.P. French Jr. and B. Raven, 'The Bases of Social Power', in D. Cartwright (ed.), *Studies in Social Power* (Ann Arbor, MI: Institute for Social Research, 1959): 150–67.

39. Michael R. Solomon, 'Packaging the service provider', *The Service Industries Journal* 5 (March 1985): 64–72.

40. Quoted in Tamar Charry, 'Advertising: Hawking, Wozniak pitch modems for U.S. robotics', *The New York Times News Service* (5 February 1997).

41. Patricia M. West and Susan M. Broniarczyk, 'Integrating multiple opinions: The role of aspiration level on consumer response to critic consensus', *Journal of Consumer Research* 25 (June 1998): 38–51.

42. Jay Rayner, 'Is it curtains for critics?', *Observer Review Cover Story* (13 July 2008): 4–7.

43. Lars Thøger Christensen and Søren Askegaard, 'Identities and images of products and organizations: A semiotic exercise', *European Journal of Marketing* 35(3/4) (2001): 292–315.

44. BBC News, 'Smoking curbs: the global picture': http://news.bbc.co.uk/1/hi/world/4016477.stm (accessed 1 March 2005); Claire Fowlder, 'Where there's smoke there's Germans', Guardian online, 8 July 2008, http://www.guardian.co.uk/commentisfree/2008/jul/08/smoking, accessed 15 July 2008.

45. Claire Fowlder 'Where there's smoke there's Germans', *ibid.*

46. Cornelia Pechmann and S. Ratneshwar, 'The effects of anti-smoking and cigarette advertising on young adolescents' perceptions of peers who smoke', *Journal of Consumer Research* 21 (September 1994): 236–51.

47. See Robert B. Cialdini, *Influence: Science and Practice*, 2nd edn (New York: Scott, Foresman, 1988) for an excellent and entertaining treatment of this process.

48. For the seminal work on conformity and social influence, see Solomon E. Asch, 'Effects of Group Pressure Upon the Modification and Distortion of Judgments', in D. Cartwright and A. Zander (eds), *Group Dynamics* (New York: Harper & Row, 1953); Richard S. Crutchfield, 'Conformity and character', *American Psychologist* 10 (1955): 191–8; Muzafer Sherif, 'A study of some social factors in perception', *Archives of Psychology* 27 (1935): 187.

49. Robert E. Burnkrant and Alain Cousineau, 'Informational and normative social influence in buyer behavior', *Journal of Consumer Research* 2 (December 1975): 206–15.

50. For a study attempting to measure individual differences in proclivity to conformity, see William O. Bearden, Richard G. Netemeyer and Jesse E. Teel, 'Measurement of consumer susceptibility to interpersonal influence', *Journal of Consumer Research* 15 (March 1989): 473–81.

51. Douglas B. Holt, Søren Askegaard and Torsten Ringberg, '7 ups and Downs', unpublished manuscript, Penn State University.

52. John W. Thibaut and Harold H. Kelley, *The Social Psychology of Groups* (New York: Wiley, 1959); W.W. Waller and R. Hill, *The Family, a Dynamic Interpretation* (New York: Dryden, 1951).

53. Bearden, Netemeyer and Teel, 'Measurement of consumer susceptibility to interpersonal influence'; Lynn R. Kahle, 'Observations: Role-relaxed consumers: A trend of the nineties', *Journal of Advertising Research* (March/April 1995): 66–71; Lynn R. Kahle and Aviv Shoham, 'Observations: Role-relaxed consumers: Empirical evidence', *Journal of Advertising Research* (May/June 1995): 59–62.

54. Leon Festinger, 'A theory of social comparison processes', *Human Relations* 7 (May 1954): 117–40.

55. Chester A. Insko, Sarah Drenan, Michael R. Solomon, Richard Smith and Terry J. Wade, 'Conformity as a function of the consistency of positive self-evaluation with being liked and being right', *Journal of Experimental Social Psychology* 19 (1983): 341–58.

56. Abraham Tesser, Murray Millar and Janet Moore, 'Some affective consequences of social comparison and reflection processes: The pain and pleasure of being close', *Journal of Personality and Social Psychology* 54(1) (1988): 49–61.

57. L. Wheeler, K.G. Shaver, R.A. Jones, G.R. Goethals, J. Cooper, J.E. Robinson, C.L. Gruder and K.W. Butzine, 'Factors determining the choice of a comparison other', *Journal of Experimental Social Psychology* 5 (1969): 219–32.

58. M.L. Richins, 'Social comparison and the idealized images of advertising', *Journal of Consumer Research* 18 (June 1991): 71–83; M.C. Martin and P.F. Kennedy, 'Advertising and social comparison: Consequences for female preadolescents and adolescents', *Psychology and Marketing* 10(6) (1993): 513–29; M.C. Martin and P.F. Kennedy, 'Social Comparison and the Beauty of Advertising Models: The Role of Motives in Comparison', in Chris T. Allen and Deborah Roedder John (eds), *Advances in Consumer Research* 21 (Provo, UT: Association for Consumer Research, 1994): 365–71; M.C. Martin and N.J. Gentry, 'Stuck in the model trap: The effects of beautiful models in ads on female preadolescents and adolescents', *Journal of Advertising* 26(2) (Summer 1997): 19–33.

59. See J.V. Wood, 'Theory and research concerning social comparisons of personal attributes', *Psychological Bulletin* 106 (September 1989): 231–48 for a detailed exposition of the evolving debates around the theory of social comparison.

60. Martin and Kennedy, 'Advertising and social comparison'; Martin and Kennedy, 'Social Comparison and the Beauty of Advertising Models'; Martin and Gentry, 'Stuck in the model trap'; Margaret K. Hogg, Margaret Bruce and Kerry Hough, 'Female images in advertising: The implications of social comparison for marketing', *International Journal of Advertising* 18(4) (1999): 445–73; Margaret K. Hogg and Aikaterini Fragou, 'Social comparison goals and the consumption of advertising: towards a more contingent view of young women's consumption of advertising', *Journal of Marketing Management* 19(7–8) (September 2003): 749–80.

61. Michael Hafner, 'How dissimilar others may still resemble the self: Assimilation and contrast after social comparison', *Journal of Consumer Psychology* 14(1 and 2) (2004): 187–96.

62. George P. Moschis, 'Social comparison and informal group influence', *Journal of Marketing Research* 13 (August 1976): 237–44.

63. Burnkrant and Cousineau, 'Informational and normative social influence in buyer behavior'; M. Venkatesan, 'Experimental study of consumer behavior conformity and independence', *Journal of Marketing Research* 3 (November 1966): 384–7.

64. J.L. Freedman and S. Fraser, 'Compliance without pressure: The foot-in-the-door technique', *Journal of Personality and Social Psychology* 4 (1966): 195–202.

65. R.B. Cialdini, J.E. Vincent, S.K. Lewis, J. Catalan, D. Wheeler and B.L. Darby, 'Reciprocal concessions procedure for inducing compliance: The door-in-the-face effect', *Journal of Personality and Social Psychology* 31 (1975): 200–15.

66. J. Craig Andrews and Richard G. Netemeyer, 'Alcohol Warning Label Effects: Socialization, Addiction, and Public Policy Issues', in Ronald P. Hill (ed.), *Marketing and Consumer Research in the Public Interest* (Thousand Oaks, CA: Sage, 1996): 153–75; 'National study finds increase in college binge drinking', *Alcoholism and Drug Abuse Weekly* (27 March 2000): 12–13; Emma Banister and Maria Piacentini, ' "Binge Drinking: Do They Mean Us?" Living Life to the Full in Students' Own Words', in C. Pechmann and L. Price (eds), *Advances in Consumer Research* 33 (forthcoming).

67. Maria Piacentini and Emma N. Banister, 'Getting hammered? . . . Students coping with alcohol', *Journal of Consumer Behaviour* 5(2) (Spring 2006).

68. BBC Online, http://www.bbc.co.uk/insideout/southeast/series2/nhs_binge_drinking_alcohol_abuse_drunk_alcoholism.shtml (17 February 2003); *Guardian*, http://society.guardian.co.uk/drugsandalcohol/story/0,8150,874700,00.html (14 January 2003).

69. B. Latane, K. Williams and S. Harkins, 'Many hands make light the work: The causes and consequences of social loafing', *Journal of Personality and Social Psychology* 37 (1979): 822–32.

70. S. Freeman, M. Walker, R. Borden and B. Latane, 'Diffusion of responsibility and restaurant tipping: Cheaper by the bunch', *Personality and Social Psychology Bulletin* 1 (1978): 584–7.

71. Nathan Kogan and Michael A. Wallach, *Risk Taking* (New York: Holt, Rinehart & Winston, 1964).

72. Nathan Kogan and Michael A. Wallach, 'Risky shift phenomenon in small decision-making groups: A test of the information exchange hypothesis', *Journal of Experimental Social Psychology* 3 (January 1967): 75–84; Kogan and Wallach, *Risk Taking*; Arch G. Woodside and M. Wayne DeLozier, 'Effects of word-of-mouth advertising on consumer risk taking', *Journal of Advertising* (Fall 1976): 12–19.

73. Roger Brown, *Social Psychology* (New York: The Free Press, 1965).

74. David L. Johnson and I.R. Andrews, 'Risky shift phenomenon tested with consumer product stimuli', *Journal of Personality and Social Psychology* 20 (1971): 382–5; see also Vithala R. Rao and Joel H. Steckel, 'A polarization model for describing group preferences,' *Journal of Consumer Research* 18 (June 1991): 108–18.

75. Donald H. Granbois, 'Improving the study of customer in-store behavior', *Journal of Marketing* 32 (October 1968): 28–32.

76. Len Strazewski, 'Tupperware locks in new strategy', *Advertising Age* (8 February 1988): 30.

77. Quoted in Melanie Wells, 'Smooth operator', *Forbes* (13 May 2002): 167–8.

78. Gergen and Gergen, *Social Psychology*.

79. L.J. Strickland, S. Messick and D.N. Jackson, 'Conformity, anticonformity and independence: Their dimensionality and generality', *Journal of Personality and Social Psychology* 16 (1970): 494–507.

80. Jack W. Brehm, *A Theory of Psychological Reactance* (New York: Academic Press, 1966).

81. R.D. Ashmore, V. Ramchandra and R. Jones, 'Censorship as an Attitude Change Induction', paper presented at meeting of Eastern Psychological Association, New York, 1971; R.A. Wicklund and J. Brehm, *Perspectives on Cognitive Dissonance* (Hillsdale, NJ: Erlbaum, 1976).

82. C.R. Snyder and H.L. Fromkin, *Uniqueness: The Human Pursuit of Difference* (New York: Plenum Press, 1980).

83. Quoted in Raymond Serafin, 'Non-conformity sparks Saab', *Advertising Age* (3 April 1995): 27.

84. See for instance the *Daily Princetonian*'s editorial about Thefacebook.com as 'possibly the biggest word-of-mouth trend to hit campus since St Ives Medicated Apricot Scrub found its ways into the women's bathroom', cited by Peter Applebome, 'On campus, hanging out by logging on', *NYT Online* (1 December 2004); see also note 99.

85. Johan Arndt, 'Role of product-related conversations in the diffusion of a new product', *Journal of Marketing Research* 4 (August 1967): 291–5.

86. ' "Word-of-mouth" to become true measure of ads', *Marketing* (9 February 1995): 7.

87. Quoted in Barbara B. Stern and Stephen J. Gould, 'The consumer as financial opinion leader', *Journal of Retail Banking* 10 (Summer 1988): 43–52.

88. Douglas R. Pruden and Terry G. Vavra, 'Controlling the grapevine', *MM* (July–August 2004): 23–30.

89. Andrew D. Gershoff, Ashesh Mukherjee and Anirban Mukhopadjyay, 'Few ways to love, but many ways to hate: Attribute ambiguity and the positivity effect in agent evaluation', *Journal of Consumer Research* 33 (March 2007): 499–505.

90. Elihu Katz and Paul F. Lazarsfeld, *Personal Influence* (Glencoe, IL: Free Press, 1955).

91. John A. Martilla, 'Word-of-mouth communication in the industrial adoption process', *Journal of Marketing Research* 8 (March 1971): 173–8; see also Marsha L. Richins, 'Negative word-of-mouth by dissatisfied consumers: A pilot study', *Journal of Marketing* 47 (Winter 1983): 68–78.

92. Arndt, 'Role of product-related conversations in the diffusion of a new product', *op. cit.*

93. James H. Myers and Thomas S. Robertson, 'Dimensions of opinion leadership', *Journal of Marketing Research* 9 (February 1972): 41–6.

94. James F. Engel, Robert J. Kegerreis and Roger D. Blackwell, 'Word-of-mouth communication by the innovator', *Journal of Marketing* 33 (July 1969): 15–19.

95. 'Black sheep of the Theakston family', *Marketing* (3 December 1992): 24.

96. Kimberley Paterson, 'Giving a boost to word-of-mouth advertising', *Rough Notes Co. Inc.* (April 1999).

97. Sonia Murray, 'Street marketing does the trick', *Advertising Age* (20 March 2000): S12.

98. Quoted in 'Taking to the streets', *Newsweek* (2 November 1998): 70–3, at 71.

99. Constance L. Hays, 'Guerrilla marketing is going mainstream', *New York Times on the Web* (7 October 1999).

100. Cathy Horyn, 'A store made for right now: You shop until it's dropped', *NYT Online* (17 February 2004).

101. Wayne Friedman, 'Street marketing hits the internet', *Advertising Age* (1 May 2000): 32; Erin White, 'Online buzz helps album skyrocket to top of charts', *Wall Street Journal Interactive Edition* (5 October 1999).

102. Jared Sandberg, 'The friendly virus', *Newsweek* (12 April 1999): 65–6.

103. See also for instance Thefacebook.com which was launched by five Harvard students and had attracted over 1 million students from 300 US universities within the space of ten months to sign up. Peter Applebome, 'On campus, hanging out by logging on', *NYT Online* (1 December 2004).

104. Karen J. Bannan, 'Marketers try infecting the internet', *New York Times on the Web* (22 March 2000).

105. Peter Landau, 'A.I. promotion', *Mediaweek* (12 November 2001).

106. Bill Barol, 'Batmania', *Newsweek* (26 June 1989): 70.

107. Dorothy Leonard-Barton, 'Experts as negative opinion leaders in the diffusion of a technological innovation', *Journal of Consumer Research* 11 (March 1985): 914–26.

108. Chip Walker, 'Word-of-mouth', *American Demographics* (July 1995): 38–44.

109. Richard J. Lutz, 'Changing brand attitudes through modification of cognitive structure', *Journal of Consumer Research* 1 (March 1975): 49–59; for some suggested remedies to bad publicity, see Mitch Griffin, Barry J. Babin and Jill S. Attaway, 'An Empirical Investigation of the Impact of Negative Public Publicity on Consumer Attitudes and Intentions', in Rebecca H. Holman and Michael R. Solomon (eds), *Advances in Consumer Research* 18 (Provo, UT: Association for Consumer Research, 1991): 334–41; Alice M. Tybout, Bobby J. Calder and Brian Sternthal, 'Using information processing theory to design marketing strategies', *Journal of Marketing Research* 18 (1981): 73–9; see also Russell N. Laczniak, Thomas E. DeCarlo and Sridhar N. Ramaswami, 'Consumers' responses to negative word-of-mouth communication: An attribution theory perspective', *Journal of Consumer Psychology* 11(1) (2001): 57–74.

110. Gulden Asugman, 'An Evaluation of Negative Word-of-Mouth Research for New Extensions', in B. Englis and A. Olofsson (eds), *European Advances in Consumer Research* 3 (Provo, UT: Association for Consumer Research, 1998): 70–5.

111. Robert E. Smith and Christine A. Vogt, 'The effects of integrating advertising and negative word-of-mouth communications on message processing and response', *Journal of Consumer Psychology* 4(2) (1995): 133–51; Paula Fitzgerald Bone, 'Word-of-mouth effects on short-term and long-term product judgments', *Journal of Business Research* 32 (1995): 213–23.

112. 'Dunkin' donuts buys out critical web site', *The New York Times on the Web* (27 August 1999); for a discussion of ways to assess negative WOM online, see David M. Boush and Lynn R. Kahle, 'Evaluating negative information in online consumer discussions: From qualitative analysis to signal detection', *Journal of EuroMarketing* 11(2) (2001): 89–105.

113. James C. Ward and Amy L. Ostrom, 'Complaining to the masses: The role of protest framing in customer-created complaint web sites', *Journal of Consumer Research* 33(2) (2006): 220.

114. Charles W. King and John O. Summers, 'Overlap of opinion leadership across consumer product categories', *Journal of Marketing Research* 7 (February 1970): 43–50.

115. John Leo, 'Psst! Wait 'till you hear this: A scholar says rumors reveal our fears and desires', *Time* (16 March 1987): 76.

116. T.M. Pavia and M.J. Mason (2004), 'The reflexive relationship between consumer behavior and adaptive coping', *Journal of Consumer Research* 31(2): 441–54.

117. 'Beware Yanks bearing drinks', *Marketing* (5 March 1992): 23–4.

118. Everett M. Rogers, *Diffusion of Innovations*, 3rd edn (New York: Free Press, 1983).

119. Leonard-Barton, 'Experts as negative opinion leaders in the diffusion of a technological innovation', *op. cit.*; Rogers, *Diffusion of Innovations, ibid.*

120. Herbert Menzel, 'Interpersonal and Unplanned Communications: Indispensable or Obsolete?' in *Biomedical Innovation* (Cambridge, MA: MIT Press, 1981): 155–63.

121. Meera P. Venkatraman, 'Opinion leaders, adopters, and communicative adopters: A role analysis', *Psychology and Marketing* 6 (Spring 1989): 51–68.

122. Rogers, *Diffusion of Innovations, op. cit.*

123. Niraj Dawar, Philip M. Parker and Lydia J. Price, 'A cross-cultural study of interpersonal information exchange', *Journal of International Business Studies* (3rd quarter 1996): 497–516.

124. Robert Merton, *Social Theory and Social Structure* (Glencoe, IL: Free Press, 1957).

125. King and Summers, 'Overlap of opinion leadership across consumer product categories', *op. cit*; see also Ronald E. Goldsmith, Jeanne R. Heitmeyer and Jon B. Freiden, 'Social values and fashion leadership', *Clothing and Textiles Research Journal* 10 (Fall 1991): 37–45; J.O. Summers, 'Identity of women's clothing fashion opinion leaders', *Journal of Marketing Research* 7 (1970): 178–85.

126. Duncan J. Watts and Peter Sheridan Dodds, 'Influentials, Networks, and Public Opinioin Formation' *Journal of Consumer Research* 34 (December 2007) 442.

127. Duncan J. Watts and Peter Sheridan Dodds, *ibid*.

128. Duncan J. Watts and Peter Sheridan Dodds, *ibid*.

129. Duncan J. Watts and Peter Sheridan Dodds, *ibid.*, 441–58.

130. Gerrit Antonides and Gulden Asugman, 'The communication structure of consumer opinions', in Flemming Hansen (ed.), *European Advances in Consumer Research* 2 (Provo, UT: Association for Consumer Research, 1995): 132–7.

131. Steven A. Baumgarten, 'The innovative communicator in the diffusion process,' *Journal of Marketing Research* 12 (February 1975): 12–18.

132. Laura J. Yale and Mary C. Gilly, 'Dyadic perceptions in personal source information search', *Journal of Business Research* 32 (1995): 225–37.

133. Russell W. Belk, 'Occurrence of Word-of-Mouth Buyer Behavior as a Function of Situation and Advertising Stimuli', in Fred C. Allvine (ed.), *Combined Proceedings of the American Marketing Association series*, no. 33 (Chicago: American Marketing Association, 1971): 419–22.

134. Lawrence F. Feick, Linda L. Price and Robin A. Higie, 'People Who Use People: The Other Side of Opinion Leadership', in Richard J. Lutz (ed.), *Advances in Consumer Research* 13 (Provo, UT: Association for Consumer Research, 1986): 301–5.

135. For discussion of the market maven construct, see Lawrence F. Feick and Linda L. Price, 'The market maven', *Managing* (July 1985): 10; scale items adapted from Lawrence F. Feick and Linda L. Price, 'The market maven: A diffuser of marketplace information', *Journal of Marketing* 51 (January 1987): 83–7.

136. Michael R. Solomon, 'The missing link: Surrogate consumers in the marketing chain', *Journal of Marketing* 50 (October 1986): 208–18.

137. Andra Adelson, 'A french skin-care line seeks to take America by first winning over pharmacists', *New York Times* (14 February 1994): D7.

138. Sarah Boseley and Rob Evans, 'Drug giants accused over doctors' perks', *The Guardian*, 23 August 2008: 1–2.

139. Stern and Gould, 'The consumer as financial opinion leader', *op. cit*.

140. William R. Darden and Fred D. Reynolds, 'Predicting opinion leadership for men's apparel fashions', *Journal of Marketing Research* 1 (August 1972): 324–8. A modified version of the opinion leadership scale with improved reliability and validity can be found in Terry L. Childers, 'Assessment of the psychometric properties of an opinion leadership scale', *Journal of Marketing Research* 23 (May 1986): 184–8.

141. Gina Kolata, 'Find Yourself Packing It On? Blame Friends', *New York Times Online Edition* (26 July 2007)

142. 'Referrals top ads as influence on patients' doctor selections', *Marketing News* (30 January 1987): 22.

143. Peter H. Reingen and Jerome B. Kernan, 'Analysis of referral networks in marketing: Methods and illustration', *Journal of Marketing Research* 23 (November 1986): 370–8.

144. Peter H. Reingen, Brian L. Foster, Jacqueline Johnson Brown and Stephen B. Seidman, 'Brand congruence in interpersonal relations: A social network analysis', *Journal of Consumer Research* 11 (December 1984): 771–83; see also James C. Ward and Peter H. Reingen, 'Sociocognitive analysis of group decision-making among consumers', *Journal of Consumer Research* 17 (December 1990): 245–62.

145. Jeff Surowiecki, *The Wisdom of Crowds* (New York: Anchor, 2005); Jeff Howe, 'The Rise of Crowdsourcing', *Wired* (June 2006): 176(8).

146. Thomas E. Weber, 'Viral marketing: Web's newest ploy may make you an unpopular friend', *The Wall Street Journal Interactive Edition* (13 September 1999).

11

European family structures, household decision-making and age cohorts

Although it was still three days before Christmas, Joost was intent on making a large cauldron of Dutch pea soup, while his Dutch Indonesian girlfriend Sadyah was in the process of chopping ingredients for several Indonesian dishes. They agreed that all these dishes taste best if they are cooked a few days before actually eating them.

Although pea soup isn't always a part of Christmas dinner in Holland, it definitely has its place in the Dutch 'winter menu'. The best pea soup is thick in texture with peas, potatoes, celery root, onions, leek, carrots, and generous chunks of ham. Hot pea soup and dark bread topped with thinly sliced bacon (*Snert met roggebrood en spec*) leaves everyone feeling warm and content. The only concession to 'store bought' ingredients that Joost will make is to add a sliced Unox rookworst (sausage) on the day the soup is served. Sadyah, on the other hand, turns her nose up at the very idea of using anything from a package. While many Dutch rely on prepared Indonesian seasoning from Conimex, Sadyah's family expects only traditional, freshly prepared dishes, which means lots of chopping, blending, mixing, and marinating for days!

As in many other European countries, Christmas is a busy family time in Holland. Everyone has social events to attend, some of which are personal and joyful, while others seem more 'obligatory'. For Joost and Sadyah, the Dutch tradition of celebrating two Christmas days (December 25 and 26) is particularly helpful as they try to find time to visit everyone. Joost's parents divorced 18 years ago, and his mother lives in the east of Holland, while his father is two hours away in Amsterdam. In addition to Joost's parents, there is also Sadyah's family. For Sadyah, the notion of what constitutes immediate family goes way beyond the nuclear family of Mum, Dad and siblings, and includes dozens of extended family members who all get together at Christmas. Family, food, and lots of train travel . . . all part of the Christmas season for Joost and Sadyah.

Dutch pea soup.
Alamy Images/OnWhite

INTRODUCTION

Joost and Sadyah's efforts to celebrate Christmas with their families is fairly typical of the joint nature of many consumer decisions. The individual decision-making process we described in detail in Chapter 9 is, in many cases, overly simplistic. This is because more than one person often participates in the problem-solving sequence, from initial problem recognition and information search to evaluation of alternatives and product choice. To further complicate matters, these decisions often include two or more people, or families, all with differing expectations, who may not have the same level of investment in the outcome, the same tastes and preferences, or the same consumption priorities.

Whether they are choosing a can of tuna or buying a new multimedia entertainment system for the home, consumers commonly work together. This section of the chapter examines issues related to *collective decision-making*, where more than one person is involved in the purchasing process for products or services that may be used by multiple consumers. We focus specifically on one of the most important organizations to which we all claim membership – the family unit. We will consider how members of a family negotiate among themselves, and how important changes in the modern family structure are affecting this process. The chapter concludes by discussing how we use age in consumer research as a predictor of behaviour, and the appeals that marketers make to diverse age subcultures.

THE FAMILY

Constructing and deconstructing the family in Europe

While it might still be too early to draw definite conclusions, it is reasonable to speculate that historians will regard the period from the 1990s to 2005 as one of the most politically, socially and economically turbulent timeframes in modern history. Radical political and market changes throughout Western and Eastern Europe are reflections and outcomes of intense social change in European societies that have been under way since the 1950s. While the extent and pace of changes and the national perceptions of social change have differed from one country to another, it is clear that many of our social institutions have been altered over the past four decades, not least of which is the notion of 'family'. In 2010 the population of the EU-27 will reach almost 492 million, the third largest population of any political entity after China (1,283 million) and India (1,041 million).[1] While the newest EU member countries have more similarities than differences with the 'former 15' EU members in terms of family structure, there are some important trends in age distributions, marriage patterns, employment, salary rates between men and women and ageing of the populations of our individual member states which will have a major impact on consumer consumption patterns of European families in the decades to come.

Before moving on to a discussion of the forces that have changed our notions of family, and what these changes mean in terms of consumer behaviour, we need to spend a moment tackling the thorny question, 'What is the family, and how do we gather data about it?' There is a great deal of family diversity throughout Europe, and the conceptualization of *family* is based on ideology, popular mythology and conventions that are firmly rooted in each country's historical, political, religious, economic and cultural traditions. Certainly, European governments have had a strong history of requiring regular and up-to-date socio-demographic information on the behaviour of families (birth rates, fertility rates, divorce rates), and about family forms (size, structure and organization). This sort of information is an essential component in governments' policy-making processes.

Figure 11.1 Women and men aged 18–24 living in parental home, 2005[3]

IE: unreliable data; PL, SE: no data; EU-25: estimate

Source: Eurostat, LFS.

Source: Eurostat, LFS.

Yet, despite a long history of international collaboration and the growing need for reliable information about demographic trends in Europe, by the mid-1990s data on households and families in the EU were still far from comparable.[2] Attempts to standardize data collection methods across countries have had to deal with issues such as national political priorities and ideologies, the centralization and autonomy of the organizations responsible for data collection, and the reluctance of some governments to accept decisions taken at the supranational level. As an example of the problems of comparing families across Europe, consider the problem of dealing with the *age of children living at home*. In most EU member states, no age limit was applied during the 1991 census. However, in Denmark, Finland and Sweden, children were considered as part of the family up to the age of 18, and in Luxembourg to 25. France applied a limit of 25 years until 1982, but this was abolished for the 1991 census, which increased the proportion of lone-parent families by 35 per cent! In today's Europe, increasing migration rates, falling fertility rates, and delaying marriage until later in life (or cohabitation instead of marriage) all influence the reporting and analyses of statistics used to paint a portrait of the European family. As Europe moves on into the new millennium, more standardized and comparable forms of data about the family will be collected (see Figure 11.1).

From both a statistical as well as a sociological perspective, 'family' is hard to nail down. However, one thing is certain – the concept of family will continue to exist and will manifest itself in varying forms over time and across countries throughout Europe. Figure 11.2 provides an overview of the many components which make up our notion of a European household.

Defining the modern family

Some experts have argued that as traditional family living arrangements have declined, people are placing even greater emphasis on the role of siblings, close friends and other relatives to provide companionship and social support.[4] In the US, some people are even joining 'intentional families', groups of strangers who meet regularly for meals and who spend holidays together. Over 500 of these communities currently operate in the US.[5]

Many marketers have focused on the renewed interest in family life brought about by the more flexible definitions of what constitutes a family. Recent research on the family has shown this social unit to be of key importance in providing insights for

Figure 11.2 Components of the 'modern family'

marketers in understanding the strength of relationships in family structure, and how this understanding leads to better development of the key value propositions that need to be offered in the marketing of goods and services to the family such as vacations and mobile phones.[6] While families were indeed out of fashion in the 1960s and 1970s, being seen by some as an infringement of personal freedom, 90 per cent of the respondents in one recent survey confirmed that family life was one of the most important things to

► them.[7] The extended family was once the most common family unit. It consisted of three generations living together and often included not only the grandparents, but aunts,

► uncles and cousins. The nuclear family, a mother and a father and one or more children (perhaps with a dog thrown in for good measure), became the model family unit over time.

Just what is a household?

For statistical purposes, Eurostat has implemented the United Nation's definition of the family unit based on the 'conjugal family concept'. *The family* is defined in the narrow sense of a family nucleus as follows: 'The persons within a private or institutional household who are related as husband and wife or as parent and never-married child by blood or adoption.' Thus, a family nucleus comprises a married couple without children or a married couple with one or more never-married children of any age, or one parent with one or more never-married children of any age. The definition tries to take into account whenever possible, couples who report that they are living in consensual unions, regardless of whether they are legally married. Under the more recent European

► Community Household Panel, a family household is more broadly defined, as a 'shared residence and common housekeeping arrangement'. Marketers are interested in both of these units, not only for their similarities, but as a way of understanding differences. Changes in consumers' family structures, such as cohabitation, delayed marriage and delayed childbirth, the return of mothers to the workforce and the upheaval caused by divorce, often represent opportunities for marketers as normal purchasing patterns become unfrozen and people make new choices about products and brands.[8]

Age of the family

Since 1960 the EU has seen a trend of falling numbers of marriages and an increase in the number of divorces. Moreover, people are remarrying more often than they did before the 1960s, and men are more likely to form a new family than women. Couples marry youngest in Portugal and oldest in Denmark, and the greatest age difference between husbands and wives is to be found in Greece. Overall, consumers aged between 35 and 44 were responsible for the largest increase in the number of households, growing by almost 40 per cent since 1980.[9] Half of all family householders fell into this age group in the year 2000. A key segment to change in the coming 20 years will be the significant increase in adults living alone – a segment which will increase to over 62 million households by 2025.[10]

Family size

Worldwide, surveys show that almost all women want smaller families than they did a decade ago. In 1980, the average European household contained 2.8 people, but today that number has slipped to 2.6 people. Furthermore, the current average number of children per woman is below the generational replacement threshold level, with a fertility rate for Europe of 1.44 children per woman in 1993 (compared to almost double this in 1964). A UK study predicts that one in five women born in the 1960s to 1980s will remain

▶ childless – a halving of the birth rate of their mother's generation.[11] The **fertility rate** is determined by the number of births per year per 1,000 women of childbearing age. For several decades now fertility rates in the EU have remained clearly below replacement levels of 2.1, a trend which is reinforced by the enlargement of the EU to the EU-27. Among the new member states only Cyprus (1.57 children per woman) and Malta (1.51) are a little above the average for EU-15 (1.47).[12] A variety of European studies on the dynamics that underlie family size show that size is dependent on such factors as educational level, the availability of birth control and religion.

Recent research has also shown that the division of labour within the household between partners (husband and wife, or however the relationship is defined) also matters in Europe. Consider the situation of women in Italy and The Netherlands. While there is a greater percentage of Dutch women than Italian women in the workforce, the fertility rate in the Netherlands is significantly higher (1.73 in The Netherlands, compared to 1.33 in Italy). In both countries, people tend to have traditional views about gender roles, but Italian society is considerably more conservative in this regard, and this seems to be a decisive difference. Women who do more than 75 per cent of the housework and child care are less likely to want to have another child than women whose husbands or partners share the load. Put differently, Dutch fathers change more nappies, pick up more kids after soccer practice and clean up the living room more often than Italian fathers; therefore, relative to the population, there are more Dutch babies than Italian babies being born. In Europe, many countries with greater gender equality have a greater social commitment to day care and other institutional support for working women, which gives those women the possibility of having second or third children.[13]

Marketers keep a close eye on the population's birth rate to gauge how the pattern of births will affect demand for products in the future. Even when a married couple does live with children, families are shrinking. The number of European households comprising one or two people is increasing (from 22 per cent to 26 per cent during 1980–90) and the number of households with four or more people is falling (from 34 per cent to 25 per cent during 1980–90).[14] The number of unmarried adults and one-person households is steadily rising (they now account for 26 per cent of European households, and are projected to be the fastest growing segment through to the year 2025). Some marketers are beginning to address the fact that this group is under-represented in advertising.[15] Gold Blend coffee built a very popular TV ad campaign around a romance between two single neighbours, while Procter & Gamble introduced Folger's Singles 'single-serve' coffee bags for people who live alone and don't need a full pot.[16] On the other hand, many singles report that they avoid buying single-size food portions or eating alone in restaurants since both remind them of their unattached status – they prefer takeaway food.[17]

Single men and women constitute quite different markets. More than half of single men are under the age of 35, while among people over age 65 women account for 80 per cent of one-person households. Despite single males' greater incomes, single women dominate many markets because of their spending patterns. Single women are more likely than single men to own a home, and they spend more on housing-related items and furniture. Single men, in contrast, spend more overall in restaurants and on cars. However, these spending patterns are also significantly affected by age: middle-aged single women, for example, spend *more* than their male counterparts on cars.[18]

Consumer behaviour as I see it . . .

Family Matters

Marketers have long been interested in how to drive brand loyalty. Brands compete for 'share of market', 'share of mind', 'share of wallet', and more recently 'share of heart'. When marketers refer to 'share of heart', they are asking, 'Compared to my competitors, where is my brand in consumers' hearts?' In an effort to better capture consumers' hearts much recent consumer research has stressed the significance of affective, identity-affirming bonds between consumers and their brands. This research encourages marketers to ask, 'How can I make my brand central to the identity of my consumers?' Brand communities that emerge around brands such as Harley-Davidson, Jones Soda, Threadless, and Apple underscore the powerful loyalty potential and customer lifetime value of brands that capture the hearts and support the identities of consumers. Certainly, firms should pay attention to developing and nurturing these affective bonds!

Linda L. Price
University of Arizona

But ask a room full of consumers, even young global consumers, how many of them are active participants in even one brand community and you'll find that only a few hands go up. Now ask a room full of consumers what they are loyal to and care about, and there's a good chance not even one consumer will mention a brand or commercial service. You may capture more share of heart than your competitor but often it is still a pretty miniscule share – brands are not nearly as important to consumers as the family dog or cat. If you ask consumers what they do care about, family and family relationships are far and away most important. For companies, there's a simple metric, 'Where is your brand in what matters most to consumers?' This is an entirely different way of thinking about 'share of heart'. To answer this question, marketers need to examine how their brands and services help consumers: 'be a family' – to reconcile individual work ambitions and family goals; 'be a couple' – with young children underfoot and competing individual pursuits. Simply stated, families are trying to manage individual, relational and family goals and identities and they give their hearts to the brands and services that help them juggle their complicated, bundled lives. In mundane oversimplified terms, families are trying to fit in some exercise time for Mom, get John home from soccer practice, make sure the family eats dinner together, homework gets done and parents save a little couple time to keep the marriage alive. Marketers have to think about how they are a resource in the family ties that truly do bind consumers' everyday lives. It may not matter if you own Mom's favourite restaurant if no one else in the family will eat there. From a network perspective, what matters is how central and unique your brand or service is as a relational resource. If you are the 'go to' resource for the relationships that matter to consumers you may come out on top of individually preferred alternatives again and again. If your brand helps families navigate their individual, relational and collective goals you can truly earn a meaningful share of heart.

Much of my research over the past 15 years has dealt with family consumption and the important roles that families play in what consumers buy, integrate into family practices, come to love and pass forward to the next generation. If you've ever watched, The Antiques Road Show, you've met consumers who discover Great Grandma's hope chest is worth a lot of money, but they would never sell it because it is 'priceless' – it has come to represent the history, values, and future of the family, and perhaps most especially the women in the family. It's quite likely that you are already the recipient or the intended recipient of a family

Consumer behaviour as I see it . . . (continued)

treasure – an object that simply must 'remain in the family'. Maybe you recall preparing or eating family recipes that replicate traditions, rituals, and practices passed down through generations to preserve and define your family. But now turn your attention to more mundane and everyday consumption choices. How do you use cell phones, Face Book, e-mail and even television to manage family relationships? What sort of cell phone plan would work best for your family? For example, if we define a cell phone as a close relationship management device, how would we design and market it? When your family takes a vacation, how important is 'being a family' in choosing where to go and what to do? How does your family balance individual, relational and collective interests and goals in vacation travel? If we define 'being a family' as a primary vacation goal, how do we design our offerings? Many business opportunities are lurking hidden in the goals and practices of family networks.

It's ironic that even though family is extremely important to most consumers relatively little consumer research and marketing effort focuses on studying family identity as a source of insight into consumer loyalty. Most research has instead focused on individual identity or how a group (such as a brand community) is important to an individual's identity. Perhaps the relative neglect of family research is in part because families are more fluid, elective and difficult to define than they were in the past. Increasingly common blended, single-parent, bi-cultural, and gay family forms may depart from dominant discourses about family. However, despite varied and elective types most people believe they belong to a family uniquely defined by structure, character and generations over time and this collective dramatically shapes the brands, objects, activities and services they consume (Epp and Price 2008). The time is ripe for consumer researchers to reconsider family consumption with new methods and perspectives. To do this we need to move beyond our conventional understandings of family, family life cycle and family decision making and question our stereotypes about what strengthens and weakens family communications.

* Not so coincidentally, my research on family consumption began about the same time I became a parent. My research was also vitally inspired by and co-created with many wonderful co-authors especially Carolyn Folkman Curasi, Amber M. Epp and Eric J. Arnould. For more information see Amber M. Epp and Linda L. Price (2008), 'Family Identity: A framework of identity interplay in consumption practices', Journal of Consumer Research, June: 50–70.

Non-traditional family structures

The European Community Household Panel regards any occupied housing unit as a household, regardless of the relationships among people living there. Thus, one person living alone, three room-mates or two lovers all constitute households. Less traditional households will rapidly increase these if trends persist. One-parent households are increasing steadily throughout Europe (most common in the UK, Denmark and Belgium, least common in Greece). Although these households are in the majority of cases headed by women, there is also an increasing trend for fathers to take on this role.[19] In the US, 10 million children live with a step-parent or with children who are not full brothers or sisters, and 24 per cent of all children live in one-parent families.[20]

Effects of family structure on consumption

A family's needs and expenditures are affected by such factors as the number of people (children and adults) in the family, their ages, and whether one, two or more adults are employed outside of the home.

Two important factors determining how a couple spend time and money are whether they have children and whether the woman works. Couples with children generally have higher expenses, and not just for the 'basics' such as food and utilities bills. Studies in the UK estimate that the costs of keeping a teenager 'in the style to which they aspire' run close to £66,000, and the costs of getting a child to the teen years is approaching £33,000.[21] In addition, a recently married couple make very different expenditures compared with people with young children, who in turn are quite different from a couple with children in college, and so on. Families with working mothers must often make allowances for such expenses as nursery care and a working wardrobe for the woman.

▶ **Multicultural dimensions**

The Euro-housewife: considerable differences between EU member states

- The percentage of women aged between 25 and 59 who describe themselves as housewives varies considerably between member states. While the EU average is 33 per cent, it ranges from a high of 60 per cent in Ireland (Spain, Greece, Italy and Luxembourg are also high), to a mere 4 per cent in Denmark.
- Barely 6 per cent of women between 25 and 39 without children stay at home, compared with 36 per cent with one child under 5 and 52 per cent with at least two children under 5.
- EU-wide, only 7 per cent of today's housewives stopped working because of marriage – but this

- number peaked at 15 per cent in Greece and 14 per cent in Spain. However, 42 per cent stop because of children.
- Family obligations, such as housework, caring for children or others are the main reason why 84 per cent of housewives are not looking for work.
- Being a housewife is strongly related to the level of education. Housewives represent 45 per cent of EU women aged from 25 to 59 with lower secondary education, 26 per cent with upper secondary education, and only 13 per cent of women with higher educational levels.[22]

The family life cycle

▶ Recognizing that family needs and expenditures change over time, the concept of the **family life cycle (FLC)** has been widely used by marketers. The FLC combines trends in income and family composition with the changes in demands placed upon this income. As we grow older, our preferences for products and activities tend to change. In many cases, our income levels tend to rise (at least until retirement), so that we can afford more as well. In addition, many purchases that must be made at an early age do not have to be repeated very often. For example, we tend to accumulate durable goods, such as furniture, and only replace them as necessary.

A life-cycle approach to the study of the family assumes that pivotal events alter role relationships and trigger new stages of life which modify our priorities. These events include the birth of a first child, the departure of the last child from the house, the death of a spouse, retirement of the principal wage earner and divorce.[23] Movement through these life stages is accompanied by significant changes in expenditures on leisure, food, durables and services, even after the figures have been adjusted to reflect changes in income.[24]

This focus on longitudinal changes in priorities is particularly valuable in predicting demand for specific product categories over time. For example, the money spent by a couple with no children on eating out and holidays will probably be diverted for quite different purchases after the birth of a child. While a number of models have been proposed to describe family life cycle stages, their usefulness has been limited because in many cases they have failed to take into account such important social trends as the changing role of women, the acceleration of alternative lifestyles, childless and delayed-child marriages and single-parent households.

Four variables are necessary to describe these changes: age, marital status, the presence or absence of children in the home, and their ages. In addition, our definition of marital status (at least for analysis purposes) must be relaxed to include any couple living together who are in a long-term relationship. Thus, while room-mates might not be considered 'married', a man and a woman who have established a household would be, as would two homosexual men or women who have a similar understanding.

Table 11.1 The family life cycle: an updated view

	Age of head of household		
	Under 35	**35–64**	**Over 64**
One adult in household	Bachelor I	Bachelor II	Bachelor III
Two adults in household	Young couple	Childless couple	Older couple
Two adults plus children in household	Full nest I	Delayed full nest	
	Full nest II	Full nest III	

Source: Adapted from Mary C. Gilly and Ben M. Enis, 'Recycling the Family Life Cycle: A Proposal for Redefinition', in Andrew A. Mitchell, (ed.), *Advances in Consumer Research 9* (Ann Arbor, MI: Association for Consumer Research, 1982): 274, Figure 1.

When these changes are considered, this approach allows us to identify a set of categories that include many more types of family situations.[25] These categories, which are listed in Table 11.1, are derived by dividing consumers into groups in terms of age, whether there is more than one adult present, and whether there are children. For example, a distinction is made between the consumption needs of people in the Full nest I category (where the youngest child is under 6), the Full nest II category (where the youngest child is over 6), the Full nest III category (where the youngest child is over 6 and the parents are middle-aged), and the Delayed full nest (where the parents are in their forties but the youngest child is under 6).

Life cycle effects on buying

As might be expected, consumers classified into these categories show marked differences in consumption patterns. Young bachelors and newlyweds have the most 'modern' sex-role attitudes, are the most likely to exercise regularly, to go to pubs, concerts, the cinema and restaurants, and to go dancing; and they consume more alcohol. Families with young children are more likely to consume health foods such as fruit, juice and yogurt, while those made up of single parents and older children buy more junk foods. The monetary value of homes, cars and other durables is lowest for bachelors and single parents, but increases as people go through the full nest and childless couple stages. Perhaps reflecting the bounty of wedding gifts, newlyweds are the most likely to own appliances such as toasters, ovens and electric coffee grinders. Babysitter and day care usage is, of course, highest among single-parent and full nest households, while home maintenance services (e.g. lawnmowing) are most likely to be employed by older couples and bachelors. Recent studies have shown that families also place a significant emotional and financial attachment to possessions that they own when those possessions are part of the family's bonding, and history. This goes well beyond our earlier notion of the importance of 'inheritance', and considers our sense of family well-being, continuity, history, and important role as 'caretaker' of the family's identity over generations.[26]

The growth of these additional categories creates many opportunities for enterprising marketers. For example, divorced people undergo a process of transition to a new social role. This change is often accompanied by the disposal of possessions linked to the former role and the need to acquire a set of possessions that help to express the person's new identity as they experiment with new lifestyles.[27]

THE INTIMATE CORPORATION: FAMILY DECISION-MAKING

The decision process within a household unit in some ways resembles a business conference. Certain matters are put up for discussion, different members may have different priorities and agendas, and there may be power struggles to rival any tale of corporate intrigue. In just about every living situation, whether a conventional family, students sharing a house or apartment, or some other non-traditional arrangement, group members seem to take on different roles just as purchasing agents, engineers, account executives and others do within a company.

Household decisions

▶ Two basic types of decisions are made by families.[28] In a **consensual purchase decision**, the group agrees on the desired purchase, differing only in terms of how it will be achieved. In these circumstances, the family will probably engage in problem-solving and consider alternatives until the means for satisfying the group's goal is found. For example, a household considering adding a dog to the family but concerned about who will take care of it might draw up a chart assigning individuals to specific duties.

▶ Unfortunately, life is not always that easy. In an **accommodative purchase decision**, group members have different preferences or priorities and cannot agree on a purchase that will satisfy the minimum expectations of all involved. It is here that bargaining, coercion, compromise and the wielding of power are all likely to be used to achieve agreement on what to buy or who gets to use it. Family decisions are often characterized by an accommodative rather than a consensual decision. Conflict occurs when there is incomplete correspondence in family members' needs and preferences. While money is the most common source of conflict between marriage partners, television choices come a close second![29] Some specific factors determining the degree of family decision conflict include the following:[30]

- *Interpersonal need* (a person's level of investment in the group): a child in a family situation may care more about what their family buys for the house than a college student who is living in student accommodation.

- *Product involvement and utility* (the degree to which the product in question will be used or will satisfy a need): a family member who is an avid coffee drinker will obviously be more interested in the purchase of a new coffeemaker to replace a malfunctioning one than a similar expenditure for some other item.

- *Responsibility* (for procurement, maintenance, payment, and so on): people are more likely to have disagreements about a decision if it entails long-term consequences and commitments. For example, a family decision about getting a dog may involve conflict regarding who will be responsible for walking and feeding it.

- *Power* (or the degree to which one family member exerts influence over the others in making decisions): in traditional families, the husband tends to have more power than the wife, who in turn has more than the oldest child, and so on. In family decisions, conflict can arise when one person continually uses the power they have within the group to satisfy their priorities.

In general, decisions will involve conflict among family members to the extent that they are important or novel and/or if individuals have strong opinions about good and bad alternatives. The degree to which these factors generate conflict determines the type of decision the family will make.[31]

Sex roles and decision-making responsibilities

▶ Traditionally, some buying decisions, termed **autocratic decisions**, were made by one spouse. Men, for instance, often had sole responsibility for selecting a car, while most decorating choices fell to women. Other decisions, such as holiday destinations, were made
▶ jointly; these are known as **syncratic decisions**. According to a study conducted by Roper Starch Worldwide, wives tend to have the most say when buying groceries, children's toys, clothes and medicines. Syncratic decisions are common for cars, holidays, homes,

appliances, furniture, home electronics, interior design and long-distance phone services. As the couple's education increases, more decisions are likely to be made together.[32]

Identifying the decision-maker

The nature of consumer decision-making within a particular product category is an important issue for marketers, so that they know who to target and whether or not they need to reach both spouses to influence a decision. Researchers have paid special attention ► to which spouse plays the role of what has been called the **family financial officer (FFO)**, who keeps track of the family's bills and decides how any surplus funds will be spent. Among newlyweds, this role tends to be played jointly, and then over time one spouse or the other tends to take over these responsibilities.[33] Spouses usually exert significant influence on decision-making, even after one of them has died. An Irish study found that many widows claim to sense the continued presence of their dead husband, and to conduct 'conversations' with them about household matters.[34]

In traditional families (and especially those with low educational levels), women are primarily responsible for family financial management. While the man is usually the wage earner, the woman in these traditional family structures typically decides how the money is spent.[35] Each spouse 'specializes' in certain activities.[36] The pattern is different among families where spouses adhere to more modern sex-role norms. These couples believe that there should be more shared participation in family maintenance activities. In these cases, husbands assume more responsibility for laundering, house cleaning, day-to-day shopping, and so on, in addition to such traditionally 'male' tasks as home maintenance and waste removal.[37] Of course, cultural background is an important determinant of the dominance of the husband or wife. Husbands tend to be more dominant in decision-making among couples with a strong Mediterranean ethnic identification.[38] Even in northern Europe, the pattern of traditional 'male' and 'female' roles is still fairly strong.

Four factors appear to determine the degree to which decisions will be made jointly or by one or the other spouse:[39]

1 *Sex-role stereotypes*: Couples who believe in traditional sex-role stereotypes tend to make individual decisions for sex-typed products (i.e. those considered to be 'masculine' or 'feminine').

2 *Spousal resources*: The spouse who contributes more resources to the family has the greater influence.

3 *Experience*: Individual decisions are made more frequently when the couple has gained experience as a decision-making unit.

4 *Socio-economic status*: More joint decisions are made by middle-class families than in either higher- or lower-class families.

Despite recent changes in decision-making responsibilities, women are still primarily ► responsible for the continuation of the family's **kin network system**: they perform the rituals intended to maintain ties among family members, both immediate and extended. This function includes such activities as co-ordinating visits among relatives, phoning and writing to family members, sending greetings cards, making social engagements, and so on.[40] This organizing role means that women often make important decisions about the family's leisure activities, and are more likely to decide with whom the family will socialize.

Heuristics in joint decision-making

The *synoptic ideal* calls for the husband and wife to take a common view and act as joint decision-makers. According to this ideal, they would very thoughtfully weigh alternatives, assign to one another well-defined roles, and calmly make mutually beneficial consumer decisions. The couple would act rationally, analytically and use as much information as possible to maximize joint utility. In reality, however, spousal decision-making is often characterized by the use of influence or methods that are likely to reduce conflict. A couple 'reaches' rather than 'makes' a decision. This process has been described as 'muddling through'.[41]

One common technique for simplifying the decision-making process is the use of *heuristics* (see Chapter 9). Some decision-making patterns frequently observed when a couple makes decisions in buying a new house illustrate the use of heuristics:

- The couple's areas of common preference are based upon salient, objective dimensions rather than more subtle, hard-to-define cues. For example, a couple may easily agree on the number of bedrooms they need in the new home, but will have more difficulty achieving a common view of how the home should look.

- The couple agrees on a system of *task specialization*, where each is responsible for certain duties or decision areas and does not interfere in the other's. For many couples, these assignments are likely to be influenced by their perceived sex roles. For example, the wife may seek out houses in advance that meet their requirements, while the husband determines whether the couple can obtain a mortgage.

- Concessions are based on the intensity of each spouse's preferences. One spouse will yield to the influence of the other in many cases simply because their level of preference for a certain attribute is not particularly intense, where in other situations they will be willing to exert effort to obtain a favourable decision.[42] In cases where intense preferences for different attributes exist, rather than attempt to influence each other, spouses will 'trade off' a less-intense preference for a more strongly felt one. For example, a husband who is indifferent to kitchen design may yield to his wife, but expect that in turn he will be allowed to design his own garage workshop. It is interesting to note that many men apparently want to be very involved in making some decorating decisions and setting budgets – more than women want them to be. According to one survey, 70 per cent of male respondents felt the husband should be involved in decorating the family room, while only 51 per cent of wives wanted them to be.[43]

CHILDREN AS DECISION-MAKERS: CONSUMERS-IN-TRAINING

Anyone who has had the 'delightful' experience of supermarket shopping with one or more children knows that children often have a say in what their parents buy, especially for products like breakfast cereal.[44] In addition, children increasingly are being recognized as a potential market for traditionally adult products. For example, Kodak is putting a lot of promotional effort into encouraging children to become photographers. Most children nowadays own or have access to a digital camera, and taking photos is seen as a cool pursuit. Websites which will post photos and mail printed photos to children are flourishing, as children take more control of their own photo collections.

▶ **Parental yielding** occurs when a parental decision maker is influenced by a child's request and 'surrenders'. The likelihood of this occurring is partly dependent on the dynamics within a particular family – as we all know, parental styles range from permissive to strict, and they also vary in terms of the amount of responsibility children are given to make decisions.[45] The strategies children use to request purchases were documented in one study. While most children simply asked for things, other common tactics included saying they had seen it on television, saying that a sibling or friend had it, or bargaining by offering to do chores. Other actions were less innocuous; they included directly placing the object in the trolley and continuous whining – often a 'persuasive' behaviour![46]

Consumer socialization

Children do not spring from the womb with consumer skills already in memory.
▶ **Consumer socialization** has been defined as the process 'by which young people acquire

Children begin making
selections and purchases
of products at an early age.
By the time they reach
their teens, the process
of socialization and peer
influence is well underway.

Photo: Gary Bamossy

skills, knowledge, and attitudes relevant to their functioning in the marketplace'.[47] Where does this knowledge come from? Friends and teachers certainly participate in this process. For instance, children talk to one another about consumer products, and this tendency increases with age.[48] Especially for young children, though, the two primary socialization sources are the family and the media.

Influence of parents

Parents' influences in consumer socialization are both direct and indirect. They deliberately try to instil their own values about consumption in their children ('you're going to learn the value of the pound/euro'). Parents also determine the degree to which their children will be exposed to other information sources, such as television, salespeople and peers.[49] Grown-ups serve as significant models for observational learning (see Chapter 7). Children learn about consumption by watching their parents' behaviour and imitating it. This modelling is facilitated by marketers who package adult products in child versions.

The process of consumer socialization begins with infants, who accompany their parents to shops where they are initially exposed to marketing stimuli. Within the first two years of life, children begin to make requests for desired objects. As children learn to walk, they also begin to make their own selections when they are in shops. By the age of 5, most children are making purchases with the help of parents and grandparents, and by 8 most are making independent purchases and have become fully-fledged consumers.[50]

 Marketing pitfall

Three dimensions combine to produce different 'segments' of parental styles. Parents characterized by certain styles have been found to socialize their children differently.[51] 'Authoritarian parents', who are hostile, restrictive and emotionally uninvolved, do not have warm relationships with their children, are active in filtering the types of media to which their children are exposed, and tend to have negative views about advertising. 'Neglecting parents' also do not have warm relationships, but they are more detached from their children and exercise little control over what their children do. In contrast, 'indulgent parents' communicate more with their children about consumption-related matters and are less restrictive. They believe that children should be allowed to learn about the marketplace without much interference.

European and global brands are part of the social expression of young children, as well as their parents!

The Advertising Archives

Influence of television: 'the electric babysitter'

It is no secret that children watch a lot of television. As a result, they are constantly bombarded with messages about consumption, both contained in commercials and in the programmes themselves. The medium teaches people about a culture's values and myths. The more a child is exposed to television, whether the programme is a local 'soap' or *Baywatch*, the more they will accept the images depicted there as real.[52] In Britain, *Teletubbies* went a step further – it was made for viewers from 3 months to 2 years old. It is unclear if this show would succeed in the US, since babies are not seen as a lucrative market for advertising messages (yet).[53]

In addition to the large volume of programming targeted directly at children, children also are exposed to idealized images of what it is like to be an adult. Since children over the age of 6 spend about a quarter of their television viewing during prime-time, they are affected by programmes and commercials targeted at adults. For example, young girls exposed to adult lipstick commercials learn to associate lipstick with beauty.[54]

Sex-role socialization

Children pick up on the concept of gender identity at an earlier age than was previously believed – perhaps as young as age 1 or 2. By the age of 3, most children categorize driving a truck as masculine and cooking and cleaning as feminine.[55] Even cartoon characters who are portrayed as helpless are more likely to wear frilly or ruffled dresses.[56] Toy companies perpetuate these stereotypes by promoting gender-linked toys with commercials that reinforce sex-role expectations through their casting, emotional tone and copy.[57]

One function of child's play is to rehearse for adulthood. Children 'act out' different roles they might assume later in life and learn about the expectations others have of them. The toy industry provides the props children use to perform these roles.[58] Depending on which side of the debate you are on, these toys either reflect or teach children about what society expects of males versus females. While pre-school boys and girls do not exhibit many differences in toy preferences, after the age of 5 they part company: girls tend to stick with dolls, while boys gravitate towards 'action figures' and high-tech diversions. Industry critics charge that this is because the toy industry is dominated by males, while toy company executives counter that they are simply responding to children's natural preferences.[59]

Often 'traditional' sex roles are stressed in children's products; the same item may be designed and positioned differently for boys and girls. Huffy, for example, manufactures bicycles for both boys and girls. The boys' versions have names such as 'Sigma' and 'Vortex', and they are described as having 'maxed-out features that'll pump your pulse'. The girls' version is more demure. It is called 'Sweet Style', and comes in pink or purple. As a company executive described it in contrast to the boys' bikes, the girls' model 'is a fashion bike. It's not built for racing or jumping – just the look'.[60]

Cognitive development

The ability of children to make mature, 'adult' consumer decisions obviously increases with age (not that grown-ups always make mature decisions). Children can be segmented by age in terms of their **stage of cognitive development**, or ability to comprehend concepts of increasing complexity. Some recent evidence indicates that young children are able to learn consumption-related information surprisingly well, depending on the format in which the information is presented (for instance, learning is enhanced if a videotaped vignette is presented to small children repeatedly).[61]

The foremost proponent of the idea that children pass through distinct stages of **cognitive development** was the Swiss psychologist Jean Piaget, who believed that each stage is characterized by a certain cognitive structure the child uses to handle information.[62] In one classic demonstration of cognitive development, Piaget poured the contents of a short, squat glass of lemonade into a taller, thinner glass. Five-year-olds, who still believed that the shape of the glass determined its contents, thought this glass held more liquid than the first glass. They are in what Piaget termed a *preoperational stage of development*. In contrast, 6-year-olds tended to be unsure, but 7-year-olds knew the amount of lemonade had not changed.

Many developmental specialists no longer believe that children necessarily pass through these fixed stages at the same time. An alternative approach regards children as differing in information-processing capability, or the ability to store and retrieve information from memory (see Chapter 7). The following three segments have been identified by this approach:[63]

1 *Limited*: Below the age of 6, children do not employ storage and retrieval strategies.

2 *Cued*: Children between the ages of 6 and 12 employ these strategies, but only when prompted.

3 *Strategic*: Children aged 12 and older spontaneously employ storage and retrieval strategies.

This sequence of development underscores the notion that children do not think like adults, and they cannot be expected to use information in the same way. It also reminds us that they do not necessarily form the same conclusions as adults do when presented with product information. For example, children are not as likely to realize that something they see on television is not 'real', and as a result they are more vulnerable to persuasive messages. The remaining section of this chapter also considers the role that age plays in our consumption, but from the perspective of how age groups (cohorts) influence our behaviours, and how consumers from different generations truly differ in their approaches to consumption.

AGE AND CONSUMER IDENTITY

The era in which a consumer grows up creates for that person a cultural bond with the millions of others born during the same time period. As we grow older, our needs and preferences change, often in unison with others who are close to our own age. For this reason, a consumer's age exerts a significant influence on their identity. All things being equal, we are more likely than not to have things in common with others of our own age. In the remaining section of this chapter, we explore some of the important characteristics of some key age groups, and consider how marketing strategies must be modified to appeal to diverse age subcultures.

Age cohorts: 'my generation'

► An **age cohort** consists of people of similar ages who have undergone similar experiences. They share many common memories about cultural heroes (e.g. Clint Eastwood vs. Brad Pitt, or Frank Sinatra vs. Kurt Cobain), important historical events (e.g. the 1968 student demonstrations in Paris vs. the fall of the Berlin Wall in 1989), and so on. Although there is no universally accepted way to divide people into age cohorts, each of us seems to have a pretty good idea of what we mean when we refer to 'my generation'.

Marketers often target products and services to one or more specific age cohorts. They recognize that the same offering will probably not appeal to people of different ages, nor will the language and images they use to reach them. In some cases separate campaigns are developed to attract consumers of different ages. For example, travel agencies throughout Europe target youth markets during the months of May and June for low-cost summer holidays to Mallorca, and then target middle-aged, more affluent consumers for the same destination during September and October. What differs in the two campaigns are the media used, the images portrayed and the prices offered.

The appeal of nostalgia

Because consumers within an age group confront crucial life changes at roughly the same time, the values and symbolism used to appeal to them can evoke powerful feelings of nostalgia. Adults aged 30+ are particularly susceptible to this phenomenon.[64] However, young people as well as old are influenced by references to their past. In fact, research indicates that some people are more disposed to be nostalgic than others, regardless of age.

 Multicultural dimensions

Warsaw

The taste of home is here, behind a cold steel counter dominated by a serving lady with an impassive, lined face and a white apron. Tangy pickled cabbage, steaming potatoes, and the watery red slosh of beet soup . . . a timeless combination that has warmed the hearts of generations of Poles, through centuries of hardship and four grim decades of Soviet rule.

To the untrained eye, Warsaw, Poland's gleaming capital, appears to be caught up in a mad race to out-Westernize the West. Here, capitalism is king – skyscrapers plastered in garish billboards dominate the city centre, while European chains like H&M and Zara have taken over brand-new shopping malls, where 20-somethings strut, sipping blended coffees.

> ## ▶ Multicultural dimensions (*continued*)
>
> For a country so recently freed from the clutches of communism, the transformation is astounding. But behind the glittering façade beats the heart of a very different Poland. Milk bars (*bar mleczny*), bare-bones cafés set up by the communist authorities in the 1950s to ensure that everyone had at least one hot meal a day, have somehow managed to survive the onslaught of capitalism. In fact, they are thriving, even in Warsaw's most fashionable districts, and to many Poles they represent a part of Polish culture that all the wonders of the free market can never replace.
>
> Eating in a milk bar is a far cry from fine dining, but for many Poles the experience is priceless. It's a scene that harks back to the days when shiny shopping malls and designer brands were nothing more than vague rumours from the other side of the Iron Curtain. But despite the changes sweeping through Poland, milk bars still attract a fiercely loyal following. At mealtimes the lines can stretch out the door.
>
> Most milk bars seem to have been frozen in time. The interiors, while clean, range from basic to downright drab. Some offer little décor aside from a handful of sturdy potted plants, whitewashed walls, and a menu of classic Polish dishes posted beside the cash register. The staff are apathetic, sometimes even rude. Customers order, are given a ticket to present at the kitchen window, then wait beside the steel-topped counter for their meals to appear.
>
> Incomes have been rising rapidly, and with an abundance of new restaurants cropping up across the country, the Polish government has begun to question the need for milk bars. But Poles refuse to let them go.
>
> Alicja Samarcew, a psychologist who still frequents milk bars about once a week, always makes a point of taking foreign visitors there because, she says, 'It's something really Polish'. Ms Samarcew has her own theories on why these spare cafés are still relevant in Poland, and how an institution imposed by a repressive regime could remain so firmly rooted in the country's collective self-image. 'For one thing, it's a place to socialize,' she says. 'I still meet people there that I've seen for years. They tell the same stories, and everybody knows them. It provides a sense of continuity in people's lives.'
>
> But, she points out, milk bars play an even more important social role. 'I wouldn't say it's real because there are poor people, it's not about that. But you are exposed to different categories of people in a milk bar, and I think this is really important. Old people come, often alone and lonely, and it can be hard to see. When we go to a restaurant, it's easy for us in the middle class to think we're the only people in the city. But when you go to a milk bar, that illusion is gone. Maybe it's something really Polish that we don't isolate these people in ghettos.'[65]

Product sales can be dramatically affected by linking a brand to vivid memories and experiences, especially for items that are associated with childhood or adolescence. Vespa scooters, Hornby electric trains and the coupon 'saving points' from Douwe Egberts coffee are all examples of products that have managed to span two or more generations of loyal consumers, giving the brand a strong equity position in competitive and crowded markets.

Many advertising campaigns have played on the collective memories of consumers by using older celebrities to endorse their products, such as American Express' campaign which featured Eric Clapton and Lou Reed. In Japan, Ringo Starr (the Beatles' drummer) is used to help promote demand for apples. The target market is middle-aged consumers, and it doesn't hurt that, phonetically, 'Ringo' means *apple* in Japanese. To assess just how pervasive nostalgia is, pay attention to television commercials, and notice how often they are produced against a background of 'classic songs'. *Memories* magazine, which was founded to exploit the nostalgia boom, even offers advertisers a discount if they run old ads next to their current ones.

THE TEEN MARKET: IT TOTALLY RULES

With a spending capacity of more than 61 billion euros per year, the European youth market of teens is a powerful demographic and an important culture to understand intimately for businesses looking to grow and maintain relevancy in the future. In 1956, the label 'teenage' first entered the (American) vocabulary, as Frankie Lymon and the

Teenagers became the first pop group to identify themselves with this new subculture. The concept of teenager is a fairly new cultural construction; throughout most of history a person simply made the transition from child to adult (often accompanied by some sort of ritual or ceremony, as we will see in a later chapter). As anyone who has been there knows, puberty and adolescence can be both the best of times and the worst of times. Many exciting changes happen as individuals leave the role of child and prepare to assume the role of adult. These changes create a lot of uncertainty about the self, and the need to belong and to find one's unique identity as a person becomes extremely important. At this age, choices of activities, friends and 'looks' are crucial to social acceptance. Teenagers actively search for cues from their peers and from advertising for the 'right' way to look and behave. Advertising geared to teenagers is typically action-oriented and depicts a group of 'in' teenagers using the product. Teenagers use products to express their identities, to explore the world and their new-found freedom in it, and also to rebel against the authority of their parents and other socializing agents. Marketers often do their best to assist in this process. The range of consumer products targeted at teenagers (and particularly young ones) is greater than ever. Then again, so is teenagers' disposable income from part-time jobs and weekly pocket money.[66]

Teenagers in every culture grapple with fundamental developmental issues as they make the transition from childhood to adult. According to research by Saatchi & Saatchi, there are four themes of conflict common to all teens:

1 *Autonomy vs. belonging.* Teenagers need to acquire independence so they try to break away from their families. On the other hand, they need to attach themselves to a support structure, such as peers, to avoid being alone. A thriving Internet subculture has developed to serve this purpose, as has text messaging via mobile phones.[67] The Net (World Wide Web) has become the preferred method of communication for many young people, since its anonymity makes it easier to talk to people of the opposite sex, or of different ethnic and racial groups.[68]

2 *Rebellion vs. conformity.* Teenagers need to rebel against social standards of appearance and behaviour, yet they still need to fit in and be accepted by others. Cult products that cultivate a rebellious image are prized for this reason. Skeleteens, a line of natural soft drinks in flavours like Brain Wash, Black Lemonade and DOA, developed such a following thanks to its 'dangerous' mystique. This underground product was first discovered by California bikers in America, who were drawn to the images of skulls and crossbones on the labels.[69]

3 *Idealism vs. pragmatism.* Teenagers tend to view adults as hypocrites, while they see themselves as being sincere. They have to struggle to reconcile their view of how the world should be with the realities they perceive around them.

4 *Narcissism vs. intimacy.* Teenagers can be obsessed with their appearance and needs. On the other hand, they also feel the desire to connect with others on a meaningful level.[70]

Teenagers throughout history have had to cope with insecurity, parental authority and peer pressure. At the start of the new millennium, however, these issues are compounded by concerns about the environment, racism, AIDS and other pressing social problems. Today's teenagers often have to cope with additional family pressures as well, especially if they live in non-traditional families where they must take significant responsibility for shopping, cooking and housework. Marketers have a difficult time 'defining' the values of today's European teens, perhaps because they are living in such socially dynamic and demanding times. A study among 500 young opinion leaders aged 14–20 across 16 European countries suggests that this age group's credo should be: 'Don't define us – we'll define ourselves'. Respondents were asked their opinions on a wide range of subjects, from new technology to family relationships, divorce, drugs, alcohol, politics, fashion, entertainment, sex and advertising. Some of the highlights of this study[71] are:

- Living life to the 'fullest' is mandatory; ambition drives them, as does the fear of failure. Young eastern Europeans strongly believe that hard work will give them a high standard of living and education is their passport to this better life.

- They perceive the 'digitized' future as one that lacks warmth – something Europe's teenagers, a divorce-experienced generation, is actively seeking.

- New technology which allows for '24-hour commerce' will lead to further stress for this generation, and a blurring of home/office means they will work longer and harder than any previous generation.

- The phone at home is still a central method for teens to talk to each other, although mobile phones are quickly penetrating this group's social network.

- This is a very visually literate generation, with clear understanding of a commercial's aims. Clichés will not be tolerated, and will lead to immediate rejection, particularly in the Nordic countries. Only eastern European teens have yet to achieve this level of 'advertising cynicism'.

- This generation is both brand-aware and brand-dismissive. It represents an opportunity, but not a homogeneous market. The successful marketer will be aware that for these consumers, an aspirational quality is essential, that heritage is an advantage, and that nothing is forever.

BABY BUSTERS: 'GENERATION X'

The cohort of consumers between the ages of 18 and 29 consists of over 30 million Europeans who will be a powerful force in years to come. This group, which has been ▶ labelled 'Generation X', 'slackers' or 'busters' was profoundly affected by the economic downturn in the first part of the 1990s. So-called baby busters include many people, both in and out of higher education, whose tastes and priorities are beginning to be felt in fashion, popular culture, politics and marketing. While the percentage of Europeans aged 25–29 is high in terms of completing upper secondary education (71 per cent in 1999, compared with 50 per cent of persons aged 50–59), this group also has a large drop-out rate, with one in five Europeans between the ages of 18 and 24 leaving the education system without completing a qualification beyond lower secondary schooling.[72]

Marketing to busters or marketing bust?

Although the income of this age cohort is below expectations, they still constitute a formidable market segment – partly because so many still live at home and have more discretionary income. Busters in their twenties are estimated to have an annual spending power of $125 billion, and their purchases are essential to the fortunes of such product categories as beer, fast food and cosmetics.

Because many busters have been doing the family shopping for a long time, marketers are finding that they are much more sophisticated about evaluating advertising and products. They are turned off by advertising that either contains a lot of hype or takes itself too seriously. They see advertising as a form of entertainment but are turned off by over commercialization.[73]

Perhaps one reason why marketers, efforts to appeal to Xers with messages of alienation, cynicism and despair have not succeeded is that many people in their twenties are not depressed after all! Generation Xers are quite a diverse group – they don't all wear reversed baseball caps and work in temporary, low-paid, mindless jobs. Despite the birth of dozens of magazines catering to 'riot grrrls' and other angry Xers with names like *Axcess*, *Project X* and *KGB*, the most popular magazine for 20-something women is *Cosmopolitan*. What seems to make this age cohort the angriest is constantly being labelled as angry by the media![74]

BABY BOOMERS

The baby boomers cohort (born between 1946 and 1964) are the source of many fundamental cultural and economic changes. The reason: power in numbers. As the Second World War ended, they began to establish families and careers at a record pace. Imagine a large python that has swallowed a mouse: the mouse moves down the length of the python, creating a moving bulge as it goes. So it is with baby boomers. In 2003 there were 76 million elderly people aged 65 and over in the EU-27 countries, compared with only 38 million in 1960. The baby boomers, ageing, coupled with extended longevity, and the overall lower fertility levels in the EU means that the population will continue to grow older for the coming decades.[75]

The market impact of boomers

Figure 11.3 shows a series of three age pyramids of the European population for both youth and boomers for a 40-year period, from 2010 to 2050.[76] Note how the top of the pyramid continues to get wider in each successive projection. This increase in the proportion of older citizens and decrease in the proportion of youth is often referred to as the 'greying and de-greening' of the European population, a structural trend which has major implications for the marketing of goods and services.

As teenagers in the 1960s and 1970s, this generation created a revolution in style, politics and consumer attitudes. As they have aged, their collective will has been behind cultural events as diverse as the Paris student demonstrations and hippies in the 1960s and Thatcherism and yuppies in the 1980s. Now that they are older, they continue to influence popular culture in important ways.

This 'mouse in the python' has moved into its mid-forties to early sixties, and is the age group that exerts the most impact on consumption patterns. Most of the growth in the market will be accounted for by people who are moving into their peak earning years. As one commercial for VH1, the music-video network that caters to those who are a bit too old for MTV, pointed out, 'The generation that dropped acid to escape reality . . . is the generation that drops antacid to cope with it'. Boomers tend to have different emotional and psychological needs from those who came before them, and this is being played out again throughout European markets. In the first decade of the twenty-first century, Boomers are busy rethinking their role in 'retirement' (which is to say, new identities, and new consumption activities). Boomers see themselves not so much in chronological age, but as simply entering in a new life stage which is full of new opportunities.[77]

THE GREY MARKET

The old widowed woman sits alone in her clean but sparsely furnished apartment, while the television blares out a soap opera. Each day, she slowly and painfully makes her way out of the apartment and goes to the corner shop to buy essentials, bread, milk and vegetables, always being careful to pick the least expensive offering. Most of the time she sits in her rocking chair, thinking sadly of her dead husband and the good times she used to have.

Is this the image you have of a typical elderly consumer? Until recently, many marketers did. As a result, they largely neglected the elderly in their feverish pursuit of the baby boomer market. But as our population ages and people are living longer and healthier lives, the game is rapidly changing. A lot of businesses are beginning to replace the old stereotype of the poor recluse. The newer, more accurate image is of an elderly person who is active, interested in what life has to offer, and is an enthusiastic consumer with the means and willingness to buy many goods and services.

Figure 11.3 European age pyramids, 2010–2050

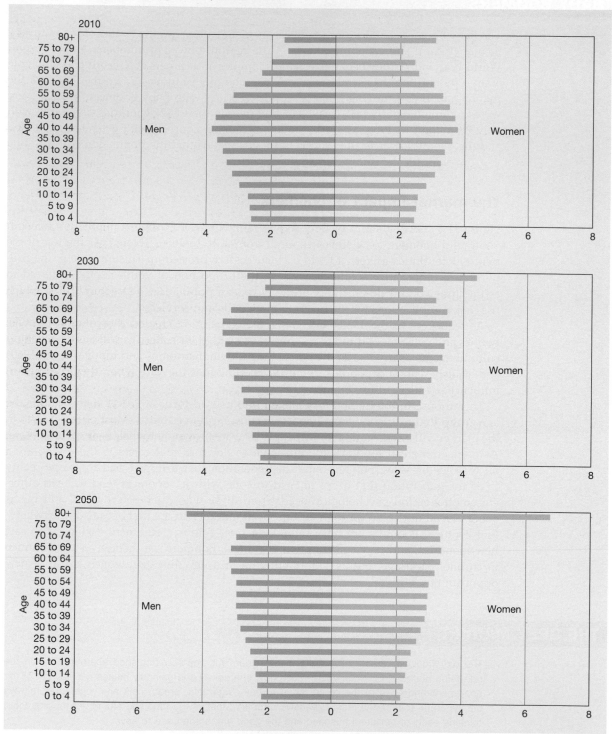

Grey power: shattering stereotypes

By the year 2010, 20 per cent of Europeans will be 62 or older. This fastest-growing age segment can be explained by the ageing of 'boomers' an increase in awareness of healthy lifestyles and nutrition, coupled with improved medical diagnoses and treatment. Over the past 50 years, life expectancy of men and women has risen steadily: by around 10 years for each sex. Throughout the EU, women live longer than men. In 1998 the life expectancy of women in the EU-15 countries was 81 years, while that for men was 75. Estimates are that the life expectancy of women and men may reach 84 and 78 years respectively by the year 2020.[78] Not only is this segment growing and living longer, but older adults have large amounts of discretionary income, since they typically have paid off their mortgage, and no longer have the expense of raising and educating children.

Most elderly people lead more active, multidimensional lives than we assume. Many engage in voluntary work, continue to work and/or are involved in daily care of a grand-child. Still, outdated images of mature consumers persist. In one survey, one-third of consumers over age 55 reported that they deliberately did *not* buy a product because of the way an elderly person was stereotyped in the product's advertising.[79]

Seniors' economic clout

There is abundant evidence that the economic health of elderly consumers is good and getting better. Some of the important areas that stand to benefit from the surging **grey market** include holidays, cars, home improvements, cruises and tourism, cosmetic surgery and skin treatments, health, finance and legal matters, and 'how-to' books for learning to cope with retirement.

It is crucial to remember that income alone does not capture the spending power of this group. As mentioned above, elderly consumers are no longer burdened with the financial obligations that drain the income of younger consumers. Elderly consumers are much more likely to own their home, have no mortgage or have a (low-cost or subsidized) rented house or apartment. Across Europe, approximately 50 per cent of pensioners'

Europe's fastest-growing age segment continues to re-define the meaning of 'ageing' by remaining active, and having multidimensional lifestyles and activities.

Saga Publishing Ltd.

Table 11.2 Amounts paid out in pensions as a percentage of final salary

Salary	€20,000	€50,000
Belgium	58%	45%
Finland	60%	59%
France	67%	51%
Germany	45%	43%
Greece	70%	48%
Ireland	53%	21%
Italy	78%	75%
The Netherlands	76%	31%
Portugal	74%	74%
Spain	94%	63%
UK	35%	14%
USA (for comparison)	71%	45%

Note: Different systems are not always directly comparable, as some base pensions on final salary, while others on average salary. Higher-income workers are treated differently, depending on country.

Sources: Fitch Investor Services; *Wall Street Journal* (30 October 2000): A21.

income still comes from state pensions, yet it is clear that older consumers are time-rich, and have a significant amount of discretionary income to spend.[80] The relatively high living standards of future retirees (the baby boomers) and the stability of public finances (until the current economic forecast) in different European states has led to an active discussion of pension reform plans throughout the EU. Nonetheless, pensions will continue to play an important role in the discretionary incomes of Europe's retired population. Table 11.2 shows the amounts paid out in pensions as a percentage of final salary. As a final note on the two major demographic trends in Europe, let's link together the 'greying' and the 'de-greening' populations. Figure 11.4 shows the dependency ratio of the number of people in the EU-27 countries over the age of 65, relative to the number of people aged 15–64 (those who are theoretically still employed).[81] While Japan (JP) faces the most critical scenario, the EU is also looking at a future with a greater percentage of the elderly, relative to a smaller percentage of younger people. This will have significant implications for social security payments, and the offerings of goods and services.

Figure 11.4 Old age dependency ratio

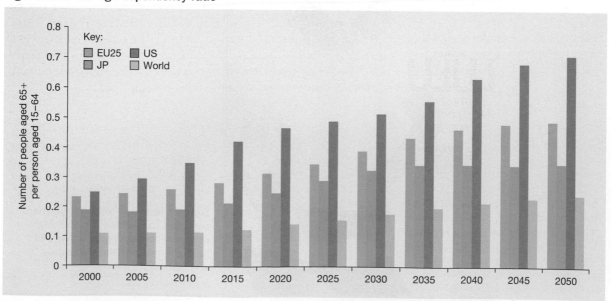

Researchers have identified a set of key values that are relevant to older consumers. For marketing strategies to succeed, they should be related to one or more of these factors:[82]

- *Autonomy.* Mature consumers want to lead active lives and to be self-sufficient. Financial services and financial planning are increasing markets for the elderly segment, who have a strong need to remain independent. While companies are the largest purchasers of cars in the UK, the majority of private buyers are 'greys' – a further sign of their financial muscle and desire for autonomy.[83]

- *Connectedness.* Mature consumers value the bonds they have with friends and family. While the 'grey' do not relate well to their own age group (most elderly report feeling on average ten years younger than they are, and feel that 'other' elderly behave 'older' than they do), they do value information which communicates clear benefits to cohorts in their age group. Advertisements which avoid patronizing stereotypes are well received.

- *Altruism.* Mature consumers want to give something back to the world. Thrifty Car Rental found in a survey that over 40 per cent of older consumers would select a rental car company if it sponsored a programme that gives discounts to senior citizens' centres. Based on this research, the company launched its highly successful 'Give a Friend a Lift' programme.

- *Personal growth.* Mature consumers are very interested in trying new experiences and developing their potential. By installing user-friendly interactive touch-screen computer stations in European stores, GNC has found that older consumers have become better educated about health issues, and are loyal to the brand.[84]

Perceived age: you're only as old as you feel

The 'grey' market does not consist of a uniform segment of vigorous, happy, ready-to-spend consumers – nor is it a group of senile, economically marginalized, immobile people. In fact, research confirms the popular wisdom that age is more a state of mind than of body. A person's mental outlook and activity level has a lot more to do with their longevity and quality of life than does *chronological age*, or the actual number of years lived. In addition to these psychological dimensions of age, there are also cultural influences on what constitutes ageing, and perceptions of what is 'elderly' across different European markets.[85]

▶ A better yardstick to categorize the elderly is **perceived age**, or how old a person feels. Perceived age can be measured on several dimensions, including 'feel-age' (how old a person feels) and 'look-age' (how old a person looks).[86] The older consumers get, the younger they feel relative to actual age. For this reason, many marketers emphasize product benefits rather than age appropriateness in marketing campaigns, since many consumers will not relate to products targeted to their chronological age.[87]

▼ Marketing pitfall

Some marketing efforts targeted at the elderly have backfired because they reminded people of their age or presented their age group in an unflattering way. One of the more infamous blunders was committed by Heinz. A company analyst found that many elderly people were buying baby food because of the small portions and easy chewing consistency, so Heinz introduced a line of 'Senior Foods' made especially for denture wearers.

Needless to say, the product failed. Consumers did not want to admit that they required strained foods (even to the supermarket cashier). They preferred to purchase baby foods, which they could pretend they were buying for a grandchild.

In Holland, a country where bicycles are an important mode of personal transportation, a specially designed 'elderly bicycle' was a resounding failure in spite of its

▶

▼ Marketing pitfall (*continued*)

competitive product benefits. While conventional marketing wisdom would suggest that a firm communicate its unique functional benefits to a target market, this wisdom backfired for the Dutch 'greys'. Positioning the bicycle as an easy-to-pedal 'senior bicycle' was met with a negative response, as the Dutch elderly who still ride a bicycle (a common sight in Holland) feel too young to be riding a 'senior' bike.[88]

Finally, there is growing evidence throughout the UK and Europe that National Health Care Programmes in these countries need to start paying more attention to the elderly with respect to informative messages regarding the risk and spread of Sexually Transmitted Infections (!). As an age cohort, Seniors are increasingly put themselves at risk by not using condoms (contraception no longer being an issue), and not knowing the sexual history of their partners. Older people are increasingly likely to be single or undergoing relationship changes and are less likely to consistently use condoms, perhaps because the risk of pregnancy no longer exists. Increased international travel, Internet dating, the growing use of drugs such as Viagra to counter erectile dysfunction and overlapping sexual networks have been identified to be factors.[89]

Segmenting seniors

The senior subculture represents an extremely large market: the number of Europeans aged 62 and over exceeds the entire population of Canada.[90] Because this group is so large, it is helpful to think of the mature market as consisting of four subsegments: an 'older' group (aged 55–64), an 'elderly' group (aged 65–74), an 'aged' group (aged 75–84) and finally a 'very old' group (85+).[91]

The elderly market is well suited for segmentation. Older consumers are easy to identify by age and stage in the family life cycle. Most receive social security benefits so they can be located without much effort, and many subscribe to one of the magazines targeted to the elderly, discussed earlier in this section. *Saga Magazine* in the UK has the largest circulation of any European magazine, with over 750,000 monthly readers. Selling holidays and insurance to the over-50s, the parent company also makes use of a database with over 4 million over-50s.

Several segmentation approaches begin with the premise that a major determinant of elderly marketplace behaviour is the way a person deals with being old.[92] *Social ageing theories* try to understand how society assigns people to different roles across the lifespan. For example, when someone retires they may reflect society's expectations for someone at this life stage – this is a major transition point when people exit from many relationships.[93] Some people become depressed, withdrawn and apathetic as they age, some are angry and resist the thought of ageing, and some appear to accept the new challenges and opportunities this period of life has to offer.

In general, the elderly have been shown to respond positively to ads that provide an abundance of information. Unlike other age groups, these consumers are not usually amused, or persuaded, by imagery-oriented advertising. A more successful strategy involves the construction of advertising that depicts the aged as well-integrated, con-tributing members of society, with emphasis on them expanding their horizons rather than clinging precariously to life.

Some basic guidelines have been suggested for effective advertising to the elderly. These include the following:[94]

- Keep language simple.
- Use clear, bright pictures.
- Use action to attract attention.
- Speak clearly, and keep the word count low.
- Use a single sales message, and emphasize brand extensions to tap consumers' familiarity.
- Avoid extraneous stimuli (excessive pictures and graphics can detract from the message).

CHAPTER SUMMARY

- Many purchasing decisions are made by more than one person. Collective decision-making occurs whenever two or more people are involved in evaluating, selecting or using a product or service.

- Demographics are statistics that measure a population's characteristics. Some of the most important of these relate to family structure, e.g. the birth rate, the marriage rate and the divorce rate. In Europe, collecting reliable and comparable data regarding the family unit has not always been a straightforward process.

- A household is an occupied housing unit. The number and type of European households is changing in many ways, for example through delays in getting married and having children, and in the composition of family households, which increasingly are headed by a single parent. New perspectives on the family life cycle, which focuses on how people's needs change as they move through different stages in their lives, are forcing marketers to consider more seriously such consumer segments as homosexuals, divorcees and childless couples when they develop targeting strategies.

- Families must be understood in terms of their decision-making dynamics. Spouses in particular have different priorities and exert varying amounts of influence in terms of effort and power. Children are also increasingly influential during a widening range of purchase decisions.

- Children undergo a process of socialization, whereby they learn how to be consumers. Some of this knowledge is instilled by parents and friends, but a lot of it comes from exposure to mass media and advertising. Since children are in some cases so easily persuaded, the ethical aspects of marketing to them are hotly debated among consumers, academics and marketing practitioners.

- Europeans have many things in common with others merely because they are about the same age or live in the same country, or same part of the country. Consumers who grew up at the same time share many cultural memories, so they may respond to marketers' *nostalgia* appeals that remind them of these experiences.

- Important age cohorts include teenagers, 18 to 29-year-olds, baby boomers and the elderly. *Teenagers* are making a transition from childhood to adulthood, and their self-concepts tend to be unstable. They are receptive to products that help them to be accepted and enable them to assert their independence. Because many teenagers receive allowances, and/or earn pocket money but have few financial obligations, they are a particularly important segment for many non-essential or expressive products, ranging from chewing gum to hair gel, to clothing fashions and music. Because of changes in family structure, many teenagers are taking more responsibility for their families, day-to-day shopping and routine purchase decisions.

- *'Gen-Xers'*, consumers aged 18–29, are a difficult group for marketers to 'get a clear picture of'. They will be a powerful force in the years to come, whose tastes and priorities will be felt in fashion, popular culture, politics and marketing.

- *Baby boomers* are the most powerful age segment because of their size and economic clout. As this group has aged, its interests have changed and marketing priorities have changed as well. The needs and desires of baby boomers have a strong influence on demands for housing, childcare, cars, clothing and so on. Only a small proportion of boomers fit into an affluent, materialistic category.

- As the population ages, the needs of *elderly* consumers will also become increasingly influential. Many marketers traditionally ignored the elderly because of the stereotype that they are inactive and spend too little. This stereotype is no longer accurate. Most of the elderly are healthy, vigorous and interested in new products and experiences – and they have the income to purchase them. Marketing appeals to this age subculture should focus on consumers, self-concepts and perceived ages, which tend to be more youthful than their chronological ages. Marketers should emphasize the concrete benefits of products, since this group tends to be sceptical of vague, image-related promotions. Personalized service is of particular importance to this segment.

▶ KEY TERMS

Accommodative purchase decision (p. 431)

Age cohort (p. 437)

Autocratic decisions (p. 431)

Cognitive development (p. 436)

Consensual purchase decision (p. 431)

Consumer socialization (p. 433)

Extended family (p. 425)

Family financial officer (FFO) (p. 432)

Family household (p. 425)

Family life cycle (FLC) (p. 429)

Fertility rate (p. 426)

Generation X (p. 440)

Grey market (p. 443)

Kin network system (p. 432)

Nuclear family (p. 426)

Parental yielding (p. 433)

Perceived age (p. 445)

Stage of cognitive development (p. 436)

Syncratic decisions (p. 431)

▶ CONSUMER BEHAVIOUR CHALLENGE

1 Review a number of popular media which are published in countries in southern Europe as well as media targeted for northern European countries. How do the ads' depictions of *family* seem to differ by region? In what sorts of consumption situations do they seem highly similar? Why?

2 For each of the following five product categories – groceries, cars, holidays, furniture and appliances – describe the ways in which you believe a married couple's choices would be affected if they had children.

3 In identifying and targeting newly divorced couples, do you think marketers are exploiting these couples' situations? Are there instances where you think marketers may actually be helpful to them? Support your answers with examples.

4 Arrange to interview two married couples, one younger and one older. Prepare a response form listing five product categories – groceries, furniture, appliances, holidays and cars – and ask each spouse to indicate, without consulting the other, whether purchases in each category are made by joint or unilateral decisions and to indicate whether the unilateral decisions are made by the husband or the wife. Compare each couples' responses for agreement between husbands and wives relative to who makes the decisions and compare both couples' overall responses for differences relative to the number of joint versus unilateral decisions. Report your findings and conclusions.

5 Collect ads for three different product categories in which the family is targeted. Find another set of ads for different brands of the same items in which the family is not featured. Prepare a report on the effectiveness of the approaches.

6 Observe the interactions between parents and children in the cereal section of a local supermarket. Prepare a report on the number of children who expressed preferences, how they expressed their preferences and how parents responded, including the number who purchased the child's choice.

7 Select a product category and, using the life cycle stages given in the chapter, list the variables that will affect a purchase decision for the product by consumers in each stage of the cycle.

8 Consider three important changes in modern European family structure. For each, find an example of a marketer who has attempted to be conscious of this change as reflected in product communications, retailing innovations, or other aspects of the marketing mix. If possible, also try to find examples of marketers who have failed to keep up with these developments.

9 Why did baby boomers have such an important impact on consumer culture in the second half of the twentieth century?

10 How has the baby boomlet changed attitudes towards child-rearing practices and created demand for different products and services?

11 Is it practical to assume that people aged 55 and older constitute one large consumer market? What are some approaches to further segmenting this age subculture?

12 What are some important variables to keep in mind when tailoring marketing strategies to the elderly?

13 Find good and bad examples of advertising targeted at elderly consumers. To what degree does advertising stereotype the elderly? What elements of ads or other promotions appear to determine their effectiveness in reaching and persuading this group?

For additional material see the companion website at **www.pearsoned.co.uk/solomon**

NOTES

1. 'Demographic Change: Challenge or Opportunity?' Eurostat, *Europe in Figures*, Eurostat yearbook: 31, 2008.
2. T. Eggerickx and F. Bégeot, 'Les recensements en Europe dans les années 1990. De la diversité des pratiques nationales à la comparabilité internationales des résulats', *Population* 41(2) (1993): 327–48. Standardization efforts continue. See *The Social Situation in the European Union*, an annual report commissioned by the European Council, and published by Eurostat.
3. *The Life of Women and Men in Europe: A Statistical Portrait* (2008), Eurostat: 22.
4. Robert Boutilier, 'Diversity in family structures', *American Demographics Marketing Tools* (1993): 4–6; W. Bradford Fay, 'Families in the 1990s: Universal values, uncommon experiences', *Marketing Research* 5 (Winter 1993) 1: 47.
5. Ellen Graham, 'Craving closer ties, strangers come together as family', *The Wall Street Journal* (4 March 1996): B1 (2).
6. Amber M. Epp and Linda L. Price (2008), 'Family identity: A framework of identity interplay in consumption practices', *Journal of Consumer Research*, June: 50–70; see also David Cheal, 'The ritualization of family ties', *American Behavioral Scientist* 31 (July/August 1988): 632.
7. 'Women and men in the European Union: a statistical portrait' (Luxembourg: Office for Official Publications of the European Communities, 1996); 'Families come first', *Psychology Today* (September 1988): 11.
8. Alan R. Andreasen, 'Life status changes and changes in consumer preferences and satisfaction', *Journal of Consumer Research* 11 (December 1984): 784–94; James H. McAlexander, John W. Schouten and Scott D. Roberts, 'Consumer behavior and divorce', *Research in Consumer Behavior* 6 (1993): 153–84.
9. 'Men and women in the European Union: a statistical portrait' (Luxembourg: Office for Official Publications of the European Communities, 1995); 'The big picture', *American Demographics* (March 1989): 22–7; Thomas G. Exter, 'Middle-aging households', *American Demographics* (July 1992): 63.
10. 'Trends in households in the European Union: 1995–2025', *Eurostat, Statistics in Focus*, Theme 3-24/2003 (Luxembourg: Office for Official Publications of the European Communities, 2004).
11. 'The population of the EU on 1 January, 1995', *Statistics in Focus. Population and Social Conditions*, no. 8 (Luxembourg: Office for Official Publications of the European Communities,

1995); Nicholas Timmins, 'One in five women to remain childless', *The Independent* (4 October 1995).
12. 'Trends in households in the European Union: 1995–2025', *op. cit.*: 14.
13. Edward del Rosario (2008), 'No Babies?' *New York Times*, 26 June 2008, http://www.nytimes.com/2008/06/29/magazine/29Birth-t.html?_r=2&oref=slogin&oref=slogin
14. 'Men and women in the European Union: a statistical portrait', *op. cit.*: 72.
15. Peg Masterson, 'Agency notes rise of singles market', *Advertising Age* (9 August 1993): 17.
16. Christy Fisher, 'Census data may make ads more single minded', *Advertising Age* (20 July 1992): 2.
17. Calmetta Y. Coleman, 'The unseemly secrets of eating alone', *The Wall Street Journal* (6 July 1995): B1 (2).
18. Stephanie Shipp, 'How singles spend', *American Demographics* (April 1988): 22–7; Patricia Braus, 'Sex and the single spender', *American Demographics* (November 1993): 28–34.
19. 'Men and women in the European Union: a statistical ortrait', *op. cit.*: 76.
20. 'Census paints a new picture of family life', *The New York Times* (30 August 1994): 22.
21. Gary Younge, 'Parents face a £66,000 bill', *The Guardian* (27 May 1996); Liz Hunt, 'The cost of growing: Schoolchildren need huge sums', *The Independent* (19 August 1996).
22. 'Trends in households in the European Union: 1995–2025', *op. cit.*
23. Mary C. Gilly and Ben M. Enis, 'Recycling the Family Life Cycle: A Proposal for Redefinition', in Andrew A. Mitchell (ed.), *Advances in Consumer Research* 9 (Ann Arbor, MI: Association for Consumer Research, 1982): 271–6.
24. Charles M. Schaninger and William D. Danko, 'A conceptual and empirical comparison of alternative household life cycle models', *Journal of Consumer Research* 19 (March 1993): 580–94; Robert E. Wilkes, 'Household life-cycle stages, transitions, and product expenditures', *Journal of Consumer Research* 22(1) (June 1995): 27–42.
25. These categories are an adapted version of an FLC model proposed by Gilly and Enis (1982). Based on a recent empirical comparison of several competing models, Schaninger and Danko found that this framework outperformed others, especially in terms of its treatment of non-conventional households, though they recommend several improvements to this model as well. See Gilly and Enis, 'Recycling the family life cycle: a proposal for redefinition', in Mitchell (ed.),

Advances in Consumer Research 9; Schaninger and Danko, 'A conceptual and empirical comparison of alternate household life cycle markets', *op. cit.*; Scott D. Roberts, Patricia K. Voli and KerenAmi Johnson, 'Beyond the Family Life Cycle: An Inventory of Variables for Defining the Family as a Consumption Unit', in Victoria L. Crittenden (ed.), *Developments in Marketing Science* 15 (Coral Gables, FL: Academy of Marketing Science, 1992): 71–5.

26. Carolyn F. Curasi, Linda L. Price, and Eric J. Arnould (2004), 'How individuals' cherished possessions become families' inalienable wealth', *Journal of Consumer Research* 31 (December): 609–22; Tonya Williams Bradford (2009), 'Intergenerationally gifted asset disposition', *Journal of Consumer Research* 36, in press.

27. James H. McAlexander, John W. Schouten and Scott D. Roberts, 'Consumer Behavior and Divorce', in *Research in Consumer Behavior* (Greenwich, CT: JAI Press, 1992); Michael R. Solomon, 'The role of products as social stimuli: A symbolic interactionism perspective', *Journal of Consumer Research* 10 (December 1983): 319–29; Melissa Martin Young, 'Disposition of Possession During Role Transitions', in Rebecca H. Holman and Michael R. Solomon (eds), *Advances in Consumer Research* 18 (Provo, UT: Association for Consumer Research, 1991): 33–9.

28. Harry L. Davis, 'Decision making within the household', *Journal of Consumer Research* 2 (March 1972): 241–60; Michael B. Menasco and David J. Curry, 'Utility and choice: An empirical study of wife/husband decision making', *Journal of Consumer Research* 16 (June 1989): 87–97; for a recent review, see Conway Lackman and John M. Lanasa, 'Family decision-making theory: An overview and assessment', *Psychology and Marketing* 10 (March/April 1993) 2: 81–94.

29. Shannon Dortch, 'Money and marital discord', *American Demographics* (October 1994): 11(3).

30. Daniel Seymour and Greg Lessne, 'Spousal conflict arousal: Scale development', *Journal of Consumer Research* 11 (December 1984): 810–21.

31. For recent research on factors influencing how much influence adolescents exert in family decision-making, see Ellen Foxman, Patriya Tansuhaj and Karin M. Ekstrom, 'Family members' perceptions of adolescents' influence in family decision making', *Journal of Consumer Research* 15 (March 1989) 4: 482–91; Sharon E. Beatty and Salil Talpade, 'Adolescent influence in family decision making: A replication with extension', *Journal of Consumer Research* 21 (September 1994) 2: 332–41.

32. Diane Crispell, 'Dual-earner diversity', *American Demographics* (July 1995): 32–7.

33. Robert Boutilier, *Targeting Families: Marketing To and Through the New Family* (Ithaca, NY: American Demographics Books, 1993).

34. Darach Turley, 'Dialogue with the departed', in F. Hansen (ed.), *European Advances in Consumer Research* 2 (Provo, UT: Association for Consumer Research, 1995): 10–13.

35. Dennis L. Rosen and Donald H. Granbois, 'Determinants of role structure in family financial management', *Journal of Consumer Research* 10 (September 1983): 253–8.

36. Robert F. Bales, *Interaction Process Analysis: A Method for the Study of Small Groups* (Reading, MA: Addison-Wesley, 1950); for a cross-gender comparison of food shopping strategies, see Rosemary Polegato and Judith L. Zaichkowsky, 'Family food shopping: Strategies used by husbands and wives', *The Journal of Consumer Affairs* 28 (1994): 2.

37. Alma S. Baron, 'Working parents: Shifting traditional roles', *Business* 37 (January/March 1987): 36; William J. Qualls, 'Household decision behavior: The impact of husbands' and wives' sex role orientation', *Journal of Consumer Research* 14 (September 1987): 264–79; Charles M. Schaninger and W. Christian Buss, 'The relationship of sex role norms to household task allocation', *Psychology and Marketing* 2 (Summer 1985): 93–104.

38. Cynthia Webster, 'Effects of Hispanic ethnic identification on marital roles in the purchase decision process', *Journal of Consumer Research* 21 (September 1994) 2: 319–31; for a recent study that examined the effects of family depictions in advertising among Hispanic consumers, see Gary D. Gregory and James M. Munch, 'Cultural values in international advertising: an examination of familial norms and roles in Mexico', *Psychology and Marketing* 14(2) (March 1997): 99–120.

39. Gary L. Sullivan and P.J. O'Connor, 'The family purchase decision process: A cross-cultural review and framework for research', *Southwest Journal of Business and Economics* (Fall 1988): 43; Marilyn Lavin, 'Husband-dominant, wife-dominant, joint', *Journal of Consumer Marketing* 10 (1993) 3: 33–42; Nicholas Timmins, 'New man fails to survive into the nineties', *The Independent* (25 January 1996). See also Roger J. Baran, 'Patterns of Decision Making Influence for Selected Products and Services Among Husbands and Wives Living in the Czech Republic', in Hansen (ed.), *European Advances in Consumer Research* 2; Jan Pahl, 'His money, her money: Recent research on financial organization in marriage', *Journal of Economic Psychology* 16 (1995): 361–76; Carole B. Burgoyne, 'Financial organization and decision-making within Western "households"', *Journal of Economic Psychology* 16 (1995): 421–30; Erich Kirchler, 'Spouses' joint purchase decisions: Determinants of influence tactics for muddling through the process', *Journal of Economic Psychology* 14 (1993): 405–38.

40. Micaela DiLeonardo, 'The female world of cards and holidays: Women, families, and the work of kinship', *Signs* 12 (Spring 1942): 440–53.

41. C. Whan Park, 'Joint decisions in home purchasing: A muddling through process', *Journal of Consumer Research* 9 (September 1982): 151–62; see also William J. Qualls and Françoise Jaffe, 'Measuring Conflict in Household Decision Behavior: Read My Lips and Read My Mind', in John F. Sherry Jr and Brian Sternthal (eds), *Advances in Consumer Research* 19 (Provo, UT: Association for Consumer Research, 1992).

42. Kim P. Corfman and Donald R. Lehmann, 'Models of cooperative group decision-making and relative influence: An experimental investigation of family purchase decisions', *Journal of Consumer Research* 14 (June 1987).

43. Alison M. Torrillo, 'Dens are men's territory', *American Demographics* (January 1995): 11(2).

44. Charles Atkin, 'Observation of parent–child interaction in supermarket decision-making', *Journal of Marketing* 42 (October 1978).

45. Les Carlson, Ann Walsh, Russell N. Laczniak and Sanford Grossbart, 'Family communication patterns and marketplace motivations, attitudes, and behaviors of children and mothers', *Journal of Consumer Affairs* 28(1) (Summer 1994): 25–53; see also Roy L. Moore and George P. Moschis, 'The role of family communication in consumer learning', *Journal of Communication* 31 (Autumn 1981): 42–51.

46. Leslie Isler, Edward T. Popper and Scott Ward, 'Children's purchase requests and parental responses: Results from a diary study', *Journal of Advertising Research* 27 (October/November 1987).

47. Scott Ward, 'Consumer Socialization', in Harold H. Kassarjian and Thomas S. Robertson (eds), *Perspectives in Consumer Behavior* (Glenville, IL: Scott, Foresman, 1980): 380.

48. Thomas Lipscomb, 'Indicators of materialism in children's free speech: Age and gender comparisons', *Journal of Consumer Marketing* (Fall 1988): 41–6.

49. George P. Moschis, 'The role of family communication in consumer socialization of children and adolescents', *Journal of Consumer Research* 11 (March 1985): 898–913.

50. James U. McNeal and Chyon-Hwa Yeh, 'Born to shop', *American Demographics* (June 1993): 34–9.

51. See Les Carlson, Sanford Grossbart and J. Kathleen Stuenkel, 'The role of parental socialization types on differential family communication patterns regarding consumption', *Journal of Consumer Psychology* 1 (1992) 1: 31–52.

52. See Patricia M. Greenfield, Emily Yut, Mabel Chung, Deborah Land, Holly Kreider, Maurice Pantoja and Kris Horsley, 'The program-length commercial: A study of the effects of television/toy tie-ins on imaginative play', *Psychology and Marketing* 7 (Winter 1990): 237–56 for a study on the effects of commercial programming on creative play.

53. Jill Goldsmith, 'Ga, ga, goo, goo, where's the remote? TV show targets tots', *Dow Jones Business News* (5 February 1997), accessed via *The Wall Street Journal Interactive Edition* (6 February 1997).

54. Gerald J. Gorn and Renee Florsheim, 'The effects of commercials for adult products on children', *Journal of Consumer Research* 11 (March 1985): 9, 62–7; for a study that assessed the impact of violent commercials on children, see V. Kanti Prasad and Lois J. Smith, 'Television commercials in violent programming: an experimental evaluation of their effects on children', *Journal of the Academy of Marketing Science* 22 (1994) 4: 340–51.

55. Glenn Collins, 'New studies on "girl toys" and "boy toys"', *New York Times* (13 February 1984): D1.

56. Susan B. Kaiser, 'Clothing and the social organization of gender perception: A developmental approach', *Clothing and Textiles Research Journal* 7 (Winter 1989): 46–56.

57. D.W. Rajecki, Jill Ann Dame, Kelly Jo Creek, P.J. Barrickman, Catherine A. Reid and Drew C. Appleby, 'Gender casting in television toy advertisements: Distributions, message content analysis, and evaluations', *Journal of Consumer Psychology* 2 (1993) 3: 307–27.

58. Lori Schwartz and William Markham, 'Sex stereotyping in children's toy advertisements', *Sex Roles* 12 (January 1985): 157–70.

59. Joseph Pereira, 'Oh boy! In toyland, you get more if you're male', *The Wall Street Journal* (23 September 1994): B1 (2); Joseph Pereira, 'Girls' favorite playthings: dolls, dolls, and dolls', *The Wall Street Journal* (23 September 1994): B1 (2).

60. Brad Edmondson, 'Snakes, snails, and puppy dogs' tails', *American Demographics* (October 1987): 18.

61. Laura A. Peracchio, 'How do young children learn to be consumers? A script-processing approach', *Journal of Consumer Research* 18 (March 1992): 4, 25–40; Laura A. Peracchio, 'Young children's processing of a televised narrative: Is a picture really worth a thousand words?' *Journal of Consumer Research* 20 (September 1993) 2: 281–93; see also M. Carole Macklin, 'The effects of an advertising retrieval cue on young children's memory and brand evaluations', *Psychology and Marketing* 11 (May/June 1994) 3: 291–311.

62. Jean Piaget, 'The child and modern physics', *Scientific American* 196 (1957) 3: 46–51; see also Kenneth D. Bahn, 'How and when do brand perceptions and preferences first form? A cognitive developmental investigation', *Journal of Consumer Research* 13 (December 1986): 382–93.

63. Deborah L. Roedder, 'Age differences in children's responses to television advertising: An information processing approach', *Journal of Consumer Research* 8 (September 1981): 1, 44–53; see also Deborah Roedder John and Ramnath Lakshmi-Ratan, 'Age differences in children's choice behavior: The impact of available alternatives', *Journal of Marketing Research* (29 May 1992): 216–26; Jennifer Gregan-Paxton and Deborah Roedder John, 'Are young children adaptive decision makers? A study of age differences in information search behavior', *Journal of Consumer Research* (1995).

64. Bickley Townsend, 'Où sont les neiges d'antan?' ('Where are the snows of yesteryear?'), *American Demographics* (October 1988): 2.

65. Adapted from: Hillary Heuler (2009), 'Poles Find Solidarity in Milk Bars', *Christian Science Monitor*, 26 January 2009, http://features.csmonitor.com/backstory/2009/01/26/poles-find-solidarity-in-milk-bars/

66. 'Same kids, more money', *Marketing* (29 June 1995): 37; see also the following websites for some overviews of allowances: http://www.kiplinger.com/drt.drthome.html and http://pages.prodigy.com/kidsmoney/.

67. Birgitte Tufte and Jeanetter Rasmussen, 'Children on the Net: State of the Art and Future Perspectives Regarding Danish Children's Use of the Internet', in Darach Turley and Stephen Brown (eds), *European Advances in Consumer Research: All Changed, Changed Utterly?* 6 (Valdosta, GA: Association for Consumer Research, 2003: 142–6; Anthony Patterson, Kim Cassidy and Steve Baron, 'Communication and Marketing in a Mobilized World: Diary Research on "Generation Txt"', in Turley and Brown (eds), *European Advances in Consumer Research*: 147–52; Hanman, Natalie, 'The kids are all writing', *The Guardian* (9 June 2005), http://www.guardian.co.uk/online/story/0,,1501803,00.html.

68. 'Same kids, more money', *op. cit.*; Scott McCartney, 'Society' subcultures meet by modem', *Wall Street Journal* (8 December 1994): B1 (2).

69. Sara Olkon, 'Black soda with skulls on label isn't aimed at the Pepsi generation', *Wall Street Journal* (24 May 1995): B1.

70. Junu Bryan Kim, 'For savvy teens: Real life, real solutions', *Advertising Age* (23 August 1993): S1 (3 pp.).

71. 'Hopes and fears: Young European opinion leaders', GfK, adapted from *Marketing Week* (25 June 1998) (study of 500 opinion leaders aged 14–20 from 16 western and eastern European countries).

72. 'Living Conditions in Europe: Statistical handbook', *Eurostat* (Luxembourg: Office for Official Publications of the European Communities, 2000): 29.

73. 'Generation next', *Marketing* (16 January 1997): 25.

74. Scott Donaton, 'The media wakes up to Generation X', *Advertising Age* (1 February 1993): 16(2); Laura E. Keeton, 'New magazines aim to reach (and rechristen) Generation X', *Wall Street Journal* (17 October 1994): B1.

75. 'Trends in households in the European Union: 1995–2025, *op. cit.*: 38.

76. 'Europe in Figures', *Eurostat Yearbook*, 2008, Figure SP.9: 29.

77. Hope Schau, Mary c. Gilly, and Mary Wolfinbarger (2009), 'Consumer identity renaissance: The resurgence of identity-inspired consumption in retirement', *Journal of Consumer Research* 36, August, in press.

78. 'Living conditions in Europe: Statistical handbook', *op. cit.*: 101.

79. 'Shades of grey', *Marketing* (24 April 1997); 'Baby boom generatie moet oud-zijn modieus maken' ['Baby boom generation has to make "old" in fashion'], *NRC Handelsblad* (2 May 1996): 7; Melinda Beck, 'Going for the gold', *Newsweek* (23 April 1990): 74.

80. 'Shades of grey', *op. cit.*

81. 'Trends in households in the European Union: 1995–2025', *op. cit.*: 93.

82. David B. Wolfe, 'Targeting the mature mind', *American Demographics* (March 1994): 32–6.

83. 'Shades of grey', *op. cit.*

84. Allyson Steward-Allen, 'Marketing in Europe to the consumer over age fifty', *Marketing News* 31(16) (4 August 1997): 18.

85. Gabriele Morello, 'Old is Gold, But What is Old?', ESOMAR seminar on 'The Untapped Gold Mine: The Growing Importance of the Over-50s' (Amsterdam: ESOMAR, 1989); Gabriele Morello, 'Sicilian time', in *Time and Society* (London: Sage, 1997): 6(1): 55–69. See also 'Living conditions in Europe: Statistical handbook', *op. cit.*: 9–21.

86. Benny Barak and Leon G. Schiffman, 'Cognitive Age: A Nonchronological Age Variable', in Kent B. Monroe (ed.), *Advances in Consumer Research* 8 (Provo, UT: Association for Consumer Research, 1981): 602–6.

87. David B. Wolfe, 'An ageless market', *American Demographics* (July 1987): 27–55.

88. 'Baby boom generatie moet oud-zijn modieus maken', *op. cit.*

89. Lisa Power and Terrence Higgins Trust (2008), 'Sex is not the preserve of the young, and gonorrhoea and syphilis are no respecters of age', BBC News, 29 June 2008, http://news.bbc.co.uk/go/pr/fr/-/2/hi/health/7477739.stm

90. 'Demographic statistics 1997', *Eurostat* (Luxembourg: Office for Official Publications of the European Communities, 1997); see also http://europa.eu.int (accessed 5 August 2005); Lenore Skenazy, 'These days, it's hip to be old', *Advertising Age* (15 February 1988).

91. This segmentation approach is based on the US population and follows William Lazer and Eric H. Shaw, 'How older Americans spend their money', *American Demographics* (September 1987): 36. See also 'Shades of grey', *op. cit.*, for a two-segment approach to the UK elderly market, and 'Living conditions in Europe: Statistical handbook', *op. cit.*: 9–21.

92. Ellen Day, Brian Davis, Rhonda Dove and Warren A. French, 'Reaching the senior citizen market(s)', *Journal of Advertising Research* (December/January 1987/88): 23–30; Warren A. French and Richard Fox, 'Segmenting the senior citizen market', *Journal of Consumer Marketing* 2 (1985): 61–74; Jeffrey G. Towle and Claude R. Martin Jr, 'The Elderly Consumer: One Segment or Many?' in Beverlee B. Anderson (ed.), *Advances in Consumer Research* 3 (Provo, UT: Association for Consumer Research, 1976): 463.

93. Catherine A. Cole and Nadine N. Castellano, 'Consumer behavior', *Encyclopedia of Gerontology* 1 (1996): 329–39.

94. J. Ward, 'Marketers slow to catch age wave', *Advertising Age* (22 May 1989): S-1.

12

Income and social class

Finally, the big day has come! David is going home with Julia to meet her parents. David had been doing some contracting work at the publishing company where Julia works, and it was love at first sight. Even though David had attended the 'School of Hard Knocks' on the streets of Liverpool, while Julia studied Classics at Trinity College, Oxford, somehow they knew they could work things out despite their vastly different social backgrounds. Julia's been hinting that the Caldwells have money from *several* generations back, but David doesn't feel intimidated. After all, he knows plenty of guys from both Liverpool and London who have wheeled-and-dealed their way into six figures; he thinks he can handle one more big shot in a silk suit, flashing a roll of bills and showing off his expensive modern furniture with mirrors and gadgets everywhere you look.

When they arrive at the family estate 90 minutes outside London, David looks for a Rolls-Royce parked at the end of the long, tree-lined driveway, but he sees only a Jeep Cherokee – which, he decides, must belong to one of the servants. Once inside, David is surprised by how simply the house is decorated and by how understated everything seems. The hall floor is covered with a faded Oriental rug, and all the furniture looks really old – in fact, there doesn't seem to be a stick of new furniture anywhere, just a lot of antiques.

David is even more surprised when he meets Mr Caldwell. He had half-expected Julia's father to be wearing a tuxedo and holding a large glass of cognac like the people on *Lifestyles of the Rich and Famous*. In fact, David had put on his best Italian silk suit in anticipation and was wearing his large cubic zirconium ring so Mr Caldwell would know that he had money too. When Julia's father emerges from his study wearing an old rumpled cardigan and plimsolls, David realizes he's definitely not in the same world . . .

CONSUMER SPENDING AND ECONOMIC BEHAVIOUR

As David's eye-opening experience at the Caldwells' suggests, there are many ways to spend money, and a wide gulf exists between those who have it and those who don't. Perhaps an equally wide one exists between those who have had it for a long time and those who made it more recently. This chapter begins by considering briefly how general economic conditions affect the way consumers allocate their money. Then, reflecting the adage, 'The rich are different', it will explore how people who occupy different positions in society consume in very different ways. Whether a person is a skilled worker like David or a child of privilege like Julia, their social class has a profound impact on what they do with money and on how consumption choices reflect the person's 'place' in society.

As this chapter illustrates, these choices play another purpose as well. The specific products and services we buy are often intended to make sure *other* people know what our social standing is – or what we would like it to be. Products are frequently bought

▶ and displayed as markers of social class: they are valued as **status symbols**. Indeed, it is quite common for a product to be positioned on the basis of its (presumed) place in the social hierarchy. The chapter continues with an assessment of the evolving natures of such status symbols, and it considers some reasons why status-driven products are not always accurate indicators of a consumer's true social standing.

The way income and social class influences consumer behaviour can be approached

▶ from an individual or a more social perspective. The field of **behavioural economics**, or economic psychology, is concerned with the 'individual' and 'psychological' side of economic decisions. Beginning with the pioneering work of the psychologist George Katona, this discipline studies how consumers' motives and their expectations about the future affect their current spending, and how these individual decisions add up to affect a society's economic welfare.[1]

Social class and income obviously also has a social side to it. The chapter is concluded with a section reflecting on the relation between social class and life style based on the work of French sociologist Pierre Bourdieu.[2] Bourdieu also has been very influential in formulating theory of practices, describing how culture is learned not so much by personal choices, nor by subjecting our selves to explicit values and norms, but by adopting routinized types of behaviour that, for us, represent the 'ways things are done'. This approach is decisive in arguing why social inequalities have a tendency to reproduce themselves in society.

Income patterns

Many Europeans would probably say that while they are comfortable, they don't earn enough money. In reality, the average European's standard of living continues to improve. Gross Domestic Product more than doubled and in some EU countries quadrupled between 1980 and 1995, although this boom was by no means shared equally among all consumer groups.[3] Individual income shifts were linked to two key factors: a shift in women's roles and increases in educational attainment.[4]

Woman's work

One reason for this increase in income is that there has also been a larger proportion of people of working age participating in the labour force. While men are more likely to have paid employment than women are, the greatest increases in paid employment in EU countries over the past decade have been among women. This steady increase in the numbers of working women is a primary cause of the increase in household incomes. Still, throughout the Union, women's average full-time earnings are less than men's, and 30 per cent of women in employment are working part-time, against only 6.5 per cent

Figure 12.1 Difference between men's and women's annual average earnings as a percentage of men's annual average earnings, 2001

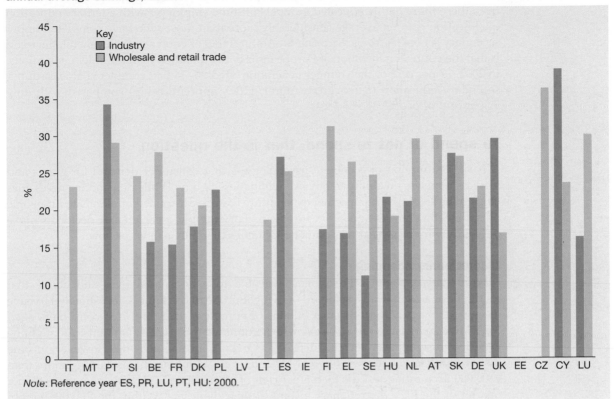

Note: Reference year ES, PR, LU, PT, HU: 2000.

Source: Based on *Eurostat, Harmonised Statistics on Earnings*, Figure 41 (Luxembourg: Office for Official Publications of the European Communities, 2004). © European Communities, 2004.

of men. Female part-time work is particularly prevalent in The Netherlands, where it accounts for almost 75 per cent of female employment, and the UK (44 per cent).[5] In 2001, the average gross monthly wage of women working on a full-time basis was 76 per cent of the earnings of a man. In Belgium, Denmark, Luxembourg and Sweden, the average wages of women are equivalent to 84–85 per cent of men's. In Ireland, The Netherlands, and the UK, on the other hand, women's wages represent only 69–70 per cent of men's.[6] The differences in pay are particularly high among older workers, the highly skilled and those employed with supervisory job status. Men are not only more concentrated in higher paid sectors and occupations, but within these sectors and occupations they are also more likely than women to hold supervisory responsibilities and if they do so the earnings are relatively higher.[7] Yet in spite of these increases in household income, women are more likely to be in part-time work, a situation which reflects the more traditional activities of caring for the household and children living at home – activities that are still seen as primarily their responsibility. As discussed in the previous chapter, family situation, the number and age of children living at home and the educational level of women heavily influence their employment activities.

Figure 12.1 shows the 'gender pay gap' between men and women in 30 countries as of 2006.

Yes, it pays to go to school!

Another factor that determines who gets a bigger slice of the pie is education. Although the expense of going to college often entails great sacrifice, it still pays in the long run. University and higher professional study graduates earn about 50 per cent more than those who have gone through secondary school only during the course of their lives. Close to half of the increase in consumer spending power during the past decade came from these more highly educated groups. Full-time employees with a tertiary education qualification earn on average considerably more than those who have completed upper secondary school (A-levels, *Baccalauréat*, Abitur, HBO or equivalent). In general, the trend is that the younger generation of Europeans is better qualified than the older generations. In 2002, 77 per cent of the younger generation aged 20–24 had completed at least upper secondary education (*Baccalauréat*, Abitur, HBO, apprenticeship) compared with only 55 per cent of people aged 50–64.[8]

To spend or not to spend, that is the question

A basic assumption of economic psychology is that consumer demand for goods and services depends on ability to buy *and* willingness to buy. While demand for necessities tends to be stable over time, other expenditures can be postponed or eliminated if people do not feel that now is a good time to spend.[9] For example, a person may decide to 'make do' with their current car for another year rather than buy a new car now.

Discretionary spending

▶ Discretionary income is the money available to a household over and above that required for a comfortable standard of living. European consumers are estimated to have discretionary spending power in billions of euros per year, and it is consumers aged 35–55 whose incomes are at a peak who account for the greatest amounts. As might be expected, discretionary income increases as overall income goes up. However, income distributions vary between different EU countries, with households earning more than €100,000 accounting for less than 5 per cent of all families. Still, they have more than a quarter of the EU's discretionary income at their disposal.[10] Within the EU, the bottom (poorest) 20 per cent of the population received only 7.6 per cent of total income in 1996, while the top (richest) 20 per cent received 39.3 per cent of total income (i.e. 5.2 times more). This gap between the most and least well-off persons (known as the *share ratio S80/S20*) is smallest in Slovenia (3.3) and Sweden (3.4). It is generally widest in the Mediterranean member states and the Baltic republics, with Portugal recording the highest ratio (6.5).[11] Figure 12.2 gives a graphic overview of disposable incomes in the income distribution for all EU member states in 2000. While discretionary income is a powerful tool for predicting certain types of consumer behaviour, it is not always a measure for which straightforward comparisons between countries can be easily made. Factors such as different levels of sales tax (VAT) or varying levels of direct family benefits for children under 19 years of age living at home in various EU countries account for differences in what constitutes true discretionary income.

Individual attitudes towards money

Many consumers are entertaining doubts about their individual and collective futures, and are anxious about holding on to what they have. A consumer's anxieties about money are not necessarily related to how much they actually have: acquiring and managing money is more a state of mind than of wallet. Money can have a variety of complex psychological meanings: it can be equated with success or failure, social acceptability, security, love or freedom.[12] Some clinical psychologists even specialize in treating money-related disorders, and report that people feel guilty about their success and deliberately make bad investments to ease this feeling! Other clinical conditions include atephobia (fear of being ruined), harpaxophobia (fear of becoming a victim of robbers), peniaphobia (fear of poverty) and aurophobia (fear of gold).[13] The Roper/Starch survey found that security was the attribute most closely linked to the meaning of money. Other significant associations included comfort, being able to help one's children, freedom and pleasure.[14]

Figure 12.2 Disposable income per capita across the EU-25, 2000

Note: Index 100 – Average all regions; NUTS 2 level except DE at NUTS 1 level: L, A, CY, SI: no data available.

Source: Eurostat, Statistics in Focus, Theme 3–7/2003 (Luxembourg: Office for Official Publications of the European Communities, 2004): 113, Map 2. © European Communities 2004.

Consumer confidence

▶ A consumer's beliefs about what the future holds is an indicator of **consumer confidence**, which reflects the extent to which people are optimistic or pessimistic about the future health of the economy and how they will fare in the future. These beliefs influence how much money a consumer will pump into the economy when making discretionary purchases.

Hence, it is no surprise that many businesses take forecasts about anticipated spending very seriously, and periodic surveys attempt to 'take the pulse' of the European consumer. The Henley Centre conducts a survey of consumer confidence, as does Eurostat and the EuroMonitor. The following are the types of attitudinal statements presented to consumers in these surveys:[15]

   'My standard of living will change for the better over the next year.'

   'My quality of life will improve over the next year.'

   'I will have a lack of money when I retire.'

   'I spend too much of my income, and intend to spend less next year.'

   'I am concerned about the amount of free time I have.'

When people are pessimistic about their prospects and about the state of the economy, they tend to cut back their spending and take on less debt. On the other hand, when they are optimistic about the future, they tend to reduce the amount they save, take
▶ on more debt and buy discretionary items. The overall **savings rate** thus is influenced by individual consumers' pessimism or optimism about their personal circumstances (for example, fear of being laid off vs. a steady increase in personal wealth due to rising real estate prices or a sudden increase in personal wealth due to an inheritance), as well

Figure 12.3 Life satisfaction by country

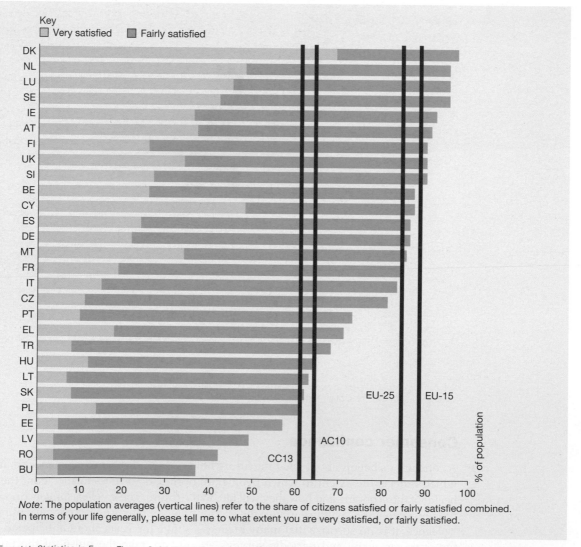

Note: The population averages (vertical lines) refer to the share of citizens satisfied or fairly satisfied combined. In terms of your life generally, please tell me to what extent you are very satisfied, or fairly satisfied.

Source: Eurostat, *Statistics in Focus*, Theme 3–24/2003 (Luxembourg: Office for Official Publications of the European Communities, 2004). © European Communities, 2004.

as by world events (for example the election of a new government or an international crisis such as the Gulf War) and cultural differences in attitudes towards saving (the Japanese have a much higher savings rate than do Europeans or Americans).[16]

The financial crisis starting in the autumn of 2008 is a good example of how mass psychology is linked to the economy. When financial markets go up, the rise is basically based on expectations (and a lot of what is bought and sold in the financial markets are expectations, and even expectations of expectations). Likewise, when the market goes down. When everybody expects greater risks of losses (rather than gains) due to bankruptcies, failing demand, unemployment, etc., investors, buyers *and* consumers become more prudent, which slows down the turnover in the marketplace and aggravates the symptoms of crisis.

Seeking value vs. quality

In an era of diminished resources, Europeans are redefining traditional relationships among price, value and quality. In the past (most notably in the 1980s), people seemed to be willing to pay almost anything for products and services. Consumers still claim to want quality – but at the right price. In surveys, most people report that they regret the conspicuous consumption of the 1980s and feel the need to live with less. The attitude of the 1990s was more practical and reflected a 'back to basics' orientation. People now want more hard news instead of 'hype' from advertising, and they appreciate ads that feature problem-solving tips or that save money or time. European youth (age range 12–24) in particular are more sceptical of advertising messages, relative to the total population.

Nonetheless, the general quality of life, and life satisfaction of European consumers is high, with some important distinctions: there are big differences between the EU-15 countries and the new member states with respect to perceived quality of life and life satisfaction. Also, levels of satisfaction are more heterogeneous among citizens of the new member states and in the EU-15. Figure 12.3 shows life satisfaction measures by country for the EU-25 countries.

 Marketing opportunity

What are the determinants of subjective quality of life and life satisfaction?

The abstract idea of what constitutes quality of life does not differ that much across Europe, and if there are differences, there is no clear divide between EU-15 countries and the new member states. The reason for this basic similarity is that the dominant concerns in all countries are income, family life and health. However, whereas abstract ideas of a good life are rather similar, actual determinants of life satisfaction are not:

- In many new member states, income satisfaction is of key importance for overall life satisfaction. Hence, improving income satisfaction is the best way to improve life satisfaction. In general, following income improvement, satisfaction with health and with family life also have a strong impact on how people evaluate their lives.
- In the old EU-15 countries, income satisfaction matters less for life satisfaction. On the whole, satisfaction with family life and social life are the

strongest determinants of subjective quality of life in these countries.
- The paramount importance of income in the East and its relative low importance in the West once again are linked with differences in economic development. Consumers in the new member states, at present, put greater emphasis on material demands, which are currently under-fulfilled in these countries to a large degree.[17]
- However, poverty is not the sole explanation for focus on income. As some research in materialism has demonstrated, the sense of relative deprivation is equally important as well as the economic history of a population. Thus, a higher degree of materialism is often found in poorer countries that have a direct way of comparing themselves to richer 'relatives', such as the Central and East European post-communist countries.[18]

SOCIAL CLASS

▶ All societies can be roughly divided into the haves and the have-nots (though sometimes 'having' is a question of degree). While social equality is a widely held value throughout Europe, the fact remains that some people seem to be more equal than others. As David's encounter with the Caldwells suggests, a consumer's standing in society, or **social class**, is determined by a complex set of variables, including income, family background and occupation.

The place one occupies in the social structure is not just an important determinant of *how much* money is spent. It also influences *how* it is spent. David was surprised that the Caldwells, who clearly had a lot of money, did not seem to flaunt it. This understated way of living is a hallmark of so-called 'old money'. People who have had it for a long time do not need to prove they have it. In contrast, consumers who are relative newcomers to affluence might allocate the same amount of money very differently.

 Marketing opportunity

'Winston Churchill preferred his with starched linen collars and loops on the shoulders to hold up his braces. Prince Charles has his fitted in the privacy of his palace, while fashion mogul Ralph Lauren – who, you'd imagine, could get them for free at his own shop – sometimes orders dozens at a time. And then there's the rather eccentric customer who wants his to resemble Australian prisoner uniforms – but made of cream-coloured silk.

What all these people have in common – the politicians and powerbrokers, royals and the slightly offbeat – is a desire for the simple luxury of a custom-made shirt. And not just any old made-to-measure shirt: these garments must be from the famous craftsmen of Jermyn Street, whose shops in London's SW1 district cater to connoisseurs with a passion for fine tailoring and a perfect fit. At prices from £100 to £155 per shirt, depending on the cloth, and with a minimum order of between four and six, you probably can't afford to wear anything else.

Jermyn Street tailors have been practising the art of fine service and attention to detail for over a century – it's what their customers expect from the place acknowledged as the world's capital of made-to-measure shirts. "We have created a unique market, and have attracted the top customers, who feel quite comfortable here", notes Paul Cuss, chief patternmaker at Turnbull and Asser, the holder of the coveted Royal Warrant for shirtmaking, and the shop that supplies

Prince Charles . . . among others. According to Mr Cuss, "It's very establishment, very clubby." With its heavy wooden furniture, stuffed hunting trophies and velvet Hapsburgian smoking jackets for sale, along with ties, bathrobes and boxer shorts and a framed picture of Winston Churchill, Turnbull and Asser's cosy emporium is a gentlemen's world straight out of *Country Life* magazine.

One can imagine the Jermyn Street of old, when landed gentry and Etonian schoolboys travelled there to buy their shirts in a rite of passage for the aristocracy, and in the process established the street's reputation. While Jermyn Street thrives on tradition, their clients come from all over the world. The French and fashion-conscious Italians come for the "tailored English look", but the shirtmakers admit to following fashion trends: among the serious solid whites and blues are a few shocking pink, lilac and dayglow orange samples.

Precise construction of the shirt also means that it takes time to have the garment finished. After measuring, there's a wait of around two weeks for a sample to be made. Then there's a trial period of washing and wearing, to see if the fit is right. Finally, the hand-cutters and sewers get to work, and in six to eight weeks the masterpiece is ready – and you can walk proudly down the street, knowing you've joined an exclusive club whose members say price doesn't matter when it comes to style.'[19]

A universal pecking order

In many animal species, a social organization develops whereby the most assertive or aggressive animals exert control over the others and have the first pick of food, living space and even mating partners. Chickens, for example, develop a clearly defined dominance–submission hierarchy. Within this hierarchy, each hen has a position in which she is submissive to all of the hens above her and dominates all of the ones below her (hence the origin of the term *pecking order*).[20]

People are no different. They also develop a pecking order where they are ranked in terms of their relative standing in society. This standing determines their access to such resources as education, housing and consumer goods. And people try to improve their ranking by moving up the social order whenever possible. This desire to improve one's lot, and often to let others know that one has done so, is at the core of many marketing strategies.

► While every culture has its **social hierarchies**, variations in terms of how explicit these distinctions are can be observed. Stratification of one sort or another is universal, even in societies that officially disdain such a process. For example, in China, a supposedly classless society, the children of top party officials, who are called *gaoganzidi*, irritate many Chinese. These offspring have a reputation for laziness, enjoying material pleasures and getting the best jobs by virtue of their family connections. They are thus a privileged class in a classless society.[21]

► Multicultural dimensions

'It is Saturday night in a club in central London. The crowd is enjoying the standard fare of nightclubs: the R&B music is loud enough to make conversation hard; the bar is doing a brisk trade in pricey drinks; and coming through the door is a steady stream of punters in designer-label plumage. Less standard is that each of these young people handing over the £10 entry fee is Asian. And, from door staff to promoter, so is nearly everyone else. This is Mumbai Rouge, self-styled "hangout for the affluent Asian professional" and the self-assurance of the phrase is matched by the confidence of the clientele. Nightclubs are only part of it. Anyone mingling with the crowd when India play cricket at the Oval or shopping in areas with a large Asian population, such as Harrow or Slough or Wolverhampton, would find ample evidence of the optimism and material aspirations of young British Asians.

The Institute of Practitioners in Advertising reported last year that Asians in the UK were far more likely to own a personal computer or a DVD player than the population overall, and that 72 per cent had pay-TV at home, compared with 39 per cent of the UK population.

On other measures, too, Asians as a group seem an attractive target for businesses. They are increasing in numbers (2.3m, according to the 2001 Census); younger than the white population overall; more likely to be found in big cities; and making important economic advances. According to the Cabinet Office, male workers of Indian origin went from earning an average 8 per cent less than their white counterparts in 1994 to earning 3 per cent more by 2000. Asians still find it more difficult to get jobs than whites, but the broad outline is of a group increasingly at home. Indeed, most of the Asian population is British-born and one, two or even three, generations removed from their countries of ancestral origin. While the first generation had to save money and establish themselves, their children and grandchildren have British roots and feel able to play hard.

Yet if the story of Asians in the UK has largely been one of integration, communications professionals have tended to put them in a niche or ignore them. In January 2003, just 2 per cent of advertising campaigns featured actors from ethnic minorities – despite blacks and Asians making up 8 per cent of the population. About five years ago, in an effort to correct this imbalance, marketing consultant Anjna Raheja coined the term "brown pound". "It was intended", she says, "to draw attention to the growing economic power of Asian – and black – consumers." It has been widely used and may have helped to increase the proportion of advertisements featuring ethnic minorities to 7 per cent by November last year. But what seems to have filled the vacuum is a cliché. As Ms Raheja notes: "There has been some trading in stereotypes." An advertisement for the Halifax Building Society this year featured a Bollywood-style troupe singing about how personal loans were "sweeter than chutney". Similarly, Walkers Crisps' campaign for Chicken Tikka Masala crisps showed Gary Lineker, the TV presenter and former soccer player, marrying an Asian granny – and getting the keys to the cornershop.'[22]

Social class affects access to resources

Just as marketers try to carve society into groups for segmentation purposes, sociologists have developed ways to describe meaningful divisions of society in terms of people's relative social and economic resources. Some of these divisions involve political power, while others revolve around purely economic distinctions. Karl Marx argued that position in a society was determined by one's relationship to the *means of production*. Some people (the haves) control resources, and they use the labour of others to preserve their privileged positions. The have-nots lack control and depend on their own labour for survival, so these people have the most to gain by changing the system. Distinctions among people that entitle some to more than others are perpetuated by those who will benefit by doing so.[23]

The sociologist Max Weber showed that the rankings people develop are not one-dimensional. Some involve prestige or 'social honour' (he called these *status groups*), some rankings focus on power (or *party*), and some revolve around wealth and property (*class*).[24]

Social class affects taste and lifestyles

The term 'social class' is now used more generally to describe the overall rank of people in a society. People who are grouped within the same social class are approximately equal in terms of their social standing in the community. They work in roughly similar occupations, and they tend to have similar lifestyles by virtue of their income levels and common tastes. These people tend to socialize with one another and share many ideas and values regarding the way life should be lived.[25] Indeed, 'birds of a feather do flock together.' We tend to marry people in a similar social class to ours, a tendency sociologists call **homogamy**, or 'assortative mating'.

▼ Marketing pitfall

'Steinar gazes over the expansive new verandah of his summer cottage on a tranquil island off Norway's south-eastern coast, chatting on his cell phone. The 50-year-old Oslo accountant recently added a host of amenities such as hot running water to his *hytte*, as Norwegians call their rustic summer cabins. Now he plans to put in a paved road to his front door and a swimming pool in the garden. "There's nothing wrong with a little comfort", says Steinar. Well, maybe not in other summer playgrounds such as France's Côte d'Azur, but here in austere Norway, the words "comfort" and "vacation" are not synonymous. Thanks to the recent oil boom, many Norwegians are spending their new-found wealth upgrading spartan summer chalets with tennis courts, jacuzzis and even helipads. But in a country where simplicity and frugality are cherished virtues, and egalitarianism is strong, the display of wealth and money is suspect. Some politicians have suggested bulldozing the houses of the wealthy if they block access to the sea, and trade union leaders have blasted a new breed of Norwegians who favour showy yachts and life in the fast lane, and who build fences around private property.

"The rich can be quite vulgar", grumbles Steinar's neighbour Brit, who demanded that he trim a metre or so off his verandah because she and her husband, Gustav, could see it from their cabin lower down the hill. Both teachers, Brit and Gustav are nearing retirement, and have a more traditional Norwegian view of how to spend their summer, and how to spend their money. At stake, many say, are Norwegian ideals of equality and social democracy. These dictate that all Norwegians should have the same quality of life and share the national wealth equally. Norwegians champion austerity because they haven't always been prosperous. Before oil was discovered about 20 years ago, only a few families were considered wealthy. This frugality is obvious even in the capital, Oslo. For all the new oil money, plus low inflation, the city isn't a brash "Kuwait of the North".

Summer chalets should reflect the spartan mood, diehards say, and vacation activities must be limited. Scraping down paint is popular, as is hammering down loose floorboards. So is swimming in lakes, fishing for supper and chopping wood. But not much else. As another neighbour, Aase, puts it: "We like to, uh, sit here. I'd like the rich to stay away from here. They would ruin the neighbourhood." '[26]

Social class is as much a state of being as it is of having: as David saw, class is also a question of what one *does* with one's money and how one defines one's role in society. Although people may not like the idea that some members of society are better off or 'different' from others, most consumers do acknowledge the existence of different classes and the effect of class membership on consumption. As one wealthy woman observed when asked to define social class: 'I would suppose social class means where you went to school and how far. Your intelligence. Where you live . . . Where you send your children to school. The hobbies you have. Skiing, for example, is higher than the snow-mobile . . . It can't be [just] money, because nobody ever knows that about you for sure.'[27]

Social stratification

In college, some students always seem to be more popular than others. They have access to many resources, such as special privileges, expensive cars, generous allowances or dates with other equally popular classmates. At work, some people are put on the fast track and are promoted to prestige jobs, given higher salaries and perhaps such perks as a parking space, a large office or the keys to the executive cloakroom.

In virtually every context, some people seem to be ranked higher than others. Patterns of social arrangements evolve whereby some members get more resources than others by virtue of their relative standing, power and/or control in the group.[28] The phenomenon ▶ of **social stratification** refers to this creation of artificial divisions in a society: 'those processes in a social system by which scarce and valuable resources are distributed unequally to status positions that become more or less permanently ranked in terms of the share of valuable resources each receives.'[29]

Achieved vs. ascribed status

If you recall groups you've belonged to, both large and small, you will probably agree that in many instances some members seemed to get more than their fair share while others were not so lucky. Some of these resources may have gone to people who earned them through hard work or diligence. This allocation is due to *achieved status*. Other

Inherited or earned wealth, there are professionals who would help you spend the money 'the right way'.

rewards may have been obtained because the person was lucky enough to be born into wealthy circles. Such good fortune reflects *ascribed status*.

Whether rewards go to the 'best and the brightest' or to someone who happens to be related to the boss, allocations are rarely equal within a social group. Most groups exhibit a structure, or status hierarchy, in which some members are somehow better off than others. They may have more authority or power, or they are simply more liked or respected.

Class structure around the world

Every society has some type of hierarchical class structure, where people's access to products and services is determined by their resources and social standing. Of course, the specific 'markers' of success depend on what is valued in each culture.

In China, an economic boom is rapidly creating a middle class of more than 130 million people that analysts project to grow to more than 400 million in 10 years. During the cultural revolution, Mao's Red Guards seized on even the smallest possessions – a pocket watch or silk scarf – as evidence of 'bourgeois consciousness'. Change came rapidly in the early 1990s, after Mao's successor Deng Xiaoping uttered the phrase that quickly became the credo of the new China: 'To get rich is glorious.' Because costs are low, a family with an annual income €10–12,000 can enjoy middle-class comforts, including stylish clothes, Chinese-made colour televisions, DVD players, and cell phones. Wealthier Chinese entrepreneurs can indulge in Cuban Cohiba cigars that sell for €20 each, a quarter of the average Chinese laborer's monthly wage. In bustling Shanghai, newly minted 'yuppies' drop their kids off for golf lessons; visit Maserati and Ferrari showrooms; buy some luxury items from Louis Vuitton, Hugo Boss, or Prada; then pick up some Häagen-Dazs ice cream before heading to an Evian spa to unwind.

Nike, which consumers in a recent survey named China's coolest brand, profits mightily from the rise of the Chinese middle class. Nike shoes are a symbol of success, and the company opens an average of 1.5 new stores a day there. The company worked for a long time to attain this status; it started by outfitting top Chinese athletes and sponsoring all the teams in China's pro basketball league. Still, becoming a fashion icon (and persuading consumers to spend twice the average monthly salary for a pair of shoes) is no mean feat in a country that is not exactly sports-crazy. So Nike affiliated with the NBA (which had begun televising games in China), bringing over players such as Michael Jordan for visits. Slowly but surely, in-the-know Chinese came to call sneakers 'Nai-ke'.[30]

Like China, India's economy has undergone a big booming period and many higher-end global brands are catching on. One of Bollywood's biggest stars, Shahrukh Khan, is 'brand ambassador' for Tag Heuer watches, which cost thousands of dollars. He gives them away on the Indian version of *Who Wants to Be a Millionaire?* India's ascendancy is fairly recent; for decades after the country became independent from Britain, its economy was a relatively closed one. Today, a lot of young consumers watch MTV, read international fashion magazines, and are embracing the power of plastic; credit-card spending in India has risen by 30 per cent a year for the past five years.[31] Not everybody is invited to the party, though. Inequality in China as well as India is out of proportion compared to what we know in the Western world, and economic development often happens at the expense of the poor population of so-called subaltern consumers, typically farmers, fishermen, unskilled workers and people of other traditional occupations.[32]

Japan is a highly status-conscious society, where upmarket, designer labels are popular and new forms of status are always being sought. To the Japanese, owning a traditional rock garden, formerly a vehicle for leisure and tranquillity, has become a coveted item. Possession of a rock garden implies inherited wealth, since aristocrats traditionally were patrons of the arts. In addition, considerable assets are required to afford the necessary land in a country where property is extraordinarily expensive. The scarcity of land also helps to explain why the Japanese are fanatical golfers: since a golf course takes up so much space, membership of a golf club is extremely valuable.[33]

In contrast to the Japanese, few Arab women work, so searching for the latest in Western luxury brands is a major leisure activity. Dressing rooms are large, with antechambers to accommodate friends and family members who often come along on shopping sprees. A major expansion of Western luxury brands is under way across the Middle East, home to some of the fashion industry's best customers. High-end retailers such as Saks Fifth Avenue and Giorgio Armani operate opulent stores to cater to this growing market. However, fashion retailers must take cultural and religious considerations into account. Missoni makes sure that collections include longer pants and skirts, and evening gowns with light shawls to cover heads or bare shoulders. And advertising and display options are more limited: erotic images don't work. In the strict religious culture of Saudi Arabia, mannequins can not reveal a gender or human shape. At Saks' Riyadh store, models are headless and do not have fingers. Half of the two-level store is off-limits to men.[34]

Here in Europe, let's take the case of England: England is also a class-conscious country, and, at least until recently, consumption patterns were pre-ordained in terms of one's inherited position and family background. Members of the upper class were educated at public schools such as Eton and Harrow, and had a distinctive accent. Remnants of this rigid class structure can still be found. 'Hooray Henrys' (wealthy young men) play polo at Windsor and at the moment hereditary peers can still take their seat in the House of Lords. The UK, together with Poland and the Baltic states, is the country in northern Europe with the highest inequality in income distribution.[35]

The dominance of inherited wealth appears to be fading in Britain's traditionally aristocratic society. According to a survey, 86 of the 200 wealthiest people in England made their money the old-fashioned way: they earned it. Even the sanctity of the Royal Family, which epitomizes the aristocracy, has been diluted because of tabloid exposure and the antics of younger family members who have been transformed into celebrities more like rock stars than royalty.[36]

► Now, some big marketers such as Unilever and Groupe Danone have set their sights on a more lower-class group the British call **chavs**. This label refers to young, lower-class men and women who mix flashy brands and accessories from big names such as Burberry

This ad demonstrates the power of the imagery of the British upper class.
The Advertising Archives

with track suits. Their style icons include soccer star David Beckham and his wife, Victoria, aka Posh Spice (both of whom made a huge splash when they moved to the US in 2007). Despite their (alleged) tackiness, marketers like chavs because they spend a lot of their disposable income on fashion, food, and gadgets. France's Danone, which makes HP Sauce, a condiment the British have poured over bacon sandwiches and fries for a century, launched a series of ads playing up to the chav culture. One features a brawl over the sauce at a wedding buffet; another includes glammy soccer players' wives mingling cattily at a party.[37] Danone found 'chavvy' people on the streets of Liverpool to star in the ads.

Social mobility

▶ To what degree do people tend to change their social class? In some traditional societies social class is very difficult to change, but in Europe, any man or woman can become prime minister. **Social mobility** refers to the 'passage of individuals from one social class to another'.[38]

This passage can be upward, downward or even horizontal. *Horizontal mobility* refers to movement from one position to another roughly equivalent in social status, like becoming a nurse instead of a junior school teacher. *Downward mobility* is, of course, not very desirable, but this pattern is unfortunately quite evident in recent years as redundant workers have been forced to join the dole queue or have joined the ranks of the homeless. In the US, a conservative estimate is that 600,000 Americans are homeless on a given day.[39]

Despite that discouraging trend, demographics decree that there must be *upward mobility* in European society. The middle and upper classes reproduce less than the lower classes (an effect known as *differential fertility*), and they tend to restrict family size below replacement level. Therefore, so the reasoning goes, positions of higher status over time must be filled by those of lower status.[40] Overall, though, the offspring of blue-collar consumers tend also to be blue-collar while the offspring of white-collar consumers tend also to be white-collar.[41] People tend to improve their positions over time, but these increases are not usually dramatic enough to catapult them from one social class to another.

Components of social class

When we think about a person's social class, there are a number of pieces of information we can consider. Two major ones are occupation and income. A third important factor is educational attainment, which is strongly related to income and occupation.

Occupational prestige

In a system where (like it or not) a consumer is defined to a great extent by what they do for a living, *occupational prestige* is one way to evaluate the 'worth' of people. Hierarchies of occupational prestige tend to be quite stable over time, and they also tend to be similar in different societies. Similarities in occupational prestige have been found in countries as diverse as Brazil, Ghana, Guam, Japan and Turkey.[42]

A typical ranking includes a variety of professional and business occupations at the top (e.g. director of a large corporation, doctor or college lecturer), while those jobs hovering near the bottom include shoeshiner, unskilled labourer and dustman. Because a person's occupation tends to be strongly linked to their use of leisure time, allocation of family resources, political orientation and so on, this variable is often considered to be the single best indicator of social class.

Income

The distribution of wealth is of great interest to social scientists and to marketers, since it determines which groups have the greatest buying power and market potential. Wealth is by no means distributed evenly across the classes. While there is a more equitable distribution of wealth across European countries relative to Latin America, Asia and America (the top fifth of the population in the US controls about 75 per cent of all assets),[43] there is still a disportionate share of wealth controlled by a small segment of the European population. As we have seen, income per se is often not a very good indicator of social class, since the way money is spent is more telling. Still, people need money to allow them to obtain the goods and services that they need to express their tastes, so obviously income is still very important.

The relationship between income and social class

Although consumers tend to equate money with class, the precise relationship between other aspects of social class and income is not clear and has been the subject of debate among social scientists.[44] The two are by no means synonymous, which is why many people with a lot of money try to use it to improve their social class.

One problem is that even if a family increases household income by adding wage earners, each additional job is likely to be of lower status. For example, a housewife who gets a part-time job is not as likely to get one that is of equal or greater status than the primary wage earner's. In addition, the extra money earned may not be pooled for the common good of the family. Instead it may be used by the individual for their own personal spending. More money does not then result in increased status or changes in consumption patterns, since it tends to be devoted to buying more of the same rather than upgrading to higher-status products.[45]

The following general conclusions can be made regarding the relative value of social class (i.e. place of residence, occupation, cultural interests, etc.) vs. income in predicting consumer behaviour:

- Social class appears to be a better predictor of purchases that have symbolic aspects, but low-to-moderate prices (e.g. cosmetics, alcohol).

- Income is a better predictor of major expenditures that do not have status or symbolic aspects (e.g. major appliances).

- Social class and income data together are better predictors of purchases of expensive, symbolic products (e.g. cars, homes, luxury goods).[46]

Measurement of social class

Because social class is a complex concept which depends on a number of factors, not surprisingly it has proved difficult to measure. Early measures included the Index of Status Characteristics developed in the 1940s and the Index of Social Position developed by Hollingshead in the 1950s.[47] These indices used various combinations of individual characteristics (such as income, type of housing) to arrive at a label of class standing. The accuracy of these composites is still a subject of debate among researchers; one recent study claimed that for segmentation purposes, raw education and income measures work as well as composite status measures.[48]

Blue-collar workers with relatively high-income jobs still tend to view themselves as working class, even though their income levels may be equivalent to those of many white-collar workers.[49] This fact reinforces the idea that the labels 'working class' or 'middle class' are very subjective. Their meanings say at least as much about self-identity as they do about economic well-being.

Problems with measures of social class

Market researchers were among the first to propose that people from different social classes can be distinguished from each other in important ways. While some of these dimensions still exist, others have changed.[50] Unfortunately, many of these measures are badly dated and are not as valid today for a variety of reasons, four of which are discussed here.[51]

Most measures of social class were designed to accommodate the traditional nuclear family, with a male wage earner in the middle of his career and a female full-time homemaker. Such measures have trouble accounting for two-income families, young singles living alone, or households headed by women which are so prevalent in today's society (see Chapter 11).

Another problem with measuring social class is attributable to the increasing anonymity of our society. Earlier studies relied on the *reputational method*, where extensive interviewing was done within a community to determine the reputations and backgrounds of individuals. This information, coupled with the tracing of interaction patterns among people, provided a very comprehensive view of social standing within a community.

This approach is virtually impossible to implement in most communities today. One compromise is to interview individuals to obtain demographic data and to combine these data with the subjective impressions of the interviewer regarding the person's possessions and standard of living. An example of this approach appears in Figure 12.4. Note that the accuracy of this questionnaire relies largely on the interviewer's judgement, especially regarding the quality of the respondent's neighbourhood. These impressions

Figure 12.4 Living room clusters and social class

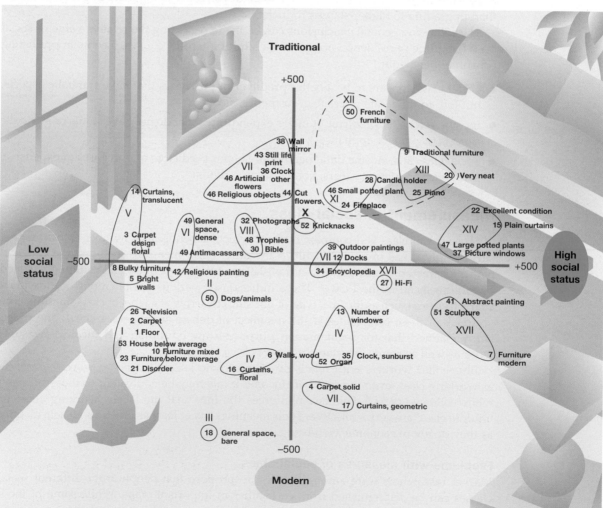

Source: Edward O. Laumann and James S. House, 'Living room styles and social attributes: The patterning of material artifacts in a modern urban community', *Sociology and Social Research 54* (April 1970): 321–42.

are in danger of being biased by the interviewer's own circumstances, which may affect their standard of comparison. This potential problem highlights the need for adequate training of interviewers, as well as for some attempt to cross-validate such data, possibly by employing multiple judges to rate the same area.

One problem with assigning people to a social class is that they may not be equal in their standing on all of the relevant dimensions. A person might come from a low-status ethnic group but have a high-status job, while another may live in a fashionable part of town but did not complete secondary school. The concept of **status crystallization** was developed to assess the impact of inconsistency on the self and social behaviour.[52] It was thought that since the rewards from each part of such an 'unbalanced' person's life would be variable and unpredictable, stress would result. People who exhibit such inconsistencies tend to be more receptive to social change than are those whose identities are more firmly rooted.

A related problem occurs when a person's social class standing creates expectations that are not met. Some people find themselves in the not unhappy position of making more money than is expected of those in their social class. This situation is known as an *overprivileged condition* and is usually defined as an income that is at least 25–30 per cent over the median for one's class.[53] In contrast, *underprivileged* consumers, who earn at least 15 per cent less than the median, must often devote their consumption priorities to sacrificing in order to maintain the appearance of living up to class expectations.

Lottery winners are examples of consumers who become overprivileged overnight. As attractive as winning is many people, it has its problems. Consumers with a certain standard of living and level of expectations may have trouble adapting to sudden affluence and engage in flamboyant and irresponsible displays of wealth. Ironically, it is not unusual for lottery winners to report feelings of depression in the months after the win. They may have trouble adjusting to an unfamiliar world, and they frequently experience pressure from friends, relatives and business people to 'share the wealth'.

One New York winner who was featured prominently in the media is a case in point. He was employed as a mail porter until he won $5 million. After winning the lottery, he divorced his wife and married his girlfriend. She wore a $12,000 gown to the ceremony and the couple arrived in a horse-drawn carriage. Other purchases included a Cadillac with a Rolls-Royce grill and a $5,000 car phone. He later denied rumours that he was heavily in debt due to his extravagant spending.[54]

The traditional assumption is that husbands define a family's social class, while wives must live it. Women borrow their social status from their husbands.[55] Indeed, the evidence indicates that physically attractive women tend to 'marry up' to a greater extent than attractive men. Women trade the resource of sexual appeal, which historically has been one of the few assets they were allowed to possess, for the economic resources of men.[56] The accuracy of this assumption in today's world must be questioned. Many women now contribute equally to the family's well-being and work in positions of comparable or even greater status than their spouses. *Cosmopolitan* magazine offered this revelation: 'Women who've become liberated enough to marry any man they please, regardless of his social position, report how much more fun and spontaneous their relationships with men have become now that they no longer view men only in terms of their power symbols.'[57]

Employed women tend to average both their own and their husband's respective positions when estimating their own subjective status.[58] Nevertheless, a prospective spouse's social class is often an important 'product attribute' when evaluating alternatives in the interpersonal marketplace (as David and Julia were to find out). *Cosmopolitan* also discussed this dilemma, implying that social class differences are still an issue in the mating game: 'You've met the (almost) perfect man. You both adore Dashiell Hammett thrillers, Mozart, and tennis. He taught you to jet ski; you taught him the virtues of tofu . . . The problem? You're an executive earning ninety-thousand dollars a year. He's a taxi driver . . .'[59]

Problems with social class segmentation: a summary

Social class remains an important way to categorize consumers. Many marketing strategies do target different social classes. However, marketers have failed to use social class information as effectively as they could for the following reasons:

- They have ignored status inconsistency.
- They have ignored intergenerational mobility.
- They have ignored subjective social class (i.e. the class a consumer identifies with rather than the one they objectively belong to).
- They have ignored consumers' aspirations to change their class standing.
- They have ignored the social status of working wives.

HOW SOCIAL CLASS AFFECTS PURCHASE DECISIONS

Different products and stores are perceived by consumers to be appropriate for certain social classes.[60] Working-class consumers tend to evaluate products in more utilitarian terms such as sturdiness or comfort rather than style or fashionability. They are less likely to experiment with new products or styles, such as modern furniture or coloured appliances.[61] In contrast, more affluent people tend to be concerned about appearance and body image, so they are more avid consumers of diet foods and drinks compared to people in small, working-class towns. These differences mean that the cola market, for example, can be segmented by social class.[62]

Class differences in worldview

A major social class difference involves the *worldview* of consumers. The world of the working class (including the lower-middle class) is more intimate and constricted. For example, working-class men are likely to name local sports figures as heroes and are less likely to take long holidays in out-of-the-way places.[63] Immediate needs, such as a new refrigerator or TV, tend to dictate buying behaviour for these consumers, while the higher classes tend to focus on more long-term goals, such as saving for college fees or retirement.[64]

Working-class consumers depend heavily on relatives for emotional support and tend to orient themselves in terms of the community rather than the world at large. They are more likely to be conservative and family oriented. Maintaining the appearance of one's home and property is a priority, regardless of the size of the house. One recent study that looked at social class and how it relates to consumers' feelings of *empowerment* reported that lower-class men are not as likely to feel they have the power to affect their outcomes. Respondents varied from those who were what the researcher calls *potent actors* (those who believe they have the ability to take actions that affect their world) to *impotent reactors* (those who feel they are at the mercy of their economic situations). This orientation influenced consumption behaviours; for example, the professionals in the study who were likely to be potent actors set themselves up for financial opportunity and growth. They took very broad perspectives on investing and planned their budgets strategically.[65]

While they would like to have more in the way of material goods, working-class people do not necessarily envy those who rank above them in social standing.[66] The maintenance of a high-status lifestyle is sometimes not seen as worth the effort. As one blue-collar consumer commented: 'Life is very hectic for those people. There are more breakdowns and alcoholism. It must be very hard to sustain the status, the clothes, the parties that are expected. I don't think I'd want to take their place.'[67]

The blue-collar consumer quoted here may be right. While good things appear to go hand in hand with higher status and wealth, the picture is not that clear. The social scientist Emile Durkheim observed that suicide rates are much higher among the wealthy. He wrote in 1897, 'the possessors of most comfort suffer most'.[68] The quest for riches has the potential to result in depression, deviant behaviour and ruin. In fact, a survey of affluent American consumers (they made an average of $176,000 a year) supports this notion. Although these people are in the top 2.5 per cent income bracket in America, only 14 per cent said they are very well off.[69]

▶ The concept of a **taste culture**, which differentiates people in terms of their aesthetic and intellectual preferences, is helpful in understanding the important yet subtle distinctions in consumption choices among the social classes. Taste cultures largely reflect education (and are also income-related).[70] A distinction is often made between low-culture and high-culture groups (this is discussed in more detail towards the end of this chapter).

While such perspectives have met with criticism due to the implicit value judgements involved, they are valuable because they recognize the existence of groupings based on shared tastes in literature, art, home decoration and so on. In one of the classic studies of social differences in taste, researchers catalogued homeowners' possessions while asking more typical questions about income and occupation. Clusters of furnishings and decorative items which seemed to appear together with some regularity were identified, and different clusters were found depending on the consumer's social status. For example, religious objects, artificial flowers and still-life portraits tended to be found together in relatively lower-status living rooms, while a cluster containing abstract paintings, sculptures and modern furniture was more likely to appear in a higher-status home (see Figure 12.4).[71] We all carry stereotypical imagery of taste cultures in our heads. If you are told about one person that they like to visit museums and attend live theatre and about another that they like camping and fishing and like to attend a wrestling match, which one would you place in the highest social class segment? You were probably right.[72]

Another approach to social class focuses on differences in the types of *codes* (the ways meanings are expressed and interpreted by consumers) used within different social strata. Discovery of these codes is valuable to marketers, since this knowledge allows them to communicate to markets using concepts and terms most likely to be understood and appreciated by specific consumers.

▶ The nature of these codes varies among social classes. **Restricted codes** are dominant among the working class, while elaborated codes tend to be used by the middle and upper classes. Restricted codes focus on the content of objects, not on relationships among
▶ objects. **Elaborated codes**, in contrast, are more complex and depend upon a more sophisticated worldview. Some differences between these two general types of codes are provided in Table 12.1. As this table indicates, these code differences extend to the way consumers approach such basic concepts as time, social relationships and objects.

Marketing appeals that are constructed with these differences in mind will result in quite different messages. For example, a life insurance ad targeted at a lower-class person might depict in simple, straightforward terms a hard-working family man who feels good immediately after purchasing a policy. An upmarket appeal might depict a more affluent older couple surrounded by photos of their children and grandchildren and contain extensive copy emphasizing the satisfaction that comes from planning for the future and highlighting the benefits of a whole-life insurance policy.

Targeting the poor

While poor people obviously have less to spend than rich ones, they have the same basic needs as everyone else. Low-income families purchase such staples as milk, bread and tea at the same rates as average-income families. And minimum-wage level households spend a greater than average share on out-of-pocket health care costs, rent and food consumed at home. In 2001, certain household types in the EU-25 countries were more likely to be at risk of poverty: single parents with dependent children (these single parents are overwhelmingly female parents), old people living alone, single females and two-adult households with three or more dependent children.[73]

Table 12.1 Effects of restricted versus elaborated codes

	Restricted codes	Elaborated codes
General characteristics	Emphasize description and contents of objects Have implicit meanings (context dependent)	Emphasize analysis and interrelationships between objects, i.e. hierarchical organization and instrumental connections Have explicit meanings
Language	Use few qualifiers, i.e. few adjectives or adverbs Use concrete, descriptive, tangible symbolism	Have language rich in personal, individual qualifiers Use large vocabulary, complex conceptual hierarchy
Social relationships	Stress attributes of individuals over formal roles	Stress formal role structure, instrumental relationships
Time	Focus on present; have only general notion of future	Focus on instrumental relationship between present activities and future rewards
Physical space	Locate rooms, spaces in context of other rooms and places: e.g. 'front room', 'corner shop'	Identify rooms, spaces in terms of usage; formal ordering of spaces: e.g. 'dining room', 'financial district'
Implications for marketers	Stress inherent product quality, contents (or trustworthiness, goodness of 'real-type'), spokesperson Stress implicit fit of product with total lifestyle Use simple adjectives, descriptors	Stress differences, advantages vis-à-vis other products in terms of some autonomous evaluation criteria Stress product's instrumental ties to distant benefits Use complex adjectives, descriptors

Source: Adapted from Jeffrey F. Durgee, 'How Consumer Sub-Cultures Code Reality: A Look at Some Code Types', in Richard J. Lutz, ed., *Advances in Consumer Research* 13 (Provo, UT: Association for Consumer Research, 1986): 332.

The unemployed do feel alienated in a consumer society, since they are unable to obtain many of the items that our culture tells us we 'need' to be successful. However, idealized advertising portrayals do not seem to appeal to low-end consumers who have been interviewed by researchers. Apparently, one way to preserve self-esteem is by placing oneself outside the culture of consumption and emphasizing the value of a simple way of life with less emphasis on materialism. In some cases, they enjoy the advertising as entertainment without actually yearning for the products; a comment by one 32-year-old British woman is typical: 'They're not aimed at me, definitely not. It's fine to look at them, but they're not aimed at me so in the main I just pass over them.'[74] A more recent study identified other coping strategies among poor people when confronted with the consumption consequences of their own poverty. Such coping strategies could be rooted in fulfilling of role expectations for example through the feeling of good mother in spite of not being able to give the children a lot in material terms, in the feeling of independence coming from not being dependent on others in spite of a low income, or in the consolation that others are worse off.[75]

Some marketers are developing products and services for low-income consumers. These strategies may be obvious in some cases (or even bordering on the insulting), as when S.C. Johnson & Son, manufacturers of Raid insect spray, regularly hosts 'cockroach evictions' at inner-city housing developments. Other strategies raise important ethical issues, especially when marketers of so-called 'sin products' such as alcohol and tobacco single out what many feel is a vulnerable audience.

Still, a lot of companies are taking a second look at marketing to the poor because of their large numbers. The economist C.K. Pralahad added fuel to this fire with his book *The Fortune at the Bottom of the Pyramid*, which argued big companies could profit and help the world's 4 billion poor or low-income people by finding innovative ways to sell them soap and refrigerators.[76]

Some companies are getting into these vast markets by revamping their distribution systems or making their products simpler and less expensive. When Nestlé Brazil shrank the package size of its Bono cookies (no relation to the U2 singer) from 200 grams to 140 grams and dropped the price, sales jumped 40 per cent. Unilever called a new soap brand Ala so that illiterate people in Latin America could easily recognize it. In Mexico, cement company Cemex improved housing in poor areas after it introduced a pay-as-you-go system for buying building supplies.[77]

 Muhammad Yunus, a Bangladeshi economist, won the 2006 Nobel Prize in Economics for pioneering the concept of **microloans**. His Grameen Bank loans small sums – typically less than $100 – to entrepreneurs in developing countries. Many of these go to 'cell-phone women', who rent time on the phones to others in their remote villages. The bank has issued about 6 million loans to date, and almost 99 per cent of recipients repay them (compared to a 50 per cent repayment rate for a typical bank in a developing country).[78]

Targeting the rich

We live in an age where elite department stores sell Donna Karan and Calvin Klein Barbies, and Mattel's Pink Splendor Barbie comes complete with crystal jewellery and a bouffant gown sewn with 24-carat threads.[79] To dress that 'living doll', Victoria's Secret offers its Million Dollar Miracle Bra, with over 100 carats of real diamonds.[80] *Somebody* must be buying this stuff . . .

Many marketers try to target affluent markets. This practice often makes sense, since these consumers obviously have the resources to expend on costly products (often with higher profit margins). *The Robb Report*, a magazine targeted at the affluent (average reader income is $755,000), in 1996 estimated that 4.8 million American households had a net worth of at least $1 million, up 118 per cent from 1992. The magazine segments the wealthy into three markets: the marginally rich (household income $70,000–$99,999), the comfortably rich (income of $100,000–$249,000), and the super rich ($250,000+).[81]

However, it is a mistake to assume that everyone with a high income should be placed in the same market segment. As noted earlier, social class involves more than absolute income: it is also a way of life, and affluent consumers' interests and spending priorities are significantly affected by such factors as where they got their money, how they got it, and how long they have had it.[82] For example, the marginally rich tend to prefer sporting events to cultural activities, and are only half as likely as the super rich to frequent art galleries or the opera.[83]

The rich *are* different. But they are different from one another as well. Income alone is not a good predictor of consumer behaviour, which reminds us that the wealthy can be further segmented in terms of attitudes, values and preferences. As David found out, one significant difference is the one between 'old' and 'new' money.

▶ Multicultural dimensions

In a land where one-child families are the rule, Chinese parents spare few expenses when bringing up baby. They want to show off their pampered child and are eager to surround their 'little emperors' with status goods. To meet this need, foreign companies are rushing in, hawking the staples of Western baby care from disposable nappies to Disney cot sheets. These items are expensive luxuries in China, and plenty of families are splurging. Chinese families spend one-third to one-half of their disposable income on their children, according to industry estimates. The Disney Babies line of T-shirts, rattles and cot linens – all emblazoned with likenesses of baby Mickey Mouse and other familiar characters – are available in department stores in a dozen or so Chinese cities. These products are true extravagances: a Disney cotton T-shirt, for example, sells for the local equivalent of about $7.25–$8.45, compared to $1.20 for a Chinese-made shirt. But as a Disney spokesman observed, 'New parents are willing to pay the extra. Mickey is portrayed as fun and intelligent in China – characteristics parents want for their children.'[84]

Old money

When people have enough money for all intents and purposes to buy just about anything they want, ironically social distinctions no longer revolve around the amount of money they have. Instead, it appears to be important to consider *where* the money came from and *how* it is spent. The 'top out-of-sight class' (such as Julia's parents) live primarily on inherited money. People who have made vast amounts of money from their own labour do not tend to be included in this select group, though their flamboyant consumption patterns may represent an attempt to prove their wealth.[85] The mere presence of wealth is thus not sufficient to achieve social prominence. It must be accompanied by a family history of public service and philanthropy, which is often manifested in tangible markers that enable these donors to achieve a kind of immortality (e.g. Rockefeller University or the Whitney Museum).[86] 'Old money' consumers tend to make distinctions among themselves in terms of ancestry and lineage rather than wealth.[87] Old money people (like the Caldwells) are secure in their status. In a sense, they have been trained their whole lives to be rich and hence feel less the urgency to demonstrate their wealth at any given occasion. As the saying goes, discretion is a matter of honour.

The *nouveaux riches*

Other wealthy people do not know how to be rich. The Horatio Alger myth, the dream of going from 'rags to riches' through hard work and a bit of luck, is still a powerful force in Western society and, more recently, in Asian societies as well. Although many people do in fact become 'self-made millionaires', they often encounter a problem (although not the worst problem one could think of!) after they have become wealthy and have changed their social status: consumers who have achieved extreme wealth and have relatively recently become members of upper social classes are known as the *nouveaux riches*, a term that is sometimes used in a derogatory manner to describe newcomers to the world of wealth.

The *nouveau riche* phenomenon is also widespread in Russia and other eastern European countries, where the transition to capitalism has paved the way for a new class of wealthy consumers who are spending lavishly on luxury items. One study of wealthy Russians identified a group of 'super-spenders', who spend as much on discretionary items as they do on rent. They would like to spend more money, but are frustrated by the lack of quality products and services available to them.[88]

 Marketing opportunity

In a sixteenth-century fortress in Florence, the semi-annual Florence children's fashion show is on, and retail buyers from around the world are moving from one designer's booth to another, putting together their Spring lines. However, down in the basement, in an isolated booth, only buyers who have RSVP'd are allowed inside, and then only after entering a security code into a computer. Once in, they are served drinks in gold-rimmed goblets, and seated in gold chairs as they view video screens showing children playing and lounging in clothes that are elegant, understated, exquisitely detailed – and priced at hundreds of euros apiece. There are no actual clothes on display in the booth, nor order forms, nor any price lists. Such commercial touches are deemed *déclassé* by the creators of I Pinco Pallino.

'Definitely to my heart, our clothes are art,' says Stefano Cavalleri, the firm's 49-year-old founder. 'Extending our image is the key point, not selling more clothes.' But Pinco is indeed selling clothes. In a market where people have more money than ever and are always looking for new ways to spend it, Pinco is suddenly hot. These aren't children's clothes for everyone, not even among the rich. The target market: mothers who, in the words of the buyers thronging the Pinco booth, regard their children as 'fashion accessories'. The fashion house turns out some of the most expensive children's clothes available anywhere. A pale green organza dress embellished with hand-embroidered silk goes for €700. Dressing a child in a complete Pinco ensemble – featuring jacket, handbag, shoes and hat in signature silks and laces with detailed embroidery and sequins – will run into well over €1,100. Already selling his creations at only the most fashionable of department stores and boutiques in Europe and America, Mr Cavalleri is working on a plan to open a Pinco boutique on Manhattan's Upper East Side, where he vows to introduce New Yorkers to his 'fairy-tale world'.[89]

Alas, many *nouveaux riches* are plagued by *status anxiety*. They monitor the cultural environment to ensure that they are doing the 'right' thing, wearing the 'right clothes', being seen in the 'right places', using the 'right' caterer, and so on.[90] Flamboyant consumption can thus be viewed as a form of symbolic self-completion, where the excessive display of symbols thought to denote 'class' is used to make up for an internal lack of assurance about the 'correct' way to behave.[91]

STATUS SYMBOLS

People have a deep-seated tendency to evaluate themselves, their professional accomplishments, their material well-being and so on, in relation to others. The popular phrase 'keeping up with the Joneses' (in Japan, 'keeping up with the Satos') refers to the comparison between one's standard of living and that of one's neighbours.

Satisfaction is a relative concept, however. We hold ourselves to a standard defined by others that is constantly changing. Unfortunately, a major motivation for the purchase and display of products is not to enjoy them, but rather to let others know that we can afford them. In other words, these products function as status symbols. The desire to accumulate these 'badges of achievement' is summarized by the slogan 'He who dies with the most toys, wins'. Status-seeking is a significant source of motivation to procure appropriate products and services that the user hopes will let others know that they have 'made it'.

Conspicuous consumption

The motivation to consume for the sake of consuming was first discussed by the social analyst Thorstein Veblen at the turn of the last century. Veblen felt that a major role of products was for invidious distinction – they are used to inspire envy in others through
▶ display of wealth or power. Veblen coined the term **conspicuous consumption** to refer to people's desire to provide prominent visible evidence of their ability to afford luxury goods. Veblen's work was motivated by the excesses of his time. He wrote in the era of the robber barons, where the likes of J.P. Morgan, Henry Clay Frick, William Vanderbilt and others were building massive financial empires and flaunting their wealth by throwing lavish parties. Some of these events of excess became legendary, as described in this account:

> there were tales, repeated in the newspapers, of dinners on horseback; of banquets for pet dogs; of hundred-dollar bills folded into guests' dinner napkins; of a hostess who attracted attention by seating a chimpanzee at her table; of centerpieces in which lightly clad living maidens swam in glass tanks, or emerged from huge pies; of parties at which cigars were ceremoniously lighted with flaming banknotes of large denominations.[92]

The trophy wife

This flaunting of one's possessions even extended to wives: Veblen criticized the 'decorative' role women were often forced to play as they were bestowed with expensive clothes, pretentious homes and a life of leisure as a way to advertise the wealth of their husbands – a sort of 'walking advertisement'. Such fashions as high-heeled shoes, tight corsets, billowing trains on dresses and elaborate hairstyles all conspired to ensure that wealthy women could barely move without assistance, much less perform manual labour. Similarly, the Chinese practice of foot-binding turned women into cripples who had to be carried from place to place.

The modern potlatch

Veblen was inspired by anthropological studies of the Kwakiutl Indians, who lived in the
▶ American Pacific Northwest. These Indians had a ceremony called a **potlatch**, a feast

where the host showed off his wealth and gave extravagant presents to the guests. The more one gave away, the better one looked to the others. Sometimes, the host would use an even more radical strategy to flaunt his wealth. He would publicly destroy some of his property to demonstrate how much he had.

This ritual was also used as a social weapon: since guests were expected to reciprocate, a poorer rival could be humiliated by being invited to a lavish potlatch. The need to give away as much as the host, even though he could not afford it, would essentially force the hapless guest into bankruptcy. If this practice sounds 'primitive', think for a moment about many modern weddings. Parents commonly invest huge sums of money to throw a lavish party and compete with others for the distinction of giving their daughter the 'best' or most extravagant wedding, even if they have to save for 20 years to do so.

The leisure class

This process of conspicuous consumption was, for Veblen, most evident among what he termed the *leisure class*, people for whom productive work is taboo. In Marxist terms, this reflects a desire to link oneself to ownership or control of the means of production, rather than to the production itself. Any evidence that one actually has to work for a living is to be shunned, as suggested by the term the 'idle rich'.

Like the potlatch ritual, the desire to convince others that one has a surplus of resources creates the need for evidence of this abundance. Accordingly, priority is given to consumption activities that use up as many resources as possible in non-constructive pursuits. This *conspicuous waste* in turn shows others that one has the assets to spare. Veblen noted that 'we are told of certain Polynesian chiefs, who, under the stress of good form, preferred to starve rather than carry their food to their mouths with their own hands'.[93]

 Marketing opportunity

Consolidating for luxury

The luxury goods sector in Europe is in the midst of an important consolidation, as smaller groups find it increasingly difficult to compete with bigger rivals in terms of advertising spending, retail networks and production capacity. As a result, groups such as French luxury goods giant LVMH, Moët Hennessy and Gucci have been buying up smaller names over the past years. Perhaps the biggest 'fashion family' is LVMH, with its stable of fashion brands including Louis Vuitton, Christian Dior, Givenchy, Christian Lacroix, Celine, Loewe, Kenzo, Fendi and Emilio Pucci.

In an effort to take full control of production in order to maintain high standards of quality and to meet rigorous delivery schedules demanded by global retail customers, Giorgio Armani SpA recently established a joint venture with Italian menswear group Ermenegildo Zagna SpA to produce one of its menswear lines. As the wealthy become more attracted to yachting, the yachtmaker Swan has been bought by fashion house Leonardo Ferragamo to close the gap between high fashion and the high seas.[94]

The death – and rebirth – of status symbols

While ostentatious products fell out of favour in the 1970s, as a result of the rebellious previous decade, the 1990s and the early part of the twenty-first century (at least until the crisis set in in 2008) has seen a resurgence of interest in luxury goods. European companies such as Hermès International, LVMH Hennesey Louis Vuitton and Baccarat enjoyed sales gains of between 13 and 16 per cent, as affluent consumers once again indulged their desires for the finer things in life. One market researcher termed this trend 'the pleasure revenge' – people were tired of buying moderately, eating low-fat foods and so on, and as a result sales boomed for self-indulgent products from fur coats to premium ice creams and caviar. As the Chairman of LVMH put it: 'The appetite for

Le vrai pouvoir ne se montre pas.

VISA INFINITE
LA SEULE LIMITE SERA VOTRE IMAGINATION.

'The real power doesn't show': As this French ad for a visa card with infinite credit underlines, there may be truth in that really high class tends to be discreet.
Carte bleue

luxury is as strong as ever. The only difference is that in the 1980s, people would put a luxury trademark on anything. Today only the best sells.'[95] Think of the earlier quote concerning the conspicuous consumption around the shift from the nineteenth to the twentieth century – which examples of similarly spectacular (and excessive?) conspicuous consumption can you find dating from the recent turn of the century?

Parody display

As the competition to accumulate status symbols escalates, sometimes the best tactic is to switch gears and go into reverse. One way to do this is to deliberately *avoid* status symbols – that is, to seek status by mocking it. This sophisticated form of conspicuous consumption has been termed **parody display**.[96] A good example of parody display is the home-furnishing style known as High Tech, which was in vogue in America a few years ago. This motif incorporated the use of industrial equipment (e.g. floors were covered with plates used on the decks of destroyers), and pipes and support beams were deliberately exposed.[97] This decorating strategy was intended to show that one is so witty and 'in the know' that status symbols are not necessary. Hence, the popularity of old, torn blue jeans and 'utility' vehicles such as jeeps among the upper classes. 'True' status is thus shown by the adoption of product symbolism that is deliberately not fashionable.

CAPITAL AND PRACTICES: CLASS-BASED LIFESTYLES

We can now try to summarize the relationship between social class and consumption, by integrating a lot of what we have described in the preceding pages into one conceptual framework. The French sociologist Pierre Bourdieu described society in terms of
▶ a competition for different types of **capital**.[98] Capital, for Bourdieu, is resources that are acknowledged and can be used as assets in various contexts. He distinguished primarily between economic (money, as well as access to money, i.e. financing possibilities), cultural (education, cultural knowledge) and social (networks, social connections) capital. Cultural capital, however, is not exclusively a matter of formal education but also, more generally speaking, a matter of 'manners'. Take the example of dining out. This is one domain (or field as Bourdieu would call it), where there can be a lot at stake. Remember that scene from *Pretty Woman*, where Julia Roberts is trying to learn which fork is used for what in a highly formal dinner setting? This is an example of trying to pick up cultural capital. But it does not have to be as high-brow as that. Just knowing a little about what to expect from an Indian versus a Thai or a Chinese restaurant, how to compose a meal from a menu, what to drink with which course – all these little 'knowledges' also constitute cultural capital. And that capital must be mobilized whenever we are eating out, whereby we reveal something about how much of it we have and which kinds of class and other distinctions are brought into play, when we sit down at the table.[99]

For Bourdieu, social life can be seen as a number of games, where people constantly lose or win. Social domination, then, is an outcome of how these resources or types of capital are distributed and brought to use strategically in the social games. Business, of course, is such a game. But family (how to make a good one) is also considered a game. As such, the games are played in different fields, such as the already mentioned business and family, but also politics, sports, news, education, entertainment, science, art and so on. Hence, it is obvious that the same types of capital do not apply in all fields – it is difficult to qualify as a sports hero based on a doctoral dissertation. But not all great sports people become sports heroes – certain of them seem have this extra 'star quality', which may be rooted in their abilities to play the games well and exploit their capital to the maximum. And speaking of sports: the notion of cultural capital was used to analyze the distinction between the inner circle of hard core football fans and the larger circle of the wider fan community in the football clubs Liverpool FC (England) and Cork City (Ireland). It was found that part of the build-up of cultural capital for the die-hard fans was through the sacrifices made for the club and for attending the matches. Thus having sacrificed a lot of time, money, effort and even family events for the club provided a particular status for the football consumers.[100]

The position of each individual in these status games and their resources constitute the
▶ basis for a person's **habitus**, a structuring set of classifications and tastes that permeates our lives and determine or ways of behaviour as well as our judgement of different social phenomena, in short, our lifestyles. These systems of judgement permeate our lives and is also what permits the lower class people to not necessarily be envious of the rich, since apart from the lack of economic worries (which, as we have seen, the lower class people also attribute to the higher class people), there is not much to be envious about. Much of the high cultural and economic capital leisurely activities appear outright boring to the lower class, just as there is a tendency to consider high class social gatherings less warm and heartfelt compared to lower class social gatherings. Hence the driver of this whole
▶ system, according to Bourdieu, is the process of **distinction**. This process works in terms of the social differences that exist in society, the aspirations to overcome them through social mobility or the aspirations to keep them (from above as well as from below) in order to reconfirm one's own social universe.

Figure 12.5 presents a simplified lifestyle mapping based on Bourdieu's work. Bourdieu distinguishes between the general level of capital (since there is a high correlation between

Figure 12.5 Bourdieu's lifestyle map with examples of leisure consumption

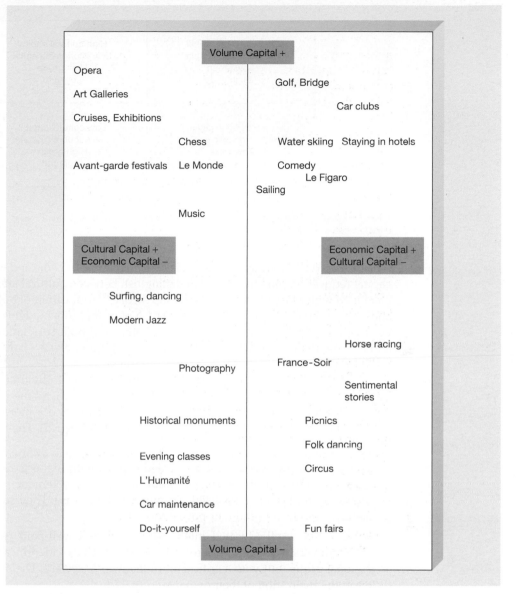

Source: Adapted from B. Moingeon, 'La sociologie de P. Bourdieu et son apport au marketing', *Recherches et Applications en Marketing*, vol. VIII no. 2 (1993) p. 123.

cultural and economic capital in society. Remember: going to school pays off) and the relative weight of cultural versus economic capital on the other. We can see the clear positioning and correlation between reading *Le Monde* (an intellectual daily newspaper), going to the opera and being a university professor, being a manager in the private sector, playing golf and reading the more conservative and business-friendly *Le Figaro*, being a worker, reading *L'Humanité* (traditionalist communist newspaper) and engaging in car repair and finally being a craftsman, reading the popular newspaper *France-Soir* and engaging in betting on horses in one's spare time.

   This approach has been applied within American consumer research to distinguish between consumer tastes among various social groupings.[101] More recently, an attempt has been made to translate Bourdieu's terms into a relatively simple lifestyle categorization

Figure 12.6 A lifestyle model based on grid-group theory and capital.

High cultural capital High economic capital Low group High grid	High cultural capital Low economic capital High group Low grid
Low cultural capital High economic capital Low group Low grid	Low cultural capital Low economic capital High group High grid

Source: Adapted from Henrik Dahl, *Hvis din nabo var en bil* (Copenhagen: Akademisk Forlag, 1997, 2nd ed. 2006).

scheme. Based on Bourdieu's notions of economic capital (income and wealth) and cultural capital (education plus the ability to distinguish between cultural styles and categories) combined with Mary Douglas's grid-group theory,[102] four different but fundamental consumer types are proposed (see Figure 12.6). Notice that this model is basically the same as in Figure 12.6 except that Bourdieu's hypothesized high correlation between cultural and economic capital has been replaced by a straightforward 2×2 matrix and the model has been turned 180 degrees around its vertical axis.

The distinction between grid and group refers to an individual's relation to their own social group and to the general social system (or grid). So the model distinguishes between people with high and low group identification and a more or less affirmative (high and low) relation to the organization of society (the grid). The model ends up with the following segments:

- *1st quadrant*: Professional, career-oriented people, with higher education and income, and with a rather individualistic attitude and an unproblematic relation to the social organization (they are responsible for much of it anyway). Their search for meaning is characterized by ambition for power and wealth.

- *2nd quadrant*: Well-educated intellectuals with less well-paid career opportunities (many university professors here), with a high degree of identification with their professional group, but with a critical attitude towards society. Their search for meaning lies in the realization of their own intellectual ideals.

- *3rd quadrant*: Relatively wealthy people, with low education and/or not so culturally interested (the stereotypical self-made (wo)man). Being preoccupied first and foremost with their own private lives, they do not show any particular interest in society, neither on a group level nor on a social level, and they may even tend to consider the rest of society (and everything strange) as relatively hostile. Often looked down upon by people from the second quadrant because of their alleged bad cultural tastes and their lack of social engagement.

- *4th quadrant*: Low on both types of capital, money and education, but with strong group affiliation and a relatively affirmative attitude towards society, these people tend to be locally oriented. The search for meaning is rooted in their daily activities and daily lives.[103]

This model has so far been applied only in Denmark. It is, however, likely to function in other countries as well, especially perhaps in more egalitarian societies than the French one, since that would possibly indicate less correlation between economic and cultural capital.

Practice theory and consumer behaviour

When Bourdieu was doing fieldwork in Algeria, he noticed the following things about the relation between what people actually did and what they said they did. First of all, as we have already discussed, there was not a very good correspondence between people's actions and their own accounts of these actions. In other words, people are not very accurate in accounting for their own behaviour. But what was more revealing was that the way people acted was not really in accordance with their own explicit values and norms either. In other words, it was as if people often behaved in ways that was difficult to explain based on their own individual accounts. In order to find a word that would take into consideration this distance between our reflections and our behaviour, Bourdieu came up with a theory of practice.

▶ Remember Bourdieu's fondness for considering social life as constituted of competitive games? **Practice theory** is normally described in terms of the sportsperson's 'feel' for the game.[104] It is very difficult for, say, a footballer to explain how to play football. It is also impossible for the same footballer to go through a lot of conscious decision processes when deciding how to move on the field, what to do with the ball, etc. There is simply no time for evaluating alternatives. Instead they act spontaneously based on experiences with how the game may unfold. That is not to say that their behaviour is determined, but it does follow certain logics or templates that the footballer can master to a larger or smaller degree.

A practice then, is, a routinised type of behaviour which involves both bodily and mental activities (the footballer moves and 'thinks' even if they do not engage in rational decision making as we have described it earlier), it involves things and their use (a football field of a certain size and design, a ball (rather important) and possibly appropriate clothes in specific colours, goals with posts, net, etc.) and some background knowledge (knowing what all this is used for, what the different lines mean, etc.).[105]

Now, the trick is to consider not just playing a football match but all our daily activities along those lines. How do we know how to go to the movies? Go to a party? To hike? To shop in the supermarket? And so on and so forth. According to practice theory, all these things are embedded in certain routines (that is we do not make decisions in the classical sense while doing them). The routines are also embedded in the things and their design. We grab a cup by its handle, because it is there – and we are made aware of this when for instance offered tea in glasses as in Turkey or elsewhere in the Middle East. This is why practice theory is especially interested in how the presence and design of the things around us influence the way we use them.[106]

Just as practice theory considers whether the design of things determine their use (rather than the other way round), so it also suggests that activities generate wants (remember the discussion of effect hierarchies). In other words, it is because we engage in certain activities that we generate personal wants and desires, not our wants and desires that make us participate in certain activities. This might not sound very revolutionary, but a lot of consumer research actually assumes that wants (motivations, that is) come first and lead us to engage in certain types of consumption. Practice theorists say that practices in many cases are more likely to come first, and then generate wants.[107] For example, if we have established certain types of cooking routines (or cooking practices) in our family (for example cooking from scratch and not relying on ready-to-eat meals), these practices generate the wants for fresh produce, etc.

Practice theory does not turn us into robots of our own social background, because the schemes of social practice are hardly ever very precise about what exactly to do. Consider how to eat 'properly'. How do we know when that practice is 'obeyed'? Not because of a very precise manual; in fact our children can point out our practices, when they act as if there is a very careful prescription of how to perform it, cutting the meat with excessively pointing little fingers, lifting the fork with great care to the mouth and slowly and without smearing anything on the side of the mouth, putting the bite in, then chewing it carefully with an exaggerated expression of satisfaction and happiness on their faces. In other words, if practices are performed consciously, they often stop being 'normal social practices' and become overdramatized performances instead. A good actor is someone who knows about this and can perform the practices of a persona in such a way that the audience cannot see that the actor is just performing a newly learned script.

Why is practice theory important to consumer research? Well, for one thing it might contribute to our understanding of why it is so difficult to alter people's consumption behaviour to more sustainable types and possibly help to solve that problem (see Alan Warde's reflections in his 'CB as I see it' column below), since a lot of our daily unsustainable consumption seems to be embedded in practices rather than deliberate choices. How many of you shower more or less 'on autopilot' in the morning, or maybe several times during the day? Do you 'choose' to shower? Well, not really, right? You just do it (as the Nike slogan goes). Not so many decades ago, showering was not a daily routine for many people, the most critical places were washed in front of the washbowl, and the weekly or so bath took care of the thorough cleaning. How did showering become such a 'normal routine' in a few decades, that we hardly think about it anymore?[108] Well, this is a good example of how practices work.

Since practices are embedded in our social background with its resources of capital, it can also profoundly alter the way we look at decision making and the way our social class background influences it. You would believe that the choice of where to study is an extremely rational one, since it basically influences your career opportunities and thereby to a large extent determines a lot of your social and economic possibilities for the rest of your life. One study examined the choice of college from a practice perspective and concluded that, especially for people of a working-class background, the fit of the school with previous life experiences was the deciding factor for choice. So students from this background tended to choose based on how much they felt 'at home' during the college visit rather than based on 'abstract information' like academic reputation, the academic quality of the curricula, etc.[109] Hence, it was the practical experience of the school 'fitting like a glove' to oneself that proved decisive. Again, this helps explain why social inequalities and class backgrounds tend to reproduce themselves from generation to generation.

Consumer behaviour as I see it . . .

Consumption and practice

Much of my research has been directed towards developing sociological explanations which go beyond models which put at their core a portrait of the consumer as an individual decision maker. It is as if both contemporary sociological and psychological ways of studying the consumer takes a point of departure in the individual, either as someone acting according to a set of norms and values, or someone acting according to theories of rational decision-making. My quest is to find much needed alternative theoretical and conceptual approaches to consumption, ones which neither turn the consumer into a dupe of the commercial and industrial system nor into a utility-maximizer. A theory of practice is a candidate.

Alan Warde
University of Manchester

The appeal of theories of practice is that they start from a look at the consumer as neither an individual decision maker, as with rational action theory, nor as someone who just obeys the norms and rules of a society or an organization. Instead, from this perspective, analysis begins from understanding the history and development of practices, for example eating or driving. The term practice implies types of behaviour collectively shared (we all do it, to some degree), historically established (we have learned it from copying others), normatively regulated (there are certain 'rights' and 'wrongs') and routinely reproduced (we don't have to think about 'how' we do it in daily life). Practices are not very precisely described, even if we all know 'how it should be done'. We also tend to pick our practices with some degree of freedom according to situation (like eating chicken with our fingers). We also tend to change practices gradually through improvisation as we go about our everyday lives.

Participants in a practice exhibit common understanding, know-how, and belief in the value of the practice. They act in accordance with a set of conventions which seem appropriate given their resources, dispositions and previous experience. Hence everyone does not perform the practice in an identical manner; there are class, gender and generational differences, and also differentiation of roles and positions based on expertise and experience within, for instance, a particular class setting.

The relevance to consumption comes from the insight that items 'consumed' are put to use in the course of engaging in particular practices and that being a competent practitioner requires appropriate consumption of goods and services. The practice, so to speak, requires that competent practitioners will avail themselves of the requisite services, possess the appropriate tools, and devote a suitable level of attention to the conduct of the practice. In this sense, practices precede individuals; practices determine the basic parameters of behaviour, including the purchase and use of commodities.

What is the use of practice theory? Well, today, malign consequences of ordinary and routine consumption associated with everyday practices have escalated into a public issue – most notably environmental sustainability. Collective bad habits, from wasting food and water, to the polluting effects of transport and energy generation, seem globally unsustainable. The principal current solutions focus on changing the behaviour of individuals. Yet changing popular expectations about the right to consume freely looks close to impossible: giving people information is not very effective in altering their behaviour; changing their values so that they wish to act better has proven extremely difficult; and they tend to resist state regulation and protest against taxation designed to reform their consumption patterns.

This is where practice theory may be of use. The principal implication of a theory of practice is that the sources of changed behaviour lie in the processes whereby practices themselves are repeated or transformed. Perhaps we can devise more effective ways of modifying or eliminating damaging behaviour by pursuing the insight that consumption exists for the sake of practices and work at that level rather than on individuals. Hence my current research objective is to understand how practices change.

CHAPTER SUMMARY

- The field of behavioural economics considers how consumers decide what to do with their money. In particular, *discretionary expenditures* are made only when people are able and willing to spend money on items above and beyond their basic needs. *Consumer confidence* – the state of mind consumers have about their own personal situation, as well as their feelings about their overall economic prospects – helps to determine whether they will purchase goods and services, take on debt or save their money.

- In the past ten years, consumers overall have been relatively pessimistic about their future prospects. A lower level of resources has caused a shift towards an emphasis on quality products that are reasonably priced. Consumers are less tolerant of exaggerated or vague product claims, and they are more sceptical about marketing activities. Consumers in their twenties are particularly sceptical about the economy and marketing targeted at their age group.

- A consumer's *social class* refers to their standing in society. It is determined by a number of factors, including education, occupation and income.

- Virtually all groups make distinctions among members in terms of relative superiority, power and access to valued resources. This *social stratification* creates a status hierarchy, where some goods are preferred over others and are used to categorize their owners' social class.

- While income is an important indicator of social class, the relationship is far from perfect since social class is also determined by such factors as place of residence, cultural interests and worldview.

- Purchase decisions are sometimes influenced by the desire to 'buy up' to a higher social class or to engage in the process of *conspicuous consumption*, where one's status is flaunted by the deliberate and non-constructive use of valuable resources. This spending pattern is a characteristic of the *nouveaux riches*, whose relatively recent acquisition of income, rather than ancestry or breeding, is responsible for their increased *social mobility*.

- Products are used as status symbols to communicate real or desired social class. *Parody display* occurs when consumers seek status by deliberately avoiding fashionable products.

- Theories of capital explains how resources come in different types and for different uses in various social settings. Most important are cultural capital (education, knowledge, manners) and economic capital (wealth or access to financing), but social capital (the networks you can draw from) is also important. Different types of capital distinguish different social classes.

- Theories of practice explain our behaviour, rooted in routinised patterns that we have learned, most significantly from our class background. Practices thus offers a different perspective on consumer behaviour that is less dependent on conscious decision making.

▶ KEY TERMS

Behavioural economics (p. 454)

Capital (p. 478)

Chavs (p. 465)

Conspicuous consumption (p. 475)

Consumer confidence (p. 457)

Distinction (p. 478)

Discretionary income (p. 456)

Elaborated codes (p. 471)

Habitus (p. 478)

Homogamy (p. 462)

Microloans (p. 473)

Parody display (p. 477)

Potlatch (p. 475)

Practice theory (p. 481)

Restricted codes (p. 471)

Savings rate (p. 458)

Social class (p. 460)

Social hierarchies (p. 461)

Social mobility (p. 466)

Social stratification (p. 463)

Status crystallization (p. 469)

Status symbols (p. 454)

Taste culture (p. 471)

▶ CONSUMER BEHAVIOUR CHALLENGE

1 The concepts *income* and *wealth* are measured in different ways throughout Europe, in spite of the standardization of currency that took place in 1999. Look through several recent issues of *Review of Income and Wealth* to get an idea of how these concepts differ across countries. For marketers, do you have any suggestions as to how to segment income groups for a Europe-wide strategy?

2 What are some of the obstacles to measuring social class in European society? Discuss some ways to get around these obstacles.

3 What consumption differences might you expect to observe between a family characterized as underprivileged vs. one whose income is average for its social class?

4 When is social class likely to be a better predictor of consumer behaviour than mere knowledge of a person's income?

5 How do you assign people to social classes, or do you at all? What consumption cues do you use (e.g. clothing, speech, cars, etc.) to determine social standing?

6 Thorstein Veblen argued that women were often used as a vehicle to display their husbands' wealth. Is this argument still valid today?

7 Given present environmental conditions and dwindling resources, what is the future of 'conspicuous waste'? Can the desire to impress others with affluence ever be eliminated? If not, can it take on a less dangerous form?

8 Some people argue that status symbols are dead. Do you agree?

9 Compile a list of occupations, and ask a sample of students who are studying a variety of subjects (both business and non-business) to rank the prestige of these jobs. Can you detect any differences in these rankings as a function of students' subjects?

10 Compile ads that depict consumers of different social classes. What generalizations can you make about the reality of these ads and about the media in which they appear?

11 Identify a current set of fraudulent status symbols, and construct profiles of consumers who are wearing or using these products. Are these profiles consistent with the images portrayed in each product's promotional messages?

12 The chapter observes that some marketers are finding 'greener pastures' by targeting low-income people. How ethical is it to single out consumers who cannot afford to waste their precious resources on discretionary items? Under what circumstances should this segmentation strategy be encouraged or discouraged?

For additional material see the companion website at www.pearsoned.co.uk/solomon

NOTES

1. Fred van Raaij, 'Economic psychology', *Journal of Economic Psychology* 1 (1981): 1–24.
2. Pierre Bourdieu, *Distinction: A Social Critique of the Judgment of Taste* (Cambridge, MA: Harvard University Press, 1984).
3. Peter S.H. Leeflang and W. Fred van Raaij, 'The changing consumer in the European Union: A meta-analysis', *International Journal of Research in Marketing* 12 (1995): 373–87.
4. Data in this section are adapted from Fabian Linden, *Consumer Affluence: The Next Wave* (New York: The Conference Board, Inc., 1994); 'Trends in households in the European Union: 1995–2025', *Eurostat, Statistics in Focus*, Theme 3–24/2003 (Luxembourg: Office for Official Publications of the European Communities, 2004).
5. 'Trends in households in the European Union: 1995–2025', *ibid.*: 51.
6. 'Living conditions in Europe: Statistical pocketbook', Earnings and Income, *Eurostat* (Luxembourg: Office for Official Publications of the European Communities, 2000): 65.
7. 'Trends in households in the European Union: 1995–2025', *op. cit.*, 'Earnings of men and women', *op. cit.*: 80; see also Hugh Muir, 'Women in less than 10 per cent of top jobs', *The Guardian* (5 January 2004), http://www.guardian.co.uk/gender/story/0,11812,1116127,00.html; Melissa Benn, 'Jobs for the Boys', *The Guardian* (5 January 2004).
8. 'Trends in households in the European Union: 1995–2025', *op. cit.*, 'Education and its outcomes', *op. cit.*: 44.
9. Christopher D. Carroll, 'How does future income affect current consumption?', *Quarterly Journal of Economics* 109 (February 1994) 1: 111–47.
10. 'Demographic statistics, 1997: Population and social conditions series', *Eurostat* (Luxembourg: Office for Official Publications of the European Communities, 1997). See also the Europa Server at: http://europa.eu.int.
11. http://epp.eurostat.ec.europa.eu/tgm/table.do?tab=table&init=1&plugin=1&language=en&pcode=tsdsc260, accessed 2 December 2008.
12. Jose J.F. Medina, Joel Saegert and Alicia Gresham, 'Comparison of Mexican-American and Anglo-American attitudes toward money', *Journal of Consumer Affairs* 30(1) (1996): 124–45.
13. Kirk Johnson, 'Sit down. Breathe deeply. This is *really* scary stuff', *New York Times* (16 April 1995): F5. For a scale that measures consumer frugality, see John L. Lastovicka, Lance A. Bettencourt, Renee Shaw Hughner and Ronald J. Kuntze, 'Lifestyle of the tight and frugal: Theory and measurement', *Journal of Consumer Research* 26 (June 1999): 85–98.
14. Robert Sullivan, 'Americans and their money', *Worth* (June 1994): 60 (12).

15. 'Frontiers: Planning or consumer change in Europe 96/97', 2 (London: The Henley Centre, 1996).

16. George Katona, 'Consumer saving patterns', *Journal of Consumer Research* 1 (June 1974): 1–12.

17. 'Trends in households in the European Union: 1995–2025', *op. cit.*, 'What the EU citizens think about their living conditions', *op. cit.*: 127.

18. Güliz Ger and Russell Belk, 'Cross-Cultural Differences in Materialism', *Journal of Economic Psychology*, 17(1) (1996): 55–77; Güliz Ger and Russell Belk, 'Accounting for materialism in four cultures', *Journal of Material Culture* 4(2) (1999): 183–204.

19. Ernest Beck, 'Why custom-made shirts are a cut above', *Wall Street Journal Europe* (4–5 April 1997): 8.

20. Floyd L. Ruch and Davidip G. Zimbardo, *Psychology and Life*, 8th edn (Glenview, IL: Scott, Foresman, 1971).

21. Louise Do Rosario, 'Privilege in China's classless society', *World Press Review* 33 (December 1986): 58.

22. Aditya Chakrabortty, 'Out with curry and Bollywood', *The Financial Times* (24 November 2004), http://news.ft.com/cms/s/54595ae4-3e4a-11d9-a9d7-00000e2511c8.html.

23. Jonathan H. Turner, *Sociology: Studying the Human System*, 2nd edn (Santa Monica, CA: Goodyear, 1981).

24. *Ibid*.

25. Richard P. Coleman, 'The continuing significance of social class to marketing', *Journal of Consumer Research* 10 (December 1983): 265–80; Turner, *Sociology, op. cit.*

26. Ernest Beck, 'Cabin fever swirls around posh cottages on Norwegian coast', *Wall Street Journal Europe* (6 August 1997): 1.

27. Quoted by Richard P. Coleman and Lee Rainwater, *Standing in America: New Dimensions of Class* (New York: Basic Books, 1978): 89.

28. *Ibid*.

29. Turner, *Sociology, op. cit.*

30. Howard W. French, 'Chinese Children Learn Class, Minus the Struggle', *New York Times Online* (22 September 2006), accessed 22 September 2006; Bay Fang, 'The Shanghai High Life', *U.S. News & World Report* (20 June 2005), www.usnews.com/usnews/biztech/articles/050620/20china.b2.htm, accessed 20 June 2005, http://travel.guardian.co.uk/cities/story/0,7450,489488,00.html, accessed 20 June 2005; Russell Flannery, 'Long Live the $25 Cigar', *Forbes* (27 December 2004): 51; Clay Chandler, 'China Deluxe', *Fortune* (26 July 2004): 149–56; Matthew Forney, 'How Nike Figured Out China', *Time* (November 2004): A10–A14; J. David Lynch, 'Emerging Middle Class Reshaping China', *USA Today* (November 12, 2002): 13A.

31. Eric Bellman, 'Name Game: As Economy Grows, India Goes for Designer Goods', *Wall Street Journal* (27 March 2007): A1.

32. Rohit Varman and Ram Manohar Vikas, 'Freedom and consumption: Towards conceptualizing systemic constraints for sualtern consumers in a capitalist society', *Consumption, Markets and Culture* 10(2) (2007): 117–31.

33. James Sterngold, 'How do you define status? A new BMW in the drive. An old rock in the garden', *New York Times* (28 December 1989): C1.

34. Cecilie Rohwedder, 'Design Houses Build Stores, Pamper Demanding Shoppers in Fashion-Industry Hot Spot', *Wall Street Journal on the Web* (23 January 2004).

35. http://epp.eurostat.ec.europa.eu/tgm/table.do?tab=table&init=1&plugin=1&language=en&pcode=tsdsc260, accessed 2 December 2008.

36. Robin Knight, 'Just you move over, 'Enry 'Iggins: A new regard for profits and talent cracks Britain's old class system', *U.S. News & World Report* 106 (24 April 1989): 40.

37. Robert Guy Matthews, 'Bawdy British Ads Target Hot Youth', *Wall Street Journal* (20 April 2005): B9.

38. Turner, *Sociology, op. cit.*: 260.

39. See Ronald Paul Hill and Mark Stamey, 'The homeless in America: An examination of possessions and consumption behaviors', *Journal of Consumer Research* 17 (December 1990): 303–21.

40. Joseph Kahl, *The American Class Structure* (New York: Holt, Rinehart & Winston, 1961).

41. Leonard Beeghley, *The Structure of Social Stratification in The United States*, 3rd edn (Allyn and Bacon, 2000).

42. Coleman and Rainwater, *Standing in America, op. cit.*: 220.

43. Turner, *Sociology, op. cit.*

44. See Coleman, 'The continuing significance of social class to marketing', *op. cit.*; Charles M. Schaninger, 'Social class versus income revisited: An empirical investigation', *Journal of Marketing Research* 18 (May 1981): 192–208.

45. Coleman, 'The continuing significance of social class to marketing', *op. cit.*

46. Bernard Dubois and Gilles Laurent, 'Is There a Euro-consumer for Luxury Goods?' in W. Fred van Raaij and Gary J. Bamossy (eds), *European Advances in Consumer Research* 1 (Provo, UT: Association for Consumer Research, 1993): 59–69; Bernard Dubois and Gilles Laurent, 'Luxury Possessions and Practices: An Empirical Scale', in F. Hansen (ed.), *European Advances in Consumer Research* 2 (Provo, UT: Association for Consumer Research, 1995): 69–77; Bernard Dubois and Patrick Duquesne, 'The market for luxury goods: Income versus culture', *European Journal of Marketing* 27(1) (1993): 35–44.

47. August B. Hollingshead and Fredrick C. Redlich, *Social Class and Mental Illness: A Community Study* (New York: John Wiley, 1958).

48. John Mager and Lynn R. Kahle, 'Is the whole more than the sum of the parts? Re-evaluating social status in marketing', *Journal of Business Psychology* 10(1) (1995): 3–18.

49. R. Vanneman and F.C. Pampel, 'The American perception of class and status', *American Sociological Review* 42 (June 1977): 422–37.

50. Donald W. Hendon, Emelda L. Williams and Douglas E. Huffman, 'Social class system revisited', *Journal of Business Research* 17 (November 1988): 259.

51. Coleman, 'The continuing significance of social class to marketing', *op. cit.*

52. Gerhard E. Lenski, 'Status crystallization: A non-vertical dimension of social status', *American Sociological Review* 19 (August 1954): 405–12.

53. Richard P. Coleman, 'The Significance of Social Stratification in Selling', in *Marketing: A Maturing Discipline, Proceedings of the American Marketing Association 43rd National Conference*, ed. Martin L. Bell (Chicago: American Marketing Association, 1960): 171–84.

54. Melinda Beck and Richard Sandza, 'The lottery craze: Multimillion dollar prizes raise new concerns that the games prey on the poor', *Newsweek* (2 September 1985): 16; Rhoda E. McKinney, 'Has money spoiled the lottery millionaires?' *Ebony* (December 1988): 150.

55. E. Barth and W. Watson, 'Questionable assumptions in the theory of social stratification', *Pacific Sociological Review* 7 (Spring 1964): 10–16.

56. Zick Rubin, 'Do American women marry up?' *American Sociological Review* 33 (1968): 750–60.

57. Sue Browder, 'Don't be afraid to marry down', *Cosmopolitan* (June 1987): 236.

58. K.U. Ritter and L.L. Hargens, 'Occupational positions and class identifications of married working women: A test of the asymmetry hypothesis', *American Journal of Sociology* 80 (January 1975): 934–48.

59. Browder, 'Don't be afraid to marry down', *op. cit.*: 236.

60. J. Michael Munson and W. Austin Spivey, 'Product and brand-user stereotypes among social classes: Implications for advertising strategy', *Journal of Advertising Research* 21 (August 1981): 37–45.

61. Stuart U. Rich and Subhash C. Jain, 'Social class and life cycle as predictors of shopping behavior', *Journal of Marketing Research* 5 (February 1968): 41–9.

62. Thomas W. Osborn, 'Analytic techniques for opportunity marketing', *Marketing Communications* (September 1987): 49–63.

63. Coleman, 'The continuing significance of social class to marketing', *op. cit.*

64. Jeffrey F. Durgee, 'How Consumer Sub-Cultures Code Reality: A Look at Some Code Types', in Richard J. Lutz, ed., *Advances in Consumer Research* 13 (Provo, UT: Association for Consumer Research, 1986): 332–7.

65. Paul C. Henry, 'Social class, market situation, and consumers' metaphors of (dis)empowerment', *Journal of Consumer Research* 31 (March 2005): 766–78.

66. David Halle, *America's Working Man: Work, Home, and Politics Among Blue-Collar Owners* (Chicago: University of Chicago Press, 1984); David Montgomery, 'America's working man', *Monthly Review* (1985): 1.

67. Quoted in Coleman and Rainwater, *Standing in America*, *op. cit.*: 139.

68. Durkheim (1958), quoted in Roger Brown, *Social Psychology* (New York: The Free Press, 1965).

69. Lenore Skenazy, 'Affluent, like masses, are flush with worries', *Advertising Age* (10 July 1989): 55.

70. Herbert J. Gans, 'Popular Culture in America: Social Problem in a Mass Society or Social Asset in a Pluralist Society?' in Howard S. Becker (ed.), *Social Problems: A Modern Approach* (New York: Wiley, 1966); Helga Dittmar, 'Material possessions as stereotypes: Material images of different socio-economic groups', *Journal of Economic Psychology* 15 (1994): 561–85; Helga Dittmar and Lucy Pepper, 'To have is to be: Materialism and person perception in working class and middle class British adolescents', *Journal of Economic Psychology* 15 (1994): 233–5.

71. Edward O. Laumann and James S. House, 'Living room styles and social attributes: The patterning of material artifacts in a modern urban community', *Sociology and Social Research* 54 (April 1970): 321–42; see also Stephen S. Bell, Morris B. Holbrook and Michael R. Solomon, 'Combining esthetic and social value to explain preferences for product styles with the incorporation of personality and ensemble effects', *Journal of Social Behavior and Personality* (1991) 6: 243–74.

72. Eugene Sivadas, George Mathew, and David J. Curry, 'A preliminary examination of the continuing significance of social class to marketing: A geodemographic replication', *Journal of Consumer Marketing* 41(6) (1997): 463–79. See also Morris B. Holbrook, Michael J. Weiss, and John Habich, 'Class-related distinctions in American cultural tastes', *Empirical Studies of the Arts* 22(1) (2004): 91–115.

73. Eurostat yearbook 2008, At-risk-of-poverty rate after social transfers, by household type, EU-25, 2005, (Luxembourg: Office for Official Publications of the European Communities, 2008): 226.

74. Quoted in Richard Elliott, 'How do the unemployed maintain their identity in a culture of consumption?' in Hansen (ed.), *European Advances in Consumer Research* 2: 1–4, at 3.

75. Kathy Hamilton and Miriam Catterell, 'I Can Do It! Consumer Coping and Poverty', in A.Y. Lee and D. Soman (eds), *Advances in Consumer Research* XXXV (2008): 551–6.

76. C.K. Pralahad, *The Fortune at the Bottom of the Pyramid: Eradicating Poverty Through Profits* (Philadelphia: Wharton School Publishing, 2004).

77. Antonio Regalado, 'Marketers Pursue the Shallow-Pocketed', *Wall Street Journal* (26 January 2007): B3.

78. www.radicalcongruency.com/20061014-microfinance-wins-the-nobel-prize (22 July 2007), accessed 24 July 2007.

79. Cyndee Miller, 'New Line of Barbie dolls targets big, rich kids', *Marketing News* (17 June 1996): 6.

78. Cyndee Miller, 'Baubles are back', *Marketing News* (14 April 1997): 1(2).

81. Anita Sharpe, 'Magazines for the rich rake in readers', *Wall Street Journal* (16 February 1996): B1 (2).

82. 'Reading the Buyer's Mind', *U.S. News & World Report* (16 March 1987): 59.

83. Rebecca Piirto Heath, 'Life on easy street', *American Demographics* (April 1997): 33–8.

84. Quoted in 'Western companies compete to win business of Chinese babies', *Wall Street Journal Interactive Edition* (15 May 1998).

85. Paul Fussell, *Class: A Guide Through the American Status System* (New York: Summit Books, 1983): 29.

86. Elizabeth C. Hirschman, 'Secular immortality and the American ideology of affluence', *Journal of Consumer Research* 17 (June 1990): 31–42.

87. Coleman and Rainwater, *Standing in America*, *op. cit.*: 150.

88. M.H. Moore, 'Homing in on Russian "Super Spenders"', *Adweek* (28 February 1994): 14–16. See also: Carol Vogel, 'Fabergé collection bought by Russian for a return home', *The New York Times* (5 February 2004), http://www.nytimes.com/2004/02/05/arts/design/05FABE.html?th=&pagewanted=print&position.

89. Monica Langley, 'Italian firm fashions a look tailor-made for indulgent parents', *Wall Street Journal* (24 August 2000): A1.

90. Jason DeParle, 'Spy anxiety: The smart magazine that makes smart people nervous about their standing', *Washingtonian Monthly* (February 1989): 10.

91. For an examination of retailing issues related to the need for status, see Jacqueline Kilsheimer Eastman, Leisa Reinecke Flynn and Ronald E. Goldsmith, 'Shopping for status: The retail managerial implications', *Association of Marketing Theory and Practice* (Spring 1994): 125–30.

92. John Brooks, *Showing off in America* (Boston: Little, Brown, 1981): 13.

93. Thorstein Veblen, *The Theory of the Leisure Class* (1899; reprint, New York: New American Library, 1953): 45.

94. Teri Agins, 'Luxury match? LVMH targets Donna Karan', *Wall Street Journal* (19 December 2000): B1; Deborah Ball, 'High style on the high seas', *Wall Street Journal* (14 September 2000): B1; Deborah Ball, 'Italy's Finpart to acquire Cerruti, Gucci set to buy Zamasport Unit', *Wall Street Journal* (9 October 2000): B16.

95. Quoted in Miller, 'Baubles are back', *op. cit.*; Elaine Underwood, 'Luxury's tide turns', *Brandweek* (7 March 1994): 18–22. See also Ball, 'Italy's Finpart to acquire Cerruti', *op. cit.*

96. Brooks, *Showing off in America*, *op. cit.*

97. *Ibid.*: 31–2.

98. Pierre Bourdieu, *La Distinction: Critique Social du Jugement* (Paris: Editions de Minuit, 1979; Eng. trans. 1984).

99. Alan Warde, Lydia Martens and Wendy Olsen, 'Consumption and the problem of variety: Cultural omnivorousness, social distinction, and dining out', *Sociology* 33(1) (1999): 105–27.

100. Brendan Richardson and Darach Turley, 'It's Far More Important Than That: Football Fandom and Cultural Capital', in S. Borghini, M.A. McGrath and C. Otnes (eds), *European Advances in Consumer Research* (Duluth, MN: Association for Consumer Research, 2008): 33–8.

101. Douglas B. Holt, 'Does cultural capital structure American consumption?' *Journal of Consumer Research* 25 (June 1998): 1–25.

102. Mary Douglas, *Natural Symbols* (New York: Random House, 1973).

103. Henrik Dahl, *Hvis din nabo var en bil* (Copenhagen: Akademisk forlag 1997), 55–81.

104. Pierre Bourdieu, *The Logic of Practice* (Stanford, CA: Stanford University Press, 1990).

105. Andreas Reckwitz, 'Toward a theory of social practices: A development in culturalist theorizing', *European Journal of Social Theory* 5(2) (2002): 243–63.

106. Elizabeth Shove, Matthew Watson, Martin Hand, and Jack Ingram, *The Design of Everyday Life* (Oxford: Berg, 2007).

107. Alan Warde, 'Consumption and theories of practice', *Journal of Consumer Culture* 5(2) (2005): 131–53.

108. Elisabeth Shove, 'Users, technologies and experiences of comfort, cleanliness and convenience', *Innovation. The European Journal of Social Science Research* 16(2) (2003): 193–206.

109. Douglas E. Allen, 'Toward a theory of consumer choice as sociohistorically shaped practical experience: The fits-like-a-glove (FLAG) framework', *Journal of Consumer Research* 28 (March 2002): 515–32.

Taking on adulthood: a story of consumption constraint

MARIA PIACENTINI, Lancaster University, UK

SALLY HIBBERT, Nottingham University, UK

MARGARET K. HOGG, Lancaster University, UK

OVERVIEW

Consumption plays an important role in identity projects (Arnould and Thompson, 2005), often representing an important source of self-esteem and self-worth. Contemporary understanding of consumption has emerged from studies of relatively privileged consumers, people who do not face major financial constraints in their daily lives. Yet, we know that a vast proportion of the world's population face great financial pressure, which affects their consumption choices (Hill, 2002). The ways in which financially constrained consumers make consumption choices is a relatively under-explored area of consumer behaviour.

Understanding of constrained consumption has primarily been informed by research into consumers living on low incomes (Hill, 2002). Impoverished consumers often struggle to meet their needs in the marketplace because there is relatively little competition for low income market segments or because the options available are low quality or otherwise unappealing. In addition, low income consumer segments often encounter further restrictions such as limited access to goods and services (due to poor transportation, lack of Internet access and limited mobility), inadequate consumer knowledge and experience and lack of social support. More recently, researchers have started to view constrained consumption more broadly and have illustrated that groups such as elderly and low literacy consumers and those undergoing transitions in their lives (e.g. moving out of the parental home, bereavement) face restrictions in the marketplace. Consumption constraints can create a great deal of stress and have negative impacts on the practical outcomes of consumption choices, how people feel in relation to particular consumption-related events and, over time, people's mental and physical health. Constrained consumers adapt to their circumstances: sometimes they demonstrate considerable resourcefulness and adopt logical strategies to meet their needs under restricted conditions; sometimes they display biased, ill-informed or irrational consumption behaviour, in just the same way as do other groups of consumers (Bertrand, Mullainathan and Shafir, 2006). They develop strategies for coping with their circumstances to meet their basic needs for food, shelter and utilities. They also use symbolic consumption to craft self-identity and thus enhance their self-esteem and self-worth. Symbolic consumption is particularly important for those consumers who are at junctures in their lives (e.g. entering the job market, becoming a parent, getting married or divorced) and face the challenge of taking on new social roles.

In this case study we focus on the consumption stories of Julie, a young woman leaving foster care and setting up a home for herself and her young daughter. Her story centres around managing her money; providing clothes for herself and her daughter; holding a birthday party celebration for her daughter; and her feelings towards her daughter as a precious possession and a symbol of her successful parenting ability. Through Julie's story, we explore the ways that consumption goods are invested with meaning, and how these meanings enable Julie to anchor her identity through material goods and precious possessions.

JULIE'S BACKGROUND

Julie is 20. She was fostered at the age of eight and had various foster placements. Julie has a three-year-old daughter, Lianne, and at the time of the interview she was pregnant with her second child. She lives with Stuart, her partner, in a one-bedroom council apartment in an economically deprived town in the North West of England. Julie and Stuart are both unemployed at present, and both rely on government welfare (benefit) payments as their main source of income. Julie is particularly close to her sister, Debra, who has temporarily moved into Julie's apartment with her partner, Paul, and their two-year-old daughter, Eva.

JULIE'S STORY

Julie story is mainly concerned with her transition to independent living, and she discussed many of the issues and challenges that she faced as she learned to live as an independent adult, after being in foster care from the age of eight. The first part of her story concerned the actual move into her new apartment:

I've been living in my own place here for about two years. When we first moved in, I thought it was fantastic; I was happy that the council had moved us here. But, three weeks after we moved in we were burgled. We had just bought a new TV; it was a 32-inch flat screen TV, with a combined DVD and video recorder. They took the TV and everything. It cost over £2,000 and we weren't insured, so it just felt like money down the drain. It was horrible. Then we found out that our neighbour was a drug dealer. He does most of his business at night, so it's not good environment for bringing up kids. I've complained to the council, but they say they can't do anything. The mailboxes keep getting ripped off too, and I'm really worried about mail going missing, so I have to get up very early in the mornings to get my mail. It's a horrible place to live, I hate it. I'm trying to get us moved somewhere else, I'm waiting for it to come through. I've been on the list for a transfer for two years.

Money management is a key concern for Julie, and much of her story related to how she managed her weekly budget and also how she accounted for special occasions, such as Christmas and birthdays.

Stuart and I take it in turns to do the food shopping because we get paid [welfare payments] in different weeks. Bills are paid monthly and I put some money away each week to pay the bills at the end of the month. Stuart wasn't really good with his money, but I taught him how to manage his money. I would say, 'You give me your money; give me £40 for food and I'll put in the same and then give me money for gas and electricity', and that's how we do it.

I start saving in January every year for the next Christmas; we save £60 every two weeks. Lianne is getting clothes for Christmas this year; she's got loads of toys already. I'll be getting her a doll, but not a doll and a pram.

For Lianne's birthday we had a big party at the Fun Factory on the promenade, and all my mum's friends came. I don't know a lot of people because I don't really associate with young people, but Stuart has got a friend called Bob and he came with his little boy. My sister Debra brought Eva to the party and my older sister came too. Lianne got loads of presents and quite a lot of money. She got £40 off my mum, £40 off my older sister, Debra bought her a new suit, my mum's friends bought her toys and dolls and things like that. Stuart and I bought her a book that reads the story and loads of new clothes. She got everything and she had a really good time. Stuart and I wanted a party for her, because Debra only had a tea party for Eva but I thought it would be nice to have a party for Lianne, so we had a big party for her. It cost me £36 for the party venue and the food cost me £40. To pay for it, I put so much away every week, like £10 every week, and went out every week and got a present for her party and put it away. So that's how I managed to do her birthday.

Julie described her approach to purchasing consumer goods, such as clothes for herself and her family.

I don't get a lot of clothes for myself, but I don't care. I tend to just wear tops and pants. I only get something new every couple of months but I don't mind because I've got a daughter now and she needs more than I need. It is difficult when you hardly have any money and you are budgeting. Sometimes people give us second-hand clothes for Lianne. At first I thought, 'Is it because I can't clothe my daughter or something?' but people explained that their kids wouldn't get any more use out of the clothes and they thought my daughter might. So, I'm not really bothered now, it's no big deal. I used to get second-hand clothes when I was a kid and I felt like people were judging me. One of my teachers used to give me clothes and things because she had a cousin the same age as me. I felt uncomfortable because she would say, 'I've got something for you', and the class would be there, and I'd feel, 'Oh, I'm getting clothes given to me. Is it because I'm a tramp or something like that?' On one hand, I was embarrassed, but then I thought that it was nice that she was thinking about me. I think it was because she knew what I had gone through, she felt sorry for me.

Another aspect of successful independent living is managing to provide healthy food for oneself and one's family, and this last part of Julie's story provides some insights into this issue.

At the community centre they put on courses about healthy eating and stuff, and they put a crèche on for our kids. It's good because you learn loads of useful things, but it's quite hard, because my daughter is very close to me, and Eva is close to Debra, so it's quite hard to get rid of them while we go . . . we have to sneak off. I suppose it is our fault, because we've mollycoddled them, but it's because we are scared that someone will take them away from us one day, so we just don't want to let them go. It puts extra pressure on you, you think any day someone can come and take your daughter. Because you know what it's like when kids are taken into foster care . . . it does add extra pressure, because you worry. You just don't want to let go of her . . .

QUESTIONS

1 What are the consumer tasks that Julie finds challenging?

2 What are the main forms of constraint that Julie faces in relation to each of these tasks? Do you think that the strategies that Julie adopts for coping with her consumption constraints are effective?

3 Which parts of Julie's story reflect symbolic consumption?

4 What does Julie's symbolic consumption tell us about her self-identity?

Sources

Arnould, E.J. and Thompson, C.J. (2005), 'Consumer culture theory', *Journal of Consumer Research*, vol. 31(4): 868–882.

Bertrand, M., Mullainathan, S. and Shafir, E. (2006), 'Behavioral economics and marketing in aid of decision making among the poor', *Journal of Public Policy and Marketing*, vol. 25(1): 8–23.

Hill, R.P. (2002), 'Stalking the poverty consumer: A retrospective examination of modern ethical dilemmas', *Journal of Business Ethics*, vol. 37(2): 209–219.

Good child, bad child: observing experiences of consumer socialization in a twenty-first century family

BEN KERRANE, Bradford University, UK

CONTEXT

Families play a large part in our lives. Indeed many decisions and purchases which we make in our adult lives are likely to be shaped and informed by our childhood experiences, and by the influence of family members. Within the family we learn to walk and talk, and how to interact with other people. We also learn about consumption in families: as children we may have been taken with our parents on many shopping trips; taught to save our pocket money and to carefully research our consumption choices; and we may have learnt how to influence the decisions of our parents and siblings. These experiences are part of the process of consumer socialization, from which we learn about consumption and acquire consumer skills. The family has therefore been described as *the* socialization unit, because it has such a tremendous influence on our consumption.

However, much of our current academic knowledge about families originates from research which was conducted in the 1960s and 1970s. These studies tended to concentrate on the experiences of husband and wives when collecting data. These studies also focused on nuclear families, comprising heterosexual couples who live in the same home with one or more children (biological or adopted). At the start of the twenty-first century many consumer researchers have called for family research to move beyond nuclear families.

Similarly, much of what we know about consumer socialization derives from research which was conducted some decades ago. This research characterized the family as being homogeneous, i.e. all the children in a family were believed to be treated in the same way by their parents. Earlier marketing research suggested that parents adopt a uniform socialization style and communication pattern when dealing with all their children.

The family story below paints a rather different picture of how children experience their family environments; and hints at some of the changes in our understanding of life in family settings.*

* The name of this family and of the individual family members are fictional.

THE BALDWIN FAMILY STORY

Carole and Ray Baldwin got married two years ago. Before this they had spent several years cohabiting. They met following the death of Carole's first husband and the breakdown of Ray's first marriage. Carole and Ray both have children from their first marriages. Ray has two non-resident children, Jamie and Andrew, who live with their mother. Carole has four children from her first marriage; three are now fully-grown adults (George, Kathy and Marie) and live away from the family home. Carole's fourth child, Jessica (aged fourteen), lives with Carole and Ray in the new family home alongside Carole and Ray's biological child, Nina (aged five).

Carole and Ray have very different opinions of Jessica and Nina. Whilst Nina is clearly the apple of her parents' eyes, Jessica is often ostracized by her mother and stepfather, and she is frequently excluded from many family activities. As Carole comments, the couple believe that they have 'a good child [Nina] and a bad child [Jessica]', with Ray going even further, claiming that 'it's not a bad child; it's a pain in the arse child'. The roles of stepparents can be very unclear, and this seems to be the case for the Baldwin family with Ray adopting a disengaged parenting style towards his stepdaughter, Jessica. Ray chooses instead to spend much of his time with Nina, his biological daughter. For example, Ray and Nina are beginning to learn Spanish together after school.

Jessica is very aware of her mother's and her stepfather's favourable opinions of Nina. Jessica reckons that Nina 'doesn't have to ask for things off Mum, she just gets them'. The ways in which Jessica and Nina attempt to ask for things, and influence their parents' behaviour, therefore differs dramatically. Jessica adopts a range of influence strategies in attempts to get her own way. These include the use of deal making, crying, and refusing to eat until she gets what she wants. Nina, in contrast, does not need to go to such great lengths.

In view of her parents' opinions, Jessica faces considerable parental resistance to her influence strategies. As a result she often uses violence and issues threats to try and get what she wants. She has realized that she stands little success in influencing her parents when she acts alone. Jessica realizes she needs to have Nina as an ally in her attempts to influence Carole and Ray. Nina, on the other hand, does not need to deploy such influence strategies. Her requests are regularly granted with minimal parental resistance. Ray, in particular, often buys Nina expensive products, much to her half-sister's annoyance. Indeed, Nina's parents often anticipate her desire for products, and purchase items for her without Nina having to instigate the process. For instance, Carole and Ray recently purchased a new mobile phone for Nina even though Jessica had been constantly asking for one for weeks before. Nina did not even ask to be bought a mobile phone. As Ray commented: 'No, Nina didn't ask for it, it was our treat. Jessica had been on at me for ages to get her one, but she goes about asking for things the wrong way. Nina just doesn't ask for things, but Jessica's like a dripping tap, and she goes on and on at you.'

Carole and Ray act as the gatekeepers of Nina and Jessica's consumption, having the ability to pay for what the children want. Carole and Ray are also therefore the recipients of their daughters' respective influence strategies, because they have the power (and money) to grant or reject their daughters' influence attempts. The relationship that the parents have with Nina and Jessica largely determines the success of the influence strategies the girls use. Realizing that alone she stands little chance of influencing her parents' decisions, Jessica recruits Nina to help her get what she wants, forming a coalition with Nina. The family recalled one occasion when Jessica wanted to purchase a toy that connected to Jessica's Sony PlayStation. Individually Jessica could not afford the toy. Jessica recognized that she would not be able to persuade her parents by herself to buy it for her. Jessica subsequently persuaded Nina to contribute towards the cost (even though Nina initially showed no interest in the product) to ensure that Jessica got the toy that she wanted. Realizing that Carole and Ray would not reject the wishes of their younger favourite daughter, and with Nina working as an intermediary for Jessica's influence strategy, Jessica got the toy that she wanted with minimal parental resistance.

Jessica, aware that her mother and stepfather spend a larger proportion of their time with her half-sister than with her, spends a great deal of time with her own friends. Consequently Jessica is often away from the family home. When Jessica is at home she spends a great deal of her time on the family computer, logged in to online chat rooms where she talks to her friends and surfs the Internet. For Jessica, her friends act as an important reference group, and they are often the source of lots of consumer information and advice. Whereas Nina is taken on shopping trips and on family days out, is involved and has an input in decisions relating to her family's consumption (particularly in terms of where they go on holiday), Jessica does not. The family, therefore, appears to be very important in Nina's consumer socialization, but plays a much less dominant role in Jessica's consumer socialization. This is perhaps not entirely surprising given Jessica's age, with adolescents often seeking consumption advice from their peers instead of their parents as it is rather uncool to be too closely associated with one's family's opinions and views as a teenager.

QUESTIONS

1 Jessica and Nina experience different environments within the family home. How and why? Identify and evaluate the features which distinguish the two environments experienced by Jessica and Nina.

2 How did the different treatment of Jessica and Nina affect their success in deploying influence strategies? How might their different experiences affect their consumer socialization?

3 Reflecting on your own family experiences, did your parents treat you and your siblings in a similar way? What influence strategies did you use to influence your parents/guardians? Do you think that these were effective, and if so, why?

4 How far can families be characterized as offering a homogeneous environment to children?

5 How far can the family be described as *the* socialization unit? Using evidence from the case, and elsewhere, justify your answer.

6 Why should marketers be interested in understanding family decision making, and in particular child consumers?

7 Traditional family decision making models assume that families have a nuclear family form.
   (a) What impact might 'alternative' families have on such models?
   (b) What role may other family members play in shaping family decision making, and the socialization of children?

Further reading

Carlson, L., and Grossbart, S. (1988), 'Parent style and consumer socialisation of children', *Journal of Consumer Research*, vol. 15: 77–94.

Carlson, L., Walsh, A., Laczniak, R.N., and Grossbart, S. (1994), 'Family communication patterns and marketplace motivations, attitudes, and behaviours of children and mothers', *The Journal of Consumer Affairs*, vol. 28(1): 25–53.

Geuens, M., Mast, G., and Pelsmacker, P. (2002), 'Children's influence on family purchase behaviour: The role of family structure', *Asia Pacific Advances in Consumer Research*, vol. 5: 130–135.

John, D.R. (1999), 'Consumer socialization of children: A retrospective look at twenty-five years of research', *Journal of Consumer Research*, vol. 26: 183–213.

McNeal, J. (1998), 'Tapping the three kids' markets', *American Demographics*, vol. 20 (April): 37–41.

Palan, K.M., and Wilkes, R.E. (1997), 'Adolescent-parent interaction in family decision making', *Journal of Consumer Research*, vol. 24: 159–169.

Ward, S. (1974), 'Consumer socialization', *Journal of Consumer Research*, vol. 2: 1–16.

To consume or not to consume: motherhood as an identity project

EMMA N. BANISTER and MANDY DIXON, Lancaster University, UK

Parenthood is viewed as a big step. It involves taking on new roles and responsibilities and is also accompanied by changing consumption patterns that can have a considerable financial impact. Estimates suggest that parents spend approximately £4,000 on 'start-up' items for the new baby in the first year (Messenger, 2007) and spend around £186,000 on raising a child from birth to the age of 21, an average of £8,859 per year, an amount that has risen substantially over the past few years and is predicted to rise further (Smithers, 2007). Some of this increase in spending could be attributed to the fact that many parents are choosing to start a family later in life and therefore have more money to spend (Messenger, 2007). It could also be claimed there is increasing pressure on parents to consume the latest thing or must-have brand, with the paraphernalia surrounding pregnancy and motherhood reflecting elements of an extended self (Belk, 1988).

However, does parenting have to be this expensive? The twenty-first century is also witnessing a considerable backlash to what some consumers see as a societal pressure to over-consume. Sometimes this backlash is demonstrated by active group membership, for example the voluntary simplifier movement (see Shaw and Newholm, 2002) or by particular behaviours such as downshifting (see Schor, 1998). Here, two mothers to be tell their own stories. Saskia and Clara focus on preparations for their new arrival with an emphasis on their consumption decisions. Both women are UK-based and in their early thirties, they have fairly modest incomes but approach parenthood, and specifically consumption decisions for parenthood, in very different ways.

SASKIA'S STORY

I just cannot wait until she's born. Yes, I already know she's a girl. I had to find out, partly because I think it will help me to bond with her but also because I want to get everything right. Like my husband said, if it's a boy, we don't want him to have a lemon room and clothes and if it's a girl I want her to be dressed in pink! Well, the nursery was the first thing we did. We didn't spend too much, but we've made sure that everything matches. It's all pink, but quite understated, you know? Plain walls and then a really pretty border and curtains. The cot is lovely – pretty simple but then we've got some really nice bedding, really quite girly – matching sheets, blankets and cot bumper. The thing was, once we'd got the nursery dresser and wardrobe of course we needed to put something in them. It's so exciting. I've washed and ironed everything and it's all folded and in the drawers waiting for her. I think she's got more clothes than me!

I've tended to buy just a few things each week so I haven't really noticed how much I've spent. I wanted all the usual vests and sleep suits and stuff but also some nice outfits for when I have visitors and want to show her off. I know people will buy us things as well, but you never know whether things will be to your taste. I've also had some people give things to me as hand-me-downs, and it's really nice of them. I have held onto stuff as it will do as back up, but you know she will be new to the world and I want her in her own stuff . . . I can't explain it really but it just doesn't seem right putting her in second-hand clothes.

In terms of equipment and other things that we need, we've tended to follow the advice of stores and websites – there's lots of checklists, so we're nearly there now – the moses basket, baby bouncer, car seat, baby bath, towels, sterilizer, bibs, scratch mits, muslin squares, blankets, sleeping bags, a cot mobile, monitor, night light . . . I think we've got most things now. The biggest decision was the pram because I wanted to try and get something that will last, but also looks good. In the end I took the advice of my cousin who's recently had a baby herself and bought a Bugaboo. She told me they are expensive but worth it. I've seen quite a few pictures of celebrities with them and they do some really great colours. I wanted to go for bright pink, but my sensible head made me go for black as I don't think we can afford to buy another one if we have another child at some point and I can't see myself pushing a boy around in a pink pram!

Next week I am having a baby shower. My best friend organized it for me. There's going to be just a few girls from work and of course all my other girlfriends. They asked me to write a wish list of gifts but I thought that was maybe a bit over the top so I've asked them just to surprise me. Mind you I wouldn't mind if they could get me a baby swing or something, I've heard they are quite good, so maybe I will drop a few hints . . .

CLARA'S STORY

I'm really looking forward to our baby being born, but that doesn't mean that I am going to rush out and spend tons of money on things that I just don't think we'll need . . . I mean the baby's not going to know is it? I do feel that there is a bit of pressure to get everything new, pristine, colour co-ordinated, and get the all-singing and dancing versions of really quite basic items. I guess you could accuse me of being a bit tight, but then on the other hand I think it's more a case of priorities. It's just not in my nature to over-consume, and I'd rather wait and spend money on things as and if we need them, when I have a better idea of what we do need and also toys and things when the baby gets a bit older and can get something out of them. Besides, it's hardly environmentally friendly is it, buying a load of stuff that is going to last you a few months – or in some cases a few weeks – just to then chuck it out or whatever?

I have done some preparation, it's not like I am closing my eyes to the possibilities. I guess I am lucky, I've got some really great friends and they've tended to give me stuff, so I've got sacks of clothes that I am going to have to sort out at some stage. I've also been given other things that might come in handy such as a sterilizer, breast pump, a sling, muslin squares, a bouncy chair, some soft toys and things . . . In fact there's not much we have had to buy ourselves. I have been doing some research about different washable nappies. I am convinced I want to go down the real nappy route. Disposable nappies just don't seem right from an environmental point of view. However, I know all babies are different and before I spend loads of money on a complete set of washable nappies I want to work out which will suit us best, so I've bought a few samples and will wait until the baby comes along – or we might go with a nappy washing service.

The pram . . . I couldn't believe it, my mum got me a pram from a charity shop the other week! It was a really lucky spot as they can be pretty expensive. What I thought was we'll use this second-hand one for now and once the baby's ready to sit up in a buggy we'll get something much smaller. We will probably need to buy that new unless we can get it off eBay or something, but by then I will have much more of a view of what will suit us best, whereas at the moment I haven't got a clue, so the pram will do us just fine. We are going to buy a new car seat ourselves . . . in fact we are going to do that this weekend. It's not that I wouldn't have one off a friend if it was offered to me, but I'm not going to buy a second-hand one off eBay or something as they say you should know its history, in case it's

been in an accident and isn't safe, that kind of thing. So that's one thing I will have bought. A friend's given me a cot and we've bought a new mattress for that as again that's the official recommendation in terms of cot death, etc.* Otherwise I can't think of anything that we've really had to buy, just everyday things like cotton wool. I wouldn't say I am taking a stance against consumption, I'm just very fortunate in terms of what I have been given and I won't just consume for the sake of it. I know this baby will end up costing me a fortune one way or another so I want to hold off as much as possible just now.

QUESTIONS

1 The case study title suggests motherhood can be viewed as an identity *project*. What is/can be meant by this? (See, for example, Arnould and Thompson, 2005: 871–3).
Consider other life transitions you have experienced – or are likely to experience in the future – and how these could be viewed as (potential) identity projects (examples might include becoming a student, entering your teenage years or entering the world of work post-graduation). What kinds of consumption choices might consumers face during these transitions?

2 Symbolic consumption suggests that we can make inferences about consumers on the basis of their consumption decisions. What can we gauge about Clara on the basis of her refusal to consume, or her refusal to consume excessively?

3 Think back to previous generations (e.g. your parents, grandparents, etc.). How has the landscape of consumption changed? Which of the products consumed by Saskia would have been considered essential in previous generations?

4 To what extent could marketers be accused of pressuring women in Saskia and Clara's position to 'over-consume'? What evidence can you find from the case to indicate the role of marketing in encouraging the consumption of particular products and brands?

5 Linked to the above, what are the different sources of information that the two women draw on? How might these different sources of information reflect their own 'particular' approach to motherhood and their attitude to consumption in general?

* Cot death is a term commonly used to describe a sudden and unexpected infant death that is initially unexplained (sudden infant death syndrome). See http://www.sids.org.uk/cot-death.html.

Sources

Arnould, E. and Thompson, C.J. (2005), 'Consumer Culture Theory (CCT): Twenty years of research', *Journal of Consumer Research*, 31 (March): 868–882.

Belk, R.W. (1988), 'Possessions and the extended self', *Journal of Consumer Research*, 15 (September): 139–168.

Messenger, C. (2007), 'The Cost of Kids', http://news.bbc.co.uk/go/pr/fr/-/1/hi/business/6407387.stm

Schor, J.B. (1998), 'Downshifters: Architects of a New American Dream', in Alba and Hutchinson (eds), *Advances in Consumer Research*, vol. XXV (Provo, Utah: Association of Consumer Research): 88–9.

Shaw, D. and Newholm, T. (2002), 'Voluntary simplicity and the ethics of consumption', *Psychology & Marketing*, 19, 2: 167–185.

Smithers, R. (2007), 'Lifetime Cost of Bringing Up Child £186,000 – and Rising', http://www.guardian.co.uk/money/2007/dec/07/parenting

Opting out, fitting in: stories from young non-drinkers

EMMA N. BANISTER and MARIA G. PIACENTINI, Lancaster University, UK

BACKGROUND

Excessive alcohol consumption is a major concern in the UK, yet it can play an important role in young people's social experience. Much research has questioned why young people consume excessive quantities of alcohol, focusing on the social facilitative role that alcohol plays, as well as the more personal benefits such as mood alteration and dealing with stress. However, there is rather less discussion of the experiences of young people who choose to opt out of, or resist, the excessive alcohol consumption culture. In this case study we focus on strategies used by three undergraduate students who do not drink alcohol (i.e. opt out), but are still keen to socialize and engage with their peers (i.e. fit in). Kelly, Alice and Jack are all very aware that their non-drinking stance is something that has to be managed and which can sometimes create tensions and challenges not faced by others within their friendship groups. However, they are proactive in making their lifestyle choice work for them, adopting practices that help alleviate these tensions in order to ensure their stance is not detrimental to their key social needs and expectations. Their stories form the basis of this case.

THE STORIES OF STUDENT NON-DRINKERS

Kelly

Kelly's decision to stop drinking was heavily influenced by some long-running problems with alcohol within her family, which have caused her to be very critical of the role of alcohol in society and what she sees as a reliance on alcohol by her peers in social situations.

> I would call quite a few of my friends alcoholics but if you ever said to them, 'I think you behave like an alcoholic' . . . they just don't associate that with what they do at all. Like they just binge and when a lot of them get drunk they get very drunk, like can't remember . . . I've never . . . they don't remember anything that's happened and it's just not anything that I fancy. They just don't see the consequences and I've obviously seen it firsthand.

Kelly describes herself as a 'control freak' and talks about not 'feeling the need' to drink. Her main strategy for dealing with her decision to opt out of drinking alcohol is to continue to participate in the drinking culture yet without consuming alcohol.

> It's funny . . . because I've been out on nights out where there's someone not drinking and everyone's shoving drinks their way more than me, they don't seem to notice that I don't drink. I think it's because I'm quite loud anyway.

In some ways, she is practising the art of 'passing' as a drinker; her strategy reflects her belief in the importance of alcohol consumption for the student experience and she attempts to 'fit in' with the social scene, while also 'opting out' of the dominant behaviour (drinking alcohol). Kelly's main tool for 'fitting in' is her lively gregarious personality which decreases the likelihood of her getting 'found out' as a non-drinker.

Kelly is, however, aware of what she sees as prevalent negative stereotypes that surround non-drinkers, particularly in the student age group (stereotypes could include the assumption that non-drinking students will prefer to study instead of socialize and are therefore less integrated into the student body than many drinkers are). In some senses Kelly successfully confronts the stereotype of the non-drinker via her personality and in so doing she ensures others do not stigmatize her as a non-drinker. As part of this rejection of what she sees as the non-drinking stereotype, she also rejects the responsible caring-type roles that become bestowed on many non-drinkers, through the nature of them being sober.

> I always say to them . . . 'I'm not taking you home or carrying you home or putting you in your bed', because that causes me huge problems.

So, although Kelly says she does not have problems with her friends drinking, and sees their consumption decisions as very much up to them, she does not like them drinking when it has an impact on her. Essentially Kelly ensures she is not marked out in order to avoid stigmatization, but also to avoid taking on additional care-giving responsibilities.

Alice

Alice had been a non-drinker prior to university and had already developed strategies with which to deal with the stance she had taken: 'I don't see the point in drinking.' However, Alice has always socialized with people who do drink alcohol, and has successfully carved out a distinct role and set of practices for herself as a non-drinker within her friendship groups. For example, before coming to university she would go out socializing with her friends from home, but would always be the designated driver and essentially took on a general carer role:

A lot of my friends were out getting drunk when they were 16/17 and I just . . . I could see absolutely no point of why you'd want to do it kind of thing . . . I was quite happy to go out with them and they would drink and I wouldn't and I was normally the one looking after them and taking them home kind of thing. And you know, I've always been that way kind of thing . . . And they kind of saw that role in me, so they were like, 'Oh Alice will always be there for us', so it kind of developed like that really.

On becoming a student, Alice became even more conscious of her non-drinking status, especially as her initial experience of university was of an extreme binge drinking culture, which highlighted how different her lifestyle was from the majority of students with whom she was coming into contact. Other students are very conscious of her non-drinking status, but in order to 'fit in', Alice's uses her non-drinking to the benefit of the wider drinking community, willingly assuming a protective and caring role when socializing around alcohol. For example, while on a study year in the USA, where the age limit for drinking alcohol is 21, she described how she assumed door duty at parties:

I always was the bouncer; that was my job, I was on the door. Like with walkie-talkies, like, 'Turn the music down please, cops are driving past'.

Another aspect of Alice's efforts to 'fit in' relate to her participation in all social activities around alcohol, substituting alcohol for a soft drink. For example, she described how she participated in various drinking games, but instead of a shot of beer, she would have a shot of a soft drink.

You're in two teams and you put basically like the equivalent of a shot in the bottom of a plastic cup and you have to down it and then put the cup on the table and flip it until it lands upside down. And then the next person in your team goes and whichever team finishes first wins. [Interviewer: And what would you drink in that game?] Diet coke.

Alice has found a way of navigating a position within the dominant drinking culture, and she has adapted the ritualistic behaviours that surround alcohol consumption (such as drinking games) to enable her participation, and has come up with non-alcoholic versions of the (alcoholic) drinking games she learned about in the USA. While she does not participate in the binge drinking culture, she is quite moderate in her approach to other students' drinking behaviour:

I don't try and press my views on them. I respect them and what they to do and they respect me kind of thing, so it's a mutual understanding . . . I feel I probably have had as many experiences as they have but I just have had them being sober and dealing with them being drunk . . .

Like Kelly, Alice still sees herself as part of the broader student drinking culture, but is confident she can participate in this without indulging in the consumption of alcohol. Unlike Kelly, she willingly takes on a supportive function caring for her friends (drinkers) on nights out.

Jack

Jack's story is very different from those of the other students in that when he first came to university he was a very heavy drinker. Jack sees alcohol as a key aspect of the university scene: 'That's what you do when you come to uni.' Jack's drinking got out of control in his first term at university, culminating in hospitalization and a permanent serious medical condition brought on by his excessive alcohol consumption. Jack has received an absolute medical warning against drinking and has had a couple of scares since this episode when he has unwittingly consumed alcohol in food.

Again Jack has continued to socialize with other students but he recognizes this might not be the path that others would follow in his position:

I suppose a lot of people were pretty much of the opinion that if that happened to them they wouldn't come out again and they would just sit in their room . . . I still go out just as much as everybody else. Like last night I went on a bar crawl with loads of people, as the sober guy and it doesn't really . . . I think it depends on your attitude, on circumstances. Like, erm, also because I've found more things to do since I stopped drinking, I don't just go to pubs all the time.

There is the indication that Jack has attempted to carve out a number of alternative identities, identities where drinking does not need to take centre stage. A key aspect to this is an element of confidence in his personal resources, the sense that Jack has enough going for him that he does not need alcohol in quite the same way as other people, or as he perhaps thought when he was a drinker. Jack acknowledges that, to some, his story has an element of coolness about it: 'I sort of established myself as being in excess of the drinking culture', and there is also little people can say if he tells them the reason why he does not drink, and he experiences little peer pressure to revert to his 'old ways'. Something else that becomes clear from Jack's story is the success with which he has also worked at establishing alternative identities wherein drinking is not necessarily core. He has become a Buddhist: 'I was kind of looking for something that made a bit more sense to me than other religions' and is also a keen musician, which takes up a lot of his time. Jack's story gives the sense that he feels lucky to be alive and that the choices available to him, concerning alcohol, are so stark that he has no choice but to abstain. His story helps him to avoid the typical non-drinker stereotype and any potential stigma that might accompany this and allows him to get on with his life.

QUESTIONS

1 Compare and contrast the ways that these three students manage their non-drinking in their everyday lives. What similarities are there? What differences?

2 From your understanding of the mechanisms of group influences, how can you explain the ways that other (drinking) students respond to these students' non-drinking? To what extent are these responses related to the youth cohort that these cases belong to? What role do the 'stories that people tell' play in the extent to which people manage to fit in with their peers while opting out?

3 Jack's story mentions the possibility of establishing alternative identities. What 'alternative identities' are open to students seeking to limit their alcohol consumption? To what extent do Kelly and Alice engage in this way of positioning themselves?

4 Based on your understanding of the stories included in this case, what recommendations would you make to health promoters who are trying to encourage people to drink less? You might want to consider how students like Kelly, Alice and Jack could feature in campaigns as non-drinking ambassadors.

5 France has traditionally been viewed as a society that handles its approach to alcohol much better than the UK. Check out and discuss the issues raised by the latest update on changing drinking habits amongst young French consumers: **http://www.guardian.co.uk/lifeandstyle/2008/aug/27/foodanddrink.france.**

Further reading

Piacentini, M.G. and Banister, E.N. (2009), 'Managing anti-consumption in an excessive drinking culture', *Journal of Business Research*, 62: 279–288.

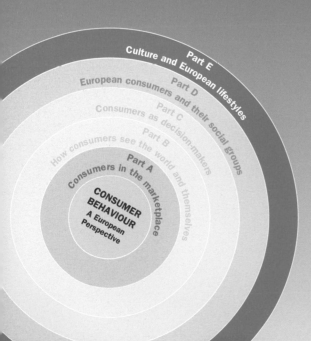

Part E
Culture and European lifestyles

Part D
European consumers and their social groups

Part C
Consumers as decision-makers

Part B
How consumers see the world and themselves

Part A
Consumers in the marketplace

CONSUMER
BEHAVIOUR
A European
Perspective

PART E

Culture and European lifestyles

The final part of this book considers consumers as members of a broad cultural system. Chapter 13 starts this part by examining some of the basic building blocks of culture and consumption, and shows how consumer behaviours and culture are constantly interacting with each other. Chapter 14 looks at the production of culture, and how the 'gatekeepers' of culture help shape our sense of fashion and consumer culture. Chapter 15 focuses on the importance of understanding consumers' lifestyles throughout Europe, and illustrates the lifestyle concept and its marketing applications with a discussion of various product categories such as, for example, food, drink and cars.

13

Culture and consumer behaviour

It's Thursday night, 7.30. Sean puts down the phone after speaking with Colum, his study partner in his consumer behaviour class. The weekly night out for the Irish marketing students has begun! Sean has just spent the summer months travelling in Europe. He was always amazed, and delighted, to find a place claiming to be an Irish pub – regardless of how unauthentic the place was, an Irish pub always sold Guinness, a true symbol of Ireland, he reflected. Sean had begun to drink when he started university. Initially, bottled beers straight from the fridge had been his preference. However, now that he's in his third year and a more sophisticated, travelled and rounded person, he feels that those beers were just a little too – well, fashionable. He has thus recently begun to drink Guinness. His dad, uncle and grandad, in fact most of the older men he knows, drink Guinness. That day in consumer behaviour the lecturer had discussed the 'Guinness Time' TV commercial which had been run the previous year. It featured a young man doing a crazy dance around a settling pint of Guinness. The young man saved his most crazed expression for the point when he took his first sip. The lecturer had pointed out that the objectives of the ad were to associate Guinness with fun – an important reason why young people drink alcohol – and to encourage them to be patient with the stout, as a good pint takes a number of minutes to settle.[1]

Sean has arranged to meet his friends in the local pub at 8.30. They will order 'three pints of the finest black stuff' and then have their own Guinness ritual. To begin, they watch it being poured and then look for the rising rings of the head – the best indication of a good pint. Once settled, a small top-up, and then ready for action. But they always wait and study their glasses before taking the first mouthful together – what a thing of beauty!

DAMIEN MCLOUGHLIN, University College, Dublin, Ireland

CULTURE AND CONSUMPTION

As we have already seen in the introductory part of this book, consumption choices cannot be understood without considering the cultural context in which they are made: culture is the 'prism' through which people view products and try to make sense of their own and other people's consumer behaviour.

Sean's beer-drinking reflects his desire to associate with and dissociate from (with help from the media and marketers) a certain style, attitude and trendiness. Being an Irishman, his attachment to Guinness has a very different meaning in his world than it would have in, for example, trendy circles in continental cities, where Guinness may be associated with the very fashionability that Sean tries to avoid.

Indeed, it is quite common for cultures to modify symbols identified with other cultures and present these to a new audience. As this occurs, these cultural products undergo a process of **co-optation**, where their original meanings are transformed and often trivialized by outsiders. In this case, an Irish beer was to a large extent divorced from its original connection with the Irish traditional working class or rurality and is now used as a trendy way of consuming 'Irishness' abroad (but without the rural or lower-class aspect).[2]

In Chapter 2, we saw how contemporary society can be regarded as a consumer society or a consumer culture – a culture in which consumption has become a central vehicle for organizing social meanings. This chapter considers culture from a somewhat broader perspective. We will take a look at how some of the characteristics not only of contemporary consumer culture but of all cultures contribute to the shaping of consumer behaviour. Myths, rituals and the sacred are not just features of so-called 'primitive' societies but are basic elements in all cultures. We will take a look at how myths and rituals of the culture in which we live create the meaning of everyday products and how these meanings move through a society to consumers.

This chapter deals mainly with the way very basic cultural values and symbols are expressed in goods and how consumers appropriate these symbols through consumption rituals. The next chapter will then take a closer look at fashion and other change processes in consumer culture. The first part of this chapter reviews what is meant by culture and how cultural priorities are identified and expressed. These social guidelines often take the form of *values*, which have already been discussed in Chapter 6. The second part considers the role of myths and rituals in shaping the cultural meaning of consumer products and consumption activities. The chapter concludes by exploring the concepts of the sacred and the profane and their relevance for consumer behaviour.

Culture, a concept crucial to the understanding of consumer behaviour, may be thought of as the collective memory of a society. Culture is the accumulation of shared meanings, rituals, norms and traditions among the members of an organization or society. It is what defines a human community, its individuals, its social organizations, as well as its economic and political systems. It includes both abstract ideas, such as values and ethics, and the material objects and services, such as cars, clothing, food, art and sports, that are produced or valued by a group of people. Thus, individual consumers and groups of consumers are but part of culture, and culture is the overall system within which other systems are organized.

Some of the pioneers of the relationship between consumption and culture were an anthropologist, Mary Douglas, and an economist, Baron Isherwood.[3] They underlined how goods are always used as social markers, not only in the traditional sense of displaying social status (although that is an important feature) but more generally by underlining, how uses of goods express particular social relationships (like friendship), particular times (like 'a party'), particular moods (like relaxation), and so on. Most importantly, these marking functions are performed through a variety of daily and not-so-daily consumption rituals. We will take a closer look at consumption rituals later in this chapter. The basic learning from this and other works on consumption and culture is that any consumption activity must be understood in the cultural context in which it is taking place.

Ironically, the effects of culture on consumer behaviour are so powerful and far-reaching that this importance is sometimes difficult to grasp or appreciate.[4] We are surrounded by a lot of practices, from seemingly insignificant behaviours like pressing the start button of our iPod to larger movements like flying to an exotic honeymoon in Thailand. What is important is that these practices have meaning to us, that we know how to interpret them. Culture is basically this interpretation system which we use to understand all

▶ those daily or extraordinary **signifying practices**[5] around us. Culture as a concept is like a fish immersed in water – we do not always appreciate this power until we encounter a different environment, where suddenly many of the assumptions we had taken for granted about the clothes we wear, the food we eat, the way we address others and so on no longer seem to apply. The effect of encountering such differences can be so great that the term 'culture shock' is not an exaggeration.

The importance of these cultural expectations is only discovered when they are violated. Several Danish companies are still trying to regain the market shares lost in the Middle East following a Danish newspaper's publication of 12 cartoons drawings of Islam's founding prophet Muhammed (in fact, not all cartoons actually portrayed the Prophet, but some other person named 'Muhammed'). Not least through the intervention of local Danish Muslim leaders, the cartoons, initially thought of as an attempt to test degrees of freedom of speech, became caught in a violent debate both in Denmark and all over Europe and the Middle East in arguments of respect for religious beliefs and feelings versus the principle of freedom of expression.[6] While we are not taking side in this debate, we use the case to illustrate that sensitivity to cultural issues, whether by journalists or by brand managers, can only come by understanding these underlying dimensions – and that is the goal of this chapter.

A consumer's culture determines the overall priorities they attach to different activities and products. It also determines the success or failure of specific products and services. A product that provides benefits consistent with those desired by members of a culture at particular time has a much better chance of attaining acceptance in the marketplace. It may be difficult to guess the success or failure of certain products. Some years ago, the American business magazine *Forbes* predicted the imminent bankruptcy of the Danish stereo manufacturer Bang & Olufsen, and advised everybody to sell off their stocks in the company. In addition, they mocked the company's new product as a ghetto blaster, with the difference that the price was $3,000 and not $300. The product was the new 'on-the-wall' stereo with automatic sliding doors – the product was an instant success and the value of Bang & Olufsen stocks multiplied by 40![7] Here was a product that was launched when the time was right – something that *Forbes* overlooked.

The relationship between consumer behaviour and culture is a two-way street. On the one hand, products and services that resonate with the priorities of a culture at any given time have a much better chance of being accepted by consumers. On the other hand, the study of new products and innovations in product design successfully produced by a culture at any point in time provides a window on the dominant cultural ideals of that period. Consider, for example, some products that reflect underlying cultural processes at the time they were introduced:

● Convenience foods and ready-to-eat meals, hinting at changes in family structure and the decline of the full-time housewife.

● Cosmetics like those of The Body Shop, made of natural materials and not tested on animals, which reflected consumers' apprehensions about pollution, waste and animal rights.

● Unisex fragrances, indicating new views on sex roles and a blurring of gender boundaries, as exemplified by Calvin Klein.

Aspects of culture

Culture is not static. It is continually evolving, synthesizing old ideas with new ones. A cultural system can be said to consist of three interrelated functional areas:[8]

1 *Ecology*: the way in which a system is adapted to its habitat. This area is shaped by the technology used to obtain and distribute resources (for example, industrialized societies vs. less affluent countries). One example is the Japanese interest in space-saving devices, since living space is often very sparse in Japanese cities.

2 *Social structure*: the way in which orderly social life is maintained. This area includes the domestic and political groups that are dominant within the culture, including for example the importance of the nuclear family vs. the extended family, different gender roles and degrees of male and female dominance in different areas of life.

3 *Ideology*: the mental characteristics of a people and the way in which they relate to their environment and social groups. This area revolves around the belief that members of a society possess a common **worldview**. They share certain ideas about principles of order and fairness. They also share an **ethos**, or a set of moral and aesthetic principles. A theme park in Bombay called Water Kingdom that caters to India's emerging middle class illustrates how distinctive a culture's worldview can be. Many consumers there are unfamiliar with mixed-sex swimming in public, so the park rents swimsuits to women who have never worn them before. No thongs here, though: the suits cover the women from wrists to ankles.[9] In Europe, contemporary Turkey is a good example of a clash of ethos within a culture, where rapid modernization and the construction of a consumer society is enchanting a lot of people but also challenging traditional pious values and thereby provoking people with a different ethos to seek alternative solutions. In a modern society, everybody wants to go on holiday. Thus, the Turkish tourist industry has provided a fancy new hotel industry for faithful Muslims with separated male and female pool and beach areas and entertainment facilities.[10]

How cultures vary

Although every culture is different, a lot of research has aimed at reducing the cultural variation to simpler principles. We have already made reference to the specificity of the Japanese relations with living space. People's culturally formed relationship to space, also called **proxemics**, is one of the fundamental distinctions between different cultures.[11] This is valid both in terms of the public space and the intimate private space immediately surrounding them. Another fundamental distinction between cultures is the relationship with time. It has been suggested that there are **monochronic** (stressing 'one thing at a time and according to schedule' principles) and **polychronic** (stressing 'several things at a time and completion of task') cultural time systems.[12] Which cultural time system do you think you belong to? Notice that when assessing such differences in cultural styles, there may not only be national cultural differences at stake here but also other kinds of cultural distinction such as urban versus rural cultures. This is one of the problems with such grand reductions of cultural differences to a simple scheme. The problem is not that proxemics or time styles are irrelevant, but that they may not be very good descriptors of what distinguishes a particular nation. It should be remembered that everyone is a member of several cultures. Your are not only British, or Swedish or . . . , but also a student (which constitutes a particular culture subdivided into subcultures), with perhaps an upper middle-class background, coming from a relatively small town, etc. As one final example, cultures also differ in their emphasis on individualism vs. collectivism. In **collectivist cultures**, people subordinate their personal goals to those of a stable in-group. By contrast, consumers in **individualist cultures** attach more importance to personal goals, and people are more likely to change memberships when the demands of the group (e.g. workplace, church, etc.) become too costly. A Dutch researcher on culture, Geert Hofstede, has proposed this and three other dimensions, the relation to differences in social power, handling of uncertainty and risk, and the degree of masculine and feminine values, to account for much of this variability.[13] However, Hofstede's and similar approaches have been much criticized. The four dimensions do not account for the differences in the meaning and the role of the concepts in each culture. That each culture has to cope with problems of power, risk and uncertainty, gender roles and the relationship between the individual and society is obvious. But that the solutions to these problems are reducible to different levels on one and the same scale is dubious, to say the least. For example, it is difficult to assume that concepts such as 'risk' or 'masculine' would mean the same in all cultures.

Although we must be able to compare behaviour across cultures by using general concepts, we must do so by initially understanding and analyzing every culture, and hence every consumer culture, on the basis of its own premises, an approach known as

▶ **ethnoconsumerism.**[14] In Figure 13.1 the principles of an ethnoconsumerist methodology are depicted. Note how central the notions of cultural categories and cultural practices are to this approach to studying consumption. To illustrate the contribution of such an approach to the study of consumer behaviour, consider a study of foreign tourist behaviour in Britain, which concluded that a sheer indication of nationality in and by itself was a bad predictor of how tourists coped with the confrontation with the (strange) British culture, whereas an ethnoconsumerist study permitted to isolate a number of cultural factors and types of behaviour that generated a much richer portrayal of touristic coping behaviour.[15] The point is that whatever consumers do, if we want to understand it fully,

Figure 13.1 Principles for an ethnoconsumerist approach to studying consumption

Source: Laurie Meamber and Alladi Venkatesh, 'Ethnoconsumerist Methodology for Cultural and Cross-Cultural Consumer Research', in R. Elliott and S. Beckmann (eds), *Interpretive Consumer Research* (Copenhagen: Copenhagen Business School Press, 2000): 87–108.

we will have to be aware of the cultural background of it. Even a simple thing like drinking a cup of coffee does not hold the same meaning in different cultures.[16]

Rules for behaviour

Values, as we saw in Chapter 6, are very general principles for judging between good and bad goals, etc. They form the core principles of every culture. From these flow norms, or rules, dictating what is right or wrong, acceptable or unacceptable. Some norms, called *enacted norms*, are explicitly decided upon, such as the rule that a green traffic light means 'go' and a red one means 'stop'. Many norms, however, are much more subtle. These *crescive norms* are embedded in a culture and are only discovered through interaction with other members of that culture. Crescive norms include the following:[17]

- A **custom** is a norm handed down from the past that controls basic behaviours, such as division of labour in a household or the practice of particular ceremonies. Offering visitors a small thing to eat or drink, such as a cup of coffee or a cup of tea, are in many cultures part of custom, whether the visit is a professional or a private one.

- **Mores** are customs with a strong moral overtone. Mores often involve a taboo, or forbidden behaviour, such as incest or cannibalism. Violation of mores often meets with strong censure from other members of a society. The rise of a highly fashion-conscious and modern Islamic consumer in Turkey (and elsewhere in the Middle East) has led to the construction of a parallel fashion scene, where the mores of displaying the female body parts are not violated.[18]

- **Conventions** are norms regarding the conduct of everyday life. These rules deal with the subtleties of consumer behaviour, including the 'correct' way to furnish one's house, wear one's clothes, host a dinner party, and so on. For example, the Chinese were grappling with a cultural problem as they prepared for the 2008 Olympics in Beijing: local habits are at odds with what foreign visitors expect to encounter. For one, there is the common Chinese habit of expressing happiness with the food through making noises that in Western context are deemed less than well mannered. Furthermore, it is common to spit on the footpath – the sinus-clearing, phlegmy pre-spit hawking sound is so common that one foreigner dubbed it 'the national anthem of China'. The government then decided to impose a hefty fine for public spitting to get people accustomed to holding in their saliva before hordes of fans descended on the city.[19]

All three types of crescive norms may operate to define a culturally appropriate behaviour. For example, mores may tell us what kind of food it is permissible to eat. Note that mores vary across cultures, so eating a dog may be taboo in Europe, while Hindus would shun beef and Muslims avoid pork products. Custom dictates the appropriate hour at which the meal should be served. Conventions tell us how to eat the meal, including such details as the utensils to be used, table etiquette, and even the appropriate apparel to be worn at dinner time.

We often take these conventions for granted, assuming that they are the 'right' things to do (again, until we are exposed to a different culture!). And it is good to remember that much of what we know about these norms is learned *vicariously* (see Chapter 7), as we observe the behaviours of actors and actresses in films and TV series, but also television commercials, print ads and other popular culture media. In the long run, marketers have a great deal to do with influencing consumers' enculturation.

MYTHS AND RITUALS

Every culture develops stories and practices that help its members to make sense of the world. When we examine these activities in other cultures, they often seem strange or even unfathomable. Yet our *own* cultural practices appear quite normal – even though a visitor may find them equally bizarre.

It works like magic!

To appreciate how so-called 'primitive' belief systems which some may consider irrational or superstitious continue to influence our supposedly 'modern', rational society, consider the avid interest of many Western consumers in magic. Marketers of health foods, anti-ageing cosmetics, exercise programmes and gambling casinos often imply that their offerings have 'magical' properties that will ward off sickness, old age, poverty or just plain bad luck. People by the millions carry lucky charms to ward off 'the evil eye', or have 'lucky' clothing or other products which they believe will bring them good fortune. Many of us have a lucky number, that we use on various occasions, such as in sports games (whether we are playing ourselves, betting, or just watching), lotteries, etc. Beliefs in magic structure major consumer events in the West as well as the East. When the calendar hit 7 July 2007 – 7/7/07 – many people in the US scrambled to take advantage of its link to lucky 777. Western culture associates the number seven with good fortune (like the seven sacraments in Roman Catholicism) and US marketers from Wal-Mart to Las Vegas casinos jumped on the bandwagon. The Mandalay Bay Casino hosted a group wedding for more than 100 couples. The New York City Ritz-Carlton even offered a Lucky Number 7 wedding package with a reception for 77, a seven-tier wedding cake, and a seven-night honeymoon at any Ritz in the world for $77,777.[20] Keep in mind that these beliefs are culturecentric so they take on different forms around the world. For

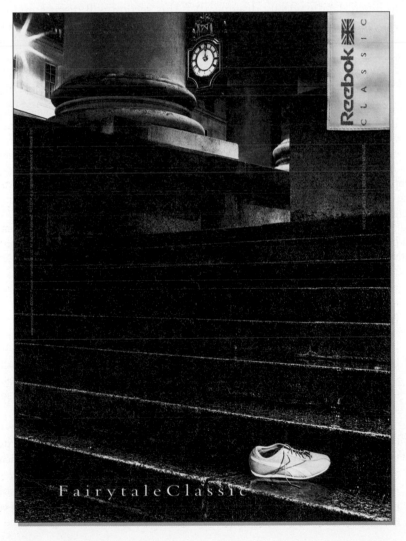

Some advertisements borrow heavily from the magical and mythological world of fairy tales. Which one is alluded to here?

example, in China 8 is the luckiest number. The Chinese word for 8 is *ba*, which rhymes with *fa*, the Chinese character for wealth. It is no coincidence that the Summer Olympics in Beijing opened on 8/8/08 at 8.08 P.M.

But the magic most prevalent in consumer culture is the magic that pertains to the transformations of our bodies. The health, wellness, and beauty industries are replete with suggestions of magical transformations of our bodies, that will help us cleanse our bodily organs, shed excess weight, restore youthful looks, and create a new and more harmonious and balanced self. Such hopes for a magic transformation lie behind a lot of contemporary consumption pertaining to the self, from the very manifest consumption of cosmetic surgery[21] to the more spiritual consumption of self-enhancement programmes.[22] Often consumers construct marketplace mythologies to serve multiple and sometimes competing ideological agendas – this is particularly true in the product categories which consumers use to deal with issues of health, healing and well-being.[23]

An interest in the occult tends to be popular, perhaps even more so when members of a society feel overwhelmed or powerless – magical remedies simplify our lives by giving us 'easy' answers. Marketing efforts are replete with more or less open references to magical practices.[24] And it is not just a matter of fooling consumers: magic is an active part also of our modern lives. Customers at river-rafting trips in America speak about the magical capacities of the river to transform their lives, heal psychological wounds and bring out the best in people.[25] Even a computer is regarded with awe by many consumers as a sort of 'electronic magician', with the ability to solve our problems (or in other cases to make data magically disappear!).[26] This section will discuss myths and rituals, two aspects of culture common to all societies, from the ancients to the modern world.

▲ Marketing opportunity

Magic is the order of the day. Never before (or at least since the Middle Ages) has the market been so populated with magicians, sorcerers, witches, spirits, druids and other beings of the magical universe. Possibly the single most influential factor here is the marketing genius of – or rather behind – Harry Potter. The completely engineered world of Harry Potter, with the cathedral of magic at Hogwarts, the variety of shops in Diagon Alley, the experience economy of Quidditch, and the plethora of sweets at Honeydukes sweetshop; all of this is based on a very enriching encounter between a society hungry for sorcery and the magic of marketing, if you are to believe one marketing wizard writing under the name of Stephen Brown. The success of the Harry Potter brand is immersed in a contemporary (postmodern?) demand for magic fairy tales and a skilful construction of a complete universe reflecting all of contemporary consumer society's wonderful and not so wonderful consequences of marketplace practices. Can we finally learn the trick? Magic matters! It is marketing for Muggles![27]

Myths

 Every society possesses a set of myths that define that culture. A **myth** is a story containing symbolic elements that expresses the shared emotions and ideals of a culture. The story may feature some kind of conflict between two opposing forces, and its outcome serves as a moral guide. In this way, a myth reduces anxiety because it provides consumers with guidelines about their world.

An understanding of cultural myths is important to marketers, who in some cases (most likely unconsciously) pattern their strategy along a mythic structure.[28] Consider, for example, the way that a company like McDonald's takes on 'mythical' qualities.[29] The golden arches are a universally recognized symbol, one that is virtually synonymous with American culture. Not only do they signify the possibility for the whole world symbolically to consume a bite of Americana and modernity, but they also offer sanctuary to Americans around the world, who know exactly what to expect once they enter. Basic struggles involving good vs. evil are played out in the fantasy world created by McDonald's advertising, as when Ronald McDonald confounds the Hamburglar. McDonald's even has a 'seminary' (Hamburger University) where inductees go to learn appropriate behaviours and be initiated into the culture. In short, McDonald's is a kind of mythical utopia representing modernity, leisurely eating and lifestyle, and the American dream – a mythical utopia it shares with other brands such as Disneyland or Disney World.[30]

Corporations often have myths and legends in their history, and some make a deliberate effort to be sure newcomers to the organization learn these. Nike (a name drawn from Greek mythology) designates senior executives as 'corporate storytellers' who explain the company's heritage to the hourly workers at Nike stores. They recount tales about the coach of the Oregon track team who poured rubber into his family waffle iron to make better shoes for his team – the origin of the Nike waffle sole. The stories emphasize the dedication of runners and coaches to reinforce the importance of teamwork. Rookies even visit the track where the coach worked to be sure they grasp the importance of the Nike legends. And rumour has it that senior Nike executives (including the CEO) have a 'swoosh' tattoo on their backsides.[31] Of course, one of the most fundamental myths of the Western world is the myth of the 'exotic Other' which is basically different from ourselves, expressed by Kipling in his lines, 'East is East and West is West, and never the twain shall meet'. This is reflected in a lot of consumer behaviour, obviously in the experiences promised by the tourist industry, where myths about destinations are sometimes supported by similar mythologies inherent in, e.g. music, or imagined lifestyles. For example, Hawaii in general[32] and surf culture[33] in particular have been studied as such mythological universes. We also find this myth, however, in more homey activities such as in the attraction to and collection of exotic goods such as Oriental carpets.[34]

The functions and structure of myths

Myths serve four interrelated functions in a culture:[35]

1 *Metaphysical*: they help to explain the origins of existence.

2 *Cosmological*: they emphasize that all components of the universe are part of a single picture.

3 *Sociological*: they maintain social order by authorizing a social code to be followed by members of a culture.

4 *Psychological*: they provide models for personal conduct.

Myths can be analyzed by examining their underlying structures, a technique pioneered by the anthropologist Claude Lévi-Strauss. Lévi-Strauss noted that many stories involve *binary opposition*, where two opposing ends of some dimension are represented (good vs. evil, nature vs. technology). Characters and products often appear in advertisements to be defined by what they *are not* rather than by what they *are* (for example, this is *not* a product for those who feel old, *not* an experience for the frightened, *not* music for the meek, etc.). Such structures have been used to analyze food categories, dividing food into hot vs. cold, for children, for adults and for old people, for men and for women etc.[36]

Recall from the discussion of Freudian theory in Chapter 6 that the ego functions as a kind of 'referee' between the opposing needs of the id and the superego. In a similar fashion, the conflict between mythical opposing forces is sometimes resolved by a *mediating figure*, who can link the opposites by sharing characteristics of each. For example, many myths contain animals that have human abilities (e.g. a talking snake) to bridge the gap between humanity and nature, just as cars (technology) are often given animal names (nature) like Jaguar or Mustang.

Myths are found everywhere in modern popular culture. While we generally equate myths with the ancient Greeks or Romans, modern myths are embodied in many aspects of popular culture, including comic books, films, holidays and even commercials. Sports consumption is replete with myths, for instance myths about 'super-athletes' or 'the eternal no. 2' – or the favourites who always fail – such as the Spanish football team until their victory in the 2008 European championship. Music is also full of myths – myths about the garage band who makes it big, or the myth of the self-destructive artist maintained by many a dead music star.[37]

Comic book superheroes demonstrate how myths can be communicated to consumers of all ages. Indeed, some of these fictional figures represent a **monomyth**, a myth that is common to many cultures.[38] The most prevalent monomyth involves a hero who emerges from the everyday world with supernatural powers and wins a decisive victory over evil forces. He then returns with the power to bestow good things on his fellow men. This basic theme can be found in such classic heroes as Lancelot, Hercules and Ulysses. The success of the Disney movie *Hercules* reminds us that these stories are timeless and appeal to people through the ages.

Comic book heroes are familiar to most consumers, and they are viewed as more credible and effective than celebrity endorsers. Film spin-offs and licensing deals aside, comic books are a multi-million dollar industry. The American version of the monomyth is best epitomized by Superman, a Christ-like figure who renounces worldly temptations and restores harmony to his community. Heroes such as Superman are sometimes used to endow a product, store or service with desirable attributes. This imagery is sometimes borrowed by marketers – PepsiCo tried to enhance its position in the Japanese market by using a figure called 'Pepsiman', a muscle-bound caricature of an American superhero in a skin-tight uniform, to promote the drink. Pepsiman even appears in a Sega game called Fighting Vipers.[39]

But there are many other, less obvious, mythological figures surrounding us. For example, the role of Einstein as a mythological figure, and one that is used for giving meaning to and promoting certain consumable objects in films or posters, or in advertisements as a sort of indirect endorsement, has been studied by consumer researchers.[40]

Many blockbuster films and hit TV programmes draw directly on mythic themes. Spiderman draws both on the myth of the superhero as well as the myth of one's eternal

In these days of marketing literacy, few will buy the message that you become a superhero through using a brand. However, we have mythologies of 'the ordinary' as well as of the extraordinary. This ad cleverly uses the eye-capturing effect of the extra-ordinary super-heroine, while underlining that the brand is targeted to 'ordinary' people – also a much larger market segment.

The Advertising Archives

fight with one's own negative sides (especially in *Spiderman 3*). So while dramatic special effects or attractive stars certainly do not hurt, a number of these films perhaps owe their success to their presentation of characters and plot structures that follow mythic patterns. Examples of these mythic blockbusters include:[41]

- *The Big Blue*. The sea is the offspring of many myths. Its inaccessibility and depth have always inspired humans to create imagery about this other world. The film depicts the search for a lost symbiosis between man and nature, where the only person with real access to this must give up his human life to become one with the purity and the graciousness of the sea, symbolized by the dolphins.

- *E.T.: The Extraterrestrial*. E.T. represents a familiar myth involving Messianic visitation. The gentle creature from another world visits Earth and performs miracles (e.g. reviving a dying flower). His 'disciples' are local children, who help him combat the forces of modern technology and an unbelieving secular society. The metaphysical function of myth is served by teaching that the humans chosen by God are pure and unselfish.

- *Easy Rider*. This 1969 cult film can be seen as the forerunner of the much-beloved road movie genre that has been among the most popular in recent decades, and which got its definitive feminist version with *Thelma and Louise*. These films feature myths of freedom and rebelliousness against the banalities of daily life (as expressed in one of the theme songs from *Easy Rider*, Steppenwolf's 'Born to be Wild'), which are recycled in a lot of commercial contexts. For instance, in a commercial for Ford's Cougar (another wild animal) model, Dennis Hopper (anno 1998) driving a Cougar raced with himself riding a motorbike in the original *Easy Rider* film.[42]

- *Jaws*. This and films constructed around similar themes draw on myths of the beast, representing the wild, dangerous, untamed nature that is culture's (human beings') enemy. Such myths are known from Christianity and other religious mythologies, such as Norse mythology (the Midgaard Snake, the Fenris Wolf), and have played a central role in the way the Western world has regarded nature over the centuries.

Also more mundane consumer objects can be the subject of mythological narratives. Furthermore, since these are culturally constructed, they change over place and time. Consider, for example, a classic study of the meanings and roles of the Italian scooter in the Italian and British market contexts. Whereas in Italy the scooter was mainly positioned as a symbol of the new, modern and liberated Italian woman, epitomized in the Italian superstar actresses of the 1950s, the scooter in Britain became caught in a cultural clash between the more 'masculine' heavy industry and the blue-collar jobs expressed in subcultural terms among the 'rockers' and their motorcycles, and the more white-collar youth subculture of the 'mods', heavily engaged in conspicuous consumption activities. The latter adopted the scooter as their prime symbol and dominant mode of transport.[43] Today, the scooter revived by consumer nostalgia and retro-marketing[44] has become a modern myth object referring to the happy and innocent 'youth' of the youth culture 40 to 50 years ago, as depicted by this bag for sale at London's Portobello Road market in 2008 (see p. 516).

Commercials as myths

Commercials can be analyzed in terms of the underlying cultural themes they represent. For example, commercials for various food products ask consumers to 'remember' the mythical good old days when products were wholesome and natural. The mythical theme of the underdog prevailing over the stronger foe (i.e. David and Goliath) has been used by the car rental firm Avis in a now classic campaign where they stated, 'We're only no. 2, we try harder'. Other figures from mythical narratives have been used by advertisers, such as the villain (a brand teasing its competitors), the hero (the brand in control) or the helper (the brand that helps you accomplish something).[45]

A bag depicting a modern myth object, the scooter.

Caroline Penhoat

This Spanish ad melds modern-day athletes with mythical figures.

Canal/ACB-Contrapunto BBDO Ad Agency

Rituals

▶ A **ritual** is a set of multiple, symbolic behaviours that occur in a fixed sequence and that tend to be repeated periodically.[46] Although bizarre tribal ceremonies, perhaps involving animal or virgin sacrifice, may come to mind when people think of rituals, in reality many contemporary consumer activities are ritualistic. Rituals are traditionally thought of as patterns of behaviour that serves to uphold the social order, but drinking rituals such as Sean's can also be thought of as transgressive and transformative, especially among younger consumers. Hence, drinking as a ritual constitutes a time and space to enter another state of being, i.e. being intoxicated! This relationship to drinking rituals is probably more characteristic of northern European consumers compared to southern Europeans.[47] A recent study the BBDO Worldwide advertising agency conducted illustrates just how crucial rituals are to many brands.[48] It labels brands that we closely link to our

▶ rituals **fortress brands** because once they become embedded in our rituals – whether brushing our teeth, drinking a beer, or shaving – we are unlikely to replace them. The study ran in 26 countries, and the researchers found that overall people worldwide practice roughly the same consumer rituals. The study claims that 89 per cent of people repeatedly use the same brand for these sequenced rituals, and three out of four are disappointed or irritated when something disrupts their ritual or their brand of choice is not available. For example, the report identifies one common ritual category it calls *preparing for battle*. For most of us this means getting ready for work. Relevant rituals include brushing teeth, taking a shower or bath, having something to eat or drink, talking to a family member or partner, checking e-mail, shaving, putting on makeup, watching TV or listening to the radio, and reading a newspaper.

Rituals can occur at a variety of levels, as noted in Table 13.1. Some of the rituals described are specifically American, but the US Super Bowl may be compared to the English FA Cup Final or the traditional ski jump competition in Austria on the first day of the new year. Some rituals affirm broad cultural or religious values, like the differences in the ritual of tea-drinking in the UK and France. Whereas tea seems a sensuous and mystical drink to the French, the drinking of coffee is regarded as having a more functional purpose. For the British, tea is a daily drink and coffee is seen more as a drink to express oneself.[49]

The ritual of going to a café with a selection of coffee opportunities was unknown outside the most metropolitan areas of the US until recent times. No longer. The Starbucks Corporation has experienced phenomenal success by turning the coffee break into a cultural event that for many has assumed almost cult-like status. The average Starbucks

Table 13.1 Types of ritual experience

Primary behaviour source	Ritual type	Examples
Cosmology	Religious	Baptism, meditation, Mass
Cultural values	Rites of passage	Graduation, marriage
	Cultural	Festivals, holidays (Valentine's Day), Super Bowl
Group learning	Civic	Parades, elections, trials
	Group	Business negotiations, office luncheons
	Family	Mealtimes, bedtimes, birthdays, Mother's Day, Christmas
Individual aims and emotions	Personal	Grooming, household rituals

Source: Dennis W. Rook, 'The ritual dimension of consumer behavior', *Journal of Consumer Research*, 12 (December 1985): 251–64. Reprinted with permission of The University of Chicago Press.

customer visits 18 times a month, and 10 per cent of the clientele stops by twice a day.[50] Starbucks has opened shops in many countries in Europe, re-exporting a new kind of coffee shop culture to places with long traditions for café culture such as France. Thus, several types of places for different 'coffee rituals' may co-exist. One study suggested at least three kinds of coffee shops in the Scandinavian context: the traditional 'Viennese' style where a lot of focus is on the baked goods, the 'starbuckified' modern coffe shop (such as Starbucks but also Baresso, etc.) and the 'local' coffee shop with a less stream-lined interior decoration than the modernist ones, and often a devoted clientele of 'alternative-minded' people.[51]

Ritual artefacts

▶ Many businesses owe their livelihoods to their ability to supply **ritual artefacts**, or items used in the performance of rituals, to consumers. Birthday candles, diplomas, specialized foods and beverages (e.g. wedding cakes, ceremonial wine, or even sausages at the stadium), trophies and plaques, band costumes, greetings cards and retirement watches are all used in consumer rituals. In addition, consumers often employ a ritual script, which identifies the artefacts, the sequence in which they are used and who uses them. The proliferation of 'manners and style' books in recent years bears witness to the renewed interest in rituals after the belief of the beat generation that they could abolish ritual behaviour and just act 'normal' and be 'natural'. Of course, such behaviour required a whole new set of rituals . . .

But rituals are not restricted to the special occasions described above. Daily life is full of ritualized behaviour. Wearing a tie on certain occasions can be seen as a ritual, for example. The significance attached to rituals will vary across cultures (Valentine's Day is slowly gaining popularity in several European countries, and in the Middle East),[52] and will often be a mixture of private and public (generally shared) symbolism.[53]

In the model of movement of meaning in the world of goods (see Chapter 4) it is suggested that there are four types of rituals that are central for consumption: possession rituals, exchange rituals, grooming rituals and divestment rituals.[54] Let us begin with considering the first and the last together, since they are logically intertwined: one con-sumer's divestment can often be linked to another consumer's taking into possession.

Possession and divestment rituals

Whether it is in the form of putting magnets on the refrigerator door, objects hanging from the mirror in the car, stickers and badges put on jackets and bags, consumers often perform various rituals that provide a certain degree of alteration to a newly purchased object. The object is thereby transformed from a mass-produced good to a personalized possession. Possession rituals mark that the object is no longer just any object, it is *my* object. The blank and boring computer screen is personalized through the installation of our background for the desktop, our own set of preferred photos as screensavers and in a multitude of other ways. We personalize the screen and the ringtones of our cellphone. Through these ritualistic inclusions of the mass-produced goods in our own little sphere of being, we are transforming them into objects that are visibly or audibly one's own and also expressions of identity, as we discussed in Chapter 5.

Since we invest personal meanings in our things, we also oftentimes invest some efforts in removing the elements of identity when we are getting rid of the things. We call these efforts rituals of disposition. When you move out of your flat, you make sure to clean it of everything that belongs to you, not only because the contract says so, but also because you do not want to allow other people a look into your private life through the personal items or traces left. You may clean it thoroughly, but possibly the new tenant will perform yet another cleaning (another divestment ritual making sure the flat is divested of you) and a possession ritual repainting in order to make sure the flat is now truly theirs. Divestment rituals also occur when cherished possessions are ritualistically transferred from one generation to the next. Such rituals of handing over things to a younger generation can contribute to lower anxieties that the new generations will cherish and protect the family heirloom as well as former generations.

Consequently, rituals of disposition are not only performed in order to remove personalization from consumer objects but, in a way, also to keep it since it confirms, if not the individual, then the family indentity. They can also be performed in order to maintain a moral identity. Consider the great efforts some consumers go through in terms of sorting their garbage for maximal recycling. We can consider this sorting behaviour an expression of environmental values, but it is also a ritual that is performed in order to divest the objects 'properly', that is in the morally and socially (and environmentally) correct way.

Grooming rituals

Whether brushing one's hair 100 strokes a day or talking to oneself in the mirror, virtually all consumers undergo private grooming rituals. These are sequences of behaviours that aid in the transition from the private self to the public self or back again. These rituals serve various purposes, ranging from inspiring confidence before confronting the world to cleansing the body of dirt and other profane materials. Traditionally a female market, the grooming sector for men is a booming business. For example, at the turn of the millennium Unilever opened a new chain of barbershops in the UK that also offer facial treatments and manicures on top of the shaves and beard trims. The adaptation to the male market is almost perfect: the waiting rooms feature PlayStations and personal CD players instead of glossy magazines.[55]

When consumers talk about their grooming rituals, some of the dominant themes that emerge from these stories reflect the almost mystical qualities attributed to grooming products and behaviours. Many people emphasize a before-and-after phenomenon, where the person feels magically transformed after using certain products (similar to the Cinderella myth).[56]

Two sets of binary oppositions that are expressed in personal rituals are *private/public* and *work/leisure*. Many beauty rituals, for instance, reflect a transformation from a natural state to the social world (as when a woman 'puts on her face') or vice versa. In these daily rituals, women reaffirm the value placed by their culture on personal beauty and the quest for eternal youth.[57] This focus is obvious in ads for Oil of Olay beauty cleanser, which proclaim: 'And so your day begins. The Ritual of Oil of Olay.' Similarly, the bath is viewed as a sacred, cleansing time, a way to wash away the sins of the profane world.[58]

Exchange rituals

It would be fair to say that the whole marketplace of exchanging goods, services and information through sharing, buying and selling is one big set of exchange rituals. However, the form of exchange rituals that most ordinary consumers would think of first and foremost is probably giving and receiving gifts. The promotion of appropriate gifts for every conceivable holiday and occasion provides an excellent example of the influence consumer rituals can exert on marketing phenomena and vice versa. In the **gift-giving ritual**, consumers procure the perfect object (artefact), meticulously remove the price tag (symbolically changing the item from a commodity to a unique good), carefully wrap it and deliver it to the recipient.[59]

Gift-giving used to be viewed by researchers primarily as a form of economic exchange, where the giver transfers an item of value to a recipient, who in turn is somehow obliged to reciprocate. However, gift-giving is interpreted increasingly as a symbolic exchange, where the giver is motivated by acknowledging the social bonds between people.[60] These might then be seen as more economic and reciprocal but may also be guided by unselfish factors, such as love or admiration, without expectations of anything in return. Some research indicates that gift-giving evolves as a form of social expression: it is more exchange-oriented (instrumental) in the early stages of a relationship, but becomes more altruistic as the relationship develops.[61] One set of researchers identified multiple ways in which giving a gift can affect a relationship.[62] These are listed in Table 13.2.

Table 13.2 Effects of gift-giving on social relationships

Relational effect	Description	Example
Strengthening	Gift-giving improves the quality of a relationship	An unexpected gift such as one given in a romantic situation
Affirmation	Gift-giving validates the positive quality of a relationship	Usually occurs on ritualized occasions such as birthdays
Negligible effect	Gift-giving has a minimal effect on perceptions of relationship quality	Non-formal gift occasions and those where the gift may be perceived as charity or too good for the current state of the relationship
Negative confirmation	Gift-giving validates a negative quality of a relationship between the gift-giver and the receiver	The selection of gift is inappropriate, indicating a lack of knowledge of the receiver. Alternatively the gift is viewed as a method of controlling the receiver
Weakening	Gift-giving harms the quality of the relationship between giver and receiver	When there are 'strings attached' or gift is perceived as a bribe, a sign of disrespect or offensive
Severing	Gift-giving harms the relationship between the giver and the receiver to the extent that the relationship is dissolved	When the gift forms part of a larger problem, such as a threatening relationship. Or when a relationship is severed through the receipt of a 'parting' gift

Source: Adapted from Julie A. Ruth, Cele C. Otnes and Frederic F. Brunel, 'Gift receipt and the reformulation of interpersonal relationships', *Journal of Consumer Research*, 25 (March 1999): 385–402, Table 1: 389.

Every culture prescribes certain occasions and ceremonies for giving gifts, whether for personal or professional reasons. The giving of birthday presents alone is a major undertaking. Business gifts are an important component in defining professional relationships, and great care is often taken to ensure that the appropriate gifts are purchased.

 Multicultural dimensions

The importance of gift-giving rituals is underscored by considering Japanese customs, where the wrapping of a gift is as important (if not more so) than the gift itself. The economic value of a gift is secondary to its symbolic meaning.[63] To the Japanese, gifts are viewed as an important aspect of one's duty to others in one's social group. Giving is a moral imperative (known as *giri*).

Highly ritualized gift-giving occurs during the giving of both household/personal gifts and company/professional gifts. Each Japanese has a well-defined set of relatives and friends with whom they share reciprocal gift-giving obligations (*kosai*).[64]

Personal gifts are given on social occasions, such as at funerals, to people who are hospitalized, to mark movements from one stage of life to another (such as weddings, birthdays) and as greetings (when one is meeting a visitor). Company gifts are given to commemorate the anniversary of a corporation's founding or the opening of a new building, as well as being a routine part of doing business, as when rewards are given at trade meetings to announce new products.

Some of the items most desired by Japanese consumers to receive as gifts include gift coupons, beer and soap.[65] In keeping with the Japanese emphasis on saving face, presents are not opened in front of the giver, so that it will not be necessary to hide one's possible disappointment with the present.

The gift-giving ritual can be broken down into three distinct stages.[66] During *gestation*, the giver is motivated by an event to procure a gift. This event may be either *structural* (i.e. prescribed by the culture, as when people buy Christmas presents), or *emergent* (i.e. the decision is more personal and idiosyncratic). The second stage is *presentation*, or the

Gift giving has long been a cultural trait among the Japanese. In recent years, it has become popular within the context of a westernised Christmas season in Japan.

Getty Images/Taxi/Gen Nishino

process of gift exchange. The recipient responds to the gift (either appropriately or not), and the donor evaluates this response.

In the third stage, known as *reformulation*, the bonds between the giver and receiver are adjusted (either looser or tighter) to reflect the new relationship that emerges after the exchange is complete. Negativity can arise if the recipient feels the gift is inappropriate or of inferior quality. The donor may feel the response to the gift was inadequate or insincere or a violation of the reciprocity norm, which obliges people to return the gesture of a gift with one of equal value.[67] Both participants may feel resentful for being 'forced' to participate in the ritual.[68]

People commonly find (or devise) reasons to give themselves something; they 'treat' themselves. Consumers purchase **self-gifts** as a way to regulate their behaviour. This ritual provides a socially acceptable way of rewarding themselves for good deeds, consoling themselves after negative events or motivating themselves to accomplish some goal.[69] Figure 13.2 is a projective stimulus similar to ones used in research on self-gifting. Consumers are asked to tell a story based on a picture such as this, and their responses are analyzed to discover the reasons people view as legitimate for rewarding themselves with self-gifts. For example, one recurring story that might emerge is that the woman in the picture had a particularly gruelling day at work and needed a pick-me-up in the form of a new fragrance. This theme could then be incorporated into a promotional campaign for a perfume. With the growing evidence of hedonic motives for consumption in recent decades, self-gifts may represent an increasingly important part of the overall consumption pattern.

Figure 13.2 Projective drawing to study the motivations underlying the giving of self-gifts

Source: Based on David G. Mick, Michelle DeMoss and Ronald J. Faber, 'Latent Motivations and Meanings of Self-Gifts: Implications for Retail Management' (research report, Center for Retailing Education and Research, University of Florida, 1990).

One final gift-giving ritual that is worth mentioning – since the rise of the Internet and its digitalized world has made its much easier and present in our lives – is the idea of sharing; of giving away (in a digital form) what one already possesses, but without losing it oneself. In what may well be the largest gift-giving system in history, the now bygone Napster music sharing community and its successors such as KaZaa and Morpheus have opened a whole new world of consumer exchange rituals with its own specific set of norms for reciprocity and contribution within the online community. For example, people who download files without leaving their files available to others are labelled as 'leeches'.[70] As we all know, this form of gift-giving has not been embraced by all. Copyright holders in the form of music publishers (and musicians) are generally less than amused, so since then we have witnessed what might best be desribed as a drama between producers protecting their intellectual property rights and consumers underlining their rights to do what they want with their possessions (including online sharing and community building) as long as it is remains a non-commercial activity.[71] Whose side are you on?

Holiday rituals

Holidays are important rituals in both senses of the word. Going on holiday was one of the most widespread rituals and tourism one of the biggest industries of the late twentieth century, and the trend looks set to continue.[72] On holidays consumers step back from their everyday lives and perform ritualistic behaviours unique to those times.[73] For example, going to Disneyland in Paris may mean a ritualized return to the memories of our own dreams of a totally free (of obligations, duties and responsibilities) fantasy land of play.[74] Holiday occasions are filled with ritual artefacts and scripts and are increasingly cast as a time for giving gifts by enterprising marketers. Holidays mean big business to hotels, restaurants, travel agents and so on.

Holidays also exist in terms of special celebratory occasions. For many businesses Christmas is the single most important season. Concerning the holidays of celebrations, most such holidays are based on a myth, and often a real (Guy Fawkes) or imaginary (Cupid on Valentine's Day) character is at the centre of the story. These holidays persist because their basic elements appeal to deep-seated patterns in the functioning of culture.[75]

The Christmas holiday is bursting with myths and rituals, from adventures at the North Pole to those that occur under the mistletoe. One of the most important holiday rituals involves Santa Claus, or an equivalent mythical figure, eagerly awaited by children the world over. Unlike Christ, this person is a champion of materialism. Perhaps it is no coincidence, then, that he appears in stores and shopping centres – secular temples of consumption. Whatever the origins of Santa Claus, the myth surrounding him serves the purpose of socializing children by teaching them to expect a reward when they are good and that members of society get what they deserve. Needless to say, Christmas, Santa Claus and other attached rituals and figures change when they enter into other cultural settings. In the Netherlands he has to compete with Sint Niklaas, who basically is his own doppelganger, and who even has his own day of celebration on 6 December. In Denmark, Norway and Sweden, Santa Claus competes or is confused with Julenissen (in Sweden, Jultomten), who is a kind of amalgamation between gnomes from ancient pagan beliefs and a contemporary Santa Claus figure. Some of the transformations of Santa Claus in a Japanese context include a figure called 'Uncle Chimney', Santa Claus as a stand-in for the newborn Christ and Santa Claus crucified at the entrance of one department store with the words 'Happy Shopping' written above his head.[76] What does this tell us about the globalization process?

On Valentine's Day, standards regarding sex and love are relaxed or altered as people express feelings that may be hidden during the rest of the year. In addition to cards, a variety of gifts are exchanged, many of which are touted by marketers to represent aphrodisiacs or other sexually related symbols. It seems as if many people in consumer societies are always on the lookout for new rituals to fill their lives. This ritual was once virtually unknown in Scandinavia but is slowly becoming part of their consumption environment.[77] Also, the American ritual of celebrating Halloween is now becoming fashionable in Europe, where the French in particular have adopted it as an occasion for festivities, dancing and the chance to show off new fashions (but see Case Study 18, p. 625).[78] Also in Denmark, Halloween has become a significant consumer ritual. Between 2005 and 2008 the sales of scary stuff from toy stores has gone up 10 to 20 per cent each year, and the sale of pumpkins (which Danes generally do not eat) has multiplied by 30 between 1999 and 2008.[79] As for many modern rituals, supermarket chains and other commercial agents have played a significant role in spreading these occasions for having a good time but also for boosting sales across borders (cf. Case Study 22, p. 640).

Rites of passage

What does a dance for recently divorced people have in common with 'college initiation ceremonies'? Both are examples of modern **rites of passage**, or special times marked by a change in social status. Every society, both primitive and modern, sets aside times where such changes occur. Some of these changes may occur as a natural part of consumers' life cycles (puberty or death), while others are more individual in nature (divorce and re-entering the dating market). As we saw with some of the other rituals, there seems to be a renewed interest in transition rites. They are increasingly becoming consumption objects in themselves as well as occasions for consumption. In order to satisfy the 'need' for rituals, not only do we import new ones from abroad, as we have seen, but in times of globalization many cultures also experience a renewed interest in the old rituals that have traditionally framed the cultural identity.[80]

Some marketers attempt to reach consumers on occasions in which their products can enhance a transition from one stage of life to another.[81] A series of Volkswagen ads underlined the role of the car in the freedom of women who were leaving their husbands or boyfriends.

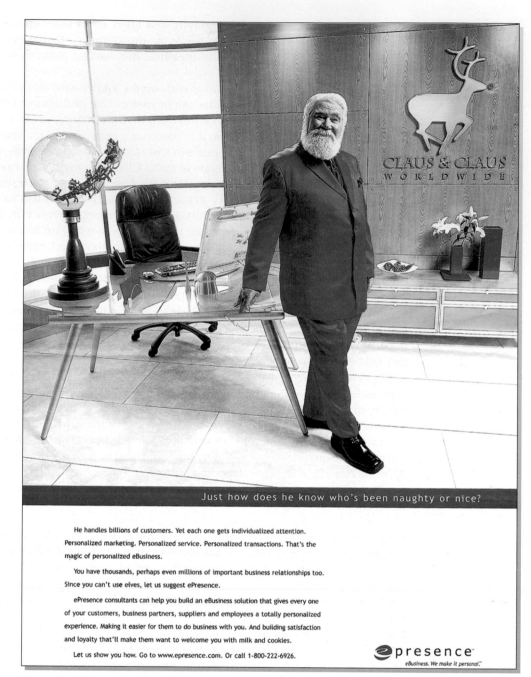

The myth of Santa Claus permeates our culture and marks the biggest consumption ritual in today's world.

Stages of role transition   Much like the metamorphosis of a caterpillar into a butterfly, consumers' rites of passage consist of three phases.[82] The first stage, *separation*, occurs when the individual is detached from their original group or status (for example, the first-year university student leaves home). *Liminality* is the middle stage, where the person is literally in between statuses (the new arrival on campus tries to work out what is happening during orientation week). The last stage, *aggregation*, takes place when the person re-enters society after the rite of passage is complete (the student returns home for the Christmas holiday as a 'real university student'). Rites of passage mark many consumer activities, as exemplified by confirmation or other rites of going from the world of the child to the world of the adult. A similar transitional state can be observed when people are prepared for certain occupational roles. For example, athletes and fashion models typically undergo a 'seasoning' process. They are removed from their normal surroundings (athletes are taken to training camps, while young models are often moved to Paris or Milan), indoctrinated into a new subculture and then returned to the real world in their new roles.

The final passage: marketing death The rites of passage associated with death support an entire industry. Death themes are replete in marketing.[83] Survivors must make expensive purchase decisions, often at short notice and driven by emotional and superstitious concerns. Funeral ceremonies help the living to organize their relationships with the deceased, and action tends to be tightly scripted down to the costumes (the ritual black attire, black ribbons for mourners, the body in its best suit) and specific behaviours (sending condolence cards or holding a wake). (However, more and more seem to emphasize a certain personal touch to commemorate the individuality of the deceased.) Mourners 'pay their last respects', and seating during the ceremony is usually dictated by mourners' closeness to the individual. Even the cortège is accorded special status by other motorists, who recognize its separate, sacred nature by not overtaking as it proceeds to the cemetery.[84]

Funeral practices vary across cultures, but they are always rich in symbolism. For example, a recent study of funeral rituals in Ghana found that the community there determines a person's social value after he has died; this status depends on the type of funeral his family gives him. One of the main purposes of death rituals is to negotiate the social identities of deceased persons. This occurs as mourners treat the corpse with a level of respect that indicates what they think of him. The Asante people who were the subjects of the study do not view death as something to fear but rather as a part of a broader, ongoing process of identity negotiation.[85]

SACRED AND PROFANE CONSUMPTION

As we saw when considering the structure of myths, many types of consumer activity involve the demarcation, or binary opposition, of boundaries, such as good vs. bad, male vs. female – or even 'regular' vs. 'low-fat'. One of the most important of these sets of boundaries is the distinction between the sacred and the profane. **Sacred consumption** involves objects and events that are 'set apart' from normal activities, and are treated with some degree of respect or awe. They may or may not be associated with religion, but most religious items and events tend to be regarded as sacred. **Profane consumption** involves consumer objects and events that are ordinary, everyday objects and events that do not share the 'specialness' of sacred ones. (Note that profane does not mean vulgar or obscene in this context.)

Domains of sacred consumption

Sacred consumption events permeate many aspects of consumers' experiences. We find ways to 'set apart' a variety of places, people and events. In this section, we will consider some examples of ways that 'ordinary' consumption is sometimes not so ordinary after all.

Sacred places

Sacred places have been 'set apart' by a society because they have religious or mystical significance (e.g. Bethlehem, Mecca, Stonehenge) or because they commemorate some aspect of a country's heritage (e.g. the Kremlin, Versailles, the Colosseum in Rome).

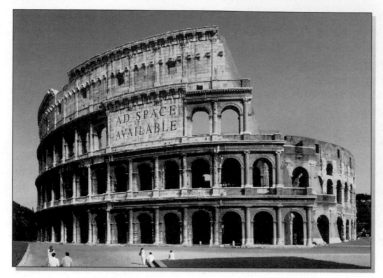

Sacred places are revered, not only in 'real life' but also in advertising, since they are immediately recognizable, highly visible and normally connote positive values. The present mythologies of the grandeur of antiquity and more generally myths attached to sacred places of world heritage are used here in a humorous (but also sacrilegious?) way for maximum attention and mind-provocation.

During 2008, there was quite a debate in Denmark whether to temporarily move the Copenhagen landmark, 'The Little Mermaid', to China for a world exhibit. The marketing people of the Danish tourist industries as well as the export organization thought it would be a scoop to present 'the real thing' to the Chinese visitors at the exhibit, but many Danes felt that it is a degradation of a sacred piece of art and a part of the 'soul' of Copenhagen for a marketing gimmick. The marketers got their way. Remember that in many cases the sacredness of these places is due to the property of contamination – that is, something sacred happened on that spot, so the place itself takes on sacred qualities. There is a plethora of sacred places to be 'consumed' around the world, and we are not only thinking world famous cathedrals. One study investigated consumer behaviour at St Brigid's Holy Well in Ireland. The study reported a plethora of holy but also secular objects left there by pilgrims, often with a little story attached explaining the magical belief in the wish for some kind of transformation, like curing an illness or blessing a relationship or children.[86] Tourism is one of the most common and rapidly spreading forms of consuming the sacred.[87]

Other places are created from the profane world and imbued with sacred qualities. When Ajax, the local football team of Amsterdam, moved from their old stadium, De Meern, to a larger, more modern stadium (De Arena), the turf from the old stadium was carefully lifted from the ground and sold to a local churchyard. The churchyard offers the turf to fans willing to pay a premium price to be buried under authentic Ajax turf!

Even the modern shopping centre can be regarded as a secular 'cathedral of consumption', a special place where community members come to practise shopping rituals.[88] Theme parks are a form of mass-produced fantasy that takes on aspects of sacredness. In particular, the various Disneylands are destinations for pilgrimages from consumers around the globe. Disneyland displays many characteristics of more traditional sacred places, especially for Americans, but Europeans too may consider these parks the quintessence of America. It is even regarded by some as the epitome of child(ish) happiness. A trip to a park is the most common 'last wish' for terminally-ill children.[89]

In many cultures, the home is a particularly sacred place. It represents a crucial distinction between the harsh, external world and consumers' 'inner space'. In northern and western Europe the home is a place where you entertain guests (in southern Europe it is more common to go out), and fortunes are spent each year on interior decorators and home furnishings; the home is thus a central part of consumers' identities.[90] But even here there are vast differences between, for example, the dominant traditionalist style of British homes and the modernist style of Danish homes.[91] Consumers all over the world go to great lengths to create a special environment that allows them to create the quality of homeliness. This effect is created by personalizing the home as much as possible, using such devices as door wreaths, mantel arrangements and a 'memory wall' for family photos.[92] Even public places, like various types of cafés and bars, strive for a home-like atmosphere which shelters customers from the harshness of the outside world.

Sacred people

People themselves can be sacred, when they are idolized and set apart from the masses. Souvenirs, memorabilia and even mundane items touched or used by sacred people take on special meanings and acquire value in their own right. Indeed, many businesses thrive on consumers' desire for products associated with famous people. There is a thriving market for celebrity autographs, and objects once owned by celebrities, whether Princess Diana's gowns or John Lennon's guitars, are often sold at auction for astronomical prices. A store called 'A Star is Worn' sells items donated by celebrities – a black bra autographed by Cher sold for $575. As one observer commented about the store's patrons, 'They want something that belonged to the stars, as if the stars have gone into sainthood and the people want their shrouds.'[93] More recently, the UK firm of ASOS (As Seen On Screen) has started a thriving online business targeted at 18 to 30-year-olds (primarily female) which offers for sale products that are identical to products that are seen in television shows. The company owners got the idea after reading an article reporting that the broadcasters of *Friends* (the television show) received over 28,000 telephone calls enquiring about a lamp that had appeared in one of the characters' apartments.[94]

Sacred events

Many consumers' activities have taken on a special status. Public events in particular resemble sacred, religious ceremonies, as exemplified by the playing of the national anthems before a game or the reverential lighting of matches and lighters at the end of a rock concert.[95]

For many people, the world of sport is sacred and almost assumes the status of a religion. The roots of modern sports events can be found in ancient religious rites, such as fertility festivals (e.g. the original Olympics).[96] Indeed, it is not uncommon for teams to join in prayer prior to a game. The sports pages are like the Scriptures (and we describe ardent fans as reading them 'religiously'), the stadium is a house of worship, and the fans are members of the congregation. After the first Scottish victory in many years in a football match against England at Wembley Stadium, Scottish fans tore down the goals to bring pieces back home as sacred relics. Indeed, grass from stadiums of important matches, like World Cup finals, has been sold in small portions at large prices.

Devotees engage in group activities, such as tailgate parties (eating and drinking in bars or even the car park prior to the event) and the 'Mexican Wave', where (resembling a revival meeting) participants on cue join the wave-like motion as it makes its way around the stadium. The athletes that fans come to see are godlike; they are reputed to have almost superhuman powers (especially football stars in southern Europe and Latin America). Athletes are central figures in a common cultural myth, the hero tale. As exemplified by mythologies of the barefoot Olympic marathon winner (Abebe Bikila from Ethiopia, 1960), or of boxing heroes (legally) fighting their way out of poverty and misery, often the heroes must prove themselves under strenuous circumstances. Victory is achieved only through sheer force of will. Of course, sports heroes are popular endorsers in commercials, but only a few of these sports personalities 'travel' very well, since sports heroes tend to be first and foremost national heroes. However, a few people are known worldwide, at least within the key target for the ads, so that they can be used in international campaigns.

If sport is one domain that is becoming increasingly sacred (see the section on sacralization below), then the traditionally sacred realm of fine arts is considered by some in danger of desacralization. In a sale of a publishing company of classical music, various representatives voiced the fear that a takeover by one of the giants such as Sony, Polygram or EMI would mean the introduction of a market logic that would destroy its opportunities to continue to sponsor unknown artists and make long-term investments in them. It is argued that classical music is not a product that can be handled by any marketer, but requires special attention and a willingness to accept financial losses in order to secure artistic openness and creativity.[97] Such reactions (as justified as they may be) indicate that artists and managers conceive of themselves as dealing with sacred objects that cannot be subjugated to what is conceived as the profane legitimacy of the market.[98] Indeed, art and marketing is the subject of study for more and more marketing and consumer researchers, for example in considering art as a kind of service.[99] Famous film directors make commercial campaigns and music videos (and music video-makers turn into great film directors), while commercial film-makers celebrate each other with their own sets of prizes for creativity. And consider 'art placement': one artist proposed a series of films featuring a mysterious 'Mr Who' engaging in a lot of daily consumption activities and used clippings from commercials to portray Mr Who's consumer universe.[100] Art and marketing, in short, are becoming increasingly blurred.[101]

Tourism is another example of a sacred, non-ordinary experience of extreme importance to marketers. When people travel on holiday, they occupy sacred time and space. The tourist is continually in search of 'authentic' experiences which differ from their normal world (think of Club Med's motto, 'The antidote to civilization').[102] This travelling experience involves binary oppositions between work and leisure and being 'at home' vs. 'away'. Norms regarding appropriate behaviour are modified as tourists scramble for illicit experiences they would not dream of engaging in at home.

The desire of travellers to capture these sacred experiences in objects forms the bedrock of the souvenir industry, which may be said to be in the business of selling sacred memories. Whether a personalized matchbook from a wedding or a little piece of the Berlin Wall, souvenirs represent a tangible piece of the consumer's sacred experience.[103]

In addition to personal mementoes, such as ticket stubs saved from a favourite concert, the following are other types of sacred souvenir icons:[104]

- Local products (such as goose liver from Périgord or Scotch whisky).
- Pictorial images (postcards).
- 'Piece of the rock' (seashells, pine cones). Sometimes this can be problematic, however. For example, it is forbidden to bring home corals and seashells from a lot of diving places around the world, in order to prevent tourists from 'tearing down' the coral reef. But temptations are great. Even at Nobel Prize dinners, approximately 100 of the noble guests each year cannot resist bringing home something, typically a coffee spoon, as a souvenir.[105]
- Symbolic shorthand in the form of literal representations of the site (a miniature London double-decker bus, Little Mermaid or Eiffel Tower).
- Markers (Hard Rock Café T-shirts).

Increasingly, we see peculiar blends of the sacred and the secular in tourism and in sacred places promoting themselves. One such case is the town of Glastonbury, England. Being an ancient site for pagan as well as Christian worship, it today profiles itself on an amalgamation of 'serious' New Age beliefs and tongue-in-cheek promotion of experience economy witchcraft à la Harry Potter.[106]

Consumer behaviour as I see it . . .

Given the omnipotent prevalence of consumption in public and private life, I think consumer researchers should, and increasingly are, examining issues of significant social and human impact. An obvious domain is sustainable consumption, from the perspective of both the consumer and the firm. We consumer researchers need to study the firm's decisions and actions as well as those of the consumers since the two inform and are informed by each other. For example, what are the motivators and the conditions for each party to engage in activities that will entail sustainable options? I have been working on collecting success stories of firms acting responsibly and making a difference. My former research on consumer desires and legitimizations of materialism provide important hints for some of the conditions under which consumers will buy into ecologically-friendly consumption.

Güliz Ger
Bilkent University,
Ankara

Politics and religion are some other domains that have a major impact on how consumers think, feel and behave. Markets are embedded in politics just as much as they are in economics and culture. While spirituality may appear to counter consumption, we see that globally, religious fundamentalism is on the rise along with consumption. Özlem Sandikci and I have been studying the interplay of religion and consumption in the case of Islamic fashions. We demonstrate that faithful consumers' dress choices require a lot of work and serve to negotiate ethics, aesthetics, and politics. Richard Wilk and I have been studying the material objects of Christianity, Islam and Buddhism and we find the meanings of such objects to be mobile.

While everyone says we cannot understand the present without understanding the past, only recently consumer researchers have begun to study the historical underpinnings of consumption. Eminegül Karababa and I examined the emergence of consumer culture in the seventeenth century Ottomans and show how consumers, markets, religion, and the state interact with each other. Russell Belk and I have been comparing seventeenth century China and The Netherlands; we find both important similarities as well as differences in these consumer cultures. Apparently, both today and in the past, consumers and consumer cultures in different parts of the world are constituted not only by Western influences but also by the local conditions.

From sacred to profane, and back again

Just to make life interesting, in recent times many consumer activities have moved from one sphere to the other. Some things that were formerly regarded as sacred have moved into the realm of the profane, while other, everyday phenomena are now regarded as sacred.[107] Both these processes are relevant to our understanding of contemporary consumer behaviour. A recent study of tea preparation in Turkey illustrates this movement. Although we are more likely to think of thick Turkish coffee, in reality Turks consume more tea per capita than any other country. In this culture people drink tea continuously, like (or instead of) water. Tea is an integral part of daily life; many households and offices boil water for tea in the traditional *çaydanlik* (double teapot) first thing in the morning, and keep it steaming all day so that the beverage is ready at any time. The tea drinking process links to many symbolic meanings – including the traditional glasses, clear to appreciate the tea's colour, and hourglass-shaped like a woman's body – and rituals, such as blending one's own tea, knowing how finely to grind the tea leaves, and how long to steep the tea for optimal flavour. When Lipton introduced the modern tea bag in 1984, Turkey was intent on modernization and soon consumers were buying electric *çaydanlik*, and mugs instead of small, shapely tea glasses. Tea became a symbol of the quick and convenient and the drinking act became more of a fashion statement – it was desacralized. Now, the authors report that many Turkish consumers opt to return to the sacred, traditional rituals as a way to preserve authenticity in the face of rapid societal changes.[108]

Desacralization

▶ **Desacralization** occurs when a sacred item or symbol is removed from its special place or is duplicated in mass quantities, becoming profane as a result. For example, souvenir reproductions of sacred monuments such as the Leaning Tower of Pisa or the Eiffel Tower, 'pop' artworks of the *Mona Lisa* or adaptations of important symbols such as the Union flag by clothing designers, tend to eliminate their special aspects by turning them into inauthentic commodities, produced mechanically and representing relatively little value.[109]

Religion itself has to some extent been desacralized. Religious symbols, such as stylized crosses or New Age crystals, have moved into the mainstream of fashion jewellery.[110] What used to be deeply religious expressions thus become fashion. In fact, religion itself becomes fashion. We witness an interesting period, where a lot of religions are competing with each other for the consumers' interest. Not all of these are New Age creations based on some sympathetic Asian philosophy. In Iceland and Norway, the ancient Norse viking religion worshipping Thor and Odin is a recognized religious community, and it has asked for recognition in Denmark as well. Even in deeply Catholic Italy, there is a revived pagan community of believers in ancient magic and mystery.[111]

▼ Marketing pitfall

'Brand new Dolce & Gabbana rosary beads. These are becoming increasingly sought after. The item is brand new with all of the original tags and box. The authenticity hologram, and the serial number are integral – Jesus is on a cross. Virgin Mary is in the middle of the necklace and at the end a metal Dolce & Gabbana tag. Fabulous necklaces. Worn by super stars like David Beckham, Britney Spears and also seen on Bono of U2.'[112]

Rosary beads as a style statement, not a prayer ritual, are hot fashion with celebrities, again. In the mid-1980s, Madonna, who was brought up a Catholic, raised eyebrows and launched a fashion craze by wearing crucifixes and rosaries with corsets. Eventually, the look became 'cheesy' and faded away. But, like many '80s trends, rosaries 'are cool again' with celebs. Britney Spears and Marlon Wayans have been spotted by paparazzi wearing rosary beads with several chains and necklaces, and David Beckham, soccer's hunky Brit, was photographed for the cover of the July 2004 issue of *Vanity Fair* with them. He brought along his own rosary beads by Dolce & Gabbana, the favourite designers of Beckham and wife Victoria 'Posh Spice' Beckham.[113] Sales of rosary beads have been very strong across the UK and Italy in the past years, and this has not gone unnoticed by officials of the Catholic Church. In the UK, one priest pointed out that while this fashion trend is 'not doing wicked things and leading us astray, I am sorry that people are wearing them as fashion accessories and are not mindful of their religious significance'.[114] As an accessory line for men, rosaries have been very successfully promoted by Dolce & Gabanna. The significant difference in wearing the rosaries is that men adorn themselves with rosaries as necklaces, rather than carrying them in their hand, which is the more traditional use. Having rosaries displayed in a stylish context of a high fashion store window alongside other fashion items such as shirts and sunglasses serves to move the rosary beads from one (religious) meaning to another (commercial and fashionable) context.[115]

Religious holidays, particularly Christmas, are regarded by many (and criticized by some) as having been transformed into secular, materialistic occasions devoid of their original sacred significance. Benetton, the Italian clothing manufacturer, has been at the forefront in creating vivid (and often controversial) messages that expose us to our cultural categories and prejudices, but at times they have touched upon the issue of desacralization.[116]

Even the clergy are increasingly adopting secular marketing techniques. Especially in the US, televangelists rely upon the power of television, a secular medium, to convey their messages. The Catholic Church generated a major controversy after it hired a prominent public relations firm to promote its anti-abortion campaign.[117] Nonetheless, many religious groups have taken the secular route, and are now using marketing

Religious symbols have become fashion symbols for many. Celebrity users, such as Madonna, have speeded up the transition, moving the original meaning of sacred objects to a popular culture context, where the meaning is no longer religious, but is, instead, associated with secular goods.

Corbis/Neal Preston

techniques to increase the number of believers. A Danish bishop addressed a number of major food producing companies for a joint venture in profiling Pentecost as a holiday season equally as important as Christmas and Easter.[118] The question is whether the use of marketing changes the 'product' or 'service' of the churches.[119]

▶ Multicultural dimensions

The American 'market for religious belief' with its televangelists and its heavy promotion of various churches and sects is a very exotic experience for many Europeans. The ad below for a Minneapolis church to help recruit worshippers is typical of the American trend towards secular practices being observed by many organized religions. It even uses a pun (on the curing of a headache) to pass on the message of salvation.

Sacralization

 Sacralization occurs when objects, events and even people take on sacred meaning to a culture or to specific groups within a culture. For example, events like the Cannes Film Festival or Wimbledon and people like Elvis Presley or Princess Diana have become sacralized to some consumers. But the process of sacralization can be used to understand more mundane phenomena than such super-events or popular culture heroes. An interesting study of devoted fans of the Apple corporation and its Macintosh computers concluded that the devotion of the Apple fans was comparable to a religious feeling, portraying Steve Jobs, co-founder and later re-installed CEO of Apple, as a kind of prophet with a message of salvation for the 'chosen few' in a PC-dominated world.[120]

Objectification occurs when sacred qualities are attributed to mundane items. One way that this process can occur is through *contamination*, where objects associated with sacred events or people become sacred in their own right. This explains the desire by many

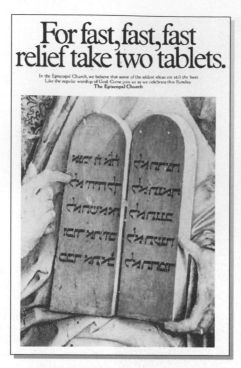

For fast, fast, fast relief take two tablets.

In the Episcopal Church, we believe that some of the oldest ideas are still the best.
Like the regular worship of God. Come join us as we celebrate this Sunday.
The Episcopal Church

The ad for the Episcopal church discussed in the multicultural dimensions box on p. 531.

Church Ad Project, 1021 Diffley, Eagen, MN 55123

fans for items belonging to, or even touched by, famous people. One standard procedure through which objects become sacralized occurs when they become included in the collection of a museum.

In addition to museum exhibits displaying rare objects, even mundane, inexpensive things may be set apart in private *collections*, where they are transformed from profane items to sacred ones. An item is sacralized as soon as it enters a collection, and it takes on special significance to the collector that, in some cases, may be hard to comprehend

▶ by the outsider. **Collecting** refers to the systematic acquisition of a particular object or set of objects, and this widespread activity can be distinguished from hoarding, which is merely unsystematic collecting.[121] Collecting typically involves both rational and emotional components, since collectors are fixed by their objects, but they also carefully organize and exhibit them.[122]

Name an item, and the odds are that a group of collectors are lusting after it. The contents of collections range from various popular culture memorabilia, rare books and autographs, to Barbie dolls, tea bags, lawnmowers and even junk mail.[123] The 1,200 members of the American McDonald's Collectors' Club collect 'prizes' like sandwich wrappers and Happy Meal trinkets – rare ones like the 1987 Potato Head Kids' Toys sell for $25.[124] Consumers are often ferociously attached to their collections; this passion is exemplified by the comment made in one study by a woman who collects teddy bears: 'If my house ever burns down, I won't cry over my furniture, I'll cry over the bears.'[125]

Some consumer researchers feel that collectors are motivated to acquire their 'prizes' in order to gratify a high level of materialism in a socially acceptable manner. By systematically amassing a collection, the collector is allowed to 'worship' material objects without feeling guilty or petty. Another perspective is that collecting is an aesthetic experience: for many collectors the pleasure emanates from being involved in creating the collection, rather than from passively admiring the items one has scavenged or bought. Whatever the motivation, hard-core collectors often devote a great deal of time and energy to maintaining and expanding their collections, so for many this activity becomes a central component of their extended selves (see Chapter 5).[126]

Marketing opportunity

Make your brand a collectable, and enhance your exposure and your brand loyalty. Certain products and brands become cult objects for devoted collectors. In the early 1990s, 'Swatch fever' infected many people. The company made more than 500 different models, some of which were special editions designed by artists. Collectors' interest made a formerly mundane product into a rare piece of art (e.g. a 'Jelly Fish' that originally sold for $30 was sold at auction for $17,000). Although thousands of people still collect the watches, the frenzy began to fade by around 1993.[127] Some collectors' items are more stable. One of the corporations exploiting this opportunity to its fullest is the Coca-Cola Company. With the plethora of Coca-Cola collectables, a lot of devoted and often highly specialized collectors have been created all over the world. They appear as 'spokespersons' for the brand when they account for their sometimes fabulous collections in the media, and they create a lot of extra and extremely positive exposure for the brand. As one researcher noted: 'These are brand owners. Coca-Cola is theirs.'[128]

CHAPTER SUMMARY

- A society's *culture* includes its values, ethics and the material objects produced by its people. It is the accumulation of *shared meanings* and traditions among members of a society. A culture can be described in terms of ecology (the way people adapt to their habitat), its social structure and its ideology (including people's moral and aesthetic principles). This chapter describes some aspects of culture and focuses on how cultural meanings are created and transmitted across members of a society.

- Members of a culture share a system of *beliefs* and *practices*, including *values*. The process of learning the values of one's culture is called enculturation. Each culture can be described by a set of core values. Values can be identified by several methods, though it is often difficult to apply these results directly to marketing campaigns due to their generality.

- *Myths* are stories containing symbolic elements that express the shared ideals of a culture. Many myths involve some binary opposition, where values are defined in terms of what they are and what they are not (e.g. nature vs. technology). Modern myths are transmitted through advertising, films and other media.

- A *ritual* is a set of multiple, symbolic behaviours which occur in a fixed sequence and tend to be repeated periodically. Rituals are related to many consumption activities which occur in popular culture. These include holiday observances, gift-giving and grooming.

- A *rite of passage* is a special kind of ritual which involves the transition from one role to another. These passages typically entail the need to acquire products and services, called ritual artefacts, to facilitate the transition. Modern rites of passage include graduations, initiation ceremonies, weddings and funerals.

- Consumer activities can be divided into *sacred* and *profane* domains. Sacred phenomena are 'set apart' from everyday activities or products. People, events or objects can become sacralized. *Objectification* occurs when sacred qualities are ascribed to products or items owned by sacred people. *Sacralization* occurs when formerly sacred objects or activities become part of the everyday, as when 'one-of-a-kind' works of art are reproduced in large quantities. *Desacralization* occurs when objects that previously were considered sacred become commercialized and integrated into popular culture.

- *Collecting* is one of the most common ways of experiencing sacred consumption in daily life. It is simultaneously one of the domains where consumption and passions are most heavily intertwined.

- The importance of consumption for understanding social interactions is now so big that we have begun to talk about our own societies as *consumer societies*, indicating that consumption might well be the single most important social activity.

▶ **KEY TERMS**

Collecting (p. 532)

Collectivist cultures (p. 508)

Conventions (p. 510)

Co-optation (p. 506)

Culture (p. 506)

Custom (p. 510)

Desacralization (p. 530)

Ethnoconsumerism (p. 509)

Ethos (p. 508)

Fortress brands (p. 517)

Gift-giving ritual (p. 519)

Individualist cultures (p. 508)

Monochronic (p. 508)

Monomyth (p. 514)

Mores (p. 510)

Myth (p. 512)

Polychronic (p. 508)

Profane consumption (p. 525)

Proxemics (p. 508)

Rites of passage (p. 523)

Ritual (p. 517)

Ritual artefacts (p. 518)

Sacralization (p. 531)

Sacred consumption (p. 525)

Self-gifts (p. 521)

Signifying practices (p. 507)

Worldview (p. 508)

▶ **CONSUMER BEHAVIOUR CHALLENGE**

1 Culture can be thought of as a society's personality. If your culture were a person, could you describe its personality traits?

2 What is the difference between an enacted norm and a crescive norm? Identify the set of crescive norms operating when a man and woman in your culture go out for dinner on a first date. What products and services are affected by these norms?

3 How do the consumer decisions involved in gift-giving differ from other purchase decisions?

4 The chapter argues that not all gift-giving is positive. In what ways can this ritual be unpleasant or negative?

5 Construct a ritual script for a wedding in your culture. How many artefacts can you list that are contained in this script?

6 What are some of the major motivations for the purchase of self-gifts? Discuss some marketing implications of these.

7 Describe the three stages of the rite of passage associated with graduating from university.

8 Identify the ritualized aspects of various kinds of sports that are employed in advertising.

9 Some people have raised objections to the commercial exploitation of cultural figures. For example, in the US many consumers deplored the profits that film-makers and business people made from films such as *Malcolm X* (e.g. by selling a 'Malcolm X' air freshener). Others argued that this commercialization merely helps to educate consumers about what such people stood for, and is inevitable in our society. More recently, the 'close-up' portrait of the British royal family in the critically acclaimed movie *The Queen* stirred quite some discussion about how close you should go. What do you think?

10 Interview two or three of your fellow students about collecting, talking about either their own collections or a collection of somebody they know of. Use concepts about the sacred to analyze the responses.

For additional material see the companion website at **www.pearsoned.co.uk/solomon**

NOTES

1. According to tradition, the slow pour takes exactly 119.5 seconds as the bartender holds the glass at a 45-degree angle, fills it three-quarters full, lets it settle and tops it off with its signature creamy head. When Guinness tried to introduce *FastPour*, an ultrasound technology that dispenses the dark brew in just 25 seconds, to make the pull faster and thus increase the number of drinks staff can pour on a busy night, the brewer had to scrap the system when drinkers resisted the innovation. Note: Diageo (which owns Guinness) hasn't given up and is experimenting with other techniques in markets where this ritual isn't so inbred. A system under test in Tokyo called *Guinness Surger* is intended for bars that are too small to accommodate kegs. It lets a bartender pour a pint from a bottle, place the glass on a special plate, and zap it with ultrasound waves that generate the characteristic head. See Dennis W. Rook, 'The ritual dimension of consumer behavior', *Journal of Consumer Research* 12 (December 1985): 251–64; Mary A. Stansfield Tetreault and Robert E. Kleine III, 'Ritual, Ritualized Behavior, and Habit: Refinements and Extensions of the Consumption Ritual Construct', in Marvin Goldberg, Gerald Gorn, and Richard W. Pollay (eds), *Advances in Consumer Research* 17 (Provo, UT: Association for Consumer Research, 1990): 31–8; Deborah Ball, 'British drinkers of Guinness say they'd rather take it slow', *The Wall Street Journal on the Web* (22 May 2003).

2. See for example, A. Fuat Firat, 'Consumer Culture or Culture Consumed', in Janeen A. Costa and G. Bamossy (eds), *Marketing in a Multicultural World: Ethnicity, Nationalism, and Cultural Identity* (Thousand Oaks, CA: Sage, 1995): 105–25.

3. Mary Douglas and Baron Isherwood, *The World of Goods*, 2nd edn (London: Routledge, 1996).

4. A classic work on this is, for example, Edward T. Hall, *The Silent Language* (New York: Doubleday, 1959).

5. Paul du Gay, Stuart Hall, Linda Janes, Hugh MacKay and Keith Negus, *Doing Cultural Studies: The Story of the Sony Walkman* (London: Sage, 1997).

6. Hans Rask Jensen, 'The Mohammed cartoons controversy and the boycott of Danish products in the Middle East', *European Business Review* 20(3), 2008: 275–89.

7. Personal communication with Jens Bernsen, 29 October 1997.

8. Clifford Geertz, *The Interpretation of Cultures* (New York: Basic Books, 1973); Marvin Harris, *Culture, People and Nature* (New York: Crowell, 1971); John F. Sherry Jr, 'The Cultural Perspective in Consumer Research', in Richard J. Lutz (ed.), *Advances in Consumer Research* 13 (Provo, UT: Association for Consumer Research, 1986): 573–5.

9. Celia W. Dugger, 'Modestly, India Goes for a Public Swim', *New York Times on the Web* (5 March 2000).

10. Güliz Ger and Özlem Sandikci, 'In-Between Modernities and Postmodernities: Theorizing Turkish Consumptionscape', in S. Broniarczyk and K. Nakamoto (eds), *Advances in Consumer Research* 29 (Valdosta, GA: Association for Consumer Research, 2002): 465–70.

11. Edward T. Hall, *The Hidden Dimension* (New York: Doubleday, 1966).

12. Edward T. Hall, *The Dance of Life. The Other Dimension of Time* (New York: Doubleday 1983).

13. Geert Hofstede, *Culture's Consequences* (Beverly Hills, CA: Sage, 1980); see also Laura M. Milner, Dale Fodness and Mark W. Speece, 'Hofstede's Research on Cross-Cultural Work-Related Values: Implications for Consumer Behavior', in W.F. van Raaij and G. Bamossy (eds), *European Advances in Consumer Research* 1 (Provo, UT: Association for Consumer Research, 1993): 70–6.

14. Alladi Venkatesh, 'Ethnoconsumerism: A Proposal for a New Paradigm to Study Cross Cultural Consumer Behavior', in Costa and Bamossy (eds), *Marketing in a Multicultural World*: 26–67.

15. Andrea Davies and James Fitchett, 'Crossing culture: A multi-method enquiry into consumer behaviour and the experience of cultural transition', *Journal of Consumer Behaviour* 3(4) (2006): 315–30.

16. Brad Weiss, 'Coffee Breaks and Coffee Connections: The Lived Experience of a Commodity in Tanzanian and European Worlds', in D. Howes (ed.), *Cross-Cultural Consumption* (London: Routledge, 1996): 93–105.

17. George J. McCall and J.L. Simmons, *Social Psychology: A Sociological Approach* (New York: The Free Press, 1982).

18. Özlem Sandikci and Güliz Ger, 'Constructing and representing the Islamic consumer in Turkey', *Fashion Theory* 11(2/3) (2007): 189–210.

19. Jim Yardley, 'No Spitting on the Road to Olympic Glory, Beijing Says,' *New York Times Online* (17 April 2007), accessed 17 April 2007.

20. Laura Petrecca, 'Ad Track: Marketers Bet on lucky 777; That's July 7, 2007', *USA Today Online* (29 May 2007), accessed 29 May 2007.

21. Søren Askegaard, Martine Cardel Gertsen and Roy Langer, 'The body consumed: Reflexivity and cosmetic surgery', *Psychology & Marketing* 19(10) (2002): 793–812.

22. Jennifer Rindfleisch, 'Consuming the self: New age spirituality as "social product" in consumer society', *Consumption, Markets and Culture* 8(4) (2005): 343–60.

23. Craig J. Thompson, 'Marketplace mythology and discourses of power', *Journal of Consumer Research* 31 (June 2004): 162–80. The author formulates the construct of marketplace mythology to explore how cultural myths are used to create marketplace mythologies that serve multiple and often competing ideological agendas. He develops his arguments within the context of the natural health market. While this market is positioned as alternative to mainstream scientific medicine, both practitioners' and consumers' quest for scientific support to validate their holistic healing treatments generate a fundamental paradox. This paper examines the mythic constructions of nature, technology, and science and their relations to both natural health's marketplace mythology of holistic well-being and key competitive forces.

24. Eric Arnould, Cele Otnes and Linda Price, 'Magic in the Marketing Age', in S. Brown, A.M. Doherty and B. Clarke (eds), *Proceedings of the Marketing Illuminations Spectacular* (Belfast: University of Ulster, 1997): 167–78.

25. Eric Arnould and Linda Price, 'River magic: Extraordinary experience and the extended service encounter', *Journal of Consumer Research* 20 (June 1993): 24–45.

26. Molly O'Neill, 'As life gets more complex, magic casts a wider spell', *New York Times* (13 June 1994): A1 (2).

27. Stephen Brown, *Wizard. Harry Potter's Brand Magic* (London: Cyan books, 2005).

28. Douglas B. Holt and Craig J. Thompson, 'Man-of-Action heroes: the pursuit of heroic masculinity in everyday consumption', *Journal of Consumer Research* 31 (September 2004): 425–40.

29. Conrad Phillip Kottak, 'Anthropological Analysis of Mass Enculturation', in Conrad P. Kottak (ed.), *Researching American Culture* (Ann Arbor, MI: University of Michigan Press, 1982): 40–74.

30. Benoît Heilbrunn, 'Brave New Brands. Cultural Branding between Utopia and A-topia', in J. Schroeder and M-Salzer-Mörling (eds), *Brand Culture* (London: Routledge, 2006): 103–17.

31. Eric Ransdell, 'The Nike Story? Just Tell It!' *Fast Company* (January–February 2000): 44.

32. Jonathan E. Schroeder and Janet L. Borgerson, 'Packaging Paradise: Consuming Hawaiian Music', in Eric Arnould and Linda Scott (eds), *Advances in Consumer Research* 26 (Provo, UT: Association for Consumer Research, 1999): 46–50.

33. Robin Canniford and Avi Shankar, 'Marketing the Savage: Appropriating Tribal Tropes', in B. Cova, R. Kozinets and A. Shankar (eds), *Consumer Tribes* (London: Butterworth Heinemann, 2007): 35–48.

34. Güliz Ger and Fabian Csaba, 'Flying Carpets: The Production and Consumption of Tradition and Mystique', in S. Hoch and R. Meyer (eds), *Advances in Consumer Research* 27 (Provo, UT: Association for Consumer Research, 2000): 132–7.

35. Joseph Campbell, *Myths, Dreams, and Religion* (New York: E.P. Dutton, 1970).

36. Sidney J. Levy, 'Interpreting consumer mythology: A structural approach to consumer behavior', *Journal of Marketing* 45 (Summer 1981): 49–61.

37. Alan Bradshaw and Morris Holbrook, 'Remembering Chet: Theorizing the mythology of the self-destructive bohemian artist as self-producer and self-consumer in the market for romanticism', *Marketing Theory* 7(2) (2007): 115–36.

38. Jeffrey S. Lang and Patrick Trimble, 'Whatever happened to the man of tomorrow? An examination of the American monomyth and the comic book superhero', *Journal of Popular Culture* 22 (Winter 1988): 157.

39. Yumiko Ono, 'PepsiCo's "American" superhero in Japanese ads is alien to U.S.', *Wall Street Journal Interactive Edition* (23 May 1997).

40. James Fitchett, Douglas Brownlie and Michael Saren, 'On the Cultural Location of Consumption: The Case of Einstein as a Commodity', in *Marketing for an Expanding Europe*, Proceedings of the 25th EMAC Conference (ed.) J. Berács, A. Bauer and J. Simon (Budapest: Budapest University of Economic Sciences, 1996): 435–53; James Fitchett and Michael Saren, 'Consuming Einstein: The Nine Billion Names of the Commodity', in Brown, Doherty and Clarke (eds), *Proceedings of the Marketing Illuminations Spectacular*: 252–63.

41. Elizabeth C. Hirschman, 'Movies as Myths: An Interpretation of Motion Picture Mythology', in Jean Umiker-Sebeok (ed.), *Marketing and Semiotics: New Directions in the Study of Signs for Sale* (Berlin: Mouton de Guyter, 1987): 335–74.

42. *Markedsføring* 1 (1999): 18.

43. Dick Hebdige, 'Object as Image: The Italian Scooter Cycle', in J.B. Schor and D.B. Holt (eds), *The Consumer Society Reader* (New York: The New Press, 2000): 117–54.

44. Stephen Brown, 'Retro-marketing: Yesterday's tomorrows, today', *Marketing Intelligence and Planning* 17(7) (1999): 363–76.

45. Benoît Heilbrunn, 'My Brand the Hero? A Semiotic Analysis of the Consumer-Brand Relationship', in M. Lambkin *et al.* (eds), *European Perspectives on Consumer Behaviour* (London: Prentice-Hall, 1998): 370–401.

46. See Rook, 'The ritual dimension of consumer behavior', *op. cit.*; Tetreault and Kleine, 'Ritual, ritualized behavior, and habit', *op. cit.*

47. Kieran Tucker, 'The Value of Ritual Theory for Understanding Alcohol Consumption Behaviours', in K. Ekström and H. Brembeck (eds), *European Advances in Consumer Research* 7 (Duluth, MN: Association for Consumer Research, 2006): 635–640; Emma Banister and Maria Piacenitini, 'Drunk and (Dis)Orderly: The Role of Alcohol in Supporting Liminality' in A.Y. Lee and D. Soman (eds), *Advances in Consumer Research* XXXV (Duluth, MN: Association for Consumer Research, 2008): 311–18.

48. Karl Greenberg, 'BBDO: Successful Brands Become Hard Habit for Consumers to Break', *Marketing Daily* (14 May 2007), available from http://www.mediapost.com, accessed 14 May 2007.

49. 'The skill of the chase', *Marketing Week* (30 April 1993): 38–40.

50. Bill McDowell, 'Starbucks is ground zero in today's coffee culture', *Advertising Age* (9 December 1996): 1 (2 pp.). For a discussion of the act of coffee drinking as ritual, see Susan Fournier and Julie L. Yao, 'Reviving Brand Loyalty: A Reconceptualization within the Framework of Consumer–Brand Relationships', working paper 96–039, Harvard Business School, 1996.

51. Dannie Kjeldgaard and Jacob Östberg, 'Coffee grounds and the global cup: Glocal consumer culture in scandinavia', *Consumption, Culture and Markets* 10(2) (2007): 175–88. See also Craig Thompson and Zeynep Arsel, 'The Starbucks brandscape and consumers' (anti-corporate) experiences of glocalization', *Journal of Consumer Research* 31 (December 2004): 631–42.

52. Farnaz Fassisi, 'As authorities frown, Valentine's Day finds place in Iran's heart', *The Wall Street Journal* (12 February 2004), http://online.wsj.com/article/0,,SB107654405884327601,00.html?mod=home%5Fpage%5Fone%5Fus.

53. Robert Grafton Small, 'Consumption and significance: Everyday life in a brand-new second-hand bow tie', *European Journal of Marketing* 27(8) (1993): 38–45.

54. Grant McCracken, *Culture and Consumption* (Bloomington, IN: Indiana University Press, 1988).

55. 'Lynx to create chain of male grooming stores', *Marketing* (24 August 2000): 5.

56. Dennis W. Rook and Sidney J. Levy, 'Psychosocial Themes in Consumer Grooming Rituals', in Richard P. Bagozzi and Alice M. Tybout (eds), *Advances in Consumer Research* 10 (Provo, UT: Association for Consumer Research, 1983): 329–33.

57. Diane Barthel, *Putting on Appearances: Gender and Attractiveness* (Philadelphia: Temple University Press, 1988).

58. Quoted in *ibid.*

59. Russell W. Belk, Melanie Wallendorf and John Sherry Jr, 'The sacred and the profane in consumer behavior: Theodicy on the odyssey', *Journal of Consumer Research* 16 (June 1989): 1–38.

60. Tina M. Lowrey, Cele C. Otnes and Julie A. Ruth, 'Social influences on dyadic giving over time: A taxonomy from the giver's perspective,' *Journal of Consumer Research* 30 (March 2004): 547–58.

61. Russell W. Belk and Gregory S. Coon, 'Gift giving as agapic love: An alternative to the exchange paradigm based on dating experiences', *Journal of Consumer Research* 20 (December 1993) 3: 393–417.

62. Julie A. Ruth, Cele C. Otnes and Frederic F. Brunel, 'Gift receipt and the reformulation of interpersonal relationships', *Journal of Consumer Research* 25 (March 1999): 385–402.

63. Colin Camerer, 'Gifts as economic signals and social symbols', *American Journal of Sociology* 94 (Supplement 1988): 5180–214.

64. Robert T. Green and Dana L. Alden, 'Functional equivalence in cross-cultural consumer behavior: Gift giving in Japan and the United States', *Psychology and Marketing* 5 (Summer 1988): 155–68.

65. Hiroshi Tanaka and Miki Iwamura, 'Gift Selection Strategy of Japanese Seasonal Gift Purchasers: An Explorative Study', paper presented at the Association for Consumer Research, Boston, October 1994.

66. John F. Sherry Jr, 'Gift giving in anthropological perspective', *Journal of Consumer Research* 10 (September 1983): 157–68.

67. Daniel Goleman, 'What's under the tree? Clues to a relationship', *New York Times* (19 December 1989): C1.

68. John F. Sherry Jr, Mary Ann McGrath and Sidney J. Levy, 'The dark side of the gift', *Journal of Business Research* 28(3) (1993): 225–45.

69. David Glen Mick and Michelle DeMoss, 'Self-gifts: Phenomenological insights from four contexts', *Journal of Consumer Research* 17 (December 1990): 327; John F. Sherry Jr, Mary Ann McGrath and Sidney J. Levy, 'Egocentric Consumption: Anatomy of Gifts Given to the Self', in John F. Sherry Jr (ed.), *Contemporary Marketing and Consumer Behavior: An Anthropological Sourcebook* (Thousand Oaks, CA: Sage, 1995).

70. Markus Giesler, 'Consumer gift systems', *Journal of Consumer Research* 33 (September 2006): 283–90.

71. Markus Giesler, 'Conflict and compromise: Drama in marketplace evolution', *Journal of Consumer Research* 34 (April 2008): 739–53.

72. On tourism as a central part of modern life, see John Urry, *The Tourist Gaze: Leisure and Travel in Contemporary Societies* (London: Sage, 1990), and John Urry, *Consuming Places* (London: Routledge, 1995). Scandinavians (or those who read Swedish) may also consult Tom Odell (ed.), *Nonstop! Turist i upplevelsesindustrialismen* (Lund: Historiska Media, 1999).

73. See, for example, Russell W. Belk, 'Halloween: An Evolving American Consumption Ritual', in Pollay, Gorn and Goldberg (eds), *Advances in Consumer Research* 17: 508–17; Melanie Wallendorf and Eric J. Arnould, 'We gather together: The consumption rituals of Thanksgiving Day', *Journal of Consumer Research* 18 (June 1991): 13–31.

74. Marc Augé, 'Un ethnologue à Euro Disneyland', *Le Monde Diplomatique* (September 1994).

75. Bruno Bettelheim, *The Uses of Enchantment: The Meaning and Importance of Fairy Tales* (New York: Alfred A. Knopf, 1976).

76. Brian Moeran and Lise Skov, 'Cinderella Christmas: Kitsch, Consumerism and Youth in Japan', in D. Miller (ed.), *Unwrapping Christmas* (Oxford: Oxford University Press, 1993): 105–33.

77. *Markedsføring* 1 (1999): 4.

78. Anne Swardson, 'Trick or treat? In Paris, it's dress, dance, eat', *International Herald Tribune* (31 October 1996): 2.

79. http://www.dr.dk/Nyheder/Kultur/2008/10/29/, accessed 1 November 2008.

80. Tuba Ustuner, Güliz Ger and Douglas B. Holt, 'Consuming Ritual: Reframing the Turkish Henna-Night Ceremony', in Hoch and Meyer (eds), *Advances in Consumer Research* 27: 209–14.

81. Michael R. Solomon and Punam Anand, 'Ritual Costumes and Status Transition: The Female Business Suit as Totemic Emblem', in Elizabeth C. Hirschman and Morris Holbrook (eds), *Advances in Consumer Research* 12 (Washington, DC: Association for Consumer Research, 1985): 315–18.

82. Arnold Van Gennep, *The Rites of Passage*, trans. Maika B. Vizedom and Gabrielle L. Caffee (London: Routledge & Kegan Paul, 1960; orig. published 1908); Solomon and Anand, 'Ritual costumes and status transition', *op. cit.*

83. Stephanie O'Donohoe and Darach Turley, 'Dealing with Death: Art, Mortality and the Marketplace', in S. Brown and A. Patterson (eds), *Imagining Marketing, Art, Aesthetics, and the Avant-Garde* (London: Routledge, 2001): 86–106.

84. Walter W. Whitaker III, 'The Contemporary American Funeral Ritual', in Ray B. Browne (ed.), *Rites and Ceremonies in Popular Culture* (Bowling Green, OH: Bowling Green University Popular Press, 1980): 316–25.

85. Samuel K. Bonsu and Russell W. Belk, 'Do not go cheaply into that good night: Death-ritual consumption in Asante, Ghana', *Journal of Consumer Research* 30 (June 2003): 41–55; *cf.* also Stephanie O'Donohoe and Darach Turley, 'Till death do us part? Consumption and the negotiation of relationships following a bereavement', *Advances in Consumer Research* 32(1) (2005): 625–26.

86. Darach Turley, 'Bidding Brigid: Objects of petition and the euphemerized goddess', paper presented at the Association for Consumer Research conference, San Francisco, October 2008.

87. On sacredness in tourism, see, for example, Urry, *The Tourist Gaze* (London: Sage 1990) and Urry, *Consuming Places* (London: Routledge, 1995).

88. Robert V. Kozinets, John F. Sherry Jr, Diana Storm, Adam Duhachek, Krittinee Nuttavuthisit and Benet DeBerry-Spence, 'Ludic agency and retail spectacle', *Journal of Consumer Research* 31 (December 2004): 658–72.

89. Kottak, 'Anthropological analysis of mass enculturation', *op. cit.*: 40–74.

90. Gerry Pratt, 'The House as an Expression of Social Worlds', in James S. Duncan (ed.), *Housing and Identity: Cross-Cultural Perspectives* (London: Croom Helm, 1981): 135–79; Michael R. Solomon, 'The role of the surrogate consumer in service delivery', *Service Industries Journal* 7 (July 1987): 292–307.

91. Malene Djursaa and Simon Ulrik Kragh, 'Syntax and Creolization in Cross-Cultural Readings of Rooms', in B. Dubois, T. Lowrey, L.J. Shrum and M. Vanhuele (eds), *European Advances in Consumer Research* 4 (Provo, UT: Association for Consumer Research, 1999): 293–303.

92. Grant McCracken, ' "Homeyness": A Cultural Account of One Constellation of Goods and Meanings', in Elizabeth C. Hirschman (ed.), *Interpretive Consumer Research* (Provo, UT: Association for Consumer Research, 1989): 168–84.

93. James Hirsch, 'Taking celebrity worship to new depths', *New York Times* (9 November 1988): C1.

94. Lisa Urquhart, 'A star is worn as on-line retailer grows up', *Financial Times* (22 October 2004), http://news.ft.com/cms/s/341eec5a-23c7-11d9-aee5-00000e2511c8,dwp_uuid=43da3afc-1308-11d9-b869-00000e2511c8.html.

95. Emile Durkheim, *The Elementary Forms of the Religious Life* (New York: Free Press, 1915).

96. Susan Birrell, 'Sports as ritual: Interpretations from Durkheim to Goffman', *Social Forces* 60 (1981) 2: 354–76; Daniel Q. Voigt, 'American Sporting Rituals', in Browne (ed.), *Rites and Ceremonies in Popular Culture*: 125–40.

97. 'Sale of UK publisher of classical music strikes a sour note', *Wall Street Journal Europe* (9 September 1997): 1, 4.

98. Søren Askegaard, 'Marketing, the performing arts, and social change: Beyond the legitimacy crisis', *Consumption, Markets and Culture* 3(1) (1999): 1–25.

99. Simona Botti, 'What Role for Marketing in the Arts? An Analysis of Art Consumption and Artistic Value', in Y. Evrard, W. Hoyer and A. Strazzieri (eds), *Proceedings of the Third International Research Seminar on Marketing Communications and Consumer Behavior* (Aix-en-Provence: IAE, 1999).

100. *Markedsføring* 2 (1999): 10.

101. Brown and Patterson (eds), *Imagining Marketing, Art, Aesthetics, and the Avant-Garde* (London: Routledge, 2000).

102. Urry, *The Tourist Gaze, op. cit.*

103. Belk *et al.*, 'The sacred and the profane in consumer behavior', *op. cit.*

104. Beverly Gordon, 'The souvenir: Messenger of the extraordinary', *Journal of Popular Culture* 20 (1986) 3: 135–46.

105. 'Even at the dinner for the Nobel prizes, they steal the spoons', *Wall Street Journal* (7 December 2000): A1, A16.

106. Pauline Maclaran and Linda Scott, 'Spiritual Toursim: Mystical Merchandise and Sacred Shopping in Glastonbury', paper presented at the Association for Consumer Research conference, San Francisco (October 2008).

107. Belk *et al.*, 'The sacred and the profane in consumer behavior', *op. cit.*

108. Güliz Ger and Olga Kravets (2007), 'Rediscovering Sacred Times in the Mundane: Tea Drinking in Turkey', Consuming Routines: Rhythms, Ruptures, and the Temporalities of Consumption, International Workshop, European University Institute, Florence, Italy, 3–5 May; *cf.* also Güliz Ger 'Religion and consumption: The profane sacred', *Advances in Consumer Research* 32(1) (2005): 79–81.

109. Belk *et al.*, 'The sacred and the profane in consumer behavior', *op. cit.*

110. Deborah Hofmann, 'In jewelry, choices sacred and profane, ancient and new', *New York Times* (7 May 1989).

111. Diego Rinallo, 'Living a Magical Life: Sacred Consumption and Spiritual Experience in the Italian Neo-Pagan Community', paper presented at the Association for Consumer Research conference, San Francisco (October 2008).

112. Promotional text from 'First fashion' webpage, an online company specializing in the sale of handbags, wallets and accessories from top fashion design houses, http://www.1stinfashion.com/ProductDetails.aspx?productID=3078 (accessed 5 August 2005).

113. Karen Thomas, 'Rosary's second coming', *USA Today* (July 2004), http://www.usatoday.com/life/people/2004-06-17-rosaries_x.htm.

114. 'Church fears rosary fashion craze', *BBC News* (29 October 2004), http://news.bbc.co.uk/1/hi/business/3964667.stm.

115. For an interesting display of rosaries as fashion, see Dolce & Gabbana's website: http://www.dolcegabbana.it/, accessed 5 August 2005. Søren Askegaard and Gary Bamossy are grateful to Diego Rinallo and Stefania Borghini of Bocconi University, Milan, for their helpful insights on the discussion of rosaries as fashion.

116. Roberto Grandi, 'Benetton's Advertising: A Case History of Postmodern Communication', unpublished manuscript, Center for Modern Culture and Media, University of Bologna, 1994; Shawn Tully, 'Teens: The most global market of all', *Fortune* (16 May 1994): 90–7.

117. Quoted in 'Public relations firm to present anti-abortion effort to bishops', *New York Times* (14 August 1990): A12.

118. *Markedsføring* 4 (1999): 8.

119. Per Østergaard, 'The Broadened Concept of Marketing as a Manifestation of the Postmodern Condition', in *Marketing Theory and Applications*, Proceedings of the AMA Winter Educators Conference 4, R. Varandarajan and B. Jaworski (eds) (Chicago: American Marketing Association, 1993): 234–9.

120. Russell W. Belk and Gülnur Tumbat, 'The cult of Macintosh', *Consumption, Markets and Culture* 8(3) (2005): 205–17.

121. Dan L. Sherrell, Alvin C. Burns and Melodie R. Phillips, 'Fixed Consumption Behavior: The Case of Enduring Acquisition in a Product Category', in Robert L. King (ed.), *Developments in Marketing Science* 14 (1991): 36–40.

122. Russell W. Belk, 'Acquiring, Possessing, and Collecting: Fundamental Processes in Consumer Behavior', in Ronald F. Bushard and Shelby D. Hunt (eds), *Marketing Theory: Philosophy of Science Perspectives* (Chicago: AMA, 1982): 185–90.

123. For an extensive bibliography on collecting, see Russell W. Belk, *Collecting in a Consumer Culture* (London: Routledge, 1995), or Russell W. Belk, Melanie Wallendorf, John F. Sherry Jr and Morris B. Holbrook, 'Collecting in a Consumer Culture', in Russell W. Belk (ed.), *Highways and Buyways* (Provo, UT: Association for Consumer Research, 1991): 178–215. See also Janine Romina Lovatt, 'The People's Show Festival 1994: A Survey', in S. Pearce (ed.), *Experiencing Material Culture in the Western World* (London: Leicester University Press, 1997): 196–254; Werner Muensterberg, *Collecting: An Unruly Passion* (Princeton, NJ: Princeton University Press, 1994); Melanie Wallendorf and Eric J. Arnould, ' "My favorite things": A cross-cultural inquiry into object attachment, possessiveness, and social linkage', *Journal of Consumer Research* 14 (March 1988): 531–47.

124. Calmetta Y. Coleman, 'Just any old thing from McDonald's can be a collectible', *Wall Street Journal* (29 March 1995): B1 (2).

125. Quoted in Ruth Ann Smith, 'Collecting as Consumption: A Grounded Theory of Collecting Behavior', unpublished manuscript, Virginia Polytechnic Institute and State University, 1994: 14.

126. See Belk, *Collecting in a Consumer Culture, op. cit.*

127. 'A feeding frenzy for Swatches', *New York Times* (29 August 1991): C3; Patricia Leigh Brown, 'Fueling a frenzy: Swatch', *New York Times* (10 May 1992): 1, 9; Mary M. Long and Leon G. Schiffman, 'Swatch fever: An allegory for understanding the paradox of collecting', *Psychology and Marketing* 14 (August 1997) 5: 495–509.

128. Jan Slater, 'Collecting the Real Thing: A Case Study Exploration of Brand Loyalty Enhancement Among Coca-Cola Brand Collectors', in Hoch and Meyer (eds), *Advances in Consumer Research* 27: 202–8.

14

Cultural change processes

Joost and Lieke are riding the Intercity train from Amsterdam to Nijmegen after a fun day of shopping in Amsterdam with friends. Lieke takes out a small electronic device from her bag. 'What's that?' Joost asks. 'It's the book by Barack Obama – *The Audacity of Hope*, Lieke answers. 'What?' Joost is surprised. 'You mean that this is a book?' 'Well, not exactly,' says Lieke, 'it's an e-book. It has software that lets me download novels and other things and read them like I would read a book – no scrolling the text and all that. I got the download at Boekhandel Atheneum a few hours ago, and now he has become the president of the United States, I thought I would like to know more about what he stands for, so I wanted to start reading on the train ride home.' 'Argh!' Joost gives Lieke a look of bewilderment as Lieke puts in her iPod earpieces and listens to *Viva la Vida*, the newest Coldplay album that she legally downloaded from the Internet and settles in to 'read' her electronic version of Obama's reflections. Joost thinks to himself that this electronic book gadget and Lieke's iPod are perfect examples of brand offerings from mainstream marketing companies that he so loves to avoid. Lieke notices the look of mild contempt on Joost's face and says, 'It's just getting started, but they expect e-books to cover 10 per cent of the book market in a few years.' Joost doesn't reply. Instead he digs out his old 256 KB MP3, and starts listening to his alternative electronic music from Aphex Twin that he downloaded for free from the Internet. Never mind that their record label, Warp, accepts all major credit cards on their Website . . .

INTRODUCTION

Navel piercings. Miniskirts. Sushi. Café latte. High-tech furniture. Kitchen-and-dining-area-in-one. Bodybuilding. Personal coaching. We inhabit a world brimming with different styles and possibilities. The food we eat, the cars we drive, the clothes we wear, the places we live and work, the music we listen to – all are influenced by the ebb and flow of popular culture and fashion. Consumers may at times feel overwhelmed by the sheer choice in the marketplace. A person trying to decide on something as routine as what to have for lunch has many hundreds of alternatives from which to choose. Despite this seeming abundance, however, the options available to consumers at any point in time actually represent only a *small fraction* of the total set of possibilities. In this chapter, we shall follow marketers' and cultural gatekeepers' attempts to set their marks on which possibilities get the most attention and which trends and tendencies become victorious in the battle for a place in our minds as consumers. We will take a closer look at processes of change driving the ever-changing styles of consumption we are presented with. In Chapter 2, we saw how culture and consumption are related through a meaning system, linking culture with consumption through systems of fashion and advertising and through a variety of consumer rituals. In the last chapter, we took a closer look at the rituals, and at some of the cultural mythologies of the advertising system. In this chapter, referring back to Figure 2.1 we will look at how fashions and consumption styles spread within and among societies.

Even though most of the consumers we have been dealing with in this book may live in Western middle-class areas each with their national and local characteristics, they are often able to 'connect' symbolically with millions of other young consumers by relating to styles that originated far away – even though the original meanings of those styles may have little relevance to them. The spread of fashions in consumption is just one example of what happens when the meanings created by some members of a culture are interpreted and produced for mass consumption.

Take the example of rap music. Baggy jeans and outfits featuring gold vinyl skirts, huge gold chains and bejewelled baseball caps, which used to be seen only on the streets of impoverished urban areas, are being adapted by *haute couture* fashion designers for the catwalks of Manhattan and Paris. In addition, a high proportion of people who buy recordings of rap music are white. How did rap music and fashions, which began as forms of expression in the black urban subculture, make it to mainstream America and the rest of the world? A brief chronology is given in Table 14.1.

Table 14.1 The mainstreaming of popular music and fashion

Date	Event
1968	Bronx DJ Kool Herc invents hip-hop.
1973–8	Urban block parties feature break-dancing and graffiti.
1979	A small record company named Sugar Hill becomes the first rap label.
1980	Manhattan art galleries feature graffiti artists.
1981	Blondie's song 'Rapture' hits number one in the charts.
1985	Columbia Records buys the Def Jam label.
1988	MTV begins *Yo! MTV* Raps, featuring Fab 5 Freddy.
1990	Hollywood gets into the act with the hip-hop film *House Party*; Ice-T's rap album is a big hit on college radio stations; amid controversy, white rapper Vanilla Ice hits the big time; NBC launches a new sitcom, *Fresh Prince of Bel Air*.

Table 14.1 (*continued*)

Date	Event
1991	Mattel introduces its Hammer doll (a likeness of the rap star Hammer, formerly known as M.C. Hammer); designer Karl Lagerfeld shows shiny vinyl raincoats and chain belts in his Chanel collection; designer Charlotte Neuville sells gold vinyl suits with matching baseball caps for $800; Isaac Mizrahi features wide-brimmed caps and takeoffs on African medallions; Bloomingdale's launches Anne Klein's rap-inspired clothing line by featuring a rap performance in its Manhattan store.
1992	Rappers start to abandon this look, turning to low-fitting baggy jeans, sometimes worn backwards; white rapper Marky Mark appears in a national campaign wearing Calvin Klein underwear, exposed above his hip-hugging pants; composer Quincy Jones launches *Vibe* magazine and it wins over many white readers.[1]
1993	Hip-hop fashions and slang continue to cross over into mainstream consumer culture. An outdoor ad for Coca-Cola proclaims, 'Get Yours 24–7'. The company is confident that many viewers in its target market will know that the phrase is urban slang for 'always' (24 hours a day, 7 days a week).[2]
1994	The (late) Italian designer Versace pushes oversized overalls favoured by urban youngsters. In one ad, he asks, 'Overalls with an oversize look, something like what rappers and homeboys wear. Why not a sophisticated version?'[3]
1996	Tommy Hilfiger, a designer who was the darling of the preppie set, turns hip-hop. He gives free wardrobes to rap artists such as Grand Puba and Chef Raekwon, and in return finds his name mentioned in rap songs – the ultimate endorsement. The September 1996 issue of *Rolling Stone* features the Fugees; several band members prominently display the Hilfiger logo. In the same year the designer uses rap stars Method Man and Treach of Naughty by Nature as runway models. Hilfiger's new Tommy Girl perfume plays on his name but also is a reference to the New York hip-hop record label Tommy Boy.[4]
1997	Coca-Cola features rapper L.L. Cool J. in a commercial that debuts in the middle of the sitcom *In the House*, a TV show starring the singer.[5]
1998	In their battle with Dockers for an increased share of the khaki market, Gap launches its first global advertising campaign. One of the commercials, 'Khakis Groove', includes a hip-hop dance performance set to music by Bill Mason.[6]
1999	Rapper turned entrepreneur Sean (Puffy) Combs introduces an upscale line of menswear he calls 'urban high fashion'. New companies FUBU, Mecca and Enyce attain financial success in the multibillion-dollar industry.[7] Lauryn Hill and the Fugees sing at a party sponsored by upscale Italian clothier Emporio Armani and she proclaims, 'We just wanna thank Armani for giving a few kids from the ghetto some great suits.'[8]
2000	**360hip-hop.com**, a Web-based community dedicated to the hip-hop culture, is launched. In addition to promoting the hip-hop lifestyle, the site allows consumers to purchase clothing and music online while watching video interviews with such artists as Will Smith and Busta Rymes.[9]
2001	Hip-hop dancing becomes the rage among China's youth, who refer to it as *jiew*, or street dancing.[10]
2003	Hip-hop finds its way into toy stores. Toy manufacturers start mimicking the hip-hop practice of using the letter 'Z' instead of the letter 'S' in names. This trend started with the 1991 film *Boyz N The Hood* (a title that was itself borrowed from a 1989 song by the rap group N.W.A.).[11]
2005	The fusion of hip-hop and brand culture becomes ever more evident. The global fast-food chain McDonald's offers to pay rappers €4.15 every time a song is played which drops the name of the 'Big-Mac'. Artists who have 'referenced' well-known products include Jay-Z, 50 Cent and Snoop Dogg. Among the happy beneficiaries have been brands such as Courvoisier, Gucci, Dom Perignon, Bentley and Porsche.[12]
Until 2008	Hip-hop increasingly disengages from its American roots as artists around the world develop their own localized interpretations. An aboriginal Australian hip-hop dancer tells a crowd the FUBU brand shirt he is wearing means 'full blood'.[13] All over Europe, home-grown artists are increasingly popular. In each country and even in each region and city the hip-hop movement is inscribed in a local artistic and political context.[14] In Portugal, for example, the immigration from former colonies in Africa as well as immigration from Asia and Latin America has created a cultural mix that makes a fertile ground for a thriving hip-hop scene.[15] Also Islamic hip-hop, and rap with lyrics promoting moralities very different from the original 'booze and girls' oriented lyrics of street gang culture is becoming increasingly popular, especially in the UK.[16] However, female Muslim rappers, exemplified by the rapper Deeyah and her Sisterhood project, are also gaining momentum with rap criticizing the subservient role ascribed to women in at least certain forms of Islam.[17]

It's common for mainstream culture to modify symbols from 'cutting-edge' subcultures for a larger audience to consume. As this occurs, these cultural products undergo a pro-
▶ cess of co-optation, where outsiders transform their original meanings. This happened to rap music, which is divorced to a large extent from its original connection with the struggles of young African Americans and is now a mainstream entertainment format.[18] One writer sees the white part of the 'hip-hop nation' as a series of concentric rings. In the centre are those who actually know African Americans and understand their culture. The next ring consists of those who have indirect knowledge of this subculture via friends or relatives but who do not actually rap, spray-paint, or break-dance. Then, there are those a bit further out who simply play hip-hop between other types of music. Finally come the more suburban 'wiggers', who simply try to catch on to the next popular craze.[19] As it was mentioned in Table 14.1, these cultural expressions also change when they move from one cultural context to another. Although, on the surface of it, Afro-American and French Arab and African urban and suburban street cultures may look alike, both in terms of musical styles and an affectionate relationship with sneakers, the consumption of the sneaker which in the American context is included in the countercultural statement is more a fashion statement in the French context.[20] The spread of hip-hop fashions and music is only one example of what happens when the marketing system takes a set of subcultural meanings, reinterprets them, and produces them for mass consumption.[21]

Cultural selection

The selection of certain alternatives over others – whether cars, dresses, computers, recording artists, political candidates, religions or even scientific methodologies – is the culmination of a complex filtration process resembling a funnel, as depicted in Figure 14.1. Many possibilities initially compete for adoption, and these are steadily narrowed down as they make their way down the path from conception to consumption in a process of
▶ cultural selection.

The Internet has made the spotting and selection of the various trends and changes in society, the symbol pool, easier. New trend-watching services can be paid for scouring the world for new possibilities in colours, fabrics, designs or combinations. They can access pictures from runways of great fashion shows, look at store decorations from H&M or Zara, or look at photos of cool London/Paris/Amsterdam/Berlin youngsters sporting the latest rebellious twist to the clothing companies' standard offerings. Even though the subscription to these services is costly, many companies think they are well worth their price, because they save in business trips and other types of costly trend-spotting fieldwork.[22]

Our tastes and product preferences are not formed in a vacuum. Choices are driven by the images presented to us in mass media, our observations of those around us, and even by our desires to live in the fantasy worlds created by marketers. These options are constantly evolving and changing. A clothing style or type of cuisine that is 'hot' one year may be 'out' the next. Some general characteristics of the evolution of styles and fashions include:

● Styles are a reflection of more fundamental societal trends (e.g. politics and social conditions).

● A style begins as a risky or unique statement by a relatively small group of people and then spreads as others increasingly become aware of the style and feel confident about trying it.

● Styles usually originate as an interplay between the deliberate inventions of designers and businesspeople and spontaneous actions by ordinary consumers who modify styles to suit their own needs. Designers, manufacturers, and merchandisers who can anticipate what consumers want will succeed in the marketplace. In the process, they help to fuel the fire when they encourage distribution of the item.

Figure 14.1 The culture production process

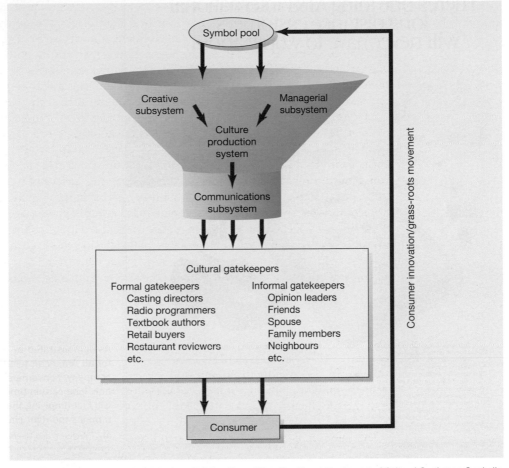

Source: Adapted from Michael R. Solomon, 'Building Up and Breaking Down: The Impact of Cultural Sorting on Symbolic Consumption', in J. Sheth and E.C. Hirschman, eds, *Research in Consumer Behavior* (Greenwich, CT: JAI Press, 1988): 325–51.

- These cultural products travel widely, often across countries and even continents.
- Influential people in the media play a significant role in deciding which will succeed.
- Most styles eventually wear out as people continually search for new ways to express themselves and marketers scramble to keep up with these desires.

Culture production systems

No single designer, company or advertising agency is solely responsible for creating popular culture. Every product, whether a hit record, a car or a new fashion, requires the input of many different participants. The set of individuals and organizations responsible for creating and marketing a cultural product is a **cultural production system (CPS)**.[23]

The nature of these systems helps to determine the types of product that eventually emerge from them. Factors such as the number and diversity of competing systems and the amount of innovation versus conformity that is encouraged are important. For example, an analysis of the Country & Western music industry has shown that the hit records it produces tend to be similar to one another during periods when it is dominated by a few large companies, whereas there is more diversity when a greater number of producers are competing within the same market.[24]

As demonstrated by this advertisement for an American telecommunications company, consumers can never be sure how long certain product types or styles will last (implying that, in contrast, AT&T remains the right choice!).

AT&T Archives and History Centre

The different members of a culture production system may not necessarily be aware of or appreciate the roles played by other members, yet many diverse agents work together to create popular culture.[25] Each member does their best to anticipate which particular images will be most attractive to a consumer market. Of course, those who are able to forecast consumers' tastes consistently will be successful over time.

Components of a CPS

A culture production system has three major subsystems: (1) a *creative subsystem* responsible for generating new symbols and/or products; (2) a *managerial subsystem* responsible for selecting, making tangible, mass-producing and managing the distribution of new symbols and/or products; and (3) a *communications subsystem* responsible for giving meaning to the new product and providing it with a symbolic set of attributes that are communicated to consumers.

An example of the three components of a culture production system for a record would be (1) a singer (e.g. Madonna, a creative subsystem); (2) a company (e.g. Atlantic Records, which manufactures and distributes Madonna's records, a managerial subsystem); and (3) the advertising and publicity agencies hired to promote the albums (a communications subsystem). Table 14.2 illustrates some of the many *cultural specialists*, operating in different subsystems, who are required to create a hit CD.

Cultural gatekeepers

Many judges or 'tastemakers' influence the products that are eventually offered to consumers. These judges, or **cultural gatekeepers**, are responsible for filtering the overflow

Table 14.2 Cultural specialists in the music industry

Specialist	Functions
Songwriter(s)	Compose music and lyrics; must reconcile artistic preferences with estimates of what will succeed in the marketplace
Performer(s)	Interpret music and lyrics; may be formed spontaneously, or may be packaged by an agent to appeal to a predetermined market (e.g. Elton John or Green Day)
Teachers and coaches	Develop and refine performers' talents
Agent	Represent performers to record companies
A&R (artist & repertoire) executive	Acquire artists for the record label
Publicists, image consultants, designers, stylists	Create an image for the group that is transmitted to the buying public
Recording technicians, producers	Create a recording to be sold
Marketing executives	Make strategic decisions regarding performer's appearances, ticket pricing, promotional strategies, and so on
Video director	Interpret the song visually to create a music video that will help to promote the record
Music reviewers	Evaluate the merits of a recording for listeners
Disc jockeys, radio programme directors	Decide which records will be given airplay and/or placed in the radio stations' regular rotations
Record shop owner	Decide which of the many records produced will be stocked and/or promoted heavily in the retail environment

of information and materials intended for consumers. Gatekeepers include film, restaurant and car reviewers, interior designers, disc jockeys, retail buyers and magazine editors. Collectively, this set of agents is known as the *throughput sector*.[26]

Speaking the language of beauty

One study of cultural gatekeepers in the fashion and beauty industry illustrates how some cultural 'products' (in this case, fashion models) are selected and championed over other stylistic possibilities.[27] Editors at such women's magazines as *Cosmopolitan*, *Marie Claire*, *Depêche Mode* and *Elle* play an important role in selecting the specific variations of beauty that will appear in the pages of these 'bibles of fashion'. These images, in turn, will be relied on by millions of readers to decide what 'look' they would like to adopt – and, of course, which particular products and services (such as hairstyles, cosmetics, clothing styles, exercise programmes) they will need to attain these images.

In this study, decision makers at a group of influential magazines identified a small set of 'looks' that characterize many of the diverse fashion models they evaluate on a daily basis – what is more, though each editor was studied independently, overall respondents exhibited a very high level of agreement among themselves regarding what the 'looks' are, what they are called, which are more or less desirable *and* which they expect to be paired with specific product advertisements. This research suggests that cultural gatekeepers tend to rely on the same underlying cultural ideals and priorities when making the selections that in turn get passed down the channel of distribution for consideration by consumers.

We have already encountered numerous examples of the minirevolution we call consumer-generated content; companies today pay attention to everyday people's opinions when they design new products, create advertising messages, or improve upon shopping experiences. The rise of social networking changes the basic process of innovation, as the consumer feedback loop in Figure 14.1 grows stronger and stronger. This shift from a top-down to a bottom-up process is a symptom of the transition from *marketerspace* where companies exert total control over the market.

▶ Instead, we now live in **consumerspace**, where customers act as partners with companies to decide what the marketplace will offer.[28] This process is becoming more and more common – in terms of your car, your cell phone and a lot of other technology products, basically in a lot of contemporary purchase processes, the consumer contributes to the
▶ end-design of the product, thereby taking the role of the **prosumer**. Even the foods you eat can be presumed. In a recent study, researchers investigated the so-called community-supported agriculture, where farmers and consumers operate on shared rewards and risks. This system, the researchers underlined, is in a way countercultural to even the organic producers, who have in many cases become too large to be seen as being close to interests of local consumers. The basic idea is that the consumer can rear their own beef, make sure that animals are living a good life, as well as support local business of high-quality and high-morality food products.[29]

High culture and popular culture

Do Beethoven and Björk have anything in common? While both the famous composer and the Icelandic singer are associated with music, many would argue that the similarity stops here. We think it doesn't. Culture production systems create many diverse kinds of products, but some basic distinctions can be offered regarding their characteristics.

Arts and crafts
▶ One distinction can be made between arts and crafts.[30] An **art product** is viewed primarily
▶ as an object of aesthetic contemplation without any functional value. A **craft product**, in contrast, is admired because of the beauty with which it performs some function (e.g. a ceramic bowl or hand-carved fishing lures). A piece of art is original, subtle and valuable, and is associated with the elite of society. A craft tends to follow a formula that permits rapid production. According to this framework, elite culture is produced in a purely aesthetic context and is judged by reference to recognized classics. It is high culture – 'serious art'.[31] However, many businesses and consumption practices operate in some grey area in between the two. Consider the tattoo business. Whereas tattooists are basicly subject to providing the tattoos the consumers order them to produce, many do consider themselves a certain group of artists and only unwillingly accept to do, for example, brand logo tattoos. They consider it a sell-out to commercial forces where the consumer could have had an artistic expression.[32]

High art vs. low art
It is not just that these grey areas exist. The whole distinction between high and low culture is not as clear as it may first appear. In addition to the possible class bias that drives such a distinction (i.e. we assume that the rich have culture while the poor do not), high and low culture are blending together in interesting ways. Popular culture reflects the world around us; these phenomena touch rich and poor. In many places in Europe, advertising is widely appreciated as an art form and the TV/cinema commercials have their own Cannes Festival. In France and the UK certain advertising executives are public figures in their respective countries. For over ten years, Europeans in different countries have paid relatively high entrance fees to watch an all-night programme in a cinema consisting of nothing but television commercials.[33]

The arts are big business. All cultural products that are transmitted by mass media become a part of popular culture.[34] Classical recordings are marketed in much the same way as Top-40 albums,[35] and museums use mass-marketing techniques to sell their wares. The Parisian museums even run a satellite gift shop at the Charles de Gaulle airport.

This advertisement demonstrates the adaptation of famous paintings ('high art') to sell products ('low art').

Used with permission of Robson Brown Advertising, Newcastle upon Tyne, England

Marketers often incorporate high art imagery to promote products. They may sponsor artistic events to build public goodwill or feature works of art on shopping bags.[36] When observers from Toyota watched customers in luxury car showrooms, the company found that these consumers tended to view a car as an art object. This theme was then used in an ad for the Lexus with the caption: 'Until now, the only fine arts we supported were sculpture, painting and music.'[37] However, the opposite also happens. Certain companies have taken to the use of consumer-generated snapshots or videos in order to generate a maximum of authenticity to their visual communication, *cf.* Jonathan Schroeder's reflections in his 'CB as I see it' below. But whether companies are using high art, street art or snapshot aesthetics, everything happens in order to create a visual gimmick that is powerful enough to break through the clutter of our contemporary over-communicating marketplace.

Consumer behaviour as I see it . . .

My interest in consumer behaviour largely focuses on visual consumption – what consumers look at, what they see, and how they make sense of the visual world. The Web, among its many influences, has put a premium on understanding visual consumption. By visual consumption, I mean not just visual oriented consumer behaviour such as surfing the Internet, watching videos, tourism, or window-shopping, but also a methodological framework to investigate the intermingling of consumption, vision, and culture, including how visual images are handled by consumer research. Thus, I pay a great deal of attention to identifying what consumers look at, how this is informed by the visual histories of contemporary images, and how those images create meaning and value. Images function within culture, and their interpretive meanings shift over time, across cultures and between consumers. My aims are interpretive rather than positive – to show how images can mean, rather than demonstrate what they mean. Image interpretation remains elusive – never complete, closed, or contained, meant to be contested and debated.

Professor Jonathan Schroeder
University of Exeter

Consumer behaviour as I see it . . . (continued)

In my research, I am particularly interested in photography – which encompasses still photography, film, and video – as a key consumer and information technology. Photography's technical ability to reproduce images makes it a central feature of visual consumption. In many ways, photography dominates how we conceive of people, places and things. However, most consumers receive little photographic training, and few consumer research studies place photography at the centre. Photography just is, apparently, its transparency falsely lulls us into believing no special tools are needed to comprehend its communicative power. We have become so used to photographic representation that it seems inevitable, a natural record of what exists or what has happened. Yet photography is not the truth, it is not a simple record of some reality. I find it useful to think of photography as a consumer behaviour as well as a central information technology. Furthermore, photographs tell us where we have been, who we are, and what we value.

A current research project centres on what I call 'snapshot aesthetics' – the use of snapshots or snapshot-like imagery for strategic communication, by both companies and consumers. Consumers post these images on social networking sites such as Facebook, Myspace, Friendster and bebo. Companies such as Volkswagen, IKEA, American Apparel, Ford Motor Company, Apple, and Coca-Cola present snapshot-like images – straightforward, generally unposed photographs of everyday life – in their print, television, and Internet communications. Many recent ads portray models in classic snapshot poses – out of focus, eyes closed, poorly framed – in contrast to more traditional and historical patterns of formal studio shots or highly posed tableaux. These 'intentional' snapshots are often characterized by 'disruptions' in formal photographic traditions – off lighting, poor focus, blurred images, awkward poses, harsh shadows, and so forth, and may appear less formal, more everyday or 'real' – more 'authentic' to consumers.

I contend that snapshot aesthetics provides an important strategic resource for marketing communication. First, these photographs appear authentic, as if they are beyond the artificially constructed world of typical advertising photography. This visual quality can be harnessed to promote brands as authentic, to invoke the 'average consumer' as a credible product endorser, and to demonstrate how the brand might fit in with the regular consumer's lifestyle. Second, snapshot aesthetics supports a casual image of brands, particularly consumer lifestyle brands. Many brands appeal to less formal consumption – from family dinners to online financial management. Popular fashion brands, in particular, court casual images for their brands and subbrands. Well-known examples include Burberry, Diesel, and Sisley – each deploy snapshot-like photographs in high profile branding campaigns for their everyday clothing lines. In this way, photographic style helps articulate market segmentation strategy. For example, Italian designer Giorgio Armani's Collezioni clothing – his most expensive ready-to-wear collection – generally appears in classically composed black-and-white promotional images, whereas the Armani Jeans line – a more recent, entry-level brand – usually features snapshot-like images of sexualized bodies. Moreover, Burberry's successful rebranding from conservative classic to contemporary cool seemed to have benefited greatly from snapshot-like photographs, featuring the likes of supermodels Kate Moss and Stella Tennant. Furthermore, many consumers are busy creating their own ads, which are often in the snapshot style. Websites such as Current TV and YouTube offer consumers a forum to try their hand at brand communication – and occasionally successful specimens are snapped up by brand managers for more conventional broadcast. Other companies sponsor consumer-generated ads, including Converse, MasterCard, and Sony.

I argue that the snapshot aesthetic embodies the experience economy by showing consumers in the midst of seemingly real, sometimes exciting, but often mundane experiences. In this way, we can think about snapshot aesthetics as an important visual aspect of documenting, marketing and understanding consumer experience.

View my research on my SSRN author page: http://ssrn.com/author=348758

Table 14.3 Cultural formulae in public artforms

Artform/genre	Classic western	Science fiction	Hard-boiled detective	Family sitcom
Time	1800s	Future	Present	Any time
Location	Edge of civilization	Space	City	Suburbs
Protagonist	Cowboy (lone individual)	Astronaut	Detective	Father (figure)
Heroine	Schoolmistress	Spacegirl	Damsel in distress	Mother (figure)
Villain	Outlaws, killers	Aliens	Killer	Boss, neighbour
Secondary characters	Townsfolk, Indians	Technicians in spacecraft	Police, underworld	Children, dogs
Plot	Restore law and order	Repel aliens	Find killer	Solve problem
Theme	Justice	Triumph of humanity	Pursuit and discovery	Chaos and confusion
Costume	Cowboy hat, boots, etc.	High-tech uniforms	Raincoat	Normal clothes
Locomotion	Horse	Spaceship	Beat-up car	Family estate car
Weaponry	Sixgun, rifle	Rayguns	Pistol, fists	Insults

Source: Arthur A. Berger, *Signs in Contemporary Culture: An Introduction to Semiotics* (New York: Longman, 1984): 86. Copyright © 1984. Reissued 1989 by Sheffield Publishing Company, Salem, WI. Reprinted with permission of the publisher.

Cultural formulae

Mass culture, in contrast, churns out products specifically for a mass market. These products aim to please the average taste of an undifferentiated audience and are predictable because they follow certain patterns. As illustrated in Table 14.3, many popular art forms, such as detective stories or science fiction, generally follow a **cultural formula**, where certain roles and props often occur consistently.[38] Computer programs even allow users to 'write' their own romances by systematically varying certain set elements of the story. Romance novels are an extreme case of a cultural formula. The romance novel and other formulae reflect the consumer society by the way consumption events and different brands play a role in the story and in the construction of the different atmospheres described.[39]

Reliance on these formulae also leads to a *recycling* of images, as members of the creative subsystem reach back through time for inspiration. Thus, young people in Britain watch retro channels like Granada Plus and UK Gold broadcasting classic decades-old soaps, and old themes are recycled for new soap series. The hippest cars for the under-30 US consumers are models often identified with the 'grandpa' generation, such as oldsmobiles and buicks from the 70s and 80s – the car are however updated with flashy paint and state-of-the-art sound systems.[40] Designers modify styles from Victorian England or colonial Africa, DJs sample sound bits from old songs and combine them in new ways, and Gap runs ads featuring now-dead celebrities including Humphrey Bogart, Gene Kelly and Pablo Picasso dressed in khaki trousers.[41] With easy access to VCRs, CD burners, digital cameras and imaging software, virtually anyone can 'remix' the past.[42]

Artists and companies in the popular music or film industry may be more guided by ideas of what could make a 'hit' than by any wish for artistic expression. And creators of aesthetic products are increasingly adapting conventional marketing methods to fine-tune their mass-market offerings. In the US, market research is used, for example, to test audience reactions to film concepts. Although testing cannot account for such intangibles as acting quality or cinematography, it can determine if the basic themes of the film strike a responsive chord in the target audience. This type of research is most appropriate for blockbuster films, which usually follow one of the formulae described earlier. In some

This ad for St Louis Zoo mimics the cultural formula of tabloid gossip as well as tabloid magazine layout in order to attract visitors.

Created by Advertising Savants Inc., St Louis, Missouri USA

cases research is combined with publicity, as when the producers of the film *Men in Black*, featuring Will Smith, showed the first 12 minutes of the film to an advance audience and then let them meet the stars to create a pre-release buzz.[43]

Even the content of films is sometimes influenced by this consumer research. Typically, free invitations to pre-screenings are handed out in shopping centres and cinemas. Attendees are asked a few questions about the film, then some are selected to participate in focus groups. Although groups' reactions usually result in only minor editing changes, occasionally more drastic effects result. When initial reaction to the ending of the film *Fatal Attraction* was negative, Paramount Pictures spent an additional $1.3 million to shoot a new one.[44] Of course, this feedback is not always accurate – before the megahit *E.T.: The Extra-Terrestrial* was released, consumer research indicated that no one over the age of four would go to see the film![45]

Reality engineering

Let us take a short trip to a cosy corner of the US. The village of Riverside, Georgia has a colourful history. You can look at the sepia photographs showing the town in the nineteenth century, or read excerpts from period novels lauding the settlement's cosmopolitan flair. You will also discover that the town was used as a Union garrison during the American Civil War. There is only one hitch: Riverside did not exist until 1998.

The account of nineteenth-century Riverside is a clever fabrication created to promote a new housing and commercial development. The story 'is a figment of our imagination', acknowledges the developer.[46]

Like Riverside, many of the environments in which we find ourselves, whether shopping centres, sports stadiums or theme parks, are composed at least partly of images and characters drawn from products, marketing campaigns or the mass media. **Reality engineering** occurs as elements of popular culture are appropriated by marketers and converted to vehicles for promotional strategies.[47] These elements include sensory and spatial aspects of everyday existence, whether in the form of products appearing in films, scents pumped into offices and shops, advertising hoardings, theme parks, video monitors attached to shopping trolleys, and so on.

The people of Disney Corporation are probably the best worldwide-known reality engineers, through their theme parks in California and Florida, and their newer parks in Japan and Europe. Disneyland-Paris got off to a problematic start when it opened in 1991. Fewer visitors and especially too few clients for the hotel and conference facilities created economic problems. But the conceptualization of the park was changed, made less American and more European, and now the park is drawing huge crowds. Also other consumption facilities and housing areas have been created around it, including a giant shopping centre where one of the streets will be a recreation of a 'typical street' of one of the local villages.[48] Other themed environments like the Asterix park, future parks or artificially created tropical environments are becoming increasingly popular for shorter holidays throughout Europe.

The mythical Simpsons family debuted in real life as 7-Eleven transformed many of its stores into Kwik-E-Marts to promote the cartoon series' movie. During the promotion customers snapped up KrustyO's cereal, Buzz Cola, and ice Squishees, all products from the show.[49] The Simpsons were also used as exemplar of particular tribal consumption patterns in one European study.[50] With the increasing importance of such media-becoming-reality and reality televisions' reality-in-the-media, no wonder consumer researchers increasingly look for clues concerning contemporary consumption patterns in the media in addition to looking at consumers.

One final recent example of reality engineering: in homage to the famous movie *Casablanca*, a former US diplomat opened a Rick's Café in that Moroccan city. The new Rick's has the same warm atmosphere as the Hollywood original (which was created on a sound stage in Hollywood). Waiters in traditional fez caps and wide-legged pants serve customers at candlelit tables. The owner commented, 'Because there has never been a Rick's Café here, I could be reasonably assured that it would succeed. It was already an institution, and it never even existed. It's not often you get a chance to turn myth into reality.'[51]

Multicultural dimensions

One of the most controversial intersections between marketing and society occurs when companies provide 'educational materials' to schools. In the US, many firms, including such companies as Nike and Nintendo, provide free book covers covered with ads. Almost 40 per cent of secondary schools in the US start the day with a 'video feed' from Channel One, which exposes students to commercials in the classroom in exchange for educational programming. Similarly, an Internet company called ZapMe! gives client schools free computers and Internet connections as well as a network of 11,000 educational sites in exchange for a promise to use the computers at least four hours a day. Commercials run continuously on the lower left-hand quarter of the screen, and the company has permission to monitor the students' browsing habits, breaking down the data by age, sex, and zip code. In a few cases companies are contracting with schools to run focus groups with their students during the school day in order to get reactions to new product ideas. Coca-Cola signed a ten year $8 million exclusive beverage contract with the Colorado Springs, Colorado school system. In some schools 9-year-olds practise maths by counting Tootsie Rolls (a brand of sweets),

Multicultural dimensions (*continued*)

and use reading software that sports logos from KMart, Coke, Pepsi and Cap'n Crunch cereal.

Corporate involvement with schools is hardly new – in the 1920s Ivory Soap sponsored soap-carving competitions for students. But, the level of intrusion is sharply increasing as companies scramble to compensate for the decrease in children's viewership of television on Saturday mornings and weekday afternoons and find themselves competing with videos and computer games for their attention. Many

educators argue that these materials are a godsend for resource-poor schools that otherwise would have hardly any other way to communicate with students. What do you think?[52]

Nor is this a purely American phenomenon any longer. The Danish consumer 'ombudsman' attacked a new series of mathematics books for primary schools for including references to brand names. The publishers defended themselves with the argument that it was to provide more realistic cases for the school children.

Product placement

Reality engineering is accelerating due to the current popularity of product placements by marketers. It is quite common to see real brands prominently displayed or to hear them discussed in films and on television. In many cases, these 'plugs' are no accident. ▶ **Product placement** refers to the insertion of specific products and/or the use of brand names in film and TV scripts. Today most major releases are brimming with real products. Directors like to incorporate branded props because they contribute to the film's realism. When Stephen Spielberg made the film *Minority Report* he used such brands as Nokia, Lexus, Pepsi, Guinness, Reebok and American Express to lend familiarity to the plot's futuristic settings. Lexus even created a new sports car model called the Maglev just for the film.[53]

Some researchers claim that product placement can aid in consumer decision-making because the familiarity of these props creates a sense of cultural belonging while generating feelings of emotional security.[54] Another study found that placements consistent with a show's plot do enhance brand attitudes, but incongruent placements that are not consistent with the plot affect brand attitudes *negatively* because they seem out of place.[55] On the other hand, a majority of consumers polled believe the line between advertising and programming is becoming too fuzzy and distracting (though, as might be expected, concerns about this blurring of boundaries rose steadily with the age of respondents).[56] For better or worse products are popping up everywhere. Worldwide product placement in all media was worth $3.5 billion in 2004, a 200 per cent increase from 1994. In the US. there were 117,976 brand occurrences on cable and broadcast networks during the first three months of 2008 alone.[57]

▲ **Marketing opportunity**

Product placement in the news broadcast? The idea may seem strange to most Europeans, but the increased strain on advertising budgets and doubts about standard advertising's effectiveness has introduced product placement in the news. The channel network Fox and McDonald's has made a six-month

deal which places two cups of McDonald's frappucinos in front of news anchors Jason Feinberg and Monica Jackson. They do not sip it, however, since it is a fake product with bogus icecubes that don't melt. Unthinkable in Europe? One would think not. Not for all channels at least![58]

Product placement has been a Western phenomenon – until recently. In China, product placement is emerging as a new way to get noticed. Most commercials on Chinese state-run TV play back-to-back in ten-minute segments, making it difficult for any one 30-second ad to attract attention. So, enterprising marketers are embedding product messages in the shows instead. A soap opera called *Love Talks* features such products as Maybelline lipstick, Motorola mobile phones and Ponds Vaseline Intensive Care lotion.[59]

In India, the booming Bombay film industry (known as Bollywood) is discovering the potential of films to expose viewers to brand names (Indian cinema attracts huge local audiences, even in villages where television is not available). Coca-Cola paid to have its local soft drink, Thums Up, prominently featured in a Hindi-language remake of the Quentin Tarantino classic *Reservoir Dogs*. Just in case the audience misses the placements, in one scene just before bullets start flying a group of slickly dressed gangsters flash each other the thumbs-up sign.[60]

A few further examples to illustrate the power of product placement:

- Although IBM sells a lot more computers, Apples are seen in many more TV shows and films such as *Mission Impossible* and *Independence Day*. Producers like to use the Apple because its image is more hip – you will remember from Chapter 13 that its followers come close to constituting a sect of believers. But Apple will only let that happen if the brand is identified onscreen.[61]

- Philip Morris paid to place Marlboro cigarettes and signs in *Superman* movies and doled out $350,000 to have Lark cigarettes featured in the James Bond film *Licence to Kill*.[62]

- In *Shrek 2*, the ogre and his bride-to-be drive through a town that has a Baskin-Robbins storefront. Out in the real world, the ice cream retailer created three flavours – Fiona's Fairytale, Puss in Boots Chocolate Mousse, and Shrek's Swirl – named for characters in the film.

- The Chinese talent programme *Lycra My Show* is partly funded by Invista, the maker of Lycra fabric, so contestants sing while wearing stretchy Lycra-based clothing. Ford produced a *Survivor* clone called *Ford Maverick Beyond Infinity* where 12 contestants on a tropical island hunt for treasure in a Ford Maverick sport utility vehicle, leap onto rafts while wearing Nike clothing, and cool off with Nestlé drinks. Ford's marketing director in China noted, 'We really built the show around the product.'[63]

- In an episode on Spain's top-rated television show, *Aqui no hay Quien Viva (No One Can Live Here)*, two characters stage a wedding as a ruse to get gifts from their friends. Instead of having a fancy reception, they drive their Hummer up to a McDonald's drive-through window.[64]

▼ Marketing pitfall

Product placement can also be non-intended from the corporate perspective and detrimental too. One little sentence in the blockbuster *Sideways* from 2004 has virtually destroyed the American market for Merlot wines, 'If anybody's drinking Merlot, I'm outta here. I am not drinking any f . . . Merlot,' exclaimed the self-designated wine connoisseur Miles in one scene in the movie. This has led to a veritable flight from Merlot wines from American consumers and a lot of producers have instead tried to sell their Merlot wines overseas – some have even removed Merlot from their fields and started to plant other types of grapes.[65]

▶ As gaming goes mass market, marketers turn to **advergaming**, where online games merge with interactive advertisements that let companies target specific types of consumers. Clearly, computer gaming is not what it used to be. Not long ago, the typical players were scruffy teenage boys shooting at TV screens in their basements. But with the online gaming explosion of recent years (the industry rakes in more than €10 billion per year in global revenue), gamers have become a more sophisticated lot and are now more representative of the general population. There are about 36 million people in the US playing personal computer or console games at least five hours a week. More women are participating, as well as older people and professionals. About half a per cent of people older than age 30 play online games.

Why is this new medium so hot? For one thing, compared to a 30-second TV spot, advertisers can get viewers' attention for a much longer time: players spend an average of five to seven minutes on an advergame site. Also, they can tailor the nature of the game and the products in it to the profiles of different users. For example, they can direct strategy games to upscale, educated users, while at the same time gearing action games to younger users.

Media images significantly influence consumers' perceptions of reality, affecting viewers' notions about such issues as dating behaviour, racial stereotypes and occupational status.[66] Studies of the cultivation hypothesis, which relates to media's ability to shape consumers' perceptions of reality, have shown that heavy television viewers tend to overestimate the degree of affluence in the country, and these effects also extend to such areas as perceptions of the amount of violence in one's culture.[67] Others have underlined the role of media and celebrity spokespersons – in this particular case David Beckham – in shaping children's moral attitudes.[68] Also, the depiction of consumer environments in programmes and advertisements may lead to further marginalization of, for example, unemployed people, who cannot afford to buy into the depicted lifestyle,[69] or to outright addicted consumers, who cannot refrain from constantly buying various goods, although they may not use these at all.

THE DIFFUSION OF INNOVATIONS

New products and styles termed innovations constantly enter the market. An innovation is any product or service that is perceived to be new by consumers. These new products or services occur in both consumer and industrial settings. Innovations may take the form of a clothing or fashion accessory style (such as the Croc, the lightweight sandal/ shoe), a new manufacturing technique (for example, a new technique now permits the Danish dairy company Thise to produce a completely fat free milk), or a novel way to deliver a service (for example through ordering online and then picking up the goodies at certain pick-up points). If an innovation is successful (most are not), it spreads through the population. First it is bought and/or used by only a few people, and then more and more consumers decide to adopt it, until, in some cases, it seems that almost everyone has bought or tried the innovation. Diffusion of innovations refers to the process whereby a new product, service or idea spreads through a population. There is a tendency for technical goods especially to diffuse more rapidly these days. Sixteen per cent of the Swedish population possessed a mobile phone in 1994 – six years later, in 2000, the number was 80 per cent. Likewise, the number of Swedes with Internet access was 74 per cent in 2004, up from 55 per cent in 2000.[70]

Adopting innovations

A consumer's adoption of an innovation may resemble the decision-making sequence discussed in Chapter 9. The person moves through the stages of awareness, information search, evaluation, trial and adoption, although the relative importance of each stage may differ depending on how much is already known about a product,[71] as well as on cultural factors that may affect people's willingness to try new things.[72] A study of 11 European countries found that consumers in individualistic cultures are more innovative than consumers in collective cultures.[73]

One of the more curious large-scale product adoptions in recent history is the victorious introduction of bottled water in modern consumer markets. Based on a variety of mythological beliefs about nature, purity, cleansing, and health, as well as the increased demand for portable drinks in our highly mobile and efficient society – notice how we have also adopted the American habit of 'coffee to go' in Europe. In spite of the fact that numerous studies have demonstrated that in a lot of places there is no particular reason why we should

Table 14.4 Global bottled water market: per capita consumption by leading countries 1998–2003(P)

2003 Rank	Countries	Gallons per capita	
		1998	2003(P)
1	Italy	35.9	48.1
2	Mexico	29.2	41.5
3	France	29.5	39.1
4	United Arab Emirates	28.1	38.1
5	Belgium–Luxembourg	30.7	35.1
6	Germany	26.4	33.1
7	Spain	25.1	30.2
8	Switzerland	23.8	25.4
9	Lebanon	16.2	25.3
10	Saudi Arabia	18.9	23.3
11	Cyprus	17.2	22.8
12	Austria	19.8	22.7
13	United States	15.3	22.6
14	Czech Republic	15.4	22.2
15	Portugal	17.2	20.6
	Global average	3.9	6.0

(P) Preliminary

Source: Beverage Marketing Corporation. Adapted from Richard Wilk, 'Bottled water: The pure commodity in the age of branding' *Journal of Consumer Culture*, vol. 6 no. 3 (2006): 304.

drink bottled water rather than tap water, the bottled water has become a symbol of the modern, healthy lifestyle. As the advertisement demonstrates, it also becomes associated with particular cultural ways of life – in this case living the Italian way. In fact, as Table 14.4 demonstrates, Italians are also the world's leading consumers of bottled water.[74]

However, even within the same culture, not all people adopt an innovation at the same rate. Some do so quite rapidly, and others never do at all. Consumers can be placed into approximate categories based upon the likelihood of adopting an innovation. The categories of adopters, shown in Figure 14.2, can be related to phases of the product life cycle concept used widely by marketing strategists.

As can be seen in Figure 14.2, roughly one-sixth of the population (innovators and early adopters) is very quick to adopt new products, and one-sixth of the people (laggards) is

Figure 14.2 Types of adopter

Vivre en Italien

Living the Italian way . . . includes drinking a lot of bottled water!

very slow. The other two-thirds are somewhere in the middle, and these majority adopters represent the mainstream public. In some cases people deliberately wait before adopting an innovation because they assume that its technological qualities will be improved or that its price will fall after it has been on the market.[75] Keep in mind that the proportion of consumers falling into each category is an estimate; the actual size of each depends upon such factors as the complexity of the product, its cost and other product-related factors, but possibly also varies from country to country.

Even though innovators represent only 2.5 per cent of the population, marketers are always interested in identifying them. According to standard theory, these are the brave souls who are always on the lookout for novel developments and will be the first to try a new offering. Just as generalized opinion leaders do not appear to exist, innovators tend to be category-specific. A person who is an innovator in one area may even be a laggard in another. For example, someone who prides themselves on being at the cutting edge of fashion may have no conception of new developments in recording technology and stereo equipment.

Despite this qualification, some generalizations can be offered regarding the profile of innovators.[76] Not surprisingly they tend to have more favourable attitudes towards taking risks. They are also, at least in an American context, likely to have higher educational and income levels and to be socially active. However, in a European study of the fashion and clothing market, the same correlation between socio-demographic variables and innovative or early adopting behaviour could not be found.[77] On the other hand, a Spanish study, perhaps not surprisingly, concluded that innovators tend to be younger and, more interestingly, that publicity and advertisement would have the biggest influence on product adoption in the early years of commercialization of a product, whereas word-of-mouth and other non-producer controlled information becomes more important thereafter.[78]

How do we locate innovators? Ad agencies and market research companies are always on the prowl for people who are on top of developing trends. One ad agency surveys taxi drivers about what they see on the streets everyday. Others get more sophisticated and use the Internet and their global networks to monitor what 'people in the know' do. The agency DDB runs a service it calls SignBank, which collects thousands of snippets of information from its 13,000 employees around the world about cultural change in order to advise their clients on what it all means for them.[79]

▶ **Early adopters** share many of the same characteristics as innovators, but an important difference is their degree of concern for social acceptance, especially with regard to expressive products such as clothing, cosmetics and so on. Generally speaking, an early adopter is receptive to new styles because they are involved in the product category and also place high value on being in fashion. The universality of the dichotomy of innovators and adopters has been challenged by research pertaining to health foods, suggesting that (1) three groups can be distinguished, namely innovators, more-involved adopters and less-involved adopters, and (2) there is not a big difference between the purchase rate of new products between innovators and adopters; rather the difference lies in the kind of innovations tried and the approach to trying new products.[80] Table 14.5 gives a brief description of the different types of consumers and their approach to new product trials.

Table 14.5 Decision styles of market segments based on adoption, innovation and personal involvement

Adoption decision process stage	Less-involved adopters	Innovators	More-involved adopters
Problem recognition	Passive, reactive	Active	Proactive
Search	Minimal, confined to resolution of minor anomalies caused by current consumption patterns	Superficial but extensively based within and across product class boundaries	Extensive within relevant product category; assiduous exploration of all possible solutions within that framework
Evaluation	Meticulous, rational, slow and cautious; objective appraisal using tried and tested criteria	Quick, impulsive, based on currently accepted criteria; personal and subjective	Careful, confined to considerations raised by the relevant product category: but executed confidently and (for the adopter) briskly within that frame of reference
Decision	Conservative selection within known range of products, continuous innovations preferred	Radical: easily attracted to discontinuously new product class and able to choose quickly within it. Frequent trial, followed by abandonment	Careful selection within a product field that has become familiar through deliberation, vicarious trial, and sound and prudent pre-purchase comparative evaluation
Post-purchase evaluation	Meticulous, tendency to brand loyalty if item performs well	Less loyal; constantly seeking novel experiences through purchase and consumption innovations	Loyal if satisfied but willing to try innovations within the prescribed frame of reference; perhaps tends towards dynamically-continuous

Source: Gordon R. Foxall and Seema Bhate, 'Cognitive style and personal involvement as explicators of innovative purchasing of health food brands', *European Journal of Marketing*, 27(2) (1993): 5–16. Used with permission.

Xerox is a traditional company that is now leading the charge toward consumerspace. It is intent on using voice of the consumer data in its R&D process, which means that it solicits feedback from end customers well before it puts a new product on the market. The company's standard development process is to design and build a prototype and *then* get customer feedback. Now Xerox is shifting to what it calls 'customer-led innovation', which encourages engineers to 'dream with the customer'. Xerox encourages the engineers to meet face-to-face with some of the 1,500 to 2,000 customers who visit showrooms at the company's four global research facilities each year. Others work on-site for a week or two with a customer, observing how they behave with the product. A team of ethnographers also observes people in real situations to see how they actually use the company's products.[81] Welcome to consumerspace.

Innovative companies understand the value of involving their most forward-thinking customers in business decisions before they introduce the final product. More than 650,000 customers tested a beta version of Microsoft Windows 2000. Many were even prepared to pay Microsoft a fee to do this because working with the program would help them understand how it could create value for their own businesses. The value of the research and development investment by customers to Microsoft was more than $500 million.

This approach is more prevalent in high-tech industries that consult their lead users about ideas; these are very experienced and knowledgeable customers. Indeed, it is common for these people to propose product improvements – because they have to live with the consequences. According to one estimate, users rather than manufacturers developed 70 per cent of the innovations in the chemical industry![82]

Types of innovations

Innovations can contain a technological level and involve some functional change (for example, car air bags) or be of a more intangible kind, communicating a new social meaning (like a new hairstyle). However, contrary to what much literature states,[83] both are symbolic in the sense that one refers to symbols of technical performance and safety and the other to less tangible symbols, such as courage and individuality. Both types refer to symbols of progress.[84] New products, services and ideas have characteristics that determine the degree to which they will probably diffuse. Innovations that are more novel may be less likely to diffuse, since they require bigger changes in people's lifestyles and thus more effort. On the other hand, most innovations are close to being of the 'me too' kind, and thus do not necessarily possess qualities that would persuade the consumer to shift from existing product types. In any case, it should be noted that in spite of all the good intentions of the marketing concept to ensure that there is a market before the product is developed, the failure rate of new products is as high as ever, if not higher.[85]

Behavioural demands of innovations

Innovations can be categorized in terms of the degree to which they demand changes in behaviour from adopters. Three major types of innovation have been identified, though these three categories are not absolutes. They refer, in a relative sense, to the amount of disruption or change they bring to people's lives.

A continuous innovation refers to a modification of an existing product, as when a breakfast cereal is introduced in a sugar-coated version, or Levi's promoted 'shrink-to-fit' jeans. This type of change may be used to set one brand apart from its competitors. The launch of Coke Zero was such a continuous innovation, where the idea was to produce a sugar-fee cola targeted to men as opposed to the Diet Coke that was mainly popular among the female segment. This was the idea; however, in many countries, including

Denmark, Coke Zero has gained as much popularity among the women as the men.[86] Most product innovations are evolutionary rather than revolutionary. Small changes are made to position the product, add line extensions or merely to alleviate consumer boredom.

Consumers may be lured to the new product, but adoption represents only minor changes in consumption habits, since innovation perhaps adds to the product's convenience or to the range of choices available. A typewriter company, for example, many years ago modified the shape of its product to make it more user friendly. One simple change was the curving of the tops of the keys, a convention that was carried over on today's computer keyboards. One of the reasons for the change was that secretaries with long fingernails had complained about the difficulty of typing on the flat surfaces.

▶ A **dynamically continuous innovation** is a more pronounced change in an existing product, as represented by self-focusing cameras or touch-tone telephones. These innovations have a modest impact on the way people do things, creating some behavioural changes, although the touch-tone telephone is an expression of a larger innovation involving many discontinuous renewals of daily life: the digitalization of communication. When introduced, the IBM electric typewriter, which used a 'golf ball' rather than individual keys, enabled typists to change the typeface of manuscripts simply by replacing one ball with another.

▶ A **discontinuous innovation** creates major changes in the way we live. Major inventions, such as the aeroplane, the car, the computer and television have radically changed modern lifestyles, although, as can be seen from these examples, major changes normally take some time from the point of introduction. The personal computer has, in many cases, supplanted the typewriter, and it has created the phenomenon of 'telecommuters' by allowing many people to work from their homes. Of course, the cycle continues, as new innovations like new versions of software are constantly being made; dynamically continuous innovations such as the 'mouse' and trackballs compete for adoption, and discontinuous innovations such as streaming video transmitted on cell phones start to appear in stores.

▲ Marketing opportunity

These years, nanotechnology is finding its way to consumer products. Not only can nanotechnology provide hardware so small that it basically becomes invisible without losing processing power, various experiments are also being undertaken with nanocoating of existing consumer objects. Such surface treatment might provide us with car windows that do not fog, paint that does not get scratches, and shirts that do not get stains. Or what about anti-bacteria coated kitchenware and door knobs? Or anti-graffiti paint.[87] Do you have any ideas that would make consumer lives better through nano-coating?

Prerequisites for successful adoption

Regardless of how much behavioural change is demanded by an innovation, several factors are desirable for a new product to succeed:[88]

● *Compatibility*. The innovation should be compatible with consumers' lifestyles. As an illustration, a manufacturer of personal care products tried unsuccessfully several years ago to introduce a hair remover cream for men as a substitute for razors and shaving cream. This formulation was similar to that used widely by women to remove hair from their legs. Although the product was simple and convenient to use, it failed because men were not interested in a product they perceived to be too feminine and thus threatening to their masculine self-concepts.

● *Trialability*. Since an unknown is accompanied by high perceived risk, people are more likely to adopt an innovation if they can experiment with it prior to making a commitment. To reduce this risk, companies often choose the expensive strategies of distributing free 'trial-size' samples of new products. For example, the Swedish coffee brand Gevalia has distributed free samples targeted especially at young people, because there is some evidence that fewer young people are drinking coffee, and those that do begin later in life.

- *Complexity.* The product should be low in complexity. A product that is easier to understand and use will often be preferred to a competitor. This strategy requires less effort from the consumer, and it also lowers perceived risk. Manufacturers of DVD players, for example, have put a lot of effort into simplifying usage (such as on-screen programming) to encourage adoption.

- *Observability.* An innovation that is easily observable is more likely to spread, since this quality makes it more likely that other potential adopters will become aware of its existence. The rapid proliferation of 'bum bags' (pouches worn around the waist in lieu of wallets or purses) was due to their high visibility. It was easy for others to see the convenience offered.

- *Relative advantage.* Most importantly, the product should offer relative advantage over alternatives. The consumer must believe that its use will provide a benefit other products cannot offer. For example, the success of many environmentally friendly product alternatives may be due to the fact that, once consumers have been convinced about the environmental advantages of the product, it is a clear and easily under-standable advantage compared to competing products.

The social context of innovations

One critical but relatively little researched aspect is the importance of the social context of product adoption behaviour.[89] This is linked to the importance of visibility of the product innovation as well as the influence of the reference group which is seen as related to the new product. For example, Western products are admired in many contexts in Asia and Africa, or the marketizing economies of Eastern Europe, for the sole reason of being linked to the status of the Western world, which is seen as 'better', more 'developed' and generally of a higher status.[90] Likewise, in Europe the association of new products with the American way of life will have a significant impact on the adopting behaviour of various groups in society but will differ in different European countries.

Another aspect of the social dimension of innovation is the pitfall of being caught up in too many continuous innovations due to an ever finer market segmentation and customization approach. This may take resources away from more strategic considera-tions of changing 'the way things are done'.[91] For example, a British bank had created such a complex structure of financial services and accounts, as well as charges attached to these services, that customers began to complain about waiting time and lack of under-standing of their own financial affairs. The bank simplified the structure to one account type and a much simpler charge system and successfully made this a unique selling proposition in a market dominated by more complex offerings.[92]

THE FASHION SYSTEM

▶ The **fashion system**[93] consists of all those people and organizations involved in creating symbolic meanings and transferring these meanings to cultural goods. Although people tend to equate fashion with clothing, be it *haute couture* or street wear, it is important to keep in mind that fashion processes affect *all* types of cultural phenomena from the more mundane (what do you think of high fashion nappy bags in unisex style?)[94] to high art, including music, art, architecture and even science (i.e. certain research topics and scientists are 'hot' at any point in time). Even business practices are subject to the fashion process; they evolve and change depending on which management techniques are in vogue, such as total quality management or 'the learning organization'.

Fashion can be thought of as a *code*, or language, that helps us to decipher these meanings.[95] However, fashion seems to be *context-dependent* to a larger extent than language. That is, the same item can be interpreted differently by different consumers and in different situations.[96] In semiotic terms, *cf.* Chapter 2, the meaning of many products is *undercoded* – that is, there is no one precise meaning, but rather plenty of room for interpretation among perceivers.

▶ At the outset, it may be helpful to distinguish among some confusing terms. **Fashion** is the process of social diffusion by which a new style is adopted by some group(s) of consumers. In contrast, *a fashion* (or style) refers to a particular combination of attributes. And, to be *in fashion* means that this combination is currently positively evaluated by some reference group. Thus, the term *Danish Modern* refers to particular characteristics of furniture design (i.e. a fashion in interior design); it does not necessarily imply that Danish Modern is a fashion that is currently desired by consumers.[97]

Collective selection

Fashions tend to sweep through countries; it seems that all of a sudden 'everyone' is doing the same thing or wearing the same styles. Some sociologists view fashion as a form of *collective behaviour*, or a wave of social conformity. How do so many people get tuned in to the same phenomenon at once, as happened with hip-hop styles? However, it has also been shown how fashion magazines were helpful in teaching women around the late nineteenth and early twentieth century to conceive of themselves as free and self-determining individuals.[98] We see here again how fashion is a process that links the macro-level cultural changes with micro-level individual behaviour.

Remember that creative subsystems within a culture production system attempt to anticipate the tastes of the buying public. Despite their unique talents, members of this subsystem are also members of mass culture. Like the fashion magazine editors discussed earlier, cultural gatekeepers are drawing from a common set of ideas and symbols, and are influenced by the same cultural phenomena as the eventual consumers of their products.

The process by which certain symbolic alternatives are chosen over others has been
▶ termed **collective selection**.[99] As with the creative subsystem, members of the managerial and communications subsystems also seem to develop a common frame of mind. Although products within each category must compete for acceptance in the marketplace, they can usually be characterized by their adherence to a dominant theme or motif – be it the grunge look, sixties nostalgia, Danish Modern or *nouvelle cuisine*.

Behavioural science perspectives on fashion

Fashion is a very complex process which operates on many levels. At one extreme, it is a macro, societal phenomenon affecting many people simultaneously. At the other, it exerts a very personal effect on individual behaviour. A consumer's purchase decisions are often motivated by their desire to be in fashion. Fashion products are aesthetic objects, and their origins are rooted in art and history. For this reason, there are many perspectives on the origin and diffusion of fashion. Although these cannot be described in detail here, some major approaches can be briefly summarized.[100]

Psychological models of fashion

Many psychological factors help to explain why people are motivated to be in fashion. These include conformity, variety-seeking, personal creativity and sexual attraction. For example, many consumers seem to have a 'need for uniqueness': they want to be different, but not too different.[101] For this reason, people often conform to the basic outlines of a fashion, but try to improvise and make a personal statement within these guidelines.

ISN'T IT NICE TO LIVE IN A TIME WHEN WOMEN
AREN'T BEING PUSHED AROUND SO MUCH ANYMORE?
Women have spent the last ten centuries conforming to their lingerie. Fortunately, lingerie has finally gotten around to conforming to women.
M A I D E N F O R M

This ad for Maidenform illustrates that fashions have accentuated different parts of the female anatomy throughout history.

Copyright © 1994 by Maidenform, Inc.

One of the earliest theories of fashion proposed that 'shifting **erogenous zones**' (sexually arousing areas of the body) accounted for fashion changes. Different parts of the female body are the focus of sexual interest, and clothing styles change to highlight or hide these parts. For example, people in the Victorian era found shoulders exciting, a 'well-turned ankle' was important at the beginning of the twentieth century, while the back was the centre of attention in the 1930s.

While these shifts may be due to boredom, some have speculated that there are deeper reasons for changes in focus; body areas symbolically reflect social values. In medieval times, for example, a rounded belly was desirable. This preference was most likely a reflection of the fact that multiple pregnancies were necessary to maintain population growth in an age when infant mortality was high. Interest in the female leg in the 1920s and 1930s coincided with women's new mobility and independence, while the exposure of breasts in the 1970s signalled a renewed interest in breastfeeding.[102] Breasts were de-emphasized in the 1980s as women concentrated on careers, but some analysts have theorized that a larger bust size is now more popular as women try to combine professional activity with child-rearing. Now, some suggest that the current prevalence of the exposed midriff reflects the premium our society places on fitness.[103] It is important to note that until very recently the study of fashion focused almost exclusively on its impact on women. More recently, consumer researchers have started to focus also on fashion consumers among other groups. First and foremost, men are not excempt from being 'fashion victims', and especially the rise of the 'metrosexual man'[104] has underlined for marketers as well as for researchers the importance of gaining insight into male fashion consumption.

Psychological research suggests that it is possible to distinguish between two different personality types, respectively more or less sensitive to the opinion of their social surroundings (also called high and low self-monitors). The high self-monitors have been demonstrated to stress the brand of a consumer good (specifically clothing) more than low self-monitors, who are on the other hand more positive to functional product attributes.[105]

Economic models of fashion

Economists approach fashion in terms of the model of supply and demand. Items that are in limited supply have high value, while those readily available are less desirable. Rare items command respect and prestige.

▶ Veblen's notion of **conspicuous consumption** proposed that the wealthy consume to display their prosperity, for example by wearing expensive (and at times impractical) clothing. The functioning of conspicuous consumption seems more complex in today's society, since wealthy consumers often engage in *parody display*, where they deliberately adopt formerly low status or inexpensive products, such as jeeps or jeans. On the other hand, new hierarchies develop between generic jeans signalling a traditional, work-oriented, classless or lower-class environment, and designer jeans expressing an urban, upmarket, class-distinctive and more contemporary lifestyle.[106] Other factors also influence the demand curve for fashion-related products. These include a *prestige-exclusivity effect*, where high prices still create high demand, and a *snob effect*, where lower prices actually reduce demand ('only a cheapskate would pay so little for that!').[107]

Sociological models of fashion

The collective selection model discussed previously is an example of a sociological approach to fashion. This perspective focuses on a subculture's adoption of a fashion (idea, style, etc.) and its subsequent diffusion into society as a whole. This process often begins with youth subcultures such as the hip-hop segment. Another current example is the integration of Goth culture into the mainstream. This fashion started as an expression of rebellion by young outcasts who admired nineteenth-century romantics and who defied conventional styles with their black clothing (often including over-the-top fashion statements such as Count Dracula capes, fishnet stockings, studded collars, and black lipstick) and punk music from bands such as Siouxsie & the Banshees and Bauhaus. Today, you can buy vampire-girl lunchboxes, and mall outlets sell tons of clunky cross jewellery and black lace. Hard-core Goths are not amused, but hey, that's fashion for you.[108]

▶ In addition, much attention has been focused on the relationship between product adoption and class structure. The **trickle-down theory**, first proposed in 1904 by Georg Simmel, has been one of the most influential approaches to understanding fashion. It states that there are two conflicting forces that drive fashion change. First, subordinate groups try to adopt the status symbols of the groups above them as they attempt to climb up the ladder of social mobility. Dominant styles thus originate with the upper classes and *trickle down* to those below. However, this is where the second force comes into play: those people in the superordinate groups are constantly looking below them on the ladder to ensure that they are not imitated. They respond to the attempts of lower classes to 'impersonate' them by adopting even *newer* fashions. These two processes create a self-perpetuating cycle of change – the engine that drives fashion.[109]

A contemporary version of conspicuous consumption and the trickle-down effect is the online shopping Website ASOS (As Seen On Screen, or As Seen On Star), where consumers can check out styles worn on the big screen, on TV or in other public contexts by celebrities like Cameron Diaz, Paris Hilton or Victoria Beckham. The basic message is: 'Now you too can look like Victoria Beckham.'[110]

The trickle-down theory was quite useful for understanding the process of fashion changes when applied to a society with a stable class structure, which permitted the easy identification of lower versus upper-class consumers. This task is not so easy in modern times. In contemporary Western society, then, this approach must be modified to account for new developments in mass culture.[111]

● A perspective based on class structure cannot account for the wide range of styles that are simultaneously made available in our society. Modern consumers have a much greater degree of individualized choice than in the past because of advances

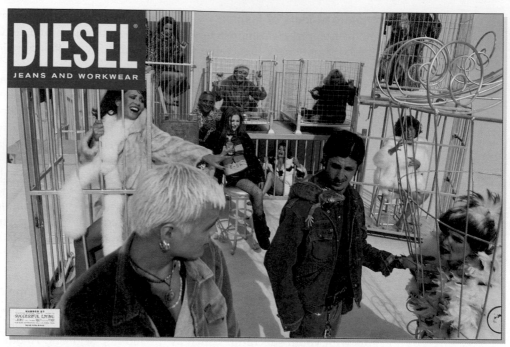

Some people argue that consumers are at the mercy of fashion designers. One study argued that both consumers and fashion designers feel like victims of each other – designers say that consumer demand and taste is very hard to predict, and consumers say the designers' ever-changing stylistic universes force them into renewing their wardrobe every so often.[112] What do you think?
Diesel S.p.A.

in technology and distribution. Just as an adolescent is almost instantly aware of the latest style trends by watching MTV, *elite fashion* has been largely replaced by *mass fashion*, since media exposure permits many groups to become aware of a style at the same time. Stores such as Zara and H&M can replenish their inventories in weeks rather than months, and the 'fast-fashion' market has become the fastest growing within the clothing sector.[113]

- Consumers tend to be more influenced by opinion leaders who are similar to them. As a result each social group has its own fashion innovators who determine fashion trends. It is often more accurate to speak of a *trickle-across effect*, where fashions diffuse horizontally among members of the same social group.[114]

- Anybody who has been on a skiing holiday will have noticed the *subcultural fashions* demonstrated among the skiers. In fact, more and more consumption-based subcultures, sailing enthusiasts for instance, adopt their own fashions in order to reinforce their community feeling and distinguish themselves from outsiders.[115]

- Finally, current fashions often originate with the lower classes and *trickle up*. Grassroots innovators are typically people who lack prestige in the dominant culture (like urban youth). Since they are less concerned with maintaining the status quo, they are more free to innovate and take risks.[116] Whatever the direction of the trickling, one thing is sure: that fashion is always a complex process of variation, of imitation and differentiation, of adoptions and rejections in relation to one's social surroundings.[117]

This blurring of origins of fashion has been attributed to the condition of post-modernity when there is no fashion, only fashions, and no rules, only choices,[118] and where the norms and rules can no longer be dictated solely from the haute couture or other cultural gatekeepers but where the individual allows themselves more freedom in creating a personal look by mixing elements from different styles.[119] This obviously has the consequence that the relatively linear models of fashion cycles discussed below become less able to predict actual fashion developments.[120]

A French researcher followed the development in the editorial content of a French fashion magazine since 1945. It turned out that the content became more global and less 'French' over the years, but also that the magazine gradually shifted away from a dictate of one certain fashion style at each point in time to an approach in the 1990s where several styles were promoted in each issue and consumers were invited to mix and match and create their own personal style independently of high fashion.[121] A similar blurring of high and low fashion was demonstrated by a prize-winning campaign, where a charity organization used former international top model Renee Toft Simonsen for promoting clothes from their second-hand shops.[122] Neither she nor the agency received any payment for their participation. The latest craze among Bristish fashion-hungry women is going to a *swishing party*. It is a kind of clothes swapping meeting, where the participants can nibble a little something to eat and sip a glass of wine while checking out the garments brought by other participants. The VISA corporation has stepped in with an organizing principle securing points given for what you hand in, and those can then be used for taking away clothes. This ensures that the swapping does not end up in chaos and free-riding behaviour but becomes a true fashion event. Hence, your access is dependent on bringing a clean, good quality garment, or shoes, that has just spent a little too much time in the wardrobe. This is both economical and environmental, underline the patrons. A total of 900,000 tons of clothing and shoes are thrown away each year in the UK. A swishing party allows people to recycle and embellish themselves at the same time – and it is a cozy event where they meet new friends who are also into fashion.[123]

The fashion system, then, is becoming increasingly complex. Brands may be very significant to consumers and they may be less ashamed to admit that than previously but they are less committed to any one brand over a longer period. The fashion industry is trying to compensate for this by overexposing their brands, putting the brand name very conspicuously all over clothing, bags, accessories, etc. in order to get a maximum of exposure out of the 'catch'.[124] The fashion industry is also exploring the individual styles for new market opportunities and new meanings of fashion goods for wider distribution.[125]

Swishing parties have become highly popular among female British fashion consumers.

David Cox

Even those trying to rebel against fashion dictates by turning to ugliness as a motif for their choice of 'look' cannot escape. Ugliness in a variety of forms is becoming increasingly fashionable; as one consumer said: 'These shoes were so ugly I just had to have them.'[126] The ugly and disgusting seems to form a specific trend in certain companies' marketing strategies.[127]

A 'medical' model of fashion

For years and years, the lowly Hush Puppy was a shoe for nerds. Suddenly – almost overnight – the shoe became a chic fashion statement even though its manufacturer did nothing to promote this image. Why did this style diffuse through the population so quickly? **Meme theory** explains this process with a medical metaphor. A *meme* is an idea or product that enters the consciousness of people over time – examples include tunes, catch-phrases ('You're fired!'), or styles such as the Hush Puppy. In this view, memes spread among consumers in a geometric progression just as a virus starts off in a small way and steadily infects increasing numbers of people until it becomes an epidemic. Memes 'leap' from brain to brain via a process of imitation.

The memes that survive tend to be distinctive and memorable, and the hardiest ones often combine aspects of prior memes. For example, the *Star Wars* movies evoked prior memes relating to the legend of King Arthur, religion, heroic youth, and 1930s adventure serials. Indeed, George Lucas studied comparative religion and mythology as he prepared his first draft of the *Star Wars* saga, 'The Story of Mace Windu'.[128]

The diffusion of many products in addition to Hush Puppies seems to follow the same basic path. A few people initially use the product, but change happens in a hurry when the process reaches the moment of critical mass – what one author calls the **tipping point**. For example, Sharp introduced the first low-priced fax machine in 1984 and sold about 80,000 in that year. There was a slow climb in the number of users for the next three years. Then, suddenly, in 1987 enough people had fax machines that it made sense for everyone to have one – Sharp sold a million units. Cell phones followed a similar trajectory.[129]

ABSOLUT LATEST.

Cell phones have become a fashion statement – and a technological gizmo for showing off among peer groups. This is so obvious for most consumers that it can be used by a compelety different company for selling a completely different product.

Cycles of fashion adoption

In 1997, a little digital animal swept across the planet. After enjoying considerable success in Japan in 1996 with about three million units sold, it spread throughout the world during 1997 where the population by the summer had increased to a total of seven million with approximately twice that number in back orders. The Tamagochi, as it is known, is an electronic pet that must be nurtured, played with and taken care of just as a living being. Failure to do so means it will weaken and show signs of maltreatment until it eventually dies. That is, in the Japanese version it dies. This unhappy ending did not appeal to Americans who therefore created their own version where it flies off to another planet if not treated well. Needless to say, the Japanese 'authentic' versions quickly became collectors' items (cf. the discussion of collections in the previous chapter). Today, many consumers might not know what a Tamagochi is, but anybody with children will know what a Pokémon is.

The stories of the Tamagochi or the Pokémon show how quickly a consumer craze can catch on globally. Although the longevity of a particular style can range from a month to a century, fashions tend to flow in a predictable sequence. The **fashion life cycle** is quite similar to the more familiar product life cycle. An item or idea progresses through basic stages from birth to death, as shown in Figure 14.3.

Variations in fashion life cycles

The diffusion process discussed earlier in this chapter is intimately related to the popularity of fashion-related items. To illustrate how this process works, consider how the **fashion acceptance cycle** works in the popular music business. In the *introduction stage*,

Figure 14.3 A normal fashion cycle

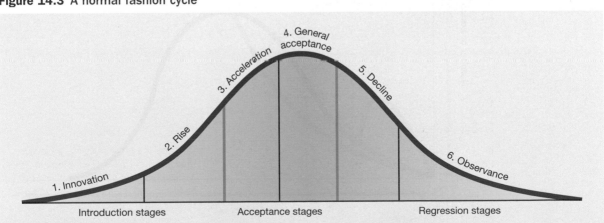

Source: Susan Kaiser, *The Social Psychology of Clothing* (New York: Macmillan, 1985). Reprinted with permission.

a song is listened to by a small number of music innovators. It may be played in clubs or on 'cutting-edge' radio stations, which is exactly how 'grunge rock' groups such as Nirvana got their start. During the *acceptance stage*, the song enjoys increased social visibility and acceptance by large segments of the population. A record may get wide airplay on 'Top-40' stations, steadily rising up the charts 'like a bullet'. This process may of course be supported or even generated by marketing efforts from the record company.

In the *regression stage*, the item reaches a state of social saturation as it becomes overused, and eventually it sinks into decline and obsolescence as new songs rise to take its place. A hit record may be played once an hour on a Top-40 station for several weeks. At some point, though, people tend to get sick of it and focus their attention on newer releases. The former hit record eventually winds up in the discount rack at the local record store.

Not everybody shares the same musical tastes. Nor, as we discussed above, is everybody necessarily influenced by the same fashion in clothing anymore. As society may become more characterized by lifestyles than by generalizable consumption patterns spreading through social classes as in the class-based fashion models, the social groups in question may consist more of a particular lifestyle than actual social classes. For example, one may distinguish generally between the more risk-prone and the more prudent fashion consumers, and each of these two groups have their own independent fashion cycles that do not necessarily influence the other groups.[131]

Figure 14.4 illustrates that fashions are characterized by slow acceptance at the beginning, which (if the fashion is to 'make it') rapidly accelerates and then tapers off. Different classes of fashion can be identified by considering the relative length of the fashion acceptance cycle. While many fashions exhibit a moderate cycle, taking several years to work their way through the stages of acceptance and decline, others are extremely long-lived or short-lived.

► A **classic** is a fashion with an extremely long acceptance cycle. It is in a sense 'anti-fashion', since it guarantees stability and low risk to the purchaser for a long period of time. Keds sneakers, classic so-called 'tennis shoes' introduced in the US in 1917, have been successful because they appeal to those who are turned off by the high-fashion,

Figure 14.4 Comparison of the acceptance cycle of fads, fashions and classics

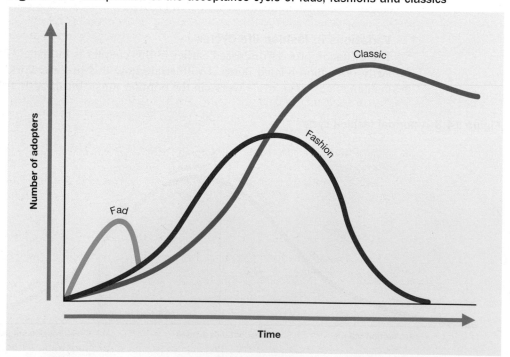

Source: Susan Kaiser, *The Social Psychology of Clothing* (New York: Macmillan, 1985). Reprinted with permission.

Figure 14.5 The behaviour of fads

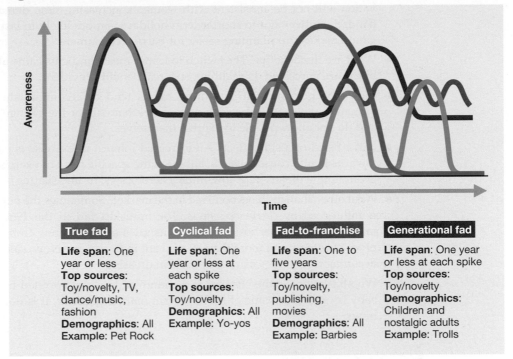

trendy appeal of L.A. Gear, Reebok and others. When consumers in focus groups were asked to project what kind of building Keds would be, a common response was a country house with a white picket fence. In other words, the shoes are seen as a stable, classic product. In contrast, Nikes were often described as steel-and-glass skyscrapers, reflecting their more modernistic image.[132]

A **fad** is a very short-lived fashion. Fads are usually adopted by relatively few people. Adopters may all belong to a common subculture, and the fad 'trickles across' members but rarely breaks out of that specific group.[133] Indeed, others are likely to ridicule the fad (which may add fuel to the fire). For example, a pair of researchers recently studied adults who resist the Harry Potter craze. They find some of these consumers avoid the Hogwarts world because they pride themselves on 'not being taken in'. These adults react negatively to the 'evangelical' enthusiasts who try to convert them to fandom. They recount the resentment of one newlywed on her honeymoon (as related in an essay by her new husband): 'My new page-turning obsession did not go down too well with my new life partner. When on our first night in the Maldives and expecting some form of conjugal rites [she found] herself in second place to a fictional 11-year-old trainee wizard and something called the Sorting Hat.'[134]

Fads are not 'one size fits all' in terms of spread and impact. Figure 14.5 illustrates different types of fads. However, whatever the fad cycle, some key characteristics of fads include:

● The fad is non-utilitarian – that is, it does not perform any explicit purpose function.

● The fad is often adopted on impulse; people do not undergo stages of rational decision-making before joining in.

● The fad diffuses rapidly, gains quick acceptance, and is short-lived.

Distinguishing beforehand between fads or more lasting tendencies of change is not easy, and many consulting agencies make a living out of being trend-spotters. However, here are a few points that may be helpful in distinguishing short-lived fads from longer-lasting innovations:[135]

- Does it fit with basic lifestyle changes? If a new hairstyle is hard to care for, this innovation will not be consistent with women's increasing time demands. On the other hand, the movement to shorter-term holidays is more likely to last because this innovation makes trip planning easier for harried consumers.

- What are the benefits? The switch to leaner meats and cuts came about because these meats are perceived as healthier, so a real benefit is evident.

- Can it be personalized? Enduring trends tend to accommodate a desire for individuality, whereas styles such as mohawk haircuts or the grunge look are inflexible and do not allow people to express themselves.

- Is it a trend or a side effect? An increased interest in exercise is part of a basic trend towards health consciousness, although the specific form of exercise that is 'in' at any given time will vary (e.g. low-impact aerobics vs. in-line skating).

- What other changes have occurred in the market? Sometimes the popularity of products is influenced by *carry-over effects*. The miniskirt fad in the 1960s brought about a major change in the hosiery market, as sales of tights grew from 10 per cent of this product category to more than 80 per cent in two years. Now, sales of these items are declining due to the casual emphasis in dressing.

- Who has adopted the change? If the innovation is not adopted by working mothers, baby boomers, or some other important market segment, it is not likely to become a trend.

CHAPTER SUMMARY

- The styles prevalent in a culture at any point in time often reflect underlying political and social conditions. The set of agents responsible for creating stylistic alternatives is termed a culture production system. Factors such as the types of people involved in this system and the amount of competition by alternative product forms influence the choices that eventually make their way to the marketplace for consideration by end consumers.

- Culture is often described in terms of high (or elite) forms and low (or popular) forms. Products of popular culture tend to follow a cultural formula and contain predictable components. On the other hand, these distinctions are blurring in modern society as imagery from 'high art' is increasingly being incorporated into marketing efforts and marketed products (or even marketing products like advertisements) are treated and evaluated as high art.

- The *diffusion of innovations* refers to the process whereby a new product, service or idea spreads through a population. A consumer's decision to adopt a new item depends on their personal characteristics (if they are inclined to try new things) and on the characteristics of the item. Products sometimes stand a better chance of being adopted if they demand relatively little change in behaviour from consumers and are compatible with current practices. They are also more likely to diffuse if they can be tested prior to purchase, if they are not complex, if their use is visible to others, and, most importantly, if they provide a relative advantage vis-à-vis existing products.

- The fashion system includes everyone involved in the creation and transference of symbolic meanings. Meanings that express common cultural categories (for instance, gender distinctions) are conveyed by many different products. New styles tend to be adopted by many people simultaneously in a process known as collective selection. Perspectives on motivations for adopting new styles include psychological, economic and sociological models of fashion.

- Fashions tend to follow cycles that resemble the product life cycle. The two extremes of fashion adoption, classics and fads, can be distinguished in terms of the length of this cycle.

► KEY TERMS

Advergaming (p. 553)

Art product (p. 546)

Classic (p. 568)

Collective selection (p. 561)

Conspicuous consumption (p. 563)

Consumerspace (p. 546)

Continuous innovation (p. 558)

Co-optation (p. 542)

Craft product (p. 546)

Cultivation hypothesis (p. 554)

Cultural formula (p. 549)

Cultural gatekeepers (p. 544)

Cultural production system (CPS) (p. 543)

Cultural selection (p. 542)

Discontinuous innovation (p. 559)

Dynamically continuous innovation (p. 559)

Early adopters (p. 557)

Erogenous zones (p. 562)

Fad (p. 569)

Fashion (p. 561)

Fashion acceptance cycle (p. 567)

Fashion life cycle (p. 567)

Fashion system (p. 560)

Innovation (p. 554)

Lead users (p. 558)

Meme theory (p. 566)

Product placement (p. 552)

Prosumer (p. 546)

Reality engineering (p. 551)

Tipping point (p. 566)

Trickle-down theory (p. 563)

Voice of the consumer (p. 558)

► CONSUMER BEHAVIOUR CHALLENGE

1 Construct a 'biography' of a product, tracing its progress from the time it was introduced. How long did it take to diffuse to the mass market? Do the same consumers use the product now as those who first adopted it? What are its future prospects – is it destined for obsolescence? Would you characterize the product as either a classic or a fad?

2 Some consumers complain that they are 'at the mercy' of designers: they are forced to buy whatever styles are in fashion because nothing else is available. Do you agree that there is such a thing as a 'designer conspiracy'?

3 What is the basic difference between a fad, a fashion and a classic? Provide examples of each.

4 What is the difference between an art and a craft? Where would you characterize advertising within this framework?

5 Think about some innovative products that you can remember, but which disappeared. Try to reflect on the reasons why these innovations failed.

6 Then try to remember some successful innovations. What characteristics made them successful? Do the successes and failures fit with the criteria mentioned in this chapter?

7 The marketing opportunity of introducing product placements in, e.g. news programmes, may have some problematic ethical and political side effects? Would you be comfortable with product placement in the news? Why, or why not?

8 The chapter mentions some instances where market research findings influenced artistic decisions, as when a film ending was reshot to accommodate consumers' preferences. Many people would oppose this use of consumer research, claiming that books, films, records or other artistic endeavours should not be designed merely to conform to what people want to read, see or hear. What do you think?

9 Many are claiming a more individualistic style of fashion these years. Discuss whether individualism in style and fashion has actually increased or whether we are being conformist in new ways.

For additional material see the companion website at www.pearsoned.co.uk/solomon

NOTES

1. Nina Darnton, 'Where the homegirls are', *Newsweek* (17 June 1991): 60; 'The idea chain', *Newsweek* (5 October 1992): 32.

2. Cyndee Miller, 'X marks the lucrative spot, but some advertisers can't hit target', *Marketing News* (2 August 1993): 1.

3. Ad appeared in *Elle* (September 1994).

4. Marc Spiegler, 'Marketing street culture: Bringing hip-hop style to the mainstream', *American Demographics* (November 1996): 23–7; Joshua Levine, 'Badass sells', *Forbes* (21 April 1997): 142–8.

5. Jeff Jensen, 'Hip, wholesome image makes a marketing star of rap's LL Cool J', *Advertising Age* (25 August 1997): 1.

6. Alice Z. Cuneo, 'Gap's 1st global ads confront dockers on a khaki battlefield', *Advertising Age* (20 April 1998): 3–5.

7. Jancee Dunn, 'How hip-hop style bum-rushed the mall', *Rolling Stone* (18 March 1999): 54–9.

8. Quoted in Teri Agins, 'The rare art of "gilt by association": How Armani got stars to be billboards', *The Wall Street Journal Interactive Edition* (14 September 1999).

9. Eryn Brown, 'From rap to retail: Wiring the hip-hop nation', *Fortune* (17 April 2000): 530.

10. Martin Fackler, 'Hip hop invading China', *The Birmingham News* (15 February 2002): D1.

11. Maureen Tkacik, ' "Z" zips into the zeitgeist, subbing for "S" in hot slang', *The Wall Street Journal Interactive Edition* (4 January 2003); Maureen Tkacik, 'Slang from the 'hood now sells toyz in target', *The Wall Street Journal Interactive Edition* (30 December 2002).

12. 'Return of the Mac – coming soon' (29 March 2005), http://news.bbc.co.uk/2/hi/business/4389751.stm.

13. Arthur, Damien, 'Authenticity and consumption in the Australian hip hop culture', *Qualitative Market Research* 9(2) (2005): 140.

14. Bennett, Andy, 'Hip-Hop am Main, Rappin' on the Tyne: Hip-hop Culture as a Local Construct in Two European Cities', in *That's the Joint!: The Hip-hop Studies Reader* (London: Routledge, 2004).

15. http://www.icce.rug.nl/~soundscapes/DATABASES/MIE/Part2_chapter08.shtml; https://sdumail.sdu.dk/exchweb/bin/redir.asp? URL=http://www.icce.rug.nl/~soundscapes/DATABASES/MIE/Part2_chapter08.shtml, accessed 9 April 2009.

16. Danmarks Radio, P1, 5 November 2008.

17. Johanne Mygind, 'Sing it out – Muslim sisters', *Information*, 7 November 2008.

18. Elizabeth M. Blair, 'Commercialization of the rap music youth subculture', *Journal of Popular Culture* 27 (Winter 1993): 21–34; Basil G. Englis, Michael R. Solomon and Anna Olofsson, 'Consumption imagery in music television: A bi-cultural perspective', *Journal of Advertising* 22 (December 1993): 21–34.

19. Marc Spiegler, 'Marketing street culture: Bringing hip-hop style to the mainstream', *American Demographics* (November 1996): 29–34.

20. Janice Brace-Govan and Hélène de Burgh-Woodman, 'Sneakers and street culture: A postcolonial analysis of marginalized cultural consumption', *Consumption, Markets and Culture* 11(2) (2008): 93–112.

21. See for example Thomas Frank, *The Conquest of Cool* (Chicago: University of Chicago Press, 1997).

22. Teri Agins, 'To track fickle fashion, apparel firms go online', *The Wall Street Journal* (11 May 2000): B1.

23. Richard A. Peterson, 'The Production of Culture: A Prolegomenon', in Richard A. Peterson (ed.), *The Production of Culture*, Sage Contemporary Social Science Issues (Beverly Hills, CA: Sage, 1976) 33: 7–22.

24. Richard A. Peterson and D.G. Berger, 'Entrepreneurship in organizations: Evidence from the popular music industry', *Administrative Science Quarterly* 16 (1971): 97–107.

25. Elizabeth C. Hirschman, 'Resource exchange in the production and distribution of a motion picture', *Empirical Studies of the Arts* 8 (1990) 1: 31–51; Michael R. Solomon, 'Building Up and Breaking Down: The Impact of Cultural Sorting on Symbolic Consumption', in J. Sheth and E.C. Hirschman (eds), *Research in Consumer Behavior* (Greenwich, CT: JAI Press, 1988): 325–51.

26. See Paul M. Hirsch, 'Processing fads and fashions: An organizational set analysis of cultural industry systems', *American Journal of Sociology* 77 (1972) 4: 639–59; Russell Lynes, *The Tastemakers* (New York: Harper & Brothers, 1954); Michael R. Solomon, 'The missing link: Surrogate consumers in the marketing chain', *Journal of Marketing* 50 (October 1986): 208–19.

27. Michael R. Solomon, Richard Ashmore and Laura Longo, 'The beauty match-up hypothesis: Congruence between types of beauty and product images in advertising', *Journal of Advertising* 21 (December 1992): 23–34.

28. Michael R. Solomon, *Conquering Consumerspace: Marketing Strategies for a Branded World* (New York: AMACOM, 2003).

29. Craig J. Thompson and Gökcen Coskuner-Balli, 'Countervailing market responses to corporate co-optation and the ideological recruitment of consumption communities', *Journal of Consumer Research* 34(2) (August 2007): 135–52.

30. Howard S. Becker, 'Arts and crafts', *American Journal of Sociology* 83 (January 1987): 862–89.

31. Herbert J. Gans, 'Popular Culture in America: Social Problem in a Mass Society or Social Asset in a Pluralist Society?' in Howard S. Becker (ed.), *Social Problems: A Modern Approach* (New York: Wiley, 1966).

32. Anders Bengtsson, Jacob Östberg and Dannie Kjeldgaard, 'Prisoners in paradise: Subcultural resistance to the marketization of tattooing', *Consumption, Markets and Culture* 8(3) (2005): 261–74.

33. Peter S. Green, 'Moviegoers devour ads', *Advertising Age* (26 June 1989): 36.

34. Michael R. Real, *Mass-Mediated Culture* (Englewood Cliffs, NJ: Prentice-Hall, 1977).

35. For some websites that show 'Top-40' music sales in Europe and North America, see: http://top40–charts.com/, and http://www.bbc.co.uk/radio1/chart/singles.shtml (accessed 5 August 2005).

36. Annetta Miller, 'Shopping bags imitate art: Seen the sacks? Now visit the museum exhibit', *Newsweek* (23 January 1989): 44.

37. Kim Foltz, 'New species for study: Consumers in action', *New York Times* (18 December 1989): A1.

38. Arthur A. Berger, *Signs in Contemporary Culture: An Introduction to Semiotics* (New York: Longman, 1984).

39. Stephen Brown, 'Psycho shopper: A comparative literary analysis of "the dark side" ', in Flemming Hansen (ed.),

European Advances in Consumer Research 2 (Provo, UT: Association for Consumer Research, 1995): 96–103; Stephen Brown, 'Consumption Behaviour in the Sex'n'Shopping Novels of Judith Krantz: A Post-structuralist Perspective', in J. Lynch and K. Corfman (eds), *Advances in Consumer Research* 23 (Provo, UT: Association for Consumer Research, 1996): 96–103.

40. 'Hip to be Square: Why Young Buyers Covet "Grandpa" Cars', *Wall Street Journal* (9 May 2006): A, p. 1.

41. Randall Frost, 'Staying power: Surviving the limelight', http://www.brandchannel.com/features_effect.asp?pf_id=215#more (accessed 5 August 2005), and Jonathan Guthrie, 'Why using a dead celebrity sells', *Financial Times* (26 April 2005), http://news.ft.com/cms/s/f93e84d2-b675-11d9-aebd-00000e2511c8.html.

42. Michiko Kakutani, 'Art is easier the 2d time around,' *The New York Times* (30 October 1994): E4. See also Stephen Brown, *Retro-Marketing* (London: Routledge, 2001).

43. Nigel Andrews, 'Filming a blockbuster is one thing; striking gold is another', *Financial Times*, accessed via Simon & Schuster College Newslink (20 January 1998).

44. Helene Diamond, 'Lights, camera . . . research!', *Marketing News* (11 September 1989): 10.

45. Nigel Andrews, 'Filming a blockbuster is one thing; striking gold is another', *op. cit.*

46. 'A brand-new development creates a colorful history', *The Wall Street Journal Interactive Edition* (18 February 1998).

47. Michael R. Solomon and Basil G. Englis, 'Reality engineering: Blurring the boundaries between marketing and popular culture', *Journal of Current Issues and Research in Advertising* 16 (Fall 1994) 2: 1–17.

48. 'Hollywood-sur-brie', *Le Nouvel Observateur* (14 November 1996): 18–19.

49. Nina M. Lentini, 'Doh! Looks Like 7-Eleven Stores May Get Homered', *Marketing Daily* (30 March 2007), available from www.mediapost.com, accessed 30 March 2007.

50. Steve Cooper, Damien McLoughlin and Andrew Keating, 'Individual and neo-tribal consumption: Tales from the Simpsons of Springfield', *Journal of Consumer Behaviour* 4(5) (2005): 330–44.

51. Nicolas Marmie, 'Casablanca Gets a Rick's', *Montgomery Advertiser* (9 May 2004): 3AA.

52. Suzanne Alexander Ryan, 'Companies teach all sorts of lessons with educational tools they give away', *The Wall Street Journal* (19 April 1994): B1 (2); Cyndee Miller, 'Marketers find a seat in the classroom', *Marketing News* (20 June 1994): 2.

53. Wayne Friedman, ' "Minority report" stars Lexus, Nokia', *Advertising Age* (17 June 2002): 41.

54. Denise E. DeLorme and Leonard N. Reid, 'Moviegoers' experiences and interpretations of brands in films revisited', *Journal of Advertising* 28(2) (1999): 71–90.

55. Cristel Antonia Russell, 'Investigating the effectiveness of product placement in television shows: The role of modality and plot connection congruence on brand memory and attitude', *Journal of Consumer Research* 29 (December 2002): 306–18.

56. Claire Atkinson, 'Ad intrusion up, say consumers', *Advertising Age* (6 January 2003): 1.

57. http://www.marketingcharts.com/television/product-placements-up-6-in-first-quarter-4477/, accessed 29 March 2009.

58. John Walsh, 'As seen on screen. Whatever next fro product placement', *The Independent*, 24 July 2008, accessed on http://www.independent.co.uk/news/media/as-seen-on-screen-whatever-next-for-product-placement-875704.html, 12 November 2008.

59. Peter Wonacott, 'Chinese TV is an eager medium for (lots of) product placement', *The Wall Street Journal Interactive Edition* (26 January 2000).

60. Gabriel Kahn, 'Product placement booms in new Bollywood films', *The Wall Street Journal Interactive Edition* (30 August 2002).

61. Jennifer Tanaka and Marc Peyser, 'The apples of their eyes', *Newsweek* (30 November 1998): 58.

62. Nancy Marsden, 'Lighting up the big screen', *San Francisco Examiner* (4 August 1998).

63. Geoffrey A. Fowler, 'New Star on Chinese TV: Product Placements', *Wall Street Journal Online Edition* (2 June 2004): B1.

64. Aaron O. Patrick and Keith Johnson, 'Spanish Television Reigns as King of Product Plugs It's Hard to Tell Where Shows Stop and Ads Begin; In 3 Hours, 105 Mentions', *Wall Street Journal* (2 February 2007): A1.

65. 'Filmreplik ødelagde Merlot i USA', *Berlingske Kultur*, 15 April 2008: 3.

66. George Gerbner, Larry Gross, Nancy Signorielli and Michael Morgan, 'Aging with television: Images on television drama and conceptions of social reality', *Journal of Communication* 30 (1980): 37–47.

67. Stephen Fox and William Philber, 'Television viewing and the perception of affluence', *Sociological Quarterly* 19 (1978): 103–12; W. James Potter, 'Three strategies for elaborating the cultivation hypothesis', *Journalism Quarterly* 65 (Winter 1988): 930–9; Gabriel Weimann, 'Images of life in America: The impact of American T.V. in Israel', *International Journal of Intercultural Relations* 8 (1984): 185–97.

68. Patricia Gaya Wicks, Agnes Nairn and Christine Griffin, 'The role of commodified celebrities in children's moral development: The case of David Beckham', *Consumption, Culture and Markets* 10(4) (2007): 401–24.

69. Stephanie O'Donohue, 'On the Outside Looking In: Advertising Experiences Among Young Unemployed Adults', in Flemming Hansen (ed.), *European Advances in Consumer Research* 2 (Provo, UT: Association for Consumer Research): 264–72; Richard Elliott, 'How Do the Unemployed Maintain Their Identity in a Culture of Consumption?' in Hansen (ed.), *European Advances in Consumer Research* 2: 273–6.

70. 'Mobilen har blivit en vardagspryl', *Info* 9 (2000): 52–4; Internet Usage in the European Union, 2005, http://www.internetworldstats.com/stats4.htm#eu.

71. Susan B. Kaiser, *The Social Psychology of Clothing* (New York: Macmillan, 1985); Thomas S. Robertson, *Innovative Behavior and Communication* (New York: Holt, Rhinehart & Winston, 1971).

72. Eric J. Arnould, 'Toward a broadened theory of preference formation and the diffusion of innovations: Cases from Zinder Province, Niger Republic', *Journal of Consumer Research* 16 (September 1989): 239–67.

73. Jan-Benedict E.M. Steenkamp, Frenkel ter Hofstede and Michel Wedel, 'A cross-national investigation into the individual and national cultural antecedents of consumer innovativeness', *Journal of Marketing* 63(2) (1999): 55–69.

74. Richard Wilk, 'Bottled water: The pure commodity in the age of branding', *Journal of Consumer Culture* 6(3) (2006): 303–25.

75. Susan L. Holak, Donald R. Lehmann and Farena Sultan, 'The role of expectations in the adoption of innovative consumer durables: Some preliminary evidence', *Journal of Retailing* 63 (Fall 1987): 243–59.

76. Hubert Gatignon and Thomas S. Robertson, 'A propositional inventory for new diffusion research', *Journal of Consumer Research* 11 (March 1985): 849–67.

77. Frank Huber, 'Ein konzept zur ermittlung und bearbeitung des frühkäufersegments im bekleidungsmarkt', *Marketing ZFP* 2 (2nd Quarter 1995): 110–21.

78. Eva Martinez, Yolanda Polo and Carlos Flavián, 'The acceptance and diffusion of new consumer durables: Differences between first and last adopters', *Journal of Consumer Marketing* 15(4) (1998): 323–42.

79. Sofie Møller Bjerrisgaard, 'The Global Construction of the Consumer', PhD project, Dept. of Marketing and Management, University of Southern Denmark, Odense. See also John A. McCarthy, Martin I. Horn, Mary Kate Szenasy and Jocelyn Feintuch, 'An exploratory study of consumer style: Country differences and international segments', *Journal of Consumer Behaviour* 6(1) (January–February 2007): 48–59.

80. Gordon R. Foxall and Seema Bhate, 'Cognitive style and personal involvement as explicators of innovative purchasing of health food brands', *European Journal of Marketing* 27(2) (1993): 5–16.

81. C.K. Prahalad and Venkatram Ramaswamy, 'Co-opting customer competence', *Harvard Business Review* (January–February 2000): 79–87; Eric von Hipple, 'Users as innovators', *Technology Review* 80 (January 1978): 3–11; Jakki Mohr, *Marketing of High-Technology Products and Services* (Upper Saddle River, NJ: Prentice Hall, 2001).

82. Byrnes, Nanette, 'Xerox' New Design Team: Customers', *Business Week* (7 May 2007): 72.

83. Elizabeth C. Hirschman, 'Symbolism and Technology as Sources of the Generation of Innovations', in Andrew Mitchell (ed.), *Advances in Consumer Research* 9 (Provo, UT: Association for Consumer Research, 1982): 537–41.

84. Søren Askegaard and A. Fuat Firat, 'Towards a Critique of Material Culture, Consumption and Markets', in Susan M. Pearce (ed.), *Experiencing Material Culture in the Western World* (London: Leicester University Press, 1997): 114–39.

85. Stephen Brown, *Postmodern Marketing* (London: Routledge, 1995).

86. 'Mange kvinder er begyndt at drikke mandecola', *Berlingske Tidende* (19 August 2008), Business: 11.

87. http://www.nanotechproject.org/inventories/consumer/, accessed 7 November 2008.

88. Everett M. Rogers, *Diffusion of Innovations*, 3rd edn (New York: Free Press, 1983).

89. Robert J. Fisher and Linda L. Price, 'An investigation into the social context of early adoption behavior', *Journal of Consumer Research* 19 (December 1992): 477–86.

90. Güliz Ger and Russell W. Belk, 'I'd like to buy the world a Coke: Consumptionscapes of the "less affluent world"', *Journal of Consumer Policy* 19 (1996): 271–304; Robin A. Coulter, Linda L. Price and Lawrence Feick, 'Rethinking the origins of involvement and brand commitment: Insights from postsocialist Central Europe', *Journal of Consumer Research* 30 (September 2003): 151–69.

91. W. Chan Kim and Renée Mauborgne, 'Value innovation: The strategic logic of high growth', *Harvard Business Review* (January–February 1997): 103–12.

92. 'Dare to be different', *Marketing* (13 February 1997): 22–3.

93. Roland Barthes, *Système de la mode* (Paris: Seuil, 1967), English: Roland Barthes, *The Language of Fashion* (Oxford: Berg Publishers 2006).

94. 'Diaper bag double take', *Discount Merchandiser* (March 2000).

95. Umberto Eco, *A Theory of Semiotics* (Bloomington, IN: Indiana University Press, 1979).

96. Fred Davis, 'Clothing and Fashion as Communication', in Michael R. Solomon (ed.), *The Psychology of Fashion* (Lexington, MA: Lexington Books, 1985): 15–28.

97. Melanie Wallendorf, 'The Formation of Aesthetic Criteria Through Social Structures and Social Institutions', in Jerry C. Olson (ed.), *Advances in Consumer Research* 7 (Ann Arbor, MI: Association for Consumer Research, 1980): 3–6.

98. Christine Delhaye, 'The development of consumption culture and the individualization of female identity', *Journal of Consumer Culture* 6(1) (2006): 87–115.

99. Herbert Blumer, *Symbolic Interactionism: Perspective and Method* (Englewood Cliffs, NJ: Prentice-Hall, 1969); Howard S. Becker, 'Art as collective action', *American Sociological Review* 39 (December 1973); Richard A. Peterson, 'Revitalizing the culture concept', *Annual Review of Sociology* 5 (1979): 137–66.

100. For more details, see Kaiser, *The Social Psychology of Clothing*, op. cit.; George B. Sproles, 'Behavioral Science Theories of Fashion', in Solomon (ed.), *The Psychology of Fashion*, op. cit.: 55–70.

101. C.R. Snyder and Howard L. Fromkin, *Uniqueness: The Human Pursuit of Difference* (New York: Plenum Press, 1980).

102. Alison Lurie, *The Language of Clothes* (New York: Random House, 1981).

103. Linda Dyett, 'Desperately seeking skin', *Psychology Today* (May/June 1996): 14.

104. Diego Rinallo, 'Producing and Consuming the Metrosexual', in S. Borghini, M.A. McGrath and C. Otnes (eds), *European Advances in Consumer Research* (Duluth, MN: Association for Consumer Research, 2008): 306–08.

105. Susan Auty and Richard Elliott, 'Social Identity and the Meaning of Fashion Brands', in B. Englis and A. Olofsson (eds), *European Advances in Consumer Research* 3 (Provo, UT: Association for Consumer Research, 1998): 1–10.

106. John Fiske, *Understanding Popular Culture* (Boston: Unwin Hyman, 1989): especially 1–21.

107. Harvey Leibenstein, *Beyond Economic Man: A New Foundation for Microeconomics* (Cambridge, MA: Harvard University Press, 1976).

108. Nara Schoenberg, 'Goth Culture Moves into Mainstream', *Montgomery Advertiser* (9 January 2003): 1G.

109. Georg Simmel, 'Fashion', *International Quarterly* 10 (1904): 130–55.

110. www.asos.com, accessed 12 November 2008.

111. Grant D. McCracken, 'The Trickle-Down Theory Rehabilitated', in Solomon (ed.), *The Psychology of Fashion*, op. cit.: 39–54.

112. Søren Askegaard, Deniz Atik and Stefania Borghini, 'The Interplay of Institutional Forces and Consumer Desires in the Moulding of Fashion', in S. Borghini, M.A. McGrath and C. Otnes (eds), *European Advances in Consumer Research* (Duluth, MN: Association for Consumer Research, 2008): 306.

113. 'Fast Fashion in 11 per cent Sales Surge', *Marketing* (20 April 2005): 14.

114. Charles W. King, 'Fashion Adoption: A Rebuttal to the "Trickle-Down" Theory', in Stephen A. Greyser (ed.), *Toward Scientific Marketing* (Chicago: American Marketing Association, 1963): 108–25.

115. Gillian Hogg, Suzanne Horne and David Carmichael, 'Fun, Fashion, or Just Plain Sailing? The Consumption of Clothing in the Sailing Community', in B. Dubois, T. Lowrey, L.J. Shrum and M. Vanhuele (eds), *European Advances in Consumer Research* 4 (Provo, UT: Association for Consumer Research, 1999): 336–40.

116. Alf H. Walle, 'Grassroots innovation', *Marketing Insights* (Summer 1990): 44–51.

117. Patrick Hetzel, 'The Role of Fashion and Design in a Postmodern Society: What Challenges for Firms?' in M.J. Baker (ed.), *Perspectives on Marketing Management* 4 (London: John Wiley & Sons, 1994): 97–118.

118. Stuart and Elizabeth Ewen, cited in Mike Featherstone, *Consumer Culture and Postmodernism* (London: Sage, 1993): 83.

119. Patrick Hetzel, 'The role of fashion and design in a postmodern society: what challenges for firms?' *op. cit.*

120. Anne F. Jensen, 'Acknowledging and Consuming Fashion in the Era after "Good Taste" – From the Beautiful to the Hideous', Doctoral Dissertations from the Faculty of Social Science, no. 40 (Odense: University of Southern Denmark, 1999).

121. Patrick Hetzel, 'A Socio-Semiotic Analysis of the Media/Consumer Relationships in the Production of Fashion Systems: The Case of the "Elle-France" Magazine', in Englis and Olofsson (eds), *European Advances in Consumer Research* 3: 104–7.

122. 'Topmodel i genbrugstøj', *Fyens Stiftstidende*, Erhverv (1 November 2000): 1.

123. http://news.bbc.co.uk/2/hi/uk_news/magazine/7563318.stm and http://www.guardian.co.uk/lifeandstyle/2007/may/18/fashion.ethicalliving, both accessed 12 November 2008.

124. 'Panik i mode-fabrikken', Intervju med Alladi Venkatesh, *Dagens Nyheter* (27 June 2000): B1.

125. Don Slater, *Consumer Culture and Modernity* (Cambridge: Polity Press, 1997).

126. Anne F. Jensen and Søren Askegaard, 'In Pursuit of Ugliness. Searching for a Fashion Concept in the Era After Good Taste', Working Paper in Marketing, no. 17 (Odense: Odense University, 1998).

127. Anonymous, 'FCUK Consumer Research: On Disgust, Revulsion and Other Forms of Offensive Advertising', paper submitted to the 2001 Association for Consumer Research European Conference (Berlin, 20–23 June).

128. Robert V. Kozinets, 'Fandoms' menace/pop flows: Exploring the metaphor of entertainment as recombinant/memetic engineering', *Association for Consumer Research* (October 1999). The new science of memetics, which tries to explain how beliefs gain acceptance and predict their progress, was spurred by Richard Dawkins who in the 1970s proposed culture as a Darwinian struggle among 'memes' or mind viruses. See Geoffrey Cowley, 'Viruses of the Mind: How Odd Ideas Survive', *Newsweek* (14 April 1997): 14.

129. Malcolm Gladwell, *The Tipping Point* (New York: Little, Brown and Co., 2000).

130. Robin Givhan, 'Designers caught in a tangled web', *The Washington Post* (5 April 1997): C1 (2 pp.).

131. Anne F. Jensen and Per Østergaard, 'Dressing for Security or Risk? An Exploratory Study of Two Different Ways of Consuming Fashion', in Englis and Olofsson (eds), *European Advances in Consumer Research* 3: 98–103.

132. Anthony Ramirez, 'The pedestrian sneaker makes a comeback', *New York Times* (14 October 1990): F17.

133. B.E. Aguirre, E.L. Quarantelli and Jorge L. Mendoza, 'The collective behavior of fads: The characteristics, effects, and career of streaking', *American Sociological Review* (August 1989). 569.

134. Quoted in Stephen Brown and Anthony Patterson, ' "You're a Wizard, Harry!" Consumer responses to the Harry Potter phenomenon', *Advances in Consumer Research* 33 (2006): 155–60.

135. Martin G. Letscher, 'How to tell fads from trends', *American Demographics* (December 1994): 38–45.

15

New times, new consumers

Chloe and Poppy are both executives in an advertising agency. After a particularly gruelling week, they are looking forward to a well-deserved weekend off. Chloe is enthusiastically telling Poppy about her plans. Since she won't have to get up early in the morning, she's going to sleep late in her new flat. Then she's planning to go window-shopping and maybe meet some friends for lunch in one of the cafés where she knows that some of them will be. Then she'll go back and rest in the afternoon until it's time to join her friend Isabella to go to the new techno and rave place, which she heard about the other day. There, they'll dance away all night long.

Poppy just smiles to herself: while Chloe's wasting her time in bed in the city, *she's* going to get up early to join a tour to a nearby bird sanctuary organized by the environmental group of which she's a member. She has heard that it will also be possible to see some rare orchids. By four o'clock, she plans to be comfortably planted in front of the computer in order to write an open letter to the municipal authorities concerning the current debate on whether to stop using pesticides in public parks and along the roadsides. Then she'll just sit back and relax, perhaps watch a rented video of one of the good films she missed due to lack of time.

Poppy is sometimes amazed at how different she is from Chloe, though both think of themselves as sophisticated and in touch with the times. They also earn the same salary and do almost the same things at work all week long. How can their tastes be so different at the weekend? 'Oh well,' Poppy sighs to herself, 'that's why they make chocolate *and* vanilla ice cream.'

LIFESTYLES AND CONSUMPTION CHOICES

Poppy and Chloe strongly resemble one another demographically. They were both raised in middle-class households, have similar educational backgrounds, are about the same age and they share the same occupation and income. However, as their leisure choices show, it would be a mistake to assume that their consumption choices are similar as well. Poppy and Chloe each choose products, services and activities that help them define a unique *lifestyle*. This chapter first explores how marketers approach the issue of lifestyle and then how they use information about these consumption choices to tailor products and communications to individual lifestyle segments. It then considers how lifestyle choices are affected by where people live, and it considers some issues that occur when firms attempt to market their products in unfamiliar cultures.

Lifestyle: who we are, what we do

In traditional societies, class, caste, village or family largely dictate a person's consumption options. In a modern consumer society, however, people are freer to select the products, services and activities that define themselves and, in turn, create a social identity they communicate to others. One's choice of goods and services makes a statement about who one is and about the types of people with whom one wishes to identify – and even some whom we wish to avoid.

▶ **Lifestyle** refers to a pattern of consumption that reflects a person's choices about how they spend time and money, but in many cases it also refers to the attitudes and values attached to these behavioural patterns. Many of the factors discussed in this book, such as a person's self-concept, reference group and social class, are used as 'raw ingredients' to fashion a unique lifestyle. In an economic sense, your lifestyle represents the way you elect to allocate income, both in terms of relative allocations to different products and services, and to specific alternatives within these categories.[1] Other somewhat similar distinctions describe consumers in terms of their broad patterns of consumption, such as those differentiating people by those who devote a high proportion of their total expenditure to food, or advanced technology, or to such information-intensive goods as entertainment and education. Often, these allocations create a new kind of status system based less on income than on accessibility to information about goods and how these goods function as social markers.[2]

Lifestyles may be considered as group identities. Marketers use demographic and economic approaches in tracking changes in broad societal priorities, but these approaches do not begin to embrace the symbolic nuances that separate lifestyle groups. Lifestyle is more than the allocation of discretionary income. It is a statement about who one is in society and who one is not. Group identities, whether of hobbyists, athletes, footballers (e.g. Bobbie's friends in Chapter 10) or drug users, take their form based on acts of expressive symbolism. The self-definitions of group members are derived from the common symbol system to which the group is dedicated. Such self-definitions have been described by a number of terms, including *lifestyle*, *public taste*, *consumer group*, *symbolic community* and *status culture*.[3]

Many people in similar social and economic circumstances may follow the same general consumption pattern. Still, each person provides a unique 'twist' to this pattern which allows them to inject some individuality into a chosen lifestyle. For example, a 'typical' student (if there is such a thing) may dress much like their friends, go to the same places and like the same foods, yet still indulge a passion for running marathons, stamp collecting or community service, activities which make them unique.

Lifestyles don't last forever, and are not set in stone. Unlike deep-seated values (discussed in Chapter 6), people's tastes and preferences evolve over time, so that consumption patterns that were viewed favourably at one point in time may be laughed at or sneered at a few years later. If you don't believe that, simply think back to what you, your friends and your family were wearing, doing and eating five or ten years ago: where *did* you find those clothes? Because people's attitudes regarding physical fitness, social activism, sex roles for men and women, the importance of home life and family, and many other things, do change, it is vital for marketers to monitor the social landscape continually to try to anticipate where these changes will lead.

LIFESTYLE MARKETING

The lifestyle concept is one of the most widely used in modern marketing activities. It provides a way to understand consumers' everyday needs and wants, and a mechanism to allow a product or service to be positioned in terms of how it will allow a person to
▶ pursue a desired lifestyle. A lifestyle marketing perspective recognizes that people sort themselves into groups on the basis of the things they like to do, how they like to spend their leisure time and how they choose to spend their disposable income.[4] These choices in turn create opportunities for market segmentation strategies that recognize the potency of a consumer's chosen lifestyle in determining both the types of products purchased and the specific brands more likely to appeal to a designated lifestyle segment.

Products are the building blocks of lifestyles

To study lifestyles is to appreciate the profoundness of the superficial, as one lifestyle analyst has put it.[5] According to a German survey of 291 of the biggest marketing research and advertising agencies, 68 per cent of them used lifestyle research of some kind, mostly for the sectors of food, cosmetics, cars, drinks and fashion and clothing.[6] Consumers often choose products, services and activities over others because they are associated with a certain lifestyle. For this reason, lifestyle marketing strategies attempt to position a product by fitting it into an existing pattern of consumption. That explains why cool restaurants, bars, and hotels like the Buddha Bar and Man Ray in Paris are branching out by selling CDs featuring the music playing on site. Aspiring lounge lizards can recreate the 'insider' experience without leaving home.[7]

Because a goal of lifestyle marketing is to provide consumers with opportunities to pursue their chosen ways to enjoy their lives and express their social identities, a key aspect of this strategy is to focus on product usage in desirable social settings (see Chapter 10). The goal of associating a product with a social situation is a long-standing one for advertisers, whether the product is included in a round of golf, a family dinner or a night at a glamorous club surrounded by the hip-hop elite or sporting and football stars.[8] Thus people, products and settings are combined to express a certain consumption style, as shown in Figure 15.1.

Product complementarity

The adoption of a lifestyle marketing perspective implies that we must look at *patterns* of behaviour to understand consumers. We can get a clearer picture of how people use products to define lifestyles by examining how they make choices in a variety of product categories. Indeed, many products and services do seem to 'go together', usually because they tend to be selected by the same types of people. In many cases, products do not seem to 'make sense' if unaccompanied by companion products (e.g. fast food and paper plates, or a suit and tie) or are incongruous in the presence of others (e.g. a big, upholstered chair in a high-tech office or the IKEA ad, shown opposite). Therefore, an important part of lifestyle marketing is to identify the *set* of products and services that seems to be linked in consumers' minds to a specific lifestyle. As one study noted, 'all goods carry meaning, but none by itself . . . The meaning is in the relations between all the goods, just as music is in the relations marked out by the sounds and not in any one note.'[9]

Figure 15.1 Linking products to lifestyle

This ad illustrates how a product offering can be highly complementary to the lifestyle of the decision maker – in this case, the wife.

S, C, P, F . . . , Patricia Luján, Carlitos. Photo: Biel Capllonch

▶ **Product complementarity** occurs when the symbolic meanings of different products are related to each other.[10] Bacardi rum and Coca-Cola have for some time advertised their products together. And, research evidence suggests that even a relatively unattractive product becomes more appealing when evaluated with other, liked products.[11] Some marketers have gone as far as putting their brands on the same product, a phenomenon known as *co-branding*.[12] For example, in various European countries one product variant of Häagen-Dazs ice cream was co-branded with Bailey's Irish Cream liqueur. Another venture was Courvoisier's entry into the world of fashion with the parent company Allied Domecq (the world's second-largest spirits company) launching a collection of luxury sportswear for men and women in its 'Atelier Courvoisier' collection, and planning similar extensions for its other brands (such as Stolichnaya vodka and Malibu coconut

579

rum).[13] Most often, though, consumers themselves, inspired by opinion leaders and other parts of the culture production system (see Chapters 10 and 13 as well), will construct the product complementarities themselves.

▶ These sets of products, termed **consumption constellations**, are used by consumers to define, communicate and perform social roles.[14] For example, the (American) 'yuppie' of the 1980s was defined by such products as a Rolex watch, BMW car, Gucci briefcase, a squash racket, fresh pesto, white wine and brie. Sometimes these constellations do actually take the form of anti-constellations from the very beginning, at least for some consumer segments. That is, people define their own style more in terms of what they are not, through a set of non-choices (due to lack of affordability, accessibility or availability) or anti-choices (due to abandonment, avoidance or aversion) of products and/or brands.[15] What positive and/or negative consumption constellations might characterize you and your friends today?

Psychographics

As Chloe and Poppy's lifestyle choices demonstrated, consumers can share the same demographic characteristics and still be very different people. For this reason, marketers need a way to 'breathe life' into demographic data to identify, understand and target consumer segments that will share a set of preferences for their products and services. Chapter 5 discussed some of the important differences in consumers' self-concepts and personalities that play a big role in determining product choices. When marketers combine personality variables with knowledge of lifestyle preferences, they have a powerful

▶ lens that they can focus on consumer segments. This tool is known as **psychographics**, which involves the description of consumers based mainly on such psychological and social psychological factors as values, beliefs and attitudes, and is used to explain why these consumers have a propensity to consume certain products or brands, use certain services, devote time to certain activities and use certain media.[16]

Psychographic research was first developed in the 1960s and 1970s to address the shortcomings of two other types of consumer research: motivational research and quantitative survey research. *Motivational research*, which involves intensive personal interviews and projective tests, yields a lot of information about individual consumers. The information gathered, however, was often idiosyncratic and deemed not very useful or reliable.[17] At the other extreme, *quantitative survey research*, or large-scale demographic surveys, yields only a little information about a lot of people. As some researchers observed, 'The marketing manager who wanted to know why people ate the competitor's cornflakes was told "32 per cent of the respondents said *taste*, 21 per cent said *flavour*, 15 per cent said *texture*, 10 per cent said *price*, and 22 per cent said *don't know* or *no answer*".'[18]

In many applications, the term 'psychographics' is used interchangeably with 'lifestyle' to denote the separation of consumers into categories based on differences in choices of consumption activities and product usage. While there are many psychographic variables that can be used to segment consumers, they all share the underlying principle of going beyond surface characteristics to understand consumers' motivations for purchasing and using products. Demographics allow us to describe *who* buys, but psychographics helps us understand *why* they buy.

Conducting a psychographic analysis

Some early attempts at lifestyle segmentation 'borrowed' standard psychological scales (often used to measure pathology or personality disturbances) and tried to relate scores on these tests to product usage. As might be expected, such efforts were largely disappointing (see Chapter 5). These tests were never intended to be related to everyday consumption activities and yielded little in the way of explanation for purchase behaviours. The technique is more effective when the variables included are more closely related to actual consumer behaviours. If you want to understand purchases of household cleaning products, you are better off asking people about their attitudes towards household cleanliness than testing for personality disorders.

Psychographic studies can take several different forms:

- A *lifestyle profile* looks for items that differentiate between users and non-users of a product.
- A *product-specific profile* identifies a target group and then profiles these consumers on product-relevant dimensions.
- A *general lifestyle segmentation* places a large sample of respondents into homogeneous groups based on similarities of their overall preferences.
- A *product-specific segmentation* tailors questions to a product category. For example, if a researcher wants to conduct research for a stomach medicine, they might rephrase the item, 'I worry too much' as, 'I get stomach problems if I worry too much'. This allows them to more finely discriminate among users of competing brands.[19]

AIOs

Most contemporary psychographic research attempts to group consumers according to some combination of three categories of variables – **a**ctivities, **i**nterests and **o**pinions – which are known as **AIOs**. Using data from large samples, marketers create profiles of customers who resemble each other in terms of their activities and patterns of product usage.[20] The dimensions used to assess lifestyle are listed in Table 15.1.

To group consumers into common AIO categories, researchers give respondents a long list of statements, and respondents are asked to indicate how much they agree with each one. Lifestyle is thus teased out by discovering how people spend their time, what they find interesting and important and how they view themselves and the world around them, as well as demographic information.

Typically, the first step in conducting a psychographic analysis is to determine which lifestyle segments are producing the bulk of customers for a particular product. Researchers attempt to determine who uses the brand and try to isolate heavy, moderate and light users. They also look for patterns of usage and attitudes towards the product. In some cases, just a few lifestyle segments account for the majority of brand users.[21] Marketers primarily target these heavy users, even though they may constitute a relatively small number of total users.

After marketers identify and understand their heavy users, they consider more specifically how these customers relate to the brand. Heavy users may have quite different

Table 15.1 Lifestyle dimensions

Activities	Interests	Opinions	Demographics
Work	Family	Themselves	Age
Hobbies	Home	Social issues	Education
Social events	Job	Politics	Income
Holiday	Community	Business	Occupation
Entertainment	Recreation	Economics	Family size
Club membership	Fashion	Education	Dwelling
Community	Food	Products	Geography
Shopping	Media	Future	City size
Sports	Achievements	Culture	Stage in life cycle

Source: William D. Wells and Douglas J. Tigert, 'Activities, interests and opinions', *Journal of Advertising Research* 11 (August 1971): 27–35.

reasons for using the product; they can be further subdivided in terms of the *benefits* they derive from using the product or service. For instance, marketers at the beginning of the walking shoe craze assumed that purchasers were basically burned-out joggers. Subsequent psychographic research showed that there were actually several different groups of 'walkers', ranging from those who walk to get to work to those who walk for fun. This realization resulted in shoes aimed at different segments.

Uses of psychographic segmentation

Psychographic segmentation can be used in a variety of ways.

- *To define the target market.* This information allows the marketer to go beyond simple demographic or product usage descriptions (such as, middle-aged men or frequent users).

- *To create a new view of the market.* Sometimes marketers create their strategies with a 'typical' customer in mind. This stereotype may not be correct because the actual customer may not match these assumptions. For example, marketers of a facial cream for women were surprised to find their key market was composed of older, widowed women who turned out to be their heavy users, rather than the younger, more sociable women to whom they were pitching their appeals.

- *To position the product.* Psychographic information can allow the marketer to emphasize features of the product that fit in with a person's lifestyle. A company that wants to target people whose lifestyle profiles show a high need to be around other people might focus on its product's ability to help meet this social need.

- *To better communicate product attributes.* Psychographic information can offer very useful input to advertising creatives who must communicate something about the product. The artist or writer obtains a much richer mental image of the target consumer than they can obtain through simply looking at dry statistics, and this insight improves their ability to 'talk' to that consumer.

- *To develop overall strategy.* Understanding how a product fits, or does not fit, into consumers' lifestyles allows the marketer to identify new product opportunities, chart media strategies and create environments most consistent and harmonious with these consumption patterns. For example, inexpensive airline tickets have become very popular in Germany, with intra-country fares often lower than the price of a train ticket. The increase in flights has sparked concern of environmental worries among 'the greens', even though the greens are one of the market segments most likely to book the low fare airline tickets. Research has shown that conflicting values (in this case, low fares vs. air pollution and the carbon footprint) can be addressed in promotions by better understanding the motives that cause the tensions.[22]

- *To market social and political issues.* Psychographic segmentation can be an important tool in political campaigns and policymakers can also employ the technique to find similarities among types of consumers who engage in destructive behaviours, such as drug use, excessive gambling or binge drinking. A psychographic study of men aged 18 to 24 who drink and drive highlighted the potential for this perspective to help in the eradication of harmful behaviours. Researchers divided this segment into four groups: 'good timers', 'well adjusted', 'nerds', and 'problem kids'. They found that one group in particular – 'good timers' – is more likely to believe that it is fun to be drunk, that the chances of having an accident while driving drunk are low, and that drinking increases one's appeal to the opposite sex. Because the study showed that this group is also the most likely to drink at rock concerts and parties, is most likely to watch MTV, and tends to listen to album-oriented rock radio stations, reaching 'good timers' with a prevention campaign was made easier because messages targeted to this segment could be placed where these drinkers were most likely to see and hear them.[23]

Lifestyle segmentation typologies

Marketers are constantly on the lookout for new insights that will allow them to identify and reach groups of consumers that are united by a common lifestyle. To meet this need, many research companies and advertising agencies have developed their own *segmentation typologies* which divide people into segments. Respondents answer a battery of questions that allow the researchers to cluster them into a set of distinct lifestyle groups. The questions usually include a mixture of AIOs, plus other items relating to their perceptions of specific brands, favourite celebrities, media preferences and so on. These systems are usually sold to companies wanting to learn more about their customers and potential customers.

At least at a superficial level, many of these typologies are fairly similar to one another, in that a typical typology breaks up the population into roughly five to ten segments. Each cluster is given a descriptive name, and a profile of the 'typical' member is provided to the client. Lifestyle categories in this system include such segments as 'avant-gardians' (interested in change), 'pontificators' (traditionalists, very British), 'chameleons' (follow the crowd) and 'sleepwalkers' (contented underachievers). Unfortunately, it is often difficult to compare or evaluate different typologies, since the methods and data used to devise these systems are frequently *proprietary* – this means that the information is developed and owned by the company, and the company feels that it would not be desirable to release this information to outsiders.

Lifestyle analyses are widely used in Europe. Below we will provide some examples of such international lifestyle segmentation efforts.

RISC

Since 1978, the Paris-based Research Institute on Social Change (RISC) has conducted international measurements of lifestyles and socio-cultural change in more than 40 countries, including most European countries. The long-term measurement of the social climate across many countries makes it possible to give more qualified guesses and anticipations of future change. It makes it possible to see signs of change in one country before it eventually spreads to other countries. For example, concern for the environment appeared in Sweden in the early 1970s, then in Germany in the late 1970s, in France at the beginning of the 1980s and in Spain in the early 1990s.[24]

RISC asks a battery of questions to identify people's values and attitudes about a wide range of issues. It combines the answers to measure 40 'trends' such as 'spirituality' or 'blurring of the sexes'. Based on statistical analysis of the respondents' scores on each trend, each individual is located in a virtual space described by three axes, representing the three most discriminating dimensions in the data material. RISC then divides the population into ten segments referring to their position in this virtual space. The three axes are:

1 *Exploration/stability*: the vertical axis separates people motivated by change, creativity, volatility and openness from people motivated by stability, familiarity, tradition and structure.

2 *Social/individual*: the horizontal axis distinguishes people oriented towards collective needs from people oriented more towards satisfaction of individual needs.

3 *Global/local*: the third axis indicates a distance between people who are comfortable with broad and unfamiliar environments, multiple loose connections and large-scale networking from people preferring close-knit relationships and a desire for the elements of life to be connected in a predictable manner. Figure 15.2 illustrates the ten segments (G for global, L for Local (behind)) and their main life aspirations.

Each of the 40 trends can also be located in the space according to the gravity point of the people who scored highest on the particular trend. Trends that are related to exploration will thus be located near the top of the map, individualism trends to the right,

Figure 15.2 The ten RISC segments

Source: *RISC Methodology* (Paris: RISC International, 1997): 14.

locality trends are smaller because they are at the back, and so on. While the position of the trends tends not to vary greatly, the percentage of various populations (countries, age groups, heavy users of a brand) supporting each trend will differ greatly. In the example in Figure 15.3, the indices are for the UK as compared to the European total. Darker colours indicate the trends that are more important in Britain as compared to the European average: cultural mobility, expanding vitality, narrow bounds, law and leaders, social recognition, well-being and epicurism (a quality-of-life orientation towards 'the finer things' in life).

The use of RISC typically involves identifying users of a brand and understanding those users better; it is also used to monitor changes in the profiles of users over time. Furthermore, potential target groups, the product benefits and the kind of communication that would attract and reach them can be indicated by systems such as RISC. In the example in Figure 15.4 we see the lifestyle profiling of German car brand B (approximately 21 per cent of the population) and car brand M (approximately 19 per cent) as their first, second or third choice if they were going to buy a new car. Car brand B has a strong profile, individual and experimental, with both global and local orientations. Car brand M, in contrast, has a more uniform profile, with evidence of popularity across all segments of the population. However, there is a very strong presence in cell 1, the group that is most interested in new designs, technologies and functions.

CCA socio-styles

A Paris-based agency, the CCA (Centre de Communication Avancé), introduced a European lifestyle typology in the early 1990s. Although the mapping principle of this lifestyle typology is similar to that of most other typologies, they use a somewhat different methodological approach since their questionnaires are not attitude-based, but use a variety of question formats and also projective techniques, such as various scenario descriptions of future social forms or consumption types that the respondent must relate to, or suggestive drawings and vignettes.[25]

The CCA study divided the European population into 16 lifestyles, regrouped into 6 so-called 'mentalities'. The resulting lifestyle map, presented in the usual suggestive vignette format, is seen in Figure 15.5. One of the advantages of this system was that

Figure 15.3 Trend map of the UK

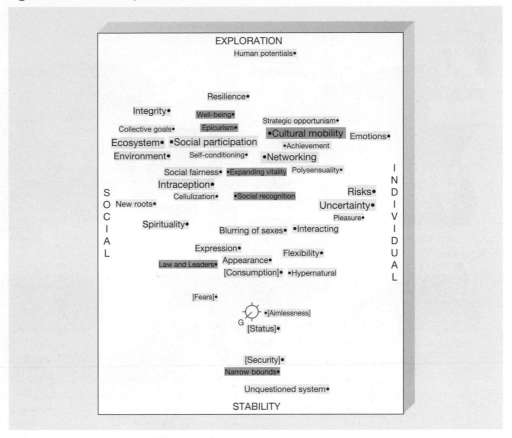

Source: *RISC Methodology* (Paris: RISC International, 1997).

Figure 15.4 Choice of brand for the next new car, Germany, brand B/brand M, 1995

Source: *RISC Methodology* (Paris: RISC International, 1997).

the 16 individual lifestyles could be gathered in other larger groups rather than just the mentalities to form marketing segments specifically adapted to a specific product sector. So some lifestyles would be grouped to form food segments, others to form car segments. In terms of innovative approaches used for lifestyle segmentation, this is probably one of the more interesting ones.[26]

Figure 15.5 CCA Eurostyles, 16 lifestyles in 6 mentalities

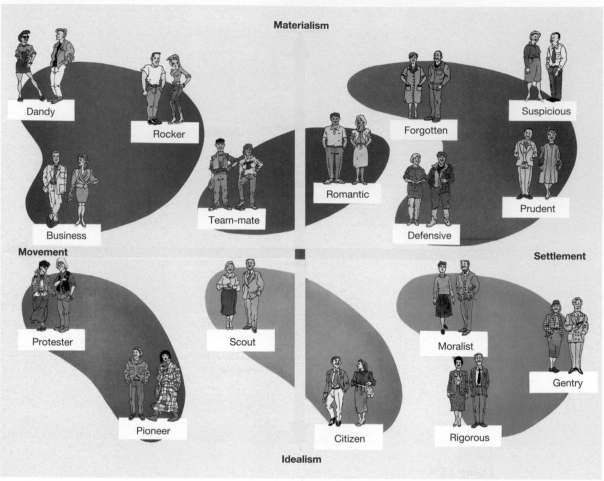

Source: CCA, Paris, 1990.

Lifestyles outside western Europe

VALS

▶ The most well-known and widely used segmentation system in America is **VALS (Values and Lifestyles System)**, developed at SRI International and now operated out of SRI Consulting Business Intelligence in California.[27] Originally, VALS combined two perspectives to create lifestyle clusters. One was based on Maslow's hierarchy of needs (discussed in Chapter 6). Maslow's hierarchy stipulates that people's needs must be satisfied sequentially – that is, companionship is not a priority until physical needs are met, and so on. The second perspective was based on the distinction made by the sociologist David Riesman between *inner-directed* people, who value personal expression and individual taste, and *outer-directed* people, who tend to be swayed by the behaviour and reactions of others.

Responding to criticisms of the VALS model, as well as to changing social values, the developers updated the system. Increasing social diversity made social values less effective as predictors of consumer behaviour. The current VALS system measures consumer behaviour on the basis of psychological dimensions, which are more resilient in periods of social change, and key demographics.

Figure 15.6 VALS segments

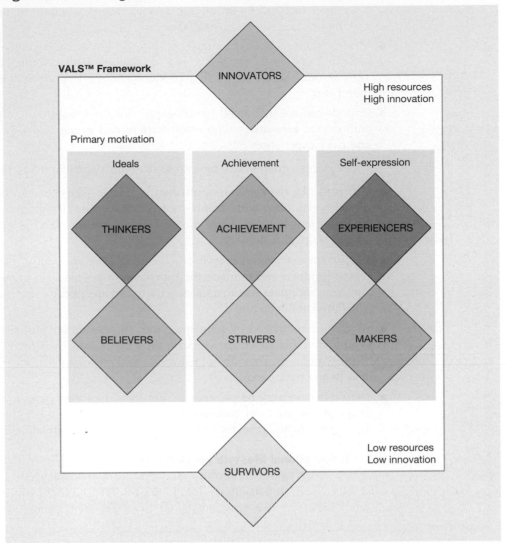

The current VALS system divides US adults into eight groups determined both by psychological characteristics and 'resources', which include such factors as income, education, energy levels and eagerness to buy. In the VALS structure, groups are arrayed vertically by resources and horizontally by primary motivation, as shown in Figure 15.6. Three self-orientations comprise the horizontal dimension. Consumers with an *ideals* orientation rely on a belief system to make purchase decisions, and they are not concerned with the views of others. People with an *achievement* orientation are more competitive; they take into account what their peers will think about their decisions and how these choices will reflect upon them. Finally, those with a *self-expression* orientation are more concerned with the emotional aspects of purchases and the satisfaction they will personally receive from products and services.

'*Innovators* are at the top of the figure because they have the highest level of resources. Innovators are characterized by success, sophistication, high self-esteem and by a "take-charge" attitude to life. They are very open to new ideas and technology, being active consumers with cultivated tastes for up-market, niche products and services. The next three groups also have sufficient resources but differ in their primary motivation':[28]

- *'Thinkers* are driven primarily by ideals. They are satisfied, reflective and comfortable. They tend to be well-educated and actively seek out information in the decision-making process'.[29]

- *'Achievers* are motivated by the desire for achievement; have goal-oriented lifestyles and prefer consensus, predictability and stability over risk, intimacy and self-discovery. They favour established, prestige products and services which demonstrate success to their peers'.[30]

- *'Experiencers* are motivated by self-expression, and tend to be impulsive, young and enthusiastic consumers who enjoy variety and excitement especially new, offbeat and risky experiences'.[31]

The next three groups have fewer resources but also differ in their primary motivation:

- *'Believers*, like thinkers, are motivated by ideals. They tend to be conservative and conventional, often with deeply rooted moral codes. Family, home and community are important to them. They choose familiar products and established brands, and tend to be loyal customers'.[32]

- *'Strivers'* primary motivation is achievement. They are trendy and fun-loving, favour stylish products and emulate the purchases of people with greater material wealth. For them, shopping is both a social activity and an opportunity to demonstrate to their peers their ability to buy'.[33]

- *'Makers* are motivated by self-expression. They value self-sufficiency. They are more likely than other groups to work on their cars, bottle their own vegetables, or build their own houses. They do not value material possessions, prefer value to luxury and tend to buy basic products'.[34]

- *'Survivors* have very few resources, and their main concerns are safety and security. Because they are most concerned with meeting needs rather than fulfilling desires, they do not have a primary motivation. They are cautious consumers.'[35]

Other international lifestyle segmentations

Japanese culture values conformity; one way to refer to the desire to fit in is *hitonami consciousness*, which translates as 'aligning oneself with other people'. Despite this overall emphasis, there is a growing segment of Japanese consumers who are swimming against the tide. These people have been called 'life designers' to reflect their interest in crafting their own lifestyle patterns. One Japanese segmentation scheme divides consumers into 'tribes' and includes among others the 'crystal tribe' (which prefers well-known brands), 'my home tribe' (family oriented) and 'impulse buyer tribe'.[36]

The value of lifestyle typologies

Generally, lifestyle analyses of consumers are exciting because they seek to provide a sort of complete sociological view of the market and its segments and trends, but their general character is their biggest weakness, since the underlying assumption – that these general segments have relatively homogeneous patterns of consumer behaviour – is far from proven.[37] One needs only to consider the index numbers in Figure 15.4 to realize that the predictive power of this typology is not extraordinary. Add to this the generally weak theoretical foundation and the problems of reliability and validity linked to the large-scale questionnaires and to the operationalization of complex social processes in simple variables, and it is understandable why some marketers see lifestyles more as a way of 'thinking the market' and as an input to creative strategies than as descriptions of segments defined by their consumer behaviour.[38]

One attempt to overcome the problem of generally defined segments is the introduction of sectorial lifestyles, an idea proposed by the CCA in the 1980s. The principle behind sectorial lifestyles is that only variables (attitudes, behaviour, etc.) that are considered relevant to a specific domain of consumption are included in the survey. The lifestyles defined on the basis of such an approach thus pertain to this specific sector of consumption only.

Syndicated surveys

A number of companies who track changes in values through large-scale surveys sell the results of these studies to marketers, who often also pay a fee to receive regular updates on changes and trends. This approach originated in the mid-1960s. It is often useful to go beyond simple demographics like a person's age to understand the values and preferences a group of people might have in common. This philosophy applies to understanding the youth market – as much as adults would like to lump all young people together, in fact there are important differences among them in terms of what they value and these priorities may mean that they have more in common with a young person halfway around the globe than with the person next door.

Behavioural targeting

▶ The latest and hottest extension of lifestyle marketing is **behavioural targeting**, which refers to presenting people with advertisements based on their Internet use. In other words, with today's technology it has become fairly easy for marketers to tailor the ads you see to websites you have visited. Some critics feel this is a mixed blessing because it implies that big companies are tracking where we go and keeping this information.

Indeed, there are important privacy issues still to be resolved, but interestingly many consumers seem more than happy to trade off some of their personal information in exchange for information they consider more useful to them. A 2006 survey on this issue reported that 57 per cent of the consumers it polled say they are willing to provide demographic information in exchange for a personalized online experience. And three-quarters of those involved in an online social network felt that this process would improve their experience because it would serve to introduce them to others who share their tastes and interests. However, a majority still express concern about the security of their personal data online.[39] Pro or con, it is clear that behavioural targeting is starting to take off in a big way:

- Microsoft combines personal data from the 263 million users of its free Hotmail e-mail service – the biggest in the world – with information it gains from monitoring their searches. When you sign up for Hotmail, the service asks you for personal information including your age, occupation, and address (though you are not required to answer). If you use Microsoft's search engine it calls Live Search, the company keeps a record of the words you search for and the results you clicked on. Microsoft's behavioural targeting system will allow its advertising clients to send different ads to each person surfing the Web. For instance, if a 25-year-old financial analyst living in a big city is comparing prices of cars online, BMW could send them an ad for a Mini Cooper. But it could send a 45-year-old suburban businessperson with children who is doing the same search an ad for the X5 SUV.[40]

- Claria released its PersonalWeb service that allows people to download a piece of tracking software and receive a home page filled with news stories and other information tailored to their interests. If a man, for example, downloaded the software for and surfed through stories about the UEFA cup and car reviews, his PersonalWeb home page would reflect those interests the next time he clicked on it. It might also include ads from car companies and from stores selling merchandise for his favourite football team.

- **Blockbuster.com** uses software that recommends video to a customer based on attributes the flick shares with other movies they have already ordered. This results in some suggestions that may not be immediately obvious. For example, someone who watched *Crash* might receive a recommendation for *Little Miss Sunshine* because both involve dysfunctional social groups, dynamic pacing and an interdependent ensemble cast. Blockbuster says the service has increased its average customer's 'to watch list' by almost 50 per cent.[41]

- MySpace uses personal details users put on their profile pages and blogs to sell highly targeted advertising in ten broad categories such as finance, autos, fashion, and music. Facebook is hard at work on a similar system, and it hopes to use sophisticated software to decide how receptive a user will be to an ad based not only on their personal information but that of their friends – even if they haven't explicitly expressed interest in that topic.[42]

 However, behavioural lifestyle marketing brings threats was well as opportunities for consumers, as represented by **cybercrime** (see Marketing threat box).

▶ Marketing threat

Threats to the consumer from cybercrime

'The large-scale computer virus attacks of the 1990s, and the internet "worms" that were prevalent at the beginning of this decade have largely been brought under control. At the same time, firewalls and other perimeter security measures have reduced the number of hacking attacks carried out against enterprises. But this does not mean that either consumers, or companies, can afford to be complacent.

"Consumers don't understand the larger definition of being safe," says Janice Chaffin, group president of the consumer division at security vendor, Symantec. "Virus threats have been mediated but phishing, being spoofed or [inadvertently] sharing information online are not protected by anti-virus measures. Consumer behaviour has to change." For Ms Chaffin, the consumers most at risk online fall into one of two categories: the naïve, and those who think they know better.

 There is the consumer who thinks he or she is protected, because they have installed some virus-scanning software, but who remains vulnerable to **phishing** and other social engineering attacks.

But more dangerous still is the consumer who actively shuns protection, because it slows down their computers. Hard-core gamers are a particularly troublesome group, Ms Chaffin says. "We have to take care of both types of consumers . . ."

The first group is more exposed to both data loss and security threats simply because they are on the road. The second can be a highly effective way of bringing vulnerabilities into even the most well-protected enterprise IT environment . . . For Ms Chaffin, education is the main way to reduce these risks. And it is also the best way, she believes, to tackle the downside of the so-called consumerisation of IT, and especially, the trend for people to use personal devices at and for work . . .

"The biggest thing that drives adoption is threats," Ms Chaffin points out. "If a threat occurs people start buying security. So education comes in to play here, educating people about what kind of security they need to have. I think CIOs have up until now thought about barriers, about keeping things out, as the best form of protection. It is giving consumers the right practices so that the chances of them becoming a carrier of an infection, so to speak, are smaller." . . .

Ms Chaffin believes that responsibility for the security of consumers is shared between the computer operating system vendors, internet service providers, security specialists and companies that do business online. Once again, it is education holds the key.

"Today we are at an inflexion point. Millions of people are doing things online, and it would not be hard for someone to steal vast amounts of information from people, so they're very hesitant to do things online," she cautions. "We have a responsibility to make sure we can keep people safe online, whether they are dealing with enterprises or dealing with their peers." '[43]

Source: 'Consumers hold key to securing the net', 4 July 2008 (Pritchard, S.), Copyright Guardian News & Media Ltd 2008.

▲ Marketing opportunity

Connectivity for the vacationing consumer

'The temptation to throw the laptop and the BlackBerry in with the suntan lotion, sunglasses and bathing costume is irresistible for many business people – even when the trip they are about to take is supposed to be holiday rather than work . . . Leif-Olof Wallin of Gartner, the IT consultancy notes that "we see more and more people bringing along a notebook on vacation".

So what options does the vacationing business traveller have for staying in touch with the office? Staying connected while on holiday has become easier in recent years thanks to the expanding range of portable hardware devices and the growing penetration of wireless e-mail and data services including cellular and Wi-Fi-based services . . .

The choice of what hardware to travel with is an important consideration, but arguably ensuring connectivity while outside the office is even more crucial. Fortunately the spread of Wi-Fi hotspots and the advent of 3G broadband wireless services have made this easier . . .

Mobile phone owners can use one of the new internet-based mobile VoIP (voice over internet protocol) services such as Jajah (**www.jajah.com**), Yeigo (**www.yeigo.com**) or Rebtel (**www.rebtel.com**) to cut call costs, or use a PC with an internet connection, Skype software and a headset or USB phone to make a call.

For international travellers with access to a Wi-Fi connection . . . another alternative is to carry a Skype-based Wi-Fi handset . . . Most network equipment makers and others including Apple also offer portable Wi-Fi routers which can be plugged into a hotel Ethernet connection and enable the user to set up an instant and secure in-room Wi-Fi "hotspot" that can be used for data or VoIP voice communications.

If you already carry a 3G cellular wireless data card for use in a laptop, you can also add a wireless datacard mobile router such as Kyocera's KR2 (**www.kyocera.com**). This clever device enables users to create an instant Wi-Fi hotspot anywhere there is a 3G signal simply by plugging a 3G datacard or USB device into the box.

. . . Enabling allows users to stay connected to the corporate network via their mobile device while

Staying connected in all areas of personal and professional life.

Getty Images

on holiday poses several challenges . . . [including] manageability and security. "By allowing these devices to be remotely updated, locked or wiped, enables greater confidence in organisations to empower employees to work from anywhere at anytime."

And that includes the beach.'[44]

Source: 'Staying connected: Technology on holiday', 8 August 2008 (Taylor, P.).

GEOGRAPHIC INFLUENCES ON LIFESTYLES

The consumption patterns of different areas of Europe as well as of the different countries (and their regions) have been shaped by unique climates, cultural influences and resources. These differences at the macro, national and regional levels can exert a major impact on consumers' lifestyles, since many of our preferences in foods, entertainment and so on are dictated by local customs and the availability of some diversions rather than others. The lifestyles of people in each part of Europe (e.g. Western Europe, Eastern Europe and Southeastern Europe), as well as in each country and each region differ in a variety of ways, some quite subtle and some quite noticeable, some easy to explain and some not so obvious. Many companies operating in Europe consider Scandinavia (Denmark, Norway and Sweden) or the Benelux (Belgium, the Netherlands and Luxembourg) to be more or less one market due to the perceived similarities between the countries. Similarly, Southeast Europe (SEE) which comprises Albania, Bosnia and Herzegovina, Croatia, former Yugoslav Republic of Macedonia; and Serbia and Montenegro[45]. Eastern Europe, in turn, consists of Belarus, Republic of Moldova, Russian Federation, and the Ukraine. That there are relative similarities between these countries is a matter of fact. However, marketers should beware of overestimating the homogeneity of such macro-regions. Portraits of macro-regions can be drawn with rough strokes only with a very big brush. In the following section we will look at a couple of examples of such macro-regions in Europe.

In addition, we should be careful of assuming homogeneity within national borders, because between northern and southern Italy, northern and southern Germany, Paris and Provence, London and Scotland there may be large differences in terms of consumption patterns and lifestyles and, consequently, in marketing and marketing research practices.[46] We examine some of the important macro-level aspects of life for European consumers below.

Europe: macro-level consumption differences

Europe consists of over 30 countries with populations that vary from the Russian Federation (143 million) to Liechtenstein (33 thousand); and all in different stages of economic and social development. Table 15.2 summarizes the population and GDP details for member states of the European Energy Agency.

Consumer lives in the European Union

We begin by sketching in the political and economic geography before examining some pictures of consumer lives in the European Union (see Figure 15.7). The EU consists of 27 member states (Austria, Belgium, Bulgaria, Cyprus, the Czech Republic, Denmark, Estonia, Finland, France, Germany, Greece, Hungary, Ireland, Italy, Latvia, Lithuania, Luxemburg, Malta, the Netherlands, Poland, Portugal, Rumania, Slovakia, Slovenia, Spain, Sweden and the United Kingdom) with 23 languages.[47] There are three official candidate

Figure 15.7 Map of European Union Member and Candidate States (2008)

Source: https://www.cia.gov/library/publications/the-world-factbook/geos/ee.html.

Table 15.2 Population and GDP for EEA member countries 2003

Country	Population (1,000s)	GDP (million EUR)	
Germany	82,551	2,072,162	Over 70 million inhabitants
Turkey	70,712	166,092	
France	59,725	1,407,304	
United Kingdom	59,280	1,078,600	
Italy	57,646	944,770	
Spain	41,101	582,408	Over 30 million inhabitants
Poland	38,195	141,807	
Romania	22,200	29,598	
Netherlands	16,215	385,436	
Greece	10,680	120,249	
Belgium	10,348	249,185	
Czech Republic	10,202	49,084	10 million inhabitants
Portugal	10,191	100,758	
Hungary	10,120	46,002	
Sweden	8,956	232,716	
Austria	8,059	217,399	
Bulgaria	7,824	10,959	
Switzerland	7,344	275,660	
Denmark	5,387	162,099	
Slovakia	5,381	20,066	5 million inhabitants
Finland	5,210	131,784	
Norway	4,560	141,203	
Ireland	3,947	94,404	
Lithuania	3,454	7,473	
Latvia	2,321	6,007	
Slovenia	1,964	20,548	
Estonia	1,350	4,515	
Cyprus	770	9,132	
Luxembourg	448	20,823	
Malta	399	3,095	Under 1 million inhabitants
Iceland	286	7,088	
Liechtenstein	33		

Note: These figures, from the EEA data service, are those used as the normalising variables in the scorecard.
Data Sources: GDP 1995 constant prices: Eurostat; Population: the World Bank.

Source: European Environment Agency, 2005. *The European environment – State and outlook 2005*, Copenhagen: 433.

Figure 15.8 Age pyramid in the EU 25 1990 and 2005

% of total population

Men, 1990[1]   Men, 2005   Women, 1990[1]   Women, 2005

Note: 1 EU-25: estimate   *Source*: Eurostat, DEMO database.

Source: Eurostat *The life of women and men in Europe* 2008 edition KS-80-07-135-EN-C page.

countries (Croatia, Turkey, and the former Yugoslav Republic of Macedonia); whilst Albania, Bosnia and Herzegovina, Montenego, and Serbia are recognized as potential candidates, along with Kosovo. The EU population totals over 495 million (2008) and is predicted to reach 505 million by 2060.[48] The population is split approximately in age bands of: nearly 16 per cent between 0 and 14 years old; two-thirds between 15 and 64; and 17 per cent aged 65 and over (Figure 15.8). The EU covers an area of over two-and-a-half million square miles; and has a labour force of 222.5 million (2006 estimate).

McDonald's hamburgers are only part of the offering to consumers in China. The restaurants' western styling and western food are as much of an attraction as the hamburgers themselves.

Corbis/Danny Lehman

Agriculture represents about 2 per cent of GDP in the EU, and employs just over 4 per cent of the labour force; industry represents about 27 per cent of the GDP and employs about 27 per cent of the labour force; and services represent over 70 per cent of the GDP (2006 estimate) and accounts for about 67 per cent of employment.[49]

Sub-regions within the EU are taken increasingly seriously by marketers. Since food consumption is traditionally linked to geographical conditions such as climate, or distance from the sea or mountains, the importance of local or regional patterns of consumption across national borders has been compared to national consumption patterns.[50] The results of an analysis of 138 food-related variables from 15 countries, however, showed that national or linguistic borders seem more significant in defining patterns of food consumption. Figure 15.9 illustrates the 12 general food cultures in Western Europe

Figure 15.9 Twelve possible European food cultures?

Source: Søren Askegaard and Tage Koed Madsen, 'The local and the global: Exploring traits of homogeneity and heterogeneity in European food cultures', *International Business Review* 7(6) (1998).

suggested by this study. To list a few of the defining characteristics of some of the food cultures, the French/French–Swiss, Wallonian and Italian clusters are characterized by, among other things, the importance of sensory pleasure and the high consumption of red wine; the Germanic cluster of countries by a high degree of health consciousness; the Portuguese and Greek food cultures by relatively traditional eating patterns with a fascination for new 'global' food; the Norwegian and Danish food cultures by their openness to convenience products (and, for the Danes, also the love of beer); and the British and Irish for their extraordinary desire for sweets and tea. One large Dutch travel firm has even developed and promoted a resort hotel in Turkey where all the rooms are done in 'Amsterdam style' and, of course, the hotel's menu consists of Dutch favourites.[51]

Interestingly, it is predominantly in the centre of Western Europe that food cultures exhibit overlapping national borders (France–Switzerland; Germany–Switzerland–Austria; the Netherlands–Flanders), the only exception being the British–Irish food culture. The more geographically peripheral countries of Western Europe (Scandinavia, Iberia, Italy and Greece) show 'national food cultures'. Is this due to more exchange and interrelationship historically among the people in the 'crossroads of Europe'? Or is it language that decides basic cultural patterns? If so, this would confirm the famous Whorf–Sapir hypothesis that language is not only a means for expressing culture but actually creates it by instituting certain schemes of classification of events, things and people. The fact that the food cultures defined in this study exactly follow linguistic lines of division (with the exception of there being two French-speaking clusters) could point in that direction. Or it could reflect the simple fact that the language of the questionnaire is very decisive for the response pattern. If the latter is the case, then it would be a strong criticism of the way in which marketers use surveys as a cross-national research instrument.[52] The truth probably lies somewhere between the two.

Grand traits of differences can be located between certain regions in Europe, for instance a distinction between Teutonic, Gallic and Anglo-Saxon styles of communicating,[53] stressing the logical strictness of the argument, its rhetorical qualities and its empirical validity respectively. Such grand traits of similarities do not necessarily permit us to conclude that there are broad similarities in the food consumption or other consumption areas as well. Obviously it is a matter of scope. Certain parts of Europe tend to have consumption patterns similar to each other compared with China, for example. But whether these similarities are detailed enough to be useful to marketers other than in a very broad sense is another question.

Consumer lives in Southeast Europe and Eastern Europe

Following the breakup of the former Soviet Union and Yugoslavia, a number of states have emerged on the European scene which are rapidly converting from central command economies to capitalist-based marketing systems (e.g. decentralization and privatization) and are characterized by growing consumer demand. Table 15.3 illustrates the considerable differences among these countries in terms of population, e.g. Macedonia with 2 million people and the Russian Federation with 143 million; population density, e.g. 9 people per square kilometre in the Russian Federation compared with 128 in the Republic of Moldova; and GDP per capita from 1,900 US dollars per head in the Republic of Moldova to 13,200 US dollars per capita purchasing power parity (PPP) in Croatia. There are also considerable differences in land mass, with Albania and FYR Macedonia covering fewer than 30,000 square kilometres compared with 16.4 million square kilometres in the Russian Federation.[54]

After a difficult period of economic restructuring in the early 1990s, exacerbated by conflicts in the Balkan states of the former Yugoslavia (e.g. Bosnia and Kosovo) and the economic crisis in the Russian Federation (1997/1988), the economies in this region grew

Table 15.3 Area, population and GDP (2005) Eastern and Southeastern Europe

	Population	Land area	Population density	GDP purchasing power parity (PPP)		Agricultural land use*		
	Million	Thousand sq km	People per sq km	Thousand million constant 2000 int. USD	Thousand constant 2000 int. USD per capita	Thousand sq km	% of total land area	Sq km per 1,000 population
Eastern Europe	**204.2**	**17,201**	**12**	**1,758**	**9.6**	**2,684**	**16%**	**13**
Belarus	9.8	207	47	69	7.9	89	43%	9
Republic of Moldova	4.2	33	128	7	1.9	25	77%	6
Russian Federation	143.2	16,381	9	1,395	10.9	2,157	13%	15
Ukraine	47.1	579	81	287	6.8	413	71%	9
Southeastern Europe	**21.7**	**262**	**83**	**–**	**–**	**128**	**49%**	**6**
Albania	3.1	27	114	15	5.3	11	41%	4
Bosnia and Herzegovina	3.9	51	76	27	7.6	21	42%	5
Croatia	4.4	56	79	52	13.2	27	48%	6
Macedonia, FYR of	2.0	25	80	13	7.1	12	49%	6
Serbia and Montenegro	8.2	102	80	–	–	56	55%	7

Data sources: World Bank, 2006 and * FAOSTAT, 2006.

Source: European Environment Agency, 'Sustainable consumption and production in South East Europe and Eastern Europe, Caucasus and Central Asia: Joint UNEP-EEA report on the opportunities and lessons learned', Copenhagen and Geneva EEA Report 3/2007, Table 2.1: 20.

rapidly in the late 1990s (e.g. about 4 to 5 per cent per annum in Southeast Europe and 6 to 8 per cent in Eastern Europe). Growth has not been even across all the economic sectors. The industry and service sectors grew everywhere except for the Republic of Moldova; whilst agricultural growth has generally been limited (see Figure 15.10). Services now represent more than 50 per cent of economic activity in all the economies in Eastern Europe and SEE.[55]

Economic growth has brought increased well-being (e.g. improved levels of life expectancy, literacy, education and standards of living) since the mid-1990s. However the improvements in the quality of life have not been evenly distributed, and the gap between the poorest and the wealthiest sections of society are significantly greater compared with pre-transition times. In Russia the poorest 20 per cent of society received 12 per cent of the total national income in 1991, and the richest 20 per cent of the population shard 31 per cent of the total national wealth (Simai, 2006).[56] By 2003 the poorest section of society (20 per cent) shared only 6 per cent of the wealth, whilst 47 per cent of the wealth went to the richest groups (20 per cent) (World Bank, 2006).[57] The urban-rural gap also remains substantial in terms of income levels, actually widening in Moldova and Russia in this period, but falling in Belarus. Residents in rural areas have limited access to clean energy sources (most notably water), and in Moldova over 50 per cent of the population use wood or coal on open fires or basic ovens. In the large cities a growing urban middle class and nouveau riche is starting to emerge, characterized by

Figure 15.10 Growth in the main economic sectors (Southeast and Eastern Europe: 1995–2005)

Data Source: World Bank, 2006.[58]

Source: European Environment Agency 'Sustainable consumption and production in South East Europe and Eastern Europe, Caucasus and Central Asia: Joint UNEP-EEA report on the opportunities and lessons learned', Copenhagen and Geneva EEA Report 3/2007 Extracts from Figure 2.2: 21.

increasing consumption of private vehicles, meat and detached housing. Evidence of increasing material prosperity can be seen from the increased purchasing power of households compared with the growth in GDP (see Figure 15.11).

Socio-demographic trends (Table 15.4) show falling population levels for a variety of reasons, e.g. increasing mortality rates and a declining birth rate have meant population decline in Russia (Lissovolik, 2005);[59] while mass emigration of workers has caused population decline in Moldova. In line with the rest of Europe, these states are witnessing the same overall demographic trend of a declining birth rate combined with an increasing number of residents aged 65 and over, most notably in Russia. Most of Eastern Europe (with the exception of Moldova) is highly urbanized. 'Dense urban areas can benefit from more efficient provision of services such as multi-apartment housing, heating, collective transport, or waste collection and treatment. On the other hand, in sprawling urban areas the demand for transport can be high and the provision of collective services more difficult to organize. In addition, consumption of processed food and goods, electronics etc; and the generation of household waste is generally higher in urban than in rural areas.'[60]

Household consumption grew by more than 80 per cent between 1995 and 2005 in Eastern and Southeastern Europe. Between 2000 and 2005 basic food and clothing still

Figure 15.11 Household expenditure and government expenditure as a percentage of GDP in Southeast and Eastern European countries

Note: The graph does not include all elements contributing to GDP: exports, imports and investment are not shown. Hence the two bars shown here can add up to less than or be greater than 100%.

Data Source: World Bank, 2006.[61]

Source: European Environment Agency 'Sustainable consumption and production in South East Europe and Eastern Europe, Caucasus and Central Asia: Joint UNEP-EEA report on the opportunities and lessons learned', Copenhagen and Geneva EEA Report 3/2007 Extracts from Figure 2.10: 27.

absorbed most household spending, but the proportion of expenditure on these items fell from 65 to 48 per cent. The additional discretionary spending was used for housing and utilities, transport and communication, home appliances and recreation. Patterns of household consumption varied widely across these countries (see Figure 15.12). Croatian and Serbian households approach the consumption patterns found in EU households much more closely than the other Southeast and Eastern European states. Croatians spend 33 per cent of their household budget on food (the lowest proportion of all these states); and the highest on transport and communication and recreation, culture and healthcare.[62]

In the new emerging European economies many marketers are exploring ways to segment these increasingly consumption-oriented societies. The D'Arcy Masius Benton & Bowles Advertising Agency conducted a psychographic study of Russian consumers, and argued that the country's 150 million consumers can be divided into five segments, including 'Cossacks' (status-seeking nationalists who drive BMWs, smoke Dunhill cigarettes and drink Rémy Martin cognac), 'Kuptsi' (merchants who value practical products and tend to drive Volkswagens, smoke Chesterfields and drink Stolichnaya vodka) and 'Russian Souls' (passive consumers who drive Lada cars, smoke Marlboros and drink Smirnoff).[63]

Table 15.4 Socio-demographic trends in EECCA and SEE countries (1995–2005)

	Population change 1995–2005	Per cent population under 14		per cent population over 65		Urban population %		Housing space per capita m²		Change in total housing space
		1995	2005	1995	2005	1995	2005	1995	2005	
Eastern Europe	−5%	21%	15%	12%	14%	71%	71%	18.4	21.2	10.1%
Belarus	−4%	22%	15%	13%	15%	68%	72%	19.5	22.6	11.1%
Republic of Moldova	−3%	27%	18%	9%	10%	46%	47%	19.9	21.4	4.2%
Russian Federation	−3%	21%	15%	12%	14%	73%	73%	18	20.9	12.2%
Ukraine	−9%	20%	15%	14%	16%	67%	68%	19.2	22	4.8%
Southeast Europe	−9%	23%	19%	10%	14%	50%	52%	–	–	–
Albania	0%	32%	27%	6%	8%	39%	45%	–	–	–
Bosnia and Herzegovina	14%	22%	17%	8%	14%	41%	46%	–	–	–
Croatia	−5%	19%	16%	13%	17%	55%	57%	–	–	–
Macedonia	4%	25%	20%	9%	11%	61%	69%	–	–	–
Serbia and Montenegro	−23%	22%	18%	11%	14%	51%	52%	–	–	–

Data sources: World Bank, 2006;[64] CISSTAT, 2006.[65]

Source: European Environment Agency, 'Sustainable consumption and production in South East Europe and Eastern Europe, Caucasus and Central Asia: Joint UNEP-EEA report on the opportunities and lessons learned', Copenhagen and Geneva EEA Report 3/2007, extracts from Table 2.2: 29.

▲ Marketing future/marketing opportunity

Will nanofoods will be everywhere one day?

After the backlash against GM foods, will consumers accept the idea of nanotechnology into the world of food or is nano set to become the next kitchen battleground . . . ? This is the question posed by Steve Boggan: 'How do you fancy tucking into a bowl of ice cream that has no more fat than a carrot? Or eating a burger that will lower your cholesterol? If you are allergic to peanuts, perhaps you'd like to fix your food so that any nut traces pass harmlessly through your body. Welcome to the world of nanofoods, where almost anything is possible . . . In food, however, the excitement [about developments in nanotechnology] is being matched by health and environmental concerns at all three stages of production: farming, processing and packaging . . .

Nano-futurists don't dispute that, one day, nanofoods will be everywhere . . . But there is a problem. There are signs that consumers will recoil from any food to which this new technology is applied.

However, one firm of German technology analysts, the Helmut Kaiser Consultancy, estimates that hundreds of food companies are conducting research

into nanotechnology. Its latest report says: "The nanofood market [soared] from $2.6bn in 2003 to $5.3bn in 2005 and is expected to reach $20.4bn in 2010. The nano-featured food-packaging market will grow from $1.1bn in 2005 to $3.7bn in 2010. More than 400 companies around the world are active in research, development and production. The US is the leader, followed by Japan and China. By 2010, Asia, with more than 50 per cent of the world population, will become the biggest market for nanofood, with China in the leading position." . . .

In Europe, any nanofoods would have to gain approval under a European Commission directive on new foods and ingredients that was introduced in 1997 to regulate genetically modified products or those manipulated at a molecular level. The directive requires such products to be assessed by member states before a licence can be granted. In Britain, the EU and the US, moves have been made to introduce voluntary codes of practice for research and manufacturing in nanotechnology, but hard legislation is lagging behind . . .

Figure 15.12 Patterns of household expenditure in individual countries in Southeast and Eastern Europe (2005)

Data Sources: CIAATAT, 2006[66]; Statistical Office of Serbia, 2006[67]; Croatian Central Bureau of Stats, 2006.[68]

Source: European Environment Agency 'Sustainable consumption and production in South East Europe and Eastern Europe, Caucasus and Central Asia: Joint UNEP-EEA report on the opportunities and lessons learned', Copenhagen and Geneva EEA Report 3/2007 Extracts from Figure 2.13: 31.

Whether nano-engineered foodstuffs land on our tables will, to a large extent, depend on consumers. If it proves as controversial as GM to many food buyers and environmentalists, then marketing it could be difficult – something of which the industry is well aware. Unilever's Gaudefroy says: "There are areas where debate is vital and it is only just beginning. Much of this is driven by what happened with GM.

We have to explain to consumers the good side of nanotechnology and what benefits it can bring them. Food regulations, in particular the EU's novel-foods directive, prescribe stringent environmental and safety evaluation before anything is introduced to the market."[69]

European advertising preferences and regulations

Consumers in different countries are accustomed to different forms of advertising. In many cases, advertising content is regulated by the government. For example, tobacco advertising in Denmark is not allowed to depict young people, and Swedish tobacco advertising targeted at end-users must not show any people at all. The European Commission in Brussels has taken initiatives to impose even stricter controls on advertising, introducing among other things a total ban on tobacco advertising in Europe.

In Germany, pricing is controlled, and special sales can be held only for a particular reason, such as going out of business or the end of the season. Advertising also focuses more on the provision of factual information rather than on the aggressive hard sell. Indeed, it is illegal to mention the names of competitors.[70] Unlike the Anglo-Saxon advertising culture, comparative advertising is banned in most Latin and Germanic countries in Europe.

But the differences among European countries are not restricted to the legal area. There are also differences concerning which type of television advertising spots and print ads will work best in various European countries. A comparative study of French and German TV spots revealed a distinct profile of the ads in these two countries. French TV ads tended to have less product information, to have a less direct way of communicating about socially sensitive topics, to rely more on non-verbal and implicit communication types and to present women in a more seductive and sexually alluring manner.[71] The same differences concerning the general image of French communication as seductive and imaginative vs. a more factual and sober German style were confirmed when looking at other types of communication such as television news programmes and news magazines. Another study of all ads sent out on a couple of channels in each country confirmed this difference, stressing the more frequent use of puns and the more rapid and personalized rhythm of the French ads, although no difference in information level was found.[72] Surprisingly, in the latter study not one single common ad was sampled in Germany and France. It seems that the use of pan-European advertising is still limited.

▶ One possible explanation for this difference may be due to the distinction between **low-context** and **high-context cultures**.[73] In a high-context culture, messages tend to be more implicit and built into the communication context, whereas communication in low-context cultures tends to be more explicit, specific and direct. France, according to this perspective of classifying culture, is relatively high-context compared with Germany, which belongs among the most low-context cultures in the world.

In comparison, the British have a more favourable attitude to advertising than either the French or the Germans. They tend to think of advertising as a humorous and entertaining part of daily life, and have fewer concerns about its manipulative capacities.[74] Indeed, the British ads may be funnier. One study found a relatively big difference between the degree to which humour is used in televised advertising. Humour was used in 88.8 per cent of British ads compared to 74.5 per cent in France and only 61 per cent in Germany. And in a sample of internationally used ads, the share of humorous ads dropped to 32.2 per cent.[75] It seems that humour is still a very national thing. Or maybe

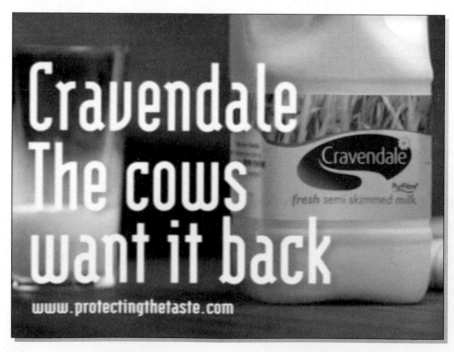

This ad for Cravendale Milk illustrates the use of humour in an advertising message.
The Advertising Archives

there are other explanations? These findings are supported by another source which concluded that, relative to Americans, the British tended to regard advertising as a form of entertainment. Compared with the US, British television commercials also contained less information.[76] One advertising executive stated outright that from watching a sample reel of German and British car ads respectively, it would be evident that the German ones would be much more rational and the British ones much more emotional.[77]

Not only do attitudes about ads vary across Europe, the same can be said for preferences for media. For example, in France outdoor posters are a highly developed and popular medium for creative campaigns. Cinema advertising is also enjoyable to the French. In the UK, adverts in daily newspapers are more important compared with other European countries, and in Germany the radio medium is more important than elsewhere.[78] But the use of various media is difficult to compare among countries due to variations in the regulation of media use: interrupting programmes with advertising is not permitted in Scandinavian countries, for example, and is not practised on German public TV channels.

Cultural differences may influence actual reader comprehension of a certain advertisement. Most of these studies have concluded that ads, like other pictures or communications, are understood culturally, and that readership is so different that a standardized execution of the ad becomes problematic.[79] When two different TV spots (called 'Hitchhiker' and 'Quackers') for the chocolate bar KitKat were tested in six different countries, the consumers (all younger people) showed significant differences in what they retained as the main idea of the ad and the main product characteristic (see Table 15.5).[80]

The variations could be explained by different factors such as relative familiarity with the product concept (in Italy), the small size of the product in relation to local competitors (the Netherlands), popularity of English-style humour (Germany) and the prevailing

Table 15.5 Differences in message decoding of two ads in six European countries

	Main ideas		
	Hitchhiker		**Quackers**
Belgium	Product for young people		You can share it
England		A break with KitKat	
Holland	Product for young people		A break with KitKat
Italy		Product quality	
Germany	To relax		A break with KitKat
France	'Magic effect'		To relax

© Copyright GfK
Source: ESOMAR, Madrid, 1992.

	Main product characteristics		
	Hitchhiker		**Quackers**
Belgium	Good product		Crispy bar
England	Chocolate bar with wafer		A snack
Holland		Little	
Italy		Good product	
Germany	Relax with KitKat		Chocolate bar
France	Crispy bar		Good product

© Copyright GfK
Source: ESOMAR, Madrid, 1992.

Source: J. Andrew Davison and Erik Grab, 'The contributions of advertising testing to the development of effective international advertising: The KitKat case study', *Marketing and Research Today* (February 1993): 15–24. Used with permission.

advertising style in the country (France). It is probably safe to conclude that, although there are often certain similarities in the way ads are understood across cultures, the readership tends to focus on different themes in different countries.[81]

A recent worldwide study by Leo Burnett found that women are 'underserved by our [advertising] industry, at least in terms of being approached with advertising that motivates and moves them in ways they find relevant and meaningful . . . they're tuning out ads that don't present women in realistic and believable ways'.[82] Their research suggested that 'changing perceptions of money, sex, humor, emotion and authenticity' meant that advertisers were having increasing difficulty in reaching this key group which is responsible for up to 80 per cent of consumer decision-making.[83]

Consumer behaviour as I see it . . .

The Latino/a market is one of the fastest growing in the United States. Numbering almost 46 million persons and with annual spending predicted to top 1.1 billion by 2010, it has certainly come into its own over the past two decades. No longer do advertisers have to convince marketers to target this group; the list of firms targeting Latinos/as with products and services includes most major US and other multinational producers and distributors of consumer products and services across the spectrum, including appliances, fast foods and beverages, entertainment, finance, health care, and communications devices and media. Yet although it is gratifying to see Latinos/as in more and more ad campaigns, films, music, and so on, is it possible to use this marketing and media activity to encourage the development of Latino/a communities? The median family income for Hispanics is $34,968, compared to $55,885 for whites, and rates of poverty follow a similar pattern, with almost 40 per cent of Hispanic families living in poverty compared to 20 per cent of white families.

Professor Lisa Peñaloza
École des Hautes Études Commerciales du Nord (EDHEC), Lille, Nice, and Paris, France

Many scholars assert that we live in a consumer society. Although consumption is increasingly a major part of our lives, I suggest that our understanding remains in its adolescence, roughly comparable to views of labour in the decades following the Industrial Revolution. Like workers then, most people now don't look at themselves primarily as consumers; nor do they think a lot about the ways consumption behaviour influences social relations. Instead, most of us tend to think of consumption as satisfying functional needs and symbolic needs limited to status for individuals, without considering how these choices collectively impact relations between minority groups and the mainstream in the US as well as in other nations.

At the time of the Industrial Revolution, workers organized themselves according to their interests, raising consciousness for a greater share in the distribution of resources. Today, consumers appeal to firms for fair trade, decent working conditions, and healthy environmental protections across the world, yet all too often their causes are isolated and geographically dispersed. Although there has been some attention to the increasing demands of consumers in self-service kiosks at airports, grocery stores, and banks, and in benefiting more from marketers' use of cultural meanings fashioned by consumers, we as professors, practitioners, and students have much more work to do to fully develop understanding and consumer consciousness of how consumption factors into minority/mainstream group relations.

Consider tourism. Consumers spend billions every day in places such as San Antonio or Albuquerque consuming culture, which effectively reaffirms and legitimizes Latino/a culture. Yet what does it do for Latino/a people and the development of their communities? A tourist tax is often part of the solution to siphon money back to the community, yet it often goes to the 'squeaky wheels', those best able to advance their causes through city government. Might there be additional ways of encouraging community organizations, artists, musicians, and theater groups to use city facilities in providing consumers more culturally authentic experiences that at the same time develop Latino/a communities in more organically connected tourist markets? This essay asks you to think more deeply and critically about how tourism specifically, and consumption more generally plays a role in the development of what is considered mainstream and minority in the US and in other nations.

Regional consumption differences

Geo-demography

▶ The term **geo-demography** refers to analytical techniques that combine data on consumer expenditures and other socio-economic factors with geographic information about the areas in which people live in order to identify consumers who share common consumption patterns.

Geo-demography is based on the assumption that 'birds of a feather flock together' – that people who have similar needs and tastes tend to live near one another. Given this, it should be possible to locate 'pockets' of like-minded people who can then be reached more economically by direct mail and other methods. Important dimensions in differentiating between neighbourhoods, suburbs, inner-city areas or towns are factors such as income level, ethnic background and demographics (most notably age). Geographic information is increasingly being combined with other data to paint an even more complete picture of the consumer. Several marketing research ventures now
▶ employ **single-source data** where information about a person's actual purchasing history is combined with geo-demographic data, thus allowing marketers to learn even more about the types of marketing strategies that motivate some people to respond.

ETHNIC AND RELIGIOUS SUBCULTURES

 Multicultural dimensions

Sevgi, waking up early on Saturday morning, braces herself for a long day of errands and chores. As usual, her mother expects her to do the shopping while she is at work, and then help prepare the food for the big family get-together tonight. Of course, her older brother would never be asked to do the shopping or help out in the kitchen – these are women's jobs.

Family gatherings make a lot of work, and Sevgi wishes that her mother would use prepared foods once in a while, especially on a Saturday when Sevgi has errands of her own to do. But no, her mother insists on preparing most of her food from scratch; she rarely uses any convenience products, to ensure that the meals she serves are of the highest quality.

Resigned, Sevgi watches TRTint on the family's cable-TV while she's getting dressed, and then she heads down to the local newsagent in 'De Pijp' to buy a magazine – there are dozens of Turkish magazines

and newspapers for sale and she likes to pick up new ones occasionally. Then Sevgi buys the grocery items her mother wants; the Islamic *halal* butcher is a long-time family friend and already has the cuts of lamb prepared for her. The vendors at the open air stalls in the Albert Cuyp Market where she and her mother shop all the time know her, and provide her with choice quality olives and vegetables. One quick stop at the local sweetshop to pick up the family's favourite *drop* (liquorice) and she's almost done. With any luck, she'll have a few minutes to stop at the music shop and pick up the latest Black Eyed Peas CD. She really liked their music on Bob Geldof's Live8 concert worldwide telecast. She'll listen to it in the kitchen while she chops, peels and stirs. Sevgi smiles to herself: despite a busy day preparing the house and meal for the family party, she feels that Amsterdam is a great place to live.

Subcultures and consumer identity

Yes, Sevgi lives in Amsterdam, not Istanbul. However, this consumer vignette could just as easily have taken place in London, Berlin, Stockholm, Marseilles or thousands of other cities throughout Europe. There are well over 25 million Europeans who belong to an ethnic sub-group, and in several European countries such as France, Belgium and Germany, they collectively account for around 10 per cent of the total population. In the UK, the ethnic communities represented are forecast to double in population to over 6 million within the next 30 years.[84]

This picture of Star Trek fans (Trekkies) shows the key role played by microcultures in defining the extended self.

Corbis/Mark Peterson

Turkish consumers have much in common with members of other racial and ethnic groups who live in Europe. These groups of consumers observe the same national holidays, their expenditures are affected by the country's economic health and they may join together in rooting for their host country's national team in the football World Cup. Nevertheless, while European residency (and in most cases European citizenship) provides the raw material for some consumption decisions, others profoundly affect and are profoundly affected by the enormous variations in the social fabric of the country where they live.

Consumers' lifestyles are affected by group memberships *within* the society at large.
▶ These groups are known as subcultures, whose members share beliefs and common experiences that set them apart from others. While subcultural group memberships often have a significant impact on consumer behaviour, some subcultural identifications are more powerful than others. Every one of us belongs to many subcultures. These memberships can be based on similarities in age (major subcultural consumer groups based on age have already been discussed in Chapter 11), race or ethnic background, place of residence. In contrast to larger, demographically based subcultures, people who
▶ are part of a micro-culture, freely choose to identify with a lifestyle or aesthetic preference. Whether 'Dead Heads', 'Netizens', or skinheads, each group exhibits its own unique set of norms, vocabulary and product insignias (such as the British Lonsdale sports and fashion clothier, whose sweatshirts signify white racists to many youths in the Netherlands).[85] These micro-cultures or 'communities' can even gel around fictional characters and events. Many devotees of *Star Trek*, for example, immerse themselves in a make-believe world of starships, phasers, and Vulcan mind melds.[86] Our subcultures and micro-cultures often play a key role in defining the extended self (see Chapter 5) and micro-cultures typically command fierce loyalty.

Ethnic and racial subcultures

Ethnic and religious identity is a significant component of a consumer's self-concept.
▶ An ethnic or racial subculture consists of a self-perpetuating group of consumers who are held together by common cultural and/or genetic ties, and is identified both by its members and by others as being a distinguishable category.[87]

In some countries, such as Japan, ethnicity is almost synonymous with the dominant culture, since most citizens claim the same homogeneous cultural ties (although Japan has sizeable minority populations, most notably people of Korean ancestry). In heterogeneous societies like those found in the US and some parts of Europe, many different cultures are represented, and consumers may expend great effort to keep their subcultural identification from being submerged into the mainstream of the dominant society.

Ethnicity and marketing strategies

Although some companies may feel uncomfortable at the notion that people's racial and ethnic differences should be explicitly taken into account when formulating marketing strategies, the reality is that these subcultural memberships are frequently paramount in shaping people's needs and wants. Research indicates, for example, that membership of these groups is often predictive of such consumer variables as level and type of media exposure, food preferences, the wearing of distinctive apparel, political behaviour, leisure activities and even willingness to try new products.

Furthermore, research evidence indicates that members of minority groups are more likely to find an advertising spokesperson from their own group to be more trustworthy, and this enhanced credibility in turn translates into more positive brand attitudes.[88] In addition, the way marketing messages should be structured depends on subcultural differences in how meanings are communicated. As mentioned earlier in this chapter, sociologists make a distinction between *high-context cultures* and *low-context cultures*. In a high-context culture, group members tend to be tightly knit, and they are likely to infer meanings that go beyond the spoken word. Symbols and gestures, rather than words, carry much of the weight of the message. Many minority cultures are high-context and have strong oral traditions, so perceivers will be more sensitive to nuances in advertisements that go beyond the message copy.[89]

To be or not to be: that is the answer

One important way to distinguish between members of a subculture is to consider the extent to which they retain a sense of identification with their country of origin vs. their host country. As people move from place to place, they may quickly assimilate to their new homes or they may resist the blending process and choose to insulate themselves from the mainstream culture. **Acculturation** refers to the process of movement and adaptation to one country's cultural environment by a person from another country.[90] As Figure 15.13 shows, many factors affect the nature of this transition process. Individual differences, such as whether the person speaks the host country language, influence how difficult the adjustment will be. This is a very important issue for marketers because of our increasingly global society.

The person's contacts with **acculturation agents** – people and institutions that teach the ways of a culture – are also crucial. Some of these agents are aligned with the *culture of origin* (in Sevgi's case, Turkey). These include family, friends, the mosque, local businesses and Turkish-language media that keep the consumer in touch with their country of origin. Other agents are associated with the *culture of immigration* (in this case, the Netherlands), and help the consumer to learn how to navigate in the new environment. These include state schools and Dutch-language media.

As immigrants adapt to their new surroundings, several processes come into play. *Movement* refers to the factors motivating people to uproot themselves physically from one location and go to another. Although many ethnic members throughout Europe are second generation (born in the country where they live), their parents are more likely to have been the first to arrive in the new country. On arrival, immigrants encounter a need for *translation*. This means attempting to master a set of rules for operating in the new environment, whether learning how to decipher a different currency or understanding

Figure 15.13 A model of consumer acculturation

Source: Adapted from Lisa Peñaloza, 'Atravesando fronteras/border crossings: A critical ethnographic exploration of the consumer acculturation of Mexican immigrants', *Journal of Consumer Research* 21 (June 1994): 32–54.

the social meanings of unfamiliar clothing styles. This cultural learning leads to a process of *adaptation*, where new consumption patterns are formed.

As consumers undergo acculturation, several things happen. Many immigrants undergo (at least to some extent) *assimilation*, where they adopt products that are identified with the mainstream culture. At the same time, there is an attempt at *maintenance* of practices associated with the culture of origin. Immigrants stay in touch with people in their country, and many continue to eat ethnic foods and read ethnic newspapers. Their continued identification with their home culture may cause *resistance*, as they resent the pressure to submerge their identities and take on new roles. Finally, immigrants (voluntarily or not) tend to exhibit *segregation*; they are likely to live and shop in places physically separated from the host community. These processes illustrate that ethnicity is a fluid concept and that members of a subculture are constantly recreating its boundaries. Figure 15.13 provides an overview of the processes involved in consumer acculturation.

An *ethnic pluralism* perspective argues that ethnic groups differ from the mainstream in varying degrees, and that adaptation to the larger society occurs selectively. Research evidence argues against the notion that assimilation necessarily involves losing identification with the person's original ethnic group. For example, Sevgi feels comfortable in expressing her 'Turkishness' in a variety of consumption-related ways: the magazines she buys, the TV programmes on the Turkish network she chooses to watch, her choice of ethnically appropriate gifts for events such as weddings and *bayram* (religious holidays).[91] Alternatively, she has no problems at all in expressing consumption behaviours of the mainstream culture – she loves eating *drop* (Dutch liquorice), buys 'Western' music and has her favourite outfits for going out to the cinema and clubs. The best indicator of ethnic assimilation, these researchers argue, is the extent to which members of an ethnic group have social interactions with members of other groups in comparison with their own.[92]

▶ The **progressive learning model** helps us to understand the acculturation process. This perspective assumes that people gradually learn a new culture as they increasingly come in contact with it. Thus, we expect that when people acculturate they will mix the
▶ practices of their original culture with those of their new or **host culture**.[93] Research generally supports this pattern when it examines such factors as shopping orientation, the importance people place on various product attributes, media preference, and brand loyalty.[94] When researchers take into account the intensity of ethnic identification, they find that consumers who retain a strong ethnic identification differ from their more assimilated counterparts in these ways:[95]

- They have a more negative attitude toward business in general (probably caused by frustration as a result of relatively low income levels).
- They are higher users of media that's in their native language.
- They are more brand loyal.
- They are more likely to prefer brands with prestige labels.
- They are more likely to buy brands that specifically advertise to their ethnic group.

The acculturation process embraces all kinds of moves, including those that involve relocating from one place to another within the same country. If you have ever moved (and it is likely you have), you no doubt remember how difficult it was to give up old habits and friends and adapt to what people in your new location do. A recent study of Turkish people who move from the countryside to an urban environment illustrates how people cope with change and unfamiliar circumstances. The authors describe a
▶ process of **warming**, which involves transforming objects and places into those that feel cozy, hospitable, and authentic. The study's informants described the process of turning a cold and unfamiliar house into a home as *güzel* ('beautiful and good', 'modern and warm'). In this context that means incorporating symbols of village life into their new homes by blanketing them with the embroidered, crocheted, and lace textiles that people traditionally make by hand for brides' dowries in the villages. The researchers reported that migrants' homes contained far more of these pieces than they would have in their village homes because they used them to adorn the modern appliances they acquired. The dowry textiles symbolize traditional norms and social networks composed of friends and family in the villages, so they link the 'cold' modern objects with the owner's past. Thus, the unfamiliar becomes familiar.[96]

Another group of researchers examined the plight of people who were forced to leave their homes and settle in a foreign country with little planning and few possessions.[97] As 'strangers in a strange land', they must essentially start over and completely resocialize. The authors did an in-depth study of refugees from a number of countries who lived in an Austrian refugee shelter. They found, for example, that teenagers are traumatized by their experience and turn to adaptive consumption strategies to cope. For example, the adolescents (including the boys) all have stuffed animals they use to comfort themselves. And all of the teenage boys wore earrings as a way to create their own community.

A recent ethnographic study of Turkish women squatters has proposed a new model, 'dominated consumer acculturation' (Figure 15.14), in contrast to the model of post-modern consumer acculturation covered by earlier research. The goal of these authors was to identify the role played by particular socio-cultural structures in acculturation by examining Turkish women peasants who were part of the widespread global phenomenon of mass migration of the rural poor into urban areas. In contrast to earlier studies, this research allowed for a more contextual model of acculturation which took account of the variety of acculturation outcomes. This model proposed 'three modes of acculturation structured by this context: migrants reconstitute their village culture in the city, shutting out the dominant ideology; or they collectively pursue the dominant ideology as a myth through ritualized consumption; or they give up on both pursuits, resulting in a shattered identity project.'[98]

Figure 15.14 Dominated consumer acculturation

Source: Tuba Ustuner and Douglas B. Holt 'Dominated Consumer Acculturation: The Social Construction of Migrant Women's Consumer Identity Projects in a Turkish Squatter' *Journal of Consumer Research* 34 (June 2007) Figure 2: 53.

Religious subcultures

In recent years, we have witnessed an explosion of religion and spirituality in popular culture including the box office success of Mel Gibson's movie *The Passion of the Christ* and the tremendous popularity and controversy surrounding the book *The Da Vinci Code*.[99] You do not have to be active in an organized religion to 'worship' products. A study of a brand community centered on the Apple Newton illustrates how religious themes can spill over into everyday consumption, particularly in the case of 'cult products.' Apple abandoned the Newton PDA years ago, but many avid users still keep the faith. The researchers examined postings in chat rooms devoted to the product. They found that many of the messages have supernatural, religious, and magical themes, including the miraculous performance and survival of the brand, as well as the return of the brand creator. The most common postings concerned instances where dead Newton batteries magically come back to life.[100]

The impact of religion on consumption

Religion *per se* has not been studied extensively in marketing, possibly because it is seen as a taboo subject. The very low-key or non-existent approach by large multinational or pan-European companies reflects the same sort of caution that these companies have in targeting ethnic groups – companies are having to decide whether religiously or ethnically-tailored programmes foster greater brand loyalty or whether any advantage is outweighed by the risks of misreading the target market and causing offence. Without question, the most successful companies targeting and serving both ethnic and religious segments are small businesses, whose managers and owners are often members of the group.[101] However, the little evidence that has been accumulated indicates that religious affiliation has the *potential* to be a valuable predictor of consumer behaviour.[102] Religious subcultures have been shown to exert an impact on such consumer variables as personality, attitudes towards sexuality, birth rates and household formation, income and political attitudes.

Putting together descriptive demographic profiles of Europe's major religious groups is not an exact science. For example, French law prohibits any question on religion in national censuses, although with an estimated 4 to 5 million Muslim inhabitants France undoubtedly has the biggest Islamic community in western Europe. As a faith, Islam is now second only to Roman Catholicism in France.[103] Similar problems with taking a census are found in the UK. Britain's 1.6 million-strong Muslim population is small, but has the fastest growth rate of all religions in the country. The thousand or so existing mosques are likely to be converted warehouses, churches or community halls. The hundreds of new mosques being built feature traditional Islamic domes and minarets – a trend which signals the growing economic vitality of British Muslims, as well as local authorities' growing acceptance of mosques.[104] While Islam is the fastest-growing religion in Europe, it is difficult to generalize about Muslims beyond belief in the teachings of the Koran, identifying holidays and periods of fasting such as Ramadan, and certain dietary restrictions. Coming from more than 120 countries and a variety of ethnic groups (Blacks, Asians, Arabs, Europeans), they are like many groups of consumers in Europe – diverse in their celebrations of consumption habits.

Christianity has dominated the history and cultural development of Europe, and has played an important role in the shaping of the European continent. While the many denominations of Christians make it the largest religious grouping in Europe (roughly 600 million), active membership is on the decline, with fewer and fewer adults attending services on any given Sunday.[105] In response to this trend, the Vatican has been involved in a variety of events aimed at developing closer and more active relationships with Europe's youth. Enlisting French fashion designers for World Youth Day, having Bob Dylan perform at a Vatican-sponsored rock concert, and having Easter Mass and information about the Vatican on a Website are recent attempts to get youth involved with the church.[106] Divided roughly into the more Protestant North and the predominantly Catholic South, Christianity still makes up the majority religion in Europe in terms of claimed membership. Its major holidays of Easter and Christmas and celebrations such as 'Carnival' (*Faschung* in Germany) are celebrated or observed to such an extent that large industries such as travel and retailing rely on these seasons as the times of the year when they earn the most revenues.

THE NEW EURO-CONSUMERS

There are a number of common trends, but there are also big differences in the local contexts in which these trends are found, as well as differences in the degree to which the trend is significant in each individual country. A number of trends seem to be valid for consumer markets in the EU.[107] These include:

- a tendency to more unevenly distributed income;
- an increasing number of older people;
- a decrease in household size;
- a growing proportion of immigrants;
- increase in environmental concern and consumption of 'green' products;
- relatively increasing consumption of services compared to durable goods.

Many European managers expect an increase in the importance of Euro-brands and Euro-consumers.[108] However, *why* and *when* companies should or could adopt pan-European strategies or not remains a complex matter. One study suggested 21 influencing factors on pan-European marketing standardization, including management characteristics, firm characteristics, industry characteristics and government characteristics, but not market characteristics![109]

We believe that consumer behaviour analysis must play an important role in the decision to standardize or adapt marketing strategies. All consumers will differ to some extent in what they buy, why they buy, who makes the purchase decision, how they buy, when they buy and where they buy.[110] Some of these differences may be explained at the lifestyle level and less so on the national level, and some are very obviously related to national or regional differences. It is also obvious that some differences are disappearing, due to the increasingly international supply of goods and the increasing internationalization of the retailing system in Europe.[111] However, not even the fact that similar goods are bought in similar stores across European countries permits us to confirm the existence of just one variety of a Euro-consumer. Product usage and knowledge, and to a certain extent imagery, may be relatively shared among Europeans, but as soon as one takes the contexts of acquisition, consumption and disposal into account, the actual role and meaning of the product in daily life becomes coloured by the local culture. No lifestyle survey has yet demonstrated a truly European profile in any of the lifestyles; European segments continue to be defined in rather abstract common denominators.

It is often asserted that segments such as international business people, or younger people mainly influenced by trends from MTV and other 'global youth culture' phenomena, are especially prone to standardized marketing. European managers are people who tend to be prime consumers of pan-European media, like business magazines or CNN (in hotel rooms).[112] So there may be a tendency to a higher degree of internationalization among younger, wealthier and more educated people. The question is how deep the similarity really is. A study of consumption of luxury goods in five major European markets concluded that the pan-European consumer of luxury brands is between 35 and 49 years old, lives in a major city, has a high income and a university education, and occupies a managerial job. On the other hand, there were big differences between the various countries in the level of brand awareness and purchase level, and the degree of significance of socio-economic factors for purchase of luxury brands. For example, Spain and Italy are strongly segmented due to socio-economic differences, while in France, the UK and Germany these socio-economic differences are less useful in explaining luxury consumption. The level of purchase and awareness was found to be high in France, the UK and Italy, and low in Germany and Spain. The most 'mature' market for luxury brands was France, the UK and a narrow Italian segment, whereas the rest of the Italians lacked the money, the Germans lacked the motivation and the Spanish lacked both.[113]

In general, the absence of one identifiable Euro-consumer does not mean that Svensson of Sweden, Smith of the UK, Smit of Holland, Simón of Spain, Schultz of Germany and Salciuviene of Lithuania cannot have more in common in certain aspects than they have with their compatriots. But it means that these similarities can be analyzed and understood only with methods that are also able to take the differences into consideration. Hence the call for an understanding of the new cultural units that make up today's marketplace of international lifestyles, global issues, national rituals and local habits.[114]

Changing nature of the marketplace

What we can identify is the changing nature of the marketplace for consumers across Europe. One of the most significant trends is the increasing convergence of new technology with consumption: 466 million mobile phones were in use in 2005 and there were 247 million Internet users in 2006.[115] Despite the increasing use of the Internet, television is still the main media. Europeans spend nearly two hours a day watching TV, which is 'three times as much time watching programmes as going online'.[116] There are variations in television consumption across the Europe (e.g. average watching time in the UK and Greece is more than 2.5 hours a day, compared with Austria, Sweden and Switzerland where the average tends to be less than two hours a day, see Figure 15.15).[117]

However, the Internet has an increasing presence in consumer lives both for information search and for purchase (Figure 15.16), although significant barriers remain to buying via the Internet (e.g. lack of credit card for payment; perceived lack of security of payment systems; long delivery times; difficulties of returning goods and seeking redress; low levels of Internet connections (Figure 15.17).[118]

▶ However it is the lack of e-skills which restricts opportunities for many consumers. This means that the increasing importance of electronic technology will work to the

Figure 15.15 Total television consumption in Europe by country

Mean number of total hours people claim to spend watching television on an average weekday
'On an average weekday, how much time, in total, do you spend watching television?'

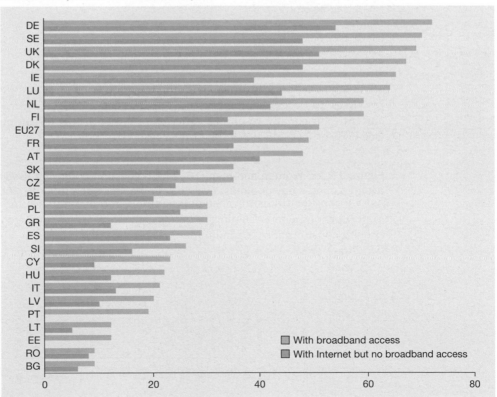

Base: 2,000 per country aged 15+

Source: European Social Survey/nVision.

Sources: Lutz Stobbe EuP Preparatory Studies 'Televisions' (Lot 5) Final Report on Task 3 'Consumer Behaviour and Local Infrastructure' (TREN/D1/40 lot 5-2005), Compiled by Deutsche Umwelthilfe and Fraunhofer IZM, Contractor: Fraunhofer Institute for Reliability and Microintegration, IZM, Berlin, 2 August 2007: 10; nVision/Future Foundation 'Media Consumption in the EU 25'.

Figure 15.16 Percentage of EU individuals who ordered goods or services over the Internet for private use in the last year

Data Source: Eurostat, 2006.

Source: *The Consumer Markets Scoreboard: Monitoring Consumer Outcomes in the Single Market* COM (2008) 31, European Communities, Luxembourg, 2008, Figure 36: 47.

Figure 15.17 Perceived barriers to buying/ordering over the Internet for EU consumers

Data Source: Eurostat, 2006.

Source: *The Consumer Markets Scoreboard: Monitoring Consumer Outcomes in the Single Market* COM (2008) 31, European Communities, Luxembourg, 2008, Figure 42: 50.

▶ advantage of those consumers with the requisite level of **digital literacy** and sufficient resources to access computers and the Internet. However, Euro-consumers are not currently all equally resourced in terms of either access to computers or the Internet (see Figures 15.18, 15.19, 15.20), or their level of e-skills.

Figure 15.18 Women and men (16–24, EU consumers) having used the Internet on average once a day or almost every day in the last three months, 2006

Source: Figure 33 Eurostat *The life of women and men in Europe* 2008 edition KS-80-07-135-EN-C page 40.

Figure 15.19 Women and men (25–54, EU consumers) having used the Internet on average every day or almost every day in the last three months, 2006

MT, RO: no data   *Source*: Eurostat, Community survey on ICT usage in households and by individuals.

Source: Figure 114 Eurostat *The life of women and men in Europe* 2008 edition KS-80-07-135-EN-C page 105.

Figure 15.20 Women and men (55–74, EU consumers) having used the Internet on average every day or almost every day in the last three months, 2006

MT, RO: no data; PT: no data for women   *Source*: Eurostat, Community survey on ICT usage in households and by individuals.

Source: Figure 160 Eurostat *The life of women and men in Europe* 2008 edition KS-80-07-135-EN-C page 149.

 Marketing opportunity or pitfall?

'How skilled are Europeans in using computers and the Internet?

One of the most remarkable developments over the past ten years has probably been the way in which the Internet – previously known only to a small circle of scientists and university students – has infiltrated, and become an important part of, our everyday lives. The Internet is not only changing our way of communicating with friends, relatives and colleagues, but also our way of working and shopping. Many traditional services are slowly being replaced by their electronic or online counterparts: banking, ticket sales, travel and holiday information, contacts with public administration, etc. This rapid growth faces a barrier, however; namely the capability of citizens or the labour force to understand and use the applications or, more generally, their ability to use Information and Communication Technologies.

E-skills at a glance
Graph 1 [Figure 15.21] shows the skill levels of different subgroups of the EU:

▲ Marketing opportunity or pitfall? (*continued*)

Figure 15.21 Individuals' level of basic computer skills (2005), EU-25
(as a percentage of the total number of individuals aged 16 to 74)

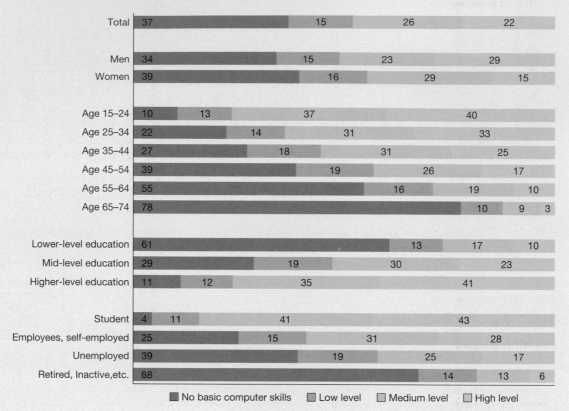

Legend: ■ No basic computer skills   ■ Low level   ☐ Medium level   ☐ High level

Source: Eurostat, Community survey on ICT usage in households and by inviduals.

Source: http://epp.eurostat.ec.europa.eu/cache/ITY_OFFPUB/KS-NP-06-017/EN/KS-NP-06-017-EN.PDF, accessed 12 August 2008.

- a first observation is that 37 per cent have no computer skills whatsoever, while only 22 per cent seem to be acquainted with a wide range of computer activities.
- as expected, educational level is an important factor: while only 11 per cent of people with a higher education have no basic e-skills, this applies to more than 60 per cent of people not educated beyond lower secondary level.
- as regards age, more than 3 out of 4 people over 65 years of age have no computer skills at all, but even among young people aged 16 to 24, about 10 per cent appear to have no basic e-skills.

Digital literacy is a problem for a large part of the population
Digital literacy involves the confident and critical use of Information Communication Technology (ICT)

for work, leisure and communication . . . These basic ICT e-skills cover a wide range of activities from basic skills in computer to Internet. As seen in Graph 1, a considerable proportion of European citizens have no computer skills at all. The fact that 37 per cent of the population lack basic computer skills is not so surprising when considering Graph 2 [Figure 15.22], which shows that more than one in three (34 per cent) of EU residents have *never* used a computer, ranging from 8 per cent in the Nordic countries Sweden, Denmark and Iceland to 65 per cent in Greece. It is clear that a lack of e-skills will prevent these people from participating fully in the information society. In the same graph, we see that a majority of 57 per cent do *not regularly* use the Internet. About 43 per cent have never used it (not in the graph). In Greece, only 18 per cent of people aged 16 to 74 are regularly online (i.e. on average at least once a week).'[119]

Figure 15.22 Individuals not using computers or the Internet (2005)
(as a percentage of the total number of individuals aged 16 to 74)

Notes: Data on computer use not available for Belgium (percentage not regularly using the Internet: 47%); no data available for France and Malta.

Source: Eurostat, Community survey on ICT usage in households and by individuals.

Source: http://epp.eurostat.ec.europa.eu/cache/ITY_OFFPUB/KS-NP-06-017/EN/KS-NP-06-017-EN.PDF, accessed 12 August 2008.

▶ The marketing future?

Looking ahead – into the clouds

'Cloud computing – just a buzz phrase or perhaps the biggest thing to happen in computing since e-commerce? **Gartner**, the research firm says cloud computing heralds an evolution that is no less influential than e-business. **Yahoo** has announced a re-organisation that includes "developing a world-class cloud-computing and storage infrastructure" and **Microsoft** says cloud computing is behind its acquisition of MobiComp, which offers back-up technology for mobile data.

In case cloud computing sounds a bit nebulous . . . Gartner defines it as "a style of computing where massively scalable IT-related capabilities are provided 'as a service', using internet technologies, to multiple external customers" . . .

What seems to be different . . . is the far greater scale that is being attempted. Big companies are involved and they are offering not just services but platforms on which they are encouraging developers to create services and applications. What is being planned is expected to encompass everyone from major enterprises to small start-ups and individual consumers. Hardware companies will vie for the business of equipping massive data farms around the world, while fearing for their PC businesses . . .

While it is easy to imagine enterprises replacing employees' desktop PCs with dumb terminals running applications from the cloud, there are also signs of how consumers will opt for this model. Look at how everything can be done in the browser now and stored in the cloud, from e-mail to word-processing and photo and video editing and storage . . .

Google, with its web-based services and massive infrastructure, seems certain to be a cloud-computing leader, but there are also less likely candidates. The online retailer **Amazon** has shown others the way in cloud computing, selling its expertise in infrastructure through its Amazon Web Services for the past two years and developing its Elastic Compute Cloud, Simple Storage and database services. Gartner says a company such as **Wal-Mart**, with its supply chain expertise, could lease its core competencies as a cloud-computing service in similar fashion . . . Fears about reliability, security and performance levels, however, remain as barriers to adoption by businesses.'[120]

Source: 'Valley view: The IT world pokes its head in the cloud', 9 July 2008 (Nuttall, C.).

CHAPTER SUMMARY

- Consumers' lifestyles are key to many marketing strategies.

- A consumer's *lifestyle* refers to the ways they choose to spend time and money and how their consumption choices reflect these values and tastes. Lifestyle research is useful to track societal consumption preferences and also to position specific products and services to different segments. Marketers segment based on lifestyle differences, often grouping consumers in terms of their AIOs (activities, interests, and opinions).

- A set of techniques called *geo-demography* analyzes consumption patterns using geographical and demographic data, and identifies clusters of consumers who exhibit similar psychographic characteristics.

- Where one comes from is often a significant determinant of lifestyle. Many marketers recognize national or regional differences in product preferences, and develop different versions of their products for different markets.

- Psychographics go beyond simple demographics in helping marketers understand and reach different consumer segments. *Psychographic* techniques classify consumers in terms of psychological, subjective variables in addition to observable characteristics (demographics). Marketers have developed a variety of systems, such as VALS, to identify consumer 'types' and to differentiate them in terms of their brand or product preferences, media usage, leisure time activities, and attitudes toward broad issues such as politics and religion.

- Identifying patterns of consumption can be superior to knowledge of individual purchases when crafting a lifestyle marketing strategy.

- We associate interrelated sets of products and activities with social roles to form *consumption constellations*. People often purchase a product or service because they associate it with a *constellation* that, in turn, they link to a lifestyle they find desirable.

- Consumers identify with many groups that share common characteristics and identities. Subcultures are large groups that exist within a society and membership in them often gives marketers a valuable clue about individuals' consumption decisions. A person's ethnic origins, racial identity, and religious background are often major components of their identity.

- Recently, several minority groups have caught the attention of marketers as their economic power has grown. Segmenting consumers by their *ethnicity* can be effective, but care must be taken not to rely on inaccurate (and sometimes offensive) ethnic stereotypes.

- The growing numbers of people who claim multi-ethnic backgrounds are beginning to blur the traditional distinctions drawn among these subcultures.

- Because a consumer's culture exerts such a big influence on their lifestyle choices, marketers must learn as much as possible about differences in cultural norms and preferences when marketing in more than one country. One important issue is the extent to which marketing strategies must be tailored to each culture, rather than standardized across cultures in the European marketplace.

- Micro-cultures are communities of consumers who participate in or otherwise identify with specific art forms, popular culture movements, and hobbies.

- Marketing messages are increasingly appealing to ethnic and racial identity.

- Marketers increasingly use religious and spiritual themes when they talk to consumers. The impact of religious identification on consumer behavior is not clear, however some differences among religious subcultures do emerge. The quest for spirituality influences demand in product categories including books, music, and cinema. Marketers need to consider the sensibilities of believers carefully when they use religious symbolism to appeal to members of different denominations.

- Given that we, as consumers, must take part in many activities that reflect our local cultures, Euro-consumers as an overall segment do not exist. The existence of a Euro-consumer is at best limited to certain segments of the population, the young and the (international) managerial class, and to certain situations.

- Varying levels of resources (e.g. digital literacy; e-skills; access to computers and the Internet) mean that some Euro-consumers have greater opportunities to benefit from the convergence of consumption and the new electronic technologies than others.

▶ KEY TERMS

Acculturation (p. 607)

Acculturation agents (p. 607)

AIOs (p. 581)

Behavioural targeting (p. 589)

Cloud computing (p. 617)

Consumption constellations (p. 580)

Cybercrime (p. 590)

Digital literacy (p. 614)

E-skills (p. 612)

Ethnic subculture (p. 606)

Food culture (p. 595)

Geo-demography (p. 605)

High-context culture (p. 602)

Host culture (p. 609)

Lifestyle (p. 577)

Lifestyle marketing perspective (p. 578)

Low-context culture (p. 602)

Micro-culture (p. 606)

Nanotechnology (p. 600)

Phishing (p. 590)

Product complementarity (p. 579)

Progressive learning model (p. 609)

Psychographics (p. 580)

Racial subculture (p. 606)

Single-source data (p. 605)

Subcultures (p. 606)

VALS (Values and Lifestyles System) (p. 586)

Warming (p. 609)

▶ CONSUMER BEHAVIOUR CHALLENGE

1 Compare and contrast the concepts of lifestyle and social class. How does lifestyle differ from income?

2 Define psychographics, and describe three ways that marketers might use it.

3 In what situations is demographic information likely to be more useful than psychographic data, and vice versa?

4 Geo-demographic techniques assume that people who live in the same neighbourhood have other things in common as well. Why do they make this assumption, and how accurate is it?

5 Behavioural targeting techniques give marketers access to a wide range of information about a consumer by telling them what Websites they visit. Do you believe this 'knowledge power' presents any ethical problems with regard to consumers' privacy? Should the government regulate access to such information? Should consumers have the right to limit access to these data?

6 Discuss some concrete situations in which international similarities in lifestyles may be more relevant than national cultural differences for market segmentation and for the understanding of consumer behaviour.

7 What is the basic philosophy behind a lifestyle marketing strategy?

8 Compile a set of recent ads that attempt to link consumption of a product with a specific lifestyle. How is this goal usually accomplished?

▶ **CONSUMER BEHAVIOUR CHALLENGE** (*continued*)

9 The chapter mentions that psychographic analyses can be used to market politicians. Conduct research on the marketing strategies used in a recent, major election. How were voters segmented in terms of values? Can you find evidence that communications strategies were guided by this information?

10 Construct separate advertising executions for a cosmetics product targeted to three of the RISC segments: ethics and universalism; appearance and international symbol status; and action and personal drive. How would the basic appeal differ for each group?

11 Using media targeted to the group, construct a consumption constellation for the social role of university students. What set of products, activities and interests tend to appear in advertisements depicting 'typical' university students? How realistic is this constellation?

12 If you were segmenting European consumers in terms of their relative level of materialism, how might your advertising and promotional strategy take this difference into account? Construct two versions of an ad for a suntan lotion, one to appeal to a high materialism country and one to appeal to a low materialism country (under the untenable assumption of all other things being equal).

13 What is the difference between a high-context and low-context culture? How would the differences between high and low context cultures affect marketing campaigns?

14 What is a subculture? How does it differ from a micro-culture?

15 What is acculturation? How does it differ from enculturation? Who are acculturation agents?

16 Describe the processes involved when a person assimilates to a new host culture.

17 Describe the progressive learning model and discuss why this perspective is important when marketing to subcultures.

18 There are, of course, people of most lifestyle types in all European countries, but their numbers vary. Try to determine which lifestyles are the most common in some European countries that you know.

19 If you have access to foreign TV channels, try to compare the advertising in the ones from your own country with the foreign ones. Are the styles different? Are the predominant products different? Is the use of a certain style of advertisement for a certain type of product similar or dissimilar?

20 Extreme sports. Chat rooms. Vegetarianism. Can you predict what will be 'hot' in the near future? Identify a lifestyle trend that is just surfacing in your universe. Describe this trend in detail, and justify your prediction. What specific styles and/or products are part of this trend?

21 Locate one or more consumers (perhaps family members) who have emigrated from another country. Interview them about how they adapted to their host culture. In particular, what changes did they make in their consumption practices over time?

22 Locate current examples of marketing stimuli that depend on an ethnic or religious stereotype to communicate a message. How effective are these appeals?

23 Religious symbolism is being used increasingly in advertising, even though some people object to this practice. For example, the French fashion house Marithe and François Girbaud used a poster of well-dressed women posed in a version of Leonardo da Vinci's *The Last Supper*; the poster was banned in Milan.[121] In another example, a French Volkswagen ad for the relaunch of the Golf showed a modern version of *The Last Supper* with the tag line, 'Let us rejoice, my friends, for a new Golf has been born'.[122] A group of clergy in France sued the company and the ad had to be removed from 10,000 hoardings. One of the bishops involved in the suit said, 'Advertising experts have told us that ads aim for the sacred in order to shock, because using sex does not work any more.' Do you agree? Should religion be used to market products? Do you find this strategy effective or offensive? When and where is this appropriate, if at all?

For additional material see the companion website at **www.pearsoned.co.uk/solomon**

NOTES

1. Pierre Valette-Florence, *Les styles de vie* (Paris: Nathan, 1994); Benjamin Zablocki and Rosabeth Moss Kanter, 'The differentiation of life-styles', *Annual Review of Sociology* (1976): 269–97.

2. Mary T. Douglas and Baron C. Isherwood, *The World of Goods* (New York: Basic Books, 1979).

3. Richard A. Peterson, 'Revitalizing the culture concept', *Annual Review of Sociology* 5 (1979): 137–66.

4. Søren Askegaard, 'Livsstilsundersøgelser: henimod et teoretisk fundament', doctoral dissertation, School of Business and Economics: Odense University, 1993.

5. Henrik Dahl, *Hvis din nabo var en bil* (Copenhagen: Akademisk Forlag, 1997).

6. Thomas Drieseberg, 'Lebensstile in der marktforschung – eine empirische bestandsaufnahme', *Soziologie – Planung und Analyze* 5 (1992): 18–26.

7. Julia Cosgrove, 'Campari and CD?' *Business Week* (1 July 2002): 14.

8. William Leiss, Stephen Kline and Sut Jhally, *Social Communication in Advertising* (Toronto: Methuen, 1986).

9. Douglas and Isherwood, *op. cit.*, *The World of Goods*: 72–3.

10. Michael R. Solomon, 'The role of products as social stimuli: A symbolic interactionism perspective', *Journal of Consumer Research* 10 (December 1983): 319–29.

11. Christopher K. Hsee and France Leclerc, 'Will products look more attractive when presented separately or together?' *Journal of Consumer Research* 25 (September 1998): 175–86.

12. Anders Bengtsson, *Consumers and Mixed-Brands: On the Polysemy of Brand Meaning*, doctoral dissertation, Lund: Lund Business Press; Anders Bengtsson, 'Unnoticed Relationships: Do Consumers Experience Co-branded Products?' in Susan Broniarczyk and Kent Nakamoto (eds), *Advances in Consumer Research* 29 (Provo, UT: Association for Consumer Research, 2002): 521–7.

13. Vanessa O'Connell, 'Courvoisier to launch clothing line: Luxury sportswear plans to transform liquor label into lush lifestyle brand', *The Wall Street Journal Online* (13 February 2004).

14. Michael R. Solomon and Henry Assael, 'The Forest or the Trees? A Gestalt Approach to Symbolic Consumption', in Jean Umiker-Sebeok (ed.), *Marketing and Semiotics: New Directions in the Study of Signs for Sale* (Berlin: Mouton de Gruyter, 1988): 189–218; Michael R. Solomon, 'Mapping product constellations: A social categorization approach to symbolic consumption', *Psychology and Marketing* 5(3) (1988): 233–58; see also Stephen C. Cosmas, 'Life styles and consumption patterns', *Journal of Consumer Research* 8(4) (March 1982): 453–5.

15. Margaret Hogg, 'Anti-Constellations: Conceptualization and Content', in B. Englis and A. Olofsson (eds), *European Advances in Consumer Research* 3 (Provo, UT: Association for Consumer Research, 1998): 44–9.

16. Askegaard, 'Livsstilsundersøgelser: henimod et teoretisk fundament', *op. cit.*: 103–5.

17. Bill Schlackman, 'An Historical Perspective', in S. Robson and A. Foster (eds), *Qualitative Research in Action* (London: Edward Arnold, 1989): 15–23.

18. William D. Wells and Douglas J. Tigert, 'Activities, interests, and opinions', *Journal of Advertising Research* 11 (August 1971): 27.

19. Piirto Heath, 'Psychographics: "Q'est-ce que c'est"?' *American Demographics* (November 1995).

20. Alfred S. Boote, 'Psychographics: Mind over matter', *American Demographics* (April 1980): 26–9; William D. Wells, 'Psychographics: A critical review', *Journal of Marketing Research* 12 (May 1975): 196–213.

21. Joseph T. Plummer, 'The concept and application of life style segmentation', *Journal of Marketing* 38 (January 1974): 33–7.

22. J.E. Burroughs and A. Rindfleisch, 'Materialism and well-being: a conflicting values perspective', *Journal of Consumer Research* 29(3): 348–70; Hugh Williamson, 'All the rage in Germany: Cheap flights', *Financial Times* (26 March 2004), http://news.ft.com/servlet/Content Server?pagename=FT.com/StoryFT/FullStory&c=StoryFT&cid=1079419851116&p=1079419860606.

23. John L. Lastovicka, John P. Murry, Erich A. Joachimsthaler, Gurav Bhalla and Jim Scheurich, 'A lifestyle typology to model young male drinking and driving', *Journal of Consumer Research* 14 (September 1987): 257–63.

24. Internal document, RISC.

25. Bernard Cathelat, *Socio-Styles-Système* (Paris: Editions D'Organisation, 1990).

26. Askegaard, 'Livsstilsundersøgelser: henimod et teoretisk fundament', *op. cit.*: 67–77.

27. http://www.sric-bi.com/VALS/types.shtml, accessed 23 July 2008.

28. http://www.sric-bi.com/VALS/types.shtml, accessed 23 July 2008; see also Martha Farnsworth Riche, 'VALS 2', *American Demographics* (July 1989): 25.

29. http://www.sirc-bi.com/VALS/types.shtml, *op. cit.*

30. *Ibid.*

31. *Ibid.*

32. *Ibid.*

33. *Ibid.*

34. *Ibid.*

35. *Ibid.*; see also Martha Farnsworth Riche, 'VALS 2', *op. cit.*

36. Leiss *et al.*, Social Communication in Advertising, *op. cit.*

37. Valette-Florence, *Les styles de vie, op. cit.*

38. Askegaard, 'Livsstilsundersøgelser: henimod et teoretisk fundament', *op. cit.*

39. 'Consumers Willing to Trade Off Privacy for Electronic Personalization', available from www.mediapost.com, accessed 23 January 2007.

40. Aaron O. Patrick, 'Microsoft Ad Push Is All about You: "Behavioral Targeting" Aims to Use Customer Preferences to Hone Marketing Pitches', *Wall Street Journal* (26 December 2006): B3; Brian Steinberg, 'Next Up on Fox: Ads That Can Change Pitch', *Wall Street Journal* (21 April 2005): B1; Bob Tedeschi, 'Every Click You Make, They'll Be Watching You', *New York TimesOnline* (3 April 2006); David Kesmodel, 'Marketers Push Online Ads Based on Your Surfing Habits', *Wall Street Journal on the Web* (5 April 2005).

41. Sarah McBride and Vauhini Vara, 'We Know What You Ought to Be Watching This Summer', *Wall Street Journal* (31 July 2007): D1.

42. Associated Press, 'MySpace Launches Targeted Ad Program', *New York Times Online* (18 September 2007), accessed 18 September 2007; Vauhini Vara, 'Facebook Gets Personal with Ad Targeting Plan', *Wall Street Journal* (23 August 2007): B1.

43. Stephen Pritchard, 'Consumers hold key to securing the net', *ft.com* (4 July 2008) http://www.ft.com/cms/s/0/fb94e152-43a0-11dd-842e-0000779fd2ac,dwp_uuid=

4dce8136-4a24-11da-b8b1-0000779e2340.html, accessed 11 August 2008.

44. Paul Taylor, 'Staying connected: Technology on holiday', *ft.com* (8 July 2008) http://www.ft.com/cms/s/0/e7cc05be-4c11-11dd-96bb-000077b07658,dwp_uuid=3d14c83a-4429-11dd-b151-0000779fd2ac.html accessed August 11, 2008.

45. European Environment Agency, 'Sustainable consumption and production in South East Europe and Eastern Europe, Caucasus and Central Asia: Joint UNEP-EEA report on the opportunities and lessons learned', Copenhagen and Geneva EEA Report 3/2007.

46. 'Going it alone', *Marketing News* (11 September 2000).

47. The EU grew from 15 to 25 with 10 new member states joining in 2004: Cyprus, Czech Republic, Estonia, Hungary, Latvia, Lithuania, Malta, Poland, Slovakia and Slovenia. In 2007 Bulgaria and Romania joined to bring total EU membership to 27 states. These most recent 12 members are 'less advanced technologically and economically than the other 15', https://www.cia.gov/library/publications/the-world-factbook/geos/ee.html

48. Ian Traynor, 'Europe of the future: Germany shrinks, France grows but U.K. population booms', *The Guardian*, 27 August 2008, http://www.guardian.co.uk/world/2008/aug/27/population.eu, accessed 27 August 2008.

49. https://www.cia.gov/library/publications/the-world-factbook/geos/ee.html

50. Søren Askegaard and Tage Koed Madsen, 'The local and the global: Patterns of homogeneity and heterogeneity in European food cultures', *International Business Review* 7(6) (1998): 549–68.

51. Pieter van Erven Dorens, 'Hollandse hap aan Turkse kust' ('Dutch bit on the Turkish coast'), *Reiskrant* (4 January 2005), http://reiskrant.nl/reiskrant/reisnieuws/16943671/Hollandse_hap_in_Turks_hotel.html.

52. See discussions in the following: Alladi Venkatesh, 'Ethnoconsumerism: A New Paradigm to Study Cultural and Cross-Cultural Consumer Behaviour', in Janeen A. Costa and G. Bamossy (eds), *Marketing in a Multicultural World* (Thousand Oaks, CA: Sage, 1995): 26–67; Jean-Claude Usunier, *Marketing Across Cultures*, 3rd edn (London: Prentice-Hall, 2000); Askegaard and Madsen, 'The local and the global: Patterns of homogeneity and heterogeneity in European food cultures', *op. cit.*; Klaus Grunert, Suzanne Grunert and Sharon Beatty, 'Cross-cultural research on consumer values', *Marketing and Research Today* 17 (1989): 30–9.

53. Usunier, *Marketing Across Cultures*, *op. cit.*

54. European Environment Agency, 'Sustainable consumption and production in South East Europe and Eastern Europe, Caucasus and Central Asia: Joint UNEP-EEA report on the opportunities and lessons learned', Copenhagen and Geneva EEA Report 3/2007, Table 2.1: 20.

55. European Environment Agency, 'Sustainable consumption and production in South East Europe and Eastern Europe, Caucasus and Central Asia: Joint UNEP-EEA report on the opportunities and lessons learned', Copenhagen and Geneva EEA Report 3/2007, Figure 2.2: 21.

56. Simai, M., 'Poverty and Inequality in Eastern Europe and the CIS Transition Economies', UN Department of Economic and Social Affairs Working Paper No. 17, ST/ESA/2006/DWP/17, http://www.un.org/esa/desa/papers/2006/wp17_2006.pdf, cited in EEA Report 2007.

57. World Bank, 'World Development Indicators 2006', World Bank, Washington, cited in EEA Report 2007.

58. World Bank, 'World Development Indicators 2006', World Bank, Washington, cited in EEA Report 2007.

59. Lissovolik, Y., *Migration: A blessing for Russia* (2005), online article by Yaroslav Lissovolik, chief economist at Deutsche UFG for Prime-Tass Business News Agency, Moscow. Downloaded from http://www.prime-tass.com/news/show.asp?topicid=65&id=377133 April, 2007, cited in EEA Report 2007.

60. European Environment Agency, 'Sustainable consumption and production in South East Europe and Eastern Europe, Caucasus and Central Asia: Joint UNEP-EEA report on the opportunities and lessons learned', Copenhagen and Geneva EEA Report 3/2007: 28.

61. *Ibid.*

62. European Environment Agency 'Sustainable consumption and production in South East Europe and Eastern Europe, Caucasus and Central Asia: Joint UNEP-EEA report on the opportunities and lessons learned', Copenhagen and Geneva EEA Report 3/2007: 29–30.

63. Stuart Elliott, 'Sampling tastes of a changing Russia', *New York Times* (1 April 1992) 2: D1.

64. World Bank, 'World Development Indicators 2006', World Bank, Washington, cited in EEA Report 2007.

65. CISSTAT, 2006. *Interstate Statistical Committee of the Commonwealth of Independent States – 15 years of the Commonwealth Independent States*. CD published 2006-11, cited in EEA Report 2007.

66. CISSTAT, 2006. *Interstate Statistical Committee of the Commonwealth of Independent States – 15 years of the Commonwealth Independent States*. CD published 2006-11, cited in EEA Report 2007.

67. Statistical Office of Serbia, *Household Budget Survey 2006*, National accounts statistics. Statistical Office of the Republic of Serbia, Belgrade, (2006) http://webrzs.statserb.sr.gov.yu/axd/en/index.php, cited in EEA (2006) Report 2007.

68. Croatian Central Bureau of Statistics (2006), *Statistical Yearbook 2006*, sub-chapter on personal consumption, cited in EEA Report 2007.

69. Steve Boggan, 'Once bitten . . . The science of nanotechnology', *The Guardian*, 26 March 2008, http://www.guardian.co.uk/science/2008/mar/26/nanotechnology.food

70. Matthias D. Kindler, Ellen Day and Mary R. Zimmer, 'A Cross-Cultural Comparison of Magazine Advertising in West Germany and the U.S.', unpublished manuscript, University of Georgia, Athens, 1990.

71. Michael Schroeder, 'Germany – France: Different Advertising Styles – Different Communication Concepts', in W.F. van Raaij and G. Bamossy (eds), *European Advances in Consumer Research* 1 (Provo, UT: Association for Consumer Research, 1993): 77–83.

72. Björn Walliser and Fabienne Moreau, 'Comparaison du style français et allemand de la publicité télévisée', *Cahiers du CESAG* 98 1/11 (1998).

73. Edward T. Hall, *Beyond Culture* (New York: Doubleday, 1976).

74. Hans Heyder, Karl Georg Musiol and Klaus Peters, 'Advertising in Europe – attitudes towards advertising in certain key East and West European countries', *Marketing and Research Today* (March 1992): 58–68.

75. Ullrich Appelbaum and Chris Halliburton, 'How to develop international advertising campaigns that work: The example of the European food and beverage sector', *International Journal of Advertising* 12(3) (1993): 223–41.

76. Marc G. Weinberger and Harlan E. Spotts, 'A situational view of information content in TV advertising in the U.S. and U.K.', *Journal of Marketing* 53 (January 1989): 89–94; see also Abhilasha Mehta, 'Global markets and standardized advertising: Is it happening? An analysis of common brands in USA and UK', in *Proceedings of the 1992 Conference of the American Academy of Advertising* (1992): 170.

77. 'Abroadminded', *Marketing* (24 April 1997): 20–1.

78. Heyder, Musiol and Peters, 'Advertising in Europe', *op. cit.*

79. Wendelin G. Müller, 'Die Standardisierbarkeit internationaler Werbung: Kulturen verlangen Adaptionen', *Marketing ZFP* 3 (3rd Quarter 1996): 179–90.

80. J. Andrew Davison and Erik Grab, 'The contributions of advertising testing to the development of effective international advertising: The KitKat case study', *Marketing and Research Today* (February 1993): 15–24.

81. Eduardo Camargo, 'The Measurement of Meaning: Sherlock Holmes in Pursuit of the Marlboro Man', in Umiker-Sebeok (ed.), *Marketing and Semiotics*: 463–83.

82. Cheryl Berman quoted in 'Leo Burnett discovers ads aimed at women fall short on five counts', Leo Burnett Press Release (24 June 2004), http://www.leoburnett.com/news/press_releases/2004/prjul09–13743.asp.

83. *Ibid.*

84. Demographic Statistics 1997: Population and Social Conditions Series (Luxembourg: Office for Official Publications of the European Communities, 1997); 'Colour Blind', *Marketing Week* (21 June 1996): 38–40.

85. 'Groninger discotheken verbieden omstreden kleding (Groningen disco forbids controversial clothing), *De Telegraaf* (11 January 2005), http://www2.telegraaf.nl/binnenland/17132161/Groninger_discotheken_verbieden_omstreden_kleding.html.

86. Erik Davis, 'tlhIngan Hol Dajatlh'a?' (Do You Speak Klingon?)', *Utne Reader* (March/April 1994): 122–29; additional material provided by personal communication, Prof. Robert V. Kozinets, Northwestern University, October 1997; and adapted from Philip Kotler, Gary Armstrong, Peggy H. Cunningham and Robert Warren, *Principles of Marketing*, 3rd Canadian edn (Scarborough, Ontario: Prentice Hall Canada, 1997): 96.

87. See Frederik Barth, *Ethnic Groups and Boundaries: The Social Organization of Culture Difference* (London: Allen & Unwin, 1969); D. Bell, 'Ethnicity and Social Change', in N. Glazer and D.P. Moynihan (eds), *Ethnicity: Theory and Experience* (Cambridge, MA: Harvard University Press, 1975): 141–74; D.L. Horowitz, 'Ethnic Identity', in *ibid.*: 109–40; J. Kotkin, *Tribes* (New York: Random House, 1993); Venkatesh, 'Ethnoconsumerism', *op. cit.*; Michel Laroche, Annamma Joy, Michael Hui and Chankon Kim, 'An Examination of Ethnicity Measures: Convergent Validity and Cross-Cultural Equivalence', in Rebecca H. Holman and Michael R. Solomon (eds), *Advances in Consumer Research* 18 (Provo, UT: Association for Consumer Research, 1991): 150–7; Melanie Wallendorf and Michael Reilly, 'Ethnic migration, assimilation, and consumption', *Journal of Consumer Research* 10 (December 1983): 292–302; Milton J. Yinger, 'Ethnicity', *Annual Review of Sociology* 11 (1985): 151–80.

88. Rohit Desphandé and Douglas M. Stayman, 'A tale of two cities: distinctiveness theory and advertising effectiveness', *Journal of Marketing Research* 31 (February 1994): 57–64; Stephen Riggins, 'The Media Imperative: Ethnic Minority Survival in the Age of Mass Communication', in S.H. Riggins (ed.), *Ethnic Minority Media: An International Perspective* (London: Sage, 1992): 1–22.

89. Steve Rabin, 'How to sell across cultures', *American Demographics* (March 1994): 56–7.

90. See Lisa Peñaloza, '*Atravesando fronteras*/border crossings: A critical ethnographic exploration of the consumer acculturation of Mexican immigrants', *Journal of Consumer Research* 21(1) (June 1994): 32–54.

91. Gokcen Coskuner and Ozlem Sandikci, 'New Clothing: Meanings and Practices', in Barbara E. Kahn and Mary Frances Luce (eds), *Advances in Consumer Research* 31 (Valdosta, GA: Association for Consumer Research, 2004): 285–90.

92. A. Fuat Firat, 'Consumer Culture or Culture Consumed?' in Costa and Bamossy (eds), *Marketing in a Multicultural World*: 105–25; Michael Laroche, Chankon Kim, Michael K. Hui and Annamma Joy, 'An empirical study of multidimensional ethnic change: The case of the French Canadians in Quebec', *Journal of Cross-Cultural Psychology* 27(1) (January 1996): 114–31.

93. Melanie Wallendorf and Michael Reilly, 'Ethnic migration, assimilation, and consumption', *Journal of Consumer Research* 10 (December 1983): 292–302.

94. Ronald J. Faber, Thomas C. O'Guinn, and John A. McCarty, 'Ethnicity, acculturation and the importance of product attributes', *Psychology & Marketing* 4 (Summer 1987): 121–34; Humberto Valencia, 'Developing an Index to Measure Hispanicness', in Elizabeth C. Hirschman and Morris B. Holbrook (eds), *Advances in Consumer Research* 12 (Provo, Utah: Association for Consumer Research, 1985): 118–21.

95. Rohit Deshpande, Wayne D. Hoyer, and Naveen Donthu, 'The intensity of ethnic affiliation: A study of the sociology of hispanic consumption', *Journal of Consumer Research* 13 (September 1986): 214–20.

96. Ger, Güliz, 'Warming: Making the new familiar and moral', *Journal of European Ethnology* (special issue of the journal *Ethnologia Europea*), Richard Wilk and Orvar Lofgren (eds) (forthcoming) check.

97. Elisabeth Kriechbaum-Vitellozzi and Robert Kreuzbauer, 'Poverty consumption: Consumer behavior of refugees in industrialized countries', *Advances in Consumer Research* 33(1) (2006); *cf.* also L. Wamwara-Mbugua, T. Wakiuru, Bettina Cornwell, and Gregory Boller, 'Triple acculturation: The role of African Americans in the consumer acculturation of Kenyan immigrants', *Advances in Consumer Research* 33(1) (2006).

98. Tuba Ustuner and Douglas B. Holt, 'Dominated consumer acculturation: The social construction of poor migrant women's consumer identity projects in a Turkish squatter', *Journal of Consumer Research* 34 (June 2007): 41.

99. Dan Brown, *The Da Vinci Code* (New York: Doubleday, 2003).

100. Albert M. Muñiz Jr and Hope Jensen Schau, 'Religiosity in the abandoned Apple Newton brand community', *Journal of Consumer Research* 31 (March 2005): 737–47.

101. Elizabeth C. Hirschman, 'Religious Affiliation and Consumption Processes: An Initial Paradigm', in *Research in Marketing* (Greenwich, CT: JAI Press, 1983): 131–70.

102. See, for example, Nejet Delener, 'The effects of religious factors on perceived risk in durable goods purchase decisions', *Journal of Consumer Marketing* 7 (Summer 1990): 27–38.

103. 'The Muslims in France: Rejecting their ancestors the Gauls', *The Economist* (16 November 1996): 113–14.

104. Clare Garner, 'Builders answer Islam's growing call to prayer', *The Independent* (4 February 1997): 7.

105. Madeline Bunting, 'Churchgoing bottoms out', *The Guardian* (10 August 1996): 2; 'Catholic Church loses mass appeal', *The Guardian* (30 January 1996): 4; 'België is niet langer katholiek (Belgium is no longer Catholic)', *Trouw* (19 September 1996); Madeline Bunting, 'Revolving door throws doubt on evangelical churches' revival', *The Guardian* (28 August 1996); for a comprehensive website on the world's religions and their populations, see: http://www.adherents.com/Religions_By_Adherents.html.

106. Amy Barrett, 'John Paul II to share stage with marketers', *Wall Street Journal Europe* (19 August 1997): 4; see also www.mix.it/rai/papa.

107. Leeflang and van Raaij, 'The changing consumer in the European Union: A "Meta-Analysis"'.

108. Massoud Saghafi and Donald Sciglimpaglia, 'Marketing in an Integrated Europe', in M. Bergadaà (ed.), *Marketing Today and for the 21st Century* 1 (ESSEC: Proceedings of the 24th EMAC Conference, 1995): 1069–76.

109. Fred van Eenennaam, 'Standardization of International Marketing Processes in a Pan-European Context: Some Research Hypotheses', in Bergadaà (ed.), *Marketing Today and for the 21st Century* 2, *ibid.*: 1221–41.

110. Vern Terpstra and Kenneth David, *The Cultural Environment of International Business*, 2nd edn (Cincinnati: Southwestern, 1985).

111. André Tordjman, 'European Retailing: Convergences, Differences, and Perspectives', in P.J. McGoldrick and G. Davies (eds), *International Retailing: Trends and Strategies* (London: Pitman, 1995): 17–50.

112. 'Abroadminded'.

113. Bernard Dubois and Gilles Laurent, 'Is There a Euroconsumer for Luxury Goods?' in van Raaij and Bamossy (eds), *European Advances in Consumer Research* 1: 58–69.

114. Susan P. Douglas and C. Samuel Craig, 'The changing dynamic of consumer behavior: Implications for cross-cultural research', *International Journal of Research in Marketing* 14 (1997): 379–95.

115. https://www.cia.gov/library/publications/the-world-factbook/geos/ee.html

116. Lutz Stobbe, EuP Preparatory Studies 'Televisions' (Lot 5) Final Report on Task 3 'Consumer Behaviour and Local Infrastructure', (TREN/D1/40 lot 5-2005), compiled by Deutsche Umwelthilfe and Fraunhofer IZM, contractor: Fraunhofer Institute for Reliability and Microintegration, IZM, Berlin (2 August 2007): 10.

117. Lutz Stobbe, *ibid.*

118. 'The Consumer Markets Scoreboard: Monitoring Consumer Outcomes in the Single Market', COM (2008) 31, European Communities, Luxembourg, 2008: 50.

119. Christophe Demunter, 'Statistics in focus: Industry, trade and services/population and social conditions/science and technology: E-skills at a glance; digital literacy', (17/2006) Eurostat KS-NP-06-017-EN-N, http://epp.eurostat.ec.europa.eu/cache/ITY_OFFPUB/KS-NP-06-017/EN/KS-NP-06-017-EN.PDF, accessed 12 August 2008.

120. Chris Nuttall, 'Valley view: The IT world pokes its head in the cloud', *ft.com* (8 July 2008), http://www.ft.com/cms/s/0/d880ee1c-4a45-11dd-891a-000077b07658,dwp_uuid=3d14c83a-4429-11dd-b151-0000779fd2ac.html, accessed 11 August 2008.

121. Sophie Arie, 'Supper is off: Milan bans Da Vinci parody', *The Guardian* (4 February 2005): 15.

122. Claudia Penteado, 'Brazilian ad irks Church', *Advertising Age* (23 March 2000): 11.

When the pumpkins deflate: from the introduction of Hallowe'en to the autopsy of a failure

DOMINIQUE ROUX, IRG-University Paris 12, France

Festive rituals, whether Christian or pagan, are topics of particular interest to consumer researchers. As well as revealing the social and cultural dimensions of the various groups and different peoples practising them, they also throw light on how different patterns of consumption are implicated in rituals (Levinson *et al.*, 1992). Hallowe'en (Belk, 1990; Levinson *et al.*, 1992), like other similar events such as Christmas (Belk, 1987, 1989) and Thanksgiving (Wallendorf and Arnould, 1991) has been analyzed not only historically, but also in terms of its contemporary function within the family, peer groups and jointly produced events. The items bought and consumed during these rituals play a major part in the performance of the ceremonial and help give expression to the genre, the role or the specific characteristics of the participants.

Socio-cultural analysis of these events takes a particularly interesting turn when their focal point is displaced and translated into foreign contexts, beyond their place of origin. Due to the fact that marketing values and devices have become familiar to an increasing number of people, globalization and its production of common reference points facilitate the commercial dissemination of a ritual, just like any other product. However, despite this homogenization of reference points, cultures remain localized and retain in part an attachment to their own distinctive place, country and customs. They produce substrata of identification and differentiation that are primarily linguistic but are also traditional in their modes of transmission. Marketing and naturalizing a foreign festival is thus something of an oxymoron, as the example of the introduction of Hallowe'en into France illustrates.

THE CONTEXT

Until the early 1990s, Hallowe'en was unknown to most French people. The introduction of this festival into France began with the acquisition, in 1992, by the French costume and fancy dress company Masport of its competitor César, which was present in the US market (Le Guay, 2002). Beginning in 1992, Masport/César arranged to set up a stand at Printemps, one of the best known Paris department stores. This initiative was repeated in following years through events held in fashionable outlets throughout the capital city, until in 1996 the company decided to supply its professional clientele with the whole range of items it produced – masks, fancy dress outfits, and accessories. But it was in 1997, under the impetus of France Telecom, that the festival took off. Looking for a marketing gimmick for the launch of its new Olaween* cell phone, France Telecom placed 8,500 pumpkins next to the Eiffel Tower. Contrary to all expectations, these pumpkins were not taken away by the refuse collection vehicles hired to remove them, but by Parisians attracted by the event. Before long, the pumpkin became a cult item. It had powerful allies in the form of the media, which were to play a key role in its implantation strategy. As the pumpkins' spokespersons (Latour, 1987), journalists became the promoters of Hallowe'en's little-known origins, (re)constructed the festival's European lineage, and gave it an indisputable cultural legitimacy (Le Guay, 2002). From the United States, Hallowe'en seems to imply a return to roots and a connection to its Celtic origins. Successfully commercializing the ritual though involves hiding the workings of the market in order to create the appearance of that which is not called into question, namely authenticity.

Hallowe'en in France enjoyed a sustained rise in popularity in the first five years following its introduction. Many companies took advantage of the fad and contributed to the spread of the event. However, its growth turned to equally rapid decline after 2001. Since 2006, the Hallowe'en festival has passed almost unnoticed in mass distribution outlets. The publicity events and media coverage associated with the end of October have subsided, an indication of the general loss of interest. Why did such a high-profile craze decline as quickly as it had arisen?

The reasons for its failure to catch on in France can be seen in the role played by the various actors involved in spreading or discrediting the event. Originally, companies and the media were the main instigators in creating interest among consumers. In opposition, the spokespeople of various Christian groups mounted an

---

* France Telecom poster campaign for the Ola cell phone in the autumn of 1997.

acrimonious crusade against Hallowe'en. However, the eventual loss of interest of the consumers themselves was the result of their increasing view that the festival was 'fabricated', commercial, inauthentic and, not least, imported. In addition, the event did not succeed in distracting attention from the difficult overall economic situation in France.

PUMPKIN SPOKESPEOPLE CONTRA RELIGIOUS SPOKESPEOPLE

Hallowe'en's close proximity to All Saints' Day and Christmas was a primary reason for concern on the part of many groups of Catholic persuasion, who were amongst the most eminent detractors of Hallowe'en ever since it had reached French shores. The 'No to Hallowe'en' collective organized protests against this pagan ceremony which was suspected of diverting or distracting the faithful from the traditional Christian commemoration of the dead. Over and beyond its position in the calendar, there was an even more profound concern about the values promoted by Hallowe'en. A festival of fear; a celebration of the omnipotence of sorcery and evil powers; a metaphysics of fate and cynicism (Le Guay, 2002): Hallowe'en is seen as radically opposed to Christian values. In its temporal proximity to All Saints' Day, it impinges on relations with death, which, instead of being associated with sanctity and ecumenicism, becomes, as in carnivals, inverted, deprived of any sacred aura and rendered anonymous. Hallowe'en replaces the reference points and beliefs anchored in a conception of man as fearful in the face of his own death with an absence of all belief when confronted by a parodic, disincarnated and distanced version of death. The opposition critique primarily turned, in an implicit way, on the symbolic undercurrents that the festival activated. They also targeted the ways in which Hallowe'en had emerged. Both the commercial motives underpinning it and also its spurious perceived authenticity were called into question. 'Saint Pumpkin' thus appeared as the latest fashion or trend devised by frivolous marketing departments, to provide even greater incentives, if such were ever needed, for households to spend money. This suspicion, independent of any religious conviction, spread progressively through the broad mass of consumers who, without any particular spokespeople, began to show increasing and persistant resistance to infection by this new ritual.

CONSUMER RESISTANCE: DENOUNCING INAUTHENTICITY, UNMASKING BUSINESS

This case study draws on respondents' views from a series of in-depth interviews carried out in 2006 among 18 individual consumers and 5 mini-groups, to identify four main motives which explain the growing

disaffection with Hallowe'en: the 'foreign' nature of an event imported from the United States; the absence of local cultural roots; the emphasis given to predominantly commercial goals; and the difficult economic conjuncture and growing insecurity with regard to the future.

First of all, the authenticity which claimed to be based on Halloween's Celtic origins did not manage to dispel the obvious facts: the festival was imported from the United States and, as such, was considered to be an artefact of American culture. Mouloud, a 36-year-old Parisian grocer, expressed it thus: 'For me, it's a religious festival invented in America. It's nothing to do with French culture. It's been parachuted in like all their products, Coca-Cola, hamburgers, and the rest.' Curiously, the reference to parachuting is not an oblique recollection of the Allied landings in France, but is here associated with products usually viewed as symbols of American commercial hegemony. Another respondent, Joël, aged 32, a software engineer, emphasized the cultural distance separating the two countries and brandished the 'French cultural exception' as a reason for rejecting Hallowe'en. 'It pushes people to consume, especially kids. But it's certainly not because it's American. The French are resistant to everything that's American. They feel superior, it's the French cultural exception.'

Over and beyond such nationalist clichés, the festival was condemned above all for its commercial dimension. Some respondents referred to it as a 'racket'. A temporary flood of Hallowe'en-themed objects as well as new or repackaged products appeared in retail outlets. Joël pointed out that 'it was an occasion to make people spend more and more money'. Claire, a 42-year-old teacher, saw it as 'an incongruous festival in France because it was imported for commercial reasons'. Unlike Christmas, which for her evoked 'dreams, myths and gentleness', 'Hallowe'en was imposed brutally, cynically, as a commercial ploy'. She said she respected the festival when it took place in the United States, but not in France where its meaning had been hijacked: 'For me, Hallowe'en can be summed up as the manipulation of children. It takes advantage of their naïvety to make a profit. Children like pumpkins, candy and fancy dress, and therefore they put pressure on their parents, who as loving parents, will give in and buy them what they want. And so the stores win out'. A storekeeper himself, Mouloud sided without hesitation with the denunciation of the manipulation, insisting that he had no wish to make a profit from it and that he had never wanted to use this festival to make money or increase his sales. 'One shouldn't blindly follow the herd just because they say so. If children come to me asking for candy, I give it to them. Because they're kids, not because it's Hallowe'en.'

In fact, the 'commercial racket' referred to by the respondents brings out the festive dimension that was the basis of the advertising for Hallowe'en, rather than emphasizing the origins and cultural roots of the festival. Moreover, questioning respondents about the origins of Hallowe'en yielded unambiguous results. For some of them, there was apparently no doubt at all. In response to the question, 'In your opinion, where does Hallowe'en come from?' the reply invariably attributed an American origin to the festival. Catherine, a bank employee, commented: 'For me, as I said, it's a festival that they've brought over from the USA. It has nothing to do with our traditions. It's relayed by the media, but it's totally articificial. That's the reason it's not caught on here.' On the other hand, for the less resistant respondents and for those willing to play the game, particularly to give pleasure to children, knowledge of the real origins of Hallowe'en was of no interest. Olivier, a 62-year-old retiree, summed it up thus: 'Since it's not a French festival, many French people attach little importance to the origin of the event. They see only the festive side, the surface of Hallowe'en in fact. Other people simply treat it as a joke.' The ludic aspect overrides the authenticity aspect. The superficial and ephemeral nature of the phenomemon tends progressively to diminish the interest it aroused initially. The ritual failed to establish itself, all the more so since it was based primarily on a self-interested commercial initiative. Sonia, a 26-year-old doctoral student in history, described it thus: 'At the beginning, it worked because it had the appeal of the unknown. It was fun having another reason to party. But I think that for most people, Hallowe'en has simply become pointless. Even if there are people who reject it because they're anti-American, the problem with Hallowe'en isn't only anti-Americanism. It suffers from the fact that it's devoid of meaning here and that it doesn't fit in with people's habits.'

As well as the sense of inauthenticity about a festival imported from the United States, its lack of cultural roots, and its strongly commercialized character, there is a further reason linked to the economic and social context in which the importation of Hallowe'en took place. Not only is Hallowe'en very close to Christmas, which by tradition absorbs a large proportion of the resources destined for gifts and festive meals, but its arrival coincided with a time of financial hardship and uncertainty with regard to the future. 'If this festival had arrived 10 or 15 years ago,' commented Maria, a 55-year-old administrative manager, 'it would have been different. Today people have a sense of growing insecurity and the declining purchasing power of households is clearly reflected in reduced consumption. Young people, in particular, are worried about the future. They want a great deal, but finally they realize that they don't have much.' However, in disadvantaged neighbourhoods, people seemed less reluctant to take advantage of an excuse for a party than elsewhere. As Rachid, aged 32 and unemployed, from a 'problem' housing project, commented, Hallowe'en is an accessible festival, especially for children who 'can buy stuff cheaply and have a ball'. Moreover, the event often falls during the school holidays. For children who do not go away on vacation, it can be a timely collective substitute offering a playful, carnival atmosphere.

Overall, although our respondents accepted the idea of 'a party for the sake of a party', 'one more way of amusing oneself' or 'a festive digression for children', most did not manage to appropriate a ritual which they considered to be 'superficial' and from which they kept a distance. The promotion of Hallowe'en as 'a children's festival' was criticized and denounced for its lack of values; its morbid liking for the occult; and its pandering to the all-powerful sovereign child. The event became less significant with each passing year. 'Hallowe'en declared Dead in France' (Olson, 2006) is an indication of the about-turn taken by consumers and the media to an event that had been applauded less then ten years previously. Like other attempts to market foreign festivals and rituals such as Saint Valentine's Day and more recently Saint Patrick's Day, the transplanting of 'Saint Pumpkin', with its masks, lanterns and witches, failed to flourish in French cultural soil.

QUESTIONS

1 Identify and assess the main arguments for the failure of Hallowe'en to take root in a French context.

2 Are these arguments exclusively French and based on the specific cultural context or are they likely to be seen and found in other countries? What reasons support their possible general application (or lack of it) to other contexts?

3 Are the features of Hallowe'en in the case study applicable to other types of 'product'? What are the limits to generalizing from this case study in terms of the characteristics of such products?

4 Discuss the opportunities for and limits of cultural globalization. To what extent can global cultural phenomena be established (or not, as the case may be)? And by which countries and cultures? And which other countries and cultures are likely to be the recipients of attempts at cultural globalization, and for what reasons?

5 What does this case study teach us about consumer resistance in the context of globalization? What does it teach us about the persistence of a culture's distinctive characteristics?

Sources

Belk, Russell W. (1987), 'A child's Christmas in America: Santa Claus as deity, consumption as religion', *The Journal of American Culture*, 10(1): 87–100.

Belk, Russell W. (1989), 'Materialism and the modern U.S. Christmas', *Interpretive Consumer Research*, Elizabeth Hirschman (ed.) (Provo, Association for Consumer Research): 115–135.

Belk, Russell W. (1990), 'Halloween: An evolving American consumption ritual', *Advances in Consumer Research*, 17(1): 508–517.

Latour, Bruno (1987), *Science in Action: How to Follow Scientists and Engineers through Society* (Cambridge, MA: Harvard University Press).

Le Guay, Damien (2002), *La Face cachée d'Halloween* (Paris: Le Cerf).

Levinson, Stacey, Stacey Mack, Dan Reinhardt, Helen Suarez, and GraceYeh (1992), 'Halloween as a consumption experience', *Advances in Consumer Research*, 19(1): 219–228.

Wallendorf, Melanie and Eric J. Arnould (1991), '"We gather together": Consumption rituals of Thanksgiving Day', *Journal of Consumer Research*, 18(1): 13–31.

Firing enthusiasm: increasing acceptance of cremation and the implications for consumer behaviour

DARACH TURLEY, Dublin City University, Ireland
STEPHANIE O'DONOHOE, The University of Edinburgh, Scotland

Some difficult consumer decisions often have to be made at distressing times, when consumers may lack the desire as well as the physical, emotional and financial resources to deal with them as they would normally. The death of a loved one is particularly demanding and traumatic, yet in the midst of their grief bereaved survivors are expected to select an undertaker, arrange a funeral, and oversee the disposal of possessions and property belonging to the deceased. Another decision at this time concerns how to dispose of the dead person's body. In most European countries this is a recent issue. Up to the 1980s, most funerals ended in some form of burial or internment. The precise nature of the burial was typically determined by family circumstance, fame, faith and social standing. However, the overall process was the same; the remains were placed where dust could return to dust at a pace dictated by the laws of nature. Cremation challenged this disposal ritual radically, significantly affecting survivors, the funeral industry and public authorities.

The history of cremation in Europe is a telling example of the 'trickle down' theory of adoption in consumer behaviour. Most members of the British Cremation Society, founded in 1874, hailed from the more educated, avant garde, unorthodox and privileged strata of society, as did those who joined the French, German and Italian cremation societies established soon after. They questioned prevailing social and religious values relating to disposal of the dead, and had the means to conduct cremations on their own estates or abroad.

Failure to fit comfortably with existing social values is critical for most consumer adoptions, and the introduction of cremation proved to be no exception. The values in question here centered on the prevailing Christian belief in the resurrection of the body. In the second half of the nineteenth century funeral services, sermons, graveyards, headstones and memorial literature were shot through with the metaphor of rest, feeding into the deeply-held Christian belief that the graveyard was merely a temporary resting place, that the bodies of those buried there would somehow rise, refreshed and renewed, on the Last Day. So, it was no surprise that there was a concerted religious backlash to what appeared at the time to be a serious challenge to a core Christian belief. Remains remain. However, if they were not allowed to do so, if bodies were to be incinerated, how could they rise?

Changing social values and the impact of two World Wars, particularly WWI, changed matters significantly. Europe's battlefields were strewn with millions of military and civilian dead, many of whom could not be retrieved, identified or repatriated. As a result, funerals were often conducted in the absence of any corpse. This forced survivors to decouple both their grief and their hopes for the dead person's future from their mortal remains. In addition to these dramatic events, other social developments helped change people's perceptions of cremation. As the twentieth century progressed, many European countries witnessed a growth in secularism that challenged core religious beliefs including belief in a future bodily resurrection. Wider availability of both electricity and running water fuelled consumers' growing preoccupation with cleanliness and sanitation. For consumers with such a mindset, cremation seemed a more efficient and hygienic option. Rapid urban expansion put pressure on the availability of land for new cemeteries. The search for work often required geographic mobility, and so survivors had to travel further to visit graves. Finally, in the UK the widespread immigration of Hindus, Sikhs and Buddhists – faiths that enjoy a historical and religiously sanctioned tradition of cremating their dead – served to make cremation more visible and to promote it as a viable and acceptable mode of disposal.

1885 saw the opening of the first UK crematorium in Woking, Surrey; three bodies were cremated that year. Early crematoria – both interiors and exteriors – were deliberately constructed to look like churches. The coffin also descended downwards on a lift rather than horizontally on a belt as they do today, in order to resemble the process of burial more closely. By 1914, 0.2 per cent of UK funerals involved a cremation; the current figure is 75 per cent. So, today, cremation is by far the most preferred option for dealing with the remains of the deceased in Britain.

There are currently about 250 crematoria in the UK, mostly run by local authorities although a few are operated by private companies. The cost of a typical cremation is £350–400, before adding the fees of the funeral director typically employed by bereaved survivors. Directors seem anxious to promote cremation funerals as essentially the same as a traditional cemetery burial, just with a different ending, and their pricing strategy reflects this. While the choice of cremation or burial is the principal disposal decision to be made, some further decisions need to be made once the cremation option has been chosen. First is the choice between a direct and a non-direct cremation. In a direct cremation the remains are removed from where the person died – usually a hospital – and taken straightaway to the crematorium. When survivors are given the ashes they can dispose of them as they wish, with or without incorporating this into some form of service.

A non-direct cremation means that a coffin containing the body is present during the funeral home viewing and/or funeral service and is subsequently taken to a crematorium for incineration. This non-direct option includes a subsidiary option where survivors can choose to either purchase or rent the coffin. Some consumers do not see the point of purchasing an expensive coffin only to have it literally go up in smoke a few days later. Funeral directors can offer these clients the option of 'renting' a coffin between the time of death and final cremation. Recyclable caskets hold an inner cardboard coffin that can slide out the folding back end of the casket at the crematorium. Most funeral directors also offer a range of urns made of wood, metal, marble or stone in which the ashes can be either retained or buried. The main savings of a cremation are the cost of a cemetery gravesite (often up to £5,000) and, in the case of a recycled coffin, the price of a coffin that can vary from several hundred to tens of thousands of pounds.

Once the ashes have been returned to the next of kin, the question of what to do with the ashes arises. Sixty per cent of UK mourners choose to take the ashes away with them rather than have them buried or pigeon-holed in cemetery columbaria. No statistics are available as to where and how these ashes are disposed of; nor indeed whether or not this had been planned for by the deceased. Anecdotal evidence suggests that prime locations for 'scattering of the ashes' are gardens, golf courses, hilltops, former holiday destinations and beaches. Tales of more elaborate if somewhat furtive disposals are not uncommon. According to a recent US newspaper report, attendants watching security monitors at Disneyland noticed a woman dumping a powdery substance from a boat going through the darkened 'Pirates of the Caribbean' cavern. When they confronted her, she told them it was only baby powder; however, it later turned out to be the cremated remains of a human being.

However unusual the chosen site(s), disposal of the ashes still represents a new and, for most families, an uncharted area of ritual possibility and creativity. Anthropologists see it as an example of a wider phenomenon called 'double ritual' in the funeral practices of other cultures. In the case of cremation, a funeral service around the time of death can be followed by a second ceremony – the scattering of the ashes – that can take place months or maybe years after the first ritual, giving bereaved survivors more time to decide what they want the disposal to mean and what it says about the deceased.

Scattering the ashes is perceived by most Europeans as a relatively new activity. It is also a secular ritual, created collectively by bereaved families and friends. Understandably survivors want 'to do things properly', but this can be difficult when the ground rules are still quite fluid. This is compounded by the fact that ashes can travel in a way that corpses never could. They can also be divided and apportioned to a number of different people, giving rise to the possibility of multiple rituals at a variety of sites. Common issues that arise include: who should attend the scattering – friends, family or both? Is one occasion more suitable than another? Should anything be said and, if so, by whom? Should the ashes be buried or simply scattered? Who should perform this final act?

As a ritual, scattering ashes should say something about the life and impact of the deceased. However, the persuasive power of this ritual may be compromised if it is carried out in an arbitrary, 'anything goes' fashion or is seen to be too contrived. Of particular importance is what some researchers have called 'using the incorrect idiom of relatedness'; the power of a ritual may suffer if it is not carried out by someone suitably related or close to the deceased – for example, if golfing buddies take over from the family in scattering the ashes over the eighteenth green. These factors may explain the popularity of accounts of scatterings that went awry, of winds that blew the ashes back on attendees, of angry park attendants or greenkeepers remonstrating and interrupting the proceedings.

Ritual considerations apart, there are a number of additional features of cremation that seem to make it particularly appealing to bereaved people today. First, it has a certain democratic character. Parodying the American Declaration of Independence, 'all men are cremated equal'. The same ovens are used to incinerate all remains. Ashes also tend not to give rise to some of the more ostentatious headstones and statuary that often adorn graves. Some commentators have also remarked on how cremation suits a generation that has benefited so much from scientific and technological control over nature. In a sense, the technology of cremation cheats nature by destroying the body before its features fade and decay. Cremation also sits well with consumers concerned with their 'green' credentials, since it offers the prospect of recycling coffins and a cheaper, more environmentally-friendly funeral overall.

The increasing availability of crematoria has also benefited religious groups for whom cremation is an integral part of their funeral ritual. For example, Hindu families may have the eldest son witness a parent's body being placed in the oven; he can also press the start button thereby fulfilling his *dharma* or sacred duty to light the funeral pyre. In addition, Hindus in Europe can have the ashes of their deceased sent to India for scattering on the Holy River Ganges. Cremations also allow survivors to keep what remains of their loved ones close to them; visits to a cemetery are no longer required. However, this advantage is not without its downside. Survivors who bury ashes in the family garden may find themselves in a quandary should they decide to move house, for example, and having a couple's ashes scattered at a similar location may lack the perceived intimacy of being buried in the same grave. Indeed, ashes do not appear to 'anchor' the dead as does a grave. Research on cemetery behaviour has noted how graves act as physical focal points for a wide range of memorial consumer behaviours. Headstones can be erected, flowers can be placed, plaques can be added, photographs can be mounted, relatives can visit and new family members can be brought and 'introduced' to the deceased.

While cremation is now firmly established as the preferred mode of disposal for the vast majority of Britain's departed, a number of core consumer behaviour and marketing issues remain for the funeral industry. Viewers of *Six Feet Under* will remember that the family running the funeral home were at pains to separate the front stage of their business – reception, viewing rooms, chapel – from its more day-to-day workings in the embalming area downstairs. This distinction between front stage and back stage is critical for many service providers. While the backstage area is, in a sense, 'out of bounds' for customers, understandably they still wonder what precisely goes on there. In traditional funerals this already applied. Mourners wondered what had gone on in that critical interval between the body being collected by the funeral director and the moment when they first viewed the deceased dressed and often embalmed. However, the advent of widespread cremation has added a further, and possibly more critical dimension, to this front stage–back stage divide. Survivors seem to harbour a mixture of curiosity and concern over what exactly happens once the conveyer belt glides the coffin through the Final Curtain after the service. For example, where exactly are the ovens? Precisely when will the cremation take place? Will everything be burned? In a culture that lays so much emphasis on individuality, people want to be assured that the ashes of their loved one will be properly identified and will not be mixed with those of another person. In a word, integrity of the ashes remains a key concern.

The industry's green credentials are also being called into question. Emissions of all descriptions are becoming matters of acute environmental and political concern. Not only do residents feel uncomfortable at having a crematorium located near their homes but public authorities are also anxious that the thousands of vaporized mercury fillings that result do not become an environmental and health hazard. Cremation costs in the UK are set to rise by £100 to finance the installation of new filters to prevent any such toxic emissions. The growth in popularity of 'woodland', all-natural funerals is also impacting on the industry. Cemeteries that allow no engine-driven hearses, no headstones, and only permit biodegradable coffins mark a challenge to the traditional revenue sources of funeral directors. On a broader level, the increasing use of recycled coffins prior to cremation also represents further possible revenue loss.

In the United States, similar developments have prompted funeral homes to diversify. Examples include increased promotion of pre-planned funerals, financial service provision, bereavement counselling, property and downsizing advice as well as monthly gatherings for single survivors who wish to establish or broaden their social horizons. One funeral home has taken this last offering a step further by organizing holidays to a variety of European destinations for their bereaved clientele. Many directors have also sought to widen the range of options available to mourners for retaining the ashes of their loved one. A firm in upstate New York called Eternity Glass (**www.eternityglass.com**) makes fine quality hand-blown, hand-crafted glass sphere urns with a small quantity of cremains preserved inside. Also available are spheres and pendants in which the ash is encased in opaque glass.

QUESTIONS

1 How well do models of consumer decision-making processes account for the choices made by consumers in the immediate aftermath of bereavement? Are there any other life course events that may have a disruptive effect on consumption patterns and practices?

2 The growth in the acceptability of cremation is a notable example of an innovation that succeeds despite being so at odds with people's prevailing mindsets at the outset. Discuss the factors influencing adoption rates for this innovation.

3 Scattering of the dead person's ashes was described above as an emergent consumer ritual, a ritual 'in the making'. Can you think of any other such emergent rituals? Are there any products or services associated with these rituals? What factors might influence the design of such rituals and the degree of satisfaction experienced by key participants?

4 Cremation is now firmly established as the preferred mode of disposal for the vast majority of Britain's departed. Discuss the implications of this for funeral directors.

5 Is there anything funeral directors can do to allay consumer concerns about backstage issues such as maintaining the 'integrity' of the cremains?

Sources and further reading

Cook, E. (2006), 'Saying Goodbye Our Way', *The Guardian*, 14 August, http://www.guardian.co.uk/lifeandstyle/2006/aug/19/familyandrelationships.family

Davies, D. (1997), *Death, ritual and belief: The rhetoric of funerary rites*. London: Cassell.

Jupp, P. (2006), *From dust to ashes: Cremation and the British way of death*. Basingstoke: Palgrave Macmillan.

Owen, R. (2008), 'Burial is best – but you can scatter your ashes if you must, rules Vatican,' *Times Online*, 11 January, http://www.timesonline.co.uk/tol/news/world/europe/article3168478.ece

Yoshino, K. (2007), 'Woman seen scattering ashes at Disneyland', *Los Angeles Times*, 14 November, http://travel.latimes.com/articles/la-trw-disney14nov14

Commercialization of rituals: Ramadan celebrations in Turkey

ÖZLEM SANDIKCI and ŞAHVER ÖMERAKI, Bilkent University, Turkey

Each year, during the ninth month of the lunar calendar, Muslims perform their religious obligation of Ramadan fasting. For a whole month, from sunrise to sunset, adult Muslims whose health permits abstain from food, drink, and sexual activity. The sunset prayer announces the end of fasting and the beginning of post-sunset dinner (*iftar*) which is followed by special night prayers. Many Muslims consider Ramadan as the most significant of the ritual duties. Ramadan signifies a time for reflection and spiritual discipline, for expressing gratitude for God's guidance and forgiveness of past sins, for acknowledgment of human dependence on God, as well as remembering and responding to the needs of the poor and hungry.

However, across the Muslim world, there are several signs that Ramadan, a time of fasting, prayer and reflection, is changing from a religious month to a holiday marked by consumption. The spirit of capitalism is felt in practices ranging from the marketing of specialty items (e.g. fasting calendars and lanterns) emblazoned with company logos to luxurious Ramadan feasts promoted by restaurants and hotels, Ramadan greeting cards, and Ramadan sweepstakes. It appears that Ramadan is taking on the commercial trappings of Christmas and Hanukah and becoming an increasingly commercialized ritual.

Similar developments are visible in Turkey. Ramadan celebrations now take place more in the public space – especially in retail environments – and in a visibly consumption-oriented manner. For instance, five-star hotels offer lavish Ramadan feasts, Ramadan festivals take place in high-traffic historical sites, and shopping malls transform themselves into Ramadan themed environments offering a variety of shopping and entertainment experiences. Underlying such changes are both state agencies and private companies who co-operate with each other to revive interest in the public celebrations of Ramadan and attract visitors. More and more, Ramadan looks like other Western-originated holiday rituals such as New Year, St. Valentine's Day, and Mother's and Father's Days that are already celebrated in Turkey but almost exclusively as holidays of consumption.

There are three important contexts where new consumption-oriented forms of Ramadan celebrations take place: Ramadan festivals organized by the municipalities, shopping malls, and hotels and restaurants. In each of these contexts theming operates as the key marketing instrument to attract visitors and educate them on how to celebrate Ramadan away from home. Retailers in these setting use several cultural motifs in order to invoke the Ottoman past and seek to create environments that look like old Ottoman streets and neighbourhoods. The Ottoman theming invokes nostalgia for a bygone age and offers a new interpretation of many forgotten rituals.

Municipalities in Istanbul, Ankara and other big cities organize Ramadan festivals. In the 1992 local elections the Islamist party took over the governance of many municipalities in Turkey including Istanbul. The very first Ramadan festival was organized by the Istanbul municipality in the same year. Soon festivals spread to different neighbourhoods in Istanbul and other cities. Although there are some variations across the festivals conducted at different locations, what these festivals commonly involve are a wide selection of food and ample opportunities for shopping and entertainment. Municipalities promote the festivals as an attempt to revive the spirit of 'old' Ramadans by constructing temporary consumption spaces that foster participation of different segments of society in these collective celebrations. As no entrance fee is charged, even people with limited incomes can visit the festival areas. However, in order to participate in the joy of the festivals one needs to spend money, i.e. on food and certain entertainment activities. Religious and tourist areas transform into big marketplaces, packed with several stands selling food and beverages as well as all kinds of paraphernalia. On each day of the Ramadan month, thousands of consumers crowd the festival places and wait until the time that the daily fasting will be over. After the call of the prayer that announces the end of the fast, entertainment begins. The activities include religious panels addressing different aspects of Ramadan and Islam as well as artistic performances. The performances mostly include traditional art forms, such as *karagöz* (traditional shadow show) and *meddah* (an earlier form of stand-up show), which were very popular during the time of the Ottoman Empire but had been long forgotten in the modern era. On the other hand, for those interested in shopping, the stands, which are built in the form of traditional Ottoman houses, offer a wide range of selections from religious objects, such as Qurans and spiritual books, to electronic appliances and Chinese-made decorative ornaments. Moreover, several local and global companies promote their products by distributing samples and other promotional materials. For example, one year Unilever distributed bowls of its newly launched instant soup and cups of Lipton brand flavoured teas. Retailers also indulge themselves in the same spirit by wearing the attire of the Ottoman era. Taken as a whole, municipalities, by creating these festive consumption spaces, make Ramadan an attractive event for companies, retailers, residents, and tourists. In the meantime, the municipality also profits as it collects rents from companies and retailers participating in the event.

Shopping malls become another site for the revival of the Ramadan ritual. During the holy month, shopping malls turn into festive places themed with Ottoman symbols. For example, during Ramadan the interior of a shopping mall was once decorated with lively coloured *fezzes*, which were initially used by the Ottoman soldiers and then were adopted as an everyday hat by Ottoman men. Corridors were also decorated by lanterns, which connote the lanterns used to light the streets in the Ottoman Empire. Similar to the festivals organized by municipalities, the malls after *iftar* provide live music, shadow shows, and plays for children. Traditional coffeehouses with their stools and small tables are also placed in most of the malls, offering a nostalgic place to relax and drink coffee or tea after the feast. Additionally, small stands are located all over the mall, which sell nostalgic candies and beverages (e.g. candyfloss or cotton candy; toffee apples; cotton halva [rather like candyfloss or cotton candy]). Shopping malls, similar to the municipality festivals, seek to reconstruct the spirit of the publicly-celebrated Ramadan experience, an experience that had lost its public appeal during the making of the modern Turkish republic. The Ottoman theming allows consumers to experience the collective but forgotten past through fantasy, similar to the role of Disney's Main Street in US culture.

Restaurants, from fast food chains like McDonald's to luxurious five-star hotels, offer different *iftar* menus in a variety of price ranges. The most conspicuous consumption of *iftar* feasts occurs in five-star hotels and restaurants, which use advertising to try and create an alternative 'elite spirit' of Ramadan. The market offers to its elite Muslim followers the ability to experience the sacredness of the month in an exclusive environment. However, rather than being available to everyone, luxurious hotels and restaurants reproduce differences in class positions, as *iftar* dinners cost $30 or more per person. The Ramadan feasts at the five-star hotels and up-market restaurants include a plethora of dishes, starters, main dishes and sweets, which reflect the abundance of choices presented to the modern consumer. Consumers partake of their *iftar* dinners either in set menus or in American style buffets. The choice of dinner menus is not limited to a single fixed menu. Rather, hotels and restaurants offered at least four different menus in order to cater for their customers' tastes. In addition, individuals can create their own customized menus. The food offered usually includes a combination of the rich cuisine of the Ottoman Empire and a variety of options from amongst Turkish and world cuisines (e.g. Mexican, Italian and Greek cuisine). The consumer is not limited to the local tastes of their country; rather, food acquires a global taste. The choice of food dishes and also the presentation combine to create an elite feast. The food is often served on copper dishes, which used to be the tableware in the Ottoman Empire. Live traditional Turkish music is also performed throughout the feast. In some of the restaurants, even *Whirling Dervish* performances are carried out. Some restaurants have revived traditions that were long forgotten, such as *Diş Kirası*. During the Ottoman times, when a family invited visitors for the *iftar* feast, the hosts also gave small gifts to their guests. Modernizing this ritual, an up-market restaurant offers gifts like silver cigarette cases and amber rosaries to its patrons. Through their sophisticated decorations, selection of dishes and entertainment activities, the restaurants and hotels have all attempted to create a simulation of the elite Ramadan celebrations of the sultans in the Ottoman palace.

Western holidays like Christmas, Valentine's Day and Hallowe'en, rather than displacing traditional local holidays, might have acted to revive and modify existing local rituals. The commercialization of ritual is attained through two processes that complement each other in order to revive and spread the ritual. On the one hand, at the symbolic level, there are distinctive characteristics that differentiate the ritual of Ramadan from other holidays and provide a unique experience for consumers. Different forms of post-sunset *iftar* feasts and celebrations, together with the use of the symbols from the Ottoman Ramadan festivals, encourage a local heterogeneity. On the other hand, rituals are still developed and embellished with the needs of the profit-oriented industries in mind. The global consumerist ideology facilitates and strengthens the consumption of 'sacralized' commodities in the form of products, services, places, and experiences, and offer consumers a new occasion for shopping and leisure. Ramadan turns into a commercialized ritual, combining a variety of symbols connoting religious values and beliefs as well as markers of the global consumption ethos. Theming, which underlies all three contexts, operates as a major instrument of commercialization.

Local municipalities and the market forge close ties for the revival of Ramadan. Municipalities transform religious and historical places into temporary commercial markets. While the local government profits from organizing the sites, retailers profit by finding another channel through which to market their products. However, what underlies this co-operation is not only the profit motive, but also the state's political ambitions. The Islamist party, which controls the governance of major cities as well as the country, emphasizes both the religious and Ottoman values for the contemporary Turkish identity and takes advantage of any incidence that can be converted into some form of cultural and religious propaganda.

On the other hand, social structures also create a restricted experience of the ritual for many individuals. For example, the luxurious feasts in five-star hotels and restaurants and certain forms of entertainment in the municipality festivals, which require payment of a cover fee, limit accessibility. Rather than acting as a ritual that emphasizes ultimate unity and equality of all believers before God, Ramadan festivals reinforce and reproduce accepted social hierarchies.

QUESTIONS

1 Which agents play a role in the transformation of Ramadan celebrations? What are their motives?

2 What is the role of globalization in the revival and execution of Ramadan rituals?

3 How might social class affect the execution of the ritual?

4 What are the possible positive and negative effects of the commercialization of rituals?

Case study 21

I hate Christmas! Resisting the norms of the festival

ILONA MIKKONEN and JOHANNA MOISANDER, Helsinki School of Economics, Finland

CONTEXT

Celebrated all over the world, Christmas is central to the retail calendar (McKechnie and Tynan, 2006) and represents the 'distilled essence of contemporary consumption' (Belk and Bryce, 1993). The economic importance of Christmas to the retail sector is undeniable: during the Christmas season 2007, for example, Europeans were estimated to have spent €51 billion on online sales alone (Forrester Research). UK based Halifax Credit Cards' research indicates that the average British shopper spends £384 on Christmas presents (the report is available at **http://www.hbosplc.com/home/home.asp**). The top European Christmas spenders are, however, the Irish, according to Deloitte's annual survey: in 2007 Irish households were estimated to spend €1,431 on average, an increase of 6.9 per cent on 2006 (**www.deloitte.com**).

Christmas, like other festive celebrations, such as Thanksgiving, Hallowe'en and Valentine's Day, is not only a major retail event. Christmas is full of meanings that derive from and reinforce culture (Fischer and Arnold, 1990). Christmas could, in fact, be described as a *cultural model* (Thompson and Arsel, 2004), a cultural construct which involves shared notions of what is correct and normal behaviour in a given social situation. These models provide individuals with frames, or boundaries, for possible and acceptable ways of behaving and thinking. Thus the cultural model of Christmas conveys the ideal image of how Christmas should be celebrated, including ritualistic consumption practices such as gift giving and family dinners.

Cultural models do not only contain rituals and scripts, however, but also norms. While most of the norms regarding Christmas take the form of customs and conventions, for which the 'punishments' for non-compliance are rather mild, they also include customs with moral overtones, especially when it comes to the religious aspects of the holiday. Norms can be very useful in creating group cohesion, but they can also help institutionalize certain ways of thinking and talking about phenomena, and certain ways of doing things within a society. Institutionalization means that these thinking–talking–behaving patterns become taken for granted. Some of the most profound institutions within society are social institutions that govern and give structure to social order and co-operation. Monetary and education systems are social institutions, as is marriage.

All over the world, there are different conventions and customs associated with celebrating Christmas. In Finland, for example, the season starts with an almost ritualistic cleaning of the house that has to be completed by 24 December, which is the most important day of the Christmas festival in Finland. The Christmas tree is usually decorated after breakfast on 24 December, and at noon 'The Declaration of Christmas Peace' is broadcast on radio and television from the city of Turku. While devoid of any legal meaning since 1889, it still marks the transition from the ordinary to the special time of the year. Other important parts of the script include the Christmas sauna, family dinner, and, as the highlight of the evening, a visit by Santa Claus who, according to Finnish folklore, lives in Korvatunturi, a fjeld (rocky plateau) in Finnish Lapland.

While many of the Christmas customs seem at first to take place on a tangible level of gift giving, decorations, and cuisine traditions, they can also be examined on a more abstract level. There seem to be strong, socially enforced rules for not only expressing love and affection for friends and family with suitable gifts, but also for being filled with a 'Christmas spirit' (Clarke, 2007). Being able to perform the expected behaviours may not be sufficient – enjoying these behaviours is also required for the norm to be fulfilled.

As a cultural phenomena Christmas is a particularly intriguing blend of the sacred and profane, materialism and spiritualism, hedonism and communal values (Fischer and Arnold, 1990), and often represents a site for tensions between selfishness and generosity as compared to other holidays like Thanksgiving, which more openly celebrates material abundance. Academic consumer research has suggested that Christmas has lost much of its spiritual import in Western commercial culture because of materialism, hedonism, and commercialism (see for example Belk, Wallendorf and Sherry, 1989; Belk and Bryce, 1993; and McKechnie and Tynan, 2006). Thus, Christmas may not stand for the jolly, sharing and caring holiday for all: instead it can be full of discrepancies between the idyllic model and the reality as perceived and experienced. As such

Christmas has provided a fertile breeding ground for consumer resistance and attempts to breach the norms associated with Christmas.

REFUSAL TO CONFORM – THE CHRISTMAS RESISTANCE MOVEMENT

Christmas summons images of family gathered around a decorated tree, of music and light and the comforting smell of a special dinner cooking on a snowy winter day [. . .] But is this the Christmas we actually experience? How many people standing in the line at the malls would say that their Christmas season is replete with warmth, affection, and neighbourliness? In fact, Christmas is experienced by most adults as a time of intensified stress . . . The result is often 'holiday blues' and even severe depression.

(Horsley and Tracy, 2001: 1)

As the above excerpt from Horsley and Tracy's (2001) *Christmas unwrapped: Consumerism, Christ, and Culture* suggests, Christmas is indeed not only a happy time for singing carols and eating turkey with loved ones. Christmas is also the most likely time of the year for people to experience symptoms of depression, not least because of the financial burdens and stress associated with Christmas, but also because of the pressures to perform as a family. Consequently, Christmas has not only passionate fans, but also avid adversaries.

If you type the words 'Christmas resistance' or 'Christmas sucks' into an Internet search engine, you will instantly receive more than a million hits. Every year during the Christmas season, hundreds of people log into the discussion forums to complain that Christmas has lost its meaning and degenerated into a senseless marketing frenzy.

One of the most organized forms of this online opposition is The Christmas Resistance Movement (http://www.xmasresistance.org/) that calls for a boycott of 'Christmas Shopping, Christmas decorations, Christmas cards, and every variety of Christmas Crap'. The not-for-profit anti-consumerism organization Adbusters asks people to 'carry the spirit of Buy Nothing Day into the holiday season by taking back Christmas'. Most of the criticism is, however, voiced in the various forums and blogs of the cyber world from behind a screen name:

I vehemently resent all the expectations and demands placed on me at Christmas. Christmas has become the antithesis of itself. It is supposed to be an attitude from the heart of sharing, reflection, and spending time with the ones you love. Instead, everybody rushes around going through the motions out of a sense of duty. They want to appear as though they have the Christmas spirit but instead are just mindlessly complying with all the demands and obligations that bombard us from every direction.

(Sailorman, 9 December 2006 at I Hate This Blog)

I despise the pre-Christmas frenzy, the stupid, pathetic decorations, the blind consumer run for gifts, gifts, gifts. More shit to buy, more shit to sell, yupee . . . P.S.: Do you really need a special day to show your dear ones that you care about them?! I don't.

(Nicola, 30 December 2006 at Sketches and Scrawls)

Both Sailorman's and Nicola's accounts resonate with the central criticism against contemporary Christmas: the 'real' meaning of Christmas has been lost to commercialism. The marketplace has invaded the private sphere of the home to the point where material abundance has become a measure of the success of the family and gift giving is an indication of mutual love and affection.

However, standing out against the norms of Christmas is not always easy because the pressure to conform is high. Even if there are no formal penalties for not liking Christmas, the fear of deviance drives the Scrooges to the Internet. As Lowrey and Otnes (2004) pointed out, the risk of being found out by others of not celebrating Christmas in a genuine festive spirit often outweighs the possible inconvenience that may result from participating. Consequently many online writers, like Jenny and sherri, feign the Christmas spirit in order to avoid discomfort, and to please family members, particularly children:

I have 2 children and a husband that think x-mas is so great. I have to put on my fake holiday smile when I would like to hibernate until New Year is over.

(Jenny, 21 November 2006 at Tribe.net)

I can relate. This time of year always caused such stress. My husband loves [Christmas], and with a small child, you have to play the game. I absolutely hate the bullshit. I just want to go to sleep and wake up on December 31.

(sherri, 26 November 2006)

ONLINE SCROOGES

Think of the reaction people get if they say they don't like this season, the names they are called: Scrooge. Grinch. Not exactly 'nice' characters you'd like to invite over for dinner.

(Epstain, Deviant Christmas, 2001, http://www.suite101.com/article.cfm/crime_deviance/87049)

Ebenezer Scrooge is the main character in Charles Dickens' novel *A Christmas Carol*; a cold-hearted and selfish man with a particular aversion to the gaiety and merriment of Christmas. Although Scrooge's opposition to Christmas as 'humbug' is reversed by the end of the story, when he becomes the very model of unselfishness and ethics, his last name has become a byword for or reference to not only exaggerated frugality, but also hatred and unfriendliness. The cartoon character Grinch is not a Christmas lover either: in the Dr. Seuss classic *How the Grinch Stole Christmas*, the hero/villain sets out to sabotage the holiday but like Scrooge ends up transforming from an unpleasant grouch into a loving and kind person touched by the Christmas spirit.

Both Dickens' and Dr. Seuss's stories, although representing different literary genres (Dickens' *Christmas Carol* being a classic, while Grinch's adventures take place in a children's picture book), underline the idea that there is something wrong with not celebrating or not liking Christmas and thus reinforcing the social norm. Nevertheless the participants in the anti-Christmas discussions seem to have adopted quite a different reading of both stories and their central characters: Scrooge and the Grinch are free from succumbing to the game, free from compliance with the empty rituals of pretending to enjoy Christmas food, the present company, and the unwanted gifts. The following anonymous accounts acknowledge the emancipatory power of 'Scroogeness':

> so maybe i am just a scrooge, but i would rather be scrooge than broke and over fed with over cooked turkey and those 'oh-so-happy-to-see-you-smiles' and the 'I love the reindeer sweaters'.
>
> (Rip's Domain, 14 December 2006)

For the online posters the Grinch and Scrooge have become representatives for standing one's ground, and being a Scrooge can actually be a source of pleasure, as suggested by Joseph (30 November 2000 at Fortunecity.com); before turning on the fake smile which he will need to sport as Father Christmas for the sake of his children when they are old enough to understand, he is going to 'enjoy being a Scrooge one last time'.

Scrooge and the Grinch are not the only fictional characters mentioned on these sites: Ozzie and Harriet of the 1950s' sitcom *The Adventures Of Ozzie And Harriet*, and Carolyn Burnham, the control-freak wife of 1999 family tragi-comedy *American Beauty* (played by Annette Bening), also become comparison points for the family parties.

In *The Adventures*, Ozzie and Harriet Nelson portray, together with their two sons, a fictional Nelson family which 'embodied wholesome, "normal" American existence so conscientiously (if blandly) that their name epitomized upright, happy family life for decades' (Weisblat, 2007). Despite their arguable innocence, even naïvety, the Nelsons – with a sweet homemaker mother, a head-of-the-household, breadwinner father, and their two responsible, talented sons who both grow up to be lawyers – sum up what continues to be the cultural family ideal in the Western world.

The Burnhams of *American Beauty*, on the other hand, are a typical case of family dysfunction. The father, Lester, is having a midlife-crisis and a crush on his teenage daughter Jane's cheerleader friend, while the mother, Carolyn, is much more interested in her career as a real-estate agent and the façade of happy family life than the actual family she has. In the discussion forums it is the Nelsons who personify the disillusions of the perfect family Christmas; when the reality unavoidably falls short of the expectations, the letdown brings in the Burnhams:

> Well, so far, my cousin is crying, laying on the couch having a meltdown. She's the Annette Bening character in 'American Beauty.' She expects Ozzy & Harriet holidays every year. And, for some reason, those never morph beyond the screamfests. Mom is not speaking to me, shoving wrapping paper around angrily and blasting Xmas music to drown me out. Other cousins (family drunks) have begun the binging and won't stop until after New Year. Isn't this a lovely season. Grab your popcorn and watch the show.
>
> (sherri, 12 December 2006 at Tribe.net)

INTERNET SAFE HAVEN FOR CHRISTMAS HATERS

In the global networks of the Internet, consumers are able to congregate with like-minded people to criticize social conventions without running the risk of being positioned as outsiders in their immediate social environments. Very few of the people participating in the anti-Christmas discussions mention actually refusing to celebrate Christmas, or even attempting to find alternative ways of spending the holiday season. Consider these following posts by candice and mita, who seem to be leading a double life of celebrating Christmas while secretly hating it online:

> Well, today is the day. Doesn't matter how much we wish it would disappear and still it shows up. Hubby and I started off the day with the annual Christmas Day Fight. Followed by the 'I hate you and I don't want your gift . . . We spend every year worshipping the Santa-god and bowing down to a dead tree that's got plastic spheres on it. And then what do we do??? Light it up to display our stupidness. Here the neighbor comes to see my dead tree; ain't it purdy? We then get to celebrate even more by eating dead fowl and pig.
>
> (candice, 25 December 2006 at Rip's Domain)

> thank god for alcohol – it's the only thing that has enabled me to cope with being incarcerated for days with my mother
>
> (mita, 30 December 2006 at Rip's Domain)

The online environments make it possible to form alternative selves while at the same time maintaining the more conforming everyday identities that reflect certain cultural models. Internet communities thus seem to grant Christmas adversaries a sort of a safe haven, not only for venting their frustrations, but also for anonymous and safe breaching of the social standard.

Overall, online environments seem to allow individuals a new type of flexibility in their identities, enabling them to occupy multiple subject positions simultaneously; in the case of Christmas one can still sing the carols and carve the turkey with loved ones, while joining another social grouping in the virtual world.

This case study is based on Ilona Mikkonen and Johanna Moisander (2008): 'Cynical identity project as consumer resistance: Constructing Scrooge in online anti-Christmas sites', paper presented at Consumer Culture Theory conference, 19–22 July 2008, Boston, USA.

QUESTIONS

1 Do you agree with the notion that Christmas has become too commercialized? If so, what kind of role do you see marketers having in this process? What do you think could and should be done about the situation?

2 What other cultural models can you think of? What kind of consumption patterns are associated with them?

3 Thinking about your own experiences of Christmas, which theoretical concepts might apply in explaining consumer behaviour within the context of Christmas (e.g. rituals; gift giving; identity and symbolic consumption)?

Sources

Belk, R.W., and Bryce, W. (1993), 'Christmas shopping scenes: From modern miracle to postmodern mall', *International Journal of Research in Marketing*, 10(3): 277.

Belk, R.W., Wallendorf, M., and Sherry Jr., John F. (1989), 'The sacred and the profane in consumer behavior: Theodicy on the odyssey', *Journal of Consumer Research*, 06(1).

Clarke, P. (2007), 'A measure for Christmas spirit', *Journal of Consumer Marketing*, 24(1): 8.

Fischer, E., and Arnold, S.J. (1990), 'More than a labor of love: Gender roles and Christmas gift shopping', *Journal of Consumer Research*, 17(3).

Horsley, R., and Tracy, J. (eds) (2001), Introduction in *Christmas unwrapped: Consumerism, Christ, and Culture*. (Harrisburgh, PA: Trinity Press International.)

Lowrey, T.M., and Otnes, C.C. (2004), 'Consumer fairy tales of the perfect Christmas: Villains and other dramatis personae', in C. Otnes (ed.), *Contemporary consumption rituals: A research anthology*. (Mahwah, NJ, USA: Lawrence Erlbaum Associates, Incorporated): 99–122.

McKechnie, S., and Tynan, C. (2006), 'Social meanings in Christmas consumption: An exploratory study of UK celebrants' consumption rituals', *Journal of Consumer Behaviour*, 5(2): 130.

Thompson, C.J., and Arsel, Z. (2004), 'The Starbucks brandscape and consumers' (anticorporate) experiences of glocalization', *Journal of Consumer Research*, 31: 631–642.

Further reading

Close, A. (2006), 'A holiday loved and loathed: A consumer perspective of Valentine's day', *Advances in Consumer Research*, 33: 353.

Hollenbeck, C.R., and Zinkhan, G.M. (2006), 'Consumer activism on the internet: The role of anti-brand communities', *Advances in Consumer Research*, 33(1): 479.

Miller, D. (ed.) (1993), *Unwrapping Christmas*. (Oxford, Clarendon Press.)

Rook, D.W. (1985), 'The ritual dimension of consumer behavior', *Journal of Consumer Research*, 12: 251.

Schau, H.J., and Gilly, M.C. (2003), 'We are what we post? Self-presentation in personal web space', *Journal of Consumer Research*, 30(3): 385–404.

Wallendorf, M., and Arnould, E.J. (1991), ' "We gather together": Consumption rituals of Thanksgiving day', *Journal of Consumer Research*, 18 (June): 13.

' 'Tis the season . . .': brand ritualization of Xmas beer consumption

DANNIE KJELDGAARD and MATTHIAS BODE, University of Southern Denmark

When does the Christmas season begin? For Danes, the answer is easy: at 8.59 P.M. on the first Friday in November. It starts with a nationwide event called *J-Dag* (Yule-Day), when the new Christmas beer is released. When Lorenzo, an Italian exchange student at the University of Southern Denmark in Odense, heard his Danish friends talking about this day weeks before the actual celebration, he was curious. Although he had only lived in Denmark for a few months, he had quickly learnt that beer drinking is more important for Danes than for his friends at home, in Italy. But why should a whole nation celebrate beer? And what does it have to do with Christmas? He was determined to find out for himself.

This year J-Dag was on November 2nd (it is normally the first Friday of November) and I celebrated it in the bar at my university, so I spent that day with many other exchange students as well as with my Danish friends. We met just an hour before the celebration started (Christmas beer can't be sold before 8.59 P.M., so people usually go to the bars and pubs at 8 o'clock so that they can wait all together until the moment when the beer arrives and is opened).

The first thing that surprised me was how the bar was decorated: there were lights and decorations everywhere, as well as many Christmas beer advertisements. The funniest thing was that the bartenders were dressed up like Santa Claus; everything seemed to recall the real Christmas except for the prevailing colour of the decorations: they were blue and not red as they would usually be at Christmastime. As I found out later, blue is the brand colour of the Christmas beer.

We were standing at the bar and as 8.59 P.M. got closer and closer I started feeling the general excitement growing in the crowd round me. A few seconds before 8.59 P.M. the countdown started (just like on New Year's Eve). Finally, the first beer was opened, the new Christmas decorations were suddenly everywhere, and the music in the bar changed to Danish and international Christmas songs. The party could begin. Everyone tried to get at least one of the free bottles of Christmas beer (this kind of beer is a little bit stronger than normal beer and a lot more festive). The beer we got was the local Albani Christmas beer; there were two kinds of that Christmas beer, the blue label Christmas beer

is much stronger than the red label Christmas beer which has a lower percentage of alcohol and is for women.

The atmosphere was very strange. It was more like a religious celebration (Christmas or Easter). Everybody was shouting good wishes to everybody else and the word you could hear the most was *skål* (cheers). Another bizarre thing was that some people were wearing strange hats. It did not take long to find out its special meaning. The tradition is that people with that hat on their head have to be kissed by all the other people they meet. Being kissed by strangers could seem rather weird and inappropriate behaviour but beer, especially Christmas beer (that is, as I said before, very strong), makes it just very funny and a way to socialize with other people.

After a few hours almost everyone was drunk but I could understand that there was nothing wrong in this, it is just part of the celebration: people celebrate Christmas beer and the best way to celebrate it is to get drunk on it.

The first supply of free Christmas beer ran out after just a few minutes. Exactly an hour later more boxes of Christmas beer were opened and the celebration continued until the morning.

This was a memorable experience for Lorenzo. As an outsider he soon felt like an active participant as the events of the evening unfolded. He learnt fast and enjoyed himself. Maybe next year, when he is back in Italy, he might even miss the J-Dag. Then he will feel more like his Danish friends, for whom the ritual starts with the build up of expectations and anticipation long before the first Friday of November, when the actual release of Christmas beers onto the Danish market takes place.

As a seasonal ritual, the J-Dag can be said to be the first of the Christmas celebrations in Denmark and is mainly carried out by young people. It resembles many of the carnivalesque celebrations in medieval times when rituals and holidays were more part of a public community matter than a private, family matter. The brands' appearance in November is associated with nostalgia and acts to co-structure seasonal dimensions of consumer culture. While a plethora of competing brands exists, the Tuborg Christmas beer brand holds a dominant market share as well as playing a defining cultural role for brand competition within this product category.

The build-up begins in late October with the release of the, by now, classic television and cinema commercials from the Tuborg brewery. They show Santa Claus chasing a beer truck on his sleigh – all on a blue and white background. The commercial continues to be used and has become a cultural icon that serves the function of announcing the approaching Christmas season. Tuborg first used this commercial successfully in 1980. The next year, in 1981, the ad agency and brand manager decided to launch a Christmas beer from Tuborg inspired by the concept of the commercial that would be able to compete with the other Christmas beers on the market. Inspired by the release of Easter beers (which the brand Carlsberg had successfully initiated in 1953), in 1990 Tuborg decided to release the beer on a specific date in bars where customers would be able to have a free sample. Today this event is known as J-Dag and is surrounded by a variety of print advertisements, TV and cinema commercials and billboard ads that forecast that a 'snow storm' will descend on the first Friday of November and announce the date and the time of arrival of the beer to the public.

In the present form of the ritual, the Christmas beer from Tuborg is released in bars and shops around the country, and J-Dag is celebrated by giving away free Christmas beers at 20.59. The ritual is mainly performed by young people, many of whom have developed their own 'warm up' rituals during the day. The other beer brands also release their beer on the same day and in some cases the day before. Nevertheless, the sheer size of the advertising effort of the Tuborg brand makes 20.59 on the first Friday of November the J-Dag. As Lorenzo mentioned, the colours are blue and white even if the beer served is from a competing brewery using alternative colour branding and labelling schemes.

Consumers crowd the bars across the cities of Denmark from late afternoon and await the official moment of release. Many will have been given or buy various merchandise such as blue and white Santa hats, ties, socks, shirts, etc. or small flashing pins for their jacket lapels primarily from the main brand Tuborg but also from regional brands such as the Albani brand from Funen (which has the 'blue' and 'red' beer versions mentioned by Lorenzo) and other merchandise paraphernalia. Snow machines spray fake snow in the streets. There are Santa's helpers in the form of scantily-clad women and dwarfs, and also advertisements and billboards from several breweries. People celebrate in bars and in the street in a spirit of frivolity and excess – to the extent that the day after there are always worried media reports about excess drinking by young people. Initially the release was on the first Wednesday of November but media panics and complaints from educational institutions about hungover students made the Tuborg brand change the release date to a Friday in 1999.

After the J-Dag the general season of frivolous Christmas parties begins – many of which are celebrated by a much older audience than those at the J-Dag – but all the more frivolous for it. The season progresses to the family-based and children-oriented Christian celebration around December 24 and finally ends with the global event of New Year – which in the Danish context is primarily an adult event where excess and transgression of regular consumption norms are the standard.

CONSTRUCTING CULTURAL RITUALS – A STRAIGHTFORWARD STRATEGIC EXERCISE?

The success and vitality of this brand-constructed ritual raises the question of whether or not it is that easy for a company to invent a ritual that can achieve a nationwide reach, and be accepted as part of the national culture. Not all brand initiated occasions for hedonic and experiential consumption necessarily achieve institutionalization as a cultural ritual. What is seemingly an advertising ploy needs to be seen in terms of a longer historical perspective. Across Europe since the middle ages, and in northern Europe since the Vikings, there has been a tradition of making stronger seasonal brews to celebrate the turn of the sun (solstice) or the fertility of land and animals (such as the spring around Easter or the harvest in the autumn). In the dim and distant past of Viking times the term for the celebration of the pre-Christian Christmas was 'to drink Yule'. The construction of the brand rituals by Tuborg is therefore by no means coincidental. Tuborg (knowingly or unknowingly) has been able to tap into historically established seasonal variations and ritualizations that can make a brand iconic. It could be said to be a contemporary manifestation of an historical ritual that is meant to mark the transition from one season to the other – hence a rite of the passage of seasons. In this way, brands can co-structure seasonal patterns of consumer culture. The development of the ritual, however, happens in interaction with official authorities, consumers, media and retailers and the culture at large.

QUESTIONS

1 How does it help to use the 'ritual' concept to understand J-Dag (in addition to product placement or sponsorship)?

2 What do you think competing beer companies should do: join the Tuborg initiated J-Dag, oppose it, or is it viable for them to create their own rituals?

3 Consider what kind of seasonal consumer culture rituals there are in your own culture. What role do brands play?

4 The J-Dag can be said to be a very local phenomenon marking the seasonality of Danish consumer culture. Could Tuborg leverage the success of the ritual for its brand in other markets?

Sources

Holt, Douglas B. (2006), '"Jack Daniels" America', *Journal of Consumer Culture*, vol. 6, no. 3: 355–377.

Kjeldgaard, Dannie and Bode, Matthias, notes from participant observation, netnographic material and consumer interviews for a research project carried out between 2007 and 2008.

Rook, Dennis W. (1985), 'The ritual dimension of consumer research', *Journal of Consumer Research*, vol. 12, no. 3: 251–264.

Glossary

ABC model of attitudes a multidimensional perspective stating that attitudes are jointly defined by affect, behavior, and cognition (p. 277)

Absolute threshold the minimum amount of stimulation that can be detected on a sensory channel (p. 128)

Accommodative purchase decision the process to achieve agreement among a group whose members have different preferences or priorities (p. 431)

Acculturation the process of learning the beliefs and behaviours endorsed by another culture (pp. 200, 607)

Acculturation agents friends, family, local businesses and other reference groups which facilitate the learning of cultural norms (p. 607)

Activation models of memory approaches to memory stressing different levels of processing that occur and activate some aspects of memory rather than others, depending on the nature of the processing task (p. 259)

Activity stores a retailing concept that lets consumers participate in the production of the products or services being sold in the store (p. 82)

Actual self a person's realistic appraisal of his or her qualities (p. 145)

Adaptation the process that occurs when a sensation becomes so familiar that it is no longer the focus of attention (p. 130)

Advergaming online games merged with interactive advertisements that let companies target specific types of consumers (p. 533)

Affect the way a consumer feels about an attitude object (p. 277)

Affluenza a term used to describe what some critics see as the negative side effects for consumers' mental and physical health of an excessive focus on consumption; and the underlying assumption of an inverse relationship between happiness and concern with material goods (p. 49)

Age cohort a group of consumers of the same approximate age who have undergone similar experiences (p. 437)

Agentic goals goals that stress self-assertion and mastery and are associated with males (p. 154)

AIOs (Activities, Interests and Opinions) the psychographic variables used by researchers in grouping consumers (p. 581)

Androgyny the possession of both masculine and feminine traits (p. 155)

Antibrand communities groups of consumers who share a common disdain for a celebrity, store, or brand (p. 387)

Appeal the basis of the persuasive message in an advertisement which can be linked to a range of emotions (e.g. fear) and message types (e.g. humour) (p. 300)

Approach–approach conflict a person must choose between two desirable alternatives (p. 182)

Approach–avoidance conflict a person desires a goal but wishes to avoid it at the same time (p. 183)

Art product a creation viewed primarily as an object of aesthetic contemplation without any functional value (p. 546)

Aspirational reference group high-profile athletes and celebrities used in marketing efforts to promote a product (p. 387)

Atmospherics the use of space and physical features in store design to evoke certain effects in buyers (p. 82)

Attention the assignment of cognitive capacity to selected stimuli (p. 130)

Attitude a lasting, general evaluation of people (including oneself), objects or issues (p. 275)

Attitude object (A_o) anything towards which one has an attitude (p. 275)

Attitude towards the act of buying (A_{act}) the perceived consequences of a purchase (p. 291)

Attitude towards the advertisement (A_{ad}) a predisposition to respond favourably to a particular advertising stimulus during an exposure situation (p. 280)

Autocratic decisions purchase decisions that are made exclusively by one spouse (p. 431)

Avatar manifestation of a Hindu deity in superhuman or animal form. In the computing world it has come to mean a cyberspace presence represented by a character that you can move around inside a visual, graphical world (p. 147)

Avoidance reference groups are reference groups which a consumer specifically chooses not to be associated with via his/her consumption choices (p. 387)

Avoidance–avoidance conflict when we desire a goal but wish to avoid it at the same time (p. 184)

B2C e-commerce businesses selling to consumers through electronic marketing (p. 15)

Balance theory considers relations among elements a person might perceive as belonging together and people's tendency to change relations among elements in order to make them consistent or balanced (p. 286)

Behaviour a consumer's actions with regard to an attitude object (p. 277)

Behavioural economics the study of the behavioural determinants of economic decisions (p. 454)

Behavioural influence perspective the view that consumer decisions are learned responses to environmental cues (p. 317)

Behavioural learning theories the perspectives on learning that assume that learning takes place as the result of responses to external events (p. 246)

Behavioral targeting the appearance and personality a person takes on as an avatar in a computer-mediated environment like Second Life (p. 589)

Being space a retail environment that resembles a residential living room where customers are encouraged to congregate (p. 80)

Bitcoms a new way to boost viewers' retention of a set of ads inserted within a TV show; the commercials are preceded with a stand-up comedian (perhaps an actor in the show itself) who performs a small set that leads into the actual ads (p. 262)

Blogosphere the universe of active weblogs (online diaries) (p. 389)

Body cathexis a person's feelings about aspects of his or her body (p. 160)

Body image a consumer's subjective evaluation of his or her physical appearance (p. 160)

Brand the name associated by a manufacturer with their product in order to distinguish their product from similar products in the marketplace; it can often also be a trademark (p. 37)

Brand communities a set of consumers who share a set of social relationships based on usage or interest in a product (pp. 37, 391)

Brand equity a brand that has strong positive associations and consequently commands a lot of loyalty (p. 252)

Brand-fests usually organized by companies to promote and celebrate their brands; and often used to encourage the development of brand communities in order to build brand loyalty and reinforce group membership (p. 392)

Brand loyalty a pattern of repeat product purchases accompanied by an underlying positive attitude towards the brand (p. 349)

Buzz word of mouth that is viewed as authentic and generated by customers (p. 299)

C2C e-commerce consumer-to-consumer activity through the Internet (p. 15)

Capital Following Bourdieu, capital involves a variety of resources (e.g. economic, cultural and social) that can be used as assets in various contexts (p. 478)

Carbon footprint the impact human activities have on the environment in terms of the amount of greenhouse gases they produce; measured in units of carbon dioxide (p. 211)

Chavs British term that refers to young, lower-class men and women who mix flashy brands and accessories from big names such as Burberry with track suits (p. 465)

Classic a fashion with an extremely long acceptance cycle (p. 568)

Classical conditioning the learning that occurs when a stimulus eliciting a response is paired with another stimulus which initially does not elicit a response on its own but will cause a similar response over time because of its association with the first stimulus (p. 247)

Cloud computing computing that involves massively scalable IT-related capabilities and internet technologies and which thereby provides companies with services, platforms or software that give access to multiple external customers…. (p. 617)

Co-consumers other patrons in a consumer setting (p. 64)

Coercive power influencing a person by social or physical intimidation (p. 395)

Cognition the beliefs a consumer has about an attitude object (p. 277)

Cognitive development the ability to comprehend concepts of increasing complexity as a person ages (p. 436)

Cognitive learning the learning that occurs as a result of internal mental processes (p. 250)

Collecting the accumulation of rare or mundane and inexpensive objects, which transforms profane items into sacred ones (p. 532)

Collective selection the process whereby certain symbolic alternatives tend to be chosen jointly in preference to others by members of a group (p. 561)

Collectivist culture a cultural orientation which encourages people to subordinate their personal goals to those of a stable in-group (p. 508)

Communal goals goals that stress affiliation and the fostering of harmonious relations and are associated with females (p. 154)

Communities of practice groups of people engaged in some mutual endeavour or activity (p. 392)

Comparative influence the process whereby a reference group influences decisions about specific brands or activities (p. 384)

Compensatory decision rules allow information about attributes of competing products to be averaged; poor standing on one attribute may be offset by good standing on another (p. 351)

Compulsive buying is a physiological and/or psychological dependency on products or services. The act of shopping can be an addictive experience for some consumers (p. 49)

Conformity a change in beliefs or actions as a reaction to real or perceived group pressure (p. 396)

Conscientious consumerism a new value that combines a focus on personal health with a concern for global health (p. 208)

Consensual purchase decision a decision in which the group agrees on the desired purchase and differs only in terms of how it will be achieved (p. 431)

Consideration set the products a consumer actually deliberates about choosing (p. 334)

Conspicuous consumption the purchase and prominent display of luxury goods as evidence of the consumer's ability to afford them (pp. 475, 563)

Consumer behaviour the processes involved when individuals or groups select, purchase, use or dispose of products, services, ideas or experiences to satisfy needs or desires (p. 6)

Consumer confidence the state of mind of consumers relative to their optimism or pessimism about economic decisions; people tend to make more discretionary purchases when their confidence in the economy is high (p. 457)

Consumer culture the relationship between market forces, consumption processes and the key characteristics of what is normally understood to be 'a culture' (p. 32)

Consumer hyperchoice a condition where the large number of available options forces us to make repeated choices that drain psychological energy and diminish our ability to make smart decisions (p. 315)

Consumer policy Concern of public bodies (including many national and international agencies) to oversee consumer-related activities for the welfare of consumers e.g. health and safety issues around the consumption of legal and illegal substances such as alcohol, cigarettes and drugs; sustainability issues and the environment (p. 17)

Consumer satisfaction/dissatisfaction (CS/D) the overall attitude a person has about a product after it has been purchased (p. 86)

Consumer socialization the process by which people acquire skills that enable them to function in the marketplace (p. 433)

Consumer society is a society where the social life is organized less around our identities as producers or workers in the production system, and more according to our roles as consumers in the consumption system (p. 32)

Consumer tribe group of people who share a lifestyle and who can identify with each other because of a shared allegiance to an activity or a product (p. 392)

Consumption constellations a set of products and activities used by consumers to define, communicate and perform social roles (p. 580)

Continuous innovation a product change or new product that requires relatively little adaptation in the consumer's behaviour (p. 558)

Convention norms regarding the conduct of everyday life (p. 510)

Co-optation a cultural process where the original meaning of a product or other symbol associated with a subculture is modified by members of mainstream culture (pp. 506, 542)

Core values common general values held by a culture (p. 198)

Corporate paradox the more involved a company appears to be in the dissemination of news about its products, the less credible it becomes (p. 299)

Corporate social responsibility (CSR) addresses two kinds of responsibility: companies' commercial responsibility to run their businesses successfully; and their social responsibilities to their local communities and wider society (p. 53)

Craft product a creation valued because of the beauty with which it performs some function; this type of product tends to follow a formula that permits rapid production; it is easier to understand than an art product (p. 546)

Cult products items that command fierce consumer loyalty and devotion (p. 193)

Cultivation hypothesis a perspective emphasizing media's ability to distort consumers' perceptions of reality (p. 554)

Cultural categories the grouping of ideas and values that reflect the basic ways members of society characterize the world (p. 35)

Cultural formula where certain roles and props often occur consistently in many popular art forms, such as detective stories or science fiction (p. 549)

Cultural gatekeepers individuals who are responsible for determining the types of message and symbolism to which members of mass culture are exposed (p. 544)

Cultural selection the process where some alternatives are selected in preference to those selected by cultural gatekeepers (p. 542)

Culture the values, ethics, rituals, traditions, material objects and services produced or valued by members of society (p. 506)

Culture production system (CPS) the set of individuals or organizations responsible for creating and marketing a cultural product (p. 543)

Custom a norm that is derived from a traditional way of doing something (p. 510)

Cybercrime involves illegal activities undertaken on the internet and can include risks of identity theft and data loss to consumers (p. 590)

Cyberspace refers to the virtual world created by the internet where individuals can engage in a variety of activities including the buying and selling of goods and services; and also games playing (p. 74)

Database marketing involves tracking consumers' buying habits and crafting products and information tailored to people's wants and needs (p. 14)

Decision polarization the process whereby individuals' choices tend to become more extreme (polarized), in either a conservative or risky direction, following group discussion of alternatives (p. 399)

De-individuation the process whereby individual identities are submerged within a group, reducing inhibitions against socially inappropriate behaviour (p. 398)

Demographics the observable measurements of a population's characteristics, such as birth rates, age distribution or income (p. 9)

Desacralization the process that occurs when a sacred item or symbol is removed or is duplicated in mass quantities and as a result becomes profane (p. 530)

Desire to wish or long for consumer goods which contribute to the formation of consumers' self-image; also refers to the sociogenic nature of needs (p. 190)

Determinant attributes the attributes actually used to differentiate among choices (p. 338)

Differential threshold the ability of a sensory system to detect changes or differences among stimuli (p. 128)

Digital literacy involves a set of requisite I.T skills, at a sufficient level of capability, in order to be able to access, navigate and use the internet; and thus enable individuals to participate fully in the information society of the twenty-first century (p. 614)

Discontinuous innovation a product change or new product that requires a significant amount of adaptation of behaviour by the adopter (p. 559)

Discretionary income the money available to an individual or household over and above that required for maintaining a standard of living (p. 456)

Dissociative reference groups are reference groups with which a consumer does not want to be linked; and therefore the consumer usually avoids products and services (or brand imagery) linked to these groups (p. 387)

Divestment rituals the steps people take to gradually distance themselves from things they treasure so that they can sell them or give them away (p. 219)

Downshifting reducing reliance on possessions and learning to get by with less (p. 208)

Drive theory focuses on the desire to satisfy a biological need in order to reduce physiological arousal (p. 179)

Drive the desire to satisfy a biological need in order to reduce physiological arousal (p. 177)

Dynamically continuous innovation a product change or new product that requires a moderate amount of adaptation of behaviour by the adopter (p. 559)

Early adopters people receptive to new styles because they are involved in the product category and place high value on being fashionable (p. 557)

Elaborated codes the ways of expressing and interpreting meanings that are complex and depend on a sophisticated worldview; they tend to be used by the middle and upper classes (p. 471)

Elaboration likelihood model (ELM) the approach that one of two routes to persuasion (central vs. peripheral) will be followed, depending on the personal relevance of a message; the route taken determines the relative importance of message contents vs. other characteristics, such as source attractiveness (p. 304)

Electronic recommendation agent a software tool that tries to understand a human decision maker's multiattribute preferences for a product category by asking the user to communicate his or her preferences. Based on that data, the software then recommends a list of alternatives sorted by the degree that they fit with the person's preferences (p. 341)

Emic perspective an approach to studying cultures that stresses the unique aspects of each culture (p. 42)

Encoding the process in which information from short-term memory is entered into long-term memory in recognizable form (p. 257)

Enculturation the process of learning the beliefs and behaviours endorsed by one's own culture (p. 199)

Erogenous zones areas of the body considered by members of a culture to be foci of sexual attractiveness (p. 562)

Ethnic subculture a self-perpetuating group of consumers held together by common cultural ties (p. 606)

Ethnocentrism the belief in the superiority of one's own country's practices and products (p. 346)

Ethnoconsumerism the understanding and analysis of each culture, including consumer culture, on the basis of its own premises (p. 509)

Ethos a set of moral, aesthetic and evaluative principles (p. 508)

Etic perspective an approach to studying culture that stresses the commonalities across cultures (p. 42)

Evaluative criteria the dimensions used by consumers to compare competing product alternatives (p. 337)

Evoked set those products already in memory plus those prominent in the retail environment that are actively considered during a consumer's choice process (p. 260, 334)

Exchange the process whereby two or more organizations or people give and receive something of value (p. 7)

Exchange theory the perspective that every interaction involves an exchange of value (p. 85)

Expectancy disconfirmation model the perspective that consumers form beliefs about product performance based on prior experience with the product and/or communications about the product that imply a certain level of quality; their actual satisfaction depends on the degree to which performance is consistent with these expectations (p. 87)

Expectancy theory the perspective that behaviour is largely 'pulled' by expectations of achieving desirable 'outcomes' or positive incentives, rather than 'pushed' from within (p. 179)

Experiential perspective an approach stressing the gestalt or totality of the product or service experience, focusing on consumers' affective responses in the marketplace (p. 317)

Expert power authority derived from possessing a specific knowledge or skill (p. 394)

Exposure an initial stage of perception where some sensations come within range of consumers' sensory receptors (p. 129)

Extended family traditional family structure where several generations and/or relatives such as aunts, uncles and cousins live together (p. 425)

Extended problem-solving an elaborate decision-making process often initiated by a motive that's fairly central to the self-concept and accompanied by perceived risk; the consumer tries to collect as much information as possible and carefully weighs product alternatives (p. 319)

Extended self the definition of self created by the external objects with which one surrounds oneself (p. 152)

Extinction the process whereby learned connections between a stimulus and response are eroded so that the response is no longer reinforced (p. 248)

Fad a short-lived fashion (p. 569)

Family financial officer (FFO) the family member who is in charge of making financial decisions (p. 432)

Family household a housing unit containing at least two people who are related by blood or marriage (p. 425)

Family life cycle (FLC) a classification scheme that segments consumers in terms of changes in income and family composition and the changes in demands placed on this income (p. 429)

Fashion the process of social diffusion by which a new style is adopted by a group or groups of consumers (p. 561)

Fashion acceptance cycle the diffusion process of a style through three stages: introduction, acceptance and regression (p. 567)

Fashion life cycle the 'career' or stages in the life of a fashion as it progresses from launch to obsolescence (p. 567)

Fashion system those people or organizations involved in creating symbolic meanings and transferring these meanings to cultural goods (p. 560)

Feature creep trend toward an increasing number of options a product offers that make it more difficult for consumers to decide among competitors (p. 377)

Fertility rate a rate determined by the number of births per year per 1,000 women of child-bearing age (p. 426)

Figure-ground principle the gestalt principle whereby one part of a stimulus configuration dominates a situation while other aspects recede into the background (p. 134)

Flow state situation in which consumers are truly involved with a product, an ad, or a Web site (p. 193)

Food culture pattern of food and beverage consumption that reflects the values of a social group (p. 595)

Foot-in-the-door technique based on the observation that a consumer is more likely to comply with a request if he or she has first agreed to comply with a smaller request (p. 285)

Fortress brands brands that consumers closely link to rituals; this makes it unlikely they will be replaced (p. 517)

Freecycling the practice of giving away useful but unwanted goods to keep them out of landfills (p. 218)

Freegans a takeoff on *vegans*, who shun all animal products; anticonsumerists who live off discards as a political statement against corporations and materialism (p. 214)

Frequency marketing a marketing technique that reinforces regular purchasers by giving them prizes with values that increase along with the amount purchased (p. 255)

Functional theory of attitudes a pragmatic approach that focuses on how attitudes facilitate social behaviour; attitudes exist because they serve some function for the person (p. 275)

Generation X (Gen-Xers or baby busters) the cohort of consumers aged 18–29, who were profoundly affected by the economic recession of the early 1990s (p. 440)

Geo-demography techniques that combine consumer demographic information with geographic consumption patterns to permit precise targeting of consumers with specific characteristics (p. 605)

Gestalt psychology a school of thought that maintains people derive meaning from the totality of a set of stimuli rather than from an individual stimulus (p. 133)

Gift-giving ritual the events involved in the selection, presentation, acceptance and interpretation of a gift (p. 519)

Global consumer culture a culture in which people around the world are united through their common devotion to brand name consumer goods, movie stars, celebrities, and leisure activities (p. 14)

Goal a consumer's desired end-state (p. 177)

Grey market term used to describe the phenomenon of a fast-growing segment of consumers aged 62 or older (p. 443)

Guerrilla marketing promotional strategies that use unconventional locations and intensive word-of-mouth campaigns (p. 403)

Habitual decision-making the consumption choices that are made out of habit, without additional information search or deliberation among products (p. 319)

Habitus systems of classification of phenomena adopted from our socialization processes (p. 478)

Hedonic consumption the multisensory, fantasy and emotional aspects of consumers' interactions with products (p. 121)

Heuristics the mental rules of thumb that lead to a speedy decision (p. 342)

Hierarchy of effects a fixed sequence of steps that occurs during attitude formation; this sequence varies depending on such factors as the consumer's level of involvement with the attitude object (p. 277)

High-context culture group members tend to be tightly knit and messages and meanings are implicit and built into the communication context (p. 602)

Homeostasis the state of being where the body is in physiological balance; goal-oriented behaviour attempts to reduce or eliminate an unpleasant motivational state and returns to a balanced one (p. 179)

Home shopping parties a gathering where a company representative makes a sales presentation to a group of people who have gathered in the home of a friend or acquaintance (p. 400)

Homogamy the tendency for individuals to marry others similar to themselves (p. 462)

Homophily the degree to which a pair of individuals is similar in terms of education, social status, and beliefs (p. 408)

Host culture a new culture to which a person must acculturate (p. 609)

Hype corporate propaganda planted by companies to create product sensation – dismissed as inauthentic by customers (p. 299)

Hyperreality a phenomenon associated with modern advertising in which what is initially stimulation or hype becomes real (pp. 39, 137)

Icon a sign that resembles the product in some culturally meaningful way (p. 135)

Impulse buying a process that occurs when the consumer experiences a sudden urge to purchase an item that he or she cannot resist (p. 83)

Index a sign that is connected to a product because they share some property (p. 135)

Individualist culture a cultural orientation that encourages people to attach more importance to personal goals than to group goals; values such as personal enjoyment and freedom are stressed (p. 508)

Inertia the process whereby purchase decisions are made out of habit because the consumer lacks the motivation to consider alternatives (pp. 192, 349)

Information power power given simply because one knows something others would like to know (p. 393)

Information search the process whereby a consumer searches for appropriate information to make a reasonable decision (pp. 313, 314)

Informational social influence the conformity that occurs because the group's behaviour is taken as evidence about reality (p. 396)

Innovation a product or style that is perceived as new by consumers (p. 554)

Innovative communicators opinion leaders who are also early purchasers (p. 409)

Instrumental values those goals that are endorsed because they are needed to achieve desired end-states or terminal values (p. 203)

Intelligent agents software programs that learn from past user behavior in order to recommend new purchases (p. 341)

Interactive mobile marketing real-time promotional campaigns targeted to consumers' cell phones (p. 195)

Interference a process whereby additional learned information displaces earlier information resulting in memory loss for the item learned previously (p. 263)

Interpretant the meaning derived from a symbol (p. 134)

Interpretation the process whereby meanings are assigned to stimuli (p. 132)

Interpretivism a research perspective that produces a 'thick' description of a consumer's subjective experiences and stresses the importance of the individual's social construction of reality (p. 25)

Involvement the motivation to process product-related information (p. 191)

JND (just noticeable difference) the minimum change in a stimulus that can be detected by a perceiver (p. 128)

Kin network system the rituals intended to maintain ties among family members, both immediate and extended (p. 432)

Knowledge structures organized systems of concepts relating to brands, stores and other concepts (pp. 259, 335)

Laddering a technique for uncovering consumers' associations between specific attributes and general consequences (p. 204)

Lateral cycling a process where already purchased objects are sold to others or exchanged for other items (p. 214)

Latitudes of acceptance and rejection formed around an attitude standard; ideas that fall within a latitude will be favourably received, while those falling outside this zone will not (p. 285)

Lead users involved, experienced customers (usually corporate customers) who are very knowledgeable about the field (p. 558)

Learning a relatively permanent change in a behaviour as a result of experience (p. 246)

Lifestyle a set of shared values or tastes exhibited by a group of consumers especially as these are reflected in consumption patterns (p. 577)

Lifestyle marketing perspective a perspective that recognizes that people are increasingly conscious that we sort ourselves and each other into groups on the basis of the things we/they like to do and how we/they spend our/their disposable income (p. 578)

Limited problem-solving a problem-solving process in which consumers are not motivated to search for information or evaluate rigorously each alternative; instead they use simple decision rules to arrive at a purchase decision (p. 319)

List of Values (LOV) scale identifies consumer segments based on the values members endorse and relates each value to differences in consumption behaviors (p. 203)

LOHAS an acronym for 'lifestyles of health and sustainability'; a consumer segment that worries about the environment, wants products to be produced in a sustainable way, and who spend money to advance what they see as their personal development and potential (p. 208)

Long-term memory the system that allows us to retain information for a long period (p. 259)

Looking-glass self the process of imagining the reaction of others towards oneself (p. 148)

LOV (List of Values) a scale developed to isolate values with more direct marketing applications (p. 203)

Low-context culture messages tend to be more explicit, specific and direct (p. 602)

Low-literate consumer people who read at a very low level; tend to avoid situations where they will have to reveal their inability to master basic consumption decisions such as ordering from a menu (p. 329)

Market beliefs the specific beliefs of decision rules pertaining to marketplace phenomena (p. 343)

Market maven a person who often serves as a source of information about marketplace activities (p. 410)

Market segmentation strategies targeting a brand only to specific groups rather than to everybody (p. 8)

Masculinism study devoted to the male image and the cultural meanings of masculinity (p. 158)

Mass customization the personalization of products and services for individual customers at a mass-production price (p. 194)

Materialism the importance consumers attach to worldly possessions (p. 206)

Means–end chain a research approach that assumes that very specific product attributes are linked at levels of increasing abstraction to terminal values (p. 204)

MECCAs (Means-end Conceptualization of the Components of Advertising Strategy) a research approach in which researchers generate a map depicting relationships between functional product or service attributes and terminal values and then use this information to develop advertising strategy (p. 206)

Membership reference group ordinary people whose consumption activities provide informational social influence (p. 388)

Meme theory a perspective that uses a medical metaphor to explain how an idea or product enters the consciousness of people over time, much like a virus (p. 566)

Memory a process of acquiring information and storing it over time (p. 257)

Mental accounting principle that states that decisions are influenced by the way a problem is posed (p. 326)

Metrosexual a straight, urban male who exhibits strong interests and knowledge regarding product categories such as fashion, home design, gourmet cooking, and personal care that run counter to the traditional male sex role (p. 158)

Micro-culture groups that form around a strong shared identification with an activity or art form (p. 619)

Microloans Small sums – typically less than $100 – banks lend to entrepreneurs in developing countries (p. 473)

Monomyth a myth with basic characteristics that are found in many cultures (p. 514)

Mores norms with strong moral overtones (p. 510)

Motivation an internal state that activates goal-oriented behaviour (p. 177)

Motivational research a qualitative research approach based on psychoanalytical (Freudian) interpretations with a heavy emphasis on unconscious motives for consumption (p. 188)

Multi-attribute attitude models those models that assume that a consumer's attitude (evaluation) of an attitude object depends on the beliefs he or she has about several or many attributes of the object; the use of a multiattribute model implies that an attitude towards a product or brand can be predicted by identifying these specific beliefs and combining them to derive a measure of the consumer's overall attitude (p. 288)

Myth a story containing symbolic elements which expresses the shared emotion and ideals of a culture (p. 512)

Need a basic biological motive (p. 177)

Negative reinforcement the process whereby a negative reward weakens responses to stimuli so that inappropriate behaviour is avoided in the future (p. 249)

Negative word-of-mouth the passing on of negative experiences involved with products or services by consumers to other potential customers to influence others' choices (p. 404)

Netnography a research technique that adapts ethnographic techniques anthropologists use to study real-world cultures to understand the social dynamics of virtual communities (p. 391)

Neuromarketing a new technique that uses a brain scanning device called functional magnetic resonance imaging (fMRI), that tracks blood flow as people perform mental tasks. Scientists know that specific regions of the brain light up in these scans to show increased blood flow when a person recognizes a face, hears a song, makes a decision, senses deception, and so on. Now they are trying to harness this technology to measure consumers' reactions to movie trailers, choices about automobiles, the appeal of a pretty face, and loyalty to specific brands (p. 339)

Non-compensatory decision rules a set of simple rules used to evaluate competing alternatives; a brand with a low standing on one relevant attribute is eliminated from the consumer's choice set (p. 351)

Normative influence the process in which a reference group helps to set and enforce basic standards of conduct (p. 384)

Normative social influence the conformity that occurs when a person alters his or her behaviour to meet the expectations of a person or group (p. 396)

Norms the informal rules that govern what is right and wrong (p. 396)

Nostalgia a bittersweet emotion when the past is viewed with sadness and longing; many 'classic' products appeal to consumers' memories of their younger days (p. 264)

Nuclear family a contemporary living arrangement composed of a married couple and their children (p. 426)

Object a semiotic term, the product that is the focus of the message (p. 134)

Observational learning the process in which people learn by watching the actions of others and noting the reinforcements they receive for their behaviours (p. 251)

Operant conditioning the process by which the individual learns to perform behaviours that produce positive outcomes and to avoid those that yield negative outcomes (p. 248)

Opinion leaders those people who are knowledgeable about products and who are frequently able to influence others' attitudes or behaviours with regard to a product category (p. 407)

Opinion seekers usually opinion leaders who are also involved in a product category and actively search for information (p. 409)

Paradigm a widely accepted view or model of phenomena being studied. The perspective that regards people as *rational information processors* is currently the dominant paradigm, though this approach is now being challenged by a new wave of research that emphasizes the frequently subjective nature of consumer decision-making (p. 24)

Parental yielding the process that occurs when a parental decision-maker is influenced by a child's product request (p. 433)

Parody display the deliberate avoidance of widely used status symbols, whereby the person seeks status by mocking it (p. 477)

Pastiche the playful and ironic mixing of existing categories and styles (p. 40)

Perceived age how old a person feels rather than his or her chronological age (p. 445)

Perceived risk the belief that use of a product has potentially negative consequences, either physical or social (p. 328)

Perception the process by which stimuli are selected, organized or interpreted (p. 118)

Perceptual map a research tool used to understand how a brand is positioned in consumers' minds relative to competitors (p. 120)

Perceptual selectivity the process in which people attend to only a small portion of the stimuli to which they are exposed (p. 129)

Persuasion an active attempt to change attitudes (p. 296)

Pluralism the coexistence of various styles, truths and fashions (p. 39)

Point-of-purchase stimuli (POP) the promotional materials that are deployed in shops or other outlets to influence consumers; decisions at the time products are purchased (p. 84)

Political consumer the political consumer uses his or her buying pattern as a weapon against or support for companies which share the person's own values (p. 50)

Popular culture the music, films, sports, books, celebrities and other forms of entertainment consumed by the mass market (p. 33)

Pop-up stores temporary locations that allow a company to test new brands without a huge financial commitment (p. 80)

Positive reinforcement the process whereby rewards provided by the environment strengthen response to stimuli (p. 249)

Positivism a research perspective that relies on the principles of the 'scientific method' and assumes that a single reality exists; events in the world can be objectively measured; and the causes of behaviour can be identified, manipulated and predicted (p. 25)

Postmodernism a theory that questions the search for universal truths and values and the existence of objective knowledge (p. 38)

Potlatch a Kwakiutl Indian feast at which the host displays his wealth and gives extravagant gifts (p. 475)

Priming the process in which certain properties of a stimulus are more likely to evoke a schema than others (p. 132)

Principle of closure implies that consumers tend to perceive an incomplete picture as complete (p. 133)

Principle of cognitive consistency the belief that consumers value harmony among their thoughts, feelings and behaviours and that they are motivated to maintain uniformity among these elements (p. 282)

Principle of similarity the gestalt principle that describes how consumers tend to group objects that share similar physical characteristics (p. 134)

Problem recognition the process that occurs whenever the consumer sees a significant difference between his or her current state and some desired or ideal state; this recognition initiates the decision-making process (p. 320)

Product complementarity the view that products in different functional categories have symbolic meanings that are related to one another (p. 579)

Product placement the process of obtaining exposure for a product by arranging for it to be inserted into a film, television programme or some other medium (p. 552)

Product signal communicates an underlying quality of a product through the use of aspects that are only visible in the ad (p. 342)

Profane consumption the process of consuming objects and events that are ordinary or of the everyday world (p. 525)

Progressive learning model the perspective that people gradually learn a new culture as they increasingly come in contact with it; consumers assimilate into a new culture, mixing practices from their old and new environments to create a hybrid culture (p. 609)

Prospect theory a descriptive model of how people make choices (p. 327)

Psychographics the use of psychological, sociological and anthropological factors to construct market segments (p. 9, 580)

Psychophysics the science that focuses on how the physical environment is integrated into the consumer's subjective experience (p. 128)

Punishment the process or outcome that occurs when a response is followed by unpleasant events (p. 249)

Purchase momentum initial impulses to buy in order to satisfy our needs increase the likelihood that we will buy even more (p. 315)

Racial subculture a self-perpetuating group held together by ties of common culture and/or genetics, identified by its members and others as a distinguishable category (p. 606)

Rational perspective a view of the consumer as a careful, analytical decision-maker who tries to maximize utility in purchase decisions (p. 315)

Reactance a boomerang effect that may occur when consumers are threatened with a loss of freedom of choice; they respond by doing the opposite of the behaviour advocated in a persuasive message (p. 401)

Reality engineering the process whereby elements of popular culture are appropriated by marketers and become integrated into marketing strategies (e.g. product placement) (p. 551)

Reference group an actual or imaginary individual or group which has a significant effect on an individual's evaluations, aspirations or behaviour (p. 384)

Referent power the power of prominent people to affect others' consumption behaviours by virtue of product endorsements, distinctive fashion statements or championing causes (p. 393)

Relationship marketing the strategic perspective that stresses the long-term, human side of buyer/seller interactions (p. 13)

Response bias a form of contamination in survey research where some factor, such as the desire to make a good impression on the experimenter, leads respondents to modify their true answers (p. 267)

Restricted codes the ways of expressing and interpreting meanings that focus on the content of objects and tend to be used by the working class (p. 471)

Retail theming strategy where stores create imaginative environments that transport shoppers to fantasy worlds or provide other kinds of stimulation (p. 79)

Retrieval the process whereby desired information is accessed from long-term memory (p. 257)

RFID (response frequency identification device) a small plastic tag that holds a computer chip capable of storing a small amount of information, along with an antenna that lets the device communicate with a computer network. These devices are being implanted in a wide range of products to enable marketers to track inventory more efficiently (p. 14)

Risky shift group members show a greater willingness to consider riskier alternatives following group discussions than they would if each member made his or her own decision without prior discussion (p. 399)

Rites of passage sacred times marked by a change in social status (p. 523)

Ritual a set of multiple, symbolic behaviours that occur in fixed sequence and that tend to be repeated periodically (p. 517)

Ritual artefacts items or consumer goods used in the performance of rituals (p. 518)

Role theory the perspective that much of consumer behaviour resembles action in a play (p. 6)

Rumour a word-of-mouth campaign to promote one product and criticize its competitors (p. 404)

Sacralization a process that occurs when ordinary objects, events or people take on sacred meaning to a culture or to specific groups within a culture (p. 531)

Sacred consumption the process of consuming objects and events that are set apart from normal life and treated with some degree of respect or awe (p. 525)

Savings rate the amount of money saved for later use influenced by consumers' pessimism or optimism about their personal circumstances and perceptions of the economy (p. 458)

Schema an organized collection of beliefs and feelings represented in a cognitive category (pp. 119, 261)

Search engines software (such as Google) that helps consumers access information based upon their specific requests (p. 323)

Self-concept the attitude a person holds to him- or herself (p. 144)

Self-gifts the products or services bought by consumers for their own use as a reward or consolation (p. 521)

Self-image congruence models the approaches based on the prediction that products will be chosen when their attributes match some aspect of the self (p. 151)

Self-perception theory an alternative explanation of dissonance effects; it assumes that people use observations of their own behaviour to infer their attitudes towards an object (p. 285)

Semiotics a field of study that examines the correspondence between a sign and the meaning(s) it conveys (p. 134)

Sensation the immediate response of sensory receptors to such basic stimuli as light, colour and sound (p. 118)

Sensory memory the temporary storage of information received from the senses (p. 258)

Sex-typed traits characteristics that are stereotypically associated with one sex or another (p. 154)

Shopping orientation a consumer's general attitudes and motivations regarding the act of shopping (p. 71)

Short-term memory the system that allows us to retain information for a short period (p. 259)

Sign the sensory imagery that represents the intended meanings of the object (p. 134)

Signifying practices practices that have meaning to individuals, who know how to interpret them, thanks to the understanding of culture as the interpreting system (p. 507)

Single-source data a compilation of information that includes different aspects of consumption and demographic data for a common consumer segment (p. 605)

Social class the overall rank of people in society; people who are grouped within the same social class are approximately equal in terms of their social standing, occupations and lifestyles (p. 460)

Social comparison theory the perspective that people compare their outcomes with others as a way to increase the stability of their own self-evaluation, especially when physical evidence is unavailable (p. 397)

Social hierarchy a ranking of social desirability in terms of consumers' access to such resources as money, education and luxury goods (p. 461)

Social judgement theory the perspective that people assimilate new information about attitude objects in the light of what they already know or feel; the initial attitude as a frame of reference and new information are categorized in terms of this standard (p. 285)

Social loafing the tendency for people not to devote as much to a task when their contribution is part of a larger group effort (p. 399)

Social marketing the promotion of causes and ideas (social products), such as energy conservation, charities and population control (p. 19)

Social mobility the movement of individuals from one social class to another (p. 466)

Social networking a growing practice whereby Web sites let members post information about themselves and make contact with others who share similar interests and opinions or who want to make business contacts (p. 415)

Social power the capacity of one person to alter the actions or outcome of another (p. 393)

Social stratification the process in a social system by which scarce and valuable resources are distributed unequally to status positions which become more or less permanently ranked in terms of the share of valuable resources each receives (p. 463)

Sociometric methods the techniques for measuring group dynamics that involve tracing of communication patterns in and among groups (p. 412)

Source attractiveness the dimensions of a communicator which increase his or her persuasiveness; these include expertise and attractiveness (p. 297)

Source credibility a communication source's perceived expertise, objectivity or trustworthiness (p. 297)

Spacing effect the tendency to recall printed material to a greater extent when the advertiser repeats the target item periodically rather than presenting it over and over at the same time (p. 261)

Stage of cognitive development segmentation of children by age or their ability to comprehend concepts of increasing complexity (p. 436)

Status crystallization the extent to which different indicators of a person's status are consistent with one another (p. 469)

Status symbols products that are purchased and displayed to signal membership in a desirable social class (p. 454)

Stimulus discrimination the process that occurs when behaviour caused by two stimuli is different as when consumers learn to differentiate a brand from its competitors (p. 248)

Stimulus generalization the process that occurs when the behaviour caused by a reaction to one stimulus occurs in the presence of other, similar stimuli (p. 248)

Storage the process that occurs when knowledge entered in long-term memory is integrated with what is already in memory and 'warehoused' until needed (p. 257)

Store gestalt consumers' global evaluation of a store (p. 82)

Store image the 'personality' of a shop composed of attributes such as location, merchandise suitability and the knowledge and congeniality of the sales staff (p. 82)

Subculture a group whose members share beliefs and common experiences that set them apart from the members of the main culture (p. 606)

Surrogate consumer a professional who is retained to evaluate and/or make purchases on behalf of a consumer (p. 410)

Symbol a sign that is related to a product through either conventional or agreed-on associations (p. 135)

Symbolic interactionism a sociological approach stressing that relationships with people play a large part in forming the self; people live in a symbolic environment and the meaning attached to any situation or object is determined by a person's interpretation of those symbols (p. 148)

Symbolic self-completion theory the perspective that people who have an incomplete self-definition in some context will compensate by acquiring symbols associated with a desired social identity (p. 150)

Syncratic decisions purchase decisions that are made jointly by spouses (p. 431)

Taste culture a group of consumers who share aesthetic and intellectual preferences (p. 471)

Terminal values end-states desired by members of a culture (p. 203)

Theory of cognitive dissonance a theory based on the premise that people have a need for order and consistency in their lives and that a state of tension is created when beliefs or behaviours conflict with one another (p. 182)

Theory of reasoned action a version of the Fishbein multi-attitude theory that considers such factors as social pressure and the attitude towards the act of buying a product rather than attitudes towards just the product itself (p. 291)

Theory of trying states that the criterion of behavior in the reasoned action model of attitude measurement should be replaced with *trying* to reach a goal (p. 293)

Time poverty a feeling of having less time available than is required to meet the demands of everyday living (p. 66)

Time style determined by an individual's priorities, it incorporates such dimensions as economic time, past or future orientation, time submissiveness and time anxiety (p. 65)

Tipping point moment of critical mass (p. 566)

Transitional economies countries that are in the process of transforming their economic system from a controlled, centralized system to a free market one (p. 48)

Tribal marketing linking a product's identity to an activity-based 'tribe' such as basketball players (p. 392)

Trickle-down theory the perspective that fashions spread as a result of status symbols associated with the upper classes trickling down to the other social classes as these consumers try to emulate those with higher status (p. 563)

U-commerce the use of ubiquitous networks that will slowly but surely become a part of us, such as wearable computers or customized advertisements beamed to us on our cell phones (p. 14)

Underground economy secondary markets (such as flea markets) where transactions are not officially recorded (p. 218)

Uses and gratifications theory argues that consumers are an active, goal-directed audience who draw on mass media as a resource to satisfy needs (p. 297)

Value a belief that some condition is preferable to its opposite (p. 198)

Value system a culture's ranking of the relative importance of values (p. 199)

Values and Lifestyles (VALS) a psychographic segmentation system used to categorize consumers into clusters (p. 586)

Variety seeking the desire to choose new alternatives over more familiar ones (p. 324)

Viral marketing the strategy of getting customers to sell a product on behalf of the company that creates it (p. 403)

Virtual community of consumption a collection of people whose online interactions are based on shared enthusiasm for and knowledge of a specific consumption activity (p. 389)

Virtual identities the appearance and personality a person takes on as an avatar in a computer-mediated environment like Second Life (p. 147)

Voice of the consumer an approach to new product development that solicits feedback from end customers well before the company puts a new product on the market (p. 558)

Want the particular form of consumption chosen to satisfy a need (p. 177)

Warming process of transforming new objects and places into those that feel cozy, hospitable and authentic (p. 609)

Weber's Law the principle that the stronger the initial stimulus, the greater its change must be for it to be noticed (p. 129)

Weblog online personal journal (p. 389)

Word-of-mouth communication (WOM) the information transmitted by individual consumers on an informal basis (p. 401)

Worldview the ideas shared by members of a culture about principles of order and fairness (p. 508)

Index

AUTHOR INDEX

PRODUCT/COMPANY/NAME INDEX

SUBJECT INDEX

Bold page numbers indicate terms emboldened in text or defined in glossary.

O. o1